The **19th Century**

1801-1900

The 19th Century

1801-1900

Volume 1
1801-1835

Editor

John Powell

Oklahoma Baptist University

SALEM PRESS

Pasadena, California   Hackensack, New Jersey

Editor in Chief: Dawn P. Dawson

Editorial Director: Christina J. Moose — *Indexing:* R. Kent Rasmussen

Managing Editor: R. Kent Rasmussen — *Graphics and Design:* James Hutson

Manuscript Editors: Desiree Dreeuws, Andy Perry — *Layout:* William Zimmerman

Production Editor: Joyce I. Buchea — *Photo Editor:* Cynthia Breslin Beres

Research Supervisor: Jeffry Jensen — *Acquisitions Editor:* Mark Rehn

Research Assistant Editor: Rebecca Kuzins — *Editorial Assistant:* Dana Garey

Cover photos (pictured clockwise, from top left): Rodin's *The Thinker* (The Granger Collection, New York); Immigrants on ship, 1887 (The Granger Collection, New York); Shaka Zulu (The Granger Collection, New York); Hokusai print (The Granger Collection, New York); Eiffel Tower (PhotoDisc); Mexican flag (The Granger Collection, New York)

∞ The paper used in these volumes conforms to the American National Standard for Permanence of Paper for Printed Library Materials, Z39.48-1992 (R1997).

Some of the essays in this work originally appeared in the following Salem Press sets: *Chronology of European History: 15,000 B.C. to 1997* (1997, edited by John Powell; associate editors, E. G. Weltin, José M. Sánchez, Thomas P. Neill, and Edward P. Keleher); *Great Events from History: North American Series, Revised Edition* (1997, edited by Frank N. Magill); *Great Events from History II: Science and Technology* (1991, edited by Frank N. Magill); *Great Events from History II: Human Rights* (1992, edited by Frank N. Magill); *Great Events from History II: Arts and Culture* (1993, edited by Frank N. Magill); and *Great Events from History II: Business and Commerce* (1994, edited by Frank N. Magill). New material has been added.

Library of Congress Cataloging-in-Publication Data

Great events from history. The 19th century, 1801-1900 / editor, John Powell.

    p. cm.

Some of the essays in this work appeared in various other Salem Press sets.

Includes bibliographical references and index.

ISBN-13: 978-1-58765-297-4 (set : alk. paper)

ISBN-10: 1-58765-297-8 (set : alk. paper)

ISBN-13: 978-1-58765-298-1 (v. 1 : alk. paper)

ISBN-10: 1-58765-298-6 (v. 1 : alk. paper)

[etc.]

  1. Nineteenth century. I. Powell, John, 1954- II. Title: 19th century, 1801-1900. III. Title: Nineteenth century, 1801-1900.

D358.G74 2006

909.81—dc22

2006019789

First Printing

CONTENTS

Publisher's Note xi
Contributors xv
Keyword List of Contents xxi
List of Maps, Tables, and Sidebars lxix
Maps of the Nineteenth Century lxxix

1800's

19th century, Arabic Literary Renaissance 1
19th century, Development of Working-Class Libraries 3
19th century, Spread of the Waltz 6
1801, Emergence of the Primitives 9
c. 1801-1810, Davy Develops the Arc Lamp 11
c. 1801-1850, Professional Theaters Spread Throughout America 14
January 1, 1801, First Asteroid Is Discovered 17
February 17, 1801, House of Representatives Elects Jefferson President 20
Summer, 1801-Summer, 1805, Tripolitan War 23
December 6, 1801-August, 1803, Flinders Explores Australia 26
1802, Britain Adopts Gas Lighting 29
January, 1802, Cobbett Founds the *Political Register* 32
March 16, 1802, U.S. Military Academy Is Established 35
March 24, 1802, Trevithick Patents the High-Pressure Steam Engine 38
April 10, 1802, Lambton Begins Trigonometrical Survey of India 40
1803-1808, Dalton Formulates the Atomic Theory of Matter 43
1803-1812, Elgin Ships Parthenon Marbles to England 46
February 24, 1803, *Marbury v. Madison* 49
May 9, 1803, Louisiana Purchase 51
September 7, 1803, Great Britain Begins Colonizing Tasmania 55
1804, British and Foreign Bible Society Is Founded 57
1804, Saussure Publishes His Research on Plant Metabolism 59
January, 1804, Ohio Enacts the First Black Codes 62
May 14, 1804-September 23, 1806, Lewis and Clark Expedition 65
September 25, 1804, Twelfth Amendment Is Ratified 69
December 2, 1804, Bonaparte Is Crowned Napoleon I 72
March, 1805-September 1, 1807, Burr's Conspiracy 75
April 7, 1805, Beethoven's *Eroica* Symphony Introduces the Romantic Age . . 78
May 4, 1805-1830, Exploration of West Africa 80
October 21, 1805, Battle of Trafalgar 83
December 2, 1805, Battle of Austerlitz 86
July 15, 1806-July 1, 1807, Pike Explores the American Southwest 90
1807, Bowdler Publishes *The Family Shakespeare* 93
1807-1834, Moore Publishes *Irish Melodies* 96
1807-1850, Rise of the Knickerbocker School 99
March 2, 1807, Congress Bans Importation of African Slaves 103

April, 1807, Hegel Publishes *The Phenomenology of Spirit*. 106
August 17, 1807, Maiden Voyage of the *Clermont* 111
1808-1826, Ottomans Suppress the Janissary Revolt 114
April, 1808, Tenskwatawa Founds Prophetstown 116
April 6, 1808, American Fur Company Is Chartered 119
May 2, 1808, Dos de Mayo Insurrection in Spain 122
May 2, 1808-November, 1813, Peninsular War in Spain 125
1809, Lamarck Publishes *Zoological Philosophy* 128

1810's

March 16, 1810, *Fletcher v. Peck* 131
September 8, 1810-May, 1812, Astorian Expeditions Explore the Pacific Northwest Coast 134
September 16, 1810, Hidalgo Issues El Grito de Dolores 138
September 16, 1810-September 28, 1821, Mexican War of Independence 140
1811-1818, Egypt Fights the Wahhābīs 143
1811-1840, Construction of the National Road 146
March 1, 1811, Muḥammad ʿAlī Has the Mamlūks Massacred 149
March 11, 1811-1816, Luddites Destroy Industrial Machines. 151
September 20, 1811, Krupp Works Open at Essen 154
November 7, 1811, Battle of Tippecanoe 157
1812-1815, Brothers Grimm Publish Fairy Tales 160
March 22, 1812, Burckhardt Discovers Egypt's Abu Simbel 163
June 18, 1812-December 24, 1814, War of 1812 166
June 23-December 14, 1812, Napoleon Invades Russia. 170
July 22, 1812, Battle of Salamanca 173
September 7, 1812, Battle of Borodino 176
1813, Founding of McGill University 179
March, 1813-December 9, 1824, Bolívar's Military Campaigns 181
July 27, 1813-August 9, 1814, Creek War. 185
October 5, 1813, Battle of the Thames 188
October 16-19, 1813, Battle of Leipzig 191
1814, Fraunhofer Invents the Spectroscope 194
1814, Scott Publishes *Waverley* 196
1814-1879, Exploration of Arabia. 199
March, 1814, Goya Paints *Third of May 1808: Execution of the Citizens of Madrid* 203
Spring, 1814-1830, Communitarian Experiments at New Harmony 206
April 11, 1814-July 29, 1830, France's Bourbon Dynasty Is Restored 210
August 13, 1814, Britain Acquires the Cape Colony 213
September 15, 1814-June 11, 1815, Congress of Vienna 216
December 15, 1814-January 5, 1815, Hartford Convention. 219
c. 1815-1830, Westward American Migration Begins. 221
c. 1815-1848, Biedermeier Furniture Style Becomes Popular. 225
January 8, 1815, Battle of New Orleans 227
February 17, 1815, Treaty of Ghent Takes Effect 230
April 5, 1815, Tambora Volcano Begins Violent Eruption 234
June 1, 1815-August, 1817, Red River Raids 236
June 8-9, 1815, Organization of the German Confederation 239

CONTENTS

June 18, 1815, Battle of Waterloo 243
November 20, 1815, Second Peace of Paris 247
1816, Laënnec Invents the Stethoscope 250
February 20, 1816, Rossini's *The Barber of Seville* Debuts 252
April, 1816, Second Bank of the United States Is Chartered 255
April 9, 1816, African Methodist Episcopal Church Is Founded 257
May 8, 1816, American Bible Society Is Founded 260
December, 1816, Rise of the Cockney School 263
1817, Ricardo Identifies Seven Key Economic Principles 267
c. 1817-1828, Zulu Expansion 270
January 18, 1817-July 28, 1821, San Martín's Military Campaigns 273
November 5, 1817-June 3, 1818, Third Maratha War 276
November 21, 1817-March 27, 1858, Seminole Wars 278
1818-1854, Search for the Northwest Passage 282
1819, Schopenhauer Publishes *The World as Will and Idea* 285
1819-1820, Irving's *Sketch Book* Transforms American Literature 288
1819-1833, Babbage Designs a Mechanical Calculator 291
February 22, 1819, Adams-Onís Treaty Gives the United States Florida 293
March 6, 1819, *McCulloch v. Maryland* 296
May, 1819, Unitarian Church Is Founded 299
May 22-June 20, 1819, *Savannah* Is the First Steamship to Cross the Atlantic 303
December 11-30, 1819, British Parliament Passes the Six Acts 305

1820's

1820's, China's Stele School of Calligraphy Emerges 307
1820's-1830's, Free Public School Movement 310
1820's-1850's, Social Reform Movement 312
1820, Jesuits Are Expelled from Russia, Naples, and Spain 315
1820-early 1840's, Europeans Explore the Antarctic 317
c. 1820-1860, *Costumbrismo* Movement 320
February 23, 1820, London's Cato Street Conspirators Plot Assassinations 323
March 3, 1820, Missouri Compromise 325
April 24, 1820, Congress Passes Land Act of 1820 328
July 2, 1820-March, 1821, Neapolitan Revolution 330
November 6, 1820, Ampère Reveals Magnetism's Relationship to Electricity 334
March 7, 1821-September 29, 1829, Greeks Fight for Independence from the Ottoman Empire 336
September, 1821, Santa Fe Trail Opens 339
1822-1831, Jedediah Smith Explores the Far West 342
1822-1874, Exploration of North Africa 345
September 7, 1822, Brazil Becomes Independent 348
October 20-30, 1822, Great Britain Withdraws from the Concert of Europe 350
1823-1831, Hokusai Produces *Thirty-Six Views of Mount Fuji* 353
May, 1823, Hartford Female Seminary Is Founded 356
October 5, 1823, Wakley Introduces *The Lancet* 358
December 2, 1823, President Monroe Articulates the Monroe Doctrine 361
1824, British Parliament Repeals the Combination Acts 365
1824, Paris Salon of 1824 368

1824, Ranke Develops Systematic History 371
February 20, 1824, Buckland Presents the First Public Dinosaur Description 374
March 2, 1824, *Gibbons v. Ogden* 376
May 7, 1824, First Performance of Beethoven's Ninth Symphony 380
December 1, 1824-February 9, 1825, U.S. Election of 1824 383
1825-1830, Great Java War 386
September 27, 1825, Stockton and Darlington Railway Opens 388
October 26, 1825, Erie Canal Opens. 391
December 26, 1825, Decembrist Revolt 395
c. 1826-1827, First Meetings of the Plymouth Brethren. 398
1826-1842, Young Germany Movement 400
1828-1834, Portugal's Miguelite Wars 403
1828-1842, Arnold Reforms Rugby School 406
February 21, 1828, *Cherokee Phoenix* Begins Publication 408
April 26, 1828-August 28, 1829, Second Russo-Turkish War. 412
May 9, 1828-April 13, 1829, Roman Catholic Emancipation 414
November, 1828, Webster Publishes the First American Dictionary of English 418
December 3, 1828, U.S. Election of 1828 421
1829-1836, Irish Immigration to Canada 423
September 24, 1829, Treaty of Adrianople 426
December 4, 1829, British Abolish Suttee in India 428

1830's

1830's-1840's, Scientists Study Remains of Giant Moas 432
c. 1830's-1860's, American Renaissance in Literature 435
1830-1842, Trail of Tears 438
c. 1830-1865, Southerners Advance Proslavery Arguments 442
c. 1830-1870, Barbizon School of Landscape Painting Flourishes 445
January 7, 1830, Baltimore and Ohio Railroad Opens 447
January 19-27, 1830, Webster and Hayne Debate Slavery and Westward Expansion 451
March 3, 1830, Hugo's *Hernani* Incites Rioting. 454
April 6, 1830, Smith Founds the Mormon Church 457
May 28, 1830, Congress Passes Indian Removal Act 460
June 14-July 5, 1830, France Conquers Algeria 464
July, 1830, Lyell Publishes *Principles of Geology* 467
July 29, 1830, July Revolution Deposes Charles X 470
August 25, 1830-May 21, 1833, Belgian Revolution 474
October-December, 1830, Delacroix Paints *Liberty Leading the People* 476
November 29, 1830-August 15, 1831, First Polish Rebellion 479
1831, Mazzini Founds Young Italy 482
1831-1834, Hiroshige Completes *The Tokaido Fifty-Three Stations* 484
January 1, 1831, Garrison Begins Publishing *The Liberator* 487
March 18, 1831, and March 3, 1832, Cherokee Cases 491
May, 1831-February, 1832, Tocqueville Visits America 493
Summer, 1831, McCormick Invents the Reaper. 496
August 21, 1831, Turner Launches Slave Insurrection 499
October, 1831, Faraday Converts Magnetic Force into Electricity 502

CONTENTS

1832-1841, Turko-Egyptian Wars 505

1832-1847, Abdelkader Leads Algeria Against France 508

March 12, 1832, *La Sylphide* Inaugurates Romantic Ballet's Golden Age 511

June 4, 1832, British Parliament Passes the Reform Act of 1832 514

July 10, 1832, Jackson Vetoes Rechartering of the Bank of the United States 518

November 24, 1832-January 21, 1833, Nullification Controversy 521

1833, British Parliament Passes the Factory Act 525

January, 1833, Great Britain Occupies the Falkland Islands 527

July 14, 1833, Oxford Movement Begins 530

August 28, 1833, Slavery Is Abolished Throughout the British Empire 533

September 3, 1833, Birth of the Penny Press 536

September 29, 1833-1849, Carlist Wars Unsettle Spain 539

December, 1833, American Anti-Slavery Society Is Founded 542

December 3, 1833, Oberlin College Opens 546

January 1, 1834, German States Join to Form Customs Union 549

April 14, 1834, Clay Begins American Whig Party 551

August 14, 1834, British Parliament Passes New Poor Law 554

October 14, 1834, Blair Patents His First Seed Planter 557

1835, Finney Lectures on "Revivals of Religion" 560

PUBLISHER'S NOTE

Great Events from History: The Nineteenth Century, 1801-1900, is the sixth installment in Salem Press's ongoing *Great Events from History* series, which was initiated in 2004 with the two-volume *Great Events from History: The Ancient World, Prehistory-476*, followed by *The Middle Ages, 477-1453* (2 vols., 2005), *The Renaissance & Early Modern Era, 1454-1600* (2 vols., 2005), *The Seventeenth Century, 1601-1700* (2 vols., 2006), and *The Eighteenth Century, 1701-1800* (2 vols., 2006). When completed, the series will extend through the twentieth century and contain more than 5,000 essays covering the milestones of world history.

EXPANDED COVERAGE

Like the rest of the series, the four current volumes represent both a revision and a significant expansion of the material on the nineteenth century in the twelve-volume *Great Events from History* (1972-1980). The present set incorporates virtually all the essays on the nineteenth century from the *Chronology of European History: 15,000 B.C. to 1997* (3 vols., 1997); *Great Events from History: North American Series, Revised Edition* (4 vols., 1997); and *Great Events from History II* (20 vols., 1991-1995). These volumes form the foundation on which the new and greatly expanded series is built. However, that foundation now forms only a fraction of the whole. Across the entire new series, more than one-third of the text is completely new. In addition, the new series adds hundreds of illustrations, tables, primary source documents, lists, appendixes, and finding aids in the form of keyword, geographic, categorized, personage, and subject indexes.

The new content in *Great Events from History: The Nineteenth Century* constitutes more than one-half of the set: To the 307 original essays we have added 360 completely new essays—commissioned especially for the new series and appearing here for the first time—for a total of 667 essays. Bibliographies for all the old essays have been expanded and updated. All essays are cross-referenced both internally, to one another, and externally, to the companion essays in *Great Lives from History: The Nineteenth Century* (4 vols., 2007). A section containing maps of world regions in the nineteenth century, plus new appendixes, numerous sidebars, quo-

tations from primary source documents, lists, maps, and illustrations have been included.

SCOPE OF COVERAGE

The nineteenth century receives worldwide coverage with the priority of meeting the needs of history students at the high school and undergraduate levels. The events covered include the curriculum-oriented geopolitical events of the era—from the Napoleonic Wars, the revolutions of 1848, and the U.S. Civil War to the partition of Africa and China's Boxer Rebellion. Essays also address important social and cultural developments in daily life: major literary movements, significant developments in art and music, trends in immigration, and progressive social legislation. Among the many broad subjects that receive extensive coverage are Europe's changing political divisions and shifting alliances, the struggles to end slavery and extend full citizenship to African Americans in the United States, the steady expansion of democracy in the Western world, the liberation of Latin America from European rule, the exploration of Africa, and the expansion of European imperialism in Africa and Asia.

The nineteenth century was also a time of immense advances in science and technology. Indeed, the advances seen in the nineteenth century world rival those of the twentieth century for the fundamental changes they brought to daily lives. At the beginning of the century, steam-powered transportation was in its infancy, electricity was little understood, and medicine had made little significant progress since the time of Galen (129-199 C.E.). By the end of the century, railroads crisscrossed every inhabited continent, steamships had displaced sailing vessels, automobiles were starting to appear, and aviation was in its infancy. Electricity was well understood and was being used for artificial lighting, machinery, and telegraphic and telephonic communication. Emblematic of broad advances in science, medicine had moved out of the dark ages with revolutionary advances in surgical techniques, anesthesia, antisepsis, and immunization.

By category, the contents of the set include events that fall into one or more of the following areas (many essays are counted under more than one category): agriculture (14), anthropology (2), archaeology (5), architecture

(21), art (28), astronomy (2), atrocities and war crimes (14), banking and finance (6), biology (19), business and labor (29), cartography (2), chemistry (12), civil rights and liberties (40), colonization (32), communications (13), crime and scandals (11), cultural and intellectual history (14), dance (5), diplomacy and international relations (57), disasters (6), earth science (13), economics (31), education (16), engineering (30), environment and ecology (12), expansion and land acquisition (88), exploration and discovery (29), fashion and design (4), genetics (10), geography (14), geology (5), government and politics (137), health and medicine (24), historiography (4), human rights (10), immigration (23), indigenous people's rights (23), inventions (41), journalism (8), laws, acts, and legal history (79), literature (38), manufacturing (10), marketing and advertising (4), mathematics (13), military history (6), motion pictures (3), music (17), natural disasters (4), organizations and institutions (63), philosophy (16), photography (9), physics (10), psychology and psychiatry (2), radio and television (3), religion and theology (35), science and technology (70), social issues and reform (72), sociology (3), space and aviation (1), sports (5), terrorism and political assassination (7), theater (19), trade and commerce (43), transportation (30), wars, uprisings, and civil unrest (154), and women's issues (25).

The scope of this set is equally broad geographically, with essays on events associated with these modern countries and world regions: Afghanistan (1), Africa (35), Algeria (4), Antarctica (1), the Arctic (2), Argentina (3), Armenia (1), Australia (6), Austria (16), Balkans (1), Belgium (4), Benin (1), Bolivia (2), Brazil (2), British Empire (48), Bulgaria (1), Cambodia (1), Canada (33), Central America and the Caribbean (25), Central Asia (1), Chile (3), China (21), Colombia (1), Congo (2), Cuba (5), Denmark (3), Ecuador (1), Egypt (9), Eritrea (1), Ethiopia (2), Europe (6), France (67), Germany (55), Ghana (1), Great Britain (105), Greece (7), Honduras (1), Hungary (2), India (9), Indonesia (4), Iraq (2), Ireland (10), Italy (20), Jamaica (1), Japan (12), Kenya (1), Korea (3), Lesotho (1), Liberia (1), Libya (1), Malaysia (1), Mali (1), Mediterranean (15), Mexico (12), Middle East (9), Morocco (2), Netherlands (5), New Zealand (2), Nicaragua (1), Nigeria (2), North Africa (3), Norway (3), Ottoman Empire (11), Paraguay (1), Peru (3), Philippines (2), Poland (3), Polynesia (4), Portugal (3), Russia (27), Saudi Arabia (3), Scandinavia (7), Solar system (1), South Africa (12), South America (10), Southeast Asia (7), Spain (22), Sudan (3), Sweden (3), Switzerland (5), Tanzania (2), Tunisia (1), Turkey (9), Uganda (1), Ukraine (5), United States (279), Uruguay (1), Venezuela (1), Vietnam (2), Zambia (1), and Zimbabwe (2).

ESSAY LENGTH AND FORMAT

The essays have an average length of 1,600 words (4-8 columns) and adhere to a uniform format. The ready-reference top matter of every essay prominently displays the following information:

- the most precise *date* (or date range) of the event
- the *common name* of the event
- a *summary paragraph* that identifies the event and encapsulates its significance
- where appropriate, any *also-known-as* name for the event
- the *locale*, or where the event occurred, including both nineteenth century and, as relevant, modern place-names
- the *categories*, or the type of event covered, from Art to Government to Military History to Transportation
- *Key Figures*, a list of the major people involved in the event, with birth and death dates, brief descriptors, and regnal dates or terms of office where applicable

The text of each essay is divided into these sections:
- *Summary of Event*, devoted to a chronological description of the facts of the event
- *Significance*, assessing the event's historical impact
- *Further Reading*, an annotated list of sources for further study
- *See also*, cross-references to other essays within the *Great Events* set, and
- *Related articles*, which lists essays of interest in Salem's companion publication, *Great Lives from History: The Nineteenth Century, 1801-1900* (4 vols., 2007).

SPECIAL FEATURES

A section of historical maps appears in the front matter of each volume, displaying world regions in the nineteenth century to assist in placing the events' locales. Accompanying the individual essays are an additional 82 maps, quotations from primary source documents, lists, and time lines—as well as more than 500 illustrations: images of artworks, battles, buildings, people, and other icons of the period.

Because the set is ordered chronologically, a *Keyword List of Contents* appears in the front matter to each volume that lists all essays alphabetically, permuted by all keywords in the essays' titles, to assist in locating events by name.

In addition, several research aids appear as appendixes at the end of Volume 4:

- The *Time Line* lists major events in the nineteenth century; in contrast to the Chronological List of Entries that follows later, the Time Line is a detailed chronological listing of events that lists not only those events covered in the set but also many other key developments during the nineteenth century.
- The *Glossary* defines terms and concepts associated with the period.
- The *Bibliography* cites major sources on the period.
- *Electronic Resources* provides URLs and descriptions of Web sites and other online resources devoted to period studies.
- The *Chronological List of Entries* organizes the contents chronologically in one place for ease of reference.

Four indexes round out the set:

- The *Geographical Index* lists essays by regions and countries.
- The *Category Index* lists essays by types of event, such as Agriculture, Architecture, and Art.
- The *Personages Index* includes major personages discussed throughout.
- The *Subject Index* includes persons, concepts, terms, battles, works of literature, inventions, organizations, artworks, musical compositions, and many other topics of discussion.

USAGE NOTES

The worldwide scope of *Great Events from History* often results in the inclusion of names and words that must be transliterated from languages that do not use the Roman alphabet, and in some cases, more than one system of transliteration exists. In many cases, transliterated words in this set follow the American Library Association and Library of Congress (ALA-LC) transliteration format for that language. However, if another form of a name or word is judged to be more familiar to the general audience, it is used instead. Pinyin transliterations are used for Chinese topics, with Wade-Giles variants provided for major names and dynasties; in a few cases, common names that are not Pinyin are used. Sanskrit and other South Asian names generally follow the ALA-LC transliteration rules, although again, more familiar forms of words are used when deemed appropriate for general readers.

Titles of books and other literature appear, upon first mention in each essay, with their full publication and translation data as known: an indication of the first date of publication or appearance, followed by the English title in translation and its first date of appearance in English; if no translation has been published in English, and if the context of the discussion does not make the meaning of the title obvious, a "literal translation" appears in roman type.

In the listing of Key Figures and in parenthetical material within the text, "r." stands for "reigned," "b." for "born," "d." for "died," and "fl." for flourished. Wherever date ranges, such as "1823-1877," appear appended to names with none of these designators, readers may assume that they signify birth and death dates or, where the contexts indicate, terms of office not considered "reigns."

THE CONTRIBUTORS

Salem Press would like to extend its appreciation to all who have been involved in the development and production of this work. Special thanks go to Dr. John Powell, Associate Professor of History at Oklahoma Baptist University, who developed the contents list and coverage notes for contributing writers to ensure the set's relevance to the high school and undergraduate curricula. The essays were written and signed by 330 historians, political scientists, and scholars of regional studies as well as independent scholars. Without their expert contributions, a project of this nature would not be possible. A full list of their names and affiliations appears in the front matter of this volume.

CONTRIBUTORS

McCrea Adams
Independent Scholar

Richard Adler
University of Michigan, Dearborn

Peggy E. Alford
Eastern Oregon University

William Allison
Weber State University

Thomas L. Altherr
Metropolitan State College of Denver

Stephen E. Ambrose
*Louisiana State University,
  New Orleans*

Michael S. Ameigh
*University of New York College,
  Oswego*

Nicole Anae
University of Tasmania

Debra D. Andrist
University of St. Thomas

Mary Welek Atwell
Radford University

James A. Baer
*Northern Virginia Community
  College*

Charles F. Bahmueller
Center for Civic Education

Sue Bailey
Tennessee Technological University

Christopher Baker
Armstrong Atlantic State University

Anita Baker-Blocker
Independent Scholar

John W. Barker
University of Wisconsin, Madison

David Barratt
Independent Scholar

Erika Behrisch
Royal Military College of Canada

Alvin K. Benson
Utah Valley State College

Donna Berliner
University of Texas, Dallas

Milton Berman
University of Rochester

Cynthia A. Bily
Adrian College

Nicholas Birns
New School University

Michael S. Bisesi
Medical College of Ohio

Kent Blaser
Wayne State University

Arnold Blumberg
Towson University

Devon Boan
Belmont University

Steve D. Boilard
*California Legislative Analyst's
  Office*

James J. Bolner
*Louisiana State University, Baton
  Rouge*

Gordon L. Bowen
Mary Baldwin College

Anthony Brundage
*California Polytechnic University,
  Pomona*

Jeffrey L. Buller
Mary Baldwin College

Michael A. Buratovich
Spring Arbor University

Joseph P. Byrne
Belmont University

Gary A. Campbell
Michigan Technological University

Edmund J. Campion
University of Tennessee

Byron Cannon
University of Utah

Kay J. Carr
*Southern Illinois University,
  Carbondale*

Kathleen Carroll
John A. Logan College

Jack Carter
University of New Orleans

Ranes C. Chakravorty
University of Virginia

John G. Clark
University of Kansas

Lawrence I. Clark
Independent Scholar

Michael D. Clark
*Louisiana State University,
  New Orleans*

David Coffey
Texas Christian University

Richard H. Collin
*Louisiana State University,
  New Orleans*

Bernard A. Cook
Loyola University

James J. Cooke
University of Mississippi

William J. Cooper, Jr.
*Louisiana State University,
  Baton Rouge*

David A. Crain
South Dakota State University

Stephen Cresswell
West Virginia Wesleyan College

Norma Crews
Independent Scholar

Tyler T. Crogg
Southern Illinois University,
Carbondale

Richard A. Crooker
Kutztown University

Edward R. Crowther
Adams State College

David H. Culbert
Independent Scholar

LouAnn Faris Culley
Kansas State University

Marsha Daigle-Williamson
Spring Arbor University

Sudipta Das
Southern University, New Orleans

Edward J. Davies II
University of Utah

John H. DeBerry
Memphis State University

Judith Boyce DeMark
Northern Michigan University

Charles A. Desnoyers
LaSalle University

Thomas E. DeWolfe
Hampden-Sydney College

M. Casey Diana
University of Illinois, Urbana-
Champaign

Stephen B. Dobrow
Farleigh-Dickinson University

Margaret A. Dodson
Independent Scholar

Martin L. Dolan
Northern Michigan State University

Maurice T. Dominguez
Tulane University

Matthias Dörries
University of California, Berkeley

Daniel J. Doyle
Pennsylvania College of Technology

Thomas Drucker
University of Wisconsin, Whitewater

John Duffy
University of Maryland

Brian R. Dunn
Clarion University

John P. Dunn
Valdosta State University

Steven I. Dutch
University of Wisconsin, Green Bay

Jodella K. Dyreson
Weber State University

Jennifer Eastman
Clark University

H. J. Eisenman
University of Missouri, Rolla

Robert P. Ellis
Independent Scholar

Linda Eikmeier Endersby
Thomas A. Edison Papers

Robert F. Erickson
Southern Illinois University

Thomas L. Erskine
Salisbury University

Cecil L. Eubanks
Louisiana State University,
Baton Rouge

John L. Farbo
University of Idaho

James J. Farsolas
Coastal Carolina University

Randall Fegley
Pennsylvania State University

Anne-Marie E. Ferngren
Oregon State University

James E. Fickle
Memphis State University

John W. Fiero
University of Louisiana, Lafayette

Brian L. Fife
Ball State University

James F. Findlay, Jr.
University of Rhode Island

Michael Shaw Findlay
California State University, Chico

Michael S. Fitzgerald
Pikeville College

Richard D. Fitzgerald
Onondaga Community College

Miletus L. Flaningam
Purdue University

George J. Flynn
State University of New York,
Plattsburgh

Michael J. Fontenot
Southern University, Baton Rouge

Charles H. Ford
Norfolk State University

Robert J. Forman
St. John's University, New York

Donald R. Franceschetti
University of Memphis

John C. Fredriksen
Independent Scholar

C. George Fry
Winebrenner Theological Seminary

Gloria Fulton
Humboldt State University

William Gahan
University of California,
Santa Barbara

Michael J. Galgano
James Madison University

John G. Gallaher
Southern Illinois University,
Edwardsville

Francesca Gamber
Southern Illinois University, Carbondale

John C. Gardner
Louisiana State University, Baton Rouge

Keith Garebian
Independent Scholar

Matthew R. Garrett
University of Nebraska, Lincoln

Mark Golden
University of Winnipeg

Sheldon Goldfarb
University of British Columbia

Nancy M. Gordon
Independent Scholar

Margaret Bozenna Goscilo
University of Pittsburgh

Lewis L. Gould
University of Texas, Austin

Hans G. Graetzer
South Dakota State University

Mary M. Graham
York College of Pennsylvania

Harold J. Grau
University of Virgin Islands

Ronald Gray
Beijing Language & Cultural University

Jack H. Greising
Northern Michigan State University

Christopher E. Guthrie
Tarleton State University

James M. Haas
Southern Illinois University

Michael Haas
College of the Canyons

William I. Hair
Florida State University

Irwin Halfond
McKendree College

Stanley Harrold
South Carolina State University

James Hayes-Bohanan
Bridgewater State College

Pamela Hayes-Bohanan
Bridgewater State College

Peter B. Heller
Manhattan College

Joyce E. Henry
Ursinus College

Mark C. Herman
Edison College

Jane F. Hill
Independent Scholar

Kay Hively
Independent Scholar

Russell Hively
Independent Scholar

John R. Holmes
Franciscan University of Steubenville

Earl G. Hoover
Independent Scholar

Lisa Hopkins
Sheffield Hallam University

Graham G. Hunt
University of Texas, Arlington

William E. Huntzicker
University of Minnesota

Raymond Pierre Hylton
Virginia Union University

John Quinn Imholte
University of Minnesota, Morris

Margot Irvine
University of Guelph

W. Turrentine Jackson
Independent Scholar

Robert Jacobs
Central Washington University

Duncan R. Jamieson
Ashland University

Elizabeth Jarnagin
Drew University

Joseph C. Jastrzembski
Minot State University

Robert L. Jenkins
Mississippi State University

Albert C. Jensen
Central Florida Community College

Jeffry Jensen
Independent Scholar

K. Sue Jewell
Ohio State University

Jane Anderson Jones
Manatee Community College

Philip Dwight Jones
Bradley University

Christopher J. Kauffman
Marillac College

Edward P. Keleher
Purdue University, Calumet

Jeffrey Kimball
Miami University of Ohio

Leigh Husband Kimmel
Independent Scholar

Richard D. King
Ursinus College

James Knotwell
Wayne State College

Gayla Koerting
University of South Dakota

Grove Koger
Boise Public Library, Idaho

Jeri Kurtzleben
University of Northern Iowa

Ralph L. Langenheim, Jr.
University of Illinois, Urbana

Eugene Larson
Pierce College

Sharon L. Larson
University of Nebraska, Lincoln

Nathan J. Latta
Independent Scholar

Anne Leader
City College of New York, City University of New York

Linda Ledford-Miller
University of Scranton

Joseph Edward Lee
Winthrop University

Gregory A. Levitt
University of New Orleans

Thomas Tandy Lewis
St. Cloud State University

Roger D. Long
Eastern Michigan University

John L. Loos
Louisiana State University, Baton Rouge

Anne C. Loveland
Louisiana State University, Baton Rouge

Eric v.d. Luft
State University of New York, Upstate Medical University

R. C. Lutz
CII

William M. McBride
U.S. Naval Academy

Sandra C. McClain
James Madison University

Branden C. McCullough
Southern Illinois University, Carbondale

Grace McEntee
Appalachian State University

James Edward McGoldrick
Greenville Presbyterian Theological Seminary

Roderick E. McGrew
Temple University

Angela S. McMullen
University of Nebraska, Lincoln

Paul Madden
Hardin-Simmons University

Russell M. Magnaghi
Northern Michigan State University

Edward J. Maguire
St. Louis University

Bill T. Manikas
Gaston College

Nancy Farm Mannikko
National Park Service

Carl Henry Marcoux
University of California, Riverside

Chogollah Maroufi
California State University, Los Angeles

Thomas C. Maroukis
Capital University

Paul T. Mason
Dusquesne University

Laurence W. Mazzeno
Alvernia College

Daniel J. Meissner
University of Wisconsin, Madison

Maurice K. Melton
Andrew College

Doris H. Meriwether
University of Louisiana, Lafayette

Joan E. Meznar
Eastern Connecticut State University

Diane P. Michelfelder
Utah State University

Liesel Ashley Miller
Mississippi State University

Randall L. Milstein
Oregon State University

William V. Moore
College of Charleston

Gordon R. Mork
Purdue University

Michele Mock Murton
Indiana University of Pennsylvania

Bert M. Mutersbaugh
Eastern Kentucky University

Alice Myers
Simon's Rock College of Bard

John E. Myers
Simon's Rock College of Bard

Bryan Ness
Pacific Union College

Charles H. O'Brien
Western Illinois University

Gary A. Olson
San Bernardino Valley College

Adrianna M. Paliyenko
Colby College

Robert J. Paradowski
Rochester Institute of Technology

William A. Pelz
Institute of Working Class History

Jan Pendergrass
University of Georgia

Marilyn Elizabeth Perry
Independent Scholar

Nis Petersen
New Jersey City University

Erika E. Pilver
Westfield State College

Marguerite R. Plummer
Louisiana State University, Shreveport

Mark A. Plummer
Illinois State University

Marjorie J. Podolsky
*Behrend College, Pennsylvania State
University, Erie*

Laurence M. Porter
Michigan State University

Clifton W. Potter, Jr.
Lynchburg College

Dorothy T. Potter
Lynchburg College

John Powell
Oklahoma Baptist University

Tessa Li Powell
Independent Scholar

Tina Powell
Fordham University

Christina Proenza-Coles
Virginia State University

Francis P. Prucha
Marquette University

Edna B. Quinn
Salisbury University

Steven J. Ramold
Eastern Michigan University

P. S. Ramsey
Independent Scholar

R. Kent Rasmussen
Independent Scholar

E. A. Reed
St. Mary's College of California

Germaine M. Reed
Georgia Institue of Technology

Merl E. Reed
Georgia State University

Kevin B. Reid
Henderson Community College

Rosemary M. Canfield Reisman
Charleston Southern University

Bernd Renner
*Brooklyn College, City University of
New York*

Betty Richardson
*Southern Illinois University,
Edwardsville*

Douglas W. Richmond
University of Texas, Arlington

Edward A. Riedinger
Ohio State University Libraries

Thomas D. Riethmann
St. Louis University

R. Todd Rober
*West Chester University of
Pennsylvania*

Charles W. Rogers
*Southwestern Oklahoma State
University*

Carl Rollyson
*Baruch College, City University of
New York*

John Alan Ross
Eastern Washington University

Robert Ross
Independent Scholar

Mary Ellen Rowe
Central Missouri State University

Dorothy C. Salem
Cuyahoga Community College

José M. Sánchez
St. Louis University

Vicki A. Sanders
Riverside Military Academy

Wayne D. Santoni
Southern Illinois University

Richard Sax
Fort Lewis College

Elizabeth D. Schafer
Independent Scholar

Randy P. Schiff
*University of California, Santa
Barbara*

Glenn Schiffman
Independent Scholar

Helmut J. Schmeller
Fort Hays State University

Beverly E. Schneller
Millersville University

Harold A. Schofield
Colorado Women's College

John Richard Schrock
Emporia State University

Larry Schweikart
University of Dayton

Elizabeth L. Scully
University of Texas, Arlington

Rose Secrest
Independent Scholar

Terry L. Seip
*Louisiana State University, Baton
Rouge*

Gustav L. Seligman
North Texas State University

Martha A. Sherwood
University of Oregon

R. Baird Shuman
*University of Illinois, Urbana-
Champaign*

Narasingha P. Sil
Western Oregon University

Donald C. Simmons, Jr.
South Dakota Humanities Council

Sanford S. Singer
University of Dayton

Shumet Sishagne
Christopher Newport University

Emilie B. Fitzhugh Sizemore
Pepperdine University

Anna Sloan
Mt. Holyoke College

Gary Scott Smith
Grove City College

Richard L. Smith
Ferrum College

Sonia Sorrell
Pepperdine University

Joseph L. Spradley
Wheaton College

James Stanlaw
Illinois State University

August W. Staub
University of Georgia

James H. Steinel
St. John's University, New York

David L. Sterling
University of Cincinnati

Pamela R. Stern
University of Arkansas

Bruce S. Stewart
Southern Illinois University, Carbondale

Dion C. Stewart
Georgia Perimeter College

Toby Stewart
Independent Scholar

Geralyn Strecker
Ball State University

Fred Strickert
Wartburg College

Taylor Stults
Muskingum College

Donald Sullivan
University of New Mexico

Glenn L. Swygart
Tennessee Temple University

Stephen G. Sylvester
Montana State University, Northern

James Tackach
Roger Williams University

Gerardo G. Tango
Independent Scholar

Susan M. Taylor
Indiana University, South Bend

J. W. Thacker
Western Kentucky University

Emory M. Thomas
University of Georgia

Ann Thompson
Independent Scholar

Jonathan L. Thorndike
Belmont University

Vincent Michael Thur
Wenatchee Valley College

Leslie V. Tischauser
Prairie State College

Brian G. Tobin
Lassen College

Frank Towers
Clarion University

Anh Tran
Wichita State University

Paul B. Trescott
Southern Illinois University, Carbondale

Marcella Bush Trevino
Barry University

Anne Trotter
Memphis State University

William M. Tuttle
University of Kansas

Paul Varner
Oklahoma Christian University

Kevin B. Vichcales
Western Michigan University

Mary E. Virginia
Independent Scholar

Harry E. Wade
East Texas State University

Meaghan G. Wagner
Pace University

Matthew Walker
University of Nebraska, Lincoln

Thomas J. Edward Walker
Pennsylvania College of Technology

William T. Walker
Chestnut Hill College

Sharon B. Watkins
Western Illinois University

Shawncey Webb
Taylor University

Marcia J. Weiss
Point Park College

Henry G. Weisser
Colorado State University

Winifred O. Whelan
St. Bonaventure University

Richard Whitworth
Ball State University

Edwin G. Wiggins
Webb Institute

Thomas A. Wikle
Oklahoma State University

Major L. Wilson
Memphis State University

Raymond Wilson
Fort Hays State University

Sharon K. Wilson
Fort Hays State University

Theodore A. Wilson
University of Kansas

Michael Witkoski
University of South Carolina

Cynthia Gwynne Yaudes
Indiana University

Kristen L. Zacharias
Albright College

Yunqiu Zhang
North Carolina A&T State University

KEYWORD LIST OF CONTENTS

Abdelkader Leads Algeria Against France
(1832-1847). 508

Abdicates, Hawaii's Last Monarch (Jan. 24,
1895) 1797

Abel and Takamine Isolate Adrenaline
(1897-1901) 1869

Abolish Suttee in India, British (Dec. 4,
1829) 428

Abolished Throughout the British Empire,
Slavery Is (Aug. 28, 1833) 533

Abu Simbel, Burckhardt Discovers Egypt's
(Mar. 22, 1812). 163

Academy Is Established, U.S. Military
(Mar. 16, 1802) 35

Acquires Oregon Territory, United States
(June 15, 1846) 718

Acquires the Cape Colony, Britain (Aug. 13,
1814) 213

Act, Arthur Signs the Chinese Exclusion
(May 9, 1882) 1558

Act, British North America (July 1, 1867) 1219

Act, British Parliament Passes Municipal
Corporations (Sept. 9, 1835) 575

Act, British Parliament Passes the Factory
(1833). 525

Act, British Parliament Passes the Matrimonial
Causes (Aug. 28, 1857). 952

Act, Canada's Indian (1876) 1437

Act, Congress Passes Dingley Tariff (July 24,
1897) 1880

Act, Congress Passes Indian Removal (May 28,
1830) 460

Act, Congress Passes the Kansas-Nebraska
(May 30, 1854) 891

Act, Grant Signs Indian Appropriation (Mar. 3,
1871) 1355

Act, Harrison Signs the Sherman Antitrust
(July 20, 1890) 1712

Act, Interstate Commerce (Feb. 4, 1887). 1655

Act, Lincoln Signs the Homestead (May 20,
1862) 1064

Act, Lincoln Signs the Morrill Land Grant
(July 2, 1862) 1066

Act Erodes Indian Tribal Unity, General
Allotment (Feb. 8, 1887) 1657

Act Fosters Canadian Settlement, Dominion
Lands (1872) 1369

Act of 1820, Congress Passes Land (Apr. 24,
1820) 328

Act of 1832, British Parliament Passes the
Reform (June 4, 1832) 514

Act of 1841, Congress Passes Preemption
(Sept. 4, 1841) 653

Act of 1866, Civil Rights (Apr. 9, 1866) 1175

Act of 1867, British Parliament Passes the
Reform (Aug., 1867) 1222

Act of 1884, British Parliament Passes the
Franchise (Dec. 6, 1884) 1627

Act Reforms the Federal Civil Service,
Pendleton (Jan. 16, 1883) 1577

Acts, British Parliament Passes the Six
(Dec. 11-30, 1819) 305

Acts, British Parliament Repeals the
Combination (1824) 365

Acts, Congress Passes the National Bank
(Feb. 25, 1863-June 3, 1864) 1093

Adams-Onís Treaty Gives the United States
Florida (Feb. 22, 1819) 293

Addams Opens Chicago's Hull-House
(Sept. 18, 1889) 1692

Administration, Scandals Rock the Grant
(Sept. 24, 1869-1877) 1296

Adopts a New Constitution, Japan (Feb. 11,
1889) 1683

Adopts Gas Lighting, Britain (1802) 29

Adrenaline, Abel and Takamine Isolate
(1897-1901) 1869

Adrianople, Treaty of (Sept. 24, 1829). 426

Advance Proslavery Arguments, Southerners
(c. 1830-1865) 442

Advances His Theory of Positivism, Comte
(1851-1854). 833

Advances the Cellular Theory of Immunity,
Metchnikoff (1882-1901) 1545

Adventures of Huckleberry Finn, Twain
Publishes (Dec., 1884-Feb., 1885) 1624

Advocates Artificial Fertilizers, Liebig
(1840). 638

Aesthetic Movement Arises (1870's). 1310

Affair, Dreyfus (October, 1894-July, 1906) . . . 1788

Afghan War, First (1839-1842) 617
Africa, Berlin Conference Lays Groundwork
    for the Partition of (Nov. 15, 1884-
    Feb. 26, 1885) 1619
Africa, Exploration of East (1848-1889) 756
Africa, Exploration of North (1822-1874) 345
Africa, Exploration of West (May 4, 1805-
    1830) 80
Africa's Congo Basin, Exploration of
    (1873-1880) 1382
Africa's Great Trek Begins, South (1835) 563
African American University Opens, First
    (Jan. 1, 1857) 936
African Methodist Episcopal Church Is
    Founded (Apr. 9, 1816) 257
African Resistance in Rhodesia, British Subdue
    (October, 1893-October, 1897) 1763
African Slaves, Congress Bans Importation of
    (Mar. 2, 1807) 103
African War, South (Oct. 11, 1899-May 31,
    1902) 1932
Afternoon of a Faun Premieres, Debussy's
    Prelude to the (Dec. 22, 1894) 1791
Age, Beethoven's Eroica Symphony
    Introduces the Romantic (Apr. 7, 1805) 78
Age, La Sylphide Inaugurates Romantic Ballet's
    Golden (Mar. 12, 1832) 511
Age of Flamenco Begins, Golden (c. 1869) . . . 1282
Air Brake, Westinghouse Patents His
    (Apr., 1869) 1287
Akron Woman's Rights Convention
    (May 28-29, 1851) 843
Alaska to the United States, Russia Sells
    (Mar. 30, 1867) 1213
Algeria, France Conquers (June 14-July 5,
    1830) 464
Algeria Against France, Abdelkader Leads
    (1832-1847) 508
Alliance, Bakunin Founds the Social
    Democratic (1868) 1235
Alliance, Franco-Russian (Jan. 4, 1894) 1776
Alliance Is Formed, Triple (May 20, 1882) 1561
Allotment Act Erodes Indian Tribal Unity,
    General (Feb. 8, 1887) 1657
Amalgamates Kimberley Diamondfields,
    Rhodes (Mar. 13, 1888) 1674
Amendment, Suffragists Protest the Fourteenth
    (May 10, 1866) 1181
Amendment Is Ratified, Fourteenth (July 9,
    1868) 1261

Amendment Is Ratified, Thirteenth (Dec. 6,
    1865) 1167
Amendment Is Ratified, Twelfth (Sept. 25,
    1804) 69
America, Establishment of the Confederate
    States of (Feb. 8, 1861) 1022
America, Professional Theaters Spread
    Throughout (c. 1801-1850) 14
America, Tocqueville Visits (May, 1831-
    Feb., 1832) 493
America Wins the First America's Cup Race
    (Aug. 22, 1851) 846
American Anti-Slavery Society Is Founded
    (Dec., 1833) 542
American Bible Society Is Founded (May 8,
    1816) 260
American Buffalo Slaughter, Great (c. 1871-
    1883) 1343
American Circus, Barnum Creates the First
    Modern (Apr. 10, 1871) 1360
American Congress, First Pan- (October,
    1889-Apr., 1890) 1695
American Dictionary of English, Webster
    Publishes the First (Nov., 1828) 418
American Era of "Old" Immigration (1840's-
    1850's) 631
American Federation of Labor Is Founded
    (Dec. 8, 1886) 1652
American Fur Company Is Chartered (Apr. 6,
    1808) 119
American Library Association Is Founded
    (Oct. 4-6, 1876) 1467
American Literature, Irving's Sketch Book
    Transforms (1819-1820) 288
American Literature Flourishes, Brahmin
    School of (1880's) 1520
American Migration Begins, Westward
    (c. 1815-1830) 221
American Renaissance in Literature
    (c. 1830's-1860's) 435
American Southwest, Pike Explores the
    (July 15, 1806-July 1, 1807) 90
American War, Spanish- (Apr. 24-Dec. 10,
    1898) 1903
American West, Frémont Explores the
    (May, 1842-1854) 660
American West, Powell Publishes His Report
    on the (1879) 1504
American Whig Party, Clay Begins (Apr. 14,
    1834) 551

America's "New" Immigration Era Begins
(1892) 1730

America's Cup Race, *America* Wins the First
(Aug. 22, 1851) 846

Amerika Shipping Line Begins, Hamburg-
(1847) 740

Amistad Slave Revolt (July 2, 1839) 622

Ampère Reveals Magnetism's Relationship to
Electricity (Nov. 6, 1820) 334

Amsterdam, First Birth Control Clinic Opens
in (1882) 1542

Analysis of Logic, Boole Publishes *The*
Mathematical (1847) 737

Ancient Troy, Schliemann Excavates (Apr.,
1870-1873) 1321

Andersen Publishes His First Fairy Tales
(May 8, 1835) 570

Andrew Johnson, Impeachment of (Feb. 24-
May 26, 1868) 1245

Anesthesia Is Demonstrated, Safe Surgical
(Oct. 16, 1846) 735

Anglo-Sikh War, Second (Apr., 1848-Mar.,
1849) 779

Announces Closing of the Frontier, U.S.
Census Bureau (1890) 1705

Announces His Discovery of the Tuberculosis
Bacillus, Koch (Mar. 24, 1882) 1550

Antarctic, Europeans Explore the (1820-
early 1840's) 317

Anthony Is Tried for Voting (June 17-18,
1873) 1404

Anti-Irish Riots Erupt in Philadelphia
(May 6-July 5, 1844) 681

Anti-Japanese Yellow Peril Campaign Begins
(May 4, 1892) 1742

Antiobscenity Law, Congress Passes the
Comstock (Mar. 3, 1873) 1394

Antiquities, Stephens Begins Uncovering
Mayan (Nov., 1839) 628

Antiseptic Procedures, Semmelweis Develops
(May, 1847) 745

Antiseptic Surgery, Lister Publishes His
Theory on (1867) 1204

Anti-Slavery Society Is Founded, American
(Dec., 1833) 542

Anti-Socialist Law, Germany Passes (Oct. 19,
1878) 1499

Antitoxin, Behring Discovers the Diphtheria
(Dec. 11, 1890) 1715

Antitrust Act, Harrison Signs the Sherman
(July 20, 1890) 1712

Apache and Navajo War (Apr. 30, 1860-
1865) 1005

Apache Wars (Feb. 6, 1861-Sept. 4, 1886) 1019

Appears on U.S. Coins, "In God We Trust"
(Apr. 22, 1864) 1119

Appears to Bernadette Soubirous, Virgin Mary
(Feb. 11-July 16, 1858) 958

Appomattox and Assassination of Lincoln,
Surrender at (Apr. 9 and 14, 1865) 1146

Appropriation Act, Grant Signs Indian (Mar. 3,
1871) 1355

Arabia, Exploration of (1814-1879) 199

Arabic Literary Renaissance (19th cent.) 1

Arc Lamp, Davy Develops the (c. 1801-1810) . . . 11

Archaeopteryx Lithographica Is Discovered
(1861) 1014

Arguments, Southerners Advance Proslavery
(c. 1830-1865) 442

Arises, Aesthetic Movement (1870's) 1310

Arises, China's Self-Strengthening Movement
(1860's) 995

Arises in New England, Transcendental
Movement (1836) 581

Armenians, Ottomans Attempt to Exterminate
(1894-1896) 1773

Army, Booth Establishes the Salvation (July,
1865) 1155

Army Besieges Paris, Prussian (Sept. 20, 1870-
Jan. 28, 1871) 1331

Arnold Reforms Rugby School (1828-1842) . . . 406

Aroostook War (1838-1839) 600

Art Movement, Courbet Establishes Realist
(1855) 911

Art Opens, Metropolitan Museum of (Feb. 20,
1872) 1372

Art Theater Is Founded, Moscow (Oct. 14,
1898) 1910

Arthur," Tennyson Publishes "Morte d'
(1842) 655

Arthur Signs the Chinese Exclusion Act
(May 9, 1882) 1558

Articulates "Open Door" Policy Toward China,
Hay (Sept. 6, 1899-July 3, 1900) 1928

Articulates the Monroe Doctrine, President
Monroe (Dec. 2, 1823) 361

Articulation of Quantum Theory (Dec. 14,
1900) 1980

Artificial Fertilizers, Liebig Advocates
(1840). 638

Arts and Crafts Movement, New Guilds
Promote the (1884) 1597

Ashanti War, Second British- (Jan. 22, 1873-
Feb. 13, 1874). 1389

Ashburton Treaty Settles Maine's Canadian
Border, Webster- (Aug. 9, 1842) 666

Asia, Przhevalsky Explores Central
(1871-1885). 1346

"Aspirin" Is Registered as a Trade Name
(Jan. 23, 1897). 1875

Assassination of Lincoln, Surrender at
Appomattox and (Apr. 9 and 14, 1865) 1146

Assassinations, London's Cato Street
Conspirators Plot (Feb. 23, 1820) 323

Association Forms, San Francisco's Chinese
Six Companies (Nov. 12, 1882). 1569

Association Is Founded, American Library
(Oct. 4-6, 1876) 1467

Associations Begin Forming, Woman Suffrage
(May, 1869) 1290

Associations Unite, Women's Rights (Feb. 17-
18, 1890) 1709

Assyrian Ruins, Layard Explores and Excavates
(1839-1847). 619

Asteroid Is Discovered, First (Jan. 1, 1801). 17

Astorian Expeditions Explore the Pacific
Northwest Coast (Sept. 8, 1810-
May, 1812) 134

At the Moulin Rouge, Toulouse-Lautrec Paints
(1892-1895) 1734

Atlanta Compromise Speech, Washington's
(Sept. 18, 1895) 1811

Atlantic, Savannah Is the First Steamship to
Cross the (May 22-June 20, 1819) 303

Atomic Theory of Matter, Dalton Formulates
the (1803-1808) 43

Attempt to Exterminate Armenians, Ottomans
(1894-1896). 1773

Attempts to Reach the North Pole, Nansen
(1893-1896). 1754

Ausgleich, Austrian (May 29, 1867) 1216

Austerlitz, Battle of (Dec. 2, 1805) 86

Australia, Flinders Explores (Dec. 6, 1801-
Aug., 1803) 26

Australia, Is Founded, Melbourne, (Aug. 16,
1835) 573

Australia, Last Convicts Land in Western
(1868) 1238

Austria and Prussia's Seven Weeks' War
(June 15-Aug. 23, 1866). 1190

Austrian Ausgleich (May 29, 1867) 1216

Automatic Dial Telephone System, Strowger
Patents (Mar. 11, 1891) 1724

Automobile, Benz Patents the First Practical
(Jan. 29, 1886). 1640

Babbage Designs a Mechanical Calculator
(1819-1833). 291

Bacillus, Koch Announces His Discovery of
the Tuberculosis (Mar. 24, 1882) 1550

Baháʾiism Takes Form (1863) 1078

Bakunin Founds the Social Democratic
Alliance (1868) 1235

Balaklava, Battle of (Oct. 25, 1854) 900

Ballet's Golden Age, La Sylphide Inaugurates
Romantic (Mar. 12, 1832) 511

Baltimore and Ohio Railroad Opens (Jan. 7,
1830) 447

Bank Acts, Congress Passes the National
(Feb. 25, 1863-June 3, 1864) 1093

Bank of the United States, Jackson Vetoes
Rechartering of the (July 10, 1832) 518

Bank of the United States Is Chartered, Second
(Apr., 1816). 255

Bans Importation of African Slaves, Congress
(Mar. 2, 1807) 103

Barbed Wire, Glidden Patents (Nov. 24,
1874) 1416

Barber of Seville Debuts, Rossini's The
(Feb. 20, 1816) 252

Barbizon School of Landscape Painting
Flourishes (c. 1830-1870) 445

Barcelona's Templo Expiatorio de la Sagrada
Família, Gaudí Begins (Nov. 3, 1883) 1592

Barnum Creates the First Modern American
Circus (Apr. 10, 1871) 1360

Baseball Begins, Modern (c. 1845) 693

Baseball's First Professional Club Forms
(1869) 1276

Basin, Exploration of Africa's Congo (1873-
1880) 1382

Basketball, Naismith Invents (1891) 1721

Basuto War (1865-1868) 1141

Battle of Austerlitz (Dec. 2, 1805). 86

Battle of Balaklava (Oct. 25, 1854) 900

Battle of Borodino (Sept. 7, 1812) 176

Battle of Bull Run, First (July 21, 1861) 1045

Battle of Chapultepec (Sept. 12-13, 1847) 751

Battle of Königgrätz (July 3, 1866) 1193
Battle of Leipzig (Oct. 16-19, 1813) 191
Battle of New Orleans (Jan. 8, 1815) 227
Battle of Palo Alto (May 8, 1846) 707
Battle of Salamanca (July 22, 1812) 173
Battle of Sedan (Sept. 1, 1870) 1328
Battle of Solferino (June 24, 1859) 976
Battle of Tel el Kebir (Sept. 13, 1882) 1566
Battle of the Little Bighorn (June 25, 1876) . . . 1454
Battle of the *Monitor* and the *Virginia*
 (Mar. 9, 1862) 1061
Battle of the Thames (Oct. 5, 1813) 188
Battle of Tippecanoe (Nov. 7, 1811) 157
Battle of Trafalgar (Oct. 21, 1805) 83
Battle of Waterloo (June 18, 1815) 243
Battles of Gettysburg, Vicksburg, and
 Chattanooga (July 1-Nov. 25, 1863) 1102
Battles of Isandlwana and Rorke's Drift
 (Jan. 22-23, 1879) 1507
Bay Rebellion, Morant (Oct. 7-12, 1865) 1161
Beethoven's *Eroica* Symphony Introduces the
 Romantic Age (Apr. 7, 1805) 78
Beethoven's Ninth Symphony, First
 Performance of (May 7, 1824) 380
Begin Forming, Woman Suffrage Associations
 (May, 1869) 1290
Begin Immigrating to California, Chinese
 (1849) 793
Begin Migration to Utah, Mormons (Feb. 4,
 1846) 703
Begin Modernization of Korean Government,
 Kabo Reforms (July 8, 1894-Jan. 1,
 1896) 1782
Begin Ravaging Easter Island, Slave Traders
 (Nov., 1862) 1076
Begin Settling Western Canada, Immigrant
 Farmers (1896) 1831
Begins, America's "New" Immigration Era
 (1892) 1730
Begins, Anti-Japanese Yellow Peril Campaign
 (May 4, 1892) 1742
Begins, California Gold Rush (Jan. 24, 1848) . . 763
Begins, Clipper Ship Era (c. 1845) 690
Begins, Commercial Oil Drilling (Aug. 27,
 1859) 985
Begins, Fraser River Gold Rush (Mar. 23,
 1858) 960
Begins, Golden Age of Flamenco (c. 1869) . . . 1282
Begins, Hamburg-Amerika Shipping Line
 (1847) 740

Begins, Klondike Gold Rush (Aug. 17,
 1896) 1857
Begins, Modern Baseball (c. 1845) 693
Begins, Naturalist Movement (c. 1865) 1138
Begins, Oxford Movement (July 14,
 1833) 530
Begins, Panic of 1837 (Mar. 17, 1837) 591
Begins, Pre-Raphaelite Brotherhood (Fall,
 1848) 790
Begins, Scramble for Chinese Concessions
 (Nov. 14, 1897) 1888
Begins, Second Riel Rebellion (Mar. 19,
 1885) 1633
Begins, South Africa's Great Trek (1835) 563
Begins, Westward American Migration
 (c. 1815-1830) 221
Begins American Whig Party, Clay (Apr. 14,
 1834) 551
Begins Barcelona's Templo Expiatorio de la
 Sagrada Família, Gaudí (Nov. 3, 1883) 1592
Begins Colonizing Tasmania, Great Britain
 (Sept. 7, 1803) 55
Begins Developing Germ Theory and
 Microbiology, Pasteur (1857) 933
Begins London Exile, Mazzini (Jan. 12,
 1837) 589
Begins Publication, *Cherokee Phoenix*
 (Feb. 21, 1828) 408
Begins Publishing *The Liberator*, Garrison
 (Jan. 1, 1831) 487
Begins Trigonometrical Survey of India,
 Lambton (Apr. 10, 1802) 40
Begins Uncovering Mayan Antiquities,
 Stephens (Nov., 1839) 628
Begins Violent Eruption, Tambora Volcano
 (Apr. 5, 1815) 234
Behring Discovers the Diphtheria Antitoxin
 (Dec. 11, 1890) 1715
Beijerinck Discovers Viruses (1898) 1892
Belgian Revolution (Aug. 25, 1830-May 21,
 1833) 474
Bell Demonstrates the Telephone (June 25,
 1876) 1457
Benz Patents the First Practical Automobile
 (Jan. 29, 1886) 1640
Bequeaths Funds for the Nobel Prizes, Nobel
 (Nov. 27, 1895) 1817
Berlin, Congress of (June 13-July 13,
 1878) 1492

Berlin Conference Lays Groundwork for the
Partition of Africa (Nov. 15, 1884-Feb. 26,
1885) 1619

Bernadette Soubirous, Virgin Mary Appears to
(Feb. 11-July 16, 1858). 958

Besieges Paris, Prussian Army (Sept. 20, 1870-
Jan. 28, 1871) 1331

Bessemer Patents Improved Steel-Processing
Method (1855) 909

Bible and Tract Society Is Founded, Watch
Tower (1870-1871) 1316

Bible Society Is Founded, American (May 8,
1816) 260

Bible Society Is Founded, British and Foreign
(1804) 57

Biedermeier Furniture Style Becomes Popular
(c. 1815-1848) 225

Bighorn, Battle of the Little (June 25, 1876) . . . 1454

Bill, Indian Legislative Council Enacts the
Ilbert (Jan. 25, 1884) 1606

Biogeography, Wallace's Expeditions Give
Rise to (1854-1862) 885

Birth Control Clinic Opens in Amsterdam,
First (1882) 1542

Birth of the Ku Klux Klan (1866). 1169

Birth of the Penny Press (Sept. 3, 1833) 536

Birth of the People's Party (July 4-5, 1892) . . . 1745

Birth of the Republican Party (July 6, 1854). . . . 894

Bismarck Becomes Prussia's Minister-
President (Sept. 24, 1862). 1073

Bismarck Introduces Social Security Programs
in Germany (1881-1889) 1534

Bizet's Carmen Premieres in Paris (Mar. 3,
1875) 1420

Bjerknes Founds Scientific Weather
Forecasting (July, 1897-July, 1904). 1877

Black Code, Mississippi Enacts First Post-
Civil War (Nov. 24, 1865) 1164

Black Codes, Ohio Enacts the First (Jan.,
1804). 62

Black Voters, Mississippi Constitution
Disfranchises (1890) 1702

Blair Patents His First Seed Planter (Oct. 14,
1834) 557

Blanc Publishes The Organization of Labour
(1839). 610

Bleak House, Dickens Publishes (Mar., 1852-
Sept., 1853). 855

Bleeding Kansas (May, 1856-Aug., 1858). 919

Bloody Island Massacre, California's (May 6,
1850) 820

Boer War, First (Dec. 16, 1880-Mar. 6,
1881) 1531

Bolívar's Military Campaigns (Mar., 1813-
Dec. 9, 1824) 181

Bonaparte Becomes Emperor of France,
Louis Napoleon (Dec. 2, 1852). 861

Bonaparte Is Crowned Napoleon I (Dec. 2,
1804) 72

Boole Publishes The Mathematical Analysis
of Logic (1847) 737

Booth Establishes the Salvation Army (July,
1865). 1155

Border, Gadsden Purchase Completes the
U.S.-Mexican (Dec. 31, 1853) 882

Border, Webster-Ashburton Treaty Settles
Maine's Canadian (Aug. 9, 1842) 666

Borodino, Battle of (Sept. 7, 1812). 176

Boulanger Crisis, French Right Wing Revives
During (Jan., 1886-1889) 1638

Bourbon Dynasty Is Restored, France's
(Apr. 11, 1814-July 29, 1830) 210

Bowdler Publishes The Family Shakespeare
(1807) 93

Boxer Rebellion (May, 1900-Sept. 7, 1901) . . . 1961

"Boycott," Irish Tenant Farmers Stage First
(Sept.-Nov., 1880). 1528

Brahmin School of American Literature
Flourishes (1880's) 1520

Brake, Westinghouse Patents His Air (Apr.,
1869) 1287

Brazil Becomes Independent (Sept. 7, 1822) . . . 348

Brethren, First Meetings of the Plymouth
(c. 1826-1827) 398

Bridge Opens, Brooklyn (May 24, 1883) 1580

Britain, Fashoda Incident Pits France vs.
(July 10-Nov. 3, 1898) 1908

Britain, Gladstone Becomes Prime Minister of
(Dec. 3, 1868-Feb. 20, 1874) 1274

Britain, Treaty of Washington Settles U.S.
Claims vs. (May 8, 1871) 1363

Britain Acquires the Cape Colony (Aug. 13,
1814) 213

Britain Adopts Gas Lighting (1802). 29

Britain Begins Colonizing Tasmania, Great
(Sept. 7, 1803) 55

Britain Establishes Penny Postage, Great
(Jan. 10, 1840) 641

Britain Occupies the Falkland Islands, Great
(Jan., 1833) 527

Britain Strengthens Its Royal Navy, Great
(1889). 1680

Britain Withdraws from the Concert of Europe,
Great (Oct. 20-30, 1822) 350

Britain's First Trades Union Congress Forms,
Great (June 2, 1868). 1255

British Abolish Suttee in India (Dec. 4, 1829) . . . 428

British-Ashanti War, Second (Jan. 22, 1873-
Feb. 13, 1874) 1389

British Canada, Rebellions Rock (Oct. 23-
Dec. 16, 1837) 595

British Empire, Slavery Is Abolished
Throughout the (Aug. 28, 1833) 533

British Expedition to Ethiopia (Apr., 1868) . . . 1250

British Houses of Parliament Are Rebuilt
(Apr. 27, 1840-Feb., 1852) 643

British Labour Party Is Formed (Feb. 27,
1900) 1954

British North America Act (July 1, 1867) 1219

British Parliament, Rothschild Is First Jewish
Member of (July 26, 1858) 966

British Parliament Passes Municipal
Corporations Act (Sept. 9, 1835) 575

British Parliament Passes New Poor Law
(Aug. 14, 1834) 554

British Parliament Passes the Factory Act
(1833). 525

British Parliament Passes the Franchise Act
of 1884 (Dec. 6, 1884) 1627

British Parliament Passes the Matrimonial
Causes Act (Aug. 28, 1857) 952

British Parliament Passes the Reform Act of
1832 (June 4, 1832). 514

British Parliament Passes the Reform Act of
1867 (Aug., 1867). 1222

British Parliament Passes the Six Acts
(Dec. 11-30, 1819) 305

British Parliament Repeals the Combination
Acts (1824) 365

British Parliament Repeals the Corn Laws
(June 15, 1846) 715

British Politics, Irish Home Rule Debate
Dominates (June, 1886-Sept. 9, 1893) 1645

British Subdue African Resistance in Rhodesia
(October, 1893-October, 1897) 1763

Brooklyn Bridge Opens (May 24, 1883) 1580

Brooks Brothers Introduces Button-Down
Shirts (1896). 1828

Brotherhood Begins, Pre-Raphaelite (Fall,
1848) 790

Brothers Grimm Publish Fairy Tales (1812-
1815) 160

Brothers Introduces Button-Down Shirts,
Brooks (1896) 1828

Brownie Cameras, Kodak Introduces
(Feb., 1900). 1950

Brown's Raid on Harpers Ferry (Oct. 16-18,
1859) 988

Brunel Launches the SS *Great Eastern*
(Jan. 31, 1858) 955

Buckland Presents the First Public Dinosaur
Description (Feb. 20, 1824) 374

Buffalo Slaughter, Great American
(c. 1871-1883). 1343

Building Opens, New Library of Congress
(Nov. 1, 1897) 1886

Built, First U.S. Petroleum Refinery Is
(1850) 807

Built, World's First Skyscraper Is
(1883-1885) 1575

Bulgarian Revolt Against the Ottoman Empire
(May, 1876) 1445

Bull Run, First Battle of (July 21, 1861) 1045

Burckhardt Discovers Egypt's Abu Simbel
(Mar. 22, 1812) 163

Bureau, Congress Creates the Freedmen's
(Mar. 3, 1865) 1143

Bureau Announces Closing of the Frontier,
U.S. Census (1890) 1705

Burlesque and Vaudeville, Rise of (1850's-
1880's) 803

Burlingame Treaty (July 28, 1868) 1264

Burr's Conspiracy (Mar., 1805-Sept. 1, 1807) . . . 75

Burton Enters Mecca in Disguise (Sept. 12,
1853) 873

Business, Ward Launches a Mail-Order
(Aug., 1872) 1378

Button-Down Shirts, Brooks Brothers
Introduces (1896) 1828

Cabin, Stowe Publishes *Uncle Tom's* (1852) . . . 852

Cable Is Completed, First Transatlantic
(July 27, 1866). 1196

Calculator, Babbage Designs a Mechanical
(1819-1833). 291

California, Chinese Begin Immigrating to
(1849) 793

California and the Southwest, United States Occupies (June 30, 1846-Jan. 13, 1847) 722

California Gold Rush Begins (Jan. 24, 1848) . . . 763

Californians Form Native Sons of the Golden State, Chinese (May 10, 1895) 1806

California's Bloody Island Massacre (May 6, 1850) 820

Calligraphy Emerges, China's Stele School of (1820's) 307

Cameras, Kodak Introduces Brownie (Feb., 1900) 1950

Campaign Begins, Anti-Japanese Yellow Peril (May 4, 1892) 1742

Campaigns, Bolívar's Military (Mar., 1813-Dec. 9, 1824) 181

Campaigns, San Martín's Military (Jan. 18, 1817-July 28, 1821) 273

Canada, Immigrant Farmers Begin Settling Western (1896) 1831

Canada, Irish Immigration to (1829-1836). 423

Canada, Rebellions Rock British (Oct. 23-Dec. 16, 1837) 595

Canada, Ukrainian Mennonites Begin Settling in (1873). 1380

Canada Forms the North-West Mounted Police (May 23, 1873) 1401

Canada Is Established, Supreme Court of (1875) 1418

Canada Is Founded, National Council of Women of (Oct. 27, 1893) 1768

Canada Unite, Upper and Lower (Feb. 10, 1841) 650

Canada's Grand Trunk Railway Is Incorporated (Nov. 10, 1852). 858

Canada's Indian Act (1876). 1437

Canada's Mackenzie Era (Nov. 5, 1873-Oct. 9, 1878). 1407

Canada's Prime Minister, Macdonald Returns as (Sept., 1878) 1496

Canada's Responsible Government, First Test of (Apr. 25, 1849) 797

Canadian Border, Webster-Ashburton Treaty Settles Maine's (Aug. 9, 1842) 666

Canadian Prime Minister, Laurier Becomes the First French (July 11, 1896). 1854

Canadian Settlement, Dominion Lands Act Fosters (1872). 1369

Canal Opens, Erie (Oct. 26, 1825) 391

Canal Opens, Germany's Kiel (June 20, 1895) 1808

Canal Opens, Suez (Nov. 17, 1869) 1301

Cape Colony, Britain Acquires the (Aug. 13, 1814) 213

Carlist Wars Unsettle Spain (Sept. 29, 1833-1849) 539

Carlyle Publishes *Past and Present* (1843) 669

Carmen Premieres in Paris, Bizet's (Mar. 3, 1875) 1420

Carolinas, Sherman Marches Through Georgia and the (Nov. 15, 1864-Apr. 18, 1865) 1127

Carrie, Dreiser Publishes *Sister* (Nov. 8, 1900) 1976

Cart War, Texas's (August-Dec., 1857) 950

Cases, Cherokee (Mar. 18, 1831, and Mar. 3, 1832) 491

Cases, Civil Rights (Oct. 15, 1883). 1586

Catholic, Newman Becomes a Roman (Oct. 9, 1845) 700

Catholic Church in Germany, Kulturkampf Against the (1871-1877) 1340

Catholic Emancipation, Roman (May 9, 1828-Apr. 13, 1829) 414

Cato Street Conspirators Plot Assassinations, London's (Feb. 23, 1820). 323

Cell Theory, Schwann and Virchow Develop (1838-1839). 602

Cellular Theory of Immunity, Metchnikoff Advances the (1882-1901) 1545

Celluloid Film, Goodwin Develops (May, 1887) 1663

Census Bureau Announces Closing of the Frontier, U.S. (1890) 1705

Centennial Exposition, Philadelphia Hosts the (May 10-Nov. 10, 1876). 1451

Central Asia, Przhevalsky Explores (1871-1885) 1346

Cereal Industry, Kellogg's Corn Flakes Launch the Dry (1894-1895) 1770

Champlain and St. Lawrence Railroad Opens (July 21, 1836) 587

Chapultepec, Battle of (Sept. 12-13, 1847) 751

Charles X, July Revolution Deposes (July 29, 1830) 470

Charter Oath, Promulgation of Japan's (Apr. 6, 1868) 1253

Chartered, American Fur Company Is (Apr. 6, 1808). 119

Chartered, Second Bank of the United States Is (Apr., 1816). 255

Chartist Movement (May 8, 1838-
    Apr. 10, 1848) 605
Chattanooga, Battles of Gettysburg, Vicksburg,
    and (July 1-Nov. 25, 1863) 1102
Cherokee Cases (Mar. 18, 1831, and Mar. 3,
    1832) 491
Cherokee Phoenix Begins Publication
    (Feb. 21, 1828) 408
Chicago Fire, Great (Oct. 8-10, 1871) 1366
Chicago World's Fair (May 1-
    Oct. 30, 1893) 1757
Chicago's Hull-House, Addams Opens
    (Sept. 18, 1889) 1692
Children Opens, New York Infirmary for
    Indigent Women and (May 12, 1857) 947
China, Hay Articulates "Open Door" Policy
    Toward (Sept. 6, 1899-July 3, 1900) 1928
China, Muslim Rebellions in (Winter, 1855-
    Jan. 2, 1878) 917
China's Self-Strengthening Movement Arises
    (1860's) 995
China's Stele School of Calligraphy Emerges
    (1820's) 307
China's Taiping Rebellion (Jan. 11, 1851-
    late summer, 1864) 836
Chinese Begin Immigrating to California
    (1849) 793
Chinese Californians Form Native Sons of
    the Golden State (May 10, 1895) 1806
Chinese Concessions Begins, Scramble for
    (Nov. 14, 1897) 1888
Chinese Exclusion Act, Arthur Signs the
    (May 9, 1882) 1558
Chinese Six Companies Association Forms,
    San Francisco's (Nov. 12, 1882) 1569
Chisholm Trail Opens (1867) 1201
Christian Science Movement, Eddy
    Establishes the (Oct. 30, 1875) 1431
Church, Smith Founds the Mormon (Apr. 6,
    1830) 457
Church in Germany, Kulturkampf Against the
    Catholic (1871-1877) 1340
Church Is Founded, African Methodist
    Episcopal (Apr. 9, 1816) 257
Church Is Founded, Unitarian (May, 1819) 299
Circulation War, Hearst-Pulitzer (1895-
    1898) 1794
Circus, Barnum Creates the First Modern
    American (Apr. 10, 1871) 1360
Civil Rights Act of 1866 (Apr. 9, 1866) 1175

Civil Rights Cases (Oct. 15, 1883) 1586
Civil Service, Pendleton Act Reforms the
    Federal (Jan. 16, 1883) 1577
Civil War, Díaz Drives Mexico into (1871-
    1876) 1338
Civil War, U.S. (Apr. 12, 1861-Apr. 9,
    1865) 1036
Civil War Black Code, Mississippi Enacts
    First Post- (Nov. 24, 1865) 1164
Civilization, Evans Discovers Crete's Minoan
    (Mar. 23, 1900) 1956
Cixi's Coup Preserves Qing Dynasty Power
    (Nov. 1-2, 1861) 1055
Claims vs. Britain, Treaty of Washington
    Settles U.S. (May 8, 1871) 1363
Clark Expedition, Lewis and (May 14, 1804-
    Sept. 23, 1806) 65
Clausius Formulates the Second Law of
    Thermodynamics (1850-1865) 813
Clay Begins American Whig Party (Apr. 14,
    1834) 551
Clermont, Maiden Voyage of the (Aug. 17,
    1807) 111
Clinic Opens in Amsterdam, First Birth
    Control (1882) 1542
Clipper Ship Era Begins (c. 1845) 690
Closing of the Frontier, U.S. Census Bureau
    Announces (1890) 1705
Club Forms, Baseball's First Professional
    (1869) 1276
Coast, Astorian Expeditions Explore the
    Pacific Northwest (Sept. 8, 1810-
    May, 1812) 134
Cobbett Founds the *Political Register*
    (Jan., 1802) 32
Coca-Cola, Pemberton Introduces (May 8,
    1886) 1643
Cockney School, Rise of the (Dec., 1816) 263
Code, Mississippi Enacts First Post-Civil
    War Black (Nov. 24, 1865) 1164
Codes, Ohio Enacts the First Black
    (Jan., 1804) 62
Coins, "In God We Trust" Appears on U.S.
    (Apr. 22, 1864) 1119
College Opens, Oberlin (Dec. 3, 1833) 546
College Opens, Vassar (Sept. 26, 1865) 1158
Colonizing Tasmania, Great Britain Begins
    (Sept. 7, 1803) 55
Colored People Is Founded, National Council
    of (July 6, 1853) 870

Colt Patents the Revolver (Feb. 25, 1836) 584

Combination Acts, British Parliament Repeals the (1824) 365

Commerce Act, Interstate (Feb. 4, 1887) 1655

Commercial Oil Drilling Begins (Aug. 27, 1859) 985

Commercial Projection of Motion Pictures, First (Dec. 28, 1895) 1820

Commonwealth v. Hunt (Mar., 1842) 658

Commune, Paris (Mar. 18-May 28, 1871) 1358

Communist Manifesto, Marx and Engels Publish *The* (Feb., 1848) 767

Communitarian Experiments at New Harmony (Spring, 1814-1830) 206

Company Is Chartered, American Fur (Apr. 6, 1808) 119

Company Is Incorporated, Standard Oil (Jan. 10, 1870). 1318

Completed, First Transatlantic Cable Is (July 27, 1866). 1196

Completed, First Transcontinental Railroad Is (May 10, 1869) 1293

Completed, Transcontinental Telegraph Is (Oct. 24, 1861) 1048

Completes the First Flying Dirigible, Zeppelin (July 2, 1900) 1969

Completes *The Tokaido Fifty-Three Stations*, Hiroshige (1831-1834) 484

Completes the U.S.-Mexican Border, Gadsden Purchase (Dec. 31, 1853) 882

Compromise, Missouri (Mar. 3, 1820). 325

Compromise of 1850 (Jan. 29-Sept. 20, 1850). . . 816

Compromise Speech, Washington's Atlanta (Sept. 18, 1895) 1811

Comstock Antiobscenity Law, Congress Passes the (Mar. 3, 1873) 1394

Comte Advances His Theory of Positivism (1851-1854). 833

Conan Doyle Introduces Sherlock Holmes (Dec., 1887) 1666

Concert of Europe, Great Britain Withdraws from the (Oct. 20-30, 1822) 350

Concessions Begins, Scramble for Chinese (Nov. 14, 1897) 1888

Concessions to Irish Nationalists, Kilmainham Treaty Makes (May 2, 1882) 1556

Confederate General to Surrender, Watie Is Last (June 23, 1865). 1153

Confederate States of America, Establishment of the (Feb. 8, 1861). 1022

Confederation Is Formed, North German (1866-1867) 1173

Confederation Is Formed, Swiss (Sept. 12, 1848) 787

Conference, First Hague Peace (May 18-July, 1899) 1926

Conference Lays Groundwork for the Partition of Africa, Berlin (Nov. 15, 1884-Feb. 26, 1885). 1619

Confronts the Nian Rebellion, Qing Dynasty (1853-1868). 864

Congo Basin, Exploration of Africa's (1873-1880) 1382

Congress, First Pan-American (October, 1889-Apr., 1890) 1695

Congress Bans Importation of African Slaves (Mar. 2, 1807) 103

Congress Building Opens, New Library of (Nov. 1, 1897). 1886

Congress Creates the Freedmen's Bureau (Mar. 3, 1865) 1143

Congress Enacts the Page Law (Mar. 3, 1875) 1423

Congress Is Founded, Indian National (1885) 1630

Congress of Berlin (June 13-July 13, 1878) . . . 1492

Congress of Vienna (Sept. 15, 1814-June 11, 1815) 216

Congress Passes Dingley Tariff Act (July 24, 1897) 1880

Congress Passes Indian Removal Act (May 28, 1830) 460

Congress Passes Land Act of 1820 (Apr. 24, 1820) 328

Congress Passes Preemption Act of 1841 (Sept. 4, 1841) 653

Congress Passes the Comstock Antiobscenity Law (Mar. 3, 1873) 1394

Congress Passes the Kansas-Nebraska Act (May 30, 1854) 891

Congress Passes the National Bank Acts (Feb. 25, 1863-June 3, 1864) 1093

Conquers Algeria, France (June 14-July 5, 1830) 464

Conspiracy, Burr's (Mar., 1805-Sept. 1, 1807) . . . 75

Conspirators Plot Assassinations, London's Cato Street (Feb. 23, 1820). 323

Constitution, Japan Adopts a New (Feb. 11, 1889) 1683

Constitution Disfranchises Black Voters,
Mississippi (1890). 1702
Constitution of 1876, Spanish (1876). 1440
Construction of the National Road
(1811-1840). 146
Controversy, Nullification (Nov. 24, 1832-
Jan. 21, 1833). 521
Convention, Akron Woman's Rights
(May 28-29, 1851) 843
Convention, Hartford (Dec. 15, 1814-
Jan. 5, 1815) 219
Convention, Seneca Falls (July 19-20,
1848) 784
Converts Magnetic Force into Electricity,
Faraday (October, 1831) 502
Convicts Land in Western Australia, Last
(1868) 1238
Corn Flakes Launch the Dry Cereal Industry,
Kellogg's (1894-1895) 1770
Corn Laws, British Parliament Repeals the
(June 15, 1846). 715
Coronation, Queen Victoria's (June 28,
1838) 608
Corporations Act, British Parliament Passes
Municipal (Sept. 9, 1835) 575
Costumbrismo Movement (c. 1820-1860) 320
Council Enacts the Ilbert Bill, Indian
Legislative (Jan. 25, 1884) 1606
Council of Colored People Is Founded,
National (July 6, 1853) 870
Council of Women of Canada Is Founded,
National (Oct. 27, 1893) 1768
Coup Preserves Qing Dynasty Power, Cixi's
(Nov. 1-2, 1861). 1055
Courbet Establishes Realist Art Movement
(1855). 911
Court of Canada Is Established, Supreme
(1875) 1418
Crafts Movement, New Guilds Promote the
Arts and (1884) 1597
Created, U.S. Department of Education Is
(Mar. 2, 1867). 1210
Creates the First Modern American Circus,
Barnum (Apr. 10, 1871). 1360
Creates the Freedmen's Bureau, Congress
(Mar. 3, 1865). 1143
Creek Massacre, Sand (Nov. 29, 1864). 1130
Creek Treaty, Medicine Lodge (Oct. 21,
1867) 1228
Creek War (July 27, 1813-Aug. 9, 1814) 185

Crete's Minoan Civilization, Evans Discovers
(Mar. 23, 1900) 1956
"Crime of 1873" (Feb. 12, 1873) 1392
Crimea, Nightingale Takes Charge of Nursing
in the (Nov. 4, 1854) 903
Crimean War (Oct. 4, 1853-Mar. 30, 1856) 876
Crisis, French Right Wing Revives During
Boulanger (Jan., 1886-1889) 1638
Cro-Magnon Remains, Lartet Discovers the
First (Mar., 1868) 1247
Cross the Atlantic, Savannah Is the First
Steamship to (May 22-June 20, 1819) 303
Crowned Napoleon I, Bonaparte Is
(Dec. 2, 1804) 72
Crushes Polish Rebellion, Russia (Jan. 22-
Sept., 1863) 1090
Cuban War of Independence (Feb. 24, 1895-
1898) 1802
Cuba's Ten Years' War (Oct. 10, 1868-
Feb. 10, 1878). 1269
Cup Race, America Wins the First America's
(Aug. 22, 1851). 846
Customs Union, German States Join to Form
(Jan. 1, 1834). 549
Cycle, First Performance of Wagner's Ring
(Aug. 13-17, 1876) 1464
Cylinder Phonograph, Edison Patents the
(Dec. 24, 1877) 1484

Daguerre and Niépce Invent Daguerreotype
Photography (1839). 613
Daguerreotype Photography, Daguerre and
Niépce Invent (1839) 613
Dahomey-French Wars (Nov., 1889-
Jan., 1894). 1697
Dalton Formulates the Atomic Theory of
Matter (1803-1808) 43
Dance, Joplin Popularizes Ragtime Music
and (1899). 1917
Danish-Prussian War (Feb. 1-Oct. 30, 1864) . . . 1117
Darlington Railway Opens, Stockton and
(September 27, 1825). 388
D'Arthur," Tennyson Publishes "Morte
(1842). 655
Darwin Publishes On the Origin of Species
(Nov. 24, 1859). 991
Darwin Publishes The Descent of Man
(1871) 1334
Darwinism, Spencer Introduces Principles of
Social (1862) 1058

Das Kapital, Marx Publishes (1867) 1207

Davy Develops the Arc Lamp (c. 1801-1810). . . . 11

Debate Dominates British Politics, Irish
Home Rule (June, 1886-Sept. 9, 1893) 1645

Debate Slavery and Westward Expansion,
Webster and Hayne (Jan. 19-27, 1830). 451

Debates, Lincoln-Douglas (June 16-Oct. 15,
1858) 963

Debussy's *Prelude to the Afternoon of a Faun*
Premieres (Dec. 22, 1894). 1791

Debuts, Rossini's *The Barber of Seville*
(Feb. 20, 1816) 252

Debuts, Wagner's *Flying Dutchman* (Jan. 2,
1843) 672

Decadent Movement Flourishes
(c. 1884-1924). 1600

Decembrist Revolt (Dec. 26, 1825) 395

Declaration of the Rights of Women (July 4,
1876) 1460

Decrees Papal Infallibility Dogma, Vatican I
(Dec. 8, 1869-Oct. 20, 1870) 1307

Decrees the Immaculate Conception Dogma,
Pius IX (Dec. 8, 1854) 906

Dedicated, Eiffel Tower Is (Mar. 31, 1889) . . . 1686

Dedicated, Statue of Liberty Is (Oct. 28,
1886) 1649

Defines "Eugenics," Galton (1883). 1572

Delacroix Paints *Liberty Leading the People*
(October-Dec., 1830). 476

Democratic Alliance, Bakunin Founds the
Social (1868) 1235

Democratic Labor Party Is Formed, Russian
Social- (Mar., 1898). 1895

Demonstrated, Safe Surgical Anesthesia Is
(Oct. 16, 1846) 735

Demonstrates the Incandescent Lamp, Edison
(Oct. 21, 1879) 1517

Demonstrates the Telephone, Bell (June 25,
1876) 1457

Department of Education Is Created, U.S.
(Mar. 2, 1867). 1210

Department Store Opens in Paris, First
Modern (1869) 1279

Deposes Charles X, July Revolution
(July 29, 1830) 470

Depot Opens, Ellis Island Immigration
(Jan. 1, 1892) 1737

Descent of Man, Darwin Publishes *The*
(1871) 1334

Description, Buckland Presents the First
Public Dinosaur (Feb. 20, 1824) 374

Design Firm, Morris Founds (1861) 1016

Designs a Mechanical Calculator, Babbage
(1819-1833). 291

Destroy Industrial Machines, Luddites
(Mar. 11, 1811-1816) 151

Develop Cell Theory, Schwann and Virchow
(1838-1839). 602

Developing Germ Theory and Microbiology,
Pasteur Begins (1857) 933

Development of Working-Class Libraries
(19th cent.) 3

Develops Antiseptic Procedures, Semmelweis
(May, 1847). 745

Develops Celluloid Film, Goodwin
(May, 1887) 1663

Develops New Integration Theory, Lebesgue
(1900) 1941

Develops Systematic History, Ranke (1824). . . . 371

Develops the Arc Lamp, Davy (c. 1801-1810) . . . 11

Develops the Periodic Table of Elements,
Mendeleyev (1869-1871) 1284

Develops the Theory of Mitosis, Roux
(1880's) 1523

Dial Telephone System, Strowger Patents
Automatic (Mar. 11, 1891) 1724

Diamondfields, Rhodes Amalgamates
Kimberley (Mar. 13, 1888) 1674

Díaz Drives Mexico into Civil War (1871-
1876) 1338

Dickens Publishes *Bleak House* (Mar., 1852-
Sept., 1853). 855

Dictionary of English, Webster Publishes
the First American (Nov., 1828) 418

Diesel Engine, Diesel Patents the (Feb.,
1892) 1740

Diesel Patents the Diesel Engine (Feb.,
1892) 1740

Dingley Tariff Act, Congress Passes
(July 24, 1897) 1880

Dinosaur Description, Buckland Presents
the First Public (Feb. 20, 1824). 374

Diphtheria Antitoxin, Behring Discovers
the (Dec. 11, 1890) 1715

Dirigible, Zeppelin Completes the First Flying
(July 2, 1900) 1969

Discovered, *Archaeopteryx Lithographica* Is
(1861) 1014

Discovered, First Asteroid Is (Jan. 1, 1801). . . . 17

Discovered, Stratosphere and Troposphere Are
(Apr., 1898-1903) 1900

Discovered in New South Wales, Gold Is
(1851) 828

Discovered in the Transvaal, Gold Is
(June 21, 1884) 1612

Discovers Crete's Minoan Civilization, Evans
(Mar. 23, 1900) 1956

Discovers Egypt's Abu Simbel, Burckhardt
(Mar. 22, 1812) 163

Discovers the Diphtheria Antitoxin, Behring
(Dec. 11, 1890) 1715

Discovers the First Cro-Magnon Remains,
Lartet (Mar., 1868) 1247

Discovers Viruses, Beijerinck (1898) 1892

Discovers X Rays, Röntgen (Nov. 9, 1895) . . . 1814

Discovery of the Tuberculosis Bacillus,
Koch Announces His (Mar. 24, 1882) 1550

Disfranchises Black Voters, Mississippi
Constitution (1890) 1702

Disguise, Burton Enters Mecca in (Sept. 12,
1853) 873

Docks at Mobile, Last Slave Ship
(July, 1859) 979

Doctrine, President Monroe Articulates the
Monroe (Dec. 2, 1823) 361

Dogma, Pius IX Decrees the Immaculate
Conception (Dec. 8, 1854) 906

Dogma, Vatican I Decrees Papal Infallibility
(Dec. 8, 1869-Oct. 20, 1870) 1307

Doll's House Introduces Modern Realistic
Drama, A (1879) 1501

Dolores, Hidalgo Issues El Grito de (Sept. 16,
1810) 138

Dominates British Politics, Irish Home Rule
Debate (June, 1886-Sept. 9, 1893) 1645

Dominion Lands Act Fosters Canadian
Settlement (1872) 1369

Dorr Rebellion, Rhode Island's (May 18,
1842) 664

Dos de Mayo Insurrection in Spain (May 2,
1808) 122

Dostoevski Is Exiled to Siberia (Dec., 1849) . . . 800

Douglas Debates, Lincoln- (June 16-Oct. 15,
1858) 963

Douglass Launches The North Star (Dec. 3,
1847) 753

Doyle Introduces Sherlock Holmes, Conan
(Dec., 1887) 1666

Draft Law, Union Enacts the First National
(Mar. 3, 1863) 1095

Drama, A Doll's House Introduces Modern
Realistic (1879) 1501

Dreams, Freud Publishes The Interpretation
of (1900) 1938

Dred Scott v. Sandford (Mar. 6, 1857) 938

Dreiser Publishes Sister Carrie (Nov. 8,
1900) 1976

Dreyfus Affair (October, 1894-July, 1906) 1788

Drilling Begins, Commercial Oil (Aug. 27,
1859) 985

Dry Cereal Industry, Kellogg's Corn Flakes
Launch the (1894-1895) 1770

Dunlop Patents the Pneumatic Tire
(Dec. 7, 1888) 1677

Dutchman Debuts, Wagner's Flying
(Jan. 2, 1843) 672

Dynamite, Nobel Patents (October, 1867) 1226

Dynasty, Greece Unifies Under the Glücksburg
(1863-1913) 1081

Dynasty Confronts the Nian Rebellion, Qing
(1853-1868) 864

Dynasty Is Restored, France's Bourbon
(Apr. 11, 1814-July 29, 1830) 210

Dynasty Power, Cixi's Coup Preserves Qing
(Nov. 1-2, 1861) 1055

East Africa, Exploration of (1848-1889) 756

Easter Island, Slave Traders Begin Ravaging
(Nov., 1862) 1076

Economic Principles, Ricardo Identifies
Seven Key (1817) 267

Economist, Wilson Launches The (Sept. 2,
1843) 678

Eddy Establishes the Christian Science
Movement (Oct. 30, 1875) 1431

Edison Demonstrates the Incandescent Lamp
(Oct. 21, 1879) 1517

Edison Patents the Cylinder Phonograph
(Dec. 24, 1877) 1484

Education Is Created, U.S. Department of
(Mar. 2, 1867) 1210

Egypt Fights the Wahhābīs (1811-1818) 143

Egyptian Wars, Turko- (1832-1841) 505

Egypt's Abu Simbel, Burckhardt Discovers
(Mar. 22, 1812) 163

Eiffel Tower Is Dedicated (Mar. 31, 1889) 1686

1812, War of (June 18, 1812-Dec. 24, 1814) . . . 166

1820, Congress Passes Land Act of (Apr. 24,
   1820) 328
1824, Paris Salon of (1824) 368
1824, U.S. Election of (Dec. 1, 1824-Feb. 9,
   1825) 383
1828, U.S. Election of (Dec. 3, 1828) 421
1832, British Parliament Passes the Reform Act
   of (June 4, 1832) 514
1837 Begins, Panic of (Mar. 17, 1837). 591
1840, U.S. Election of (Dec. 2, 1840) 646
1848, Italian Revolution of (Jan. 12, 1848-
   Aug. 28, 1849) 760
1848, Paris Revolution of (Feb. 22-June,
   1848) 773
1848, Prussian Revolution of (Mar. 3-Nov. 3,
   1848) 776
1850, Compromise of (Jan. 29-Sept. 20,
   1850) 816
1867, British Parliament Passes the Reform
   Act of (Aug., 1867) 1222
1868, Spanish Revolution of (Sept. 30,
   1868) 1266
1873," "Crime of (Feb. 12, 1873). 1392
1876, Spanish Constitution of (1876). 1440
1884, U.S. Election of (Nov. 4, 1884) 1615
El Grito de Dolores, Hidalgo Issues (Sept. 16,
   1810) 138
Elected President, McKinley Is (Nov. 3,
   1896) 1860
Elected U.S. President, Lincoln Is (Nov. 6,
   1860) 1010
Election of 1824, U.S. (Dec. 1, 1824-Feb. 9,
   1825) 383
Election of 1828, U.S. (Dec. 3, 1828) 421
Election of 1840, U.S. (Dec. 2, 1840) 646
Election of 1884, U.S. (Nov. 4, 1884) 1615
Electricity, Ampère Reveals Magnetism's
   Relationship to (Nov. 6, 1820) 334
Electricity, Faraday Converts Magnetic Force
   into (October, 1831) 502
Elects Jefferson President, House of
   Representatives (Feb. 17, 1801) 20
Elements, Mendeleyev Develops the Periodic
   Table of (1869-1871) 1284
Elevator, Otis Installs the First Passenger
   (Mar. 23, 1857). 942
Elgin Ships Parthenon Marbles to England
   (1803-1812) 46
Ellis Island Immigration Depot Opens
   (Jan. 1, 1892) 1737

Ellis Publishes Sexual Inversion (1897) 1867
Emancipation, Roman Catholic (May 9, 1828-
   Apr. 13, 1829) 414
Emancipation of Russian Serfs (Mar. 3,
   1861) 1026
Emancipation Proclamation, Lincoln Issues
   the (Jan. 1, 1863) 1084
Emergence of the Primitives (1801) 9
Emerges, China's Stele School of Calligraphy
   (1820's). 307
Emperor of France, Louis Napoleon Bonaparte
   Becomes (Dec. 2, 1852) 861
Emperors' League Is Formed, Three (May 6-
   Oct. 22, 1873) 1398
Empire, Bulgarian Revolt Against the Ottoman
   (May, 1876) 1445
Empire, German States Unite Within German
   (Jan. 18, 1871). 1349
Empire, Greeks Fight for Independence
   from the Ottoman (Mar. 7, 1821-
   Sept. 29, 1829) 336
Empire, Slavery Is Abolished Throughout the
   British (Aug. 28, 1833) 533
Enacts First Post-Civil War Black Code,
   Mississippi (Nov. 24, 1865). 1164
Enacts the First Black Codes, Ohio (Jan.,
   1804). 62
Enacts the First National Draft Law, Union
   (Mar. 3, 1863). 1095
Enacts the Ilbert Bill, Indian Legislative
   Council (Jan. 25, 1884). 1606
Enacts the Page Law, Congress (Mar. 3,
   1875) 1423
Encyclical on Labor, Papal (May 15, 1891) . . . 1727
Ends Mexican War, Treaty of Guadalupe
   Hidalgo (Feb. 2, 1848) 770
Engels Publish The Communist Manifesto,
   Marx and (Feb., 1848) 767
Engine, Diesel Patents the Diesel (Feb.,
   1892) 1740
Engine, Lenoir Patents the Internal Combustion
   (1860). 998
Engine, Otto Invents a Practical Internal
   Combustion (May, 1876) 1449
Engine, Trevithick Patents the High-Pressure
   Steam (Mar. 24, 1802). 38
England, Elgin Ships Parthenon Marbles to
   (1803-1812) 46
England's Poet Laureate, Tennyson Becomes
   (Nov. 5, 1850) 825

English, Webster Publishes the First American Dictionary of (Nov., 1828) 418

Enters Mecca in Disguise, Burton (Sept. 12, 1853) 873

Episcopal Church Is Founded, African Methodist (Apr. 9, 1816) 257

Era, Canada's Mackenzie (Nov. 5, 1873-Oct. 9, 1878) 1407

Era Begins, America's "New" Immigration (1892) 1730

Era Begins, Clipper Ship (c. 1845) 690

Era of "Old" Immigration, American (1840's-1850's) 631

Erie Canal Opens (Oct. 26, 1825) 391

Erodes Indian Tribal Unity, General Allotment Act (Feb. 8, 1887) 1657

Eroica Symphony Introduces the Romantic Age, Beethoven's (Apr. 7, 1805) 78

Errors, Pius IX Issues the Syllabus of (Dec. 8, 1864) 1133

Erupt in Philadelphia, Anti-Irish Riots (May 6-July 5, 1844) 681

Eruption, Tambora Volcano Begins Violent (Apr. 5, 1815) 234

Erupts, Krakatoa Volcano (Aug. 27, 1883) . . . 1583

Essen, Krupp Works Open at (Sept. 20, 1811) . . . 154

Established, Supreme Court of Canada Is (1875) 1418

Established, Third French Republic Is (Feb. 13, 1871-1875) 1353

Established, U.S. Military Academy Is (Mar. 16, 1802) 35

Establishes Malaria's Transmission Vector, Ross (Aug. 20, 1897) 1883

Establishes Penny Postage, Great Britain (Jan. 10, 1840) 641

Establishes Realist Art Movement, Courbet (1855) 911

Establishes the Christian Science Movement, Eddy (Oct. 30, 1875) 1431

Establishes the Salvation Army, Booth (July, 1865) 1155

Establishment of Independent U.S. Treasury (Aug. 1, 1846) 726

Establishment of the Confederate States of America (Feb. 8, 1861) 1022

Ethiopia, British Expedition to (Apr., 1868) 1250

Ethiopia Repels Italian Invasion (Mar. 1, 1896) 1842

"Eugenics," Galton Defines (1883) 1572

Europe, Great Britain Withdraws from the Concert of (Oct. 20-30, 1822) 350

Europeans Explore the Antarctic (1820-early 1840's) 317

Evans Discovers Crete's Minoan Civilization (Mar. 23, 1900) 1956

Examined, Strauss Publishes *The Life of Jesus Critically* (1835-1836) 566

Excavates Ancient Troy, Schliemann (Apr., 1870-1873) 1321

Excavates Assyrian Ruins, Layard Explores and (1839-1847) 619

Exclusion Act, Arthur Signs the Chinese (May 9, 1882) 1558

Exhibition, First Impressionist (Apr. 15, 1874) 1410

Exhibits *The Thinker*, Rodin (1888) 1669

Exile, Mazzini Begins London (Jan. 12, 1837) 589

Exiled to Siberia, Dostoevski Is (Dec., 1849) . . . 800

Expands into Korea, Japan (1870's) 1313

Expansion, Webster and Hayne Debate Slavery and Westward (Jan. 19-27, 1830) . . . 451

Expansion, Zulu (c. 1817-1828) 270

Expedites Transcontinental Mail, Pony Express (Apr. 3, 1860-Oct. 26, 1861) 1001

Expedition, Lewis and Clark (May 14, 1804-Sept. 23, 1806) 65

Expedition to Ethiopia, British (Apr., 1868) . . . 1250

Expeditions Explore the Pacific Northwest Coast, Astorian (Sept. 8, 1810-May, 1812) 134

Expeditions Give Rise to Biogeography, Wallace's (1854-1862) 885

Expelled from Russia, Naples, and Spain, Jesuits Are (1820) 315

Experiments at New Harmony, Communitarian (Spring, 1814-1830) 206

Exploration of Africa's Congo Basin (1873-1880) 1382

Exploration of Arabia (1814-1879) 199

Exploration of East Africa (1848-1889) 756

Exploration of North Africa (1822-1874) 345

Exploration of West Africa (May 4, 1805-1830) 80

Explore the Antarctic, Europeans (1820-early 1840's) 317

Explore the Pacific Northwest Coast, Astorian Expeditions (Sept. 8, 1810-May, 1812) 134

Explores and Excavates Assyrian Ruins, Layard (1839-1847) 619

Explores Australia, Flinders (Dec. 6, 1801-Aug., 1803) 26

Explores Central Asia, Przhevalsky (1871-1885) 1346

Explores the American Southwest, Pike (July 15, 1806-July 1, 1807) 90

Explores the American West, Frémont (May, 1842-1854) 660

Explores the Far West, Jedediah Smith (1822-1831) 342

Exposition, Philadelphia Hosts the Centennial (May 10-Nov. 10, 1876) 1451

Exterminate Armenians, Ottomans Attempt to (1894-1896) 1773

Fabian Society Is Founded (Jan., 1884). 1603

Factory Act, British Parliament Passes the (1833). 525

Fair, Chicago World's (May 1-Oct. 30, 1893) 1757

Fair, London Hosts the First World's (May 1-Oct. 15, 1851). 840

Fairy Tales, Andersen Publishes His First (May 8, 1835). 570

Fairy Tales, Brothers Grimm Publish (1812-1815) 160

Falkland Islands, Great Britain Occupies the (Jan., 1833) 527

Falls, First U.S. Hydroelectric Plant Opens at Niagara (Nov. 16, 1896) 1863

Falls, Livingstone Sees the Victoria (Nov. 17, 1853) 879

Family Shakespeare, Bowdler Publishes The (1807) 93

Famine, Great Irish (1845-1854). 696

Far West, Jedediah Smith Explores the (1822-1831) 342

Faraday Converts Magnetic Force into Electricity (October, 1831) 502

Farmers Begin Settling Western Canada, Immigrant (1896) 1831

Farmers Stage First "Boycott," Irish Tenant (Sept.-Nov., 1880). 1528

Fashoda Incident Pits France vs. Britain (July 10-Nov. 3, 1898) 1908

Faun Premieres, Debussy's Prelude to the Afternoon of a (Dec. 22, 1894) 1791

Federal Civil Service, Pendleton Act Reforms the (Jan. 16, 1883). 1577

Federation of Labor Is Founded, American (Dec. 8, 1886) 1652

Female Seminary Is Founded, Hartford (May, 1823) 356

Female Seminary Opens, Mount Holyoke (Nov. 8, 1837) 597

Fenian Risings for Irish Independence (June, 1866-1871) 1184

Ferguson, Plessy v. (May 18, 1896) 1848

Fertilizers, Liebig Advocates Artificial (1840). 638

Fetterman Massacre (Dec. 21, 1866) 1199

Fever, Suppression of Yellow (June, 1900-1904) 1966

Fifty-Three Stations, Hiroshige Completes The Tokaido (1831-1834). 484

Fight for Independence from the Ottoman Empire, Greeks (Mar. 7, 1821-Sept. 29, 1829) 336

Fights the Wahhābīs, Egypt (1811-1818) 143

Film, Goodwin Develops Celluloid (May, 1887) 1663

Finney Lectures on "Revivals of Religion" (1835). 560

Fire, Great Chicago (Oct. 8-10, 1871) 1366

Firm, Morris Founds Design (1861) 1016

First Afghan War (1839-1842). 617

First African American University Opens (Jan. 1, 1857) 936

First American Dictionary of English, Webster Publishes the (Nov., 1828) 418

First America's Cup Race, America Wins the (Aug. 22, 1851). 846

First Asteroid Is Discovered (Jan. 1, 1801) 17

First Battle of Bull Run (July 21, 1861) 1045

First Birth Control Clinic Opens in Amsterdam (1882) 1542

First Black Codes, Ohio Enacts the (Jan., 1804). 62

First Boer War (Dec. 16, 1880-Mar. 6, 1881) 1531

First "Boycott," Irish Tenant Farmers Stage (Sept.-Nov., 1880). 1528

First Commercial Projection of Motion Pictures (Dec. 28, 1895). 1820

First Cro-Magnon Remains, Lartet Discovers the (Mar., 1868) 1247

First Fairy Tales, Andersen Publishes His
(May 8, 1835). 570

First Flying Dirigible, Zeppelin Completes the
(July 2, 1900) 1969

First French Canadian Prime Minister, Laurier
Becomes the (July 11, 1896) 1854

First Hague Peace Conference (May 18-
July, 1899). 1926

First Impressionist Exhibition (Apr. 15,
1874) 1410

First International Is Founded (Sept. 28,
1864). 1124

First Jewish Member of British Parliament,
Rothschild Is (July 26, 1858). 966

First Labour Member, Hardie Becomes
Parliament's (Aug. 3, 1892). 1748

First Meetings of the Plymouth Brethren
(c. 1826-1827) 398

First Minstrel Shows (Feb. 6, 1843) 675

First Modern American Circus, Barnum
Creates the (Apr. 10, 1871) 1360

First Modern Department Store Opens in
Paris (1869) 1279

First National Draft Law, Union Enacts the
(Mar. 3, 1863). 1095

First Opium War (Sept., 1839-Aug. 29, 1842). . . 625

First Pan-American Congress (October, 1889-
Apr., 1890) 1695

First Passenger Elevator, Otis Installs the
(Mar. 23, 1857). 942

First Performance of Beethoven's Ninth
Symphony (May 7, 1824) 380

First Performance of Wagner's Ring Cycle
(Aug. 13-17, 1876) 1464

First Polish Rebellion (Nov. 29, 1830-Aug. 15,
1831) 479

First Post-Civil War Black Code, Mississippi
Enacts (Nov. 24, 1865) 1164

First Practical Automobile, Benz Patents the
(Jan. 29, 1886). 1640

First Professional Club Forms, Baseball's
(1869) 1276

First Public Dinosaur Description, Buckland
Presents the (Feb. 20, 1824) 374

First Riel Rebellion (Oct. 11, 1869-July 15,
1870) 1299

First Seed Planter, Blair Patents His (Oct. 14,
1834) 557

First Skyscraper Is Built, World's (1883-
1885) 1575

First Steamship to Cross the Atlantic, Savannah
Is the (May 22-June 20, 1819) 303

First Telegraph Message, Morse Sends
(May 24, 1844) 684

First Test of Canada's Responsible Government
(Apr. 25, 1849) 797

First Trades Union Congress Forms, Great
Britain's (June 2, 1868) 1255

First Transatlantic Cable Is Completed (July 27,
1866). 1196

First Transcontinental Railroad Is Completed
(May 10, 1869) 1293

First Underground Railroad Opens in London
(Jan. 10, 1863). 1087

First U.S. Hydroelectric Plant Opens at Niagara
Falls (Nov. 16, 1896) 1863

First U.S. National Park, Yellowstone Becomes
the (Mar. 1, 1872) 1375

First U.S. Petroleum Refinery Is Built (1850) . . . 807

First World's Fair, London Hosts the (May 1-
Oct. 15, 1851). 840

Flamenco Begins, Golden Age of (c. 1869) . . . 1282

Flaubert Publishes Madame Bovary (Oct. 1-
Dec. 15, 1856) 926

Fletcher v. Peck (Mar. 16, 1810). 131

Flinders Explores Australia (Dec. 6, 1801-
Aug., 1803) 26

Flood, Johnstown (May 31, 1889) 1689

Florida, Adams-Onís Treaty Gives the United
States (Feb. 22, 1819) 293

Flourishes, Barbizon School of Landscape
Painting (c. 1830-1870). 445

Flourishes, Brahmin School of American
Literature (1880's) 1520

Flourishes, Decadent Movement (c. 1884-
1924) 1600

Flourishes, Underground Railroad (c. 1850-
1860) 809

Flying Dirigible, Zeppelin Completes the First
(July 2, 1900) 1969

Flying Dutchman Debuts, Wagner's (Jan. 2,
1843) 672

Force into Electricity, Faraday Converts
Magnetic (October, 1831) 502

Forecasting, Bjerknes Founds Scientific
Weather (July, 1897-July, 1904) 1877

Foreign Bible Society Is Founded, British and
(1804) 57

Form, Bahā'īism Takes (1863) 1078

Form Customs Union, German States Join to
(Jan. 1, 1834) 549

Form Native Sons of the Golden State,
Chinese Californians (May 10, 1895) 1806

Formed, British Labour Party Is (Feb. 27,
1900) 1954

Formed, National Grange Is (Dec. 4, 1867) . . . 1231

Formed, North German Confederation Is (1866-
1867). 1173

Formed, Russian Social-Democratic Labor
Party Is (Mar., 1898) 1895

Formed, Swiss Confederation Is (Sept. 12,
1848) 787

Formed, Three Emperors' League Is (May 6-
Oct. 22, 1873) 1398

Formed, Triple Alliance Is (May 20, 1882). . . . 1561

Former Samurai Rise in Satsuma Rebellion
(Jan.-Sept. 24, 1877) 1469

Forming, Woman Suffrage Associations Begin
(May, 1869) 1290

Forms, Baseball's First Professional Club
(1869) 1276

Forms, Great Britain's First Trades Union
Congress (June 2, 1868). 1255

Forms, San Francisco's Chinese Six
Companies Association (Nov. 12, 1882) . . . 1569

Forms the North-West Mounted Police, Canada
(May 23, 1873) 1401

Formulates the Atomic Theory of Matter,
Dalton (1803-1808) 43

Formulates the Second Law of Thermodynamics,
Clausius (1850-1865). 813

Fosters Canadian Settlement, Dominion Lands
Act (1872). 1369

Found in Germany, Neanderthal Skull Is
(Aug., 1856) 923

Foundations of Geometry, Hilbert Publishes
The (1899). 1913

Founded, African Methodist Episcopal Church
Is (Apr. 9, 1816) 257

Founded, American Anti-Slavery Society Is
(Dec., 1833). 542

Founded, American Bible Society Is
(May 8, 1816). 260

Founded, American Federation of Labor Is
(Dec. 8, 1886) 1652

Founded, American Library Association Is
(Oct. 4-6, 1876) 1467

Founded, British and Foreign Bible Society Is
(1804) 57

Founded, Fabian Society Is (Jan., 1884) 1603

Founded, First International Is (Sept. 28,
1864). 1124

Founded, Hartford Female Seminary Is (May,
1823) 356

Founded, Indian National Congress Is
(1885) 1630

Founded, Melbourne, Australia, Is (Aug. 16,
1835) 573

Founded, Modern New York Times Is
(Sept. 18, 1851). 849

Founded, Moscow Art Theater Is (Oct. 14,
1898) 1910

Founded, National Council of Colored People
Is (July 6, 1853) 870

Founded, National Council of Women of
Canada Is (Oct. 27, 1893) 1768

Founded, Smithsonian Institution Is (Aug. 10,
1846) 729

Founded, Theosophical Society Is (Sept.,
1875) 1429

Founded, Unitarian Church Is (May,
1819) 299

Founded, Watch Tower Bible and Tract
Society Is (1870-1871) 1316

Founding of McGill University (1813). 179

Founds Design Firm, Morris (1861) 1016

Founds Prophetstown, Tenskwatawa (Apr.,
1808) 116

Founds Scientific Weather Forecasting,
Bjerknes (July, 1897-July, 1904) 1877

Founds the Mormon Church, Smith (Apr. 6,
1830) 457

Founds the Political Register, Cobbett (Jan.,
1802). 32

Founds the Social Democratic Alliance,
Bakunin (1868) 1235

Founds the Zionist Movement, Herzl
(Feb., 1896-Aug., 1897). 1836

Founds Young Italy, Mazzini (1831). 482

Fourteenth Amendment, Suffragists Protest the
(May 10, 1866) 1181

Fourteenth Amendment Is Ratified (July 9,
1868) 1261

France, Abdelkader Leads Algeria Against
(1832-1847). 508

France, Louis Napoleon Bonaparte Becomes
Emperor of (Dec. 2, 1852) 861

France and Spain Invade Vietnam (Aug.,
1858) 968

France Conquers Algeria (June 14-July 5, 1830) 464

France Occupies Mexico (Oct. 31, 1861-June 19, 1867). 1051

France vs. Britain, Fashoda Incident Pits (July 10-Nov. 3, 1898) 1908

France's Bourbon Dynasty Is Restored (Apr. 11, 1814-July 29, 1830) 210

Franchise Act of 1884, British Parliament Passes the (Dec. 6, 1884) 1627

Francis Joseph I Meet at Villafranca, Napoleon III and (July 11, 1859). 982

Franco-Prussian War (July 19, 1870-Jan. 28, 1871) 1325

Franco-Russian Alliance (Jan. 4, 1894). 1776

Fraser River Gold Rush Begins (Mar. 23, 1858) 960

Fraunhofer Invents the Spectroscope (1814). . . . 194

Free Public School Movement (1820's-1830's) 310

Freedmen's Bureau, Congress Creates the (Mar. 3, 1865) 1143

Frémont Explores the American West (May, 1842-1854) 660

French Indochina War (Apr., 1882-1885) 1553

French Republic Is Established, Third (Feb. 13, 1871-1875) 1353

French Right Wing Revives During Boulanger Crisis (Jan., 1886-1889). 1638

French Wars, Dahomey- (Nov., 1889-Jan., 1894). 1697

Freud Publishes *The Interpretation of Dreams* (1900) 1938

Frontier, U.S. Census Bureau Announces Closing of the (1890) 1705

Fugitive Slave Law, Second (Sept. 18, 1850) . . . 822

Fuji, Hokusai Produces *Thirty-Six Views of Mount* (1823-1831). 353

Funds for the Nobel Prizes, Nobel Bequeaths (Nov. 27, 1895) 1817

Fur Company Is Chartered, American (Apr. 6, 1808) 119

Furniture Style Becomes Popular, Biedermeier (c. 1815-1848) 225

Gadsden Purchase Completes the U.S.-Mexican Border (Dec. 31, 1853) 882

Galloping Horse, Muybridge Photographs a (1878) 1487

Galton Defines "Eugenics" (1883) 1572

Galveston Hurricane (Sept. 8, 1900) 1972

Games Are Inaugurated, Modern Olympic (Apr. 6, 1896) 1845

Garibaldi's Redshirts Land in Sicily (May-July, 1860). 1008

Garrison Begins Publishing *The Liberator* (Jan. 1, 1831) 487

Gas Lighting, Britain Adopts (1802) 29

Gaudí Begins Barcelona's Templo Expiatorio de la Sagrada Família (Nov. 3, 1883) 1592

General Allotment Act Erodes Indian Tribal Unity (Feb. 8, 1887). 1657

General Electric Opens Research Laboratory (Dec. 15, 1900) 1983

General to Surrender, Watie Is Last Confederate (June 23, 1865) 1153

Geology, Lyell Publishes *Principles of* (July, 1830) 467

Geometry, Hilbert Publishes *The Foundations of* (1899). 1913

Georgia and the Carolinas, Sherman Marches Through (Nov. 15, 1864-Apr. 18, 1865) . . . 1127

Germ Theory and Microbiology, Pasteur Begins Developing (1857) 933

German Confederation, Organization of the (June 8-9, 1815) 239

German Confederation Is Formed, North (1866-1867) 1173

German Empire, German States Unite Within (Jan. 18, 1871). 1349

German States Join to Form Customs Union (Jan. 1, 1834) 549

German States Unite Within German Empire (Jan. 18, 1871). 1349

Germany, Bismarck Introduces Social Security Programs in (1881-1889) 1534

Germany, Kulturkampf Against the Catholic Church in (1871-1877) 1340

Germany, Neanderthal Skull Is Found in (Aug., 1856) 923

Germany Movement, Young (1826-1842). 400

Germany Passes Anti-Socialist Law (Oct. 19, 1878) 1499

Germany's Kiel Canal Opens (June 20, 1895) 1808

Gettysburg, Vicksburg, and Chattanooga, Battles of (July 1-Nov. 25, 1863) 1102

Ghent Takes Effect, Treaty of (Feb. 17, 1815). . . 230

Giant Moas, Scientists Study Remains of (1830's-1840's) 432

Gibbons v. Ogden (Mar. 2, 1824) 376

Gives the United States Florida, Adams-Onís Treaty (Feb. 22, 1819) 293

Gives Women the Vote, Wyoming (Dec., 1869) 1304

Gladstone Becomes Prime Minister of Britain (Dec. 3, 1868-Feb. 20, 1874) 1274

Glidden Patents Barbed Wire (Nov. 24, 1874) 1416

Glücksburg Dynasty, Greece Unifies Under the (1863-1913) 1081

God We Trust" Appears on U.S. Coins, "In (Apr. 22, 1864) 1119

Gold Is Discovered in New South Wales (1851). 828

Gold Is Discovered in the Transvaal (June 21, 1884) 1612

Gold Rush Begins, California (Jan. 24, 1848) . . . 763

Gold Rush Begins, Fraser River (Mar. 23, 1858) 960

Gold Rush Begins, Klondike (Aug. 17, 1896) 1857

Golden Age, *La Sylphide* Inaugurates Romantic Ballet's (Mar. 12, 1832) 511

Golden Age of Flamenco Begins (c. 1869). . . . 1282

Golden State, Chinese Californians Form Native Sons of the (May 10, 1895) 1806

Goodwin Develops Celluloid Film (May, 1887) 1663

Goodyear Patents Vulcanized Rubber (June 15, 1844) 687

Government, First Test of Canada's Responsible (Apr. 25, 1849) 797

Government, Kabo Reforms Begin Modernization of Korean (July 8, 1894-Jan. 1, 1896). 1782

Goya Paints *Third of May 1808: Execution of the Citizens of Madrid* (Mar., 1814) 203

Grand Trunk Railway Is Incorporated, Canada's (Nov. 10, 1852) 858

Grange Is Formed, National (Dec. 4, 1867) . . . 1231

Grant Administration, Scandals Rock the (Sept. 24, 1869-1877) 1296

Grant Signs Indian Appropriation Act (Mar. 3, 1871) 1355

Great American Buffalo Slaughter (c. 1871-1883) 1343

Great Britain Begins Colonizing Tasmania (Sept. 7, 1803) 55

Great Britain Establishes Penny Postage (Jan. 10, 1840) 641

Great Britain Occupies the Falkland Islands (Jan., 1833) 527

Great Britain Strengthens Its Royal Navy (1889) 1680

Great Britain Withdraws from the Concert of Europe (Oct. 20-30, 1822) 350

Great Britain's First Trades Union Congress Forms (June 2, 1868) 1255

Great Chicago Fire (Oct. 8-10, 1871). 1366

Great Eastern, Brunel Launches the SS (Jan. 31, 1858) 955

Great Irish Famine (1845-1854) 696

Great Java War (1825-1830). 386

Great Sioux War (Aug. 17, 1862-Dec. 28, 1863) 1070

Great Trek Begins, South Africa's (1835) 563

Greco-Turkish War (Jan. 21-May 20, 1897) . . . 1872

Greece Unifies Under the Glücksburg Dynasty (1863-1913) 1081

Greeks Fight for Independence from the Ottoman Empire (Mar. 7, 1821-Sept. 29, 1829) 336

Grimm Publish Fairy Tales, Brothers (1812-1815) 160

Grito de Dolores, Hidalgo Issues El (Sept. 16, 1810) 138

Ground Is Broken for the Washington Monument (July 4, 1848). 781

Guadalupe Hidalgo Ends Mexican War, Treaty of (Feb. 2, 1848) 770

Guilds Promote the Arts and Crafts Movement, New (1884) 1597

Gun, Maxim Patents His Machine (1884) 1594

Hague Peace Conference, First (May 18-July, 1899). 1926

Hamburg-Amerika Shipping Line Begins (1847). 740

Happersett, Minor v. (Mar. 9, 1875) 1426

Hardie Becomes Parliament's First Labour Member (Aug. 3, 1892) 1748

Harpers Ferry, Brown's Raid on (Oct. 16-18, 1859) 988

Harrison Signs the Sherman Antitrust Act (July 20, 1890) 1712

Hartford Convention (Dec. 15, 1814-Jan. 5, 1815) 219

Hartford Female Seminary Is Founded (May,
1823) 356

Hawaii's Last Monarch Abdicates (Jan. 24,
1895) 1797

Hay Articulates "Open Door" Policy Toward
China (Sept. 6, 1899-July 3, 1900) 1928

Hayes Becomes President (Mar. 5, 1877) 1472

Hayne Debate Slavery and Westward
Expansion, Webster and (Jan. 19-27,
1830) 451

Hearst-Pulitzer Circulation War (1895-
1898) 1794

Hegel Publishes *The Phenomenology of Spirit*
(Apr., 1807). 106

Hereditary Theory, Rediscovery of Mendel's
(1899-1900) 1920

Heredity, Mendel Proposes Laws of (1865) . . . 1135

Hernani Incites Rioting, Hugo's (Mar. 3,
1830) 454

Herzl Founds the Zionist Movement
(Feb., 1896-Aug., 1897). 1836

Hidalgo Ends Mexican War, Treaty of
Guadalupe (Feb. 2, 1848). 770

Hidalgo Issues El Grito de Dolores (Sept. 16,
1810) 138

High-Pressure Steam Engine, Trevithick Patents
the (Mar. 24, 1802) 38

Hilbert Publishes *The Foundations of Geometry*
(1899) 1913

Hill Launches Housing Reform in London
(1864) 1114

Hiroshige Completes *The Tokaido Fifty-Three
Stations* (1831-1834) 484

History, Ranke Develops Systematic (1824). . . . 371

Hokusai Produces *Thirty-Six Views of Mount
Fuji* (1823-1831) 353

Holmes, Conan Doyle Introduces Sherlock
(Dec., 1887) 1666

Holyoke Female Seminary Opens, Mount
(Nov. 8, 1837) 597

Home Rule Debate Dominates British Politics,
Irish (June, 1886-Sept. 9, 1893). 1645

Homestead Act, Lincoln Signs the (May 20,
1862) 1064

Horse, Muybridge Photographs a Galloping
(1878) 1487

Hosts the Centennial Exposition, Philadelphia
(May 10-Nov. 10, 1876) 1451

Hosts the First World's Fair, London (May 1-
Oct. 15, 1851). 840

House Introduces Modern Realistic Drama,
A Doll's (1879) 1501

House of Representatives Elects Jefferson
President (Feb. 17, 1801) 20

Houses of Parliament Are Rebuilt, British
(Apr. 27, 1840-Feb., 1852) 643

Housing Reform in London, Hill Launches
(1864) 1114

Howe Patents His Sewing Machine (Sept. 10,
1846) 732

Huckleberry Finn, Twain Publishes *Adventures
of* (Dec., 1884-Feb., 1885) 1624

Hugo's *Hernani* Incites Rioting (Mar. 3,
1830) 454

Hull-House, Addams Opens Chicago's
(Sept. 18, 1889) 1692

Hunt, Commonwealth v. (Mar., 1842) 658

Hurricane, Galveston (Sept. 8, 1900) 1972

Hydroelectric Plant Opens at Niagara Falls,
First U.S. (Nov. 16, 1896). 1863

Ilbert Bill, Indian Legislative Council Enacts
the (Jan. 25, 1884). 1606

Immaculate Conception Dogma, Pius IX
Decrees the (Dec. 8, 1854) 906

Immigrant Farmers Begin Settling Western
Canada (1896). 1831

Immigrating to California, Chinese Begin
(1849). 793

Immigration, American Era of "Old" (1840's-
1850's) 631

Immigration Depot Opens, Ellis Island
(Jan. 1, 1892) 1737

Immigration Era Begins, America's "New"
(1892) 1730

Immigration to Canada, Irish (1829-1836). 423

Immunity, Metchnikoff Advances the Cellular
Theory of (1882-1901) 1545

Impeachment of Andrew Johnson (Feb. 24-
May 26, 1868). 1245

Importation of African Slaves, Congress Bans
(Mar. 2, 1807) 103

Impressionist Exhibition, First
(Apr. 15, 1874) 1410

Impressionist Movement Begins, Post- (Late
1870's) 1434

Improved Steel-Processing Method, Bessemer
Patents (1855) 909

"In God We Trust" Appears on U.S. Coins
(Apr. 22, 1864) 1119

Inaugurated, Modern Olympic Games Are
(Apr. 6, 1896) 1845

Inaugurated President, Lincoln Is (Mar. 4,
1861) 1028

Inaugurates Romantic Ballet's Golden Age,
La Sylphide (Mar. 12, 1832) 511

Incandescent Lamp, Edison Demonstrates the
(Oct. 21, 1879) 1517

Incident Pits France vs. Britain, Fashoda
(July 10-Nov. 3, 1898) 1908

Incites Rioting, Hugo's *Hernani* (Mar. 3,
1830) 454

Incorporated, Canada's Grand Trunk Railway Is
(Nov. 10, 1852) 858

Incorporated, Standard Oil Company Is (Jan. 10,
1870) 1318

Independence, Cuban War of (Feb. 24, 1895-
1898) 1802

Independence, Fenian Risings for Irish (June,
1866-1871) 1184

Independence, Liberia Proclaims Its (July 26,
1847) 748

Independence, Mexican War of (Sept. 16, 1810-
Sept. 28, 1821) 140

Independence from the Ottoman Empire,
Greeks Fight for (Mar. 7, 1821-
Sept. 29, 1829) 336

Independent, Brazil Becomes (Sept. 7, 1822) . . . 348

Independent U.S. Treasury, Establishment of
(Aug. 1, 1846) 726

India, British Abolish Suttee in (Dec. 4,
1829) 428

India, Lambton Begins Trigonometrical Survey
of (Apr. 10, 1802) 40

Indian Act, Canada's (1876) 1437

Indian Appropriation Act, Grant Signs
(Mar. 3, 1871) 1355

Indian Legislative Council Enacts the Ilbert
Bill (Jan. 25, 1884) 1606

Indian National Congress Is Founded (1885). . . 1630

Indian Removal Act, Congress Passes
(May 28, 1830) 460

Indian Tribal Unity, General Allotment Act
Erodes (Feb. 8, 1887) 1657

Indigent Women and Children Opens, New
York Infirmary for (May 12, 1857) 947

Indochina War, French (Apr., 1882-1885) 1553

Industrial Machines, Luddites Destroy
(Mar. 11, 1811-1816) 151

Industry, Kellogg's Corn Flakes Launch the
Dry Cereal (1894-1895) 1770

Infallibility Dogma, Vatican I Decrees Papal
(Dec. 8, 1869-Oct. 20, 1870) 1307

Infirmary for Indigent Women and Children
Opens, New York (May 12, 1857) 947

Installs the First Passenger Elevator, Otis
(Mar. 23, 1857) 942

Institution Is Founded, Smithsonian (Aug. 10,
1846) 729

Insurrection, Philippine (Feb. 4, 1899-July 4,
1902) 1922

Insurrection, Turner Launches Slave (Aug. 21,
1831) 499

Insurrection in Spain, Dos de Mayo (May 2,
1808) 122

Integration Theory, Lebesgue Develops New
(1900) 1941

Internal Combustion Engine, Lenoir Patents the
(1860) 998

Internal Combustion Engine, Otto Invents a
Practical (May, 1876) 1449

International Is Founded, First (Sept. 28,
1864) 1124

International Red Cross Is Launched (Aug. 22,
1864) 1122

Interpretation of Dreams, Freud Publishes *The*
(1900) 1938

Interstate Commerce Act (Feb. 4, 1887) 1655

Introduces Brownie Cameras, Kodak (Feb.,
1900) 1950

Introduces Button-Down Shirts, Brooks
Brothers (1896) 1828

Introduces Coca-Cola, Pemberton (May 8,
1886) 1643

Introduces Modern Realistic Drama, *A Doll's
House* (1879) 1501

Introduces Principles of Social Darwinism,
Spencer (1862) 1058

Introduces Sherlock Holmes, Conan Doyle
(Dec., 1887) 1666

Introduces Social Security Programs in
Germany, Bismarck (1881-1889) 1534

Introduces *The Lancet*, Wakley (Oct. 5, 1823). . . 358

Introduces the Romantic Age, Beethoven's
Eroica Symphony (Apr. 7, 1805) 78

Invade Vietnam, France and Spain (Aug.,
1858) 968

Invades Nicaragua, Walker (June 16, 1855-
May 1, 1857) 914

Invades Russia, Napoleon (June 23-Dec. 14, 1812) 170

Invasion, Ethiopia Repels Italian (Mar. 1, 1896) 1842

Invent Daguerreotype Photography, Daguerre and Niépce (1839) 613

Invents a Practical Internal Combustion Engine, Otto (May, 1876) 1449

Invents Basketball, Naismith (1891) 1721

Invents the Inverted Pendulum Seismograph, Wiechert (1900) 1944

Invents the Reaper, McCormick (Summer, 1831) 496

Invents the Spectroscope, Fraunhofer (1814) . . . 194

Invents the Stethoscope, Laënnec (1816) 250

Inverted Pendulum Seismograph, Wiechert Invents the (1900) 1944

Irish Famine, Great (1845-1854) 696

Irish Home Rule Debate Dominates British Politics (June, 1886-Sept. 9, 1893) 1645

Irish Immigration to Canada (1829-1836) 423

Irish Independence, Fenian Risings for (June, 1866-1871) 1184

Irish Melodies, Moore Publishes (1807-1834) . . . 96

Irish Nationalists, Kilmainham Treaty Makes Concessions to (May 2, 1882) 1556

Irish Riots Erupt in Philadelphia, Anti- (May 6-July 5, 1844) 681

Irish Tenant Farmers Stage First "Boycott" (Sept.-Nov., 1880) 1528

Irving Manages London's Lyceum Theatre (1878-1899) 1490

Irving's *Sketch Book* Transforms American Literature (1819-1820) 288

Isandlwana and Rorke's Drift, Battles of (Jan. 22-23, 1879) 1507

Island, Slave Traders Begin Ravaging Easter (Nov., 1862) 1076

Island, Stevenson Publishes *Treasure* (July, 1881-1883) 1537

Island Immigration Depot Opens, Ellis (Jan. 1, 1892) 1737

Islands, Great Britain Occupies the Falkland (Jan., 1833) 527

Isolate Adrenaline, Abel and Takamine (1897-1901) 1869

Issues El Grito de Dolores, Hidalgo (Sept. 16, 1810) 138

Issues the Emancipation Proclamation, Lincoln (Jan. 1, 1863) 1084

Issues the Syllabus of Errors, Pius IX (Dec. 8, 1864) 1133

Italian Invasion, Ethiopia Repels (Mar. 1, 1896) 1842

Italian Revolution of 1848 (Jan. 12, 1848-Aug. 28, 1849) 760

Italy, Mazzini Founds Young (1831) 482

Italy Is Proclaimed a Kingdom (Mar. 17, 1861) 1032

Jackson Vetoes Rechartering of the Bank of the United States (July 10, 1832) 518

Jameson Raid (Dec. 29, 1895-Jan. 2, 1896) . . . 1824

Janissary Revolt, Ottomans Suppress the (1808-1826) 114

Japan Adopts a New Constitution (Feb. 11, 1889) 1683

Japan Expands into Korea (1870's) 1313

Japan to Western Trade, Perry Opens (Mar. 31, 1854) 888

Japanese Rule, Korean Military Mutinies Against (July 23, 1882-Jan. 9, 1885) 1563

Japanese War, Sino- (Aug. 1, 1894-Apr. 17, 1895) 1784

Japanese Yellow Peril Campaign Begins, Anti- (May 4, 1892) 1742

Japan's Charter Oath, Promulgation of (Apr. 6, 1868) 1253

Japan's Meiji Restoration (Jan. 3, 1868) 1242

Java War, Great (1825-1830) 386

Jedediah Smith Explores the Far West (1822-1831) 342

Jefferson President, House of Representatives Elects (Feb. 17, 1801) 20

Jesuits Are Expelled from Russia, Naples, and Spain (1820) 315

Jesus Critically Examined, Strauss Publishes *The Life of* (1835-1836) 566

Jewish Member of British Parliament, Rothschild Is First (July 26, 1858) 966

Johnson, Impeachment of Andrew (Feb. 24-May 26, 1868) 1245

Johnstown Flood (May 31, 1889) 1689

Join to Form Customs Union, German States (Jan. 1, 1834) 549

Joplin Popularizes Ragtime Music and Dance (1899) 1917

Journalism, Rise of Yellow (1880's-1890's) . . . 1526

July Revolution Deposes Charles X (July 29, 1830) 470

Kabo Reforms Begin Modernization of Korean
    Government (July 8, 1894-Jan. 1, 1896) . . . 1782
Kansas, Bleeding (May, 1856-Aug., 1858) 919
Kansas-Nebraska Act, Congress Passes the
    (May 30, 1854) 891
Kapital, Marx Publishes *Das* (1867) 1207
Kellogg's Corn Flakes Launch the Dry Cereal
    Industry (1894-1895) 1770
Key Economic Principles, Ricardo Identifies
    Seven (1817) 267
Khartoum, Siege of (Mar. 13, 1884-Jan. 26,
    1885) 1609
Kiel Canal Opens, Germany's (June 20,
    1895) 1808
Kilmainham Treaty Makes Concessions to
    Irish Nationalists (May 2, 1882) 1556
Kimberley Diamondfields, Rhodes
    Amalgamates (Mar. 13, 1888) 1674
Kingdom, Italy Is Proclaimed a (Mar. 17,
    1861) 1032
Klondike Gold Rush Begins (Aug. 17, 1896). . . 1857
Klux Klan, Birth of the Ku (1866) 1169
Knickerbocker School, Rise of the (1807-
    1850) 99
Koch Announces His Discovery of the
    Tuberculosis Bacillus (Mar. 24, 1882) 1550
Kodak Introduces Brownie Cameras (Feb.,
    1900) 1950
Könniggrätz, Battle of (July 3, 1866) 1193
Korea, Japan Expands into (1870's) 1313
Korean Government, Kabo Reforms Begin
    Modernization of (July 8, 1894-Jan. 1,
    1896) 1782
Korean Military Mutinies Against Japanese
    Rule (July 23, 1882-Jan. 9, 1885) 1563
Krakatoa Volcano Erupts (Aug. 27, 1883) 1583
Krupp Works Open at Essen (Sept. 20, 1811) . . . 154
Ku Klux Klan, Birth of the (1866) 1169
Kulturkampf Against the Catholic Church in
    Germany (1871-1877). 1340

La Sylphide Inaugurates Romantic Ballet's
    Golden Age (Mar. 12, 1832) 511
Labor, Papal Encyclical on (May 15, 1891) . . . 1727
Labor Is Founded, American Federation of
    (Dec. 8, 1886) 1652
Labor Party Is Formed, Russian Social-
    Democratic (Mar., 1898) 1895
Laboratory, General Electric Opens Research
    (Dec. 15, 1900) 1983

Labour, Blanc Publishes *The Organization of*
    (1839). 610
Labour Member, Hardie Becomes Parliament's
    First (Aug. 3, 1892) 1748
Labour Party Is Formed, British (Feb. 27,
    1900) 1954
Laënnec Invents the Stethoscope (1816). 250
Lamarck Publishes *Zoological Philosophy*
    (1809). 128
Lambton Begins Trigonometrical Survey of
    India (Apr. 10, 1802). 40
Lamp, Davy Develops the Arc (c. 1801-1810) . . . 11
Lamp, Edison Demonstrates the Incandescent
    (Oct. 21, 1879) 1517
Lancet, Wakley Introduces *The* (Oct. 5, 1823). . . 358
Land Act of 1820, Congress Passes (Apr. 24,
    1820) 328
Land Grant Act, Lincoln Signs the Morrill
    (July 2, 1862) 1066
Land in Sicily, Garibaldi's Redshirts (May-
    July, 1860). 1008
Land in Western Australia, Last Convicts
    (1868) 1238
Lands Act Fosters Canadian Settlement,
    Dominion (1872) 1369
Landscape Painting Flourishes, Barbizon
    School of (c. 1830-1870) 445
Lartet Discovers the First Cro-Magnon
    Remains (Mar., 1868) 1247
Last Confederate General to Surrender,
    Watie Is (June 23, 1865) 1153
Last Convicts Land in Western Australia
    (1868) 1238
Last Monarch Abdicates, Hawaii's (Jan. 24,
    1895) 1797
Last Slave Ship Docks at Mobile (July, 1859). . . 979
Launch the Dry Cereal Industry, Kellogg's
    Corn Flakes (1894-1895) 1770
Launched, International Red Cross Is (Aug. 22,
    1864). 1122
Launches a Mail-Order Business, Ward (Aug.,
    1872) 1378
Launches Housing Reform in London, Hill
    (1864) 1114
Launches Slave Insurrection, Turner (Aug. 21,
    1831) 499
Launches *The Economist*, Wilson (Sept. 2,
    1843) 678
Launches *The North Star*, Douglass (Dec. 3,
    1847) 753

Launches the SS *Great Eastern*, Brunel (Jan. 31, 1858) 955

Laureate, Tennyson Becomes England's Poet (Nov. 5, 1850) 825

Laurier Becomes the First French Canadian Prime Minister (July 11, 1896) 1854

Law, British Parliament Passes New Poor (Aug. 14, 1834) 554

Law, Congress Enacts the Page (Mar. 3, 1875) 1423

Law, Congress Passes the Comstock Antiobscenity (Mar. 3, 1873) 1394

Law, Germany Passes Anti-Socialist (Oct. 19, 1878) 1499

Law, Second Fugitive Slave (Sept. 18, 1850) . . . 822

Law, Union Enacts the First National Draft (Mar. 3, 1863) 1095

Law of Thermodynamics, Clausius Formulates the Second (1850-1865) 813

Laws of Heredity, Mendel Proposes (1865) . . . 1135

Layard Explores and Excavates Assyrian Ruins (1839-1847) 619

Leading the People, Delacroix Paints *Liberty* (October-Dec., 1830) 476

Leads Algeria Against France, Abdelkader (1832-1847) 508

League Is Formed, Three Emperors' (May 6-Oct. 22, 1873) 1398

Lebesgue Develops New Integration Theory (1900) 1941

Lectures on "Revivals of Religion," Finney (1835) 560

Legislative Council Enacts the Ilbert Bill, Indian (Jan. 25, 1884) 1606

Leipzig, Battle of (Oct. 16-19, 1813) 191

Lenoir Patents the Internal Combustion Engine (1860) 998

Lewis and Clark Expedition (May 14, 1804-Sept. 23, 1806) 65

Liberator, Garrison Begins Publishing *The* (Jan. 1, 1831) 487

Liberia Proclaims Its Independence (July 26, 1847) 748

Liberty, Mill Publishes *On* (1859) 971

Liberty Is Dedicated, Statue of (Oct. 28, 1886) 1649

Liberty Leading the People, Delacroix Paints (October-Dec., 1830) 476

Libraries, Development of Working-Class (19th cent.) 3

Library Association Is Founded, American (Oct. 4-6, 1876) 1467

Library of Congress Building Opens, New (Nov. 1, 1897) 1886

Liebig Advocates Artificial Fertilizers (1840) . . . 638

Life of Jesus Critically Examined, Strauss Publishes *The* (1835-1836) 566

Lighting, Britain Adopts Gas (1802) 29

Lincoln, Surrender at Appomattox and Assassination of (Apr. 9 and 14, 1865) 1146

Lincoln-Douglas Debates (June 16-Oct. 15, 1858) 963

Lincoln Is Elected U.S. President (Nov. 6, 1860) 1010

Lincoln Is Inaugurated President (Mar. 4, 1861) 1028

Lincoln Issues the Emancipation Proclamation (Jan. 1, 1863) 1084

Lincoln Signs the Homestead Act (May 20, 1862) 1064

Lincoln Signs the Morrill Land Grant Act (July 2, 1862) 1066

Lister Publishes His Theory on Antiseptic Surgery (1867) 1204

Literary Renaissance, Arabic (19th cent.) 1

Literature, American Renaissance in (c. 1830's-1860's) 435

Literature, Irving's *Sketch Book* Transforms American (1819-1820) 288

Literature Flourishes, Brahmin School of American (1880's) 1520

Lithographica Is Discovered, *Archaeopteryx* (1861) 1014

Little Bighorn, Battle of the (June 25, 1876) . . . 1454

Livingstone Sees the Victoria Falls (Nov. 17, 1853) 879

Lodge Creek Treaty, Medicine (Oct. 21, 1867) 1228

Logic, Boole Publishes *The Mathematical Analysis of* (1847) 737

London, First Underground Railroad Opens in (Jan. 10, 1863) 1087

London, Hill Launches Housing Reform in (1864) 1114

London Exile, Mazzini Begins (Jan. 12, 1837) 589

London Hosts the First World's Fair (May 1-Oct. 15, 1851) 840

London's Cato Street Conspirators Plot Assassinations (Feb. 23, 1820) 323

London's Lyceum Theatre, Irving Manages
(1878-1899) 1490

London's Savoy Theatre Opens (Oct. 10,
1881) 1539

Long Walk of the Navajos (Aug., 1863-
Sept., 1866) 1105

Louis Napoleon Bonaparte Becomes Emperor
of France (Dec. 2, 1852) 861

Louisiana Purchase (May 9, 1803) 51

Lower Canada Unite, Upper and (Feb. 10,
1841) 650

Luddites Destroy Industrial Machines (Mar. 11,
1811-1816) 151

Lyceum Theatre, Irving Manages London's
(1878-1899) 1490

Lyell Publishes *Principles of Geology* (July,
1830) 467

McCormick Invents the Reaper (Summer,
1831) 496

McCulloch v. Maryland (Mar. 6, 1819) 296

Macdonald Returns as Canada's Prime Minister
(Sept., 1878). 1496

McGill University, Founding of (1813) 179

Machine, Howe Patents His Sewing (Sept. 10,
1846) 732

Machine Gun, Maxim Patents His (1884) 1594

Machines, Luddites Destroy Industrial (Mar. 11,
1811-1816) 151

Mackenzie Era, Canada's (Nov. 5, 1873-Oct. 9,
1878) 1407

McKinley Is Elected President (Nov. 3,
1896) 1860

Madame Bovary, Flaubert Publishes (Oct. 1-
Dec. 15, 1856) 926

Madison, Madison v. (Feb. 24, 1803) 49

Mafeking, Siege of (Oct. 13, 1899-May 17,
1900) 1935

Magnetic Force into Electricity, Faraday
Converts (October, 1831). 502

Magnetism's Relationship to Electricity,
Ampère Reveals (Nov. 6, 1820) 334

Maiden Voyage of the *Clermont* (Aug. 17,
1807) 111

Mail, Pony Express Expedites Transcontinental
(Apr. 3, 1860-Oct. 26, 1861) 1001

Mail-Order Business, Ward Launches a (Aug.,
1872) 1378

Maine's Canadian Border, Webster-Ashburton
Treaty Settles (Aug. 9, 1842). 666

Malaria's Transmission Vector, Ross
Establishes (Aug. 20, 1897) 1883

Mamlūks Massacred, Muḥammad ʿAlī Has the
(Mar. 1, 1811). 149

Man, Darwin Publishes *The Descent of*
(1871) 1334

Manages London's Lyceum Theatre, Irving
(1878-1899) 1490

Manifesto, Marx and Engels Publish *The
Communist* (Feb., 1848) 767

Maratha War, Third (Nov. 5, 1817-June 3,
1818) 276

Marbles to England, Elgin Ships Parthenon
(1803-1812) 46

Marbury v. Madison (Feb. 24, 1803) 49

Marches Through Georgia and the Carolinas,
Sherman (Nov. 15, 1864-Apr. 18, 1865) . . . 1127

Marconi Patents the Wireless Telegraph
(June, 1896) 1851

Marx and Engels Publish *The Communist
Manifesto* (Feb., 1848) 767

Marx Publishes *Das Kapital* (1867) 1207

Mary Appears to Bernadette Soubirous, Virgin
(Feb. 11-July 16, 1858). 958

Maryland, McCulloch v. (Mar. 6, 1819) 296

Massacre, California's Bloody Island (May 6,
1850) 820

Massacre, Fetterman (Dec. 21, 1866). 1199

Massacre, Sand Creek (Nov. 29, 1864). 1130

Massacre, Washita River (Nov. 27, 1868) 1271

Massacre, Wounded Knee (Dec. 29, 1890). . . . 1718

Massacred, Muḥammad ʿAlī Has the Mamlūks
(Mar. 1, 1811). 149

Mathematical Analysis of Logic, Boole
Publishes *The* (1847) 737

Matrimonial Causes Act, British Parliament
Passes the (Aug. 28, 1857) 952

Matter, Dalton Formulates the Atomic Theory
of (1803-1808). 43

Maxim Patents His Machine Gun (1884). 1594

Mayan Antiquities, Stephens Begins
Uncovering (Nov., 1839). 628

Mayo Insurrection in Spain, Dos de (May 2,
1808) 122

Mazzini Begins London Exile (Jan. 12, 1837). . . 589

Mazzini Founds Young Italy (1831) 482

Mecca in Disguise, Burton Enters (Sept. 12,
1853) 873

Mechanical Calculator, Babbage Designs a
(1819-1833). 291

Medicine Lodge Creek Treaty (Oct. 21,
1867) 1228

Meet at Villafranca, Napoleon III and Francis
Joseph I (July 11, 1859) 982

Meetings of the Plymouth Brethren, First
(c. 1826-1827) 398

Meiji Restoration, Japan's (Jan. 3, 1868) 1242

Melbourne, Australia, Is Founded (Aug. 16,
1835) 573

Melodies, Moore Publishes *Irish* (1807-1834) . . . 96

Melville Publishes *Moby Dick* (1851) 830

Member of British Parliament, Rothschild Is
First Jewish (July 26, 1858) 966

Memphis and New Orleans Race Riots (May
and July, 1866) 1178

Mendel Proposes Laws of Heredity (1865) 1135

Mendeleyev Develops the Periodic Table of
Elements (1869-1871) 1284

Mendel's Hereditary Theory, Rediscovery of
(1899-1900) 1920

Mennonites Begin Settling in Canada,
Ukrainian (1873) 1380

Message, Morse Sends First Telegraph
(May 24, 1844) 684

Metabolism, Saussure Publishes His Research
on Plant (1804) 59

Metchnikoff Advances the Cellular Theory of
Immunity (1882-1901) 1545

Method, Bessemer Patents Improved Steel-
Processing (1855) 909

Methodist Episcopal Church Is Founded,
African (Apr. 9, 1816) 257

Metropolitan Museum of Art Opens (Feb. 20,
1872) 1372

Metropolitan Opera House Opens in New York
(Oct. 22, 1883) 1589

Mexican Border, Gadsden Purchase Completes
the U.S.- (Dec. 31, 1853) 882

Mexican War (May 13, 1846-Feb. 2, 1848) 710

Mexican War, Treaty of Guadalupe Hidalgo
Ends (Feb. 2, 1848) 770

Mexican War of Independence (Sept. 16, 1810-
Sept. 28, 1821) 140

Mexico, France Occupies (Oct. 31, 1861-
June 19, 1867) 1051

Mexico into Civil War, Díaz Drives (1871-
1876) 1338

Microbiology, Pasteur Begins Developing
Germ Theory and (1857) 933

Migration Begins, Westward American
(c. 1815-1830) 221

Migration to Utah, Mormons Begin (Feb. 4,
1846) 703

Miguelite Wars, Portugal's (1828-1834) 403

Military Academy Is Established, U.S. (Mar. 16,
1802) 35

Military Campaigns, Bolívar's (Mar., 1813-
Dec. 9, 1824) 181

Military Campaigns, San Martín's (Jan. 18,
1817-July 28, 1821) 273

Military Mutinies Against Japanese Rule,
Korean (July 23, 1882-Jan. 9, 1885) 1563

Mill Publishes *On Liberty* (1859) 971

Minister-President, Bismarck Becomes
Prussia's (Sept. 24, 1862) 1073

Minoan Civilization, Evans Discovers Crete's
(Mar. 23, 1900) 1956

Minor v. Happersett (Mar. 9, 1875) 1426

Minstrel Shows, First (Feb. 6, 1843) 675

Mississippi Constitution Disfranchises Black
Voters (1890) 1702

Mississippi Enacts First Post-Civil War Black
Code (Nov. 24, 1865) 1164

Missouri Compromise (Mar. 3, 1820) 325

Mitosis, Roux Develops the Theory of
(1880's) 1523

Moas, Scientists Study Remains of Giant
(1830's-1840's) 432

Mobile, Last Slave Ship Docks at (July,
1859) 979

Moby Dick, Melville Publishes (1851) 830

Modern American Circus, Barnum Creates
the First (Apr. 10, 1871) 1360

Modern Baseball Begins (c. 1845) 693

Modern Department Store Opens in Paris,
First (1869) 1279

Modern *New York Times* Is Founded (Sept. 18,
1851) 849

Modern Olympic Games Are Inaugurated
(Apr. 6, 1896) 1845

Modern Realistic Drama, *A Doll's House*
Introduces (1879) 1501

Modernization of Korean Government,
Kabo Reforms Begin (July 8, 1894-
Jan. 1, 1896) 1782

Monarch Abdicates, Hawaii's Last (Jan. 24,
1895) 1797

Monitor and the *Virginia*, Battle of the (Mar. 9,
1862) 1061

Monroe Articulates the Monroe Doctrine,
President (Dec. 2, 1823) 361

Monroe Doctrine, President Monroe Articulates
the (Dec. 2, 1823). 361

Monument, Ground Is Broken for the
Washington (July 4, 1848) 781

Moore Publishes *Irish Melodies* (1807-1834). . . . 96

Morant Bay Rebellion (Oct. 7-12, 1865) 1161

Mormon Church, Smith Founds the (Apr. 6,
1830) 457

Mormons Begin Migration to Utah (Feb. 4,
1846) 703

Morrill Land Grant Act, Lincoln Signs the
(July 2, 1862) 1066

Morris Founds Design Firm (1861). 1016

Morse Sends First Telegraph Message (May 24,
1844) 684

"Morte d'Arthur," Tennyson Publishes (1842). . . 655

Moscow Art Theater Is Founded (Oct. 14,
1898) 1910

Motion Pictures, First Commercial Projection
of (Dec. 28, 1895). 1820

Moulin Rouge, Toulouse-Lautrec Paints *At the*
(1892-1895) 1734

Mount Fuji, Hokusai Produces *Thirty-Six Views
of* (1823-1831) 353

Mount Holyoke Female Seminary Opens
(Nov. 8, 1837) 597

Mounted Police, Canada Forms the North-West
(May 23, 1873) 1401

Movement, Chartist (May 8, 1838-Apr. 10,
1848) 605

Movement, *Costumbrismo* (c. 1820-1860). 320

Movement, Courbet Establishes Realist Art
(1855). 911

Movement, Eddy Establishes the Christian
Science (Oct. 30, 1875) 1431

Movement, Free Public School (1820's-
1830's) 310

Movement, Herzl Founds the Zionist
(Feb., 1896-Aug., 1897). 1836

Movement, New Guilds Promote the Arts and
Crafts (1884) 1597

Movement, Rise of the Symbolist (1886). 1636

Movement, Russian Realist (1840's-1880's) . . . 635

Movement, Social Reform (1820's-1850's) 312

Movement, Young Germany (1826-1842). 400

Movement Arises, Aesthetic (1870's) 1310

Movement Arises, China's Self-Strengthening
(1860's). 995

Movement Arises in New England,
Transcendental (1836) 581

Movement Begins, Naturalist (c. 1865). 1138

Movement Begins, Oxford (July 14, 1833) 530

Movement Begins, Post-Impressionist (Late
1870's) 1434

Movement Flourishes, Decadent (c. 1884-
1924) 1600

Muḥammad ʿAlī Has the Mamlūks Massacred
(Mar. 1, 1811). 149

Munch Paints *The Scream* (1893). 1751

Municipal Corporations Act, British Parliament
Passes (Sept. 9, 1835) 575

Museum of Art Opens, Metropolitan (Feb. 20,
1872) 1372

Music, Rise of Tin Pan Alley (1890's) 1700

Music and Dance, Joplin Popularizes Ragtime
(1899) 1917

Muslim Rebellions in China (Winter, 1855-
Jan. 2, 1878) 917

Mutinies Against Japanese Rule, Korean
Military (July 23, 1882-Jan. 9, 1885) 1563

Mutiny Against British Rule, Sepoy (May 10,
1857-July 8, 1858) 944

Muybridge Photographs a Galloping Horse
(1878) 1487

Naismith Invents Basketball (1891) 1721

Nansen Attempts to Reach the North Pole
(1893-1896). 1754

Naples, and Spain, Jesuits Are Expelled from
Russia, (1820) 315

Napoleon I, Bonaparte Is Crowned (Dec. 2,
1804). 72

Napoleon III and Francis Joseph I Meet at
Villafranca (July 11, 1859) 982

Napoleon Bonaparte Becomes Emperor of
France, Louis (Dec. 2, 1852) 861

Napoleon Invades Russia (June 23-Dec. 14,
1812) 170

National Bank Acts, Congress Passes the
(Feb. 25, 1863-June 3, 1864) 1093

National Congress Is Founded, Indian
(1885) 1630

National Council of Colored People Is
Founded (July 6, 1853) 870

National Council of Women of Canada Is
Founded (Oct. 27, 1893) 1768

National Draft Law, Union Enacts the First
(Mar. 3, 1863) 1095

National Grange Is Formed (Dec. 4, 1867) 1231

National Park, Yellowstone Becomes the
First U.S. (Mar. 1, 1872) 1375

National Road, Construction of the (1811-
1840) 146

Nationalists, Kilmainham Treaty Makes
Concessions to Irish (May 2, 1882) 1556

Native Sons of the Golden State, Chinese
Californians Form (May 10, 1895) 1806

Naturalist Movement Begins (c. 1865) 1138

Navajo War, Apache and (Apr. 30, 1860-
1865) 1005

Navajos, Long Walk of the (Aug., 1863-
Sept., 1866) 1105

Navy, Great Britain Strengthens Its Royal
(1889) 1680

Neanderthal Skull Is Found in Germany
(Aug., 1856) 923

Neapolitan Revolution (July 2, 1820-
Mar., 1821) 330

Nebraska Act, Congress Passes the Kansas-
(May 30, 1854) 891

Nervous System, Ramón y Cajal Shows How
Neurons Work in the (1888-1906) 1671

Neurons Work in the Nervous System,
Ramón y Cajal Shows How (1888-1906) . . . 1671

New Constitution, Japan Adopts a (Feb. 11,
1889) 1683

New England, Transcendental Movement
Arises in (1836) 581

New Guilds Promote the Arts and Crafts
Movement (1884) 1597

New Harmony, Communitarian Experiments at
(Spring, 1814-1830) 206

"New" Immigration Era Begins, America's
(1892) 1730

New Integration Theory, Lebesgue Develops
(1900) 1941

New Library of Congress Building Opens
(Nov. 1, 1897) 1886

New Orleans, Battle of (Jan. 8, 1815) 227

New Orleans Race Riots, Memphis and (May
and July, 1866) 1178

New Poor Law, British Parliament Passes
(Aug. 14, 1834) 554

New South Wales, Gold Is Discovered in
(1851) 828

New York, Metropolitan Opera House Opens in
(Oct. 22, 1883) 1589

New York Infirmary for Indigent Women and
Children Opens (May 12, 1857) 947

New York Times Is Founded, Modern (Sept. 18,
1851) 849

New Zealand Women Win Voting Rights
(Sept. 19, 1893) 1761

Newman Becomes a Roman Catholic (Oct. 9,
1845) 700

Nez Perce War (June 15-Oct. 5, 1877) 1479

Niagara Falls, First U.S. Hydroelectric Plant
Opens at (Nov. 16, 1896) 1863

Nian Rebellion, Qing Dynasty Confronts the
(1853-1868) 864

Nicaragua, Walker Invades (June 16, 1855-
May 1, 1857) 914

Niépce Invent Daguerreotype Photography,
Daguerre and (1839) 613

Nightingale Takes Charge of Nursing in the
Crimea (Nov. 4, 1854) 903

Ninth Symphony, First Performance of
Beethoven's (May 7, 1824) 380

Nobel Bequeaths Funds for the Nobel Prizes
(Nov. 27, 1895) 1817

Nobel Patents Dynamite (October, 1867) 1226

Nobel Prizes, Nobel Bequeaths Funds for the
(Nov. 27, 1895) 1817

North Africa, Exploration of (1822-1874) 345

North America Act, British (July 1, 1867) 1219

North German Confederation Is Formed
(1866-1867) 1173

North Pole, Nansen Attempts to Reach the
(1893-1896) 1754

North Star, Douglass Launches The (Dec. 3,
1847) 753

Northwest Coast, Astorian Expeditions Explore
the Pacific (Sept. 8, 1810-May, 1812) 134

North-West Mounted Police, Canada Forms the
(May 23, 1873) 1401

Northwest Passage, Search for the (1818-
1854) 282

Nullification Controversy (Nov. 24, 1832-
Jan. 21, 1833) 521

Nursing in the Crimea, Nightingale Takes
Charge of (Nov. 4, 1854) 903

Oath, Promulgation of Japan's Charter (Apr. 6,
1868) 1253

Oberlin College Opens (Dec. 3, 1833) 546

Occupies California and the Southwest, United
States (June 30, 1846-Jan. 13, 1847) 722

Occupies Mexico, France (Oct. 31, 1861-
June 19, 1867) 1051

Occupies the Falkland Islands, Great Britain
(Jan., 1833) 527

Ogden, Gibbons v. (Mar. 2, 1824) 376

Ohio Enacts the First Black Codes (Jan.,
1804) 62

Ohio Railroad Opens, Baltimore and (Jan. 7,
1830) 447

Oil Company Is Incorporated, Standard
(Jan. 10, 1870). 1318

Oil Drilling Begins, Commercial (Aug. 27,
1859) 985

Oil Trust Is Organized, Standard (Jan. 2,
1882) 1547

"Old" Immigration, American Era of
(1840's-1850's). 631

Olympic Games Are Inaugurated, Modern
(Apr. 6, 1896) 1845

On Liberty, Mill Publishes (1859) 971

On the Origin of Species, Darwin Publishes
(Nov. 24, 1859). 991

Onís Treaty Gives the United States Florida,
Adams- (Feb. 22, 1819) 293

Open at Essen, Krupp Works (Sept. 20, 1811). . . 154

"Open Door" Policy Toward China, Hay
Articulates (Sept. 6, 1899-July 3, 1900) . . . 1928

Opens, Baltimore and Ohio Railroad (Jan. 7,
1830) 447

Opens, Brooklyn Bridge (May 24, 1883). 1580

Opens, Champlain and St. Lawrence Railroad
(July 21, 1836) 587

Opens, Chisholm Trail (1867) 1201

Opens, Ellis Island Immigration Depot (Jan. 1,
1892) 1737

Opens, Erie Canal (Oct. 26, 1825) 391

Opens, Germany's Kiel Canal (June 20,
1895) 1808

Opens, London's Savoy Theatre (Oct. 10,
1881) 1539

Opens, Metropolitan Museum of Art (Feb. 20,
1872) 1372

Opens, Mount Holyoke Female Seminary
(Nov. 8, 1837) 597

Opens, New Library of Congress Building
(Nov. 1, 1897). 1886

Opens, New York Infirmary for Indigent
Women and Children (May 12, 1857) 947

Opens, Oberlin College (Dec. 3, 1833) 546

Opens, Paris's Salon des Refusés (May 15,
1863) 1099

Opens, Santa Fe Trail (Sept., 1821) 339

Opens, Stockton and Darlington Railway
(September 27, 1825). 388

Opens, Suez Canal (Nov. 17, 1869) 1301

Opens, Vassar College (Sept. 26, 1865) 1158

Opens at Niagara Falls, First U.S. Hydroelectric
Plant (Nov. 16, 1896) 1863

Opens Chicago's Hull-House, Addams
(Sept. 18, 1889) 1692

Opens in Amsterdam, First Birth Control Clinic
(1882) 1542

Opens in London, First Underground Railroad
(Jan. 10, 1863). 1087

Opens in New York, Metropolitan Opera
House (Oct. 22, 1883). 1589

Opens in Paris, First Modern Department Store
(1869) 1279

Opens Japan to Western Trade, Perry (Mar. 31,
1854) 888

Opens Research Laboratory, General Electric
(Dec. 15, 1900) 1983

Opera House Opens in New York, Metropolitan
(Oct. 22, 1883) 1589

Opium War, First (Sept., 1839-Aug. 29,
1842) 625

Opium War, Second (Oct. 23, 1856-Nov. 6,
1860) 930

Oregon Territory, United States Acquires
(June 15, 1846) 718

Organization of Labour, Blanc Publishes *The*
(1839). 610

Organization of the German Confederation
(June 8-9, 1815) 239

Organized, Standard Oil Trust Is (Jan. 2,
1882) 1547

Origin of Species, Darwin Publishes *On the*
(Nov. 24, 1859). 991

Otis Installs the First Passenger Elevator
(Mar. 23, 1857) 942

Otto Invents a Practical Internal Combustion
Engine (May, 1876) 1449

Ottoman Empire, Bulgarian Revolt Against the
(May, 1876) 1445

Ottoman Empire, Greeks Fight for Independence
from the (Mar. 7, 1821-Sept. 29, 1829) . . . 336

Ottomans Attempt to Exterminate Armenians
(1894-1896) 1773

l

Ottomans Suppress the Janissary Revolt (1808-1826) 114

Outlaws Slavery, Zanzibar (1873-1897) 1386

Oxford Movement Begins (July 14, 1833). 530

Pacific, War of the (Apr. 5, 1879-Oct. 20, 1883) 1514

Pacific Northwest Coast, Astorian Expeditions Explore the (Sept. 8, 1810-May, 1812). 134

Pacific Railroad Surveys (Mar. 2, 1853-1857). . . 867

Page Law, Congress Enacts the (Mar. 3, 1875) 1423

Painting Flourishes, Barbizon School of Landscape (c. 1830-1870) 445

Paints *At the Moulin Rouge*, Toulouse-Lautrec (1892-1895) 1734

Paints *Liberty Leading the People*, Delacroix (October-Dec., 1830). 476

Paints *The Scream*, Munch (1893) 1751

Paints *Third of May 1808: Execution of the Citizens of Madrid*, Goya (Mar., 1814). 203

Palo Alto, Battle of (May 8, 1846). 707

Pan-American Congress, First (October, 1889-Apr., 1890) 1695

Panic of 1837 Begins (Mar. 17, 1837) 591

Papal Encyclical on Labor (May 15, 1891). . . . 1727

Papal Infallibility Dogma, Vatican I Decrees (Dec. 8, 1869-Oct. 20, 1870) 1307

Paraguayan War (May 1, 1865-June 20, 1870). 1150

Paris, Bizet's *Carmen* Premieres in (Mar. 3, 1875) 1420

Paris, First Modern Department Store Opens in (1869). 1279

Paris, Prussian Army Besieges (Sept. 20, 1870-Jan. 28, 1871) 1331

Paris, Second Peace of (Nov. 20, 1815) 247

Paris Commune (Mar. 18-May 28, 1871). 1358

Paris Revolution of 1848 (Feb. 22-June, 1848) 773

Paris Salon of 1824 (1824). 368

Paris's Salon des Refusés Opens (May 15, 1863) 1099

Park, Yellowstone Becomes the First U.S. National (Mar. 1, 1872). 1375

Parliament, Rothschild Is First Jewish Member of British (July 26, 1858). 966

Parliament Are Rebuilt, British Houses of (Apr. 27, 1840-Feb., 1852) 643

Parliament Passes Municipal Corporations Act, British (Sept. 9, 1835) 575

Parliament Passes New Poor Law, British (Aug. 14, 1834). 554

Parliament Passes the Factory Act, British (1833). 525

Parliament Passes the Franchise Act of 1884, British (Dec. 6, 1884) 1627

Parliament Passes the Matrimonial Causes Act, British (Aug. 28, 1857). 952

Parliament Passes the Reform Act of 1832, British (June 4, 1832). 514

Parliament Passes the Reform Act of 1867, British (Aug., 1867). 1222

Parliament Passes the Six Acts, British (Dec. 11-30, 1819) 305

Parliament Repeals the Combination Acts, British (1824). 365

Parliament Repeals the Corn Laws, British (June 15, 1846) 715

Parliament's First Labour Member, Hardie Becomes (Aug. 3, 1892) 1748

Parthenon Marbles to England, Elgin Ships (1803-1812) 46

Partition of Africa, Berlin Conference Lays Groundwork for the (Nov. 15, 1884-Feb. 26, 1885) 1619

Party, Birth of the People's (July 4-5, 1892) . . . 1745

Party, Birth of the Republican (July 6, 1854) . . . 894

Party, Clay Begins American Whig (Apr. 14, 1834) 551

Party Is Formed, British Labour (Feb. 27, 1900) 1954

Party Is Formed, Russian Social-Democratic Labor (Mar., 1898) 1895

Passage, Search for the Northwest (1818-1854) 282

Passenger Elevator, Otis Installs the First (Mar. 23, 1857) 942

Passes Anti-Socialist Law, Germany (Oct. 19, 1878) 1499

Passes Dingley Tariff Act, Congress (July 24, 1897) 1880

Passes Indian Removal Act, Congress (May 28, 1830) 460

Passes Land Act of 1820, Congress (Apr. 24, 1820) 328

Passes Municipal Corporations Act, British Parliament (Sept. 9, 1835) 575

Passes New Poor Law, British Parliament (Aug. 14, 1834) 554

Passes Preemption Act of 1841, Congress (Sept. 4, 1841) 653

Passes the Comstock Antiobscenity Law, Congress (Mar. 3, 1873). 1394

Passes the Factory Act, British Parliament (1833). 525

Passes the Franchise Act of 1884, British Parliament (Dec. 6, 1884) 1627

Passes the Kansas-Nebraska Act, Congress (May 30, 1854) 891

Passes the Matrimonial Causes Act, British Parliament (Aug. 28, 1857). 952

Passes the National Bank Acts, Congress (Feb. 25, 1863-June 3, 1864) 1093

Passes the Reform Act of 1832, British Parliament (June 4, 1832) 514

Passes the Reform Act of 1867, British Parliament (Aug., 1867). 1222

Passes the Six Acts, British Parliament (Dec. 11-30, 1819) 305

Past and Present, Carlyle Publishes (1843) 669

Pasteur Begins Developing Germ Theory and Microbiology (1857) 933

Patents a Practical Typewriter, Sholes (June 23, 1868) 1258

Patents Automatic Dial Telephone System, Strowger (Mar. 11, 1891) 1724

Patents Barbed Wire, Glidden (Nov. 24, 1874) 1416

Patents Dynamite, Nobel (October, 1867) 1226

Patents His Air Brake, Westinghouse (Apr., 1869) 1287

Patents His First Seed Planter, Blair (Oct. 14, 1834) 557

Patents His Machine Gun, Maxim (1884) 1594

Patents His Sewing Machine, Howe (Sept. 10, 1846) 732

Patents Improved Steel-Processing Method, Bessemer (1855) 909

Patents the Cylinder Phonograph, Edison (Dec. 24, 1877) 1484

Patents the Diesel Engine, Diesel (Feb., 1892) 1740

Patents the First Practical Automobile, Benz (Jan. 29, 1886). 1640

Patents the High-Pressure Steam Engine, Trevithick (Mar. 24, 1802). 38

Patents the Internal Combustion Engine, Lenoir (1860). 998

Patents the Pneumatic Tire, Dunlop (Dec. 7, 1888) 1677

Patents the Revolver, Colt (Feb. 25, 1836). . . . 584

Patents the Wireless Telegraph, Marconi (June, 1896) 1851

Patents Vulcanized Rubber, Goodyear (June 15, 1844) 687

Peace Conference, First Hague (May 18-July, 1899) 1926

Peace of Paris, Second (Nov. 20, 1815) 247

Peck, Fletcher v. (Mar. 16, 1810) 131

Pemberton Introduces Coca-Cola (May 8, 1886) 1643

Pendleton Act Reforms the Federal Civil Service (Jan. 16, 1883) 1577

Pendulum Seismograph, Wiechert Invents the Inverted (1900) 1944

Peninsular War in Spain (May 2, 1808-Nov., 1813) 125

Penny Postage, Great Britain Establishes (Jan. 10, 1840) 641

Penny Press, Birth of the (Sept. 3, 1833). 536

People, Delacroix Paints *Liberty Leading the* (October-Dec., 1830) 476

People Is Founded, National Council of Colored (July 6, 1853) 870

People's Party, Birth of the (July 4-5, 1892) . . . 1745

Performance of Beethoven's Ninth Symphony, First (May 7, 1824) 380

Performance of Wagner's Ring Cycle, First (Aug. 13-17, 1876) 1464

Periodic Table of Elements, Mendeleyev Develops the (1869-1871). 1284

Perry Opens Japan to Western Trade (Mar. 31, 1854) 888

Petroleum Refinery Is Built, First U.S. (1850). . . 807

Phenomenology of Spirit, Hegel Publishes *The* (Apr., 1807). 106

Philadelphia, Anti-Irish Riots Erupt in (May 6-July 5, 1844) 681

Philadelphia Hosts the Centennial Exposition (May 10-Nov. 10, 1876) 1451

Philippine Insurrection (Feb. 4, 1899-July 4, 1902) 1922

Philosophy, Lamarck Publishes *Zoological* (1809). 128

Phoenix Begins Publication, *Cherokee* (Feb. 21, 1828) 408

Phonograph, Edison Patents the Cylinder
(Dec. 24, 1877) 1484

Photographs a Galloping Horse, Muybridge
(1878) 1487

Photography, Daguerre and Niépce Invent
Daguerreotype (1839) 613

Pictures, First Commercial Projection of Motion
(Dec. 28, 1895) 1820

Pike Explores the American Southwest (July 15,
1806-July 1, 1807) 90

Pius IX Decrees the Immaculate Conception
Dogma (Dec. 8, 1854) 906

Pius IX Issues the Syllabus of Errors (Dec. 8,
1864) 1133

Plant Metabolism, Saussure Publishes His
Research on (1804) 59

Plant Opens at Niagara Falls, First U.S.
Hydroelectric (Nov. 16, 1896) 1863

Planter, Blair Patents His First Seed (Oct. 14,
1834) 557

Plessy v. Ferguson (May 18, 1896) 1848

Plot Assassinations, London's Cato Street
Conspirators (Feb. 23, 1820) 323

Plymouth Brethren, First Meetings of the
(c. 1826-1827) 398

Pneumatic Tire, Dunlop Patents the (Dec. 7,
1888) 1677

Poet Laureate, Tennyson Becomes England's
(Nov. 5, 1850) 825

Pole, Nansen Attempts to Reach the North
(1893-1896) 1754

Police, Canada Forms the North-West Mounted
(May 23, 1873) 1401

Policy Toward China, Hay Articulates "Open
Door" (Sept. 6, 1899-July 3, 1900) 1928

Polish Rebellion, First (Nov. 29, 1830-Aug. 15,
1831) 479

Polish Rebellion, Russia Crushes (Jan. 22-Sept.,
1863) 1090

Political Register, Cobbett Founds the (Jan.,
1802) 32

Politics, Irish Home Rule Debate Dominates
British (June, 1886-Sept. 9, 1893) 1645

Pony Express Expedites Transcontinental Mail
(Apr. 3, 1860-Oct. 26, 1861) 1001

Poor Law, British Parliament Passes New
(Aug. 14, 1834) 554

Popular, Biedermeier Furniture Style Becomes
(c. 1815-1848) 225

Popularizes Ragtime Music and Dance, Joplin
(1899) 1917

Portugal's Miguelite Wars (1828-1834) 403

Positivism, Comte Advances His Theory of
(1851-1854) 833

Post-Civil War Black Code, Mississippi Enacts
First (Nov. 24, 1865) 1164

Post-Impressionist Movement Begins (Late
1870's) 1434

Postage, Great Britain Establishes Penny
(Jan. 10, 1840) 641

Powell Publishes His Report on the American
West (1879) 1504

Power, Cixi's Coup Preserves Qing Dynasty
(Nov. 1-2, 1861) 1055

Practical Automobile, Benz Patents the First
(Jan. 29, 1886) 1640

Practical Internal Combustion Engine, Otto
Invents a (May, 1876) 1449

Practical Typewriter, Sholes Patents a (June 23,
1868) 1258

Preemption Act of 1841, Congress Passes
(Sept. 4, 1841) 653

Prelude to the Afternoon of a Faun Premieres,
Debussy's (Dec. 22, 1894) 1791

Premieres, Debussy's Prelude to the Afternoon
of a Faun (Dec. 22, 1894) 1791

Premieres in Paris, Bizet's Carmen (Mar. 3,
1875) 1420

Premieres in Rome, Puccini's Tosca (Jan. 14,
1900) 1946

Pre-Raphaelite Brotherhood Begins (Fall,
1848) 790

Presents the First Public Dinosaur Description,
Buckland (Feb. 20, 1824) 374

Preserves Qing Dynasty Power, Cixi's Coup
(Nov. 1-2, 1861) 1055

President, Hayes Becomes (Mar. 5, 1877) 1472

President, House of Representatives Elects
Jefferson (Feb. 17, 1801) 20

President, Lincoln Is Elected U.S. (Nov. 6,
1860) 1010

President, Lincoln Is Inaugurated (Mar. 4,
1861) 1028

President, McKinley Is Elected (Nov. 3,
1896) 1860

President Monroe Articulates the Monroe
Doctrine (Dec. 2, 1823) 361

Press, Birth of the Penny (Sept. 3, 1833) 536

Prime Minister, Laurier Becomes the First
French Canadian (July 11, 1896) 1854

Prime Minister, Macdonald Returns as
Canada's (Sept., 1878) 1496

Prime Minister of Britain, Gladstone Becomes
(Dec. 3, 1868-Feb. 20, 1874) 1274

Primitives, Emergence of the (1801) 9

Principles, Ricardo Identifies Seven Key
Economic (1817) 267

Principles of Geology, Lyell Publishes (July,
1830) 467

Principles of Social Darwinism, Spencer
Introduces (1862) 1058

Prizes, Nobel Bequeaths Funds for the Nobel
(Nov. 27, 1895) 1817

Procedures, Semmelweis Develops Antiseptic
(May, 1847). 745

Proclaimed a Kingdom, Italy Is (Mar. 17,
1861) 1032

Proclaims Its Independence, Liberia (July 26,
1847) 748

Proclamation, Lincoln Issues the Emancipation
(Jan. 1, 1863) 1084

Professional Club Forms, Baseball's First
(1869) 1276

Professional Theaters Spread Throughout
America (c. 1801-1850) 14

Programs in Germany, Bismarck Introduces
Social Security (1881-1889) 1534

Projection of Motion Pictures, First Commercial
(Dec. 28, 1895) 1820

Promote the Arts and Crafts Movement, New
Guilds (1884) 1597

Promulgation of Japan's Charter Oath (Apr. 6,
1868) 1253

Prophetstown, Tenskwatawa Founds (Apr.,
1808) 116

Proposes Laws of Heredity, Mendel (1865) . . . 1135

Proslavery Arguments, Southerners Advance
(c. 1830-1865) 442

Protest the Fourteenth Amendment, Suffragists
(May 10, 1866) 1181

Prussian Army Besieges Paris (Sept. 20, 1870-
Jan. 28, 1871) 1331

Prussian Revolution of 1848 (Mar. 3-Nov. 3,
1848) 776

Prussian War, Danish- (Feb. 1-Oct. 30,
1864). 1117

Prussian War, Franco- (July 19, 1870-Jan. 28,
1871) 1325

Prussia's Minister-President, Bismarck Becomes
(Sept. 24, 1862) 1073

Prussia's Seven Weeks' War, Austria and
(June 15-Aug. 23, 1866). 1190

Przhevalsky Explores Central Asia (1871-
1885) 1346

Public Dinosaur Description, Buckland Presents
the First (Feb. 20, 1824) 374

Public School Movement, Free (1820's-
1830's) 310

Publication, *Cherokee Phoenix* Begins (Feb. 21,
1828) 408

Publish Fairy Tales, Brothers Grimm (1812-
1815) 160

Publish *The Communist Manifesto*, Marx and
Engels (Feb., 1848). 767

Publishes *Adventures of Huckleberry Finn*,
Twain (Dec., 1884-Feb., 1885) 1624

Publishes *Bleak House*, Dickens (Mar., 1852-
Sept., 1853). 855

Publishes *Das Kapital*, Marx (1867) 1207

Publishes His First Fairy Tales, Andersen
(May 8, 1835). 570

Publishes His Report on the American West,
Powell (1879) 1504

Publishes His Research on Plant Metabolism,
Saussure (1804) 59

Publishes His Theory on Antiseptic Surgery,
Lister (1867). 1204

Publishes *Irish Melodies*, Moore (1807-1834) . . . 96

Publishes *Madame Bovary*, Flaubert (Oct. 1-
Dec. 15, 1856) 926

Publishes *Moby Dick*, Melville (1851). 830

Publishes "Morte d'Arthur," Tennyson
(1842). 655

Publishes *On Liberty*, Mill (1859) 971

Publishes *On the Origin of Species*, Darwin
(Nov. 24, 1859). 991

Publishes *Past and Present*, Carlyle (1843) 669

Publishes *Principles of Geology*, Lyell (July,
1830) 467

Publishes *Self-Help*, Smiles (1859) . . . 974

Publishes *Sexual Inversion*, Ellis (1897) 1867

Publishes *Sister Carrie*, Dreiser (Nov. 8,
1900) 1976

Publishes *The Descent of Man*, Darwin
(1871) 1334

Publishes *The Family Shakespeare*, Bowdler
(1807) 93

Publishes the First American Dictionary of
English, Webster (Nov., 1828) 418

Publishes *The Foundations of Geometry*,
Hilbert (1899) 1913

Publishes *The Interpretation of Dreams*, Freud
(1900) 1938

Publishes *The Life of Jesus Critically Examined*,
Strauss (1835-1836) 566

Publishes *The Mathematical Analysis of Logic*,
Boole (1847) 737

Publishes *The Organization of Labour*, Blanc
(1839) 610

Publishes *The Phenomenology of Spirit*, Hegel
(Apr., 1807) 106

Publishes *The World as Will and Idea*,
Schopenhauer (1819) 285

Publishes *Treasure Island*, Stevenson (July,
1881-1883) 1537

Publishes *Uncle Tom's Cabin*, Stowe (1852) . . . 852

Publishes *Waverley*, Scott (1814) 196

Publishes *Zoological Philosophy*, Lamarck
(1809) 128

Publishing *The Liberator*, Garrison Begins
(Jan. 1, 1831) 487

Puccini's *Tosca* Premieres in Rome (Jan. 14,
1900) 1946

Pulitzer Circulation War, Hearst- (1895-
1898) 1794

Pullman Strike (May 11-July 11, 1894) 1779

Purchase, Louisiana (May 9, 1803) 51

Purchase Completes the U.S.-Mexican Border,
Gadsden (Dec. 31, 1853) 882

Qing Dynasty Confronts the Nian Rebellion
(1853-1868) 864

Qing Dynasty Power, Cixi's Coup Preserves
(Nov. 1-2, 1861) 1055

Quantum Theory, Articulation of (Dec. 14,
1900) 1980

Queen Victoria's Coronation (June 28, 1838) . . . 608

Race, *America* Wins the First America's Cup
(Aug. 22, 1851) 846

Race Riots, Memphis and New Orleans (May
and July, 1866) 1178

Ragtime Music and Dance, Joplin Popularizes
(1899) 1917

Raid, Jameson (Dec. 29, 1895-Jan. 2, 1896) . . . 1824

Raid on Harpers Ferry, Brown's (Oct. 16-18,
1859) 988

Raids, Red River (June 1, 1815-Aug., 1817) . . . 236

Railroad Flourishes, Underground (c. 1850-
1860) 809

Railroad Is Completed, First Transcontinental
(May 10, 1869) 1293

Railroad Opens, Baltimore and Ohio (Jan. 7,
1830) 447

Railroad Opens, Champlain and St. Lawrence
(July 21, 1836) 587

Railroad Opens in London, First Underground
(Jan. 10, 1863) 1087

Railroad Surveys, Pacific (Mar. 2, 1853-
1857) 867

Railway Is Incorporated, Canada's Grand Trunk
(Nov. 10, 1852) 858

Railway Opens, Stockton and Darlington
(September 27, 1825) 388

Ramón y Cajal Shows How Neurons Work in
the Nervous System (1888-1906) 1671

Ranke Develops Systematic History (1824) 371

Raphaelite Brotherhood Begins, Pre- (Fall,
1848) 790

Ratified, Fourteenth Amendment Is (July 9,
1868) 1261

Ratified, Thirteenth Amendment Is (Dec. 6,
1865) 1167

Ratified, Twelfth Amendment Is (Sept. 25,
1804) 69

Ravaging Easter Island, Slave Traders Begin
(Nov., 1862) 1076

Reach the North Pole, Nansen Attempts to
(1893-1896) 1754

Realist Art Movement, Courbet Establishes
(1855) 911

Realist Movement, Russian (1840's-1880's) . . . 635

Realistic Drama, *A Doll's House* Introduces
Modern (1879) 1501

Reaper, McCormick Invents the (Summer,
1831) 496

Rebellion, Boxer (May, 1900-Sept. 7, 1901) . . . 1961

Rebellion, China's Taiping (Jan. 11, 1851-
late summer, 1864) 836

Rebellion, First Polish (Nov. 29, 1830-Aug. 15,
1831) 479

Rebellion, First Riel (Oct. 11, 1869-July 15,
1870) 1299

Rebellion, Former Samurai Rise in Satsuma
(Jan.-Sept. 24, 1877) 1469

Rebellion, Morant Bay (Oct. 7-12, 1865) 1161

Rebellion, Qing Dynasty Confronts the Nian
(1853-1868). 864

Rebellion, Rhode Island's Dorr (May 18,
1842) 664

Rebellion, Russia Crushes Polish (Jan. 22-
Sept., 1863) 1090

Rebellion, Taos (Jan. 19-Feb. 3, 1847). 743

Rebellion Begins, Second Riel (Mar. 19,
1885) 1633

Rebellions in China, Muslim (Winter, 1855-
Jan. 2, 1878) 917

Rebellions Rock British Canada (Oct. 23-
Dec. 16, 1837) 595

Rebuilt, British Houses of Parliament Are
(Apr. 27, 1840-Feb., 1852) 643

Rechartering of the Bank of the United States,
Jackson Vetoes (July 10, 1832). 518

Reconstruction of the South (Dec. 8, 1863-
Apr. 24, 1877) 1109

Red Cloud's War (June 13, 1866-Nov. 6,
1868). 1187

Red Cross Is Launched, International (Aug. 22,
1864). 1122

Red River Raids (June 1, 1815-Aug., 1817) 236

Red River War (June 27, 1874-June 2,
1875) 1413

Rediscovery of Mendel's Hereditary Theory
(1899-1900) 1920

Redshirts Land in Sicily, Garibaldi's (May-July,
1860) 1008

Refinery Is Built, First U.S. Petroleum (1850). . . 807

Reform Act of 1832, British Parliament Passes
the (June 4, 1832). 514

Reform Act of 1867, British Parliament Passes
the (Aug., 1867). 1222

Reform in London, Hill Launches Housing
(1864) 1114

Reform Movement, Social (1820's-1850's) 312

Reforms Begin Modernization of Korean
Government, Kabo (July 8, 1894-Jan. 1,
1896) 1782

Reforms Rugby School, Arnold (1828-1842) . . . 406

Reforms the Federal Civil Service, Pendleton
Act (Jan. 16, 1883) 1577

Refusés Opens, Paris's Salon des (May 15,
1863) 1099

Registered as a Trade Name, "Aspirin" Is
(Jan. 23, 1897). 1875

Relationship to Electricity, Ampère Reveals
Magnetism's (Nov. 6, 1820) 334

Religion," Finney Lectures on "Revivals of
(1835). 560

Remains, Lartet Discovers the First Cro-
Magnon (Mar., 1868) 1247

Remains of Giant Moas, Scientists Study
(1830's-1840's). 432

Removal Act, Congress Passes Indian (May 28,
1830) 460

Renaissance, Arabic Literary (19th cent.) 1

Renaissance in Literature, American (c. 1830's-
1860's) 435

Repeals the Combination Acts, British
Parliament (1824). 365

Repeals the Corn Laws, British Parliament
(June 15, 1846) 715

Repels Italian Invasion, Ethiopia (Mar. 1,
1896) 1842

Report on the American West, Powell Publishes
His (1879). 1504

Republic Is Established, Third French (Feb. 13,
1871-1875) 1353

Republican Party, Birth of the (July 6, 1854) . . . 894

Research on Plant Metabolism, Saussure
Publishes His (1804). 59

Resistance in Rhodesia, British Subdue African
(October, 1893-October, 1897) 1763

Responsible Government, First Test of
Canada's (Apr. 25, 1849). 797

Restoration, Japan's Meiji (Jan. 3, 1868). 1242

Restored, France's Bourbon Dynasty Is
(Apr. 11, 1814-July 29, 1830) 210

Returns as Canada's Prime Minister,
Macdonald (Sept., 1878) 1496

"Revivals of Religion," Finney Lectures on
(1835). 560

Revives During Boulanger Crisis, French Right
Wing (Jan., 1886-1889) 1638

Revolt, Amistad Slave (July 2, 1839) 622

Revolt, Decembrist (Dec. 26, 1825) 395

Revolt, Ottomans Suppress the Janissary
(1808-1826). 114

Revolt, Texas's Salinero (Sept. 10-Dec. 17,
1877) 1482

Revolt Against the Ottoman Empire, Bulgarian
(May, 1876). 1445

Revolution, Belgian (Aug. 25, 1830-May 21,
1833) 474

Revolution, Neapolitan (July 2, 1820-Mar.,
1821) 330

Revolution, Texas (Oct. 2, 1835-Apr. 21, 1836) 577

Revolution Deposes Charles X, July (July 29, 1830) 470

Revolution of 1848, Italian (Jan. 12, 1848-Aug. 28, 1849) 760

Revolution of 1848, Paris (Feb. 22-June, 1848) 773

Revolution of 1848, Prussian (Mar. 3-Nov. 3, 1848) 776

Revolution of 1868, Spanish (Sept. 30, 1868) 1266

Revolver, Colt Patents the (Feb. 25, 1836). 584

Rhode Island's Dorr Rebellion (May 18, 1842) 664

Rhodes Amalgamates Kimberley Diamondfields (Mar. 13, 1888) 1674

Rhodesia, British Subdue African Resistance in (October, 1893-October, 1897). 1763

Ricardo Identifies Seven Key Economic Principles (1817) 267

Riel Rebellion, First (Oct. 11, 1869-July 15, 1870) 1299

Riel Rebellion Begins, Second (Mar. 19, 1885) 1633

Right Wing Revives During Boulanger Crisis, French (Jan., 1886-1889) 1638

Rights, New Zealand Women Win Voting (Sept. 19, 1893) 1761

Rights Associations Unite, Women's (Feb. 17-18, 1890). 1709

Rights Convention, Akron Woman's (May 28-29, 1851) 843

Rights of Women, Declaration of the (July 4, 1876) 1460

Ring Cycle, First Performance of Wagner's (Aug. 13-17, 1876) 1464

Rioting, Hugo's *Hernani* Incites (Mar. 3, 1830) 454

Riots, Memphis and New Orleans Race (May and July, 1866) 1178

Riots Erupt in Philadelphia, Anti-Irish (May 6-July 5, 1844) 681

Rise in Satsuma Rebellion, Former Samurai (Jan.-Sept. 24, 1877) 1469

Rise of Burlesque and Vaudeville (1850's-1880's) 803

Rise of the Cockney School (Dec., 1816) 263

Rise of the Knickerbocker School (1807-1850) 99

Rise of the Symbolist Movement (1886) 1636

Rise of Tin Pan Alley Music (1890's) 1700

Rise of Yellow Journalism (1880's-1890's) . . . 1526

Risings for Irish Independence, Fenian (June, 1866-1871) 1184

River Gold Rush Begins, Fraser (Mar. 23, 1858) 960

River Massacre, Washita (Nov. 27, 1868) 1271

River Raids, Red (June 1, 1815-Aug., 1817). . . . 236

River War, Red (June 27, 1874-June 2, 1875) 1413

Road, Construction of the National (1811-1840) 146

Rock British Canada, Rebellions (Oct. 23-Dec. 16, 1837) 595

Rock the Grant Administration, Scandals (Sept. 24, 1869-1877) 1296

Rodin Exhibits *The Thinker* (1888). 1669

Roman Catholic, Newman Becomes a (Oct. 9, 1845) 700

Roman Catholic Emancipation (May 9, 1828-Apr. 13, 1829) 414

Romantic Age, Beethoven's *Eroica* Symphony Introduces the (Apr. 7, 1805) 78

Romantic Ballet's Golden Age, *La Sylphide* Inaugurates (Mar. 12, 1832) 511

Rome, Puccini's *Tosca* Premieres in (Jan. 14, 1900) 1946

Röntgen Discovers X Rays (Nov. 9, 1895). . . . 1814

Rorke's Drift, Battles of Isandlwana and (Jan. 22-23, 1879) 1507

Ross Establishes Malaria's Transmission Vector (Aug. 20, 1897) 1883

Rossini's *The Barber of Seville* Debuts (Feb. 20, 1816) 252

Rothschild Is First Jewish Member of British Parliament (July 26, 1858) 966

Roux Develops the Theory of Mitosis (1880's) 1523

Royal Navy, Great Britain Strengthens Its (1889) 1680

Rubber, Goodyear Patents Vulcanized (June 15, 1844) 687

Rugby School, Arnold Reforms (1828-1842) . . . 406

Ruins, Layard Explores and Excavates Assyrian (1839-1847). 619

Rule, Sepoy Mutiny Against British (May 10, 1857-July 8, 1858) 944

Russia, Napoleon Invades (June 23-Dec. 14, 1812) 170

Russia Crushes Polish Rebellion (Jan. 22-
Sept., 1863) 1090

Russia, Naples, and Spain, Jesuits Are Expelled
from (1820) 315

Russia Sells Alaska to the United States
(Mar. 30, 1867) 1213

Russian Alliance, Franco- (Jan. 4, 1894) 1776

Russian Realist Movement (1840's-1880's) 635

Russian Serfs, Emancipation of (Mar. 3,
1861) 1026

Russian Social-Democratic Labor Party Is
Formed (Mar., 1898) 1895

Russo-Turkish War, Second (Apr. 26, 1828-
Aug. 28, 1829) 412

Russo-Turkish War, Third (Apr. 24, 1877-
Jan. 31, 1878) 1476

Safe Surgical Anesthesia Is Demonstrated
(Oct. 16, 1846) 735

Salamanca, Battle of (July 22, 1812) 173

Salinero Revolt, Texas's (Sept. 10-Dec. 17,
1877) 1482

Salon des Refusés Opens, Paris's (May 15,
1863) 1099

Salon of 1824, Paris (1824) 368

Salvation Army, Booth Establishes the
(July, 1865) 1155

Samurai Rise in Satsuma Rebellion, Former
(Jan.-Sept. 24, 1877) 1469

San Francisco's Chinese Six Companies
Association Forms (Nov. 12, 1882) 1569

San Martín's Military Campaigns (Jan. 18,
1817-July 28, 1821) 273

Sand Creek Massacre (Nov. 29, 1864) 1130

Sandford, Dred Scott v. (Mar. 6, 1857) 938

Santa Fe Trail Opens (Sept., 1821) 339

Satsuma Rebellion, Former Samurai Rise in
(Jan.-Sept. 24, 1877) 1469

Saussure Publishes His Research on Plant
Metabolism (1804) 59

Savannah Is the First Steamship to Cross the
Atlantic (May 22-June 20, 1819) 303

Savoy Theatre Opens, London's (Oct. 10,
1881) 1539

Scandals Rock the Grant Administration
(Sept. 24, 1869-1877) 1296

Schliemann Excavates Ancient Troy
(Apr., 1870-1873) 1321

School, Arnold Reforms Rugby (1828-1842) . . . 406

School, Rise of the Cockney (Dec., 1816) 263

School, Rise of the Knickerbocker
(1807-1850) 99

School Movement, Free Public (1820's-
1830's) 310

School of American Literature Flourishes,
Brahmin (1880's) 1520

School of Calligraphy Emerges, China's Stele
(1820's) 307

School of Landscape Painting Flourishes,
Barbizon (c. 1830-1870) 445

Schopenhauer Publishes The World as Will and
Idea (1819) 285

Schwann and Virchow Develop Cell Theory
(1838-1839) 602

Scientific Weather Forecasting, Bjerknes
Founds (July, 1897-July, 1904) 1877

Scientists Study Remains of Giant Moas
(1830's-1840's) 432

Scott Publishes Waverley (1814) 196

Scramble for Chinese Concessions Begins
(Nov. 14, 1897) 1888

Scream, Munch Paints The (1893) 1751

Search for the Northwest Passage (1818-
1854) 282

Second Anglo-Sikh War (Apr., 1848-
Mar., 1849) 779

Second Bank of the United States Is Chartered
(Apr., 1816) 255

Second British-Ashanti War (Jan. 22, 1873-
Feb. 13, 1874) 1389

Second Fugitive Slave Law (Sept. 18, 1850) . . . 822

Second Law of Thermodynamics, Clausius
Formulates the (1850-1865) 813

Second Opium War (Oct. 23, 1856-Nov. 6,
1860) 930

Second Peace of Paris (Nov. 20, 1815) 247

Second Riel Rebellion Begins (Mar. 19,
1885) 1633

Second Russo-Turkish War (Apr. 26, 1828-
Aug. 28, 1829) 412

Sedan, Battle of (Sept. 1, 1870) 1328

Seed Planter, Blair Patents His First (Oct. 14,
1834) 557

Sees the Victoria Falls, Livingstone (Nov. 17,
1853) 879

Seismograph, Wiechert Invents the Inverted
Pendulum (1900) 1944

Self-Help, Smiles Publishes (1859) 974

Self-Strengthening Movement Arises, China's
(1860's) 995

Sells Alaska to the United States, Russia
(Mar. 30, 1867) 1213

Seminary Is Founded, Hartford Female
(May, 1823). 356

Seminary Opens, Mount Holyoke Female
(Nov. 8, 1837) 597

Seminole Wars (Nov. 21, 1817-Mar. 27,
1858) 278

Semmelweis Develops Antiseptic Procedures
(May, 1847). 745

Sends First Telegraph Message, Morse
(May 24, 1844) 684

Seneca Falls Convention (July 19-20,
1848) 784

Sepoy Mutiny Against British Rule (May 10,
1857-July 8, 1858) 944

Serfs, Emancipation of Russian (Mar. 3,
1861) 1026

Settlement, Dominion Lands Act Fosters
Canadian (1872). 1369

Settles Maine's Canadian Border, Webster-
Ashburton Treaty (Aug. 9, 1842). 666

Settles U.S. Claims vs. Britain, Treaty of
Washington (May 8, 1871) 1363

Settling in Canada, Ukrainian Mennonites
Begin (1873) 1380

Settling Western Canada, Immigrant Farmers
Begin (1896) 1831

Sevastopol, Siege of (Oct. 17, 1854-Sept. 11,
1855) 897

Seven Key Economic Principles, Ricardo
Identifies (1817) 267

Seven Weeks' War, Austria and Prussia's
(June 15-Aug. 23, 1866). 1190

Seville Debuts, Rossini's The Barber of
(Feb. 20, 1816) 252

Sewing Machine, Howe Patents His (Sept. 10,
1846) 732

Sexual Inversion, Ellis Publishes (1897) 1867

Shakespeare, Bowdler Publishes The Family
(1807) 93

Sherlock Holmes, Conan Doyle Introduces
(Dec., 1887) 1666

Sherman Antitrust Act, Harrison Signs the
(July 20, 1890) 1712

Sherman Marches Through Georgia and the
Carolinas (Nov. 15, 1864-Apr. 18, 1865). . . 1127

Ship Docks at Mobile, Last Slave (July,
1859) 979

Ship Era Begins, Clipper (c. 1845). 690

Shipping Line Begins, Hamburg-Amerika
(1847). 740

Ships Parthenon Marbles to England, Elgin
(1803-1812) 46

Shirts, Brooks Brothers Introduces Button-
Down (1896) 1828

Sholes Patents a Practical Typewriter (June 23,
1868) 1258

Shows, First Minstrel (Feb. 6, 1843). 675

Siberia, Dostoevski Is Exiled to (Dec.,
1849) 800

Sicily, Garibaldi's Redshirts Land in (May-
July, 1860). 1008

Siege of Khartoum (Mar. 13, 1884-Jan. 26,
1885) 1609

Siege of Mafeking (Oct. 13, 1899-May 17,
1900) 1935

Siege of Sevastopol (Oct. 17, 1854-Sept. 11,
1855) 897

Signs Indian Appropriation Act, Grant
(Mar. 3, 1871). 1355

Signs the Chinese Exclusion Act, Arthur
(May 9, 1882) 1558

Signs the Homestead Act, Lincoln (May 20,
1862) 1064

Signs the Morrill Land Grant Act, Lincoln
(July 2, 1862) 1066

Signs the Sherman Antitrust Act, Harrison
(July 20, 1890) 1712

Sikh War, Second Anglo- (Apr., 1848-Mar.,
1849) 779

Sino-Japanese War (Aug. 1, 1894-Apr. 17,
1895) 1784

Sioux War (1876-1877). 1442

Sioux War, Great (Aug. 17, 1862-Dec. 28,
1863) 1070

Sister Carrie, Dreiser Publishes (Nov. 8,
1900) 1976

Six Acts, British Parliament Passes the
(Dec. 11-30, 1819) 305

Sketch Book Transforms American Literature,
Irving's (1819-1820) 288

Skull Is Found in Germany, Neanderthal
(Aug., 1856) 923

Skyscraper Is Built, World's First (1883-
1885) 1575

Slaughter, Great American Buffalo (c. 1871-
1883) 1343

Slave Insurrection, Turner Launches
(Aug. 21, 1831). 499

Slave Law, Second Fugitive (Sept. 18, 1850) 822

Slave Revolt, *Amistad* (July 2, 1839) 622

Slave Ship Docks at Mobile, Last (July, 1859) 979

Slave Traders Begin Ravaging Easter Island (Nov., 1862). 1076

Slavery, Zanzibar Outlaws (1873-1897) 1386

Slavery and Westward Expansion, Webster and Hayne Debate (Jan. 19-27, 1830) 451

Slavery Is Abolished Throughout the British Empire (Aug. 28, 1833) 533

Slavery Society Is Founded, American Anti- (Dec., 1833). 542

Slaves, Congress Bans Importation of African (Mar. 2, 1807) 103

Smiles Publishes *Self-Help* (1859). 974

Smith Explores the Far West, Jedediah (1822-1831) 342

Smith Founds the Mormon Church (Apr. 6, 1830) 457

Smithsonian Institution Is Founded (Aug. 10, 1846) 729

Social Darwinism, Spencer Introduces Principles of (1862) 1058

Social Democratic Alliance, Bakunin Founds the (1868) 1235

Social-Democratic Labor Party Is Formed, Russian (Mar., 1898) 1895

Social Reform Movement (1820's-1850's) 312

Social Security Programs in Germany, Bismarck Introduces (1881-1889) 1534

Socialist Law, Germany Passes Anti- (Oct. 19, 1878) 1499

Society Is Founded, American Anti-Slavery (Dec., 1833). 542

Society Is Founded, American Bible (May 8, 1816) 260

Society Is Founded, British and Foreign Bible (1804) 57

Society Is Founded, Fabian (Jan., 1884) 1603

Society Is Founded, Theosophical (Sept., 1875) 1429

Solferino, Battle of (June 24, 1859) 976

Sons of the Golden State, Chinese Californians Form Native (May 10, 1895) 1806

Soubirous, Virgin Mary Appears to Bernadette (Feb. 11-July 16, 1858). 958

South, Reconstruction of the (Dec. 8, 1863-Apr. 24, 1877) 1109

South African War (Oct. 11, 1899-May 31, 1902) 1932

South Africa's Great Trek Begins (1835) 563

Southerners Advance Proslavery Arguments (c. 1830-1865) 442

Southwest, Pike Explores the American (July 15, 1806-July 1, 1807). 90

Southwest, United States Occupies California and the (June 30, 1846-Jan. 13, 1847) 722

Spain, Carlist Wars Unsettle (Sept. 29, 1833-1849) 539

Spain, Dos de Mayo Insurrection in (May 2, 1808) 122

Spain, Jesuits Are Expelled from Russia, Naples, and (1820) 315

Spain, Peninsular War in (May 2, 1808-Nov., 1813) 125

Spain Invade Vietnam, France and (Aug., 1858) 968

Spanish-American War (Apr. 24-Dec. 10, 1898) 1903

Spanish Constitution of 1876 (1876) 1440

Spanish Revolution of 1868 (Sept. 30, 1868). . . 1266

Species, Darwin Publishes *On the Origin of* (Nov. 24, 1859). 991

Spectroscope, Fraunhofer Invents the (1814) . . . 194

Speech, Washington's Atlanta Compromise (Sept. 18, 1895) 1811

Spencer Introduces Principles of Social Darwinism (1862). 1058

Spirit, Hegel Publishes *The Phenomenology of* (Apr., 1807). 106

Spread of the Waltz (19th cent.) 6

Spread Throughout America, Professional Theaters (c. 1801-1850) 14

St. Lawrence Railroad Opens, Champlain and (July 21, 1836) 587

St. Petersburg, Tchaikovsky's *Swan Lake* Is Staged in (Jan. 27, 1895) 1800

SS *Great Eastern*, Brunel Launches the (Jan. 31, 1858) 955

Stage First "Boycott," Irish Tenant Farmers (Sept.-Nov., 1880). 1528

Staged in St. Petersburg, Tchaikovsky's *Swan Lake* Is (Jan. 27, 1895) 1800

Standard Oil Company Is Incorporated (Jan. 10, 1870). 1318

Standard Oil Trust Is Organized (Jan. 2, 1882) 1547

States Join to Form Customs Union, German (Jan. 1, 1834) 549

States of America, Establishment of the Confederate (Feb. 8, 1861) 1022

States Unite Within German Empire, German (Jan. 18, 1871). 1349

Stations, Hiroshige Completes *The Tokaido Fifty-Three* (1831-1834) 484

Statue of Liberty Is Dedicated (Oct. 28, 1886) 1649

Steam Engine, Trevithick Patents the High-Pressure (Mar. 24, 1802). 38

Steel-Processing Method, Bessemer Patents Improved (1855) 909

Stele School of Calligraphy Emerges, China's (1820's). 307

Stephens Begins Uncovering Mayan Antiquities (Nov., 1839) 628

Stethoscope, Laënnec Invents the (1816) 250

Stevenson Publishes *Treasure Island* (July, 1881-1883) 1537

Stockton and Darlington Railway Opens (September 27, 1825). 388

Store Opens in Paris, First Modern Department (1869) 1279

Stowe Publishes *Uncle Tom's Cabin* (1852). . . . 852

Stratosphere and Troposphere Are Discovered (Apr., 1898-1903) 1900

Strauss Publishes *The Life of Jesus Critically Examined* (1835-1836) 566

Street Conspirators Plot Assassinations, London's Cato (Feb. 23, 1820). 323

Strengthens Its Royal Navy, Great Britain (1889) 1680

Strike, Pullman (May 11-July 11, 1894) 1779

Strowger Patents Automatic Dial Telephone System (Mar. 11, 1891) 1724

Study Remains of Giant Moas, Scientists (1830's-1840's). 432

Style Becomes Popular, Biedermeier Furniture (c. 1815-1848) 225

Subdue African Resistance in Rhodesia, British (October, 1893-October, 1897) 1763

Sudanese War (Mar., 1896-Nov., 1899) 1839

Suez Canal Opens (Nov. 17, 1869) 1301

Suffrage Associations Begin Forming, Woman (May, 1869) 1290

Suffragists Protest the Fourteenth Amendment (May 10, 1866) 1181

Suppress the Janissary Revolt, Ottomans (1808-1826). 114

Suppression of Yellow Fever (June, 1900-1904) 1966

Supreme Court of Canada Is Established (1875) 1418

Surgery, Lister Publishes His Theory on Antiseptic (1867) 1204

Surgical Anesthesia Is Demonstrated, Safe (Oct. 16, 1846) 735

Surrender, Watie Is Last Confederate General to (June 23, 1865) 1153

Surrender at Appomattox and Assassination of Lincoln (Apr. 9 and 14, 1865). 1146

Survey of India, Lambton Begins Trigonometrical (Apr. 10, 1802). 40

Surveys, Pacific Railroad (Mar. 2, 1853-1857) 867

Suttee in India, British Abolish (Dec. 4, 1829) 428

Swan Lake Is Staged in St. Petersburg, Tchaikovsky's (Jan. 27, 1895) 1800

Swiss Confederation Is Formed (Sept. 12, 1848) 787

Syllabus of Errors, Pius IX Issues the (Dec. 8, 1864). 1133

Sylphide Inaugurates Romantic Ballet's Golden Age, *La* (Mar. 12, 1832) 511

Symbolist Movement, Rise of the (1886). 1636

Symphony, First Performance of Beethoven's Ninth (May 7, 1824) 380

Symphony Introduces the Romantic Age, Beethoven's *Eroica* (Apr. 7, 1805) 78

Systematic History, Ranke Develops (1824). . . . 371

Table of Elements, Mendeleyev Develops the Periodic (1869-1871) 1284

Taiping Rebellion, China's (Jan. 11, 1851-late summer, 1864) 836

Takamine Isolate Adrenaline, Abel and (1897-1901) 1869

Tales, Andersen Publishes His First Fairy (May 8, 1835). 570

Tales, Brothers Grimm Publish Fairy (1812-1815) 160

Tambora Volcano Begins Violent Eruption (Apr. 5, 1815). 234

Taos Rebellion (Jan. 19-Feb. 3, 1847) 743

Tariff Act, Congress Passes Dingley (July 24, 1897) 1880

Tasmania, Great Britain Begins Colonizing
(Sept. 7, 1803) 55

Tchaikovsky's *Swan Lake* Is Staged in
St. Petersburg (Jan. 27, 1895) 1800

Tears, Trail of (1830-1842) 438

Tel el Kebir, Battle of (Sept. 13, 1882) 1566

Telegraph, Marconi Patents the Wireless
(June, 1896) 1851

Telegraph Is Completed, Transcontinental
(Oct. 24, 1861) 1048

Telegraph Message, Morse Sends First
(May 24, 1844) 684

Telephone, Bell Demonstrates the (June 25,
1876) 1457

Telephone System, Strowger Patents Automatic
Dial (Mar. 11, 1891). 1724

Templo Expiatorio de la Sagrada Família,
Gaudí Begins Barcelona's
(Nov. 3, 1883). 1592

Ten Years' War, Cuba's (Oct. 10, 1868-
Feb. 10, 1878) 1269

Tenant Farmers Stage First "Boycott," Irish
(Sept.-Nov., 1880). 1528

Tennyson Becomes England's Poet Laureate
(Nov. 5, 1850) 825

Tennyson Publishes "Morte d'Arthur" (1842) . . . 655

Tenskwatawa Founds Prophetstown
(Apr., 1808). 116

Test of Canada's Responsible Government,
First (Apr. 25, 1849) 797

Texas Revolution (Oct. 2, 1835-Apr. 21,
1836) 577

Texas's Cart War (August-Dec., 1857) 950

Texas's Salinero Revolt (Sept. 10-Dec. 17,
1877) 1482

Thames, Battle of the (Oct. 5, 1813) 188

Theater Is Founded, Moscow Art (Oct. 14,
1898) 1910

Theaters Spread Throughout America,
Professional (c. 1801-1850) 14

Theatre, Irving Manages London's Lyceum
(1878-1899) 1490

Theatre Opens, London's Savoy (Oct. 10,
1881) 1539

Theory, Articulation of Quantum (Dec. 14,
1900) 1980

Theory, Lebesgue Develops New Integration
(1900) 1941

Theory, Rediscovery of Mendel's Hereditary
(1899-1900) 1920

Theory, Schwann and Virchow Develop Cell
(1838-1839). 602

Theory and Microbiology, Pasteur Begins
Developing Germ (1857) 933

Theory of Immunity, Metchnikoff Advances
the Cellular (1882-1901) 1545

Theory of Matter, Dalton Formulates the
Atomic (1803-1808) 43

Theory of Mitosis, Roux Develops the
(1880's) 1523

Theory of Positivism, Comte Advances His
(1851-1854). 833

Theory on Antiseptic Surgery, Lister Publishes
His (1867) 1204

Theosophical Society Is Founded (Sept.,
1875) 1429

Thermodynamics, Clausius Formulates the
Second Law of (1850-1865) 813

Thinker, Rodin Exhibits *The* (1888) 1669

Third French Republic Is Established (Feb. 13,
1871-1875) 1353

Third Maratha War (Nov. 5, 1817-June 3,
1818) 276

*Third of May 1808: Execution of the Citizens of
Madrid*, Goya Paints (Mar., 1814) 203

Third Russo-Turkish War (Apr. 24, 1877-
Jan. 31, 1878) 1476

Thirteenth Amendment Is Ratified (Dec. 6,
1865). 1167

Thirty-Six Views of Mount Fuji, Hokusai
Produces (1823-1831) 353

Three Emperors' League Is Formed (May 6-
Oct. 22, 1873) 1398

Times Is Founded, Modern *New York* (Sept. 18,
1851) 849

Tin Pan Alley Music, Rise of (1890's) 1700

Tippecanoe, Battle of (Nov. 7, 1811) 157

Tire, Dunlop Patents the Pneumatic (Dec. 7,
1888) 1677

Tocqueville Visits America (May, 1831-
Feb., 1832) 493

Tokaido Fifty-Three Stations, Hiroshige
Completes *The* (1831-1834) 484

Tom's Cabin, Stowe Publishes *Uncle* (1852) . . . 852

Tosca Premieres in Rome, Puccini's (Jan. 14,
1900) 1946

Toulouse-Lautrec Paints *At the Moulin Rouge*
(1892-1895). 1734

Tower Is Dedicated, Eiffel (Mar. 31, 1889) . . . 1686

Tract Society Is Founded, Watch Tower Bible and (1870-1871) 1316

Trade, Perry Opens Japan to Western (Mar. 31, 1854) 888

Trade Name, "Aspirin" Is Registered as a (Jan. 23, 1897) 1875

Traders Begin Ravaging Easter Island, Slave (Nov., 1862) 1076

Trades Union Congress Forms, Great Britain's First (June 2, 1868) 1255

Trafalgar, Battle of (Oct. 21, 1805) 83

Trail of Tears (1830-1842) 438

Trail Opens, Chisholm (1867) 1201

Trail Opens, Santa Fe (Sept., 1821) 339

Transatlantic Cable Is Completed, First (July 27, 1866) 1196

Transcendental Movement Arises in New England (1836) 581

Transcontinental Mail, Pony Express Expedites (Apr. 3, 1860-Oct. 26, 1861) 1001

Transcontinental Railroad Is Completed, First (May 10, 1869) 1293

Transcontinental Telegraph Is Completed (Oct. 24, 1861) 1048

Transforms American Literature, Irving's *Sketch Book* (1819-1820) 288

Transmission Vector, Ross Establishes Malaria's (Aug. 20, 1897) 1883

Transvaal, Gold Is Discovered in the (June 21, 1884) 1612

Treasure Island, Stevenson Publishes (July, 1881-1883) 1537

Treasury, Establishment of Independent U.S. (Aug. 1, 1846) 726

Treaty, Burlingame (July 28, 1868) 1264

Treaty, Medicine Lodge Creek (Oct. 21, 1867) 1228

Treaty Gives the United States Florida, Adams-Onís (Feb. 22, 1819) 293

Treaty Makes Concessions to Irish Nationalists, Kilmainham (May 2, 1882) 1556

Treaty of Adrianople (Sept. 24, 1829) 426

Treaty of Ghent Takes Effect (Feb. 17, 1815) . . . 230

Treaty of Guadalupe Hidalgo Ends Mexican War (Feb. 2, 1848) 770

Treaty of Washington Settles U.S. Claims vs. Britain (May 8, 1871) 1363

Treaty Settles Maine's Canadian Border, Webster-Ashburton (Aug. 9, 1842) 666

Trek Begins, South Africa's Great (1835) 563

Trevithick Patents the High-Pressure Steam Engine (Mar. 24, 1802) 38

Tribal Unity, General Allotment Act Erodes Indian (Feb. 8, 1887) 1657

Tried for Voting, Anthony Is (June 17-18, 1873) 1404

Trigonometrical Survey of India, Lambton Begins (Apr. 10, 1802) 40

Triple Alliance Is Formed (May 20, 1882) 1561

Tripolitan War (Summer, 1801-Summer, 1805) 23

Troposphere Are Discovered, Stratosphere and (Apr., 1898-1903) 1900

Troy, Schliemann Excavates Ancient (Apr., 1870-1873) 1321

Trust" Appears on U.S. Coins, "In God We (Apr. 22, 1864) 1119

Trust Is Organized, Standard Oil (Jan. 2, 1882) 1547

Tuberculosis Bacillus, Koch Announces His Discovery of the (Mar. 24, 1882) 1550

Turkish War, Greco- (Jan. 21-May 20, 1897) 1872

Turkish War, Second Russo- (Apr. 26, 1828-Aug. 28, 1829) 412

Turkish War, Third Russo- (Apr. 24, 1877-Jan. 31, 1878) 1476

Turko-Egyptian Wars (1832-1841) 505

Turner Launches Slave Insurrection (Aug. 21, 1831) 499

Twain Publishes *Adventures of Huckleberry Finn* (Dec., 1884-Feb., 1885) 1624

Twelfth Amendment Is Ratified (Sept. 25, 1804) 69

Typewriter, Sholes Patents a Practical (June 23, 1868) 1258

Ukrainian Mennonites Begin Settling in Canada (1873) 1380

Uncle Tom's Cabin, Stowe Publishes (1852) . . . 852

Uncovering Mayan Antiquities, Stephens Begins (Nov., 1839) 628

Underground Railroad Flourishes (c. 1850-1860) 809

Underground Railroad Opens in London, First (Jan. 10, 1863) 1087

Unifies Under the Glücksburg Dynasty, Greece (1863-1913) 1081

Union, German States Join to Form Customs (Jan. 1, 1834) 549

Union Congress Forms, Great Britain's First
   Trades (June 2, 1868) 1255
Union Enacts the First National Draft Law
   (Mar. 3, 1863) 1095
Unitarian Church Is Founded (May, 1819) 299
Unite, Upper and Lower Canada (Feb. 10,
   1841) 650
Unite, Women's Rights Associations
   (Feb. 17-18, 1890) 1709
Unite Within German Empire, German States
   (Jan. 18, 1871) 1349
United States, Jackson Vetoes Rechartering of
   the Bank of the (July 10, 1832) 518
United States, Russia Sells Alaska to the
   (Mar. 30, 1867) 1213
United States Acquires Oregon Territory
   (June 15, 1846) 718
United States Florida, Adams-Onís Treaty
   Gives the (Feb. 22, 1819) 293
United States Is Chartered, Second Bank of the
   (Apr., 1816) 255
United States Occupies California and the
   Southwest (June 30, 1846-Jan. 13, 1847) . . . 722
United States v. Wong Kim Ark (Mar. 28,
   1898) 1897
Unity, General Allotment Act Erodes Indian
   Tribal (Feb. 8, 1887) 1657
University, Founding of McGill (1813) 179
University Opens, First African American
   (Jan. 1, 1857) 936
Unsettle Spain, Carlist Wars (Sept. 29, 1833-
   1849) 539
Upper and Lower Canada Unite (Feb. 10,
   1841) 650
U.S. Census Bureau Announces Closing of the
   Frontier (1890) 1705
U.S. Civil War (Apr. 12, 1861-Apr. 9, 1865) . . . 1036
U.S. Claims vs. Britain, Treaty of Washington
   Settles (May 8, 1871) 1363
U.S. Coins, "In God We Trust" Appears on
   (Apr. 22, 1864) 1119
U.S. Department of Education Is Created
   (Mar. 2, 1867) 1210
U.S. Election of 1824 (Dec. 1, 1824-Feb. 9,
   1825) 383
U.S. Election of 1828 (Dec. 3, 1828) 421
U.S. Election of 1840 (Dec. 2, 1840) 646
U.S. Election of 1884 (Nov. 4, 1884) 1615
U.S. Hydroelectric Plant Opens at Niagara Falls,
   First (Nov. 16, 1896) 1863

U.S.-Mexican Border, Gadsden Purchase
   Completes the (Dec. 31, 1853) 882
U.S. Military Academy Is Established
   (Mar. 16, 1802) 35
U.S. National Park, Yellowstone Becomes the
   First (Mar. 1, 1872) 1375
U.S. Petroleum Refinery Is Built, First (1850) . . 807
U.S. President, Lincoln Is Elected (Nov. 6,
   1860) 1010
U.S. Treasury, Establishment of Independent
   (Aug. 1, 1846) 726
Utah, Mormons Begin Migration to (Feb. 4,
   1846) 703

Vassar College Opens (Sept. 26, 1865) 1158
Vatican I Decrees Papal Infallibility Dogma
   (Dec. 8, 1869-Oct. 20, 1870) 1307
Vaudeville, Rise of Burlesque and (1850's-
   1880's) 803
Vetoes Rechartering of the Bank of the
   United States, Jackson (July 10, 1832) 518
Vicksburg, and Chattanooga, Battles of
   Gettysburg, (July 1-Nov. 25, 1863) 1102
Victoria Falls, Livingstone Sees the (Nov. 17,
   1853) 879
Victoria's Coronation, Queen (June 28,
   1838) 608
Vienna, Congress of (Sept. 15, 1814-June 11,
   1815) 216
Vietnam, France and Spain Invade (Aug.,
   1858) 968
Views of Mount Fuji, Hokusai Produces
   Thirty-Six (1823-1831) 353
Villafranca, Napoleon III and Francis Joseph I
   Meet at (July 11, 1859) 982
Violent Eruption, Tambora Volcano Begins
   (Apr. 5, 1815) 234
Virchow Develop Cell Theory, Schwann and
   (1838-1839) 602
Virgin Mary Appears to Bernadette Soubirous
   (Feb. 11-July 16, 1858) 958
Virginia, Battle of the Monitor and the (Mar. 9,
   1862) 1061
Viruses, Beijerinck Discovers (1898) 1892
Visits America, Tocqueville (May, 1831-Feb.,
   1832) 493
Volcano Begins Violent Eruption, Tambora
   (Apr. 5, 1815) 234
Volcano Erupts, Krakatoa (Aug. 27, 1883) 1583

Vote, Wyoming Gives Women the (Dec., 1869) 1304

Voters, Mississippi Constitution Disfranchises Black (1890). 1702

Voting, Anthony Is Tried for (June 17-18, 1873) 1404

Voting Rights, New Zealand Women Win (Sept. 19, 1893) 1761

Voyage of the *Clermont*, Maiden (Aug. 17, 1807) 111

Vulcanized Rubber, Goodyear Patents (June 15, 1844) 687

Wagner's *Flying Dutchman* Debuts (Jan. 2, 1843) 672

Wagner's Ring Cycle, First Performance of (Aug. 13-17, 1876) 1464

Wahhābīs, Egypt Fights the (1811-1818) 143

Wakley Introduces *The Lancet* (Oct. 5, 1823) . . . 358

Walk of the Navajos, Long (Aug., 1863- Sept., 1866) 1105

Walker Invades Nicaragua (June 16, 1855- May 1, 1857) 914

Wallace's Expeditions Give Rise to Biogeography (1854-1862). 885

Waltz, Spread of the (19th cent.) 6

War, Apache and Navajo (Apr. 30, 1860- 1865) 1005

War, Aroostook (1838-1839). 600

War, Austria and Prussia's Seven Weeks' (June 15-Aug. 23, 1866). 1190

War, Basuto (1865-1868) 1141

War, Creek (July 27, 1813-Aug. 9, 1814) 185

War, Crimean (Oct. 4, 1853-Mar. 30, 1856). . . . 876

War, Cuba's Ten Years' (Oct. 10, 1868- Feb. 10, 1878) 1269

War, Danish-Prussian (Feb. 1-Oct. 30, 1864). . . 1117

War, Díaz Drives Mexico into Civil (1871- 1876) 1338

War, First Afghan (1839-1842) 617

War, First Boer (Dec. 16, 1880-Mar. 6, 1881) 1531

War, First Opium (Sept., 1839-Aug. 29, 1842) 625

War, Franco-Prussian (July 19, 1870- Jan. 28, 1871) 1325

War, French Indochina (Apr., 1882-1885) 1553

War, Great Java (1825-1830) 386

War, Great Sioux (Aug. 17, 1862-Dec. 28, 1863) 1070

War, Greco-Turkish (Jan. 21-May 20, 1897) . . . 1872

War, Hearst-Pulitzer Circulation (1895- 1898) 1794

War, Mexican (May 13, 1846-Feb. 2, 1848). . . . 710

War, Nez Perce (June 15-Oct. 5, 1877). 1479

War, Paraguayan (May 1, 1865-June 20, 1870). 1150

War, Red Cloud's (June 13, 1866-Nov. 6, 1868). 1187

War, Red River (June 27, 1874-June 2, 1875) 1413

War, Second Anglo-Sikh (Apr., 1848- Mar., 1849) 779

War, Second British-Ashanti (Jan. 22, 1873- Feb. 13, 1874) 1389

War, Second Opium (Oct. 23, 1856- Nov. 6, 1860) 930

War, Second Russo-Turkish (Apr. 26, 1828- Aug. 28, 1829) 412

War, Sino-Japanese (Aug. 1, 1894-Apr. 17, 1895) 1784

War, Sioux (1876-1877) 1442

War, South African (Oct. 11, 1899-May 31, 1902) 1932

War, Spanish-American (Apr. 24-Dec. 10, 1898) 1903

War, Sudanese (Mar., 1896-Nov., 1899) 1839

War, Texas's Cart (August-Dec., 1857) 950

War, Third Maratha (Nov. 5, 1817-June 3, 1818) 276

War, Third Russo-Turkish (Apr. 24, 1877- Jan. 31, 1878) 1476

War, Treaty of Guadalupe Hidalgo Ends Mexican (Feb. 2, 1848) 770

War, Tripolitan (Summer, 1801-Summer, 1805) 23

War, U.S. Civil (Apr. 12, 1861-Apr. 9, 1865) 1036

War, Zulu (Jan. 22-Aug., 1879). 1511

War in Spain, Peninsular (May 2, 1808- Nov., 1813) 125

War of 1812 (June 18, 1812-Dec. 24, 1814). . . . 166

War of Independence, Cuban (Feb. 24, 1895- 1898) 1802

War of Independence, Mexican (Sept. 16, 1810-Sept. 28, 1821) 140

War of the Pacific (Apr. 5, 1879-Oct. 20, 1883) 1514

Ward Launches a Mail-Order Business (Aug., 1872) 1378

Wars, Apache (Feb. 6, 1861-Sept. 4, 1886) 1019

Wars, Dahomey-French (Nov., 1889-Jan., 1894) 1697

Wars, Portugal's Miguelite (1828-1834) 403

Wars, Seminole (Nov. 21, 1817-Mar. 27, 1858) 278

Wars, Turko-Egyptian (1832-1841) 505

Wars Unsettle Spain, Carlist (Sept. 29, 1833-1849) 539

Washington Monument, Ground Is Broken for the (July 4, 1848) 781

Washington Settles U.S. Claims vs. Britain, Treaty of (May 8, 1871) 1363

Washington's Atlanta Compromise Speech (Sept. 18, 1895) 1811

Washita River Massacre (Nov. 27, 1868) 1271

Watch Tower Bible and Tract Society Is Founded (1870-1871) 1316

Waterloo, Battle of (June 18, 1815) 243

Watie Is Last Confederate General to Surrender (June 23, 1865) 1153

Waverley, Scott Publishes (1814) 196

We Trust" Appears on U.S. Coins, "In God (Apr. 22, 1864) 1119

Weather Forecasting, Bjerknes Founds Scientific (July, 1897-July, 1904) 1877

Webster and Hayne Debate Slavery and Westward Expansion (Jan. 19-27, 1830) . . . 451

Webster-Ashburton Treaty Settles Maine's Canadian Border (Aug. 9, 1842) 666

Webster Publishes the First American Dictionary of English (Nov., 1828) 418

West, Frémont Explores the American (May, 1842-1854) 660

West, Jedediah Smith Explores the Far (1822-1831) 342

West, Powell Publishes His Report on the American (1879) 1504

West Africa, Exploration of (May 4, 1805-1830) 80

Western Australia, Last Convicts Land in (1868) 1238

Western Canada, Immigrant Farmers Begin Settling (1896) 1831

Western Trade, Perry Opens Japan to (Mar. 31, 1854) 888

Westinghouse Patents His Air Brake (Apr., 1869) 1287

Westward American Migration Begins (c. 1815-1830) 221

Westward Expansion, Webster and Hayne Debate Slavery and (Jan. 19-27, 1830) 451

Whig Party, Clay Begins American (Apr. 14, 1834) 551

Wiechert Invents the Inverted Pendulum Seismograph (1900) 1944

Wilson Launches *The Economist* (Sept. 2, 1843) 678

Win Voting Rights, New Zealand Women (Sept. 19, 1893) 1761

Wins the First America's Cup Race, *America* (Aug. 22, 1851) 846

Wire, Glidden Patents Barbed (Nov. 24, 1874) 1416

Wireless Telegraph, Marconi Patents the (June, 1896) 1851

Withdraws from the Concert of Europe, Great Britain (Oct. 20-30, 1822) 350

Woman Suffrage Associations Begin Forming (May, 1869) 1290

Woman's Rights Convention, Akron (May 28-29, 1851) 843

Women, Declaration of the Rights of (July 4, 1876) 1460

Women and Children Opens, New York Infirmary for Indigent (May 12, 1857) 947

Women of Canada Is Founded, National Council of (Oct. 27, 1893) 1768

Women the Vote, Wyoming Gives (Dec., 1869) 1304

Women Win Voting Rights, New Zealand (Sept. 19, 1893) 1761

Women's Rights Associations Unite (Feb. 17-18, 1890) 1709

Wong Kim Ark, United States v. (Mar. 28, 1898) 1897

Work in the Nervous System, Ramón y Cajal Shows How Neurons (1888-1906) 1671

Working-Class Libraries, Development of (19th cent.) 3

Works Open at Essen, Krupp (Sept. 20, 1811) . . . 154

World as Will and Idea, Schopenhauer Publishes *The* (1819) 285

World's Fair, Chicago (May 1-Oct. 30, 1893) 1757

World's Fair, London Hosts the First (May 1-Oct. 15, 1851) 840

World's First Skyscraper Is Built (1883-1885) 1575

Wounded Knee Massacre (Dec. 29, 1890) 1718

Wyoming Gives Women the Vote (Dec., 1869) 1304

X Rays, Röntgen Discovers (Nov. 9, 1895) 1814

Yellow Fever, Suppression of (June, 1900-1904) 1966

Yellow Journalism, Rise of (1880's-1890's) . . . 1526

Yellow Peril Campaign Begins, Anti-Japanese (May 4, 1892) 1742

Yellowstone Becomes the First U.S. National Park (Mar. 1, 1872) 1375

Young Germany Movement (1826-1842) 400

Young Italy, Mazzini Founds (1831). 482

Zanzibar Outlaws Slavery (1873-1897). 1386

Zeppelin Completes the First Flying Dirigible (July 2, 1900) 1969

Zionist Movement, Herzl Founds the (Feb., 1896-Aug., 1897). 1836

Zoological Philosophy, Lamarck Publishes (1809). 128

Zulu Expansion (c. 1817-1828) 270

Zulu War (Jan. 22-Aug., 1879) 1511

LIST OF MAPS, TABLES, AND SIDEBARS

Abolitionists of the Underground Railroad
 (*primary source*) 811
Abu Simbel in Modern Egypt (*map*) 164
Act Prohibiting the Slave Trade to the United
 States, Congressional (*primary source*) 104
Addiction to Novels, Curing Emma Bovary's
 (*primary source*) 927
Address, Jefferson's Inaugural
 (*primary source*) 21
Admission of New States, The Constitution
 and the (*primary source*) 326
Advertisement for *The Family Shakspeare*
 (*primary source*) 94
Africa, Explorers' Routes in East (*map*) 757
Africa, Explorers' Routes in North and West
 (*map*) 81
Africa at the End of the Nineteenth Century
 (*map*) . . . . 1620, 1621, lxxx
Against the Grain (*primary source*) 1601
"Ain't I a Woman?" (*primary source*) 844
Alaska Purchase Treaty (*primary source*) 1214
Alexander II on Serf Emancipation
 (*primary source*) 1027
Amendment to the U.S. Constitution,
 Fourteenth (*primary source*) 1262
Amendment to the U.S. Constitution,
 Thirteenth (*primary source*) 1167
Amendment to the U.S. Constitution,
 Twelfth (*primary source*) 70
America at the End of the Nineteenth
 Century, North (*map*) lxxxiii
American Indian Reservations in 1883
 (*map*) 1658
American Library Association Charter of
 1879 (*primary source*) 1468
American Literature? An (*primary source*) 1522
Anarchism, Bakunin's Materialist
 (*primary source*) 1236
Andrew Jackson on Indian Removal
 (*primary source*) 462
Annual Immigration to the United States,
 1821-2003, Average (*table*) 1732
Anti-Luddite Law, Lord Byron Opposes the
 (*primary source*) 153
Anti-Slavery Convention, Declaration of the
 National (*primary source*) 544

Antitrust Act, The Sherman
 (*primary source*) 1713
Aphorisms from *Self-Help* (*primary source*) . . . 975
Apology, Irving's (*primary source*) 101
Arc of the Meridian, The Great (*map*) 41
Armenian Massacres, 1894-1896 (*map*) 1774
Asia and Australasia at the End of the
 Nineteenth Century (*map*) lxxxi
Asia During the Late Nineteenth Century,
 Central (*map*) 1347
Astoria, 1810-1812, Hunt's Route from
 St. Louis to (*map*) 135
Atomic Theory, Dalton's (*sidebar*) 43
Atomic Theory, Proust's Contribution to
 (*primary source*) 44
Austerlitz, 1805, Battle of (*map*) 87
Australasia at the End of the Nineteenth
 Century, Asia and (*map*) lxxxi
Australia at the End of the Nineteenth
 Century (*map*) 1240, 1241
Average Annual Immigration to the United
 States, 1821-2003 (*table*) 1732
Axioms of Geometry, Hilbert's
 (*primary source*) 1914

Bakunin's Materialist Anarchism
 (*primary source*) 1236
Balkans at the End of the Nineteenth
 Century, The (*map*) 1447
Bank of the United States' Constitutionality,
 Jackson Questions the (*primary source*) 519
Baseball's First Official Rules
 (*primary source*) 695
Basketball's Original Rules
 (*primary source*) 1722
Bateson Defends Mendel (*primary source*) 1136
Battle of Austerlitz, 1805 (*map*) 87
Battle of Trafalgar (*map*) 84
Battle Sites in the Mexican War (*map*) 711
Beagle (*map*), Charles Darwin's Voyage
 on the 992
"Biograph: The Marvel of Science"
 (*primary source*) 1821
Black Laws, Ohio's (*primary source*) 63
"Blue Tail Fly, Jim Crack Corn: Or, The"
 (*primary source*) 677

Boudinot on Georgian Harassment
(*primary source*) 410
Bovary's Addiction to Novels, Curing Emma
(*primary source*) 927
Boxer Rebellion (*primary source*) 1963
Boxers, Words of the (*primary source*). 1963
British India at the End of the Nineteenth
Century (*map*). 1631
British Railway Network Around 1840 (*map*). . . 389
British Resolution Outlawing Suttee
(*primary source*) 430
Buchanan on Kansas Statehood, President
(*primary source*) 921
"Buckets, Cast Down Your"
(*primary source*) 1812
Burckhardt's Interview with Muḥammad
ʿAlī Pasha (*primary source*) 201
Burton's Reasons for Going to Mecca
(*primary source*) 874
Byron Opposes the Anti-Luddite Law, Lord
(*primary source*) 153

California's Gold, President Polk
Acknowledges (*primary source*) 765
Campaigns in Southern Africa, Jameson's
(*map*) 1764
Canada, 1873, The Dominion of (*map*). 1220
Canada, The Dominion of (*primary source*) . . . 1221
Canada at the End of the Nineteenth Century
(*map*) 1832, 1833
Canada in 1841, The Province of (*map*) 651
Canada's Vast Landscape (*primary source*) . . . 1370
Career in Cinema Begins, Méliès's (*primary
source*). 1823
Caribbean Theater of the Spanish-American
War (*map*). 1904
Carlyle on English Workhouses
(*primary source*) 670
"Cast Down Your Buckets"
(*primary source*) 1812
Cease-Fire Deadlines in the Treaty of Ghent
(*primary source*) 232
Cell Theory, A New 603
Central and Eastern Europe (*map*) 1399
Central Asia During the Late Nineteenth
Century (*map*). 1347
Chaotic World of Early Cinema, The
(*primary source*) 1664
"Charge of the Light Brigade, The"
(*primary source*) 901

Charter of 1879, American Library
Association (*primary source*) 1468
Chicago Tribune Report on the Fire
(*primary source*) 1367
Chief Justice Fuller's Dissent
(*primary source*) 1899
China, Foreign Concessions in (*map*). 1889
China and Japan (*map*) 1785
Chinese Exclusion Act of 1882
(*primary source*) 1560
Chinese Immigration to the United States,
1851-2003 (*table*). 795
"Christianity, Unitarian" (*primary source*). . . . 301
Cinderella's Guardian (*primary source*) 161
Cinema, The Chaotic World of Early
(*primary source*) 1664
Cinema Begins, Méliès's Career in
(*primary source*) 1823
Civil Disobedience, Thoreau on
(*primary source*) 582
Civil Rights Act of 1866 (*primary source*) 1177
Civil Rights Cases, The (*primary source*) 1587
Civil War, Time Line of the U.S. (*time line*) . . . 1039
Civil War Sites (*map*). 1037
Colleges and Universities, Major Land-Grant
(*table*) 1068
Combination Acts, The Select Committee
Reports on the (*primary source*) 366
Commodity and Its Secret, The Fetishism of
the (*primary source*) 1208
Communist Manifesto, Prologue to The
(*primary source*) 769
Compromise of 1850, The (*primary source*). . . . 818
Comstock Law, Text of the
(*primary source*) 1395
Comstockery Must Die! (*primary source*) 1396
Concessions in China, Foreign (*map*). 1889
Confederal Assembly, The German
(*primary source*) 240
Confederate and Union Territories (*map*). 1023
Confederate States to the Union,
Readmission of the (*map*) 1110
Confession, Nat Turner's (*primary source*) 501
Congo Basin, Explorers' Routes in the
(*map*) 1383
Congressional Act Prohibiting the Slave
Trade to the United States
(*primary source*) 104
Conrad's *Heart of Darkness*, X Rays and
(*primary source*) 1816

Constitution, Fourteenth Amendment to the
  U.S. (*primary source*) 1262
Constitution, Thirteenth Amendment to the
  U.S. (*primary source*) 1167
Constitution, Twelfth Amendment to
  the U.S. (*primary source*) 70
Constitution, Voting Qualifications in
  Mississippi's (*primary source*) 1703
Constitution and the Admission of New
  States, The (*primary source*) 326
Constitutionality, Jackson Questions the Bank
  of the United States' (*primary source*) 519
Crane, Ichabod (*primary source*) 289
Crete in the Modern Mediterranean Region
  (*map*) 1957
Crimean War, The (*map*) 877
Cro-Magnon Excavation Sites in Germany
  and France (*map*), Neanderthal and 1248
Cro-Magnon Remains (*primary source*) 1249
Cuban Independence, U.S. Resolution
  Recognizing (*primary source*) 1805
Culture Area, Mayan (*map*) 629
Curing Emma Bovary's Addiction to Novels
  (*primary source*) 927
Currency, Mottos of U.S. (*primary source*) 1120

Dalton's Atomic Theory (*sidebar*) 43
"Darkest England" (*primary source*) 1157
Darwin's Voyage on the *Beagle* (*map*),
  Charles 992
Darwin's Natural Selection (*primary source*) . . . 993
Deadlines in the Treaty of Ghent, Cease-Fire
  (*primary source*) 232
Death Sentence, The Horror of a
  (*primary source*) 801
Decision, *Scott v. Sandford* (*primary source*) . . . 940
Declaration of Sentiments, Garrison's
  (*primary source*) 489
Declaration of Sentiments and Resolutions
  (*primary source*) 785
Declaration of the National Anti-Slavery
  Convention (*primary source*) 544
Declaration of Women's Rights
  (*primary source*) 1462
Defining "Indian" (*primary source*) 1438
Democracy in America, Why Tocqueville
  Wrote (*primary source*) 494
Descent of Man, The (*primary source*) 1336
Development of Gas Lighting in Early
  Nineteenth Century England 30

Diplomacy, U.S. and European
  (*primary source*) 363
Discovery of Jim's Humanity, Huck's
  (*primary source*) 1625
Dissent, Chief Justice Fuller's
  (*primary source*) 1899
Dissent, Justice Harlan's (*primary source*) 1850
"Doll-Wife, I Have Been Your"
  (*primary source*) 1502
Dominion of Canada, The (*primary source*) . . . 1221
Dominion of Canada, 1873, The (*map*) 1220

Early Cinema, The Chaotic World of
  (*primary source*) 1664
East Africa, Explorers' Routes in (*map*) 757
Eastern Europe, Central and (*map*) 1399
Egypt, Abu Simbel in Modern (*map*) 164
1848, The Revolutions of (*map*) 761
Election, Votes in the 1860 Presidential
  (*map*) 1011
Election, Votes in the 1896 Presidential
  (*map*) 1862
Electric Light (*primary source*) 1519
Electric Power Plant in North America, Tesla
  on the First (*primary source*) 1865
Emancipation, Alexander II on Serf
  (*primary source*) 1027
Emancipation Proclamation
  (*primary source*) 1085
Emigration to the United States, 1820-1920,
  European (*map*) 632
Emigration to the United States in 1900,
  European (*map*) 1731
Emma Bovary's Addiction to Novels, Curing
  (*primary source*) 927
Engels on Young Germany (*primary source*) . . . 402
"England, Darkest" (*primary source*) 1157
English Workhouses, Carlyle on
  (*primary source*) 670
Erie Canal, The (*map*) 392
"Erie Canal, Fifteen Years on the"
  (*primary source*) 393
Ethiopian Empire, The Mahdist State and the
  (*map*) 1840
Eugenics, The Question of (*primary source*) . . . 1573
Europe, Central and Eastern (*map*) 1399
Europe at the End of the Nineteenth Century
  (*map*) lxxxii
European Emigration to the United States,
  1820-1920 (*map*) 632

European Immigration to the United States,
 1821-1890 (*table*). 633
European Emigration to the United States in
 1900 (*map*) 1731
Excavation Sites in Germany and France,
 Neanderthal and Cro-Magnon (*map*) 1248
Expansion and the Mfecane, Zulu (*map*). 271
Expansion into the Pacific, 1860-1898, U.S.
 (*map*) 1923
Expedition, Lewis and Clark (*map*) 66
Expedition, Nansen's Polar (*map*) 1755
Expedition to the West (*primary source*) 662
Explorations, Flinders's (*map*). 27
Explorers' Routes in East Africa (*map*) 757
Explorers' Routes in North and West Africa
 (*map*). 81
Explorers' Routes in the Congo Basin (*map*). . . 1383
Extract from "Morte d'Arthur"
 (*primary source*) 656
Extracts from the Page Law
 (*primary source*) 1424

Factory Act of 1833, Major Provisions of the
 (*sidebar*) 526
Falkland Islands, The (*map*) 528
Family Shakspeare, Advertisement for *The*
 (*primary source*) 94
Feast, Waverley's Highland (*primary source*). . . 197
Ferguson, Plessy v. (*primary source*). 1849
Fetishism of the Commodity and Its Secret,
 The (*primary source*) 1208
"Fifteen Years on the Erie Canal"
 (*primary source*) 393
Fire, *Chicago Tribune* Report on the
 (*primary source*) 1367
First Reconstruction Act, Johnson's Rejection
 of the (*primary source*) 1111
The First Sighting of Moby Dick
 (*primary source*) 832
Flight of the Nez Perce in 1877 (*map*) 1480
Flinders's Explorations (*map*). 27
Foreign Concessions in China (*map*) 1889
Fossil Sites in New Zealand, Giant Moa
 (*map*) 433
Fourteenth Amendment to the U.S.
 Constitution (*primary source*). 1262
France, Neanderthal and Cro-Magnon
 Excavation Sites in Germany and (*map*) . . . 1248
French Indochina (*map*). 1554
Frontier Thesis, Turner's (*primary source*). . . . 1707

Fuller's Dissent, Chief Justice
 (*primary source*) 1899
$F(x) = 3x + 1$, Values and Differences for
 (*table*). 291

Gadsden Purchase Territory, the (*map*) 883
Galveston Hurricane, Memorializing the
 (*primary source*) 1974
Garrison's Declaration of Sentiments
 (*primary source*) 489
Gas Lighting in Early Nineteenth Century
 England, Development of 30
Geometry, Hilbert's Axioms of
 (*primary source*) 1914
Georgian Harassment, Boudinot on
 (*primary source*) 410
German Confederal Assembly, The
 (*primary source*) 240
German Confederation, 1815, The (*map*) 241
German Immigration to the United States,
 1821-2003 (*table*). 741
Germany, Engels on Young (*primary source*) . . . 402
Germany, The Unification of (*map*) 1350
Germany and France, Neanderthal and Cro-
 Magnon Excavation Sites in (*map*) 1248
Gettysburg Address, Lincoln's
 (*primary source*). 1104
Ghent, Cease-Fire Deadlines in the Treaty
 of (*primary source*). 232
Giant Moa Fossil Sites in New Zealand (*map*). . . 433
Gladstone Informs the Queen of the Coming
 Franchise Act (*primary source*)
Gold, President Polk Acknowledges
 California's (*primary source*) 765
Grand Canyon, Powell on the Great and
 Unknown (*primary source*) 1505
Great Arc of the Meridian, The (*map*). 41
Great Britain, Madison's Case for Making
 War on (*primary source*) 168
Grieving Mother, Lincoln's Letter to a
 (*primary source*) 1042
Growth of the United States, Territorial 724
Guardian, Cinderella's (*primary source*). 161

Harlan's Dissent, Justice (*primary source*) 1850
Harmony Constitution, New (*primary source*). . . 208
"Harp That Once Through Tara's Halls, The"
 (*primary source*). 97
Hayes on the Post-Reconstruction South,
 President (*primary source*) 1474

Hay's First "Open Door" Note
(*primary source*) 1929
Her Own Words, Liliuokalani in
(*primary source*) 1798
Highland Feast, Waverley's (*primary source*) . . . 197
Hilbert's Axioms of Geometry
(*primary source*) 1914
Historical Truth and Religious Truth,
Strauss on (*primary source*) 568
"Holmes, Mr. Sherlock" (*primary source*) 1667
Homesteader Qualifications
(*primary source*) 1065
Horror of a Death Sentence, The
(*primary source*) 801
Huck's Discovery of Jim's Humanity
(*primary source*) 1625
Humanity, Huck's Discovery of Jim's
(*primary source*) 1625
Hunt's Poetics (*primary source*) 265
Hunt's Route from St. Louis to Astoria,
1810-1812 (*map*) 135
Hurricane, Memorializing the Galveston
(*primary source*) 1974
Hurstwood, Sister Carrie and
(*primary source*) 1977

"I Have Been Your Doll-Wife"
(*primary source*) 1502
Ichabod Crane (*primary source*) 289
Immigration Laws, Late Nineteenth Century
U.S. (*sidebar*) 1738
Immigration to the United States, 1821-1890,
European (*table*) 633
Immigration to the United States, 1821-2003,
Average Annual (*table*) 1732
Immigration to the United States, 1821-2003,
German (*table*) 741
Immigration to the United States, 1821-2003,
Irish (*table*) 682
Immigration to the United States, 1851-2003,
Chinese (*table*) 795
Inaugural Address, Jefferson's
(*primary source*) 21
Inaugural Address, John Quincy Adams's
(*primary source*) 384
Inaugural Address, Lincoln's First
(*primary source*) 1030
Independence, South American (*map*) 183
India at the End of the Nineteenth Century,
British (*map*) 1631

"Indian," Defining (*primary source*) 1438
Indian Removal, Andrew Jackson on
(*primary source*) 462
Indian Reservations in 1883, American
(*map*) 1658
Indian Territory in 1836, Tribal Lands in
(*map*) 461
Indochina, French (*map*) 1554
Indonesia, Krakatoa in Modern (*map*) 1584
Indonesia, Tambora in Modern (*map*) 235
Interview with Muḥammad ʿAlī Pasha,
Burckhardt's (*primary source*) 201
Ireland at the End of the Nineteenth Century
(*map*) 1647
Irish Immigration to the United States,
1821-2003 (*table*) 682
Irving's Apology (*primary source*) 101
Italy, Unification of (*map*) 1033

"J'Accuse. . . !" (*primary source*) 1790
Jackson on Indian Removal, Andrew
(*primary source*) 462
Jackson on Tariff Reduction and Nullification
(*primary source*) 523
Jackson Questions the Bank of the United
States' Constitutionality (*primary source*) . . . 519
Jameson Raid, The (*map*) 1825
Jameson's Campaigns in Southern Africa
(*map*) 1764
Japan, China and (*map*) 1785
Jarndyce and Jarndyce (*primary source*) 857
Jefferson's Inaugural Address
(*primary source*) 21
Jefferson's Instructions to Lewis and Clark
(*primary source*) 67
"Jim Crack Corn: Or, The Blue Tail Fly"
(*primary source*) 677
Jim's Humanity, Huck's Discovery of
(*primary source*) 1625
John Quincy Adams's Inaugural Address
(*primary source*) 384
Johnson's Rejection of the First
Reconstruction Act (*primary source*) 1111
Justice Harlan's Dissent (*primary source*) 1850

Kansas Statehood, President Buchanan on
(*primary source*) 921
Klondike, Routes to the (*map*) 1858
Krakatoa in Modern Indonesia (*map*) 1584

Land-Grant Colleges and Universities, Major (*table*) 1068

Lands in Indian Territory in 1836, Tribal (*map*) 461

Lands Settled by 1890, U.S. (*map*) 1706

Landscape, Canada's Vast (*primary source*) . . . 1370

Late Nineteenth Century U.S. Immigration Laws (*sidebar*) 1738

Latin America, U.S. policy on (*primary source*) 363

Laws of Thermodynamics, The (*sidebar*) 815

Leaves of Grass (*primary source*) 436

Letter to a Grieving Mother, Lincoln's (*primary source*) 1042

Lewis and Clark Expedition (*map*) 66

Library Association Charter of 1879, American (*primary source*) 1468

Light, Electric (*primary source*) 1519

"Light Brigade, The Charge of the" (*primary source*) 901

Liliuokalani in Her Own Words (*primary source*) 1798

Lincoln's First Inaugural Address (*primary source*) 1030

Lincoln's Gettysburg Address (*primary source*) 1104

Lincoln's Letter to a Grieving Mother (*primary source*) 1042

Literature?, An American (*primary source*) . . . 1522

A Little Neanderthal in Some of Us? (*primary source*) 925

Livingstone's First Visit to Victoria Falls (*primary source*) 880

Long Walk of the Navajos (*map*) 1106

Lord Byron Opposes the Anti-Luddite Law (*primary source*) 153

Louisiana Purchase, Thomas Jefferson on (*primary source*) 53

Louisiana Purchase Territory, The (*map*) 52

Luddite Law, Lord Byron Opposes the Anti- (*primary source*) 153

McCulloch v. Maryland, Marshall's Opinion in (*primary source*) 297

Madison's Case for Making War on Great Britain (*primary source*) 168

Mahdist State and the Ethiopian Empire, The (*map*) 1840

Mail Routes, Pony Express and Overland (*map*) 1002

Major Land-Grant Colleges and Universities (*table*) 1068

Major Provisions of the Factory Act of 1833 (*sidebar*) 526

Man, The Descent of (*primary source*) 1336

Manila Bay and Harbor (*map*) 1904

Marshall's Opinion in *McCulloch v. Maryland* (*primary source*) 297

"Marvel of Science, Biograph: The" (*primary source*) 1821

Maryland, Marshall's Opinion in *McCulloch v.* (*primary source*) 297

Massacres, 1894-1896, Armenian (*map*) 1774

Materialist Anarchism, Bakunin's (*primary source*) 1236

Mayan Culture Area (*map*) 629

Mecca, Burton's Reasons for Going to (*primary source*) 874

Mediterranean Region, Crete in the Modern (*map*) 1957

Mediterranean Region, Troy in the Modern (*map*) 1322

Méliès's Career in Cinema Begins (*primary source*) 1823

Memorializing the Galveston Hurricane (*primary source*) 1974

Mendel, Bateson Defends (*primary source*) 1136

Meridian, The Great Arc of the (*map*) 41

Metchnikoff's Nobel Prize (*primary source*) 1546

Mexican Territories Before the Texas Revolution 141

Mexican War, Battle Sites in the (*map*) 711

Mexican War, Time Line of the (*time line*) 712

Mfecane, Zulu Expansion and the (*map*) 271

Mississippi's Constitution, Voting Qualifications in (*primary source*) 1703

Moa Fossil Sites in New Zealand, Giant (*map*) 433

Moby Dick, The First Sighting of (*primary source*) 832

Modern Egypt, Abu Simbel in (*map*) 164

Monroe Doctrine (*primary source*) 363

"Morte d'Arthur," Extract from (*primary source*) 656

Mottos of U.S. Currency (*primary source*) 1120

"Mr. Sherlock Holmes" (*primary source*) 1667

Muḥammad ʿAlī Pasha, Burckhardt's Interview with (*primary source*) 201

Nansen's Polar Expedition (*map*) 1755
Nat Turner's Confession (*primary source*). 501
"National Apostasy" (*primary source*). 531
National Park, Yellowstone (*map*) 1376
Natural Selection, Darwin's (*primary source*) . . . 993
Navajos, Long Walk of the (*map*) 1106
Navies of the World at the End of the
    Nineteenth Century, Principal (*table*) 1681
Neanderthal and Cro-Magnon Excavation
    Sites in Germany and France (*map*). 1248
Neanderthal in Some of Us?, A Little
    (*primary source*) 925
A New Cell Theory. 603
New Harmony Constitution (*primary source*) . . . 208
New Parliamentary Oath, A (*primary source*) . . . 416
New Zealand, Giant Moa Fossil Sites in
    (*map*) 433
Newman's Change of Heart
    (*primary source*) 701
Nez Perce in 1877, Flight of the (*map*) 1480
Nobel Prize, Metchnikoff's
    (*primary source*) 1546
North America, Tesla on the First Electric
    Power Plant in (*primary source*) 1865
North America at the End of the Nineteenth
    Century (*map*) lxxxiii
North and West Africa, Explorers' Routes in
    (*map*). 81
Northwest Passage, The (*map*) 283
Novels, Curing Emma Bovary's Addiction to
    (*primary source*) 927
Nullification, Jackson on Tariff Reduction
    and (*primary source*) 523

Ohio's Black Laws (*primary source*) 63
On Sexual Inversion in Women and Men
    (*primary source*) 1868
"Open Door" Note, Hay's First
    (*primary source*) 1929
Oregon Treaty (*primary source*) 720
Outlawing Suttee, British Resolution
    (*primary source*) 430
Overland Mail Routes, Pony Express and
    (*map*) 1002

Pacific, 1860-1898, U.S. Expansion into the
    (*map*) 1923
Pacific, War of the (*map*) 1515
Page Law, Extracts from the
    (*primary source*) 1424

Panic of 1837, Van Buren's Response to the
    (*primary source*) 593
Parliamentary Oath, A New (*primary source*) . . . 416
"Pea, The Princess and the" (*primary source*) . . . 571
Peasant's Death, A (*primary source*). 636
Pendleton Act, The (*primary source*) 1578
People's Party, Platform of the
    (*primary source*) 1746
Perfection of the Details (*primary source*). 615
Pike's Expeditions, 1806-1807 (*map*) 91
Platform of the People's Party
    (*primary source*) 1746
Plessy v. Ferguson (*primary source*) 1849
Poem for the Statue of Liberty
    (*primary source*) 1650
Poetics, Hunt's (*primary source*). 265
Polar Expedition, Nansen's (*map*) 1755
Pony Express and Overland Mail Routes
    (*map*) 1002
"Poor?, Why Are the Many"
    (*primary source*) 1604
Population Centers, 1790-1890, Shifting
    U.S. (*map*) 222
Post-Reconstruction South, President Hayes
    on the (*primary source*) 1474
Post-Revolutionary Texas (*map*). 578
Powell on the Great and Unknown Grand
    Canyon (*primary source*) 1505
Power Plant in North America, Tesla on the
    First Electric (*primary source*) 1865
President Buchanan on Kansas Statehood
    (*primary source*) 921
President Hayes on the Post-Reconstruction
    South (*primary source*) 1474
President Polk Acknowledges California's
    Gold (*primary source*) 765
Presidential Election, Votes in the 1860
    (*map*) 1011
Presidential Election, Votes in the 1896
    (*map*) 1862
"Princess and the Pea, The"
    (*primary source*) 571
Principal Navies of the World at the End
    of the Nineteenth Century (*table*) 1681
Prologue to *The Communist Manifesto*
    (*primary source*) 769
Proust's Contribution to Atomic Theory
    (*primary source*) 44
Province of Canada in 1841, The (*map*) 651
Purchase Treaty, Alaska (*primary source*) 1214

Qualifications, Homesteader
  (*primary source*) 1065
Qualifications in Mississippi's Constitution,
  Voting (*primary source*) 1703
Question of Eugenics, The
  (*primary source*) 1573

Raid, The Jameson (*map*) 1825
Railroad, Abolitionists of the Underground
  (*primary source*) 811
Railroad in 1869, The, Transcontinental
  (*map*) 1294
Railway Network Around 1840, British
  (*map*) 389
Readmission of the Confederate States to the
  Union (*map*) 1110
Reasons for Going to Mecca, Burton's
  (*primary source*) 874
Reconstruction Act, Johnson's Rejection of
  the First (*primary source*) 1111
Red River War, The (*map*) 1414
Reform Act of 1867 (*primary source*) 1223
Rejection of the First Reconstruction Act,
  Johnson's (*primary source*) 1111
"Religion Is, What a Revival of"
  (*primary source*) 561
Religious Truth, Strauss on Historical Truth
  and (*primary source*) 568
Representation, Schopenhauer on
  (*primary source*) 286
Reservations in 1883, American Indian
  (*map*) 1658
Resolution Outlawing Suttee, British
  (*primary source*) 430
"Revival of Religion Is, What a"
  (*primary source*) 561
Revolution, Mexican Territories Before the
  Texas 141
Revolutions of 1848, The (*map*) 761
Routes in East Africa, Explorers' (*map*) 757
Routes in North and West Africa, Explorers'
  (*map*) 81
Routes in the Congo Basin, Explorers'
  (*map*) 1383
Routes to the Klondike (*map*) 1858

St. Louis to Astoria, 1810-1812, Hunt's
  Route from (*map*) 135
Schopenhauer on Representation
  (*primary source*) 286

"Science, Biograph: The Marvel of"
  (*primary source*) 1821
Scott v. Sandford Decision (*primary source*) . . . 940
Secret, The Fetishism of the Commodity
  and Its (*primary source*) 1208
Select Committee Reports on the
  Combination Acts, The (*primary source*) . . . 366
Self-Help, Aphorisms from (*primary source*) . . . 975
Serf Emancipation, Alexander II on
  (*primary source*) 1027
Sexual Inversion in Women and Men, On
  (*primary source*) 1868
Shakspeare, Advertisement for *The Family*
  (*primary source*) 94
"Sherlock Holmes, Mr." (*primary source*) 1667
Sherman Antitrust Act, The
  (*primary source*) 1713
Shifting U.S. Population Centers, 1790-1890
  (*map*) 222
Sister Carrie and Hurstwood
  (*primary source*) 1977
Six Acts, The (*sidebar*) 306
Slave Trade to the United States,
  Congressional Act Prohibiting the
  (*primary source*) 104
Slavery in the United States and Its
  Territories, c. 1860 (*map*) 443
Slavery Sanitized (*primary source*) 853
Socialism Through the Eyes of an Artist
  (*primary source*) 1598
South, President Hayes on the Post-
  Reconstruction (*primary source*) 1474
South African Republic, The 1613
South America at the End of the Nineteenth
  Century (*map*) lxxxiv
South American Independence (*map*) 183
Southern Africa, Jameson's Campaigns in
  (*map*) 1764
Spanish-American War, Caribbean Theater
  of the (*map*) 1904
Statehood, President Buchanan on Kansas
  (*primary source*) 921
States, The Constitution and the Admission
  of New (*primary source*) 326
States to the Union, Readmission of the
  Confederate (*map*) 1110
Statue of Liberty, Poem for the
  (*primary source*) 1650
Strauss on Historical Truth and Religious
  Truth (*primary source*) 568

Sun Writing (*primary source*) 614
Suttee, British Resolution Outlawing
(*primary source*) 430

Taiping Rebellion, The (*map*) 837
Tambora in Modern Indonesia (*map*) 235
Tariff Reduction and Nullification,
Jackson on (*primary source*) 523
Territorial Growth of the United States 724
Territories, Confederate and Union (*map*) 1023
Territories Before the Texas Revolution,
Mexican. 141
Tesla on the First Electric Power Plant in
North America (*primary source*) 1865
Texas, Post-Revolutionary (*map*) 578
Texas Revolution, Mexican Territories
Before the. 141
Text of the Comstock Law
(*primary source*) 1395
Thermodynamics, The Laws of (*sidebar*) 815
Thesis, Turner's Frontier (*primary source*). . . . 1707
Thirteenth Amendment to the U.S.
Constitution (*primary source*). 1167
Thomas Jefferson on Louisiana Purchase
(*primary source*). 53
Thoreau on Civil Disobedience
(*primary source*) 582
Time Line of the Mexican War (*time line*). 712
Time Line of the U.S. Civil War
(*time line*) 1039
Time Line of the War of 1812 (*time line*) 167
"Tippecanoe and Tyler Too"
(*primary source*) 647
Tocqueville Wrote *Democracy in America*,
Why (*primary source*) 494
Trafalgar, Battle of (*map*) 84
Trail of Tears (*map*) 440
Transcontinental Railroad in 1869, The
(*map*) 1294
Treaty, Alaska Purchase (*primary source*) 1214
Treaty of Ghent, Cease-Fire Deadlines in the
(*primary source*) 232
Tribal Lands in Indian Territory in 1836
(*map*) 461
Troy in the Modern Mediterranean Region
(*map*) 1322
Truth and Religious Truth, Strauss on
Historical (*primary source*). 568
Turner's Confession, Nat (*primary source*) 501
Turner's Frontier Thesis (*primary source*) 1707

Twelfth Amendment to the U.S. Constitution,
The (*primary source*) 70
"Twenty Years of Vaudeville"
(*primary source*) 805
Underground Railroad, Abolitionists of the
(*primary source*) 811
Underground Railroad During the 1850's,
The (*map*). 810
Unification of Germany, The (*map*) 1350
Unification of Italy (*map*). 1033
Union, Readmission of the Confederate States
to the (*map*) 1110
Union Territories, Confederate and (*map*) 1023
"Unitarian Christianity" (*primary source*) 301
United States, 1820-1920, European
Emigration to the (*map*) 632
United States, 1821-1890, European
Immigration to the (*table*) 633
United States, 1821-2003, Average Annual
Immigration to the (*table*). 1732
United States, 1821-2003, German
Immigration to the (*table*) 741
United States, 1821-2003, Irish Immigration
to the (*table*) 682
United States, 1851-2003, Chinese
Immigration to the (*table*) 795
United States, Territorial Growth of the 724
United States and Its Territories, c. 1860,
Slavery in the 443
United States in 1900, European Emigration
to the (*map*) 1731
United States v. Wong Kim Ark
(*primary source*) 1898
Universities, Major Land-Grant Colleges and
(*table*) 1068
U.S. Civil War, Time Line of the (*time line*) . . . 1039
U.S. Constitution, Fourteenth Amendment to
the (*primary source*). 1262
U.S. Constitution, Thirteenth Amendment to
the (*primary source*). 1167
U.S. Constitution, Twelfth Amendment to
the (*primary source*) 70
U.S. Currency, The Mottos of
(*primary source*). 1120
U.S. Expansion into the Pacific, 1860-1898
(*map*) 1923
U.S. Immigration Laws, Late Nineteenth
Century (*sidebar*) 1738
U.S. Lands Settled by 1890 (*map*) 1706

U.S. Population Centers, 1790-1890, Shifting
(*map*) 222
U.S. Resolution Recognizing Cuban
Independence (*primary source*) 1805

Values and Differences for F(*x*) = 3*x* + 1
(*table*) 291
Van Buren's Response to the Panic of 1837
(*primary source*) 593
"Vaudeville, Twenty Years of"
(*primary source*) 805
Victoria Falls, Livingstone's First Visit to
(*primary source*) 880
Voortrekker Routes (*map*) 564
Votes in the 1860 Presidential Election
(*map*) 1011
Votes in the 1896 Presidential Election
(*map*) 1862
Voting Qualifications in Mississippi's
Constitution (*primary source*) 1703

Walk of the Navajos, Long (*map*) 1106
War of 1812, Time Line of the (*time line*) 167
War of the Pacific (*map*) 1515
War on Great Britain, Madison's Case for
Making (*primary source*) 168
War, The Red River (*map*) 1414
Waverley's Highland Feast
(*primary source*) 197
Webster-Hayne Debates (*primary source*) 452
West, Expedition to the (*primary source*) 662

West Africa, Explorers' Routes in North and
(*map*) 81
"What a Revival of Religion Is"
(*primary source*) 561
"Why Are the Many Poor?"
(*primary source*) 1604
Why Tocqueville Wrote *Democracy in
America* (*primary source*) 494
"Woman, Ain't I a" (*primary source*) 844
Women's rights declaration, U.S.
(*primary source*) 785, 1462
Wong Kim Ark, United States v.
(*primary source*) 1898
Words of the Boxers (*primary source*) 1963
Workhouses, Carlyle on English
(*primary source*) 670
World at the End of the Nineteenth Century,
Principal Navies of the (*table*) 1681
World in 1801 (*map*) lxxix
World in 1900 (*map*) lxxix
World of Early Cinema, The Chaotic
(*primary source*) 1664
Writing, Sun (*primary source*) 614

X Rays and Conrad's *Heart of Darkness*
(*primary source*) 1816

Yellowstone National Park (*map*) 1376
Young Germany, Engels on (*primary source*) . . . 402

Zulu Expansion and the Mfecane (*map*) 271

The World in 1801

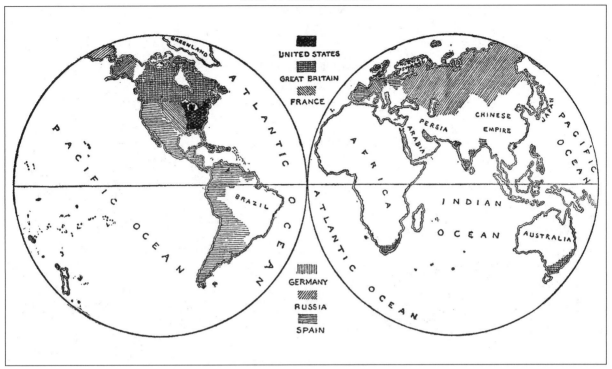

The World in 1900

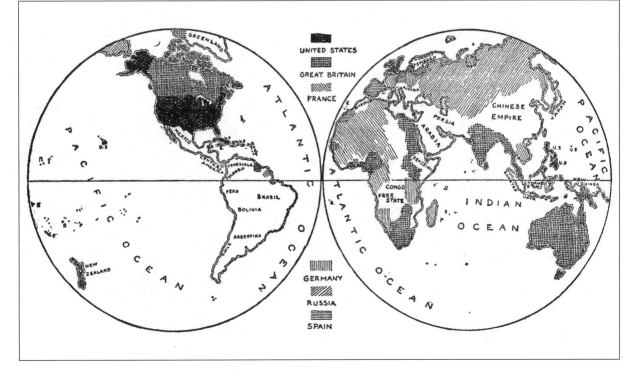

AFRICA AT THE END OF THE NINETEENTH CENTURY

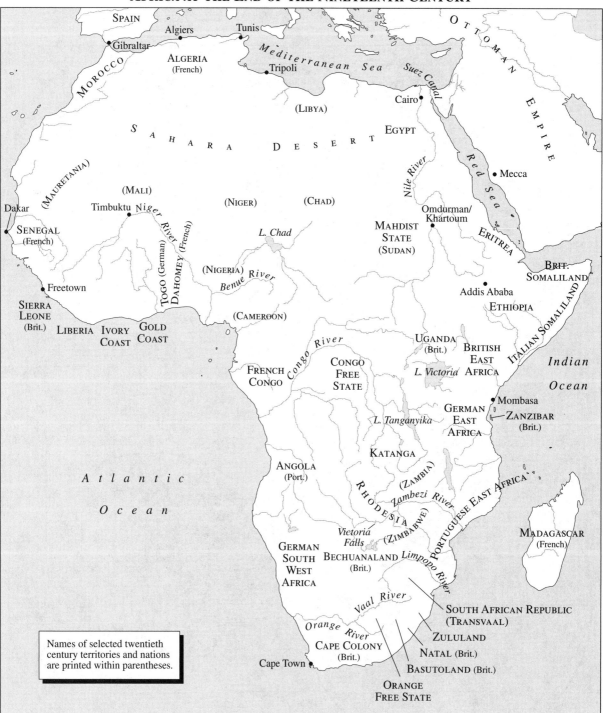

SPAIN

Gibraltar

Algiers

Tunis

MOROCCO

Mediterranean Sea

ALGERIA
(French)

Tripoli

(LIBYA)

Suez Canal

Cairo

EGYPT

OTTOMAN EMPIRE

Red Sea

Mecca

S A H A R A   D E S E R T

Nile River

(MAURETANIA)

Dakar

SENEGAL
(French)

(MALI)

Timbuktu

Niger River

(NIGER)

(CHAD)

L. Chad

MAHDIST
STATE
(SUDAN)

Omdurman/
Khartoum

ERITREA

BRIT.
SOMALILAND

TOGO (German)

DAHOMEY (French)

(NIGERIA)

Benue River

Addis Ababa

ETHIOPIA

ITALIAN SOMALILAND

Freetown

SIERRA
LEONE
(Brit.)

LIBERIA

IVORY
COAST

GOLD
COAST

(CAMEROON)

Congo River

FRENCH
CONGO

CONGO
FREE
STATE

UGANDA
(Brit.)

L. Victoria

BRITISH
EAST
AFRICA

Indian Ocean

Mombasa

GERMAN
EAST
AFRICA

ZANZIBAR
(Brit.)

L. Tanganyika

Atlantic Ocean

KATANGA

ANGOLA
(Port.)

RHODESIA

(ZAMBIA)

Zambezi River

(ZIMBABWE)

PORTUGUESE EAST AFRICA

MADAGASCAR
(French)

Victoria Falls

GERMAN
SOUTH
WEST
AFRICA

BECHUANALAND
(Brit.)

Limpopo River

Vaal River

SOUTH AFRICAN REPUBLIC
(TRANSVAAL)

ZULULAND

Orange River

CAPE COLONY
(Brit.)

Cape Town

NATAL (Brit.)

BASUTOLAND (Brit.)

ORANGE
FREE STATE

Names of selected twentieth
century territories and nations
are printed within parentheses.

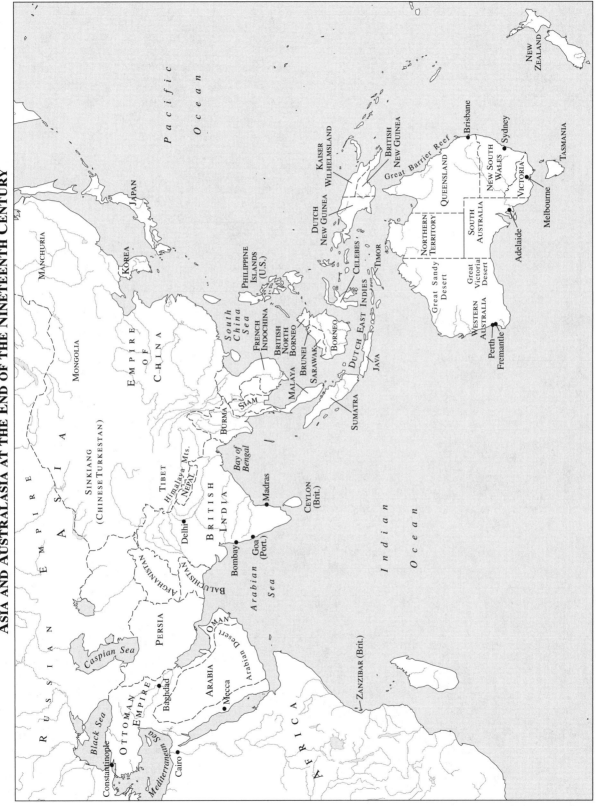

ASIA AND AUSTRALASIA AT THE END OF THE NINETEENTH CENTURY

EUROPE AT THE END OF THE NINETEENTH CENTURY

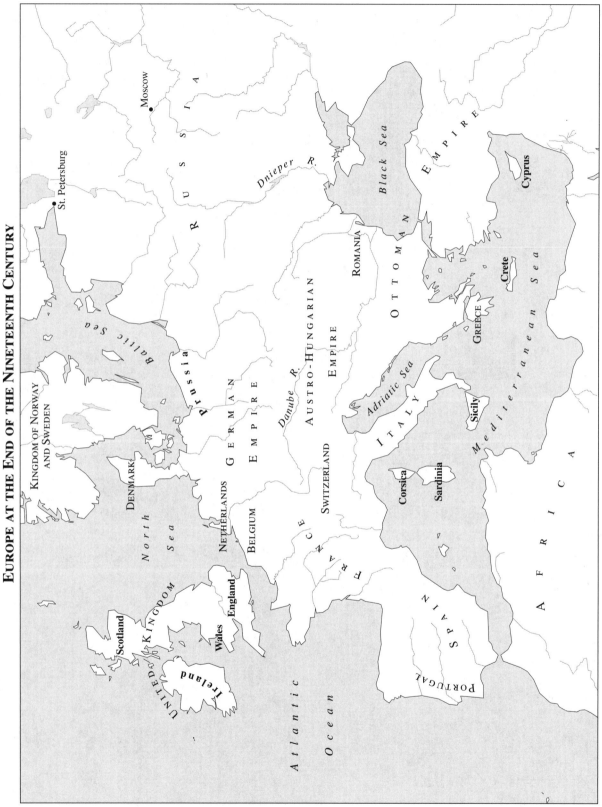

NORTH AMERICA AT THE END OF THE NINETEENTH CENTURY

Bering Sea

Bering Strait

Arctic Ocean

ALASKA

KLONDIKE

GREENLAND (Denmark)

Baffin Bay

DOMINION

Hudson Bay

OF   CANADA

St. Lawrence River

NEWFOUNDLAND

Washington

Oregon

Montana

North Dakota

Idaho

South Dakota

Wyoming

Nevada

Utah

Colorado River

California

Colorado

Nebraska

Minnesota

Wisconsin

Great Lakes

Michigan

Iowa

Kansas

Missouri River

Indiana   Ohio

Illinois

Ohio River

Maine

Vermont

New Hampshire

Massachusetts

Rhode Island

Connecticut

New York

Penn-sylvania

New Jersey

Delaware

Maryland

Arizona (terr.)

Rio Grande

New Mexico (terr.)

Oklahoma (terr.)

Arkansas River

Mississippi River

Kentucky

Tennessee

Virginia

West Virginia

North Carolina

South Carolina

Texas

Louisiana

Mississippi

Alabama

Georgia

Florida

MEXICO

Pacific Ocean

Gulf of Mexico

Atlantic Ocean

CUBA

JAMAICA

HAITI

PUERTO RICO

DOMINICAN REPUBLIC

Caribbean Sea

CENTRAL AMERICA

SOUTH AMERICA

SOUTH AMERICA AT THE END OF THE NINETEENTH CENTURY

North
Atlantic
Ocean

Caracas

BRITISH
GUIANA

DUTCH
GUIANA

FRENCH
GUIANA

VENEZUELA

Bogotá

COLOMBIA

Galápagos
Islands

Amazon River

ECUADOR — Quito

Amazon Basin

BRAZIL

São Francisco River

PERU

Andes

Lima

La Paz

BOLIVIA

Sucre

South
Pacific
Ocean

Paraná River

PARAGUAY

Rio de Janeiro

Mountains

CHILE

Santiago

ARGENTINA

URUGUAY

Buenos Aires

Montevideo

Negro River

South
Atlantic
Ocean

Falkland
Islands
(British)

Stanley

South
Georgia

Cape
Horn

The **19th Century**

1801-1900

19th century
ARABIC LITERARY RENAISSANCE

The Arabic Literary Renaissance began after the French occupation of Egypt ended and continued until Middle Eastern nationalist sentiments revived in the wake of World War I. During that long period, European modernization heavily influenced Middle Eastern literary figures and philosophers. As Arab intellectuals adjusted to these new influences, some adapted well while others repudiated modernity outright.

ALSO KNOWN AS: Arabic Literary Revival; *Naḥda*
LOCALE: Egypt, Lebanon, and other Middle Eastern countries
CATEGORY: Literature

KEY FIGURES

Napoleon Bonaparte (1769-1821), first consul of France, 1799-1804, and general who led French occupation of Egypt
Muḥammad ʿAlī Pasha (1769-1849), Albanian-born viceroy of Egypt, 1805-1848
Ismāʿīl Pasha (1830-1895), viceroy of Egypt, 1863-1879
Rifāʾah Rāfiʾ aṭ-Ṭahtawi (1801-1873), director of the Cairo School of Languages, 1836
Butrus al-Bustani (1819-1883), Lebanese lexicographer
Nāṣif Yāziji (1800-1871), Lebanese poet
Kahlil Gibran (1883-1931), Lebanese poet, philosopher, and artist
Shihāb al-Dīn Maḥmūd al-Ālūsī (1802-1854), Iraqi writer

SUMMARY OF EVENT

The Arabic Literary Renaissance marked a segment of wider political, intellectual, and cultural reform affecting the Middle East. Known as *Naḥda* in Arabic, the regional literary renaissance ended preexisting Middle Eastern literary norms, which had been largely dependent upon oral traditions. The literary symbolism, forms, and figures, as well as technological innovations, made the renaissance a conduit through which Arab culture meshed with modernity amid political and cultural conflict. Rather than submit to Western ways completely, Arabic literature adapted new styles and techniques that preserved elements of Arabic culture.

Prior to the nineteenth century, the literary period known as the Age of Depression developed themes that the Arabic Literary Renaissance repeated in new ways. Both periods emphasized romantic ideals of Arab life and a sense of ethnic pride. Although literary subjects shifted from individual achievement and heroics to everyday life, Arab identity remained a constant. Emphasis on broader social themes served as a natural reaction to French general Napoleon Bonaparte's invasion of Egypt in 1798. Napoleon brought more than a military occupation of territory; he also brought scientists and scholars to study and survey Egyptian history, culture, and topography. European efforts to learn about and exploit "orientalism" helped introduce modern concepts to the Middle East.

Although France's occupation of Egypt lasted only three years, it profoundly altered Egyptian attitudes after a new ruler, Muḥammad ʿAlī Pasha, consolidated power in 1805. Mimicking his Ottoman allies, Muḥammad Alī reformed Egypt's military and education systems along Western lines. By 1816, the transition from Egypt's religious Azhar system of education gave way to Westernized secular institutions. Muḥammad ʿAlī imported European technicians, scientists, and educators to create a modern Arab state.

Determined not to be outdone by the Lebanese, Muḥammad Alī ordered an Arabic printing press for disseminating Western knowledge as well as printing classical Arabic texts. In 1828, the Boulaq Press issued Egypt's first official newspaper. In 1835, the Cairo School of Languages began teaching French, Italian, and English. Six years later, the Cairo school helped establish the Translation Bureau, further opening Egypt to the West. Printing presses, language schools, and the Translation Bureau introduced an Arab audience to European literature, history, and technical manuals.

Additionally, the West's Christian missionaries and educational institutions infiltrated the region. Under Egyptian occupation, Syria and Lebanon became home to Western colleges. In 1847, the United States established the American College, later renamed the American University of Beirut. Missionary schools for women also began appearing in the Middle East. Later in the century, Egyptian ruler Khedive Ismāʿīl advanced modern educational reforms. Educated in France, Ismāʿīl increased educational opportunities for all, including women. He founded the Dar al-ʿUlum, a teachers' training college seeking connections between Islamic traditions and Western learning. Ismāʿīl encouraged his countrymen to wear Western apparel, adopt Western legal codes, incorporate European financial standards, and fund construction of a Cairo opera house that opened in

1869, in time to celebrate the completion of the Suez Canal with the world premiere of Giuseppe Verdi's *Aida*. All of these reforms bound Egypt more closely to European influences.

These rapid changes split Arab society and intellectuals into two factions: those repudiating modernity and those embracing it. By the mid-nineteenth century, many Arabs were taking steps to preserve their cultural identity, including their rich literary heritage. For example, the Egyptian poet Sayyid Alī al-Darwish and the Lebanese poet Nāṣīf Yāziji imitated older poetic forms dating back to the twelfth century.

Nevertheless, scholars such as Rifāʾah Rāfiʾ aṭ-Ṭahtawi, who was one of many students Muḥammad ʿAlī sent to Europe to study, followed Western ways; aṭ-Ṭahtawi became director of the Cairo School of Languages in 1836. The school's students assisted in translating more than two thousand books into Arabic. Others open to modernity included the Iraqi writer Shihāb al-Dīn al-Ālūsī, whose ode commemorating British queen Victoria's reign won popular acclaim. Interestingly, Arab literary figures developed a paradoxical relationship concerning modernity as the century progressed. While Egyptian poets born after 1850, such as Aḥmad Shawqī, Muḥammad Ḥāfiẓ Ibrāhīm, and Khalīl Maṭrān, all adopted modern literary forms, they applied them to express strong Arab nationalist sentiments.

By the late nineteenth century, another ethnic group was contesting nationalist autonomy in the Middle East and threatening Arabic notions of identity. The Viennese playwright and journalist Theodor Herzl was calling for a Jewish homeland. Herzl's 1896 book *Der Judenstaat* (the Jewish state) argued for Jewish self-determination as an alternative to persistent European anti-Semitism. The following year, Herzl joined others in galvanizing support for the Zionist movement, which specified Palestine—the future center of the modern state of Israel—as the location for this new Jewish state. Like Napoleon's invasion, Zionism invigorated Arab nationalism, combining it with reactionary expressions of political Islam.

Interpreting modernity as a threat placed Egyptians and neighboring Arabs on the defensive by forcing them to protect and further define their culture. Literary forms new to Arab culture—such as novels, short stories, essays, biographies, autobiographies, histories, literary criticism, and, most significant, dramas—conveyed a growing awareness of self-identity. Arab writers and philosophers saw modernity as a vehicle imperative for reinvigorating Arab honor and winning respect for it among the world's civilizations.

By the end of the renaissance era, a few literary figures sought compromise among competing views. For example, Butrus al-Bustani's work on an Arabic encyclopedia and dictionary defined the substantive contributions to world culture that Arabs could claim. Through art and philosophical teachings, the Lebanese writer Kahlil Gibran spread mystical concepts of human existence that challenged scientific notions of modernity. Writers such as these interpreted Arab culture and history as a vital component of the modern world. Using humanity as the constant link between antiquity and modernity, Gibran's writings defused tensions among the competing schools of thought.

SIGNIFICANCE

Throughout the nineteenth and into the twentieth century, the Arabic Literary Renaissance revealed two diverging viewpoints regarding modernity. Many Arabs accommodated change and strove to elevate the Arab role in the modern era. Muḥammad ʿAlī and his successor, Khedive Ismāʿīl, bound the Middle East more closely to Europe's modern practices by reforming Egyptian military tactics and armaments, as well as social customs and laws. Although many Arab writers and thinkers applauded these events, a substantial portion considered modernization a threat to Arab identity. Scholars such as Kahlil Gibran and Butrus al-Bustani disseminated Arab thought and accomplishments to others by redefining modernity as a reciprocal relationship wherein exchanges of knowledge and philosophy replaced assimilation and resentment. However, conflict between modernization's proponents and opponents marginalized the true significance of Gibran's and al-Bustani's work.

By the late nineteenth century, the two feuding groups and their philosophical platforms had solidified. Politically, the polarized factions continued into the twentieth century with promodernist leaders such as Egyptian prime minister and president Gamal Abdel Nasser and antimodernist groups such as the Society of the Muslim Brotherhood. Novels such as Naguib Mahfouz's Cairo Trilogy reflected the rifts pervading Arab society, and Mahfouz won the 1988 Nobel Prize in Literature. These tensions have persisted into the twenty-first century.

—*Matthew Walker*

FURTHER READING

Badawi, M. M. *A Short History of Modern Arabic Literature*. Oxford, England: Clarendon Press, 1993. This book offers an excellent introduction to period and its long-term implications.

Bakalla, M. H. *Arabic Culture Through Its Language and Literature*. Boston: Kegan Paul International, 1984. Bakalla offers a concise summary of the Arabic Literary Renaissance.

Boullata, Issa J., and Terri DeYoung, eds. *Tradition and Modernity in Arabic Literature*. Fayetteville: University of Arkansas Press, 1997. Although it focuses on a late period in the Arabic Literary Renaissance, this edited volume offers lengthy examinations of philosophers such as Kahlil Gibran.

Daly, M. W., ed. *Modern Egypt from 1517 to the End of the Twentieth Century*. Vol. 2 in *The Cambridge History of Egypt*. New York: Cambridge University Press, 1998. Chapter 6, written by Khaled Fahmy, chronicles the events and significance of Muḥammad's governorate.

Fahmy, Khaled. *All the Pasha's Men: Mehmed Ali, His Army, and the Making of Modern Egypt*. New York: Cambridge University Press, 1997. Examines Muḥammad's military reforms and recruitment policies in the context of his modernization of Egypt's government.

Gibb, H. A. R. *Arabic Literature: An Introduction*. London: Oxford University Press, 1926. Although in many ways dated, this classic study of Arabic literature remains highly respected in the field.

Haywood, John A. *Modern Arabic Literature, 1800-1970*. London: Lund Humphries, 1971. Haywood's text serves as one the cornerstones in the field of the Arabic Literary Renaissance.

Moss, Joyce, ed. *Middle Eastern Literatures and Their Times*. Vol. 6 in *World Literature and Its Times*. Detroit: Thomson Gale, 2004. Collection of authoritative essays on individual writers and works, including many from the nineteenth century.

SEE ALSO: 1811-1818: Egypt Fights the Wahhābīs; Mar. 1, 1811: Muḥammad ʿAlī Has the Mamlūks Massacred; 1814-1879: Exploration of Arabia; 1832-1841: Turko-Egyptian Wars; Nov. 17, 1869: Suez Canal Opens; Sept. 13, 1882: Battle of Tel el Kebir; Feb., 1896-Aug., 1897: Herzl Founds the Zionist Movement.

RELATED ARTICLES in *Great Lives from History: The Nineteenth Century, 1801-1900:* Muḥammad ʿAbduh; Theodor Herzl; Muḥammad ʿAlī Pasha; Napoleon I.

19th century
DEVELOPMENT OF WORKING-CLASS LIBRARIES

Beginning with the first library for the working class in Scotland in 1741 and influenced by increased popular education and the rise of a free press, libraries founded by and for the British working class thrived into the nineteenth century, satisfying reading interests and tastes before the rise of free public libraries.

LOCALE: Great Britain
CATEGORIES: Literature; cultural and intellectual history; education; organizations and institutions

KEY FIGURES
James Stirling (1692-1770), mines manager at Leadhills
Francis Place (1771-1854), English reformer
George Jacob Holyoake (1817-1906), English socialist reformer
Elizabeth Gaskell (Elizabeth Cleghorn Stevenson; 1810-1865), British writer

SUMMARY OF EVENT
A number of important changes in Great Britain in the eighteenth century led to a demand for secular literature. These changes included increased provisions for education, the growth of reading publications, and increased interest in reading. The old town and parish libraries could not satisfy the needs created by these changes, so two new kinds of subscription libraries—private and commercial—were developed to provide reading materials for different social classes. Starting with four in Scotland and two in England, the private libraries founded for and by the working class continued to grow during the nineteenth century but gradually gave way to an increasing number of free public libraries.

The library that came into being at Leadhills in Lanarkshire, Scotland, became the first private subscription library and the first library for the working class in Great Britain. The Leadhills Reading Society, as the library was originally called, was founded in 1741 by the lead miners of the Scots Mines Company. Of the twenty-three founding members, all were miners except the minister and the schoolmaster. James Stirling, mines manager, was often credited with helping establish the library. Supported by members' subscription fees (6 shillings), the library provided readings not only for leisure but also for serious study. The next three libraries also were founded in Scotland: First founded was the Wanlockhead library (a carbon copy of the Leadhills library) by the lead miners in Dumfriesshire in 1756. The Westerkirk library was founded by the antimony miners, also in Dumfriesshire, in 1792. The Langloan library was founded by the weavers and other working men in Lanarkshire in 1794. The first two working-class libraries in England were the Economical Library at Kendal (1797) and the Artizans' Library at Birmingham (1799). The former, designed for the use and instruction of the working class, proved useless. The latter, Artizans', was originally a Sunday school library.

During the nineteenth century, tradesmen, mechanics, and artisans founded a number of libraries, the best known being the Edinburgh Mechanics' Subscription Library, which formed in 1825. The Edinburgh Mechanics' Institute, originally called the Edinburgh School of Arts, provided vocational instruction for the working class. The subscription library was founded by three members of the school who wished to pursue their studies even when the school was closed in the summer. In England, libraries for mechanics and apprentices were founded at Liverpool (1823), Sheffield (1823), Kendal (1824), and Durham (1851). The Liverpool and Sheffield libraries owed their origins to the editors of the *Liverpool Mercury* and the *Sheffield Independent*, respectively. A number of smaller working-class libraries existed, but without a distinguishing title.

The Edinburgh Mechanics' Subscription Library could be considered the first of a group of libraries associated with the mechanics' institutes. Started in the 1820's, the institutes were focused on improving working-class adult education. Social reformers such as Francis Place and George Jacob Holyoake were active in promoting these institutes, believing that the institutes could serve as instruments of emancipation for the working class in their demand for social and political reform. From Edinburgh and London, the mechanics' institutes spread to the industrial areas of the north of England, the midlands, south Wales, and central Scotland. The growing economic importance of many provinces such as Liverpool, Manchester, and Glasgow was a direct result of the Industrial Revolution. By 1850, there were about seven hundred mechanics' institutes, with fifty in, mostly, the Forth-Clyde area in Scotland. The libraries at these institutes had holdings of 655,000 volumes. The largest library was at Liverpool (15,300 volumes), followed by Manchester (13,000 volumes).

Finally, certain factories and firms opened libraries for their workers. One of the best factory libraries was founded for the mill workers at W. & D. Morris factories at Chorlton-on-Medlock in Manchester in 1845. A library was founded in the Fieldhouse Institute by John Bright and Brothers at Rochdale in 1832. Still another one was established at Ipswich in 1856 for the workers of the foundry of Messrs. Ransomes and May. Elizabeth Gaskell's novel *Mary Barton: A Tale of Manchester Life* (1848) inspired the founding of factory libraries in Manchester in 1849. According to the book, working men in the manufacturing districts of Lancashire displayed real interest in book use.

Book selection at the working-class libraries reflected the social, political, and cultural influences before and during the nineteenth century, notably the lapse of government censorship and the movement for inexpensive literature. As in most of Europe, the press in Great Britain in the eighteenth century was frequently subjected to strict censorship. John Milton's plea for freedom of the press in 1644 contributed to the final lapse of the Licensing Act in 1694. As an independent press emerged during the nineteenth century, censorship gradually yielded to the demand for a free press. Additionally, born out of the Reform Act of 1832—a landmark in the turn to inexpensive publishing—a new movement provided literature that was free from religious and other propaganda at a price affordable to the working classes.

The working-class libraries were not interested in acquiring fiction and serial literature in the beginning of the century. The working people's enthusiasm for controversial religion was a major motivating factor in deciding which books to acquire. While working-class piety remained, dissident social behavior was nonetheless evident in a society influenced by moderate clergy and the patronage system. Because of the impact of the Enlightenment, the working people were interested more in social science than in vocational reading. Their preference for such socially scientific subjects as history, geography, biography, and politics reflected a change toward secular book use. About 50 percent of reading materials were works on history and religion, followed by biography and travel. The shift toward fiction by the end of the century marked the most notable change in book use and a new level of sophistication in reading.

The Scottish working class was conservative in its literary tendencies, so the libraries most often collected classical literature and were strongly influenced by the newly established Free Church of Scotland and the rising temperance movement. All fiction was excluded from the libraries until the commercial success of the Scottish poet Sir Walter Scott. His success influenced how books would be selected.

The working-class libraries originally relied on members' subscription fees for their operations. For this reason, many were small and short-lived. Their success and failure largely depended on favorable circumstances or financial support from outside sources. The Leadhills, Wanlockhead, and Westerkirk libraries were founded in well-paid mining communities. The Leadhills library was also supported by the local gentry. The Westerkirk library became a general library when the mining company there stopped its operations. The Liverpool Mechanics' and Apprentices' Library flourished under a management committee of wealthy supporters and donors. The library gradually faded with the appearance of free public libraries. A similar fate led to the slow demise of mechanics' institute libraries. By the end of the nineteenth century, there remained about eighty-three working-class libraries, which survived mostly in large villages and market towns.

SIGNIFICANCE

The development of the working-class libraries reflected a time of increasing popular education and increasing interest in book use. The libraries also helped educate the working classes in their demand for political and social reform. Side by side with the private libraries for the middle class and the clergy, the working-class libraries satisfied the growing needs for cheap and wholesome reading materials, which the government failed to provide. Finally, the working-class libraries in Scotland encouraged their patrons to participate in intellectual life and supported the rejection of a separate intellectual class.

—Anh Tran

FURTHER READING

Battles, Matthew. *Library: An Unquiet History*. New York: W. W. Norton, 2003. A history of libraries as well as the forces in history that try to destroy information and communication.

Crawford, John. "The Ideology of Mutual Improvement in Scottish Working Class Libraries." *Library History* 12, no. 1 (1996): 49-62. Contends that the Enlightenment and the idea of mutual improvement were at the core of the establishment of the Leadhills library.

Harris, Michael H. *History of Libraries in the Western World*. Metuchen, N.J.: Scarecrow Press, 1995. A general survey of library history, originally published in 1984.

Lerner, Fred. *The Story of Libraries: From the Invention of Writing to the Computer Age*. New York: Continuum, 1998. Explains how major societies used libraries and discusses how these societies were affected by the libraries they created and inherited.

Rose, Jonathan. "A Conservative Canon: Cultural Lag in British Working-Class Reading Habits." *Library and Culture* 33, no. 1 (1998): 98-104. Explores the conservative literary tastes of the working people compared to the more avant-garde preference found among the middle classes.

Vincent, David. *The Rise of Mass Literacy*. Cambridge, England: Polity, 2000. Vincent examines how eighteenth century ideas about literacy and reading were practiced well into the nineteenth century.

SEE ALSO: 1820's-1830's: Free Public School Movement; 1820's-1850's: Social Reform Movement; June 4, 1832: British Parliament Passes the Reform Act of 1832; Oct. 4-6, 1876: American Library Association Is Founded.

RELATED ARTICLES in *Great Lives from History: The Nineteenth Century, 1801-1900:* William Edward Forster; Francis Place.

19th century
SPREAD OF THE WALTZ

The waltz, which expanded from its roots in the rotating folk dances of rural Central Europe, first appeared in written music by the end of the eighteenth century. The dance, which involves couples in close contact, became extremely popular with the rising middle class and then within elite circles.

LOCALE: Vienna, Austria
CATEGORIES: Dance; music

KEY FIGURES

Johann Strauss, Jr. (1825-1899), Austrian violinist, composer, and conductor known as the Waltz King

Joseph Lanner (1801-1843), Austrian composer and conductor and early partner of Johann Strauss, Sr.

Johann Strauss, Sr. (1804-1849), Austrian composer and conductor known as the founder of the waltz

The Waltz King, Austrian composer Johann Strauss. (Library of Congress)

SUMMARY OF EVENT

Although the word *waltzen*, a modification of the Latin *volvere*, meaning to turn or rotate, had existed for many years prior to the emergence of the dance known as the waltz, it was first applied to dance during the mid-eighteenth century. For centuries, the folk dances of central Europe had included movements in lively three-beat patterns, with couples spinning around and holding each other tightly. Although similar in style, each dance, from particular regions, had a different name, including *ländler, dreher, spinner, weller, schleifer, steirer*, and others. They were also described collectively as German dances. These dizzying, intoxicating dances would have been unthinkable in the pre-nineteenth century courts of Europe, in which dancers maintained a degree of distance from each other, always stayed in strict control of themselves, and rarely made physical contact. Courtship in elite circles was closely circumscribed, and it was often connected to political allegiances, inheritance, or both. The earthy peasants, having little to gain or lose, had no such concerns.

During the late eighteenth century, political and economic transformations would affect social dancing. The rise of the middle class gave more leisure time and social mobility to large numbers of young people who were attracted to the sensuality and simplicity of the rustic dances. Also, with the influence of the French and American Revolutions, there was a trend toward the rejection of overly formal and intricate forms of interaction. Eventually, the verb describing the rotating of the dancers came to be used as a noun, and the word "waltz" began to appear in print in the 1790's as a category of dance music.

According to written accounts, the original German dances were more boisterous and a bit slower in tempo. Partners would often hop and jump, and male partners would lift their female partners. At some point during the transition from rural to urban environments, these movements were replaced by a sort of gliding and sliding, which accelerated the spinning even more, and which required a polished floor to reduce friction from the feet. The triple time was retained as a key feature of the genre. With one step to each beat of the meter, every successive measure of music placed the dancer's weight on the opposite foot, increasing momentum.

The waltz became wildly popular all over Europe, but it was not without controversy. Many believed it was undignified and was morally suspect because the partners held each other so closely. One of the earliest and best-known centers for waltzing was Vienna, Austria, which became the capital of the Austro-Hungarian Empire and one of the most prosperous and powerful cities in the world. The Viennese could afford to hire musicians for their dances, and since Vienna was surrounded by the folk cultures from which the waltz had emerged, area musicians were quite familiar with its rhythmic requirements and its potential for evoking infectious joy among dancers. In the first decade of the nineteenth century, great dance halls opened in Vienna, including the Apollosaal, which could hold up to six thousand dancers. Large groups of dancers also resulted in larger groups of musicians.

In this environment, the first great dance orchestras evolved and then developed parallel to, and sometimes overlapping with, Vienna's well-established tradition of concert music. The first two musicians to achieve great fame as composers of waltzes and leaders of dance orchestras were Johann Strauss, Sr., and Joseph Lanner. Until 1825, the two were partners and played in the same group. As composers, they contributed to the development of the waltz as a musical form, grouping waltzes together into extended pieces with introductions and recapitulations. Strauss, Sr., the founder of the waltz, introduced rhythmic variations, and Lanner was known for his beautiful melodies.

Strauss's and Lanner's orchestras were respected by concert musicians, who were impressed by the composers' high standards of ensemble precision and intonation. The two developed these standards partly from constant practice and also from receiving long-term employment in the dance halls. The music grew more and more lavish and contributed to a glamorous atmosphere far removed from the humble origins of the waltz. Well-dressed couples could almost leave the earth together and escape into a dream world as they glided through a flowing environment of visual and musical beauty, expressing a romantic yearning for emotional transcendence.

Concert musicians quickly adopted the waltz for their own purposes. Solo piano works were among the first pieces to include the term in their titles or interpretive

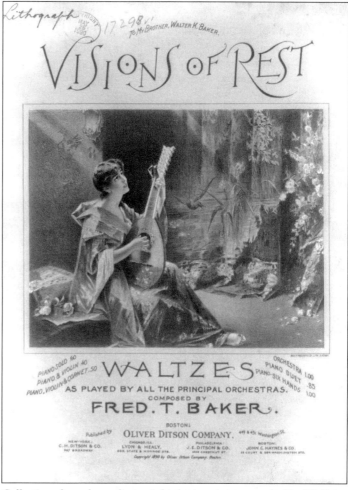

Collection of popular waltz music by the American composer Fred T. Baker first published in 1890. (Library of Congress)

instructions. Franz Schubert wrote two sets of waltzes for piano in the years 1815-1821, and Carl Maria von Weber's *Invitation to the Dance* (1819) anticipated the formal innovations of Strauss, Sr., and Lanner. A waltz melody by Anton Diabelli became the basis for elaborate variations by Ludwig van Beethoven, Franz Liszt, and Schubert. The Polish pianist Frédéric Chopin, who lived in Vienna for a time in the 1830's before relocating to Paris, made some dismissive comments about the popular waltz scene, but he would compose significant works in the form, which aside from its faster tempo bears some similarities to the *mazurka* of his homeland. Chopin's waltz pieces introduced many complex rhythms and changes of tempo. Later, Johannes Brahms, who became a friend of the Strauss family, also composed piano pieces in the waltz idiom.

In Vienna, the orchestral dance tradition continued throughout the nineteenth century. Johann Strauss, Jr., the son of the elder composer, and his brothers Josef and Eduard, were all conductors, and Johann became even more successful than his father as a composer and conductor. Of his many waltzes, *The Blue Danube* (1867) is his best-known work. In 1872, when he was billed as the Waltz King, he was engaged to conduct a performance of this piece by an orchestra of twenty thousand for an audience of one hundred thousand. Strauss later turned his attention to composing operettas, in which waltz music was an important ingredient, including *Die Fledermaus* (1874) and others. The waltz entered the world of symphonic music as well. Richard Wagner included one in his opera *Parsifal* (1882). Peter Ilich Tchaikovsky, who loved waltzes, included them in his symphonic works for ballet, including *Swan Lake* (1877), *Sleeping Beauty* (1889), and *The Nutcracker* (1892).

SIGNIFICANCE

The waltz at first heralded social transformation, but its long association with Vienna became a tradition unto itself as an ongoing source of local pride. After World War I and the end of the Austro-Hungarian Empire, the social context changed, and the waltz was preserved as a genre to be included in ballroom dancing, which became very popular internationally. In this new context, the waltz was studied along with other dances, often in schools that were partially recreational and social. Contests, too, were held. Taken from the Viennese model, the waltz became more stylized and defined.

The traditional waltz survived its inclusion in the vast nineteenth and early twentieth century repertoire for ballet, operetta, and concert music. It also was frequently included in films with historic themes. Classical composers continued to use the waltz style, sometimes as a stylistic quotation and sometimes transplanted into more modern, even disturbing settings. As a genre within the swing style, the "jazz waltz" entered the stylistic vocabulary of instrumental jazz musicians in the 1950's.

—*John E. Myers*

FURTHER READING

Carner, Mosco. *The Waltz*. London: Max Parrish, 1948. A comprehensive history of the waltz as a social and musical phenomenon, including discussion of the major composers and a section on the impact of the waltz on concert music. Illustrated. Includes music examples and an index.

Fantel, Hans. *The Waltz Kings Johann Strauss: Father and Son, and Their Romantic Age*. New York: William Morrow, 1972. A colorful descriptive language describes the musicians, their friends, families, and associates, and the world in which they lived. Illustrated.

Reeser, Educard. *The History of the Waltz*. Translated by W. A. G. Doyle-Davidson. Stockholm: Continental, 1949. A historical account and commentary, with illustrations, music examples, and a bibliography.

Schönberg, Harold C. *The Lives of the Great Composers*. 3d ed. New York: W. W. Norton, 1997. Includes a chapter that discusses the artistic impact of the waltz orchestras and anecdotes about the musicians. Illustrations, bibliography.

Wechsberg, Joseph. *The Waltz Emperors: The Life and Times and Music of the Strauss Family*. New York: G. P. Putnam's Sons, 1973. A detailed portrait of the Strauss family and its popular music reflecting a period of eighty years. Beautifully illustrated, with an index.

Yaraman, Sevin H. *Revolving Embrace: The Waltz as Sex, Steps, and Sound*. Hillsdale, N.Y.: Pendragon Press, 2002. Detailed musical analyses and social commentary. Illustrations, bibliographical references, and index.

SEE ALSO: c. 1869: Golden Age of Flamenco Begins.
RELATED ARTICLES in *Great Lives from History: The Nineteenth Century, 1801-1900:* Ludwig van Beethoven; Johannes Brahms; Frédéric Chopin; Johann Strauss; Peter Ilich Tchaikovsky; Richard Wagner; Carl Maria von Weber.

1801
EMERGENCE OF THE PRIMITIVES

A group of young French artists, the Primitives revolted against the neoclassical artistic values of their tutor, Jacques-Louis David, and embraced ancient Greek and fifteenth century Italian art. They produced little work that has survived and had only a negligible influence on later nineteenth century artists, but their unconventional attitudes and lifestyles anticipated those of the bohemians and later movements.

ALSO KNOWN AS: Les Primitifs
LOCALE: Paris, France
CATEGORY: Art

KEY FIGURES
Pierre-Maurice Quay (c. 1779-1802/1803), French
    artist and leader of the Primitives
Jacques-Louis David (1748-1825), neoclassical painter
    and Jacobin leader in the French Revolution
Jean-Pierre Franque (1774-1860),
Joseph-Boniface Franque (1774-1833), and
Jean Broc (1771-1850), students of David and
    members of the Primitives

SUMMARY OF EVENT

The French Revolution of 1789 captured the heart of France's most prominent and influential neoclassical painter, Jacques-Louis David. David's career began as the ornamental artistic style later known as rococo was still in full blossom, so David's early work—stunning and austere political paintings such as *Oath of the Horatii* (1784) and *Death of Socrates* (1787)—reflected the changing moral climate in France. When the revolution began in 1789, David quickly became its supporter. He eventually served in the National Assembly, and his art became a tool for advancing the revolution. His *Death of Marat* (1794), a heroic portrayal of his murdered friend Jean-Paul Marat, evokes the pietà, equating Marat's sacrifice with that of Christ.

When the revolution waned and its leader Robespierre was executed, David was thrown into prison, where he conceived the idea for his painting *Intervention of the Sabine Women* (1799). In his efforts to advance his revolutionary political and artistic ideas, David had taught an enormous number of students. However, after his release, he exerted an increased influence over their work, intending either to maintain control of his artistic agenda following the revolution or to supervise the work of his new generation of students more closely. Among

his students was a mysterious and only modestly talented young man still in his teens, Pierre-Maurice Quay.

Along with his friends Jean Broc and twin brothers Jean-Pierre Franque and Joseph-Boniface Franque, Quay rejected the bourgeois values that the Enlightenment had brought to European science and philosophy and demanded a return to the primitive and ancient world of Homer, Ossian, and the Bible, and to fifteenth century Italian artistic styles. The budding circle of friends associated the elaborate ornamentation of the *rocaille* style that had been popular during the eighteenth century with bourgeois values, and Quay began calling the art "rococo," a distortion of *rocaille*. They advocated going back to the primitive art of the ancient Greeks, characterized as the pure and single circuit lines seen on the vases and urns from antiquity. They believed that all art produced after the time of the Greek sculptor Phidias (fifth century B.C.E.) should be destroyed. They isolated themselves from others, grew long beards which led them to be called *Barbus* (the bearded ones), adopted vegetarian diets, and began wearing long, flowing robes like those illustrated on ancient sculptures.

When David completed *Intervention of the Sabine Women*, Quay, Broc, the Franque brothers, and several other students severely criticized his work as a representation of the stylistic boldness they so passionately rejected. In response, David expelled them from his studio. The expelled artists then formed a commune in an abandoned convent outside Paris, where they began to turn away from their admiration of ancient Greece and move toward a passion for Middle Eastern mysticism and concepts associated with the Bible.

Quay liked to be called Agamemnon, after the Greek king in Homer's epics—an acknowledgment of his admiration of antiquity and a likely reference to his self-concept as a leader. One of the few references to Quay by a near-contemporary, the French author Charles Nodier, suggests that Quay was a man of enormous charisma, far too gifted intellectually and emotionally to engage in the daily pursuits of ordinary human life. When Napoleon I asked Quay, "Why did you adopt a type of clothing which separates you from the world?" Quay answered, "In order to separate myself from the world." In spite of Quay's youth, his impact on his peers and their movement is unmistakable. The Primitives maintained a close and unbroken solidarity during his lifetime and disbanded almost immediately after his early death, sometime around

Jacques-Louis David. (Library of Congress)

the age of twenty-four. Quay's indifference to the details of life may have led him never actually to complete a painting—none of his work still exists today—yet his reputation in his own time is evidenced by the existence of a portrait of him painted in about 1800 by Henri-François Riesener that hangs in the Louvre Museum.

None of the Primitives left a portfolio of major works, though Broc and Jean-Pierre Franque were mildly successful as artists. Both had been considered by David to be very promising students, and Franque, ironically, had been asked by David to assist him in painting *Intervention of the Sabine Women*. Broc's most famous surviving work is *Death of Hyacinthus*, which he completed in 1801, though the style of the painting offers little insight into the artistic values of the Primitives. A portrayal from Greek mythology, the painting has much in common with David's early work and is similar to *Oath of the Horatii* and *Intervention of the Sabine Women*.

Franque exhibited a painting, *Dream of Love Induced by the Power of Harmony*, at the Salon of 1806. After losing to Antoine-Jean Gros in a competition to paint Na-

poleon on the battlefield at Eylau, he exhibited a strange allegorical and historical work at the Salon of 1810 depicting a voluptuous personification of a helpless France pleading with Napoleon to come to her aid. Its title, *Allegory of the Condition of France Before the Return from Egypt*, alludes to Napoleon's years campaigning in Egypt.

In addition to Quay, Broc, and the Franque brothers, the Primitives were known to include Antoine-Hilaire-Henri Périé and Joseph-Boniface Franque's wife, Lucile Messageot, both painters. Their known supporters and sympathizers included artists Paul Duqueylar and Jacques-Nicolas Paillot de Montabert, sculptor Lorenzo Bartolini, and writers Jean-Antoine "Auguste" Gleizes and Charles Nodier.

SIGNIFICANCE

Although their admiration of ancient and simple artistic values may have influenced a handful of paintings of the time, including Jean-Auguste-Dominique Ingres's *Venus Wounded by Diomedes* (1803), the Primitives had little lasting influence on nineteenth century art, primarily because they produced few works themselves. Broc's *School of Apelles*, shown at the Salon of 1800, is one of the few paintings produced during the movement's life span. Quay left no known works. Over the next hundred and fifty years, painters periodically pursued a similar interest in archaic styles of art—most notably Edward Hicks, Henri Rousseau, and Grandma Moses—and they too were called "Primitives." Any connection, however, between the Primitives and these later Primitive artists must be considered distant and indirect.

On the other hand, the unorthodox and insouciant lifestyle of the Primitives is considered a prototype of the alienated and unconventional lives of nineteenth century artists and writers who came to be called bohemians, after the Bohemian Gypsies, whose dress and behavior stood in stark contrast to conventional French society. This tradition would run through the German Nazarenes, the Pre-Raphaelites, the Arts and Crafts movement, the Symbolists, and the hippie movement of the 1960's. By the middle of the nineteenth century, the lifestyle had become so entrenched in the European mind that literary and artistic works began portraying bohemian communities, as in Henri Murger's short-story anthology *Scènes de la vie de Bohème* (1849) and Giacomo Puccini's opera *La Bohème* (1896).

—*Devon Boan*

FURTHER READING

Boime, Albert. *A Social History of Modern Art*. Vol. 1 in *Art in an Age of Revolution, 1750-1800*. Chicago: University of Chicago Press, 1990. An analysis of the social and political influences, including popular culture, on art during the period leading to the emergence of the Primitives.

Craske, Matthew. *Art in Europe, 1700-1830: A History of the Visual Arts in an Era of Unprecedented Urban Economic Growth*. Oxford, England: Oxford University Press, 1997. An examination of the influence of urbanization and rapid political and economic change on artistic production and distribution.

Lee, Simon. *David A & I: Art and Ideas*. London: Phaidon, 2004. A biography of Jacques-Louis David, who taught the young artists of the Primitives and against whom their movement was directed, with an emphasis on David's political activities and their effect on his art.

Levitine, George. *The Dawn of Bohemianism: The Barbu Rebellion and Primitivism in Neo-classical France*. University Park: Pennsylvania State University Press, 1978. The most comprehensive work available on the Primitives, with an emphasis on their influence on subsequent bohemian artists.

Rosenblum, Robert. *Transformation in Late Eighteenth-Century Art*. Princeton, N.J.: Princeton University Press, 1970. An engaging examination of the visual arts during the transition from neoclassicism to Romanticism. Offers an especially detailed account of the Primitives.

SEE ALSO: 1803-1812: Elgin Ships Parthenon Marbles to England; Mar., 1814: Goya Paints *Third of May 1808: Execution of the Citizens of Madrid*; 1824: Paris Salon of 1824; c. 1830-1870: Barbizon School of Landscape Painting Flourishes; Oct.-Dec., 1830: Delacroix Paints *Liberty Leading the People*; Fall, 1848: Pre-Raphaelite Brotherhood Begins; 1855: Courbet Establishes Realist Art Movement.

RELATED ARTICLES in *Great Lives from History: The Nineteenth Century, 1801-1900*: Jacques-Louis David; Théodore Géricault; Jean-Auguste-Dominique Ingres.

c. 1801-1810
DAVY DEVELOPS THE ARC LAMP

Through his experiments with the newly discovered voltaic battery, Humphry Davy created a brilliant light by bringing two carbon electrodes near each other. He continued to refine the design and later dramatically demonstrated his invention with increasingly powerful batteries.

LOCALE: Bristol and London, England
CATEGORIES: Inventions; science and technology; engineering

KEY FIGURES

Humphry Davy (1778-1829), English chemist, physicist, and poet
Alessandro Volta (1745-1827), Italian physicist and inventor of the battery
Antoine-Laurent Lavoisier (1743-1794), French chemist

SUMMARY OF EVENT

From the start of his scientific career, Sir Humphry Davy was fascinated by light. His interest developed from reading Antoine-Laurent Lavoisier's *Traité élémentaire de chimie* (1789; *Elements of Chemistry*, 1790) in Robert Kerr's 1790 English translation. This pivotal work of the chemical revolution contained the first table of elements, and "light" was at the top of Lavoisier's list of "simple substances," followed by "caloric," the heat substance that played a fundamental role in his analysis of the three states of matter (solid, liquid, and gas).

Influenced by Sir Isaac Newton's ideas, Davy was critical of Lavoisier, stating that light was "corpuscularian," not elemental, and that heat was not a substance but a result of the motions of material particles. He also disagreed with Lavoisier's speculations that caloric (or heat) was a modification of light. One of Davy's early investigations involved firing a gunlock in a vacuum and in carbon dioxide. Since he saw no sparks at the moment of ignition, Davy concluded that light is not caloric but a kind of matter. When he repeated the experiment in oxygen, he saw brilliant sparks. This led him to propose that Lavoisier's "oxygen" was really a composite of light and oxygen, which he named "phosoxygen," a view that he later repudiated. In 1799, Davy's "An Essay on Heat, Light, and the Combinations of Light" was published in

Thomas Beddoes's collection, *Contributions to Physical and Medical Knowledge: Principally from the West of England* (1799).

Although Lavoisier's treatise helped stimulate Davy's investigations of heat and light, the instigating event in his electrochemical studies and his invention of the arc lamp was Alessandro Volta's invention in 1800 of the electric battery (or "voltaic pile"), a device that produced a steady flow of electrical current. Volta soon communicated his discovery to the Royal Society of London, and Davy was so impressed by Volta's invention that he saw it as an "alarm-bell" for himself and other experimenters. When William Nicholson and Anthony Carlisle used a voltaic pile to decompose water into its component gases, hydrogen and oxygen, Davy became fascinated by the connection between electrical and chemical forces. He disagreed with Volta's interpretation that the electrical force was generated by contacts between dissimilar metals in the battery, arguing, instead, that a chemical reaction produced the current.

Davy began using the electric battery for various projects, but precisely when he used a voltaic pile to generate light between two charcoal rods is not clear. Most scholars suggest dates between 1800 and 1810. Pinpointing the time is complicated by events in Davy's life, as well as by his habit of revising and expanding his early work in response to later scientific observations and experiments. Davy was between positions when some of his early research was done. He had been doing important medical research on nitrous oxide at Beddoes's institute in Bristol, but, at the invitation of Benjamin Thompson, Count von Rumford, he moved to the Royal Institution in London early in 1801.

Some of Davy's experiments on "galvanic electricity" were published while he was in Bristol, including his discovery that charcoal worked as effectively as metals in producing sparks when connected to a voltaic pile. Around that time, Davy was also performing experiments that showed that silver salts were blackened by light, a process that would be central to the invention of photography by Nicéphore Niépce in 1826. He also showed that electric current from a voltaic pile could produce light when it heated thin wires of platinum or other metals to incandescence.

Some scholars assert that, before Davy moved to London, he had already noticed the light produced between two carbon rods when they were connected to a voltaic pile. Because the resulting discharge traced an arc between the rods, this device became known as an arc lamp, or arc light, and Davy has been given credit as the first

person to create such a lamp. This arc of electricity, which had high current and low voltage, was both brilliantly luminous and intensely hot. No commercial applications emerged from Davy's early research, but he did use the heat of the arc in several experiments.

Most of Davy's greatest work in electrochemistry took place at the Royal Institution of Great Britain during the first decade of the nineteenth century, when he proved himself as an outstanding lecturer, excellent fund-raiser, and innovative researcher. He published his observations about the arc light in the Royal Institution's journal in the summer of 1802. However, because of the institution's emphasis on practical research, for the next few years Davy devoted himself to applied chemistry rather than continuing his work in electrochemistry. Between 1806 and 1810, with an interruption due to illness, Davy made the discoveries for which he became best known, including further work on electrical illumination based on his access to vastly improved batteries.

During these years of productivity, the batteries that Davy used went from utilizing 250 metallic plates to utilizing 500 plates and eventually 2,000 plates—some of the most powerful batteries ever built. With such powerful sources of electricity, Davy was able to isolate, in 1807, potassium from molten potash (potassium carbonate) and sodium from molten soda (sodium carbonate). In 1808, he used electricity to separate several metals from their oxides, including magnesium, strontium, barium, and calcium. In this way, Davy proved that several substances that Lavoisier had listed as elemental, such as magnesia, were really compounds. With his battery of 2,000 plates, Davy demonstrated that muriatic acid (hydrochloric acid) contained no oxygen, contrary to Lavoisier's assertions, and that Lavoisier's "oxymuriatic radical" was really elemental chlorine.

In 1809, Davy used a bank of powerful batteries to stage a demonstration of the arc lamp. Before an audience at the Royal Institution, a brilliant, arc-shaped light was generated between two carbon rods that were a few inches apart. Some scholars call this demonstration "the birth of the arc lamp." Accounts of this demonstration are more numerous and detailed than the evidence for Davy's 1801 arc-light experiments. Witnesses in 1809 spoke of a light so intense that it rivaled the Sun's. Furthermore, the light was not confined to the area between the electrodes but spread into the air beyond the gap. However, because of the intense heat, the tips of the carbon rods were consumed, and, to maintain the light, the rods had to be carefully pushed closer together.

Some scholars state that this demonstration at the

Royal Institution occurred in 1808, while others claim that Davy's carbon electric arc lamp was first exhibited in 1810. Perhaps this confusion is due to repetitions of the dramatic experiment before different audiences. A witness to the 1810 demonstration reported that the "arch of light" was so intense that any substance introduced into it "instantly became ignited," including quartz, sapphire, and magnesia. Although Davy went on to invent the miner's safety lamp in 1815, he did not foresee any practical applications for his arc lamp. After his knighthood and marriage in 1812, his interests moved away from electrochemistry.

SIGNIFICANCE

It took several decades before the practical significance of Davy's arc lamp was realized. In order to have arc lighting available for extended use, a feed mechanism that kept the carbon electrodes at the proper distance was needed, since the rods became shorter because of combustion. After such a mechanism was developed in the 1840's, arc lamps made their appearance on the streets of Paris and in its opera house. Commercial applications of the electric arc multiplied in the 1850's. For example, an arc lamp was installed in the South Foreland Lighthouse in the English Channel, and an arc light was turned on in the Clock Tower of London's Palace of Westminster whenever Parliament was in session.

With the increased availability of powerful dynamos and with the invention of an improved form of the arc lamp known as the Jablochkov candle, whose light was less harsh than that of earlier arc lamps, cities in Europe and the United States began to light their streets and public buildings with the new devices. Gas lighting was still the largest illuminating industry, but arc-lamp systems developed by Charles F. Brush and others led to the lighting of streets in Cleveland, New York, and Washington. Arc lighting was also part of the American Centennial World's Fair in Philadelphia (1876) and the Chicago World's Columbian Exposition (1893). However, arc lights were too harsh and bright for homes and offices. Only after Thomas Alva Edison developed the first truly practicable incandescent lamp in 1879, along with a system to distribute direct-current electricity, did the electric light, which had begun so modestly in the experimental work of Davy, spread throughout the world.

—*Robert J. Paradowski*

FURTHER READING

Bowers, Brian. *A History of Electric Light and Power.* New York: Peter Peregrinus, 1982. This volume, part of a history of technology series, centers on how electricity was brought to the public. The early chapters deal with Davy and Michael Faraday. References at the ends of chapters. Index.

Fullmer, June Z. *Young Humphry Davy: The Making of an Experimental Chemist.* Philadelphia: American Philosophical Society, 2000. This book, which covers Davy's career until the start of his tenure at the Royal Institution, contains material on his early work in electricity and light. Notes to primary and secondary sources at the ends of chapters, a select bibliography, and an index.

Golinski, Jan. *Science as Public Culture: Chemistry and Enlightenment in Britain, 1760-1820.* Cambridge, England: Cambridge University Press, 1992. Chapter 7, "Humphry Davy: The Public Face of Genius," is an examination of Davy's electrochemical research with an emphasis on its practical applications and its social setting. Extensive bibliography and index.

Hartley, Harold. *Sir Humphry Davy.* Reprint. London: EP, 1973. The standard account of Davy's life. Bibliography and index.

Knight, David. *Humphry Davy: Science and Power.* 2d ed. Cambridge, England: Cambridge University Press, 1998. Based on Davy's notebooks, his formal and informal writings, and his poetry. Introduces general readers to what Knight calls "the first professional scientist." References to primary and secondary sources in the notes to the chapters, select bibliography, and an index.

Pancaldi, Giuliano. *Volta: Science and Culture in the Age of Enlightenment.* Princeton, N.J.: Princeton University Press, 2003. The interactions between Volta and Davy were many, and this life of Volta also contains interesting material on Enlightenment Europe. Extensive bibliography and index.

SEE ALSO: 1802: Britain Adopts Gas Lighting; Nov. 6, 1820: Ampère Reveals Magnetism's Relationship to Electricity; Oct., 1831: Faraday Converts Magnetic Force into Electricity; Oct. 21, 1879: Edison Demonstrates the Incandescent Lamp; Nov. 16, 1896: First U.S. Hydroelectric Plant Opens at Niagara Falls; Dec. 15, 1900: General Electric Opens Research Laboratory.

RELATED ARTICLES in *Great Lives from History: The Nineteenth Century, 1801-1900:* Sir Humphry Davy; Thomas Alva Edison; Michael Faraday; Nicéphore Niépce.

c. 1801-1850
PROFESSIONAL THEATERS SPREAD THROUGHOUT AMERICA

The establishment of professional theaters and theater companies in the United States was the first step in the development of a national American theater. At first, these theaters were dominated by European repertoires, but as the American theater-going audience expanded, American plays, operas, and minstrel shows became standard fare.

LOCALE: United States
CATEGORY: Theater

KEY FIGURES

Edwin Booth (1833-1893), American actor
William Dunlap (1766-1839), American actor, playwright, manager, and theater historian
Dan Emmett (1815-1904), American violinist and blackface entertainer
Edwin Forrest (1806-1872), first American actor to win European fame
Thomas Wignell (1753-1803), British actor and theatrical manager
Alexander Reinagle (1756-1809), British composer and theatrical manager

SUMMARY OF EVENT

By the early nineteenth century, the two premier theater sites in the United States were Philadelphia and New York. The former had largely abandoned its Quaker objections to drama by the time of the Revolutionary War, while the latter's Dutch origins fostered a tolerant, cosmopolitan atmosphere compared to New England cities such as Boston, which had no playhouse until 1794. As the nation grew and transportation improved, the number of theaters rapidly expanded. Professional dramatic productions had reached the West Coast by 1850.

Through the 1830's, Philadelphia was a major theater and publishing center. Its finest playhouse was the Chestnut Street Theatre. Built in 1794 by British composer Alexander Reinagle and actor-manager Thomas Wignell, the Chestnut Street Theatre was the first American theater to be lit by gas (starting in 1816). Rebuilt after an 1820 fire, it remained a popular site for melodramas, Italian operas in English translation, comedies, and plays of William Shakespeare. It was finally razed in 1855. Wignell and Reinagle also constructed and managed the Holliday Street Theatre in Baltimore, which operated, despite an 1873 fire, until 1917, when the building was demolished. "The Star Spangled Banner" was first sung in the Holliday Street Theatre in 1813.

Philadelphia's second playhouse, the Walnut Street Theatre, was built in 1809 as an indoor circus. It is one of America's few federal-style theaters. The opulent Academy of Music, another of the city's surviving nineteenth century landmarks, opened in 1857. Modeled on Milan's La Scala, the Academy of Music was designed to host receptions, balls, concerts, and public lectures, as well as opera and plays.

New York City's Park Theatre opened in 1798 under the leadership of actor John Hodgkinson and playwright William Dunlap. The quality of its productions, sixty of which were adapted or written by Dunlap, foreshadowed the city's future preeminence in American drama. The Park Theatre seated about two thousand people. Like the Chestnut Street Theatre, it burned in 1820, but within two years it had been rebuilt. In 1825-1826, the New Park Theatre hosted America's first season of Italian opera, including works by Gioacchino Rossini and Wolfgang Amadeus Mozart.

The New Park Theatre soon had numerous rivals, many of which would be destroyed by fire. The Bowery Theatre burned and was rebuilt five times; remarkably, its 1845 building survived until a final conflagration in 1929. Probably the nineteenth century's worst theater fire occurred on December 26, 1811, at Virginia's Richmond Theatre. An accident with a lamp during a performance led to a panic and the deaths of seventy-two patrons. A theater tragedy of a different sort, which revealed the hostility that still existed between the United States and Great Britain, was New York's Astor Place Riot. Built in 1847 as a temple of high culture, the Astor Place Opera House was soon converted to a theater. In May, 1849, a long-standing feud between British actor William Macready and his American rival Edwin Forrest led to a violent confrontation between an anti-British mob and the New York militia. Shots were fired, twenty-one people were killed, and thirty-six were wounded.

In its fourth incarnation, New York's Bowery Theatre was the site of the first minstrel show. In February, 1843, four white men led by Dan Emmett blackened their faces, sang in dialect, and danced in imitation of African American dance. Minstrel shows quickly became theatrical favorites throughout the nation, remaining popular for more than a century. They marked a shift from variety acts to specialized shows. Minstrels also parodied classical operas and famous European musicians, such as the Swedish singer Jenny Lind and the Norwegian violist Ole Bull.

Although acceptance of drama came later to Boston, its 1794 Federal Street Theatre was elegantly designed by noted architect Charles Bulfinch, and it seated nearly one thousand people. In 1827, a quarrel among its actors led to the founding of the Tremont Street Theatre; competition between the two houses ended with the closing of the older playhouse within two years. The Tremont Street Theatre lasted until 1843, when it was sold to a Baptist congregation. In 1849, the Boston Museum was the site of the first appearance of Edwin Booth, along with his father Junius, in Shakespeare's *Richard III* (pr. c. 1592-1593, revised 1623).

Even after the Louisiana Purchase (1803), New Orleans theaters continued to host French-language plays. Only by 1817 did the American Theatre, on the city's Camp Street, begin presenting plays in English. At mid-century, four theaters were active in the city. A milestone in the cultural history of New Orleans was the 1835 completion of the elaborate St. Charles Theatre, which cost

$350,000 and seated four thousand people. It burned in 1842 but was rebuilt within a year.

Although plays were given in a Washington, D.C., hotel as early as 1801—the same year a playhouse opened in Cincinnati, Ohio—the nation's capital had no permanent theater until 1804. By 1835, the capital's growing status led to the establishment of the Old Washington Theatre and the National Theatre. Ford's Theatre was originally a Baptist church from 1834 to 1859. Following the merger of two congregations, the building in 1863 became a playhouse managed by John T. Ford. After President Abraham Lincoln's assassination on April 14, 1865, the theater closed, and Ford's attempt to reopen it in June was unsuccessful. After being used for offices and storage, the building became a museum in 1931. Ford's Theatre was restored as a nineteenth century playhouse in 1967.

As America moved westward, plays were performed in Pittsburgh in 1808, Lexington, Kentucky, in 1810, and St. Louis in 1814, in a variety of buildings also used for other purposes. The St. Louis Theatre, which opened in 1837, was the first playhouse west of the Mississippi. A

Astor Place Opera House riots. (C. A. Nichols & Company)

second site, the Bates Theatre, opened in 1851 and burned in 1880. Chicago's Rialto Theatre began operations in 1838 and lasted two years; the Rice Theatre followed it in 1847. Like so many nineteenth century structures, the Rice Theatre burned in 1859. In common with their eastern counterparts, these theaters presented a mixture of melodramas, varieties, Shakespeare plays, and minstrel shows.

By eastern standards, the Eagle Theater, Sacramento, California's first playhouse (1849), was relatively primitive. Partly wood and canvas, it drew crowds of miners who applauded the melodramas performed there three times a week. In 1850 after a flood, the company moved to San Francisco, where the Jenny Lind Theatre, California's second theater, opened in October of 1850. The singer nicknamed the Swedish Nightingale captured audiences' hearts as she toured the eastern and midwestern United States between 1850 and 1852. Lind did not visit California, but such was her popularity that three of San Francisco's theaters bore her name during that period.

Unlike Jenny Lind, Edwin Booth did perform in California during the early 1850's. The Booths continued the tradition of family troupes. Three brothers—Junius Brutus, Edwin, and John Wilkes—became actors and occasionally acted together. John Wilkes Booth's assassination of Lincoln overshadowed the entire family. Edwin did not return to the stage until January, 1866. In 1869, he built Booth's Theatre in New York, where his company specialized in performing Shakespeare's plays as originally written, rather than "bowdlerized" versions. Edwin Booth elevated the quality of American theater and toured the United States and Europe until 1891.

SIGNIFICANCE

As the United States grew, plays with American themes, melodramas, minstrel shows, and adaptations of American novels such as *Uncle Tom's Cabin* (1852) vied with European operas and Shakespearean plays for popularity in U.S. theaters. Variety helped playhouses compete in large cities, but by the 1850's some venues began specializing in minstrel shows, melodramas, or broad comedies. An evening at the theater—including music before the curtains opened and an afterpiece—might last five hours. The range of choices ushered in a golden age of theater, which remained America's main source of entertainment until it was largely replaced by motion pictures in the first two decades of the twentieth century and by television during the mid-twentieth century.

—*Dorothy T. Potter*

FURTHER READING

Bank, Rosemarie, K. *Theatre Culture in America, 1825-1860.* Cambridge, England: Cambridge University Press, 1997. Focuses on the evolution of performances in response to the changing tastes of nineteenth century American audiences.

Carson, William G. B. *The Theatre on the Frontier: The Early Years of the St. Louis Stage.* New York: Benjamin Blom, 1965. Primary emphasis is on St. Louis, but the book discusses other western theaters through 1839 as well.

Glazer, Irvin R. *Philadelphia Theatres, A-Z: A Comprehensive Descriptive Record of 813 Theatres Constructed Since 1724.* New York: Greenwood Press, 1986. Extensive description of Philadelphia's performance sites, from playhouses to motion picture theaters.

Kamen, Henry A. *Music in New Orleans: The Formative Years, 1791-1841.* Baton Rouge: Louisiana State University Press, 1984. Discusses New Orleans's unique blend of cultures, music, and antebellum theater.

Mahar, William J. *Behind the Burnt Cork Mask: Early Blackface Minstrelsy and Antebellum American Culture.* Urbana: University of Illinois Press, 1999. Describes the rise of minstrelsy in both the North and the South and its relationship to other forms of theater in the United States.

Naylor, David, and Joan Dillon. *American Theatres: Performance Halls of the Nineteenth Century.* New York: John Wiley & Sons, 1997. Focuses mainly on theaters that were still extant in the 1990's, with numerous photographs and detailed descriptions of their performance spaces.

Richardson, Gary A. *American Drama from the Colonial Period Through World War I.* New York: Twayne, 1993. A concise history dealing mainly with nineteenth century theater, especially romantic plays and melodramas.

Young, William C. *Documents of American Theatre History: Famous American Playhouses, 1716-1899.* 2 vols. Chicago: American Library Association, 1973. Rich in detail; includes excerpts from diaries, letters, and newspapers, as well as more than two hundred illustrations.

SEE ALSO: 1807: Bowdler Publishes *The Family Shakespeare*; Mar. 3, 1830: Hugo's *Hernani* Incites Rioting; Feb. 6, 1843: First Minstrel Shows; 1850's-1880's: Rise of Burlesque and Vaudeville; Apr. 10,

1871: Barnum Creates the First Modern American Circus; 1878-1899: Irving Manages London's Lyceum Theatre; Oct. 22, 1883: Metropolitan Opera House Opens in New York; Oct. 14, 1898: Moscow Art Theater Is Founded.

RELATED ARTICLES in *Great Lives from History: The Nineteenth Century, 1801-1900:* Edwin Booth; Charles Bulfinch; Edwin Forrest; Abraham Lincoln; Jenny Lind; Gioacchino Rossini.

January 1, 1801
FIRST ASTEROID IS DISCOVERED

The discovery of Ceres was an accident that occurred during a large, cooperative search for what was believed to be a missing planet between the orbits of Mars and Jupiter. The discovery led to the eventual cataloging of several thousand asteroids and a rethinking of the structure of the solar system.

ALSO KNOWN AS: Discovery of Ceres

LOCALE: Palermo, Sicily, Kingdom of Naples (now Italy)

CATEGORIES: Astronomy; science and technology; exploration and discovery; photography; mathematics

KEY FIGURES

Giuseppe Piazzi (1746-1826), Italian monk and astronomer who discovered the first asteroid

Johann Titius (1729-1796), German astronomer who created an empirical formula for determining planetary distances

Johann Bode (1747-1826), German astronomer who popularized Titius's planetary formula and used it to predict a missing planet between Mars and Jupiter

William Herschel (1738-1822), German-English astronomer who discovered Uranus

Franz Xaver von Zach (1754-1832), German-Hungarian astronomer who organized a search for a missing planet between Mars and Jupiter

Carl Friedrich Gauss (1777-1855), German mathematician who calculated the orbit of the first discovered asteroid

Heinrich Olbers (1758-1840), German physician and astronomer who discovered the second and fourth asteroids

Daniel Kirkwood (1814-1895), American astronomer who discovered gaps in the distribution of asteroids

Max Wolf (1863-1932), German astronomer who applied photographic techniques to asteroid searches

SUMMARY OF EVENT

On the very first day of the nineteenth century, the Italian astronomer-monk Giuseppe Piazzi discovered the first asteroid from the observatory he had established in Palermo, Sicily. Although his discovery was accidental, it was not entirely unexpected. Toward the end of the eighteenth century, several astronomers had suspected that a "missing planet" might lie between the orbits of Mars and Jupiter. Piazzi made his discovery as astronomers were beginning to organize a systematic search for that planet.

In 1766, the German astronomer Johann Titius found that the positions of the known planets could be approximated by a simple mathematical formual. By adding the number 4 to each number in the sequence 0, 3, 6, 12, 24, 48, 96, and then dividing by 10, planetary distances from the Sun could be calculated in astronomical units (AU), with one AU representing the distance between Earth and the Sun. However, an exception occurred at the fifth position, where a gap appeared between the orbits of Mars and Jupiter at $(4 + 24)/10 = 2.8$ AU. Titius suggested that the gap might contain an unknown moon of Mars. The German astronomer Johann Bode publicized Titius's rule and predicted in 1772 that a missing planet might be found in the gap at 2.8 AU.

Bode's prediction was reinforced when the German-English astronomer Sir William Herschel discovered the planet Uranus in 1781. When the distance of Uranus was measured at about 19 AU, it was found to compare well with the Titius-Bode rule for the next logical number in the sequence, giving a distance of $(4 + 192)/10 = 19.6$ AU. On September 21, 1800, the German-Hungarian astronomer Baron Franz Xaver von Zach organized a systematic search for a planet at 2.8 AU by dividing the heavens into twenty-four equal sections and assigning each section to a different astronomer. One of the chosen astronomers was Piazzi, whose Palermo observatory was the farthest south of any European facility. Even before these twenty-four so-called "celestial police" could begin their work,

Piazzi made the accidental discovery of a faint object, which turned out to be the first asteroid.

A Theatine monk and priest, Piazzi was assigned as the chair of higher mathematics at the Academy of Palermo in 1780. There he established an observatory with the help of royal patronage from King Ferdinand III of Sicily. While checking star maps against telescopic observations on the night of January 1, 1801, Piazzi found a dim, star-like object that was not on his maps and that changed its position from night to night. After observing the object for twenty-four nights, until he became too ill to continue, he reported what he thought might be a comet.

By the time other astronomers tried to check Piazzi's results, the object he observed had receded behind the Sun. Piazzi was unable to work out the object's exact orbit but showed that it was similar to a planetary orbit and estimated the distance of the object at 2.7 AU. Piazzi's last contribution to the discovery of the object, if it could be recovered and confirmed, was to propose it be named Ceres Ferdinandea, in honor of Sicily's patron goddess of agriculture, Ceres, and Sicily's King Ferdinand III.

When the celestial police received Piazzi's report, Bode and several other astronomers immediately concluded that the object Piazzi had found was the missing planet. To facilitate recovery of the object, the young German mathematician Carl Friedrich Gauss worked out a method to determine a precise orbit from three observations. His effort required the solution of seventeen equations but led to a successful recovery of the object on December 31, 1801, by Baron von Zach one year after its initial discovery. The object's distance was measured at 2.77 AU with a period of 4.6 years, and its name was officially shortened to Ceres. When Herschel observed Ceres early in 1802, he concluded that it was only a fraction the size of Earth's Moon, much too small to be a planet, and proposed the name "asteroid" (star-like) for minor planets such as it.

Because Ceres appeared to be too small to be a planet, the celestial police continued their search. On March 28, 1802, the German astronomer Heinrich Olbers found a second small object at the same distance as Ceres but with a more eccentric orbit. He named it Pallas after Pallas Athena, the Greek goddess of wisdom. Herschel then showed that Pallas was even smaller than Ceres.

Consistent with the Titius-Bode rule, Olbers proposed in 1803 that asteroids come from an exploded

Carl Friedrich Gauss.

planet at 2.8 AU. This possibility led to a continuing search that resulted in the discovery of the asteroid Juno in 1804 by the German astronomer Karl Harding and the discovery of Vesta in 1807 by Olbers at distances of 2.67 AU and 2.36 AU. Their approximate diameters and modern designations are 580 miles (33 kilometers) for 1 Ceres, 300 miles (483 kilometers) for both 2 Pallas and 4 Vesta, and 120 miles (193 kilometers) for 3 Juno. All these bodies are much smaller than Earth's Moon, which has a diameter of about 2,135 miles (3,435 kilometers).

No additional asteroids were discovered until 1845, when the German astronomer Karl Hencke discovered 5 Astraea after fifteen years of observing. When Hencke discovered a sixth asteroid, 6 Hebe, in 1847, other astronomers returned to the search. Over the next forty-five years more than three hundred asteroids were discovered, mostly in the so-called main belt between 2.1 AU and 3.4 AU. Only the largest asteroids have spherical shapes, notably the three largest: 1 Ceres, 2 Pallas, and 4 Vesta.

In 1867, the American astronomer Daniel Kirkwood discovered gaps in the main belt in which few asteroids have been found. These so-called Kirkwood gaps occur where the periods of asteroid orbits are simple fractions of the twelve-year period of massive Jupiter at 5.2 AU, and result from repeated gravitational forces called resonances.

In 1891, the pace of asteroid discoveries accelerated with the use of photography, beginning with the work of the German astronomer Max Wolf. Wolf used long exposures in which the movements of asteroids produced light streaks. Since then, several thousand additional asteroids have been cataloged, including 248 found by Wolf himself.

SIGNIFICANCE

Asteroids provide important insights into the formation and nature of planets and meteorites. Olbers's idea that asteroids came from an exploded planet at 2.8 AU has been discredited by the fact that asteroid orbits do not intersect at this distance, even though about half of their orbits are between 2.75 AU and 2.85 AU. Furthermore, their total mass is equivalent to only about 3 percent of the Moon's mass. Astronomers now believe that asteroids are the debris left over after planet formation and that the gravitational forces caused by Jupiter's large mass depleted much of this debris and prevented the rest from combining to form a single planet. Collisions among asteroids and their resulting fragmentation are believed to be the source of most of the meteorites that reach the surface of Earth. They represent the oldest material in the solar system from shortly before planet formation.

Asteroids have played significant roles in Earth's history. Some are now known to have elliptical orbits that cross Earth's orbit, probably as a result of past collisions in the main belt. Some of these have hit Earth in the distant past and left craters more than 60 miles (96 kilometers) in diameter that have been revealed by satellite photography. It is believed that some asteroid impacts have contributed to major extinctions of species, such as the dinosaurs, and perhaps even reversals of Earth's magnetism. Astronomers now conduct regular surveys to detect such "killer asteroids" in order to provide warnings of possible collisions with Earth.

—*Joseph L. Spradley*

FURTHER READING

Hoskin, Michael, ed. *The Cambridge Concise History of Astronomy*. Cambridge, England: Cambridge University Press, 1999. Contains a useful chapter on the discovery of asteroids.

Jaki, Stanley L. "The Early History of the Titius-Bode Law." *American Journal of Physics* 40 (July, 1972): 1014-1023. This article has an interesting account of the background of the discovery of asteroids.

Kaufmann, William J., and Roger A. Freedman. *Universe*. 5th ed. New York: W. H. Freeman, 1999. Chapter 17, "Vagabonds of the Solar System," offers a good introduction to the search and discovery of asteroids.

Peebles, Curtis. *Asteroids: A History*. Washington, D.C.: Smithsonian Institution Press, 2000. A comprehensive account of the two-century history of asteroid discovery.

Watson, Fletcher G. *Between the Planets*. Cambridge, Mass.: Harvard University Press, 1956. The early chapters provide good accounts of the discovery and properties of asteroids.

SEE ALSO: 1814: Fraunhofer Invents the Spectroscope; 1839: Daguerre and Niépce Invent Daguerreotype Photography.

RELATED ARTICLES in *Great Lives from History: The Nineteenth Century, 1801-1900:* Friedrich Wilhelm Bessel; Carl Friedrich Gauss; Pierre-Simon Laplace; Simon Newcomb.

1800's

February 17, 1801

HOUSE OF REPRESENTATIVES ELECTS JEFFERSON PRESIDENT

The bloodless transfer of power from one political party to its bitter rival in the 1800 presidential election signified the success of the new two-party system in the United States, and President-Elect Thomas Jefferson would go on to oversee some of the most significant developments in his young nation's history.

ALSO KNOWN AS: Election of 1800-1801
LOCALE: United States
CATEGORY: Government and politics

KEY FIGURES
Thomas Jefferson (1743-1826), president of the United States, 1801-1809
John Adams (1735-1826), president of the United States, 1797-1801
James A. Bayard (1767-1815), Federalist congressman from Delaware
Aaron Burr (1756-1836), Republican vice presidential candidate in 1800
Alexander Hamilton (1755-1804), Federalist leader in New York
Charles Cotesworth Pinckney (1746-1825), Federalist vice presidential candidate in 1800

SUMMARY OF EVENT
The presidential campaign of 1800 pitted President John Adams, a Federalist, against Vice President Thomas Jefferson, a Republican who was an old political adversary and an even older friend of Adams. Adams had defeated Jefferson in the 1796 presidential election by the slim margin of three electoral votes. New England seemed to be solidly Federalist and the South seemed to be solidly Republican. The critical states were Pennsylvania and New York. Jefferson had carried Pennsylvania in 1796; he hoped to maintain his position there and to win New York to his side. South Carolina was also an important state, for the Federalists enjoyed strong support there.

Deteriorating U.S. relations with France dominated the Adams administration and came to a showdown over the XYZ affair—a diplomatic incident in which corrupt French officials surreptitiously demanded an apology, a large loan, and bribes from the United States. The Federalists were able to parlay U.S. indignation over the XYZ affair into strong political support for their program. Many Federalists—including Adams, for a time, in 1798-1799—were willing to declare war or force a declaration of war from France. Influential, well-to-do Fed-

eralist political activists (called High Federalists) who often distrusted President Adams, though he was a Federalist himself, realized that their continued popularity depended on maintaining public opinion at a high emotional level against the French.

For a time, in 1799, it seemed that the Republicans, damned by their opponents as pro-French, would be out of the running in the 1800 election. However, the popular mood changed as the war fever declined, as opposition to the military program and taxes increased, and as Adams himself became less aggressive, and Republican chances proportionately improved. When the president suddenly decided to send a new peace mission to France, the High Federalists realized that they were doomed. Peace was now the major theme, and the Republicans had been committed to peace all along.

Adams's peace policy split the Federalist Party. Alexander Hamilton attacked the president directly and schemed to replace him. The Republicans, united behind Jefferson, applied themselves diligently to capturing the

President Thomas Jefferson. (Library of Congress)

critical middle states, such as New York and Pennsylvania. As the election outcome would prove, the Republicans were more efficiently organized than the Federalists.

In 1800, the popular vote was conducted in the states at various times during October and November. In the majority of states, however, the state legislatures, not the voters, selected the presidential electors. Significantly, although the Federalists maintained control over the national government, in 1800 the Republicans controlled a majority of the state governments.

In New York, for example, Aaron Burr was the Republican leader and Hamilton directed the opposition. At stake was the composition of the state legislature. The party that captured that body would control the twelve electoral votes cast by New York. Burr outmaneuvered Hamilton, and the Republicans captured a majority in the state's lower house, thus giving them a majority of one in the combined vote of both houses. This defeat deflated the hopes of the Federalists. The Republicans staved off an energetic Federalist campaign in South Carolina and brought Jefferson home the victor by eight electoral votes. This margin was not impressive, but it did represent a significant shift of party strength in the crucial middle states. The Republican Party did not penetrate New England, but John Adams improved his position in some southern states. Despite a serious split in his own party, President Adams looked stronger in 1800 than he had in 1796.

The Federalist Party had a second opportunity to prevent the election of Jefferson, whom its members regarded as an "atheistic, Jacobinic, democratic" politician. In 1800, the electors did not distinguish between the president and the vice president in casting their votes. The man who received the most electoral votes became president, and the runner-up became vice president. In a display of party unity, each Republican elector cast a vote for Jefferson and a vote for Burr, the vice presidential candidate on the Republican ticket. The resulting tie meant that the decision would be made in the House of Representatives, with each state casting one vote. Enough Federalists preferred Burr to make Jefferson's election dubious.

JEFFERSON'S INAUGURAL ADDRESS

Thomas Jefferson's inaugural address, delivered on March 4, 1801, addressed the sharp division between the Federalists and the Republicans and the extremely narrow margin of Jefferson's victory in his bid to become president. He sought to reassure the public as to the strength of the union despite the rivalry of its two major parties.

During the contest of opinion through which we have passed the animation of discussions and of exertions has sometimes worn an aspect which might impose on strangers unused to think freely and to speak and to write what they think; but this being now decided by the voice of the nation, announced according to the rules of the Constitution, all will, of course, arrange themselves under the will of the law, and unite in common efforts for the common good. All, too, will bear in mind this sacred principle, that though the will of the majority is in all cases to prevail, that will to be rightful must be reasonable; that the minority possess their equal rights, which equal law must protect, and to violate would be oppression. Let us, then, fellow-citizens, unite with one heart and one mind. Let us restore to social intercourse that harmony and affection without which liberty and even life itself are but dreary things. And let us reflect that, having banished from our land that religious intolerance under which mankind so long bled and suffered, we have yet gained little if we countenance a political intolerance as despotic, as wicked, and capable of as bitter and bloody persecutions. During the throes and convulsions of the ancient world, during the agonizing spasms of infuriated man, seeking through blood and slaughter his long-lost liberty, it was not wonderful that the agitation of the billows should reach even this distant and peaceful shore; that this should be more felt and feared by some and less by others, and should divide opinions as to measures of safety. But every difference of opinion is not a difference of principle. We have called by different names brethren of the same principle. We are all Republicans, we are all Federalists. If there be any among us who would wish to dissolve this Union or to change its republican form, let them stand undisturbed as monuments of the safety with which error of opinion may be tolerated where reason is left free to combat it.

Hamilton, whose dislike of the devious Burr would later cause the famous duel in which he lost his life, supported Jefferson in the House. The Federalist Party ignored Hamilton's advice, however, in the hope that a prolonged contest would damage the Republican Party and perhaps postpone the transfer of power. The Federalists also sought some guarantees from both candidates regarding their plans for the future, but neither Jefferson nor Burr would commit himself. Finally, after thirty-five ballots, James A. Bayard, the lone representative from Delaware, decided to switch this vote, and thus his state's support, to Jefferson. Finally, on February 17, 1801, the nation had a president-elect.

SIGNIFICANCE

Jefferson considered the election of 1800 "as real a revolution in the principles of our government as that of 1776 was in its form." Jefferson's view was supported by some Federalists. Many High Federalists were positive that Jefferson would lead the nation into chaos and anarchy. However, Jefferson, in his inaugural address, spoke of conciliation and moderation rather than revolution.

The most concrete issue separating Adams's from Jefferson's policy toward France evaporated when Adams came out for peace. Jefferson, in later days, charged Adams with monarchist and antirepublican tendencies. There was little substance to those charges. Jefferson did articulate a greater confidence in popular government than did Adams, and the former was more suspicious of centrist tendencies in government. Both men were nationalists, however, devoted to representative government, determined to disengage the United States from European politics, and convinced of the future greatness of the republic. Although Adams lost the election to Jefferson, he also defeated the High Federalists in his own party. In so doing, Adams closed the already narrow gap between him and Jefferson.

Historians consider the political campaign and election of 1800 to be highly significant. The election ushered in the basic strategies of modern electoral campaigning. Jefferson, in particular, was instrumental in clearly defining the principles and objectives of Republicanism. He and his associates effectively used the press and pamphleteers to disseminate their appeals to farmers, laborers, and townsfolk. More important, the election demonstrated that the peaceful transfer of political power between rival ideologies was possible without bloodshed or revolution. The Federalists—the party that favored a strong, centralized government and served the needs of rich merchants, speculators, and landed gentry—gave way to the Republicans, who were later called Democratic Republicans and who were the forerunners of the modern Democratic Party.

Under the Republican banner, Jefferson campaigned in 1800 on a platform calling for change: promoting individual and political liberties, safeguarding states' rights against an encroaching central government, protecting the freedoms of press and religion, ensuring the right to dissent and criticize government, and encouraging free trade abroad but avoiding inappropriate alliances with European powers. During his two-term administration, Jefferson tried to keep those campaign promises.

—*John G. Clark, updated by Richard Whitworth*

FURTHER READING

Cunningham, Noble E. *In Pursuit of Reason: The Life of Thomas Jefferson.* Baton Rouge: Louisiana State University Press, 1987. Details Jefferson's public carer. Provides critical resources on Jefferson's faith in human reason, progress, and education.

Elkins, Stanley, and Eric McKitrick. *The Age of Federalism.* New York: Oxford University Press, 1993. Recreates the political climate in the 1790's leading up to the election of 1800. Focuses on the conflicting visions of Alexander Hamilton and Thomas Jefferson.

Fleming, Thomas J. *Duel: Alexander Hamilton, Aaron Burr, and the Future of America.* New York: Basic Books, 1999. Fleming sets the rivalry between Hamilton and Burr firmly within the chaotic political environment of the time.

Mayer, David N. *The Constitutional Thought of Thomas Jefferson.* Charlottesville: University Press of Virginia, 1994. Shows how Jefferson's constitutional thinking evolved from Whig to Federalist to Republican. Scholarly but highly readable.

Morgan, Edmund Sears. *The Meaning of Independence: John Adams, George Washington, Thomas Jefferson.* Rev. ed. Charlottesville: University Press of Virginia, 2004. First published in 1976, this brief volume has become a standard work on the early U.S. presidents. This edition includes a new preface in which the author reflects on his thoughts about the subject over the previous quarter century.

Randall, Willard S. *Thomas Jefferson: A Life.* New York: Henry Holt, 1993. Challenges the assumptions offered by earlier scholars on the influences of Jefferson's revolutionary political thinking.

Risjord, Norman K. *Thomas Jefferson.* Madison, Wis.: Madison House, 1994. A concise bundling of existing scholarship on Jefferson's evolving political philosophy, with Risjord's own view that Jefferson never successfully developed a coherent ideology.

Tucker, Robert, and David Hendrickson. *Empire of Liberty: The Statecraft of Thomas Jefferson.* New York: Oxford University Press, 1990. Examines Jefferson's ideas and his impact on U.S. foreign policy. Useful in understanding the American response to the world at large.

Weisberger, Bernard A. *America Afire: Jefferson, Adams, and the Revolutionary Election of 1800.* New York: William Morrow, 2000. Engagingly written analysis of the 1800 election that examines the politics and personalities of both major candidates.

SEE ALSO: Feb. 24, 1803: *Marbury v. Madison*; Sept. 25, 1804: Twelfth Amendment Is Ratified; Mar., 1805-Sept. 1, 1807: Burr's Conspiracy; Dec. 1, 1824-Feb. 9, 1825: U.S. Election of 1824; Dec. 3, 1828: U.S. Election of 1828; Dec. 2, 1840: U.S. Election of 1840.

RELATED ARTICLE in *Great Lives from History: The Nineteenth Century, 1801-1900:* Aaron Burr.

Summer, 1801-Summer, 1805
TRIPOLITAN WAR

Although a comparatively minor military conflict, the Tripolitan War was the first foreign war in which the independent United States fought. Prosecution of the war was politically controversial in the United States, but the federal government used the war to strengthen its naval forces and to create the Marine Corps.

ALSO KNOWN AS: First Barbary War; Barbary Coast War
LOCALE: North Africa
CATEGORY: Wars, uprisings, and civil unrest

KEY FIGURES
Thomas Jefferson (1743-1826), president of the United States, 1801-1809
Richard Dale (1756-1826), American naval officer who commanded the first flotilla sent to North Africa
Richard Valentine Morris (1768-1815), Dale's successor as commodore in North Africa
William Bainbridge (1774-1833), captain of the USS *Philadelphia*
Stephen Decatur (1779-1820), American naval captain
William Eaton (1764-1811), general of Hamet Karamānlī's rebels in Tripoli
Edward Preble (1761-1807), commodore of U.S. naval forces through most of the Tripolitan War
Yūsuf Karamānlī (d. 1838), pasha of Tripoli, r. 1795-1832
Hamet Karamānlī (fl. early nineteenth century), older brother of Yūsuf

SUMMARY OF EVENT
From mid-1801 to 1805, the United States used its young navy to wage its first naval war against the Barbary states of North Africa, which included the Mediterranean coastal cities of Tripoli, Morocco, Tunis, and Algiers. For years, pirate forces from these states plagued European and American merchant ships in the Mediterranean, taking money and slaves as often as they could. Moreover, the rulers of the Barbary states exacted tributes of money and arms in exchange for granting safe passage through the Mediterranean. In 1801, the pasha of Tripoli, Yūsuf Karamānlī, increased his demands on U.S. vessels. When U.S. president Thomas Jefferson refused to pay, Karamānlī declared war.

All four of the Barbary states were troublesome to the United States, but Tripoli's Yūsuf Karamānlī had one thing that the rulers of the other three states did not—a blood relative who was his rival for power. Yūsuf had driven his older brother, Hamet, into hiding before claiming power. When the U.S. government learned of this development, William Eaton, the U.S. ambassador to the Barbary region, and several others came up with the idea of helping to restore Hamet to power.

The United States first sent a flotilla of four ships, under Commodore Richard Dale, into Barbary waters to show off new American naval power. Dale was expressly ordered to defend his fleet if attacked but had no orders to take the offensive. Through the first two years of the so-called war, the only battle that took place occurred while Dale was busy setting up a blockade at Gibraltar, near the Atlantic entrance to the Mediterranean. One of Dale's commanders, Captain Andrew Sterrett of the *Enterprise*, destroyed a Tripolitan schooner. This action made negotiations between the United States and Tripoli futile. After an otherwise eventless year passed, Dale took his flotilla back to the United States because his crews' enlistments were up.

In February of 1802, the U.S. Congress passed an act that loosened some of the restrictions that Dale had faced. Richard Valentine Morris was made commodore, and sailors were conscripted for two years instead of one. For the most part, Morris seemed content to stay in Gibraltar with his family and avoid military action. Although he commanded a fleet of six intimidating ships, he did not make a single aggressive move toward Tripoli. Fed up with Morris's apparent incompetence, President Jefferson had him relieved of his duties on August 31, 1803, and replaced him with Edward Preble. Around that same time, Jefferson also made Ambassador Eaton the

U.S. bombardment of Tripoli. (C. A. Nichols & Company)

Navy Agent of the United States for the Barbary Regencies, a lengthy title that served the purpose of keeping Eaton close to the conflict.

Not long after Preble replaced Morris as commodore, one of the most notorious events of the war occurred. On October 31, 1803, the USS *Philadelphia*, the pride of the U.S. fleet under Captain William Bainbridge, grounded itself on a reef near the Tripolitan coast and resisted all efforts to free it. Tripolitan vessels surrounded the *Philadelphia*, forcing its crew to abandon the ship in such haste that the sailors failed to render the ship and its weapons useless to the enemy. Yūsuf's ships quickly captured the crew and salvaged the American ship and most of its weapons.

The American naval officers in the Mediterranean determined that Yūsuf could not be left the master of the *Philadelphia*, so a sixty-two-man force under the command of Captain Stephen Decatur was sent into Tripoli to burn the ship. On the night of February 16, 1804, the Americans sailed into the Tripolitan port aboard the *Intrepid*, a ship captured from the Tripolitan fleet, on a surprise attack. However, they encountered little resistance,

as the *Philadelphia* was not heavily guarded. After setting the ship afire, the Americans claimed a victory.

Later during that same summer, Preble tested the might of his forces in several full-scale attacks on the city of Tripoli. Meanwhile, Eaton located Hamet Karamānlī. After finding Hamet, however, Eaton was given only eight of the one hundred Marines whom he had requested for the purpose of gathering an army of Hamet supporters. Conflicts in the Mediterranean made sea travel impossible for this troop, so they walked to the city of Derna, where they hoped to recruit some of Hamet's rich friends to his cause.

Anticipating this move, Yūsuf neutralized all of Hamet's possible allies and sent a force of his own to Derna. However, Eaton's little pro-Hamet army arrived there first. On April 24, 1805, his small force took the city by surprise and astonishingly captured Derna swiftly. Two further battles in May clinched Hamet and Eaton's victory. They were now poised to move on Tripoli, but news arrived that Yūsuf had struck a deal with the United States. Yūsuf was to release all American slaves, in return for which he was to receive a tribute of sixty thousand dollars. Eaton was forced to withdraw, and Hamet and the rest of the troops were smuggled to safety, officially ending America's first war.

SIGNIFICANCE

The Tripolitan War is perhaps most famous for the birth of the U.S. Marine Corps, but other milestones were also passed in this war. The people of the United States feared having a permanent domestic military force. The instability of the new national government made Americans wary of any military force that might be used against them. The formation of the Navy was controversial, and its actual deployment was even more controversial—which was one of the reasons that Congress never officially declared war.

The Tripolitan War was the first military conflict with a foreign power in which the independent United States engaged. It was also a precursor to the War of 1812 with Great Britain. In 1801, most of the world had not even heard of the United States of America. The fact that U.S. Navy ships could take on the turbulent Barbary states proved the determination of the United States as a nation. If the conflict had not been settled diplomatically, the United States would almost certainly have won the war—a fact that played a significant role in the strengthening of U.S. maritime forces. The war gave the United States the confidence it needed to survive and helped to prepare the U.S. Navy for many later conflicts.

—*Meaghan G. Wagner*

FURTHER READING

Chidsey, Donald Barr. *The Wars in Barbary: Arab Piracy and the Birth of the United States Navy*. New York: Crown, 1971. A full look at many of the important people and events that precipitated the Tripolitan War. Follows some of the significant subsequent political events.

Crumley, B. L. *The Marine Corps: Three Centuries of Glory*. San Diego, Calif.: Thunder Bay Press, 2002. Brief but informative discussion of the U.S. Marines' involvement in the Tripolitan War and how the struggles in North Africa affected the U.S. military forces.

Macleod, Julia H., and Louis B. Wright. *The First Americans in North Africa: William Eaton's Struggle for a Vigorous Policy Against the Barbary Pirates, 1799-1805*. Princeton, N.J.: Princeton University Press, 1945. A look at the political circumstances surrounding the conflict in the Barbary states, focusing on Tunis.

Rodd, Francis Rennell. *General William Eaton*. New York: Van Rees Press, 1932. Biography of Eaton that includes a penetrating look at the U.S. naval forces. Also examines the politics that affected Eaton's career and his involvement in the conflict.

Wheelan, Joseph. *Jefferson's War: America's First War on Terror, 1801-1805*. New York: Avalon, 2003. A good look at how the events in Barbary affected the American people.

SEE ALSO: Mar. 16, 1802: U.S. Military Academy Is Established; Oct. 21, 1805: Battle of Trafalgar; June 18, 1812-Dec. 24, 1814: War of 1812; 1822-1874: Exploration of North Africa.

RELATED ARTICLES in *Great Lives from History: The Nineteenth Century, 1801-1900:* Stephen Decatur; David G. Farragut; Oliver Hazard Perry.

December 6, 1801-August, 1803
FLINDERS EXPLORES AUSTRALIA

Parts of Australia were known to European explorers as early as the mid-seventeenth century, but the fact that the continent was a single, great landmass was not understood until Matthew Flinders circumnavigated the continent and charted its coastlines. His expedition also made major contributions to natural history, and his expedition's naturalist, Robert Brown, became a prominent plant taxonomist who later influenced Charles Darwin.

LOCALE: Australia
CATEGORIES: Exploration and discovery; geography

KEY FIGURES
Matthew Flinders (1774-1814), British naval officer and explorer
Robert Brown (1773-1858), English naturalist and plant taxonomist who accompanied Flinders
George Bass (1771-1803), English naval officer and surgeon
Ferdinand Bauer (fl. early nineteenth century), botanical illustrator
Sir Joseph Banks (1743-1820), British naturalist and president of the Royal Society who organized the Flinders expedition
Nicolas Baudin (1754-1803), French naturalist who led a rival Australian expedition

SUMMARY OF EVENT

In 1800, the southern continent later known as Australia was almost unknown in Europe. When Dutch navigators had discovered the continent's barren northwestern corner in the early seventeenth century, they dubbed the territory New Holland and supposed it to be merely a large island. The Dutch explorer Abel Tasman circumnavigated Australia in 1642-1643, touching Tasmania and New Zealand and demonstrating that the southern landmass was limited in extent. However, he did not realize that the lands that he circumnavigated actually constituted a single mass. In 1770, Captain James Cook had conducted a survey of Australia's southeastern coast, which he claimed for Great Britain and named New South Wales. Based upon this survey and the recommendations of Sir Joseph Banks, Cook's naturalist, Britain established a penal colony at Port Jackson (modern Sydney) in 1788.

In 1795, Matthew Flinders arrived in the struggling penal colony as a midshipman on board a vessel that was bringing a new colonial governor. Over the next three years, Flinders commanded coasting vessels that supplied a remote penal colony on Norfolk Island, and he twice made the long and difficult run to South Africa's Cape Colony for provisions and livestock. Meanwhile, his friend and ship's surgeon George Bass explored Australia's southern coast and deduced that a strait separated Tasmania from the mainland. That strait was later named after Bass.

In 1798, with the support of the governor, Bass and Flinders set sail in a twelve-foot open boat, the *Tom Thumb*, in which they passed through Bass Strait and circumnavigated Tasmania in a counterclockwise direction, noting the positions of the island's bays and promontories. Flinders also surveyed the Furneaux Islands, at the entrance to Bass Strait. At the end of this remarkable voyage, Flinders returned to England, where he published an account of his travels.

Hoping to return to Australia at the head of a more fully equipped expedition, Flinders found a valuable ally in Sir Joseph Banks, the eminent naturalist who was president of the Royal Society. Banks had influential connections in government and understood the political importance of maritime exploration.

At that time, France and Great Britain were at war. The French naturalist Nicolas Baudin had recently applied successfully to the British government for passports guaranteeing his proposed scientific expedition to Australia immunity from British naval attack. Banks himself had misgivings about the French expedition. He suspected that Baudin's patron, Napoleon Bonaparte, had designs on New South Wales. Consequently he welcomed Flinders's proposal for a rival British expedition and pressured the stingy British Admiralty into providing Flinders with a ship, an experienced crew, and a competent scientific team. The scientific team included the naturalist Robert Brown, landscape artist William Westfall, botanical illustrator Ferdinand Bauer, and a gardener skilled in keeping plant specimens healthy on long voyages.

The *Investigator*, a hundred-foot-long converted collier, left Spithead on March 27, 1801, carrying a crew of seventy-eight, plus six members of the scientific staff. The ship arrived at Cape Leeuwin on December 6, 1801, after an uneventful voyage via the Cape of Good Hope, and immediately commenced a survey of Australia's unknown southern coast. Flinders recorded the positions of physical features so precisely that his charts were used until World War II. Meanwhile, Brown collected plant and animal specimens—many of which he preserved alive. Bauer sketched the specimens as they were collected, using an elaborate color-coding system to reproduce hues accurately at a later date. In his expedition's occasional encounters with Australia's Aboriginal peoples, Flinders respected their desire to remain unmolested. They, in turn, kept their distance, except during an episode of theft in the Gulf of Carpentaria on Australia's northern coast.

The expedition realized its hope of finding a good, well-watered bay that would be suitable as a stop for China-bound shipping when it entered Spencer Gulf, near the site of where modern Melbourne now stands,

immediately west of Bass Strait. Not long afterward, they met Baudin's expedition on the *Géographe*, which was anchored in Encounter Bay. After four months on a barren coast, the sailors of the *Investigator* were exhausted and suffering from scurvy. Baudin's crew, which had been ravaged by tropical diseases contracted in Timor, was in even worse shape. Both ships proceeded to Port Jackson for rest, recovery, and repairs.

At the end of July, the re-equipped *Investigator* sailed north, up the east coast of Australia, through the treacherous maze of islets and reefs east of the Great Barrier Reef, and entered the Gulf of Carpentaria through the Torres Strait, which separates Australia from New Guinea. Flinders sought and found the safest route through the shallow, reef-dotted strait, a valuable short-

FLINDERS'S EXPLORATIONS

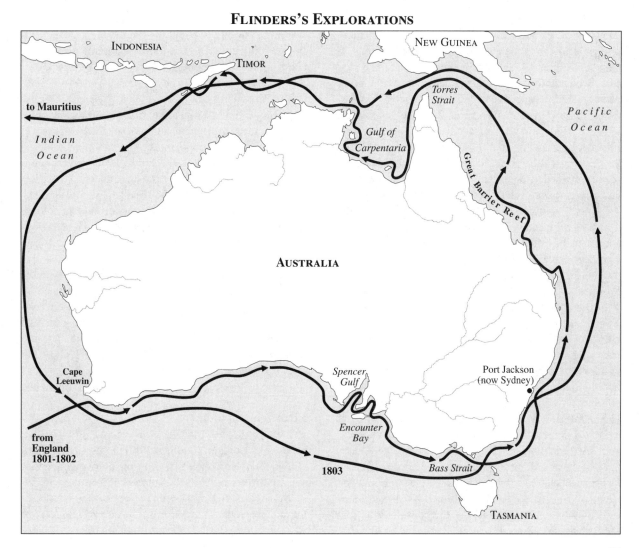

cut for China-bound shipping. At that point, an inspection of the *Investigator* revealed the ship to have become unseaworthy. Flinders decided to wait out the monsoon season in the gulf and used the time to survey its contours. He discovered that old Dutch charts showing a continuous coastline were fairly accurate and that there was definitely no sea connection between the northern Gulf of Carpentaria and the southern coast.

In March, 1803, with his crew again debilitated and the ship in danger of breaking up, Flinders sailed northward to Timor. There the Dutch governor afforded Flinders the hospitality due to his scientific passport but could provide almost nothing in the way of supplies. From Timor, Flinders sailed south, well out to sea, and arrived back at Port Jackson on June 9, after completing the first close circumnavigation of Australia in ten months and eighteen days.

After the *Investigator* was judged to be unfit for further service, Flinders transferred his crew, charts, and dried specimens to the *Porpoise* and embarked for England on August 10, accompanied by two merchant vessels. Brown and Bauer remained behind with the living plant and animal specimens they had collected. On August 17, the *Porpoise* and one of the merchant vessels struck a reef and were abandoned by the third ship. Flinders oversaw the successful transfer of most of the stricken vessels' cargoes and provisions, and all but three of the crewmen, to a sand spit. He then made a hazardous 750-mile voyage back to Port Jackson in an open boat.

Flinders returned to his marooned shipmates in the *Cumberland*, a leaky and filthy thirty-nine-ton schooner, accompanied by the *Rolla*, a China-bound merchantman. His men salvaged the scientific collections and took them back to Port Jackson, from which the collections eventually found their way to England in 1805, along with Bauer and Brown and their own collections from Norfolk Island and Tasmania. Most of the *Investigator*'s crew elected to sail on the *Rolla* and reached England a year later.

Flinders himself continued on in the *Cumberland*, hoping to secure another ship in England with which to continue his Australian explorations. However, the *Cumberland* proved so unseaworthy that he was forced to stop at the island of Mauritius, then a French possession. At that moment, Britain and France were once again at war. Mauritius's French governor, Charles Decaen, suspecting that Flinders was an intelligence agent, seized his ship and imprisoned him—a circumstance doubly galling in view of the consideration that the British had shown to Baudin in Port Jackson.

Despite determined efforts by Sir Joseph Banks and his counterparts in the French Academy of Sciences, Flinders remained interned on Mauritius until 1810. The long imprisonment delayed his promotion to post captain and so undermined his health that he never again resumed active duty. After returning to England, he devoted his remaining years to preparing an account of his travels and accompanying charts for publication. *A Voyage to Terra Australis* appeared on the day of his death, June 19, 1814.

SIGNIFICANCE

Had the British not defeated the French in 1815, the political aspects of Flinders's explorations would probably seem more important outside Australia, where he is viewed as a national hero on a par with his American contemporaries, Meriwether Lewis and William Clark. After Napoleon lost the Battle of Waterloo (1815), there was no possibility of either the French or their Dutch allies pressing claims to western Australia, and Britain's acquisition of Singapore in 1819 secured the most direct sea route between India and China.

From a scientific point of view, the voyage of the *Investigator* can be viewed as the first installment in a saga of exploration, the final installment of which is known to every Australian schoolchild. The landmarks of the south coast of Australia bear the names Investigator, Flinders, and Brown. The landmarks of Australia's northwest coast bear the names Beagle, Fitzroy, and Darwin, testifying to the much more famous voyage of discovery that three decades later would complete the survey that Flinders had begun. In his subsequent long career as Britain's most distinguished and innovative plant taxonomist, Robert Brown drew extensively on the field experience he obtained in Australia in 1801-1804. A pioneer in microscopy, he is credited with discoveries of cellular streaming, nucleation of plant cells, and Brownian motion. His data and observations figure prominently in Charles Darwin's *On the Origin of Species by Means of Natural Selection* (1859).

—*Martha A. Sherwood*

FURTHER READING

Brown, Anthony J. *Ill-Starred Captains: Flinders and Baudin*. London: Chatham, 2001. Stresses the rivalry and complementary activities of the two contemporary British and French explorers and provides a day-by-day description of Flinders's activities.

Gascoigne, John. *Science in the Service of Empire: Joseph Banks, the British State, and the Uses of Science in the Age of Revolution.* New York: Cambridge University Press, 1998. Particularly useful for the role of the East India Company in the exploration of Australasia.

Macintyre, Stuart. *A Concise History of Australia.* Cambridge, England: Cambridge University Press, 2000. Broad survey of Australia that includes a lengthy discussion of the continent's exploration.

Rice, Tony. *Three Centuries of Natural History Exploration.* New York: Clarkson N. Potter, 1999. The chapter on the Flinders expedition focuses on Robert Brown and Ferdinand Bauer and includes a number of Bauer's spectacular illustrations.

SEE ALSO: Sept. 7, 1803: Great Britain Begins Colonizing Tasmania; Aug. 16, 1835: Melbourne, Australia, Is Founded; 1851: Gold Is Discovered in New South Wales.

RELATED ARTICLES in *Great Lives from History: The Nineteenth Century, 1801-1900:* Charles Darwin; Sir John Franklin; Meriwether Lewis and William Clark; John MacArthur; Edward Gibbon Wakefield.

1802
BRITAIN ADOPTS GAS LIGHTING

F. A. Winsor and William Murdock established coal gas as an inexpensive and convenient fuel for lighting streets, factories, and public buildings. Generated from coal, the gas was a boon to commercial and manufacturing interests but was also a heavy polluter, and its use led to deteriorating working conditions.

LOCALE: England
CATEGORIES: Inventions; science and technology; business and labor

KEY FIGURES
Frederick Albert Winsor (1763-1830), founder of the London Gas Light and Coke Company
William Murdock (1754-1839), British engineer and inventor
Philippe Lebon (1767-1804), French engineer

SUMMARY OF EVENT
As the eighteenth century drew to a close, artificial lighting lagged behind other technologies of the infant Industrial Revolution. Wax candles and the best whale oil lamps, used in profusion, provided excellent illumination but were prohibitively expensive. Tallow candles, used by all but the wealthy, required constant attention and were unsuitable for large spaces or outdoor use. Light was a luxury; for the most part, eighteenth century England was a relatively dark place, especially during the winter months.

There are several competing claims for the discovery that flammable gases could be used for illumination, but the first person to demonstrate a prototype with commercial potential is usually considered to be William Murdock, an engineer employed by James Watt and Matthew Boulton in their steam engine manufactory in Birmingham, England. While setting up a satellite plant in Cornwall, Murdock devised a method of collecting waste gas from coke production and burning it in cylindrical nozzles modeled on a contemporary whale-oil lamp. With Watt's backing, he built a gas lighting system on a much larger scale at the company's Soho works in Birmingham. After being used for festive illuminations celebrating the Peace of Amiens in 1802, his system was expanded to light the factory itself in 1804. Murdock also designed a gas-generating system and persuaded a large textile mill in Manchester to convert to gas lighting. In 1806, the first year of operation, savings in labor and materials cut lighting costs by 50 percent.

At about the same time, a German-born inventor and entrepreneur, Frederick Albert Winsor, began promoting gas lighting in London. Winsor had seen French inventor Philippe Lebon demonstrate his "thermolampe" to curious crowds in Paris in 1798, and he was impressed by its potential. Failing to find commercial backers on the Continent, he traveled to England, where he met with a better reception. With whale oil becoming scarce and expensive because of the resumption of war between France and England, substitutes looked more attractive. In 1804, Winsor obtained a patent for a gas generating apparatus and set up shop in fashionable Pall Mall. He conducted public lectures and demonstrations and distributed advertisements making extravagant claims.

Winsor's gaslights illuminated Carleton House, home of the Prince of Wales, for the king's birthday in 1807. Shortly afterward he issued a prospectus for the New Patriotic Imperial and National Light and Heat Company, touting coal gas as the key to reviving a faltering econ-

DEVELOPMENT OF GAS LIGHTING IN EARLY NINETEENTH CENTURY ENGLAND

1802	Peace of Amiens celebrated by the illumination of the exterior of the Soho Foundry in Birmingham
1804	Soho Foundry converts to gas lighting
1804	F. A. Winsor patents a gas generating apparatus
1806	Gas lighting installed at a cotton mill in Manchester
1807	Illumination of Carleton House, London, the residence of the Prince of Wales
1808	W. Murdock presents paper on gas lighting to the Royal Society of London
1810	London Gas Light and Coke Company is chartered
1814	Installation of gas streetlights in Westminster (London)
1817	Drury Lane Theatre, London, installs gas lighting
1819	Manchester builds first municipal gas generating system
1822	St. Paul's Cathedral, London, installs gas lighting

omy, eliminating crime, and winning the war with Napoleon. Few people were willing to invest in so speculative a venture, so Winsor approached Parliament for a special charter. After three years of heated debate, against opposition from Watt and Murdoch, ridicule from luminaries such as inventor Sir Humphry Davy, and the protests of the whaling industry, Parliament finally granted a charter for the more modest London Gas Light and Coke Company in 1810.

Winsor's approach, which ultimately edged out Murdoch's earlier claim, relied on centralized generation of gas and distribution through pipelines to numerous customers, rather than on the sale of generators to individual factories. Gas lighting expanded rapidly. Westminster Bridge, London, was lit for New Year's Day, 1813, and the main thoroughfares of Westminster soon followed. By 1815 there were twenty-six miles of gas pipeline in London. Other British metropolitan areas followed suit. Industrial Manchester established the first municipal gas generating system in 1819. Drury Lane Theatre installed gas lighting in 1817 and St. Paul's Cathedral installed it in 1822. In the United States, several cities had gas generating plants by 1820.

As a lighting source, gas was hardly the panacea Winsor envisioned. A mixture of hydrogen, methane and short-chain hydrocarbons, and carbon monoxide, coal gas is toxic and explosive. There were numerous accidents in gas lighting's early days. Inadequate pipes cobbled together from war surplus gun barrels and fix-

tures installed by untrained workers led to frequent leaks and explosions. Fluctuating pressure caused flames to go out, and asphyxiation from carbon monoxide poisoning followed.

Hydrogen sulfide, which gives gas its characteristic rotten egg odor, produces sulfur dioxide upon combustion. Gas suppliers left in the hydrogen sulfide during the purifying process to reduce the danger from gas leaks, but the result was the generation of a corrosive pollutant in the indoor environment. Relative to the amount of light produced, gas generates more heat and depletes oxygen more rapidly than candles or whale oil, which continued to be used for most domestic lighting until kerosene became available around 1860.

Although gas itself was comparatively inexpensive, only the well-to-do could afford the costs of installation. Because pollutants from gas burning tarnished silver and rotted cloth, people with fine furnishings avoided it. The prince regent solved this dilemma by illuminating the grandly furnished public rooms of Brighton Palace with gaslights outside the windows. Gas's great virtue was its convenience. After it is turned on, a gas fixture remains lit without requiring periodic attention. This made it ideal for use in streetlights, for lighting large halls with high ceilings, and for factories.

Darkness was no longer a constraint on commerce and industry, proving a great boon for factory owners, whose machines no longer stood idle during long winter nights. Working after sundown contributed to the competitive advantage of manufacturers in England and New England. The laboring population, however, generally experienced a decline in the quality of their lives, as increased hours at work rarely translated into more remuneration, and gaslight created a stifling, unhealthful atmosphere in factories. Illumination, moreover, ended at the factory door—poor neighborhoods had no streetlights, and even tallow candles were a luxury in a working-class household.

SIGNIFICANCE

The rapid social and technological changes of the first two decades of the nineteenth century make almost impossible any assessments of the contributions, either positive or negative, that any one technological innovation made toward the whole.

On the positive side, the introduction of effective streetlights in urban areas is widely cited as having cut crime. A saying of the time was that "a streetlight is as good as a policeman." People felt safer being abroad at night. It was no longer necessary to schedule public lectures to coincide with a full moon, and shops and places of entertainment had a larger evening clientele. The crime rate in British cities fell considerably between 1815 and 1830. Claiming credit were the proponents of street lighting, those advocating measures favoring industry (and therefore full employment), those who instituted a regular police force in London, and those who revised a chaotic draconian penal code. Likewise, the differential in crime rates between poor and well-to-do neighborhoods, which persists in urban areas into the twenty-first century, cannot be ascribed entirely to superior illumination.

As a source of pollution the gas industry must rank near the top. A gas plant burned coal to fuel the refining process, consumed coal to produce its product, and spewed smoke, slag, and water used to remove some of the impurities. The toxic gas itself escaped during all phases of the delivery process, and the end product created further pollution when consumed. The nature of the product and delivery system dictated that gas plants be located near residential and commercial centers, though not in immediate proximity to the people who benefited from its consumption. Working conditions in gas plants were hellish—indeed, they helped inspire Gustave Doré's celebrated illustrations (1861) for Dante's *Inferno*.

Throughout much of the nineteenth century, gas was the usual fuel for lighting streets, theaters, large public buildings, and factories. The introduction of the incandescent gas mantle about 1880 greatly increased the intensity of illumination. The high heat to light output ratio of coal gas, coupled with its convenience, made it an ideal fuel for cooking; many urban middle-class homes had gas in their kitchens and candles in their parlors.

Domestic lighting after 1850 benefited from the rise of the petroleum industry in the United States. Kerosene—cheap, nonexplosive, and odorless compared to most alternatives—became the lighting fuel of choice for both urban and rural homes across the class spectrum. The switch to fossil fuels—first coal, then oil—occurred

at a time when rapid population growth and reliance on steam power for transportation drastically curtailed the availability of animal fats. Had the technology for producing light from fossil fuels not been in place during the mid-nineteenth century, society would have found itself in the dark.

—*Martha A. Sherwood*

FURTHER READING

Bowers, B. *Lengthening the Day: A History of Lighting Technology*. New York: Oxford University Press, 1998. A good source for the practical aspects of manufacturing and supplying gas, and for the interplay of various technologies before the adoption of electricity.

Dillon, Maureen. *Artificial Sunshine: A Social History of Domestic Lighting*. London: National Trust, 2002. Vividly describes lighting as a social phenomenon. Copiously illustrated.

Matthew, H. C. G., and Brian Harrison, eds. *Oxford Dictionary of National Biography: From the Earliest Times to the Year 2000*. New York: Oxford University Press, 2004. Has detailed entries on Frederick Albert Winsor, William Murdock, Matthew Boulton, and James Watt. An invaluable source for biographies of obscure British historical personages.

Williams, Trevor I. *A History of the British Gas Industry*. New York: Oxford University Press, 1981. Discusses the foundation of the London Gas Light and Coke Company, with an emphasis on its business aspects.

SEE ALSO: c. 1801-1810: Davy Develops the Arc Lamp; Oct., 1831: Faraday Converts Magnetic Force into Electricity; 1850: First U.S. Petroleum Refinery Is Built; Oct. 21, 1879: Edison Demonstrates the Incandescent Lamp.

RELATED ARTICLES in *Great Lives from History: The Nineteenth Century, 1801-1900:* Sir Humphry Davy; Thomas Alva Edison; Michael Faraday; Sir William Robert Grove; Étienne Lenoir; The Siemens Family; Charles Proteus Steinmetz; Joseph Wilson Swan; George Westinghouse.

January, 1802
COBBETT FOUNDS THE *POLITICAL REGISTER*

The most influential organ of radical political dissent in late Georgian England, William Cobbett's Political Register *set important precedents for future political journals. Initially patriotic in tone, the weekly gravitated toward exposure of corruption and agitation for social justice and parliamentary reform. A broadsheet version, dubbed* Cobbett's Twopenny Trash, *was the first English political periodical aimed at the working class.*

LOCALE: London, England
CATEGORIES: Communications; social issues and reform

KEY FIGURES

William Cobbett (Peter Porcupine; 1763-1835), founder, editor, and principal writer of the *Political Register*
William Windham (1750-1810), Whig politician who helped found the *Political Register*
Luke Hansard (1752-1828), printer who published the *Political Register* and *Parliamentary History*
Sir Francis Burdett (1770-1844), radical member of Parliament who helped underwrite the *Political Register*

SUMMARY OF EVENT

In January of 1802, a new weekly journal called the *Political Register* appeared on the streets of London. The journal's editor and principal writer was William Cobbett, a self-educated farm boy. Cobbett had recently returned from the United States, where he had established himself as an incisive political commentator under the pen name Peter Porcupine. The persona of Peter Porcupine was that of a thoroughgoing Tory who was both pro-English and anti-French. Cobbett's initial editorial stance in his new journal was similar. A new British government administration had recently signed a peace agreement with France. The *Political Register* filled a publishing vacuum, speaking for those who favored both social reform—traditionally a Whig or radical platform—and continuing the war with revolutionary France—a stance spearheaded by the Tories under William Pitt the Younger. Cobbett's journal was partly the brainchild of the prowar Whig radical William Windham.

The lively, provocative writing and independent spirit of the *Political Register* made it an instant success. Its circulation began at three hundred copies and grew to

more than three thousand copies by the end of 1804, despite the fact that its ten-and-one-half-pence price meant that no ordinary working person could afford a personal subscription. Indeed, Cobbett pointed with pride to the fact that the cost of his publication ensured that it had only a respectable readership.

Early issues of the journal included complete transcripts of parliamentary debates; that was a novelty at that time, but daily papers soon followed suit. In 1804 Cobbett decided to issue *Parliamentary Debates* as a separate publication and at the same time undertook his *History of Parliament* series, editing and preparing pre-1803 records for publication. He also undertook a compendium of state trials. The *Parliamentary Register* appeared under Cobbett's directorship until 1810, when he sold the rights to its printer, Luke Hansard, who continued to issue it as *Hansard's Parliamentary Debates*.

In 1804, Cobbett toured rural southern England, seeing at first hand how enclosures, wartime prices, and land speculation were devastating the lives of rural laborers. In the quarter century since he had left his family farm, large landholdings operated as businesses had prospered, while rural unemployment skyrocketed and most farm laborers became dependent on parish relief. Cobbett now saw war fever as a smokescreen for wartime profiteering, and he ascribed the nation's economic woes to oppressive taxation, excessive indebtedness, and government corruption. The solution, he concluded, was a radical reform of Parliament.

After 1804, the editorial stance of the *Political Register* moved toward the radicalism of Sir Francis Burdett and Henry "Orator" Hunt and away from Windham's more moderate Whig politics. It was never an easy alliance. The radicals' support came from urban areas, and their concerns reflected that fact. Cobbett's main goal was preserving rural English society. While the radicals clamored for universal manhood suffrage in industrial cities, Cobbett advocated abolishing all borough parliamentary seats. He eventually opposed the Corn Laws that regulated the import and export of grains but only when he became convinced that high agricultural prices mainly benefited wealthy farmers.

Another feature of the *Political Register* distinguishing it from many contemporary radical publications was its respect for the Church of England. Cobbett had no use for evangelism and Puritanism, and was quick to attack church corruption. However, he was neither an atheist nor a freethinker. On the subject of Roman Catholic emancipation, which he supported, he clashed with the Irish parliamentarian Daniel O'Connell by advocating government constraints on Roman Catholic clergy.

The *Political Register* faced its first major challenge in 1810, when the government prosecuted Cobbett for publishing an impassioned piece on soldiers who had refused to obey orders in the town of Ely. Troops from Hanover had been called in, and the ringleaders were brutally flogged. The spectacle of English soldiers being flogged by Germans appalled Cobbett. His resulting xenophobic diatribe against a British ally and apparent condoning of mutiny during wartime came under the government's definition of sedition. He was convicted and sentenced to pay a fine of one thousand pounds and spend two years in London's Newgate Prison.

While Cobbett raised money to pay his fine and cover the substantial costs that would be necessary to live in comfort in prison, he discovered that his business manager had mishandled the finances of the *Political Register* and cost him six thousand pounds. By selling the *Parliamentary Register* to Hansard and continuing to edit the *Political Register* from his prison cell, Cobbett managed to avoid bankruptcy but never fully recouped his losses. He emerged from prison two years later an angry, embittered man.

The end of the war with France in 1815 brought hard times. Sales of all periodicals dropped. Cobbett's accusation that the government had engineered Napoleon's escape from his exile on Elba in order to crush French liberty garnered derision and cost him support. A loan from Sir Francis Burdett helped Cobbett keep his journal afloat, and violent urban riots in 1816-1817 increased public demand for radical journalism. To avoid paying periodical taxes, Cobbett issued his landmark *Address to the Journeymen and Labourers of England* as a broadside, priced at two pence. This single issue sold an unprecedented 200,000 copies and grossed more than sixteen hundred pounds. Emboldened by this success, Cobbett began issuing more of his articles aimed at workingmen as broadsides and pamphlets. Some numbers of *Cobbett's Twopenny Trash* sold as many as forty thousand copies. His was the first English political publication specifically aimed at members of the working class. It remained popular because Cobbett understood the concerns of his audience and wrote in a style that appealed to them.

Responding to widespread rioting, the government suspended habeas corpus in March of 1817 and began imprisoning troublemakers without trial. Fearing incarceration, Cobbett dashed off *The Last Hundred Days of English Liberty* and then sailed for the United States, where he remained until 1820. During his absence, his journal continued to appear but lost much of its support, particularly among followers of Hunt and others who remained in England, some of whom suffered imprisonment for their actions.

The trial of Queen Caroline (1768-1821) of Brunswick, the former Princess of Wales, for adultery in 1820 provided a cause with broad popular support. Cobbett championed the queen and castigated the unpopular King George IV in the pages of his journal; he also wrote most of Caroline's petitions and public statements. Pressured by popular clamor, the House of Lords finally abandoned the prosecution. Caroline died soon afterward.

In 1821, Cobbett began the series *Rural Rides*, later collected in book form. He used it to combine his love for traditional rural life with scathing commentaries on the social forces undermining that life and appeals for parliamentary reform. Appealing to readers of all classes, *Rural Rides* remains a minor classic of English literature, securing for its author literary as well as political fame.

William Cobbett. (Library of Congress)

By the late 1820's, English reformers were concentrating on urban problems. In 1828 and 1829, the *Political Register* resounded with warnings that deteriorating conditions in rural England were likely to result in insurrection. When the so-called Swing riots broke out in southern England in 1830, the authorities suspected Cobbett of more than accurate prophecy. Brought to trial for sedition in 1831, he defended himself ably and was acquitted. He continued writing and publishing his weekly *Political Register* until his death on June 18, 1835. His journal, which was again in financial difficulties, soon ceased publication.

SIGNIFICANCE

In retrospect, the *Political Register* looms larger as a literary than a political force. Of the causes it so eloquently advocated, only Roman Catholic emancipation and parliamentary reform were realized during William Cobbett's lifetime. Morever, the form taken by parliamentary reform did virtually nothing to ameliorate the grim lives of the rural poor.

Cobbett skillfully identified and dramatized the multiple economic woes that characterized Britain in his day, but he was no economist. Had the government taken his advice and reduced taxes by defaulting on the national debt, the results would surely have been disastrous. Cobbett's preoccupation with government corruption made for entertaining reading, but he exaggerated the impact of the problem and proposed cures far worse than the disease.

The *Political Register* failed to catalyze a political revolution, but it did represent a revolution in journalism. Especially in its broadsheet form, it was the first English-language periodical to put political and social controversy into the hands of working people in language to which they could relate. Other contemporary reformers tended to be patronizing, claiming to speak for the unrepresented masses but seldom listening to those masses or explaining clearly how the proposed remedies could be expected to effect reform. Cobbett respected his audience. He addressed them directly, on their own level. Two hundred years after the founding of the *Political Register*, his lively, hard-hitting prose is still read and still resonates.

—*Martha A. Sherwood*

FURTHER READING

Burton, Anthony. *William Cobbett, Englishman: A Biography.* London: Aurum Press, 1997. A balanced treatment that discusses the background and context of key political treatises.

Dyck, Ian. "William Cobbett and the Rural Radical Platform." *Social History* 18, no. 2 (1993): 185-204. Emphasizes Cobbett's rural roots; offers a detailed treatment of the role of the *Political Register* during the Swing riots.

Green, Daniel. *Great Cobbett: The Noblest Agitator.* London: Hodder & Stoughton, 1983. Good coverage of Cobbett's two trials for libel, *Twopenny Trash*, and the trial of Queen Caroline.

Thompson, Noel, and David Eastwood, eds. *The Collected Social and Political Writings of William Cobbett.* Reprint. London: Routledge/Thoemmes Press, 1998. Seventeen volumes in facsimile, with an extensive introduction. Includes all of the widely cited articles from the *Political Register*. Arranged partly by topic and partly chronologically.

SEE ALSO: Mar. 11, 1811-1816: Luddites Destroy Industrial Machines; Dec. 11-30, 1819: British Parliament Passes the Six Acts; Feb. 23, 1820: London's Cato Street Conspirators Plot Assassinations; Oct. 5, 1823: Wakley Introduces *The Lancet*; June 4, 1832: British Parliament Passes the Reform Act of 1832; Sept. 2, 1843: Wilson Launches *The Economist*.

RELATED ARTICLES in *Great Lives from History: The Nineteenth Century, 1801-1900:* William Cobbett; Francis Place.

March 16, 1802

U.S. MILITARY ACADEMY IS ESTABLISHED

Creation of the first military academy and first engineering school in the United States helped erode Federalist domination of the army's officer corps and laid the foundation for a professionally trained officer corps.

ALSO KNOWN AS: Military Peace Establishment Act; West Point

LOCALE: West Point, New York

CATEGORIES: Education; organizations and institutions; military history; engineering

KEY FIGURES

John Adams (1735-1826), president of the United States, 1797-1801

Henry Dearborn (1751-1829), secretary of war under President Thomas Jefferson

Alexander Hamilton (1755-1804), Federalist politician who was a leading proponent of a military academy

Thomas Jefferson (1743-1826), president of the United States, 1801-1809

Henry Knox (1750-1806), former chief of artillery under General George Washington and the first U.S. secretary of war

Sylvanus Thayer (1785-1872), third superintendent of West Point

James McHenry (1753-1816), secretary of war under President John Adams

George Washington (1732-1799), first president of the United States, 1789-1797, and a persistent advocate of a military academy

Louis de Tousard (fl. early nineteenth century), French artillery officer

SUMMARY OF EVENT

Even after emerging victorious from the Revolutionary War (1775-1783), the United States faced potentially hostile forces from all directions. Monarchical European countries to the east were eager for the American experiment in democracy to fail. Native Americans menaced settlement and further advancement in the American West. Great Britain occupied the territory to the north and Spain the land to the south and southwest. The new nation obviously needed a system of national defense. However, many Americans had a strong suspicion of standing armies—a sentiment that dated back to England's civil war in the seventeenth century. Many Americans regarded an aristocracy as the most formida-

ble threat to their democracy, and they believed that aristocracies had their roots in standing armies. Some Americans thought an army of citizen-soldiers led by a trained officer corps might be the answer. The disloyal actions by Continental Army officers at Newburgh in the winter of 1782-1783 and the elitist, self-perpetuating, and politically dangerous Society of Cincinnati formed by Colonel Henry Knox, George Washington's chief of artillery, and other army officers at the end of the Revolutionary War underscored concerns of those who feared the creation of a military officer class.

Knox was one of the earliest advocates of a national military academy. In 1783, Washington had called for the establishment of one or more academies for instruction in the military arts. No action was taken, however, and by 1785 the national army had dwindled to a force with fewer than one hundred officers and men. In 1790, the federal government purchased the fort of West Point on the Hudson River for $11,085 at a moment when the United States seemed to be once again on the brink of war.

At that time, France, the U.S. ally, was at war with Great Britain and Spain, and it was apparent that the United States would have to bolster its national defenses in order to remain neutral in that conflict. On May 7, 1794, Congress authorized an increase in the Corps of Artillerists and Engineers at West Point. Congress also established the rank of cadet for junior officers assigned to West Point to be trained in the arts of war. With other duties absorbing most of their time, however, the cadets received little actual training. Meanwhile, the war in Europe continued to expand, bringing pressures in the United States not only to enlarge the army drastically but also to found a military academy. On July 16, 1798, Congress empowered President John Adams to appoint four teachers for the purpose of instructing the cadets and young officers in the Corps of Artillerists and Engineers; however, no qualified teachers were found.

At that juncture, after years of failure, Federalist leader Alexander Hamilton informed Secretary of War James McHenry that the United States needed a system of military education. He wanted an army officer school at West Point, another for artillerists and engineers, a third for cavalry and infantry, and a fourth for the Navy. In his plan, students would attend West Point for two years and then spend two more years at one of the other schools. Washington echoed Hamilton's sentiment.

West Point on the Hudson River during the mid-1870's. (Library of Congress)

Shortly before his death, he wrote that "the Establishment of an Institution of this kind . . . has ever been considered by me as an Object of primary importance to this Country."

McHenry received further advice in the form of a memorandum prepared by Louis de Tousard, a major in the First Regiment of Artillerists and Engineers. In January, 1800, McHenry consolidated the recommendations of Hamilton and Major Tousard, and President Adams sent his plan to Congress. Again, however, Congress did nothing, chiefly because of the real fear among Republicans that a trained corps of officers would threaten democracy. The use of federal troops in Pennsylvania during the so-called Fries Rebellion in 1799 had underscored Thomas Jefferson's opposition to the enlarged army Congress had authorized in 1798 and its potential to act as a domestic "spanking army."

Some historians believe that the final impetus for the establishment of the U.S. Military Academy was the desire to create a national university that would emphasize science over the classics. Thomas Jefferson, who became

president in 1801, was a leading advocate of offering more empirical courses in higher education. He believed that a military academy could fill this role and might also be supported by those who would oppose the idea of a national university. More important, Jefferson was concerned deeply with the domination of the army officer corps by Federalists and saw a military academy as a way to break Federalist power within the military by the appointment of politically reliable—presumably Republican—candidates into the army officer corps.

On March 16, 1802, Congress passed the Military Peace Establishment Act, which enpowered the president to establish a corps of engineers stationed at West Point, which would constitute a military academy. After years of efforts by Knox, Washington, Hamilton, and others, a law was finally enacted that acknowledged the need for such a civilian-controlled academy emphasizing training in the military arts.

In concert with his secretary of war, Henry Dearborn, Jefferson attempted to purge the officer corps of Federalists by restructuring and initially reducing the size of the officer corps. It was rebuilt with Antifederalist cadets drawn from Republican stock and trained at the U.S. Military Academy.

SIGNIFICANCE

Although the new U.S. Military Academy began training cadets shortly after it was created, it would be nearly two decades before it became fully professionalized under the leadership of its third superintendent, Sylvanus Thayer, who took charge in July, 1817. Before Thayer's time, the academy had no definitive administration or instructional systems and inadequate teaching materials. The absence of systematic academic instruction and laxness in supervision made cadet discipline poor. Thayer, who was well acquainted with French engineering and methods of instruction and who had a keen analytical mind and organizing abilities, brought revolutionary changes to the academy. During his sixteen years as superintendent of West Point, he undertook reforms in teaching and administration that became the basis of the modern military academy.

In the long term, the establishment of the U.S. Military Academy paved the way for the nation's modern armed forces and helped solidify the unity of the young United States. In 1846, the federal government established the U.S. Naval Academy at Annapolis, Maryland. In 1955, it opened the U.S. Air Force Academy in Colorado.

—*William M. Tuttle, updated by William M. McBride*

FURTHER READING

Ambrose, Stephen. *Duty, Honor, Country: A History of West Point*. Baltimore: Johns Hopkins University Press, 1966. A comprehensive and readable account of the history of the U.S. Military Academy up to the time of the Vietnam War that concentrates on the service of famous graduates.

Crackel, Theodore J. *Mr. Jefferson's Army: Political and Social Reform of the Military Establishment, 1801-1809*. New York: New York University Press, 1987. A well-argued and well-documented study of Jefferson's attempts to "republicanize" the army officer corps.

_____. *West Point: A Bicentennial History*. Lawrence: University Press of Kansas, 2002. Comprehensive history of the academy with generous attention to its early years.

Forman, Sidney. *West Point: A History of the United States Military Academy*. New York: Columbia University Press, 1950. A history of West Point from its beginnings as a fortification on the Hudson River to its transition to a military academy.

Kohn, Richard H. *Eagle and Sword: The Federalists and the Creation of the Military Establishment in America, 1783-1802*. New York: Free Press, 1975. A contextual study useful for understanding the founding of West Point.

Pappas, George S. *To the Point: The United States Military Academy, 1802-1902*. Westport, Conn.: Praeger, 1993. This history of the academy's early years emphasizes Thayer's efforts to make the institution a high-caliber military academy and engineering school.

SEE ALSO: Summer, 1801-Summer, 1805: Tripolitan War; June 18, 1812-Dec. 24, 1814: War of 1812; July 2, 1862: Lincoln Signs the Morrill Land Grant Act.

RELATED ARTICLE in *Great Lives from History: The Nineteenth Century, 1801-1900:* Sylvanus Thayer.

March 24, 1802
TREVITHICK PATENTS THE HIGH-PRESSURE STEAM ENGINE

The expiration of Watt's steam engine patent in 1800 opened the way for Richard Trevithick's design of the portable, high-pressure steam engine, which in turn led to the development of locomotives and railroads.

LOCALE: Great Britain
CATEGORIES: Inventions; science and technology; engineering; transportation

KEY FIGURES

Richard Trevithick (1771-1833), developer of the high-pressure steam engine
George Stephenson (1781-1848), developer of the first successful railroad locomotive
James Watt (1736-1819), proprietor, with Matthew Boulton, of the Soho Engineering Works, manufacturers of early steam engines
John Wilkinson (1728-1808), inventor of improved method of boring cannon and cylinders

SUMMARY OF EVENT

The eighteenth century saw the emergence of the steam engine, the mechanism by which artificial sources of power were to be widely applied to many forms of production. Throughout that century, use of the steam engine spread mostly in the mines of Great Britain, chiefly as a source of pumping power to empty the mines of water but also as a motive power for transporting the products of the mines, primarily coal and iron.

Nineteenth century industry expanded the use of steam power, using it to operate the machinery in the factories growing across the landscape. Most important, however, was the use of steam power to operate the locomotives that made modern railroads possible. The engines of the eighteenth century were of two kinds: those designed by Thomas Newcomen at the beginning of the century and those designed by James Watt in the latter half of the century. Both types, however, used steam to create a vacuum. (Air pressure filled the vacuum and created the motive power of these engines.) Unlike Newcomen, Watt was highly successful in gaining patent protection for his engines, which enabled him to disapprove of any developments that might increase the power of the engines, notably the use of high-pressure steam rather than a vacuum to move the piston in the cylinder.

Changes in the use of high-pressure steam were not prevented by Watt's patents alone, however; other technologies, notably in the field of metallurgy, also had to occur before the power of high-pressure steam could be put to use. One of these changes was the development of better quality cast iron so that more trustworthy cylinders could be made, cylinders with uniform dimensions in which the piston fitted tightly. This development was spearheaded by the Darby family of Coalbrookdale, whose experiments with iron ore smelted with coal led to the creation of reliable cast-iron cylinders. Furthermore, the creation of effective boring machinery, which led to the accurate boring out of a cylinder, rested on the work of John Wilkinson, whose boring machine was designed primarily to bore out cannon. Finally, the development of iron manufacture generally made possible the creation of boilers, which could raise steam to high pressure without bursting.

The expiration of Watt's patents in 1800 unleashed a flood of new, high-pressure steam engines. Richard Trevithick was the first of many to build steam engines using high-pressure steam. In 1800, he built one for Cook's Kitchen Mine, in Cornwall, proving this type of engine's usefulness. On Christmas Eve, 1801, he had completed a steam engine that ran on the roads in Cornwall, proving the usefulness of this type of engine for locomotion. He then demonstrated his engine to Count Rumford, in London, and applied for a patent, which was awarded to him on March 24, 1802.

The great advantage of Trevithick's high-pressure steam engine was that its cylinder and piston could be quite small, and because he dispensed with the condenser that was an integral part of the Watt engines, the new engine was relatively light in weight. These factors made Trevithick's engine portable. Previous versions of the steam engine, which had been used mostly in mines for pumping water or moving the mined material to the surface, had been stationary. Also, the new engines were commonly called puffers because they vented exhausted steam into the air instead of condensing the steam, as in Watt engines.

The power generated by the Trevithick engines was about ten times that of the contemporary Watt engines, even though the Trevithick engines were generally smaller. Trevithick demonstrated the potential of this great increase in power in 1804 at an iron mine near Merthyr Tydfil in Wales. One of his engines had hauled a load of ten tons for nearly ten miles at five miles per hour. As it turns out, this engine had been the first locomotive, for it ran on iron rails, was steered by one man, and it pulled five freight cars and seventy men who were on board. This demonstrated that using iron rails was the way to go: The iron rails kept the machine on the intended route, and the friction between wheel and rail helped propel the train.

The rapidly growing demands placed on England's mines propelled the new high-pressure steam engine forward. Traditionally, much of the demand had been concentrated in the ancient tin and lead mines of Cornwall. By Trevithick's time, iron and coal were needed most. Coal in particular was in high demand, because the shortage of fodder during the Napoleonic Wars constrained the supply of horses for industrial transport. Mines, with their heavy materials, needed better ways to retrieve their coal stores and move them into the transportation system. Engines began to replace horses, pulling coal cars along the rails that miners had long since found to be the easiest way to bring the coal to the surface. It was not surprising, then, that the rapidly developing coal mines in the north of England were ready to adopt the new system of transportation.

The person who made that transfer possible was George Stephenson. Stephenson began his career as a mine superintendent. In 1812 he was put in charge of a group of coal mines in the vicinity of Newcastle, called the Grand Allies. At a mine in Killingworth the previous year, Stephenson had rebuilt the pump that removed the water filling the mine; his success led to his appointment as a mine superintendent. As superintendent he devoted himself to improving the ways in which the coal was moved from the mine, using the wagon way to move the material over cast-iron rails. He soon realized, however, that wrought iron would be a better material, and that flanged wheels would link the engine securely to the rails. A portable engine with high-pressure steam, combined with the secure locomotion provided by well-placed wrought iron rails, made rail travel possible.

Trevithick's reputation was established beyond challenge when he designed and operated the Stockton and Darlington Railway. Also, an engine of his design successfully competed in the famous locomotive trials at Rainhill in October, 1829, in which Stephenson, using a tubular boiler to increase the production of steam, won the trials with his locomotive called "Rocket." Stephenson's "tubular" method became standard in steam-engine boilers. He also increased the engine's power by connecting the piston rod directly to the wheels instead of running the wheels through a system of gears. Both of these innovations became standard features of railroad locomotives.

Stephenson became, with his son Robert, a powerhouse of the railroad industry as well. The pair produced many of the engines on the early railroads of England, and their designs clearly revealed the potential of this new technology.

The first steam railroad train. (P. F. Collier and Son)

SIGNIFICANCE

In many respects the railroad was the signature technology of the nineteenth century. The work of Trevithick and Stephenson, conducted within the short span of thirty years, created a whole new industry that laid the foundation for the nineteenth century's transportation revolution.

—Nancy M. Gordon

FURTHER READING

Briggs, Asa. *The Power of Steam: An Illustrated History of the World's Steam Age.* Chicago: University of Chicago Press, 1982. A well-illustrated account of the adoption of steam power. Includes many useful diagrams.

Cardwell, D. S. L. *Turning Points in Western Technology: A Study of Technology, Science, and History.* New York: Science History, 1972. Highlights significant inventions in the history of technology in the Western world.

Derry, T. K., and Trevor L. Williams. *A Short History of Technology from the Earliest Times to A.D. 1900.* Oxford, England: Oxford University Press, 1960. Sets the important inventions in context.

Kirby, Maurice W. *The Origins of Railway Enterprise: The Stockton and Darlington Railway, 1821-1863.* New York: Cambridge University Press, 1993. A well-written study of the earliest commercial railroad.

Mokyr, Joel. *The Lever of Riches: Technological Creativity and Economic Progress.* New York: Oxford University Press, 1990. Shows how technology makes possible economic advances.

Tunzelmann, G. W. von. *Steam Power and British Industrialization to 1860.* Oxford, England: Clarendon Press, 1978. Explores steam power's role in industrialization in the first half of the nineteenth century.

SEE ALSO: September 27, 1825: Stockton and Darlington Railway Opens; Jan. 7, 1830: Baltimore and Ohio Railroad Opens; July 21, 1836: Champlain and St. Lawrence Railroad Opens; Nov. 10, 1852: Canada's Grand Trunk Railway Is Incorporated; Mar. 2, 1853-1857: Pacific Railroad Surveys; Jan. 10, 1863: First Underground Railroad Opens in London; Apr., 1869: Westinghouse Patents His Air Brake; May 10, 1869: First Transcontinental Railroad Is Completed; Feb., 1892: Diesel Patents the Diesel Engine.

RELATED ARTICLES in *Great Lives from History: The Nineteenth Century, 1801-1900:* Rudolf Diesel; George Stephenson; Richard Trevithick.

April 10, 1802
LAMBTON BEGINS TRIGONOMETRICAL SURVEY OF INDIA

The survey of India devised by William Lambton produced the Great Arc of the Meridian, a chain of measurements established from the south of India to the Himalayas. This survey of unprecedented magnitude resulted in the precise measurement of distances and heights throughout the Indian subcontinent and initiated the field of geodetic sciences in India.

ALSO KNOWN AS: Great Trigonometrical Survey; Triangulation Survey of India

LOCALE: India

CATEGORIES: Exploration and discovery; geography; cartography; mathematics; earth science

KEY FIGURES

William Lambton (1753/1769-1823), British surveyor
Sir George Everest (1790-1866), British surveyor
James Rennell (1742-1830), British cartographer

SUMMARY OF EVENT

A landmark event in colonial history, the Great Trigonometrical Survey of India was an integral part of the subcontinent's colonization during which information about the land and its population was exhaustively collected. When the survey began, colonial mapmaking had already been institutionalized under the auspices of the British East India Company. During the 1760's and 1770's, James Rennell had set the stage for this mapmaking with his general survey of Bengal. The Great Trigonometrical Survey was much more ambitious than the regional surveys undertaken by Rennell and others in the eighteenth century. It introduced new scientific methods in place of standard route surveys, which were based on the observation of hills, mountains, forts, and other landmarks visible from rivers and roads.

The prime mover behind the survey was William Lambton, a British veteran of the American Revolutionary War (1775-1783) who served as a regimental officer

THE GREAT ARC OF THE MERIDIAN

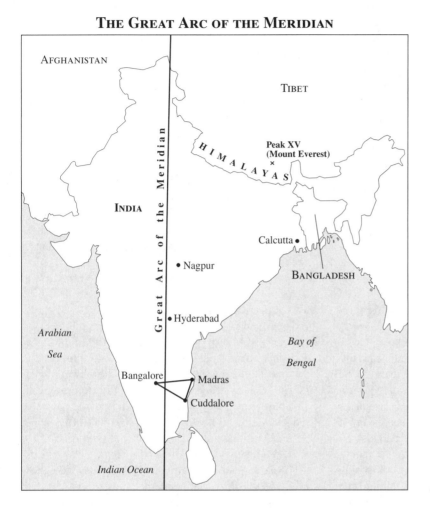

ginning with the measurement of a baseline between two points, the distance to a third point could be determined by measuring the angles with the theodolite. The newly determined sides of the triangle could then become the baselines for subsequent triangulation, and a chain of triangles could thereby be constructed. This method was used to create what was known as the Great Arc of the Meridian, a continuous chain of triangles that extended the entire length of the subcontinent, from Cape Comorin in the south of India to Mussoorie in the north. The Great Arc provided the backbone for other series of arcs, such as Lambton's Peninsular Longitudinal, constructed between 1803 and 1805, Sir George Everest's Bombay Longitudinal (1822-1823), the Calcutta Longitudinal (1825-1831), and the Northeast Longitudinal (1840-1850).

On April 10, 1802, Lambton laid out the first baseline that would serve as the anchor for the Great Trigonometrical Survey. The first full measurement of the line's seven and one-half miles required four hundred individual measurements with a one-hundred-foot chain. At each measurement, the extended chain was supported by five wooden coffers propped up with tripods. Each coffer was fitted with a thermometer, so measurements could be adjusted to take into account any expansion of the bars due to variations in temperature. It took fifty-seven days to complete the elaborate process of measuring the baseline. In September, Lambton began his triangulation, completing the short meridional arc from Madras to Cuddalore in order to determine the length of a degree of latitude. In October, 1804, after completing the series, Lambton headed westward and inland to carry the chain of triangles in the direction of Bangalore. With the onset of the monsoon season in 1805, Lambton began his major mission, the latitudinal measurement of the Great Arc of the Meridian. With the Bangalore base as their starting point, the triangles composing this arc extended north about one hundred miles to the territory of the nizam of Hyderabad and south toward the subcontinent's tip.

in India. In seeking funds for his project, Lambton argued that there was need for a mathematical and topographical survey of India "of the greatest accuracy." To many in the British East India Company, Lambton's survey was impractical, and some viewed it as a waste of time and money. In spite of his detractors, Lambton began his massive survey in 1802, ordering an enormous brass and cast-iron instrument called a theodolite from London. The instrument, which weighed about one-half ton and required twelve men to carry it, would be erected on makeshift towers or mountain peaks in order to measure the angles between markers. Foreshadowing a string of logistical and mechanical difficulties, the theodolite arrived in India only after the ship carrying it was captured by the French and taken to Mauritius.

Lambton's surveying process, known as "triangulation," used trigonometric computations to determine the position of three mutually visible reference points. Be-

In 1818, sixteen years after the beginning of the survey, the British government officially named it the Great Trigonometrical Survey (GTS). That same year, Lambton took on Sir George Everest as his chief assistant, and four years later, when Lambton died on the road while measuring triangulations between Hyderabad and Nagpur, Everest assumed control of the project. Known for his harsh temper and tenacity, Everest was forced to seek medical treatment in London briefly; however, the survey was resumed after his return. In 1832, Andrew Scott Waugh and Thomas Renny-Tailyour joined Everest to complete the northern section of the Great Arc of the Meridian. By 1834, when Everest retired, the survey had come within range of the Himalayan Mountains. The highest mountain in the range, known then as Peak XV, rose from forbidden territory on the Nepal-Tibet border, and it was therefore inaccessible to the surveyors; however, measurements taken from six different directions and averaged together determined that its height was precisely 29,000 feet. Hailed as the highest point on earth, the peak was named after Sir George Everest.

The work of surveyors in the Himalayan range led unexpectedly to new scientific findings. As the team ran the Great Arc of the Meridian into the Himalayas, they encountered curious data. Discrepancies in measurements determined by a plumb bob at different peaks displayed variations in gravity. This set of data confirmed discoveries in the Andes, where it had been shown that mountains are made of material less dense than that composing lowlands. The findings encouraged scientists to pursue the conditions of the earth's gravitational equilibrium and ultimately to develop an idea fundamental to modern geophysics that would later be known as "isostasy."

SIGNIFICANCE

The Great Arc of the Meridian was the longest measurement of the earth ever attempted, and the methods by which it was constructed represent a landmark in the field of cartography. Before the Great Trigonometrical Survey of India, maps were based largely on information derived from coastal surveys or astronomical references. By contrast, the survey created a highly accurate series of measurements based directly on the landmass. Moreover, it formed a skeletal framework that could be exploited to produce detailed localized maps and topographic analyses of specific regions as necessary. It also lent itself to the measurement of heights in the Himalayan mountain range and established that Peak XV, later named Mount Everest, was the highest point on earth.

From the eighteenth century, surveying and mapmaking had come to play an integral role in Britain's administration of India. It laid the groundwork for the construction of roads, railways, power lines, and other infrastructure, and it aided the efficiency of British revenue collection. For William Lambton, however, the prime motivation for the Great Trigonometrical Survey was scientific. At the beginning of the nineteenth century, when he devised the survey, little was known about the earth's shape and size. As he had hoped, by its completion the survey had contributed precise knowledge of the earth's curvature at various latitudes, settling an issue that had remained outstanding in the scientific community for more than seventy years. Ultimately, the survey provided some of the most significant contributions to the advancement of geodesy and general science during the nineteenth century.

—Anna Sloan

FURTHER READING

Adas, Michael. *Machines as the Measure of Men: Science, Technology, and Ideologies of Western Dominance.* Ithaca, N.Y.: Cornell University Press, 1989. Provides a broader context for the Great Trigonometrical Survey of India by exploring the impact of technology on history and its role in European expansion.

Edney, Matthew H. *Mapping an Empire: The Geographical Construction of British India, 1765-1843.* New Delhi, India: Oxford University Press, 1999. This exhaustive source on British mapping describes how British visitors used modern survey techniques both to define the spatial image of the empire and to legitimate its colonialist activities.

Everest, George. *An Account of the Measurement of an Arc of the Meridian between the Parallels of 18°3′ and 24°7′: Being a Continuation of the Grand Meridional Arc of India.* 2 vols. London: J. L. Cox, 1830. The surveyor's own account of his process.

Keay, John. *The Great Arc: The Dramatic Tale of How India Was Mapped and Everest Was Named.* New York: HarperCollins, 2000. A concise history of the surveying process, with illustrations, photographs, and a good map of the triangulations.

Phillimore, R. H. *Historical Records of the Survey of India, 1945-1958.* 5 vols. n.p.: Dehra Dun, 1950-1968. Volume 3 describes the events leading up to the survey in the years 1815-1830, while volume 4 describes the contributions of George Everest between the years 1830 and 1843. Volume 5, dealing with the contributions of Andrew Waugh, was withdrawn from mass publication.

Wilford, John Noble. *The Mapmakers*. Rev. ed. New York: Alfred A. Knopf, 2000. Chapter 11 describes the surveying methods of Lambton and Everest, as well as their contribution to general science. The text is particularly useful in describing the geodetic implications of the project.

SEE ALSO: Dec. 4, 1829: British Abolish Suttee in India; 1854-1862: Wallace's Expeditions Give Rise to Bio-geography; May 10, 1857-July 8, 1858: Sepoy Mutiny Against British Rule; Jan. 25, 1884: Indian Legislative Council Enacts the Ilbert Bill; 1885: Indian National Congress Is Founded.

RELATED ARTICLES in *Great Lives from History: The Nineteenth Century, 1801-1900:* Sir Richard Francis Burton; Sir John Franklin; Mary Kingsley; Rudyard Kipling; David Livingstone; Sir James Clark Ross; John Hanning Speke; Henry Morton Stanley.

1803-1808
DALTON FORMULATES THE ATOMIC THEORY OF MATTER

The formulation of the atomic theory of matter and the first tabulation of atomic weights by John Dalton had a profound effect on the development of both chemistry and physics. It established the basis for quantitative chemistry and provided a bridge across which chemistry and physics could relate to each other.

LOCALE: England

CATEGORIES: Chemistry; physics; science and technology

KEY FIGURES

John Dalton (1766-1844), English chemist, physicist, and meteorologist
Thomas Thomson (1773-1852), Scottish chemist and medical doctor
Antoine-Laurent Lavoisier (1743-1794), French chemist
Joseph-Louis Proust (1754-1826), French chemist
Jöns Jacob Berzelius (1779-1848), Swedish chemist
Joseph-Louis Gay-Lussac (1778-1850), French chemist and physicist

SUMMARY OF EVENT

From the time he was a young boy, John Dalton showed a keen interest in scientific observations. A poor, mostly self-taught individual, Dalton developed an intuitive ability for formulating theories to explain collections of data. Between 1787 and 1844, he kept a daily record of the weather, recording more than 200,000 meteorological observations in his notebooks. This interest led him to investigate the composition and properties of gases in the atmosphere. He realized that water could exist as a gas that mixed with air and occupied the same space as air. In 1793, he published some of his findings in *Meteorological Observations and Essays*. From 1793 until 1799, he taught chemistry and some other scientific subjects at New College in Manchester, England, where he began his quest for an atomic theory of matter.

In 1803, John Dalton wrote a classic paper titled "The Absorption of Gases by Water and Other Liquids," which was published in 1805. Near the end of the paper, he proposed an atomic theory of matter that also included the first published tabulation of atomic weights. His concept of atoms was directly related to the measurable property of mass. He had determined the relative weights of a number of atoms from chemical analyses that were available for water, ammonia, carbon dioxide, and a few other substances.

DALTON'S ATOMIC THEORY

John Dalton's atomic theory of matter can be summarized in the following five basic statements:

1. All matter is composed of small particles called atoms.
2. Atoms are the smallest entities that make up matter. They cannot be subdivided, created, or destroyed.
3. All atoms of a given element are identical in size, mass, and all other properties. Atoms of different elements differ in size, mass, and other properties.
4. The atoms of different elements can combine in simple, whole-number ratios to form chemical compounds.
5. Atoms are combined, separated, or rearranged in chemical reactions.

PROUST'S CONTRIBUTION TO ATOMIC THEORY

Joseph-Louis Proust's law of definite proportions, which stated that elements always combine in precise proportions to form compounds, was a significant influence on John Dalton's development of atomic theory, since the law was an effect of atomic interactions. In 1806, Proust summarized his law as follows:

Everything in mineralogy is not a compound [*combinaison*] . . . [T]here is a large number of substances to which this name should not be applied indiscriminately, as some authors do for want of having thought sufficiently about what is understood by this word in chemistry. Because they have not noticed that the science has made a rule of reserving its use, they have applied it indifferently to substances which it deliberately avoids describing thus. They therefore confuse compounds with certain concrete solutions, certain combinations, certain systems of compound bodies to which it attaches a quite contrary idea. Nature, for example, presents us with compounds of elements, but also with combinations formed by a multiple aggregation of these same compounds. . . .

Let us stop for a moment to satisfy an objection which d'Aubuisson certainly addresses to me, when he says in a memoir in which he so justly sees the futility of certain definitions, "The analyses of the copper ore [*cuivre gris*], which Klaproth has just published, are a new example of compounds formed in variable proportions." I would reply that the copper ore does not belong at all to the order of compounds which chemists are examining at the moment in order to unravel the principles of their formation. A compound according to our principles, as Klaproth would tell you, is something like sulphide of silver, of antimony, of mercury, of copper; it is an acidified combustible substance, etc.; it is a privileged product to which nature assigns fixed proportions; it is in a word a being which she never creates, even in the hands of man, except with the aid of a balance, *pondere et mensura*.

Source: Excerpt translated by Maurice Crosland, ed., in *The Science of Matter: A Historical Survey* (Harmondsworth, Middlesex, England: Penguin, 1971).

Dalton's primary impetus was discovered by chemist Henry Roscoe after Dalton's death. Roscoe carefully studied Dalton's lab notebooks and concluded that Dalton formulated his theory in response to his observation that gases with different densities mix together instead of separating into layers. The theory was also motivated by Joseph-Louis Proust's discovery in 1800 that elements combine in definite proportions to form compounds. Proust's concept of definite proportions enabled Dalton to associate atoms with elements, and it established that the components of chemical compounds have a fixed relation based on their mass.

Dalton's scientific experiments were carried out with crude, homemade experimental equipment that produced rather imprecise data. They were of sufficient quality, however, to provide the necessary clues that Dalton's creative mind needed to formulate the probable explanation for the observed data. Because of the many revisions that Dalton made in his lab notebooks, as well as the lack of exact dates on many of the pages, it is almost impossible to determine the exact time when he formulated the atomic theory of matter.

In 1808, Dalton published the details of his atomic theory in the first part of his *New System of Chemical Philosophy* (1808-1827, 2 vols.). The second part of volume 1 was published in 1810. Dalton defined an element as a substance composed of only one kind of atom. His theory provided a natural way to represent chemical compounds. After inventing a set of elemental symbols, he used them to combine different elements to provide schematic representations of what he believed were the molecular structures of a variety of compounds. Dalton constructed the first periodic table of elements. He used letters and symbols arranged inside of circles for his scheme. Later, Jöns Jacob Berzelius pointed out that the circles were not needed and recommended the one- or two-letter symbols that are currently used in the periodic table of elements.

Dalton assumed that chemical combination always occurred in the simplest way possible with the smallest number of atoms. This insight led him to formulate the principle that particles of different mass can combine chemically. It also led him incorrectly to assume that only one atom of hydrogen combines with oxygen to form water. As a result, he concluded that oxygen atoms weighed eight times as much as hydrogen atoms. Experiments conducted later by Joseph-Louis Gay-Lussac showed that a water molecule consists of two atoms of hydrogen combined with one oxygen atom, requiring a change in Dalton's table of atomic weights. Because Dalton was a very independent scientist who feared that others might misguide him in his research, he was reluctant to accept the findings of Gay-Lussac.

Dalton continued to develop an atomic theory of matter in a series of lectures that he presented in London in 1803, in Manchester in 1805, and in Edinburgh in 1807.

Although Dalton's atomic theory did not initially attract much attention from other scientists, his publication of *New System of Chemical Philosophy*, along with Thomas Thomson's *A System of Chemistry* (1802), stirred great interest in Dalton's theory. The atomic theory of matter allowed Dalton and others to explain many principles of chemistry with simplicity. Dalton's theory explained the fact that mass can be neither created nor destroyed in chemical or physical reactions. This is known as the law of conservation of mass, a principle first discovered by Antoine-Laurent Lavoisier around 1789.

Dalton's theory also explained Proust's law of definite proportions. The amounts of products and reactants in any particular chemical reaction always occur in the same definite proportions by volume of gases or by numbers of molecules. In the latter part of 1808, Dalton once again concentrated his efforts on meteorological research and associated investigations. He also frequently defended his atomic theory of matter in private conversations and in scientific meetings. Because he pictured atoms as hard, indivisible spheres, his theory provided no insights into the structure of an atom or into the mechanism that causes atoms to bond together. However, his theory laid the foundation for other scientists to pursue and eventually explain these phenomena.

SIGNIFICANCE

John Dalton has been called the founder of modern atomic theory. Until Dalton proposed the atomic theory of matter, the concept of atoms—which was originally stated by Leucippus and Democritus in the fourth century B.C.E.—remained a very simplistic idea. Dalton's atomic theory provided chemists with a new, enormously fruitful model of reality. It led to two fundamental laws of nature, the law of conservation of mass and the law of definite composition, which eventually led to the periodic table of elements.

Dalton's theory had significant explanatory power, leading him and his successors to develop explanations for many confirmed experimental results. Dalton's theory is still used to explain the properties of many chemicals and compounds today. His theory has also been expanded to explain new observations, including the existence of elementary particles that make up the internal structure of atoms and the existence of isotopes of atoms. A variety of isotopes can be used to trace the various steps in chemical reactions and metabolic processes in the human body. Tracer techniques have proven invaluable in the clinical diagnosis of many disorders in the body.

Dalton's theory formed the foundation for the science of chemistry. As a result, Dalton is known as the founder of modern chemistry. His atomic theory has led to myriad significant applications, including the development of the best model of the atom, the description of different phases of matter, the harnessing of atomic energy, the development of atomic weapons, the quantitative explanation of chemical reactions, and the chemistry of life. Dalton's theory established the framework for the development of biochemistry and the understanding of the bonding of carbon atoms to form chains and branching structures that are essential in the formation of sugars, fatty acids, nucleic acids, carbohydrates, proteins, and other molecular structures on which life is based.

—*Alvin K. Benson*

FURTHER READING

McDonnell, John James. *The Concept of an Atom from Democritus to John Dalton.* Lewiston, N.Y.: Edwin Mellen Press, 1991. Historical development of ideas about the fundamental makeup of matter from Democritus (460-370 B.C.E.) until Dalton's proposed atomic theory.

Smyth, A. L. *John Dalton, 1766-1844: A Bibliography of Works by and About Him.* Brookfield, Vt.: Ashgate, 1998. Contains a bibliography of works by Dalton and about Dalton, including an annotated list of his personal effects and experimental equipment that are still in existence.

Tillery, Bill W., Eldon D. Enger, and Frederick C. Ross. *Integrated Science.* New York: McGraw-Hill, 2001. Discusses the history of Dalton's formulation of the atomic theory and explains its importance in the context of chemistry and the other physical sciences.

Whiting, Jim, and Marylou Morano Kjelle. *John Dalton and the Atomic Theory.* Hockessin, Del.: Mitchell Lane, 2004. An excellent treatise on John Dalton and the steps he took in developing the fundamental concepts for his atomic theory of matter.

SEE ALSO: 1804: Saussure Publishes His Research on Plant Metabolism; 1850-1865: Clausius Formulates the Second Law of Thermodynamics; 1869-1871: Mendeleyev Develops the Periodic Table of Elements; Nov. 9, 1895: Röntgen Discovers X Rays; Dec. 14, 1900: Articulation of Quantum Theory.
RELATED ARTICLES in *Great Lives from History: The Nineteenth Century, 1801-1900:* John Dalton; Joseph-Louis Gay-Lussac; Dmitry Ivanovich Mendeleyev.

1800's

1803-1812
ELGIN SHIPS PARTHENON MARBLES TO ENGLAND

Lord Elgin's removal of large sections of sculpture to England from the Parthenon on the Acropolis of Athens began a revival of interest in classical antiquity among northern Europeans and provoked repeated international demands for the return of the artworks to Greece.

LOCALE: Athens, Greece; London, England
CATEGORIES: Architecture; art

KEY FIGURES
Seventh Earl of Elgin (Thomas Bruce; 1766-1841), British diplomat
Giovanni Battista Lusieri (1755-1821), Venetian artist and antiquarian
Philip Hunt (fl. early nineteenth century), chaplain to the British embassy in Constantinople

SUMMARY OF EVENT
In the wake of Napoleon I's occupation of Egypt in 1798, during which large amounts of Egyptian antiquities were transported to Paris's Louvre Museum, other northern European powers began extensive acquisitions of sculpture, jewelry, and even entire buildings from various historical sites around the Mediterranean basin to the more heavily populated cities in the north. Not yet clearly distinguished from antiquarianism, early nineteenth century archaeology rarely attempted to preserve the integrity of the sites being studied or to respect local peoples' interest in their own native cultures. The practice of wholesale removal of artifacts would continue through most of the nineteenth century and include such major archaeological relocations as Karl Humann's removal of the Great Altar of Pergamum from Turkey to Berlin in 1878, Heinrich Schliemann's smuggling of a vast treasure that included at least 8,750 gold rings and buttons from Troy to Germany in 1873, and Lord Elgin's removal of marble sculptures from the Acropolis in Athens to London.

Born Thomas Bruce, Lord Elgin became the seventh earl of Elgin on the death of his older brother when he was only five years old. The Bruce family had been heirs to the Elgin title since 1633, and this honor had fallen to

Face of the Parthenon from which Elgin had the marble friezes removed. (PhotoDisc/Su Davies)

Portions of the Elgin marbles as they were displayed in the British Museum during the early twentieth century. (George L. Schuman & Company)

Thomas Bruce's direct line following the death of Charles Bruce in 1647. As he entered adulthood, Elgin studied in England and France before beginning a military career that would take him to numerous cities in Europe and Turkey. From 1799 until 1803, Elgin served as British ambassador to Constantinople, the capital of the Ottoman Empire. The Turkish-based empire was then a vast power which at that time controlled all of Greece. While he was there, Elgin became fascinated by the architecture and sculpture adorning many ancient Greek cities, particularly the friezes that formed part of the classical temple to Athena, the Parthenon in Athens.

Working through his agents, the Italian artist Giovanni Battista Lusieri and the chaplain Philip Hunt, Elgin learned what permissions he needed to acquire sculptures in Athens, what powers he should request from the Ottomans, and how to deal with various political obstacles he might encounter. At that time diplomatic relationships were particularly close between Great Britain and the Ottomans, which had together driven the French out of Egypt only a few years earlier. Elgin was thus able to obtain a *firman*, or royal order, from the Ottoman Empire that allowed his representatives to study the Acropolis and to remove "extraneous" inscriptions and sculptures.

Elgin would use his liberal interpretation of the *firman*'s latter privilege to justify his removal of a large number of sculptures from the Parthenon and nearby buildings. Elgin directed his agents to remove representative samples of sculptural decoration from the Parthenon, giving special attention to the building's *metopes*—the square panels of relief sculpture depicting such scenes as the battle between the gods and the giants, the battle between the Greeks and the Amazons, and the Trojan War.

Elgin undoubtedly believed that his removal of the sculptures from the Parthenon was not mere spoliation but rather an attempt to preserve the ancient artifacts in a manner that would not be possible in Greece. The Parthenon had been badly damaged as recently as 1689 during the Turko-Venetian War, in which the Ottomans had used the ancient structure to store explosives. When their explosives were hit by a shell during a Venetian bombardment, the resulting detonation caused most of the damage currently seen in the building. Moreover, Elgin depicted the Ottomans as indifferent to the historical significance of the Acropolis. He claimed that they regarded it as a site at which idols had been worshipped and had failed to protect it during the empire's many political upheavals. Finally, Elgin probably believed that he was

47

making the cultural richness of the Parthenon available to many more people by moving parts of it from sparsely populated Greece to heavily populated London.

Despite his intentions, Elgin realized that his actions were likely to provoke protests from the Ottomans. He therefore hurried to have a large portion of the sculptures taken from Athens on the British ship *Mentor*, followed by an even larger amount of material conveyed by the British warships *Diana* and *Hydra*. The *Mentor* was wrecked in a storm before it reached England, and its cargo of antiquities had to be reclaimed from the bottom of the sea over the next several years.

The first of Elgin's shipments from Greece to England began arriving in London in 1803. When Elgin himself returned to England in 1806, he began displaying his acquisitions to his fellow countrymen, many of whom were able to see ancient Greek art for the first time. These private showings gave rise to a renewed interest in the art of the classical period, much of which had been known in England, France, and Germany only through written descriptions and often unreliable drawings.

By 1811, Elgin had suffered a number of financial reverses, causing him to offer the marbles for sale to the British government in the hope that he might recover his private investment in their transportation and begin repairs on his home, which had been suffering from years of neglect. The British government offered Elgin only half of what he requested. Elgin then embarked on a long series of negotiations to sell the sculptures for what he considered to be a fair price.

In 1812, the last of the shipments that Elgin had ordered to be sent from Athens finally arrived in London, and the Acropolis sculptures were once again together in a single location. Finally, on June 7, 1816, the House of Commons voted to purchase the marbles from Elgin for £35,000, only a moderate increase from what it had offered him five years earlier. By that time, a fierce debate was already developing between those who believed that the sculptures had been looted from Greece and should be returned and those who believed that they were likely to be better preserved in England than in Greece. The marbles were transferred to the British Museum, where they then became the centerpiece of that institution's collection of antiquities.

SIGNIFICANCE

Removal of the Elgin marbles to England gave rise to a renewed interest in ancient Greece throughout northern Europe. The classical revival of the nineteenth century differed from the neoclassicism of the eighteenth century by placing a greater emphasis on ancient Greece than on ancient Rome. This revival can be traced to the impact that the Elgin marbles had on their original audience. Although relatively few northern Europeans traveled to Greece during the early nineteenth century, many did travel to London, and the collection of the sculptures in the British Museum provided many visitors with their only direct contact with ancient Greek art.

Elgin's looting of the Acropolis also began a controversy that has continued to affect relations between Great Britain and Greece into the twenty-first century. The Ottoman and later the Greek governments have consistently argued that the removal of the Elgin marbles from Athens to London was an act of international theft, that there can be no justification for the sculptures' continued presence in the British Museum, and that the works should immediately be returned to Athens, where museum space is ready for them.

—Jeffrey L. Buller

FURTHER READING

Cosmopoulos, Michael B., ed. *The Parthenon and Its Sculptures*. New York: Cambridge University Press, 2004. Comprehensive art historical approach to the significance of the Elgin marbles as well as other sculptures associated with Athens's Parthenon.

Gallo, Luciano. *Lord Elgin in Search of Greek Architecture: The Elgin Drawings at the British Museum*. London: Philip Wilson, 2005. Includes information, not merely on the Elgin marbles themselves, but also on the larger archaeological and cultural implications of Elgin's travels in Greece.

St. Clair, William. *Lord Elgin and the Marbles*. New York: Oxford University Press, 1998. Exhaustive account of the details leading to Elgin's acquisition of the sculptures and their subsequent influence on European art and architecture.

SEE ALSO: 1801: Emergence of the Primitives; Mar. 22, 1812: Burckhardt Discovers Egypt's Abu Simbel; Mar. 7, 1821-Sept. 29, 1829: Greeks Fight for Independence from the Ottoman Empire; 1839-1847: Layard Explores and Excavates Assyrian Ruins; Nov., 1839: Stephens Begins Uncovering Mayan Antiquities; 1863-1913: Greece Unifies Under the Glücksburg Dynasty; Apr., 1870-1873: Schliemann Excavates Ancient Troy; Mar. 23, 1900: Evans Discovers Crete's Minoan Civilization.
RELATED ARTICLE in *Great Lives from History: The Nineteenth Century, 1801-1900*: Sir Arthur Evans.

February 24, 1803
MARBURY V. MADISON

One of the most important rulings in the history of the U.S. Supreme Court, Marbury v. Madison *established the Court's right of judicial review of actions by other branches of government, thereby significantly enhancing the power of the judiciary branch.*

LOCALE: Washington, D.C.
CATEGORIES: Laws, acts, and legal history; government and politics

KEY FIGURES
William Marbury (1761?-1835), appointed justice of the peace by President John Adams
John Adams (1735-1826), president of the United States, 1797-1801
Thomas Jefferson (1743-1826), president of the United States, 1801-1809
James Madison (1751-1836), secretary of state who was ordered by Jefferson to withhold Marbury's commission
John Marshall (1755-1835), chief justice of the United States, 1801-1835

SUMMARY OF EVENT
Although the power of judicial review has long been a fundamental principle of constitutional interpretation, it is not mentioned explicitly in the U.S. Constitution. The first clear case in which the U.S. Supreme Court, guided by the spirit of the Constitution's provisions, declared a congressional act void was *Marbury v. Madison.*

When President John Adams was preparing to leave office in early 1801, he regarded the transfer of his presidential power to newly elected Thomas Jefferson as a virtual revolution in United States political life. Jefferson's Republican Party represented to Adams and the Federalists not merely a different political party that had opposed the Federalists' stewardship of the federal government, but also the *enemy* of that government. The presidential election campaign of 1800 had been marked by almost hysterical appeals on both sides. The Federalists had identified themselves with government under the Constitution, while the Republicans seemed to call for a radical change in the nature of that government.

As Jefferson's inauguration neared, the Federalists feared that their work of more than a decade in establishing a strong, stable government under the Constitution was in jeopardy, as Jefferson was also sweeping into office a Republican Congress. As the defeated candidate,

Adams hoped to maintain some of his party's power by appointing sixteen new circuit judges to strengthen the Federalist complexion of the federal bench during Jefferson's administration.

Adams appointed, and the Senate confirmed, his secretary of state, John Marshall, to the vacant position of chief justice. At the same time, Congress reduced the size of the Supreme Court from six to five members upon the occasion of the next vacancy. Jefferson was thus presented with a Court that would be headed by a political enemy and a membership that he might not be able to change before the end of his term. Congress also authorized Adams to appoint up to fifty justices of the peace for the District of Columbia. Their appointments had been approved by the Senate, but Adams and Marshall did not finish having all their commissions formally delivered to the new appointees before Jefferson's inauguration on March 4, 1801. Jefferson then instructed his secretary of state, James Madison, not to deliver the remaining commissions.

In December, 1801, William Marbury, one of Adams's appointees, sued in the Supreme Court for a writ of *mandamus* (an ancient common-law writ compelling a corporation, government official, or lower court to perform a particular duty required by law) requiring Madison to deliver his commission. Marbury cited a section of the Judiciary Act of 1789 that was designed to compel the secretary of state to perform the office's duty under the law.

In its review of Marbury's case on February 24, 1803, Chief Justice Marshall, speaking for the Supreme Court, declared that Marbury did indeed have a right to the commission that should be delivered to him. However, he also ruled that Marbury could not obtain from the Court a writ of *mandamus* ordering his commission's delivery because the Court itself did not have the power to issue such a writ. The Court ruled that section 13 of the Judiciary Act of 1789, which had added authority to the original jurisdiction of the Supreme Court, was void because it violated Article II of the Constitution.

The original jurisdiction of the Supreme Court (when the Court acts as a trial court) was limited to cases "affecting ambassadors, other public ministers and consuls, and those in which a state is a party." Because Marbury fitted none of those categories and because there was no mention of the authority to issue writs of *mandamus* at the trial level, the Court refused to assume jurisdiction over his case, despite the fact that Congress had granted

Chief Justice John Marshall. (Library of Congress)

the Court such power in the Judiciary Act of 1789. In short, Marbury was requesting that the Court exercise an appellate function that was beyond its jurisdiction. Because the Judiciary Act of 1789 conflicted with the Constitution as the supreme law of the land, the former must be declared unconstitutional. Although Congress had passed a law, the Supreme Court had essentially reviewed and, in this case, rejected it. The principle of judicial review was born.

SIGNIFICANCE

The Supreme Court would not again exercise the power of judicial review until its notorious ruling in the case of *Dred Scott v. Sandford* in 1857, when it declared unconstitutional the Missouri Compromise Act of 1820, which excluded slaves from the territories. Nevertheless, since 1857, the Supreme Court and other courts have cited the rule in *Marbury v. Madison* on countless occasions. To support his position that the Supreme Court could invalidate laws of Congress, Marshall relied heavily on the arguments of Alexander Hamilton in supporting the doctrines of judicial review as set forth in *The Federalist* No.

78. Hamilton argued that it is the duty of judges, when there is doubt, to say what the law in a particular case is. The Constitution is the supreme law. If, therefore, in the consideration of a case, the Supreme Court finds a conflict between the law as passed by Congress and the supreme law as stated in the Constitution, it must, under its constitutional responsibility, apply the supreme law. Marshall thus succeeded in securing for the Court a preeminent position in the interpretation of the Constitution.

—*Edward J. Maguire, updated by Marcia J. Weiss*

FURTHER READING

Barber, Sotirios A. *On What the Constitution Means.* Baltimore: Johns Hopkins University Press, 1984. A scholarly approach to the Constitution as an entire document interpreted as an expression of ideals and a commitment to ethics and morality in society.

Choper, Jesse, H. *Judicial Review and the National Political Process: A Functional Reconsideration of the Role of the Supreme Court.* Chicago: University of Chicago Press, 1980. Advances the thesis that, although judicial review is incompatible with democracy, the Supreme Court must exercise that power when individual rights need protection within the political process. Otherwise, the Court should decline to exercise its authority, thereby reducing conflict between majoritarian democracy and judicial review. Includes references to cases and secondary legal materials.

Clinton, Robert Lowry. *"Marbury v. Madison" and Judicial Review.* Lawrence: University Press of Kansas, 1989. A review of sources that this author believes have wrongly interpreted the principle of judicial review in *Marbury v. Madison*. Extensive notes and bibliography.

Ely, John Hart. *Democracy and Distrust: A Theory of Judicial Review.* Cambridge, Mass.: Harvard University Press, 1980. Sets forth a new theory of constitutional interpretation based on principles of constitutional law. Detailed notes and citations.

Lewis, Thomas T., and Richard L. Wilson, eds. *Encyclopedia of the U.S. Supreme Court.* 3 vols. Pasadena, Calif.: Salem Press, 2001. Comprehensive reference work on the Supreme Court that contains substantial discussions of *Marbury v. Madison*, John Marshall, judicial review, and many related subjects.

Newmyer, R. Kent. *John Marshall and the Heroic Age of the Supreme Court.* Baton Rouge: Louisiana State University Press, 2001. Focuses on Marshall's legal philosophies, analyzing some of his Supreme Court decisions and placing his beliefs in historical context.

Snowiss, Sylvia. *Judicial Review and the Law of the Constitution*. New Haven, Conn.: Yale University Press, 1990. A review of the historical intent and the debate surrounding judicial review, and the controversy concerning whether the Framers intended to establish judicial review.

Wolfe, Christopher. *The Rise of Modern Judicial Review: From Constitutional Interpretation to Judge-Made Law*. New York: Basic Books, 1986. Describes and documents the transformation of constitutional interpretation and judicial power, from its initial understanding by the Founders to a natural rights theory and, ultimately, to an expansive and discretionary approach. Includes references to secondary sources and case law.

SEE ALSO: Feb. 17, 1801: House of Representatives Elects Jefferson President; Mar. 16, 1810: *Fletcher v. Peck*; Mar. 6, 1819: *McCulloch v. Maryland*; Mar. 2, 1824: *Gibbons v. Ogden*; Mar. 6, 1857: *Dred Scott v. Sandford*.

RELATED ARTICLES in *Great Lives from History: The Nineteenth Century, 1801-1900:* John Marshall; Joseph Story.

May 9, 1803
LOUISIANA PURCHASE

The single largest land acquisition in U.S. history, the Louisiana Purchase not only doubled the territory of the United States but also secured new western borders for the nation and effectively removed France as a colonial power from North America.

ALSO KNOWN AS: Louisiana Territory
LOCALE: Paris, France; Washington, D.C.
CATEGORIES: Expansion and land acquisition; diplomacy and international relations

KEY FIGURES

Napoleon I (Napoleon Bonaparte; 1769-1821), first consul of France and later emperor of the French, r. 1804-1814, 1815

François de Barbé-Marbois (1745-1837), Napoleon's minister of finance

Thomas Jefferson (1743-1826), president of the United States, 1801-1809

Sieur de La Salle (René Robert Cavelier; 1643-1687), French explorer who claimed the Louisiana Territory for France and named it

Robert R. Livingston (1746-1813), U.S. minister to France

James Monroe (1758-1831), envoy whom Jefferson sent to Paris to assist Livingston in negotiating for the purchase

Toussaint-Louverture (1743-1803), leader of the slave revolt in Santo Domingo

SUMMARY OF EVENT

The first Europeans to explore the region that became known as the Louisiana Territory were the Spanish during the sixteenth century, but they failed to occupy the area effectively. In 1682, the French explorer René Robert Cavelier, sieur de La Salle, claimed the region for France and named it in honor of King Louis XIV. The territory remained French until near the end of the Seven Years' War (known as the French and Indian War in North America) in 1763, when France ceded it to Spain in return for help in France's war against Great Britain and its allies and to compensate Spain for the loss of Florida. During the late 1790's, France began to rebuild its empire in the Western Hemisphere. Through the secret Treaty of San Ildefonso of October 1, 1800, Spain ceded Louisiana back to France.

Reports of the impending transfer of Louisiana, and perhaps even Florida, from Spain to France began to reach the United States in the spring of 1801. The Jefferson administration viewed this transfer with some alarm, because a powerful and aggressive Napoleonic France in control of the mouth of the Mississippi River would constitute a much graver threat to U.S. rights on that vital artery of commerce and communication than the presence of weak and declining Spain. Secretary of State James Madison instructed Robert R. Livingston, the U.S. minister to Paris, to investigate the continuing rumors. If Livingston found them to be true, he was to try to acquire the Floridas (or at least West Florida) if they were part of the cession. If Spain had not ceded the Floridas to France, the United States would attempt to obtain them from Spain. Livingston learned that France had acquired Louisiana and New Orleans, but not the Floridas. His discussions with the French government were otherwise inconclusive.

THE LOUISIANA PURCHASE TERRITORY

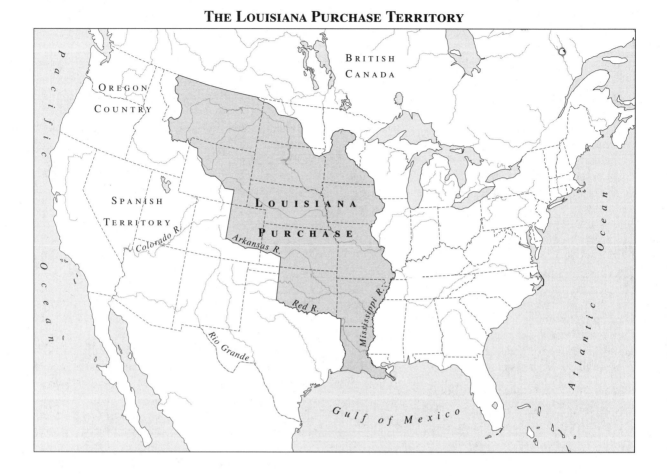

On October 16, 1802, the Spanish administrator of Louisiana at New Orleans, Juan Ventura Morales, issued a proclamation withdrawing from the United States the right to deposit goods at New Orleans for transshipping, as the Pinckney Treaty of 1795 with Spain had provided. This meant that U.S. boats coming down the Mississippi River could no longer unload their goods at New Orleans for reloading aboard oceangoing vessels sailing to the East Coast and foreign ports. The United States blamed the French for this Spanish edict, although France had not yet taken possession of Louisiana.

When news of the suspension reached westerners who depended on the Mississippi River and the use of the port of New Orleans as their commercial lifeline, they were greatly aroused, as were their spokespersons in Congress. There was a real possibility that armed westerners might march on New Orleans and seize it. In response to their demands for action to protect U.S. rights on the Mississippi River and at New Orleans, President Thomas Jefferson sent James Monroe as his envoy to

France to help Livingston in the negotiations with the French government. Livingston and Monroe were authorized to try to acquire, at most, only New Orleans and the Floridas, should they belong to France, and the right of the free navigation of the Mississippi River.

Meanwhile, Napoleon's plans for restoring the French Empire in North America depended on subjugating slaves on the West Indian island of Santo Domingo (Hispaniola) who were in revolt under the leadership of Pierre Dominique Toussaint Louverture. The sugar, coffee, indigo, and cotton produced on that island were important to the French economy, and the island might serve as a staging ground for any projected French invasion of the North American continent. Napoleon realized that if the French could not control the island, Louisiana would be of little value to him. Despite the expenditure of many lives, thousands of French troops, and enormous sums of money, the slaves were far from subdued at the end of 1802, and Santo Domingo was in ruins. Napoleon decided to abandon the island. As Louisiana would have served mainly as a granary and supply region for that island, it would be of little worth to France. Napoleon, therefore, elected to sell Louisiana to the United States.

Napoleon had several other reasons for making the sale. Determined to resume war against Great Britain and other European powers, he needed funds to restock his army after the military debacle in Santo Domingo. He also feared that Great Britain might simply take Louisiana from France and thought that he could forestall the formation of an alliance between the United States and Great Britain and even perhaps build up the United States as a rival that would check British expansion. He probably also was aware of the difficulties that Spain had had in dealing with the numerous Native American societies in the region since 1762 and expected that France might have no better luck. Finally, he wished to avert war with an expanding United States, whose government appeared set to empower its president to seize New Orleans by force.

On April 11, 1803, Napoleon ordered his minister of finance, the marquis de Barbé-Marbois, to negotiate the sale of the entire territory of Louisiana, not only New Orleans and its environs. Although they had no authorization to purchase all Louisiana, Livingston and Monroe entered into the bargaining and, after some haggling over price, came to terms. The negotiations were completed on May 9, although the treaty and two conventions making up the agreement bore the date April 30. Under the agreement, the United States acquired "Louisiana," including New Orleans, but its boundaries were only vaguely defined. In return, the United States agreed to pay approximately fifteen million dollars, assume the debts that French citizens owed to the United States (roughly one-quarter of the purchase price), and incorporate all inhabitants of Louisiana—except indigenous peoples and slaves—as citizens of the United States. The news reached the United States around July 4, adding extra jubilation to the patriotic mood on the nation's independence day.

Although Jefferson had some grave doubts about the constitutionality of the purchase because the Constitution did not expressly grant the president or Congress the power to acquire foreign territory, he approved it. He mulled over the idea of proposing an amendment to legitimize the purchase and any future territorial acquisition. After further reflection, Jefferson realized that with the exception of a few Federalists who worried that the nation would grow too large for an effective democracy, the majority of both Congress and the people of the United States enthusiastically supported the purchase. Jefferson decided to draw on a so-called "higher laws doctrine" and found enough justification for the purchase in the preamble to the U.S. Constitution, which states as one of its purposes the need to "promote the general Welfare."

The U.S. Senate ratified the agreements on October 20, and the president proclaimed them to be in effect the next day. The formal transfer of the southern portion of the territory from Spain to France—despite the Treaty of San Ildefonso—occurred on November 30, 1803, and the transfer from France to the United States occurred on December 20. The northern segment was transferred to the United States on March 10, 1804,

THOMAS JEFFERSON ON THE LOUISIANA PURCHASE

Thomas Jefferson's message to Congress regarding the Louisiana Purchase, January 16, 1804:

In execution of the act of the present session of Congress for taking possession of Louisiana, as ceded to us by France, and for the temporary government thereof, Governor Claiborne, of the Mississippi Territory, and General Wilkinson were appointed commissioners to receive possession. They proceeded with such regular troops as had been assembled at Fort Adams from the nearest posts and with some militia of the Mississippi Territory to New Orleans. To be prepared for anything unexpected which might arise out of the transaction, a respectable body of militia was ordered to be in readiness in the States of Ohio, Kentucky, and Tennessee, and a part of those of Tennessee was moved on to the Natchez. No occasion, however, arose for their services. Our commissioners, on their arrival at New Orleans, found the Province already delivered by the commissioners of Spain to that of France, who delivered it over to them on the 20th day of December, as appears by their declaratory act accompanying this. Governor Claiborne, being duly invested with the powers heretofore exercised by the governor and intendant of Louisiana, assumed the government on the same day, and for the maintenance of law and order immediately issued the proclamation and address now communicated.

On this important acquisition, so favorable to the immediate interests of our Western citizens, so auspicious to the peace and security of the nation in general, which adds to our country territories so extensive and fertile and to our citizens new brethren to partake of the blessings of freedom and self-government, I offer to Congress and our country my sincere congratulations.

one day after Spain had returned it to France. A little less than one year after Napoleon had proposed the sale, Louisiana was the property of the United States.

SIGNIFICANCE

Acquisition of the Louisiana Territory virtually doubled the territorial extent of the United States, giving the new nation what then seemed to be almost limitless room for expansion. It also made possible the nation's later expansion to the Pacific Ocean. The purchase also set a precedent for obtaining foreign territory and peoples by treaty, and it increased nationalist feelings in the country and helped undercut secessionist intrigues in the West. It did not solve all the problems of the West, but it redirected their nature. Friction with New Spain—which was soon to become Mexico—and the various Great Plains and Texas Native Americans increased, but the French were no longer a complicating factor.

Within a few decades, the new territory would provoke major debates over the future expansion of slavery there and the removal of Native Americans to a newly created Indian Territory. In 1803, the purchase demarcated a reserve for Native Americans west of the Mississippi River and provided a place for the eventual relocation of most eastern tribal peoples in the ensuing four decades. Meanwhile, the federal government undertook to survey the extent of its new territories by having Meriwether Lewis and William Clark lead a major expedition of exploration.

—John L. Loos, updated by Thomas L. Altherr

FURTHER READING

Balleck, Barry J. "When the Ends Justify the Means: Thomas Jefferson and the Louisiana Purchase." *Presidential Studies Quarterly* 22, no. 4 (1992): 679-696. Argues that Jefferson's support of the purchase was consistent with his constitutional views.

Carson, David A. "The Role of Congress in the Acquisition of the Louisiana Territory." *Louisiana History* 26, no. 4 (1985): 369-383. Asserts that Napoleon was aware of unpassed congressional resolutions to authorize the president to employ force to seize New Orleans.

Cerami, Charles A. *Jefferson's Great Gamble: The Remarkable Story of Jefferson, Napoleon, and the Men Behind the Louisiana Purchase.* Naperville, Ill.: Sourcebooks, 2003. Admirably clear and engaging history of the Louisiana Purchase that examines all the figures who played a role in that event.

Flemingo, Thomas. *Louisiana Purchase.* New York: John Wiley & Sons, 2003. Brief study of the Louisiana Purchase, emphasizing the diplomatic negotiations, that is well suited for high school students.

Kukla, Jon. *A Wilderness so Immense: The Louisiana Purchase and the Destiny of America.* New York: Alfred A. Knopf, 2003. Beautifully written and well-illustrated scholarly study of the Louisiana Purchase that examines the event from all perspectives.

Lyon, E. Wilson. *Louisiana in French Diplomacy, 1759-1804.* Norman: University of Oklahoma Press, 1934. The second half of the book gives a detailed account of French viewpoints leading to the sale of Louisiana.

Peterson, Merrill D. *Thomas Jefferson and the New Nation.* New York: Oxford University Press, 1970. This spirited interpretation demonstrates that Jefferson was more than a passive player in the negotiations to secure Louisiana.

Sheehan, Bernard W. *Seeds of Extinction: Jeffersonian Philanthropy and the American Indian.* Chapel Hill: University of North Carolina Press, 1973. Places the Louisiana Purchase within the context of Jeffersonian-era attitudes about removal of eastern Native Americans to the West.

Skolnik, Richard, comp. *1803: Jefferson's Decision: The United States Purchases Louisiana.* New York: Chelsea House, 1969. Reprints many of the primary sources pertinent to the purchase.

SEE ALSO: May 14, 1804-Sept. 23, 1806: Lewis and Clark Expedition; Dec. 2, 1804: Bonaparte Is Crowned Napoleon I; Mar., 1805-Sept. 1, 1807: Burr's Conspiracy; July 15, 1806-July 1, 1807: Pike Explores the American Southwest; c. 1815-1830: Westward American Migration Begins; Feb. 22, 1819: Adams-Onís Treaty Gives the United States Florida; June 15, 1846: United States Acquires Oregon Territory; Dec. 31, 1853: Gadsden Purchase Completes the U.S.-Mexican Border.

RELATED ARTICLES in *Great Lives from History: The Nineteenth Century, 1801-1900:* Henri Christophe; Meriwether Lewis and William Clark; Napoleon I.

September 7, 1803
GREAT BRITAIN BEGINS COLONIZING TASMANIA

After the British established a settlement on mainland Australia, they moved to occupy Tasmania, motivated partly by their fear of French annexation, and brought devastation to the island's native peoples.

LOCALE: Van Diemen's Land (now Tasmania); Australia

CATEGORIES: Exploration and discovery; expansion and land acquisition

KEY FIGURES

Abel Janszoon Tasman (1603-1659), Dutch explorer who claimed Tasmania for the Netherlands in 1642

James Cook (1728-1779), English navigator who charted the coast of New South Wales in 1770

Philip Gidley King (1758-1808), second British governor of New South Wales, 1800-1806

John Bowen (1751-1835), British army lieutenant who was commissioned to establish a settlement in Tasmania

David Collins (1756-1810), British judge-advocate assigned to Tasmania

SUMMARY OF EVENT

Tasmania, the Australian island first called Anthony van Diemensland, or Van Diemen's Land, was claimed soon after it was sighted in 1642 by the Dutch navigator Abel Tasman. Tasman formally proclaimed the island to be under the flag of the Dutch prince Frederich Henry, but the Dutch did little to further that claim. More than a century later, the English navigator Captain James Cook explored the eastern coast of mainland Australia. On April 30, 1770, he anchored in Botany Bay, where British colonization work began after the British government took up James Maria Matra's proposal to colonize the continent in 1783. In 1787, the British sent eleven ships to Australia. The little fleet included six transports carrying about seven hundred convicts, and the colony of Sydney was founded in 1788.

At that time, Australia was not known to be a single landmass and Tasmania was believed to be connected to the eastern part of the continent, which the British called New South Wales. That theory was dashed when George Bass and Matthew Flinders circumnavigated Tasmania in October, 1798. The large ocean passage separating Tasmania from New South Wales became known as Bass Strait. The island then became popular to European seamen because of its nearness to offshore seal and whale colonies. However, the decision to claim Tasmania for Great Britain arose from the race for strategic strongholds against the French.

British fears of French territorial expansion were strong at the turn of the nineteenth century, when Britain and France were engaged in a large-scale war. The appearance of French navigators, such as Thomas Nicolas Baudin, in Australian waters in 1802 therefore fostered

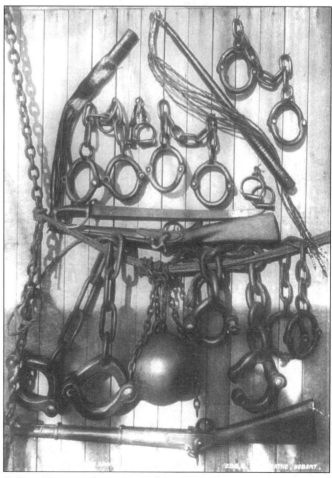

Relics of Tasmania's convict era housed in a Hobart museum. The items include whips, shackles, guns, and an iron ball. (Library of Congress)

fears that France had designed on Tasmania. Soon afterward, Philip Gidley King, the British governor of New South Wales, appointed Lieutenant John Bowen to establish a British colony on Tasmania.

The date the first new settlement was established on the island is generally given as September 7, 1803—the day on which the *Lady Nelson* dropped its anchor in Risdon Cove, an inlet on the eastern shore of Tasmania, by the mouth of Derwent River. Bowen's party was small. It consisted of a medical officer, Jacob Mountgarrett; a store-keeper named Wilson; a small body of soldiers; a number of free settlers; and an assortment of male and female convicts. In February, 1804, Lieutenant Governor David Collins decided that Risdon Cove was a poor landing site, so he moved the site to Sullivan's Cove, on the eastern bank of the Derwent River. The colony established there later became Tasmania's capital city, Hobart.

On December 5, 1804, William Paterson founded a second settlement at Port Dalrymple, on the Tamar River. Like Risdon Cove, it too was shifted to another site more conducive to the development of a productive town. That settlement later became the city of Launceston. Meanwhile, in August, 1804, Collins took over Bowen's command and became the first governor of Van Diemen's Land. Bowen's colony had not fared well. In May, 1804, while Bowen was away from his colony, a violent clash between European settlers and local Aborigines had left many dead and wounded. The conflict was made more disturbing because until that time, the Aboriginal community had appeared shy, if not suspicious of the colonials, but never aggressive. What triggered the attack and how many people died can only be guessed because contemporary eyewitness reports accounts are contradictory.

From that time, violence between settlers and indigenous communities became more frequent. Aboriginal people responded to settler violence with violence of their own, and reports of convicts being speared were made in 1805 and 1807. However, Aboriginal spears offered little protection against the more lethal firearms of the settlers. Colonial authorities of the day tried various strategies to counter the negative effects of European settlement. In 1810, Governor Collins ordered that any settler found recklessly firing on Aborigines would be legally punished. However, the fact that many offenders, particularly those known as bushrangers, remained outside the law meant that Collins's order carried little force. Later, European sealers and whalers also attacked Aborigines as the trade in skins and oil became more lucrative.

In March, 1829, the Tasmanian government engaged George Augustus Robinson to establish a mission at which all indigenous Tasmanians were to reside. Robinson's intentions were benevolent, and his Calvinist beliefs assured him he was accomplishing God's will. However, the period during which he undertook his challenge fell during a particularly turbulent time in Tasmanian history. The consequences of European settlement on the indigenous populations of both Tasmania and Australia were devastating. Violence and resettlement, coupled with introduced diseases and infections, took a deathly toll from which the Aboriginal communities never fully recovered.

European settlers in Tasmania also eventually turned against one another. Some settlers hired convicts to work as hunters; the knowledge of the Tasmanian landscape that the convicts acquired while hunting helped train them for criminal bushranging activities after they escaped from their overlords. Some fugitives voluntarily turned themselves in and endured severe floggings and imprisonment, but others mobilized in groups. Two men remembered only as Lemon and Brown were among the first recorded bushrangers in Tasmania. In 1808, they were captured after killing three soldiers and an indentured convict. Lemon was shot and decapitated, and Brown was forced to carry the head of his companion to Hobart. He was later tried and hung in chains in Sydney. Bushranging eventually threatened the Tasmania colonies to such an extent that Governor Lachlan Macquarie offered clemency in 1814 to all the absconders—except murderers—who returned to their duties within six months.

SIGNIFICANCE

Great Britain annexed Tasmania principally because of its fears that France would seize the island. Modern place names in and around the island, such as D'Entrecasteaux Channel, Furneaux Islands, and Freycinet Peninsula, attest to the important contributions made by French navigators in the region. However, there is little documented evidence to suggest that the French actually intended occupying Tasmania themselves.

British colonization policy fostered trouble. The British government initially saw settlement of Tasmania as a means of ridding the British Isles of convicts and rebels—who were mostly Irish. Consequently, a large portion of Tasmania's first colonists were proven troublemakers. Violence was thus a natural by-product of European settlement, and the island's indigenous peoples paid a heavy price for colonization.

—*Nicole Anae*

FURTHER READING

Bonwick, James. *The Bushrangers: Illustrating the Early Days of Van Diemen's Land.* Hobart, Tasmania: Fullers Bookshop, 1967. Facsimile of the original edition published in 1856; a colorful account of the early years of British settlement of Tasmania.

Cox, Robert. *Steps to the Scaffold: The Untold Story of Tasmania's Black Bushrangers.* Pawleena, Australia: Cornhill, 2004. Revisionist account of indigenous communities, bushrangers, and European settlers in Tasmania.

Giblin, R. W. *The Early History of Tasmania.* 2 vols. Melbourne, Australia: Melbourne University Press, 1939. Extensively researched account of the early history of Tasmania.

Tardif, Phillip. *John Bowen's Hobart: The Beginning of European Settlement in Tasmania.* Sandy Bay, Tasmania: Sandy Bay Tasmanian Historical Research Association, 2003. Important examination of Bowen's role in the settlement of the island.

Twain, Mark. *Following the Equator.* Reprint. New York: Oxford University Press, 1996. Facsimile reprint of Twain's 1897 account of his round-the-world lecture tour, during which he spent more than two months in Australia. Quoting freely from earlier published sources, Twain offers a scathing indictment of British mistreatment of Aborigines in Australia and Tasmania but praises the work of George Augustus Robinson. Chapter 29 contains Twain's own firsthand description of Tasmania in 1895.

West, John. *The History of Tasmania.* Sydney: Angus & Robertson, 1971. Reprint edition of a history of Tasmania first published in 1852.

Windschuttle, Keith. *The Fabrication of Aboriginal History.* Paddington, Tasmania: Macleay Press, 2002. Modern thesis examining the effects of Tasmanian settlement on the island's indigenous peoples.

SEE ALSO: Dec. 6, 1801-Aug., 1803: Flinders Explores Australia; 1820-early 1840's: Europeans Explore the Antarctic; Aug. 16, 1835: Melbourne, Australia, Is Founded; 1851: Gold Is Discovered in New South Wales; 1868: Last Convicts Land in Western Australia.

RELATED ARTICLES in *Great Lives from History: The Nineteenth Century, 1801-1900:* John MacArthur; A. B. Paterson; Edward Gibbon Wakefield.

1804
BRITISH AND FOREIGN BIBLE SOCIETY IS FOUNDED

The rise of Christian evangelicalism in the late eighteenth and early nineteenth centuries brought with it a number of religious societies established to spread Protestant Christianity and exert European influence throughout the world. The British and Foreign Bible Society was an important example of that trend.

LOCALE: London, England

CATEGORIES: Organizations and institutions; religion and theology

KEY FIGURES

Thomas Charles (1755-1814), founder of the Welsh Calvinist Methodists who cofounded the Bible society

Joseph Hughes (1769-1833), Baptist minister who founded the Religious Tract Society and cofounded the Bible society

Mary Jones (1784-1866), Welsh woman who inspired the Bible society

SUMMARY OF EVENT

The British and Foreign Bible Society (BFBS) was founded in 1804 with the seemingly simple aim of providing Bibles for as many people as possible in their native languages with neither commentaries nor notes. In the process of fulfilling this goal, the society had a significant impact on the British printing industry and translated the Bible into many languages.

A devout and determined Welsh teenager is credited with inspiring the society's founding. When Mary Jones (later Lewis) was sixteen, she saved money to purchase a Bible in Welsh and walked twenty-five miles to another town, Bala, to purchase one. Until then, she had to walk two miles to a neighbor's home each time she wanted to read the Bible, as her family did not own a copy. The Welsh Bible was both expensive and difficult to obtain. As she had been warned, all the copies in Bala had been claimed. Upon hearing her story, however, the Reverend Thomas Charles gave her one of the claimed copies. Several years later, in 1802, Charles shared Jones's story with his fellow members of the Religious Tract Society and suggested that they form a society to provide Bibles to the people of Wales. The Reverend Joseph Hughes is credited with expanding Charles's idea by asking, "Why just Wales? Why not the world?"

The effort brought together members of the Church of England and Dissenters (non-Anglican Protestants). The committee established to govern the BFBS was deliberately designed to reflect the society's ecumenical and international aspirations, with secretaries being named from Anglicans, Dissenters, and foreigners. One foundational guideline was to exclude commentary and notes from the society's Bibles in an effort to remain as ecumenical, or broad-spirited, as possible within a Protestant context. It can be seen as a tribute to BFBS influence and importance that other societies brought out competing versions of the Bible in line with their own particular doctrines and traditions. One early example of a "what to include" controversy the BFBS faced involves the Apocrypha, a set of texts included in Roman Catholic Bibles. Lutheran and Anglican Bibles included the Apocrypha in a separate section, whereas groups with Calvinist leanings excluded it completely. After much debate, BFBS officials decided to exclude the Apocrypha from future editions of the Bible.

Before Bibles could be printed and distributed, they had to be translated into the languages of their intended audiences. Sometimes translators had to create a written form of a spoken language or dialect before the translation work could begin. Hence translation was key to the society's mission. Books commemorating the society's milestones, such as its 1904 centennial, devote much space to stories of dedicated translators spending years living with a population in order to learn the intricacies of its language fully enough to make the Bible come alive within that language.

The society soon developed a reputation among its paper suppliers, printers, and book binders as a demanding customer. It could well afford to be, given the high volume of orders it placed. BFBS organizers took full advantage of emerging technologies available to them and experimented with new means and methods of production, such as using machines instead of artisans to bind Bibles. They were also early adaptors of more rapid and efficient printing technologies, such as the steam press.

Within England, people usually had to pay for BFBS Bibles, with society representatives coming to their homes on a regular basis to collect installments. Only after all or most of the price had been paid were Bibles delivered. These prices, however, were subsidized—

sometimes heavily in the case of the poor. Several rationales lay behind the payment plan for the so-called lower classes. It was thought that recipients would value their Bibles more if they had to sacrifice a little to obtain them and that setting aside a little each week toward a goal would instill fiscal discipline. Also, as with other social and moral reform movements, it was thought that regular contact with middle-class volunteers who collected for and distributed the Bibles would have an uplifting influence on those in poverty.

Distribution within England was handled through volunteers, associations, and sometimes small storefront shops. (During the 1850's, the domestic volunteer visitors would be largely supplanted by colportage, a system in which paid agents visited homes and sold the Bibles.) Abroad, the political and economic climate affected the society's activities. French emperor Napoleon I was threatening to conquer Great Britain. The Irish were contending with famine and economic hardship. The British Empire and its influence were spreading.

These realities affected the society in direct and indirect ways. For example, the BFBS made sure to produce a French-language edition to benefit French prisoners of war, and it also worked to place English-language Bibles in the hands of British prisoners. Just as the domestic poor of Britain were viewed as "benighted" and in need of uplifting contact with their supposed social betters as well as with the Word of God, the world beyond Britain's shores was often viewed as being in dire need of Christianity and the "civilizing" influence of British culture. Therefore, sea captains, adventurers, and merchants, as well as colporteurs, were engaged to distribute Bibles. In some cases, Bibles would precede missionaries by years, so when the missionaries finally arrived in a given area, they would find the people already familiar with the basic story and precepts of Christianity.

The activities of the BFBS were very expensive, despite the cost-cutting efforts and technical prowess of the society's officials. Therefore, the society sought donations, and some of its supporting members found unique ways to support the cause of spreading the Christian message by providing Bibles. One supporter even taught a pet parrot to ask passersby for contributions and placed a small bag outside the bird's cage to collect these donations. When the bird died, a sign asking for donations was hung in the cage and the bag remained.

SIGNIFICANCE

More than two hundred years after its founding, the BFBS continues to distribute Bibles worldwide, maintaining its traditions of utilizing the newest technologies available to produce and distribute the Bible and of making Scripture available to as many people as possible in as many forms as possible. The society now uses machine-assisted translation to increase the number of languages in which its text is available. It also produces audio and video versions of the Bible in various languages.

—*Elizabeth Jarnagin*

FURTHER READING

Batalden, Stephen K., and Kathleen Cann, eds. *Sowing the Word: The Cultural Impact of the British and Foreign Bible Society, 1804-2004*. Sheffield, South Yorkshire, England: Sheffield Phoenix, 2004. A collection of nineteen academic papers discussing the society's impact on various countries it has worked, stories of Bible translators, the role of women in the society, and other issues.

Cain, Peter, and Tony Hopkins. *British Imperialism, 1688-2000*. 2d ed. New York: Longman, 2001. Analyzes British imperialism by reference to the unique features of Great Britain's economic development.

Canton, William. *The Story of the Bible Society*. New York: E. P. Dutton, 1904. Written to commemorate the society's centennial, this book maintains a laudatory tone.

Howsam, Leslie. *Cheap Bibles: Nineteenth-Century Publishing and the British and Foreign Bible Society*. New York: Cambridge University Press, 1991. Examines the relationships between the BFBS, its suppliers, and its customers between 1804 and the 1860's. Traces the economics and changing technologies involved in large-scale production and distribution of Bibles as well as its cultural implications.

McDannell, Colleen. *Material Christianity: Religion and Popular Culture in America*. New Haven, Conn.: Yale University Press, 1996. A chapter titled "The Bible in the Victorian Home" looks at the Bible as an element of American popular culture, particularly during the Victorian era.

SEE ALSO: May 8, 1816: American Bible Society Is Founded; c. 1826-1827: First Meetings of the Plymouth Brethren; July 14, 1833: Oxford Movement Begins; 1835-1836: Strauss Publishes *The Life of Jesus Critically Examined*; Sept., 1875: Theosophical Society Is Founded.

RELATED ARTICLES in *Great Lives from History: The Nineteenth Century, 1801-1900:* William Booth; William Carey; Samuel Ajayi Crowther; David Livingstone; Napoleon I.

1804
SAUSSURE PUBLISHES HIS RESEARCH ON PLANT METABOLISM

Nicolas-Théodore de Saussure's research helped establish the basis of plant metabolism. He discovered that the gain in dry matter by growing plants far exceeds the weight of the carbon dioxide that they absorb, and that water is the major contributor to the gain. He also showed that plants obtain nitrogen and various minerals from the soil and demonstrated that minerals are essential for plant growth.

LOCALE: Geneva, Switzerland
CATEGORIES: Biology; environment and ecology; chemistry

KEY FIGURES

Nicolas-Théodore de Saussure (1767-1845), Swiss chemist and plant physiologist
Jan Baptista van Helmont (1580-1644), Belgian chemist, physiologist, and physician

Stephen Hales (1677-1761), English botanist, physiologist, and clergyman
Joseph Priestley (1733-1804), English clergyman and chemist
Jan Ingenhousz (1730-1799), Dutch-born physician and chemist
Antoine-Laurent Lavoisier (1743-1794), French chemist
Jean Senebier (1742-1809), Swiss clergyman and naturalist

SUMMARY OF EVENT

Swiss chemist and plant physiologist Nicolas-Théodore de Saussure built his work on seventeenth and eighteenth century research and experimentation, leading to a series of insights into plant nutrition and respiration. Earlier scientists had learned that the green tissues of a plant use two simple, inorganic raw materials, water and carbon dioxide, and, in the presence of light, assimilate carbon into the plant's dry matter. (It was later learned that the carbon is fixed as carbohydrate.) Scientists also found that, in the process of carbon assimilation, oxygen gas is released as a waste product. This understanding of photosynthesis replaced the belief that plants obtain all their nutrition from the soil, in a manner analogous to an animal's ingestion of food.

Along with this insight came an understanding of the countervailing process called respiration. In a modern, cellular sense, during respiration an organism uses oxygen to break down organic compounds to meet its needs for energy and building blocks for other organic molecules. In respiration, carbon dioxide is released. The processes of photosynthesis and respiration are opposed.

The development of this new understanding of plant physiology began in the early seventeenth century, when Jan Baptista van Helmont concluded from an experiment that water rather than soil was the source of the gain in dry weight by growing plants. He was incorrect in concluding that water was the sole source, however.

During the early eighteenth century, Stephen Hales correctly surmised that plants derive some of their nutrition from "air" (in modern terms, from atmospheric carbon dioxide). Then, in 1771, Joseph Priestley showed that growing plants release oxygen. In 1779, Jan Ingenhousz demonstrated that plants require light in order to release oxygen and that only the green parts of plants emit this gas. Ingenhousz also established that plants, like animals, respire. Swiss naturalist Jean Senebier, who was Saussure's teacher, demonstrated that the amount of oxygen that plants liberate is related to the amount of available carbon dioxide. Ingenhousz subsequently established that plants retain weight from the carbon in the carbon dioxide that they absorb.

The contributions by Saussure to advancing the understanding of plant physiology owed much to his use of, to a greater extent than his predecessors, the quantitative physical and chemical methods pioneered by eighteenth century French chemist Antoine-Laurent Lavoisier. Each of Saussure's experiments had a specific goal. He used replicates and control plants and repeated his experiments with different species. In addition, unlike his predecessors, he had a greater appreciation of the importance of growing experimental plants in a normal cycle of light and darkness.

Saussure was the first to use direct chemical methods to show that, in a photosynthesizing leaf, fixed carbon appears at the same time that carbon dioxide is lost from the surrounding atmosphere and replaced by oxygen. He demonstrated that, even though the atmosphere contains only a trace of carbon dioxide, plant leaves assimilate large amounts of carbon directly from that source. Saussure thereby disproved Senebier's contention that plants obtain carbon dioxide from water absorbed from the soil by the roots, or from dew by the leaves. Saussure also showed that respiration is as essential to plants as it is to animals, and that physiologically active parts of plants, such as green leaves and opening flowers, need more oxygen for respiration than do other plant parts.

In plant respiration, the carbon dioxide formed by the combination of oxygen with carbon is emitted by green parts of the plant in the dark and by nongreen parts all the time, in contrast to the release of oxygen by illuminated green parts. Saussure demonstrated that plants fix carbon dioxide photosynthetically with an efficiency greatly exceeding that of the countervailing process of respiration and that, consequently, the net effect of growing plants on the atmosphere is the fixation of carbon dioxide and the evolution of oxygen.

Saussure also discovered that the dry weight gained by a growing plant equals roughly twice the weight of carbon fixed. He then reasoned correctly—like van Helmont—that water is a plant nutrient. It is now known that water contributes the large amount of hydrogen present in plant dry matter. (Water is the basic medium of living cells, but the meaning here is of incorporation into the structural and functional building blocks, not the watery matrix, of the cell.)

Saussure also identified the route by which plants obtain nitrogen, which is as essential a constituent of plants as it is of animals. Previous researchers such as Priestley and Ingenhousz had supposed that plants get this nutrient from the atmosphere, which consists of 78 percent nitrogen by volume. Saussure demonstrated that plants absorb nitrogen only in a chemically combined form, in aqueous solution from the soil, via their roots. In addition, by showing that plants grew poorly if kept in distilled water (which has no minerals), Saussure established that minerals such as potassium, phosphorus, sodium, calcium, magnesium, iron, and manganese are essential for plant growth, even though they account for only a very small proportion of plant dry matter. Before this discovery, most scientists thought that the minerals absorbed by a plant from the soil were just a chance, nutritionally inconsequential, occurrence.

In 1804, Saussure published his findings in plant metabolism as *Recherches chimiques sur la végétation* (chemical research on vegetation). This work, which consists of research papers, established the theoretical basis of plant nutrition and the methodology of plant physiology. He had previously published three articles on carbon dioxide and its fixation in plant tissues in the journal *Annales de Chimie* (annals of chemistry).

SIGNIFICANCE

Saussure's book *Recherches chimiques sur la végétation* culminated a revolution in the understanding of plant nutrition and physiology that had taken two centuries to achieve. He identified the source and route of supply of nearly all the major elements that had been shown to occur in mature plants. Although knowledge was still rudimentary, his publication marked the establishment of plant physiology as a science.

Saussure's discoveries were fundamental to later work in plant physiology, but, immediately after him, there was a thirty-year lull in interest in the quantitative study of carbon assimilation and the synthesis of organic compounds by plants. Then, during the mid-nineteenth century, there were advances in understanding of the steps in carbohydrate formation by photosynthetic activity. Toward the end of the nineteenth century, the idea that carbohydrate formation is the starting point for the synthesis of the other organic constituents of a plant began to gain adherents.

During the early twentieth century came the insight that the oxygen released in photosynthesis is derived from the splitting of water, not from carbon dioxide as Saussure and other previous researchers had thought. As of the early twenty-first century, at least fifty intermediate steps in photosynthesis had been identified, and the discovery of many more was fully anticipated. Scientists had determined that cellular respiration, too, is complex, involving numerous chemical steps.

—*Jane F. Hill*

FURTHER READING

Epstein, Emanuel, and Arnold J. Bloom. *Mineral Nutrition of Plants: Principles and Perspectives*. 2d ed. Sunderland, Mass.: Sinauer Associates, 2005. Describes how plants acquire and use mineral nutrients.

Galston, Arthur W. *Life Processes of Plants*. New York: Scientific American Library, 1994. An easy-to-read overview of plant physiological processes. Chapter 1 explores photosynthesis.

Govindjee, J. T. Beatty, H. Gest, and J. F. Allen, eds. *Discoveries in Photosynthesis*. Berlin: Springer, 2005. An encyclopedic volume detailing the history of photosynthesis research.

Hall, David O., and Krishna Rao. *Photosynthesis*. 6th ed. New York: Cambridge University Press, 1999. A concise introduction to the complexities of photosynthesis. Chapter 2 provides a historical overview.

Morton, A. G. *History of Botanical Science: An Account of Botany from Ancient Times to the Present Day*. London: Academic Press, 1981. Chapter 8 of this comprehensive volume includes details about Saussure's work.

Nash, Leonard K. *Plants and the Atmosphere*. Harvard Case Histories in Experimental Science. Cambridge, Mass.: Harvard University Press, 1952. A well-written, authoritative account of the basic discoveries in photosynthesis from about 1650 to 1804.

Reed, Howard S. *A Short History of the Plant Sciences*. Waltham, Mass.: Chronica Botanica, 1942. Includes a detailed account of the development of the understanding of plant nutrition.

SEE ALSO: 1803-1808: Dalton Formulates the Atomic Theory of Matter; 1838-1839: Schwann and Virchow Develop Cell Theory; 1840: Liebig Advocates Artificial Fertilizers; Nov. 24, 1859: Darwin Publishes *On the Origin of Species*.

RELATED ARTICLES in *Great Lives from History: The Nineteenth Century, 1801-1900:* Luther Burbank; Ferdinand Julius Cohn; Charles Darwin; Joseph-Louis Gay-Lussac; Asa Gray; Justus von Liebig.

January, 1804
OHIO ENACTS THE FIRST BLACK CODES

Although "black codes" that discriminated against African Americans are generally associated with the post-Civil War South, the first such laws were enacted in the northern state of Ohio, most of whose white citizens wished to discourage fugitive slaves and free blacks from entering their state.

ALSO KNOWN AS: Black laws
LOCALE: Ohio
CATEGORIES: Laws, acts, and legal history; civil rights and liberties

KEY FIGURE
Edward Tiffin (1766-1829), Virginian who acted as president of Ohio's 1802 constitutional convention and later became governor of Ohio

SUMMARY OF EVENT
The Northwest Territory that was created by the Northwest Ordinance in 1787 was eventually divided into the states of Ohio, Indiana, Michigan, Illinois, and Wisconsin. In 1800, what was to become the state of Ohio separated from the rest of the territory. Two years later, Ohio elected delegates to a constitutional convention in preparation for a statehood petition, which the U.S. Congress approved in 1803.

Although the Northwest Ordinance prohibited slavery in the Northwest Territory, Ohio's constitutional convention debated the issue during its sessions. With the slaveholding states of Virginia on Ohio's eastern boundary and Kentucky on its southern boundary, there was considerable pressure for Ohio to recognize slavery. Many immigrants to Ohio came from slave states and saw nothing wrong with the institution. However, while many southern Ohioans did not object to slavery, residents of the northern part of Ohio were more inclined to oppose it. Immigrants from New England, New York, and Pennsylvania tended to accept the concepts of the Enlightenment, as expressed in Thomas Paine's *The Rights of Man* (1791-1792) and the Declaration of Independence, which proclaimed the concepts of liberty and equality for all people. Northern Ohioans, many of whom had had little contact with either free or enslaved African Americans, usually opposed slavery from an idealistic perspective. Thus, a geographic division with regard to slavery existed within Ohio from the first.

Delegates at the 1802 constitutional convention debated several questions that focused on African Americans, including the issue of whether slavery should be permitted within Ohio. If slavery were prohibited, should the new state permit indentured servitude? Regardless of the outcome of those discussions, the place of African Americans in the new state had to be defined: Should African Americans be allowed to vote? Should they be granted civil rights? Should they be encouraged to immigrate to Ohio?

Edward Tiffin served as president of the convention. Before leaving Virginia, he had freed his own slaves, but he did not necessarily support the concept of equal rights for African Americans. When the convention had a tie vote on the question of granting African Americans the right to vote, Tiffin cast the deciding negative vote on the issue.

There was little strong feeling for instituting slavery in Ohio. There was, however, a strong sentiment in favor of granting limited rights for African Americans. At the moment Ohio's constitutional convention opened in Chillicothe on November 1, approximately five hundred African Americans lived in the Ohio territory. African Americans constituted approximately 10 percent of Ohio's total population, but none of them was represented in the constitutional convention because none could meet the property qualifications required for voting. After a major debate over allowing African Americans to vote at the convention, it was decided not to delete the word "white" from the qualifications for the franchise. Nevertheless, Ohio's African American population grew from five hundred in 1800 to nearly two thousand by 1810. Most of this growth probably occurred before the passage of the first Ohio black codes.

Former southerners living in Ohio were primarily responsible for the state's black codes. In 1804, the legislature debated and passed the first of these laws, which was titled An Act to Regulate Black and Mulatto Persons. The intent of this legislation was clearly to discourage African Americans from moving into Ohio and to encourage those already there to leave. Many delegates from parts of Ohio near Virginia and Kentucky undoubtedly supported the codes because of their geographic locations. Ohio shared a 375-mile border with the two southern states, and many legislators did not want to see a mass influx of black people into Ohio. Early Ohioans generally rejected slavery but not strongly enough to protest against it. At the same time, they opposed African Americans living in Ohio as free citizens.

1800's

The first Ohio black code, which went into force in January, 1804, had several provisions designed to control African Americans. First, no black or mulatto person could settle in Ohio without a certificate of freedom from a United States court. African Americans and mulattoes already residing in Ohio had until June 1, 1804, to produce such certificates. The certificates cost twelve and one-half cents each and were required of children as well as adults.

The law made it a criminal offense for a white person to employ for more than one hour any black person who did not have the appropriate certificate. Fines ranged from ten to fifty dollars for each offense, with half the money going to the informants who reported violations of the law. The law also required that an additional fifty cents per day was to be paid by white employers to the owners of the black people whom they hired, as it assumed that any black person who did not have a certificate must be a slave. Penalties for aiding fugitives from slavery remained the same, but fines for assisting slaves attempting to escape from the state could be as much as one hundred dollars.

At the convention, the vote on this issue was split, with those in the northern half of the state opposed to placing restrictions on African American employment, while delegates from southern Ohio supported them. The bill eventually passed in Ohio's lower house by a vote of nineteen to eight and in its upper house by a vote of nine to five, although the geographic lines in the state senate were not as clearly drawn as they were in the lower house.

A few years later, an even stronger bill to restrict African Americans was presented in Ohio's state senate. In its final version, it forbade African Americans from settling in Ohio unless they could post five-hundred-dollar bonds and present affidavits signed by two white men that attested to their good character. Fines for helping fugitive slaves were doubled. A final provision of the law barred African Americans from testifying against white defendants in court. There is no record of the vote in the state senate, but the bill passed the House by a vote of twenty to nine and became law in January, 1807.

As restrictive as the original black codes were, the new law was far worse. It stripped African Americans of legal protections and placed them at the mercy of whites. Whites, on the other hand, did not need to fear being tried for their own offenses against black people, unless white witnesses were available to testify against them. In at least one instance, an African American was murdered by whites when the only witnesses were black people who could not testify against

OHIO'S BLACK LAWS

SECTION 1. Be it enacted by the General Assembly of the State of Ohio, That from and after the first day of June next. no black or mulatto person shall be permitted to settle or reside in this state, unless he or she shall first produce a fair certificate from some court within the United States, of his or her actual freedom, which certificate shall be attested by the clerk of said court, and the seal thereof annexed thereto, by said clerk.

SECTION 2. And be it further enacted, That every black or mulatto person residing within this state, on or before the fifth day of June, one thousand eight hundred and four, shall enter his or her name, together with the name or names of his or her children, in the clerk's office in the county in which he, she or they reside, which shall be entered on record by said clerk, and thereafter the clerk's certificate of such record shall be sufficient evidence of his, her or their freedom . . .

SECTION 3. And be it further enacted, That no person or persons residents of this state, shall be permitted to hire, or in any way employ any black or mulatto person, unless such black or mulatto person shall have one of the certificates as aforesaid . . .

SECTION 4. And be it further enacted, That if any person or persons shall harbour or secret any black or mulatto person, the property of any person whatever, or shall in any wise hinder or prevent the lawful owner or owners from retaking and possessing his or her black or mulatto servant or servants, shall, upon conviction thereof, by indictment or information, be fined in any sum not less than ten nor more than fifty dollars . . .

SECTION 5. And be it further enacted, That every black or mulatto person who shall come to reside in this state with such certificate as is required in the first section of this act, shall, within two years, have the same recorded in the clerk's office, in the county in which he or she means to reside . . .

SECTION 6. And be it further enacted, That in case any person or persons, his or their agent or agents, claiming any black or mulatto person that now are or hereafter may be in this state, may apply, upon making satisfactory proof that such black or mulatto person or persons is the property of him or her who applies, to any associate judge or justice of the peace within this state, the associate judge or justice is hereby empowered and required, by his precept, to direct the sheriff or constable to arrest such black or mulatto person or persons and deliver the same in the county or township where such officers shall reside . . .

the culprits. At such times when cases involving African Americans did go to court, they were heard by all-white juries before white judges. Because they also could not vote, African Americans had no legal means of protesting against the discriminatory black codes.

SIGNIFICANCE

Ohio's 1804 and 1807 black codes were enforced only infrequently, but they were laws on the books and as such were constant reminders that African Americans had only the barest minimum of human and civil rights in Ohio, and that those rights existed only at the whim of white society. Ohio's laws gradually fell into disuse and finally were repealed in 1849, long after the abolitionist movement, with its western center located in Oberlin, Ohio, was well under way, and long after the Underground Railroad had opened several stations in Ohio. After the Civil War (1861-1865) and the abolition of slavery throughout the United States, the former slave states of the South took up Ohio's earlier example by enacting even more severe black codes of their own in efforts to strip newly free slaves of their rights as American citizens.

—*Duncan R. Jamieson*

FURTHER READING

Bankston, Carl L., III, ed. *African American History*. 3 vols. Pasadena, Calif.: Salem Press, 2006. Encyclopedic work on all aspects of African American history, including the black codes.

Bell, Howard H. "Some Reform Interests of the Negro During the 1850's as Reflected in State Conventions." *Phylon* 21, no. 2 (1960): 173-181. Brief study of discriminatory laws that includes information on Ohio's black codes.

Erickson, Leonard. "Politics and the Repeal of Ohio's Black Laws, 1837-1849." *Ohio History* 82, nos. 3/4 (1973): 154-175. Discusses the movement to repeal Ohio's black codes beginning in the 1830's. Maps, tables, and notes.

Franklin, John Hope, and Alfred A. Moss, Jr. *From Slavery to Freedom*. 8th ed. Boston: McGraw-Hill, 2000. The standard history of African Americans, from the earliest days of slavery to the present.

Knepper, George W. *Ohio and Its People*. Kent, Ohio: Kent State University Press, 1989. A thorough history of Ohio, including a significant amount of material on African Americans.

Rasmussen, R. Kent. *Farewell to Jim Crow: The Rise and Fall of Segregation in America*. New York: Facts On File, 1997. Written for young adults, this brief but comprehensive history of segregation in U.S. history places Ohio's black codes in a broad perspective.

Rodabaugh, James H. "The Negro in the Old Northwest." In *Trek of the Immigrants: Essays Presented to Carl Wittke*. Rock Island, Ill.: Augustana College Library, 1964. Discusses the antislavery movement among the New Englanders who settled in the Western Reserve, and the work of the Underground Railroad in bringing escaped slaves into Ohio.

Wilson, Charles Jay. "The Negro in Early Ohio." *Ohio Archeological and Historical Quarterly* 39, no. 4 (1930). Now difficult to find, but the most complete analysis of Ohio's black codes.

SEE ALSO: Dec. 3, 1833: Oberlin College Opens; c. 1850-1860: Underground Railroad Flourishes; Nov. 24, 1865: Mississippi Enacts First Post-Civil War Black Code; Apr. 9, 1866: Civil Rights Act of 1866; Oct. 15, 1883: Civil Rights Cases.

RELATED ARTICLE in *Great Lives from History: The Nineteenth Century, 1801-1900:* Frederick Douglass.

May 14, 1804-September 23, 1806
LEWIS AND CLARK EXPEDITION

The first major transcontinental exploratory expedition in North America, the Lewis and Clark expedition, opened the Louisiana Territory to settlement and trade and reinforced U.S. claims to the Oregon region on the Pacific coast.

ALSO KNOWN AS: Corps of Discovery
LOCALE: Western United States
CATEGORIES: Exploration and discovery; geography

KEY FIGURES
Meriwether Lewis (1774-1809) and
William Clark (1770-1838), leaders of the expedition
Sacagawea (c. 1788-1812), Shoshone woman whose presence with the expedition facilitated the Rocky Mountain portage
George Drouillard (c. 1773-1810), hunter, sign language specialist, and interpreter for the expedition
Toussaint Charbonneau (b. c. 1759), French husband of Sacagawea and interpreter for the expedition
York (1770-1806), Clark's slave, whom Clark freed after the expedition

Thomas Jefferson (1743-1826), president of the United States, 1801-1809

SUMMARY OF EVENT
Meriwether Lewis, William Clark, and their companions were the first Europeans to cross the western half of what became the continental United States. They traveled through the future states of Missouri, Kansas, Nebraska, South Dakota, North Dakota, Montana, Idaho, Washington, and Oregon. Their two-year-long expedition was the concluding act in the long and fruitless search for a water route through the continent—a northwest passage—that had begun soon after Christopher Columbus discovered the New World at the end of the fifteenth century.

The instigator of the expedition was President Thomas Jefferson, who first thought of such an undertaking around the time that the United States achieved its independence in 1783. During the ensuing decade he twice tried unsuccessfully to launch a transcontinental exploring party. Not until he assumed the presidency in 1801, however, was he in a position to have his plan implemented. On January 18, 1803, the president asked Congress to authorize an appropriation of twenty-five hundred dollars to send a military expedition to explore the Missouri River up to its source in the Rocky Mountains, and then down the nearest westward-flowing streams to the Pacific Ocean. Jefferson gave two reasons for the proposed expedition: to prepare the way for the extension of the American fur trade to the Native American peoples throughout the area to be explored and to advance geographical knowledge of the continent.

When Jefferson sent his message to Congress, none of the territory that he proposed to explore lay within the United States. At that time, the immense region between the Mississippi River and the Rocky Mountains—all of which was collectively known as Louisiana—belonged to France. Parts of the Pacific Northwest were claimed by Great Britain, Spain, Russia, and the United States. While Jefferson was developing his plans for a transcontinental exploring

Meriwether Lewis (left) and William Clark (right).

LEWIS AND CLARK EXPEDITION, 1804-1806

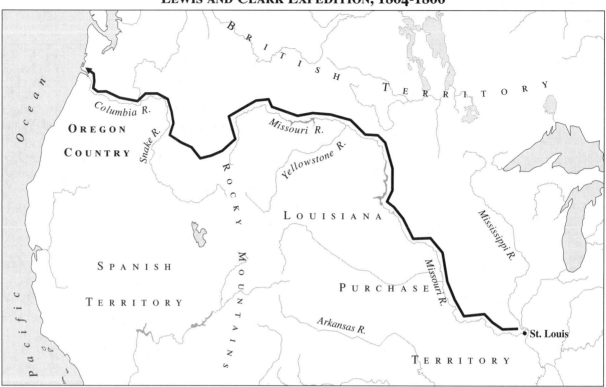

expedition, however, he also was overseeing negotiations with the French government of Napoleon Bonaparte. These talks resulted in the purchase of Louisiana from France through a treaty signed in May, 1803. Thus, by the time the expedition was finally launched, it not only explored U.S. territory but also strengthened the U.S. claim to the region beyond the Rocky Mountains.

To command the expedition, Jefferson chose his private secretary, Captain Meriwether Lewis. With Jefferson's approval, Lewis then invited his longtime friend William Clark to be his coleader. After making initial preparations in the East, Lewis traveled to Wood River, Illinois, opposite the mouth of the Missouri River. Clark and several recruits joined him on the way down the Ohio River. Lewis and Clark then spent the winter of 1803-1804 at Camp Wood River recruiting and training their men, gathering additional equipment and supplies— which included fourteen bales of trade goods—and collecting information about the Missouri River from traders and boatmen.

The expedition party eventually included twenty-seven young, unmarried soldiers; a mixed-blood hunter and interpreter named George Drouillard; Clark's black slave, York; and Lewis's big Newfoundland dog, Scammon. An additional body comprising an army corporal, five privates, and several French boatmen was to accompany the main expedition party through its first season and then return down the Missouri River with the expedition's records, sketches, and scientific specimens.

Officially known as the Corps of Discovery, the expedition began its historic journey at the confluence of the Missouri and Mississippi Rivers. On May 14, 1804, it started traveling up the Missouri River in a fifty-five-foot keelboat and two dugout canoes. The expedition reached the villages of the Mandan and Minnataree people, near the mouth of the Knife River in the future state of North Dakota, at the end of October after traveling about 1,600 miles (2,575 kilometers). There the explorers built a log stronghold called Fort Mandan and went into winter quarters.

During the long, frigid winter that followed, Lewis and Clark made copious notes in their journals, drew maps of their route, and met with numerous Native American visitors. From the Minnatarees, especially, they obtained invaluable information about the course of the Missouri River and the country through which it ran.

The contributions of these and other Native Americans to the success of the exploration cannot be overstated. Finally, on April 7, 1805, the expedition resumed its journey. The party now numbered only thirty-three persons. In addition to the permanent detachment, the party included the French interpreter Toussaint Charbonneau; his young Shoshone wife, Sacagawea; and their two-month-old son, Jean Baptiste, who was nicknamed Pompey. After passing through country never before visited by Europeans, the expedition reached the navigable limits of the Missouri River on August 17.

With Sacagawea's help, Lewis and Clark purchased horses from her brother Cameahwai of the Shoshone people and began their journey through the Rocky

---

JEFFERSON'S INSTRUCTIONS TO LEWIS AND CLARK

Excerpts from Thomas Jefferson's letter of June 20, 1803, to Meriwether Lewis regarding the exploratory expedition that Lewis was about to undertake with William Clark.

Instruments for ascertaining, by celestial observations, the geography of the country through which you will pass, have already been provided. Light articles for barter and presents among the Indians, arms for your attendants, say from ten to twelve men, boats, tents, and other traveling apparatus, with ammunition, medicine, surgical instruments and provisions, you will have prepared. . . .

The object of your mission is to explore the Missouri River, and such principal streams of it, as, by its course and communication with the waters of the Pacific Ocean, whether the Columbia, Oregan [*sic*], Colrado [*sic*], or any other river, may offer the most direct and practible water-communication across the continent, for the purposes of commerce. . . .

The commerce which may be carried on with the people inhabiting the line you will pursue, renders a knowledge of those people important. You will therefore endeavour to make yourself acquainted, as far as a diligent pursuit of your journey shall admit, with the names of the nations and their numbers:

The extent and limits of their possessions;

Their relations with other tribes or natins [*sic*];

Their language, traditions, monuments;

Their ordinary occupations in agriculture, fishing, hunting, war, arts, and the implements for these;

Their food, clothing, and domestic accommodations:

The diseases prevalent among them, and the remedies they use;

Moral and physical circumstances which distinguish them from the tribes we know;

Peculiarities in their laws, customs, and dispositions;

And articles of commerce they may need or furnish, and to what extent.

And, considering the interest which every nation has in extending and strengthening the authority of reason and justice among the people around them, it will be useful to acquire what knowledge you can of the state of morality, religion, and information amoung them; as it may better enable those who may endeavour to civilize and instruct them, to adapt their measures to the existing notions and practices of those on whom they are to operate.

Other objects worthy of notice will be;

The soil and face of the country, its growth and vegetable productions, especially those not of the United States;

The animals of the country generally, and expecially those not known in the United States

The remains and accounts of any which may be deemed rare or extinct;

The mineral productions of every kind, but more particularly metals, lime-stone, pit-coal, and saltpetre; salines and mineral waters, noting the temperature of the last, and such circumstances as may indicate their character;

Volcanic appearances;

Climate, as characterized by the thermometer, by the proportion of rainy, cloudy, and clear days; by lightning, hail, snow, ice; by the access and recess of frost; by the winds prevailing at different seasons; the dates at which particular plants put forth, or lose their flower or leaf; times of appearance of particular birds, reptiles or insects.

Mountains. Three years earlier, Sacagawea had been captured by a Minnataree raiding party, which carried her east to the prairie, where Charbonneau had purchased her for his wife. The chance meeting of Sacagawea and her brother, who had become the chief of their clan, was a convenient opportunity for the expedition. Along with the horses, Lewis and Clark were given travel instructions and lent a guide, called Toby, to assist them through the mountains. After crossing the mountains, the explorers descended the Clearwater, Snake, and Columbia Rivers to the Pacific Ocean, where they arrived in mid-November.

After a dreary winter at Fort Clatsop, south of the Columbia River, the explorers started for home on March 23, 1806. Other than fighting to keep warm and searching for food, the highlight of their Pacific coast stay was a visit to the remains of a beached whale, from which they obtained 300 pounds (136 kilograms) of blubber and oil. They were anxious to return east, as they saw the sun only on six days during their stay at Fort Clatsop.

On their return journey, the party divided temporarily. Lewis and a small party explored the Marias River, while Clark and the rest of the expedition descended the Yellowstone River. The entire expedition reunited below the mouth of the Yellowstone, then hurried down the Missouri and arrived in St. Louis on September 23, 1806.

SIGNIFICANCE

The Lewis and Clark expedition accomplished its mission with remarkable success. During more than twenty-eight months, it traveled more than 8,000 miles (12,875 kilometers). During the entire journey, only one man, Sergeant Charles Floyd, lost his life—apparently from a ruptured appendix. Although the explorers met thousands of Native Americans, they had only one violent encounter with them. That incident occurred while Lewis was high up the Marias River and resulted in the death of two Piegan members of the Blackfoot Confederacy.

The total expense of the undertaking, including the special congressional appropriation of $2,500, was $38,722.25. Charbonneau collected $500.33 for his and Sacagawea's services. For this comparatively small cost to the federal government, Lewis and Clark and their companions took the first giant step in opening the West to the American people.

—*John L. Loos, updated by Russell Hively*

FURTHER READING

Ambrose, Stephen E. *Undaunted Courage: Meriwether Lewis, Thomas Jefferson, and the Opening of the American West*. New York: Simon & Schuster, 1996. Best-selling account by a prominent historian who retraced the expedition's route to the Pacific and painstakingly re-created the activities and discoveries of the journey.

Biddle, Nicholas, and Paul Allen, eds. *History of the Expedition Under the Command of Captains Lewis and Clark*. 2 vols. Philadelphia: J. B. Lippincott, 1961. Prepared between 1810 and 1814 by Nicholas Biddle, a young Philadelphia lawyer, this work is based on both Lewis's and Clark's journals.

De Voto, Bernard, ed. *The Journals of Lewis and Clark*. Boston: Houghton Mifflin, 1953. A one-volume condensation of the *Original Journals of Lewis and Clark Expedition*. Includes maps.

Jones, Landon Y. *William Clark and the Shaping of the West*. New York: Hill & Wang, 2004. Focuses on Clark's private life and public career in the thirty years following his expedition with Lewis. Includes discussions of Clark's duties in the Kentucky militia, his service as governor of the Missouri Territory, and his role as superintendent of Indian affairs at St. Louis.

McGrath, Patrick. *The Lewis and Clark Expedition*. Morristown, N.J.: Silver Burdett, 1985. A simple but complete telling of the Lewis and Clark adventure for younger readers.

Ronda, James P. *Lewis and Clark Among the Indians*. Lincoln: University of Nebraska Press, 1984. An important and engaging ethnohistorical study, this work chronicles the daily contact between the explorers and Indians and shows that the expedition initiated important economic and diplomatic relations with them.

Slaughter, Thomas P. *Exploring Lewis and Clark: Reflections on Men and Wilderness*. New York: Random House, 2003. A revisionist view of the expedition in which Slaughter attempts to correct the myths and legends that he believes have surrounded it.

Tourtellot, Jonathan B., ed. "Meriwether Lewis/William Clark." In *Into the Unknown: The Story of Exploration*. Washington, D.C.: National Geographic Society, 1987. A thirty-four-page chapter devoted to the Lewis and Clark expedition.

SEE ALSO: May 9, 1803: Louisiana Purchase; July 15, 1806-July 1, 1807: Pike Explores the American Southwest; Apr. 6, 1808: American Fur Company Is Chartered; Sept. 8, 1810-May, 1812: Astorian Expeditions Explore the Pacific Northwest Coast; c. 1815-1830: Westward American Migration Begins; Feb.

22, 1819: Adams-Onís Treaty Gives the United States Florida; 1822-1831: Jedediah Smith Explores the Far West; June 15, 1846: United States Acquires Oregon Territory; 1879: Powell Publishes His Report on the American West.

RELATED ARTICLES in *Great Lives from History: The Nineteenth Century, 1801-1900:* Meriwether Lewis and William Clark; Zebulon Pike; Sacagawea; Jedediah Smith; David Thompson.

1800's

September 25, 1804
TWELFTH AMENDMENT IS RATIFIED

The Twelfth Amendment to the U.S. Constitution simplified the procedures for electing the president and vice president and helped to avert repetitions of the potentially disruptive confusion that had occurred in the previous two presidential elections.

LOCALE: Washington, D.C.
CATEGORIES: Laws, acts, and legal history; government and politics

KEY FIGURES
John Adams (1735-1826), president of the United States, 1797-1801
Aaron Burr (1756-1836), third vice president of the United States, 1801-1805
Thomas Jefferson (1743-1826), president of the United States, 1801-1809
James Madison (1751-1836), secretary of state in 1804 and later president, 1809-1817
Thomas Pinckney (1750-1828), unsuccessful candidate for vice president in 1796
John Taylor (1753-1824), senator from Virginia who advocated the Twelfth Amendment

SUMMARY OF EVENT
The Twelfth Amendment to the U.S. Constitution was necessitated by a basic flaw in the original document. Article II, section 1, clause 3 of the Constitution had established a complicated and confusing procedure for electing presidents and vice presidents. That procedure required elections to be determined by votes of an electoral college made up of electors from each of the states, each of which was entitled to the same number of electors as it had representatives in Congress. Appointed in whatever manner the individual state legislatures chose, the electors were to vote for two persons, presumably one for president and the other for vice president; however, the ballots were not so labeled. The candidate receiving the highest number of votes—provided that the number constitute a majority of the electoral votes—was

elected president. The candidate with the next highest number of votes was elected vice president.

In elections contested by more than two major candidates for either the presidency or the vice presidency, it was possible that none of the candidates would receive a clear majority of the electoral vote. In such situations, the House of Representatives was to elect the president from among the five candidates receiving the most votes. Two-thirds of the members constituted a quorum for this purpose, and each state was to have a single vote—a measure designed to ensure that the smaller states had equal weight. A simple majority vote in the House was required for election. If the same situation occurred in the vice presidential election, the Senate was to elect the vice president from the top two vote-getters by a majority vote. One vote was to be allowed for each senator, and a quorum was to be two-thirds of the Senate. If the president-elect were to die or become disabled between the time of the popular election and the determination of the electoral vote, the vice president-elect was to become president. This procedure was similar to that applying to presidents who died during their terms of office.

When the Constitution was written, it was presumed that many worthy candidates would receive electoral votes and that seldom, if ever, would any candidate receive a majority of the electoral vote. Thus, the electoral college was, in effect, intended to serve only as a nominating procedure to provide up to five good candidates for consideration by the House of Representatives. The Framers of the Constitution did not anticipate the development of political parties, which began forming in the 1790's. The election of 1796 found Federalist John Adams of Massachusetts opposed by Republican Thomas Jefferson of Virginia. Adams won the election, but his running mate, Thomas Pinckney of South Carolina, finished in third place, nine votes behind Jefferson, so Jefferson became vice president. That unusual election resulted in a situation in which rival presidential candidates representing different political parties were

THE TWELFTH AMENDMENT TO THE U.S. CONSTITUTION

The Electors shall meet in their respective states, and vote by ballot for President and Vice President, one of whom, at least, shall not be an inhabitant of the same state with themselves; they shall name in their ballots the person voted for as President, and in distinct ballots the person voted for as Vice-President, and they shall make distinct lists of all persons voted for as President, and of all persons voted for as Vice-President, and of the number of votes for each, which lists they shall sign and certify, and transmit sealed to the seat of the government of the United States, directed to the President of the Senate;—The President of the Senate shall, in the presence of the Senate and House of Representatives, open all the certificates and the votes shall then be counted;—The person having the greatest number of votes for President, shall be the President, if such number be a majority of the whole number of Electors appointed; and if no person have such majority, then from the persons having the highest numbers not exceeding three on the list of those voted for as President, the House of Representatives shall choose immediately, by ballot, the President. But in choosing the President, the votes shall be taken by states, the representation from each state having one vote; a quorum for this purpose shall consist of a member or members from two-thirds of the states, and a majority of all the states shall be necessary to a choice. And if the House of Representatives shall not choose a President whenever the right of choice shall devolve upon them, before the fourth day of March next following, then the Vice-President shall act as President, as in the case of the death or other constitutional disability of the President.—The person having the greatest number of votes as Vice-President, shall be the Vice-President, if such number be a majority of the whole number of Electors appointed, and if no person have a majority, then from the two highest numbers on the list, the Senate shall choose the Vice-President; a quorum for the purpose shall consist of two-thirds of the whole number of Senators, and a majority of the whole number shall be necessary to a choice. But no person constitutionally ineligible to the office of President shall be eligible to that of Vice-President of the United States.

finally tipped the scales in favor of Jefferson. In the prolonged voting that took place in the House of Representatives, Jefferson was finally elected on the thirty-sixth ballot on a date dangerously close to inauguration day.

The odd results of the elections of 1796 and 1800 brought forth a demand for a fundamental change in the electoral system. Congressman John Taylor and other Jeffersonian Republicans prepared a series of resolutions suggesting an appropriate amendment to the Constitution. Their resolutions were introduced into Congress, where support from several states was immediately evident.

The only major objection to changes in the electoral college came from smaller states and from the Federalists. Representatives from the smaller states feared that their states' role in the presidential elections might be diminished if the electoral college were abandoned. The Federalists merely hoped to disrupt or confuse the election of 1804. After much debate, agreement was finally reached in Congress in December of 1803. An amendment was written and sent to the states for ratification. Within a year, the necessary number of states, thirteen out of seventeen, had ratified the amendment. On September 25, 1804, Secretary of State James Madison announced the adoption of the Twelfth Amendment in time for the election of 1804.

forced to serve four years together as president and vice president.

A different, but equally awkward, result came out of the electoral balloting in the 1800 presidential election. In that contest, Jefferson and his vice presidential running mate, Aaron Burr of New York, received the same number of votes. This election went into the House of Representatives, where Federalist opposition to Jefferson was strong. Although it was common knowledge that the electors who voted for Jefferson and Burr intended to place Jefferson in the top position, many die-hard Federalists were determined to thwart their intentions by putting Burr into the presidency. Moderate Federalists, influenced by Burr's home-state rival Alexander Hamilton,

SIGNIFICANCE

Although the Twelfth Amendment did not abolish the electoral college or radically change the method of electing the president and vice president, it did remedy some basic defects. Separate ballots were provided for the election of president and vice president, thus preventing the bizarre result of 1796. Provision was also made for the vice president to take over as acting president if the House should delay too long in selecting a president—something that almost occurred after the election of 1800.

In situations in which no candidate received a majority vote in the electoral college, the House of Representatives was to choose a president from the three candidates who received the most votes, rather than from among five. Equality among the states was maintained when presidential or vice presidential elections went into the House or the Senate. Since then, three presidents have been elected despite receiving fewer popular votes than their opponents. In the first instance, in 1876, Rutherford B. Hayes assumed the presidency after an election so close that ballots from at least four states were in dispute. A special commission was set up to decide the outcome. The second time, in 1888, Grover Cleveland had a majority of the vote but lost the presidency to Benjamin Harrison. The third instance occurred in 2000, when the U.S. Supreme Court intervened in favor of Republican candidate George W. Bush before charges of voting irregularities in Florida could be resolved.

Since the early nineteenth century, discussions about amending the Twelfth Amendment to prevent candidates who receive majority popular votes from losing the electoral vote have periodically arisen. The most common proposal is to have the electoral vote be counted in proportion to the popular vote. For example, if there were two candidates for president and a state had ten electoral votes, the candidate receiving 60 percent of the popular vote in the state would receive six electoral votes, and the candidate receiving 40 percent of the popular vote would receive four electoral votes.

—*Edward J. Maguire, updated by Susan M. Taylor*

FURTHER READING

Dershowitz, Alan M. *Supreme Injustice: How the High Court Hijacked Election 2000*. New York: Oxford University Press, 2001. Critical analysis by a distinguished legal authority on the Supreme Court's role in the 2000 presidential election, with close attention to the constitutional basis of U.S. election law.

Hockett, Homer C. *The Constitutional History of the United States*. Vol. 1. New York: Macmillan, 1939. Contains pertinent information regarding the demand for and the adoption of the Twelfth Amendment.

Holder, Angela Roddey. *The Meaning of the Constitution*. New York: Barron's, 1987. Provides concise, comprehensive explanations of the significance of the words and clauses of the Constitution. Includes a good working bibliography.

Kuroda, Tadahisa. *The Origins of the Twelfth Amendment: The Electoral College in the Early Republic, 1787-1804*. Westport, Conn.: Greenwood Press, 1994. Outlines the election history of the United States and argues the need for a change in the electoral college.

Luttbeg, Norman R. *American Electoral Behavior, 1952-1992*. 2d ed. Itasca, Ill.: F. E. Peacock, 1995. Contrasts more recent electoral behavior with past electoral behavior. Includes some discussion of a possible amendment to the Twelfth Amendment.

Posner, Richard A. *Breaking the Deadlock: The 2000 Election, the Constitution, and the Courts*. Princeton, N.J.: Princeton University Press, 2001. Study by a legal scholar and federal judge of the Constitution and U.S. election law, with special attention on the 2000 presidential election.

Roseboom, Eugene H. *A Short History of Presidential Elections*. New York: Collier Books, 1967. Provides a brief account of the presidential elections from George Washington to Lyndon Johnson and explains the need for the Twelfth Amendment.

Rule, Wilma, and Joseph Zimmerman. *Electoral Systems in Comparative Perspective: Their Impact on Women and Minorities*. Westport, Conn.: Greenwood Press, 1994. Discusses elections and cross-cultural studies of the need for change.

Wright, Russell O. *Presidential Elections in the United States: A Statistical History, 1860-1992*. Jefferson, N.C.: McFarland, 1995. Discusses the history of the elections process and provides some interesting statistics.

SEE ALSO: Feb. 17, 1801: House of Representatives Elects Jefferson President; Dec. 1, 1824-Feb. 9, 1825: U.S. Election of 1824; Dec. 3, 1828: U.S. Election of 1828; Dec. 2, 1840: U.S. Election of 1840; Nov. 6, 1860: Lincoln Is Elected U.S. President; Mar. 5, 1877: Hayes Becomes President; Nov. 4, 1884: U.S. Election of 1884; Nov. 3, 1896: McKinley Is Elected President.

RELATED ARTICLES in *Great Lives from History: The Nineteenth Century, 1801-1900:* Aaron Burr; Benjamin Harrison; Rutherford B. Hayes.

December 2, 1804
BONAPARTE IS CROWNED NAPOLEON I

Napoleon Bonaparte's coronation as emperor of France marked a fundamental symbolic break with the republican and egalitarian forces of revolution that had brought him to power, while visibly confirming his absolute control of France.

ALSO KNOWN AS: France's First Empire
LOCALE: Paris, France
CATEGORY: Government and politics

KEY FIGURES
Napoleon I (Napoleon Bonaparte; 1769-1821), French first consul, 1799-1804, and emperor, r. 1804-1814, 1815
Emmanuel-Joseph Sieyès (1748-1836), French legislator, 1795-1814, consul, 1799-1804, and imperial count, 1808-1814
Joséphine (1763-1814), wife of Napoleon and empress of France
Letizia Bonaparte (1750-1836), mother of Napoleon, later titled Madame Mère
Lucien Bonaparte (1775-1840), brother of Napoleon
Duc d'Enghien (Louis Antoine Henri de Condé; 1772-1804), cousin of the late King Louis XVI
Pius VII (Barnaba Gregorio Chiaramonti; 1742-1823), Roman Catholic pope, 1800-1823

SUMMARY OF EVENT
The coronation of Napoleon Bonaparte as French emperor Napoleon I on December 2, 1804, marked the official beginning of France's First Empire; however, the actual establishment of his regime dated from the coup d'état of November 9, 1799 (commonly referred to as 18 Brumaire, the date according to the revolutionary calendar). In that coup, a group of conspirators including Napoleon, Lucien Bonaparte, Emmanuel-Joseph Sieyès, and Talleyrand had overthrown the Directory (the executive body of the nation). Within a month, a consulate had been established. Under the Constitution of Year VIII, Napoleon Bonaparte was named first consul and, in effect, given dictatorial powers for ten years.

This constitution, originally a complicated system of checks and balances, was the work of the political theorist Sieyès. It was altered by Bonaparte to concentrate far-reaching powers in the office of first consul, while maintaining the trappings of republicanism. After some disagreements and political maneuvering, Sieyès and his fellow consul, Pierre-Roger Ducos, retired to the senate.

They were replaced by Jean-Jacques-Régis de Cambacérès and Charles François Lebrun, second and third consuls who had very limited responsibilities.

Bonaparte made much of the fact that the new constitution restored universal manhood suffrage. All male citizens age twenty-one or above did have the right to vote if they met the residence requirement, but there was no direct representation in either of the two houses of the legislature, whose members were chosen by the first consul from national lists. The electorate voted only for candidates whose names would be put on such lists. Thus Napoleon, who had once declared that "a constitution should be short and obscure," controlled the legislature to a large extent. Coupled with the executive powers he possessed as first consul, he virtually consolidated all power in his own person. In February, 1800, a majority of nearly three million voters accepted the new government, endorsing Napoleon's usurpation of power.

During the first years of the Consulate, Bonaparte used his power to solve five major problems facing France. Through a combination of concessions and toughness, he put an end to a civil war in the conservative Vendée region that had been raging with varying intensity since early in 1793. Freedom of worship was restored, and royalists were encouraged to make their peace with the government. To eliminate factionalism, Napoleon invited able men of all political persuasions to join the consular civil service, and a number of former monarchists, Girondins, and Jacobins accepted. Napoleon's second Italian campaign destroyed the Second Coalition at the Battle of Marengo (June 14, 1800) and led to the Treaty of Lunéville in 1801. There followed the Treaty of Amiens with Great Britain in 1802. For the first time in nine years, France was at peace with all other nations.

During the summer of 1801, Napoleon signed a concordat with Pope Pius VII. The agreement ended the breach that had been initiated by the revolutionary government's nationalization of lands belonging to the Roman Catholic Church in 1789 and that had continued with the adoption of the Civil Constitution of the Clergy in 1791. Although probably a Deist or even an agnostic himself, Napoleon recognized the centrality of the Catholic faith to the majority of France's peasant farmers, who had never accepted the Jacobin cult of reason.

France's financial problems, which had been a major cause of the revolution, were also put in better order, partly through the elimination of corruption in government contracts (which had been widespread during the Directory), the establishment of the Bank of France, and the appointment of more competent officials to oversee the Treasury. Law and order were restored at both local and national levels, and a recodification of the Civil Code—renamed the Napoleonic Code (*Code Napoléon*) in 1807—was initiated in 1801.

These measures seemed to justify the trust and power that the vast majority of French people had placed in their first consul. To them, Napoleon had become the man who had built peace and harmony out of revolutionary chaos. His popularity grew, and in August, 1802, an overwhelming majority of French citizens voted to offer him the title of first consul for life with the power to nominate his successor. In May of 1804, despite a renewal of war with Great Britain, the senate voted to give Napoleon the title of emperor and to establish the succession to the throne through the male line of the Bonaparte family.

In the so-called Opera Plot of 1800, a wagon full of explosives was set off prematurely when Napoleon and Joséphine Bonaparte were on their way to the opera to hear Joseph Haydn's *The Creation*. Napoleon used the incident as an excuse to eliminate the remains of the Jacobin faction, although the police determined that it was actually the work of Royalists subsidized by the British government. Napoleon had attempted to neutralize the Royalist opposition by granting an amnesty to all but approximately one thousand émigrés who would settle for nothing less than a Bourbon restoration. Convinced by information from Joseph Fouché, the minister of police, that a Bourbon prince was at the heart of the conspiracy, Napoleon authorized the kidnapping from Baden and execution by firing squad of the duc d'Enghien, a cousin of Louis XVI. The execution, achieved in March of 1804, shocked Europe, because Enghien apparently had nothing to do with plots to assassinate Bonaparte. Despite public condemnation, Napoleon remained determined to establish a hereditary monarchy, and the overall success of his domestic and foreign policies seemed to prove that an empire would fulfill the needs of France.

Events surrounding the coronation were a curious mixture of dignity and farce. The site was moved from the Hôtel des Invalides to Notre-Dame de Paris to accommodate the crowds and the large number of participants. The pope agreed to participate in the ceremony and that Napoleon would crown himself and Joséphine, but he refused to recognize the Bonapartes' civil marriage, insisting they must first be remarried according to the rites of the Roman Catholic Church.

Napoleon's brothers Lucien and Jérôme were not present at the coronation, because each had married a woman whom their brother considered unsuitable. Letizia Bonaparte deliberately remained in Italy with Lucien, attempting to effect a reconciliation between him and Napoleon. Hurt and annoyed, Napoleon ordered that his formidable mother be included in the official coronation painting by Jaques-Louis David. While his brothers sulked, Napoleon's sisters Elisa, Pauline, and Caroline quarreled over their titles and about having to help bear the train of their hated sister-in-law. Amazingly, the ceremony took place without serious incident.

SIGNIFICANCE

Although personally of simple tastes, Napoleon viewed elaborate ceremonials and titles as means of binding sub-

Napoleon crowning Josephine empress immediately after he was crowned emperor of France. (The S. S. McClure Company)

ordinates to his regime. Perhaps he also hoped that the creation of a monarchical system would make him more acceptable to the monarchs whose armies he had so often defeated. This reasoning was mistaken. Napoleon had underestimated the damage to his reputation resulting from Enghien's execution. Europe's hereditary kings and emperors continued to regard Napoleon as an upstart and a product of revolution.

In the decade to come, the emperor's actions would largely confirm Europe's opinion of him. Having achieved absolute power in France, the only logical next step as far as Napoleon was concerned was to extend his power to cover the continent. He began a series of wars of imperial conquest that, despite his eventual defeat, would permanently alter the map of Europe.

—*John G. Gallaher, updated by Dorothy T. Potter*

FURTHER READING

Bonaparte, Napoleon. *Napoleon on Napoleon: An Autobiography of the Emperor*. Edited by Somerset de Chair. London: Cassell, 1992. Edited from Napoleon's various autobiographical writings, this work provides the emperor's account of events leading up to his coronation, particularly the Enghien incident.

Holtman, Robert B. *The Napoleonic Revolution*. Philadelphia: J. B. Lippincott, 1967. Emphasizes Napoleon's innovations in a number of specific areas, including the law, education, religion, and nationalism, as well as his military achievements.

Johnson, Paul. *Napoleon*. New York: Viking Press, 2002. Concise biography, providing an overview of Napoleon's life and career. Johnson portrays Napoleon as an opportunist, whose militarism and style of governance planted the seeds for warfare and totalitarianism in the twentieth century.

Lefebvre, Georges. *Napoleon: From 18 Brumaire to Tilsit, 1799-1807*. Translated by Henry F. Stockhold. New York: Columbia University Press, 1969. Lefebvre considers Napoleon's rule to have been a logical result of the events of the French Revolution. Creation of an empire did not consolidate Napoleon's power but rather (in Lefebvre's view) widened the gulf between the emperor and the nation.

Markham, Felix. *The Bonapartes*. New York: Taplinger, 1975. Describes the complex and frequently stormy relations among the Bonapartes, a family in which the women, particularly Napoleon's mother Letizia and his wife Joséphine, played more meaningful parts than did several of his brothers.

_____. *Napoleon*. New York: New American Library, 1964. Provides a succinct and balanced account of the emperor's private and public lives.

Méneval, Claude-François. *Napoleon: An Intimate Account of the Years of Supremacy, 1800-1814*. Edited by Proctor Jones, with assistance by Charles-Otto Zieseniss. New York: Random House, 1992. Drawn from the memoirs of Napoleon's secretary, the Baron de Méneval, and his valet Constant, this lavishly illustrated book pays particular attention to the personal aspects of life at the consular and later imperial court.

Schom, Alan. *Napoleon Bonaparte*. New York: Harper-Collins, 1997. Scholarly, detailed biography covering all facets of Napoleon's life and career. Schom is unusually candid about his subject's character flaws and failures.

Van Deusen, Glyndon G. *Sieyès: His Life and His Nationalism*. Reprint. New York: AMS Press, 1968. Focuses on Sieyès's intellectual contributions to the revolutionary process and his motivation for helping to bring Napoleon to power.

SEE ALSO: Oct. 21, 1805: Battle of Trafalgar; May 2, 1808-Nov., 1813: Peninsular War in Spain; June 23-Dec. 14, 1812: Napoleon Invades Russia; Apr. 11, 1814-July 29, 1830: France's Bourbon Dynasty Is Restored; Sept. 15, 1814-June 11, 1815: Congress of Vienna; June 18, 1815: Battle of Waterloo; Nov. 20, 1815: Second Peace of Paris; Dec. 2, 1852: Louis Napoleon Bonaparte Becomes Emperor of France; Feb. 13, 1871-1875: Third French Republic Is Established.

RELATED ARTICLES in *Great Lives from History: The Nineteenth Century, 1801-1900:* Jacques-Louis David; Joséphine; Napoleon I; Napoleon III.

March, 1805-September 1, 1807
BURR'S CONSPIRACY

In one of the least understood events in early American national history, Aaron Burr plotted to invade Mexico and detach the Mississippi Valley from the United States. His challenge to the territorial integrity of the new Union failed, but from it emerged a Supreme Court decision that mere intent cannot in itself be considered treasonous.

LOCALE: Ohio and Mississippi Valleys
CATEGORIES: Government and politics; wars, uprisings, and civil unrest; crime and scandals

KEY FIGURES

Aaron Burr (1756-1836), vice president of the United States, 1801-1805

Theodosia Burr Alston (1783-1813), Burr's daughter and only confidant

Harman Blennerhassett (1765-1831), Irish immigrant who supported Burr's expeditionary force

Andrew Jackson (1767-1845), major general of Tennessee militia and later president of the United States, 1829-1837

Thomas Jefferson (1743-1826), president of the United States, 1801-1809

John Marshall (1755-1835), chief justice of the United States, 1801-1835, who presided over Burr's trial

Marqués de Casa Yrujo (Carlos Martínez de Yrujo y Tacón; 1763-1824), Spanish minister to the United States, 1796-1806

Anthony Merry (1756-1835), British minister to the United States from whom Burr solicited financial and military assistance

James Wilkinson (1757-1825), commanding general of the U.S. Army and Burr's coconspirator

SUMMARY OF EVENT

From 1804 through 1806, Aaron Burr promoted, organized, and led an expedition into the Mississippi Valley. Although his purpose remains unclear, he may have intended to invade Spanish Mexico, detach several western states from the union, colonize in what is now northwestern Louisiana, or some combination of these goals. In addition, he was accused of plotting to overthrow the U.S. government and seize Washington, D.C.

Burr had been prominent in the American Revolution (1775-1783) and was a generally successful politician noted for ambition, elegance, womanizing, and opportunism. After he was rejected for a second term as vice president by Thomas Jefferson and the Republicans, he was defeated in a bid for governor of New York in 1804. Shortly thereafter, James Wilkinson, commanding general of the Army, requested a visit and surreptitiously spent the night at Burr's residence. What transpired is unclear, but it is thought they laid plans to conquer Texas and northern Mexico, and may have discussed separating the western lands from the United States.

Angered by Alexander Hamilton's derogatory personal remarks during the gubernatorial campaign, Burr challenged Hamilton to a duel and killed him on July 11, 1804. The election and duel effectively terminated Burr's political career. To escape arrest, Burr fled to Philadelphia, where he met Charles Williamson, an old friend and a British agent. He discussed his western plans with Williamson, who presented them to Anthony Merry, the British minister to the United States. Merry forwarded Burr's plan to detach the western states and invade Mexico to his superiors in London, who were uninterested. Many historians believe Burr also met Wilkinson in Philadelphia and, at that time, concocted his conspiracy. Wilkinson's presence in Philadelphia, however, is unverified in public accounts. Burr resumed his vice presidential duties on November 4, 1804, in spite of outstanding indictments for murder in New York and New Jersey. Apparently furthering his plans, Burr influenced Jefferson to appoint Wilkinson governor of the northern part of the District of Louisiana at St. Louis.

On March 2, 1805, Burr withdrew from the Senate. He then met with Merry and offered to detach Louisiana (at that time, the huge region extending from the Great Lakes to the Gulf of Mexico, bordered on the east by the Mississippi River and on the west by the Great Plains) from the United States. His price for doing so would be one-half million dollars and British naval support in the Gulf of Mexico. Merry again wrote to his superiors on March 29, but received no response.

On April 23, Burr set out for Pittsburgh and the Ohio and Mississippi Valleys, seeking support and widely discussing his various plans. On his way down the Ohio River, he visited the estate of Harman Blennerhassett, a wealthy and idealistic Irish expatriate, who subsequently became one of Burr's principal supporters. He also met twice with Andrew Jackson, who commanded the Tennessee militia at Nashville, enlisting his support for a campaign against the Spanish lands. He conferred with Wilkinson at Fort Massac, just below the junction of the

Cumberland and Ohio Rivers, on June 6 and probably refined the plan to invade Mexico. In New Orleans, he contacted the Mexican Associates, a group of Creoles and the bishop of New Orleans, securing encouragement for an expedition against Mexico. On his return trip, Burr spent several days with Wilkinson in St. Louis in September, 1805, and apparently made more detailed plans for invading Mexico.

After returning to Washington in November, 1805, Burr and his associates unsuccessfully sought aid from the Marqués de Casa Yrujo, the Spanish minister to the United States, to dismember the union and establish an independent western confederacy. In July, 1806, Burr purchased the Bastrop lands, about four hundred thousand acres on the Washita River in northwestern Louisiana. He then went west again to recruit volunteers and support for a military expedition down the Mississippi River, which he planned for late fall.

As Burr was developing his plans, President Jefferson ignored the detailed reports he was receiving of Burr's activities. Nevertheless, on November 4, Burr was brought before a grand jury in Frankfort, Kentucky, charged with preparing a military expedition against Mexico but was declared innocent the next day. In the meantime, Harman Blennerhassett converted his island estate on the Ohio River opposite what is now Parkers-burg, West Virginia, into a supply depot and rendezvous site for Burr's recruits. This activity attracted the attention of the governor of Ohio, who sent the state militia to seize the island and most of Blennerhassett's supplies on December 5. Meanwhile, Burr went to Nashville, reassured Andrew Jackson, obtained boats from Jackson, and rejoined his group at the mouth of the Cumberland River on December 27. Accompanied by about sixty men on December 29, he appeared below Fort Massac, explaining that his purpose was to colonize the Bastrop lands that he had legally purchased.

Meanwhile, Wilkinson apparently lost confidence in Burr's plan and informed Jefferson of the scheme to dismember the United States. Wilkinson also sent Jefferson a "cipher letter," purportedly from Burr, detailing Burr's plans. He also declared martial law in Louisiana and arrested some of Burr's associates. Jefferson then ordered the arrest of anyone conspiring to attack Spanish territory. Learning of the president's order at Natchez, Burr attempted to flee to Spanish Florida. He was arrested near Mobile, brought to Richmond, Virginia, and arraigned on charges of treason for attempting to dismember the union and of the misdemeanor of organizing an expedition against Spanish territory.

Chief Justice John Marshall, who presided over Burr's subsequent trial, interpreted the U.S. Constitution

Dispersal of Burr's expedition. (C. A. Nichols & Company)

narrowly, ruling that the mere expression of intent to divide the union did not constitute an overt act of treason. Government witnesses, some of whom were successfully contradicted, and the "cipher letter" failed to demonstrate overt acts of treason by Burr, so Marshall dismissed the treason charge against Burr. The government was unable to prove that Burr's expedition had been military or had been directed against Spanish territory, so the misdemeanor charge was dropped as well.

After his release, Burr spent four years in Europe lobbying the British and French governments to support his Mexican plans. After returning to the United States, he practiced law in New York. Wilkinson was investigated by Congress and court-martialed by the army but was cleared and retained his command.

SIGNIFICANCE

Although Burr discussed his plans with hundreds of people, the true story of his conspiracy remains controversial. Until his death, he continued to promote diverse settlement schemes and expeditions into Spanish and Mexican territory. Documents relating to his plans that have survived are wildly contradictory, unreliable, and incomplete. His daughter, Theodosia Burr Alston, the only person whom he fully trusted, was lost at sea with a large collection of his papers in 1813. Burr willed his other personal papers to Matthew L. Davis, a politician, journalist, and friend, but they were partly destroyed and lost.

Burr's alleged goals were by no means unique. Secession was repeatedly proposed to advance regional interests until the Civil War (1861-1865). Private American filibustering excursions into Spanish and Mexican territory persisted until after the Spanish American War (1898). A mature sense of national identity did not come to the United States until the late nineteenth and early twentieth centuries.

Burr's case also had important constitutional ramifications. Chief Justice Marshall's ruling in Burr's favor preserved the right of Americans to voice opposition to the government without fear of being charged with treason and further defined the independent scope of the judicial and executive branches of government.

—*Ralph L. Langenheim, Jr.*

FURTHER READING

Adams, Henry. *History of the United States of America During the Administrations of Jefferson and Madi-*son. 9 vols. New York: Charles Scribner's Sons, 1889-1891. After examining English and Spanish archives, Adams concluded that Burr conspired to dismember the union; his conclusion gained wide acceptance.

Brodie, Fawn M. *Thomas Jefferson: An Intimate History.* New York: Bantam, 1974. This distinguished biography of Jefferson suggests that Burr's many conflicting purported plots and unfounded claims resulted from mental imbalance on his part.

Fleming, Thomas J. *Duel: Alexander Hamilton, Aaron Burr, and the Future of America.* New York: Basic Books, 1999. Lively study of the political rivalry between Burr and Hamilton that is placed firmly within the chaotic political environment of the time.

Lomask, Milton. *Aaron Burr: The Conspiracy and Years of Exile, 1805-1806.* New York: Farrar, Straus and Giroux, 1982. Based on primary documents and scholarly analyses of older records, including a discrediting of Burr's purported "cipher letter" to Wilkinson.

Melton, Buckner F., Jr. *Aaron Burr: Conspiracy to Treason.* New York: John Wiley & Sons, 2002. Study of Burr's plot to set up an independent republic in the western United States or Mexico. A constitutional law expert, Melton provides a detailed account of Burr's treason trial.

Montgomery, M. R. *Jefferson and the Gun-men: How the West Was Almost Lost.* New York: Crown, 2000. Popular account of Burr's conspiracy.

Parmet, Herbert S., and Marie B. Hecht. *Aaron Burr: Portrait of an Ambitious Man.* New York: Macmillan, 1967. A well-documented biography of one of the most enigmatic figures in American history.

Vidal, Gore. *Burr.* New York: Random House, 1973. Well-documented historical novel, in which fact and fiction are clearly separated. Re-creates the contemporary social and political environment during Burr's lifetime. Vidal is remotely related to Burr.

SEE ALSO: Feb. 17, 1801: House of Representatives Elects Jefferson President; May 9, 1803: Louisiana Purchase; May 30, 1854: Congress Passes the Kansas-Nebraska Act; June 16, 1855-May 1, 1857: Walker Invades Nicaragua.

RELATED ARTICLES in *Great Lives from History: The Nineteenth Century, 1801-1900:* Aaron Burr; Andrew Jackson; John Marshall; Zebulon Pike.

April 7, 1805
BEETHOVEN'S *EROICA* SYMPHONY INTRODUCES THE ROMANTIC AGE

Ludwig van Beethoven's Third Symphony, the Eroica, *introduced an innovative approach to the symphonic form and, in spite of its negative reception, inspired a generation of composers whose creative musical forms and techniques characterized the period that came to be known as the Romantic era.*

ALSO KNOWN AS: Beethoven's Third Symphony; *Sinfonia eroica*; Heroic Symphony
LOCALE: Theater-an-der-Wien, Vienna, Austria
CATEGORY: Music

KEY FIGURES
Ludwig van Beethoven (1770-1827), German composer
Napoleon I (1769-1821), emperor of France, r. 1804-1814
Hector Berlioz (1803-1869), French composer of program music
Franz Schubert (1797-1828), Austrian composer
Felix Mendelssohn (1809-1847), German composer
Frédéric Chopin (1810-1849), Polish composer known for innovative piano techniques
Franz Liszt (1811-1886), Hungarian composer who developed the symphonic poem
Johannes Brahms (1833-1897), German composer

SUMMARY OF EVENT
Ludwig van Beethoven began composing music at a time when mainstream musical taste valued disciplined structures, simple melodies and textures, and emotional restraint. Beethoven studied briefly with Joseph Haydn, one of the classical era's most creative composers, so his early compositions, including two symphonies, were rooted in the styles and traditions of the time. In 1803, however, he began envisioning a symphony that would be dramatically different—longer, with richer textures and more extensive instrumentation. The recent ascent of Napoleon Bonaparte—who arose from the ranks of the common people and became first consul of the French Republic in 1799—epitomized the ideals that were sweeping Europe following the French Revolution (1789), so Beethoven decided to compose this new symphony in honor of the general whose heroic leadership he admired. When, however, in 1804 Napoleon had himself crowned Emperor Napoleon I, Beethoven felt betrayed and marked out the general's name on the symphony's title page with such anger that he broke his pen. He retitled

his Third Symphony *Sinfonia eroica*, or the Heroic Symphony. It was now, according to Beethoven, composed to celebrate the memory of a great man.

The work premiered at the Theater-an-der-Wien on April 7, 1805. It was groundbreaking in its creativity, opening with two powerful staccato chords then progressing through four movements that ranged from a celebratory military piece to a mournful dirge, evoking a hero's ascent, death, and rebirth. Its themes recurred throughout the four movements, surprising a listener with a slow passage where a spirited one might have been expected, as in the final movement, or adding a militaristic undertone to the funeral march, as in the second movement.

The final result was often unexpectedly noisy and possessed none of the unity among its movements that contemporary concertgoers expected. Even worse for these confused concertgoers, at almost an hour in length, the *Eroica* Symphony carried on long after other symphonies would have ended. The audience grew restless, and one patron is reported to have shouted, "I'll pay another kreutzer if they will just stop playing!" Early reviews acknowledged the mixed reception the symphony received, and the work was only periodically performed during the rest of Beethoven's life, but the new Romantic style it introduced would quickly find its way into the work of other composers.

Romanticism acquired its name from its evocation of the medieval romances, epic poems about heroic figures, exotic lands, and unrequited love. The Romantic era proved to be a period of sweeping musical innovation. At the center of the movement was an emotional depth imparted to music by composers who sought to express subjective, personal emotions in musical form. As a result of this expressionistic drive, the texture of Romantic music became richer. Melodies became longer, more dramatic, and more emotional. Tempos grew more extreme. Harmonies moved toward a fuller sound, sometimes even into dissonance, to create more volume and a wider range of expression. Composers even began using newly invented instruments to expand the creative possibilities of musical composition.

The values at the center of the movement—emotional intensity, the beauty of nature, the power of the imagination—had begun to emerge in combination with nationalistic themes in the Sturm und Drang literature that swept Germany a generation before. Indeed, Sturm und

Drang's most renowned writers, Friedrich Schiller and Johann Wolfgang von Goethe, were major influences on Beethoven and other Romantic composers and writers. A decade before the *Eroica* Symphony was performed, William Wordsworth and Samuel Taylor Coleridge had published the first great work of Romantic literature, *Lyrical Ballads* (1798), and had given the movement a literary direction that would shape a generation of poets and authors.

Beethoven's *Eroica* Symphony offered a similar direction to a new generation of musical composers. The year after Beethoven died, an eccentric young composer named Hector Berlioz heard several of his symphonies and was inspired to compose a macabre autobiographical work entitled *Episode in the Life of an Artist: A Fantastic Symphony*, better known by its French title, *Symphonie fantastique*. Rooted in Berlioz's fascination with Goethe's *Faust: Eine Tragödie* (pb. 1808; *The Tragedy of Faust*, 1823), the symphony recounted the tragedy of a lovesick musician who attempted to poison himself but instead fell into a deep sleep in which his passions played themselves out through strange visions. The symphonic form Berlioz used came to be called "program music," because it told a story in a purely instrumental form. To heighten the narrative effect, Berlioz introduced a technique called the *idée fixe* (fixed idea), a recurring musical theme designed to convey the same character or concept each time it was played.

Several of Beethoven's successors in the Romantic movement are now considered to be among music history's most creative and renowned figures. Franz Schubert, who never acquired a patron and was forced to compose his music in tandem with a teaching career, wrote what some consider the first true Romantic symphony, the *Unfinished Symphony*. Felix Mendelssohn's overture for *A Midsummer Night's Dream* is considered the standard for orchestral overtures, and his *Scottish Symphony* and *Italian Symphony* are renowned for their evocation of geographic settings. Frédéric Chopin's technical brilliance on the piano, as well as his sensitive and expressive compositions, made him one of the most popular figures of his day. Franz Liszt is often considered the era's most innovative stylist. An admirer of Berlioz's program music and its foremost practitioner after Berlioz, Liszt pioneered the symphonic poem and bold approaches to harmony and motivic transformation. Two generations after Beethoven, Johannes Brahms sought to merge the musical values of the classical era with Romantic tastes, and his First Symphony is sometimes called "Beethoven's Tenth Symphony."

SIGNIFICANCE

Beethoven's popularity after composing the *Eroica* Symphony allowed him to become the first prominent composer to earn his living from a broader audience: Lessons, the sale of his compositions as sheet music, and ticket sales for his public performances contributed to his income. The resulting financial independence allowed Beethoven to pursue his own creative vision instead of depending upon a wealthy patron, as had Joseph Haydn, Wolfgang Amadeus Mozart, and other composers of the Baroque and classical periods. As a result, Beethoven's symphonies evolved to showcase his extraordinary creativity. His Symphony No. 9, his last and the product of years of experimentation, pushed the creative boundaries far beyond the *Eroica* Symphony, not only through its length and complexity but also through its use of a full choir and vocal soloists in its dramatic final movement. Such a radical departure from tradition paved the way for the next generation of composers to experiment with even more original forms, as Berlioz demonstrated less than a decade later with his *Symphonie fantastique*.

Beethoven and his Romantic successors brought about an apotheosis for orchestral music. Public concerts

Hector Berlioz. (Library of Congress)

become a popular amusement for the emerging middle class, and such audiences preferred works that appealed to their emotions rather than their understanding of musical technique or themes. As a result, not only audiences but also critics and subsequent composers came to consider symphonic music superior to sonatas, chamber works, and other popular musical forms of the period. Eventually, the heightened interest in music led to an increase in musical education and ultimately created a wider audience for sophisticated piano and concert pieces, concerti, "tone poems," and opera.

—*Devon Boan*

FURTHER READING

Abraham, Gerald, ed. *Romanticism, 1830-1890.* Vol. 9 in *The New Oxford History of Music.* New York: Oxford University Press, 1990. An exhaustive, scholarly critical survey detailing the diverse musical styles of the Romantic era's most renowned composers.

Bent, Ian, ed. *Music Theory in the Age of Romanticism.* Cambridge, England: Cambridge University Press, 1996. A series of essays by music historians exploring the manner in which audiences and musicians of the Romantic era would have heard and interpreted music, including the *Eroica* Symphony. The authors utilize a variety of social and cognitive perspectives to provide their analyses.

Cooper, Barry. *The Beethoven Compendium: A Guide to*

Beethoven's Life and Music. New York: Thames and Hudson, 1996. A detailed and well-organized encyclopedia of Beethoven and his life and works. Includes a broad overview of the time period and social context in which Beethoven wrote, as well as information on the development of musical instruments and musicology in Beethoven's time.

Lockwood, Lewis. *Beethoven: The Music and the Life.* New York: W. W. Norton, 2003. Aimed at the general reader, this biography focuses on Beethoven's compositions, placing them within a musical and historical context.

Stanley, Glenn, ed. *The Cambridge Companion to Beethoven.* New York: Cambridge University Press, 2000. Series of essays analyzing Beethoven's personality and musical compositions.

SEE ALSO: May 7, 1824: First Performance of Beethoven's Ninth Symphony; Mar. 12, 1832: *La Sylphide* Inaugurates Romantic Ballet's Golden Age; Aug. 13-17, 1876: First Performance of Wagner's Ring Cycle; Dec. 22, 1894: Debussy's *Prelude to the Afternoon of a Faun* Premieres.

RELATED ARTICLES in *Great Lives from History: The Nineteenth Century, 1801-1900:* Ludwig van Beethoven; Hector Berlioz; Johannes Brahms; Frédéric Chopin; Franz Liszt; Felix Mendelssohn; Napoleon I; Franz Schubert; Robert Schumann.

May 4, 1805-1830
EXPLORATION OF WEST AFRICA

After the British abolition of the Atlantic slave trade, British and French explorers began pushing into West Africa in earnest, seeking geographical knowledge, commercial possibilities, and individual glory. Their explorations had no immediate important consequences, but the areas they traversed anticipated the later imperial division of West Africa.

LOCALE: West Africa
CATEGORIES: Exploration and discovery; geography

KEY FIGURES
Mungo Park (1771-1806), Scottish physician who was the first European to explore the Niger River fully
Hugh Clapperton (1788-1827), Scottish explorer who was the first European to describe northern Nigeria
Alexander Gordon Laing (1793-1826), Scottish

explorer who was the first European to visit Timbuktu
René-Auguste Caillié (1799-c. 1838), French explorer who was the first European to reach Timbuktu and return

SUMMARY OF EVENT

After centuries of trading—mainly for slaves—along the west and equatorial coasts of Africa, Europeans knew almost nothing about the interior of Africa. That situation began to change during the early nineteenth century. On May 4, 1805, the Scottish explorer Mungo Park started inland from the Senegal coast leading an expedition of forty-five, most of whom were British soldiers. A decade earlier, Park had become the first European to see the Upper Niger River during an exploratory mission up the

EXPLORERS' ROUTES IN NORTH AND WEST AFRICA

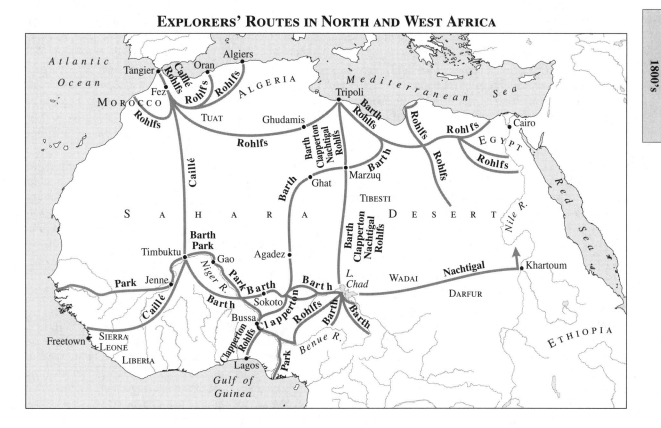

Gambia River that he had undertaken on his own under the auspices of a private organization, the African Association. During the interval the British government had become concerned that the French might establish a protectorate stretching from their coastal colony in Senegal to the Niger. In fact, the French had no such intention. Nevertheless, Park was sent back with instructions to explore the entire course of West Africa's longest river.

Park's second mission was a disaster. Most of the soldiers serving under him died of fever before they even reached the Niger River. After reaching the river in late November, 1805, the survivors built a boat and sailed downstream. During an approximately one-thousand-mile journey, as they passed through various territories, Park and his men often fired on anyone they suspected of having hostile intentions toward them. The result was a running series of engagements that finally culminated at the village of Bussa in what became Nigeria, where Park and his men were killed in early 1806.

Park's tragedy did little to dampen British public enthusiasm for West African exploration. After Britain declared the slave trade to be illegal in 1807, business and government leaders saw a new need to penetrate the inte-

rior of West Africa and seek out new products. West Africa was thought to be a good place to do business although there was little tangible evidence to support such an assumption. Others, the so-called humanitarian lobby, proclaimed that Great Britain had a moral obligation to bring Christianity and Western civilization to the Africans. Several exploratory attempts from the west and south ended in disaster with most of the men dying of disease. Officials in London decided to turn to North Africa in the hope of finding a better way into the interior.

In February, 1822, two British army officers, Dixon Denham and Hugh Clapperton, set out from the Mediterranean port of Tripoli for Lake Chad on what became known as the Bornu Mission. They were instructed to check out information the British had received that the Niger River flowed into Lake Chad. When they arrived, the men split up. Denham vainly sought a connection between the Niger River and Lake Chad, while Clapperton traveled on to Sokoto, the capital of the Fulani Empire of Hausaland, where he established relations with the local government. The two men subsequently joined together again and returned to Tripoli in January, 1825.

After Clapperton and Denham's explorations, it was

logical to follow the trip south to Lake Chad with a trip southwest to the Niger Bend. The choice fell to another British soldier, Alexander Gordon Laing, who was instructed to head for Timbuktu, a town on the Upper Niger, then follow the river down to the coast. Laing led a small expedition in which he was the only European; he later admitted to preferring that arrangement, so he would not have to share the glory of any discoveries he made. Britain regarded the expedition as urgent after collecting information about two French agents headed for Timbuktu in native disguise. This information was inaccurate, but it heightened British fears that the French were out to claim the interior of Africa for themselves. On July 18, 1825, Laing and a small party rode out of Tripoli and into the Sahara.

Laing harbored an envy of Clapperton that became an obsession as his journey proceeded. He wrote letters to his wife and others in which he sneered at Clapperton's accomplishments and claimed that the Niger River and Timbuktu were destined for himself alone. However, Laing did not know that five months after he had left Tripoli, Clapperton was sent on a new expedition inland from the Guinea coast with the intention of visiting Sokoto and Timbuktu and discovering the Niger's outlet. Clapperton himself died from a fever in Sokoto in April, 1827, but his servant, Richard Lander, eventually did accomplish the last of his mission's goals.

Laing would soon have more important matters to deal with than the specter of Clapperton. In the middle of the Sahara Desert, at a place called Wadi Ahennet, he was attacked by Tuaregs. Several of his men were killed and others were wounded, including Laing himself, who suffered a total of twenty-four wounds. Later, while visiting the camp of a friendly Kunta marabout, the rest of his men died of yellow fever. Nevertheless, Laing finally reached Timbuktu on August 13, 1826. He was the first European in the modern era to visit that fabled city. He stayed in Timbuktu for five weeks, but during his return home, his African guide murdered him about thirty miles north of Timbuktu.

Laing was the first European known to reach Timbuktu, but a Frenchman, René-Auguste Caillié, was the first to visit that city and return safely. Of humble origins, Caillié had some previous experience traveling in the interior of Senegal and was determined to win a gold medal and money offered by the Paris Geographical Society to the first person to return from Timbuktu. After his proposals for an expedition were turned down by both the French and British governments, he set out from the west coast on his own on April 19, 1827. He disguised himself

as an Egyptian who had been carried to France as a slave and was now trying to return home and to embrace Islam again.

Caillié traveled with various merchant caravans on a circuitous route since he had no real idea as to where he was going. Along the way he suffered from scurvy and an infection that almost cost him a foot. In March, 1828, he visited Jenne, becoming the first European to visit that major Niger River city. A month later, he arrived in Timbuktu, where he remained for two weeks. During that time he collected much information on the city and its commerce, finally dispelling the myth of Timbuktu the Golden that had originated with Leo Africanus in the sixteenth century. Still in disguise, he joined a caravan to Morocco and in Tangier was able to sneak aboard a French ship. After returning home, he published an account of his travels.

SIGNIFICANCE

Laing's death, which became known through various avenues, had immediate repercussions. The British consul in Tripoli, who also happened to be Laing's father-in-law, accused the French consul and the vizier of the Bashaw, the local ruler, of stealing Laing's journal and ultimately of complicity in his death. Although the latter charge was unfounded, what happened to Laing's journal has never been satisfactorily resolved. Ultimately the British withdrew their support of the Bashaw, which weakened his government and allowed the Turks to reassert their control over Tripoli.

Caillié returned to Europe as the Laing affair was reaching its climax. In Britain, sorrow over Laing's death was easily misdirected into public animosity against Caillié, who, it was charged, was a fraud. Meanwhile, Caillié's trip failed to stimulate French interest in West Africa. In 1830, the year in which Caillié's account of his journey was published, French armies invaded Algiers for reasons that had nothing to do with Caillié or West African exploration. Over the next half century, the French focused their imperial designs on expanding into the Algerian hinterland.

The British continued to be more interested than the French in sub-Saharan Africa but focused most of their attention on the continent's eastern and central regions. The midcentury mission of Heinrich Barth, a German who traveled under the sponsorship of the British government, remained the one great achievement of exploration left for West Africa. Barth was able to show conclusively that Caillié's claims were valid. Perhaps ironically, when virtually all of West Africa fell victim to

European imperialism during the late nineteenth century, the British ended up controlling some of the territory first explored by Clapperton and Lander, while most of the lands traversed by Park, Laing, and Caillié went to France.

—*Richard L. Smith*

FURTHER READING

Bovill, E. W. *The Niger Explored*. London: Oxford University Press, 1968. Thorough account covering West African explorations from Park's second trip through Laing, including the political and diplomatic setting for West African exploration.

Duffill, Mark. *Mungo Park*. Edinburgh: National Museums of Scotland, 1999. Park's memoir of his first expedition is still in print, but this short biography provides a more general look at this complicated man.

Gramont, Sanche de. *The Strong Brown God: The Story of the Niger River*. Boston: Houghton Mifflin, 1976. Written in a journalistic style but satisfactorily researched, this book covers the whole nineteenth century and is especially useful for Park, Clapperton, and Lander.

La Gueriviere, Jean de. *The Exploration of Africa*. Translated by Florence Brutton. Woodstock, N.Y.: Duckworth, 2003. General overview of nineteenth century exploration and its impact on the European popular imagination.

Welch, Galbraith. *The Unveiling of Timbuctoo: The Astounding Adventures of Caillié*. New York: Carroll & Graf, 1991. Voluminous work on Caillié's explorations that is still useful although it was written in 1939 in what may today appear a somewhat turgid style.

SEE ALSO: Mar. 22, 1812: Burckhardt Discovers Egypt's Abu Simbel; 1822-1874: Exploration of North Africa; 1848-1889: Exploration of East Africa; Nov. 17, 1853: Livingstone Sees the Victoria Falls; 1873-1880: Exploration of Africa's Congo Basin; Nov. 15, 1884-Feb. 26, 1885: Berlin Conference Lays Groundwork for the Partition of Africa; Nov., 1889-Jan., 1894: Dahomey-French Wars.

RELATED ARTICLES in *Great Lives from History: The Nineteenth Century, 1801-1900:* Samuel Ajayi Crowther; Mary Kingsley.

October 21, 1805
BATTLE OF TRAFALGAR

A decisive British naval victory off the southern coast of Spain, the Battle of Trafalgar crushed French and Spanish naval power, thereby ensuring British security during the Napoleonic Wars and making possible British naval dominance throughout the nineteenth century.

LOCALE: Off Cape Trafalgar, Spain
CATEGORIES: Wars, uprisings, and civil unrest; military history

KEY FIGURES

Lord Nelson (Horatio Nelson; 1758-1805), overall commander of the British fleet
Napoleon I (Napoleon Bonaparte; 1769-1721), emperor of France, r. 1804-1814, 1815
Pierre-Charles-Jean-Baptiste-Silvestre de Villeneuve (1763-1806), commander of the combined French/Spanish fleet
Cuthbert Collingwood (1750-1810), commander of the second British battle line

SUMMARY OF EVENT

After the brief respite provided by the Treaty of Amiens (1802), the Napoleonic Wars flared up again in 1805. Napoleon I's primary objective was an invasion of Great Britain, the sole European power not under his control. The powerful British Royal Navy, however, prevented the French from gaining even temporary control of the English Channel, negating Napoleon's powerful army. As he could not defeat the Royal Navy, Napoleon conceived a plan to deceive it long enough for his naval forces to gain control of the English Channel. France's navy alone could not defeat the British, but an alliance with Spain gave Napoleon control of the Spanish fleet as well. Napoleon conceived a plan to confuse and deceive the British, set for March, 1805.

In the first step of Napoleon's plan, the combined French and Spanish fleets would slip out of port unnoticed and launch a combined raid on British possessions in the West Indies. This raid, it was hoped, would convince the British that the combined fleet intended to stay in the Caribbean Sea for an extended period, which

THE BATTLE OF TRAFALGAR

would lure the Royal Navy across the Atlantic Ocean in its pursuit. Having achieved this deception, the combined fleet would then return across the Atlantic Ocean, leaving the British fruitlessly to search for them in the Caribbean Sea. While the Royal Navy looked for the combined fleet in the Caribbean Sea, the French and Spanish fleet would arrive in the English Channel to escort Napoleon's 350,000-man army on its invasion of England.

Napoleon's plan soon fell apart. The French and Spanish fleets met at the arranged point, but Admiral Pierre-Charles-Jean-Baptiste-Silvestre de Villeneuve, the commander of the combined fleet, could not elude the British blockade at Toulon commanded by the British admiral, Lord Nelson. The combined fleet sailed for the Caribbean Sea, but with Nelson in hot pursuit. Unable to raid British possessions in the Caribbean successfully, Villeneuve decided to return to Europe, specifically the Spanish port of Cádiz. Nearing Cádiz, the combined fleet engaged a British squadron at Cape Finisterre on July 22. Villeneuve lost two ships and retired into Cádiz to replenish his fleet.

Thwarted in his invasion of England, Napoleon ordered Villeneuve to take the combined fleet into the Mediterranean Sea to support his operations against the Austrians. Cowed by his losses at Cape Finisterre, however, Villeneuve remained at Cádiz for the entire summer, under the constant watch of Admiral Nelson and the British battle fleet. Finally, threatened with dismissal,

Villeneuve ordered the combined fleet into the Mediterranean. On October 20, 1805, Villeneuve, with thirty-three ships (eighteen French and fifteen Spanish) mounting 2,640 guns, headed southeast toward the Strait of Gibraltar. Before Villeneuve could reach Gibraltar, however, Nelson's battle fleet of twenty-seven ships mounting 2,138 guns cut off their advance, forced Villeneuve to turn northward in an attempt to flee back into Cádiz, and prepared to engage the French and Spanish fleet.

Under normal circumstances, Villeneuve would have escaped Nelson and reached Cádiz safely. French ships tended to be faster and more maneuverable than their British counterparts, and traditional linear tactics usually worked in France's favor. In linear tactics, opposing forces would array their ships in lines opposite each other and battle in a straightforward manner, with each individual ship engaging the enemy ship opposite it. In this type of engagement, the French, with their faster ships, could choose to stay in a fight if they had the upper hand or could disengage and retreat if threatened with defeat.

Two things prevented Villeneuve from escaping in the present confrontation. First, the fast French ships had to stay with their slower Spanish allies, negating their speed advantage. Second, Nelson had no intention of engaging in linear tactics. Nelson wanted to cut the formidable combined fleet into sections, which his superior gunnery could then destroy piecemeal. To accomplish this goal, Nelson split his own force into two squadrons. Nelson, leading the first squadron from his flagship HMS *Victory*, would form the squadron into a line at right angles to the French and Spanish line and would slam into the middle of them, while Admiral Cuthbert Collingwood, leading the other squadron from his flagship HMS *Royal Sovereign*, would hit the rearward third of the combined fleet, also at a right angle. If the gambit was successful, the foremost one-third of the combined fleet would escape, but Nelson could defeat two-thirds of the French and Spanish fleet.

On October 21, 1805, with Villeneuve retreating northward to Cádiz, Nelson put his plan into action. Nearing the French and Spanish fleet from the west, Nelson ordered his men to battle by sending by flag signal to all ships the message "England expects that every man will do his duty." Nelson's unexpected approach surprised Villeneuve, but the tactic entailed a huge risk for the British fleet. By sailing directly toward the combined fleet, the British prevented themselves from firing at the enemy. The French and Spanish, however, could fire full broadsides of cannon at their approaching enemy. For nearly two hours, the English fleet had to endure a steady cannonading while unable to return fire itself. By early afternoon, however, the British columns had reached the combined fleet, smashed into its formation, and turned the tables. Now in the midst of the combined fleet, the English could fire full broadsides into the enemy, and it was the French and Spanish fleet, now immobilized to avoid collisions, that could not return fire.

The battle soon became a melee, with ships firing upon every enemy vessel that came into view. Nelson led *Victory* directly toward Villeneuve's flagship *Bucentaure* and engaged in a furious gun battle at close range. At the same time, Collingwood directed *Royal Sovereign* toward the Spanish flagship *Santissima Trinidad* and soon left the Spanish vessel a flaming wreck that later exploded when the flames reached the powder magazine.

The battle raged for four hours, as each English ship passed through the French and Spanish line, adding to the carnage inflicted by the earlier Royal Navy ships. The forward one-third of Villeneuve's ships attempted to turn about to aid their countrymen, but unfavorable winds, English warships, and recognition of defeat led the forward segment to retreat to safety. By late afternoon, Villeneuve struck his flag as a symbol of surrender and the battle ended with the total defeat of the combined fleet. Nelson, however, did not live to savor his victory.

In mid-afternoon, while *Victory* engaged the French vessel *Redoubtable*, a French rifleman caught sight of Nelson, in full dress uniform with medals and regalia, and shot him through the spine.

Nelson lingered long enough to know that he had achieved a great victory but succumbed to his wound at approximately the time the French and Spanish fleet surrendered. His victory, if Pyrrhic from a personal standpoint, was absolute. While *Victory* and other British ships sustained considerable damage, no English ship was lost. Of the thirty-three ships of the combined fleet, eleven fled back to Cádiz, two sank, and the other twenty fell into British hands. English casualties totaled fifteen hundred killed and wounded, compared to nearly seven thousand French and Spanish casualties with another seven thousand sailors taken prisoner.

SIGNIFICANCE

With the loss of his fleet, Napoleon was unable to invade England, which greatly contributed to his eventual defeat at Waterloo in 1815. Even beyond Napoleon's empire, French naval power never recovered. Before the Battle of Trafalgar, France was the only real threat to the Royal Navy. Afterward, the French navy lagged behind the British in prestige, numbers, and technology. Without any serious rival, Great Britain established itself as the

British ships of the line at Trafalgar. (P. F. Collier and Son)

world's dominant naval power for the next century, threatened only by the rise of the German navy in the early twentieth century. British dominance of the seas translated into growing economic power and expanding colonial influence, as Great Britain remained the world's leading nineteenth century superpower.

—*Steven J. Ramold*

FURTHER READING

Coleman, Terry. *The Nelson Touch: The Life and Legend of Horatio Nelson*. New York: Oxford University Press, 2002. Well-researched, balanced biography of Nelson, whom the author describes as "a paramount naval genius and a natural born predator."

Howarth, David. *Trafalgar: The Nelson Touch*. New York: Atheneum, 1969. Concentrates on the admiral's last campaign. Howarth provides specific details; he also covers Nelson's close relations with the men who served under him. An excellent index and many maps and drawings enhance the scholarly nature of this work.

Keegan, John. *The Price of Admiralty: The Evolution of Naval Warfare*. New York: Penguin Books, 1990. An outstanding blow-by-blow account of Trafalgar, with a comparison of the battle to other important naval engagements.

Pocock, Thomas. *The Terror Before Trafalgar: Napoleon, Nelson, and the Secret War*. New York: W. W. Norton, 2003. A discussion of how the battle might

have changed the outcome of the Napoleonic Wars if the French had won.

Schom, Alan. *Trafalgar: Countdown to Battle, 1803-1805*. New York: Atheneum, 1990. A full discussion of the political and military events that led to the decisive battle in 1805.

Warner, Oliver. *Nelson's Battles*. New York: Macmillan, 1965. Warner provides detailed information about Nelson's major engagements; an appendix lists all the ships and captains who served with Nelson at Aboukir Bay, Copenhagen, and Trafalgar. Excellent maps, many portraits, and frequent quotations from Nelson and his contemporaries.

_____. *Victory: The Life of Lord Nelson*. Boston: Little, Brown, 1958. A well-written, detailed life of Nelson in which considerable emphasis is placed upon personalities as well as major campaigns. Includes an extensive bibliography and a most complete index.

SEE ALSO: Dec. 2, 1805: Battle of Austerlitz; May 2, 1808-Nov., 1813: Peninsular War in Spain; June 23-Dec. 14, 1812: Napoleon Invades Russia; Oct. 16-19, 1813: Battle of Leipzig; Sept. 15, 1814-June 11, 1815: Congress of Vienna; June 18, 1815: Battle of Waterloo; Nov. 20, 1815: Second Peace of Paris; 1889: Great Britain Strengthens Its Royal Navy.

RELATED ARTICLES in *Great Lives from History: The Nineteenth Century, 1801-1900:* Napoleon I; Lord Nelson.

December 2, 1805
BATTLE OF AUSTERLITZ

A major turning point in the Napoleonic Wars, France's rout of the Russian army at Austerlitz closely followed its rout of the Austrian army at Ulm. These allied setbacks destroyed the Third Coalition and moved the wavering Prussians to seek peace terms with France.

LOCALE: Austerlitz (now Slavkov u Brna, Czech Republic)

CATEGORY: Wars, uprisings, and civil unrest

KEY FIGURES

Napoleon I (Napoleon Bonaparte; 1769-1821), emperor of the French, r. 1804-1814, 1815

Alexander I (1777-1825), czar of Russia, r. 1801-1825

Jean-Baptiste-Jules Bernadotte (1763-1844), French

marshal at Austerlitz who became Charles XIV John, crown prince of Sweden, in 1810

Louis Davout (1770-1823), commander of France's Third Corps at Austerlitz

Francis II (1768-1835), Holy Roman Emperor, 1792-1806

Karl Mack von Leiberich (1752-1828), commander of the Austrian army that capitulated at Ulm

Nicholas-Jean de Dieu Soult (1769-1851), commander of France's Fourth Corps at Austerlitz

SUMMARY OF EVENT

In 1805, Great Britain, Austria, Russia, Sweden, and Naples joined to form the Third Coalition against France. Two earlier international coalitions had joined to combat revolutionary France. The Third Coalition was the first to oppose France after Napoleon Bonaparte had himself crowned Emperor Napoleon I in December, 1804. In May, 1803, Britain had broken the unfavorable Peace of Amiens. While Napoleon was seriously contemplating an invasion of Britain, Austria and Russia declared war on his new empire. Russia's Czar Alexander I joined the coalition mainly for philosophical reasons, picturing himself in the role of the savior of Europe. His fear of French influence in the eastern Mediterranean was a secondary reason. Austria, on the other hand, had more forceful reasons for fighting France. The treaties of Campo Formio (1797) and Lunéville (1801) had humiliated Austria by reducing the size of its empire and by eliminating its influence in Germany and Italy.

Throughout the summer of 1805, the French army was poised along the English Channel, waiting for Napoleon's navy to gain at least temporary control of the short expanse of ocean between Calais and Dover. In late August, however, Napoleon turned his back on the English Channel in order to meet a new and more dangerous threat developing on the Upper Danube. Without waiting for their Russian allies to arrive, the Austrians decided to open their campaign without delay and catch the French off guard. However, they made two fatal errors. They concentrated their strength in Italy, believing that the major fighting would take place there, as it had in two previous campaigns, and they underestimated the speed at which the French army could move. Napoleon moved six army corps to the upper Danube so fast that he was able to shatter the Austrian army in southern Germany and force Baron Karl Mack von Leiberich to surrender his army with twenty thousand men at Ulm on October 20, 1805. This victory opened the road to Vienna, which the French captured in mid-November.

By late November, the Russian army had gathered in substantial force at Moravia, to the north of Vienna. There they were joined by fragments of the Austrian army. However, the principal Austrian forces, commanded by their talented general, Archduke Charles, were still far south of the Danube River, retiring eastward. At that moment, Alexander I, who had joined his army, decided to give battle despite a warning from his chief military adviser that such a move would be disastrous. The Russian forces outnumbered the French, and the czar believed that he would win, especially as he had chosen a favorable battlefield. Furthermore, at that time, the Prussian government was in the process of joining the coalition, and if Alexander could defeat Napoleon at Austerlitz, the Prussian army would march south and cut

BATTLE OF AUSTERLITZ, 1805

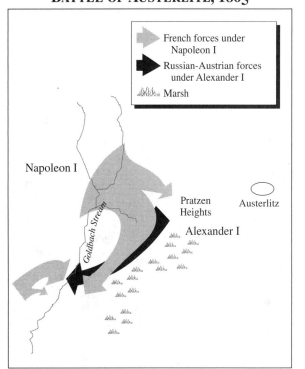

off the French retreat. The war would be brought to a victorious conclusion for the allies, and Alexander would be the hero of all Europe. Such was not to be the case, however, at least not for another six years.

Moving rapidly, Napoleon's army occupied the Pratzen Heights, which was the best strategic position on the field. Feigning weakness, Napoleon ordered his forces to withdraw. The Russian army then seized the initiative by moving in to occupy the Pratzen Heights and surrounding area. Believing that the Russians would concentrate their attack against his right, Napoleon placed Marshal Louis Davout's Third Corps there and ordered Marshal Nicholas-Jean de Dieu Soult's Fourth Corps to hold his extended center. By the time Napoleon had finished his dispositions, his army, consisting of 73,200 men, was defending a position stretching more than five miles, south from the Brünn-Austerlitz road to Menitz Pond behind Goldbach Brook. After checking all of his preparations, Napoleon visited with his soldiers and was greeted with cheers and an impromptu torchlight parade.

Meanwhile, the predominantly Russian army of 85,700 men attacked the French position on the morning of December 2, 1805. Napoleon had concentrated his

Napoleon I (on white horse) at the Battle of Austerlitz. (The S. S. McClure Company)

strength in the center and on his left flank. The Russians massed against his right. After having marched seventy miles from Vienna, the Third Corps under the command of Marshal Davout defended a three-mile front on Napoleon's right. Although overextended and outnumbered four to one, Davout's infantry held against repeated Russian assaults.

By 10:00 A.M., the half-frozen marshes along the Goldbach were covered with Russian dead and wounded. Despite the heavy losses, the czar ordered his army to continue the assault on the French front right. When Napoleon saw that the enemy was committed to the turning of his right flank, he ordered Soult to retake the Pratzen Heights occupied by the Russian center. Soult's Fourth Corps immediately attacked but was driven back by a fierce counterattack by the Russian Imperial Guards. Napoleon then ordered the cavalry of the Imperial Guard to reinforce Soult, and the Pratzen Heights was secured.

At 11:00 A.M., after further strengthening Soult's forces, Napoleon ordered an attack southward against the Russians. By 1:00 P.M., Davout's Third Corps as well as Marshal Jean-Baptise Bernadotte's First Corps on the left flank were moving forward. By 2:00 P.M., the Rus-

sian army had been split into two parts and both were in full retreat. The divisions commanded by Soult had moved to the high ground in the center and then pivoted upon Davout's soldiers so that the Russian forces were driven onto the half-frozen lakes of Menitz and Satschan, which had bounded the French right flank. The Russian army lost 27,000 men, killed and wounded, while the French suffered only 1,300 killed, 6,490 wounded, and 500 missing. The French also captured 180 cannons and 45 enemy colors.

SIGNIFICANCE

After the battle, Alexander was led from the battlefield in tears, as his brave but poorly led troops fled eastward in disorder. The French victory was complete, and the enemy was no longer capable of giving battle. Francis II, the ruler of the Holy Roman Empire, immediately asked for an armistice, and later signed the Peace of Pressburg, which put an end to the Third Coalition. Alexander did not sign a peace treaty but led the remnants of his army back to Russia to reorganize. When news of the battle reached Berlin, the Prussians (who had been preparing to enter the struggle by attacking the French lines of communication) at once sent an envoy to Napoleon to discuss terms. Napoleon's hold on Italy and Germany was reconfirmed and strengthened, while Austria's western boundary was pushed still farther to the east.

—*John G. Gallaher, updated by J. W. Thacker*

FURTHER READING

Bowden, Scotty. *Napoleon and Austerlitz: An Unprecedentedly Detailed Combat Study of Napoleon's Epic Ulm-Austerlitz Campaigns of 1805.* Chicago: Emperor's Press, 1997. One of the best detailed expositions of the combat in the Battles of Ulm and Austerlitz.

Chandler, David G. *The Campaigns of Napoleon.* New York: Macmillan, 1966. Standard work on Napoleon's military career, containing clear descriptions of all Napoleon's battles.

Connelly, Owen. *Blundering to Glory: Napoleon's Military Campaigns.* Wilmington, Del.: Scholarly Resources, 1987. Although lacking detailed descriptions of Napoleon's battles, this study provides perhaps the best critical analysis of Napoleon's career as a military commander.

Esposito, Vincent J., and John Robert Elting. *A Military History and Atlas of the Napoleonic Wars.* New York: Frederick A. Praeger, 1964. While the narrative descriptions of Napoleon's campaigns and battles are rather brief, the maps are among the best available in any published work.

Goetz, Robert. *1805, Austerlitz: Napoleon and the Destruction of the Third Coalition.* Mechanicsburg, Pa.: Stackpole Books, 2005. About one-half of this book provides a detailed analytical reconstruction of the Battle of Austerlitz that does a good job in explaining how Napoleon was able to defeat the larger Russian force. The rest of the book discusses the events before and after the battle.

Hourtoulle, François Guy. *Austerlitz: The Eagle's Sun.* Paris: Histoire & Collections, 2003. Lavishly illustrated book designed for amateur military historians interested in such matters as detailed pictures of uniforms and equipment.

Johnson, Paul. *Napoleon.* New York: Viking Press, 2002. Concise biography, providing an overview of Napoleon's life and career. Johnson portrays Napoleon as an opportunist, whose militarism and style of governance planted the seeds for warfare and totalitarianism in the twentieth century.

Marceron, Claude. *Austerlitz: The Story of a Battle.* Translated by George Unwin. New York: W. W. Norton, 1966. Although uncritical of Napoleon, this study provides a complete narrative of the Battle of Austerlitz.

Schom, Alan. *Napoleon Bonaparte.* New York: HarperCollins, 1997. Scholarly, detailed biography covering all facets of Napoleon's life and career. Schom is unusually candid about his subject's character flaws and failures.

SEE ALSO: Dec. 2, 1804: Bonaparte Is Crowned Napoleon I; Oct. 21, 1805: Battle of Trafalgar; May 2, 1808-Nov., 1813: Peninsular War in Spain; June 23-Dec. 14, 1812: Napoleon Invades Russia; July 22, 1812: Battle of Salamanca; Sept. 7, 1812: Battle of Borodino; Oct. 16-19, 1813: Battle of Leipzig; June 18, 1815: Battle of Waterloo.

RELATED ARTICLES in *Great Lives from History: The Nineteenth Century, 1801-1900:* Alexander I; Charles XIV John; Napoleon I.

1800's

July 15, 1806-July 1, 1807
PIKE EXPLORES THE AMERICAN SOUTHWEST

After the Lewis and Clark expedition explored the northwestern part of the Louisiana Territory, Zebulon Pike led an expedition into the Southwest that paved the way to open a trade route to Santa Fe, while creating a myth that branded the Southwest as the "Great American Desert."

LOCALE: American Southwest
CATEGORIES: Exploration and discovery; trade and commerce

KEY FIGURES

Zebulon Pike (1779-1813), army lieutenant who led the expedition
James Wilkinson (1757-1825), commanding general of the Western Army of the United States
John Hamilton Robinson (fl. early nineteenth century), Pike's civilian companion on the expedition
Facundo Melgares (fl. early nineteenth century), Spanish lieutenant who led an expedition that nearly intercepted Pike

SUMMARY OF EVENT

On July 15, 1806, Lieutenant Zebulon Pike of the Western Army of the United States set out from St. Louis with a party of twenty-two men with orders to locate and explore the headwaters of the Arkansas and Red Rivers. His plan was to ascend the Arkansas River, cross over to the Red River, and then descend that river to its junction with the Mississippi River. After the United States purchased the Louisiana Territory from France in 1803, the boundary line between its territories and the Spanish Empire in the Southwest was undetermined. The Spanish were naturally prepared to resist any attempts by the United States to encroach on land that they claimed.

The farther west Pike moved, the more likely he was to encounter trouble, as the Spanish furiously tried to protect their northern borderlands from encroachment. Already experienced in reconnaissance work, Pike had recently returned from a successful exploration to the upper Mississippi River, where he had negotiated land concessions from the Sioux and protested the presence of British fur posts in the Minnesota region. On his expedition into the Southwest, Pike's first concern was to negotiate a peace between the Osage and Pawnee tribes.

Pike ascended the Missouri and Osage Rivers to the Osage villages, where he obtained horses. Then he moved on to the Pawnee villages on the Republican River. There he found the Pawnees ready to resist further American advances to the west because they had recently been visited by a more impressive Spanish expedition that had been sent out to defend New Spain's northern borders from U.S. encroachment.

Leading a force of six hundred men and driving two thousand horses and mules, Don Facundo Melgares had distributed Spanish flags and medals among the Pawnees, captured U.S. traders in the region, and urged the Pawnees to turn back other Americans who tried to travel farther west. Contrary to a historical legend that later arose, Melgares did not know that Pike's expedition was coming. He was hoping to push the Lewis and Clark expedition farther north. However, it appears higher Spanish officials had been informed of the Pike expedition by Pike's own commander, General James Wilkinson, who was also Special Agent Number 13 for the Spanish intelligence service. Whether, and to what degree, Pike was involved in Wilkinson's intrigues in the Southwest has remained an area of fierce debate.

Zebulon Pike. (Library of Congress)

PIKE'S EXPEDITIONS, 1806-1807

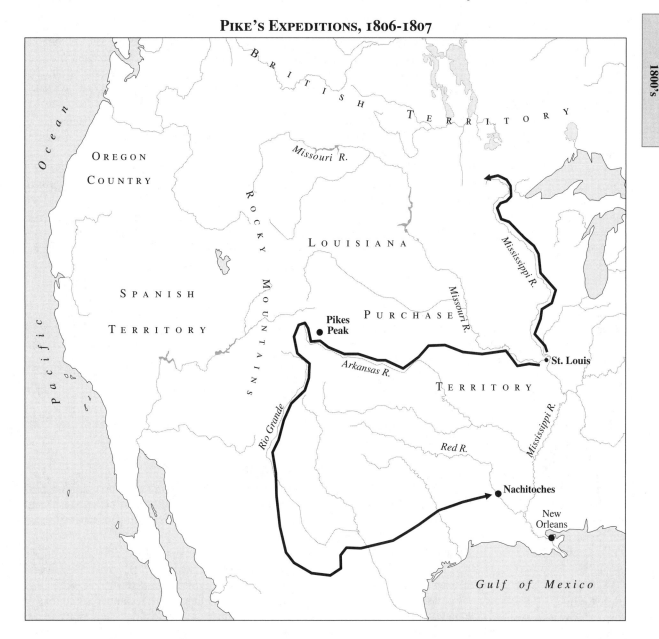

Pike's near miss with Melgares's expedition proved to be a stroke of good fortune for Pike, who had moved so slowly that he had avoided an encounter with the superior Spanish detachment. After the Pawnees were pacified, he could follow Melgares's route into the Rockies. With a display of force, Pike's troops intimidated the Pawnees, then pressed on to the Big Bend of the Arkansas River. There six men descended the river in two canoes fashioned from cottonwood logs and buffalo skins and returned to the United States.

Following the return route of Melgares, Pike's trail led up the Arkansas River. In November, 1806, Pike's party spotted the Rocky Mountains for the first time. From an encampment near the site of present-day Pueblo, Colorado, Pike and three companions set out to climb the peak now bearing Pike's name. Armpit-deep snows and the lack of winter clothing prevented Pike from making a successful ascent of the peak himself, but what he wrote about the massive pinnacle—now called Pikes Peak—permanently established his identification with it. During the next two months, he explored the Colorado country, reaching the site of present-day Leadville, Colorado, while hunting in vain for the headwaters of the Red River. With several men in his band suffering from frostbite, Pike established a winter camp at the Royal Gorge on the Arkansas River.

After leaving two men in a log shelter at this camp to guard the exhausted horses and a portion of the expedition's baggage, Pike and his few remaining men headed into the Wet Mountain Valley, crossed the rugged Sangre de Cristo Mountains into the San Luis Valley. There they spied one of the wonders of Colorado, the massive dunes that later became part of the Sand Dunes National Park. Moving southwest, Pike stood at the foot of Mount Blanca and through his glass viewed a watercourse that he believed to be the Red River. What he had actually found was the Rio Grande.

Pike then headed south, crossed the Rio Grande, and built a shelter near the confluence of the Rio Conejos and the Rio Grande, just south of the site of present-day Sanford, Colorado. The weather was bitterly cold during this February journey, and Pike's men waged a grim struggle with hunger. Although Pike did not know exactly where he was, he alleged that he was still on U.S. soil.

From the encampment on the Rio Grande, the enigmatic Dr. John H. Robinson, a civilian who had joined the expedition some time after its departure, set out for Santa Fe, professing to have a commission to collect a debt for a friend in Illinois. Robinson's arrival in Santa Fe made Pike's presence in Spanish territory known to Spanish authorities, and the Nyuutsiyu (Utes) Indians told them Pike's precise location. On February 26, 1807, one hundred Spanish troops appeared in Pike's camp. They arrested Pike and his men and escorted them to Santa Fe.

The Spanish were uncertain whether the explorers' presence in Spanish territory was accidental or purposeful, and they were perplexed about what they should do with them. After seizing Pike's maps and papers and examining them, they became convinced that Pike was a spy. They then escorted Pike's party to Chihuahua City and detained them there for several months. Nemesio Salcedo, who commanded the Spanish army in the northern provinces, finally decided to deport the group to the United States. Under escort, Pike and his men were taken by way of San Antonio, Texas, to Natchitoches, then a trading post on the Louisiana border, and there turned over to U.S. troops on July 1, 1807, thus ending Pike's expedition.

SIGNIFICANCE

From the time he left Santa Fe, Pike took voluminous notes on the country through which he passed and concealed them skillfully to make certain that they would not be confiscated. Although he failed to carry out his assignment to locate the headwaters of the Red River and descend that river, he incorporated the information he had obtained in a report he subsequently published in 1810, thereby adding to American knowledge of the Southwest. As a result of the publication, Pike gained national fame; editions also appeared in French, German, and Dutch.

Pike was such a keen observer that when he returned to the United States, he was able to provide precise figures on the numbers and types of troops stationed in the northern provinces of the Spanish Empire, as well as information concerning the character and personality of the Spanish military officers. His reports showed Spain's New Mexico territory to be poorly defended and only adequately governed. In addition to this intelligence, Pike declared that the Great Plains were "sandy deserts" similar to those in Africa. Thus he originated what proved to be the "Great American Desert" myth. Finally, he pointed out in great detail the potential value of trade between the United States and Santa Fe.

—W. Turrentine Jackson,
updated by Edward R. Crowther

FURTHER READING

Carter, Carrol Joe. *Pike in Colorado*. Fort Collins, Colo.: Old Army Press, 1978. Brief but excellent and accurate study of Pike's passage through the Centennial State.

Cook, Warren L. *Flood Tide of Empire: Spain and the Pacific Northwest, 1543-1819*. New Haven, Conn.: Yale University Press, 1973. Outstanding account of the political, diplomatic, and economic conditions of the northern provinces of Spain's New World empire, including General Wilkinson's involvement in Spanish policy during the early nineteenth century.

Hollon, W. Eugene. *The Lost Pathfinder: Zebulon Montgomery Pike*. Norman: University of Oklahoma Press, 1949. An older but excellent full-scale biography of Pike. Still frequently cited as the most authoritative study of Pike's career.

Hyslop, Stephen G. "An Explorer or a Spy?" *American History* 37, no. 3 (August, 2002): 58. Describes Pike's Western explorations, including his alleged espionage activities for Aaron Burr, who was plotting to seize part of Spanish territory around the same time.

Montgomery, M. R. *Jefferson and the Gun-Men: How the West Was Almost Lost.* New York: Crown, 2000. Chronicle of Burr's conspiracy that covers Pike's and Wilkinson's involvement in the abortive scheme.

Pike, Zebulon Montgomery. *Journals with Letters and Related Documents.* Edited by Donald Jackson. Norman: University of Oklahoma Press, 1966. The easiest to use of the many editions of Pike's journals. For many years the standard edition of Pike's expedition journals was *The Expeditions of Zebulon Montgomery Pike* (3 vols., New York: Francis P. Harper, 1895), edited by Elliott Coues.

Sanford, William R., and Carl R. Green. *Zebulon Pike: Explorer of the Southwest.* Springfield, N.J.: Enslow, 1996. Biography intended for general readers; part of the Legendary Heroes of the Wild West series.

SEE ALSO: May 9, 1803: Louisiana Purchase; May 14, 1804-Sept. 23, 1806: Lewis and Clark Expedition; Mar., 1805-Sept. 1, 1807: Burr's Conspiracy; Sept., 1821: Santa Fe Trail Opens; 1822-1831: Jedediah Smith Explores the Far West; May, 1842-1854: Frémont Explores the American West; June 30, 1846-Jan. 13, 1847: United States Occupies California and the Southwest; Mar. 2, 1853-1857: Pacific Railroad Surveys; 1867: Chisholm Trail Opens; 1879: Powell Publishes His Report on the American West.

RELATED ARTICLES in *Great Lives from History: The Nineteenth Century, 1801-1900:* Aaron Burr; Meriwether Lewis and William Clark; Zebulon Pike; Jedediah Smith.

1800's

1807
BOWDLER PUBLISHES *THE FAMILY SHAKESPEARE*

Representing a heightened British delicacy regarding sexual morality that came to be known as "Victorian," the English physician Thomas Bowdler published an expurgated version of William Shakespeare's works that removed what he deemed "vulgar parts." His attempt to sanitize literature for middle-class readers gave birth to the term for all such attempts, "bowdlerization."

LOCALE: England
CATEGORY: Literature

KEY FIGURES
Thomas Bowdler (1754-1825), English physician, writer, and editor
Henrietta Maria Bowdler (1754-1830), English writer and sister of Thomas
William Shakespeare (1564-1616), English playwright

SUMMARY OF EVENT
Along with Charles C. Boycott and the earl of Sandwich, Thomas Bowdler is responsible for one of the most recognized eponyms in the English language, "to bowdlerize." He certainly did not assume that his name would come to denote an obsessively prudish act of censorship. However, after his death his edition of the works of William Shakespeare, expunged of what Bowdler deemed objectionable content, became one of the most notable examples of rewriting an author to suit an audience. It

was used as an illustration of the moral priggishness later suggested by pejorative uses of the term "Victorian."

The first edition of *The Family Shakespeare: In Which Nothing Is Added to the Original Text, but Those Words and Expressions Are Omitted Which Cannot with Propriety Be Read Aloud in a Family*, containing twenty plays, appeared anonymously in 1807, hiding the fact that it was largely the work of Henrietta Maria Bowdler, Thomas's sister. In 1818, Thomas, presumably wishing to protect his sister's reputation from those who would judge her for having worked so intimately with such "offensive" passages, published the work in ten volumes under his own name. The 1818 edition included all of Shakespeare's plays, although the language of *Othello, the Moor of Venice* (pr. 1604, rev. 1623) forced Bowdler to "advise the transferring it from the parlour to the cabinet."

Thomas Bowdler generally continued Henrietta's omission of sexually suspicious words or passages. Romeo's statement about Juliet in *Romeo and Juliet* (pr. c. 1595-1596) that she would not "ope her lap to saint-seducing gold" was stricken, while Iago's notorious reference to Othello and Desdemona making the "beast with two backs" became "your daughter and the Moor are now together." Profanities such as "'Sblood" for "by God's blood" were cut. Bowdler restored some scenes that Henrietta had deemed irrelevant to several plots, but Doll Tearsheet disappeared entirely from *Henry IV,*

ADVERTISEMENT FOR *THE FAMILY SHAKSPEARE*

This advertisement appeared in *The Times of London* on December 15, 1818. The quote is credited to Bowdler's Preface:

THE FAMILY SHAKSPEARE; in which nothing is added to the original text; but those words and expressions are omitted which cannot with propriety be read aloud in a family. By THOMAS BOWDLER, Esq. F.R.S. and S.A. In 10 vols. . . .

"My great objects in this undertaking are to remove from the writings of Shakspeare some defects which diminish their value, and at the same time to present to the public an edition of his plays, which the parent, the guardian, and the instructor of youth may place without fear in the hands of the pupil; and from which the pupil may derive instruction as well as pleasure; may improve his moral principles while he refines his taste; and, without incurring the danger of being hurt with any indelicacy of expression, may learn in the fate of Mackbeth, that even a kingdom is dearly purchased, if virtue be the price of the acquisition."—Preface.

Part II (pr. 1598), along with most of the Porter's scene in *Macbeth* (pr. 1606) and all of Katherine's bawdy English lesson in act 3 of *Henry V* (pr. c. 1598-1599).

In the Bowdlers' editions, Henry IV called Owen Glendower "vile Glendower" rather than "damned Glendower," Falstaff's "belly" became his "body," and in *Measure for Measure* (pr. 1604) Lucio's "He hath got his friend with child" was changed to "His friend's with child by him." This particular play demanded a separate preface, in which Bowdler announced that

the indecent expressions with which many of the scenes abound are so interwoven with the story, that it is extremely difficult to separate one from the other. I trust, however, that I have succeeded in doing it. . . .

In all, Bowdler removed more than 10 percent of the text of Shakespeare's plays; *Hamlet, Prince of Denmark* (pr. c. 1600-1601) and *Romeo and Juliet* each received more than one hundred alterations.

The earliest edition of *The Family Shakespeare* was published at a time when Romantic poets such as Lord Byron and Percy Bysshe Shelley were challenging conventional moral and political attitudes, almost thirty years before Queen Victoria ascended the throne. However, rather than influence intellectuals, Bowdler sought to shield the sensibilities of Shakespeare's middle-class readers. The work's subtitle announced this ethical goal. Bowdler contributed to the popular desire for "improved" literature and continued an older tendency to re-

vise Shakespeare to suit prevailing tastes. He later published bowdlerized versions of the Old Testament and of Edward Gibbon's *The History of the Decline and Fall of the Roman Empire* (1776-1788).

Altered versions of Shakespeare had already appeared in the late seventeenth century. For example, William Davenant and John Dryden revised *The Tempest* (pr. 1611) in 1667, Davenant adapted *Macbeth* in 1674, and Nahum Tate's revised *King Lear* (pr. c. 1605-1606), in which Cordelia survives to marry Edgar, appeared in 1687 (and became the only stage version of that play for well more than a century). These alterations were made largely for aesthetic, not moral or religious, reasons; it was thought that Shakespeare's "untutored" genius needed refining to please the neoclassical preferences of Enlightenment audiences.

This desire for a more "beautified" Shakespeare was influenced by the eighteenth century emphasis on "sensibility." Persons of delicate taste, especially young women, were believed to be too sensitive to experience whatever was deemed violent, gross, or obscene. No moral person would wish to be offended even by the printed page; therefore, editions designed to protect tender sensibilities became popular, especially anthologies of inoffensive passages such as Vicesimus Knox's *Elegant Extracts* (1784), William Dodd's *Beauties of Shakespeare* (1752), and Elizabeth Griffiths's *The Morality of Shakespeare's Drama* (1775). As Bowdler himself asserted, in capitals, in 1823:

IF ANY WORD OR EXPRESSION IS OF SUCH A NATURE, THAT THE FIRST IMPRESSION WHICH IT EXCITES IS AN IMPRESSION OF OBSCENITY, THAT WORD OUGHT NOT TO BE SPOKEN, OR WRITTEN, OR PRINTED: AND IF PRINTED, IT OUGHT TO BE ERASED.

A third factor in Bowdler's success was the influence of evangelical Christianity, especially in regard to the proper upbringing of children. In 1806, for example, a Methodist minister had announced that Shakespeare's work was filled with "Barefaced obscenities, low vulgarity, and nauseous vice." In 1841, the Protestant author

Charlotte Elizabeth Browne Tonna recalled happening upon *The Merchant of Venice* (pr. c. 1596-1597) at the age of seven and tasting the "pernicious sweets" of "this ensnaring book!" Evangelical readers thus welcomed Bowdler's work as a guard against the corruption of the young. Said one approving reviewer, "It is scarcely possibly for a young person of fervid genius to read Shakespeare without a dangerous elevation of fancy." In 1821, Francis Jeffrey in the *Edinburgh Review* praised Bowdler's cutting of offending passages, noting that "those who recollect such scenes must all rejoice that Mr. Bowdler has provided a security against their recurrence." This concern for the moral protection of youth had also helped popularize Charles and Mary Lamb's famous 1807 volume *Tales from Shakespeare: Designed for the Use of Young Persons*.

Not everyone was pleased with Bowdler's work. In 1818, the *Monthly Review* lamented that Bowdler had "omitted many phrases as containing indelicacies which we cannot see, and of the guilt of which our bard, we think, is entirely innocent." In April, 1822, the *British Critic* summarized the damage done to Shakespeare by the Bowdlers: "Emendations, curtailments, corrections (*all for his own good*) have been multiplied to infinity. . . . They have purged and castrated him, and tattooed and beplaistered him, and cauterized and phlebotomized him."

The verb "bowdlerize" first appeared as a derogatory term in 1836 and came to describe all forms of literary emasculation. Nevertheless, between 1829 and 1899, seventy editions of *The Family Shakespeare* appeared, and Bowdler's influence spread to imitators. The first American expurgation of Shakespeare was published in 1849, and more than forty different expurgated versions of Shakespeare were available in England by 1894. In the preface to *Sylvie and Bruno* (1889), Lewis Carroll even observed that Bowdler had not gone far enough: "neither Bowdler's, Chambers's, Brandram's, nor Cundell's 'Boudoir' Shakespeare, seems to me to meet the want: they are not sufficiently 'expurgated.'" Shortly thereafter, in an 1894 essay titled "Social Verse," the poet Algernon Charles Swinburne neatly summarized the Victorians' approval of Bowdler's work:

> More nauseous and more foolish cant was never chattered than that which would deride the memory or depreciate the merits of Bowdler. No man ever did more service to Shakespeare than the man who made it possible to put him into the hands of intelligent and imaginative children.

SIGNIFICANCE

For Bowdler's defenders, then and now, his censorship of Shakespeare was mitigated by the resulting wider readership for the dramatist, especially among youth who might not otherwise have come to know him in print. It is also true that, compared to some other contemporary expurgators, Bowdler was more lenient; for example, John Philip Kemble's acting version of *Othello* excised more than one-third of the play. Bowdler also never altered the plot or the characterization of the plays, as the Reverend James Plumptre's *The English Drama Purified* (1812) had done. If the Shakespeare that Bowdler produced was an emasculated and benign dramatist whose main purpose was to avoid offending women and children, epitomize English creativity, and arouse patriotic literary pride, he was nevertheless, according to Marvin Rosenberg, "the most nearly authentic Shakespeare virtuous females were then likely to hear."

—*Christopher Baker*

FURTHER READING

Dobson, Michael. "Bowdler and Britannia: Shakespeare and the National Libido." In *Shakespeare and Race*, edited by Catherine M. S. Alexander and S. Wells. Cambridge, England: Cambridge University Press, 2000. Contends that Bowdler's edition promoted the dramatist as a model of both national pride and sexual propriety.

Franklin, Colin. "The Bowdlers and Their *Family Shakespeare*." *The Book Collector* 49 (2000): 227-243. Summarizes Bowdler's social context and his edition. Defends his efforts to popularize Shakespeare while guarding young readers from his bawdiness.

Perrin, Noel. *Dr. Bowdler's Legacy: A History of Expurgated Books in England and America*. 3d ed. Boston: David R. Godine, 1991. A popularly written and well-documented account of Bowdler's work and influence.

Price, Leah. "The Poetics of Pedantry from Thomas Bowdler to Susan Ferrier." *Women's Writing* 7 (2000): 75-88. Argues that the novels of Susan Ferrier (1782-1854), which are composed largely of extracts and quotes from famous authors, follow Bowdler's practice of altering texts for reading aloud in polite, mixed company.

Rosenberg, Marvin. "Reputation, Oft Lost Without Deserving. . . ." *Shakespeare Quarterly* 9 (Autumn, 1958): 499-506. Summarizes Bowdler's work and defends him by comparing him to more stringent expurgators of his time and earlier.

SEE ALSO: Dec., 1816: Rise of the Cockney School; May 8, 1835: Andersen Publishes His First Fairy Tales; June 28, 1838: Queen Victoria's Coronation; c. 1884-1924: Decadent Movement Flourishes; Nov. 8, 1900: Dreiser Publishes *Sister Carrie*.

RELATED ARTICLES in *Great Lives from History: The Nineteenth Century, 1801-1900:* Hector Berlioz; Sarah Bernhardt; Edwin Booth; Lord Byron; Lewis Carroll; Henry Irving; Fanny Kemble; William Charles Macready; Percy Bysshe Shelley; Ellen Terry; Queen Victoria.

1807-1834
MOORE PUBLISHES *IRISH MELODIES*

Already one of the most popular poets and songwriters of his age, Thomas Moore became a household name after the far-reaching popularity of his Irish Melodies. *His work earned him acclaim as Ireland's national bard.*

LOCALE: Dublin, Ireland
CATEGORIES: Literature; music

KEY FIGURE
Thomas Moore (1779-1852), Irish poet and satirist

SUMMARY OF EVENT
Thomas Moore's youth coincided with upheavals that were to influence the future course of Irish history. The dominant Anglican ascendancy had come under attack from both Protestant Dissenters (mainly Presbyterians) and Roman Catholics. Discontent was first publicly aired in Presbyterian Ulster, under the enlightened leadership of Henry Grattan (1746-1820), but Dublin Castle and Westminster failed to meet Grattan even halfway. Had they done so, and had his message been heeded, there might have emerged some reconciliation of sectarian and ethnic strife in a common Irish patriotism.

Reconciliation was not to be, although 1793 saw the repeal of some of the harshest and most discriminatory penal laws. In 1798, a largely Roman Catholic revolt, inspired by an anticipated but aborted French invasion, resulted in savage repression and permanent alienation of Irish from English, and Irish Catholics from Irish Protestants, eventually leading to the emergence of the Orange Lodges to counter the ideal of a united republican—and essentially Roman Catholic—Ireland.

On January 1, 1801, the British government pushed through Parliament an Act of Union of the English and Irish parliaments that, while intended as a step forward, in effect disempowered the Dublin parliament while failing to serve Irish interests in Westminster because the Catholic majority was still disenfranchised. By that time, Grattan's moderate and patient leadership had been replaced by the firebrand oratory of Daniel O'Connell (1775-1847), whose founding of the Catholic Association of 1823 aimed to will into being a Catholic nation. These heady events form the backdrop to Moore's *Irish Melodies*, which he began publishing in 1807.

The *Irish Melodies* may have been inspired during Moore's days at Trinity College, Dublin, when he and his

Thomas Moore. (R. S. Peale/J. A. Hill)

friend Edward Hudson played airs together and discussed the misfortunes of Ireland. Moore ever after noted that his passion for Irish music was directly inspired by Hudson, who collected airs (Hudson, however, was arrested in 1798 for activities with the United Irishmen). Moore also was influenced by the 1792 festival of nine Irish harpers, the only nine who could be located. James MacDonnell had organized the festival in Belfast and Edward Bunting transcribed the music. Bunting thereafter traveled throughout Ulster, Munster, and Connaught, assembling a collection he published in 1796 as *A General Collection of the Ancient Irish Music*. Moore obtained a copy of Bunting's work and was inspired to write lyrics for traditional airs.

The festival and Bunting's transcriptions were part of a larger movement to rescue, restore, and codify national music. Other collections of Irish melodies had been published, including *Historical Memoirs of the Irish Bards* (1786) by J. C. Walker (d. 1810), *Celebrated Irish Tunes* by James Jackson, *Curious Selection of Favorite Scenes* by J. Brysson, *Hibernian Muse* (anon.), and *The Repository of Scots and Irish Airs* by J. McFayden. England saw the publication of E. T. Warren's thirty-two-volume collection of popular songs, including glees, madrigals, and canons, and John Stafford Smith's *Ancient Songs* (1799) and *Musica Antiqua* (1812). In Scotland, George Thomson published the six-volume *Selected Collection of Original Scottish Airs for the Voice* (1793) and Sir Walter Scott published his *Minstrelsy of the Scottish Border* (1802-1803). Glee clubs and madrigal societies proliferated in this era, called the age of the Celtic Revival, groups of individuals who loved to play and sing popular music.

Within the year following Moore's infamous duel with Lord Jeffrey (interrupted by Bow Street police) over Jeffrey's scathing review of Moore's *Epistles, Odes, and Other Poems* (1806) in the *Edinburgh Review*, Moore was approached by the Dublin music publisher William Power, who, aware of Moore's talent and reputation, asked him to write lyrics to traditional Irish melodies, a proposal he accepted with pleasure in that it seemed "so truly National." When Moore met his future musical collaborator Sir John Stevenson, he recited odes from his 1800 work *Odes of Anacreon* (a work so acclaimed that he was long afterward referred to as "Anacreon Moore"), from which Stevenson later composed several glees.

Moore's *Irish Melodies* had become a sensation not only because Moore was a talented musician but also because he was a talented poet who could create songs in which poetry and music coalesced. His aesthetic agenda

---

"THE HARP THAT ONCE THROUGH TARA'S HALLS"

The harp that once thro' Tara's halls
    The soul of music shed,
Now hangs as mute on Tara's walls,
    As if that soul were fled. —
So sleeps the pride of former days,
    So glory's thrill is o'er,
And hearts, that once beat high for praise,
    Now feel that pulse no more.

No more to chiefs and ladies bright
    The harp of Tara swells;
The chord alone, that breaks at night,
    Its tale of ruin tells.
Thus Freedom now so seldom wakes,
    The only throb she gives,
Is when some heart indignant breaks,
    To show that still she lives.

Source: Thomas Moore, *The Complete Poems of Thomas Moore* (n.d.).

---

promoted the idea not only that a sound should seem like an echo of the sense but also that sound and sense, music and lyrics, should be one. Also, at a time when Irish relations with the English were poisoned by rebellions and repressions, Moore was able to give voice to Irish feelings in the idiom of his time: motifs of sentiment, sensibility, nostalgia for a golden past, desire for freedom and equality, and reverence for the beauties of nature. He did so in a way—often allegorically and never overtly threatening to the English—that made his songs accepted, adored, and performed in homes across Great Britain.

Because part of his contractual obligation was that he should himself perform the *Irish Melodies*, he wrote the lyrics for his own voice. They showed his talent not merely for poetry but also for writing words that enhanced the beauty of the sung lyric. As a biographer noted, "No one has ever so considered the voice" nor so brilliantly suited the words to the lyrical cadences of the airs.

Moore had his critics, however. Some accused him of being unfaithful to his Irish heritage and to the cause of Ireland by living among the well-to-do in London and becoming more a Whig than an Irish nationalist. Other critics compared the *Irish Melodies* unfavorably to the works of the major Romantics. Moore, however, wrote *Irish Melodies* for song, not to be read as poems; criticism leveled against him as a poet based on silent reading of the words was necessarily erroneous. Contemporaries also charged that he had tampered with the purity of a national treasure by altering the airs to suit his own voice, changing the character of the traditional melodies.

Bunting's collection was transcribed from contemporary harpers' performances—and there can never be "authorized versions" of folk music; Moore previously knew some of the airs. When they had preexisting Gaelic lyrics, Moore was able to adapt them, but he did so intuitively, for he knew no Gaelic. His technical collaborator, Stevenson, made his own changes, and he did so to the disapproval of Moore.

An academic musician, Stevenson arranged the airs for piano, which Moore himself did not use when performing. Moore lamented that "the hand that corrects their [the airs'] errors is almost sure to destroy their character, and the few little flowers they boast are pulled away with the weeds." He resented the academic hand of Stevenson, but knew that he could not execute the arrangements himself. In Moore's notes to performers, he instructed them that the timing ought to be secondary to other matters, so that the timing would not detract from the lyrical expression and the "curve" of the air. The debate over Moore's respect for the integrity of the original airs, and of Stevenson's part in their formal arrangement, faded into an uneasy consensus: Moore's project was so well executed that the point was moot.

Despite the overt Irish nationalism of the first two installments of the series, which included songs commemorating the 1798 and 1803 rebellions, Moore received critical and popular acclaim. By 1810, though, he found himself on the defensive against charges of "mischievous" politics, and, thereafter, his nationalism was couched in allegory.

SIGNIFICANCE

Thomas Moore provided a fresh infusion of pure lyric into British poetry, a process that began with his *Odes of Anacreon* and was crystallized in the *Irish Melodies*, injecting pure musicality and the cadences of Irish folk song into English poetry. Considered a major poet by his contemporaries, he was read by many Romantics, and his influence can be seen in their works. His personal and literary relationship with Lord Byron is well known. Indeed, the *Irish Melodies* influenced Byron's *Hebrew Melodies* (1815), wherein Moore's "The Harp That Once Through Tara's Hall," for instance, becomes Byron's harp of King David, and Moore's Romantic Irish nationalism, with its themes of exile and repression, defiance and melancholy, colored Byron's work.

A master craftsman, Moore brought into English-language poetry the lilt of Irish song and the atmosphere of Celtic magic. His far-reaching influence is unmistakable in the works of the younger Romantics in England, in the anapestic feet of the American gothic poems of Edgar Allan Poe, in the images of the Pre-Raphaelite poems of Dante Gabriel Rossetti, and in the works of the great Irish modernist William Butler Yeats, whose poems have been a schoolroom for much of the best lyric poetry of the twentieth century.

Some said that although Moore never participated actively in the cause of Irish nationalism, he did more for the cause through his literary work than he could have done in any other way, for his immense popularity throughout Great Britain brought the Irish and their problems into parlors across the isles in the most endearing and enduring of manners.

—*Donna Berliner*

FURTHER READING

Davis, Leith. *Music, Postcolonialism, and Gender: The Construction of Irish National Identity, 1724-1874.* Notre Dame: University of Notre Dame Press, 2006. A history of Irish nationalism that takes into account gender identity and popular culture. Includes the chapters "A 'Truly National' Project: Thomas Moore's *Irish Melodies* and the Gendering of the British Cultural Marketplace" and "In Moore's Wake: Irish Music in Ireland After the *Irish Melodies.*"

DeFord, Miriam Allen. *Thomas Moore.* New York: Twayne, 1967. A good background work on Moore's career. Contains a chapter on the *Irish Melodies.*

Jones, Howard Mumford. *The Harp That Once: A Chronicle of the Life of Thomas Moore.* New York: Henry Holt, 1937. Critical biography that portrays Moore as the national bard of Ireland.

Jordan, Hoover H. "Thomas Moore: Artistry in the Song Lyric." *SEL* 2 (1962): 403-440. Detailed study of Moore's aesthetics from a technical standpoint.

McMahon, Sean. *The Minstrel Boy: Thomas Moore and His Melodies.* Cork, Ireland: Mercier Press, 2001. An updated biography of Moore, with a focus on his classic work. Includes selections of Moore's verse.

Moore, Thomas. *Irish Melodies: The Illustrated 1846 Edition.* Mineola, N.Y.: Dover, 2000. A reprint of Moore's classic work, with illustrations by Daniel Maclise.

Strong, Leonard A. G. *The Minstrel Boy: A Portrait of Tom Moore.* New York: Alfred A. Knopf, 1937. Critical biography that examines Moore's aesthetics.

Tessier, Thérèse. *The Bard of Erin: A Study of Thomas Moore's "Irish Melodies," 1808-1834.* Salzburg, Austria: Institut für Anglistik und Amerikanistic, 1981. Detailed examination of the *Irish Melodies.*

SEE ALSO: 1807-1850: Rise of the Knickerbocker School; 1812-1815: Brothers Grimm Publish Fairy Tales; 1814: Scott Publishes *Waverley*; 1819-1820:

Irving's *Sketch Book* Transforms American Literature; c. 1820-1860: *Costumbrismo* Movement; May 8, 1835: Andersen Publishes His First Fairy Tales.

RELATED ARTICLES in *Great Lives from History: The Nineteenth Century, 1801-1900:* Lord Byron; Stephen Collins Foster; Edvard Grieg; Washington Irving.

1807-1850
RISE OF THE KNICKERBOCKER SCHOOL

Taking their nickname from the costume of the original Dutch settlers of Manhattan, the Knickerbockers were a group of young New York City writers, led by Washington Irving, who created the first truly national literature in the United States and helped to free American culture from Europe.

LOCALE: New York State
CATEGORY: Literature

KEY FIGURES

Washington Irving (1783-1859), creator of the fictional Diedrich Knickerbocker

James Fenimore Cooper (1789-1851), the first professional American novelist

James Kirke Paulding (1778-1860), cofounder, with Irving, of the periodical *Salmagundi*

William Cullen Bryant (1794-1878), American poet and editor of the *New York Evening Post*

Fitz-Greene Halleck (1790-1867), coauthor of *The Croaker Poems*

SUMMARY OF EVENT

Before the turn of the nineteenth century, Americans were too much concerned with settling their new land and establishing their independence from Great Brtain to spare much interest in a national literature. Moreover, New World writers had scant American history to draw upon, no kings or lords to people their works, no wealthy patrons to support them, and no apparent way to compete with popular British imports. Why, many of them wondered, would anyone want to read an American book, and what would such a boook be about? During the first decades of the nineteenth century, the so-called Knickerbockers answered such questions. Several Knickerbockers were native New Yorkers, but others were latecomers

to New York City. They differed greatly among themselves in their religious faiths, politics, and backgrounds, but they shared a belief in the possibility of an authentic native literature.

In 1807, *Salmagundi: Or, The Whim-Whams of Opinions of Launcelot Langstaff, Esq. and Others* announced the arrival of this new group. A series of twenty pamphlets written by Washington Irving, his brother William, and William's brother-in-law James Kirke Paulding, *Salmagundi* contained satirical sketches, poems, theatrical criticism, and witty essays that described life in New York City and opposed Jeffersonian democracy.

In December, 1809, Washington Irving published *A History of New York from the Beginning of the World to the End of the Dutch Dynasty*, as written by Diedrich Knickerbocker, and supposedly found among his papers by his landlord. Drawing upon history, fable, and his own imagination, Irving used his imaginary Knickerbocker—as unreliable a narrator as any of his eighteenth century forebears—to satirize the stolid Dutch settlers of New York. He also drew parallels between the history of New Netherlands and the United States and ridiculed not only history itself and the epic narrative style commonly used to write it, but also American political parties and even Thomas Jefferson, as the inventor of useless contrivances. However, beneath the satire, Irving, who preferred the picturesque past to the then current world of trade and speculation, revealed an early awareness of contradictions in American society between idealism and materialism.

In 1819, a series of playful, satirical poems was published anonymously in the *New York Evening Post*. Their authors were Fitz-Greene Halleck of Connecticut and Joseph Rodman Drake, a true New Yorker. Drake met an early death in 1825, but Halleck went on to become New York's favorite poet, a friend of William Cullen Bryant, and the author of light lyrical poems satirizing authors, politicians, men of science, and the affectations of the nouveau riche. These early efforts found great favor with New York readers.

Meanwhile, Irving was cementing an international reputation as well as his claim upon posterity with publication of *The Sketch Book of Geoffrey Crayon, Gent.* (1819-1820), which was highly praised in both America and England. It contained the now-famous tales "Rip Van Winkle" and "The Legend of Sleepy Hollow"— both narrated by Diedrich Knickerbocker, the old Dutch gentleman from the Catskills. Thereafter, "Knickerbocker" became synonymous not only with the group of writers but also with New York City and New Yorkers. Irving's Father Knickerbocker became New York's most popular symbol during the late nineteenth and early twentieth centuries. Irving's considerable literary output included sketches of England, histories, and biographies

of figures such as George Washington and Christopher Columbus. After spending seventeen years in Europe, as a diplomatic attaché, secretary to the American legation, and later as minister to Spain, Irving retired to his home in Tarrytown, overlooking the Hudson River, where he enjoyed the affection and celebrity that his literary career afforded him.

James Fenimore Cooper, another Knickerbocker transplant to New York City, became one of the most influential American novelists of the nineteenth century. Cooper's family had been wealthy landowners in Otsego, New York, and Cooper envisioned an America governed by a landed aristocracy. When his family's fortunes collapsed, he was forced to entertain other possibilities, although his belief in the superiority of a white landed class never faltered. His first novel, *Precaution*, set in England and published anonymously in 1820, sold poorly, but his second novel, *The Spy* (1821), was

1. Henry T. Tackerman	6. Henry Wadsworth Longfellow	11. Ralph Waldo Emerson
2. Oliver Wendell Holmes	7. Nathaniel Parker Willis	12. William Cullen Bryant
3. William Gilmore Simms	8. William H. Prescott	13. John P. Kennedy
4. Fitz-Greene Halleck	9. Washington Irving	14. J. Fenimore Cooper
5. Nathaniel Hawthorne	10. James K. Paulding	15. George Bancroft

Washington Irving and his literary friends. (P. F. Collier and Son)

deliberately patriotic and spectacularly successful, as was *The Pilot* (1823), the first American sea story.

Although Cooper wrote more than forty books of fiction and nonfiction, he is remembered mostly for his five Leatherstocking Tales: *The Pioneers* (1823), *The Last of the Mohicans* (1826), *The Prairie* (1827), *The Pathfinder* (1840), and *The Deerslayer* (1841). His great contribution to American literature was the creation of the archetypal American hero in the character of Natty Bumppo, who was also known as Leatherstocking, Hawkeye, Deerslayer, Long Rifle, and the Trapper. A silent and rootless loner, Bumppo has fled from society and sought the isolation of the natural world. Quick on the trigger when necessary, he operates in an environment beyond the law and according to his own moral values. He is accompanied by Chingachgook, the embodiment of the so-called noble savage, equally brave and moral, but doomed, as his race is doomed. These two companions— one white, the other dark, one from the natural world, the other from the so-called civilized world—encounter the violence and terror manifest as white people press ever farther into the wilderness, and the march of modern progress exacts its toll. Their literary and dramatic descendants can be seen in films and on television to this day.

In his prime, James Kirke Paulding ranked in popularity alongside Irving and Cooper as a storyteller who combined narrative skill with enthusiastic nationalism. At the age of eighteen, after growing up in Tarrytown, he moved to New York City, where he collaborated with Irving on *Salmagundi*. From his childhood, when members of his family were forced to leave their home in fear of the Tories, he detested the British. In 1812, as tensions between the United States and Great Britain increased, he published a sharp satire, *The Diverting History of John Bull and Brother Jonathan*. He followed it with *The Lay of the Scottish Fiddle* (1813), a parody of Sir Walter Scott's *The Lay of the Last Minstrel* (1805). After the War of 1812 brought the threat of British invasion to American shores, Paulding enlisted in the New York state militia as a major.

Paulding strongly advocated a native literature that would use the language and materials indigenous to the

---

IRVING'S APOLOGY

In 1848, Washington Irving wrote an apology—an explanation of his motives—for Knickerbocker's History of New York, *which was published at the beginning of subsequent editions of the work. As the apology makes clear, Irving was concerned with the creation of a distinctively American literature, tied both in content and in form to the United States, its land, and its people.*

The main object of my work, in fact, had a bearing wide from the sober aim of history, but one which, I trust, will meet with some indulgence from poetic minds. It was to embody the traditions of our city in an amusing form; to illustrate its local humors, customs and peculiarities; to clothe home scenes and places and familiar names with those imaginative and whimsical associations so seldom met with in our new country, but which live like charms and spells about the cities of the old world, binding the heart of the native inhabitant to his home.

In this I have reason to believe I have in some measure succeeded. Before the appearance of my work the popular traditions of our city were unrecorded; the peculiar and racy customs and usages derived from our Dutch progenitors were unnoticed, or regarded with indifference, or adverted to with a sneer. Now they form a convivial currency, and are brought forward on all occasions; they link our whole community together in good-humor and good-fellowship; they are the rallying points of home feeling; the seasoning of our civic festivities; the staple of local tales and local pleasantries; and are so harped upon by our writers of popular fiction that I find myself almost crowded off the legendary ground which I was the first to explore by the host who have followed in my footsteps.

Source: Washington Irving, *Knickerbocker's History of New York: Complete* (New York: G. P. Putnam's Sons, 1894).

New World and not be a servile imitation of British imports. Throughout his life, which included government service under Presidents James Madison, James Monroe and Martin Van Buren, Paulding continued to write. He published numerous tales, poems, and essays, and five novels: *Konigsmarke* (1823), *The Dutchman's Fireside* (1831), *Westward Ho* (1832), *The Old Continental* (1846), and *The Puritan and His Daughter* (1849).

William Cullen Bryant joined the Knickerbocker group during the late 1820's, when he moved from Massachusetts to New York City to edit the *New York Review*. Already celebrated as a poet on the basis of his poem "Thanatopsis" (1817), he was accepted immediately into the New York literary circle. He became editor and owner of the *Evening Post*, and through fifty years as a journalist and critic he commented on all matters political, cultural, and economic. An unabashed liberal, he was critical of American capitalism. He was also a vigorous opponent of slavery, a campaigner for the creation of New York City's Central Park, and a champion of unpopular causes. Although literature was only an occasional pursuit for Bryant, he claimed that America had landscapes and subjects as worthy of celebration as any that Europe could offer. His life was long, extending from the beginning of Romanticism to the beginning of realism.

The year 1830 brought *The Knickerbocker Magazine*. Until its demise in 1865, this magazine published the works of almost every living American writer of note. However, by midcentury, as the Civil War (1861-1865) loomed, both literary tastes and concerns of the writers were changing, and the popularity of the Knickerbockers diminished.

SIGNIFICANCE

The Knickerbockers' great contribution was the creation of a new literature that was national in scope with an artistry that was sufficiently high to command respect not only from their fellow countrymen in the New World but also from England and the Continent. The Knickerbockers produced essays, novels, and poetry that stimulated and entertained, using American material, landscapes, and language. They defined American character and humor, and paved the way for such major nineteenth century literary figures as Nathaniel Hawthorne, Ralph Waldo Emerson, Herman Melville, and Mark Twain.

—*Joyce E. Henry*

FURTHER READING

Aderman, Ralph, ed. *Critical Essays on Washington Irving*. Boston: G. K. Hall, 1990. Anthology of contemporary reviews and essays of Irving's work and twentieth century essays.

Bryant, William Cullen. *Power for Sanity: Selected Editorials of William Cullen Bryant, 1829-1981*. Edited by William Cullen Bryant II. New York: Fordham University Press, 1994. Eclectic collection, helpfully annotated, demonstrating Bryant's passion for free commerce, free speech, and free soil and his skillful prose style.

Link, Earl Carl. "American Nationalism and the Defense of Poetry." *Southern Quarterly* 41, no. 2 (2003): 48-59. A brief description of Bryant's ideas of poetry as set forth in his lectures before the New York Athenaeum.

Parrington, Vernon L. *The Romantic Revolution in America, 1800-1860*. New York: Harcourt, Brace & World, 1927. An old but still useful work discussing early American literature from a regional perspective, with excellent discussions of all the Knickerbockers.

Reid, Margaret. *Cultural Secrets as Narrative Form: Story Telling in Nineteenth-Century America*. Columbus: Ohio State University Press, 2004. Examines the roles of experience, language and secrecy in the works of James Fenimore Cooper, Nathaniel Hawthorne, and Owen Wister.

Taylor, Alan. "Fenimore Cooper's America." *History Today* 46, no. 2 (1996): 21-27. A good overview of Cooper's personal life, his social concerns and ambitions, and the connection with his novels.

SEE ALSO: 1814: Scott Publishes *Waverley*; Dec., 1816: Rise of the Cockney School; 1819-1820: Irving's *Sketch Book* Transforms American Literature; c. 1830's-1860's: American Renaissance in Literature; 1880's: Brahmin School of American Literature Flourishes; Dec., 1884-Feb., 1885: Twain Publishes *Adventures of Huckleberry Finn*.

RELATED ARTICLES in *Great Lives from History: The Nineteenth Century, 1801-1900:* William Cullen Bryant; James Fenimore Cooper; Nathaniel Hawthorne; Washington Irving.

March 2, 1807
CONGRESS BANS IMPORTATION OF AFRICAN SLAVES

When the U.S. Congress formally outlawed the slave trade into the United States, the law proved to be a symbolic act rather than a practical end to the trade, and the difficulties of both passing and enforcing the act reflected the young nation's moral ambiguity about freedom and slavery.

LOCALE: Washington, D.C.

CATEGORIES: Human rights; trade and commerce; laws, acts, and legal history; atrocities and war crimes

KEY FIGURES

Stephen Row Bradley (1754-1830), Vermont senator who introduced the first bill on this subject

Barnabas Bidwell (1763-1833), Massachusetts representative who drafted anti-slave-trade legislation in the House of Representatives

Thomas Jefferson (1743-1826), president of the United States, 1801-1809

SUMMARY OF EVENT

Because the essence of slavery is to regard human beings as property, the buying and selling of slaves is implicit in the institution; therefore, the slave trade is as old as slavery itself. In the ancient Mediterranean world, slaves were obtained from many locations, including North Africa. As early as 1444, the Portuguese began importing African slaves, and at the end of the same century, Christopher Columbus took a few black slaves born in Spain to Hispaniola, the first European New World colony. At first, the Spaniards intended to use native Caribbean peoples as slaves, but by the sixteenth century, the native Caribbeans had proved unsatisfactory as slaves, and most of them were dying off from smallpox, syphilis, influenza, measles, and other diseases introduced by European contact. The Caribbean peoples who remained proved rebellious, physically unsuitable for agricultural exploitation, and quick to disappear into familiar surrounding forests. Early in the six-

teenth century, Spain began importing black African slaves to its New World colonies.

The Netherlands and France also took up the practice of importing African slaves in their New World possessions. During the seventeenth century, England had begun to gain commercial ascendancy by developing the notorious "triangular trade," which linked equatorial Africa, the Caribbean, and its North American colonies. By the time Great Britain's American colonies revolted and established the United States of America, the triangular trade had reached its peak. In 1790, approximately three-quarters of a million people of black African descent were living in the United States. Almost nine-tenths of them labored as slaves in the southern states, with Virginia alone claiming three hundred thousand slaves. About 28 percent of African Americans in the northern states were free, but only one major American city, Boston, had no black slaves at all. The American struggle for political independence did not effect freedom for the slaves and their offspring.

Antislavery sentiment in North America was growing at the time of the American Revolution but needed competent leadership to challenge the long-standing practice

Although Congress banned the importation of slaves in 1807, the slave trade within the United States flourished until the time of the Civil War (1861-1865). The Alexandria, Virginia, slave-dealing firm in this photograph operated only a few miles from the nation's capital during the 1850's. (National Archives/Mathew Brady Collection)

CONGRESSIONAL ACT PROHIBITING THE SLAVE TRADE TO THE UNITED STATES

The following passage is excerpted from the 1807 act of Congress that banned the importation of African slaves to the United States and its territories.

An act to prohibit the importation of slaves into any port or place within the jurisdiction of the United States. . . .

Be it enacted, That from and after the first day of January, one thousand eighteen hundred and eight, it shall not be lawful to import or bring into the United States or the territories thereof, from any foreign kingdom, place, or country, any negro, mulatto, or person of color, with intent to hold, sell, or dispose of such negro, mulatto, or person of color, as a slave, or to be held to service or labor.

SECTION 2: *And be it further enacted,* That no citizen or citizens of the United States, or any other person, shall . . . for himself, or themselves, or any other person whatsoever, either as master, factor, or owner, build, fit, equip, load, or otherwise prepare any ship or vessel, in any port or place within the jurisdiction of the United States, nor shall cause any ship or vessel to sail from any port or place within the same, for the purpose of procuring any negro, mulatto, or person of color, from any foreign kingdom, place, or country, to be transported to any port . . . within the United States, to be held, sold, or disposed of as slaves, or to be held to service or labor. . . .

Approved, March 2, 1807

of people enslaving their fellow humans. The Society of Friends (Quakers), some of whose members had a long history of opposition to slavery, led the antislavery, or abolitionist, movement in Pennsylvania, beginning shortly before the outbreak of the revolution, and a few clergymen of other religious congregations in England and America took up the cause. Arguments against slavery at the Constitutional Convention of 1787 foundered on threats that delegates from South Carolina and Georgia would ratify no constitution that outlawed the slave trade. In the end, the convention wrote into Article I of the Constitution the vaguely worded promise that Congress would not move to end the slave trade before 1808:

The Migration or Importation of such Persons as any of the States now existing shall think proper to admit, shall not be prohibited by the Congress prior to the Year one thousand eight hundred and eight, but a Tax or duty may be imposed on such Importation, not exceeding ten dollars for each Person.

Opposition to slavery was not all high-minded. The French Revolution of 1789 had helped inspire a bloody slave revolt in France's Caribbean colony of Saint Domingue on the island of Hispaniola that eventually led to the creation of independent, black-ruled Haiti. In the United States, fear of similar slave uprisings was probably a more powerful motive for opposing the slave trade than democratic or humanitarian sentiments in the antislavery agitation of the 1790's.

By the 1790's, several northern states had outlawed slavery, sometimes through legislation that instituted abolition gradually or at least banned traffic in slaves. Maryland, Massachusetts, Connecticut, New York, and New Jersey had all passed anti-slave-trade legislation in the 1780's, as did even South Carolina for a few years. However, such piecemeal legislation could not stop the trade in human beings, particularly after 1793, when the invention of the cotton gin suddenly made cotton a far more profitable crop in the South by greatly increasing the speed at which seeds could be separated from the picked cotton, thus increasing plantation owners' desire for more cotton pickers. It has been said that slavery might have simply died out in the United States, had it not been for the invention of the cotton gin.

Northern merchants, although not slave owners themselves, had few scruples about supplying new slaves for southern cotton-growing states, and the delight of New England textile mill owners over the newly burgeoning supply of cotton was not likely to make them support abolition. At the turn of the nineteenth century, the slave trade to the United States was far from waning. It has been estimated that no fewer than twenty thousand new slaves were imported in Georgia and South Carolina in 1803.

In December, 1805, Senator Stephen R. Bradley of Vermont introduced federal legislation that would prohibit the slave trade beginning in 1808—the earliest date allowed by the Constitution. However, the bill was stalled for some months. A similar bill was offered in the House of Representatives by Barnabas Bidwell of Massachusetts, again to no effect. Later that year, President Thomas Jefferson urged passage of the bill in his message to Congress. On March 2, 1807, Congress enacted a law specifying a twenty-thousand-dollar fine and forfeiture of ship and cargo for importing slaves, as well as other penalties for acts ranging from equipping a slave ship to knowingly buying an imported slave. The disposition of illegally imported slaves was left to the states, however. The law also prohibited coastal trade in slaves carried on in vessels smaller than forty tons. Enforcement of the law was delegated first to the secretary of the Treasury and later to the secretary of the Navy.

Antislavery forces rejoiced in this new and symbolically important law, but its enforcement proved weak. An exhaustive census of the slave trade published in 1969 estimated that 1.9 million slaves were illegally imported into the United States between 1811 and 1870. Later research has called that estimate low. Probably one-fifth of the Africans who became American slaves arrived in the United States *after* 1808, when the federal law took effect.

Although more than one hundred slave vessels were seized and their officers arrested in the years between 1837 and 1862, and nearly the same number of cases were prosecuted, convictions were difficult to obtain. Moreover, when convictions were obtained, judges often pronounced light sentences. Meanwhile, because of meager press coverage of the slave trade, few Americans were aware of the extent of the violations. During the decades following the 1807 law, most Americans thought of slave importation as something of the past. Some people, particularly in the South, continued to sympathize with the slave trade.

Another weakness of the 1807 law was that it permitted the continuation of slave traffic among states. Slave owners were permitted to take their slaves into other slave states or, according to the Missouri Compromise of 1820, into a western territory south of 36°30′, an area greatly increased by the annexation of Texas in 1845. Moreover, runaway slaves were not out of danger when they entered so-called free states. Nearly one-half century after the 1807 law, the Fugitive Slave Law of 1850 obligated all those who captured fugitive slaves *anywhere* in the United States to return the slaves to their owners.

SIGNIFICANCE

It was morally important that Stephen Bradley and Barnabas Bidwell took initiatives to end the sanctioning of U.S. participation in the Atlantic slave trade. It was also important that President Thomas Jefferson, who owned slaves and whose ambiguous attitude toward slavery has continued to cause debate among historians, used his influence to secure passage of the law.

The law was an important step in the direction of creating a truly free society. If it was not a highly effective step, it was at least a necessary one in a new nation that could not agree to condemn slavery outright at that nation's birth or in its early decades. However, the underlying problem with the law forbidding importation of slaves was the institution of slavery itself. As long as a person could be someone else's property, that person would almost inevitably be subject to slave trade of some sort. It was illogical to try to restrict the buying and selling of men, women, and children so long as slavery itself continued to be legal. Nothing better illustrates the problems of compromise between holders of diametrically opposed convictions than the long series of compromises over slavery. Ultimately, the nation could find no better solution for its ambiguous struggle with slavery than the bloody Civil War of 1861-1865.

—*Robert P. Ellis*

FURTHER READING

Barry, Boubacar. *Senegambia and the Atlantic Slave Trade*. Translated by Ayi Kwei Armah. New York: Cambridge University Press, 1998. Originally published in French in 1988, this book provides a meticulously detailed examination of four centuries of the slave trade from a region that supplied many slaves to North America.

Blackburn, Robin. *The Overthrow of Colonial Slavery, 1776-1848*. New York: Verso, 1988. Chapter 7 treats the U.S. experience, with emphasis on politically expedient motives for containing the growth of slavery.

Davis, David Brion. *Slavery and Human Progress*. New York: Oxford University Press, 1984. In arguing that much of what is called progress rests on slavery and the slave trade, contends that abolitionists' most difficult opponents were progressives.

Eltis, David, and James Walvin, eds. *The Abolition of the Atlantic Slave Trade: Origins and Effects in Europe, Africa, and the Americas*. Madison: University of Wisconsin Press, 1981. Part 4, "American Demographic and Cultural Responses," contains four essays, including one studying the effect of U.S. abolition on African American culture.

Franklin, John Hope, and Alfred A. Moss, Jr. *From Slavery to Freedom: A History of African Americans*. 8th ed. Boston: McGraw-Hill, 2000. Pioneering study by an African American historian, first published in 1947. Contains historical background and succinct summary of the enactment of the 1807 law and its aftermath.

Howard, Warren S. *American Slavers and the Federal Law, 1837-1862*. Berkeley: University of California Press, 1963. A copiously documented study of violations of the 1807 law during the quarter century before the outbreak of the Civil War.

Rawley, James A. *The Transatlantic Slave Trade: A History*. New York: W. W. Norton, 1981. Surveys the slave trade from its fifteenth century beginnings and places U.S. involvement in its international context. Revises upward previous estimates, but asserts that the U.S. slave trade was a small percentage of the whole.

Thomas, Hugh. *The Slave Trade: The Story of the Atlantic Slave Trade, 1440-1870*. New York: Simon & Schuster, 1999. A massive volume that offers a comprehensive survey of almost every aspect of the slave trade but one that younger readers will find readily accessible.

SEE ALSO: 1820's-1850's: Social Reform Movement; Mar. 3, 1820: Missouri Compromise; Aug. 28, 1833: Slavery Is Abolished Throughout the British Empire; Dec., 1833: American Anti-Slavery Society Is Founded; July 2, 1839: *Amistad* Slave Revolt; July, 1859: Last Slave Ship Docks at Mobile; Dec. 6, 1865: Thirteenth Amendment Is Ratified; 1873-1897: Zanzibar Outlaws Slavery.

RELATED ARTICLES in *Great Lives from History: The Nineteenth Century, 1801-1900:* Sir Thomas Fowell Buxton; Samuel Ajayi Crowther; Paul Cuffe.

April, 1807
HEGEL PUBLISHES *THE PHENOMENOLOGY OF SPIRIT*

Georg Wilhelm Friedrich Hegel's The Phenomenology of Spirit, *published just twenty-six years after* Immanuel Kant's Critique of Pure Reason, *sought to complete Kant's philosophical system. By expanding that system to include human social structures, as well as the history of philosophy,* The Phenomenology of Spirit *became one of the foundational texts in continental philosophy, one of the two strands of philosophy that define post-Kantian thought.*

ALSO KNOWN AS: *Die Phänomenologie des Geistes*; *The Phenomenology of Mind*
LOCALE: Bamberg and Würzburg, Bavaria (now in Germany)
CATEGORY: Philosophy

KEY FIGURES
Georg Wilhelm Friedrich Hegel (1770-1831), German absolute Idealist philosopher
Immanuel Kant (1724-1804), German founder of critical philosophy
Friedrich Wilhelm Joseph von Schelling (1775-1854), German Romantic Idealist philosopher
Johann Gottlieb Fichte (1762-1814), German subjective Idealist philosopher
Friedrich Immanuel Niethammer (1766-1848), German businessman, civil servant, and philosopher
Hermann Friedrich Wilhelm Hinrichs (1794-1861), German "Old Hegelian" philosopher

Alexandre Kojève (1902-1968), French Hegelian philosopher
Jean-Jacques Rousseau (1712-1778), French-Swiss social philosopher
George Berkeley (1685-1753), bishop of Cloyne and Anglo-Irish empiricist philosopher

SUMMARY OF EVENT
In 1781, Immanuel Kant revolutionized philosophy with his publication of *Kritik der reinen Vernunft* (*Critique of Pure Reason*, 1838), which asked how knowledge is possible and challenged nearly every philosophical idea that had been established up to that time. The Kantian revolution in philosophy has been compared to the Copernican revolution in cosmology, because just as Nicolaus Copernicus placed a new object—the Sun—at the center of the cosmos, Kant placed a new object—the human mind—at the center of epistemological inquiry. Kant's "Copernican turn inward" was based on his argument that the way to understand how knowledge is possible is to subject the mind itself to a critical examination. Kant analyzed the structures of the mind that turn experience into knowledge and that therefore determine what knowledge looks like and how it functions. He sought thereby to ground knowledge, that is, to provide it with some measure of objective validity.

German Idealism, which also gave the "I" or the mind pride of place, emerged in the 1790's, mostly as an attempt to build upon Kant's critical philosophy and to resolve some of its perceived problems. Johann Gottlieb Fichte's *Grundlage der gesamten Wissenschaftslehre* (1794; *The Science of Knowledge*, 1868) turned Idealism in a subjectivist direction, while Friedrich Wilhelm Joseph von Schelling's *System des transzendentalen Idealismus* (1800; *Introduction to Idealism*, 1871) tried to synthesize Fichtean subjectivism with German Romanticism to see all reality subsumed in a mystical identity with the absolute. Georg Wilhelm Friedrich Hegel, who would become the most famous of the German Idealists, saw his own work as another attempt to correct and complete Kant's project using phenomenology, that is, the study of experience.

Even though Schelling and Hegel had been schoolmates at Tübingen and although Schelling was five years younger than Hegel, Schelling considered himself Hegel's mentor during the late 1790's and early nineteenth century. Whether Hegel ever considered himself Schelling's protégé or disciple remains uncertain. Schelling brought Hegel to the University of Jena in January, 1801, and in September Hegel's first philosophical book appeared: *Differenz des Fichte'schen und Schelling'schen Systems der Philosophie* (1801; *The Difference Between Fichte's and Schelling's Systems of Philosophy*, 1977). In 1802 and 1803, Hegel and Schelling edited a philosophical journal together. However, Hegel grew dissatisfied with the lack of rigor in Schelling's thought and began to discern ways to improve it. When Schelling left Jena for Würzburg in 1803, Hegel's independent thought began in earnest. In 1804, Hegel started working on *Die Phänomenologie des Geistes* (1807; *The Phenomenology of Spirit*, 1868; also known as *The Phenomenology of Mind*, 1910), which would mark his final break with Schelling.

On the same day that Hegel finished writing the book, he saw Napoleon I, whom he called "the world-soul on horseback," reconnoitering for the Battle of Jena (October 13-14, 1806). As a result of that battle, Hegel was out of a job and impoverished. In March, 1807, he moved to Bamberg to become a newspaper editor. Josef Anton Goebhardt published *The Phenomenology of Spirit* in April, 1807, in Bamberg and Würzburg with financing guaranteed by Hegel's best friend, Friedrich Immanuel Niethammer.

The topic of *The Phenomenology of Spirit* is *Geist*, an untranslatable term that can mean either spirit or mind but in German often also suggests culture or intellectual life. Translating the term is complicated by the fact that Hegel argues in his book that *Geist* is, in fact, everything that exists. The book is primarily a work of epistemol-

Georg Wilhelm Friedrich Hegel. (Library of Congress)

ogy, because it aims to show how *Geist* comes to know itself, that is, how human consciousness, which is one component of *Geist*, comes to know itself as human self-consciousness, as well as how it comes to know the physical world of objects. It is crucial that for Hegel, those two processes are one and the same.

Because *Geist* is constantly in motion toward self-knowledge, empirical knowledge, and absolute knowledge, it is always entering new relationships and assimilating old relationships into its conscious fabric. This process is its growth or development (*Entwicklung*). It begins for Hegel, as it does for Kant, with the interior of the indivudual human mind, but in Hegel's analysis the process quickly expands from interior mental life to exterior social life and comes to define the historical changes in society.

Indeed, because the process of *Entwicklung* defines the entirety of existence, Hegel believes that the movement of *Geist* toward self-knowledge and self-fulfillment is nothing less than the totality of history. *Geist* is everything that ever was, and at any given stage it is potentially everything that ever will be. Thus, truth is not static but dynamic: The truth, for Hegel, names the process of coming to understand the truth and not merely the

CONTENTS OF *THE PHENOMENOLOGY OF SPIRIT*

Georg Wilhelm Friedrich Hegel's The Phenomenology of Spirit *charts the evolution of consciousness from its most primitive to its most advanced form. The table of contents of the book is thus an important blueprint of Hegel's argument: It presents an outline of the stages through which Hegel believes consciousness must pass in order to achieve what he calls "absolute knowing." A simplified version of the table of contents appears below.*

A. Consciousness

    I. Sense-Certainty: Or, The "This" and "Meaning"

    II. Perception: Or, The Thing and Deception

    III. Force and the Understanding: Appearance and the Supersensible World

B. Self-Consciousness

    IV. The Truth of Self-Certainty

        A. Independence and dependence of self-consciousness: Lordship and bondage

        B. Freedom of self-consciousness: Stoicism, scepticism, and the unhappy consciousness

C. (AA.) Reason

    V. The Certainty of Truth and Reason

        A. Observing reason

        B. The actualization of rational self-consciousness through its own activity

        C. Individuality which takes itself to be real in and for itself

(BB.) Spirit

    VI. Spirit

        A. The *true* Spirit. The ethical order

        B. Self-Alienated Spirit. Culture

        C. Spirit that is certain of itself. Morality

(CC.) Religion

    VII. Religion

        A. Natural religion

        B. Religion in the form of art

        C. The revealed religion

(DD.) Absolute Knowing

    VIII. Absolute Knowing

Source: G. W. F. Hegel, Hegel's Phenomenology of Spirit. *Translated by A. V. Miller (New York: Oxford University Press, 1977), pp. xxxiii-xxxv.*

becoming conscious of it, but that raising of consciousness is not easy.

The mechanism of *Geist*'s evolution is another untranslatable German term, *Aufhebung*, which is most often rendered in English as either "overcoming" or "sublation," and which is meant to indicate a process in which the useful aspect of a thing is retained and the useless aspect is left behind. Each stage in the evolution of *Geist* seeks to attain perfect or absolute knowledge, according to that stage's own model of perfection. Each model of knowledge contains its own *Maßstab* (yardstick) by which to measure its own success or failure. According to Hegel, each stage before the ultimate one fails its own test, and it is "sublated" or "overcome" (*aufgehoben*), transitioning to the next stage.

As the bud becomes the blossom and then the fruit, or as the child grows into the adolescent and then the adult, each new phase is both the same as and different from the last one. Because it retains its identity through its changes, each phase is *aufgehoben*, simultaneously preserved, canceled, and raised to a higher level. Thus, individuals are preserved in the absolute. By contrast, Hegel satirized Schelling's absolute identity theory as "the night in which all cows are black," that is, in which individuals lose their individuality. For Hegel, each individual self-consciousness is an indissoluble unit and a free spirit, even though its being must always be harmonized with other self-consciousnesses and with absolute spirit.

final conclusion. It is achieved at each stage only with gradually received prerequisites, meaning that each step in the process is necessary and none can be skipped. For Hegel, "the actual is rational," meaning that history is a logical process that makes sense and that evolves in the way it must in order for *Geist* fully to express and to understand itself. *Geist* actualizes its potentiality simply by

Hegel rejected the respective idealisms of Fichte, George Berkeley, and Kant in favor of a dialectical idealism grounded in solid empirical fact. The dialectic includes logical, historical, psychological, and several other kinds of transitions. *The Phenomenology of Spirit* criticizes the Enlightenment for its one-sided reliance on cold reason but at the same time criticizes Romanticism for discarding reason in favor of feeling. All aspects of *Geist* must be present and reconciled if any resulting synthesis is to be valid.

The sections in *The Phenomenology of Spirit* dealing with political thought and history carried an implicit criticism of Jean-Jacques Rousseau's social contract theory, which Hegel developed further in his later *Grundlinien der Philosophie des Rechts* (1821; *The Philosophy of Right*, 1855). Hegel generally supported the French Revolution but argued that absolute freedom leads ineluctably to terror, as was shown historically from 1792 to 1794. His analysis of Sophocles' drama *Antigonē* (441 B.C.E.; *Antigone*, 1729) showed that the disagreeing parties in basic existential conflicts between divine law and human law could each be in the right and that such disagreements were permanently and tragically unresolvable.

Hegel savaged the then popular pseudoscience of phrenology for its material reductionism, the reductio ad absurdum of empiricism, but he depicted it as the ashes from which the phoenix of self-conscious *Geist* emerges. *Geist* and all its phenomena necessarily appear in time. Everything changes except change itself, since the essence of *Geist* is to change. *Geist* can neither annul time nor comprehend itself apart from time. The final stages of Hegel's dialectic before the achievement of absolute knowing interrelate the three highest manifestations of *Geist*: art, religion, and philosophy. The content of each is the same, absolute spirit, but art presents it for the senses, religion for the emotions, and philosophy for reason.

Hegel wanted *The Phenomenology of Spirit* to explain the entire progress of *Geist* from the most primitive kinds of consciousness to absolute knowledge. For him, each phase of *Geist*'s evolution related dialectically to every other phase and could not be understood apart from its universal context. This concrete interrelationship of dialectical phases was what Hegel called mediation (*Vermittlung*). Because truth was only the whole, any partial or isolated truth was demonstrably false in some of its contexts. The adequate concept (*Begriff*) of any phase necessarily involved its entire mediation. In other words, the truth of Hegel's book, like the truth of history, was to be found in its entirety, from beginning to end, and not in any of its isolated parts.

Many of Hegel's interpreters have erred by trying to interpret the whole book in terms of only one of its parts or themes. For example, Hegel's own student Hermann Friedrich Hinrichs saw *The Phenomenology of Spirit* only as the progress of religious consciousness, and the twentieth century French leftist Alexandre Kojève interpreted it all in terms of the master-slave dialectic, an early phase of Hegel's psychosocial history. Kojève's misinterpretation was particularly important, because his lectures influenced many of the most important and influential French thinkers of their generation, all of whom understood Hegel through his warped lens. These thinkers included Jean-Paul Sartre, Jacques Lacan, Maurice Merleau-Ponty, Louis Althusser, and Henry Bataille.

SIGNIFICANCE

Hegel's *The Phenomenology of Spirit* was one of the most original, pivotal, influential, and controversial Western philosophical books of all time. It is notoriously difficult, but that has not detracted from its intellectual appeal. Since its publication, rightists and leftists, libertarian individualists and social progressives, republicans and communists, conservatives and liberals, traditionalists and feminists, Nazis and Zionists, theists and atheists have all, either legitimately or illegitimately, found inspiration in *The Phenomenology of Spirit*. So many diametrically opposed parties each claiming Hegel as its antecedent does not mean that Hegel's thought is inconsistent, but rather that it is, as Hegel intended, universally applicable and relevant to the encounter with any worldly or spiritual situation.

Almost all Western philosophy since Kant can be thought of as post-Kantian, in the sense that it continues, modifies, or confronts and rejects Kant's model. The two major schools of post-Kantian philosophy are analytic philosophy and continental philosophy, and Hegel may be seen as one of the founders of the latter school. Hegel's most important contribution to philosophy is arguably to be found in his twin assertions that the history of philosophy is itself an integral part of philosophy and that epistemology is inseparable from social philosophy. Hegel argued that it is impossible to ground knowledge in the structure of the individual mind, as Kant had tried to do, because knowledge is an inherently social phenomenon that can be understood only within a social and historical context. Moreover, he argued, because truth is a historical process, rather than a static set of facts, it is not the same in all times and places. Thus, truth must be understood as changing rather than eternal. These two Hegelian insights—that knowledge is social and that truth is historical—arguably form the basis of continental philosophy.

—*Eric v.d. Luft*

1800's

FURTHER READING

Harris, Henry Silton. *Hegel's Development: Night Thoughts, Jena, 1801-1806*. Oxford, England: Clarendon Press, 1983. A biographical investigation of the genesis of *The Phenomenology of Spirit* by one of the world's greatest Hegel scholars.

_____. *Hegel's Ladder: A Commentary on Hegel's "Phenomenology of Spirit."* 2 vols. Indianapolis: Hackett, 1997. A detailed and scrupulous labor of love, thirty-five years in the making.

Hegel, G. W. F. *Phenomenology of Spirit*. Translated by A. V. Miller. Oxford, England: Clarendon Press, 1977. The standard English translation but flawed by inconsistent renderings of key terms, failure to recognize some terms as systematic, and frequent paraphrase. Findlay's paragraph-by-paragraph summaries are the most useful part of the book.

Houlgate, Stephen. *An Introduction to Hegel: Freedom, Truth, and History*. 2d ed. Malden, Mass.: Blackwell, 2005. Includes chapters on various aspects of Hegel's thought, including his philosophy of logic, religion, aesthetics, phenomenology, nature, and the subjective spirit. Relates Hegel to other thinkers and discusses his relevance to current philosophical debates.

Lauer, Quentin. *A Reading of Hegel's "Phenomenology of Spirit."* New York: Fordham University Press, 1982. An idiosyncratic but well-respected interpretation.

Loewenberg, Jacob. *Hegel's "Phenomenology": Dialogues on the Life of Mind*. La Salle, Ill.: Open Court, 1965. Still widely esteemed as one of the best commentaries on *The Phenomenology of Spirit*.

Pinkard, Terry. *Hegel: A Biography*. Cambridge, England: Cambridge University Press, 2000. The standard biography, built on thorough and insightful research.

Pippen, Robert B. *Hegel's Idealism: The Satisfactions of Self-Consciousness*. New York: Cambridge University Press, 1989. Extremely lucid explication of Hegelian philosophy. A must for those struggling with *The Phenomenology of Spirit*.

Russon, John. *Reading Hegel's "Phenomenology."* Bloomington: Indiana University Press, 2004. A selective interpretation of particular sections rather than the whole book, loosely tied together by a study of the nature of human experience.

Stern, Robert. *Routledge Philosophy Guidebook to Hegel and "The Phenomenology of Spirit."* London: Routledge, 2002. A clear and accessible but not simplistic introduction to one of the most difficult books in Western philosophy.

Westphal, Merold. *History and Truth in Hegel's "Phenomenology."* Bloomington: Indiana University Press, 1998. A brief but solid commentary that emphasizes the interplay between subjectivity and social history.

SEE ALSO: 1819: Schopenhauer Publishes *The World as Will and Idea*; 1824: Ranke Develops Systematic History; 1836: Transcendental Movement Arises in New England; 1839: Blanc Publishes *The Organization of Labour*; Feb., 1848: Marx and Engels Publish *The Communist Manifesto*; 1851-1854: Comte Advances His Theory of Positivism; 1859: Mill Publishes *On Liberty*; 1867: Marx Publishes *Das Kapital*; 1900: Freud Publishes *The Interpretation of Dreams*.

RELATED ARTICLES in *Great Lives from History: The Nineteenth Century, 1801-1900:* Georg Wilhelm Friedrich Hegel; Karl Marx; Napoleon I; Friedrich Wilhelm Joseph von Schelling.

August 17, 1807
MAIDEN VOYAGE OF THE *CLERMONT*

The maiden voyage of the first commercially successful steam-powered riverboat launched a new era in transportation that would have a profound impact on the opening of the North American continent, whose extensive river systems offered a network of ready-made highways well suited for steamboat traffic.

LOCALE: Hudson River, New York
CATEGORIES: Trade and commerce; engineering; transportation; inventions

KEY FIGURES

Robert Fulton (1765-1815), American inventor who designed and built the *Clermont*
Robert R. Livingston (1746-1813), Fulton's financial backer
Henry Miller Shreve (1785-1851), another developer of steamboats
Richard Wilson (fl. early nineteenth century), African American cook on the *Clermont*'s first voyage

SUMMARY OF EVENT

During the mid-1790's, Robert R. Livingston, a wealthy and famous Hudson Valley landowner, persuaded the New York State legislature to grant him exclusive rights to operate steam-powered boats on the Hudson River, which was then known as the North River, from 1798 to 1818. The terms of this agreement required Livingston to produce within one year a boat that would run at 4 miles (6.4 kilometers) an hour. His attempts to satisfy this requirement failed, and he went to France as the United States minister. There he met Robert Fulton, a U.S. citizen who was studying and working on inventions in the field of submarines and torpedoes.

Livingston persuaded Fulton to devote his efforts to designing and building a steamboat. Like Livingstone's earlier effort, Fulton's own first attempt, on France's Seine River in 1803, was a failure. During a storm, the heavy engine and boilers of his boat broke through the bottom of the boat and sank it. Fulton learned much from this failure, however, and in 1806, he and Livingston decided to return to the United States to build a steamboat for the North River.

A steam engine that the two men ordered from the British firm of Boulton and Watt arrived in New York in November, 1806. The engine's cylinder was 2 feet (0.6 meters) in diameter, and its piston stroke was 4 feet (1.2 meters). Fulton arrived from Europe during the follow-

ing month but seemed to be in no hurry to get on with building a boat in which to put the engine. Meanwhile, the New York legislature granted Livingston an extension of the monopoly that it had granted him earlier.

The hull of Fulton's boat was built by Charles Brown at Corlears Hook on New York's East River. Fulton then had the finished hull towed to Paulus Hook Ferry, where he set up his shop and began to install the machinery. There is some disagreement about the dimensions of the boat's hull, which appears to have been about 130 feet (39.6 meters) long and 15 feet (4.57 meters) wide. The vessel's keel reached three or four feet below the surface of the water. The hull was sharply pointed at both its bow and its stern. Its only deck was just a few feet above the waterline. The engine and boiler were installed on the deck, and the engine drove large paddle wheels on both sides of the vessel. The wheels were fifteen feet in diameter and four feet wide. As they rotated, their paddle blades dipped two feet into the water.

Fulton was one of the first steamboat designers to use scientific methods. He successfully calculated that the Boulton and Watt engine could move the vessel at a speed of about five miles (eight kilometers) per hour. Although modern theories would give a slightly different estimate, his calculations were nearly correct.

Although some work on the boat remained to be completed, Fulton decided to make a short test voyage on Sunday, August 9, 1807. He set out from Brown's wharf and ran the boat about one mile up the East River to a point about even with what is now Houston Street in Manhattan. The boat achieved a speed of 3 miles (4.8 kilometers) per hour this run, even though its paddle wheels were not completed. A week later, with the paddle wheels fully equipped, Fulton moved the boat around the Battery at the southern tip of Manhattan to a wharf on the North River. Passengers aboard the boat on this short trip included U.S. senator Samuel Latham Mitchill and Dr. William McNiven, the dean of Ripon Cathedral in England.

At about one o'clock of the following afternoon, on August 17, the steamboat set out for Albany. The chief engineer was a Scot named George Jackson, and the captain was Davis Hunt. Food and drink had been brought on board, and an African American man named Richard Wilson served as the cook. Forty passengers, mostly members of the Livingston family, were on board. They reached Haverstraw Bay by nightfall and arrived at Livingston's estate above Kingston twenty-four hours after leaving New York. The distance covered was 110 miles (177 kilometers). The name of this estate was Clermont—which became the name by which the steamboat was afterward known. Throughout his life, Fulton himself called his boat simply "the steamboat" or "the North River steamboat." The name *Clermont* seems to have been first used by Cadwallader D. Colden in *The Life of Robert Fulton* (1817), which he published two years after Fulton died.

On the morning of August 19, Fulton's steamboat set out from Clermont to cover the remaining forty miles (sixty-four kilometers) to Albany, where it arrived shortly after 5:00 P.M. Although the governor of New York was among the welcoming crowd when the boat arrived, the event was not mentioned in the day's newspapers. Chief engineer Jackson got so drunk in Albany that Fulton fired him and placed his assistant, Charles Dyke, in charge for the return journey to New York. A few paying passengers embarked for the return journey at a fare of seven dollars each, more than double what sailing vessels charged to make the same trip. Leaving Albany at 9:00 A.M. on Thursday, August 20, the steamboat arrived in New York at 4:00 P.M. on Friday, August 21. There

were some twenty newspapers in New York at the time, but only one, *The American Citizen*, took note of Fulton's accomplishment. After further improvements to cabins and decks, the steamboat entered full commercial service on September 2, 1807. The number of paying passengers grew rapidly. On October 1, sixty passengers paid to ride the boat from Albany to New York; on October 2, ninety passengers went to Albany.

Regular steamboat service between New York City and Albany, which began in 1807, continued until 1948. On September 13 of that year, the steamboat *Robert Fulton* of the Hudson River Day Line made the last steamboat trip over this route.

SIGNIFICANCE

It is no exaggeration to say that Fulton's voyage opened a new era in transportation. Steamboat transportation was especially important in the United States, whose immense river systems provided major transportation routes throughout the country. Especially important was the Mississippi-Missouri river system, which drains virtually the entire region between the Appalachian and Rocky Mountains.

Fulton's first steamboat. (C. A. Nichols & Company)

In June, 1816, Henry Shreve sailed from Wheeling, Virginia (now in West Virginia), in his steamboat *Washington* and went down the Mississippi River to New Orleans. This was no great feat, however, as keelboats and flatboats had been going downriver for many years. However, Shreve then returned 1,500 miles (2,415 kilometers) *up* the river to Louisville, Kentucky, in twenty-four days—a journey that keelboats propelled by men using poles took four to six months to make. Upriver voyages at reasonable speeds created a flourishing trade between New Orleans and cities such as Cincinnati, Louisville, and St. Louis.

In 1824, the U.S. Supreme Court struck down state-sponsored monopolies such as Livingston's in its *Gibbons v. Ogden* decision. This action fostered competition in steamboat transportation that led to rapid improvements in technology and service. By the 1830's, the internal waterways of the United States were crowded with steamboats of various shapes and sizes. After the Erie Canal from Albany to Buffalo opened in 1825 and the Welland Canal between Lake Erie and Lake Ontario opened in 1833, steamboats could sail from New York to ports on the Great Lakes.

—*Edwin G. Wiggins*

FURTHER READING

Baxter, Maurice G. *The Steamboat Monopoly: "Gibbons v. Ogden," 1824*. New York: Alfred A. Knopf, 1970. A narrative and assessment of the case in which the Supreme Court had its first opportunity to interpret the commerce clause of the Constitution.

Buckman, D. L. *Old Steamboat Days on the Hudson River*. New York: Grafton Press, 1907. Appreciative history of early steamboas written just one hundred years after the *Clermont*'s first voyage, at a time when steamboats were still working the Hudson River.

Donovan, Frank. *River Boats of America*. New York: Thomas Y. Crowell, 1966. Discusses the *Clermont* briefly, while providing broad coverage of steam-powered riverboats throughout the United States.

Hutcheon, Wallace. *Robert Fulton, Pioneer of Undersea Warfare*. Annapolis, Md.: Naval Institute Press, 1981. Puts Fulton's steamboat in perspective with regard to his other inventions.

Morgan, John S. *Robert Fulton*. New York: Mason/Charter, 1977. A biography covering all aspects of Fulton's life. Index.

Philip, Cynthia Owen. *Robert Fulton*. New York: Franklin Watts, 1985. Biography of Fulton that includes a full chapter about the *Clermont*.

Ringwald, D. C. *Hudson River Day Line*. 2d ed. New York: Fordham University Press, 1990. A profusely illustrated, large-format book covering the Hudson River Day Line from the *Clermont* to the last Hudson River steamboat trip in 1948.

Sale, Kirkpatrick. *The Fire of His Genius: Robert Fulton and the American Dream*. New York: Free Press, 2001. Well-written and balanced biography that describes how Fulton's steamboat transformed nineteenth century America.

Shagena, Jack L. *Who Really Invented the Steamboat? Fulton's Clermont Coup: A History of the Steamboat Contributions of William Henry, James Rumsey, John Fitch, Oliver Evans, Nathan Read, Samuel Morey, Robert Fulton, John Stevens, and Others*. Amherst, N.Y.: Humanity Books, 2004. Shagena, a retired aerospace engineer, traces the technological contributions of the many inventors, including Fulton, who helped create the steamboat.

SEE ALSO: c. 1815-1830: Westward American Migration Begins; May 22-June 20, 1819: *Savannah* Is the First Steamship to Cross the Atlantic; Mar. 2, 1824: *Gibbons v. Ogden*; Oct. 26, 1825: Erie Canal Opens; July 21, 1836: Champlain and St. Lawrence Railroad Opens; Jan. 31, 1858: Brunel Launches the SS *Great Eastern*.

RELATED ARTICLES in *Great Lives from History: The Nineteenth Century, 1801-1900:* Robert Fulton; Mark Twain.

1808-1826
OTTOMANS SUPPRESS THE JANISSARY REVOLT

Sultan Mahmud II faced considerable opposition to his efforts to reform the Ottoman Empire. The Ottoman military, which included the powerful yet corrupt Janissary corps, championed reactionary policies until its destruction.

LOCALE: Anatolia and the Balkans; Constantinople (now Istanbul, Turkey)

CATEGORIES: Wars, uprisings, and civil unrest; government and politics; social issues and reform

KEY FIGURES
Mahmud II (1785-1839), Ottoman sultan, r. 1808-1839
Selim III (1761-1808), Ottoman sultan, r. 1789-1807

SUMMARY OF EVENT
At the beginning of the nineteenth century, the Ottoman Empire was on the verge of collapse. Enemies, both foreign and domestic, carved off Ottoman territory, while internal unrest made normal government functions ineffectual. Ottoman leaders recognized the need for change, but they had great difficulties promoting reforms of government and military affairs. Reforms began during the reign of Selim III, who argued that the state needed a new military capable of fighting like the best of the European powers. Such a strategy required the importation of Western ideas and technology, and doing so placed Selim on a collision course with archconservatives. The opponents, an alliance of politicians, religious leaders, and soldiers, are best represented by the Yeni Çeri, or Janissary corps.

Historian David Nicolle succinctly defines nineteenth century Janissaries as "the Empire's most important infantry corps, and its greatest military weakness." Once the sultan's shock troops, by the eighteenth century the Janissaries had devolved into a near-parasite class of armed rentiers. Unwilling to embrace new technology or ideas, they were a powerful faction with garrison units in most important cities, and a major presence in the empire's capital, Constantinople.

Since the early eighteenth century, Janissaries had played a considerable role in Ottoman politics. Their status as the empire's main infantry force provided a vehicle that allowed them to veto government actions and even obtain the execution of their political opponents. Although doggedly opposed to military reform, Janissary leaders were often adroit politicians. The key to their success was not only holding a monopoly on military power but also having extensive familial, business, and social connections with middle- and lower-class city folk. These alliances included important conservative leaders within the ulama, a body of scholar-officials that regulated Muslim life throughout the empire.

No longer made up predominantly of Christian children from the Balkans, the Janissaries now recruited relatives and business associates to fill their ranks. They were a corrupt lot, maintaining fictitious members to increase company payrolls and collecting bribes and protection money from local merchants. As they seldom engaged the sultan's many foreign enemies, this was a coveted career, which partially explains the constant growth of the corps in the late eighteenth and early nineteenth centuries. By 1808, the Janissaries numbered 140,000 men, but of this number, probably no more than 10 percent were trained soldiers.

The corps developed a notorious reputation. In Constantinople, for example, where they also served as a fire brigade, corps members often set fires and then demanded bribes to put out the blazes. The year 1810 witnessed more than two thousand incidents of that nature. In Jerusalem, the Janissaries sold surplus weapons to local rebels, while in Cairo their protection rackets directed against local businessmen impressed even the corrupt Mamlūks.

A contemporary observer, John Moore, gave one explanation why such a depraved and useless military could survive. Writing in 1799, he described the Janissaries as the "only professional soldiers" in the Ottoman army. Janissaries thus, were the "best of the worst," but the sultans could not dispense with their limited services until a substitute was available. Selim III's answer was his *nizam-ul Cedid* (new order), an infantry force designed to fight like European regulars. For a decade (1791-1801), this new corps increased in size and prestige, but not without also attracting the attention of Janissary leaders and their allies.

Conservative forces could draw on legal, religious, and social arguments to attack the sultan. The Ottoman Empire was an Islamic state, where good government meant there was a just sovereign who upheld the Sharia, Islamic religious law. Selim's importation of European ideas and technology was a much debated concept, and was seen by many as a step away from good government. Muslims, after all, lived in a world of perfection, while Europe, part of the non-Muslim *dar al-harb* (house of conflict or war), could only provide confusion and dilute Islamic purity. This argument appealed to influential religious authorities, while the simple fact that *nizam-ul Cedid* forces drained away revenues made the Janissary rank-and-file fearful of losing their monopoly on power.

On March 26, 1807, angered by these military reforms and higher taxes, Janissaries and their urban allies attacked *nizam-ul Cedid* troops, starting a year-long series of coups and counter-coups. In the end, Selim was deposed and then murdered and replaced briefly with a half-witted cousin named Mustafa IV. Mustafa IV, too, was murdered, leaving only one surviving male member from the imperial family, Mahmud II.

Learning from the disasters of 1807, the new sultan approached change with caution. At the same time, Mahmud had little doubt of the need for reforms. Between 1808 and 1826, the Ottoman government fought against Russian and Persian invaders, plus Serbian, Greek, and Arab rebels. At best, Mahmud's soldiers could fight to a stalemate, and, more often, they suffered defeat. Simultaneously, political maneuvers in the capital pitted the sultan's desire for reform against archconservatives and their Janissary backers.

By the early 1820's, Mahmud had cleverly isolated Janissaries from their allies within the ulama by coopting the latter into a new governmental department of religion. Mahmud also was adroit at publicizing Janissary misdeeds, so as to alienate the corps from Constantinople's urban mob. Equally important was the creation of a new artillery corps, which, as it did not seem to have an infantry function, caused little concern to the Janissaries.

The new gunners, however, were trained not only in artillery drill but also as foot soldiers. By 1826, they numbered fourteen thousand and were probably the best troops in the empire. In June, the sultan ordered selected men from every Janissary regiment to train in Western drill. As he expected, Janissary opposition was quick and violent. On June 14, each Constantinople unit overturned their soup kettles, a traditional call for insurrection. Expecting an alliance with the city's urban rabble, the Janissaries instead ran into an Ottoman version of Napoleon Bonaparte's "whiff of grapeshot."

The new artillery units ravaged the rebels, forcing them to retreat into a vast wooden barracks. The gunners followed this up with incendiary rounds that quickly set the building on fire. The fire destroyed the barracks and almost every man hiding inside. The rebellion lasted less than three hours. Hunted down without mercy, the rebellious Janissaries obtained the same treatment they had meted out so often in the past. In Constantinople alone,

thousands were killed in what was soon dubbed the *vaka-I hayriye* (auspicious event or incident). An eyewitness described the Sea of Mammara "mottled with dead bodies." Massacres on a smaller scale took place at Vidin, Izmit, and Edirne.

SIGNIFICANCE

Despite the poor showing of new, reformed Ottoman troops in the Russo-Turkish War and again in the Egyptian-Turkish Wars of 1831 and 1839, Mahmud II's destruction of the Janissary corps was a singular event in Ottoman history. By removing these military reactionaries, he was now able to improve not only the army but also civil government and education. The destruction of the Janissaries marked a decisive break with the past and allowed Mahmud and his successors to instigate reforms that strengthened the state, improved military efficiency, and thus allowed the "sick man of Europe" to move into the twentieth century.

—*John P. Dunn*

FURTHER READING

Assad Effendi. *Précis historique de la destruction du corps des Janissaries par le Sultan Mahmoud, en 1826*. Paris: Firmins Didot, 1833. The author, who was a government worker, provides the "official" history of the Janissary corps' destruction. In French.

Goodwin, Godfrey. *The Janissaries*. London: Saqi, 1997. A history of the Janissary corps, from its beginnings in the fifteenth century to the early twentieth century. Includes bibliographical references and an index.

Levy, Avigdor. "Military Policy of Sultan Mahmud II, 1808-1839." Unpublished Ph.D. dissertation. Harvard University, 1968. A massive work that examines Sultan Mahmud II's military reforms. Based on a vast array of archival sources.

Lewis, Bernard. *The Emergence of Modern Turkey*. New York: Oxford University Press, 2002. Extensive coverage of the problems and solutions of Sultan Selim III and Sultan Mahmud II in developing a modernized Turkey.

Nicolle, David. *Armies of the Ottoman Empire, 1775-1820*. London: Osprey, 1998. An excellent introduction to the Ottoman military that stresses the challenges facing military reformers.

Shaw, Stanford, and Ezel Shaw. *History of the Ottoman Empire and Modern Turkey*. 2 vols. New York: Cambridge University Press, 1978. A well-written standard account that provides considerable coverage of nineteenth century Ottoman civil and military reforms.

SEE ALSO: Mar. 1, 1811: Muḥammad ʿAlī Has the Mamlūks Massacred; Apr. 26, 1828-Aug. 28, 1829: Second Russo-Turkish War; Sept. 24, 1829: Treaty of Adrianople; May, 1876: Bulgarian Revolt Against the Ottoman Empire; Apr. 24, 1877-Jan. 31, 1878: Third Russo-Turkish War.

RELATED ARTICLE in *Great Lives from History: The Nineteenth Century, 1801-1900:* Muḥammad ʿAlī Pasha.

April, 1808
TENSKWATAWA FOUNDS PROPHETSTOWN

Ultimately an abject failure, this attempt by the Shawnee spiritual leader and his brother Tecumseh to build a pantribal confederacy was part of the last concerted effort of Native Americans to resist Anglo-American expansion east of the Mississippi River.

LOCALE: Northwestern Indiana
CATEGORIES: Social issues and reform; indigenous people's rights

KEY FIGURES

Main Poc (1760?-1816), Potawatomi shaman and war chief
Tecumseh (1768-1813), Shawnee war chief and diplomat
Tenskwatawa (Shawnee Prophet; 1768-1837), Shawnee spiritual leader
William Henry Harrison (1773-1841), governor of Indiana and later president of the United States, 1841

SUMMARY OF EVENT

At least as early as the 1730's, Native American leaders west of the Appalachian Mountains advocated an alliance of tribes to resist the expanding British settlements and the powerful Iroquois Confederacy. Tribal prophets preached a radical idea, the beginning of a new movement: All native peoples, despite their diverse languages and cultures and ancient tribal rivalries, were really one people, separate and distinct from the Europeans, and never meant to live with the Europeans or to adopt their ways.

By 1795, disagreements over strategy, factional strife within tribes, failing support from European allies, and military defeats had badly disrupted the budding nativist movement. Tribal leaders willing to accept compromise signed treaties with the new U.S. government, surrendering millions of acres of land. In return, the U.S. government supported these so-called government chiefs, hoping that through them it could control the tribes and prevent organized resistance. Many Indian communities now faced desperate struggles for survival.

Frontiersmen settling old grudges freely hunted and raided on tribal lands. Indians could not testify in U.S. courts and had no protection under U.S. law. Native people often took their own forms of revenge, escalating the violence. Anglo-American squatters crowded onto tribal lands, openly violating treaties. Displaced refugees fled to the remaining tribal lands, further straining already depleted game supplies and farmlands. Many tribesmen had become dependent on the fur trade for the necessities of life, and cheap liquor had become a basic fur trade commodity. By 1800, alcoholism had reached epidemic proportions among the northwestern tribes. European diseases, against which the native peoples had neither biological immunity nor medical remedies, ravaged tribes. For native peoples throughout the trans-Appalachian West, it was a time of despair, starvation, and social chaos.

In April, 1805, an aging alcoholic known as Lalawethika ("Rattle" or "Noisemaker" because of his bragging and belligerent behavior) collapsed in a Shawnee village, apparently dead. Although of no use as a hunter or warrior, Lalawethika had studied with the noted doctor Penagashea. His teacher had died in 1804, however, and working alone, Lalawethika had failed to stop an epidemic that struck his village in early 1805. Now it appeared that he too was dead. However, before his funeral could take place, he suddenly returned to life. He told his amazed neighbors that he was sent back from the spirit world with a mission. The alcoholic braggart was dead, he said; he had been born again as Tenskwatawa, the "Open Door," to lead his people in a spiritual renewal.

Tenskwatawa preached that the use of alcohol and other vices must stop. Violence among neighbors and the greedy accumulation of material wealth must also stop. The people must restore traditional communal values, living in peace with all other tribes. Native people were children of the Master of Life, but Europeans came from the Great Serpent, the Destroyer, and corrupted all they touched. The people must have nothing more to do with Europeans or their goods. If the people purified themselves and faithfully performed the new rituals explained in Tenkswatawa's visions, they would restore the spiritual power of the tribes, the earth would be renewed, and the white invaders would disappear forever.

News of the Shawnee Prophet, as Tenskwatawa came to be known, spread among the tribes of the region. His message was believable, not only because Tenskwatawa seemed infused with magnetism and power but also because three generations of prophets among the tribes had reported similar visions. Followers gathered around Tenskwatawa in 1805, hoping that he might be able to make the promise of spiritual renewal finally a reality. During the summer of 1805, Tenskwatawa established a new village at Greenville, Ohio, on the U.S. side of a boundary line set by the 1795 Treaty of Greenville. Because the new site was not associated with any specific tribe, Tenskwatawa expected that it would be easier to establish a great village of all tribes there. This new, independent village

Shawnee spiritual leader Tenskwatawa. (Courtesy, California State University at Long Beach)

would not be controlled by any of the government chiefs, and its location openly defied the hated treaty.

Through the fall and winter of 1805, Tenskwatawa met delegations from many tribes and cultivated alliances with Native American leaders throughout the region. Seven treaties signed by the government chiefs between 1804 and 1807 ceded millions of acres of tribal land to the United States and sent many angry, disillusioned tribesmen into Tenskwatawa's camp. Disciples and allied prophets carried Tenskwatawa's message throughout the Great Lakes region and to the tribes of the south. The powerful Potawatomi shaman and war chief Main Poc, probably the most influential native leader in the region, journeyed to Greenville in the fall of 1807 to confer with Tenskwatawa. Main Poc favored the movement but planned a regional confederacy, rather than a union of all native peoples. He also firmly refused to give up his old blood feud with the Osage or his fondness for alcohol. On other crucial points, however, he and Tenskwatawa agreed and joined as allies.

Hundreds of people from a dozen tribes gathered at Greenville. Tenskwatawa, increasingly occupied with his duties as spiritual leader, delegated diplomatic missions to his older brother Tecumseh, who was a gifted orator with a wide network of contacts among leaders of both northern and southern tribes. Tecumseh was also a respected war chief and a confirmed nativist. Of intertribal heritage himself—his mother was Creek, his father Shawnee— Tecumseh had traveled widely among the tribes and knew their common problems and the need for common solutions. He opposed U.S. expansion; treaty land cessions in which he had had no voice had cost him his home. His father and two brothers died fighting Euro-Americans, and he made his reputation as a warrior in battle against that same enemy.

By 1807, Tecumseh had become his brother Tenskwatawa's adviser and representative abroad, while Tenskwatawa concentrated on the problems at Greenville. Relations with Shawnee government chief Black Hoof and his followers deteriorated rapidly, and a violent clash seemed likely. The small cornfields and depleted game around Greenville could not feed the village. The site was far from the northwestern tribes, now Tenskwatawa's strongest supporters. U.S. frontiersmen were alarmed by the rapidly growing village so near their settlements, and ugly incidents between Indians and white settlers escalated.

As rumors spread of an impending military campaign against the village, Main Poc urged Tenskwatawa to move the village to Potawatomi territory, where the people would find better hunting and more land for their gardens. They would also be farther from enemies and closer to friends. In January, 1808, Tenskwatawa agreed. Through February and March, his followers gathered supplies and prepared for the move. In the first week of April, they burned their old village and started west. Miami government chief Little Turtle, who claimed authority over the region into which Tenskwatawa was moving, attempted to prevent establishment of the new village. Tenskwatawa informed Little Turtle that the Master of Life had chosen the place. There, a great union of all native peoples would guard the boundary between Indian and U.S. lands and prevent further U.S. expansion.

In April, while Tecumseh visited Canada to get supplies of food and ammunition for firearms from the British, Tenskwatawa supervised the construction of the new village. Called Prophetstown by white settlers, the village was situated on the northwest bank of the Wabash River, just below the mouth of the Tippecanoe River, in northwestern Indiana. The site quickly became a focal point for the nativist movement. With a population of more than four hundred in June, and more arriving daily, food and other supplies remained a pressing problem. While Tecumseh was working to persuade the British to help, Tenskwatawa tricked Indiana governor William Henry Harrison into supplying corn.

The overconfident Harrison now believed he could control Tenskwatawa and his followers. The winter of 1808-1809 was unusually hard, and Prophetstown suffered severely from food shortages and a devastating epidemic. Many people went back to their old villages, bitterly disillusioned with Tenskwatawa. By the summer, Harrison believed that Tenskwatawa's influence was broken and thought that he himself could push another land cession on the tribes of the region. On September 30, 1809, government chiefs of the Miami, Potawatomi, and Lenni Lenape signed the Treaty of Fort Wayne, ceding millions of acres of land for about two cents an acre.

Members of Tenskwatawa's movement were outraged by the treaty. The widespread anger revitalized the movement, and people again flocked to Prophetstown. While Tenskwatawa remained the spiritual leader of the movement, Tecumseh emerged as the political and military leader. When Tecumseh traveled south to confer with the Creek, Choctaw, Chickasaw, and others, Harrison decided the time to strike had come. He burned Prophetstown after the Battle of Tippecanoe on November 7-8, 1811.

The destruction of Prophetstown left Tenskwatawa discredited as a religious leader. Afterward, he lived with a small band of his remaining followers in the Wabash River Valley, but American government pressure forced him to flee to Canada. He lived in Canada until 1825, when he returned to live among the Ohio Shawnee. He aided Governor Lewis M. Cass of the Michigan Territory in his efforts to persuade the Ohio Shawnee to move west across the Mississippi. In 1827, he established his home on the Shawnee Reservation in Kansas, where he lived out the remainder of his life.

SIGNIFICANCE

A central reason that Harrison attacked Tippecanoe was to prevent Tecumseh and Tenskwatawa's confederacy from developing into a serious threat against white settlements. In this he succeeded, particularly as Tenskwatawa's prophecy that Indians would be immune to bullets from their enemies' guns was a disastrous mistake. Afterward, Tenskwatawa's influence was broken, and even his brother Tecumseh no longer trusted him. Tecumseh himself, however, remained fiercely opposed to further white encroachments into Indian lands and was prepared to carry on the military struggle. However, he was killed in Canada at the Battle of the Thames in 1813.

One of the most important results of the destruction of Prophetstown and the defeat of Tecumseh in the Battle of Tippecanoe was the elevation of William Henry Harrison to the status of a national hero in the United States. In 1840, he would parlay his popularity into election as president. However, he died after only one month in office and left no legacy in national politics.

—Mary Ellen Rowe

FURTHER READING

Allen, Robert S. *His Majesty's Indian Allies*. Toronto: Dundurn Press, 1992. Presents material from British sources neglected by U.S. historians.

Cleaves, Freeman. *Old Tippecanoe: William Henry Harrison and His Times*. 1939. Reprint. Newtown, Conn.: American Biography Press, 1990. Full and detailed biography of Harrison that contains a colorful account of Harrison's campaign against the Indian confederation.

Dowd, Gregory Evans. *A Spirited Resistance*. Baltimore: Johns Hopkins University Press, 1992. Traces the nativist movement from the 1730's, providing the ideological and historical context for Prophetstown.

Drake, Benjamin. *Life of Tecumseh*. 1858. Reprint. New York: Arno Press, 1969. Biography using primary documents and interviews with individuals who knew Tecumseh.

Edmunds, R. David. *The Shawnee Prophet*. Lincoln: University of Nebraska Press, 1983. Carefully researched and objective biography of Tenskwatawa that also says much about Tecumseh and shows how the lives of the two brothers were intertwined.

_____. *Tecumseh and the Quest for Indian Leadership*. Boston: Little, Brown, 1984. Thorough research separates fact from fiction in this balanced biography of the famous Shawnee leader.

Sugden, John. *Tecumseh: A Life*. New York: Henry Holt, 1998. Definitive biography of Tecumseh, placing his life within the context of Shawnee and general Native American history. Sugden details Tecumseh's failed attempts to create a pan-Indian resistance movement.

SEE ALSO: Nov. 7, 1811: Battle of Tippecanoe; June 18, 1812-Dec. 24, 1814: War of 1812; July 27, 1813-Aug. 9, 1814: Creek War; Oct. 5, 1813: Battle of the Thames.

RELATED ARTICLES in *Great Lives from History: The Nineteenth Century, 1801-1900:* William Henry Harrison; Tecumseh.

April 6, 1808

AMERICAN FUR COMPANY IS CHARTERED

In creating the American Fur Company John Jacob Astor built the first commercial monopoly in U.S. history, and his company and its offshoots played a major role in the opening of the western United States to trade and settlement.

LOCALE: Albany, New York

CATEGORIES: Trade and commerce; fashion and design

KEY FIGURES

John Jacob Astor (1763-1848), organizer of and principal stockholder in the American Fur Company

Ramsay Crooks (1787-1859), Astor's chief assistant in the western fur trade and president of the American Fur Company during its final days

Robert Stuart (1785-1848), one of Astor's lieutenants in the fur trade

Wilson Price Hunt (1783-1842), leader of the overland expedition to Astoria in 1811-1812

Manuel Lisa (1772-1820), Missouri River explorer and founder of the Missouri Fur Company

SUMMARY OF EVENT

On April 6, 1808, New York's state legislature granted a charter to the American Fur Company for a period of twenty-five years. The company's capital stock was not to exceed one million dollars until two years had passed, and thereafter it was not to exceed two million dollars. The sole stockholder was John Jacob Astor, who in 1783 had come to the United States as an impoverished twenty-year-old immigrant from Germany. After serv-ing as an assistant to a fur merchant in New York City, Astor entered the business on his own and soon began to trade with China and other areas of eastern Asia. By the early nineteenth century he had become one of the richest and most powerful men in the United States.

In 1808, Astor was pondering the possibilities for a fur-trading empire in the recently purchased Lousiana Territory and regions farther west. He decided to challenge Canada's North West Company and the Michilimackinac Company, which had long exploited the trade in those areas. Astor was encouraged by the breakthrough efforts of St. Louis explorer and entrepreneur Manuel Lisa, who had built a trading post on the Missouri River at the mouth of the Bighorn River in 1807 and later a fort at Omaha and had created the Missouri Fur Company. Astor sensed that the time was ripe for aggressive American expansion up the Missouri River.

Astor envisioned American control of the fur trade in the mountain regions of the Northwest all the way to the Pacific coast. He dreamed of extending that trade across the Pacific to China and other markets. His traders would take the furs to eastern Asia and trade for spices, silks, teas, and other commodities. His scheme called for a huge company with trading posts along the shores of the Great Lakes and the Missouri and Columbia Rivers. First, however, he had to consolidate his own holdings and obtain new capital, preferably with the blessings of the state or federal government. He therefore engineered the chartering of the American Fur Company in 1808 and similarly the creation of the Pacific Fur Company two years later. He controlled both companies and inter-

1800's

John Jacob Astor. (Library of Congress)

peoples when the outbreak of the War of 1812 between the United States and Great Britain foiled their endeavors.

Astor feared a British seizure of his Columbia River post, so he elected to sell the project to the rival North West Company in 1813 and abandoned his plans in the Pacific Northwest. The activities of his parties, however, had contributed greatly to Euro-American knowledge of the region, and had incidentally helped to reinforce American claims to the Oregon territory.

The War of 1812 also affected Astor's considerable operations in the Midwest. In 1811 the American Fur Company had merged with the North West and Michilimackinac Companies to form the South West Fur Company, which was to confine its activities to the Great Lakes south of the Canadian border. Although the war interrupted the company's operations, the company later thrived. In 1817, Astor was able to buy out his partners. He established the Northern Department of the American Fur Company with headquarters at Michilimackinac. Because Congress excluded foreign traders from the territory during the same year, Astor achieved a monopoly of the fur trade in the Great Lakes region.

Astor then moved to gain control of trade in the Upper Missouri River region. In 1817, he arranged a working agreement with powerful firms in St. Louis to set up the Western Department of the American Fur Company. In 1822, Congress abolished federally sponsored trading posts in tribal territories, part of the "factory system" that had been in operation since 1796. Using his considerable political influence, Astor undercut this program. Agents of the American Fur Company extended their sphere of influence in the upper Missouri area, crushing opposition ruthlessly. In 1827, Astor's company absorbed its greatest competitor, the Columbia Fur Company, and afterward operated between the upper Mississippi and the upper Missouri as the Upper Missouri Outfit. By 1828, the American Fur Company commanded an overwhelming share of the fur trade on the northern plains and in the Northwest.

Meanwhile, Mexican, French Canadian, and American trappers continued to maintain a brisk commerce in furs out of Taos, in what is now New Mexico, and a consortium of traders who would organize the Rocky Mountain Fur Company were consolidating control of trade in the central Rocky Mountains.

changed their resources so that the firms were virtually indistinguishable.

After Astor established the Pacific Fur Company, he made plans to dispatch two parties to the Columbia River. One party arrived by sea at the mouth of the Columbia in March, 1811. Work promptly began on a post called Astoria on the lower Columbia River. The second party, under the command of Wilson Price Hunt, departed overland from St. Louis in March, 1811. This group experienced terrible hardships along the way and the few members of the group who survived did not reach their objective until February, 1812. Uncertain about the practicality of ocean trade routes, the Astorians sent Robert Stuart east to find an easier overland trail. The Astorians were winning their struggle for survival and had established trade with the local indigenous tribal

At the peak of his fortunes, Astor retired and his company split. One group included some ten stockholders of the Northern Department under Ramsay Crooks, Astor's chief assistant. It assumed the name of the American Fur Company and became one of the first large American trusts. However, the company broke up in 1834 at the onset of the decline of the fur trade. Furs were becoming scarce as the "factors," the "mountain men" and trappers, overtrapped many of the furbearers' streams and ponds.

During the late 1830's, the demand for fur garments also declined as fashions changed in Europe and the eastern United States. Under Crooks, the American Fur Company survived the Panic of 1837 but lingered only as a much smaller concern in the 1840's. Small companies and freelance trappers continued to mop up the shrinking trade in northern New Mexico, but for the most part they could only watch as new waves of settlers and miners arrived to exploit the agricultural and mineral resources of the trans-Mississippi West.

SIGNIFICANCE

John Jacob Astor built his fur-trading empire at a time of unique opportunity in American history. The West was opening up to trade and settlement, fur-bearing animals were abundant, and there was a great demand for furs in the eastern United States and Europe. With his exceptional business acumen and willingness to act aggressively, Astor was able brilliantly to capitalize on the opportunities and enjoyed remarkable success. However, Astor is remembered primarily for building the first private monopoly in United States history. Through a decade and a half, his American Fur Company almost totally dominated the fur trade throughout the United States. As the fur trade declined after his retirement, his company ceased to be the power that it had been under his control. However, his acquisition of large tracts of Manhattan and his wise investments in banking, insurance, and government stocks ensured that the Astor family would play a major role in American business into the twentieth century.

—*James E. Fickle, updated by Thomas L. Altherr*

FURTHER READING

Chittenden, Hiram M. *The American Fur Trade of the Far West.* New York: Press of the Pioneers, 1935. Reprint. Stanford, Calif.: Academic Reprints, 1985. Nearly exhaustive study of the history of the fur trade in the western United States, with considerable attention to Astor's enterprises.

Haeger, John D. *John Jacob Astor: Business and Finance in the Early Republic.* Detroit: Wayne State University Press, 1991. A detailed economic history of Astor's ventures in the midwestern and western fur trade and other businesses in the East.

Jones, Robert F., ed. *Astorian Adventure: The Journal of Alfred Seton, 1811-1815.* New York: Fordham University Press, 1993. A fascinating account of daily life at Astoria by one of the company's clerks.

Madsen, Axel. *John Jacob Astor: America's First Multimillionaire.* New York: John Wiley & Sons, 2001. Full biography of Astor's life and his involvement in the fur trade.

Oglesby, Richard E. *Manuel Lisa and the Opening of the Missouri Fur Trade.* Norman: University of Oklahoma Press, 1963. This volume documents Lisa's importance in the expansion of American trade enterprises in the Upper Missouri River Valley.

Philips, Paul C. *The Fur Trade.* 2 vols. Norman: University of Oklahoma Press, 1961. A massive history of the North American fur trade from the beginning of the seventeenth century to the middle of the nineteenth, with Astor playing a leading role in the second volume.

Ronda, James P. *Astoria and Empire.* Lincoln: University of Nebraska Press, 1990. The most complete account of the founding of Astoria and its decline during the War of 1812; the book places Astor's efforts within an overall imperialist context.

Wishart, David J. *The Fur Trade of the American West, 1807-1840.* Lincoln: University of Nebraska Press, 1992. This slender treatise examines the effects of western geography on the process of establishing and expanding the fur trade.

SEE ALSO: May 9, 1803: Louisiana Purchase; May 14, 1804-Sept. 23, 1806: Lewis and Clark Expedition; Sept. 8, 1810-May, 1812: Astorian Expeditions Explore the Pacific Northwest; c. 1815-1830: Westward American Migration Begins; June 1, 1815-Aug., 1817: Red River Raids; Sept., 1821: Santa Fe Trail Opens; 1822-1831: Jedediah Smith Explores the Far West; June 15, 1846: United States Acquires Oregon Territory.

RELATED ARTICLES in *Great Lives from History: The Nineteenth Century, 1801-1900:* John Jacob Astor; Meriwether Lewis and William Clark; Zebulon Pike; Jedediah Smith; David Thompson.

May 2, 1808
DOS DE MAYO INSURRECTION IN SPAIN

The Dos de Mayo insurrection in Spain, a rebellion first against the incompetent Spanish monarchy and then against France, resulted in the defeat of French emperor Napoleon I. Napoleon had infuriated the Spanish people by refusing to accept the ascension of Ferdinand VII as king of Spain in his bid to take control of Spain and advance his own empire.

LOCALE: Madrid, Spain
CATEGORY: Wars, uprisings, and civil unrest

KEY FIGURES
Joseph Bonaparte (1768-1844), brother of Napoleon I and king of Spain, r. 1808-1813
Napoleon I (Napoleon Bonaparte; 1769-1821), emperor of France, r. 1804-1814, 1815
Charles IV (1748-1819), Bourbon king of Spain, r. 1788-1808
Ferdinand VII (1784-1833), Bourbon king of Spain, r. 1808, 1813-1833
Manuel de Godoy (1767-1851), chief minister of Charles IV
Francisco de Goya (1746-1828), painter to the Spanish court after 1789
Joachim Murat (1767-1815), commander of French forces in Spain
María Luisa (1751-1819), queen of Spain and wife of Charles IV

SUMMARY OF EVENT
With the French Bourbons ascending the throne of Spain in 1700, a close alliance formed between France and Spain. Throughout the eighteenth century, Spain and France often fought against their common enemy, England. When the French Revolution (1789) broke out, however, the Spanish crown supported the French monarchy against the revolutionaries; after Louis XVI was executed, the Spaniards joined the First Coalition against France. Following the return of more conservative governments in France, Spanish policy once again veered toward an alliance with France against England.

Spanish policy in the 1790's was controlled by Manuel de Godoy, the so-called Prince of the Peace, chief minister of King Charles IV, and the lover of María Luisa, Charles's wife. Charles was a weak, incompetent monarch, completely dominated by his wife and her lover. Many of the reforms initiated by the earlier Bourbons and carried through by Charles III were ignored or

allowed to lapse by Godoy, who was chiefly interested in his own advancement. Godoy intended to use the French alliance to procure power and wealth for himself.

In 1799, Napoleon Bonaparte came to power in France and in 1804 made himself emperor of the French. In his ambitions to control Europe, he saw the possibility of using Godoy's avarice to take over Spain. Through a series of alliances concluded during the early nineteenth century. Spain became closely tied to France and subservient to Napoleon. Spanish naval strength was drained to serve France's needs, while Godoy enriched himself.

By 1807, Napoleon believed that the time had come to take over Spain completely. Both Spain and Portugal were weak links in his Continental System (trade embargo against the British), and the Anglo-Portuguese alliance bothered him. In 1807 he concluded a treaty with Godoy that allowed French troops passage through northern Spain into Portugal. By late 1807, the French forces had driven the Portuguese royal family out of the country and had occupied some of the fortresses of northern Spain.

All the pent-up, anti-French feelings in Spain now rallied to Ferdinand VII, son of Charles IV and heir to the throne. He was popular with those Spaniards who were offended by the scandalous character of Queen María Luisa and by the incompetence of the king as well as Godoy. Ferdinand hoped to obtain aid from Napoleon to overthrow his father and Godoy, and he promised Napoleon that he would marry a Bonaparte princess in return for help.

Napoleon, however, intended to eliminate the Spanish Bourbons and place his brother Joseph Bonaparte on the throne of Spain. In February, 1808, he sent Marshal Joachim Murat with a large army toward Madrid. The Spanish populace welcomed the move, believing that the French were there to help Ferdinand secure the throne. Shortly before Murat entered Madrid, a mob attacked Godoy on March 19, 1808, and demanded both his resignation and the abdication of Charles in favor of Ferdinand. Charles abdicated, named Ferdinand king, and made plans to leave for America. Napoleon, pleased with Charles's abdication, found that the popular support for Ferdinand upset his plans and therefore ordered Murat not to recognize Ferdinand. Murat persuaded Charles to retract his abdication and place himself in Napoleon's hands.

The French also committed a major blunder. Anticipating the restoration of Charles when Ferdinand would abdicate, Murat announced that Charles IV was the king of Spain. Therefore, Murat appeared to protect both Godoy and Charles even though Ferdinand had begun to place his uncle Antonio in charge of a junta to rule Spain.

Napoleon next invited Ferdinand and Charles to come to Bayonne to settle the dispute. Cleverly putting pressure on both and taking advantage of a disgraceful family quarrel, he persuaded Charles and Ferdinand to abdicate in favor of any person whom he nominated, but on the condition that the Spanish Empire would remain intact and that Roman Catholicism would remain the state religion of Spain. Napoleon then gave both men estates in France and named his brother Joseph as king of Spain.

When news of the dethroning of the Bourbons reached Madrid, the populace turned against Napoleon and the French. On May 2 (Dos de Mayo), 1808, a large crowd sullenly watched the members of the Spanish royal family prepare to leave the palace for their journey to France. As the royal coach prepared to depart, one of the younger children in it cried out at leaving, and the crowd became a mob. They attacked the French guard

and massacred them. Murat ordered the French troops to fire on the mob, and martial law was proclaimed. Madrid had erupted against the French. When news of the uprising reached the rest of Spain, there were similar uprisings against French garrisons.

The famous riot became immortalized by Francisco Goya, a visionary artistic genius who is considered to be one of the founders of modern art. Goya mastered the use of bright colors when he was a young artist. As painter to the Spanish court after 1789, a profound event occurred when syphilis took away Goya's hearing in 1792. The supernatural aspect of Goya's work became pronounced as Goya withdrew into melancholy. By now a liberal who idealized French culture, Goya began to attack the king and believed ardently in the ideals of the French Revolution (1789).

The French invasion in 1808 jolted Goya's life and art. His moving painting, *The Second of May 1808: The Charge of the Mamelukes* (1814), preserves brilliantly the attack by mostly unarmed Spanish patriots upon Napoleon's well-armed cavalry. More astounding is *Third of May 1808: Execution of the Citizens of Madrid*

Reception at the court of King Charles IV. (Francis R. Niglutsch)

(1814), which contains all the romantic horror that fascinated Goya.

SIGNIFICANCE

By May 30, all Spain was in rebellion against the French. Napoleon had to send more troops to fight the Spaniards, but he was not able to defeat them. The fighting and the disruption of authority in Spain caused a political, social, economic, and religious revolution whose reverberations continued into the twentieth century.

—*José M. Sánchez, updated by Douglas W. Richmond*

FURTHER READING

Altamira, Rafael. *A History of Spain; From the Beginnings to the Present Day.* Translated by Muna Lee. 1949. Reprint. Princeton, N.J.: D. Van Nostrand, 1966. A general history of Spain that considers the results of the insurrection.

Carr, Raymond. *Spain, 1808-1975.* 2d ed. New York: Oxford University Press, 1982. Carr's study of nineteenth and twentieth century Spain covers the uprising of 1808 in detail and includes an excellent analysis of the factions involved in both the uprising and the events immediately preceding it.

Chastenet, Jacques. *Godoy, Master of Spain, 1792-1808.* Translated by J. F. Huntington. London: Batchworth Press, 1953. An excellent biography of Godoy and a study of his part in the events preceding the insurrection.

Esdaile, Charles J. *Fighting Napoleon: Guerillas, Bandits, and Adventurers in Spain, 1808-1814.* New Haven, Conn.: Yale University Press, 2004. Focuses on the Spanish peasants, bandits and other guerrilla fighters who attacked the French army, assessing the contributions they made to the Peninsular War.

Herr, Richard. *The Eighteenth Century Revolution in Spain.* Princeton, N.J.: Princeton University Press, 1958. This work is one of the best books ever written on this period in Spanish history.

Hilt, Douglas. *The Troubled Trinity: Godoy and the Spanish Monarchs.* Tuscaloosa: University of Alabama Press, 1987. A revisionist study of the Spanish leader that effectively synthesizes modern scholarship.

Lovett, Gabriel H. *Napoleon and the Birth of Modern Spain.* 2 vols. New York: New York University Press, 1965. This two-volume study of the events of the war in Spain is the most detailed and comprehensive study of the period.

Lynch, John. *Bourbon Spain, 1700-1808.* Oxford, England: Basil Blackwell, 1989. Lynch provides an insightful and comprehensive overview of the crises facing the Bourbon monarchy in Spain. The book contains a bibliographic essay on different aspects of the Spanish Bourbon regime.

Ramos Oliveira, Antonio. *Politics, Economics, and Men of Modern Spain, 1808-1916.* Translated by Teener Hall. London: Victor Gollancz, 1946. A socioeconomic history of the results of the insurrection written by Spain's noted Marxist historian.

Smith, Rhea Marsh. *Spain: A Modern History.* Ann Arbor: University of Michigan Press, 1965. A general history of Spain that also considers the results of the insurrection.

SEE ALSO: Dec. 2, 1804: Bonaparte Is Crowned Napoleon I; May 2, 1808-Nov., 1813: Peninsular War in Spain; July 22, 1812: Battle of Salamanca; Mar., 1814: Goya Paints *Third of May 1808: Execution of the Citizens of Madrid*; Apr. 11, 1814-July 29, 1830: France's Bourbon Dynasty Is Restored; Sept. 29, 1833-1849: Carlist Wars Unsettle Spain; Sept. 30, 1868: Spanish Revolution of 1868; 1876: Spanish Constitution of 1876.

RELATED ARTICLES in *Great Lives from History: The Nineteenth Century, 1801-1900:* Napoleon I; La Saragossa.

May 2, 1808-November, 1813
PENINSULAR WAR IN SPAIN

The Peninsular War, in which the British military was primarily responsible for driving the French out of Spain, marked French emperor Napoleon I's first major setback, while demonstrating the strength of the British army and revealing the weakness of Spain's monarchy and the political divisions within Spain.

ALSO KNOWN AS: Spanish War of Independence
LOCALE: Spain; Portugal
CATEGORY: Wars, uprisings, and civil unrest

KEY FIGURES

Napoleon I (Napoleon Bonaparte; 1769-1821),
    emperor of the French, r. 1804-1814, 1815
Duke of Wellington (Arthur Wellesley; 1769-1852),
    British military commander in Spain, r. 1812-1813
Joseph Bonaparte (1768-1844), Napoleon's brother
    and the French-imposed king of Spain, r. 1808-1813
Ferdinand VII (1784-1833), Bourbon heir to the Spanish
    crown and king of Spain, r. 1808, 1813-1833

SUMMARY OF EVENT

The Peninsular War, sometimes known as the War of Independence in Spain, changed Spain irrevocably. As one phase of the continental war against France, the Peninsular War was the arena in which the French emperor Napoleon I first tasted a serious military defeat. The war was touched off by the insurrection of May 2, 1808, in Madrid, in which the Spanish army and guerrilla forces turned against the French occupation forces. British intervention eventually provided the military force needed to drive out the French. Meanwhile, liberal leaders redefined the nature of the Hispanic monarchy.

The need to coordinate military activities, together with the demand from the British for a formal government with which to ally, led to the formation of a central government in Spain known as the First Junta on May 25, 1808. Following the Spanish army's great victory over the French in July, 1808, the insurgents organized the Junta Supreme Central in December, 1808. The junta signed a formal alliance with Great Britain on January 14, 1809.

As the war against the French continued, the Spanish monarchy's lack of prestige provoked demands for the enactment of radical measures in the form of a constitution. The junta then transformed itself into a Council of Regency, acting in behalf of the Spanish Prince Ferdinand, who was being held captive in France. It also con-

voked the Spanish Cortes (legislature) to write a new constitution. The Cortes met in the port of Cádiz, one of the few cities not controlled by Napoleon's forces. There an elected body of one hundred representatives declared that "national sovereignty resides in the Cortes." As revolts against Spanish colonial rule in the Americas began breaking out in 1810, debate over Spain's new constitution went on from August, 1811, until its promulgation on March 19, 1812.

The impact of the 1812 constitution had wide-ranging repercussions. Since it was written in a merchant stronghold, the Cádiz constitution overrepresented the ideology of liberals, who stressed individual rights and limits on the power of the monarchy. As a reaction against the centralization of both the Bourbon and Habsburg Dynasties, the 1812 constitution limited the right of the state to intervene in the economy and politics. Reflecting the power of new commercial and industrial groups, the document also maintained that sovereignty resided in the Cortes, not in the three estates or the Crown. The new charter also proclaimed universal male suffrage and ended entailed estates and aristocratic privileges. It required the king to represent, as well as defend, the people's interests as represented by the Cortes.

Although the members of the Cortes had no concern for peasants and common workers since it was made up of wealthy members of the bourgeoisie, Spain's new constitution was by far the most democratic charter in Europe, and it established primary schools in hundreds of newly created municipalities. Moreover, the 1812 constitution mandated free elections in the colonies. The liberals also wanted to neutralize military influence in domestic politics. To do that, the Cortes abolished the previously rigid distinctions between soldiers and officers. The deputies wanted to indoctrinate the troops with liberal civic virtue. As a result, the Cortes also created a National Guard in 1814 that was wholly under the control of civilian authorities, particularly newly created political bosses (*jefes politicos*) to whom the generals were subordinated. The Cortes also removed exemptions from civil law and favored guerrilla leaders. Spain's so-called War of Independence was thus also an ideological struggle against privilege and the traditional state.

Meanwhile, Emperor Napoleon I appointed his brother, Joseph Bonaparte, the king of Spain, and Joseph claimed that his government was based upon a constitution. That document had been drafted in Bayonne,

The duke of Wellington (left) entering Badajoz after his troops breached its walls and recaptured the Spanish city from the French in March, 1812. (Francis R. Niglutsch)

France, not in Spain, but was nevertheless the first written constitution to be applied to Spain. Spanish support for Joseph Bonaparte, who was also known as José I in Spain, came from opportunistic bureaucrats and several army officers who claimed to be following orders from Prince Ferdinand. The most radical wing of the liberals, the *afrancesados*, also backed Joseph because they concluded that the Spanish monarchy could not be trusted to enact serious reforms. Therefore, the Peninsular War was not only an international conflict but also a civil war. Traditional aristocrats as well as the generally conservative masses soon identified change with foreign invaders.

The war itself caused enormous destruction of property and life. Society began to break down because the nature of guerrilla warfare weakened the fabric of personal and collective relationships. French troops inflicted cruel atrocities and burned many villages. The brutality of the French forces became immortalized by the shocking etchings of the Spanish painter Francisco de Goya. Guerrilla fighters were effective against the

French in the countryside but could not protect city dwellers from French reprisals. As a consequence, the urban population often became indifferent to the rural mobilization against the French.

In developing his plan for Spain, Napoleon seriously misjudged the Spanish character. The sheer tenacity of Spanish resistance forced him to use three hundred thousand troops to garrison every possible area in Spain. At that time, Napoleon was invading Russia, and most of the French soldiers used in Spain were conscripts instead of seasoned professionals. Meanwhile, a British army commanded by Lord Wellington liberated Portugal and marched into Madrid on August 12, 1812.

Soon afterward, the British army lifted the French siege of Cádiz. Meanwhile, guerrilla forces and bandits attacked French forces incessantly. Many Spanish priests claimed that killing French soldiers would not be a sin and that Spanish patriots could enter Heaven without question. Priests and monks also spread rumors that Napoleon had imprisoned the pope and reduced clerical privileges. By the summer of 1812, the French did not have enough forces to contain the Spanish and Anglo-Portuguese armies as well as guerrilla onslaughts. Short of money and equipment, the Spanish government offered command of its own armies to Wellington, who crushed Bonaparte's forces at the Battle of Vitoria on June 21, 1813, and drove the French north, across the Pyrenees.

Spanish forces played only an auxiliary role in Wellington's campaign. The revolts in Spanish America were limiting Spain's ability to participate with Great Britain in the Peninsular War. Between November, 1811, and October, 1813, the Spanish regency government sent thousands of troops to pacify its American colonies. Spain restored order to New Spain (Mexico) for the time being, but its control of Argentina, Chile, and much of Venezuela began to slip away. The American revolts also disrupted critical gold shipments to Spain with devastating financial results.

Spanish and British forces did not cooperate well or greatly respect each other during the war. The bankruptcy of the Spanish government resulted in poorly equipped and badly commanded Spanish units that often disappointed the British. Wellington demanded a wide range of powers to subordinate both the Spanish army and Spanish provincial authorities to his command. The British government sent huge amounts of equipment and clothing to Spain. It angered Wellington to see Spanish soldiers begging in the streets, despite the provisions they were being given by the British. Fed up with the attempts of Spanish liberals to restrict his power, Wellington resigned his command in August, 1813, but the Cortes soon reinstated him. When Wellington invaded France at the end of 1813, however, he did not want Spanish troops to accompany him for fear that they would intensify resistance by French civilians.

SIGNIFICANCE

Final victory in the Peninsular War did not improve relations between Spain and Great Britain. After the Spanish army had utterly humiliated itself during its 1812 and 1813 campaigns, Spanish officers became bitterly jealous over the success of the British forces as well as tactless British suggestions that British officers should lead Spanish armies. Many Spaniards were also embarrassed at not being able to participate in the invasion of France. Moreover, the liberals as well as the monarchists feared that Britain would encourage Spanish colonies to fight for their independence from Spain. Finally, Britain made no secret of its desire for free trade and better access to Spanish American markets and resources. A new treaty

between Spain and Britain in 1814 mandated that Spain would never again ally with France, in return for a British promise to remain neutral in the Spanish American wars for independence.

In a desperate bid to regain influence in Spain, Napoleon released Ferdinand VII, who received a rapturous welcome when he crossed the Catalonian frontier into Spain in March, 1814. As the French hoped, Ferdinand arrested liberal leaders in May, 1814, and reestablished the monarchy. Rather uneasily, Ferdinand swore allegiance to the 1812 constitution. He eventually withdrew his recognition of the constitution, but the old regime of Spain's authoritarian monarchy was gone forever and liberals would become a dynamic force in modern Spain.

—*Douglas W. Richmond*

FURTHER READING

Alexander, D. W. *Rod of Iron: French Counter-insurgency Policy in Aragón During the Peninsular War.* Wilmington, Del.: Scholarly Resources, 1985. A careful analysis of the efforts of French commanders, primarily Suchet and Reille, to subjugate Aragón, obtain supplies for French forces, and prepare the area for annexation to France. The valuable insights of this study are also applicable to other Spanish provinces.

Carr, Raymond. *Spain, 1808-1975.* 2d ed. New York: Oxford University Press, 1982. Broad history of Spain that contends that the aristocracy and regular clergy instigated agitation in favor of Ferdinand and against the French invaders.

Christiansen, E. *The Origins of Military Power in Spain, 1800-1854.* London: Oxford University Press, 1967. Strongly critical view of the Spanish military, with attention to its undistinguished role in the Peninsular War.

Corrigan, Gordon. *Wellington: A Military Life.* London: Hambledon and London, 2001. A former soldier, Corrigan examines Wellington's claims to military greatness, concluding that he was the first modern general.

Esdaile, Charles J. *The Peninsular War: A New History.* New York: Palgrave Macmillan, 2003. Well-written and comprehensive history of the Peninsular War that covers all aspects of the war, from lively descriptions of individual battles to incisive analyses of political and social issues.

_____. *The Spanish Army in the Peninsular War.* New York: Manchester University Press, 1988. The author traces the composition, organization, and general outlook of the Spanish army during a total breakdown of central authority.

1800's

Gates, David. *The Spanish Ulcer: A History of the Peninsular War*. New York: W. W. Norton, 1986. Emphasizes the role of the regular Spanish armies but makes little effort to describe and evaluate the role of the guerrillas.

Lovett, Gabriel H. *Napoleon and the Birth of Modern Spain*. 2 vols. New York: New York University Press, 1965. Lovett concludes that the common people of Spain initiated a national campaign against the French.

Weller, Jac. *Wellington in the Peninsula*. Harrisburg, Pa.: Stackpole Books, 1999. Lavishly illustrated popular history of Wellington's campaigns in the Peninsular War.

SEE ALSO: May 2, 1808: Dos de Mayo Insurrection in Spain; Sept. 16, 1810-Sept. 28, 1821: Mexican War of Independence; June 23-Dec. 14, 1812: Napoleon Invades Russia; July 22, 1812: Battle of Salamanca; Mar., 1813-Dec. 9, 1824: Bolívar's Military Campaigns; Mar., 1814: Goya Paints *Third of May 1808: Execution of the Citizens of Madrid*; Jan. 18, 1817-July 28, 1821: San Martín's Military Campaigns.

RELATED ARTICLES in *Great Lives from History: The Nineteenth Century, 1801-1900:* Napoleon I; José de San Martín; Duke of Wellington.

1809
LAMARCK PUBLISHES *ZOOLOGICAL PHILOSOPHY*

In Zoological Philosophy, *Jean-Baptiste Lamarck proposed a pre-Darwinian theory of organic evolution, or transmutation of species, and explained it by the twofold mechanism of natural progress and the inheritance of acquired characteristics.*

LOCALE: Paris, France
CATEGORIES: Biology; genetics

KEY FIGURES

Jean-Baptiste Lamarck (1744-1829), French naturalist
Edward Drinker Cope (1840-1897), American paleontologist
Georges Cuvier (1769-1832), French naturalist, comparative anatomist, and paleontologist
Comte de Buffon (Georges Louis Leclerc; 1707-1788), French naturalist and encyclopedist of natural history
Carolus Linnaeus (1707-1778), Swedish taxonomist
Erasmus Darwin (1731-1802), English physician, grandfather of Charles Darwin
Jean-Baptiste Bory de Saint-Vincent (1778-1846), French botanist
Charles Darwin (1809-1882), English naturalist

SUMMARY OF EVENT

The eighteenth century saw a number of naturalists, including the great taxonomist Carolus Linnaeus and, in later life, naturalist Georges Leclerc, comte de Buffon, question the immutability of species. According to the time period's common understanding, any new forms resulted from either hybridization or degeneration of type. The idea of unlimited change found expression in the

works of mathematician Pierre-Louis Moreau de Maupertuis in the early eighteenth century and others, including naturalists Jean-Baptiste Robinet and Charles Bonnet. The latter theories, however, did not find many adherents and were not grounded in the systematic study of organic beings.

Before 1800, Lamarck himself accepted the immutability of species, though his attempts to discover a natural classification of plants in his first book, published in 1779, became important when he later conceived of the evolutionary process. During the 1790's, he worked on the classification of invertebrates, which had all been lumped together into one group. He also did research on physicochemical problems and attempted to convince his contemporaries that his chemistry was superior to the new chemistry of Antoine-Laurent Lavoisier.

Before publishing *Philosophie zoologique: Ou, Exposition des considérations relative à l'histoire naturelle des animaux* (1809; *Zoological Philosophy: An Exposition with Regard to the Natural History of Animals*, 1914), Lamarck had explored the principles of organic change, described in his *Recherches sur l'organisation des corps vivans* (1802; studies on the organization of living bodies). The principles include spontaneous generation at the lowest levels of the plant and animal kingdoms, the natural production of increasingly complex organisms from simpler ones, and the influence of the environment, which altered the natural progress toward ever-increasing complexity.

Two issues led Lamarck to the idea of the mutability of species. First was his rejection of the extinction of spe-

LAMARCK ON INHERITED TRAITS

In his Zoological Philosophy *(1809), excerpted here, Jean-Baptiste Lamarck makes his case for the heritability of traits.*

Circumstances have an influence on the form and the organic structure of animals. What this means is that by undergoing significant change, the circumstances proportionally alter, over time, both the form and the organic structure itself. . . .

Thus, efforts made in any direction whatever . . . enlarge these parts and make them acquire dimensions and a shape which they would never have attained if these efforts had not become the habitual action of the animals which carried them out. Observations undertaken on all the known animals provide examples of this everywhere.

Is it possible that there is a more striking one than the kangaroo? . . . 1. Its front limbs . . . have remained thin, very small, and almost without force. 2. The back limbs . . . have, by contrast, undergone a considerable development and have become very large and very powerful. 3. Finally, the tail . . . has acquired at its base an extremely remarkable thickness and power. . . .

Conclusion Accepted Up Until Today: Nature (or its author), in creating the animals, anticipated all the possible sorts of circumstances in which they would have to live and gave to each species a fixed organic structure, as well as a determined and invariable form for its parts, which forces each species to live in those places and climates where it is located and to maintain there the habits which we know it has.

My Personal Conclusion: Nature, by producing in succession all the animal species and beginning with the most imperfect or the simplest, gradually made the organic structure more complicated; as these animals generally spread out into all the habitable regions of the world, from the influence of the circumstances which each species encountered, it acquired the habits which we know in it and the modifications in its parts which observation reveals to us in that species. . . .

Could there be in natural history a more important conclusion, one to which we ought to give more attention, than the one I have just revealed?

Source: Jean-Baptiste Lamarck, *Zoological Philosophy* (1809), chapter 7. Translated by Ian Johnston. (Nanaimo, B.C.: Malaspina University-College, 2000).

cess of life. Lamarck's experience in classification supported his idea that nature progressed from simple to complex in the production of living beings. His theory of evolution rested on a phylogenetic (historical) interpretation of the gradation of organic beings. Also, whereas individuals could not be placed linearly on the scale, the large groups could be.

The fact of organic transformation required a cause. During the eighteenth century the idea of the march of human history had developed, that is, a natural course of progress, which circumstances modified. Along similar lines, Lamarck proposed two quite different causes for organic diversity. The first and more important cause was the tendency of nature to cause an increase in the complexity of organization of animals. The second cause was the influence of the environment upon heredity.

In chapter 7 of *Zoological Philosophy*, Lamarck elucidates the two laws of inheritance: first, continuous use strengthens an organ and continuous disuse weakens it until it ultimately disappears; second, through long-term environmental influences organisms developed needs that occasioned inherited changes in organs through use or disuse. These laws formed his principle of the inheritance of acquired characteristics.

cies, a phenomenon that had been suspected but not convincingly demonstrated until the 1790's. As an adherent of geological uniformitarianism, the idea that geological changes were slow and steady, he rejected the explanation proposed by Georges Cuvier and others that geological catastrophes had erased entire species. Lamarck asserted that the forms no longer in existence had changed into present forms.

Second, Lamarck devised a theory of spontaneous generation to account for the origins of the simplest living forms. The causes of spontaneous generation were entirely physical: Light, combined with certain elements—for example, caloric and electric—occasioned the organization of inorganic matter and excited the pro-

Lamarck was inconsistent in his assertions concerning the necessity of both causes. In some places he argued that evolution occurred even in the absence of environmental effects; in others, having noted that when species reproduce in an unchanging environment they do not change, he seemed to deny the inevitability of progress. Lamarck provided three pages of speculations concerning how structures might change. For example, the membranes between the toes of a bird stretched until the webbed foot formed in waterfowl. The horns and antlers of male ruminants formed in response to the excess flow of inner fluids stirred up by fits of anger.

Lamarck had worked out these views by 1802 but published them seven years later in *Zoological Philoso-*

phy, which contains three parts. Part 1 presents his views on the natural classification of animals, and that classification reveals increasing complexity, which is interrupted by environmental factors leading to the inheritance of acquired characteristics. Part 2 details Lamarck's materialistic definition of life and his views on spontaneous generation. Part 3 encompasses his views on the nature of the nervous system, again explained in terms of physical causes. One of the functions of the nervous system was to create unconscious needs or instincts, the actions of which could change habits and lead to deviations from the progressive plan of nature.

Instincts are not universal in all species. Lamarck believed that the most important features of animals were the nervous, respiratory, and circulatory systems, in that order. On the linear scale of organisms, descending from the top position, occupied by humans, to the lowest, the infusoria, one could observe the simplification and finally the disappearance of these systems. In species with little-developed nervous systems in particular (and in plants), habits formed from the direct influence of the external fluids upon the internal organization, while in more advanced organisms, the nonconscious "internal sentiment" mediated the influence of the external fluids.

Lamarck's ideas gathered a few adherents. However, even before the publication of *Zoological Philosophy*, Georges Cuvier, the most important comparative anatomist and paleontologist in France at the time, attacked Lamarck's system. He rejected Lamarck's geological uniformitarianism and organic transformationism and interpreted geological history as a series of alternations of catastrophes that caused extinction and creations of new species. Furthermore, he believed in a very tight or rigid organization of the organism, in which all structures worked together to perform the functions necessary to life. Any change in structure beyond the normal bounds would result in death. When *Zoological Philosophy* appeared, the general public as well as the scientific community largely ignored it.

SIGNIFICANCE

Lamarck's work represents one of the earliest attempts to explore species inheritance, the mutability of species, and organic evolution. Several years earlier, in the 1790's, Erasmus Darwin, the grandfather of Charles Darwin, published a theory of organic transmutation, in which he also argued for natural progression and presented a view similar to the inheritance of acquired characteristics. Lamarck, however, viewed the latter mechanism as secondary, and the overemphasis on its importance stemmed

from Cuvier's ridicule of Lamarck's bird examples and his focus on it in his obituary of Lamarck.

During the 1820's several minor figures and a more important one, Jean-Baptiste Bory de Saint-Vincent, attempted to gain adherents to Lamarck's views. Although their views sometimes bore little resemblance to Lamarck's actual works, the idea of organic transformation lived on. Lamarck's idea that evolution did occur, moreover, may have paved the way for the acceptance of Charles Darwin's theory, especially in Italy. Lamarckianism also had adherents outside the realm of biology. It influenced the social evolution theories of Herbert Spencer, for example, and had a number of proponents, such as the neo-Lamarckian American paleontologist Edward Drinker Cope, who liked the idea that organisms themselves drove their own destiny.

Charles Darwin was well aware of Lamarck's work. His conception of evolution, however, differed greatly from the earlier one. Unlike Lamarck, Darwin did not consider evolution to be progressive. Moreover, Darwin's mechanism for evolutionary change—natural selection—bore no resemblance to the inheritance of acquired characteristics. However, in the absence of an understanding of genetics, Darwin did speculate that the use and disuse of parts and the influence of habits of life and the environment might cause variations in individuals, variations on which natural selection operated.

—*Kristen L. Zacharias*

FURTHER READING

Bowler, Peter J. *Evolution, The History of an Idea*. Rev. ed. Berkeley: University of California Press, 1989. Lengthy work examining theories of earth history and evolution from the sixteenth to the twentieth centuries. Highly useful for placing the work of Lamarck in its larger context.

Burkhardt, Richard W., Jr. *The Spirit of System: Now with "Lamarck in 1995."* Cambridge, Mass.: Harvard University Press, 1995. A reprint of Burkhardt's authoritative 1977 book, along with a lengthy introductory essay assessing scholarship since its original publication.

Corsi, Pietro. *The Age of Lamarck: Evolutionary Theories in France, 1790-1830*. Berkeley: University of California Press, 1988. A study focusing on Lamarck's earlier scientific study of the organization of living bodies (1802), which contained most of his ideas on transmutation, and the reaction to his evolutionary theory by Cuvier and others.

Gould, Stephen Jay. "A Division of Worms." *Natural History* 108, no. 1 (February, 1999). Argues that

Lamarck's theory has been misread and that he modified his ideas during his studies after the publication of *Zoological Philosophy*.

Lamarck, Jean-Baptiste. *Lamarck's Open Mind: The Lectures*. Gold Beach, Oreg.: High Sierra Books, 2004. A reissue of six lectures given by Lamarck, including two relating to his theory of transmutation.

_____. *Zoological Philosophy: An Exposition with Regard to the Natural History of Animals*. Translated by Hugh Elliot. Chicago: University of Chicago Press, 1984. The introductory essays by David L. Hull and Richard W. Burkhardt, Jr., provide an overview of the development and impact of Lamarck's thought.

SEE ALSO: Feb. 20, 1824: Buckland Presents the First Public Dinosaur Description; July, 1830: Lyell Publishes *Principles of Geology*; 1854-1862: Wallace's Expeditions Give Rise to Biogeography; Nov. 24, 1859: Darwin Publishes *On the Origin of Species*; 1861: *Archaeopteryx Lithographica* Is Discovered; 1865: Mendel Proposes Laws of Heredity; 1871: Darwin Publishes *The Descent of Man*.

RELATED ARTICLES in *Great Lives from History: The Nineteenth Century, 1801-1900*: Louis Agassiz; Karl Ernst von Baer; Samuel Butler; Georges Cuvier; Charles Darwin; Asa Gray; Ernst Haeckel; Thomas Henry Huxley; Sir Charles Lyell; Herbert Spencer.

1810's

March 16, 1810
FLETCHER V. PECK

In this ruling, the U.S. Supreme Court's broad construction of the Constitution's contracts clause enhanced protection from legislative interference for vested rights in private property. For the first time, moreover, the Court declared that a state law was unconstitutional and therefore invalid.

ALSO KNOWN AS: Yazoo affair
LOCALE: Washington, D.C.
CATEGORIES: Laws, acts, and legal history; economics

KEY FIGURES

John Peck (fl. early nineteenth century), seller of a small tract of the Yazoo lands

Robert Fletcher (fl. early nineteenth century), New Hampshire resident who bought the Yazoo tract and then demanded a refund

Alexander Hamilton (1755-1804), secretary of the Treasury, 1789-1795

John Quincy Adams (1767-1848), son of president John Adams and Fletcher's attorney

Luther Martin (1748-1826), member of the Constitutional Convention who represented Peck

Gideon Granger (1767-1822), postmaster general under Jefferson

John Marshall (1755-1835), chief justice of the United States, 1801-1835

John Randolph (1773-1833), opponent of the United States paying investors in Yazoo lands

SUMMARY OF EVENT

Although it is almost axiomatic that many cases from which great constitutional principles are derived have sordid backgrounds, few can match the comic-opera corruption behind the U.S. Supreme Court's March 16, 1810, *Fletcher v. Peck* decision, a case that began fifteen years earlier.

On January 7, 1795, the Georgia legislature passed a bill permitting the sale of some thirty-five million acres of fertile, well-watered land for $500,000, payable over a five-year period. The purchasers were four land companies that had been formed to speculate in western lands. The fact that the state of Georgia itself did not have clear title to the lands apparently did not bother the state's legislature because, with one exception, every member of the legislature had been bribed. The problem of unclear title also did not trouble Georgia's governor, who signed the legislation into law.

To be sure, the legislature's action was not without some benefits to Georgia. The state needed the money, and the problem of wresting the title to the land from the Native American tribes through action by the federal government now became the concern of the speculators. The state had sold a slightly smaller tract to other speculators six years earlier with a similarly clouded title and on inferior terms, and the electorate of the state had not been disturbed. In the interval, however, Eli Whitney had invented the cotton gin, which revolutionized the cotton industry. Now, the same lands would be in great demand for the production of cotton, assuming that their Native American residents could be removed.

ARTICLE I, SECTION 10 OF THE U.S. CONSTITUTION

The decision of the U.S. Supreme Court in Fletcher v. Peck *revolved around Article I, section 10, of the Constitution, reproduced below. In particular, the Court made reference to the prohibitions on states from impairing the obligation of contracts and from passing laws ex post facto.*

No State shall enter into any Treaty, Alliance, or Confederation; grant Letters of Marque and Reprisal; coin Money; emit Bills of Credit; make any Thing but gold and silver Coin a Tender in Payment of Debts; pass any Bill of Attainder, ex post facto Law, or Law impairing the Obligation of Contracts, or grant any Title of Nobility.

No State shall, without the Consent of the Congress, lay any Imposts or Duties on Imports or Exports, except what may be absolutely necessary for executing it's inspection Laws: and the net Produce of all Duties and Imposts, laid by any State on Imports or Exports, shall be for the Use of the Treasury of the United States; and all such Laws shall be subject to the Revision and Control of the Congress.

No State shall, without the Consent of Congress, lay any Duty of Tonnage, keep Troops, or Ships of War in time of Peace, enter into any Agreement or Compact with another State, or with a foreign Power, or engage in War, unless actually invaded, or in such imminent Danger as will not admit of delay.

The gross dishonesty of the whole transaction upset many conscientious citizens. As a consequence, in 1796, a new legislature was elected in which every member pledged to vote for the repeal of the act of sale. On February 13, the state passed the Rescinding Act. So strong was the feeling in the state that a formal ceremony was held on the steps of the state house, during which a copy of the initial bill was formally burned. The fraud became known as the Yazoo affair.

However, as quick as Georgia's efforts to undo the fraudulent deal had been, they did not come in time to prevent the sale of certain of the lands to presumably innocent third parties. It was over these titles that the legal and political battles took place. The land companies involved in the transactions did not consider the Rescinding Act to be valid, and they continued to sell the land. Most of the purchasers lived in the Middle Atlantic and New England states, and they were greatly concerned as to the validity of their purchases. To defend their purchases, the New England-Mississippi Company was formed to protect the rights of investors. The company sought an opinion from Secretary of the Treasury Alexander Hamilton concerning the legality of the land claims. Hamilton did not attempt to investigate the question of Georgia's title to the land but, in a pamphlet published in 1796, stated that if the titles were valid, the Re-

scinding Act was void and in his opinion, the courts would so rule. Armed with an opinion from one of the country's most distinguished public servants, the company continued to offer its lands to both prospective settlers and speculators.

At the same time that the New England-Mississippi Company was selling its lands, a proposal was made to the U.S. Congress, with the full backing of the Jefferson administration, that the United States should enter into an arrangement whereby Georgia would cede its claims to the lands in question to the federal government in return for compensation. In addition, the federal government would handle the claims to the area of the several Native American tribes and the Spanish government. This proposal became law. The report of the commissioners whom Jefferson appointed to study the problem proposed that five million acres of the lands be retained and the proceeds from their sale be used to indemnify the Yazoo land purchasers. Although the claims of the speculators, in the commissioners' opinion, could not be supported, they proposed the indemnity for them to ensure "the tranquility of those who may hereafter inhabit the territory," and argued that the federal government should enter into a compromise on reasonable terms.

The federal action caused a political fight of major proportions. When the commissioners' proposal reached the floor of the House of Representatives, it was attacked by a wildly indignant Congressman John Randolph, who was determined to defeat it by any means possible. Randolph's motives were partly ideological and partly emotional. He had been in Georgia when the Rescinding Act had been passed and had been present at the burning ceremony. He apparently believed that he understood the depths of the popular opposition to the grant in Georgia. He contended that Georgia had no initial right to make the sale, that the sale was firmly rooted in fraud and corruption so as to make it invalid, and that it was legally impossible to sell a third purchaser a better title.

Randolph was opposed in the House by Gideon Granger, the postmaster general, who was lobbying with his considerable ability in favor of the measure. After four days of intensive debate, Randolph's eloquence won and the measure was defeated. Afterward, supporters of the legislation brought up the measure annually for several years, only to be defeated each time. Eventually, the purchasers followed the implicit advice given earlier by Alexander Hamilton by seeking relief through the courts.

The "friendly" suit of *Fletcher v. Peck* originated in the sale made by John Peck of Massachusetts to Robert Fletcher of New Hampshire of fifteen thousand acres of Yazoo lands. It was Fletcher's intention to test the legality of his purchase. Because the litigants lived in different states, the case was heard in the federal courts. After Justice William Cushing of the Supreme Court, acting in his capacity as a circuit judge, found for Peck in October, 1807, the case was appealed to the Supreme Court.

Supreme Court justice William Johnson later said in a concurring opinion that the controversy had the appearance of a feigned case, but that his admiration for the attorneys involved in the case had induced him "to abandon [his] scruples, in the belief that they would never consent to impose a mere feigned case upon this Court." Luther Martin, Peck's attorney, contended that the several states were free, sovereign, and independent entities, and that "the sovereignty of each, not of the whole, was the principle of the Revolution." Consequently, Martin argued, the federal courts had no jurisdiction in the matter. John Quincy Adams, who was later replaced by Joseph Story, the future Supreme Court justice, based his own case on Hamilton's old opinion that the grant was a contract, and under Article I, section 10 of the U.S. Constitution, it could not be rescinded.

The issue in *Fletcher v. Peck* was essentially a question of public welfare versus public confidence in the sanctity of land grants. To refuse to allow the states the authority to repeal the land grant, especially in the context of an obvious fraud, would undermine the public welfare and invite land speculators to corrupt state legislatures. At the same time, to give the state legislature the right to revoke the land grant would jeopardize public confidence in all public grants, and in turn would discourage investment and the exploitation of land.

"That corruption," John Marshall wrote at the beginning of his opinion in *Fletcher v. Peck*, "should find its way into the governments of our infant republics and contaminate the very source of legislation . . . [is a circumstance] deeply to be to be deplored." Despite this, the Rescinding Act of the Georgia legislature was still void.

Marshall did not clearly establish the reasons that the repeal of the land grant was constitutionally infirm. At one point in his opinion, he argued that the 1796 act of the Georgia legislature impaired the obligation of a contract in violation of Article I, section 10 of the Constitution; elsewhere, he suggested that the Georgia act was a violation of the ex post facto clause of the same article and section. "The rescinding act," he wrote, "would have the effect of an ex post facto decision. It forfeits the estate of Fletcher for a crime not committed by himself, but from those from who he purchased." This argument had the defect of ignoring the fact that the ex post facto clause had been held applicable only to criminal cases in *Calder v. Bull* in 1798, and the law in *Fletcher* dealt solely with a civil subject.

Elsewhere in the opinion, following one of the arguments of Alexander Hamilton, Marshall intimated that the Rescinding Act was invalid because it conflicted with the nature of society and government. At the conclusion of his opinion, Marshall said that "the state of Georgia was restrained by general principles which are common to our free institutions or by the particular provisions of the Constitution."

SIGNIFICANCE

Despite the ambiguity and shortcomings of Marshall's opinion, *Fletcher v. Peck* was the first clear precedent for the assertion by the Supreme Court of a power to declare state laws unconstitutional. Its immediate practical effect was negligible; Georgia no longer owned the Yazoo lands, as they had been ceded to the federal government. However, *Fletcher* did lay the foundations for using the contract clause of the Constitution to protect private property interests against the vagaries of state legislatures. As such, it is a reflection of the overall strategy of the Marshall Court to facilitate investment and energize the U.S. economy.

Although the speculators had won in the Supreme Court, they were not to secure a congressional, or monetary, victory until 1814, when Congress, after John Randolph's failure to win reelection, passed an appropriation of five million dollars to buy up their now untarnished titles.

—*Gustav L. Seligman, updated by David L. Sterling*

FURTHER READING

Beveridge, Albert J. *Conflict and Construction, 1800-1815*. Vol. 4 in *The Life of John Marshall*. Boston: Houghton Mifflin, 1919. This classic biography of Marshall devotes almost sixty pages to a discussion of *Fletcher v. Peck*.

Haines, Charles G. *The Role of the Supreme Court in American Government and Politics, 1789-1835*. Berkeley: University of California Press, 1944. A study of

1810's

the Supreme Court in its formative period. Gives adequate coverage to *Fletcher v. Peck* and places it in the framework of the Court's development.

Hunting, Warren B. *The Obligation of Contracts Clause of the United States Constitution*. Baltimore: Johns Hopkins University Press, 1919. Contains a technical discussion of an important phase of U.S. constitutional history. Detailed coverage of *Fletcher v. Peck*.

Lewis, Thomas T., and Richard L. Wilson, eds. *Encyclopedia of the U.S. Supreme Court*. 3 vols. Pasadena, Calif.: Salem Press, 2001. Comprehensive reference work on the Supreme Court that contains substantial discussions of *Fletcher v. Peck*, contracts, John Marshall, Joseph Story, and many related subjects.

Newmyer, R. Kent. *John Marshall and the Heroic Age of the Supreme Court*. Baton Rouge: Louisiana State University Press, 2001. Examination of Chief Justice Marshall's legal philosophy, as it was expressed in his Court decisions, that places his beliefs in historical context.

_____. *Supreme Court Justice Joseph Story: Statesman of the Old Republic*. Chapel Hill: University of

North Carolina Press, 1985. A comprehensive, analytical biography of Story, one of the lawyers in *Fletcher v. Peck* and a future associate of John Marshall.

White, G. Edward. *The Marshall Court and Cultural Change, 1815-1835*. Abridged ed. New York: Oxford University Press, 1991. Although abridged, this study of the record of the Marshall Court contains almost eight hundred pages of text and almost eighty pages on the contract clause cases.

Wright, Benjamin F., Jr. *The Contract Clause of the Constitution*. Cambridge, Mass.: Harvard University Press, 1938. A more detailed study of the contract clause than Hunting's and broader in scope.

SEE ALSO: Feb. 24, 1803: *Marbury v. Madison*; Mar. 6, 1819: *McCulloch v. Maryland*; Mar. 2, 1824: *Gibbons v. Ogden*; May 28, 1830: Congress Passes Indian Removal Act.

RELATED ARTICLES in *Great Lives from History: The Nineteenth Century, 1801-1900:* John Quincy Adams; John Marshall; Joseph Story.

September 8, 1810-May, 1812
ASTORIAN EXPEDITIONS EXPLORE THE PACIFIC NORTHWEST COAST

The expeditions that John Jacob Astor sent to the Pacific coast to establish permanent trading posts ultimately failed, but the effort launched a new phase in the escalating American-British contest for control of the Pacific Northwest.

LOCALE: Pacific Northwest
CATEGORIES: Expansion and land acquisition; exploration and discovery

KEY FIGURES
John Jacob Astor (1763-1848), American entrepreneur who originated the Astorian venture
Comcomly (1765?-1830), Chinook chief
William Price Hunt (1783-1842), leader of the overland expedition
Duncan McDougall (d. 1818) and
Robert Stuart (1785-1848), leaders of the sea expedition
David Mackenzie (fl. early nineteenth century), first to arrive from the overland expedition
David Thompson (1770-1857), North West Company partner, explorer, and fur trader

SUMMARY OF EVENT
In 1784, John Jacob Astor emigrated from Germany to the United States to make his fortune in a new land. Beginning as a clerk in a New York City furrier's shop, he eventually became a major fur dealer and one of the most successful entrepreneurs in the United States. By 1800, he realized that further expansion of his business would bring him into direct competition with the great British fur companies of Canada—the Hudson's Bay Company and the North West Company—and that much more than his personal fortune was at stake. Where the trading companies built posts, the governments of their nations would follow, establishing outposts and claiming the region. Over the next few years, Astor devised a plan to create a transcontinental U.S. company that could compete with the British trading companies, establish a fur trade monopoly across the center of the North American continent, and extend beyond to control trade with China and Russian Alaska. Astor's new company would not only make him a leader of the international fur industry but also establish the sovereignty of the United States in its trading sphere and prevent British expansion from Canada.

HUNT'S ROUTE FROM ST. LOUIS TO ASTORIA

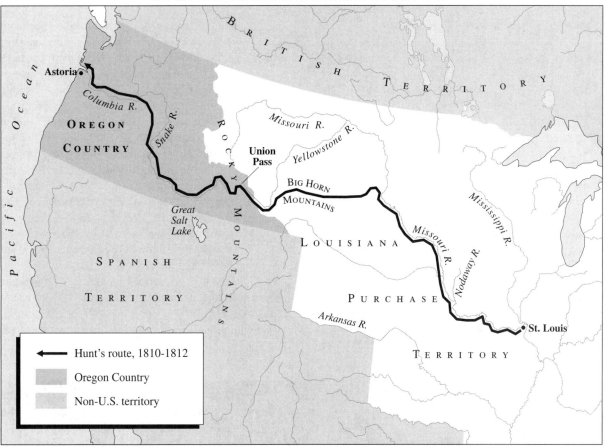

In 1808, Astor incorporated the American Fur Company and then proceeded to set up subsidiary regional companies to carry out specific parts of his plan. One of these, the Pacific Fur Company, formally organized in the summer of 1810, was to establish a base of operations on the northwest coast of what would later become the western United States, explore and establish a trade monopoly in the rich fur regions west of the Rocky Mountains, manage a monopoly on trade with the Russian settlements in Alaska, and corner the market on the fur trade with China. To initiate this ambitious project, two expeditions of "Astorians" started out in 1810. One expedition, led by Duncan McDougall and Robert Stuart, was to travel by sea around South America to the mouth of the Columbia River. In addition to clerks, craftsmen, and laborers, the expedition would take the tools and supplies needed to build and maintain a trading post on the Columbia. The second expedition, led by William Price Hunt, was to travel overland from St. Louis, blazing a

trail to the Columbia River and selecting sites for the network of trading posts that Astor intended to build across the continent.

McDougall and Stuart's expedition boarded the ship *Tonquin* and sailed from New York City on September 8, 1810. The voyage was plagued by bad luck, delays, and increasingly bitter quarrels between the *Tonquin*'s overbearing captain and the Astorians. In February, 1811, the *Tonquin* laid over in the Hawaiian Islands, taking on stores of food, water, and additional laborers and livestock to support the new trading post. After battling ocean storms and the sand bars, whirlpools, and treacherous currents at the mouth of the Columbia River, the *Tonquin* finally found safe harbor in the river on March 24. McDougall and Stuart selected a site on the river's south bank, and the heavy work of clearing away the dense forest began. By April 19, actual construction on the new post of Astoria had commenced.

Meanwhile, Hunt's overland party was delayed by recruiting and supply problems and did not leave St. Louis until October 21, 1810. Facing the onset of winter after a grueling trip up the Missouri River and uncertain about the best route west, the expedition camped on the Nodaway River, about five hundred miles above St. Louis. In March, 1811, the Astorians resumed their journey; however, poor luck with weather, equipment, and travel routes exacerbated personnel problems and slowed the expedition's progress. A bit of good luck came from encounters with native communities, which provided food and geographical information.

Hunt followed native trade routes to the Rocky Mountains, crossing present-day South Dakota and Wyoming. West of the Continental Divide, the expedition got lost and suffered terribly from hunger, harsh weather, rough terrain, and the dangers of trying to navigate the wild Snake River. In late October, 1811, Hunt divided his party into smaller groups to search for food and the best route to the Columbia River. The group led by David Mackenzie finally reached Astoria on January 18, 1812. On February 15, Hunt and forty-five of the original sixty members of the main party arrived there after a difficult and dangerous overland journey during which Shoshone Indians helped them. The remaining overlanders straggled in a few weeks later.

By that time, Astoria was a growing trading post with a large store, living quarters, a blacksmith shop, and storage sheds, all enclosed in a ninety-foot-square palisade. McDougall and the other Pacific Fur Company partners were planning to expand Astoria and establish satellite posts around the region. They, too, had been hampered by bad luck. Their lifeline to the outside world, the ship *Tonquin*, had left Astoria June 1, 1811, to trade with Indian communities along the coast. By early July, rumors reached them that Indians on Vancouver Island had destroyed the ship and its crew in revenge for the captain's insults to their chief. A lone survivor eventually reached Astoria to confirm that the story was true.

Although tribes on the lower Columbia River welcomed the traders, the Astorians remained nervous about their neighbors' intentions, particularly as they depended on the local people for food as well as furs. Although the newcomers immediately planted a garden at their post, it took time for them to learn how to grow crops in the unfamiliar climate and soil. Meanwhile, rations were short at Astoria. This situation suited the local Chinook chief,

British fur traders securing a peaceful surrender at Astoria. (Francis R. Niglutsch)

Comcomly. As the most powerful native leader in the region, he claimed a monopoly on trade with Astoria. Through the traders' first year, Comcomly saw to it that they had just enough food to survive and just enough trade to keep them from leaving, while ensuring that they remained dependent on him. Although the Astorians resented Comcomly's manipulation of their business, they could rarely outwit him and dared not oppose him openly.

To further Astor's grand plan and to break Comcomly's control, Hunt, McDougall, and the other partners planned expeditions to establish trading posts inland. Before they could act, however, a new challenge appeared. David Thompson, a North West Company partner, suddenly arrived at Astoria, on July 15, 1811. Renowned as an explorer of the far Northwest, Thompson had discovered the source of the Columbia River in 1807. In 1811, he became the first European to follow the river from its headwaters to its mouth. He had claimed the country he traversed for his company and Great Britain.

This unexpected appearance of an archrival spurred the Astorians to action: One Astorian led an expedition up the Columbia River to hold the region against the North West Company. Other parties explored the terrain and trade prospects up the coast and up the Willamette River. In May, 1812, a long-overdue supply ship arrived with abundant material and more people. Operations expanded rapidly west of the Rockies, while Robert Stuart started eastward with a party to find a good overland express route to St. Louis. During their crossing, east of Jackson's Hole, they would discover the crucial South Pass through the Rockies, which would later open the floodgates to the settlement of the Oregon territory.

Fortune again turned against the Astorians, however. On June 18, 1812, the United States declared war on Great Britain. In January, 1813, that news reached Astoria, with reports that the North West Company and the British Royal Navy planned joint expeditions to capture the U.S. outpost. Knowing that they could expect no help from Astor while the British controlled the seas, the partners began negotiations to sell Astoria to the North West Company before it was taken by force. The British sloop *Raccoon* arrived in November, 1813, and took possession of the post. In April, 1814, the Americans returned east. Most Astorians were Canadian, however, and many were former employees of the North West Company, who now went back to work for their old company.

SIGNIFICANCE

After the North West Company took over Astoria, its leaders renamed the post Fort George and made it their West Coast headquarters. Although Astor failed to establish his trade empire, he did provoke U.S. concern about British expansion in the Northwest. The U.S. government based future claims to the region in part on the U.S. occupation at Astoria. Returning Astorians brought back a wealth of information about the Far West, and the route pioneered by Robert Stuart's 1812-1813 expedition would later become the famous Oregon Trail. In 1846, the United States and Great Britain would finally work out a settlement by which Oregon became U.S. territory.

—*Mary Ellen Rowe*

FURTHER READING

Haeger, John Denis. *John Jacob Astor: Business and Finance in the Early Republic*. Detroit: Wayne State University Press, 1991. Study of Astor's career as a merchant, fur trader, and speculator to examine American economic development between 1790 and 1860.

Irving, Washington. *Astoria: Or, Anecdotes of an Enterprise Beyond the Rocky Mountains*. Philadelphia: Carey, Lea and Blanchard, 1836. Available in many modern editions, this history was written from interviews and diaries of participants by one of the great authors in the United States.

Jaeger, John D. "Business Strategy and Practice in the Early Republic: John Jacob Astor and the American Fur Trade." *Western Historical Quarterly* 19, no. 2 (May, 1988): 183-202. Compares Astor's business strategy with modern business practices.

Lavender, David. *The Fist in the Wilderness*. Garden City, N.Y.: Doubleday, 1964. Examines the history of the American Fur Company and the Pacific Fur Company.

Madsen, Axel. *John Jacob Astor: America's First Multimillionaire*. New York: John Wiley & Sons, 2001. A conventional biography of Astor, with considerable attention to his business enterprises.

Pole, Graeme. *David Thompson: The Epic Expeditions of a Great Canadian Explorer*. Canmore, Alta.: Altitude Publishing Canada, 2003. Examination of Thompson's twenty-eight years in the western fur trade.

Rollins, Phillip A., ed. *The Discovery of the Oregon Trail: Robert Stuart's Narrative of His Overland Trip Eastward from Astoria in 1812-13*. New York:

1810's

Edward Eberstadt & Sons, 1935. Contains the overland diaries of Hunt and Stuart and other useful material.

Ronda, James P. *Astoria and Empire*. Lincoln: University of Nebraska Press, 1990. Analyzes Astoria's role in the struggle for national sovereignty in the Northwest.

Ross, Alexander. *Adventures of the First Settlers on the Oregon or Columbia River, 1810-1813*. Lincoln: University of Nebraska Press, 1986. Ross, one of the original clerks at Astoria, gives a colorful firsthand account of the venture.

SEE ALSO: May 14, 1804-Sept. 23, 1806: Lewis and Clark Expedition; Apr. 6, 1808: American Fur Company Is Chartered; 1822-1831: Jedediah Smith Explores the Far West; May, 1842-1854: Frémont Explores the American West; Aug. 9, 1842: Webster-Ashburton Treaty Settles Maine's Canadian Border; June 15, 1846: United States Acquires Oregon Territory; 1879: Powell Publishes His Report on the American West.

RELATED ARTICLES in *Great Lives from History: The Nineteenth Century, 1801-1900:* John Jacob Astor; Jedediah Smith; David Thompson.

September 16, 1810
HIDALGO ISSUES EL GRITO DE DOLORES

Although the revolt led by Miguel Hidalgo was crushed, Hidalgo's call for independence began the first stage in Mexico's ultimately successful struggle for independence from Spain.

ALSO KNOWN AS: Hidalgo revolt
LOCALE: Dolores, Guanajuato, Mexico
CATEGORY: Wars, uprisings, and civil unrest

KEY FIGURES

Miguel Hidalgo y Costilla (1753-1811), leader of the movement for Mexican independence from Spain
Ignacio de Allende (1779-1811), Mexican army officer who led the movement to overthrow Spanish rule
Félix María Calleja del Rey (1759-1828), leader of the Spanish forces that fought against the revolution

SUMMARY OF EVENT

In 1810, the composition of Mexican society exhibited profound ethnic and caste distinctions. At the top of the population of six million people, fifteen thousand Spaniards from Spain, or *peninsulares*, monopolized the highest political and clerical positions in the colony. Below them were 1,092,367 *criollos*, or people of Spanish blood born in Mexico. Although physically indistinguishable from *peninsulares*, the *criollos* were relegated to lower political offices and the ranks of the lower to middle clergy. As a result, most *criollos* devoted themselves to economic pursuits. Next were the *mestizos*, or persons of mixed Spanish and American Indian or Spanish and African blood, who numbered 1,328,706. They were, for the most part, socioeconomically inferior to both *criollos* and *peninsulares*. Although Mexican Indi-

ans constituted the largest population group in the colony, with 3,676,281 people, they occupied the lower rungs of society and were subject to restrictions not applied to other groups.

As the largest and most economically significant of Spain's overseas possessions, Mexico entered the nineteenth century influenced by liberal and political currents in Europe. The Enlightenment, the American and French Revolutions, and the Napoleonic invasion of Spain had persuaded disaffected *criollos* to question Mexico's colonial status and, in some cases, to advocate Mexico's independence from Spain. Father Miguel Hidalgo y Costilla emerged as a principal leader of a nascent group espousing independence.

Born in 1753, Hidalgo began his religious studies at an early age, first under the Jesuits, until the order's expulsion from Mexico in 1767, then at the diocesan College of San Nicolás Obispo in Valladolid. Following a course of study in rhetoric, Latin, Thomistic theology, music, and Indian languages, Hidalgo took his bachelor's degree in 1774. He then began preparations for the priesthood and celebrated his ordination in 1778. Rising in his profession, Hidalgo became a rector at San Nicolás in 1790, only to resign his position two years later because of possible financial mismanagement of college funds, religious unorthodoxy, and charges of gambling and fornication. Like many other Mexican curates of the time, Hidalgo had several relationships with women and fathered three illegitimate children during his career. Although none of the charges against him was proven, Hidalgo subsequently held only rural curacies, culminating in his transfer to the small parish of Dolores in 1803. At

Dolores, he introduced industrial innovations in the production of pottery, olive oil, and other items, and made his residence a center for musical, literary, and intellectual gatherings.

While at Dolores, Hidalgo became acquainted with Ignacio de Allende, a captain of the queen's cavalry regiment, who brought him into the so-called Querétaro Conspiracy, a plot to overthrow Spanish rule and allow the *criollos* to take control of the country. Other conspirators included Juan de Aldama, Miguel Domínguez and his wife, Josefa Ortiz de Domínguez, and Mariano Galván. To offset Spanish superiority in arms, ammunition, and organization, the conspirators decided to appeal to the Indian and mestizo masses to join their revolt, which they set for December 8, 1810. Before that date, however, Galván betrayed the conspiracy and viceregal authorities began to make arrests. Forewarned of his impending arrest on September 16, Hidalgo decided to begin the revolt at once, ringing the bells of the Dolores church and summoning his parishioners.

Although the exact words Hidalgo used in his *grito* (literally "shout") are not known, it is generally believed that he launched the revolt in the name of King Ferdinand VII, who had been deposed by the French, and exhorted his Indian and mestizo followers to reclaim their lands, defend their rights and religion, and put an end to bad government. Already suffering from the effects of a bad corn harvest in 1809 and the economic dislocations that triggered in other areas of the economy, the people were predisposed to heed Hidalgo's words. Aroused, a force of between five hundred and eight hundred, led by Hidalgo and Allende, marched on San Miguel, a larger town in the vicinity and Allende's birthplace. Passing through the village of Atotonilco along the way, Hidalgo entered the church and took up a banner of Our Lady of Guadalupe, making the Indian Virgin the emblem of a revolt that would rely heavily on Indian and mestizo support.

An appeal to the disaffected masses added a social and ethnic dimension to the revolt that only became clear during the capture of San Miguel, when Hidalgo's forces degenerated into a destructive mob intent on sacking the city and persecuting its Spanish minority. Although Allende managed to reestablish order, the problem reasserted itself at the capture of Celaya, on September 21. The turmoil was seen even more dramatically at the important mining center of Guanajuato, where miners and the city's lower classes joined the rebels in storming the city's granary, where most of the local Spaniards had taken refuge. Breaching the walls, the rebels massacred the defenders before looting the city over two days.

By mid-October, Hidalgo's forces numbered between sixty and eighty thousand people, and their attack on Mexico City, the capital, began. Royalist forces met Hidalgo's army at Monte de las Cruces on October 30, 1810. Although vastly outnumbered, the highly disciplined and well-armed royalist forces inflicted severe casualties on Hidalgo's army before retreating back toward the city. Overruling Allende and other rebel leaders, Hidalgo forbade a final assault, possibly to recoup his losses and to avoid a repetition of the chaos at Guanajuato on a much larger scale if the capital fell to the insurgents.

Retreating toward the northwest, the rebels reconstituted their forces at Guadalajara. Royalist forces under General Félix María Calleja del Rey met Hidalgo's new army on January 17, 1811. Although once more outnumbered, royalist forces under Calleja again demonstrated the organization and skill lacking in Hidalgo's army. Nevertheless, the issue was in doubt until a chance cannonball struck a rebel ammunition wagon. The resulting explosion and spreading fire created havoc and led to a general rout of Hidalgo's forces.

Fleeing northward, Hidalgo and other rebel leaders were eventually captured by royalist forces at Monclava, Coahuila. Because he was a priest, Hidalgo avoided immediate execution and instead stood trial before the Inquisition. He was found guilty of treason and heresy, and the court remanded him to the secular authorities. On July 30, 1811, Hidalgo met his death before a firing squad.

SIGNIFICANCE

Hidalgo's death marked the end of the first phase of the Mexican War of Independence. Guerrilla forces fought on through much of the decade, but with little *criollo* support. Most of the *criollos* were disillusioned by the anarchy and racial conflict they perceived in Hidalgo's revolt and the inability or unwillingness of the Indian and mestizo insurgents to distinguish between Spaniard and *criollo*. The majority of the *criollos* were social conservatives and preferred an independence that would guarantee them political power. Only when they perceived that Spain suddenly was following a liberal course counter to their own did these *criollos* throw their support to independence in 1820-1821, supporting a political, if not a social, revolution.

Hidalgo's revolt is commemorated annually as part of Mexico's independence day celebrations, which are held on September 15 and 16. A traditional part of the celebration has Mexico's president reenact the Grito de Dolores.

—*Joseph C. Jastrzembski*

1810's

FURTHER READING

Hamill, Hugh M., Jr. "Caudillismo and Independence: A Symbiosis." In *The Independence of Mexico and the Creation of the New Nation*, edited by Jaime E. Rodriguez O. Los Angeles: University of California at Los Angeles, Latin American Center Publications, 1989. Contrasts the leadership styles and abilities of Hidalgo and Calleja.

_____. *The Hidalgo Revolt: Prelude to Mexican Independence*. Gainesville: University Press of Florida, 1966. The standard English-language account of the Hidalgo Revolt.

Leone, Bruno. *The Mexican War of Independence*. San Diego, Calif.: Lucent Books, 1996. Brief young-adult history of the Mexican struggle for independence, with many sidebars, notes, and guides to further readings.

Lynch, John. *The Spanish American Revolutions, 1808-1826*. New York: W. W. Norton, 1973. Excellent overview of all the independence movements occurring in the Spanish American colonies. Highlights the social implications of the early Mexican movement.

Meyer, Michael C., and William H. Beezley, eds. *The Oxford History of Mexico*. New York: Oxford University Press, 2000. Comprehensive history of Mexico written by twenty-one specialists in the field who take into account the latest developments in research.

Meyer, Michael C., and William L. Sherman. "The Wars for Independence." In *The Course of Mexican History*. 5th ed. New York: Oxford University Press, 1995.

Highly readable account of the independence period. Contains suggestions for further reading. Illustrated.

Van Young, Eric. "Quetzalcóatl, King Ferdinand, and Ignacio Allende Go to the Seashore: Or, Messianism and Mystical Kingship in Mexico, 1800-1821." In *The Independence of Mexico and the Creation of the New Nation*, edited by Jaime E. Rodriguez O. Los Angeles: University of California at Los Angeles, Latin American Center Publications, 1989. Discusses how Indian messianism functioned as an element of popular ideology in the Mexican Revolution.

Villoro, Luis. "The Ideological Currents of the Epoch of Independence." In *Major Trends in Mexican Philosophy*. Notre Dame: University of Notre Dame Press, 1966. Surveys the intellectual underpinnings of the various Mexican independence phases.

SEE ALSO: Mar., 1805-Sept. 1, 1807: Burr's Conspiracy; Sept. 16, 1810-Sept. 28, 1821: Mexican War of Independence; Mar., 1813-Dec. 9, 1824: Bolívar's Military Campaigns; Jan. 18, 1817-July 28, 1821: San Martín's Military Campaigns; Sept. 7, 1822: Brazil Becomes Independent; May 13, 1846-Feb. 2, 1848: Mexican War; 1871-1876: Díaz Drives Mexico into Civil War.

RELATED ARTICLES in *Great Lives from History: The Nineteenth Century, 1801-1900:* Simón Bolívar; Fanny Calderón de la Barca; José de San Martín; Antonio López de Santa Anna.

September 16, 1810-September 28, 1821
MEXICAN WAR OF INDEPENDENCE

Mexico's war of independence ultimately achieved an end to Spanish rule in New Spain; in the process, it also brought about the ascendancy of the military in Mexican politics for the next century.

LOCALE: Mexico
CATEGORIES: Wars, uprisings, and civil unrest; colonization; expansion and land acquisition

KEY FIGURES

Miguel Hidalgo y Costilla (1753-1811), Mexican cleric and nationalist leader
Agustín de Iturbide (1783-1824), Mexican soldier and later emperor of Mexico as Agustín I, r. 1822-1823
Ferdinand VII (1784-1833), king of Spain, r. 1808, 1814-1833

José María Morelos (1765-1815), Mexican cleric and nationalist leader
Félix María Calleja del Rey (1759-1828), Spanish military commander
Vicente Guerrero (1783-1831), Mexican guerrilla soldier and later vice president, 1824-1828, and president, 1829
Guadalupe Victoria (Manuel Félix Fernández; 1786-1843), Mexican insurgent and later president, 1824-1829

SUMMARY OF EVENT

The beginning of Mexico's War of Independence is generally dated to El Grito de Dolores, the proclamation of Father Miguel Hidalgo y Costilla in the town of Dolores on September 16, 1810. Certain *criollos* (Spaniards born in the New World) of the intellectual class had been agitating for some time against the Crown in favor of an independent Mexico. When the royal authorities uncovered a plot by Father Hidalgo and his cohorts in Querétaro, Father Hidalgo defied the government openly and headed an insurrection composed of *criollo* liberals, mestizos (Mexican residents of mixed European and African or American Indian descent), and various American Indian groups. His army, which resembled a mob more than a proper military force, won stunning victories initially. Father Hidalgo committed a strategic error, however, by not capitalizing on his momentum to seize the capital, Mexico City. As a result, he was eventually captured, tried by the Inquisition, and executed in 1811.

Following Father Hidalgo's death, leadership of the independence movement fell to another parish priest, the mestizo José María Morelos. The *criollos* distrusted the insurgency, especially after Father Morelos began to espouse land redistribution and racial equality. Although much more gifted with military acumen than Father Hidalgo, Morelos resorted to guerrilla warfare because of the small size of his army. His tactics worked. By the spring of 1813, his forces encircled Mexico City. Morelos occupied himself with the political issues of the structure of government after independence. Six months later, royalist forces under General Félix María Calleja del Rey shattered the encircled rebel troops. In the fall of 1815, Morelos was captured. Like Father Hidalgo before him, Morelos was tried, defrocked, and executed.

Only two vestiges of the independence movement remained: the rebel guerrilla forces under chieftain general Guadalupe Victoria (who had changed his name from Manuel Félix Fernández), striking from the mountains of Puebla and Veracruz, and a thousand troops in Oaxaca, led by Vicente Guerrero. By 1819, the viceroy of New Spain reported to King Ferdinand VII that the insurrection was effectively finished and offered a pardon to the last renegades. Assistance for independence then came from an unexpected source—the mother country.

When the Spanish monarchy was exiled and imprisoned during the period of Napoleonic control of Spain, the Central Junta in Cádiz instituted a governing body of elected representatives called the Cortes. The Cortes presided in 1812 over the writing of Spain's first liberal constitution, which included some modest anticlerical clauses. Upon his restoration in 1814, Ferdinand VII immediately revoked the constitution, suspended the Cortes, imprisoned or exiled liberal opponents, and prepared an army to crush revolutionary movements in

Mexican Territories Before the Texas Revolution

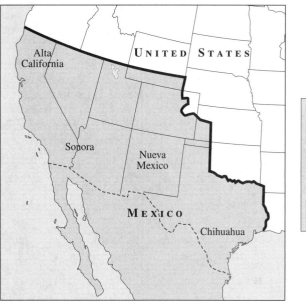

1810's

Spanish America. By 1820, Spanish opposition to Ferdinand's reactionism resulted in Colonel Rafael Riego leading thousands of army troops to force the monarch to accept the Constitution of 1812 and reestablish the Cortes.

The Cortes built upon the foundation of the 1812 constitution to end clerical privileges, reduce the tithe, order the sale of church property, abolish the Inquisition, suppress the monastic order, and expel the Jesuits. The conservative *criollos* in New Spain violently opposed this liberalization. The clergy of New Spain viewed the Constitution and the Cortes as blasphemous, and the wealthy *criollos* relied upon the church for their mortgages. The entire social and economic system of New Spain was threatened: Independence would solve their problem. What was needed was a royalist who could be persuaded to betray the Crown.

Born to wealthy *criollo* parents, Agustín de Iturbide entered the royalist army at a young age and gained the reputation as a formidable, if ruthless, commanding officer against the armies of independence. After the defeat of Morelos, Iturbide's military as well as his financial fortune waned. By 1820, after leading a dissolute life in Mexico City, he was penniless and eager for an opportunity to salvage his future. When the viceroy (perhaps upon the advice of the conspiring clerics) chose him to lead twenty-five hundred royalist forces against Vicente

Modern rendering of Mexican insurgents in 1814. (The Institute of Texan Cultures, San Antonio, Texas)

The new viceroy, Juan O'Donojú, assessed the situation quickly: New Spain was lost. The Treaty of Córdoba, signed by both Iturbide and O'Donojú on August 24, 1821, provided for the peaceful removal of royalist forces and acceptance of most of the terms of the Plan de Iguala. Iturbide had made one important addition to the plan: If no European prince accepted the throne of Mexico, a Mexican could be designated as emperor. On September 27, 1821, Iturbide, at the head of the Army of the Three Guarantees, made his triumphal entry into Mexico City on his thirty-eighth birthday. The next day, September 28, Iturbide, as spokesperson for the governing junta, declared Mexico an independent nation.

SIGNIFICANCE

The independence of Mexico, once the prize possession of the Spanish crown, foreshadowed Spain's decline as a global empire. The Mexican War of Independence created Mexico's gallery of historical heroes and villains, but it also ushered in a tradition of military intervention to achieve political goals—a legacy due to which Mexico has spent much of its national period suffering. For the common people, rural and illiterate, life changed very little as a result of independence. The constant bloodshed that followed throughout the next decade and a half reinforced the powerlessness of Mexican peasants to change their fates.

—*Jodella K. Dyreson*

Guerrero, Iturbide promptly opened negotiations with the rebel forces to effect independence. Guerrero, although suspicious, agreed to Iturbide's Plan de Iguala, issued on February 12, 1821.

The Plan de Iguala proposed to unite all classes and races under the "three guarantees" which, in reality, served to benefit the *criollos*. First, Mexico would be an independent constitutional monarchy. The crown would be offered to Ferdinand VII or another European royal. Second, Roman Catholicism would remain the sole religion, with its clerical privileges left intact. Third, all citizens were to be equal regardless of class or race. The *criollos* especially meant this to apply to their status compared to that of the *peninsulares* (residents of New Spain born in Spain), whose privileges the *criollos* resented. The plan interfered with no property rights. The viceroy, whose replacement from Spain was already en route, resigned after only a few skirmishes.

FURTHER READING

Anna, Timothy E. *The Mexican Empire of Iturbide*. Lincoln: University of Nebraska Press, 1990. A political history of Mexico at the time of independence, with special emphasis on the statecraft of Agustín de Iturbide. Attempts to alter the traditional villainous view of the emperor by a more sympathetic and complex one.

Archer, Chirston I., ed. *The Birth of Modern Mexico, 1780-1824*. Wilmington, Del.: Scholarly Resources, 2003. Collection of articles by various scholars concentrating on conditions and strategies for Mexican independence, placing the ideas and actions of Hidalgo and others in historical context.

Bazant, Jan. *A Concise History of Mexico from Hidalgo to Cárdenas, 1805-1940*. New York: Cambridge University Press, 1977. A highly quoted narrative history of the formative years of Mexico. Not highly analytical, especially concerning the war for independence, but includes fascinating anecdotes.

Flores Caballero, Romeo. *Counterrevolution: The Role of the Spaniards in the Independence of Mexico, 1804-1838.* Translated by Jaime E. Rodriguez. Reprint. Lincoln: University of Nebraska Press, 1974. Presents the role of the Spaniards in Mexico as the principal leaders of the colonial economy and the events that resulted in their replacement by the *criollos.* Refutes the common assumption that the expulsion of the Spaniards after Independence caused the bankruptcy of the Mexican economy.

Meyer, Michael C., William L. Sherman, and Susan M. Deeds. *The Course of Mexican History.* 7th ed. New York: Oxford University Press, 2003. A comprehensive, well-balanced history of Mexico. Discusses the impact of events on society, including repercussions of independence for the common folk.

Miller, Robert Ryal. *Mexico: A History.* Norman: University of Oklahoma Press, 1985. Highly readable, concise introduction to Mexican history from pre-Columbian times to the 1980's. Emphasizes the nineteenth century and revolutionary periods.

Robertson, William Spence. *Iturbide of Mexico.* Durham, N.C.: Duke University Press, 1952. A standard biography of Iturbide, based on extensive primary sources in Mexico. Reinforces the traditional portrait of Iturbide as a less-than-admirable figure in Mexican independence. Directly refuted by Anna's study on Iturbide.

Ruiz, Ramón Eduardo. *Triumphs and Tragedy: A History of the Mexican People.* New York: W. W. Norton, 1992. A passionate narrative on Mexican history. Often supplies different perspectives from those of the standard surveys.

SEE ALSO: May 2, 1808: Dos de Mayo Insurrection in Spain; May 2, 1808-Nov., 1813: Peninsular War in Spain; Sept. 16, 1810: Hidalgo Issues El Grito de Dolores; Mar., 1813-Dec. 9, 1824: Bolívar's Military Campaigns; Jan. 18, 1817-July 28, 1821: San Martín's Military Campaigns; Sept. 7, 1822: Brazil Becomes Independent; Oct. 2, 1835-Apr. 21, 1836: Texas Revolution; May 13, 1846-Feb. 2, 1848: Mexican War; Oct. 31, 1861-June 19, 1867: France Occupies Mexico; 1871-1876: Díaz Drives Mexico into Civil War. **RELATED ARTICLES** in *Great Lives from History: The Nineteenth Century, 1801-1900:* Fanny Calderón de la Barca; Miguel Hidalgo y Costilla; Benito Juárez; Maximilian; Antonio López de Santa Anna.

1811-1818
EGYPT FIGHTS THE WAHHĀBĪS

Egypt's war with the Wahhābīs exemplified the complex political relationships affecting the Arab world and its transition into the modern era. Although the Egyptians eventually subdued the Wahhābīs in battle, these Arab nomads spread a theocratic political philosophy that swept through the Middle East. The Wahhābī vision of Islamic governance helped foster modern political Islam, simultaneously influencing the later creation of Saudi Arabia.

LOCALE: Egypt; Ottoman Empire
CATEGORIES: Wars, uprisings, and civil unrest; religion and theology; government and politics; expansion and land acquisition

KEY FIGURES
Muḥammad ʿAlī Pasha (1769-1849), Albanian-born Ottoman viceroy of Egypt, 1805-1848
Ibrāhīm Paṣa (1789-1848), son of Muḥammad ʿAlī and Egyptian military commander

Mahmud II (1785-1839), Ottoman sultan, r. 1808-1839
Muḥammad ibn ʿAbd al-Wahhāb (1703-1792), Islamic scholar and founder of Wahhābīism
Muḥammad ibn Saʿūd (d. 1765), head of the Saʿudi family that allied with the Wahhābīs

SUMMARY OF EVENT
Six years after consolidating his political power, the Ottoman viceroy of Egypt, Muḥammad ʿAlī Pasha, began a series of military campaigns designed to expand his influence in the Middle East. After having relied on the Ottoman Turks to quash domestic resistance to attain his power, Muḥammad ʿAlī secretly hoped to make Egypt independent from the declining empire. In 1811, he seized upon such an opportunity by invading the Hijaz and Najd regions of modern Saudi Arabia. The political tensions between Egyptians and Ottoman Turks; the causes, course, and consequences of the war; and the Wahhābīs' political orientation and alliances make the

Egyptian war with the Wahhābīs a small but pivotal event in the course of modern history.

Muḥammad ʿAlī proved himself an ambitious and conniving politician. His experience as an Albanian officer in the Ottoman army provided him with a decidedly Western perspective that embraced modernity. After he was appointed the Ottoman viceroy, or pasha, of Egypt in 1805, he oversaw military and civil reforms that he hoped would translate into greater Egyptian autonomy. Before enhancing his image abroad, however, he faced stiff opposition from domestic political rivals.

Prior to Napoleon's intervention in Egypt in 1798, numerous wealthy landowning families, known as the Mamlūks, or Mamelukes, governed Egypt on behalf of the Ottoman Turks. Egypt's political power remained decentralized under this feudal-like bureaucracy. Initially, Muḥammad ʿAlī tried cajoling these barons. However, many resented his dictatorial power and his modern reforms. In 1811, to ensure their compliance, he lured opposing Mamlūks to a meeting at which he had them massacred. After consolidating his power at home, he pursued expansion abroad.

The Ottoman Turks feared regional competition from Egypt. Too weak to engage Muḥammad ʿAlī directly, Sultan Mahmud II requested that he quell the rebelling Wahhābīs in Arabia's Hijaz and Najd regions. Mahmud hoped that Egypt's expenditure of men and resources in Arabia would check Muḥammad ʿAlī's regional ambition while providing security in an area vital to Turkish trade. The ensuing conflict then devolved into a war of attrition.

After the Battle of al-Khaif, Muḥammad ʿAlī's Albanian infantry deserted his army, making him rely more heavily upon his Egyptian contingents. Muḥammad ʿAlī's son Ibrāhīm Paşa commanded the expedition and, after eight arduous years, succeeded in conquering the Wahhābīs, breaking their rule over Medina and Mecca. Muḥammad ʿAlī then appointed Ibrāhīm governor in Arabia—an act that implied Egyptian, rather than Ottoman, control. In response, the Turks incited a revolt in Cairo that Muḥammad ʿAlī suffocated by uniting Egyptian public opinion behind his new invasion of the Sudan, to the south. Meanwhile, Muḥammad ʿAlī's actions in

Muḥammad ʿAlī Pasha. (Library of Congress)

Arabia agitated Turks to the north in addition to provoking the enmity of the Wahhābīs to the east.

More than a simple band of Bedouins creating havoc, the Wahhābīs represented a powerful Islamic philosophy. Within Islam, discrepancies between social lifestyle and religious authority remain highly contested. The Wahhābīs interpreted Islamic law, or Sharia, in strict, puritanical terms devoid of any dissent. The Sunni theological scholar Muḥammad ibn ʿAbd al-Wahhāb spread these views in his Ḥanbalite schools. Witnessing the growing corruption of traditional social standards resulting from an external invasion of modernity and an internal manifestation of paganism, the Wahhābīs championed traditional norms. They repudiated pagan rituals and iconoclastic worship, defied Muslims who advocated rationalism, and mutinied against Sufi doctrines on mysticism. ʿAbd al-Wahhāb interpreted these Islamic derivatives as heretical and stressed the individual's responsibility to follow divine will as determined by the Qurʾān. During the late eighteenth century, the Saʿūdi family, under Muḥammad ibn Saʿūd and his sons, incorporated these teachings into their Hijaz and Najd provinces.

By the nineteenth century the Wahhābī-Saʿūdi alliance had expanded aggressively between the Red Sea and the Persian Gulf. The Wahhābīs began harassing Ottoman provinces by sacking Karbala in what is now Iraq and conquering Mecca, Islam's most revered city. Additionally, the Saʿūdi emir labeled the Ottoman sultan a heretic and usurper. Against Wahhābī fervor backed by Saʿūdi force, outlying Ottoman provinces capitulated, bringing puritanical Islam into direct conflict with Arabs espousing modernity. During the war with the Egyptians, the Wahhābī yielded ground only after exerting determined tenacity. Despite its political and military defeat, Wahhābīism remained as a vibrant philosophical alternative to modern reform.

Historians debate the extent to which modernity influenced Wahhābīism. The movement evolved from an Islamic reformation challenging new interpretations of faith and theocratic government. From this perspective, the Muslim world faced growing social and political stratification. Stress among competing economic interests polarized Egyptian society and politics. On one hand, Arabia's Hijaz region opened trade with eastern lands stretching to India. On the other hand, Upper Egypt prospered from thriving trade with both Great Britain and France.

Rather than enhance Egypt's regional standing, these competing commercial interests pitted a burgeoning class of wealthy merchants against an established class of wealthy landowners. Although modernity had little impact on Wahhābī teachings during the eighteenth century, the fundamentalist sect countered the region's hasty adoption of Western reforms by the nineteenth century. Soon after the end of the war in 1818, Wahhābī schools spread to Cairo. Over the course of the nineteenth and into the twentieth century, Egypt wrestled with Wahhābī- and Western-oriented factions and the volatile environment they created.

Significance

The events surrounding the Egyptian war with the Wahhābīs exhibited a lasting set of intersecting factors that persist in the modern world. First, Muḥammad ʿAlī's ambition launched Egypt on a rendezvous with Western modernity. The war initiated expansionist expeditions that challenged both Ottoman hegemony and provincial rulers who enforced traditional social practices. The war also contributed to the Ottoman Empire's impotent image. By 1811, the sultan's viceroys, such as Muḥammad

ʿAlī, were acting with increasing autonomy. The empire limped into the twentieth century, during which World War I delivered the coup de grâce in 1918.

Wahhābīism's emergence as a militant, puritanical sect reflected a tumultuous era within the history of Islam. Throughout the nineteenth century, the Ottomans retreated from their position as sole representative of an autonomous Muslim world. Islam experienced a bloody reformation in which the powerful Saʿūdi family spread radical fundamentalist teachings. By the 1930's, the Saʿūdi family had consolidated political power once again and succeeded in forming modern Saudi Arabia, in which Wahhābīism remains the official state religion. Finally, Wahhābīism challenged modernity as Western reforms infiltrated the Middle East. After the war, Wahhābīism took root in Egypt and other areas where modern reforms disenfranchised the established social order. Ultimately, succeeding rulers and generations struggled to resolve these volatile issues, which were evident during the early twenty-first century's conflict with Osama Bin Laden's Wahhābī sect.

—*Matthew Walker*

Further Reading

Cleveland, William L. *A History of the Modern Middle East*. Boulder, Colo.: Westview Press, 1994. Excellent overview of Muḥammad ʿAlī's rise to power and imperialist exploits.

Harris, Christina P. *Nationalism and Revolution in Egypt: The Role of the Muslim Brotherhood*. London: Mouton, 1964. Discussion of Wahhābīism that serves as an insightful reference with a thorough understanding of the movement within an Islamic context.

Hassan, Hassan. *In the House of Muhammad Ali: A Family Album, 1805-1952*. Cairo, Egypt: American University in Cairo Press, 2000. Lavishly illustrated memoir of life within Egypt's ruling family by a member of the family. Although the author's firsthand observations are limited to the twentieth century, he also provides an intimate look at Muḥammad ʿAlī's family during the nineteenth century.

Lawson, Fred H. *The Social Origins of Egyptian Expansionism During the Muḥammad ʿAlī Period*. New York: Columbia University Press, 1992. Detailed account of Egyptian foreign policymaking as well as a rich record of Egypt's domestic situation during the war with the Wahhābīs.

Marsot, Afaf Lutfi al-Sayyid. *A Short History of Modern Egypt*. New York: Cambridge University Press, 1985. Like Cleveland's book, Marsot's narrative provides a concise overview with specific attention paid to Egyptian bureaucracy.

Pollard, Lisa. *Nurturing the Nation: The Family Politics of Modernizing, Colonizing, and Liberating Egypt.* Berkeley: University of California Press, 2005. Study of family and gender issues in Egyptian politics leading up to the revolution of 1919.

Yapp, M. E. *A History of the Near East: The Making of the Modern Near East, 1792-1923.* New York: Longman, 1987. Yapp provides a thorough explanation of

the Wahhābīs complete with highly detailed regional maps.

SEE ALSO: 19th cent.: Arabic Literary Renaissance; Mar. 1, 1811: Muḥammad ʿAlī Has the Mamlūks Massacred; 1814-1879: Exploration of Arabia; 1832-1841: Turko-Egyptian Wars.

RELATED ARTICLES in *Great Lives from History: The Nineteenth Century, 1801-1900:* Muḥammad ʿAlī Pasha; Napoleon I.

1811-1840
CONSTRUCTION OF THE NATIONAL ROAD

The first federally financed interstate transportation project, the National Road helped to link the states, but it was so politically controversial that the federal government did not again participate in highway development until the twentieth century.

ALSO KNOWN AS: National Pike; Cumberland Road

LOCALE: Betweeen Cumberland, Maryland, and Wheeling, Virginia

CATEGORIES: Expansion and land acquisition; transportation; engineering

KEY FIGURES
Albert Gallatin (1761-1849), secretary of the Treasury under Thomas Jefferson

Thomas Jefferson (1743-1826), president of the United States, 1801-1809

Ebenezer Zane (1747-1812), pioneer road builder who laid out Zane's Trace, later part of the National Road

SUMMARY OF EVENT
As the United States expanded westward into the Ohio Valley, transportation became increasingly difficult. Much of the commerce of the eastern seaboard relied upon rivers for transportation, but no existing water routes cut through the Appalachian Mountains to the Northwest Territory. Roads were needed both for economic reasons and for military security. Recognizing the need for internal improvements, Congress passed a bill authorizing the construction of a road from Cumberland, Maryland, to Ohio in 1806.

Construction began in 1811, and the road reached Wheeling, Virginia, on the Ohio River in 1818. It was

130 miles long and cost, on the average, thirteen thousand dollars per mile. As the first federally mandated highway, it became known as the National Road. Construction continued intermittently until 1840, when the road reached Vandalia, Illinois. By then, railroads and canals had eclipsed turnpikes in transporting freight, and construction on the National Road ended. The federal government did not become involved in road construction again until the twentieth century.

Construction of the National Road coincided with a report that Albert Gallatin, secretary of the Treasury under President Thomas Jefferson, submitted to Congress on the transportation needs of the nation. Gallatin recommended that the central government expend some twenty million dollars to develop a comprehensive and national transportation network. He was well aware that private or state capital, without the active financial aid of the federal government, could not accomplish such a vast undertaking. Gallatin recommended the construction of both roads and canal systems to link the expanding frontier with the more developed eastern states. Approval of the National Road project seemed to indicate that Gallatin's proposed system had taken the first momentous step.

Construction of the road from Cumberland, Maryland, a city located on the upper reaches of the Potomac River, to Wheeling, Virginia, a site on the Ohio River, would link the two river systems and make transportation of freight and people from the mid-Atlantic states to the interior of the growing country easier. Cutting through the ridges of the Appalachian Mountains would prove a daunting task. After five years of extensive surveys to determine the best route, road crews commenced preparing a sixty-six-foot-wide right-of-way. The thickly forested hills were cleared, and workers excavated a road-bed twelve to eighteen inches deep. The roadbed was filled with broken stones and rolled to form a level surface. Stone and masonry bridges were constructed to cross the numerous streams and small rivers common in the mountains.

In 1818, when the road reached Wheeling, it became a major trade route to the West. Large numbers of travelers left testimony to the economic importance of the road. Goods from Baltimore could now reach the Ohio River via wagon, at a considerable savings in freight. The road gave Baltimore a decided but brief commercial advantage over its major competitor to the north, Philadelphia. Philadelphia was to feel increasingly pressed by its competitors, for in 1817, the state of New York authorized the construction of the Erie Canal. Thus, both Baltimore and New York City would be directly linked to the West. To maintain its commercial position, Philadelphia, with the aid of Pennsylvania, launched its own system of internal transportation improvements in the direction of Pittsburgh.

Meanwhile, enormous quantities of goods and large numbers of people passed over the National Road. Cattle from the Ohio Valley, Monongahela flour, and spiritous liquors passed over the road to market. Taverns and grazing stations sprang up along the road to serve the wagoners, drovers, and immigrants who moved along the route. Wheeling boomed, as did many towns located along the National Road. Supporters of the road wanted to extend it across Ohio, but the Panic of 1819 brought construction to a halt for seven years while Congress debated funding. Critics of federal involvement in internal improvements believed that the road had already served its purpose, and that any additional improvements should be left to the states or private enterprise.

In 1825, Congress finally voted to allocate additional funds, and construction of the road proceeded across Ohio into Illinois. The new road first followed and improved upon a crude public road developed by an Ohio pioneer, Ebenezer Zane, and then cleared a new path as it stretched toward the Mississippi River. It appeared to be a successful first step in federal efforts to link sections of the nation together.

Two specific actions, one occurring during the presidency of James Madison and the other during that of James Monroe, contributed to the federal government's assuming a passive and nondirective role in meeting the nation's transportation requirements. Both involved presidential vetoes.

The logistic problems of the War of 1812 and the

Albert Gallatin. (Library of Congress)

rapid movement of population into the West aroused considerable support for federal activity in internal improvements. To meet the demand both of citizens and of national security, John C. Calhoun, a representative from South Carolina, introduced the Bonus Bill into Congress in 1817. This bill was designed to provide a permanent fund for the construction of internal improvements, and it passed both houses of Congress.

Although President James Madison had publicly called for such a system, he vetoed the bill on strict constructionist grounds. He argued that the Constitution was made up of enumerated powers, that federal activity in internal improvements was not one of those powers, and that to justify such activity under the "general welfare" clause was to make the government the judge of its own powers. Madison maintained that a constitutional amendment was required before the government could operate in the area of internal improvements. Five years later, President James Monroe vetoed a bill authorizing repair of the National Road to be financed by the collection of tolls. The general tenor of his veto message was similar to that of Madison. These vetoes, coupled with the rising sectional antagonisms that eventually culminated in the Civil War (1861-1865), put an end to the

147

hopes that the federal government would provide leadership and support in transportation.

SIGNIFICANCE

The National Road was the last federal highway project for almost a century, as many Americans believed that the federal government lacked the constitutional authority to finance and build internal improvements. The constitutional barrier proved to be an obstacle that could not be overcome. Supporters of the National Road eventually were able to extend it a total of six hundred miles to a terminus at Vandalia, Illinois, but no other roads were funded. The states were thrown back on their own resources, as the federal government relinquished its responsibilities in this critical area.

In 1824, Congress passed the General Survey Act, which enabled the president to plot out a comprehensive system of roads and canals, but the battle was already lost. Nothing came of this legislation. The federal government thereafter confined itself to the granting of alternate sections of public lands along the route of intended canals and railroads. New York, as early as 1817, had anticipated this outcome and proceeded to construct the Erie Canal with state funds. State funds and private capital, both domestic and foreign, provided the financial support required to construct the canals and railroads that eventually bound the nation together. The National Road faded into obscurity, until the rise of bicycles and automobiles revived its usage. In 1926, the National Road became part of the U.S. Highway 40 and served as a major east-west artery until construction of Interstate 70.

—*John G. Clark, updated by Nancy Farm Mannikko*

FURTHER READING

Aitken, Thomas. *Albert Gallatin: Early America's Swiss-Born Statesman.* New York: Vantage Press, 1985. Biography of the secretary of the Treasury whose report on the transportation needs of the nation proved pivotal in planning the National Road.

Ierley, Merritt. *Traveling the National Road: Across the Centuries on America's First Highway.* Reprint. Woodstock, N.Y.: Overlook Press, 1993. Interesting general history of the National Road.

Raitz, Karl B. *A Guide to the National Road.* Baltimore: Johns Hopkins University Press, 1996. Modern travel guide to each segment of the National Road. Lavishly illustrated with maps and photographs.

Schneider, Norris F. *The National Road: Main Street of America.* Columbus: Ohio Historical Society, 1975. History of the National Road, emphasizing the role the highway played in Ohio's development.

Searight, Thomas B. *The Old Pike: A History of the National Road.* Berryville, Va.: Prince Maccus, 1983. Colorful history of the National Road with an emphasis on its early years.

Smith, Barry. *Cumberland Road.* Boston: Houghton Mifflin, 1989. History of U.S. Highway 40, with an emphasis on the portion of the highway that passed through Maryland and Virginia to the Ohio River.

Vivian, Cassandra. *The National Road in Pennsylvania.* Charleston, S.C.: Arcadia, 2003. Illustrated guide to sites along the stretch of the National Road that went through Pennsylvania.

SEE ALSO: c. 1815-1830: Westward American Migration Begins; Oct. 26, 1825: Erie Canal Opens; Jan. 7, 1830: Baltimore and Ohio Railroad Opens; July 21, 1836: Champlain and St. Lawrence Railroad Opens; Nov. 10, 1852: Canada's Grand Trunk Railway Is Incorporated.

RELATED ARTICLES in *Great Lives from History: The Nineteenth Century, 1801-1900:* Albert Gallatin; James Monroe.

March 1, 1811
MUḤAMMAD ʿALĪ HAS THE MAMLŪKS MASSACRED

Despite their defeat by Napoleon Bonaparte's invading French army in 1798, the Mamlūks continued to threaten Muḥammad ʿAlī, Egypt's Ottoman-appointed governor, until he effectively liquidated them, making himself uncontested ruler of Egypt.

LOCALE: Cairo, Egypt

CATEGORIES: Atrocities and war crimes; government and politics

KEY FIGURES

Mahmud II (1785-1839), Ottoman sultan and caliph, r. 1808-1839, who condoned the Mamlūk Massacre

Muḥammad ʿAlī Pasha (1769-1848), Ottoman-appointed governor-general of Egypt, 1805-1848

Ahmad Tusun (Tosun Pasha; c. 1793/1798-1816), second son of Muḥammad ʿAlī

Khusrau Pasha (c. 1756-1855), Muḥammad ʿAlī's predecessor as governor of Egypt, 1802-1803

SUMMARY OF EVENT

Originally a Circassian military slave dynasty, the Mamlūks ruled Egypt between 1250 and 1517, when they were defeated by the Ottoman Turks. In 1798, they were again defeated, by Napoleon Bonaparte's invading French. However, after the turn of the nineteenth century, they managed to regroup once again and threatened the power of the Ottoman viceroy. In 1804, the head of the Ottoman's Albanian-staffed cavalry, Muḥammad ʿAlī, collaborated with the Mamlūks in a power play to secure the governorship of Egypt. Afterward, however, Muḥammad ʿAlī's suspicions of the Mamlūks caused him to induce a number of their leaders to set up residence in Giza, just outside Cairo, so that he could keep a watchful eye on their activities.

The Mamlūks themselves were far from unified. As a group they had tried to play off, just as Muḥammad ʿAlī was to do, the different centers of power—the religious clerics (*ulama*), the merchants, the Ottomans, eventually the French and the British—against

one another and to exploit the country economically to their advantage, as they had long done. All of this occurred under the nominal rule of the Ottoman sultan in Constantinople. However, by the early nineteenth century, internecine rivalry among the Mamlūk military households and European intervention had reduced but not eliminated their power.

Early in 1811, Muḥammad ʿAlī responded to a request from Sultan Mahmud II to send his second son, Ahmad Tusun, with an expeditionary force to Arabia's Hijaz re-

The massacre of the Mamlūks. (Francis R. Niglutsch)

149

gion to suppress the Wahhābīs' fundamentalist Islamic revolt. Although wishing to comply, the Egyptian governor was apprehensive about being left without the several thousand men and equipment that his son would take out of the country. Muḥammad ʿAlī contrived a plot to eliminate what he believed to be the Mamlūk threat against his authority.

On March 1, 1811, Muḥammad ʿAlī invited all the Mamlūk notables to a reception and parade at the Citadel, his fortified residence on hills overlooking Cairo. The ostensible occasion was the investiture of his son Ahmad Tusun as pasha of Jidda on the eve of his departure for Arabia. Estimates of the numbers of Mamlūks who showed up at the reception vary greatly. Some run into the hundreds, but it appears that only twenty-four Mamlūk notables under their leader, Shahin Bey, and sixty underlings appeared. They came in full regalia, along with their decorated mounts. During the ceremonial procession of troops loyal to Muḥammad ʿAlī, the Mamlūks were wedged into the middle of the parade line. At the point where the route led through a narrow alleyway carved into rock and enclosed within high walls, loyal Albanian troops under Salih Koch barred the exit gate and took up their positions at the top of the wall, from which they opened fire upon the Mamlūks. Shahin was slain outright, as were most of the others. Those who survived were beheaded. During the weeks that followed, many more Mamlūks were killed in Cairo and Upper Egypt. Their lands were then confiscated.

Congratulations on his exploit reached Muḥammad ʿAlī from various sources, including Sultan Mahmud II. Fifteen years later, Mahmud emulated his underling's deed by eliminating his own crack Janissary infantry in 1826. There were, however, differences between the Mamlūk and Janissary Massacres. For example, whereas the Janissaries integrated themselves into Ottoman society, the Mamlūks had isolated themselves from all levels of Egyptian society for centuries while remaining as an exploitative military aristocracy. Muḥammad ʿAlī's elimination of the Mamlūk threat helped to restore order and security in Egypt, leaving him the undisputed master of Egypt. By contrast, Constantinople remained unstable even after the Janissary Massacre of 1826.

SIGNIFICANCE

The period between Napoleon's 1798 invasion of Egypt and 1811 witnessed a see-saw in the struggle for power in Egypt, but the Mamlūk Massacre ordered by Muḥammad ʿAlī put a definitive end to that source of instability. Nevertheless, although the Citadel Massacre marked the

termination of any effective claim to Mamlūk power, some survivors were later incorporated into the hierarchy, serving in high military or administrative positions throughout the reign of Muḥammad ʿAlī and beyond.

Two major explanations have been given to explain the brutal 1811 massacre by a man who was not, by nature, bloodthirsty. The first is that the Mamlūks were, indeed, conspiring to unseat the Egyptian governor. Also, Muḥammad ʿAlī wanted to ensure the stability of both his own rule and that of his successors by putting an end to a disruptive and dangerous element. In any case, brutally repressive measures were common in the Ottoman Empire at that time. Muḥammad ʿAlī's predecessor as governor, Khusrau Pasha, had been ordered to get rid of the troublesome Mamlūks—but had failed. It is reasonable to assume that the Mamlūks would have engineered Muḥammad ʿAlī's destruction with as little compunction as he had in planning theirs.

—*Peter B. Heller*

FURTHER READING

Cameron, Donald A. *Egypt in the Nineteenth Century: Or, Mehemet Ali and His Successors Until the British Occupation in 1882*. London: Smith, Elder, 1898. In addition to a separate chapter on the Mamlūks, this work by a British scholar contains the most graphic account of the 1811 Mamlūk Massacre, even though the author's highly inflated figures of the number of victims were modified by later research.

Daly, Martin W., ed. *The Cambridge History of Egypt: Modern Egypt from 1517 to the End of the Twentieth Century*. Vol. 2. New York: Cambridge University Press, 1998. Puts the 1811 massacre into the broader contexts of Egyptian and Ottoman history.

Dodwell, Henry. *The Founder of Modern Egypt: A Study of Muhammad Ali*. New York: Cambridge University Press, 1977. Originally published in 1931, this well-written British classic focuses on Muḥammad ʿAlī's role in history.

Fahmy, Khaled. *All the Pasha's Men: Mehmed Ali, His Army, and the Making of Modern Egypt*. New York: Cambridge University Press, 1997. Contrasts Muḥammad ʿAlī's Mamlūk Massacre in Egypt with Sultan Mahmud II's elimination of the Janissary threat to his power in Constantinople.

Hunter, F. Robert. *Egypt Under the Khedives, 1805-1879: From Household Government to Modern Bureaucracy*. Pittsburgh: University of Pittsburgh Press, 1988. Pinpoints the Mamlūks' role in Egyptian society.

Marsot, Afaf Lutfi al-Sayyid. *Egypt in the Reign of Mu-hammad Ali*. New York: Cambridge University Press, 1984. Dispassionate explanation of Muḥammad ʿAlī's uncharacteristically brutal act in eliminating the Mam-lūk threat to his rule.

Philipp, Thomas, and Ulrich Haarmann, eds. *The Mam-luks in Egyptian Politics and Society*. Cambridge, En-gland: Cambridge University Press, 1998. Examina-tion of how the Mamlūks managed to continue to wield political, military, and economic power in Egypt after their defeat by the Ottomans in 1517.

Sonbol, Amira el-Azhary. *The New Mamluks: Egyptian* *Society and Modern Feudalism*. Syracuse, N.Y.: Syr-acuse University Press, 2000. Study of how the Mamlūks exploited Egypt to their own advantage be-fore their destruction as a center of power in 1811.

SEE ALSO: 19th cent.: Arabic Literary Renaissance; 1808-1826: Ottomans Suppress the Janissary Revolt; 1811-1818: Egypt Fights the Wahhābīs; 1832-1841: Turko-Egyptian Wars; Sept. 13, 1882: Battle of Tel el Kebir.

RELATED ARTICLES in *Great Lives from History: The Nineteenth Century, 1801-1900:* Muḥammad ʿAlī Pa-sha; Napoleon I.

March 11, 1811-1816
LUDDITES DESTROY INDUSTRIAL MACHINES

At the height of Great Britain's involvement in the Napoleonic Wars, an epidemic of machine breaking and industrial sabotage swept textile industries in northern England. Claiming allegiance to the mythical "General Ludd," workmen took up arms against the Industrial Revolution. Never a coordinated movement, Luddism had minimal impact on English society, but it survives in popular imagination as a model of futile opposition to progress.

LOCALE: Northern England
CATEGORY: Wars, uprisings, and civil unrest

KEY FIGURES
George Mellor (c. 1790-1813), Yorkshire wool worker and Luddite leader
Gravener Henson (1785-1852), Nottingham labor activist and author
Sir Thomas Maitland (1760-1824), British general who led the campaign against the Luddites

SUMMARY OF EVENT
On March 11, 1811, a band of armed English workers at-tacked a stocking factory in Arnold, near Nottingham. Claiming to be under the direction of a leader named "General Ludd," they proceeded to destroy knitting ma-chines, or frames, of a new type designed to produce wide fabric for cheap seamed stockings. Through the months that ensued, their action was repeated in forays of escalating scope and violence, first in the hosiery shops around Nottingham, then in the woolen mills of the West Riding of Yorkshire, and finally in the cotton mills around Manchester. Slow to react at first, the British gov-ernment eventually dispatched some thirteen thousand troops to restore order. By December of 1812, the main wave of frame-breaking had subsided, partly because of vigorous suppression and partly because of improved economic conditions. However, isolated incidents of in-dustrial sabotage by Luddites continued to occur until 1816, and Luddism—in the more general sense of vio-lent opposition to technological change—experienced a resurgence among British agricultural workers in 1830.

Several factors contributed to severe economic dis-tress among textile workers in the north of England in 1811. The previous two decades had seen an exponential expansion in the cotton and hosiery industries that was due to the mechanization of spinning. Cheap cotton thread opened up a tremendous domestic and export mar-ket for cotton cloth, stockings, and lace, all of them made on hand-operated machinery in small workshops. Men flocked to the textile trades. As long as markets were ex-panding, modest innovations increasing worker produc-tivity passed without protest. In the woolen industry, power-operated cropping frames and gig mills used in finishing cloth had existed since the mid-eighteenth cen-tury, but skilled workmen and operators of small shops had succeeded in blocking their adoption.

Great Britain had been at war with revolutionary France since 1793. In 1809, in response to Napoleon's Continental System, the British parliament adopted the Orders in Council, effectively cutting off any continental export trade and straining trade relations with the United States. The Americans retaliated with the Non-Inter-course Act (1809). Goods piled up in warehouses. Fac-tories laid off workers and cut the wages of those still working to the point where they could not afford basic necessities. Poor harvests in 1810 and 1811, coupled with barriers to importation, caused food prices to sky-rocket. New machinery was only one of the factors making the life of textile workers unbearable, but it was a convenient available target in a country where working men could not vote and strikes were illegal.

Because many of the Luddite attacks were individually well coordinated, demonstrating a knowledge of military tactics, and because incidents were accompanied by threatening letters and proclamations issued in the name of "General Ludd," the Home Office, successively under the direction of Dudley Ryder and Lord Sidmouth, had good reason to fear a coordinated movement abetted by the French. Despite an extensive network of spies, no French connection was found, and only the Yorkshire croppers had an identifiable local leader. As for General Ludd, said to have been an apprentice named Ned Ludlum who initiated the movement by smashing a wide stocking frame in his father's shop, he was never apprehended and probably never existed.

Luddism has been equated in the popular imagination with opposition by workers to the Industrial Revolution, but this association applies strictly only to the disturbances in Yorkshire. The machines smashed in Nottingham were of Elizabethan design, and, although workmen

were invariably the agents of destruction, competition between mill owners may have been a factor, especially in the destruction of John Heathcote's lace mill in 1816. Because of a wide franchise and a radical town council, Luddites who were apprehended fared better in Nottingham than elsewhere. Nottingham workmen also had an effective leader in Gravener Henson, who was committed to legal avenues of redress and succeeded in getting Parliament to consider a bill prohibiting some of the most obnoxious manufacturing abuses. (Henson is sometimes incorrectly supposed to have been General Ludd.)

In Yorkshire, the Luddites were led by George Mellor, a skilled workman who made his living cropping, that is, using massive shears to finish woolen cloth. He organized his fellow croppers to smash cropping frames and went one step further, advocating the assassination of recalcitrant factory owners. He and two others actually ambushed and killed a manufacturer, William Horsefall, and went on to lead a band of one hundred men in an attack on William Cartwright's fortified mill in Rawlfolds on April 11, 1812. Brought to trial for both crimes at the York Assizes on January 6, 1813, Mellor was convicted and executed along with sixteen other men convicted of crimes related to Luddism. This brutal retribution shocked many at the time and now seems utterly disproportionate to the crimes of those who only damaged property.

In the cotton-manufacturing areas, Luddism was only one ingredient in a mass of unrest ranging from food riots spawned of sheer desperation to middle-class political radicalism. Factories housing power looms became targets, not so much because power looms were seen as a threat to individual workmen as because these were the largest establishments. In Lancaster, a sort of female Robin Hood led a mob that seized provision carts on their way to market and sold the food at bargain prices in Manchester. The decision at the 1812 Lancaster Assizes to execute her for her crime passed into folklore as "hanging a poor starving woman for stealing potatoes."

Although the government dispatched large numbers of troops to the north under the command of the able and brutal Sir Thomas Maitland,

Contemporary engraving of rioting Luddites drawn by Phiz (Hablot Knight Browne; 1815-1882). (Hulton Archive/Getty Images)

the military was of limited use against Luddite raids. Luddites assembled in secret, struck at night, and fled before troops could be deployed. Neither spies nor accused men provided much useful information, mainly because the movement was so decentralized and indefinite in extent.

Economic factors sparked the outbreak of Luddism, and economic factors hastened its decline. A good harvest in 1812 brought food prices down. The war against Napoleon, which had seemed interminable at the beginning of 1811, was well on the way to being won by the middle of 1813. Military orders, reopened export markets, and general optimism revived the textile business. It is noteworthy that rates of property crimes in general peaked in the same period, declined, and then peaked again during the postwar depression of 1816-1817, coinciding then with outbreaks of violent political radicalism.

SIGNIFICANCE

Luddism caught the popular imagination, but its immediate impact was not great. A total of forty-eight people died, including two managers and eleven attackers killed in raids and thirty-five people executed. Half of those executed had committed property crimes such as looting that were probably incidental to actual anti-industrial sabotage. The economic impact of property destruction was dwarfed by larger economic cycles relating to the export market. Unlike the disturbances of 1816-1817 and 1819, Luddism failed to provoke a strong response in Parliament; laws specifically against frame-breaking were passed, but there was no general and systematic erosion of personal liberty. Luddism did lend fuel to the successful campaign to repeal the Orders in Council in 1812, but even this supposed victory for the northern manufacturing interests failed to achieve its aim of preventing war with the United States.

The main impact of Luddism lay in its utter failure to achieve its main aim of derailing the progress of mechanization in industry. The term "Luddite" became in subsequent generations emblematic of misguided attempts by production workers to prevent erosions of their liveli-

---

LORD BYRON OPPOSES THE ANTI-LUDDITE LAW

In a letter to Lord Holland, poet Lord Byron offered his opposition to a law that was soon to pass in Britain that made the destruction of frames (or knitting machines) punishable by death. In the excerpt here, Byron wrote that although the actions of the workers are condemnable, the reason for their violence is nonetheless understandable and should be met with "pity" and not "punishment."

For my own part, I consider the manufacturers as a much injured body of men, sacrificed to the views of certain individuals who have enriched themselves by those practices which have deprived the frame-workers of employment. For instance;—by the adoption of a certain kind of frame, one man performs the work of seven—six are thus thrown out of business. But it is to be observed that that work thus done is far inferior in quality, hardly marketable at home, and hurried over with a view to exportation. Surely, my Lord, however we may rejoice in any improvement in the arts which may be beneficial to mankind, we must not allow mankind to be sacrificed to improvements in mechanism. The maintenance and well-doing of the industrious poor is an object of greater consequence to the community than the enrichment of a few monopolists by any improvement in the implements of trade, which deprives the workman of his bread, and renders the labourer "unworthy of his hire."

My own motive for opposing the bill is founded on its palpable injustice, and its certain inefficacy. I have seen the state of these miserable men, and it is a disgrace to a civilized country. Their excesses may be condemned, but cannot be the subject of wonder. The effect of the present bill would be to drive them into actual rebellion. . . . Condemning, as every one must condemn, the conduct of these wretches, I believe in the existence of grievances which call rather for pity than punishment.

Source: Lord Byron, Letter to Lord Holland, February 25, 1812.

---

hood brought on by increases in efficiency—from agricultural laborers who burned ricks and destroyed farm machinery during the Swing Riots in southern England in 1830-1831 to disgruntled downsized white-collar professionals who propagate computer viruses in the twenty-first century.

—*Martha A. Sherwood*

FURTHER READING

Bailey, Brian. *The Luddite Rebellion.* New York: New York University Press, 1998. A clear nonscholarly account with numerous illustrations.

Binfield, Kevin, ed. *Writings of the Luddites.* Baltimore: Johns Hopkins University Press, 2004. A collection of anonymous letters, petitions, and manifestoes, with a lengthy, informative introduction and annotations explaining the context in which they appeared.

Carpenter, Kenneth, ed. *The Luddites: Three Pamphlets, 1812-1839.* New York: Arno Press, 1972. One of the pamphlets is the complete proceedings of the

1813 Luddite trials in York. A critical primary reference.

Reid, Robert William. *Land of Lost Content: The Luddite Revolt, 1812*. London: Heinemann, 1986. Aimed at the general reading public. Core of the book is a narrative description of the disturbances in Yorkshire, with emphasis on individuals on both sides of the conflict.

Sale, Kirkpatrick. *Rebels Against the Future: The Luddites and Their War on the Industrial Revolution—Lessons for the Computer Age*. Reading, Mass.: Addison-Wesley, 1995. Emphasizes the role of technological change and draws parallels with the present day.

Thomas, Malcolm I. *The Luddites: Machine-Breaking in Regency England*. Brookfield, Vt.: Ashgate, 1993. Emphasizes economic factors and discusses origins of Luddism in the eighteenth century.

SEE ALSO: Jan., 1802: Cobbett Founds the *Political Register*; Feb. 23, 1820: London's Cato Street Conspirators Plot Assassinations; 1824: British Parliament Repeals the Combination Acts; 1839: Blanc Publishes *The Organization of Labour*; June 2, 1868: Great Britain's First Trades Union Congress Forms.

RELATED ARTICLES in *Great Lives from History: The Nineteenth Century, 1801-1900:* William Cobbett; Napoleon I.

September 20, 1811
KRUPP WORKS OPEN AT ESSEN

Despite the company's slow beginning, the opening of the Krupp Works presaged the dominance of heavy industry, especially the manufacture of steel, in the industrialization of the European continent, and the Krupp Works eventually played a major role in the European arms race.

LOCALE: Ruhr River Valley, western Germany
CATEGORIES: Manufacturing; business and labor; trade and commerce

KEY FIGURES
Benjamin Huntsman (1704-1776), inventor of cast steel through the crucible method
Friedrich Krupp (1787-1826), founder of the Krupp Works
Alfred Krupp (1812-1887), Friedrich's grandson
Friedrich Alfred Krupp (1854-1902), Alfred's son
Helene Amalie Ascherfeld Krupp (1732-1810), grandmother of Friedrich and major financier

SUMMARY OF EVENT
The Industrial Revolution has long been regarded as the seminal development of nineteenth century Europe. A central role in Europe's industrialization was the emergence of the steel industry. The major force behind the transformation of the European steel industry was the emergence of the Krupp Works of Essen, Germany, as one of the Continent's leading producers of steel.

At the beginning of the nineteenth century, the pre-dominant industrial metal was iron, both cast and wrought—not its stronger alloy, steel. Great Britain was the major iron producer, and steel products represented only a tiny component of its iron industry, largely used in the manufacture of springs for clocks and expensive table utensils. British steel production was concentrated at Sheffield, in northern England, and benefited from the work of the chemist Benjamin Huntsman, who in the middle of the eighteenth century devised a better and more reliable method of making steel than that heretofore used. Huntsman's method was to heat pig iron ingots in clay pots, or crucibles, that absorbed the excess carbon of the pig iron and produced, with only one reheating, steel that could be manipulated to make goods that were in heavy demand.

The Huntsman technique was kept secret in Sheffield, but the city's manufacturers of steel products that were superior to anything else then available took advantage of their reputation and their products were admired throughout Europe. However, by the early nineteenth century, some knowledge of the crucible methodology had begun to leak out, and European manufacturers attempted to duplicate it. That, in fact, was exactly the intent of the German Friedrich Krupp, who on September 20, 1811, set up a small steelworks on the banks of Germany's Berne River, a tributary of the Ruhr, in the provincial town of Essen. At that time, the German states, like the rest of continental Europe, were cut off from importing British products by France's Napoleon I. A major stimulus to Krupp was the offer of a substantial prize to the German who devised a method of making crucible steel comparable to the Sheffield product.

It eventually took more than twenty years for the small Krupp enterprise to master the crucible steelmaking technique. Meanwhile, the number of men working for Krupp varied from one to seven, and Krupp himself—who had no particular expertise in this field—experimented and hawked the results of his experiments around the small principalities of western Germany. During this crucial phase, Krupp was sustained by the substantial economic resources of his grandmother, Helene Amalie Ascherfeld Krupp, and by the Krupp family business, which had been trading successfully for more than two centuries in western Germany. Krupp himself was never to reap the rewards of his efforts, as he died a discouraged man in 1826.

It was Krupp's teenage grandson, Alfred Krupp, who built the Krupp Works into the monolithic business that it later became. The younger Krupp achieved this success largely because he was a remarkably effective marketer. However, he also made good use of the vast economic resources of his mostly female relatives. In fact, there are those who maintain that it was the female Krupps, not the male members of the family, who were the true founders of the business. The role of the women, however, remained largely hidden.

Krupp Works exhibit at the 1893 Chicago World's Fair. The center of the exhibit is a massive wheeled cannon. (Library of Congress)

The first steel products of the Krupp Works to benefit from the marketing skills of the family were molds sold to the small principalities of western Germany for making coins. These high-quality molds established Krupp's reputation. The market for steel then expanded with the creation of the Zollverein, a customs union encompassing much of central Germany in 1834. After it was formed, Alfred Krupp rushed to market his products throughout Germany. When railroads began to be built in Germany during the 1840's and 1850's, Krupp expanded his operation greatly, and the numbers of Krupp employees grew from single to double digits. By 1849, the Krupp Works had perfected steel springs and axles for railroad cars, and Krupp began marketing steel railroad-car wheels that were cast as a single piece. This innovation played a major part in the expansion of the business during the second half of the century, along with the replacement of iron rails of the earliest railroads with steel rails. Production of railroad supplies remained a major component of Krupp's business and included much of the equipment and rails used on Canadian and early U.S. railroads.

It was the arms business, however, that made Krupp the powerhouse that it was to become by the end of the century. Alfred applied his considerable marketing skills to winning over the Prussian government and selling it ever-larger weapons. When these helped Prussia win battles during its brief war with Austria in 1866 and its 1870 war with France, Krupp's dominance of the arms market became unrivaled. Krupp then became a major contributor to the European arms race that characterized the last years of the nineteenth century, spilling over from artillery pieces that grew ever larger and more destructive to increasingly powerful naval vessels. Krupp also developed nickel steel that made possible relatively lightweight armor for the new fleet that the ambitious German emperor, William II, was building to keep up with Great Britain's Royal Navy.

Through the rest of his life, Alfred Krupp steadfastly refused to convert his family business from a sole proprietorship to a corporation. During the 1860's, he created the Prokura, a five-person management unit that ran much of the firm's day-to-day business. However, at his death in 1887, control of the entire firm passed to his son, Friedrich (Fritz) Alfred Krupp. Although the younger Krupp was not highly regarded by his fellows, he proved to be an effective manager of his inheritance. Under his direction, the Krupp Works continued to expand. By 1871, it had 10,000 employees; by the end of the century it had about 43,000. Fritz abolished the Prokura and replaced it with a management board, but final decisions always rested with him. What he did not do was produce a male heir who could take over the firm on his death in 1902. He was survived by two teenage daughters. Almost unavoidably, the firm became a corporation. However, almost all its shares were held in trust for the elder of Fritz Krupp's daughters.

SIGNIFICANCE

The Krupp Works has been much demonized, especially for its role in providing war materiel to Germany's government during World War I and World War II. Nevertheless, it was not fundamentally different from similar industrial empires elsewhere in the world, notably in the United States. Krupp rode the wave of industrialization during the early nineteenth century, when it was immeasurably assisted by the dominance of steel as the raw material of modern industry.

In some respects Krupp was a model of corporate welfare, as the company created a host of services to its employees: housing, insurance, health services, even grocery stores. The extent to which the company promoted large industry, and especially the production of armaments, has permanently tarnished its reputation, and may well have inspired the heir to the Krupp fortune voluntarily to give much of it up in 1965.

—*Nancy M. Gordon*

FURTHER READING

Batty, Peter. *The House of Krupp*. Rev. ed. Lanham, Md.: Cooper Square Press, 2002. First published in 1967, this survey of the Krupp dynasty from its founding to mid-twentieth century provides the most readable and concise study. Batty thoroughly investigates Alfred Krupp's youth and is adroit at displaying the youthful factors that later played a role in his direction of the firm.

Henderson, W. O. *The Rise of German Industrial Power*. Berkeley: University of California Press, 1975. A comprehensive history of Germany's rise to industrial preeminence in nineteenth century Europe.

Landes, David. *The Wealth and Poverty of Nations: Why Some Nations Are So Rich and Some So Poor*. New York: W. W. Norton, 1998. Major work by America's preeminent historian of technology that gives a concise explanation of the problem of making steel during the early years of the nineteenth century.

Manchester, William. *The Arms of Krupp, 1587-1968*. Boston: Little, Brown, 1968. A massive account by an American writer of popular histories. Manchester demonizes the firm, but he did consult the Krupp archives.

Showalter, Dennis E. *Railroads and Rifles: Soldiers, Technology, and the Unification of Germany*. Hamden, Conn.: Archon Books, 1975. A close study of Krupp's role in the unification of Germany. The author focuses on Krupp's early years of business and his successful association with the Prussian government through the acquisition of government contracts. Especially well covered are Krupp's armaments contracts during the critical period of German unification during the 1860's and 1870's.

SEE ALSO: 1855: Bessemer Patents Improved Steel-Processing Method; June 15-Aug. 23, 1866: Austria and Prussia's Seven Weeks' War; July 19, 1870-Jan. 28, 1871: Franco-Prussian War; May, 1876: Otto Invents a Practical Internal Combustion Engine; Jan. 29, 1886: Benz Patents the First Practical Automobile; 1889: Great Britain Strengthens Its Royal Navy; Feb., 1892: Diesel Patents the Diesel Engine.

RELATED ARTICLES in *Great Lives from History: The Nineteenth Century, 1801-1900:* Carl Benz; Sir Henry Bessemer; Rudolf Diesel; Alfred Krupp.

November 7, 1811
BATTLE OF TIPPECANOE

The Battle of Tippecanoe has been credited with breaking an incipient Native American confederation, triggering the War of 1812, and giving William Harrison the reputation that would later make him president. However, the battle itself was actually little more than a skirmish that signaled the last gasp of Native American resistance to white encroachment east of the Mississippi River.

LOCALE: Northwestern Indiana
CATEGORIES: Wars, uprisings, and civil unrest; indigenous people's rights

KEY FIGURES
William Henry Harrison (1773-1841), governor of the Indiana Territory and later president of the United States, 1841
Tecumseh (1768-1813), political and military leader of the American Indian tribes of the Northwest
Tenskwatawa (Shawnee Prophet; 1768-1837), Shawnee spiritual leader and brother of Tecumseh

SUMMARY OF EVENT
When William Henry Harrison was governor of the Indiana Territory, he was determined to provoke a fight with the Native American tribes living within the territory recently ceded to the United States. The main tribal leaders, Tecumseh and his brother, Tenskwatawa—who was known as the Shawnee Prophet—hoped to avoid such a fight. They had established their capital, Prophetstown, at the village of Tippecanoe, 80 miles (128 kilometers) south of Lake Michigan near the confluence of the Tippecanoe and Wabash Rivers in present-day northwestern Indiana. There, members of a growing Native American movement had flocked to join their community. Despite a message of peace from the Prophet, Harrison moved up the Wabash River with one thousand troops on September 26 and headed toward Prophetstown. On November 6, the U.S. troops encamped twelve miles (nineteen kilometers) from Tippecanoe.

Tecumseh and Tenskwatawa had hoped to avoid bloodshed, but reckless members of their movement forced the issue by attacking the U.S. camp in the predawn hours of November 7. Roused from his sleep, Harrison immediately rallied his men and reinforced his overrun flank. The forest and nearby river bottoms echoed with the sounds of screams, musket and rifle fire, shouted curses and commands, and the cries of fright-

ened, wounded, and dying men and animals. Two of Harrison's close friends, Major Jo Daviess and Thomas Randolph, were among the dead. Harrison promised Randolph he would look after the dying man's young child, a promise that he kept.

Harrison managed to hold his troops together in time to drive the attackers back. Two hours later, all was again relatively calm. Harrison's force surveyed its position and discovered nearly two hundred casualties, accounting for one-fifth of his force. More than sixty of his men were dead or dying. The Native Americans, who had been driven back into the swamps and river bottoms, had left behind thirty-eight of their own dead. Two days later, Harrison's men entered a deserted Tippecanoe, found food and British rifles, and burned the village. Such were the immediate results of the widely heralded Battle of Tippecanoe, which many historians consider to have been of fundamental importance in breaking Tecumseh's plan for a western Indian confederation, speeding the outbreak of the War of 1812, and contributing to Harrison's election as president in 1840.

In broad terms, the clash at Tippecanoe was the almost inevitable result of two vastly different cultures struggling for domination of the North American continent. In a more immediate sense, the conflict stemmed from the differing drives, personalities, and objectives of two significant western leaders: the great Shawnee chieftain Tecumseh and the aspiring politician and military man William Henry Harrison. The clash at Tippecanoe was a single episode in a long series of confrontations between Native Americans and Europeans that stretched back to the early days of European colonization in North America. Conflict rather than cooperation between the races was the rule, and the Battle of Tippecanoe represents one of the last stands east of the Mississippi River for the Native Americans as they were pushed farther and farther west by the encroachments of European civilization and institutions.

For the Native Americans, the Battle of Tippecanoe was simply one round in a long struggle in which they were poorly matched against the land-hungry and grasping white settlers. The Indians were dependent on the whites for arms and ammunition; many had been weakened by addiction to alcohol obtained from frontier bootleggers; and they lacked strong organization and unity of purpose. Tecumseh, the political and military leader of the tribes of the Northwest, and his brother Tenskwatawa, the Prophet, sought to overcome these weaknesses by calling on their people to reject the white man's culture, reassert their independence, and unite to drive the whites back across the Ohio River. Since 1808, they had attempted to form a confederacy in response to movement of Europeans into the Ohio Valley. By 1811, however, only four thousand Native Americans remained in the region, which now had one hundred thousand white settlers.

Harrison's attack at Tippecanoe had been intended to shatter the confederacy and the influence of the Prophet. In this, it was partially successful. The Prophet had promised his followers immunity from the white man's bullets. Instead, the enemies' bullets had brought death and suffering, and the Prophet's spell was broken. Tecumseh failed to rally the Sauk and Osage tribes to the south into his cause. Instead of terrifying Tecumseh, however, Harrison had stirred him to fury.

Despite the Indian defeat at Tippecanoe, the idea of confederation continued until Tecumseh, allied with the British in the War of 1812, was killed on Canadian soil at the Battle of the Thames River, across Lake Erie in October, 1813. The Indians had resisted white aggrandize-

ment for a quarter of a century, but it was Tippecanoe that brought the Prophet's career into eclipse. He was never again trusted by his brother, and he drifted into obscurity.

Harrison's later career was largely built around the conflict at Tippecanoe. He was an ambitious man who extracted every ounce of glory that could be gained from his success in the battle. His version of the episode depicted the policies of the U.S. government toward Indians as enlightened and compassionate. U.S. settlers were admittedly encroaching on tribal lands, but those lands were legitimately acquired through treaties with the old village chiefs. Furthermore, Harrison argued, the settlers were making efforts to uplift and civilize Indians. If the Indians, particularly Tecumseh and the Prophet, resisted these policies and the almost inevitable U.S. expansion, then it was because of their savage nature or, still worse, the result of British influence.

Harrison's views were not universally accepted by his own people, who heatedly debated everything about the Battle of Tippecanoe, but Harrison was so widely accepted as the Hero of Tippecanoe that he was given the opportunity of winning more military honors during the

General Harrison's charge at the Battle of Tippecanoe. (Francis R. Niglutsch)

War of 1812, and he parlayed his military reputation into political offices, culminating in his election to the presidency.

SIGNIFICANCE

The impact of the Battle of Tippecanoe on public sentiment was perhaps most important as a precursor to the War of 1812. Feelings between the United States and Great Britain were running high in 1811, and tempers were close to the breaking point. Many people in the United States believed, with some justification, that the British were stirring up trouble among the tribes. The discovery of British arms at the Battle of Tippecanoe was widely accepted as proof of a British-Native American conspiracy that threatened U.S. security and violated the rights of the United States as a sovereign nation. The fact that the British had actually attempted to restrain Tecumseh and the Prophet was either unknown or ignored. The important fact is that many people in the United States were highly incensed by the Battle of Tippecanoe; that bad feeling became part of the package of western grievances and ambitions that helped to trigger the War of 1812.

—*James E. Fickle, updated by Richard Adler*

FURTHER READING

Berton, Pierre. *The Invasion of Canada, 1812-1813.* Boston: Little, Brown, 1980. First volume of a two-volume account of the War of 1812 from a Canadian perspective. An excellent description of the Battle of Tippecanoe and its long-term significance.

Cleaves, Freeman. *Old Tippecanoe: William Henry Harrison and His Times.* 1939. Reprint. Newtown, Conn.: American Biography Press, 1990. One of the few major biographies of Harrison. Includes an excellent account of the Battle of Tippecanoe.

Dangerfield, George. *The Era of Good Feeling.* New York: Harcourt, Brace & World, 1952. Pulitzer-Prize-winning account of the early nineteenth century. Places the war and the Battle of Tippecanoe within the larger perspective.

Elting, John. *Amateurs to Arms! A Military History of the War of 1812.* New York: Da Capo Press, 1995. A detailed military view of an unpopular, badly fought, and arguably unnecessary war. Highlights the military campaigns.

Hickey, Donald. *The War of 1812.* Chicago: University of Illinois Press, 1990. An overview of the causes of the war. Concludes that the war was important in promoting nationalism and maintaining a sense of manifest destiny.

Klinck, Carl F. *Tecumseh: Fact and Fiction in Early Records.* Englewood Cliffs, N.J.: Prentice-Hall, 1961. A biographical sketch of Tecumseh based on relevant documentation.

Sugden, John. *Tecumseh: A Life.* New York: Henry Holt, 1998. A full and nearly definitive biography of Tecumseh that considers his life within the broader context of early nineteenth century Native American history.

_____. *Tecumseh's Last Stand.* Norman: University of Oklahoma Press, 1985. A straightforward account of Tecumseh's role in the War of 1812, emphasizing the period leading up to his death in battle.

SEE ALSO: Apr., 1808: Tenskwatawa Founds Prophetstown; June 18, 1812-Dec. 24, 1814: War of 1812; July 27, 1813-Aug. 9, 1814: Creek War; Oct. 5, 1813: Battle of the Thames; Jan. 8, 1815: Battle of New Orleans; Apr. 14, 1834: Clay Begins American Whig Party; Dec. 2, 1840: U.S. Election of 1840.

RELATED ARTICLES in *Great Lives from History: The Nineteenth Century, 1801-1900:* William Henry Harrison; Tecumseh.

1812-1815
BROTHERS GRIMM PUBLISH FAIRY TALES

The appearance of the first volume of Jacob and Wilhelm Grimm's Kinder- und Hausmärchen *continued the English and German Romantics' elevation of folk materials to literary status and popularized folktales for a broad audience.*

LOCALE: Berlin, Prussia (now in Germany)
CATEGORY: Literature

KEY FIGURES
Jacob Grimm (1785-1863), German grammarian, mythographer, and lexicographer
Wilhelm Grimm (1786-1859), German antiquarian and lexicographer
Clemens Brentano (1778-1842), German Romantic poet

SUMMARY OF EVENT
When the first volume of their extraordinary collection of German *Märchen*, or fairy tales, appeared in 1812 as *Kinder- und Hausmärchen* (revised 1815; *German Pop-*

ular Stories, 1823-1826), the Grimm brothers were not yet well known. They would not begin work on their famous dictionary for another quarter century, and the first edition of Jacob's groundbreaking *Deutsche Grammatik* (German grammar), which introduced Grimm's law, would not appear until 1819. Their only publication before the fairy tales was a collection of Danish hero-songs by Wilhelm and an essay on old German songs by Jacob, both published only a year earlier (1811).

German readers were ready for exactly the sort of folk materials they found in the Grimms' tales. German Romanticism had eroded, if not eradicated, the Enlightenment notion of the preeminence of classical literary forms (that is, following Greek and Roman models). An antiquarian spirit that preceded Romanticism in England, which had produced such folk-ballad collections as Bishop Thomas Percy's *Reliques of Ancient English Poetry* (1765), prompted German readers to look to their own native tradition for literary materials. A leading German literary critic of the late eighteenth century, Johann Gottfried Herder, in *Von deutscher Art und Kunst* (1773; on German manners and art) called for a rediscovery of authentic German folk literature. Johann Karl Augustus Musäus responded with *Volksmärchen der Deutschen* (5 volumes, 1782-1786; popular fairy tales of the Germans), although instead of transcribing tales from the oral tradition, as Herder's manifesto called for, Musäus made up original tales in the folktale manner, creating the genre of *Kunstmärchen* (artistic fairy tales) rather than the longed-for *Volksmärchen*.

As the German Romantic movement appeared at the turn of the century, the taste for authentic German folk literature grew. Romantics Achim von Arnim and Clemens Brentano disguised their imitations of folk-style lyrics as folklore collections in *Des Knaben Wunderhorn* (1805-1808; *The Boy's Magic Horn*, 1805-1808). About the same time (1806), the Grimm brothers began collecting stories to give the German reading public exactly what it was yearning for. When the first volume of the Grimms' collection appeared in 1812, it was something of a compromise between the *Kunstmärchen* of the Romantics and the true folk collection Herder wanted. The prefaces to *Kinder-*

Jacob Grimm (left) and Wilhelm Grimm. (Library of Congress)

Brothers Grimm Publish Fairy Tales

CINDERELLA'S GUARDIAN

The versions of the fairy tales published originally by Jacob and Wilhelm Grimm are often quite moralistic. Evil—particularly greed—is punished, and virtue and work are rewarded. For example, the Grimms' Cinderella is watched over, not by a "fairy godmother" who happens to find her, but by a white bird who sits in a tree she has planted and grown with her own tears.

It happened that the father was once going to the fair, and he asked his two step-daughters what he should bring back for them. "Beautiful dresses," said one, "Pearls and jewels," said the second. "And thou, Cinderella," said he, "what wilt thou have?" "Father, break off for me the first branch which knocks against your hat on your way home." So he bought beautiful dresses, pearls and jewels for his two step-daughters, and on his way home, as he was riding through a green thicket, a hazel twig brushed against him and knocked off his hat. Then he broke off the branch and took it with him. When he reached home he gave his step-daughters the things which they had wished for, and to Cinderella he gave the branch from the hazel-bush. Cinderella thanked him, went to her mother's grave and planted the branch on it, and wept so much that the tears fell down on it and watered it. And it grew, however, and became a handsome tree. Thrice a day Cinderella went and sat beneath it, and wept and prayed, and a little white bird always came on the tree, and if Cinderella expressed a wish, the bird threw down to her what she had wished for.

Source: Grimm Brothers, "Cinderella." *Household Tales by the Brothers Grimm.* Translated by Margaret Hunt (London: George Bell and Sons, 1884).

The German reader's thirst for authentic German tales was made even more acute by a groundswell of ethnic consciousness brought on by the Napoleonic Wars. King Jérôme, the youngest brother of Napoleon, was officially Jacob's employer at the library. The German name of the town, Wilhelmshöhe, was changed to Napoleonshöhe, and the superiority of French culture was everywhere proclaimed—creating a political need for German folk literature where there was already a personal one.

When the first volume of *Kinder- und Hausmärchen* appeared in 1812, the Napoleonic suppression of German culture had already waned; the French occupation would last only one more year, ending in 1813, and the Grimms would publish their second volume just as Napoleon met his final defeat in 1815. Jacob's preface to both volumes would sound the proclamation of German-ness. To the Grimms, the simple tales of the German peasants represented the last echoes of Germanic mythology poised, with the advent of modern industrial Europe, to disappear. Jacob opens his preface with something of a fairy tale of his own: an allegory of a farmer whose entire crop has been destroyed by a storm. Looking closely at a small area protected by a hedge, he realizes that the destruction has not been absolute after all: A few stalks remain, to be nurtured to full growth. This was Jacob's metaphor for the tales he and his brother offered the German people: a carefully preserved remnant of a once great crop, dim remnants of a once great Germanic mythology nearly destroyed by French cultural chauvinism.

The reaction to *Kinder- und Hausmärchen* was immediate and sensational. Not only the popular audience but also German intellectuals recognized the volume as an answer to Herder's call, nearly forty years earlier, for authentic German folktales. Both scholar and burgher warmed to the homely appeal of the tales and the preface, which—far from touting them as polished literary pieces—valued them for their rustic honesty. As a result, Jacob's preface almost guaranteed critical success for the tales: Not even the stuffiest, most Frenchified critic could fault a work that aimed only at being simple and German. Each volume went through a number of print-

und Hausmärchen implied that it was purely a work of research and collection, an implication that would lead not a few twentieth century critics and historians to accuse the Grimm brothers of fraudulently passing off their quite ingenious inventive powers as merely mechanical anthologizing.

Such controversies, however, lay far in the future when Jacob and Wilhelm Grimm set about collecting their stories—for they did begin as collectors, however the final product was judged. Jacob was in fact employed as a librarian during most of his time spent on the collection, giving him unlimited access to the rich holdings of the royal library at Wilhelmshöhe. With only nominal official duties, he had ample time to write and edit—and to visit the peasant storytellers. The Grimms became friendly with the Romantic Brentano, whose folk song collection had led him to announce his intention to follow up with a collection of tales. With Brentano's blessing, the Grimms took up the task, and with an archivist's diligence spent six years in preparing the first volume.

ings before the second (and not the final) edition of 1819. The initial success of the tales is all the more extraordinary when one considers that the first edition was presented as a literary text, with notes and scholarly apparatus, and no illustrations.

SIGNIFICANCE

The two volumes of *Kinder- und Hausmärchen*, 1812 and 1815, contained more than two hundred tales. In the remaining half century of their lives, the Grimms continued to refine their stories (and to some extent edit them, removing language and content deemed objectionable for children). Although the German audience hailed them as authentic German folk matter, the larger world recognized their universality. They became a major work of world literature, translated into seventy languages. The first English volume, translated by Edgar Taylor as *German Popular Stories*, appeared in 1823, with comic illustrations by the popular London illustrator George Cruikshank.

Although the Grimms continued to collaborate on their historical and philological scholarship, particularly their *Deutsches Wörterbuch* (1852-1862; German dictionary), a massive three-volume historical dictionary begun in 1838 and not completed until a century after their deaths, it would be the fairy tales for which the world would remember them. The continued status of the stories as literary masterpieces has much to do with the fact that the Grimms did encounter them as authentic folk stories that reflected basic archetypes of the human imagination, yet they had the sensibility to shape them into patterns that emphasized their affinities with other classics of world literature. Because so many of the tales were about children coming of age, the volumes offered insight into developmental psychology, a field that would not develop until nearly a century later.

—*John R. Holmes*

FURTHER READING

Bettelheim, Bruno. *The Uses of Enchantment: The Meaning and Importance of Fairy Tales*. New York: Alfred A. Knopf, 1976. Since its first appearance, this psychoanalytic study of fairy tales by an eminent psychologist has been indispensable to a study of the Grimms' tales.

Ellis, John M. *One Fairy Story Too Many*. Chicago: University of Chicago Press, 1983. A thorough exploration of the premise that the Grimms perpetrated a fraud in presenting their own compositions as authentic folk material.

McGlathery, James M., ed. *The Brothers Grimm and Folktale*. Urbana: University of Illinois Press, 1988. This collection of scholarly articles is for the advanced researcher and tends to favor psychoanalytic and folkloric interpretations.

Tatar, Maria. *The Hard Facts of the Grimms' Fairy Tales*. Rev. ed. Princeton, N.J.: Princeton University Press, 2003. A scholarly presentation of the evidence for the Grimms' falsification of the "collection" process for the tales.

_____. *The Annotated Brothers Grimm*. New York: W. W. Norton, 2004. Detailed notes on forty-six of the most analyzed tales, with generous background essays, a biography of the Grimms, and a thorough bibliography.

SEE ALSO: 1807-1834: Moore Publishes *Irish Melodies*; May 8, 1835: Andersen Publishes His First Fairy Tales; 1842: Tennyson Publishes "Morte d'Arthur"; 1886: Rise of the Symbolist Movement.

RELATED ARTICLES in *Great Lives from History: The Nineteenth Century, 1801-1900:* Hans Christian Andersen; L. Frank Baum; Lewis Carroll; Jacob and Wilhelm Grimm; Engelbert Humperdinck; Noah Webster.

March 22, 1812
BURCKHARDT DISCOVERS EGYPT'S ABU SIMBEL

The young Swiss explorer Johann Ludwig Burckhardt made one of the great archaeological discoveries of all time when he happened, almost by accident, on the colossal statues that Pharaoh Ramses II had erected in his own honor during the thirteenth century B.C.E.

LOCALE: Southern Egypt
CATEGORIES: Exploration and discovery; art

KEY FIGURES
Ramses II (1300-1213 B.C.E.), pharoah of Egypt, r. 1279-1213 B.C.E.
Johann Ludwig Burckhardt (John Lewis Burckhardt; 1784-1817), Swiss explorer and Arabist
Sir Joseph Banks (1743-1820), English intellectual who served as president of the Royal Society
William George Browne (1768-1813), English explorer
Friedrich Konrad Hornemann (1772-1801), German explorer sponsored by the African Association
Giovanni Battista Belzoni (1778-1823), Italian Egyptologist who excavated at Abu Simbel

SUMMARY OF EVENT
Johann Ludwig Burckhardt was born into a prominent Swiss family in Berne. However, his family fell into political disfavor after the French Revolution (1789), and his father was unfairly discredited while Burckhardt was still in his teens. This change caused a precipitous decline in the family's fortunes. Burckhardt left Switzerland for England in 1806, shortly after completing his studies at the German universities of Leipzig and Göttingen. While his money was running low in London, he met the intellectual Sir John Banks, who introduced him to the writings of William George Browne, a noted English explorer of Africa.

Through Banks, Burckhardt learned that the Association for Promoting the Discovery of Interior Parts of Africa was in the enviable position of having a large credit balance. Consequently, it was prepared to award a substantial sum to someone who would be willing to spend ten years or more

exploring in North Africa and the Middle East. The recipient was expected to send regular reports back to the association. At that time, most of Europe was caught up in an enthusiastic tide of curiosity about everything Arabic and Egyptian.

Burckhardt had been attending public gatherings that focused on Arabic culture, and he applied for the grant, for which there was only one other contender. In early 1808, he learned that he had won the award and requested the committee's permission to attend Cambridge University in preparation for his travels. During the spring, he began his work at Cambridge, where he concentrated on Arabic and other languages and on Arab history. He was already fluent in five European languages.

In January, 1809, Burckhardt left for Syria, where he spent two years in Aleppo, working on his Arabic until he

Abu Simbel during the early twentieth century. The man standing on the lap of one of the statues makes it possible to appreciate the colossal scale of the sculptures. (Library of Congress)

ABU SIMBEL IN MODERN EGYPT

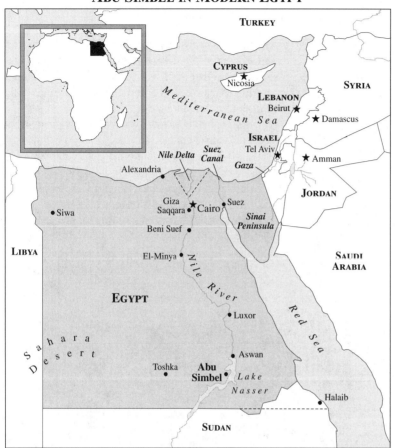

is now Libya. He was expected to follow the route plotted by Friedrich Konrad Hornemann, a German explorer who had devised a detailed plan for exploring the region but died before he could implement it. As Burckhardt traveled from Aleppo to Cairo, he passed through present-day Jordan. Following information he gleaned from people he met on his travels, he explored an area that Europeans had not yet discovered: the ancient city of Petra, one of the world's most significant archaeological sites.

Burckhardt continued to Cairo, hoping to join a caravan going to Fezzan. Finally, when hope of joining such a caravan faded, he sailed south on the Nile River toward Sudan. After reaching Aswan, he continued his journey south to a point about twenty-five miles north of Egypt's modern border with Sudan, where he made an amazing find. Protruding from sands that had drifted around them for centuries were four colossal stone heads. Below them, unseen by Burckhardt, was a temple that had been built to honor Egypt's Pharaoh Ramses II between 1260 and 1250 B.C.E. The temple's great hall was 115 feet (35 meters) wide and 98 feet (29.8 meters) high.

Also unseen by Burckhardt on the same site was another smaller temple honoring the memory of Ramses' queen, Nefertari, that remained completely covered. Burckhardt made his initial discovery on March 22, 1812, but could do little except to report it. He certainly could not begin a project as complicated as excavating the temple, and he did not realize the full extent of his find. In fact, he would die five years later without ever knowing that a second temple stood on the site.

The slow and arduous process of excavating the site was begun in 1816 by the Italian Egyptologist Giovanni Battista Belzoni. By 1850, only two of the four colossi that had revealed the site were been completely uncovered. It was not until the twentieth century that excavation of the entire site was completed, but then it was threatened with destruction when the Egyptian government erected the Aswan High Dam in 1952. A worldwide

spoke it flawlessly. He also immersed himself in Arab religion, history, dress, daily life, rituals, customs. During his years in England, he had already adopted Arab dress. In Syria he went further in adopting Muslim ways. He mingled with the poor, lived as they did, sleeping on earthen floors, eating their food, and generally fitting into the culture so fully that he eventually could pass as a Muslim. That ability made it possible for him to travel through the desert with Arab caravans, which would be necessary to the work he was committed to doing. Out of this experience grew Burckhardt's detailed book on Muslim life, *Notes on the Bedouins and Wahabys* (1831). This study became the most complete account in print about Arab culture and is still an informative source for those wishing to learn more about the Middle East and Muslim culture.

In 1812, the association sponsoring Burckhardt suggested that he travel to the regions south of the Sahara Desert by way of Fezzan in the southeastern part of what

effort saved Abu Simbel by having it moved and reassembled, stone by stone, on a higher site.

Meanwhile, in 1813, Burckhardt became the first European who is known to have visited the holy city of Mecca, where he had to pass as a Muslim. He continued his explorations and writing but suffered from recurring illnesses. He finally died in Cairo on October 17, 1817, after suffering from persistent dysentery. He was accorded a Muslim funeral and buried the same evening in a Muslim grave. He lived only thirty-three years.

SIGNIFICANCE

Working in a solitary situation without direct supervision, Burckhardt was supported decently by his grant. He used this money conscientiously and to full advantage, becoming a virtual citizen of the Middle East, blending into its culture as few Europeans could have done, and learning about it as an insider.

Burckhardt bequeathed his papers, including many Arab manuscripts, to Cambridge University, where this valuable collection is available to scholars. His writings, all published posthumously, include *Travels in Nubia* (1819), *Travels in Syria and the Holy Land* (1822), *Travels in Arabia* (1829), *Notes on the Bedouins and Wahabys* (1831), and *Arabic Proverbs* (1972). Few nineteenth century European explorers made Johann Ludwig Burckhardt's broad range of discoveries and contributions, but the English explorer and Arabist Richard Francis Burton matched some of his achievements.

—*R. Baird Shuman*

FURTHER READING

Burckhardt, John Lewis. *Arabic Proverbs: Or, the Manners and Customs of the Modern Egyptians*. Piscataway, N.J.: Georgias Press, 2002. Collection of proverbs collected and translated by Burckhardt. Valuable for Burckhardt's preface and a penetrating introduction by Egyptologist C. E. Bosworth.

_____. *Notes on the Bedouins and Wahabys*. 2 vols.

New York: Johnson Reprint, 1967. This reprinting of Burckhardt's 1831 book contains a modern preface by Egyptologist William Ouesley and presents information about a world little known to nineteenth century Europeans. Its chapters on Bedouin attire, robbery and theft, government, blood revenge, and burial of the dead present detailed insights into nineteenth century Muslim life.

Hallett, Robin. *The Penetrating of Africa: European Exploration in North and West Africa to 1815*. New York: Frederick A. Praeger, 1965. Chapter three of this detailed book begins with a lengthy and illuminating section on Burckhardt. The accompanying maps of Burckhardt's travels are especially useful.

Jones, Charles H. *Africa: The History of Exploration and Adventure as Given in the Leading Authorities from Herodotus to Livingstone*. Reprint. Westport, Conn.: Negro University Press, 1970. Jones presents a brief biographical sketch of Burckhardt in a useful discussion of North African exploration.

Sim, Katharine. *Desert Traveller: The Life of Jean Louis Burckhardt*. London: Phoenix Press, 2000. This new edition of the only full biography of Burckhardt is comprehensive, readable, and well presented. An essential resource.

SEE ALSO: 1803-1812: Elgin Ships Parthenon Marbles to England; 1814-1879: Exploration of Arabia; 1822-1874: Exploration of North Africa; 1839-1847: Layard Explores and Excavates Assyrian Ruins; Nov., 1839: Stephens Begins Uncovering Mayan Antiquities; Sept. 12, 1853: Burton Enters Mecca in Disguise; Apr., 1870-1873: Schliemann Excavates Ancient Troy; Mar. 23, 1900: Evans Discovers Crete's Minoan Civilization.

RELATED ARTICLES in *Great Lives from History: The Nineteenth Century, 1801-1900:* Sir Arthur Evans; Sir Richard Francis Burton.

1810's

June 18, 1812-December 24, 1814
WAR OF 1812

This first major war waged by the United States under its new Constitution was militarily inconclusive, but it tested the republic's sovereignty and generated a sense of nationalism.

LOCALE: United States; Canada
CATEGORY: Wars, uprisings, and civil unrest

KEY FIGURES

John Quincy Adams (1767-1848), principal U.S. peace negotiator at Ghent and later president of the United States, 1825-1829

George Canning (1770-1827), foreign secretary of Great Britain

Henry Clay (1777-1852), Speaker of the House of Representatives and leader of the War Hawks

George Erskine (fl. early nineteenth century), British minister to the United States

Thomas Jefferson (1743-1826), president of the United States, 1801-1809

James Madison (1751-1836), president of the United States, 1809-1817

Napoleon I (Napoleon Bonaparte; 1769-1821), emperor of the French, r. 1804-1814, 1815

SUMMARY OF EVENT

The War of 1812 was an outgrowth of events in the Napoleonic Wars in Europe that occurred during the first decade of the nineteenth century. After war broke out between France and Great Britain in 1793, the United States tried, with some success, to follow a policy of neutrality toward both belligerents. It avoided a struggle with Great Britain through Jay's Treaty of 1794 and ended a war crisis with France in 1800 through the Convention of Mortefontaine. In 1805, however, the Napoleonic Wars took a new turn, placing U.S. neutrality on a precarious basis. With Napoleon dominating the European continent and the British controlling the seas, the struggle turned into an economic squeeze, with the United States in the middle.

In an attempt to starve the other into submission, each side began to harass and seize U.S. ships. By the Order in Council of 1806, Great Britain declared a paper blockade of the European coast from Denmark to Brittany and required U.S. ships to be searched for contraband. France countered with the Berlin Decree, which authorized the seizure of all ships going to England before landing at continental ports. When Great Britain responded by issuing a second order in council requiring neutral vessels destined for continental ports to stop in England first, Napoleon issued the Milan Decree, ordering the seizure of any neutral vessel that submitted to British search.

Because the British dominated the seas, their restrictions on U.S. shipping were more effective than those of

The U.S. frigate Constitution *(foreground) defeating the British frigate HMS* Guerriere *off the coast of Canada on August 19, 1812. The British ship was so badly damaged that it was scuttled the next day, after its crewmen were safely removed.* (C. A. Nichols & Company)

TIME LINE OF THE WAR OF 1812

1803-1812	Great Britain's Royal Navy impresses approximately six thousand American sailors to serve on British ships.
1807-1812	British and French seize at least nine hundred American ships, increasing American animosity toward the British.
1812	U.S. forces attempt three unsuccessful invasions of Canada.
June 18, 1812	United States declares war on Great Britain to force the British to stop impressing American sailors and to recognize the neutral maritime rights of the United States.
Aug. 16, 1812	U.S. army in Detroit is forced to surrender, leaving the Upper Northwest entirely in British control.
Oct. 13, 1812	Battle of Queenston Heights: British and Canadian forces defeat a charge by the Americans.
Jan. 22, 1813	Battle of Frenchtown: Small U.S. force is massacred.
Apr. 27, 1813	Battle of York: U.S. troops capture and burn York.
May 27, 1813	Battle of Fort George: Colonel Winfield Scott's troops, in cooperation with the U.S. fleet, capture Fort George, causing the British to abandon the entire Niagara front.
May 28-29, 1813	Battle of Sackett's Harbor: General Jacob J. Brown repels a major British offensive on Sackett's Harbor, the main U.S. naval base on Lake Ontario.
June 6, 1813	Battle of Stony Creek: British regain initiative and most of the west bank of the Niagara.
Sept. 10, 1813	Battle of Lake Erie: Captain Oliver Hazard Perry leads U.S. forces in victory over a British naval attack.
Oct. 5, 1813	Battle of the Thames: General William Henry Harrison leads U.S. forces to victory in the northwestern theater. The defeat of the British and the multitribal alliance led by Tecumseh enables the United States to regain control of territory in the Detroit area that was lost in earlier defeats.
Nov. 11, 1813	Battle of Chrysler's Farm: U.S. force is defeated.
Dec. 29-30, 1813	British troops burn Buffalo.
Mar. 27, 1814	Battle of Horseshoe Bend: Andrew Jackson defeats Creeks and seizes Creek lands.
July, 1814	Battles of Chippewa, Lundy's Lane, and Ft. Erie.
Aug. 24, 1814	Battle of Bladensburg: British rout U.S. army and capture Washington, D.C., burning important public buildings; President James Madison leads U.S. countercharge through the streets of the capital city.
Sept. 11, 1814	Battle of Lake Champlain: British squadron surrenders to American force and retreats to Canada.
Sept. 12-14, 1814	Battle of Baltimore: Britain is unable to capture this important military target and the failure at Baltimore strongly influences the outcome of the War of 1812.
Dec. 24, 1814	United States and Great Britain sign Treaty of Ghent.
Jan. 8, 1815	Battle of New Orleans: Last battle of the war ends in British defeat.
Feb. 17, 1815	Treaty of Ghent: Represents the formal end to the war.

1810's

France. Moreover, the British practice of impressing seamen sailing under the U.S. flag, claiming they were deserters from the Royal Navy, was an affront to the honor of the United States and a challenge to its sovereignty. As a result, war almost erupted between the United States and Great Britain in the spring of 1807, when British seamen from HMS *Leopard* boarded the USS *Chesapeake*, after firing a broadside, and seized the alleged deserters on board. Outraged, President Thomas Jefferson barred British ships from U.S. waters and obtained another embargo, confining all U.S. shipping to port. By thus withholding needed supplies from the belligerents, he hoped to gain their recognition of U.S. neutrality.

Jefferson's embargo was the first of a series of coercive economic measures adopted by the United States in an attempt to avoid war. Because the embargo seriously depressed the economy, which was dependent on the export trade, it was replaced in 1809 by the Non-Intercourse Act, which cut off shipping with Great Britain and France only. This measure was superceded the following year by Macon's Bill Number Two, restoring complete freedom of trade but providing that if the belligerent nations should recognize the neutral rights of the United States, nonintercourse would be revived against the other belligerent. When Napoleon pretended to revoke the Berlin and Milan Decrees, President James Madison revived the policy of nonintercourse against Great Britain.

MADISON'S CASE FOR MAKING WAR ON GREAT BRITAIN

In his fourth state of the union address to the U.S. Congress in late 1812, President James Madison defended American involvement in the unpopular War of 1812.

The situation of our country, fellow citizens, is not without its difficulties, though it abounds in animating considerations, of which the view here presented of our pecuniary resources is an example. With more than one nation we have serious and unsettled controversies, and with one, powerful in the means and habits of war, we are at war. The spirit and strength of the nation are nevertheless equal to the support of all its rights, and to carry it through all its trials. They can be met in that confidence.

Above all, we have the inestimable consolation of knowing that the war in which we are actually engaged is a war neither of ambition nor of vain glory; that it is waged not in violation of the rights of others, but in the maintenance of our own; that it was preceded by a patience without example under wrongs accumulating without end, and that it was finally not declared until every hope of averting it was extinguished by the transfer of the British scepter into new hands clinging to former councils, and until declarations were reiterated to the last hour, through the British envoy here, that the hostile edicts against our commercial rights and our maritime independence would not be revoked; nay, that they could not be revoked without violating the obligations of Great Britain to other powers, as well as to her own interests.

To have shrunk under such circumstances from manly resistance would have been a degradation blasting our best and proudest hopes; it would have struck us from the high rank where the virtuous struggles of our fathers had placed us, and have betrayed the magnificent legacy which we hold in trust for future generations. It would have acknowledged that on the element which forms three-fourths of the globe we inhabit, and where all independent nations have equal and common rights, the American people were not an independent people, but colonists and vassals.

It was at this moment and with such an alternative that war was chosen. The nation felt the necessity of it, and called for it. The appeal was accordingly made, in a just cause, to the Just and All-powerful Being who holds in His hand the chain of events and the destiny of nations.

It remains only that, faithful to ourselves, entangled in no connections with the views of other powers, and ever ready to accept peace from the hand of justice, we prosecute the war with united counsels and with the ample faculties of the nation until peace be so obtained. . . .

Despite U.S. efforts at economic coercion, the British refused to change their maritime policies. In 1809, an agreement was worked out between the British minister to the United States, George Erskine, and Secretary of State James Madison, whereby Great Britain would abandon its orders in council and the United States would suspend nonintercourse. However, Erskine was recalled from his post by George Canning, the foreign secretary of Great Britain, who pursued a hard line toward the United States. As a result of this diplomatic fiasco, relations between Great Britain and the United States deteriorated, with each side believing that it had been deceived by the other.

The failure of the Erskine agreement placed the United States firmly on the road to war. In 1810, a new Congress was elected. When it took office at the end of 1811, it brought into positions of leadership a group of young Republicans who were impatient with pacific responses to humiliation abroad. Angered by the British challenge on the seas to their country's sovereignty, these War Hawks, as they were known, also were incensed by news of secret British aid to the American Indians in the Northwest. After naming Henry Clay as Speaker of the House, the War Hawks passed a series of resolutions to enlarge the Army and Navy and arm the militia. In April, 1812, the Madison administration boosted war sentiment in Congress by requesting a thirty-day embargo on U.S. shipping as a prelude to war. In June, Madison asked Congress to declare war against Great Britain. In a close vote that revealed sharp opposition to war, especially in the Northeast, Congress responded affirmatively on June 18.

In Great Britain, opposition to the orders in council had mounted sharply. Two days before the United States declared war, the British government announced its intention to repeal the orders. Even so, Madison refused to end the struggle as long as the issue of impressment of sailors remained unresolved.

Despite their bellicosity, the Jeffersonian Republicans had neglected their army and militia forces, which were unprepared for military operations. The war itself proved indecisive, and neither side was able to inflict a mortal blow on the other. The United States was able to control the northern Great Lakes and Northwest through most of the war, but its strategy of invading Upper Canada proved a dismal failure. An army under General Stephen Van Rensselaer was forced to surrender to the British at Queenston Heights in 1812. The United States did invade Canada the following year, burning the provincial capital of York (now Toronto) and defeating a combined Indian and British force at the Battle of the Thames in 1813. However, U.S. forces never established real control over Canadian soil.

By 1814, the performance of the U.S. Army had improved significantly. U.S. forces scored several hard-fought victories along the Niagara frontier, including at Chippewa, Lundy's Lane, and Fort Erie, but they lacked adequate resources to sustain the effort. Although the Navy won several skirmishes, most notably the sinking of HMS *Guerriere* by the USS *Constitution*, the British were able to drive most U.S. shipping off the seas. They were far less successful in containing U.S. privateers, however, and these raided British commerce with impunity and much profit.

Napoleon's downfall in 1814 and the subsequent reinforcement of Canada seriously jeopardized the strategic position of the United States. Many members of Britain's Parliament began calling for punitive operations. However, the British strategy of launching a three-pronged attack against the United States also proved unsuccessful. In 1814, a British armada entered Chesapeake Bay and, in retaliation for the burning of York, burned Washington, D.C. The British forces failed in their second objective of taking Baltimore, despite an all-night bombardment of Fort McHenry in Baltimore Harbor.

A second British drive across northern New York was repulsed at Plattsburg. A third British force suffered a major defeat at the Battle of New Orleans, as it tried to secure control of the Mississippi River. Ironically, this most bitter struggle of the war took place two weeks after peace had been concluded in Europe between the belligerent powers. By dint of skillful negotiating at Ghent in Belgium, the U.S. delegation under John Quincy Adams achieved its aim of preserving the prewar conditions, despite negotiating from a position of weakness. The accord, signed on Christmas Eve, 1814, reflected both Adams's unwillingness to compromise the national interest and British preoccupation with European events.

SIGNIFICANCE

When viewed against the backdrop of the immensely larger Napoleonic Wars, the War of 1812 appears little more than a backwoods, frontier skirmish. Despite its inconclusive nature, however, this conflict exercised direct and salutary effects upon the development of North America. The United States had commenced the war in a fractured condition politically, yet emerged with a degree of consolidation and consensus it had not possessed before. The Federalists, by dint of their strident opposition, were thoroughly discredited and began a slide into obscurity. The prevailing nationalism also launched a new generation of political leadership. At least three presidents—John Quincy Adams, Andrew Jackson, and William Henry Harrison—owed their elections, in part, to wartime activities. The U.S. Army was drastically reformed during the postwar era and made great strides in proficiency and professionalism. The bitter legacy of defeats forced a Jeffersonian rapprochement with the military establishment and adoption of more rational defense policies.

The War of 1812 made indelible marks upon the inhabitants of Canada as well. Defeat of U.S. forces stimulated the Canadians' first surge of national consciousness and, abetted by patriotic organizations such as the United Empire Loyalists, Canadians undertook a political and cultural evolution entirely different from their southern neighbor. If the War of 1812 had any clear losers, they were the Native American peoples. Crushing defeats north and south presaged their ultimate removal and accelerated the pace of white expansion on the frontier.

—Emory M. Thomas, updated by John C. Fredriksen

FURTHER READING

Borneman, Walter R. *1812: The War That Forged a Nation.* New York: HarperCollins, 2004. Comprehensive study of the war that pays special attention to the conflict's contribution to unifying the United States.

Elting, John R. *Amateurs to Arms! A Military History of the War of 1812.* Chapel Hill, N.C.: Algonquin Books, 1991. A revealing discussion of the factors surrounding U.S. military ineptitude; good coverage of obscure actions.

Hickey, Donald R. *The War of 1812: A Forgotten Conflict.* Urbana: University of Illinois Press, 1989. A broad synthesis of the political and diplomatic concerns that underscored U.S. political infighting.

Remini, Robert V. *Andrew Jackson*. 3 vols. Baltimore: Johns Hopkins University Press, 1998. The first volume of this nearly definitive biography covers Jackson's military career and his role in territorial expansion.

Stagg, J. C. A. *Mr. Madison's War: Politics, Diplomacy and Warfare in the Early American Republic, 1783-1830*. Princeton, N.J.: Princeton University Press, 1983. Portrays the war as James Madison's ideological crusade to save republicanism; detailed notes and imaginative use of primary sources.

Stanley, George F. G. *The War of 1812: Land Operations*. Toronto: Macmillan of Canada in collaboration with the National Museum of Man, National Museums of Canada, 1983. Modern Canadian perspective on a variety of strategic and political considerations usually overlooked by U.S. scholars.

Watts, Steven. *The Republic Reborn: War and the Making of Liberal America, 1790-1820*. Baltimore: Johns Hopkins University Press, 1987. Argues that the war and its aftermath were a reaffirmation of revolutionary principles and a factor in expanding them for posterity.

SEE ALSO: Summer, 1801-Summer, 1805: Tripolitan War; May 2, 1808-Nov., 1813: Peninsular War in Spain; Nov. 7, 1811: Battle of Tippecanoe; July 27, 1813-Aug. 9, 1814: Creek War; Oct. 5, 1813: Battle of the Thames; Jan. 8, 1815: Battle of New Orleans; Feb. 17, 1815: Treaty of Ghent Takes Effect; Feb. 22, 1819: Adams-Onís Treaty Gives the United States Florida; 1838-1839: Aroostook War.

RELATED ARTICLES in *Great Lives from History: The Nineteenth Century, 1801-1900:* John Quincy Adams; George Canning; Henry Clay; Francis Scott Key; James Monroe; Napoleon I.

June 23-December 14, 1812
NAPOLEON INVADES RUSSIA

Napoleon's disastrous attempt to invade Russia led to the near destruction of his army and began the fall of his empire.

LOCALE: European Russia
CATEGORIES: Expansion and land acquisition; wars, uprisings, and civil unrest

KEY FIGURES

Napoleon I (Napoleon Bonaparte; 1769-1821), emperor of the French, r. 1804-1814, 1815

Alexander I (1777-1825), czar of Russia, r. 1801-1825

Pyotr Ivanovich Bagration (1765-1812), commander of the Russian Second Army

Mikhail Bogdanovich Barclay de Tolly (1761-1818), Russian field marshal of Scottish descent who commanded the Russian Army of the West

Mikhail Ilarionovich Kutuzov (1745-1813), Barclay de Tolly's successor as commander in chief of the Russian armies

SUMMARY OF EVENT

On June 23, 1812, the French emperor Napoleon I crossed the Niemen River with 440,000 troops to open a campaign against Russia. France and Russia had been allied since 1807, but their relationship had never been cordial and had degenerated rapidly since 1809. The Russian court and Russian commercial opinion had both opposed the alliance from the start, and Russia's Czar Alexander I had refused to give political, military, or economic cooperation to Napoleon. In 1809, the Russians had given no effective aid to the French in the war with Austria, even though the alliance committed Russia to support France. Moreover, the Russian czar had been lax in enforcing Napoleon's embargo against British goods, and, in 1810, Russia levied special customs duties that affected French trade adversely.

Alexander had refused to negotiate a marriage between Napoleon and the Grand Duchess Anna Pavlovna. Serious political difficulties concerning Turkey, Prussia, and the remnants of Poland increased the tension between France and Russia. In 1811, when Napoleon seized the grand duchy of Oldenburg—whose integrity he had guaranteed when he met Alexander at Tilsit—the diplomatic crisis broke, and war began a year later.

Because Alexander knew that war was imminent, he made peace with Turkey and formed an alliance with Sweden. His attempts to win Prussia, Austria, and the grand duchy of Warsaw failed, however, and the British could provide no effective military aid. For all practical purposes, Russia was forced to stand alone against the French. By contrast, Napoleon was able to recruit and arm his forces from almost the whole of Europe. Includ-

French troops burning their flags for warmth during their disastrous retreat from Moscow. (Francis R. Niglutsch)

ing his reserves, he could send 600,000 men against Moscow. The Russian armies that faced him totaled only 153,000 men with reserves of 30,000, even though the Russians had suffered 40,000 casualties before the Battle of Smolensk. The French held a heavy numerical superiority at the start, but their numerical advantage was offset to some extent by problems of logistics and diversions that prevented them from concentrating their forces. Moreover, the large proportion of non-French elements in Napoleon's Grand Army made discipline difficult and desertions a serious problem.

Napoleon's Russian campaign proved to be a bitter, bloody struggle. The first Russian commander, Prince Mikhail Bogdanovich Barclay de Tolly, retreated from a confrontation with Napoleon's vastly superior forces, and the war became a series of vicious rearguard actions carried on in blistering heat with both armies suffering from lack of water and supplies. The situation worsened for the French when they left the Russo-Polish borderlands, for the Russian peasants fled, burning their homes and destroying their crops. Napoleon tried desperately to

prevent the Russian Second Army, under the command of Prince Pyotr Ivanovich Bagration, from joining Barclay, but he failed.

Napoleon then sought a final, crushing engagement with the Russians, but in this he also failed. On the Russian side, disorder was as threatening as were the French. The supply service broke down, sufficient food and fodder were not available, and men and animals alike suffered and died. Furthermore, a bitter rivalry between Barclay and Bagration, as well as intrigues at the Russian court, disrupted the war effort. Alexander was finally persuaded to appoint Mikhail Ilarionovich Kutuzov as commander in chief, although the czar personally loathed him. A septuagenarian with less than one year to live, Kutuzov was both shrewd and able, and he planned to continue the campaign as Barclay had begun it.

The First and Second Russian Armies joined together, Smolensk was abandoned in flames to the invaders, and Kutuzov chose a position near the small village of Borodino to fight the battle he knew was needed before he could again retreat. The Battle of Borodino began on

September 7. When it ended, the Russian army had checked Napoleon's advance. Both sides suffered terrible casualties, but the Russians were able to withdraw in order. Kutuzov enraged his officers and scandalized St. Petersburg when he refused to attack the French the morning after Borodino. Furthermore, he threw the country into despair by refusing to defend Moscow.

Napoleon expected to have victory in hand and enjoy peace by the time he reached Moscow, but all he found when he entered the ancient city on September 14 was emptiness and dismal silence. Soon, the city began to burn. Night after night the destructive flames soared upward as the wind aided patriotic arsonists, until the French were left occupying a smoking shell. Moreover, the Russians ignored French overtures to negotiate, and finally even Napoleon had to admit defeat. With his original forces now reduced to 110,000 men, Napoleon evacuated Moscow on October 19, 1812. Five days later, after declining another battle at Borodino, he turned away from Kaluga and retraced the old, wasted route to Smolensk.

According to contemporary accounts, Napoleon's leadership seems to have been sapped by the series of misfortunes that had confronted him since the beginning of the Russian campaign and had steadily increased since the failure to force the czar to sue for peace. Instead of striking at vulnerable Russian forces close to the French lines, Napoleon merely ordered the army to continue its withdrawal, hardly bothering to order the most elementary precautions to defend his flanks or rear.

The retreat had begun; it soon became a rout. Lacking adequate clothing and food, and with Cossacks and peasant irregulars harrying its flanks, the Grand Army entered its death agony. Discipline collapsed, and between Smolensk and the border, the winter struck in all its fury. Nevertheless, the disaster could have been worse; instead of pressing his advantage, Kutuzov allowed Napoleon to escape. This decision was not entirely a matter of choice, for the Russians had suffered grievous losses, and the bitter cold greatly reduced their own effectiveness.

The final and single most disastrous calamity befell the Grand Army late in November when it reached the Beresina River to find that the Russians had seized a key position overlooking the crossing. At last stirred into action, Napoleon ordered his engineers to construct a bridge across the icy stream. During the retreat, however, Russian artillery hampered the crossing and eventually found the range of the bridge. Those French troops not killed or wounded in the bombardment were forced to try

fording the river, and thousands more died. Both the campaign and Napoleon's army essentially came to an end.

Meanwhile, Napoleon heard disturbing news from France. On October 24, a conspiracy had struck, spreading word of Napoleon's alleged death and attempting to seize control of the government. Although officers and troops loyal to Napoleon had moved to crush the uprising, the situation was clearly desperate. On December 6, Napoleon left the remnants of his army behind and went on to Paris, where he arrived at midnight on December 18. His arrival had been preceded by an announcement in the *Moniteur*, the official government news organ, which blamed the French defeat not on the Russian army but instead on the Russian winter. The announcement concluded with a stunning tribute to Napoleon's egotism: "His Majesty's health has never been better."

SIGNIFICANCE

On December 14, Marshall Ney crossed the Niemen River with the tattered remains of an army. It is estimated that a mere thirty thousand men returned from the Russian campaign. An army of half a million men had been nearly annihilated. Despite these terrible losses, Napoleon and France continued to fight for fifteen months longer. However, the invasion of Russia proved to be Napoleon's most serious error. The road that led to his final defeat at Waterloo in 1815 began at the gates of Moscow.

—John G. Gallaher, updated by Michael Witkoski

FURTHER READING

Cate, Curtis. *The War of the Two Emperors: The Duel Between Napoleon and Alexander, Russia, 1812.* New York: Random House, 1985. Study of the Russian campaign that views the conflict as essentially a personal one between two headstrong monarchs, each bent on imposing his view on Europe.

Esposito, Vincent. *Military History and Atlas of the Napoleonic Wars.* New York: AMS Press, 1978. Excellent source for a basic understanding of the military nature of the ill-fated invasion and how the campaign was played out.

Johnson, Paul. *Napoleon.* New York: Viking Press, 2002. Concise biography of Napoleon that offers an overview of both his life and his career. Johnson portrays Napoleon as an opportunist whose militarism and style of governance planted the seeds for warfare and totalitarianism in the twentieth century.

Klimenko, Michael. *Alexander I, Emperor of Russia: A*

Reappraisal. Tenafly, N.J.: Hermitage, 2002. A full-length account of Alexander's life written by a professor of Russian history.

Marris, Albert. *Napoleon and the Napoleonic Wars.* New York: Viking, 1991. Places the Russian debacle within the context of the overall history of Napoleon's military campaigns.

Nafziger, George. *Napoleon's Invasion of Russia.* Novato, Calif.: Presidio Press, 1988. A thorough examination of the Russian campaign from a primarily military point of view.

Nicolson, Nigel. *Napoleon, 1812.* London: Weidenfeld & Nicolson, 1985. Concentrates on the campaign from Napoleon's angle of vision and what he intended to accomplish.

Riehn, Richard. *1812: Napoleon's Russian Campaign.* New York: McGraw-Hill, 1990. A generally balanced and fair appraisal of the events, including an assessment of the Russian army and its commanders.

Schom, Alan. *Napoleon Bonaparte.* New York: Harper-Collins, 1997. Detailed scholarly biography covering all facets of Napoleon's life and career. Schom is unusually candid about his subject's character flaws and failures.

Tarle, Eugene. *Napoleon's Invasion of Russia, 1812.* New York: Oxford University Press, 1942. A detailed account of Napoleon's invasion, campaign, and retreat from Russia.

SEE ALSO: May 2, 1808-Nov., 1813: Peninsular War in Spain; July 22, 1812: Battle of Salamanca; Sept. 7, 1812: Battle of Borodino; Oct. 16-19, 1813: Battle of Leipzig; Sept. 15, 1814-June 11, 1815: Congress of Vienna; June 18, 1815: Battle of Waterloo; Nov. 20, 1815: Second Peace of Paris.

RELATED ARTICLES in *Great Lives from History: The Nineteenth Century, 1801-1900:* Alexander I; Napoleon I; Michel Ney.

July 22, 1812
BATTLE OF SALAMANCA

The pivotal battle in the Peninsular War against Napoleon's French occupation army, the Battle of Salamanca in Spain was fought by an army of British, Portuguese, and Spanish troops against a French army known as the Army of Portugal. Although the armies were fairly evenly matched initially, tactical errors by the French commander led to a rout.

LOCALE: Arapiles, near Salamanca, Spain
CATEGORY: Wars, uprisings, and civil unrest

KEY FIGURES
Arthur Wellesley (1769-1852), earl and later duke of Wellington and British commander on the Iberian Peninsula
Auguste Marmont (1774-1852), duc de Raguse and commander of the Army of Portugal
Bertrand Clauzel (1772-1842), French military commander
Sir Edward Pakenham (1778-1815), British military commander
Sir Benjamin D'Urban (1777-1849), British general
Joseph Bonaparte (1768-1844), king of Spain, r. 1808-1813
Napoleon I (1769-1821), emperor of France and brother of Joseph

SUMMARY OF EVENT

Napoleon I's coronation as emperor of France in 1804 strengthened his resolve to take over Europe and intensified his ongoing conflict with the British, whose commerce was being ruined by his blockades and who feared his continued progress toward his goal. The French armies had taken Spain in 1808, but they fought ongoing battles known as the Peninsular War against rebellious Spaniards and their allies, the British and the Portuguese. Early in 1812, Napoleon decided to attack the Russians, too, diverting French troops from Spain and heartening the resistance. By mid-July, Marshal Auguste Marmont—the commander of the so-called Army of Portugal, comprising about fifty-two thousand French troops and eighty cannons in the Iberian Peninsula—was under significant pressure. Both Joseph Bonaparte, the French-imposed king of Spain, and his own troops wanted Marmont to do something about the resistance. A seesaw of hostilities ensued.

By that time, Arthur Wellesley, who was then the earl of Wellington, had entered Salamanca without incident, occupying the city with an army of fifty thousand British, Portuguese, and Spanish troops and fifty-four guns on June 27, 1812. Marmont's army was east of the city, between Toros and Tordesillas, as the combined troops commanded by Wellington were making their way toward him on July 13 via Ciudad Rodrigo. On July 15, Marmont surprised Wellington, necessitating the latter's retreat to Salamanca. On July 16, Wellington came into possession of a letter from King Joseph to Marmont, promising him thirteen thousand reinforcements with Joseph himself at their head plus the cavalry and guns of a French general named Caffarelli. This forced Wellington to hasten his plans.

By July 18, the opposing armies faced each other on either side of the Guarena River. Both crossed the River Tormes on July 21 and camped. During that same night, a terrible lightning storm killed some British troops and stampeded some of their horses. The next morning, July 22, Marmont's plan was to cut off the British access to the road to Ciudad Rodrigo at the point of two distinctive hills, the Lesser and the Greater Arapiles. He managed to defeat a Portuguese brigade and took possession of the Greater Arapil, but Wellington held the Lesser Arapil.

Marmont then made the first of several crucial mistakes. He mistook dust visible beyond the hills for a sign of Wellington's retreat, even though British troops were still visible in the hills opposite the French troops. Marmont believed that he could overwhelm what he anticipated was a small rearguard force. However, when he sent some of his troops to divide what he thought were two British divisions at the chapel of Nostra Señora de la Peña from what he thought was the retreating main force, he spread himself too thinly and exposed his own flanks. A gap was formed between two French infantry divisions, which were named Thomiere and Maucune, after their commanding officers.

Wellington, who had moved hidden soldiers to his advantage before he stopped for lunch in the town of Arapiles, literally saw his opportunity in the gap. He immediately attacked to the far side, just as a division commanded by his brother-in-law, Sir Edward Pakenham, and General Sir Benjamin D'Urban's Portuguese cavalry entered the fray head-on. They attacked from all sides, and the French fell back. Thomiere was killed and his troops scattered. In response, Maucune defensively chose to group his troops densely, and they were cut down by British fire. They, too, fled, but the British cavalry, commanded by General John Le Marchant, then

Street fighting in the Battle of Salamanca. (Francis R. Niglutsch)

overran the retreating French infantry, though the general himself was killed in the effort.

Early in the battle, Marmont had been wounded and his deputy general killed, so Marshal Bertrand Clauzel took over command of the French troops. He very nearly saved the day by combining infantry and cavalry attacks. Wellington took advantage of the French troops' progress into the midst of his troops, however, and caught them in a cross fire. Casualties were heavy on both sides. Wellington then counterattacked and scattered the opposition. By nightfall, the French were in full retreat across the river. Had a Spanish force commanded by Carlos de España not withdrawn from the bridge at Alba de Tormes, this would have prevented the French from escaping, and Clauzel's entire army would have been trapped. As it was, about seven thousand French were killed and wounded, and another seven thousand were taken prisoner, in addition to the capture of twenty big guns. The victors' casualties were slightly less than half that number, but half of those came from just two divisions.

SIGNIFICANCE

The Battle of Salamanca is known for the catastrophic strategic errors committed by Auguste Marmont that led to the defeat of the French. It is also remembered for the short duration (about forty minutes) of main battle prior to Clauzel's rally, for the horrific casualties on the French side—about 25 percent of the force, including the three most senior commanders—and for the definitive final victory of the British-led troops, which set the stage for the end of the Peninsular War. The loss of French men, equipment, land, and pride at the Battle of Salamanca was an important step toward thwarting Napoleon's ambitions. As a direct result of the July 22 battle, the British, Portuguese, and Spanish army marched into Madrid, Spain's capital, on August 12. This entrance into the capital symbolically freed the Spanish for the first time since 1808 and persuaded the British government to continue the war in Spain, though Wellington then headed to Burgos and near disaster.

Even so, the Battle of Salamanca was definitive for Wellington personally. Previously thought of as too cautious in battle, fighting with defensive strategies, and requiring an overwhelming strength of numbers to succeed, Wellington was now judged aggressive and decisive. He was raised to duke as a reward. The storm the night before the Battle of Salamanca became a pattern in the campaign against Napoleon, with another happening just before the battle at Sorauren and again before Waterloo. The British troops began to believe that such storms were harbingers of victory.

Today, the battlefield, not far from the University of Salamanca, remains essentially unchanged from the time of the battle. There is a memorial to the battle on the crest of the higher hill and a museum in the town of Arapiles itself.

—*Debra D. Andrist*

FURTHER READING

Muir, Rory. *Salamanca, 1812.* New Haven, Conn.: Yale University Press, 2001. Detailed account of the battle.

Oman, Sir Charles. *A History of the Peninsular War.* Vol. 5. London: Greenhill Books, 1995. An overview of the efforts to stop Napoleon's conquest of Europe, though with details of all the aspects.

Parkinson, Roger. *The Peninsular War.* Edited by Ludovic Kennedy. Ware, England: Wordsworth Military Library, 2000. Detailed guide to the entire period of which the Battle of Salamanca was part.

Weller, Jac. *Wellington in the Peninsula, 1808-1814.* London: Greenhill Books, 1992. Includes Wellington's own words about the battle via his reports and letters, in addition to third-person commentary.

SEE ALSO: May 2, 1808: Dos de Mayo Insurrection in Spain; May 2, 1808-Nov., 1813: Peninsular War in Spain; June 23-Dec. 14, 1812: Napoleon Invades Russia; Sept. 7, 1812: Battle of Borodino; Oct. 16-19, 1813: Battle of Leipzig; June 18, 1815: Battle of Waterloo; Nov. 20, 1815: Second Peace of Paris.

RELATED ARTICLES in *Great Lives from History: The Nineteenth Century, 1801-1900:* Napoleon I; Duke of Wellington.

1810's

September 7, 1812
BATTLE OF BORODINO

In the Battle of Borodino, Napoleon's French army engaged and defeated Russia's army in a bloody battle of attrition outside Moscow. Because the Russians retreated and left Moscow open to occupation, Napoleon claimed a victory. His inability to destroy the Russian army, however, left him unable to dictate terms and brought about his eventual defeat.

LOCALE: Borodino, Russia
CATEGORY: Wars, uprisings, and civil unrest

KEY FIGURES
Napoleon I (Napoleon Bonaparte; 1769-1821),
   emperor of France, r. 1804-1814, 1815
Mikhail Ilarionovich Kutuzov (1745-1813), Russian
   general and honorary prince
Mikhail Bogdanovich Barclay de Tolly (1761-1818),
   Russian general
Pyotr Ivanovich Bagration (1765-1812), Russian
   prince and general
Louis Davout (1770-1823), marshal of France, 1804-
   1814, duke of Auerstädt, prince of Eckmül, and
   later minister of war, 1815

SUMMARY OF EVENT
Napoleon I's invasion of Russia in 1812 was a consequence of his desire to control continental trade and to remove a potential ally for Britain. In previous campaigns, Napoleon's formula had been to march rapidly into enemy territory, draw the enemy army into a major battle, and then rely upon high French morale, skill, and concentrated artillery to destroy the opposing force. After a nation's field army was effectively destroyed, Napoleon could dictate the terms of peace. In 1806, for example, the twin battles of Jena and Auerstädt had crippled the Prussian army and resulted in Prussia's surrender and its subsequent incorporation into Napoleon's system of alliances.

When he attacked Russia in 1812, Napoleon's strategy appears to have been based on the expectation of fighting a decisive battle near the frontier that would have allowed him to repeat his formula for success. While French forces had been successful in earlier battles, however, the cumulative costs of Napoleon's campaigns since 1796 had reduced the available manpower in France. To compensate, Napoleon created the famous Grand Armée (great army), an amalgam of French and French-allied forces. Large contingents from Prussia, Westphalia, Austria, Poland, and Italy provided more than half of the Grand Armée's 614,000 troops.

In Russia, meanwhile, the drift toward war had not resulted in coherent planning. Divisions within the Russian leadership affected operations throughout 1812. The two principal commanders in the field, General Prince Pyotr Ivanovich Bagration and General Mikhail Bogdanovich Barclay de Tolly, promoted different strategies. Barclay proposed a slow withdrawal to lure Napoleon into the vastness of Russia, where French logistic limitations would cripple the Grand Armée. Bagration sought early battle, but when the French advance began in June, 1812, it soon separated the two Russian commanders and forced them to retreat. Throughout June, July, and August, the Russian retreat continued.

In August, Barclay attempted an unsuccessful stand near Smolensk, but he was again forced to withdraw after suffering significant casualties. In frustration, the Russian czar, Alexander I, promoted General Mikhail Ilarionovich Kutuzov to the honorary rank of prince and gave him overall command of Russian forces. Kutuzov chose to make a stand at the small village of Borodino, eighty-one miles west of Moscow. Borodino was located at a choke point on the road to the great city, and the nearby terrain would allow Russian defenders to claim the high ground and use it to obstruct the French advance. Napoleon would be forced into a disadvantageous battle against fire from prepared Russian positions.

Although the summer had seen continued Russian defeats, it had also seen a diminution of the Grand Armée. Throughout the Napoleonic Wars, logistics were an Achilles heel of the French forces. On campaign, the French fed themselves by scavenging and requisitioning from farms en route. Because Russia was both poorly developed and thinly settled, this method was insufficient. The army's rations grew increasingly sparse. Moreover, ordinary Russians saw these "requisitions" as depredations, so French logistic inadequacies not only weakened the army but also created a deep reservoir of ill will among the Russian populace.

Because Napoleon failed to trap and destroy the Russian army, he was repeatedly forced to leave large garrisons behind to hold major cities and crossroads. Thus, by the time Kutuzov decided to stand at Borodino, the Grand Armée had fallen from 614,000 men to approximately 126,000. The continued advance had been especially hard on the French cavalry, which lost large numbers of valuable horses. The lack of horses markedly reduced the efficiency of French scouting and the French ability to use cavalry rapidly to exploit any battlefield victory—key factors in Napoleon's normal tactics.

The Russian army had also suffered during the summer, and Kutuzov's forces were down to perhaps 120,000 effective soldiers. To augment these troops, the Russians raised militia forces and also strengthened their position at Borodino by constructing a number of hasty fortifications. On the north end of their position, they built what became known as the Raevsky, or Great Redoubt. This was an earthwork position, with a ditch backed by walls composed of piled-up earth. Within these walls were eighteen heavy cannon sited to overlook a long, open slope. The Russians anticipated that the main attack would come at the Great Redoubt, so they stationed the bulk of their forces and reserves on the north end of their line. During the middle of the field, the homes of the hamlet of Semenovskaya—southeast of Bordino—were disassembled to provide timbers for the creation of three "fletches." These were arrowhead-shaped earthworks that were open in the back. Each fletch was established on higher ground near obstacles preventing movement to either side of the approach. Thus, any attack by the French would be forced directly into the fletches' lines of fire.

Not only were Napoleon's forces depleted, but many of his men also were suffering from the rigors of months of hard marching on an insufficient diet. They were both hungry and thirsty as a result of poor logistic preparations. Napoleon himself was ill, suffering from dysuria, a condition in which urine is very concentrated and any movement—especially urination—is very painful. Thus, Napoleon, a man famous as an active commander who was often present on the battlefield, proved remarkably passive and stationary during the battle. Kutuzov proved equally unwilling to leave his headquarters, so throughout the day key decisions were made by subordinates and junior officers at the front with surprisingly little supervision from their commanders.

The Russians expected an attack in the north. When

The Battle of Borodino. (Hulton Archive/Getty Images)

the attack finally came, however, on September 7, 1812, it began in the south: The French intended to encircle the Russians. Napoleon's most capable marshal, Louis Davout, had recommended a strong envelopment, but Napoleon refused, apparently fearing that any delay would allow the Russians to retreat again. Inadequate French reconnaissance failed to identify all the fletches, and throughout the morning, stubborn fighting in and around these field works drew in more and more of both sides' reserves. Attacks in the center of the line also bogged down among the ruins of Semenovskaya. Corps and division commanders continued to persevere with attacks, and some positions changed hands a number of times, resulting in the loss of many fine officers on both sides.

In the north, the French attack began late in the morning, and the straight-on attacks again resulted in high casualties. Kutuzov allowed a force of Cossacks and cavalry to ride toward the French supply train, and as a result, Napoleon held back his cavalry, which was forming for a mass assault on the Great Redoubt. The massed French cavalry waited for more than two hours to launch its attack. It had massed within range of the heavy artillery in the redoubt and suffered very heavy casualties. Finally, the cavalry charged. It managed to push the Russians out of the redoubt, but only after heavy hand-to-hand combat.

By evening, the Russians had been forced out of both the Great Redoubt and the fletches, but they retreated in good order and maintained cohesion. Although the French had now gained the upper hand, Napoleon refused to send in his major reserves, the Imperial Guard, to capitalize on the Russian withdrawal. Napoleon's comment at the time indicated that he wanted to preserve the Imperial Guard as a reserve force for the rest of the campaign. Without the pressure of continued French attacks, however, the Russian army was able to withdraw intact, and Napoleon's opportunity to destroy the army was lost. His own Grand Armée had shown great courage and determination and ultimately held the field, but the cost was huge. Of the French forces, 6,967 were killed and 21,453 were wounded—including one marshal, fourteen lieutenant generals, and thirty-three major generals. The Russians lost approximately 17,000 dead and 30,126 wounded. Napoleon had sought a battle to destroy the Russians, but his lack of tactical finesse at Borodino prevented his troops from encircling the Russians effectively enough to destroy them. It also caused his own army heavy casualties.

SIGNIFICANCE

For Napoleon's invasion of Russia to succeed, he would have had to force the Russian czar to surrender and to follow Napoleon's dictates. The losses suffered by the Russian army at the Battle of Borodino were insufficient to force surrender. Even worse, those losses were heavy enough—especially in combination with the depredations of French scavengers—to incite great resentment among the Russian people. They fueled a Russian nationalism that refused surrender. Despite Napoleon's nominal victory, then, Borodino contributed to his ultimate failure in Russia.

Borodino proved to be the climactic battle of Napoleon's Russian campaign, and it is particularly telling that the battle progressed in a manner so contrary to the emperor's accustomed military experiences. It was fought deep inside Russia rather than at the border, and the exhausted Grand Armée was unable to encircle and destroy the opposing force as it had done in Napoleon's earlier campaigns. Instead, Napoleon's direct attacks against entrenchments resulted in heavy losses and a grudging but orderly Russian retreat. As a result of Napoleon's insistence on direct attacks, his losses were nearly as crippling as those suffered by the Russians. He failed to destroy the Russian army, and as a result he was not in the position of overwhelming superiority he had hoped to achieve. Napoleon's plan was to dictate the terms of surrender. Instead, he was unable to force Russia even to offer to surrender. Ultimately, the heavy casualties the Grand Armée suffered at Borodino meant that a French tactical victory was also a significant strategic defeat.

—*Kevin B. Reid*

FURTHER READING

Duffy, Christopher. *Borodino and the War of 1812*. New York: Charles Scribner's Sons, 1973. Classic study of the Battle of Borodino. Duffy's insight into the commanders and their plans is essential for understanding the battle.

Riehn, Richard K. *1812: Napoleon's Russian Campaign*. New York: John Wiley & Sons, 1991. Accessible and thorough; a masterful study of Napoleon's most crucial campaign.

Rothenberg, Gunther E. *The Napoleonic Wars*. London: Cassell, 1999. Provides a good basic understanding of Napoleon's style of generalship and the role that the Russian campaign played in his ultimate defeat.

Zamoyski, Adam. *Moscow, 1812: Napoleon's Fatal March*. New York: HarperCollins, 2004. Provides a good soldier's-eye view of the campaign and the sacrifices made before, during, and after the Battle of Borodino.

SEE ALSO: Dec. 2, 1805: Battle of Austerlitz; May 2, 1808-Nov., 1813: Peninsular War in Spain; June 23-Dec. 14, 1812: Napoleon Invades Russia; July 22, 1812: Battle of Salamanca; Oct. 16-19, 1813: Battle of Leipzig; June 18, 1815: Battle of Waterloo; Nov. 20, 1815: Second Peace of Paris.
RELATED ARTICLES in *Great Lives from History: The Nineteenth Century, 1801-1900:* Alexander I; Napoleon I.

1813
FOUNDING OF McGILL UNIVERSITY

The institution of higher learning that was launched by James McGill's bequest of land and money began slowly but eventually developed into one of the leading universities in North America and one particularly noted for its medical school.

LOCALE: Montreal, Quebec
CATEGORIES: Education; organizations and institutions

KEY FIGURES
James McGill (1744-1813), colonial Canadian merchant and politician
John Bethune (1791-1872), principal of McGill College, 1835-1846
John William Dawson (1820-1899), principal of McGill College, 1855-1893, and of McGill Normal School, 1857-1870

SUMMARY OF EVENT
During James McGill's lifetime as a fur trader and merchant in colonial Montreal, the Canadian Education Act of 1801 established the Royal Institution for the Advancement of Learning, which theoretically provided for the future establishment of Canadian institutions of secondary education and higher learning. However, it was not until McGill's death in 1813 and the probating of his will that this provision showed some promise of fruition. McGill left his estate of Burnside, a forty-six-acre plot with a manor house valued at £15,000, as well as £10,000 in cash, to serve as an endowment for a nondenominational, anglophone college, provided that a university or college was established within ten years of his death. The founding of McGill University is officially remembered as coinciding with the date of McGill's will.

François Desrivières, a nephew of Mrs. McGill's first husband, contested the will. While the case was in court, however, a governing board of the Royal Institution was set up in 1818, and a royal charter was obtained for the proposed college in 1821, within the ten-year period provided in McGill's will. The land and estate were finally surrendered on March 16, 1829, but the endowment funds were not settled until 1835.

In 1829, Archdeacon George Jehoshaphat Mountain became the first principal of McGill College and stated that his first intention was to "engraft" a medical institution to the proposed faculty of arts. There had been a Montreal General Hospital since 1815, and in 1823, it had been renamed the Montreal Medical Institution and moved to a building at 20 St. James Street, which served as the formally organized teaching arm of the hospital. In 1832, the hospital and the college formally merged, and the doctors of the former were constituted as the faculty of medicine of the latter. The medical program was the only successful academic program of the institution until 1835.

John Bethune, rector of the parish of Montreal, was appointed principal of McGill College in 1835 and served in that position for the next decade. He and his family occupied the Burnside estate in 1836 as the Principal's House. The manor house would later serve as both a faculty and a student residence. The medical faculty lapsed between 1836 and 1838 as a result of political troubles, but medical instruction resumed in 1838. The arts faculty at McGill College was formally inaugurated in 1843, though by 1844, student enrollment had declined to only nine students. A reorganization of the Board of the Royal Institution for the Advancement of Learning forced out Bethune, though he provided for the development of a future faculty of law with the appointment to the faculty of Justice William Badgley in 1844.

Edinburgh University graduate William Turnbull Leach was appointed as the first professor of classical literature in 1846, and Dr. Abraham de Sola, rabbi of the Montreal Spanish and Portuguese Jewish congregation, was appointed as lecturer in Hebrew and oriental languages in 1848, becoming a professor in 1853. As the only nondenominational institutions in Canada, McGill College and Dalhousie University in Nova Scotia admitted students and appointed professors of various faiths.

Although many administrative records were lost when the medical building was destroyed by fire in 1907, it is known that McGill College awarded its first medical degree in 1833, and there seem to have been between thirty and fifty-six medical students enrolled throughout the 1840's. The charter was amended and a new board of governors appointed in 1852, and a new building, Burnside Hall (named in honor of the original McGill manor house), was constructed to house a new high school department, as well as the faculty of arts. Members of the medical faculty had already, at their own expense, erected a medical facility at 15 Cote Street, which they then rented back to the college.

An 1853 prospectus defined McGill College as anglophone, broadly Protestant, and focused on professional education. John William Dawson became principal of McGill College and guided the opening of McGill Normal School in 1857. It was later renamed the Macdonald School for Teachers, then the Institute of Education, and then the Faculty of Education. Thirty-five of the initial forty students of the Normal School were women,

even though women were not admitted to other programs of the college for several decades.

At the time that Canada gained its independence in 1867, 48 students were enrolled in the law school, 68 students were in the arts, and 177 were in the school of medicine, reflecting the preeminence of the medical program at McGill. Indeed, beginning in the later decades of the nineteenth century and continuing into the twenty-first century, the McGill School of Medicine attracted and graduated significant numbers of American, and later international, students to study in its acclaimed medical programs.

SIGNIFICANCE

Although 1813 remains the official date of the founding of McGill University, it took two decades for the college to begin holding classes, when an existing medical institution was "engrafted" into the college and began educating future doctors. The college had no students in the arts for another decade thereafter. The original charter of the institution provided for only five faculty members, including the principal—a limitation that, combined with Desrivières's lawsuits, artificially constricted the development of the young school.

The McDonald Engineering Building of McGill University toward the end of the nineteenth century. (Library of Congress)

Despite this slow beginning, McGill University developed into one of the leading universities in North America by the end of the nineteenth century, noted especially for its medical and law schools. Located in a traditionally bilingual province, McGill is also notable for being primarily an anglophone institution in a primarily French-speaking city. Although at times throughout its history it has defined itself as broadly Protestant, in fact it has been a remarkably nondenominational institution that has attracted faculty, staff, and students from a variety of religious traditions and ethnic backgrounds. The old McGill Burnside estate, whose boundary ran down the middle of the present University Street, has developed into a downtown campus of 104 buildings on eighty acres. James McGill, the Scottish immigrant and benefactor who came to political and economic prominence in colonial Montreal and whose name will forever be identified with the university, is buried in front of the steps to the arts building.

—*Richard Sax*

FURTHER READING

Frost, Stanley Brice. *McGill University: For the Advancement of Learning, 1895-1971.* 2 vols. Montreal: McGill-Queen's University Press, 1980-1984. The definitive history of McGill University, written by a retiring vice principal who also served as dean of the faculty of divinity (later the Religious Studies Department) and dean of the faculty of graduate studies and research.

Gillett, Margaret, and Ann Beer, eds. *Our Own Agendas: Autobiographical Essays by Women Associated with McGill University.* Montreal: McGill-Queen's University Press, 1995. First-person narratives written by women of the faculty, staff, and student body of the university.

Ross, Murray G. *The University: The Anatomy of Academe.* New York: McGraw-Hill, 1976. Includes discussion of distinctly nondenominational character of McGill and Dalhousie Universities, as opposed to most other institutions in the Canadian provinces in the first half of the nineteenth century.

Wilson, J. Donald., et al., eds. *Canadian Education: A History.* Scarborough, Ont.: Prentice-Hall/Canada, 1970. Includes valuable discussion of the Canadian Education Act of 1801, which provided an unfunded mandate for schools of higher education throughout Canada.

SEE ALSO: Mar. 16, 1802: U.S. Military Academy Is Established; 1820's-1830's: Free Public School Movement; May, 1823: Hartford Female Seminary Is Founded; Dec. 3, 1833: Oberlin College Opens; Nov. 8, 1837: Mount Holyoke Female Seminary Opens; Jan. 1, 1857: First African American University Opens; Sept. 26, 1865: Vassar College Opens.

RELATED ARTICLES in *Great Lives from History: The Nineteenth Century, 1801-1900:* First Earl of Durham; Sir William Osler.

1810's

March, 1813-December 9, 1824
BOLÍVAR'S MILITARY CAMPAIGNS

The flamboyant and energetic revolutionary leader Simón Bolívar waged a long series of military campaigns during which he experienced drastic shifts in fortune but throughout which he never abandoned his commitment to rid South America of Spanish rule. His audacity, brilliance, and persistence resulted in the liberation of what would become five independent South American countries in the northern part of the continent.

LOCALE: Northern South America

CATEGORIES: Wars, uprisings, and civil unrest; colonization; government and politics; expansion and land acquisition

KEY FIGURES

Simón Bolívar (1783-1830), Venezuelan Creole revolutionary leader and ruler of Gran Colombia, 1822-1830

Francisco de Paula Santander (1792-1840), rebel general, vice president of Gran Colombia, 1821-1828, and later president of Colombia, 1832-1837

José Antonio Páez (1790-1873), *llanero* warlord allied to Bolívar and later president of Venezuela, 1830-1846 and 1861-1863

Pablo Morillo (1778-1837), Spanish royalist general

Antonio José de Sucre (1795-1830), general in Bolívar's service and later president of Bolivia, 1826-1828

José de San Martín (1778-1850), Argentinian general
   who liberated Chile
José Tomás Boves (1782-1814), *llanero* warlord
   opposed to Bolívar
José de la Serna (1770-1832), last Spanish viceroy of
   Peru
Ferdinand VII (1784-1833), king of Spain, r. 1808 and
   1813-1833
Manuela Sáenz (1797-1856), mistress to Bolívar and
   an unofficial member of his staff

SUMMARY OF EVENT

By 1813, the liberal Creole leader Simón Bolívar had experienced much frustration in his attempts to win independence for his native Venezuela from its Spanish colonial government. From 1810 to 1812, he had taken a
leading part in Francisco de Miranda's abortive independence movement. He had then left Venezuela for the
neighboring province of New Granada, where he had
served as a military commander for the rebel government
in the city of Bogotá. However, he soon became restless
and pleaded with the Bogotá regime to allow him to invade Venezuela. He finally secured permission, took

Statue of Simón Bolívar in Caracas, Venezuela. (Library of Congress)

five hundred soldiers, and launched his military expedition in March, 1813.

The ensuing campaign established Bolívar's reputation. Outmaneuvering his numerically superior adversaries and collecting new recruits as he went from one
success to the next, Bolívar entered the Venezuelan capital of Caracas in July, 1813, and was awarded the title by
which he would thenceforth be known: the Liberator. After proclaiming the Second Republic of Venezuela, however, he soon committed grave political blunders, the
most serious of which was alienating the tough, fiercely
independent *llaneros*, cowboys of the Venezuelan
plains. Laws restricting *llanero* freedoms, requiring
them to hold identification papers and to be tied to laboring for large ranchers, threatened their way of life. Led
by a Spanish transplant, José Tomás Boves, the plains-
men proved to be redoubtable opponents. Boves, a ruthless individual known as the Asturian Tiger, proved to be
more than a match for Bolívar, routing his forces at the
Battle of La Puerta on June 15, 1814.

Shortly thereafter, the tide began turning even more
decisively as a result of developments in Spain. As the
Napoleonic Wars wound down, French occupation troops
fighting in the Peninsular War were driven
from Spain by combined British forces and
Spanish guerrillas, and King Ferdinand VII
was restored to the throne. Ferdinand was determined to crush all Latin American insurrections, and Napoleon I's defeat freed more
Spanish troops for that purpose. In July of
1814, Bolívar evacuated Caracas and fled to
Colombia. Boves destroyed his last remaining
supporters at the Battle of Urica on December 5, 1814. However, Boves was slain during
the battle, an event that would hold portent for
the future.

From Colombia, Bolívar escaped to Cura-
çao, Jamaica, then to Haiti, where he received
money, supplies, and assistance from Haitian
president Alexandre Pétion. During the course
of 1815, Venezuela and Colombia were effectively won back to the royalist cause through
the efforts of the able Spanish general Pablo
Morillo, known as the Pacifier. After two
failed attempts to land on the west coast of
Venezuela, Bolívar made landfall in September, 1816, at Angostura on the Orinoco River.
His revived movement was strengthened from
two significant directions. First, English, Scottish, and Irish veterans of the Napoleonic Wars

SOUTH AMERICAN INDEPENDENCE

PANAMA
1903

Caracas

GUIANA
1966

North Atlantic Ocean

VENEZUELA
1830

SURINAME
1975

FRENCH
GUIANA
(France)

Bogotá

COLOMBIA
1819

ECUADOR
1822

Quito

Amazon River

BRAZIL
1822

Lima

PERU
1821–1824

La Paz

BOLIVIA
1825

South Pacific Ocean

PARAGUAY
1811

Asunción

Rio de Janeiro

CHILE
1818

ARGENTINA
1816

URUGUAY
1828

Santiago

Buenos Aires

Montevideo

South Atlantic Ocean

PATAGONIA

(Divided between Chile and Argentina in 1881.)

■ = Gran Colombia

■ = United Provinces of La Plata

1819 = Year of independence

1810's

183

joined Bolívar's forces and forged a formidable unit called the British Legion. Second, Bolívar gained the support of the new *llanero* warlord, José Antonio Páez.

In 1819, Bolívar launched his greatest coup: While Páez held Morillo's attention in Venezuela, Bolívar led his forces on a dangerous and exhausting march across the Andes into Colombia. This daring gamble paid huge dividends when Bolívar staged a surprise attack at Boyaca on August 7, 1819. The much larger Spanish force was shattered, and an independent government was established at Bogotá, with Bolívar as president. Leaving the administration in the hands of the vice president, Francisco de Paula Santander, Bolívar sped back to confront Morillo in Venezuela.

The situation there developed into a stalemate, until news of a coup by a junta of liberal army officers on January 1, 1820, altered the balance. In compliance with the junta's wishes, Morillo halted aggressive operations against the rebels, signed a cease-fire with Bolívar on November 25, 1820, and returned to Spain, his departure removing the most imposing obstacle to independence. Bolívar and Páez capitalized on the opportunity provided by Morillo's absence, and on June 24, 1821, at the Battle of Carabobo, royal troops were cleared from Venezuela. Bolívar then turned his attention to Ecuador and Peru, still in Spanish hands. He dispatched his ablest lieutenant, General Antonio José de Sucre, to the city of Guayaquil, Ecuador, which quickly surrendered. The inland city of Quito, however, sheltered a Spanish garrison that was determined to resist the revolutionaries.

It was at this juncture that the two major South American independence movements converged. José de San Martín's Army of the Andes, which had crossed the mountains from Argentina to liberate Chile, was now pressing into Peru, and San Martín was near enough at hand to lend Sucre reinforcements. While Bolívar fought his way down the Cauca Valley, Sucre climbed the heights before Quito and took the city after a battle at Mount Pichincha (May 24, 1822). It was during his triumphant procession into Quito that Bolívar encountered the vivacious Manuela Sáenz, who would soon become his mistress and lifelong companion.

From July 26 to July 27, 1822, the two great leaders, Bolívar and San Martín, met privately at Guayaquil. After their conference, San Martín withdrew from Peru, leaving its final liberation to Bolívar and Sucre. In Peru, the last bastions of royalist resitance, under General José de Canterac and Viceroy José de la Serna, doggedly held on to portions of what are now Peru and Bolivia. On August 6, 1824, Canterac's army was beaten at the Battle of

Junin. Then, on December 9, 1824, Sucre inflicted the final, most devastating defeat on the royalists at Ayacucho, where Serna was captured and effective resistance came to an end.

SIGNIFICANCE

The lengthy independence struggle and Bolívar's stellar role in it enabled the Liberator to set forward his plan for a unified South American republic. Called Gran Colombia, the republic encompassed present-day Colombia, Venezuela, Panama, and Ecuador. Within a scant seven years, however, both Bolívar and Sucre were dead, and Gran Colombia was no more, having split into its component regions. Thereafter, disunity and recurrent coups d'état led by military strongmen known as *caudillos* became pervasive features of the Latin American sociopolitical landscape. Bolívar brought about South American independence, but his vision of a grand South American republic was never realized.

—*Raymond Pierre Hylton*

FURTHER READING

Anna, Timothy E. *The Fall of the Royal Government in Peru.* Lincoln: University of Nebraska Press, 1979. Takes the point of view that the crucial elements of South American indepedence lay in royalist weaknesses adeptly exploited by Bolívar and Sucre.

Bierck, Harold A., Jr., ed. *Selected Writings of Simón Bolívar.* Compiled by Vicente Lecunam and translated by Lewis Bertrand. 2 vols. New York: Colonial Press, 1951. Enlightening listing of primary documents, mainly composed of letters of Bolívar during various stages of his struggle.

Earle, Rebecca A. *Spain and the Independence of Colombia, 1810-1825.* Exeter, England: University of Exeter Press, 2000. Focuses on the vagaries of political events in Spain, how they affected Colombia, and the inability of Spanish governments to form policies based on reality.

Graham, Richard. *Independence in Latin America: A Comparative Approach.* New York: McGraw-Hill, 1994. Examines parallels and contrasts between the various freedom movements in the different regions and provinces of Latin America.

Herring, Hubert. *A History of Latin America from the Beginnings to the Present.* New York: Alfred A. Knopf, 1967. Classic study that includes an account of the independence struggles of the 1810's and 1820's.

Keen, Benjamin. *A History of Latin America.* Boston: Houghton Mifflin, 1996. The pages dealing with the wars of independence compare quite favorably with those of Herring in their flow and clarity.

O'Leary, General Daniel Florencio. *Bolívar and the War of Independence*. Translated by Robert F. McNerney, Jr. Austin: University of Texas Press, 1970. Firsthand account by an officer in Bolívar's British Legion who was handpicked by Bolívar to write his biography. As may be expected, it is highly complimentary to the Liberator.

Safford, Frank, and Marco Palacios. *Colombia: Fragmented Land, Divided Society*. New York: Oxford University Press, 2002. Two chapters are devoted to describing and analyzing the liberation struggle and the collapse of Bolívar's grand design.

Stoan, Stephen K. *Pablo Morillo and Venezuela, 1815-1820*. Columbus: Ohio State University Press, 1974.

Unusual account about the only Spanish general who had a chance to defeat the independence movement.

SEE ALSO: May 2, 1808-Nov., 1813: Peninsular War in Spain; Sept. 16, 1810: Hidalgo Issues El Grito de Dolores; Sept. 16, 1810-Sept. 28, 1821: Mexican War of Independence; Jan. 18, 1817-July 28, 1821: San Martín's Military Campaigns; Sept. 7, 1822: Brazil Becomes Independent; Jan., 1833: Great Britain Occupies the Falkland Islands; June 16, 1855-May 1, 1857: Walker Invades Nicaragua; May 1, 1865-June 20, 1870: Paraguayan War; Apr. 5, 1879-Oct. 20, 1883: War of the Pacific.

RELATED ARTICLES in *Great Lives from History: The Nineteenth Century, 1801-1900:* Simón Bolívar; Napoleon I; José de San Martín; Antonio José de Sucre.

1810's

July 27, 1813-August 9, 1814
CREEK WAR

During the Creek War, the federal government broke the power of the Creek nation, seized Creek lands, and opened Alabama to white settlement. The war also launched Andrew Jackson's military career, which put him on the road to the U.S. presidency.

ALSO KNOWN AS: Creek Indian War; Muscogee War
LOCALE: Alabama
CATEGORIES: Expansion and land acquisition; wars, uprisings, and civil unrest; indigenous people's rights

KEY FIGURES

Big Warrior (d. 1825), chief of the Upper Creeks and leader of the progressive peace party

Andrew Jackson (1767-1845), major general of Tennessee militia whose forces destroyed the Red Stick movement

Peter McQueen (d. 1818), mixed-race planter, chief, and leader of the Red Stick faction

William Weatherford (c. 1780-1824), mixed-race son of a Scots trader and leader of the Red Stick faction

Josiah Francis (d. c. 1818), mixed-race Creek warrior

William McIntosh (c. 1775-1825), Creek ally of the U.S. government

SUMMARY OF EVENT

Among all the American Indian peoples at the turn of the nineteenth century, the people who seemed most likely

to assimilate into the advancing white culture were the Muscogee, whom whites called Creeks. Colonial deerskin traders from Charleston, South Carolina, married into this matrilineal native culture, establishing kinship ties with their wives' families throughout the Muscogee nation and siring mixed-race children who became the nation's cultural and political elite. Alexander McGillivray—of Scottish, French, and Muscogee background—was educated in Charleston and became one of the most powerful and influential chiefs (micos) in the culture's history. William Weatherford, William McIntosh, and others born to both cultures remained influential in the tribe through and beyond the coming Creek War.

President George Washington appointed Revolutionary War veteran Benjamin Hawkins as Indian agent to the Muscogee, whom Hawkins attempted to teach European-derived farming techniques. With well-established agricultural traditions of their own, the Muscogee took easily to the teachings of both Hawkins and their own mixed-race people. The Muscogees established within their nation a subculture that featured frame houses, fenced fields, domesticated animals, adoption of European clothing and technology, and most other vestments of the traditional frontier South, including cotton production with African American slave labor for the wealthy.

The Muscogee cultural transition was not entirely smooth, however. One problem was the continued encroachment of advancing white civilization. So relentless were the demands of state governments for cessions of Muscogee lands that the Muscogee named one Tennessee governor the Dirt King and gave a Georgia governor the name Always Asking for Land.

Meanwhile, as buckskin breeches went out of fashion in Europe, the market for American deerskins evaporated. The Muscogee had traded heavily in deerskins, and they now found themselves with nothing to trade for European clothing, weapons, household utensils, and other goods to which they had become accustomed. By continuing to buy these goods on credit, they fell deeply into debt to U.S. and British trading houses. The Jefferson administration, through Hawkins, encouraged the paying off of these debts through cessions of land. The Muscogee strenuously objected to this plan, even when the U.S. government offered perpetual annuities to the tribe and bonuses to local chiefs who signed land treaties. The pressure on Muscogee hunting grounds intensified,

and the chiefs who ceded land became enemies in the eyes of many of their kinsmen.

More sinister than the insatiable land hunger of the United States was its innate distrust of American Indians and its general desire to eliminate rather than assimilate them. Some segment of the native population—Iroquois, Shawnee, Cherokee, Muscogee—seemed to be constantly at war with the frontiersmen. For whites, these violent clashes supported their belief that American Indians were dangerous savages in need of extermination. Another problem was the strength and depth of the Muscogees' own native culture. Their relationship to their environment and their tribal traditions had been deeply satisfying. Although white culture made life more comfortable, it did not resolve any life-threatening problems for the Muscogee. Thus, it was a luxury, not a necessity.

The pressure of encroaching white settlement continued to increase all along the U.S. frontier during the early

In August, 1813, the Creeks made a successful attack on Fort Mims, in lower Alabama, that provoked heavy U.S. reprisals. (Library of Congress)

186

nineteenth century, prompting the Shawnee chief Tecumseh to attempt an alliance of all Native American tribes so that they might together resist further white advances and save American Indian lands and culture. When Tecumseh and his brother, Tenskwatawa, known as the Shawnee Prophet, visited the Muscogee tribal council to urge an alliance with the Shawnee, head chief Big Warrior rejected the idea and called for continued peace with white Americans. A movement—part spiritual, part political—was already growing among the Muscogee, however, calling for a return to the roots of Muscogee tradition and a rejection of the values and material goods of white society.

The traditionalists were primarily young. Among their leaders were men who had successfully assimilated white culture—half-white cotton planters such as Peter McQueen, and such white traders' sons as William Weatherford and Josiah Francis. The leaders of the progressive, assimilationist wing were often older. Some, such as William McIntosh, lived like white men. Others, such as Big Warrior, maintained a traditional Muscogee lifestyle yet accepted the inevitability of progress.

On July 27, 1813, this cultural and political dispute broke into open warfare, a civil war within the nation over the direction the culture should take: toward the European style of life or back to the purity and spirituality of Muscogee life. The reactionary wing, led by a reluctant Weatherford, a vengeful Francis, and McQueen, became known, from the red color symbolic of war, as Red Sticks.

The war spilled over into white society with the killing of isolated settlers in southern Tennessee and the massacre of two large numbers of white, black, and Creek people at Forts Sinquefield and Mims in lower Alabama. These killings brought U.S. major general Andrew Jackson into the conflict with an army of Mississippi, Georgia, and Tennessee militia, joined by progressive Muscogee, Choctaw, and Cherokee allies.

Jackson's early campaign was tedious and unsuccessful. With winter approaching, pay in arrears, little to eat, and enlistments expiring, many militiamen prepared to go home. Jackson branded them all mutineers and arrested and executed six leaders, cowing the frontiersmen into remaining to continue the fight. Through hard marching and sporadic fighting, the allied force of frontiersmen and progressive Native Americans chased and battled the Red Sticks across Alabama, finally cornering a large contingent at Tohopeka (Horseshoe Bend) on the Tallapoosa River. In this battle, more than five hundred Red Sticks were killed, destroying Red Stick resistance.

SIGNIFICANCE

In the ensuing Treaty of Horseshoe Bend, signed on August 9, 1814, Jackson took approximately twenty-five million acres of land from both Red Stick insurgents and his Muscogee, Choctaw, and Cherokee allies. The cession opened the land to immediate white and African American settlement and created the heart of the cotton South. The Creek War left Andrew Jackson with a veteran and victorious army well positioned to block the British invasion of New Orleans, giving the United States its most impressive land victory in the War of 1812 and opening the path to the White House for Andrew Jackson.

For the Muscogee, the defeat spelled the beginning of the end of their existence in their homeland. Within two decades, they and most other surviving members of the South's Five Civilized Tribes were banished to the Indian Territory, Oklahoma.

—*Maurice K. Melton*

FURTHER READING

Barrett, Carole, and Harvey Markowitz, eds. *American Indian Biographies.* Rev. ed. Pasadena, Calif.: Salem Press, 2005. Collection of nearly four hundred biographies of Native Americans, including more than a dozen Creeks.

Braund, Kathryn E. Holland. *Deerskins and Duffels: The Creek Indian Trade with Anglo-America, 1685-1815.* Lincoln: University of Nebraska Press, 1993. Describes the competitors, pricing, credit policies, markets, and distribution of the Muscogee deerskin trade; provides a detailed look at Muscogee life.

George, Noah Jackson. *A Memorandum of the Creek Indian War.* Meredith, N.H.: R. Lothrop, 1815. 2d ed. Edited by W. Stanley Hoole. University, Ala: Confederate Publishing Company, 1986. Based on General Jackson's reports and correspondence, this pamphlet gives a battle-by-battle account of the campaign from the U.S. perspective. Written amid the passions of the War of 1812, it asserts that the Red Sticks were tools of the British.

Griffith, Benjamin W., Jr. *McIntosh and Weatherford, Creek Indian Leaders.* Tuscaloosa: University of Alabama Press, 1988. A highly readable account of the war. Argues that Weatherford was a most reluctant Red Stick, knowing from the outset that the movement was doomed.

Halbert, Henry Sale, and T. H. Ball. *The Creek War of 1813 and 1814.* Chicago: Donohue and Henneberry, 1895. Reprint with introduction and annotation by

Frank L. Owsley, Jr. University: University of Alabama Press, 1969. Provides a lengthy discussion of the causes of the war, presenting it as an intertribal difference that would have been resolved had whites not interfered.

Hudson, Charles M. *The Southeastern Indians*. Knoxville: University of Tennessee Press, 1976. Places the Muscogee within the larger framework of the native population of the area. One of several excellent volumes on southeastern American Indians by ethnologist Hudson.

Martin, Joel. *Sacred Revolt: The Muscogees' Struggle for a New World*. Boston: Beacon Press, 1991. Emphasizes the importance of spirituality in Muscogee life, in the evolution of the Red Sticks' back-to-our-culture campaign, and in their warmaking.

O'Brien, Sean Michael. *In Bitterness and in Tears: Andrew Jackson's Destruction of the Creeks and Seminoles*. Guilford, Conn.: Lyons Press, 2005. Engagingly written history of Andrew Jackson's role as a military commander in the Creek War of 1813-1814 and the First Seminole War of 1818.

Remini, Robert V. *Andrew Jackson*. 3 vols. Baltimore: Johns Hopkins University Press, 1998. The first volume of this distinguished biography covers Jackson's military activities and career before he became president of the United States.

Woodward, Thomas S. *Woodward's Reminiscences of the Creek, or Muscogee Indians, Contained in Letters to Friends in Georgia and Alabama*. Tuscaloosa: Alabama Book Store, 1859. Reprint. Mobile, Ala.: Southern University Press, 1965. A veteran of the war, Woodward knew many Muscogee leaders and their culture. Although written with the wisdom and common sense of later years, this entertaining little volume has its errors and must be read with a critical eye.

SEE ALSO: Apr., 1808: Tenskwatawa Founds Prophetstown; Nov. 7, 1811: Battle of Tippecanoe; June 18, 1812-Dec. 24, 1814: War of 1812; Oct. 5, 1813: Battle of the Thames; Nov. 21, 1817-Mar. 27, 1858: Seminole Wars.

RELATED ARTICLES in *Great Lives from History: The Nineteenth Century, 1801-1900:* Andrew Jackson; Osceola.

October 5, 1813
BATTLE OF THE THAMES

The Battle of the Thames was one of the most decisive U.S. land victories during the War of 1812, and it also brought the death of the Shawnee chief Tecumseh and contributed to the decline of his multitribal Native American alliance.

LOCALE: Ontario, Canada
CATEGORIES: Wars, uprisings, and civil unrest

KEY FIGURES
Tecumseh (1768-1813), Shawnee war chief
William Henry Harrison (1773-1841), commander of U.S. forces at the battle and later president, 1841
Richard Mentor Johnson (1780-1850), Kentucky congressman who was credited with killing Tecumseh
Henry Procter (1763-1822), commander of the British forces at the battle

SUMMARY OF EVENT
The Battle of the Thames was an important United States victory in the northwestern theater during the War of 1812 with Great Britain. The battle took place on the northern bank of the Thames River near Moraviantown in Upper Canada (now southern Ontario Province). On September 10, 1813, U.S. naval forces had won control of Lake Erie in the Battle of Put-In Bay. This prevented reinforcement and resupply of the British army at the lake's western end, in the vicinity of Detroit and Fort Malden.

When a superior U.S. force under William Henry Harrison crossed the lake on September 27, Major General Henry Procter, the British commander in Upper Canada, began withdrawing toward the east along the Thames River. Procter's Native American allies, who made up the bulk of his forces, angrily protested the abandonment of their homelands in Michigan. Procter reassured the Shawnee chief Tecumseh, who was the leader of an alliance of warriors from many tribes, that a stand soon would be made against Harrison's advancing army. However, Procter's retreat up the Thames was mismanaged and slow, and most of his spare ammunition and other supplies were lost. Harrison's faster-moving

Commodore Perry at the Battle of Put-In Bay, in which the United States won naval control of Lake Erie. Painted in c. 1911 by Percy Moran (1862-1935). (Library of Congress)

army overtook the British on October 5, forcing Procter to turn and fight before he had reached the defensive position that was being prepared at Moraviantown.

The British force included five hundred warriors of Tecumseh's alliance. In addition to Tecumseh's fellow Shawnees (then dwelling principally in Indiana), this body included warriors from the Sac, Fox, Ottawa, Ojibwa, Wyandot, Potawatomi, Winnebago, Lenni Lenape, and Kickapoo nations, all from the Northwest Territory, and a small band of Creeks from the South. Their women and children accompanied the still-loyal warriors. Approximately one thousand of Tecumseh's followers, angered by Procter's retreat from Michigan, had abandoned the British. Procter's forces totaled more than a thousand, including 450 regulars of the Forty-first Regiment of Foot and some Canadian militia.

The U.S. army under Harrison numbered about three thousand troops. One 120 of these troops were infantrymen from the regular army; the rest were Kentucky mounted militia volunteers. A one-thousand-man militia regiment commanded by Colonel Richard Mentor Johnson played a decisive part in the battle. There were also 260 American Indians in Harrison's force, including about forty Shawnees.

Outnumbered three to one by the U.S. troops, Procter's British and American Indian force took a position across a road that ran along the north bank of the Thames River. With the river protecting his left flank and a wooded swamp his right, Procter placed his British regulars in two parallel lines one hundred yards apart. On his left, commanding the road, Procter positioned his only cannon, a six-pounder. Tecumseh's warriors were placed in the swamp on the British right flank. The swamp slanted away at an angle that would enable the Indians to fire into the left flank of U.S. troops advancing toward the British infantrymen. Because Procter expected Harrison to send his mounted units, as usual, against the Native Americans, he dispersed the two lines of British soldiers thinly, sheltering behind scattered trees in open order, several feet apart. Only when infan-

try were positioned almost shoulder-to-shoulder, however, could they effectively repel a cavalry charge. When
Harrison noticed this inviting disposition, he sent Colonel Johnson's mounted regiment to attack the British infantry, while his other forces, dismounted as infantry,
marched against the Indians on the American left. The
small force of regular U.S. infantry was assigned to rush
the single British cannon.

Colonel Johnson's well-drilled mounted regiment,
organized in columns, galloped through the two lines of
thinly spread British infantry to their rear. The militiamen then dismounted and began to fire. The British, demoralized and hungry after not having eaten in more than
fifty hours, quickly surrendered. Each line of British soldiers seems to have fired a single volley and panicked.
The crew working Procter's cannon fled without firing a
single shot. This part of the battle lasted less than five
minutes.

The infantry units on the U.S. troops' left were having
less success against Tecumseh's warriors in the swamp.
The poorly disciplined militia infantry, now on foot,
were initially repulsed and driven back by the Indians.
The collapse of the main British position enabled Johnson to swing part of his regiment leftward to attack the
Indians' flank. At this point, where Tecumseh's warriors
joined the right of the British soldiers, Tecumseh and the
Shawnees had taken their position. Led by Johnson and a
small, select group that called itself the Forlorn Hope,
Johnson's regiment dismounted and pushed into the
woods. Heavy firing erupted, and most of the twenty men
in the Forlorn Hope were killed or wounded. Colonel
Johnson was hit by five bullets, his horse by seven. Early
in this intense action, Tecumseh fell, killed by a shot near
his heart.

With the death of their leader, the warriors in this part
of the swamp, on the Indians' left, began to fall back. Demoralization spread, and this, coupled with the continuing advance of the U.S. forces, brought an end to the
fighting. Although Procter himself had fled after a brief
effort to rally his troops, Tecumseh had stood his ground
and died fighting, as he had sworn to do. The Native
American warriors had fought on for more than thirty
minutes after the British regulars had given up, but now
they slipped away through the woods to find their families. The victory of Harrison's army was complete.

Because of mismanagement of the retreat and his poor
handling of the battle, Major General Procter was court-
martialed and publicly reprimanded. Harrison, on the
other hand, became a national hero, as did Colonel Johnson, who was widely credited with killing Tecumseh.

Twelve British troops were killed, 22 were wounded, and
601 were captured. Harrison reported a count of 33 Indian bodies on the field. Contradictory records suggest
that on the U.S. side, as many as 25 were killed or mor-
tally injured, and 30 to 50 wounded.

SIGNIFICANCE

The Battle of the Thames enabled the United States to regain control of territory in the Detroit area that had been
lost in earlier defeats, ended any British threat at the
western end of Lake Erie, and greatly reduced the danger
of tribal raids in the Northwest. Another important result
of the battle was the decline of the multitribal alliance
that Tecumseh had fashioned and brilliantly led. Native
Americans continued to take the field in support of British operations, but now their support became sporadic
and ineffective. Tecumseh's strategy of protecting tribal
lands through military cooperation with Great Britain
had failed.

On the northern shore of Lake Erie, the Canadian right
flank, a stalemate developed. Harrison's army disinte-
grated as the enlistments of his militiamen expired and
they returned to Kentucky. The weakened U.S. troops
were unable to advance eastward toward Burlington and
York, or to threaten British-held Michilimackinac to the
north. However, U.S. naval control of Lake Erie prevented fresh initiatives in the area by the British.

—*Bert M. Mutersbaugh*

FURTHER READING

Antal, Sandy. *A Wampum Denied: Procter's War of
1812.* East Lansing: Michigan State University Press,
1997. Chronicles the battle on the Detroit frontier, led
by British commander Henry Procter, during the War
of 1812. Details Tecumseh's role in assisting the
British.

Borneman, Walter R. *1812: The War That Forged a Nation.* New York: HarperCollins, 2004. Comprehensive study of the war that pays special attention to the
conflict's contribution to unifying the United States.

Dowd, Gregory Evans. *A Spirited Resistance: The North
American Indian Struggle for Unity, 1745-1815.* Baltimore: Johns Hopkins University Press, 1992. Explains the Shawnee leaders' struggles as part of a
larger pattern of cultural revitalization and military
resistance.

Edmunds, R. David. *The Shawnee Prophet.* Lincoln:
University of Nebraska Press, 1983. An insightful
study of the Shawnee society that produced Tecumseh and his alliance. Argues that Tecumseh's brother,

Tenskwatawa, the Prophet, originated the alliance, which Tecumseh took over as Tenskwatawa's influence faded.

_____. *Tecumseh and the Quest for Indian Leadership*. Boston: Little, Brown, 1984. A brief treatment that concentrates on the warrior brother.

Gilpin, Alec R. *The War of 1812 in the Old Northwest*. East Lansing: Michigan State University Press, 1958. A scholarly, well-written study that puts Harrison's 1813 campaign and the Battle of the Thames into context of the entire war in the northwestern theater.

Sugden, John. *Tecumseh: A Life*. New York: Henry Holt, 1998. The best biography of Tecumseh to date. Does an especially good job of placing Tecumseh's life

within the wider context of Shawnee and Native American history.

_____. *Tecumseh's Last Stand*. Norman: University of Oklahoma Press, 1985. Detailed analysis of the battle and the campaign that preceded it. Examines the question of who actually killed Tecumseh.

SEE ALSO: Apr., 1808: Tenskwatawa Founds Prophetstown; Nov. 7, 1811: Battle of Tippecanoe; June 18, 1812-Dec. 24, 1814: War of 1812; July 27, 1813-Aug. 9, 1814: Creek War.

RELATED ARTICLES in *Great Lives from History: The Nineteenth Century, 1801-1900:* Sir Isaac Brock; William Henry Harrison; Tecumseh.

1810's

October 16-19, 1813
BATTLE OF LEIPZIG

The Battle of Leipzig, also known as the Battle of the Nations, resulted in the defeat of Napoleon's army by a combined allied force and marked the decline of the French emperor's fortunes.

ALSO KNOWN AS: Battle of the Nations
LOCALE: Leipzig (now in Germany)
CATEGORY: Wars, uprisings, and civil unrest

KEY FIGURES
Napoleon I (Napoleon Bonaparte; 1769-1821), emperor of the French, r. 1804-1814, 1815
Jean-Baptiste-Jules Bernadotte (1763-1844), crown prince of Sweden, commander of the Army of the North, and later king of Sweden and Norway as Charles XIV John, r. 1818-1844
Gebhard Leberecht von Blücher (1742-1819), Prussian commander of the Army of Silesia
Karl Philipp zu Schwarzenberg (1771-1820), Austrian military commander

SUMMARY OF EVENT
Napoleon I's failure to impose a French peace on Czar Alexander I of Russia and the destruction of his vast army during its retreat from Moscow in the fall of 1812 led to the formation of the sixth and final coalition against France. As the Russian army advanced westward into central Europe, the nations that had been held in submission by Napoleon's military might prepared for what is sometimes called the "War of Liberation." Prussia and Sweden were the first to join Russia and Great Britain;

Prussia, to regain its position as a major state in Europe, and Sweden to acquire Norway and glory.

By April, 1813, Napoleon was able to field a respectable army in southern Germany along the Elbe River. By June, he had won several minor battles and had driven the allied armies back to the Oder River. An armistice halted operations during most of the summer, but since neither side was really interested in peace without military victory, both gave more time and energy to reorganizing and reinforcing their respective armies than to peace talks. The resumption of hostilities in mid-August, however, brought the advantage to the allies. Perceiving that the time had come to end French domination on the Continent, Austria joined the Coalition.

The opening of the final phase of the campaign found allied armies on three sides of Napoleon, with a numerical superiority of two to one. Nevertheless, Napoleon had the advantage of a centralized command and internal lines of communication, which enabled him to deal effectively with the separated and poorly coordinated allied armies for two months. Gradually, however, the allied forces began to draw closer. By mid-October, the three allied armies had crossed the Elbe and were converging on the French forces near Leipzig. The main allied force, commanded by Karl Philipp zu Schwarzenberg, was moving up from the south; the Army of the North, commanded by Jean-Baptiste-Jules Bernadotte, crown prince of Sweden, was moving in from the north; and the Army of Silesia, commanded by Gebhard Leberecht von Blücher, was approaching from the northwest.

Czar Alexander I meeting the rulers of Austria and Prussia at Leipzig.
(Francis R. Niglutsch)

Napoleon believed that he could concentrate against Schwarzenberg south of Leipzig and defeat his combined Austro-Russian army before Blücher and Bernadotte could arrive to support him. On the morning of October 16, 1813, the allied army attacked the French position five miles south of Leipzig. By noon, the allied attack had been halted and the French were advancing along the whole front. The numerical strength of both armies was about equal, with the allies having had an advantage in the morning and the French at noon. The day's fighting ended without a definite decision.

On October 17, there was little combat as both sides prepared for the final round. As the day wore on, it became increasingly obvious to Napoleon that he could not hold his Leipzig position and, with Blücher and Berna-

dotte closing in on him from the north, he would have to retreat through the city of Leipzig and along the main road to Erfurt. During the predawn hours of October 18, the French army withdrew to a preselected perimeter about Leipzig. The allied high command ordered an all-out attack, hoping to crush the French by sheer weight of numbers now that they enjoyed a superiority of two to one. However, their attack was neither concentrated on any one point of the French line nor energetically carried out by all commanders. The French stood their ground.

During the night of October 18-19, the French army began a methodical evacuation of the right bank of the Elster River, including the city of Leipzig. The operation went well through the morning of October 19, but as the allies closed in on the bridgehead, a nervous corporal blew up the only bridge linking Leipzig with the west bank of the Elster while it was still crowded with French troops and in no immediate danger of falling into enemy hands. This premature destruction of the only escape route for the French rear guard turned the brilliant defensive operation into a clear-cut defeat.

Napoleon's strategic plan during the 1813 German campaign was twofold. On the political side, he sought to retain control of the German states and, if possible, force Prussia and Austria to withdraw from the Coalition against him. Militarily, he understood the need to defeat in detail the various allied armies converging against him before they had the opportunity to unite their overwhelming forces and smash his army, terribly weakened both in morale and matériel from the disastrous Russian campaign of 1812. He failed in both efforts.

Politically, Napoleon underestimated both the power of German nationalism, which had grown steadily during the years of French dominance, and the determination of the allies to put an end to Napoleon's mastery of Europe. In June, 1813, Napoleon had rejected an offer from Metternich, the Austrian foreign minister, for a negotiated peace that would have greatly reduced French territory but left Napoleon the French throne. Rightly or wrongly, Napoleon believed that his security, and French greatness, depended solely upon continued military dominance of central Europe. His attitude hardened the allied determination and led to unprecedented cooperation among his enemies.

These political calculations heavily influenced Napoleon's military decisions in 1813. After winning the battle of Bautzen (May 19, 1813) for example, he accepted a seven-week armistice with the Prussians, rather than crushing their defeated army. Elsewhere throughout Germany, Napoleon's troops were scattered in garrisons rather than united in a powerful striking force. Holding territory, especially the German state of Saxony, rather than defeating the enemy's main armies, became a prime component of Napoleon's strategic plan. The combination of these miscalculations, political and military, placed Napoleon into his desperate position at Leipzig. Faced with allied armies approaching him from all points of the compass, he fought an essentially defensive battle that turned into defeat because of ill luck and poor coordination.

SIGNIFICANCE

The Battle of Leipzig was a decisive victory for the allies that broke Napoleon's hold on Germany and forced the French armies back behind the Rhine. The aura of invincibility that had attached to Napoleon before Leipzig was based at least as much on his brilliant manipulation of public perception as on the reality of his military prowess, but it was nonetheless an important aspect of his success as a conqueror. After Leipzig, that aura was gone. In the campaign of 1814 that followed, the allies would press their advantage of numbers and position until Napoleon's own marshals forced him to admit defeat and abdicate the throne.

—*John G. Gallaher, updated by Michael Witkoski*

FURTHER READING

Brett-James, Antony. *Europe Against Napoleon: The Leipzig Campaign, 1813*. London: Macmillan, 1970. Study of the campaign and the battle, much of it drawn from eyewitness accounts.

Britt, Albert Sidney. *The Wars of Napoleon*. Wayne, N.J.: Avery Publishing Group, 1985. One in the West Point military history series, this volume offers a comprehensive, illustrated view of Napoleon's career, with a fine section on Leipzig.

Connelly, Owen. *Blundering to Glory: Napoleon's Military Campaigns*. Wilmington, Del.: Scholarly Resources, 1987. Argues that Napoleon's victories were the result of brilliant improvisation and that, when this genius faltered, defeats such as Leipzig resulted.

Esposito, Vincent. *Military History and Atlas of the Napoleonic Wars*. New York: AMS Press, 1978. A good basic history that provides background and visuals to understand the battle.

Johnson, Paul. *Napoleon*. New York: Viking Press, 2002. Concise biography, providing an overview of Napoleon's life and career. Johnson portrays Napoleon as an opportunist whose militarism and style of governance planted the seeds for warfare and totalitarianism in the twentieth century.

Marshall-Cornwall, James. *Napoleon as Military Commander*. London: D. Van Nostrand, 1967. Argues that Napoleon was no innovator in military practice but instead raised conventional practice to its logical conclusion.

Schom, Alan. *Napoleon Bonaparte*. New York: HarperCollins, 1997. Scholarly, detailed biography covering all facets of Napoleon's life and career. Schom is unusually candid about his subject's character flaws and failures.

SEE ALSO: Dec. 2, 1805: Battle of Austerlitz; May 2, 1808-Nov., 1813: Peninsular War in Spain; June 23-Dec. 14, 1812: Napoleon Invades Russia; July 22, 1812: Battle of Salamanca; Sept. 7, 1812: Battle of Borodino; June 18, 1815: Battle of Waterloo; Nov. 20, 1815: Second Peace of Paris.

RELATED ARTICLES in *Great Lives from History: The Nineteenth Century, 1801-1900:* Alexander I; Gebhard Leberecht von Blücher; Charles XIV John; Napoleon I.

1810's

1814
FRAUNHOFER INVENTS THE SPECTROSCOPE

Joseph von Fraunhofer discovered that sunlight, when passed through a glass prism or a grating, produced a spectrum of colors that contained numerous dark lines. Later investigators showed that these dark lines were produced by specific chemical elements.

LOCALE: Bavaria (now in Germany)
CATEGORIES: Inventions; physics; chemistry; astronomy; photography; mathematics

KEY FIGURES
Joseph von Fraunhofer (1787-1826), German glass maker who invented the spectroscope
Gustav Robert Kirchhoff (1824-1887) and
Robert Bunsen (1811-1899), German scientists who used the spectroscope to show that chemical elements emit unique spectral patterns
William Hyde Wollaston (1766-1828), British scientist
Thomas Young (1773-1829), British scientist who first determined the wavelength of light waves

SUMMARY OF EVENT
In 1704, the renowned British physicist Sir Isaac Newton published *Optiks*, which described his wide-ranging investigations into the properties of light. He measured the angular dispersion of sunlight into a spectrum of colors by using a triangular glass prism. He also gave a mathematical explanation for the creation of the rainbow due to refraction of sunlight by water droplets in the atmosphere.

About one hundred years later, British scientist William Hyde Wollaston saw something in the spectrum of sunlight that neither Newton nor anyone else had noted before. Wollaston's experiment involved sunlight moving through a narrow slit into a dark room, where the sunlight struck a prism. The resulting spectrum was observed from ten feet away. At that distance the colors from red to violet were greatly spread out. Wollaston noticed that the continuous spectrum of the sun had some narrow, dark lines in it. Whereas an ordinary light source viewed through a prism emits a truly continuous spectrum of colors, sunlight appears to have some missing wavelengths. He reported finding seven dark lines but had no explanation for what caused them.

In 1814, twelve years after Wollaston's discovery, Joseph von Fraunhofer independently discovered through his own experimentation the dark lines in the spectrum of the sun. He devised a special apparatus, the spectroscope, that enabled him to catalog more than five hundred dark lines, now called Fraunhofer lines. The spectroscope had a lens that could be pointed at the sun or any other source of light, followed by a narrow slit. The incoming light beam struck a prism made of flint glass that produced a relatively large angular separation of colors. The spectrum was viewed through an eyepiece attached to a platform that could be rotated, allowing the angle of view to be measured with high precision. The most prominent dark lines were given letter names. Fraunhofer noted that the "D" line in the solar spectrum exactly matched the angle of sodium light that had been observed previously. However, he was not able to determine the significance of this observation.

The British scientist Thomas Young earlier had shown that a light beam, when passed through two slits that are very close together, produced an interference pattern of bright and dark images on a screen. He explained this pattern using the wave theory of light: When two waves are in step, their amplitudes will add to produce a brightness, but when they are half a wavelength out of step, their amplitudes will cancel to produce darkness. Young developed a mathematical formula that used the distance between the two slits and the angles of maximum brightness to calculate the wavelength of the light. Fraunhofer improved on Young's double slit by making a grating, consisting of a large number of closely spaced parallel slits. He wound a thin metal wire back and forth between two threaded screws. By advancing from one thread to the next one, he obtained a closely spaced mesh of wires.

Fraunhofer replaced the prism in his spectroscope with such a grating. The angular separation of colors, or dispersion, was not much better than his result had been with the prism. To improve his observations further, he needed to make the slits in the grating even closer together. As part owner of a glassworks company, Fraunhofer had access to a machine shop. A new grating was made by scribing hundreds of evenly spaced parallel lines on a piece of glass. Light came through the spaces to form a spectrum with high dispersion. With this device, he was able to measure the wavelength of yellow light from a sodium flame with a precision that agrees within 1 percent of the modern accepted value.

Fraunhofer was not an academic scientist. He was a craftsman skilled in making glass lenses for optical instruments. He used the solar dark lines as fixed calibration points to measure how the index of refraction of glass varied throughout the spectrum. He learned how to combine lenses of different glass composition into an achromatic system that gave the sharpest possible images. He became famous throughout Europe as the premier supplier of lenses for large telescopes.

Gustav Robert Kirchhoff, a physicist, and Robert Bunsen, the chemist of Bunsen burner fame, were colleagues at the University of Heidelberg in Germany. During the 1850's, they were studying the spectra of flames that contained various chemicals such as sodium, potassium, and copper salts. Using a grating in a spectroscope, they observed that each element had a unique spectrum of bright lines. These emission spectra provided them with an unambiguous identification, like a fingerprint, for each element. Kirchhoff and Bunsen were aware of Fraunhofer's work thirty-five years earlier on dark lines in the spectrum of sunlight. In trying to understand these lines, Kirchhoff set up a crucial experiment. Using a laboratory lamp, he showed that it had a true continuous spectrum with no dark lines. Then he placed a sodium flame between the lamp and the grating. This time the continuous spectrum had a dark line in the yellow region, just at the known wavelength of sodium. Evidently, sodium vapor was absorbing its particular wavelength out of the continuous spectrum.

Kirchhoff and Bunsen proposed the idea that atoms have an absorption spectrum that matches their emission spectrum. They were able to show that three prominent Fraunhofer dark lines in the solar spectrum exactly matched the emission wavelengths of potassium. They concluded that light from the surface of the sun was being absorbed at fixed wavelengths by sodium, potassium, and other atoms in the sun's outer atmosphere.

SIGNIFICANCE

The Fraunhofer dark lines have led to some interesting results. Sir John Lockyer, a British astronomer, speculated in 1868 that a prominent dark line in the solar spectrum, which did not match any element known on Earth, might be caused by a new element found only on the sun. He named it "helium," after the Greek word for the sun. Some thirty years later, helium gas eventually was found on Earth in deep mineshafts. Helium has become a valuable resource for various technological applications, as well as for lighter-than-air balloons.

Fraunhofer dark lines are found not only in the spectrum of the sun but also in all stars. Astronomers can use telescopes to focus on one star at a time and can record its spectrum on photographic film. In some cases, the Fraunhofer lines show shifts toward longer wavelengths, that is, toward the red end of the spectrum. "Red shift"

occur when stars are moving away from the earth at high speeds. This phenomenon is like the drop in frequency that one hears when an ambulance with a siren is traveling away from the listener. The red shift in the Fraunhofer lines from distant stars is the primary evidence for an expanding universe.

Spectroscopy has been extended to other parts of the electromagnetic spectrum as new instrumentation became available. For example, infrared spectra are the primary means to obtain information about the structure of molecules. Gamma ray spectroscopy has become a highly developed method of analysis that can detect impurities in materials as small as a few parts per billion. Fraunhofer's spectroscope was the starting point for many practical applications in analytical chemistry, astronomy, medical research, and other technologies.

—*Hans G. Graetzer*

FURTHER READING

Connes, Pierre. "How Light Is Analyzed." *Scientific American* (September, 1968): 72-82. Gives line drawings and photographs that show how the prism and grating are used for optical spectroscopy. Includes a section on modern instrumentation.

Jackson, Myles. *Spectrum of Belief: Joseph Fraunhofer and the Craft of Precision Optics*. Cambridge, Mass.: MIT Press, 2000. A thoroughly researched book on the life and work of Fraunhofer, containing an appendix with explanatory notes and an extensive bibliography.

Jenkins, Reese V. "Fraunhofer, Joseph." In *Dictionary of Scientific Biography*. Vol. 5. New York: Charles Scribner's Sons, 1981. An authoritative compilation of biographies, with several pages devoted to Fraunhofer's career.

Taylor, Lloyd W. *Physics, the Pioneer Science*. Cambridge, Mass.: Riverside Press, 1941. An excellent introductory physics textbook with much historical information on scientists. Out of print but likely available in academic libraries.

Walker, James S. *Physics*. 2d ed. Upper Saddle River, N.J.: Pearson/Prentice Hall, 2004. A college-level textbook explaining interference of light waves, including Thomas Young's use of the double slit and Fraunhofer's grating.

SEE ALSO: Jan. 1, 1801: First Asteroid Is Discovered; Nov. 6, 1820: Ampère Reveals Magnetism's Relationship to Electricity.

RELATED ARTICLE in *Great Lives from History: The Nineteenth Century, 1801-1900:* Friedrich Wilhelm Bessel.

1810's

1814
SCOTT PUBLISHES *WAVERLEY*

Waverley was the first of a long series of novels that made Sir Walter Scott one of the most widely read authors in the world. It is often considered the first historical novel, a genre in which real historical events and figures are portrayed from the point of view of a fictional, minor participant in those events.

LOCALE: Edinburgh, Scotland
CATEGORY: Literature

KEY FIGURE
Sir Walter Scott (1771-1832), Scottish novelist and poet

SUMMARY OF EVENT
Walter Scott began writing *Waverley: Or, 'Tis Sixty Years Since* in 1805 and first published it anonymously in 1814. At first, he did not want to acknowledge writing the novel, because he did not want to jeopardize his high standing as a popular Romantic poet. Scott's poetic powers were waning, however, and he faced increasing competition from others, especially Lord Byron. He therefore decided on a prose form that would reflect his deep reading in history, his readers' love of exotic locales, and their nostalgia for the heroic world of the past.

Waverley takes place, as its subtitle indicates, sixty years before Scott began work on it, in 1745. It therefore also takes place roughly sixty years after the Stuart king James II was deposed as a result of his adherence to Roman Catholicism and his belief in the divine right of kings. James's deposition in the Glorious Revolution (1688) was decried by many Scots, and those who remained loyal to James and to the Stuart Dynasty were called Jacobites. Scott set his novel during the Jacobite Rebellion of 1745, which sought to return the Stuarts to the British throne. *Waverley* proved to be such a success that Scott went on to publish a series of novels based on the history of Scotland and of Europe during the Middle Ages and other periods of interest to the Romantics.

Through the first four decades of the eighteenth century, the two parliamentary parties, the Whigs and the Tories, continued to quarrel over the rights of the Stuarts. Certain Tories conspired to restore the Stuarts, while the Whigs—aiming to enhance the power of Parliament—favored a Protestant succession to the throne of England, even if it meant securing a sovereign from Germany who was related to the British royal family. In 1714, the Whigs triumphed, installing the Protestant king George I, the elector of Hanover, on the British throne. A Hanoverian monarchy seemed more likely to preserve the power of Parliament, which the Stuarts had threatened by continuing to claim that the sovereign had absolute power. The Tories and their supporters continued to agitate for a Stuart return, placing their hopes on Prince Charles Edward (Bonnie Prince Charlie), who lived in exile in France.

Often considered the first historical novel, *Waverley* was the first of a long series of historical novels that made Sir Walter Scott one of the most widely read authors in the world. Before Scott, novels had certainly dealt with the past, but in the English novel, historical periods were merely an aspect of setting and theme—as in gothic fiction. The past was mysterious, a curiosity, or even an exotic costume drama, but it was not valued in its own right.

Sir Walter Scott. (R. S. Peale/J. A. Hill)

Scott's historical novels reflect the transition from the Age of Reason to the age of Romanticism. In the former, humanity's increasing rationalism—its ability to think for itself and to contest the dogmas of the past—meant that history was significant insofar as it led to the present or had been displaced by human progress. In the latter, the past became part of the quest of people to know themselves. The past became an object of nostalgia as well, since progress had its costs, which included the breakdown of the traditional ways of living that had produced stable communities.

While Scott endorsed the Hanoverian succession, his novels appealed to his readers' feeling that something had been lost as well as gained in the course of history. A pastoral way of life, an absolute devotion to the monarchy, and the survival of a hardy individualism all seemed threatened in the first decades of the nineteenth century, as England gathered itself to encounter an age of reform and the Industrial Revolution. Scott's heroes find themselves poised at this transition from the age of chivalry—depicted glowingly in *Ivanhoe* (1819) and *Quentin Durward* (1823), for example—to one that calls for prudent adjustments to the realities of modern life. In this sense, Scott's novels are also criticisms of the very Romanticism he had conjured in his popular books of poetry, such as *Marmion: A Tale of Flodden Field* (1808).

The protagonist of *Waverley*, Edward Waverley, the prototype of Scott's callow heroes, visits the estate of Baron Bradwardine. He is enchanted with his surroundings, which give him ample room to indulge his Romantic imagination. At the same time, however, the novel's narrator presents a more realistic picture of Scottish Highland life—the slovenliness of the villages and a provincialism that does nothing to enrich Waverley's education or to sober his rather wild yearning for adventure. Scott's hero is a Romantic idealist, and the idea of the "lost cause"—the plot to restore the Stuart ruler, Bonnie Prince Charlie, to the throne—appeals to him. The Highlanders are a rugged people who seem to Waverley to

---

WAVERLEY'S HIGHLAND FEAST

In Waverley, *Sir Walter Scott portrays the rustic people of the Scottish Highlands as somewhat savage, while assigning to those Scots of highest rank the dignity he believed inherent to nobility. The Highland feast attended by Waverley presents a literal embodiment of this principle, as the Highlanders at the feast become more rustic and less dignified as a direct function of their distance from their chieftain's place at table.*

The hall, in which the feast was prepared, occupied all the first story of Ian nan Chaistel's original erection, and a huge oaken table extended through its whole length. The apparatus for dinner was simple, even to rudeness, and the company numerous, even to crowding. At the head of the table was the Chief himself, with Edward, and two or three Highland visitors of neighbouring clans; the elders of his own tribe, wadsetters and tacksmen, as they were called, who occupied portions of his estate as mortgagers or lessees, sat next in rank; beneath them, their sons and nephews and foster-brethren; then the officers of the Chief's household, according to their order; and lowest of all, the tenants who actually cultivated the ground. Even beyond this long perspective, Edward might see upon the green, to which a huge pair of folding doors opened, a multitude of Highlanders of a yet inferior description, who, nevertheless, were considered as guests, and had their share both of the countenance of the entertainer and of the cheer of the day. In the distance, and fluctuating round this extreme verge of the banquet, was a changeful group of women, ragged boys and girls, beggars, young and old, large greyhounds, and terriers, and pointers, and curs of low degree; all of whom took some interest, more or less immediate, in the main action of the piece.

Source: Walter Scott, *Waverley: Or, 'Tis Sixty Years Since* (Boston: Estes and Lauriat, 1893), chapter 20.

---

represent a kind of authenticity and austerity lacking in his comfortable and complacent upbringing.

Waverley's nascent politics become intertwined with his personal feelings when he abandons his love for the sedate Rose Bradwardine and becomes enamored of the fiery Flora MacIvor, whom he encounters while visiting Glennaquoich, the Highland hideaway of the rogue Donald Bean Lean. The susceptible Edward becomes involved in the treasonable Jacobite plot, although like all of Scott's protagonists, he is no fanatic but rather an earnest young man carried away by his emotions and looking for excitement. What the impressionable Waverley finds so attractive about these Highland Jacobites is their fervor and dedication to a cause. Their convictions are a welcome antidote to his tepid English upbringing. The Highlander Jacobites are loyal to their chieftains and to the Stuart family, even when the odds are against them. Their moral clarity and courage contrast with the rather insipid character of the civilized life that has formed Waverley.

Scott, however, emphasized Edward's youth and ignorance. The young Waverley has not yet come to grips with an adult world that requires not only bravery but also compromise—and a recognition of when to abandon lost causes. Scott's readers in 1814 knew that Waverley was, in fact, embracing a doomed way of looking at the world that had since been relegated to Great Britain's past. They might have empathized with Waverley (a great many Englishmen felt nostalgic about the Stuarts but did not want them to return to the throne), but they realized his Romantic feelings were a kind of self-indulgence that could not prevail in a world far more complex than the Jacobite Highlanders were willing to acknowledge.

Edward's involvement with the Jacobites leads to the loss of his commission in the British army and to his imprisonment for treason against the Hanoverian government. Rose Bradwardine rescues him from prison, and he rejoins the Jacobite forces. Fortunately for Waverley, at the Battle of Prestonpans (1745; a Jacobite victory), he rescues a Colonel Talbot, who in gratitude secures a pardon for Waverley and the Bradwardines after the decisive Jacobite defeat at the Battle of Culloden (1746).

The pardon provides Waverley with the opportunity to rehabilitate himself—especially after Flora MacIvor, grieving over her brother's execution for treason, rejects Waverley and enters a convent, freeing him to marry the more sensible Rose, whose temperament suits the chastened protagonist. Waverley and Rose then retire to her father's estate, where Waverley busies himself in the work of restoring it.

SIGNIFICANCE

Although *Waverley* appeared decades after the Jacobite rebellions of 1715 and 1745, British readers remained fascinated with the lost cause and admired the vitality of the doomed Highlanders. The world portrayed by Scott was a simpler world of pure moral conviction that made for exciting reading, especially since Scott provided extraordinary descriptions of Highland landscapes, villages, and characters.

To European and American readers, Scott offered a new form of the novel: He combined the *Bildungsroman* (literally, "education novel," a story focusing on a character's psychological growth) with a depiction and interpretation of history. The hallmark of this new form, the historical novel, was that it portrayed real events in the past through the eyes of a fictional hero—a hero of lesser rank and lesser importance than the famous historical figures whom he observed.

Waverley and his later works made Scott not only a best-selling novelist in Europe and America but also a commanding cultural figure. His historical novels provided a rationale for change while honoring the past. Edward Waverley, for example, must move beyond his Jacobite sentimentality, but that sentimentality is given full value. In other words, Scott's readers could revel in the past while simultaneously recognizing the need to abandon it. It is significant that Waverley relinquishes his Jacobite politics but restores Baron Bradwardine's estate. Respect for the past is here fused with the need for renewal. Progress depends on revering yet redeeming the past.

To call Scott's novels historical, however, does not quite do justice to their significance. Novels like *Waverley* were also superb examples of travel writing and sociology. Scott showed how cultural habits and manners evolved over time. His precise descriptions brought to the novel an ability to document the past that inspired such other novelists as James Fenimore Cooper and Honoré de Balzac.

—*Carl Rollyson*

FURTHER READING

Hayden, John O., ed. *Scott: The Critical Heritage*. London: Routledge & Kegan Paul, 1970. Includes the most important reviews of Scott's work, presented in chronological order.

Johnson, Edgar. *Sir Walter Scott: The Great Unknown*. London: Hamish Hamilton, 1970. Hailed as the definitive biography of Scott, this two-volume study is a meticulous study of the writer's life and work; it remains an important guide that has influenced several generations of critics.

Lukács, Georg. *The Historical Novel*. 1937. Reprint. Lincoln: University of Nebraska Press, 1983. Still one of the most important studies of Scott's historical novels. Lukács's work is largely responsible for inventing the historical novel as a distinct and significant literary genre in the eyes of critics.

Millgate, Jane. *Walter Scott: The Making of a Novelist*. Toronto: University of Toronto Press, 1984. The best study of Scott's development as a novelist.

Shaw, Harry E., ed. *Critical Essays on Sir Walter Scott*. New York: Twayne, 1996. An important collection of criticism on Scott.

Sutherland, John. *Walter Scott: A Critical Biography*. London: Basil Blackwell, 1995. This volume's strength is the author's ability to relate Scott's life to his work.

SEE ALSO: 1807-1834: Moore Publishes *Irish Melodies*; 1807-1850: Rise of the Knickerbocker School; 1819-1820: Irving's *Sketch Book* Transforms American Literature; May 8, 1835: Andersen Publishes His First Fairy Tales; 1842: Tennyson Publishes "Morte d'Arthur"; Mar., 1852-Sept., 1853: Dickens Publishes *Bleak House*; Oct. 1-Dec. 15, 1856: Flaubert Publishes *Madame Bovary*; July, 1881-1883: Stevenson Publishes *Treasure Island*.

RELATED ARTICLES in *Great Lives from History: The Nineteenth Century, 1801-1900:* Honoré de Balzac; Lord Byron; Samuel Taylor Coleridge; James Fenimore Cooper; John Keats; Sir Walter Scott; William Wordsworth.

1814-1879
EXPLORATION OF ARABIA

Acting with the encouragement of their governments and upon a variety of personal motives, a growing number of European explorers began penetrating the vast Arabian Peninsula, a region then little known to the outside world.

LOCALE: Arabian Peninsula
CATEGORY: Exploration and discovery

KEY FIGURES

Johann Ludwig Burckhardt (1784-1817), Anglo-Swiss explorer
Sir Richard Francis Burton (1821-1890), British explorer and writer
Charles Montagu Doughty (1843-1926), British explorer and writer
Wilfrid Scawen Blunt (1840-1922), British explorer, husband of Anne Blunt
Anne Isabella Blunt (1837-1917), British explorer, wife of Wilfrid Blunt
William Gifford Palgrave (1826-1888), British army officer and explorer
James Wellsted (1805-1842), British naval officer and explorer
Carlo Guarmani (1828-1884), Italian horse dealer and explorer
George Foster Sadlier (1789-1859), British army officer and explorer

SUMMARY OF EVENT

At the beginning of the nineteenth century, Europeans knew little about Arabia. That Middle Eastern peninsula's extremely harsh climate and desert terrain, coupled with the hostility of its inhabitants toward Christian interlopers, had discouraged contact through more than a millennium. During the eighteenth century, however, the pattern had begun to change, and during the nineteenth century European explorers, acting from a variety of motives, traveled into and sometimes across Arabia. Several Europeans even disguised themselves in order to visit the holy city of Mecca, a pilgrimage to which was required of every able-bodied Muslim man.

During the nineteenth century, Arabia was wracked by turmoil as a result of a movement initiated by eighteenth century Muslim reformer Muḥammad ibn ʿAbd al-Wahhāb. Believing that they were cleansing a religion grown corrupt, the Wahhābīs eventually conquered most of the peninsula, even sacking Mecca and Medina in the first decade of the nineteenth century. However, their success was checked for a time by the actions of Egyptian viceroy Muḥammad ʿAlī Pasha and his son Ibrāhīm Paṣa.

One of the first European explorers to produce an account of the Wahhābīs was Johann Ludwig Burckhardt. Commissioned by a British society known as the African Association, Burckhardt immersed himself in Muslim culture in preparation for an expedition into northwestern Africa. After studying Arabic and making an initial expedition into Jordan, Burckhardt took passage aboard a small ship crossing the Red Sea from Egypt in 1814 as "Sheikh Ibrahim."

Burckhardt reached the Arabian port of Jidda in mid-July, and after numerous difficulties he managed to enter Mecca—which lies inland from Jidda—on September 9, 1814. Although the city was once again under intermittent siege by the Wahhābīs, and although he faced a dire fate should his identity be revealed, Burckhardt enjoyed Mecca. In Medina, however, he contracted plague and was forced to return to Egypt via Yanbuʿ al Baḥr (a port north of Jidda, commonly called Yanbu). He died in Egypt in 1817. Burckhardt's posthumously published books provided Westerners with detailed descriptions of the Muslim holy cities.

Another explorer who reported on the Wahhābīs was George Foster Sadlier, an officer with the British army in

India who landed on the eastern coast of Arabia in June of 1819. Carrying offers of British assistance to Ibrāhīm Paṣa, who had recently defeated Wahhābī forces, Sadlier trailed the victorious commander from the Persian Gulf into the heart of Arabia. He observed the sacked Wahhābī capital of Ad Dirʿīyah and caught up with the Egyptian only at the outskirts of Medina. Proceeding to Yanbu, he became the first European known to have crossed the peninsula.

Some years later, James Wellsted surveyed the southern and southeastern coasts of Arabia as a naval officer with the British East India Company, identifying sites for the coaling stations necessary to refuel steamships. Wellsted visited the island of Socotra, located off the Horn of Africa and part of present-day Yemen, in 1834. The following year, he and fellow officer Charles Cruttenden discovered the ruins of the ancient city of Naqab-al-Hayar (also in present-day Yemen), built by early inhabitants of southern Arabia known as the Himyarites. In 1836, Wellsted's ship put in at the port of Masqat on the Gulf of Oman. Venturing inland, the officer became the first European to see the Rubʿ al-Khali, or

Johann Ludwig Burckhardt in traditional Arab garb. (Hulton Archive/Getty Images)

Empty Quarter (Great Sandy Desert), the desert that covers much of southeastern Arabia.

Like Wellsted, Sir Richard Francis Burton worked for the British East India Company, and like Burckhardt he visited the Muslim holy cities. On leave from the Eighteenth Bombay Light Infantry, he was commissioned by the Royal Geographical Society to explore central and eastern Arabia. After perfecting his command of Arabic, Burton sailed disguised as Afghan doctor "Sheikh Abdullah" from Port Suez in Egypt to Yanbu. After joining a camel caravan, Burton reached Medina on July 25, 1853, and subsequently accompanied another caravan of some fifty thousand pilgrims to Mecca, which he entered on September 11. Like Burckhardt, Burton feared for his life should his disguise be penetrated, but he managed to make sketches of several of the city's shrines. Although his plans to explore the Rubʿ al-Khali were thwarted by illness, he wrote one of the liveliest travel accounts of the century, *Personal Narrative of a Pilgrimage to El-Medinah and Meccah* (1855-1856). Years later, in 1877-1878, Burton would take part in an unsuccessful expedition into Midian, in northwestern Arabia, to hunt for gold.

William Gifford Palgrave reversed Sadlier's feat in 1862-1863. A Roman Catholic priest, Palgrave undertook his travels for a mixture of motives. He wanted to investigate the practicalities of missionary work in Arabia, but he had also agreed to report his findings to French emperor Napoleon III, who hoped to extend French influence in the region. In addition, Palgrave planned to help European horse dealers obtain breeding stock of Arabia's renowned horses. Disguising himself as a Syrian doctor, Palgrave set out from southern Jordan in July, 1862, crossing the An Nafūd desert and entering the central Arabian city of Riyadh. He eventually reached Masqat in 1863.

The Syrian-Italian horse dealer Carlo Guarmani shared several of Palgrave's motives. Under commission from Napoleon III and Italian king Victor Emmanuel II, Guarmani traveled to the central Arabian cities of ʿUnayzah and Ḥāʾil in 1863 to purchase horses and to report on the activities of the Wahhābīs. Borrowing heavily from the writings of those who had preceded him, he produced a colorful narrative still popular among horse enthusiasts.

Charles Montagu Doughty was in many ways the most admirable of Arabia's European explorers. After studying geology at Cambridge University and wandering through Europe, Doughty determined to make his way to Madāʿin Ṣāliḥ, an ancient city in what became

BURCKHARDT'S INTERVIEW WITH MUḤAMMAD ʿALĪ PASHA

Johann Ludwig Burckhardt presented this extract from his journals as an example of one of several meetings that he had with the khedive of Egypt during the course of his travels. The exchange includes allusions to Muḥammad ʿAlī's conflicts with the Mamlūks and Wahhābīs. Burckhardt traveled under the guise of "Sheikh Ibrahim."

Q. Sheikh Ibrahim, I hope you are well.

A. Perfectly well, and most happy to have the honour of seeing you again.

Q. You have travelled much since I saw you at Cairo. How far did you advance into the negro country?

To this question I replied, by giving a short account of my journey in Nubia.

Q. Tell me, how are the Mamelouks at Dongola?

I related what the reader will find in my *Nubian Travels.*

Q. I understand that you treated with two of the Mamelouk Beys at Ibrim; was it so?

The word treated (if the dragoman rightly translated the Turkish word), startled me very much; for the Pasha, while he was in Egypt, had heard that, on my journey towards Dongola, I had met two Mamelouk Beys at Derr; and as he still suspected that the English secretly favoured the Mamelouk interest, he probably thought that I had been the bearer of some message to them from government. I therefore assured him that my meeting with the two Beys was quite accidental that the unpleasant reception which I experienced at Mahass was on their account; and that I entertained fears of their designs against my life. With this explanation the Pasha seemed satisfied.

Q. Let us only settle matters here with the Wahabys, and I shall soon be able to get rid of the Mamelouks. How many soldiers do you think are necessary for subduing the country as far as Senaar?

A. Five hundred men, good troops, might reach that point, but could not keep possession of the country; and the expenses would scarcely be repaid by the booty.

Q. What do those countries afford?

A. Camels and slaves; and, towards Senaar, gold, brought from Abyssinia; but all this is the property of individuals. The chiefs or kings in those countries do not possess any riches.

Q. In what state are the roads from Egypt to Senaar?

A. I described the road between Asouan and Shendy, and from Souakin to the same place.

Q. How did you pass your time among the Blacks?

A. I related some laughable stories, with which he seemed greatly amused.

Q. And now, Sheikh Ibrahim, where do you mean to go?

A. I wish to perform the Hadj, return to Cairo, and then proceed to visit Persia.—(I did not think it advisable to mention my design of returning into the interior of Africa.)

Q. May God render the way smooth before you! but I think it folly and madness to travel so much. What, let me ask, is the result of your last journey?

A. Men's lives are predestined; we all obey our fate. For myself, I enjoy great pleasure in exploring new and unknown countries, and becoming acquainted with different races of people. I am induced to undertake journies by the private satisfaction that travelling affords, and I care little about personal fatigue.

Source: John Lewis Burckhardt, *Travels in Arabia: Comprehending an Account of Those Territories in Hadjaz Which the Mohammedans Regard as Sacred* (London: H. Colburn, 1829), pp. 77-78.

northwestern Saudi Arabia. He studied Arabic in Baghdad but otherwise made few practical preparations. Doughty set out in November, 1876, with a caravan that was expected to pass by the ancient city on its way to Mecca and Medina. A devout Christian, he refused to deny his religion and consequently suffered many indignities and near death. His *Travels in Arabia Deserta* (1888) is a widely admired masterpiece of English literature, drawing on Arabic as well as on the language of classic English authors Geoffrey Chaucer and Edmund Spenser.

Like Guarmani, Anne Isabella Blunt and Wilfrid Scawen Blunt were interested in horses. They traveled through what are now Iraq and Syria in early 1878 and obtained six Arabian mares. Like Doughty, they made no secret of their Christian religion, but their obvious admiration for the way of life of the desert-dwelling nomads, or bedouins, eased their passage. As a result, they also came away with the promise of safe conduct into Arabia itself, joining a caravan in late 1878 and early 1879 into the An Nafūd desert. Thanks to his experiences, Wilfrid was to become one of the earliest champions of Arab nationalism.

SIGNIFICANCE

Europeans boasted of "exploring" Arabia, but, with the possible exception of the Rubʿ al-Khali, Arabians themselves were familiar with most of their own homeland. What Europeans meant was that they were familiarizing themselves with Arabia—no small feat, as the region had long been cut off from European contact. The rise of the Wahhābīs had piqued European curiosity, and the construction of the Suez Canal, which was completed in 1869 and which linked the Mediterranean and Red Seas, increased the strategic interest of the region to Europeans.

Many of Arabia's European explorers acted out of a desire for knowledge, a motive especially evident in the case of polymath Richard Francis Burton. Others acted wholly or partially out of political concerns on behalf of their respective countries or sponsors. Some had commercial expectations, while others acted out of spiritual conviction or a keenly developed sense of adventure. With the exception of Sadlier, who apparently disliked Arabia intensely, all the European explorers seem to have found their travels exhilarating if extraordinarily difficult and dangerous. Among them, Wilfrid Blunt seems to have had the greatest sensitivity to the nationalistic impulses that would dominate the region in the following century.

—*Grove Koger*

FURTHER READING

Burton, Richard F. *Personal Narrative of a Pilgrimage to El-Medinah and Meccah.* London: Longman, Brown, Green & Longmans, 1855-1856. Burton's famous account of his penetration of the Muslim holy cities.

Doughty, Charles Montagu. *Travels in Arabia Deserta.* Cambridge, England: Cambridge University Press, 1888. Doughty's idiosyncratic re-creation of his travels.

Guarmani, Carlo. *Northern Nejd: Journey from Jerusalem to Anaiza in Kasim.* Jerusalem: Press of the Franciscan Fathers, 1866. Guarmani's account of his adventures securing Arabian horses. Usually translated as *Journey from Jerusalem to Northern Najd.*

Lovell, Mary S. *A Rage to Live: A Biography of Richard and Isabel Burton.* New York: W. W. Norton, 1998. A joint biography emphasizing the interaction between the explorer and his wife. Illustrations, map, chronology, bibliography.

Sim, Katharine. *Desert Traveller: The Life of Jean Louis Burckhardt.* London: Gollancz, 1969. Biography of the first important nineteenth century explorer of the region. Illustrations, maps, bibliography.

Taylor, Andrew. *God's Fugitive: The Life of Charles Montagu Doughty.* Hammersmith, Greater London, England: HarperCollins, 1999. Biography recounting Doughty's explorations as well as his literary career. Illustrations, maps, bibliography.

Trench, Richard. *Arabian Travellers.* Topsfield, Mass.: Salem House, 1986. An attractively produced survey supplemented with maps, numerous illustrations, a glossary, and a select bibliography.

SEE ALSO: 19th cent.: Arabic Literary Renaissance; 1811-1818: Egypt Fights the Wahhābīs; Mar. 22, 1812: Burckhardt Discovers Egypt's Abu Simbel; 1822-1874: Exploration of North Africa; 1839-1847: Layard Explores and Excavates Assyrian Ruins; Sept. 12, 1853: Burton Enters Mecca in Disguise.

RELATED ARTICLES in *Great Lives from History: The Nineteenth Century, 1801-1900:* Sir Richard Francis Burton; Napoleon III.

March, 1814
GOYA PAINTS *THIRD OF MAY 1808: EXECUTION OF THE CITIZENS OF MADRID*

One of Goya's best-known and most provocative paintings, the Third of May 1808, *dramatically presents the culmination of two violent days of bloody rioting and civilian executions that led to the Peninsular War between Spain and France.*

LOCALE: Madrid, Spain
CATEGORIES: Art; wars, uprisings, and civil unrest

KEY FIGURES
Francisco de Goya (1746-1828), Spanish painter and printmaker
Joseph Bonaparte (1768-1844), king of Naples, r. 1806-1808, king of Spain, r. 1808-1813, and brother of French emperor Napoleon I
Ferdinand VII (1784-1833), king of Spain, r. 1808, 1813-1833

SUMMARY OF EVENT

A painter to three generations of Spanish kings, Francisco de Goya is regarded as the most important Spanish artist of the late eighteenth and early nineteenth centuries. His 1814 painting *Third of May 1808* stands as one of his most powerful works of art. After King Joseph Bonaparte's departure from Spain in 1813, and the reestablishment of the Spanish regency with the accession of Ferdinand VII, Goya began two canvases in March of 1814 to record the shocking events of early May, 1808, the beginning of the Peninsular War.

Tensions between the French and the Spanish had erupted on May 2, 1808, with riots and subsequent retaliation in the streets of Madrid that left approximately four hundred persons dead. French soldiers arrested and executed scores of Spanish citizens all day and into the early hours of May 3. Bonaparte took the throne slightly more than one month later and reigned as an unwelcome monarch until March 17, 1813. Many Spaniards initially welcomed the French, hoping Napoleon's armies would oust their corrupt government, give Ferdinand VII his birthright as king, and bring much-needed social reform. Their optimism was dashed as war engulfed the country in the bloody wake of May 2 and May 3.

On March 9, 1814, Goya's petition to paint "our glorious insurrection against the tyrant of Europe" was granted by the interim Regency Council, which agreed to pay Goya for supplies and provide a monthly stipend.

Goya's two identically sized canvases, each 266 by 345 centimeters (8 feet, 9 inches by 11 feet, 4 inches), portray the fighting of one day and the gruesome aftermath of the next with broad, loose brushstrokes that heighten the sense of immediacy and action in each scene. With striking visual contrast, Goya cast the Spanish first as heroes overthrowing their French invaders and then as victims summarily punished for insurrection. May 2 is depicted as a colorful, raucous street fight with echoes of artist Peter Paul Rubens and classical battle scenes, while the predawn execution of May 3 is bleak and brutal, reminiscent of popular prints. Although the *Third of May 1808* has garnered the most critical attention, it cannot be understood effectively without considering its companion.

The *Second of May 1808* depicts one of the violent fights between Spanish civilians and French troops that erupted in the streets of Madrid after a group tried to prevent members of the Spanish royal family from abandoning the city for France. Goya chose to paint the disturbance of the Puerta del Sol, the hub of Madrilenian life. Horses, Turkish mercenaries (the much-feared Mamlūks), and Spanish citizens fill the width of the composition, which is dominated by three Mamlūk fighters on horseback, their powerful mounts suggesting the inequality between the two sides. Despite this disparity, the Spaniards appear to have the upper hand. Just right of center, a turbaned figure in golden pants and a dark jacket, dagger at the ready, is thrown off-balance as he is grabbed by the waist from behind. His widened eyes reveal that he knows he is destined to the same gruesome fate as that of his compatriot in front of him, who falls off his horse, arms thrown back, mouth open, and covered in blood. A Spanish partisan prepares to stab the fallen enemy soldier, though only for revenge because his foe is already dead.

Other soldiers, armed with swords and rifles, try to repel the menacing mob, who crowd forward from the background, watching the struggle with rapt attention. Contrary to traditional battle scenes, Goya neither glorifies nor sanitizes the bloody conflict, showing both sides enmeshed in brutal and vicious combat. The bodies of both French and Spanish fighters lie on the ground, their weapons strewn about, still and ineffective.

Goya overlays this horizontal band of activity with two dominant diagonal axes, which intersect between the

Francisco de Goya's Third of May 1808: Execution of the Citizens of Madrid. (Hulton Archive/Getty Images)

mounted mercenaries at the center of the painting. The axis that moves downward from left to right first passes over a struggle between a mounted soldier and standing civilian brightly dressed in a golden jacket and short ivory pants. The axis then moves through the body of the bloodied Mamlūk, whose sprawled legs clad in bright red dominate the center of the composition, and then to a crouching man at the lower right, whose yellow pants, white shirt, and pale green jacket draw attention to his stabbing the dead Mamlūk's horse. The man's figure bears a strong resemblance to the main character of Goya's companion painting, *The Third of May 1808*.

The excitement of *The Second of May 1808*, with its bright colors and sunlit display of Spanish resistance, is notably absent from Goya's second, better-known canvas that hauntingly depicts the events of the following morning. Day has turned to eerily quiet night, as French soldiers execute those caught with arms or suspected of participating in the previous day's riots. Goya again relies on diagonal lines for the organization of his canvas, as two groups of figures recede into space from left fore-

ground to right middle-ground before the distant, sleeping city.

On the painting's right, a tightly knit phalanx of French soldiers lunges forward with rifles raised, their sharp bayonets pointed unnecessarily close to their unarmed captives. Opposite, an inchoate mass of Spanish civilians huddles together before Madrid's Príncipe Pío hill as they await execution. Bloodied corpses fill the left foreground, piled randomly to make vivid the degrading, humiliating, and pitiless nature of their recent deaths. Just behind them, a man kneels on the bloodstained ground, surrounded by those waiting to die. His golden pants and white, long-sleeved shirt draw the viewer's attention. No longer an aggressor, he is now a victim, his empty hands thrown open in a pleading V-shaped gesture of surrender. Many have noted the similarity of his pose to that of the crucified Christ, a reference surely recognizable to the Roman Catholic Spanish audience for whom this image was intended.

The Christ-like figure wears bright colors that suggest purity and innocence, and they contrast starkly with the painting's overall gray, black, and brown tones, further tugging at the viewer's sympathy. The only other light source in the painting is a large lantern; its cold, artificial glare illuminates the cruel, predawn killings. Goya masterfully captures feelings of fear and despair through pose, expression, and gesture as those waiting to die either watch with hands clasped in horror or cover their faces, unable to look at the slaughter before them. Their inexorable destiny is further emphasized by the demeanor of the French soldiers, who stand rigidly with their backs to the viewer, anonymous members of a faceless, soulless killing machine rather than the human race. This contrast echoes the patriotic view of the uprising and subsequent war, in which the Spanish cast the rioters of May 2 as defenseless heroes and innocent, modern-day martyrs and the French as brutal oppressors.

SIGNIFICANCE

Goya's paintings influenced later nineteenth century artists, especially the French painter Édouard Manet (1832-1883), who adapted Goya's composition for his own portrayal of the *Execution of Maximillian* (1867), but it remains unclear if Goya's works were publicly shown during his lifetime. Goya had requested permission to paint these works; he was not commissioned to do so. His receipt of financial support from the interim Spanish government suggests he wanted to complete the work.

The paintings were first publicly acknowledged in 1834, when they were in storage at the El Prado Museum. They might have been displayed as part of a grand triumphal procession celebrating the return of King Ferdinand in 1813. Despite uncertainty over its immediate reception, the *Third of May 1808* is now recognized as a canonical example of Romantic painting that focuses on victimhood, the dramatic presentation of horror and violence, and the appeal to the viewer's compassion, sympathy, and emotion.

—*Anne Leader*

FURTHER READING

Castres, Juares, and Jean-Louis Auge. "Precis de composition: *Le 2 mai 1808* et *Le 3 mai 1808* de Goya." *Connaissance des Arts* 537 (March, 1997): 84-89.

Analyzes Goya's two paintings to determine how he constructed space using calculated attention to symmetry, perspective, and formal harmony.

Gassier, Pierre, and Juliet Wilson. *The Life and Complete Work of Francisco Goya.* 2d ed. New York: Harrison House, 1981. A standard monograph on Goya, first published in French in 1970. Includes a catalog of 1,870 paintings, drawings, and prints, and complemented by 2,148 illustrations.

Hofmann, Werner. *Goya: "To Every Story There Belongs Another."* Translated by David H. Wilson. London: Thames and Hudson, 2003. A well-illustrated monograph on Goya with a short discussion of his wartime works.

Symmons, Sarah. *Goya.* London: Phaidon, 1998. Part of the Art & Ideas: Major Figures series, which provides overviews of individual artists who hold an important place in art history. The reader should see, especially, the chapter "Disasters of War: War and the Artist as Witness."

Thomas, Hugh. *Goya: The "Third of May 1808."* New York: Viking Press, 1972. Part of the Art in Context series, this book places the paintings in their historical, social, cultural, and artistic contexts.

Tomlinson, Janis. *Francisco Goya y Lucientes 1746-1828.* London: Phaidon, 1994. A monograph that argues that Goya was an artist whose works had greater continuity than has been recognized.

_____. *Goya in the Twilight of the Enlightenment.* New Haven, Conn.: Yale University Press, 1992. Traces Goya's career from 1789 to about 1816. Argues that works from this period reflect important political and social changes in Spain and mark a turning point in Goya's career.

SEE ALSO: 1801: Emergence of the Primitives; May 2, 1808: Dos de Mayo Insurrection in Spain; May 2, 1808-Nov., 1813: Peninsular War in Spain; Oct.-Dec., 1830: Delacroix Paints *Liberty Leading the People*.

RELATED ARTICLE in *Great Lives from History: The Nineteenth Century, 1801-1900:* La Saragossa.

Spring, 1814-1830
COMMUNITARIAN EXPERIMENTS AT NEW HARMONY

Two experiments in communitarianism undertaken at New Harmony were responses to rapid modernization and industrialization. They enjoyed mixed success but encouraged other many cooperative living experiments among people yearning for peaceful and simple lives.

ALSO KNOWN AS: Harmonie
LOCALE: New Harmony, Indiana
CATEGORIES: Social issues and reform

KEY FIGURES

George Rapp (1757-1847), founder of the Rappites and first owner of New Harmony
Robert Owen (1771-1858), British industrialist, second owner of New Harmony
Robert Dale Owen (1801-1877), Robert's son, radical freethinker and later congressman and senator
William Maclure (1763-1840), intellectual and partner of Robert Owen
Thomas Say (1787-1834), entomologist and curator of the American Philosophical Society

SUMMARY OF EVENT

Founded in the spring of 1814, New Harmony, Indiana, was a small village located on the banks of the Wabash River in the southwestern part of the state. Its chief historical significance rests in the fact that it was the site of two experiments in communal living that reflected an important phase of U.S. social and cultural history during the pre-Civil War period. The town was founded by George Rapp, a German pietistic Lutheran and dissenter. Rapp believed in communal life and sought a place in the American West where he might implement his social theories in detail. Having already developed a flourishing settlement of German immigrants like himself in Pennsylvania, Rapp sought a new abode that would be more spacious and closer to river transportation for the many goods his followers were producing for sale to the outside world. In the spring of 1814, he purchased more than 24,000 acres of rich alluvial land near the Wabash River south of Vincennes, then the capital of Indiana Territory.

The hamlet of Harmonie, which Rapp named after the town he and his followers were abandoning in Pennsylvania, prospered under the guiding hand of the industrious Germans. Within a few short years, its colonists had placed under cultivation hundreds of acres of rich Indiana bottomlands that included large fruit orchards and an extensive grape vineyard as well as the usual farmlands. In addition, the colonists created an extensive system of small manufactures, including a gristmill, a tannery, a center for weaving, a distillery, and a cotton gin. The Rappites sold their products from farm and factory throughout the entire area and shipped quantities of goods by keelboat and flatboat down the Ohio and Mississippi Rivers to New Orleans. Private property was not allowed, and all property and profits were held in common, with all members of the community sharing equal ownership.

The social practices of the community were as interesting as their economic life was successful. Rapp ruled with an iron hand, and his decisions served as the infallible guide to daily action within the town. Men and women lived in separate dormitories, which were constructed soon after the town was established, and celibacy was strictly enforced for everyone, even married couples. The concept of family was replaced by that of community. Regular churchgoing at the two churches in Harmonie, a flourishing school system, and weekly social activities, lectures, and intellectual discussions made life in the town busy and stimulating.

Although Harmonie was prospering, there is evidence showing that as early as 1821 Rapp was planning to relocate the community. Indiana was not as ideal a place for his experiment as he had hoped, because residents of the surrounding areas were uneducated, uncultured, and resistant to new ways. In his efforts to gain recognition for his communitarian movement, Rapp moved the experiment and founded Economy, Pennsylvania, in May, 1824. Earlier that same year, Rapp had sent agents to England to seek out prospective buyers of the communal property in Indiana.

Robert Owen, the famous Welsh-Scottish philanthropist, social reformer, and textile manufacturer, showed immediate interest in the site, viewing it as an opportunity to acquire a ready-made place to implement his personal theories for social reform. Owen was an atheist who believed that humankind was basically good and, if removed from the corrupting influences of the modern world, might achieve perfection. He wanted to humanize, not reject, industry and had already created a small-scale model milltown in New Lanark, Scotland. Wanting to try his experiments on a larger scale, he personally inspected the lands in Indiana early in 1825 and purchased Harmonie for $95,000, complete with its twenty thousand acres of rich land and 180 buildings capable of providing places of business and housing for at least seven hundred people. Thereafter, he then changed the name of the town to New Harmony, by which it is best known to students of the communitarian movement in the United States.

Owen was a powerful propagandist—a man with a mission to bring reform, theoretical and practical, to the world. He wrote and traveled widely to disseminate his ideas; the purchase of New Harmony gave him a laboratory in which to experiment concretely with his theories. Within a relatively short time following the announcement of the transfer of ownership to Owen, people interested in participating in the new experiment in community living began to arrive in New Harmony. Hampered by overcrowding and by groups of people with a diversity of intentions and points of view, the New Harmony experiment struggled to keep afloat.

Lacking the cohesiveness of the German colonists who had preceded them, Owen and his supporters never experienced the economic success that had been enjoyed by the Rappites. Only the commitment of Owen's considerable personal fortune to the enterprise prevented the operation from going under quickly. At the same time, however, a substantive community life developed at New Harmony under the leadership of Owen and his son Robert Dale Owen. For a time, widely recognized intellectual leaders such as William Maclure, a famous geologist and philanthropist, and entomologist Thomas Say,

the curator of the American Philosophical Society, lived at New Harmony and participated enthusiastically in the bustling life of the experimental community.

After 1830, Robert Owen turned his attention to other reform projects. He had lost much of his fortune in financing the social experiment in Indiana, and his interest declined as debts piled up and small groups broke off from the main community of reformers. The reformist spirit symbolized by Owen continued in New Harmony long after he personally abandoned the project. Experimental efforts in public education initiated by Maclure, and the continued residence in New Harmony throughout the 1830's and 1840's of various sons of the founder, served to remind the outside world of the significant heritage demanding basic changes in society that was emanating from this obscure village on the edge of the civilized world.

New Harmony was technically a community of social equals during both Rapp's and Owen's eras. A primitive form of socialism was attempted there under Owen's leadership, but it never functioned successfully. Nevertheless, this backwoods settlement was symbolic of efforts in many other parts of the United States in the pre-Civil War era to establish small, egalitarian communities that were to serve as beacon lights of reform for American society and for the Western world in general.

Historians of this communitarian movement have identified almost one hundred of these small reformist societies that were established between 1825 and 1860,

Architect's rendering of Robert Owen's vision for his Harmony community. (Library of Congress)

NEW HARMONY CONSTITUTION

Robert Owen's New Harmony constitution, excerpted here, was adopted by the communitarian society in Indiana as a preliminary document.

This Preliminary Society is particularly formed to improve the character and conditions of its own members, and to prepare them to become associates in independent communities, having common property.

The sole objects of these communities will be to procure for all their members the greatest amount of happiness, to secure it to them, and to transmit it to their children to the latest posterity.

Persons of all ages and descriptions, exclusive of persons of color, may become members of the preliminary society. Persons of color may be received as helpers to the society, if necessary; or it may be found useful to prepare and enable them to become associates in communities in Africa, or in some other country, or in some other part of this country. . . .

All members must provide their own household and kitchen furniture, and their small tools, such as spades, hoes, axes, rakes, etc., and they may bring such provisions as they have already provided.

All members shall willingly render their best services for the good of the society, according to their age, experience and capacity, and if inexperienced in that which is requisite for its welfare, they shall apply diligently to acquire the knowledge of some useful occupation or employment.

They shall enter the society with a determination to promote its peace, prosperity and harmony, and, never, under any provocation whatever, act unkindly or unjustly towards, not speak in an unfriendly manner of, any one either in our out of the society. . . .

The members shall receive such advantages, living, comfort and education for their children as this society, and the present state of New Harmony affords.

The living shall be upon equal terms for all, with the exceptions hereafter to be mentioned.

In old age, sickness, or when an accident occurs, care shall be taken of all parties, medical aid shall be afforded, and every attention shown to them that kindness can suggest. . . .

All members shall enjoy complete liberty of conscience, and be afforded every facility for exercising those practices of religious worship and devotion which they may prefer.

Source: Robert Owen, "Constitution of the Preliminary Society of New Harmony" (1825), in *Sources of the Making of the West: Peoples and Cultures*, edited by Katharine J. Lualdi (Boston: Bedford/St. Martin's Press, 2001), vol. 2. pp. 67-70.

rest of society could be depended upon to imitate these models, somewhat more slowly over a period of time, in achieving widespread and desirable social reform.

The two communitarian experiments at New Harmony also reflect the broad historical development of the communitarian ideal. It had its origins in the religious ideology of the radical Protestant sects that appeared at the time of the Reformation—attitudes that were transferred to the United States in the colonial and early national periods by immigrants much like George Rapp and his followers from Germany. By the second quarter of the nineteenth century, however, the communitarian ideal was becoming rapidly secularized. Robert Owen, an atheist, symbolized this second phase in the development of the movement. Those attracted to New Harmony during his regime almost without exception were vitally interested in the social regeneration of humankind but saw no need to connect this concern to specific religious doctrines.

SIGNIFICANCE

The communitarian ideal received the widespread attention it did in the four decades prior to the Civil War (1861-1865) for a variety of reasons. The rapid westward expansion of the frontier during this period left the entire social structure of the country somewhat in flux. This movement seemed to give a special thrust to the work of social reformers, since their efforts might well serve as the basic institutional framework for the nation's foreseeable future as plastic institutions matured into permanence and the frontier era passed into history. The work of the communitarians also seemed attractive because alternative methods of social reform now were thought to be at a dead end. Rampant individualism seemed incapable of answering the need for some sort of collective action to deal with the ills of the nineteenth century.

chiefly in the Midwest. New Harmony, then, clearly served as a prototype for the entire movement. Communitarianism was collectivistic by nature, opposed to revolution, yet impatient with gradualism. The first purpose of the small experimental community was to implement apparently incompatible aims: to achieve immediate, root-and-branch reform by gradual, nonrevolutionary means. A second purpose was to serve as a model of peaceable change for the larger world. Microcosms of society could undergo drastic alterations, and then the

Remembering the bloodlettings of the period from 1789 to 1815 in Europe, observers suggested that revolution had revealed itself to be a dangerous two-edged sword. Moreover, the problems created by industrialization seemed already to have moved beyond gradualism as a means of solving them. Drastic reform was necessary, but drastic reform without revolution. The communitarian approach seemed a model solution to the dilemmas posed by these attitudes. It was voluntaristic, genuinely experimental, deliberately planned, rational, and nonrevolutionary. All these characteristics were immensely appealing to reformers throughout the Western world in the first half of the nineteenth century.

These tendencies, and others, provided a special appeal in the United States during the same period. Faith in the idea that communities can remake their institutions by reasoned choice seemed normal, for that is what the United States had done during the period of constitution-making. The communitarians' belief in social harmony, not class warfare, was also a deeply held American attitude. The experimentation of the communitarians found a ready response in a nation of tinkerers—a nation that was itself thought to be an experiment. Perhaps most important, the group procedure that was at the heart of the communitarian effort reflected a tendency that has revealed itself in many areas of American thought and activity.

Perhaps as a product of the frontier experience and a deeply revered democratic tradition, Americans have always placed great stress upon the development of voluntary associations. From the Mayflower Compact to the establishment of the Tennessee Valley Authority and the encouragement of grassroots community action programs, the belief in voluntary associations has asserted itself. The communitarian movement fits neatly into such an ideological framework.

—*James F. Findlay, Jr., updated by Geralyn Strecker*

FURTHER READING

Arndt, Karl J. R., ed. and comp. *A Documentary History of the Indiana Decade of the New Harmony Society, 1814-1824.* 2 vols. Indianapolis: Indiana Historical Society, 1975-1978. A vast, encyclopedic collection of letters, official documents, maps, and other records of the New Harmony Society taken from its archives. Volume 2 contains a large, detailed map of the community in 1832, with a key identifying buildings.

_____. *George Rapp's Harmony Society, 1785-1847.* Rev. ed. Rutherford, N.J.: Fairleigh Dickinson University Press, 1972. A comprehensive narrative using primary sources from the New Harmony Society's archives to let its members tell their own story. Previous historians of New Harmony did not have access to these sources; therefore, Arndt's work is far more accurate and comprehensive.

_____. *George Rapp's Successors and Material Heirs, 1847-1916.* Rutherford, N.J.: Fairleigh Dickinson University Press, 1971. Continues Arndt's volume that covered 1785-1847.

Bestor, Arthur E. *Backwoods Utopias: The Sectarian Origins and the Owenite Phase of Communitarian Socialism in America, 1663-1829.* 2d ed. Philadelphia: University of Pennsylvania Press, 1970. Situates New Harmony in the greater utopian and communal movement, paying special attention to Robert Owen's involvement with the group.

Donnachie, Ian. *Robert Owen: Owen of New Lanark and New Harmony.* 2000. Reprint. Edinburgh: Birlinn, 2005. Full biography of Owen that describes his work as a factory owner and social reformer.

Lockwood, George B. *The New Harmony Movement.* New York: Augustus M. Kelley, 1970. An early yet still useful work covering the history and sociological implications of the movement through the nineteenth century.

Royle, Edward. *Robert Owen and the Commencement of the Millennium: A Study of the Harmony Community.* New York: St. Martin's Press, 1998. Study of the Harmony community that Robert Owen established in Hampshire, England.

Taylor, Anne. *Visions of Harmony: A Study in Nineteenth-Century Millenarianism.* New York: Oxford University Press, 1987. Offers speculative biographies of George Rapp and Robert Owen, drawing heavily from materials not included in Karl J. R. Arndt's work. Some of Taylor's assertions are not supported by fact, and the work does not provide as much information on millenarianism as the title suggests.

Thompson, Brian. *Devastating Eden: The Search for Utopia in America.* London: HarperCollins, 2004. One of the fullest history to date of both of the experimental communities that were established in Harmony, Indiana. Chronicles the successes and failures of both communities.

SEE ALSO: 1820's-1850's: Social Reform Movement; 1836: Transcendental Movement Arises in New England.

RELATED ARTICLES in *Great Lives from History: The Nineteenth Century, 1801-1900:* Robert Owen; Frances Wright.

FRANCE'S BOURBON DYNASTY IS RESTORED

The restoration of the Bourbon Dynasty to the French throne placed two brothers of Louis XVI on the throne and encouraged them to attempt, with the support of foreign powers and Royalists of the old aristocracy, to reverse the revolutionary process and withdraw basic rights. After sixteen years of growing public dissatisfaction, a new revolution overthrew the Bourbons a second time.

LOCALE: France
CATEGORY: Government and politics

KEY FIGURES

Napoleon I (Napoleon Bonaparte; 1769-1821), emperor of the French, r. 1804-1814, 1815
Charles of Bourbon (1757-1836), count of Artois who became Charles X, king of France, r. 1824-1830
Charles-Ferdinand of Bourbon (duc de Berry; 1778-1820), son of the count of Artois
Comte de Provence (1755-1824), French count who later became Louis XVIII, king of France, r. 1814, 1815-1824
Marie-Louise of Habsburg (1791-1847), Austrian duchess who later became Empress Marie-Louise of France, 1810-1814, 1815
Metternich (1773-1859), Austrian foreign minister
Viscount Castlereagh (Robert Stewart; 1769-1822), British foreign secretary
Talleyrand (1754-1838), French foreign minister

SUMMARY OF EVENT

In October, 1813, after Napoleon Bonaparte was defeated by the combined coalition forces in the Battle of the Nations at Leipzig, he returned to France to consolidate his rule amid growing disillusionment with his regime. Unable to defeat the powerful coalition of Great Britain, Austria, Russia, and Prussia arrayed against France, Napoleon abdicated on April 11, 1814. The victors then debated who should head the French government. The Austrians, represented by Metternich, urged that the toddler son of Napoleon and his Austrian wife, Marie-Louise, be placed upon the French throne under coalition tutelage. The other coalition powers rejected this idea and, under British and then Russian prompting, agreed to restore the family of the guillotined King Louis XVI to rule.

Louis XVI's son had died as a child in prison in 1795 but was acknowledged by Royalists as King Louis XVII.

The succession next passed to the brothers of Louis XVI, first to the childless comte de Provence who became King Louis XVIII, and then to the comte de Artois, who became King Charles X. These two royal brothers had lived in exile in Germany, Russia, and Great Britain for almost twenty-five years. They were out of touch with the mood of the French people and were surrounded by supporters equally out of touch with the developments that had meanwhile transformed France.

Within France, enthusiastic support for the Bourbons was limited to a conservative portion of the old nobility and certain Royalist regions of France, such as the south. Most French people, however, were exhausted by long years of war, and members of the middle class wanted an end to economic disruptions caused by Napoleon's Continental System. The majority were willing to accept the Bourbons if they could provide peace, stability, prosperity, and a guarantee that the basic civil and political freedoms won during the French Revolution (1789) would be preserved.

Louis XVIII, the first brother to become king, personally sought national reconciliation through a compromise between revolutionary freedoms and royal authority. The victorious coalition leaders, especially Britain's Viscount Castlereagh, reinforced the French king's inclination toward a moderate constitutional monarchy. The royal charter issued by Louis XVIII on June 14, 1814, was not a constitution in the ordinary sense, but it did establish a government with parliamentary representation, a right to vote limited to the 1 percent of the wealthiest Frenchmen, and great powers for the Crown. Basic civil rights were guaranteed; these included equality before the law, due process of law, freedom of religious conscience, and relative freedom of speech and press.

Louis's appointment of Talleyrand, a former revolutionary and Bonapartist, as his foreign minister symbolized the new king's sincere desire for reconciliation. Talleyrand skillfully induced the coalition to grant France generous peace terms in the hope of increasing the king's popularity. The first Treaty of Paris, signed on May 30, 1814, allowed France to retain the boundaries of 1792, which included areas conquered early in the French Revolution, and did not impose a foreign occupation or payment of reparations. It soon became clear, however, that not even all Royalists accepted the king's policies. Extreme conservatives known as Ultraroyalists, or Ultras, criticized his moderation and found support from the comte de Artois. The Ultras demanded an "alliance of Throne and Altar" and revenge upon former revolutionaries. Fear of Ultraroyalism and resentment against foreign intervention motivated many of the French who supported Napoleon when he took advantage of quarrels among the coalition powers negotiating at the Congress of Vienna to escape from his exile on the Mediterranean island of Elba and resume leadership of France.

On March 1, 1815, Napoleon landed in France and began his final "Hundred Days" in power. The coalition powers quickly reunited to oppose the emperor, while the Bourbons fled France once again. Napoleon gambled that a quick victory might bring a peace settlement favorable to him. The coalition powers were gathering their forces to oppose him, so he marched into Belgium in the hope of success, only to be beaten at Waterloo in June,

Napoleon I signing his abdication at Fontainbleau. (R. S. Peale/J. A. Hill)

1815. He then retreated into France and abdicated a second time, on June 22. This time, he was exiled to St. Helena, a remote British colony in the South Atlantic from which escape was almost impossible.

Louis XVIII reentered France, this time clearly returned to the throne by virtue of foreign military conquest and against the wishes of many of the French. The second Treaty of Paris of November 20, 1815, imposed harsher terms, punishing the French for following Napoleon, and attempted to reduce French military potential. French territory was reduced to the boundaries of 1789, sizable financial reparations were imposed, and northeastern France was occupied by coalition troops for several years.

The new peace settlement made it more difficult for Louis XVIII to win support inside France. Furthermore, enraged Ultraroyalists took revenge upon revolutionaries, Bonapartists, and sometimes Protestants in the White Terror of June to November, 1815. The death toll mounted into the hundreds, about ten thousand people were arrested and tried for political crimes, and 25 to 30 percent of all government officials (at least fifty thousand) were purged from their positions and replaced by largely inexperienced Royalists. The Ultras scored a triumph in the first election held under the charter, winning a comfortable margin in the Chamber of Deputies. The result of the Hundred Days and the White Terror was to polarize political opinion further in France and for many to confirm the memory of Napoleon as a child of the French Revolution fighting against the oppression of the Bourbons.

Encouraged and supported by his British and Russian allies, the Bourbon king soon dismissed the Ultra Chamber, and a new election led to a much more moderate majority in the parliament. Between 1816 and 1820, Louis XVIII gained support for his moderate policies and political conditions liberalized. France's economy expanded, the war reparations were paid, and the occupation army departed in 1818. France again played a significant, but not dominant, role in European affairs. Although fewer than 1 percent of France's male population could vote or hold elected office, the French people gained experience in confronting issues through parliamentary debate and public discussions in the press, rather than through revolution.

A crisis occurred in 1820 that reversed these positive developments and resulted in repressive

1810's

measures and the ascendancy of the Ultras once more. An embittered Bonapartist assassinated Charles-Ferdinand of Bourbon, the son of the comte de Artois and the only hope of continuing the Bourbon line. The murderer hoped to extinguish the Bourbon Dynasty, and Royalists reacted with outrage. Government policy swung sharply to the right, with new election laws that gave Ultras a parliamentary majority and punished expression of dissenting opinion. Ultras rejoiced when a son was born posthumously to Charles-Ferdinand's wife seven months after he was killed. Louis XVIII, aged and tired of struggle, gave in to the tide of Ultraroyalism; he died in September, 1824.

Artois then ascended the throne as King Charles X and staged an elaborate coronation ceremony that recalled medieval claims of divine right monarchy and absolutism. Ultras joined in a conservative religious organization and encouraged clerical interference in government and intolerance of all who did not share their political views.

SIGNIFICANCE

During sixteen years of restored Bourbon rule, Louis XVIII and Charles X managed to alienate almost every faction in France. Under Charles X, freedom of expression disappeared. The entire middle class and French citizens who had valued the freedoms gained during the French Revolution turned against their Bourbon king. Secret underground opposition groups plotted renewed revolution, since open political dissent had been outlawed. Royal policies could scarcely have seemed better calculated to force together all factions of opinion against the Ultras and to set the stage for the violent confrontation that led to the overthrow of Charles X on July 29, 1830. No Bourbon would ever again sit on the French throne.

—Sharon B. Watkins

FURTHER READING

Alexander, Robert. *Re-Writing the French Revolutionary Tradition: Liberal Opposition and the Fall of the Bourbon Monarchy*. New York: Cambridge University Press, 2003. Expansive exploration of France's revolutionary political tradition between 1815 and 1830 that looks at all classes of French citizens.

Artz, Frederick B. *France Under the Bourbon Restoration, 1814-1830*. New York: Russell & Russell, 1931. Despite its age, this book still provides thorough, balanced coverage of the people and events that were important through the years of the Bourbon Restoration.

Bertier de Sauvigny, Guillaume de. *The Bourbon Restoration*. Philadelphia: University of Pennsylvania Press, 1966. Detailed study by a French specialist who offers a sympathetic treatment of the Bourbons.

Fraser, Elisabeth A. *Delacroix, Art, and Patrimony in Post-Revolutionary France*. New York: Cambridge University Press, 2004. Examination of the paintings that the French painter Eugène Delacroix created during the years of the Bourbon Restoration in an attempt artistically to reconcile the turmoil of the French Revolution with the events of the Restoration.

Furet, François. *Revolutionary France, 1770-1880*. Translated by Antonia Nevill. Oxford, England: Basil Blackwell, 1992. Written by a leading French historian, this work includes recent interpretations and views the Restoration as a stage in France's transition from medieval monarchy to modern democracy.

Magraw, Roger. *France, 1815-1914: The Bourgeois Century*. New York: Oxford University Press, 1986. The first chapter places the Bourbon Restoration in its context and interprets it primarily as an ill-fated last effort of the old nobility to control France.

Wright, Gordon. *France in Modern Times: From the Enlightenment to the Present*. 5th ed. New York: W. W. Norton, 1995. The chapters dealing with the end of the French Empire and the establishment of the Restoration provide an excellent starting place for those not already familiar with the period.

SEE ALSO: Dec. 2, 1804: Bonaparte Is Crowned Napoleon I; May 2, 1808: Dos de Mayo Insurrection in Spain; Sept. 15, 1814-June 11, 1815: Congress of Vienna; June 18, 1815: Battle of Waterloo; Nov. 20, 1815: Second Peace of Paris; July 2, 1820-Mar., 1821: Neapolitan Revolution; July 29, 1830: July Revolution Deposes Charles X; Oct.-Dec., 1830: Delacroix Paints *Liberty Leading the People*; Feb. 22-June, 1848: Paris Revolution of 1848; Dec. 2, 1852: Louis Napoleon Bonaparte Becomes Emperor of France; Feb. 13, 1871-1875: Third French Republic Is Established.

RELATED ARTICLES in *Great Lives from History: The Nineteenth Century, 1801-1900:* Viscount Castlereagh; Eugène Delacroix; Metternich; Napoleon I; Talleyrand.

August 13, 1814
BRITAIN ACQUIRES THE CAPE COLONY

Great Britain's acquisition of the Cape Colony was part of the peace agreements that followed the Napoleonic Wars and was motivated primarily by Britain's fear of the Cape's falling into French hands. However, the introduction of a permanent British presence in South Africa also set in motion social and political changes that would ultimately lead to the South African War.

ALSO KNOWN AS: Cape of Good Hope
LOCALE: Cape of Good Hope, South Africa
CATEGORIES: Expansion and land acquisition; colonization

KEY FIGURES

Hendrick Fagel (fl. early nineteenth century), Dutch envoy to London
Viscount Castlereagh (Robert Stewart; 1769-1822), British foreign secretary and leader of the House of Commons, 1812-1822
William I (1772-1843), prince of Orange, 1814, and later king of the Netherlands, r. 1815-1840

SUMMARY OF EVENT

Great Britain acquired the Cape Colony by the London Convention of August 13, 1814, between Britain and the Netherlands that became part of the general settlement of Europe after the Napoleonic Wars. The Congress of Vienna of 1815 took cognizance of that convention and many earlier territorial arrangements of the victors in those wars.

The Cape Colony and Ceylon (present Sri Lanka) were the only colonies captured from the Netherlands by the British that were not returned. For example, the far more valuable Dutch East Indies became Dutch again once the Napoleonic Wars were over. The reason for this was that the Netherlands, formerly a French ally by revolutionary coercion, became an enlarged entity designed to serve as a buffer against the prospect of future French aggression. For a time, the region that was later to become Belgium was incorporated into the restored kingdom of the Netherlands. The British did not want to weaken the Netherlands by depriving the reconstituted nation of the heart of its colonial empire.

Britain had been in control of the Cape of Good Hope several years before the London Convention sanctioned the arrangement. Britain first gained control in September, 1795, when an assault by sea and land under Admiral

George Keith Elphinstone, General James Craig, and General Clarke captured the Cape of Good Hope. Those British officers claimed to take the terrritory on behalf of the prince of Orange, who had been driven from the Netherlands by Dutch republican allies of revolutionary France. Actually, they took it as a strategic move in the worldwide struggle between Britain and France. The Cape of Good Hope was a vital stage on the route to India, and Britain was determined that it should not fall into enemy hands. At the Peace of Amiens of 1802, Britain returned the Cape of Good Hope to the Dutch government, which was then known as the Batavian Republic.

After war between Britain and France resumed, the British sent another expedition, under Admiral Popham and General Baird, that retook the Cape in 1806. From that date onward, the Cape Colony, known after 1910 as the Cape Province, was colonized by many British settlers and became a stronghold of British influence in Africa.

Hendrick Fagel negotiated in London in 1814 for the Dutch government, and Robert Stewart, Viscount Castlereagh, represented Britain. The Dutch envoy concentrated on retaining Dutch territory in South America and did not vigorously resist the British claim to hold the Cape of Good Hope. For his part, Castlereagh had to yield to the widespread popular British insistence calling for the retention of the Cape Colony on behalf of the security of British India, as the Cape was a vital revictualing stop on the sea route to India.

A complicated financial arrangement expedited the transfer of the Cape of Good Hope from the Netherlands to Britain. The prince of Orange, who later became King William I of the Netherlands, accepted the arrangement. In sum, Britain paid six million pounds, but only two million pounds went to the Dutch government directly; that sum was to be used to fortify the southern frontier of the enlarged Dutch state against France. Three million pounds was paid to settle a Dutch debt with Russia and one million pounds went to Sweden to settle another obligation.

While the 1814 negotiations between Fagel and Castlereagh progressed, relatively little public discussion about the Cape territory took place. Some commentators regarded the territory as advantageous for trade, others wanted the Cape territory to serve as a base in the struggle to abolish the slave trade, and still others thought it might have potential as a colony. In 1814, nobody knew about the great treasures of diamonds, gold, and rare metals that would later be discovered in the interior of South Africa.

The strategic value of the Cape of Good Hope was well known when Britain captured it, but it was not seen as a great prize for any other reason. The Africans living in the region were regarded as backward, the soil appeared to be poor for agriculture, and the location itself was too remote and too dry to attract many European settlers. The Dutch East India Company had administered the colony since an expedition had arrived at the Cape in 1652 to establish a refreshment station for Dutch ships traveling to the Dutch East Indies, the fabled Spice Islands that were later known as Indonesia. The purpose of Dutch settlement, which was originally concentrated in a compact region within about sixty miles (about one hundred kilometers) of Cape Town, was to replenish long-distance shipping with wine and food. A varied population of Dutch people, detribalized Africans, and slaves developed in the colony. An important component of the population was added when numerous French Protestants, called Huguenots, fled prosecution in their home country and blended with the Dutch population.

Eventually, some Dutch-speaking farmers who felt constrained by company rule broke away and established cattle-raising operations deeper in the interior. They were known as Boers or Trekboers, after the Dutch term for farmers, but eventually preferred to be known as Afrikaners. Their ranches were huge, often around six thousand acres of generally dry grazing land. Their culture was rough and ready and based upon narrow fundamentalist Calvinistic interpretations of the Bible. The Afrikaners saw themselves as a new Chosen People and the black Africans who sought to resist their incursions as heathens who had to make way for God's people. These movements and attitudes marked the beginning of the problem of racial strife in South Africa that the British acquired along with the Cape Colony.

Some Afrikaners who had settled far in the interior had established their own republics before the British took over. One of the British governor's first responsibilities was to realign those distant settlers with the Cape government. Another problem of wars with African states on the eastern frontier was not so easily solved. By 1820, the government was sending British settlers along

Great Britain's acquisition of the Cape Colony was the first step in what became Britain's quest to colonize as much of Africa as possible. During the late nineteenth century, Cecil Rhodes dominated South African politics and helped extend British control into Central Africa. His dream was to build a British "Cape-to-Cairo" railroad. He did not realize that dream but saw the completion of a telegraphic connection between Cape Town and Cairo in 1892, as depicted in this cartoon by Linley Sambourne (1844-1910).

the frontier to act as a buffer between Africans and Afrikaners, but strife continued.

The Afrikaners at the Cape had lost their attachments to the Netherlands and did not resist the British takeover initially. Substantial immigration from the Netherlands had ceased long before the British arrived, and the frontier created a new way of life for the whites at the Cape. Even the Dutch language had evolved away from the mother tongue at the Cape, becoming Afrikaans. Moreover, the ruling Dutch East India Company had long been known as bankrupt, corrupt, restrictive, and exploitative, so its demise was welcomed by the settlers.

214

Attractive British reforms were instituted quickly. Many of the company's economic restrictions were swept away, and government officeholders had to accept salaries instead of taking fees and bribes.

SIGNIFICANCE

The Dutch capitulations to the British in 1795 and 1806 contained no guarantees that Dutch forms of government would be preserved, but the British retained familiar Roman Dutch law and many local institutions and customs as well as the Afrikaans-speaking officials who ran them. The previous experience of the British Empire with preserving French culture in Canada undoubtedly guided British efforts. There was no clamor for British laws and institutions because few British subjects wanted to emigrate to the Cape during the early period of British control.

Nevertheless, at the highest level a very new and distinctly British form of government was imposed. The Cape Colony became one of the first British Crown Colonies—a form of government that the British would later establish throughout their worldwide empire in colonies whose people the British deemed incapable of self-government or, at best, not ready for it. The prerogative of the British crown was not impaired in this form of government, and the Crown Colonies were ruled directly by governors appointed by Britain's prime minister or by the British colonial secretary acting with the prime minister's approval.

Despite these improvements, conflicts between the British administration and the Afrikaners began early. The Afrikaners regarded the British as too lenient toward African societies, too restrictive about frontier expansion, and too supportive of missionary activities. Differences between the British and the Afrikaners would escalate during the 1830's, when large numbers of Afrikaner voortrekkers (migrants) began moving deeper into the interior, where they created new republics. At the end of the nineteenth century, conflicts between the British and the Afrikaner republics would precipitate the South African (Boer) War.

—*Henry G. Weisser*

FURTHER READING

Etherington, Norman. *The Great Treks: The Transformation of Southern Africa, 1815-1854*. Harlow, England: Pearson Education, 2001. Study of the great changes in Afrikaner society after the British acquisition of the Cape, as Afrikaners moved ever farther into the interior.

Giliomee, Hermann. *The Afrikaners: Biography of a People*. Charlottesville: University Press of Virginia, 2003. An evenhanded appraisal of the construction of Afrikaner identity, which took many of its most distinctive forms during the nineteenth century, after the British occupied the Cape.

Nelson, Harold D. *South Africa: A Country Study*. Washington, D.C.: American University, Foreign Area Studies, 1981. Nelson's work has a clear and precise historical chapter on Britain's acquisition of the Cape Colony.

Wilson, Monica, and Leonard Thompson, eds. *South Africa to 1870*. Vol. 1 in *The Oxford History of South Africa*. New York: Oxford University Press, 1969. Reprinted as *A History of South Africa to 1870*. Boulder, Colo.: Westview Press, 1982. This study stresses social history rather than political history and pays special attention to the interrelationships among ethnic groups in South Africa.

SEE ALSO: Sept. 15, 1814-June 11, 1815: Congress of Vienna; c. 1817-1828: Zulu Expansion; 1835: South Africa's Great Trek Begins.
RELATED ARTICLE in *Great Lives from History: The Nineteenth Century, 1801-1900:* Viscount Castlereagh.

September 15, 1814-June 11, 1815
CONGRESS OF VIENNA

The Congress of Vienna settled European political affairs after the twenty-year struggle with Napoleon and ushered in nearly a century of general peace on the Continent.

LOCALE: Vienna, Austria
CATEGORIES: Diplomacy and international relations; wars, uprisings, and civil unrest

KEY FIGURES

Alexander I (1777-1825), czar of Russia, r. 1801-1825
Karl von Hardenberg (1750-1822), chancellor of Prussia
Metternich (1773-1859), Austrian foreign affairs minister
Viscount Castlereagh (Robert Stewart; 1769-1822), British foreign secretary
Talleyrand (1754-1838), French foreign affairs minister
Wilhelmine von Sagan (1781-1839), Metternich's beautiful and strong-willed lover

SUMMARY OF EVENT

On March 10, 1814, one month before the defeat of Napoleon I, France's four major adversaries—Great Britain, Austria, Russia, and Prussia—signed the Treaty of Chaumont. Under this treaty, the four nations agreed to remain allied until a final victory over Napoleon was achieved and then to hold a general European congress to secure the peace. In signing the first Peace of Paris on May 30, 1814, with the restored Bourbon monarchy of France, the four great powers reaffirmed their intention to hold such a congress at Vienna.

From beginning to end, the Congress of Vienna remained almost exclusively a congress of the great powers, with the smaller states being summoned to participate only in the discussion of matters that pertained to them individually. A plenary session of all the powers involved in the Napoleonic Wars was never held.

The problem of the organizational relationship between the great and the small powers, which plagued the diplomats throughout the opening months of the congress, was soon overshadowed by a serious dispute within the ranks of the four primary allies themselves concerning Poland. From the beginning of the first informal discussion in Vienna on September 15, 1814, the four great powers could not agree on the partition of Polish territory.

Czar Alexander I of Russia had been determined for some time to reconstitute the former Polish state as a Russian dependency. Prince Karl von Hardenberg, the Prussian chancellor, agreed to surrender to Alexander the Polish lands that Prussia had acquired during the eighteenth century if the czar would support the Hohenzollern claim to the whole of Saxony. Metternich, the Austrian minister of foreign affairs, and Viscount Castlereagh, the British foreign secretary, naturally regarded the Russian and Prussian demands as serious threats to the balance of power in Europe. Especially disturbing was the possibility that Russia would move deeper into Europe than ever before.

During this crucial period when the fate of post-Napoleonic Europe was being discussed, the major player at the conference, Austrian foreign minister Metternich, was terribly distracted. Although he was a married man with children, he was also an incurable womanizer who in 1814 found himself passionately in love with the beautiful Wilhelmine, duchess of the Germanic province of Sagan. At the same time, however, Wilhelmine, a strong-willed woman who prized her independence, had taken other lovers. When Metternich learned of this, he was devastated. During the fall of 1814, when Metternich needed to concentrate the most on diplomatic issues, he was obsessed with his feelings for Wilhelmine. He found it difficult to concentrate on important matters such as the fate of Poland or the relationship of Prussia and Austria in the context of Germany after Napoleon. Competing foreign ministers, such as Chancellor Hardenburg of Prussia and the shrewd Talleyrand, certainly noticed the Austrian minister's distraction and moved to profit from it.

Only after what has been called Metternich's "six weeks of hell" was Metternich able to put Wilhelmine behind him and turn to the issues of war and peace. After an exchange of letters the affair between them was declared over. It was almost as if a separate peace treaty had been negotiated between sovereign nations. However, Metternich was at last able to move to attend to larger issues.

The dispute within the allied camp was particularly welcomed by Talleyrand, the French minister of foreign affairs, who had been seeking a voice for France at the Congress of Vienna for some time. He now had his opportunity. In December of 1814, he put forward a compromise plan to Castlereagh and Metternich under which

Russia would be offered a reduced Poland and Prussia would be offered a reduced Saxony with some territory in the Rhineland. If the two countries proved to be slow in accepting the compromise, Talleyrand offered an additional plan whereby Austria and Great Britain would ally and resist, by force if necessary, the Russo-Prussian stand. Such an alliance did come into existence on January 3, 1815, but it never mobilized its forces because Prussia and Russia decided to accept a compromise solution based on Talleyrand's suggestion.

In an agreement signed on February 11, 1815, Poland was repartitioned among Austria, Prussia, and Russia. In addition, Prussia received only two-fifths of Saxony, but by way of compensation annexed parts of both the Rhineland and Westphalia. As part of the same agreement, Austria acquired Salzburg, the Tyrol, and territory along the Dalmatian (or Illyrian) coastline. Talleyrand's solution to the Polish question thus enabled the allies to heal the breach in their ranks. Moreover, his diplomacy earned for France a greater role at the Congress of Vienna than it had before, at least until Napoleon's temporary resumption of power in March of 1815.

Despite their preoccupation with Napoleon during the Hundred Days of his restoration during the spring of 1815, the allies and the lesser powers met on June 9 to sign the Final Act of the Congress of Vienna. This treaty encompassed previously concluded bilateral agreements and other measures, together with new arrangements worked out in the congress itself. Most of its provisions can be subordinated under the headings of legitimacy, security, and compensation, which were the three major principles that dominated the congress.

"Legitimacy" involved the restoration of dynasties that had been deposed during the Napoleonic period, including the restoration of the House of Orange to the throne of Holland and Bourbon lines to the thrones of France, Spain, and the kingdom of the Two Sicilies. Under the principle of "security," the states near or adjacent to France were enlarged to forestall any possible future aggression on the part of that country. As a result, Holland received the old Austrian Netherlands, Prussia obtained Rhenish and Westphalian territories, and Switzerland was perpetually neutralized and assigned three additional cantons on the French frontier.

Finally, besides embracing the territorial provisions made for security reasons, the principle of "compensation" included Russia's acquisition of Finland from Sweden, which in turn received Norway from Denmark,

1810's

Conferees at the Congress of Vienna. (Francis R. Niglutsch)

which was punished for having been a staunch Napoleonic ally. Great Britain was compensated with Malta, Ceylon, the Cape of Good Hope colony, and Dutch Guiana (Surinam), among other territories. Austria obtained Salzburg, the Tyrol, the Italian lands of Lombardy and Venetia, and districts along the Dalmatian coast. These lands, together with the accession of lesser Habsburg princedoms in the smaller north-central Italian states, compensated Austria for the surrender of the southern Netherlands to Holland.

The only major part of the settlement that did not fall within the principles enumerated above was the disposition of the Germanies. In place of the old Holy Roman Empire, which had come to an end in 1806, the allies established a confederation of some thirty-nine states under the presidency of Austria. The Diet of the German Confederation comprised diplomats speaking on behalf of their rulers, not of popularly elected representatives. The tradition of Austrian predominance over a coalition of disunified German states was preserved well into the nineteenth century.

SIGNIFICANCE

The Vienna settlement brought about the restoration of a conservative order in Europe. To preserve the arrangement, Austria, Great Britain, Russia, and Prussia signed the Quadruple Alliance later in 1815 to establish the Concert of Europe. They were joined by France in 1818. The Concert of Europe sought to preserve the Vienna settlement for at least twenty years through periodic conferences (several of which were held between 1818 and 1822) to deal with liberal-nationalist challenges to the settlement in Greece, Spain, and the Italian states. In the long run, such tests of the balance of power in Europe brought about the dissolution of the Vienna settlement and the end of the Concert of Europe.

—Edward P. Keleher, updated by Michael Witkoski

FURTHER READING

Alsop, Susan Mary. *The Congress Dances: Vienna, 1814-1815.* New York: Harper & Row, 1984. Provides an excellent account of the role played by the duchess of Sagan and other noblewomen at the conference.

Chapman, Tim. *The Congress of Vienna: Origins, Processes, and Results.* London: Routledge, 1998. Examination of the negotiations conducted at the Congress, describing the historical background for the sessions, the agreements that were reached, and the long-term consequences of these agreements.

Cook, Chris, and John Paxton. *European Political Facts, 1789-1848.* New York: Facts On File, 1981. Helps put the deliberations at Vienna within their larger historical context.

Dwyer, Philip G. *Talleyrand.* London: Longman, 2002. Biography of one of the key figures at the Congress of Vienna. Dwyer portrays Talleyrand as a pragmatic politician who was willing to mediate between various factions to achieve a compromise.

Flenley, Ralph. *Makers of Eighteenth Century Europe.* Reprint. Freeport, N.Y.: Books for Libraries Press, 1970. A reprint of the 1927 edition, this volume provides a good, traditional account of the diplomatic maneuvers at the event.

Klimenko, Michael. *Alexander I, Emperor of Russia: A Reappraisal.* Tenafly, N.J.: Hermitage, 2002. Full-length study of the czar by a specialist in Russian history.

McGuigan, Dorothy Gies. *Metternich and the Duchess: The Public and Private Lives at the Congress of Vienna.* Garden City, N.Y.: Doubleday, 1975. A thorough examination of the pivotal role Wilhelmine played during the Congress.

Nicholson, Harold. *The Congress of Vienna: A Study in Allied Unity, 1812-1822.* 1945. Reprint. New York: Grove Press, 2000. A reprint of the classic study in which Nicholson provides a comprehensive narrative of the negotiations at the Congress and the power struggle among Castlereagh and other participants.

Sauvigny, Guillaume. "Congress of Vienna." In *Historical Dictionary of France from the 1815 Restoration to the Second Empire,* edited by Edgar Newman. New York: Greenwood Press, 1985. A brief but informative overview of the diplomatic initiative that reshaped Europe for three generations.

SEE ALSO: Apr. 11, 1814-July 29, 1830: France's Bourbon Dynasty Is Restored; Aug. 13, 1814: Britain Acquires the Cape Colony; Feb. 17, 1815: Treaty of Ghent Takes Effect; June 8-9, 1815: Organization of the German Confederation; June 18, 1815: Battle of Waterloo; Nov. 20, 1815: Second Peace of Paris; July 2, 1820-Mar., 1821: Neapolitan Revolution; Oct. 20-30, 1822: Great Britain Withdraws from the Concert of Europe.

RELATED ARTICLES in *Great Lives from History: The Nineteenth Century, 1801-1900:* Alexander I; Viscount Castlereagh; Karl von Hardenberg; Metternich; Napoleon I; Talleyrand.

December 15, 1814-January 5, 1815
HARTFORD CONVENTION

Sectional divisions in the United States highlighted by the War of 1812 resulted in proposals by New England Federalists to amend the U.S. Constitution and preserve the union.

LOCALE: Hartford, Connecticut
CATEGORY: Government and politics

KEY FIGURES

George Cabot (1752-1823), Massachusetts Federalist
John Lowell (1769-1840), radical member of the extremist faction in the Federalist Party
James Madison (1751-1836), president of the United States, 1809-1817
Harrison Gray Otis (1765-1848), Massachusetts Federalist who conceived the idea of a New England convention
Caleb Strong (1745-1819), governor of Massachusetts and leader of the Federalist opposition to Madison's war policy

SUMMARY OF EVENT

The War of 1812 was never popular among New England Federalists, who called it Mr. Madison's War. New Englanders as a whole recoiled from the war of conquest preached by southerners and westerners, and Federalists were eager to find fault with the Republicans' conduct of the war. By the fall of 1814, sectional and political feelings about the war had reached alarming proportions. The U.S. invasions of Canada had been abortive. British troops had burned Washington in August, 1814. The British army occupied eastern Maine, and enemy ships hovered about the New England coast.

The Madison administration collected war taxes and militia units in New England, but it appeared that a disproportionately small share of money and men was allotted to the defense of that section. New Englanders believed that they were carrying the dual burdens of defending themselves and also supporting the war effort of an incompetent national administration that showed no concern for them. New England had been the most fiercely anti-British part of the new nation during the Revolutionary War (1775-1783). As the momentum of the nation had shifted to the western states, New England had become more conservative in nature, sympathetic to the mercantile and business classes, much as the British had been. Although the New England leaders who opposed the war had so far said or done nothing overtly

treasonous, it was suspected by many that they were using the war as an excuse to consider some sort of reunion with Great Britain. Certainly this was what was hoped by the British press and public when they heard news of the Hartford Convention.

The bad situation threatened to become worse; Congress appeared to be ready to enact a national conscription act, which presumably would remove even more of New England's defenders. The U.S. commissioners at Ghent in Belgium were making no progress toward a negotiated peace, nor were they likely to do so as long as the British enjoyed military success. New England, with good reason, was alarmed.

Fear and frustration showed plainly in the results of the elections of 1814. The Federalists gained large majorities in both state and national offices, and the party leadership interpreted its success as a mandate for action against Mr. Madison's War. The activities of Governor Caleb Strong of Massachusetts demonstrated how extreme such action might become. In November, 1814, Strong offered thinly veiled hints of a separate peace and an alliance to General Sir John Sherbrooke, the British governor of Nova Scotia. Strong's overtures to the enemy came to nothing, but they served as an index of the desperation that infected Strong's section and his party.

This same mood of desperation moved Strong to call the Massachusetts General Court, or legislature, into special session in October, 1814. It responded to the crisis by calling for a convention of delegates from the New England states to meet at Hartford, Connecticut, on December 15. According to Harrison Gray Otis, the nephew of Revolutionary War agitator James Otis and the acknowledged author of the convention plan, the delegates were to discuss ways and means of sectional defense and to take steps to revise the U.S. Constitution to accord with sectional interests.

Three of the five New England states heeded the call of Massachusetts. The legislatures of Connecticut and Rhode Island joined the Bay State in selecting delegations. Vermont and New Hampshire took no official action, but delegates chosen by local and county conventions in those states attended the Hartford sessions. Twenty-six men took part in the convention, and for the most part they were of a moderate temper. Extremists such as John Lowell and former secretary of state Timothy Pickering took no part in the proceedings and privately bewailed the convention's lack of "bold and ardent men." Well aware that a firm but fine line separated political opposition from treason in wartime, the Hartford delegates sought to play a positive, not negative, role.

This moderation was in part necessitated by the fact that New England, in political terms, was not monolithically Federalist at the time. Although the Federalists controlled the state legislatures of all five extant New England states (Maine was still a part of Massachusetts at that time), they did so by rather small margins. The national tide that had elected Thomas Jefferson and James Madison to the presidency had managed to elect a substantial minority of Democratic-Republican legislators to the New England state houses, and these, and the constituents they represented, surely would have opposed any more virulent antiwar or anti-Madison rhetoric.

The Hartford Convention, when assembled and organized, conducted most of its business in committees. George Cabot, the leader of the Massachusetts delegation who had explained that one of his objectives was to prevent "hot-heads from getting into mischief," was probably instrumental in stacking the committees with moderate men. Otis was apparently the guiding spirit of the committees and the author of the report adopted by the convention on January 3, 1815, two days before the the convention closed.

Otis's report, the product of the Hartford Convention, began by stating the mission of the convention, which was to provide for concerted sectional defense and to propose repairs to the Constitution. The report then discussed at length the circumstances that had given rise to the convention. It focused on the disaffection of extremists, and although it opposed radical solutions such as dissolving the union, it plainly implied that the union was in peril. In effect, it contained a mild ultimatum to the Madison administration to listen to the convention and its moderate solutions or be prepared to face the radicals and disunion. There followed a cataloging of the sins of Republican administrations past and present. Finally, the convention offered its solution in the form of a series of seven amendments to the Constitution, requiring that

1. the "three-fifths compromise," which allowed states to count a portion of their chattel population in determining proportionate representation in Congress and the Electoral College, be abolished

2. there be a two-thirds vote of both houses of Congress to admit new states into the union

3. no embargo be imposed for more than sixty days

4. a two-thirds vote of both houses of Congress be required to adopt declarations of war

5. a two-thirds vote of both houses of Congress be required to adopt declarations of commercial nonintercourse acts

6. naturalized citizens be ineligible for federal office, elective or appointive

7. no president might succeed himself, and that no successive presidents might be from the same state.

These provisions exhibited New England's antagonism toward southern and western states and forecast the later sectional divisions that eventually were to lead to the Civil War (1861-1865).

The work of the convention reflected a mixture of sectional complaints and political rancor. Its enemies accused the assembly of treason, yet its temper was moderate. Although the convention addressed itself to some legitimate sectional grievances, it lapsed into the rhetoric of narrow partisanship. Perhaps no individual came closer to the truth than John Adams, who described the Hartford delegates as "intelligent and honest men who had lost touch with reality."

SIGNIFICANCE

The supreme irony of the Hartford Convention was that even while the convention debated, U.S. arms won a great victory at New Orleans, and Great Britain and the United States made peace at Ghent. By the time representatives carrying the report of the Hartford Convention arrived in Washington, the country knew that peace had come. The Hartford Convention had, therefore, lost its point. Such circumstances blunted New England sectionalism, and the Federalist Party seemed treasonous, ludicrous, or both. Its demise was imminent.

—*Emory M. Thomas, updated by Nicholas Birns*

FURTHER READING

Banner, James M. *To the Hartford Convention: The Federalists and the Origins of Party Politics in Massachusetts, 1789-1815.* New York: Alfred A. Knopf, 1970. Places the convention in the context of Federalist Party history.

Buel, Richard, Jr. *America on the Brink: How the Political Struggle Over the War of 1812 Almost Destroyed the Young Republic.* New York: Palgrave Macmillan, 2005. Examines the politics surrounding the War of 1812, with a chapter on the Hartford Convention.

Elkins, Stanley M., and Eric McKitrick. *The Age of Fed-

eralism. New York: Oxford University Press, 1993. A useful discussion of the mentality of Federalism.

Hickey, Donald. *The War of 1812: A Forgotten Conflict.* Urbana: University of Illinois Press, 1989. A reliable summary of the Hartford Convention.

Morison, Samuel Eliot. *Harrison Gray Otis, 1765-1848.* Boston: Houghton Mifflin, 1969. Presents a mildly sympathetic view of the Hartford Convention.

Stagg, J. C. A. *Mr. Madison's War: Politics, Diplomacy, and Warfare in the Early American Republic, 1783-1830.* Princeton, N.J.: Princeton University Press, 1983. Places the convention in the context of the War of 1812 and presents a broad political overview.

Watts, Steven. *The Republic Reborn: War and the Making of Liberal America, 1790-1820.* Baltimore: Johns Hopkins University Press, 1987. Argues that the Hartford Convention opposed the mainstream of U.S. political development.

Wills, Garry. *A Necessary Evil: A History of American Distrust of Government.* Reprint. 1999. New York: Simon & Schuster, 2002. A history of political dissent in the United States, with a chapter on the Hartford Convention.

SEE ALSO: June 18, 1812-Dec. 24, 1814: War of 1812; c. 1815-1830: Westward American Migration Begins; Feb. 17, 1815: Treaty of Ghent Takes Effect.

RELATED ARTICLES in *Great Lives from History: The Nineteenth Century, 1801-1900:* John Quincy Adams; John C. Calhoun; Henry Clay; William Henry Harrison; James Monroe; Martin Van Buren; Daniel Webster.

1810's

---

c. 1815-1830
WESTWARD AMERICAN MIGRATION BEGINS

The early migration of American settlers to west of the Appalachian Mountains advanced American industrialization, increased a growing trend toward sectionalism, and ultimately devastated Native American populations.

LOCALE: Old Northwest and trans-Appalachian West
CATEGORIES: Immigration; expansion and land acquisition; transportation

KEY FIGURES
Meriwether Lewis (1774-1809) and
William Clark (1770-1838), leaders of the expedition commissioned to explore the Louisiana Purchase lands

SUMMARY OF EVENT

One of the great developments in the decade that followed the end of the War of 1812 was the mass migration of tens of thousands of Euro-Americans into the country west of the Appalachian Mountains. However, the West was not created overnight. Even before the American Revolution (1775-1783), American colonists had moved into the middle and upper Ohio River Valley. In 1775, Daniel Boone and thirty axmen blazed the Wilderness Road through the Cumberland Gap and founded the Kentucky settlement of Boonesborough. New settlers followed the Great Valley Road down the Shenandoah Valley to a connection with Boone's route and from there,

continued into Kentucky. To the north, routes such as Braddock's Road and Forbes's Road led to the forks of the Ohio River. By 1790, the settler population west of the mountains already totaled more than 200,000 people, but the movement had only begun.

Several forces stimulated men and women to undertake the arduous journey westward. Not the least of these were policies and programs pursued by the federal government. For example, the Harrison Land Act of 1800, including subsequent amendments in 1804, reduced the minimum amount of land that one settler could purchase to one-quarter section (160 acres) and the minimum price to $1.64 an acre, thus allowing for more individual purchases. The act also granted credit for four years. Under this act, millions of acres of land were disposed of by the United States.

As important as a liberal land policy in encouraging westward migration in the late eighteenth century was the establishment of security along the frontier. This was effected through both diplomatic and military measures. Jay's Treaty was concluded with Great Britain in 1794, and Pinckney's Treaty was concluded with Spain in 1795. Through these treaties, the borders with Canada and Florida were settled.

Around the same time, U.S. military campaigns against Native Americans both north and south of the Ohio River led to a temporary lessening of tensions between Indian communities and Euro-Americans. The

Louisiana Purchase of 1803 and the Adams-Onís Treaty of 1819 gave the United States title to the Gulf Coast west of the Sabine River, while the campaigns of the War of 1812 crushed American Indian military power in the eastern Great Lakes region. The exploratory expedition of Meriwether Lewis and William Clark in 1804-1806 was one of the first steps in opening the new lands to settlement and commercial development. With reasonable security thus obtained, the land proved more attractive to potential settlers.

Changes in technology were crucial to the movement westward. One technological development that stimulated western migration was the invention of the cotton gin in 1793. This device opened up most of the land in the South to the production of upland cotton, which found its major market in the enormous textile industry that began developing in England at the beginning of the nineteenth century. Cheap, fertile land to the west and depleted land to the east caused a great shift of cotton production into the trans-Appalachian area between 1815 and 1835.

Another major factor in westward migration was the improvement in transportation methods. The construc-

tion of the Erie Canal, which was completed in 1825, reduced the cost of travel, particularly affecting the North. Another development that affected all sections was the invention and rapid exploitation of the steamboat. The steamboat enabled the rapid movement of people and goods, which significantly advanced westward expansion. The covered wagon made the movement of families easier, because household goods and farm tools could be transported more efficiently.

All these developments and others gave rise to a new concept of the West. In 1790, about 95 percent of the total American population resided east of the Appalachian Mountains and considered those mountains as their nation's western frontier. By 1820, the number of Americans living west of the Appalachians had risen to about 20 percent of the national population.

Between 1790 and 1812, four western states were admitted to the union: Kentucky in 1792, Tennessee in 1796, Ohio in 1803, and Louisiana in 1812. Afterward, new admissions increased more rapidly—Indiana in 1816, Mississippi in 1817, Illinois in 1818, Alabama in 1819, and Missouri in 1821. Michigan and Arkansas were organized into territories in 1805 and 1819.

SHIFTING U.S. POPULATION CENTERS, 1790-1890

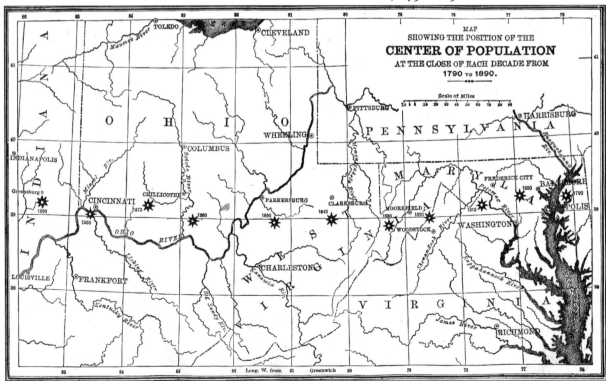

Contemporary print of a pioneer wagon train passing through a mountain range. (Library of Congress)

By 1820, the population of the United States was distributed in a vast triangle with its base along the Atlantic Ocean and its apex roughly at the confluences of the Ohio and Missouri Rivers with the Mississippi River. Along both legs of the triangle, people were spilling over—north to the upper Great Lakes and south to the Gulf of Mexico.

SIGNIFICANCE

Westward migration had momentous social, political, and economic consequences for the nation as a whole. In terms of social disruption, both Native American and African American societies were changed dramatically by the westward movement. By 1812, white settlers were encroaching upon much unceded Indian land. Eventually, several Native American tribes were relocated to Indian Territory west of the Mississippi River, thus changing the political and economic history of a large segment of the U.S. population. Many African American families were split when slaveholding white families moved west, taking their slaves with them.

The political consequences included a geographically changed U.S. Congress and a growing sectionalism. For

example, by 1820 eighteen new senators in Congress were from the West. No longer could the older regions operate in tandem or in opposition to one another without regarding western interests. The West had become a political force, and westerners were not long in taking advantage of the fact that they were being courted by both the North and South. Politics in the United States assumed an increasingly sectional tone after 1815. This sectionalism made political parties even more important than earlier, because they were the sole vehicles through which national interests could contest with sectional interests. Between 1815 and 1830, there was little apparent difference between the objectives and needs of the Northwest and the Southwest. With the assimilation of the Southwest into a greater and solid South by about 1830, the Old Northwest became even more politically significant.

Economically, the early westward migration was of vast import. New land was brought into production, towns were developed, new market patterns were established, and new industries were created. The opening of the West to Euro-American settlement was an incentive to further movement westward, and wave after wave of

1810's

223

migrants passed on, bringing with them newer needs and wants and establishing churches, schools, theaters, and prisons. Whatever was happening politically, the flow into the West of Euro-American and foreign immigrants created that mass consumer demand upon which industry could thrive and out of which the beginnings of a national economy would develop.

—John G. Clark, updated by Judith Boyce DeMark

Further Reading

Billington, Ray A. *Westward Expansion: A History of the American Frontier*. New York: Macmillan, 1967. A classic overview of the migration westward, which includes a section on the early nineteenth century process. Focuses on Euro-American men as the most significant group in the westward migration.

Hurt, Douglas. *The Ohio Frontier: Crucible of the Old Northwest, 1726-1830*. Bloomington: Indiana University Press, 1996. Comprehensive study of the early days of settlement in Ohio.

Limerick, Patricia N. *The Legacy of Conquest: The Unbroken Past of the American West*. New York: W. W. Norton, 1987. A revisionist view of the migration west that includes the experience of minority groups and women in the migratory process.

Riley, Glenda. *The Female Frontier: A Comparative View of Women on the Prairie and the Plains*. Lawrence: University Press of Kansas, 1988. Analyzes the role of women in the westward movement by looking at several areas of frontier settlement, including the farm areas of the early westward migration.

Sanford, William R., and Carl R. Green. *Zebulon Pike: Explorer of the Southwest*. Springfield, N.J.: Enslow, 1996. Popular biography of one of the earliest and most important explorers of the American Southwest.

Slaughter, Thomas P. *Exploring Lewis and Clark: Reflections on Men and Wilderness*. New York: Random House, 2003. One of many studies of the Lewis and Clark expedition published in time for the centenary of the expedition. This book offers a revisionist view of the expedition and tries to correct the many myths and legends that surround it.

Turner, Frederick Jackson. *Rise of the New West, 1819-1829*. 1906. Reprint. New York: Harper & Row, 1968. Remains the basis for study and discussion of the westward migration.

Wade, Richard C. *The Urban Frontier: The Rise of Western Cities, 1790-1830*. Cambridge, Mass.: Harvard University Press, 1959. One of the earliest and most widely read accounts of the significance of urbanization in the westward movement.

See also: May 9, 1803: Louisiana Purchase; May 14, 1804-Sept. 23, 1806: Lewis and Clark Expedition; July 15, 1806-July 1, 1807: Pike Explores the American Southwest; Aug. 17, 1807: Maiden Voyage of the *Clermont*; Apr. 6, 1808: American Fur Company Is Chartered; 1811-1840: Construction of the National Road; Feb. 22, 1819: Adams-Onís Treaty Gives the United States Florida; Oct. 26, 1825: Erie Canal Opens; Jan. 7, 1830: Baltimore and Ohio Railroad Opens; Feb. 4, 1846: Mormons Begin Migration to Utah; May 20, 1862: Lincoln Signs the Homestead Act; July 2, 1862: Lincoln Signs the Morrill Land Grant Act; 1890: U.S. Census Bureau Announces Closing of the Frontier.

Related articles in *Great Lives from History: The Nineteenth Century, 1801-1900:* Johnny Appleseed; Meriwether Lewis and William Clark; Zebulon Pike; Jedediah Smith.

c. 1815-1848
BIEDERMEIER FURNITURE STYLE BECOMES POPULAR

Focused on function and comfort and associated with the pan-German middle class, Biedermeier decorative arts grew out of the French Empire style. Initially a deprecating term, Biedermeier became a descriptor for an entire lifestyle.

LOCALE: Western Europe; United States
CATEGORIES: Art; architecture; cultural and intellectual history

KEY FIGURES

Karl Friedrich Schinkel (1781-1841), Prussian architect and designer
Josef Ulrich Danhauser (1780-1829), German cabinetmaker
Carl Leistler (1805-1857), Viennese furniture maker
Gottlob Samuel Mohn (1789-1825), German enameler
Anton Kothgasser (1769-1851), Austrian enameler
Dominik Biemann (1800-1857), Bohemian engraver
Friedrich Egermann (1777-1864), Bohemian glass inventor
Georg Friedrich Kersting (1785-1847), German painter
Franz Heinrich (1802-1890), German painter
Friedrich Muller (fl. nineteenth century), German doll maker and inventor

SUMMARY OF EVENT

The term *Biedermeier* was not used to describe a style until after 1853, after it had lost general popularity. The tongue-in-cheek origin of the term has been variously attributed to the following three sources: first, to Papa Biedermeier, a self-opinionated buffoonish cartoon character who commented on all topics, including the decorative arts, personifying middle-class taste to readers of the German humor magazine *Fliegenden Blättern* (flying sheets); second, to Gottlieb Biedermeier, a pseudonym for the collaborative work of two or more German poets, including Ludwig Eichrodt (1827-1892), based upon the German word *bieder* (plain, conventional, honest) and the common German surname Meier, a sort of "good-old-boy" image; and third, to Biedermann and Bummel-meier, two cheery comic characters who lampooned middle-class Germans in the 1830's.

Elegant yet simple, and featuring geometric designs that rely on figured veneers rather than the ornate decora-tion of the French Empire style, the less-severe Bieder-meier furniture inspired less-formal home arrangement, usually featuring a piano and knickknacks, all to give a sense of everyday family life. Derived from those classi-cal lines combined with traditional painted peasant furni-ture, Biedermeier suited the more modest size and practi-cal needs of comfortable middle-class homes, which were now set back farther from the street, symbolic of the emphasis on the personal and on privacy.

Karl Friedrich Schinkel and Josef Ulrich Danhauser were key figures in the diffusion of the style. Dan-hauser's workshop (1804-1838) produced innovations such as the sofa and more-comfortable armchairs. Fea-turing coil-spring upholstery, the furniture style was rectangular and sturdy, at first boxy but by 1840 curvy. Chairs had concave or saber-like legs, and tables usually had curves, their supports lyre- or melon-like pedestals and tops usually round. The down-to-earth woods used were farm and orchard, including apple, elm, pear, cherry, and birch, with light finishes, inlays, little or no carving, pressed brass ornaments in imitation of ormolu, painted decoration of motifs from antiquity—animal, floral, or classical vase and urn—or both. However, ma-hogany, rosewood, walnut, maple, sycamore, and poplar were used, generally with inlaid patterns of ebony or black-stained fruitwood.

Biedermeier occasional tables owe much to the de-signs of Carl Leistler. Those tables usually featured richly figured veneers of walnut and Karelian birch, re-strained ebonized or parcel-gilt decoration, and funda-mentally classical designs. They were often mounted or carved with Egyptian motifs and stood on lion's paw "feet." The fall-front secretaire-on-chest was popular, veneered in indigenous woods such as birch, poplar, ma-ple, or fruitwood, a simple classical design relying on figuring of veneers for decorative interest. There was an emphasis on smaller pieces for specific functions: ladies' writing desks, sewing tables, cheval mirrors, bookcases, small tables, pianos, and china cabinets.

Northern Germany saw less color and variety in its furniture, most often featuring mahogany with black horsehair upholstery. The Dutch preferred the restrained elegance of Biedermeier but in lighter woods such as am-boyna, ash, walnut, mahogany, and fruitwoods, with still gently curving, essentially Grecian designs.

Furniture was not the only decorative art associated with Biedermeier. Glass was characterized by elaborate surface decoration, either in a repeating pattern or applied irregularly, emphasizing the chunkiness of glass itself. Gottlob Samuel Mohn had learned from his father a thin, transparent enameling technique for tumblers and beakers. His father was a home painter in Dresden, Germany. In 1811, Mohn went to Vienna, where he met Anton Kothgasser, an Austrian painter at the royal porcelain factory. They became known as enamelers of simple, straight-sided beakers in the Biedermeier style beginning in 1814. One design was the trumpet-shaped beaker with a heavy foot, often facet-cut, called a *Ranftbecher*. Kothgasser specialized in romantic watercolors, landscapes, cityscapes, portraits, and allegorical and neoclassical subjects. Mohn specialized in silhouettes and allegorical subjects but was best known for topographical motifs: palaces, cityscapes, and tourist views, typically with gilded borders. Another design was the *Perlbecher*, a beaker with a closely woven net of multicolored glass beads around the base of a bowl and the goblet bearing portraits of monarchs or notables in sulphide cameos.

Dominik Biemann, a Bohemian glass engraver trained in Prague, worked in Silesia at Sklarzska Poreba glassworks. He was the top engraver of portraits on glass with heavy cutting on base and the gold rim typical of the period. He was one of first to follow the tourist trade, taking commissions. In 1823, Friedrich Egermann, a glassfactory owner in Blottendorf in northern Bohemia, had discovered how to produce hyalith, a dense black glass, and lithyalin, a marbled glass similar to jasper or agate, in colors from brick streaked with green to deep blues and purples. He also discovered how to stain glass with gold, using silver. This stain was frequently used by Kothgasser as a background. Another Bohemian discovery, overlaying or encasing glass vessels in opaque glass of another color and then cutting away broad facets to reveal the contrast with the panels shaped, gilded, painted, or engraved, was basic to Biedermeier-style glass.

Biedermeier style was introduced in the Meissen porcelain factory in Germany in 1830, with pieces similar in form to earlier neoclassical ones but with heavier and less-elaborate decoration, often painted with topographical views. Matthias Niedermayer (d. 1827) was the director of the state ceramic factory in Vienna when, in the 1830's, the neoclassical-restrained eighteenth century shapes were replaced by the heavier, rounded shapes of the Biedermeier style. Biedermeier-like pieces were also produced at the Tucker factory in Philadelphia from 1826 to 1838.

Paintings deemed appropriate for the "quiet happi-

ness of the domestic scene" were produced by Georg Kersting and Franz Heinrich. The most typical Biedermeier painting was the genre picture, which told a common story. Other Biedermeier-style painters included watercolorist Peter Fendi; portrait painters Erwin Speckter, Julius Oldach, and Victor Emil Janssen; and landscape artists Friedrich Wasmann, Christian Morgenstern, Jacob Gensler, and Louis Gurlitt, who painted detailed nature scenes of northern Germany, Scandinavia, and Italy. Only certain subjects could be painted, by law.

Toys, too, were touched by the style. Friedrich Muller, founder of the German Sonneberg doll industry, invented molds to mass-produce the papier-mâché dolls' heads typical of Biedermeier-style dolls. They featured elaborate hairstyles molded in papier-mâché, with features similar to the wooden dolls that preceded them, with painted eyes and eyebrows and black molded hair. The papier-mâché shoulder head was glued to a kid body (made normally from white or pink leather) with usually unjointed limbs of wood or kid, the hands typically spoon-shaped with a separate thumb, and the flat, painted shoes typical of dolls made before 1860. Biedermeier-style doll heads of china were introduced between 1845 and 1860, featuring bald heads with a black dot covered with a curled plait of real hair, fine features, and delicately painted faces. These heads were known as highbrows or highborns.

SIGNIFICANCE

The ideal that the German states would forget political differences and join in a united Germany, part of the patriotic propaganda of the post-War of Liberation (1813) period, had collapsed. Financial reforms and deflationary policies led to a shortage of money and little credit. Merchants had to contend with competition from English manufactured goods, and landowners faced the threat of imported Russian wheat. The Austrian emperor, neither a heroic figure nor in need of other than the practical, inexpensive furniture that was all his treasury allowed, led the move to a simpler style in keeping with the changed conditions. The middle-class emphasis on practicality and family life emulated the emphasis of the royal family. Biedermeier's original mockery could be attributed to the refusal of the German aristocracy and administrative and middle classes to mix; middle-class attempts to emulate the nobility led to social parody. The heroic and classical overtones of the original ideal were replaced by an almost antiheroic style linked to the middle class or bourgeoisie.

Stringent social controls had been established by rulers fearing the diffusion of the democratic ideals of the French Revolution (1789). During this period, known as *Vormärz*, lodges, clubs, and societies were shut down and members imprisoned, so people retired to the relative safety and privacy of their homes and proven friends. Intimate gatherings and dancing became the norm. Whereas Romanticism had focused on the self, Biedermeier would shift to interpersonal relationships. Because this was a period of ever-more innovative technology such as steam-powered transportation and labor-saving household appliances (sewing machines and gas lighting), and because of the introduction of mass production, the individual who was a Biedermeier preferred the personal, homey touch of craftsmen's work to machine-made items.

By 1848, the Biedermeier age was over. Another revolution had taken place in Paris, and so the Viennese demanded similar design reforms, which broke the social strata.

—Debra D. Andrist

FURTHER READING

Chase, Linda, Karl Kemp, and Lois Lammerhuber. *The World of Biedermeier*. New York: Thames and Hudson, 2001. A discussion of the history and uses of the Biedermeier style. Includes photos.

Klein, Rosemary, ed. *Encyclopedia of Antiques*. Stamford, Conn.: Longmeadow Press, 1989. Includes a historical and comparative overview of the Biedermeier style.

Miller, Judith, ed. *Miller's Antiques Encyclopedia*. London: Octopus, 1999. A historical and comparative overview of all Biedermeier decorative arts.

Rak, Jiri. *Biedermeier*. Milan, Italy: Skira, 2001. This work focuses on Biedermeier-style furniture.

SEE ALSO: 1861: Morris Founds Design Firm; 1884: New Guilds Promote the Arts and Crafts Movement.

RELATED ARTICLES in *Great Lives from History: The Nineteenth Century, 1801-1900:* Jacques-Louis David; William Morris; John Ruskin.

1810's

January 8, 1815
BATTLE OF NEW ORLEANS

Although this battle was fought after the formal conclusion of the War of 1812, the American victory over the British helped restore pride in the nation and launched General Andrew Jackson on a career that would lead him to the presidency.

LOCALE: New Orleans, Louisiana
CATEGORY: Wars, uprisings, and civil unrest

KEY FIGURES

Andrew Jackson (1767-1845), commander of the U.S. Military District Number Seven and later president of the United States, 1829-1837

Daniel T. Patterson (d. 1839), American commander of the New Orleans Naval Station

Third Earl of Bathurst (Henry Bathurst; 1762-1834), British secretary for war and the colonies

Alexander Cochrane (1758-1832), British commander of the Royal Navy's New Orleans expedition

Robert Ross (1766-1814), first British general appointed commander of the New Orleans expedition

Edward Pakenham (1778-1815), British general who succeeded Ross

SUMMARY OF EVENT

Through two years, Louisiana lay on the fringe of the southern theater of the War of 1812. The southern campaigns were waged in what was then Spanish Florida, where U.S. troops seized Mobile, and in the Mississippi Territory, where frontiersmen fought Creek Indians. The British naval blockade brought commerce to a standstill at New Orleans, but before late 1814, the war did not otherwise threaten its polyglot population. Engaged in a vast struggle with Napoleon I's France, Great Britain could barely spare enough troops to defend Canada against U.S. attack, and the British War Ministry dismissed early proposals to capture New Orleans.

Napoleon's defeat at Leipzig in October, 1813, allowed the British to begin consideration of large-scale operations against the United States. After Napoleon abdicated in April, 1814, a substantial number of British forces were released from European commitments, and the British government began preparations in earnest to tighten its blockade of the United States, raid the Atlantic coast, and invade northern New York from Canada.

In July, 1814, the British War Ministry decided to attack New Orleans and subsequently appointed Admiral Sir Alexander Cochrane and Major General Robert Ross to command the expedition. The earl of Bathurst, as secretary for war, explained the purposes of the invasion to Ross in September: to gain control over the mouth of the Mississippi River and thereby deprive trans-Appalachian Americans of their link with the sea, and to occupy a valuable land possession whose restoration would improve the terms of peace for Great Britain, or whose cession by the United States could be exacted as the price of peace. Bathurst gave Cochrane and Ross discretion to strike at New Orleans directly from the Gulf of Mexico or overland from Mobile, and he instructed Ross to aid Louisiana's Creoles if they desired to reattach their homeland to Spain. At that time, Cochrane and Ross were raiding the Chesapeake Bay area, but New Orleans was their next target.

Cochrane believed that American Indians, slaves, and pirates who sheltered at Barataria, an island in the swamps off New Orleans, would assist a Gulf coast invasion directed against New Orleans. Operating under orders that Cochrane issued before the War Ministry's decision, his subordinates occupied Spanish Pensacola in August and began to organize and arm Indians and escaped slaves. In early September, the British made overtures to the Baratarians and prepared to attack Mobile; however, that effort came to nothing.

Andrew Jackson was major general of the Tennessee militia in March, 1814, when he defeated the Creeks at Horseshoe Bend and seriously weakened their ability to continue fighting. Two months later, Jackson was appointed federal commander of Military District Number Seven, which included the Mobile-New Orleans area, as well as the U.S. Army in the Southwest. Fully aware of British activities, he went south in August to strengthen Mobile's defenses, to sever remaining British and Spanish connections with the Indians, and to secure the coast against invasion. In mid-September, his forces defeated the British attempt on Mobile, which had been made without the Baratarians, who showed no signs of cooperating. In early November, Jackson expelled both the British and Indians from Pensacola.

General Ross's death near Baltimore in September dealt British fortunes another blow. The ship carrying Major General Sir Edward Pakenham, Ross's successor, was slow in crossing the Atlantic. As a result, Pakenham

Romanticized depiction of General Andrew Jackson leading his troops in the Battle of New Orleans; from a painting by Percy Moran (1862-1935). (Library of Congress)

was not with Cochrane's powerful invasion fleet when it sailed from its Jamaica rendezvous into the Gulf of Mexico in late November or when Cochrane's sailors overcame U.S. gunboats at the mouth of Lake Borgne in December. Cochrane had decided to attack New Orleans from the Gulf of Mexico by sailing through Lake Borgne.

Meanwhile, Jackson arrived in New Orleans on December 1 and proceeded to block all invasion approaches. However, because of a subordinate's negligence, one approach was left open. On December 23, the vanguard of British troops landed, advanced along unprotected Bayou Bienvenue, and emerged from the swamps on the east bank of the Mississippi, fewer than ten miles below the city. Jackson responded quickly. That same night, he attacked the British camp, inflicting large casualties and throwing the invaders off balance. When Pakenham finally arrived on Christmas Day, he found his army in a dead end. On its right were cypress swamps; on its left were two U.S. warships and the Mississippi River; and in front, Jackson's small but growing army was constructing a mud and log breastwork on the narrow plain of Chalmett, barring the way to New Orleans.

While attempting to regain the advantage, the British destroyed one of Commandant Daniel T. Patterson's ships on December 27. During the following days, they suffered serious reverses. U.S. troops turned back a reconnaissance-in-force on December 28, 1814, and won an artillery duel on January 1, 1815, thwarting Pakenham's attempt to breach the breastwork. The only alternative left to the British was a direct assault. Pakenham developed his plan: One large column would attack the U.S. center at the edge of the swamp, a smaller column would assault the U.S. right, and a third would move to support one of the other two columns as the fighting developed. Meanwhile, a small force would attack the weak U.S. positions across the river, and the rest of Pakenham's approximately ten thousand soldiers, some of whom were veterans of the Napoleonic Wars, would form a reserve.

At daybreak, on Sunday, January 8, Pakenham gave the signal to advance. Waiting for the attack was a heterogeneous collection of about five thousand defenders—Louisiana Acadians; Anglo-Saxons; Creoles; free men of color, including Baratarians, Choctaw Indians, and French *émigrés*; Mississippi, Kentucky, and Tennessee militia; and U.S. Marines, regulars, and sailors. Only portions of the line were directly engaged, but the terrific fire from their artillery, muskets, and rifles cut down Pakenham's troops as they advanced through the mist across the rain-soaked field. Pakenham himself was killed while desperately urging his men on. Shortly after-

ward, his crippled army withdrew. The partially successful British attack on the west bank came too late to affect the outcome of the great assault. American casualties totaled only 71 men, of whom only about a dozen were killed. By contrast, the British lost 2,057 men. In the entire campaign that had begun on December 23, British dead totaled more than 2,400 men.

Because of the apparent impregnability of Jackson's lines and a shortage of supplies, the British leaders decided to retreat. The withdrawal went unimpeded, as Jackson decided against allowing his relatively undisciplined and heterogeneous collection of troops to attack what was still a trained army. The American forces thus remained behind their lines until the British had disappeared. Pakenham's forces moved through the swamp to Lake Borgne and then to Pea Island. On January 27, the remainder of the now half-starved British troops were gone from the Mississippi Delta. In a face-saving move, Cochrane attempted to level Fort St. Philip near the Gulf. After failing to accomplish even that, his fleet sailed away to attack Fort Bowyer at Mobile. After its fall, official news of the ratification of the Treaty of Ghent—which had been concluded on December 24, 1814—reached the armies. In mid-March, the British fleet returned to England.

On January 23, Jackson marched into the city of New Orleans with his troops, welcomed as a hero. However, he continued to maintain martial law until the middle of March and required the volunteers to remain under arms in the militia until he received official word of the signing of a treaty. As a consequence, when members of the Louisiana senate listed the officers to whom they extended official thanks, they omitted Jackson's name.

SIGNIFICANCE

The last major battle in the War of 1812, the Battle of New Orleans, was a British tragedy, inasmuch as it had taken place two weeks after the Treaty of Ghent had brought the war to a close. Despite the fact that the bloody engagement did not play a role in the outcome of the war, the Battle of New Orleans made Andrew Jackson a national hero. The battle's consequences stretched beyond Jackson's role. One must address the question of British goals in a war that they certainly provoked, but that was started by the United States. First, the British aimed to limit U.S. settlement beyond the Appalachian Mountains. To do so, they wanted to create an American Indian buffer state in the region beyond Ohio. Their second goal was to assuage the fear of U.S. aggression into Canada, a fear with some merit. Further, by annexing

1810's

Louisiana, they could prevent communication of the west with the sea. Along with Spanish claims to Florida, this would serve to block U.S. expansion.

Pakenham arrived in the United States with instructions to "rescue" Louisiana; he brought with him a complete governmental staff, with himself appointed as governor. Although the Treaty of Ghent was signed, it was not to take effect until ratified by all concerned. In the meantime, Pakenham would have control of Louisiana, an eventuality interrupted by his defeat and death.

—Jeffrey Kimball, updated by Richard Adler

FURTHER READING

Borneman, Walter. *1812: The War That Forged a Nation*. New York: HarperCollins, 2004. History of the War of 1812 that places it in a broad context, arguing that despite internal controversy over the necessity of the war in the United States, its prosecution ultimately united the American states into a national entity.

Brooks, Charles B. *The Siege of New Orleans*. Seattle: University of Washington Press, 1961. Detailed account of events leading up to the Battle of New Orleans.

Elting, John. *Amateurs to Arms! A Military History of the War of 1812*. New York: Da Capo Press, 1995. Military perspective on the War of 1812 that closely ex-

amines its military actions, including the Battle of New Orleans.

Hitsman, J. Mackay, and Donald Graves, eds. *The Incredible War of 1812: A Military History*. Toronto: Robin Brass Studio, 2000. Broad military history of the War of 1812 with a good account of the Battle of New Orleans.

McConnell, Roland C. *Negro Troops of Antebellum Louisiana: A History of the Battalion of Free Men of Color*. Baton Rouge: Louisiana State University Press, 1968. Contains an account of the role played by African Americans in the Battle of New Orleans.

Remini, Robert V. *Andrew Jackson*. 3 vols. Baltimore: Johns Hopkins University Press, 1998. The first volume of this nearly definitive three-volume biography of Jackson covers his military career and role in territorial expansion.

SEE ALSO: May 9, 1803: Louisiana Purchase; Nov. 7, 1811: Battle of Tippecanoe; June 18, 1812-Dec. 24, 1814: War of 1812; July 27, 1813-Aug. 9, 1814: Creek War; Feb. 17, 1815: Treaty of Ghent Takes Effect.

RELATED ARTICLES in *Great Lives from History: The Nineteenth Century, 1801-1900:* Sir Isaac Brock; Andrew Jackson; Napoleon I.

February 17, 1815
TREATY OF GHENT TAKES EFFECT

After more than four months of negotiations, British and American delegates to the Ghent peace commission drafted a mutually acceptable treaty that concluded the unpopular War of 1812 and laid a basis for more amicable British-American relations. To allow time for news of the settlement to be communicated over vast distances, the treaty's terms did not take final effect until nearly two months after they were settled.

ALSO KNOWN AS: Peace of Ghent

LOCALE: Ghent, Austrian Netherlands (now Belgium)

CATEGORIES: Diplomacy and international relations; wars, uprisings, and civil unrest

KEY FIGURES

John Quincy Adams (1767-1848), Massachusetts politician who led the U.S. peace delegation

James A. Bayard (1767-1815),

Henry Clay (1777-1852),

Albert Gallatin (1761-1849), and

Jonathan Russell (1771-1832), members of the U.S. delegation

James Madison (1751-1836), president of the United States, 1809-1817

James Monroe (1758-1831), U.S. secretary of state

Viscount Castlereagh (Robert Stewart; 1769-1822), British foreign secretary

SUMMARY OF EVENT

During the summer of 1814, the chances of the United States and Great Britain finding a negotiated, honorable peace that would end the War of 1812 appeared remote. The United States ostensibly had gone to war to protect its rights on the high seas. President James Madison and Secretary of State James Monroe had repeatedly stated that the recognition of such rights, and particularly an end to British practice of impressing

U.S. sailors into the Royal Navy, was essential to any settlement.

The British had refused to abandon impressment, and the war continued. Militarily, the conflict had been inconclusive. In many ways, the British were in the stronger position at the outset of peace talks. By the summer of 1814, they and their allies had defeated France's Napoleon I. Great Britain could then turn its attention and energies to the war with its former North American colonies. With France subdued and battle-hardened British troops available for North American duty, Britain seemed in a position to end the war by military conquest. Moreover, Americans were divided over what was called "Mr. Madison's War." The Federalist Party and New England generally had opposed the war from its beginning. The Republican administration faced the unpleasant prospects of political humiliation, military defeat, or both, should it continue to pursue its war aims.

Such were the circumstances when U.S. and British commissioners finally met in Ghent on August 9, 1814. The British had agreed to direct meetings as an alternative to mediation by Alexander I, the czar of Russia, and showed no haste to deal with the U.S. upstarts. Ghent was chosen as a convenient, easily accessible site—a pleasant, neutral city in what was then the Austrian Netherlands, soon to be part of the Kingdom of the United Netherlands and a major city in Belgium after that country's independence in 1830.

The U.S. government dispatched five commissioners who represented a broad spectrum of backgrounds to Ghent. John Quincy Adams, a Massachusetts Republican and nominally the head of the delegation, was a staunch nationalist. Henry Clay and Jonathan Russell were "war hawks" from Kentucky and Rhode Island, respectively. James A. Bayard, a Delaware Federalist, and Albert Gallatin, a Pennsylvania Republican, were moderates; the latter, because of his role as peacemaker among his colleagues, emerged as the functional leader of the U.S. delegation at Ghent. The representatives from the United States often quarreled among themselves, but they stood firmly together in the face of their British counterparts.

Adams and Russell arrived in Ghent on June 23. The other U.S. delegates were there by July 6. Because the talks were clearly going to be protracted, the U.S. delegates moved out of their hotel and into the Lovendeghem House in the heart of the city. Far from being the "five lonely Americans," as they have been often described, they became active in local intellectual and cultural life.

Formal negotiations began in an atmosphere of distrust as a result of the U.S. delegates' one-month wait for their British counterparts to arrive. The British delegation included admiralty lawyer Dr. William Adams, Vice-Admiral Lord Gambier, and Henry Goulburn of the Colonial Office. Accompanied by a secretary, Anthony J. Baker, they took up residence in a former Carthusian monastery at Meerhem. Their principal role was not so much to negotiate as to act as the messengers of Viscount Castlereagh, the British foreign secretary.

Although the United States had always tried to pose as the injured party in the conflict, the British dominated the early months of the conference. They proposed the creation of an American Indian buffer state between British and U.S. territories in the American Northwest and asked for a substantial cession of land along the border between Canada and the United States. The U.S. representatives refused. Anticipating Britain's imminent capture of New Orleans, the British delegates then suggested that each party continue to occupy the territory it held at the conclusion of hostilities (*uti possidetis*). Again, the United States refused, holding to its principle of the restoration of territories each side held prior to the outbreak of war (*status quo ante bellum*).

Finally, the constancy and apparent unanimity of the U.S. delegation bore fruit. Throughout the negotiations, the British cabinet had debated whether to conquer or conciliate the United States. Foreseeing greater good in friendship with the United States than in lasting enmity between the kindred nations, Castlereagh led the way toward compromise.

Several factors, some only vaguely relating to the war, confirmed Castlereagh's judgment. While the Ghent negotiations were proceeding, the British were having difficulties at the Congress of Vienna with their recent allies in the Napoleonic Wars. It seemed for a time that a new war with Russia might be imminent. France was restive, portending Napoleon's return from Elba in 1815. At home, the British people were war-weary and growing resentful of heavy taxation. To make matters worse for the British, the United States won a timely victory at Plattsburg on September 11, 1814. The architect of the victory over Napoleon, the duke of Wellington, estimated that a conquest of the United States would come only at a heavy cost of men, money, and time. At that juncture, the British decided to compromise.

The commissioners at Ghent still bargained hard, but the stakes were no longer as great as when the conference opened. On November 11, 1814, the United States pre-

CEASE-FIRE DEADLINES IN THE TREATY OF GHENT

When the treaty was signed on December 24, 1814, it was mutually understood that because of the slowness of long-distance communications, several months would be needed for the news of the peace settlement to reach all the combatants spread around the world. The treaty's second article acknowledged this problem by spelling out when the treaty would take effect in each war zone.

Immediately after the ratifications of this Treaty by both parties as hereinafter mentioned, orders shall be sent to the Armies, Squadrons, Officers, Subjects, and Citizens of the two Powers to cease from all hostilities: and to prevent all causes of complaint which might arise on account of the prizes which may be taken at sea after the said Ratifications of this Treaty, it is reciprocally agreed that all vessels and effects which may be taken after the space of twelve days from the said Ratifications upon all parts of the Coast of North America from the Latitude of twenty three degrees North to the Latitude of fifty degrees North, and as far Eastward in the Atlantic Ocean as the thirty sixth degree of West Longitude from the Meridian of Greenwich, shall be restored on each side:—that the time shall be thirty days in all other parts of the Atlantic Ocean North of the Equinoctial Line or Equator:—and the same time for the British and Irish Channels, for the Gulf of Mexico, and all parts of the West Indies:—forty days for the North Seas for the Baltic, and for all parts of the Mediterranean—sixty days for the Atlantic Ocean South of the Equator as far as the Latitude of the Cape of Good Hope.—ninety days for every other part of the world South of the Equator, and one hundred and twenty days for all other parts of the world without exception.

Spawning a legacy of bad feeling between Great Britain and the United States, which persisted for many years, the war gave Americans a greater feeling of national identity, simultaneously paving the way for the destruction of Native American populations. The war also stimulated the growth of manufacturing and turned Americans increasingly toward domestic matters and away from foreign affairs.

The Treaty of Ghent had a major impact on the relationships of the United States with both Canada and the Native American nations. Future wars between the United States and Britain were averted by the Rush-Bagot Agreement of 1817, which limited armaments to both sides around the Great Lakes. Boundary commissions and subsequent treaties in 1818, 1842, and 1846 fixed most of the long border between the United States and British Canada. The Red River Valley went to the United States; the borders of Alberta, Manitoba, and Saskatchewan were moved south to 49 degrees north latitude. Oregon Territory (Oregon, Washington, and British Columbia) was to be jointly administered by Great Britain and the United States.

Under the terms of the treaty, the United States agreed to exact no retribution and to take no land from the Indians who had fought for the British. However, the defeat of the British and their American Indian allies helped to open the Old Northwest and Southwest to the waves of settlement that would lead to white domination east of the Mississippi and eventually beyond.

At the time, the treaty was, in many ways, seen as a victory for neither side. However, for the United States, there was cause for rejoicing. The United States had stood firm against a great power. Castlereagh and the British had recognized U.S. military potential and decided to court instead of conquer. Most important, the peace that both sides wanted and needed was secure. The treaty provided a steady foundation for an British-American relationship that, over a century, would transform the two nations' foreign policies from suspicious opposition to firm friendship.

—Emory M. Thomas, updated by Randall Fegley

sented a proposal that would restore prewar boundaries. They agreed that the treaty would say nothing about impressment, which they believe would be unnecessary in a post-Napoleonic Europe. The British abandoned their designs on U.S. territory and their desire for an Indian buffer state; however, they still demanded the islands in Passamaquoddy Bay on the coast of Maine, the right of navigation on the Mississippi River, and prohibitions on U.S. rights to dry fish in Newfoundland.

In the end, the participants at Ghent delegated the detailed matters to commissions to resolve after peace had been concluded. The Peace of Ghent provided for a return to the *status quo ante bellum*. Both two sides signed the treaty on Christmas Eve, 1814. Because of the slow communications of the era, the treaty did not take effect until February 17, 1815, after ratification by the governments of both sides. Meanwhile, the British suffered a humiliating defeat in the Battle of New Orleans on January 8, 1815.

SIGNIFICANCE

Sometimes called America's Second War for Independence, the War of 1812 had several important results.

FURTHER READING

Bartlett, Christopher J. "Castlereagh, 1812-1822." In *The Makers of British Policy: From Pitt to Thatcher*, edited by T. G. Otte. New York: Palgrave, 2002. Essay about the diplomacy of the British foreign secretary who directed the British side of the negotiations at Ghent.

Bemis, Samuel Flagg. *John Quincy Adams and the Foundations of American Foreign Policy*. New York: Alfred A. Knopf, 1949. A diplomatic historian presents Adams's role at Ghent as part of a larger triumph in American statecraft.

Borneman, Walter. *1812: The War That Forged a Nation*. New York: HarperCollins, 2004. Study of the War of 1812 that emphasizes the conflict's diplomatic background and argues that despite the internal controversy over the necessity of the war, its prosecution ultimately united the American states into a national entity.

Coles, Harry. *The War of 1812*. Chicago: University of Chicago Press, 1965. Brief but incisive narrative of the war that includes chapters on the treaty providing a penetrating summary of the negotiations.

Elting, John. *Amateurs to Arms! A Military History of the War of 1812*. New York: Da Capo Press, 1995. Detailed military history of the War of 1812, which the author sees as having been an unpopular, badly fought, and largely unnecessary war.

Engelman, Fred. *The Peace of Christmas Eve*. New York: Harcourt, Brace & World, 1962. Written from a U.S. viewpoint, this excellent account of the negotiations and signing of the Treaty of Ghent contains much on the setting, personalities, and interaction related to the event.

Gallatin, James. *The Diary of James Gallatin*. New ed. Westport, Conn.: Greenwood Press, 1979. In this reprint of his diary, James Gallatin, secretary to and son of the U.S. delegate Albert Gallatin, observes the treaty negotiations from behind the scenes.

Horsman, Reginald. *The War of 1812*. New York: Alfred A. Knopf, 1969. General history of the war that treats the Treaty of Ghent in its broader European context.

Perkins, Bradford. *Castlereagh and Adams: England and the United States, 1812-1823*. Berkeley: University of California Press, 1964. Part of a three-volume study of early British-American diplomacy. More than half of this volume is devoted to the diplomacy surrounding the War of 1812.

Vannieuwenhuyse, Johan. *The Treaty of Ghent*. Ghent: Museum Arnold Vander Haeghen-Stadsarchief, 1989. Excellent, brief overview of the Treaty of Ghent by a Belgian scholar who presents details and sources that are frequently overlooked.

1810's

SEE ALSO: June 18, 1812-Dec. 24, 1814: War of 1812; Sept. 15, 1814-June 11, 1815: Congress of Vienna; Dec. 15, 1814-Jan. 5, 1815: Hartford Convention; Jan. 8, 1815: Battle of New Orleans; Feb. 22, 1819: Adams-Onís Treaty Gives the United States Florida; 1838-1839: Aroostook War; Aug. 9, 1842: Webster-Ashburton Treaty Settles Maine's Canadian Border; June 15, 1846: United States Acquires Oregon Territory; May 8, 1871: Treaty of Washington Settles U.S. Claims vs. Britain.

RELATED ARTICLES in *Great Lives from History: The Nineteenth Century, 1801-1900:* John Quincy Adams; Viscount Castlereagh; Henry Clay; Albert Gallatin; James Monroe.

April 5, 1815
TAMBORA VOLCANO BEGINS VIOLENT ERUPTION

The eruption of Indonesia's Tambora volcano, the largest eruption in history at that time, killed an estimated ninety-two thousand people and vented enough material into the stratosphere to cause global cooling and unusually cold summers as far as Europe and North America into the following year.

LOCALE: Island of Sumbawa, Indonesia
CATEGORIES: Disasters; natural disasters; environment and ecology; geology; earth science

KEY FIGURES
Sir Stamford Raffles (1781-1826), British lieutenant governor of Java, 1811-1816, and amateur naturalist
Heinrich Zollinger (1818-1859), Swiss biologist
William Jackson Humphreys (1862-1949), American physicist and meteorologist

SUMMARY OF EVENT

When the Indonesian volcano Tambora erupted at full force in April, 1815, it spewed about 150 cubic kilometers (36 cubic miles) of ash into the stratosphere. It also killed an estimated ninety-two thousand people on the islands of Sumbawa and Lombok. About ten thousand people died during the great eruption, and the remaining deaths resulted from disease and starvation following the cataclysm. The eruption was isolated and far from Western trade routes, ensuring that information about the event would be difficult to come by. However, Sir Stamford Raffles, the British lieutenant governor of Java at the time of the eruption, collected as many accounts of the eruption as possible, providing at least some information on the conditions following the blast.

Tambora occupies the elliptical Sanggar Peninsula on the northwest coast of the island of Sumbawa. Geologically, Sumbawa seems to have been originally an island that eventually connected to the mainland as the volcano grew. Pre-eruption descriptions of the volcano indicate that it may have been as high as 4,000 meters (more than 13,000 feet), which would have made it the highest peak in the East Indies. In modern Indonesia, only peaks in New Guinea are taller than this estimate. The volcano had not erupted in historic times, and later investigations indicate more than five thousand years may have passed since its last eruption. Little evidence exists for highly explosive eruptions before 1815, suggesting that the volcano had only recently entered a new phase in its life cycle.

Mild eruptions began at least one year, and possibly as long as three years, before the great eruption of 1815. Smaller eruptions became more violent on April 5, 1815, and they continued until the main event on April 10. On April 6, explosions reportedly were heard as far as 1,400 kilometers (900 miles) away. The main eruption started when a column of ash and hot gases rose to at least 30 kilometers (nearly 100,000 feet) altitude for about one hour. As the gas pressure beneath the volcano lessened, the column collapsed, sending pyroclastic flows of incandescent gases, ash, and pumice fragments down the mountain in all directions. On April 11 explosions were heard as far away as 2,600 kilometers (1,600 miles). The main phase of the eruption lasted only about twenty-four hours, although ash continued to fall in Java for several days and smaller eruptions continued until July. During the great eruption, the volcano lost more than 1,000 meters (3,000 feet) of its summit, which collapsed inward to form a deep basin, or caldera. It was not until 1847 that Heinrich Zollinger, a biologist, observed the caldera.

High-altitude ejecta from Tambora consisted of ash particles, or finely pulverized rock particles, and microscopic sulfuric acid droplets, or aerosols, which are much more effective than ash at intercepting sunlight and modifying climate. From June 28 to July 2, and again from September 3 to October 7, brilliantly colored sunsets were seen in London. Observers specifically noted that these sunsets differed from normal sunsets because the colors extended higher in the sky and lasted longer than usual. Many reported unusual conditions, including sunspots that were visible to the unaided eye, days where the sun was red well above the horizon, and dimmed stars near the horizon. Reports of unusual atmospheric dimming, or extinction, persisted into 1817. The eclipse of January 9-10, 1816, was noted as extremely dark, with the moon invisible to the unaided eye at totality.

Ice cores later collected in Antarctica and Greenland show the effects of Tambora in the form of unusually high sulfuric acid concentration between 1815 and 1818. If the Greenland concentration is typical of the global average, Tambora must have vented about 200 million tons of sulfuric acid. Calculations of the atmospheric effects of that much sulfuric acid are in general agreement with observations.

Pre-industrial age skies were much clearer than those of the present time. Human activities generate enough dust to reduce average visibility to less than half of what it was in pre-industrial times. Although modern humans take little notice of hazy conditions, haze that was not connected to humid weather conditions was highly unusual in the time before industrialization, and accounts of "dry fog" have proven to be valuable indicators of high altitude volcanic particles. During the year 1816, there were persistent dry fogs over much of the northeastern United States. The same year, however, became notorious for other climatic effects as well. Unusually cold weather in North America and Europe caused 1816 to be known as the "year without a summer."

Contemporary newspapers, letters, and diaries commented on the late spring of 1816. In early June, snow fell across much of northern New England and in Quebec City, and frost killed foliage and crops. In July frost struck again and caused more damage to crops. North of Quebec, lakes remained frozen into July. For the next six weeks the weather improved to near normal, although dry weather added to the stress on farmers. Just as it appeared that a good harvest was possible, an early frost struck in late August, leaving snow in the mountains of New England.

The principal recipients of the wrath of severe summer weather were corn and hay. Many newspaper reports of the time expressed more concern over the availability of fodder for livestock than over the weather's direct effect on people. The crop failure of 1816 meant not only food and fodder shortages but also lack of seed to plant in 1817. Countless farmers left Vermont and Maine to settle newly opened lands in Ohio and Indiana.

In western Europe, there were few reports of weather extremes such as summer snow, but the summer was still cold enough to lead to widespread poor harvests. Europe was just recovering from the economic and physical damage of the Napoleonic Wars and was unprepared for widespread crop failures. For Ireland, a typhus epidemic spread through Europe. Switzerland and France saw famines, inflated prices, and food riots. Areas with adequate food saw protests against requisitioning some of the food supply to starved areas. Potatoes, still a less-than-preferred food for many, were used as an emergency food source.

There are debates, however, about whether or not Tambora's eruption had any role in the global cholera pandemic that began in India in 1816. It has been suggested that the eruption caused famine in India, which in turn led to a local cholera outbreak that spread among a population with lowered resistance, eventually reaching beyond India to become global.

SIGNIFICANCE

During the early twentieth century, American physicist and meteorologist William J. Humphreys was one of the first to document links between volcanic emissions and climate change. He collected sunspot, climatic, and volcanic data to show that atmospheric dust had a more important effect on climate than solar activity, and he suggested a link between the Tambora eruption and the severe and cold weather of 1816.

Tambora's great eruption marks one of the clearest and even most recent examples of how a volcano affects global climates. Conditions similar to those from Tambora, especially dry fogs and unusual cold weather, were found in other records and were used to infer the dates of

TAMBORA IN MODERN INDONESIA

large eruptions in areas that were either unexplored or without written records. Tambora is also a benchmark for computer modeling of the effects of large eruptions, and it was widely cited as a natural analogue for the climatic effects of a so-called nuclear winter that could follow a global nuclear war.

Tambora's eruption also shows how difficult it is to infer environmental cause and effect. Although 1816 was the coldest summer on record in some places around the world, that year does not appear, in other locations, to be dramatically different from earlier cold years without summer snowfalls. The ambiguities in interpreting the effects of the largest eruption in historic times illustrate how difficult it can be to establish cause and effect for more subtle climatic changes.

—*Steven I. Dutch*

FURTHER READING

Botkin, Daniel B., ed. *Forces of Change: A New View of Nature*, Washington, D.C.: National Geographic Society, 2000. Prominent scientists offer perspectives on global change and the processes that shape it, including the role of volcanic eruptions.

Francis, Peter. *Volcanoes: A Planetary Perspective*. New York: Oxford University Press, 1993. Presents a global history of volcanoes and volcanic eruptions.

Self, S., M. R. Rampino, M. S. Newton, and J. A. Wolff. "Volcanological Study of the Great Tambora Eruption of 1815." *Geology* 12 (1989): 659-663. A summary of the eruption of 1815, describing ash layers and the summit collapse.

Stommel, Henry, and Elizabeth Stommel. *Volcano Weather: The Story of 1816, the Year Without a Summer*. Newport, R.I.: Seven Seas Press, 1983. Discussion of the climatic effects of Tambora in the year following the eruption, with emphasis on New England. Includes many newspaper and diary excerpts.

Stothers, Richard B. "The Great Tambora Eruption of 1815 and Its Aftermath." *Science* 224 (June, 1984): 1191-1198. An analysis of worldwide climatic data, with lengthy discussions of the observational evidence for global stratospheric aerosols.

Wade, Nicholas. *The "New York Times" Book of Natural Disasters*. Guilford, Conn.: Lyons Press, 2001. *New York Times* science reporters examine natural disasters, including the effects of ancient, recent, and future volcanic eruptions.

SEE ALSO: July, 1830: Lyell Publishes *Principles of Geology*; Aug. 27, 1883: Krakatoa Volcano Erupts; Apr., 1898-1903: Stratosphere and Troposphere Are Discovered; 1900: Wiechert Invents the Inverted Pendulum Seismograph.

RELATED ARTICLE in *Great Lives from History: The Nineteenth Century, 1801-1900:* Sir Charles Lyell.

June 1, 1815-August, 1817
RED RIVER RAIDS

These small but bloody conflicts between commercial traders and their Native American allies and settlers fighting for control of the fur trade in southern Manitoba were ultimately inconclusive but retarded the development of the region.

LOCALE: Red River Colony, Manitoba, Canada

CATEGORIES: Wars, uprisings, and civil unrest; trade and commerce

KEY FIGURES

Fifth Earl of Selkirk (Thomas Douglas; 1771-1820), founder of the Red River Colony

Miles Macdonell (1769-1828), first governor of Assiniboia, 1811-1815

Robert Semple (1777-1816), second governor of Assiniboia, 1815-1816

SUMMARY OF EVENT

In 1811, Thomas Douglas, fifth earl of Selkirk, bought a large number of shares in the Hudson's Bay Company, England's largest fur-trading company. In return, he received 116,000 square miles of land in the Red River Valley in what is now southern Manitoba, immediately north of the Dakota Territory of the United States. In this huge territory, he planned to build a community called Assiniboia, after the name of a local river. Its colonists were to grow food, mainly potatoes, for Hudson's Bay Company trappers but would not be allowed to trap or trade in furs. Selkirk hoped to recruit farmers suffering from an agricultural depression in his native Scotland to settle the land.

Selkirk sent an advance party, led by Miles Macdonell, a retired army officer from Scotland, to establish an initial base and appointed Macdonell the colony's first governor. Macdonell's party of thirty-six Scottish and Irish farmers arrived on August 29, 1812. They settled near the junction of the Red and Assiniboine Rivers, in what is now Winnipeg. The settlement, called Point Douglas, was only a few miles from a North West Company post known as Fort Gibraltar.

Selkirk's original settlement had great difficulty surviving its first years on the prairie. Only help from fur traders and Metis working for the North West Company, the Hudson's Bay Company's major rival for furs in the region, enabled Macdonell's group to survive. The term Metis, from a French word meaning "mixed," was used to describe people of French-Indian or English-Indian descent. (Sometimes these people were also called the Bois Brulés.) Written with a small *m*, the word refers to all persons of mixed blood, but with a capital *M*, it signifies a distinct cultural and ethnic group living in the region of southern Manitoba. These people were descended from marriages between Native American women and European fishermen on Canada's Atlantic coast during the early seventeenth century. By 1810, the Metis had moved into buffalo country on the northern Great Plains. Many were employed as buffalo hunters by the North West Company to provide provisions for its trappers.

During the second year, eighty more immigrants arrived at the Red River colony. Their presence greatly increased the colony's chance for survival. They started growing wheat, barley, oats, and corn, but potatoes remained their principal crop. Some of the settlers also had brought sheep with them. They settled during the War of 1812, between Great Britain and the United States, while larger British forces were engaging Napoleon's armies in Europe.

Macdonell proved to be an arrogant and unpopular governor, and he engaged in major conflicts with North West Company trappers and Native Americans. As the population of his colony expanded to more than two hundred Europeans in 1814, he sought to prevent food shortages by prohibiting the export of pemmican from his lands. Buffalo hunters made pemmican—a key food source for trappers and Metis—from dried strips of buffalo meat that they pounded into a powder, mixed with melted fat, and stored in buffalo-skin bags.

The governor also angered local trappers and Metis by prohibiting the export of pemmican from Assiniboia after January 8, 1814. This order made it difficult for employees of the North West Company to get food, since U.S. troops had recently recaptured the company's key

Thomas Douglas, fifth earl of Selkirk. (Library and Archives Canada)

trading post of Detroit, from which food supplies for trappers had been sent west. Now both sources of provisions, Assiniboia and Detroit, were cut off. The trappers for the North West Company saw the Pemmican Proclamation as part of a Hudson's Bay Company plot to destroy their business. At a meeting in August, the company's trappers decided to destroy the Red River colony and take back control of the region. To accomplish this goal, the company needed the support of the Metis population of the upper Assiniboine River Valley.

Macdonell angered the Metis by prohibiting them from killing buffalo in his colony. By contrast, the North West Company recognized the Metis as a new nation and accepted their title to lands occupied by Selkirk's colonists. Thus, the North West Company and the Metis joined together to drive out the Assiniboia settlers. In 1815, agents of the North West Company arrested Governor Macdonell and took him to Montreal for trial. He was charged with interfering with Native American rights in what the North West Company claimed was

Indian territory. While the governor stood trial in the east, the Metis attacked the colonists along the Red River, drove them from their homes, and burned their fields.

Only one colonist remained in the community after the attack, but he managed to save some of the wheat crop. When a few new settlers, under the leadership of Colin Robertson, returned in the fall, they harvested enough grain to ensure their survival. A few weeks later, a relief party sent out by Lord Selkirk made it to the Red River. Led by the newly appointed governor, Robert Semple, the settlement began to rebuild. When news of this development reached the headquarters of the North West Company, orders were sent out to destroy the village again. Violence spread into the area again in the spring of 1816. Robertson led a force that took control of the North West Company's Fort Gibraltar in May, giving Assiniboians control of the river.

On June 1, Metis set out on the Assiniboine River in three boats filled with pemmican. When Robertson heard this news, he ordered the abandonment of Fort Gibraltar and left the colony for England. The Metis continued their journey and reached the Red River at Frog Plain, below the Hudson's Bay Company settlement. On June 19, Governor Semple set out with twenty-five colonists to intercept the Metis. At a point in the woods called Seven Oaks, the Metis confronted Semple's band. A Metis man named Boucher rode out to talk with Semple, but after they exchanged a few words, a fight broke out between them and a gun was fired. Firing then began from all sides, but the colonists quickly were surrounded by a much larger force and twenty men, including Semple, were killed. The remaining six men escaped into the woods. Only one Metis was killed. The Seven Oaks Massacre gave the North West Company control of the Red River territory once again.

Despite this setback, Lord Selkirk did not give up on his colony. He hired a band of mercenaries to recapture control. Selkirk led the force himself and in June of 1817 returned to Assiniboia after destroying a North West Company outpost. He quickly signed a treaty with local Metis allowing resettlement of the region. Fields were restored, seeds were planted, and settlers brought in a small crop before winter arrived. New colonists from Scotland's Orkney Islands then arrived, along with a small group of French Canadians. Selkirk provided money for a school and a church, and Roman Catholic and Presbyterian missionaries began to work among the Cree and Assiniboin Indians living along the Red River.

SIGNIFICANCE

The colony seemed to be at peace at last, but the following summer brought further disaster. In August, 1817, a vast swarm of locusts attacked Assiniboia. Most of the potato crop was killed, forcing many farmers to abandon their land. Locusts came again in 1819 and devastated the entire prairie. No food or seed remained in the entire valley. Settlers had to send a party all the way into the Wisconsin Territory to buy seeds for a new potato crop. Lord Selkirk's death in 1820 was another major setback for the community, and it would be several years before farmers grew enough to feed the local population. Buffalo herds continued to provide subsistence during hard times. The Metis hunted the buffalo and sold their hides and meat to the farmers. Gradually, however, the native peoples and the new settlers learned to live together and end their hostilities.

While the Red River colony was becoming a permanent part of the landscape, the right for control of the fur trade was waged in the courts. Shortages of fur-bearing animals east of the Rocky Mountains brought economic problems to both companies. In 1821, the companies merged and ended their fighting. The Seven Oaks Massacre was the worst single incident in the great battle for control of Canada's fur trade.

—Leslie V. Tischauser

FURTHER READING

Brown, Jennifer S. *Strangers in Blood: Fur Trade Families in Indian Country*. 1980. Reprint. Norman: University of Oklahoma Press, 1996. Discusses the development of the Metis people in eastern Canada and the Great Plains from the seventeenth century to the twentieth century.

Brown, Jennifer S. H., Jacqueline Peterson, Robert K. Thomas, and Marcel Giraud, eds. *New Peoples: Being and Becoming Métis in North America*. St. Paul: Minnesota Historical Society, 2001. Part of a series on the history of Manitoba's Indian societies.

Davidson, Gordon Charles. *The North West Company*. New York: Russell & Russell, 1967. A history of the development and expansion of the second largest fur company in North America.

Morton, W. L. *Manitoba: A History*. Toronto: University of Toronto Press, 1967. One chapter is devoted to the importance of the Red River colony. Presents a decidedly old-fashioned view of the métis, referring to them as "halfbreeds" and "savages."

Pritchett, John Perry. *Red River Valley, 1811-1849: A Regional Study*. New Haven, Conn.: Yale University

Press, 1942. Contains an almost minute-by-minute account of the Seven Oaks Massacre.

SEE ALSO: Apr. 6, 1808: American Fur Company Is Chartered; Oct. 11, 1869-July 15, 1870: First Riel Rebellion; c. 1871-1883: Great American Buffalo Slaughter; 1873: Ukrainian Mennonites Begin Settling in Canada; 1876: Canada's Indian Act; Mar. 19, 1885: Second Riel Rebellion Begins.
RELATED ARTICLE in *Great Lives from History: The Nineteenth Century, 1801-1900:* David Thompson.

June 8-9, 1815
ORGANIZATION OF THE GERMAN CONFEDERATION

1810's

The German Confederation replaced the medieval Holy Roman Empire, which had been dissolved by its last emperor in 1806, with a new federal organization of thirty-nine small and medium-sized German states under the leadership of Prussia and Austria.

ALSO KNOWN AS: German Federal Act
LOCALE: Vienna, Austria
CATEGORIES: Government and politics; expansion and land acquisition; diplomacy and international relations

KEY FIGURES
Freiherr vom Stein (1757-1831), German reformer
Metternich (1773-1859), Austrian minister of foreign affairs
Alexander I (1777-1825), czar of Russia, r. 1801-1825
Francis II (1768-1835), Holy Roman Emperor, r. 1792-1806, and emperor of Austria as Francis I, r. 1804-1835
Frederick William III (1770-1840), king of Prussia, r. 1797-1840

SUMMARY OF EVENT
Napoleon I's defeat at Leipzig in October, 1813, by the joint forces of Austria, Prussia, Russia, and Bavaria enabled the people of central Europe to look forward, for the first time in twenty years, to the prospect of peace and independence from French domination. This prospect spawned a multiplicity of plans as to how to reorganize politically the area in central Europe that had formerly constituted the Holy Roman Empire. One of the most indefatigable proposers was Freiherr vom Stein, the author of many reforms that modernized the Prussian state in 1807-1808.

Dismissed from office in Prussia in 1808 at the behest of Napoleon, Stein had then attached himself to the czar and helped put together the alliances that eventually led to Napoleon's defeat. As early as 1812, Stein advanced a plan that envisaged organizing Germany into two parts, one in the north under the leadership of Prussia and one in the south under the leadership of Austria. Such a plan met with opposition from Hanover, which objected to being dominated by Prussia; because the ruler of Hanover happened also to be the king of Great Britain, a major partner in the victorious alliance against Napoleon, Stein's first plan went nowhere.

In 1813, Stein came up with another proposal. He suggested that there be three German states, Prussia, Austria, and a Germany comprising all the rest of the German states but ruled by Austria's Emperor Francis II. This proposal was rejected by Metternich, acting for Austria. Such a plan, Metternich believed, would lead the smaller states to seek alliance with a rejuvenated France, whereas Metternich hoped to create a stable institution in Germany that would defend against any further French aggression. Moreover, all the smaller states in Germany were insistent on the preservation of their sovereignty, conferred on them with the 1813 dissolution of Napoleon's Confederation of the Rhine.

In 1814, the major allies against the French (Russia, Britain, Austria, Prussia) decided that Germany should be organized into a confederation whose members would be the ruling princes of the lesser German states—those, that is, that had survived Napoleon's compression of the more than three hundred petty principalities that had existed prior to 1789. Stein proposed that the confederation have a federal assembly made up of representatives of the constituent states. The confederation would be responsible for such common matters as foreign policy, defense, and the operation of a common legal system. A directory (executive committee) composed of representatives of Austria, Prussia, Bavaria, and Hanover (the four largest German powers) would provide direction for the confederation. This plan, with some modifications, was laid before the German Committee consisting of representatives of Austria, Prussia, Bavaria, Hanover, and Württemberg.

THE GERMAN CONFEDERAL ASSEMBLY

Article 4 of the German Federal Act of 1815, reproduced below, specified the makeup of the Confederal Assembly, the central legislative body of the German Confederation, as well as apportioning power within that body.

Art. 4. The affairs of the Confederation will be managed by a Confederal Assembly in which all members of that same [Confederation] shall cast through their plenipotentiaries—acting in part individually, in part jointly—the following votes, irrespective of their rank:

1) Austria	1 Vote
2) Prussia	1 Vote
3) Bavaria	1 Vote
4) Saxony	1 Vote
5) Hannover	1 Vote
6) Württemberg	1 Vote
7) Baden	1 Vote
8) Electoral Hesse (Churhesse [Hesse-Kassel])	1 Vote
9) Grand Duchy of Hesse (Großherzogtum Hessen [Hesse-Darmstadt])	1 Vote
10) Denmark on behalf of Holstein	1 Vote
11) Netherlands on behalf of the Grand Duchy of Luxemburg	1 Vote
12) The Grand Ducal and Ducal Saxon Houses	1 Vote
13) Brunswick (Braunschweig) and Nassau	1 Vote
14) Meklenburg Schwerin and Meklenburg Strelitz	1 Vote
15) Holstein-Oldenburg, Anhalt and Schwarzburg	1 Vote
16) Hohenzollern, Lichtenstein, Reuss, Schaumburg Lippe, Lippe and Waldeck	1 Vote
17) The free cities of Lübeck, Frankfurth, Bremen, and Hamburg	1 Vote
Total	**17 Votes**

this, he would need to acquire some Polish territories belonging to Prussia and Austria. In the end, he sacrificed getting Polish Austria (the province of Galicia) and settled for less than all of Polish Prussia. To get anything at all from Prussia meant compensating it with something else: An easy offer was the kingdom of Saxony, whose ruler had obstinately supported Napoleon to the bitter end.

Both Britain and Austria wanted to curb Russia's expansion into Europe. In this endeavor, they won the support of the restored Bourbon monarchy of France. As a compromise, Prussia received only half of Saxony (the kingdom's now abject ruler was able to keep half for himself) but was given an assortment of lands in western Germany that before 1789 had been a medley of tiny principalities, some of them ruled by archbishops. These had been converted into a single kingdom by Napoleon, to be ruled by one of his brothers, and now were available for reassignment. Some of the larger of these small principalities were returned to their old rulers, but the bulk of the area went to Prussia, even though they had no territorial connection with the existing kingdom of Prussia. Some other minor territories were redistributed, chiefly between Bavaria and Austria.

After these territorial distributions had been made, it became possible to return to the question of how to organize the thirty-four German states, as well as four free cities—Bremen, Hamburg, Lübeck, and Frankfurt—whose independence was negotiated by Stein. Metternich made common cause with the smaller states, which insisted upon the preservation of their sovereignty. This meant that only a federation, with very limited powers, could be imposed from above.

The German Confederation that finally emerged from the German Committee was a loose federation. Its objective was "the preservation of the external and internal security of Germany and of the independence and inviolability of the individual German states." All states pledged to protect one another from invasion if any land invaded belonged to the old empire or the new confederation. This pledge excluded Austria's Polish, Hungarian, and Italian lands, as well as Prussia's provinces of East Prussia, West Prussia, and Posen. Three foreign monarchs were also parties to the confederation by virtue of their conjoint status as rulers of German states: the British king George III (king of Hanover), the Danish king Frederick VI (duke of Holstein), and king William I of the Netherlands (grand duke of Luxembourg).

Members were not to make war on one another, nor were they to enforce their claims by violence. Instead,

Before negotiations could proceed, however, the question of a future organization of the German states fell victim to great-power politics. Czar Alexander I, conscious of the central role played by Russia in the defeat of Napoleon, wanted to acquire portions of Poland he did not already control in order to create a new kingdom of Poland with himself as its ruler. In order to do

they were to appeal to the Confederal Assembly for an impartial decision. They could make individual alliances, but in time of war they were forbidden to take part in unilateral negotiations or truces and they could not make separate peace settlements. These provisions were clearly intended to prevent a repeat of the Napoleonic ex-

perience, when the French emperor had played off one small German state against another.

The business of the German Confederation was to be managed by the Confederal Assembly, which would meet at Frankfurt and over which Austria was to preside. There were to be two kinds of procedure: the Select

THE GERMAN CONFEDERATION, 1815

Council and the Plenary Council. Routine concerns were to be handled by the Select Council, in which the eleven larger states each had one vote and the remaining twenty-eight states were divided into six curias each with one vote; decisions were to be made by a simple majority vote. The Plenary Council was to decide constitutional and religious questions, and a two-thirds majority was required for any proposal to pass. Major changes demanded unanimity.

The Confederal Assembly was granted extensive powers: It could make war and peace, maintain a federal army, make treaties, exchange ambassadors, and regulate commerce. Without an effective administrative structure, however, it had no means of enforcing its decisions. All member states were to provide representative constitutions, but few complied with this provision; the most notable to do so were Baden and Württemberg.

The German Federal Act was signed on June 8, 1815. It was incorporated into the Final Act of the Congress of Vienna the following day, June 9, 1815, thereby gaining recognition under international law. In this way, the constitution of the German Confederation was placed under the official guarantee of the signatory powers.

SIGNIFICANCE

Although Metternich did not dictate the details of the constitution of the German Confederation, it served his purposes well: A buffer state between Austria and France had been established. Since the Confederal Assembly represented the states and not the people, he could rely on the conservatism of the majority of the states, governed by monarchs primarily concerned with maintaining their sovereignty. For the Habsburg Dynasty it was a more efficient arrangement than the old empire; Habsburg security had been increased without additional expense.

Moreover, despite the ambitions of many German intellectuals, it was clear that the vast majority of the German people still saw themselves as subjects of their local ruler rather than as citizens of a national state. Before a national state could be established, Germany needed to develop as an economic unit; the confederation provided a stable, if immovable, political structure within which that economic development could take place.

—*Christopher J. Kauffman,*
updated by Nancy M. Gordon

FURTHER READING

Hertz, Frederick. *The German Public Mind in the Nineteenth Century.* Translated by Eric Northcott and edited by Frank Eyck. Totowa, N.J.: Rowman & Littlefield, 1975. Contains a chapter, "The German Bund," with a focus on the assorted proposals by Stein and others that preceded the Federal Act.

Holborn, Hajo. *A History of Modern Germany.* 3 vols. New York: Alfred A. Knopf, 1964. Written by the most eminent of the émigré historians of the 1930's, this large work includes the chapter "The Wars of Liberation and the Peace Settlement of Vienna." Holborn describes the roles played by the lesser German states in the shape of the postwar territorial and political arrangements.

John, Michael. "The Napoleonic Legacy and Problems of Restoration in Central Europe: The German Confederation." In *Napoleon's Legacy: Problems of Government in Restoration Europe,* edited by David Laven and Lucy Riall. New York: Berg, 2000. Discusses the German Confederation as a part of Napoleon's legacy to Europe.

Nipperdey, Thomas. *Germany from Napoleon to Bismarck.* Translated by Daniel Nolan. Princeton, N.J.: Princeton University Press, 1996. This book, by one of the most admired German scholars of the post-World War II period, chronicles in the fullest detail the extraordinarily complex negotiations that preceded agreement on the Federal Act. For those who want all the details.

Sagarra, Eda. *An Introduction to Nineteenth Century Germany.* Harlow, England: Longman, 1980. Contains a succinct summary of how the German Confederation came about.

Sheehan, James J. *German History, 1770-1886.* Oxford, England: Clarendon Press, 1989. Part of the Oxford History of Modern Europe series. This American scholar treats the German Confederation as part of "Restoration Politics." The events that led to the confederation are described against the background of great-power relationships.

SEE ALSO: Sept. 15, 1814-June 11, 1815: Congress of Vienna; Jan. 1, 1834: German States Join to Form Customs Union; Sept. 12, 1848: Swiss Confederation Is Formed; Feb. 1-Oct. 30, 1864: Danish-Prussian War; 1866-1867: North German Confederation Is Formed; June 15-Aug. 23, 1866: Austria and Prussia's Seven Weeks' War; Jan. 18, 1871: German States Unite Within German Empire; May 18-July, 1899: First Hague Peace Conference.

RELATED ARTICLES in *Great Lives from History: The Nineteenth Century, 1801-1900:* Alexander I; Metternich; Napoleon I; Freiherr vom Stein.

June 18, 1815
BATTLE OF WATERLOO

The final great military action of the long Napoleonic Wars, the Battle of Waterloo ended Napoleon's bid to regain his throne, led to his final and permanent exile from Europe, and left Great Britain the undisputed leading power in Europe.

LOCALE: Waterloo, Belgium
CATEGORY: Wars, uprisings, and civil unrest

KEY FIGURES

Napoleon I (Napoleon Bonaparte; 1769-1821), emperor of the French, r. 1804-1814, 1815, and commander of the French forces
Duke of Wellington (Arthur Wesley or Wellesley; 1769-1852), commander of the Anglo-allied forces at Waterloo
Gebhard Leberecht von Blücher (1742-1819), commander of the Prussian forces

Comte Jean-Baptiste Drouet d'Erlon (1765-1844), French general under Napoleon
Emmanuel de Grouchy (1766-1847), commander of detached wing of French army
Michel Ney (1769-1815), Napoleon's field commander at Waterloo

SUMMARY OF EVENT

On March 1, 1815, Napoleon Bonaparte returned to France from the island of Elba, where he had been exiled by the victorious allies after abdicating his throne. Napoleon believed correctly that the French people, especially members of the army, despised the restored Bourbon monarchy. Upon his landing, he was almost universally hailed, and thousands of troops rallied to their long-victorious standards—the imperial eagles. Even Marshal Michel Ney, who had sworn he would return with Napoleon "in an iron cage," fell under the charismatic power

1810's

British troops prepare to make their final advance against the French at Waterloo. (Francis R. Niglutsch)

243

of his former commander and deserted the Bourbon cause.

Napoleon also hoped that emerging differences between the allies—Great Britain, Prussia, Austria, and Russia—would prevent them from responding effectively to his return. There was some reason for that belief, as Austria, Russia, and Prussia had come close to going to war over the issue of controlling Poland, while Britain adopted a generally aloof and unhelpful role. The issue of Poland had been resolved, however, and so great was their mutual hatred and fear of the French emperor that the allies were determined on his destruction.

By the time Napoleon entered Paris in triumph on March 20, the allies had already begun to respond. An Austrian army of 200,000 troops was being prepared to invade France, with a Russian force of 150,000 to follow later during the summer. To the north, an Anglo-allied army under Arthur Wellesley, the duke of Wellington, was forming in the Low Countries, supported to the east by a Prussian force commanded by General Gebhard Leberecht von Blücher. After the four allied armies were ready, they would launch a coordinated attack on Napoleon, pushing him into Paris. There, he could be reduced by siege, thus denying him a chance to outwit his opponents on the battlefield, as he had so often done in the past.

Napoleon's two main options were to adopt a delaying strategy, holding off the allies until they agreed to a negotiated peace, or to take the initiative. Typically, he chose the more active course. His decision was to strike first against the Prussians and Anglo-allied forces in Belgium, defeating them before they could unite and forcing each to retreat to its base of operations—Wellington to the Channel ports, Blücher to the Rhineland. The destruction or even the disruption of these two armies would make the north secure, so Napoleon could swing to the south and east and face the Austro-Russian threat. Still married to the daughter of the Austrian emperor, Napoleon hoped the Habsburgs might be disposed to a peace treaty that would allow him to retain his throne.

After quickly raising an army of some 100,000 troops, Napoleon moved his forces skillfully and secretly to the Franco-Belgian frontier. While the allies remained unaware of Napoleon's location, he crossed the Sambre River on June 16 to a position that threatened both Wellington's and Blücher's forces. A detachment under Marshal Ney struck at the British forces in position around the village of Quatre Bras, while French troops led by Marshal Emmanuel de Grouchy fell on the Prus-

French troops retreating from Waterloo. (R. S. Peale/J. A. Hill)

French soldiers flocking to Napoleon's banner after his escape from Elba. (The S. S. McClure Co.)

1810's

sians at Ligny. Ney's attack on Wellington was inconclusive, but the British withdrew during the night to take up defensive positions near the village of Waterloo. The French defeated Blücher's troops and, although reinforcements requested from Ney were recalled before they could rout the Prussians, Napoleon believed that Blücher would continue retreating eastward and was therefore no immediate threat. As a result, he promptly turned to crush the Anglo-allied force, leaving part of his army under Grouchy to contain any Prussian countermarch.

The bulk of Wellington's army was made up not of British soldiers, but of German, Dutch, and Belgian units, many of them suspected by Wellington of being unreliable and perhaps pro-French. Wellington's doubts were reflected in his disposition of his forces in taking up a defensive position on the road to Brussels: The weaker allied units were stationed on the flanks, where they could do the least harm, while the more reliable continental troops, such as the King's German Legion, were placed among the steadier British forces in the middle. The British right flank was anchored by a strong point, the Château de Hougoumont, and the left flank by a cluster of farmhouses and cottages. Napoleon's forces were drawn up across from Wellington's army. After becom-

ing aware that Blücher had not continued his retreat and therefore was a threat, Napoleon decided against a battle of maneuver and instead opted for a direct, forceful frontal attack to break Wellington's composite army.

The battle opened just before midday on June 18, with a French advance against Hougoumont to deprive the British of that stronghold. This engagement quickly degenerated into a vicious hand-to-hand exchange which lasted throughout the rest of the battle without materially affecting it. Meanwhile, Napoleon ordered an intensive bombardment of Wellington's center by a "grand battery" of some eighty cannon. This cannonade, designed to break the morale of the allied troops, was followed by an infantry attack under General Comte Jean-Baptiste Drouet d'Erlon that bent but failed to breach the allied line. Marshal Ney, mistakenly believing the allies about to break, ordered a series of cavalry charges. The British troops quickly formed squares and repulsed the cavalry with considerable losses for the French. A countercharge by the British cavalry extended too deeply into the French lines, and the British horsemen in turn experienced heavy casualties.

As the afternoon wore on, two events brought the battle to a crisis point. In the center, the French captured the strong points of La Haye Sainte, a collection of buildings and its nearby sandpit. This development placed the already battered center of Wellington's line in great danger. To the right of the French line, Blücher's Prussians, who had not been contained by Grouchy's troops, began to drive in Napoleon's flank. Grouchy himself and the forces under his command remained out of contact with Napoleon and never appeared on the battlefield, even though Grouchy was desperately urged by his officers to "march toward the sound of the guns."

Now desperate to force a conclusion, and believing that the British center must at last be weakened to the point of collapse, Napoleon gambled on one last move. Around seven o'clock, he committed his last, and probably his best, troops, the Imperial Guard, to a frontal attack against Wellington's right center. Having carefully held his reserves intact throughout the day, Wellington was

245

able to reinforce the point of impact with relatively fresh and solid units. Concentrated and deadly British volley fire caught the soldiers of the Imperial Guard on their front and flanks, breaking their charge. When the Imperial Guard turned in retreat, Wellington sensed the tide of battle had turned irreversibly. He ordered a general advance of the entire Anglo-allied line. At the same time, the Prussians broke through Napoleon's right flank, and the French army collapsed.

During the ten-hour battle, the French lost some twenty-five thousand men killed and wounded, with nine thousand captured. Wellington's army had approximately fifteen thousand casualties, while Blücher's Prussians, coming late but decisively to the field, suffered about eight thousand casualties.

SIGNIFICANCE

The defeat at Waterloo was the end for Napoleon and his dream of empire. He attempted to raise a second army, but his marshals refused to support him and his enemies in Paris conspired against him. Abdicating again on June 21, and fearing revenge from the other allies, he surrendered directly to the British. He was then exiled—more successfully this time—to the distant south Atlantic island of St. Helena, where he died in 1821.

Wellington, already a British national hero for his earlier victories in the Napoleonic Wars, rose to an even higher level in his nation's esteem. He remained in France until 1818 as the commander of the British army of occupation. After he returned home, he entered politics and became prime minister in 1828.

—*Michael Witkoski*

FURTHER READING

Corrigan, Gordon. *Wellington: A Military Life*. London: Hambledon and London, 2001. A former soldier, Corrigan examines Wellington's claims to military greatness, concluding that he was the first modern general.

Gneisenau, August von. *The Life and Campaigns of Field Marshal Prince Blücher of Whalstaff: From the Period of His Birth and First Appointment in the Prussian Service Down to His Second Entry into Paris in 1815*. Translated by General Count Gneisenau and J. E. Marston. London: Constable, 1996. A reprint of a biography written by the chief of staff of General Blücher, the commander of the Prussian army during the Battle of Waterloo.

Hamilton-Williams, David. *Waterloo: New Perspectives*. New York: John Wiley & Sons, 1993. Uses archival and documentary evidence, much of it French and Prussian, to argue that Dutch, Belgian, and German forces have had their contributions eclipsed by a focus on the British army's role.

Hofschroer, Peter. *1815, The Waterloo Campaign: The German Victory: From Waterloo to the Fall of Napoleon*. Harrisburg, Pa.: Stackpole Books, 1999. History of Napoleon's last months in power from the German perspective.

Howarth, David. *Waterloo: A Near Run Thing*. Conshohocken, Pa.: Combined Books, 1997. A reexamination of the Battle of Waterloo by a leading authority on the campaign.

_____. *Waterloo: Day of Battle*. New York: Atheneum, 1968. A fast-paced overview of the battle that draws heavily on records and narratives of actual participants.

Keegan, John. *The Face of Battle*. New York: Viking Press, 1976. A classic study of warfare that gives a masterful presentation of the battle as it must have appeared to its participants.

Schom, Alan. *One Hundred Days: Napoleon's Road to Waterloo*. New York: Atheneum, 1992. Concentrates on Napoleon's return and the campaign prior to the battle, outlining the goals and strategy of his campaign against Wellington and Blücher.

Uffindell, Andrew. *The Eagle's Last Triumph: Napoleon's Victory at Ligny, June 1815*. London: Greenhill Books, 1994. A military history of the battle at Ligny, which occurred two days before Waterloo.

Weller, Jac. *Wellington at Waterloo*. New York: Thomas Y. Crowell, 1967. Weller presents a novel study by restricting himself to what Wellington could have known at any given moment of the battle.

SEE ALSO: Dec. 2, 1804: Bonaparte Is Crowned Napoleon I; Oct. 21, 1805: Battle of Trafalgar; Dec. 2, 1805: Battle of Austerlitz; May 2, 1808-Nov., 1813: Peninsular War in Spain; June 23-Dec. 14, 1812: Napoleon Invades Russia; July 22, 1812: Battle of Salamanca; Sept. 7, 1812: Battle of Borodino; Oct. 16-19, 1813: Battle of Leipzig; Apr. 11, 1814-July 29, 1830: France's Bourbon Dynasty Is Restored; Sept. 15, 1814-June 11, 1815: Congress of Vienna; Nov. 20, 1815: Second Peace of Paris.

RELATED ARTICLES in *Great Lives from History: The Nineteenth Century, 1801-1900:* Gebhard Leberecht von Blücher; Napoleon I; Michel Ney; Duke of Wellington.

November 20, 1815
SECOND PEACE OF PARIS

The Second Peace of Paris ended the Napoleonic Wars and established the framework for European politics for the next century.

ALSO KNOWN AS: Treaty of Paris

LOCALE: Paris, France

CATEGORIES: Diplomacy and international relations; wars, uprisings, and civil unrest

KEY FIGURES

Alexander I (1777-1825), czar of Russia, r. 1801-1825

Friedrich Gentz (1764-1832), secretary of the Congress of Vienna, 1814-1815

Karl von Hardenberg (1750-1822), chancellor of Prussia

Metternich (1773-1859), Austrian foreign affairs minister

Armand-Emmanuel du Plessis (duc de Richelieu; 1766-1822), chief minister of Louis XVIII who succeeded Talleyrand in 1815

Viscount Castlereagh (Robert Stewart; 1769-1822), British foreign secretary, 1812-1822

Talleyrand (1754-1838), French foreign affairs minister

Duke of Wellington (Arthur Wesley or Wellesley; 1769-1852), British general

SUMMARY OF EVENT

The Second Peace of Paris was the final peace treaty made between France and the victorious allies after the final defeat of Napoleon I. It was part of the general settlement made by the Congress of Vienna (1815-1816) and can be understood only in relation to that conference. The participants were the same at both conferences, but the Second Peace of Paris was made after the settlement at Vienna. The Second Peace of Paris also was linked to negotiations leading to the Quadruple Alliance of Great Britain, Prussia, Austria, and Russia. Both agreements were signed November 20, 1815.

The first Peace of Paris consisted of seven treaties signed on May 30, 1814, by the French government of the restored Bourbon king, Louis XVIII, and each of the seven belligerent powers: Great Britain, Austria, Russia, Prussia, Spain, Sweden, and Portugal. Basically generous, this treaty restored French boundaries as they had existed in 1792 with some added frontier districts and enclaves including some 450,000 people and 150 square miles. France also regained most of its colonies, except

Tobago, St. Lucia, and Mauritius, which had been seized by the British. French posts in India were restored, though without sovereign rights, and France promised to abolish the slave trade in French colonies within five years. No indemnity was imposed, and France was even allowed to keep works of art taken by Napoleon from other countries. This treaty also united Flanders with Holland and Genoa with Piedmont as buffer states against possible French expansion.

While the Congress of Vienna debated the territorial divisions of Europe, however, Napoleon returned to France from Elba on March 1, 1815. The French army and people rallied to his cause, and the restored Bourbon king, Louis XVIII, again fled into exile. Napoleon was soundly defeated at Waterloo on June 18 by an allied army under the command of the duke of Wellington, ably assisted by a Prussian army under General Gebhard Leberecht von Blücher. Napoleon's second period of rule, the Hundred Days, came to an end. He surrendered to the British, who imprisoned him first in England, and then on the island of St. Helena in the south Atlantic.

Napoleon's return resulted in a new and harsher peace treaty, since the French nation had broken the First Peace of Paris and again waged war. The fact that only the British and Prussian armies were responsible for defeating Napoleon at Waterloo and were the first to occupy France gave these two nations added bargaining power. Louis XVIII again was restored to the French throne and Talleyrand was made prime minister of France, but the French were largely excluded from the negotiations taking place at Vienna. The smaller powers played no significant role.

Negotiations continued for four months because Prussia desired a harsh treaty. Prussian pillaging and misconduct of Prussian soldiers also led to friction and objections from Wellington and the British. Some of the smaller German states and the Netherlands supported the Prussian demands. Although Prince Karl von Hardenberg, chancellor of Prussia, favored moderation, the Prussian generals largely overrode his influence. The Prussian military sought a large indemnity and the acquisition of Alsace, Lorraine, French Flanders, and Savoy, as well as the return of works of art stolen by Napoleon.

Metternich, the Austrian minister of foreign affairs, followed a somewhat hesitant course. He had to tread carefully because of hostile Austrian popular opinion. He also may have been willing to shift his position in order to gain territorial advantages for Austria. Metternich's appointee as secretary of the Congress of Vienna, Friedrich Gentz, favored a moderate peace. He closely associated himself with Robert Stewart, Viscount Castlereagh, foreign secretary of Great Britain, and was basically sympathetic with his policies. Czar Alexander I of Russia remained firmly opposed to territorial changes but favored a moderate indemnity.

Castlereagh and Wellington essentially agreed with Alexander but were under pressure from the press, public opinion, the prince regent, the prime minister, and the British cabinet to punish France severely. There was considerable agitation for punishing French military and political leaders who joined Napoleon after his return from Elba. The arrest and execution of Michel Ney tended to quiet public outcry in Great Britain for punishment.

Castlereagh, however, convinced Lord Liverpool and his cabinet that a policy of "security, not revenge" was preferable. He pointed out that a vengeful peace would lead to French attempts to regain lost territory, and that

France should be kept strong and friendly as a possible future ally. As security against possible French expansion he proposed temporary occupation of France, minor frontier adjustments, and dismantling certain French forts. He also proposed a moderate indemnity and the returning of works of art. Metternich basically agreed, and Alexander was persuaded without undue difficulty to accept this compromise. The Prussians found themselves alone and gave way. Talleyrand, however, would not accept this arrangement, and resigned. Louis XVIII replaced him with Armand-Emmanuel du Plessis, duc de Richelieu, who signed the treaty after obtaining a few minor concessions.

Territorial provisions of the Second Treaty of Paris were based on French boundaries as they existed in 1790. Compared to the earlier treaty, this took away a small area of the Netherlands frontier, gave part of the Saar in Germany (including the forts of Saarlouis and Landau) to Prussia, and annexed part of Savoy to Piedmont. The fortress of Huningen near Basel was demolished. Colonial provisions remained as in the first treaty. A F700 million

Napoleon boarding the Bellerophon, *which took him to his final exile, on the South Atlantic island of St. Helena.* (The S. S. McClure Co.)

indemnity was awarded to the allies, and F240 million was awarded to private creditors. France also had to support the Allied Army of Occupation in northern France under Wellington. Some art treasures taken by Napoleon were returned to their original owners.

SIGNIFICANCE

Although the Second Peace of Paris was harsher to France than the first treaty had been, it remained generous. The indemnity and occupation payments were less than may have been justified, for France had suffered little devastation from the Napoleonic Wars. French boundaries of 1790 were essentially restored, and France lost little land and even retained some minor acquisitions.

The lenience shown to France perhaps was the last flowering of eighteenth century balance of power diplomacy as opposed to the emotional and vengeful settlements in the Franco-Prussian War (1870-1871) and later. The wisdom of the settlement was attested by the fact that France did not attempt to retaliate and soon was admitted to the Congress of Europe. The "Congress" system, the Quadruple Alliance, and the Holy Alliance of Prussia, Austria, and Russia successfully prevented major European conflict until the Crimean War of 1854. With the decay of the Quadruple Alliance, progressive tensions arising in large part from the Italian and German wars of unification Europe led to a divisive pattern of alliances that culminated in World War I.

—José M. Sánchez,
updated by Ralph L. Langenheim, Jr.

FURTHER READING

Kissinger, Henry. *Diplomacy*. New York: Simon & Schuster, 1994. Concisely summarizes European diplomacy of the Second Treaty of Paris and thereafter.

_____. *A World Restored: Metternich, Castlereagh, and the Problems of Peace, 1815-1822*. Reprint. Boston: Houghton Mifflin, 1973. First published in 1957, Kissinger's work summarizes diplomatic maneuvering between Napoleon's final defeat until the Congress of Vienna.

Nicolson, Sir Harold. *The Congress of Vienna: A Study in Allied Unity, 1812-1822*. New York: Viking Press, 1961. Emphasizes policy and continuity from the Frankfort Proposals through the First and Second Peaces of Paris to the Congress of Vienna.

Sauvigny, Guillaume de Bertier de. *Metternich and His Times*. London: Darton, Longman & Todd, 1962. Provides background on Metternich and briefly covers his part in the Second Peace of Paris.

Sweet, Paul R. *Friedrich von Gentz, Defender of the Old Order*. Madison: University of Wisconsin Press, 1941. Reprint. Westport, Conn.: Greenwood Press, 1970. Illuminates Gentz's role in the Second Peace of Paris and at the Congress of Vienna.

Tapie, Victor-L. *The Rise and Fall of the Habsburg Monarchy*. Translated by Stephen Hardman. New York: Praeger, 1971. Tapie chronicles Austrian political and social life leading up to the Second Treaty of Paris and after.

Webster, Sir Charles. *The Foreign Policy of Castlereagh, 1812-1815*. 2 vols. London: G. Bell, 1925-1931. Webster's work includes a general account of the Second Peace of Paris centered on Castlereagh's objectives.

SEE ALSO: Dec. 2, 1804: Bonaparte Is Crowned Napoleon I; Apr. 11, 1814-July 29, 1830: France's Bourbon Dynasty Is Restored; Sept. 15, 1814-June 11, 1815: Congress of Vienna; June 18, 1815: Battle of Waterloo; Oct. 20-30, 1822: Great Britain Withdraws from the Concert of Europe; July 29, 1830: July Revolution Deposes Charles X.

RELATED ARTICLES in *Great Lives from History: The Nineteenth Century, 1801-1900:* Alexander I; Viscount Castlereagh; Karl von Hardenberg; Metternich; Napoleon I; Michel Ney; Talleyrand; Duke of Wellington.

1810's

1816
LAËNNEC INVENTS THE STETHOSCOPE

Laënnec's invention of the stethoscope enabled physicians to study the sounds of the living heart and lungs in detail. His meticulous and revolutionary two-volume description of his findings, published in 1819, marked the beginning of the modern study of chest diseases, which could be more accurately diagnosed, more clearly understood, and more effectively treated.

LOCALE: France
CATEGORIES: Inventions; health and medicine; science and technology

KEY FIGURES
René-Théophile-Hyacinthe Laënnec (1781-1826), French physician and inventor
Leopold Auenbrugger (1722-1809), Austrian physician
Jean Nicolas Corvisart des Marets (1755-1821), French physician
John Forbes (1788-1861), British physician
Pierre Adolphe Piorry (1794-1879), French physician and inventor

SUMMARY OF EVENT
During the 1750's, Leopold Auenbrugger discovered that healthy and diseased chests make different sounds when they are struck. Healthy chests, which are drier and full of air, sound like cloth-covered drums. Diseased chests contain various thick fluids and sound differently muffled, depending on the particular disease. These differences can be heard, quantified, and analyzed to reach a diagnosis, but they cannot be heard easily by an unaided human ear. Auenbrugger devised techniques of striking a patient's chest gently but firmly with his fingers. He then correlated these sounds from different parts of the chest with specific pathological implications. He named his method "percussion" and published his findings in Vienna in 1761 as *Inventum novum ex percussione thoracis humani* (*On Percussion of the Chest*, 1936).

Physicians generally ignored percussion until Baron Jean Nicolas Corvisart des Marets, Napoleon I's doctor, translated Auenbrugger's work in 1808 as *Nouvelle méthode pour reconnaitre les maladies internes de la poitrine par la percussion de cette cavité*. With the blessing of a medical mind as prominent as that of Corvisart's, percussion became immediately and almost universally accepted as a valuable diagnostic tool.

René-Théophile-Hyacinthe Laënnec was one of Corvisart's students at the Hôpital de la Charité in Paris. Both men practiced the ancient technique of "auscultation," which then meant listening to chest sounds by putting the ear directly on a patient's body. Auscultation had many problems. It did not work with obese patients, exposed physicians to lice and contagious skin conditions, and could offend female patients. Worst of all, the sounds the doctor heard were faint and unclear. Percussion helped, but not much. As diagnosticians, both Corvisart and Laënnec wanted to amplify and clarify the sounds emitted by living chests.

In 1816, Laënnec examined an overweight woman with possible heart disease, but his examination was hampered because he could not get his ear close enough to her heart to hear it clearly. Remembering the principle that sound travels better through solids than it does through air, he spontaneously rolled up a few sheets of paper tightly into a tube and put one end on her chest and the other to his ear. The sounds he heard amazed him. He heard the heart more clearly and loudly and with less background noise than he had ever heard it before.

Laënnec and Corvisart instantly knew that Laënnec had stumbled upon a historic medical advance. Believing that they could now "see" inside a person's chest with this new instrument. Laënnec named the instrument the "stethoscope," combining two Greek words *stêthos* (chest) and *skopos* (one who watches). Auscultation thereafter became either "mediate," using the stethoscope, or "immediate," using the ear alone.

Soon after making his original paper stethoscope, Laënnec began crafting the instruments from wood. The stethoscopes he made were cylindrical, were about the size of a flashlight, and were called "monaural" because they could be used by one ear only. Laënnec realized that "binaural," or two-eared, stethoscopes would be better but did not know how to create them.

Laënnec and some of his teachers, colleagues, and students were among the first scientists to understand the value of postmortem examination for studying disease. They shifted the focus of pathological research from the living to the dead, measuring their observations of cadavers against what they knew of healthy anatomy. Laënnec carefully described the chest sounds he heard in dying patients, then verified his hypotheses through autopsy and dissection, and thereby correlated specific sounds with specific diseases or conditions. His research with cadavers helped him diagnose diseases in living patients. His investigations contributed mostly to the knowledge of lung diseases, especially tuberculosis, which, ironically, is what killed him at the age of only forty-five.

After three years of this research, Laënnec categorized and published his results in 1819 in the monumental two-volume work *De l'auscultation médiate: Ou, Traité du diagnostic des maladies des poumons et du coeur.* Sir John Forbes translated the work in 1821 as *A Treatise on the Diseases of the Chest.* Laënnec's even more detailed second edition of his masterpiece appeared in 1826 and became a medical classic throughout the English-speaking world soon after Forbes's 1827 translation.

SIGNIFICANCE

In the few decades following Laënnec's invention and his discoveries, many physicians across Europe and America augmented his work, further classifying chest sounds and increasing the diagnostic power of the monaural stethoscope. One of the earliest books in this genre was Victor Collin's *Des diverses méthodes d'exploration de la poitrine et de leur application au diagnostic de ses maladies* (1824), which W. N. Ryland translated in 1829 as *Manual for the Use of the Stethoscope: A Short Treatise on the Different Methods of Investigating the Diseases of the Chest.* Pierre Adolphe Piorry reported on combined techniques of percussion and mediate auscultation in *De la percussion médiate* (1828).

Other major researchers with the monaural stethoscope were Jean-Baptiste Bouillaud, who gave a classic description of endocarditis in 1835; William Stokes and Henry Ingersoll Bowditch, who wrote introductory texts on the use of this instrument; and William Wood Gerhard, whose description of bronchitis in *Lectures on the Diagnosis, Pathology, and Treatment of the Diseases of the Chest* (1842) remains unsurpassed in accuracy and detail. The greatest of these first-generation investigators of chest diseases was Josef Skoda, whose *Abhandlung über Perkussion und Auskultation* (1839) provided such intricate classifications and fine interpretations of chest sounds that the work remains a text for physicians.

Despite the obvious diagnostic advantages of the stethoscope, many physicians from the 1820's to the 1850's were reluctant to use it because its shape prevented them from simultaneously looking at and listening to the patient. Several inventors made clumsy attempts to overcome this inconvenience, but their prim-

itive binaural stethoscopes did not transmit sound as accurately, loudly, or distinctly as the wooden monaural stethoscopes that were then common. Meanwhile, other inventors were having more success with improving the monaural stethoscope, selecting solid tubes to isolate heart sounds, using hollow tubes to isolate lung sounds, and experimenting with different kinds of wood, as well as ivory and brass.

The first successful binaural stethoscopes emerged during the 1850's through the separate efforts of Arthur Leared, George P. Cammann, and others. A century of steady technological advances after the mid-1850s led to the development of the modern binaural stethoscope, which has a chest piece with a hollow bell on one side for isolating low-frequency sounds and a flat diaphragm on its other side for isolating high-frequency sounds. The bell/diaphragm assembly and the two earpieces are connected by about 35 centimeters (14 inches) of flexible tubing.

American physician Austin Flint made so much progress with the binaural stethoscope that he was called "the American Laënnec." Among his groundbreaking works are *Physical Exploration and Diagnosis of Diseases Affecting the Respiratory Organs* (1856), *A Practical Treatise on the Diagnosis, Pathology, and Treatment of the Diseases of the Heart* (1859), and *A Manual of Auscultation and Percussion, Embracing the Physical Diagnosis of Diseases of the Lungs and Heart, and of Thoracic Aneurism* (1876).

—*Eric v.d. Luft*

FURTHER READING

Duffin, Jacalyn Mary. *To See with a Better Eye: A Life of Laënnec.* Princeton, N.J.: Princeton University Press, 1998. The standard biography on Laënnec.

Kervran, Roger. *Laënnec: His Life and Times.* New York: Pergamon, 1960. Another good biography.

Reiser, Stanley Joel. *Medicine and the Reign of Technology.* New York: Cambridge University Press, 1978. The second chapter of this work, "The Stethoscope and the Detection of Pathology by Sound," places Laënnec's invention within the context of diagnostic improvements that began in the eighteenth century.

Rogers, Spencer Lee. *The Monaural Stethoscope.* San Diego, Calif.: Museum of Man, 1972. Appraises the fundamental technology of early stethoscopes.

Sterne, Jonathan. "Mediate Auscultation, the Stethoscope, and the 'Autopsy of the Living': Medicine's Acoustic Culture." *Journal of the Medical Humanities* 22, no. 2 (June, 2001): 115-136. Sterne examines the central place of the stethoscope in nineteenth century medical thought.

SEE ALSO: Oct. 5, 1823: Wakley Introduces *The Lancet*; 1857: Pasteur Begins Developing Germ Theory and Microbiology; 1867: Lister Publishes His Theory on Antiseptic Surgery; Nov. 9, 1895: Röntgen Discovers

X Rays; 1897-1901: Abel and Takamine Isolate Adrenaline; 1898: Beijerinck Discovers Viruses.
RELATED ARTICLES in *Great Lives from History: The Nineteenth Century, 1801-1900:* Emil von Behring; Marie Anne Victorine Boivin; Robert Koch; Wilhelm Conrad Röntgen.

February 20, 1816
ROSSINI'S *THE BARBER OF SEVILLE* DEBUTS

After overcoming a terrible opening night and vocal enemies, Gioacchino Rossini's The Barber of Seville *soon became his most widely popular work. Its continued popularity over the years and the familiarity of its score have made it one of the world's most beloved and famous operas.*

ALSO KNOWN AS: *Almaviva: Ossia, L'inutile precauzione*; *Almaviva: Or, The Useless Precaution*
LOCALE: Rome (now in Italy)
CATEGORIES: Theater; music

KEY FIGURES
Gioacchino Rossini (1792-1868), Italian composer
Cesare Sterbini (1784-1831), Italian librettist
Pierre-Augustin Caron de Beaumarchais (1732-1799), French writer of the original play
Giovanni Paisiello (1740-1816), Italian composer of an earlier operatic treatment of Beaumarchais's play

SUMMARY OF EVENT
Success in opera was the avenue to fame and fortune for many composers during the nineteenth century. As a public entertainment, opera served mainly to show off the talents of popular singers. In Italy, it was a high-pressure business. Most Italian cities had opera houses, and for their "season"—the expanded *carnevale* period beginning just after Christmas and ending on *Giovedì grasso*, the night before Ash Wednesday—these houses provided productions that usually included at least one new work. Impresarios were hired to engage singers, directors, and composers.

In the largest opera houses, such as those in Milan, Venice, Rome, and Naples, impresarios wielded great patronage and influence but faced the frustrating temperaments of their artists, while also watching out for local censors and attempting to remain profitable. Expected to fit their music to the talents of the singers engaged (who

were often paid more than they were), composers could become worn-out workhorses, earning attention and a livelihood by turning out several operas each season. Many professional libretto writers were hack poets, though some were skilled at the job. Composers often took whatever texts their contract required. The formulaic nature of operatic structure at the time—display arias, duets, and ensembles, separated by keyboard-accompanied recitative—could work to a certain routine. However, audiences expected good tunes, and creative, imaginative composers had ample room in which to work.

Born in Pesaro, Italy, Gioacchino Rossini launched early into this rewarding but brutalizing business of creating operas. Both his parents were musicians, one an accomplished horn player, the other a singer in local opera companies. Their initial training was furthered in Bologna, where Gioacchino trained as a singer, a pianist, and a cellist, while composing substantial instrumental pieces by his early teens. At fifteen years of age, he composed his first opera, though it was not immediately performed. His debut came at eighteen in Venice with his first *opera buffa*, or comic opera, the farce *La cambiale di matrimonio* (1810; *The Bill of Marriage*). It won him recognition as a gifted and highly original composer with a command of vocal writing, comic style, and orchestral mastery. For Venice, he wrote four more comic operas, one-act pieces, within the next three years, as well as producing a serious opera for Ferrara. In 1812, he had a sensational success at Milan's prestigious La Scala Theater with his comedy *La pietra del paragone* (*The Touchstone*). At the age of twenty, with only two years of experience, Rossini was now a celebrity, the most promising young composer in Italy.

Rossini's timing was perfect: He came on the operatic scene when the older Italian masters were dead or moribund, while the subsequent masters—such as Gaetano

Donizetti and Vincenzo Bellini—were yet to appear, and Giuseppe Verdi as well in the future. From 1812 until he left Italy in 1823, Rossini became the most influential and successful composer in Italy, setting the course of Italian opera for the new century.

Rossini expanded his scope spectacularly with his first serious opera, the heroic melodrama *Tancredi* (1813), composed for Venice's illustrious La Fenice Theater. Only three months later, he had another comic triumph for another Venetian theater, the madcap *L'italiana in Algeri* (1813; *The Italian Girl in Algiers*). Moving back to La Scala in Milan, he produced another serious opera, *Aureliano in Palmira* (1814), followed by a sequel to his last comic opera, *Il turco in Italia* (1814; *The Turk in Italy*). This alternation between comic and serious works was dictated by the whims of the impresarios who gave Rossini his commissions, and a new commission from Venice's La Fenice produced an *opera seria* disaster in late 1814.

A new turn in Rossini's career was launched by the powerful impresario Domenico Barbaja, whose widely spread theater operations included the most important houses in Naples. Barbaja contracted Rossini to serve as his Neapolitan music director and to compose operas, using the resources of perhaps the finest company of singers in Europe. Rossini began his work for Barbaja boldly at the great San Carlo Theater with *Elisabetta, regina d'Inghilterra* (1815; *Elizabeth, Queen of England*) in October of 1815. In the title role was Isabella Colbran, previously Barbaja's mistress, now Rossini's lover, and later to become his first wife.

Rossini's contract in Naples allowed him to accept work from houses elsewhere, among them two in Rome. For the Valle Theater, he ground out a tragic opera to a libretto by a local hack, Cesare Sterbini. Its premiere in December, 1815, was a dismal failure. Then, by default, Sterbini was assigned as librettist for Rossini's other Roman commission, for the Argentina Theater. Rossini himself chose the subject, Pierre-Augustin Caron de Beaumarchais's celebrated play *Le Barbier de Séville: Ou, La Précaution inutile* (1775; *The Barber of Seville: Or, The Useless Precaution,* 1776).

It was a brash decision. There had already been some half dozen operatic treatments of Beaucarchais's play, one of them still popular with audiences at the time. The latter opera was composed in 1782 by Giovanni Paisiello, one of the most prolific and admired composers of Italian opera of his day. He was still alive, he had basked in and then survived the favor of Napoleon, and he had many fervent admirers.

Paisiello's librettist, Giuseppe Petrosellini, had drained all the satire and social criticism out of the play, turning it into simple, if delightful, farce. Rossini insisted on restoring some sharper elements in Sterbini's libretto—though not too many. Aware of his boldness, Rossini wrote to the aged Paisiello to assure him graciously that he was not deliberately trying to challenge the older master. Knowing it would appear that way, Rossini titled his opera *Almaviva: Ossia, L'inutile precauzione* (1816; *Almaviva: Or, The Useless Precaution*); only after Paisiello's death, a year later, did Rossini

During a performance of one of the earliest productions of The Barber of Seville, *Lindor (kneeling) reveals to Rosina that he is Count Almaviva.* (Hulton Archive/Getty Images)

definitively appropriate the older opera's title, renaming his work *Il barbiere di Siviglia* (*The Barber of Seville*).

Rossini always worked in a chaotic and high-speed fashion. He produced the fully orchestrated score of *The Barber of Seville* in about two weeks, not at all unusual for him. He made his usual recourse to self-borrowings. For example, after discarding the original overture (now lost) on the first night of performance, he appropriated music he had originally written for an earlier opera about a Roman emperor and then revised for another about Queen Elizabeth I, finally and decisively fixing it to *The Barber of Seville*.

The premiere of Rossini's opera was disastrous. The theater manager's death by stroke had delayed the opening. When it finally came, on February 20, 1816, the rabid fans of Paisiello, known as *paisiellisti*, rallied to jeer the young composer. Absurd accidents plagued the performance. For example, the actor playing Don Basilio fell and broke his nose before he was to sing his big aria, "Calumny"; a cat wandered onto the stage to join the singers at one point. Rossini was rightly philosophical about it all. The following night—with the new overture in place and no cats evident on stage—the audience responded to the opera's merits and acclaimed the composer.

Quickly, though not instantly, Rossini's *The Barber of Seville* was taken up not only around Italy but also around Europe, cementing his fame. The original Almaviva had been tenor Manuel Garcia; when Garcia and his family troupe introduced Italian opera to New York City in 1825, Rossini's hit was their starter. The opera's currency brought it, nevertheless, much transformation. Rossini himself took the tenor's dazzling final solo and transferred it the following year to the end of his next Roman opera, *La cenerentola* (1817; *Cinderella*). Over the years, sopranos pushed aside the high-range mezzo voice for which Rossini designed the role of Rosina and made it a high coloratura part, filling it with disfiguring embellishments; they also turned a music-lesson scene in act 2 into a blanket opportunity to interpolate all sorts of display solos from other sources.

Rossini ultimately produced a total of ten operas for Naples, including *Otello* (1816; *Othello*), *Armida* (1817), and *La donna del lago* (1819; *The Lady of the Lake*), bringing new profundity to his style, as well as six for the houses of other cities (two for La Scala). In 1823, he had a triumph in Vienna with *Semiramide*. Ready to leave Italy and drawn by greater financial prospects in

Paris, Rossini settled there in 1824, writing one Italian opera and four in French, culminating with *Guillaume Tell* (1829; *William Tell*). Then, at thirty-seven, he retired from operatic composition. He continued to compose music for his own pleasure, however, and enjoyed a plush life of celebrity leisure for his remaining thirty-nine years.

SIGNIFICANCE

Joining Wolfgang Amadeus Mozart's *Le nozze di Figaro* (1786; *The Marriage of Figaro*) as the other supreme Beaumarchais operafication, Rossini's *The Barber of Seville* did not deter at least eight other composers from trying their hand at adaptations of the play. Nevertheless, through the years when all of Rossini's other operas fell into neglect, *The Barber of Seville* retained its endless popularity and kept the composer's reputation alive, making possibile its later redemption. *The Barber of Seville* remains a staple of the opera repertoire.

—*John W. Barker*

FURTHER READING

Gossett, Philip. "Rossini." In *The New Grove Dictionary of Music and Musicians*. 2d ed. Vol. 21, edited by Stanlie Sadie. New York: Grove Press, 2001. Detailed article with extensive bibliography.

John, Nicholas, ed. *"The Barber of Seville" and "Moses."* London: John Calder, 1985. Introductory essays with full libretto.

Kendall, Alan. *Gioacchino Rossini: The Reluctant Hero*. London: Victor Gollancz, 1992. Particularly strong analysis of Rossini's personality.

Osborne, Richard. *Rossini*. Boston: Northeastern University Press, 1986. Concise biography and listener's guide to the operas.

Robinson, Paul. "Enlightenment and Reaction." In *Opera and Ideas: From Mozart to Strauss*. New York: Harper & Row, 1985. Provocative comparison of Mozart's and Rossini's Figaros.

Rosselli, John. *The Opera Industry in Italy from Cimarosa to Verdi: The Role of the Impresario*. New York: Cambridge University Press, 1984. Fascinating picture of opera as business in Rossini's day.

Stendhal. *Life of Rossini*. Translated by Richard N. Coe. Rev. ed. New York: Criterion Books, 1970. A pioneering biography, written in 1824 by the now famous novelist, a contemporaneous friend and admirer.

Weinstock, Herbert. *Rossini: A Biography*. New York: Alfred Knopf, 1968. The most comprehensive and thorough study.

SEE ALSO: c. 1801-1850: Professional Theaters Spread Throughout America; Mar. 3, 1830: Hugo's *Hernani* Incites Rioting; Jan. 2, 1843: Wagner's *Flying Dutchman* Debuts; Mar. 3, 1875: Bizet's *Carmen* Premieres in Paris; Aug. 13-17, 1876: First Performance of Wagner's Ring Cycle; Oct. 22, 1883: Metropolitan Opera House Opens in New York; Jan. 14, 1900: Puccini's *Tosca* Premieres in Rome.

RELATED ARTICLES in *Great Lives from History: The Nineteenth Century, 1801-1900:* Georges Bizet; Léo Delibes; Gaetano Donizetti; Gioacchino Rossini; Giuseppe Verdi; Richard Wagner.

April, 1816
SECOND BANK OF THE UNITED STATES IS CHARTERED

The federal government's wish to restore the monetary system to the gold standard led to the second attempt to created a national bank, but the bank was ultimately the victim of political opposition.

LOCALE: Washington, D.C.
CATEGORIES: Banking and finance; trade and commerce; organizations and institutions

KEY FIGURES

John Jacob Astor (1763-1848), New York merchant
Nicholas Biddle (1786-1844), director and third president of the Second Bank
Langdon Cheves (1776-1857), Speaker of the House of Representatives and president of the Second Bank
Stephen Girard (1750-1831), powerful Philadelphia banker and largest subscriber to the Second Bank
William Jones (1760-1831), secretary of the Navy and first president of the Second Bank
James Madison (1751-1836), president of the United States, 1809-1817

SUMMARY OF EVENT

In April, 1816, President James Madison signed a bill authorizing the establishment of the Second Bank of the United States. In January, 1817, the bank commenced operations in Philadelphia in the same building that had housed the First Bank of the United States. The First Bank had been chartered in 1791 as part of the comprehensive financial program of Treasury Secretary Alexander Hamilton. One purpose in chartering the bank was to improve the market for the newly issued securities constituting the funded national debt, for these securities could be turned in to purchase stock in the new bank. In addition, the bank was expected to enlarge credit availability substantially, as only three commercial banks existed in 1790. The Bank of the United States was also to serve as a fiscal agent for the federal government, managing its checking account, helping to issue and redeem

government securities, and paying the interest on them. However, the First Bank's charter was not renewed in 1812, despite the bank's productive and efficient existence of twenty years.

In 1812, the United States entered the War of 1812 with Great Britain. As usual, government expenditures greatly increased, and most of that increase was financed by borrowing. The federal government borrowed extensively by selling securities to state-chartered banks, which numbered about eighty-eight in 1812. To pay for these securities, the banks expanded their notes and deposits, while their specie reserves declined. In 1814, when British warships sailed up Chesapeake Bay and burned Washington, D.C., most banks outside New England suspended specie redemption of their liabilities. Suspension freed the banks to expand their credit with little restraint. As a result, many bank notes depreciated severely and commodity prices increased by about 50 percent between 1811 and 1814.

After the war ended in December, 1814, a movement to form a new Bank of the United States gained momentum. As in 1790, the federal government was burdened with a large public debt, much of it selling below face value. It was believed that if the securities could be used to pay for the stock of a new bank, their market value would rise. Furthermore, Treasury officials needed competent help in managing their funds, after having had bad experiences with state bank depositories. One of the government's most important motivations was to restore monetary order to the United States and halt the inflation process. Many businessmen, such as Stephen Girard and John Jacob Astor, believed that the banks needed to return to redeeming their notes and deposits in gold and silver on demand, as they had done before 1814. Girard and Astor also were large investors in government securities.

The new bank charter passed Congress in April of 1816. It specified the structure and operations of the bank but did not identify any public purpose that the bank was to serve. The Second Bank of the United States resembled its predecessor in many respects, although its capitalization, at thirty-five million dollars, was larger. As before, the government took one-fifth of the stock. A new feature was that one-fifth of the directors were appointed by the government. The bank provided a depository for federal funds in every state where a branch opened.

Between 1817 and 1828, twenty-eight branches were established in the major commercial cities of the nation. It was through these branches that the Second Bank was enabled to exercise control over the rapidly increasing number of state banks. The bank transferred federal funds from place to place and paid public creditors without charge to the government. The bank was authorized to issue notes that were receivable at par in all payments to the government. It was also authorized to lend money and to buy and sell bills of exchange. It became the manager of the U.S. Treasury's bank account and handled transactions involving issue, redemption, and interest payments on government securities.

The new bank was expected to lead the nation's banks back to specie redemption, aided by the Webster Resolution of 1816, which forbade the Treasury to accept notes of non-specie-paying banks. The banks nominally resumed specie payments in February, 1817, but their specie reserves were very small relative to their liabilities. The Second Bank tried to make their position easier by expanding its own credit rapidly. However, the bank was badly managed under its first president, William Jones, and made many bad loans.

In 1818, the United States experienced a large international outflow of gold. The government called on banks to redeem notes and deposits in specie. As their reserves declined, they were obliged to reduce loans, and the resulting contraction of credit led to severe deflation and economic depression. The Second Bank reduced its loans from forty-three million dollars in early 1818 to thirty-one million dollars in September, 1819, during which time its note circulation fell from ten million to four million dollars. Under fire for internal mismanagement and for the country's deflationary distress, Jones resigned as president in 1822. His successor, Langdon Cheves, concentrated on cleaning up the Second Bank's internal affairs without much concern for the nation's economy.

The Second Bank's role in the Panic of 1819 made it politically unpopular. In 1817, Maryland placed a tax upon the branch office in Baltimore. In 1819, after several other states had followed this example, Ohio and Kentucky imposed taxes of sixty thousand dollars and

fifty thousand dollars on the U.S. Bank branches in those states. However, the landmark Supreme Court decision in *McCulloch v. Maryland* (1819) held that chartering the bank was within the constitutional authority of the Congress and that state taxes could not be imposed to block federal programs.

SIGNIFICANCE

In 1823, Nicholas Biddle became president of the Second Bank. He developed many programs to expand its operation. In particular, the bank became an extensive dealer in domestic exchange. The bank made loans secured by goods (such as cotton) produced in the interior and sent to eastern cities for sale or export. These loans were repaid in the eastern cities, but the bank's interior branches could sell drafts on those funds to local people needing to make payments to the East. The process yielded revenue for the bank and helped improve the country's interregional payments system. However, Biddle and the Second Bank had many political enemies. The number of state-chartered and private banks was increasing, and they and their customers resented the competition from the Second Bank and the restraints it imposed on them. Antagonism from President Andrew Jackson ultimately led him to block recharter of the Second Bank, and its federal charter expired in 1836.

—John G. Clark, updated by Paul B. Trescott

FURTHER READING

Bodenhorn, Howard. *A History of Banking in Antebellum America: Financial Markets and Economic Development in an Era of Nation-Building.* New York: Cambridge University Press, 2000. Examination of American banking policies in the years leading up to the Civil War, with attention to the Bank of the United States.

Brown, Marion A. *The Second Bank of the United States and Ohio, 1803-1860: A Collision of Interests.* Lewiston, N.Y.: Edwin Mellen Press, 1998. Study of the conflicts between the Second Bank of the United States and the state of Ohio.

Govan, Thomas P. *Nicholas Biddle: Nationalist and Public Banker, 1786-1844.* Chicago: University of Chicago Press, 1959. This highly readable biography gives ample background on the evolution of the Second Bank and its political adventures.

Hammond, Bray. *Banks and Politics in America.* Princeton, N.J.: Princeton University Press, 1957. This breezy, entertaining book blends political and economic analysis. Criticizes the Jacksonian point of view.

Kaplan, Edward S. *The Bank of the United States and the American Economy*. Westport, Conn.: Greenwood Press, 1999. Broad, economic study of the role of the Bank of the United States in American economic history.

Redlich, Fritz. *The Molding of American Banking: Men and Ideas*. 1951. Reprint. New York: Johnson Reprint, 1968. Emphasizes the role of businessmen in the initial chartering of the Second Bank, and assesses Biddle's innovations in both commercial and central banking.

Smith, Walter B. *Economic Aspects of the Second Bank of the United States*. Cambridge, Mass.: Harvard University Press, 1953. Presents considerable statistical data and objective analysis of the Second Bank's operations.

Timberlake, Richard H. *Monetary Policy in the United States: An Intellectual and Institutional History*. Chicago: University of Chicago Press, 1993. Chapter 3 depicts the Second Bank as a rather primitive central bank, constrained by its commitment to the gold standard.

SEE ALSO: Mar. 6, 1819: *McCulloch v. Maryland*; July 10, 1832: Jackson Vetoes Rechartering of the Bank of the United States; Mar. 17, 1837: Panic of 1837 Begins; Aug. 1, 1846: Establishment of Independent U.S. Treasury; Feb. 25, 1863-June 3, 1864: Congress Passes the National Bank Acts; Apr. 22, 1864: "In God We Trust" Appears on U.S. Coins.
RELATED ARTICLES in *Great Lives from History: The Nineteenth Century, 1801-1900:* John Jacob Astor; Nicholas Biddle; Andrew Jackson.

1810's

April 9, 1816
AFRICAN METHODIST EPISCOPAL CHURCH IS FOUNDED

The African Methodist Episcopal Church was a radically distinct Protestant denomination that became an advocate for the cause of abolition and a bulwark of the African American community and set a precedent for future African American churches of other denominations.

ALSO KNOWN AS: AME Church
LOCALE: Philadelphia, Pennsylvania
CATEGORIES: Religion and theology; organizations and institutions

KEY FIGURES
Richard Allen (1760-1831), founder and first bishop of the African Methodist Episcopal Church
Francis Asbury (1745-1816), leader of the Methodist Church in America in the eighteenth century
Absalom Jones (1746-1818), first priest of African descent in the U.S. Episcopal church

SUMMARY OF EVENT
On April 9, 1816, sixteen African Methodist delegates met in Philadelphia to unite as the African Methodist Episcopal Church. Most of these delegates had gained their spiritual leadership skills through self-study and life struggles. From Philadelphia and Attleborough, Pennsylvania, delegates joined representatives from Baltimore, Wilmington, and Salem to elect a bishop.

Accounts vary as to what happened next. Some reports indicate that the Reverend Daniel Coker, a Baltimore teacher and school founder, was elected bishop but declined the office the following day in deference to Richard Allen, who had organized the convention. Other records relate that both Allen and Coker were elected; Allen saw no need for two bishops and assumed the role of vice-chair. One account states that Coker's light skin made him unacceptable as the first head of a racially separate institution. Whatever the process, the outcome was the election of Richard Allen, who was consecrated as the first bishop of the African Methodist Episcopal Church on April 11, 1816. From the original sixteen delegates in 1816, membership grew to 7,257 in the year 1822.

Philadelphia provided a receptive haven for African American leaders. Before the American Revolution (1775-1783), manumissions in that city had run high and a private school for African children had been founded. Following the Revolutionary War, city leaders such as Benjamin Franklin and Benjamin Rush established abolition societies, and the state legislature passed laws for the gradual emancipation of slaves.

Richard Allen, who has become known as the founder of African American Protestantism, was born a slave in 1760 in Philadelphia. Sold to the Stokeley plantation near Dover, Delaware, Allen attended evangelical tent meetings and experienced a religious conversion when

Bishops of the African Methodist Episcopal Church through 1876. (Library of Congress)

he was seventeen years of age. He joined the Methodist Society, which held classes in the forest under the leadership of a white man, Benjamin Wells. Allen became a convincing proselytizer, converting first his family and then his owner, who agreed to permit Allen to purchase his own freedom in 1777.

Allen worked at many jobs and preached at his regular stops, developing broad contacts through his travels. As an aide to other itinerant preachers, he met Bishop Francis Asbury, who established the first General Conference of the Methodist Church in America in 1784. When Asbury asked Allen to accompany him on a southern trip, with the stipulation that Allen must not mingle with slaves and must accept segregated accommodations, Allen refused to accompany him and returned to Philadelphia in February, 1786.

Because the church was one of the only legal meeting places for African Americans, religion became a major focus of African American life. Allen joined such Phila-

delphia leaders as former slave clerk and handyman Absalom Jones, and other members of the St. Thomas vestry: James Forten, a freeborn sailmaker; William White; Jacob Tapisco; and James Champion. Allen and Jones became lay preachers throughout the city—especially at St. George's Methodist Episcopal Church at early morning and evening services. As African American attendance at services increased, racial conflict became apparent. In November, 1786, African Americans worshiping at St. George's were ordered to sit in the gallery. After mistakenly sitting in the wrong section of the gallery, Allen, Jones, and White were physically removed while praying at the Sunday morning worship service.

The humiliation of this incident led to a mass exodus of African Americans from the church and a movement to create a separate church as an organized act of self-determination. In the spring, the African American leaders established the Free African Society, the first mutual aid society established to serve their community. By

1791, they were holding regular Sunday services, assuming lay leadership positions, and making plans for the construction of a church building. The effectiveness of the society's leadership and organization was demonstrated to white leaders during the yellow fever epidemic of 1793.

The leaders differed over the issue of church affiliation, with the majority voting to unite with the Episcopal Church. On July 17, 1794, the St. Thomas African Church was dedicated as the first African church in Philadelphia, a Protestant Episcopal church with Absalom Jones as pastor. Jones became the first African American priest in 1804.

Jones and Allen favored Methodism, but only Allen withdrew from the Free African Society to form a separate church. Bishop Asbury of the Methodist Episcopal Church presided over the dedication of Allen's creation, the Bethel African Methodist Episcopal Church, on July 29, 1794. Allen declared the church independent in management but did not sever all relations with the Methodist Episcopal Church. The articles of incorporation ensured independence by allowing membership only to people of African descent. Allen then became the first African American to receive ordination from the Methodist Episcopal Church in the United States.

Such church independence helped African Americans resist the insults and subordination resulting from slavery and racial prejudice and reflected a growing role of the church in the black community. Sermons in the church underscored the need for the African American community to become self-reliant through the church, schools, and economic organizations in order to gain group solidarity and recognition. Christian character, in turn, depended upon Christian education. In the summer of 1795, Bethel cooperated with the Society for the Improving of the Condition of the Free Blacks by arranging for the arrival, temporary housing, and placement for newly emancipated slaves.

Church trustees petitioned the African school for free instruction. Bethel not only established the first Sunday school for African Americans but also set a precedent with the 1795 opening of the first day school established by African Americans for their children. The day school was soon followed by a night school for working people. In 1798, Allen and Jones gained permission from Prince Hall of Boston to set up the Second African (Masonic) Lodge in Philadelphia. Because music was an integral part of African American worship, Allen enhanced the cultural expression of his people by compiling a collection of sixty-four hymns for his congregation in 1801.

As increasing numbers of women experienced religious conversions and entered preaching, Allen supported their spiritual growth by allowing an Englishwoman, Dorothy Ripley, to speak to his congregation in 1803. In 1804, he established the Society of Free People of Color for Promoting the Instruction and School Education of Children of African Descent. In 1809, he helped James Forten and Absalom Jones organize the Society for the Suppression of Vice and Immorality in Philadelphia, to provide community supervision of the morality of African Americans and to establish means for their moral uplift. These leaders recruited three thousand members for the Black Legion during the War of 1812. The successful functions associated with African American churches led to greater membership. By 1813, St. Thomas had a membership of 560, while Bethel Church had 1,272 communicants.

After the African Methodist Episcopal Church was established in 1816, the movement spread to other cities and along the seaboard states. Church leaders continued their pioneering efforts for group solidarity. In January, 1817, the First Negro Convention met at the Bethel Church to protest the plans of the American Colonization Society for emigration of free blacks to Africa. During that same year, Allen's church supported the first female licensed worker of the African Methodist Episcopal Church, Jarena Lee. Also in 1817, Allen and Jacob Tapisco published the *First Church Discipline* as well as a book of hymns compiled by Allen, Daniel Coker, and James Champion. After the death of Absalom Jones in 1818, Allen served as Book Steward until 1820; the position served as the foundation for the church's Book Concern, which continued to unite followers across the country through the twentieth century.

SIGNIFICANCE

In later years, the church continued to improve the conditions for African Americans. It supported the use of boycotts to protest the economic basis of slavery through the Free Produce Society of Philadelphia, which was organized at an assembly at Bethel Church on December 20, 1830, to advocate purchase only of produce grown by free labor. The First Annual Convention of the People of Color, convened in Philadelphia in 1831, elected Richard Allen as its leader shortly before his death on March 26, 1831. The African Methodist Episcopal Church has survived in the twenty-first century as an integral part of the African American community and continued its strong leadership role.

—Dorothy C. Salem

FURTHER READING

Allen, Richard. "Letters of Richard Allen and Absalom Jones." *Journal of Negro History* 1, no. 4 (October, 1916): 436-443. The common concerns of the two leaders are expressed in their correspondence.

_____. *The Life, Experience, and Gospel Labors of the Right Reverend Richard Allen.* 1833. Reprint. Nashville, Tenn.: Abingdon Press, 1983. Presents an accounting of Allen's religious life.

Angell, Stephen W., and Anthony B. Pinn, eds. *Social Protest Thought in the African Methodist Episcopal Church, 1862-1939.* Knoxville: University of Tennessee Press, 2000. Study of the role of the AME Church during the Civil War and and its aftermath.

Dodson, Jualynne E. *Engendering Church: Women, Power, and the AME Church.* Lanham, Md.: Rowman & Littlefield, 2002. Exploration of the important role of women in the African Methodist Episcopal Church; includes a history of the church.

Dvorak, Katharine L. *An African American Exodus.* Brooklyn, N.Y.: Carlson, 1991. Provides the history and theology of the nineteenth century African Methodist Episcopal Church.

George, Carol V. R. *Segregated Sabbaths: Richard Allen and the Rise of Independent Black Churches, 1760-1840.* New York: Oxford University Press, 1973. A standard account of the development of the independent churches.

Mwadilitu, Mwalimu I. [E. Curtis Alexander]. *Richard Allen: The First Exemplar of African American Education.* New York: ECA Associates, 1985. Examines Allen's educational leadership through the church.

Nash, Gary. "New Light on Richard Allen: The Early Years of Freedom." *William and Mary Quarterly* 46 (April, 1989): 332-340. Consideration of Allen's role in early national history by a leading authority on early American race relations.

Rasmussen, R. Kent. *Farewell to Jim Crow: The Rise and Fall of Segregation in America.* New York: Facts On File, 1997. Written for young adults, this history of segregation in the United States discusses the founding of the AME Church in the wider context of African American responses to segregation and points up the importance of churches in African American history.

Wesley, Charles. *Richard Allen: Apostle of Freedom.* Washington, D.C.: Associated Publishers, 1935. The standard biography of Allen.

SEE ALSO: Jan., 1804: Ohio Enacts the First Black Codes; Dec., 1833: American Anti-Slavery Society Is Founded; 1835: Finney Lectures on "Revivals of Religion"; July 6, 1853: National Council of Colored People Is Founded.

RELATED ARTICLE in *Great Lives from History: The Nineteenth Century, 1801-1900:* Paul Cuffe.

May 8, 1816
AMERICAN BIBLE SOCIETY IS FOUNDED

The founding of the American Bible Society was a major step in the Christian evangelical movement of the early nineteenth century. In addition to its own publication work, the society began providing funds to missionaries for the translation and printing of Bibles. Its goal was to provide Bibles to as many people as possible, without endorsing any particular doctrinal or denominational positions.

LOCALE: New York, New York

CATEGORIES: Religion and theology; organizations and institutions

KEY FIGURES

Elias Boudinot (1740-1821), American politician and cofounder and first president of the American Bible Society

Samuel J. Mills (1783-1818), early supporter of the American Bible Society

Jedidiah Morse (1761-1826), pastor, missionary society leader, and cofounder of the American Bible Society

John E. Caldwell (1769-1819), a leader of the New York Bible Society and later the first general agent of the American Bible Society

William Jay (1789-1858), a major proponent of a national Bible society

SUMMARY OF EVENT

The outbreak of the American Revolutionary War in 1775 brought to a halt the importation of Bibles from England. The result was a shortage of Bibles at a time when there was a strong desire to reignite the evangelistic fires of the First Great Awakening (1739-1742). In 1777, to help satisfy the growing demand for Bibles, the Second Continental Congress voted to purchase twenty thousand Bibles from Holland. A representative from New Jersey, Elias Boudinot, cast the vote of that state in favor of the purchase.

When the American Revolution ended in 1783, Bibles from England reappeared in American bookstores, but a desire to alleviate the need to import them by printing American Bibles had already been ignited. Robert Aitken had printed some in Philadelphia during the revolution, but they were more expensive than those imported from England. It was a British Bible that inspired young Abraham Lincoln in his Kentucky log cabin. American-printed Bibles soon became less expensive, however, and by the end of the eighteenth century they were being printed in cities throughout the United States. The Second Great Awakening (1790's-1830's) increased the demand for them.

In 1804, the British and Foreign Bible Society was founded in England. The vision of that organization soon spread to the entire world. Reports about its work were circulated in America in a journal called *The Panoplist*, founded in Boston in 1805 by Jedidiah Morse, who urged the formation of similar societies in the United States.

The first such U.S. society was the Philadelphia Bible Society, founded in December, 1808. Its constitution became a guide for future societies, specifying that, in order to avoid denominational and doctrinal controversy, all Bibles had to be without notes. Some felt that the Philadelphia Bible Society should expand to encompass the entire nation, but others thought that a centralized society would become unwieldy and lose its focus. The latter group believed that the proliferation of local societies would better meet the needs of the nation: Local groups could each serve their own communities while still communicating, cooperating, and possibly sharing funds to meet national needs.

Circulars were sent to leaders of various denominations throughout the country, urging them to establish local Bible societies. By 1814, there were more than one hundred state and local Bible societies in the United States. The goals of each were to provide Bibles to those too poor to buy their own and to extend their services to foreign lands when possible. The British and Foreign Bible Society sent grants of three hundred to five hundred dollars to each of the sixteen state societies and, by the end of 1816, had given more than eight thousand dollars to support the American work. The leaders in Amer-

American Bible Society poster issued during World War I to solicit public support for its program of providing servicemen with copies of the New Testament. General John J. Pershing (1860-1948) commanded the American Expeditionary Force sent to Europe in 1916. (Library of Congress)

ica rewarded the British with such titles as "Venerable Parent."

There were still many, however, who felt the need for a national Bible society. As a result, on May 8, 1816, fifty-six delegates representing state and local societies from New England to Kentucky and North Carolina met in the Garden Street Dutch Reformed Church in New York City. In addition to ministers, the delegates included lawyers, editors, judges, doctors, bankers, and businessmen. Denominations represented included Presbyterians, Congregationalists, Methodists, Episcopalians, Baptists, Quakers, and members of the Dutch

Reformed Church. Together, they decided to form the American Bible Society.

Of the delegates who met on that historic day, five men were most important. Samuel J. Mills had been among the first to raise the call for a national society. As a student at Andover Theological Seminary (founded by Jedidiah Morse in 1807), Mills had joined with like-minded students to form the American Board of Commissioners for Foreign Missions in 1810. Mills traveled widely in America for this board, especially west of the Appalachian Mountains. The moral conditions and shortage of Bibles he encountered in that area spurred his desire to help found a national Bible society. After participating in the founding of the society, Mills went to Africa to survey the need for Bibles on that continent. He died on the return trip.

After reporting on the work of the British and Foreign Bible Society in *The Panoplist*, Jedidiah Morse traveled from Massachusetts to Georgia, helping found local Bible societies. In 1809, he began urging the Philadelphia society to assume national leadership, publishing appeals from missionaries such as William Carey in India for Bibles in native languages and reporting on the travels and appeals of Samuel Mills. Morse was on the committee at the May, 1816, meeting that drafted the constitution of the American Bible Society.

The most persistent voice on behalf of a national society was that of Elias Boudinot, the president of the New Jersey Bible Society. After a long career as a national political leader, Boudinot devoted his last years to philanthropic endeavors. Much of this work involved Native American causes, such as the Brainerd Mission in Tennessee, inspiring Buck Watie, a young Cherokee, to visit Boudinot in 1818 on his way to the Foreign Mission School in Cornwall, Connecticut. Later, Watie registered at the school under the name Elias Boudinott, using two *t*'s to distinguish himself from his benefactor. During his years as a Cherokee leader, the second *t* was dropped.

In 1814, the New Jersey society appointed the first Elias Boudinot to a committee studying the need for a national society. Based on its report, a resolution was adopted on August 30 calling for the establishment of such a society. Boudinot circulated the resolution and answered in writing the objections of those opposed. In May, 1815, he won the support of the Connecticut Bible Society, and others soon followed. Finally, on January 31, 1816, Boudinot issued a call for a convention to meet in New York City in May to form a national society. However, because of illness he could not personally attend that meeting.

As the corresponding secretary of the New York Bible Society, John E. Caldwell was at first opposed to the creation of a national society, even though, after being orphaned during the American Revolution, he was raised in the household of Elias Boudinot. However, in 1815 he gave his support to Boudinot's plan, and he was the host for the May, 1816, meeting. William Jay, meanwhile, was the recording secretary of the Westchester, New York, Auxiliary Bible Society. His father, John Jay, who had been the first chief justice of the United States, was its president. In March, 1816, William Jay sent to Boudinot a sixteen-page memoir, in which he espoused the need for Bibles in both the Christian and non-Christian areas of the world. Boudinot circulated this appeal prior to the May meeting. It was reprinted by Caldwell in *The Christian Herald*, anonymously at Jay's request.

When the organizational convention of the American Bible Society began on May 8, 1816, Joshua Wallace, replacing the ailing Boudinot as the delegate from New Jersey, was elected chairman. Lyman Beecher, a young pastor from Connecticut, acted as secretary. An extremely valuable conventional delegate was Gardiner Spring, for sixty-three years pastor of the Brick Presbyterian Church in New York City. James Fenimore Cooper, the novelist, was among other well-known delegates.

In the afternoon of the opening day of the convention, without a dissenting vote, a resolution was adopted to form a national Bible society. On May 11, meeting in New York City Hall, the first officers of the new society were elected, including Elias Boudinot as the first president. By the end of 1816, the British and Foreign Bible Society had given about fourteen hundred dollars to its new American counterpart.

SIGNIFICANCE

The American Bible Society helped spread Bibles throughout the United States and the world. Upon the death of Elias Boudinot in 1821, John Jay was elected president of the society. Three U.S. presidents, John Quincy Adams, Rutherford B. Hayes, and Benjamin Harrison, later served on the board of the society, and Abraham Lincoln was a strong supporter.

The first translation printed by the society was the Book of John in the language of the Native American Delaware tribe. Other nineteenth century achievements of the society include providing Bibles to immigrants and to riders of the Pony Express. During the U.S. Civil War, a special pocket Bible was printed to give to men on both sides, with a special truce created so it could be given to Confederate soldiers. Beginning with the U.S.

Navy in 1817, society Bibles have been given to American military personnel.

—*Glenn L. Swygart*

FURTHER READING

American Bible Society. www.americanbible.org. Accessed December 15, 2005. Provides the mission statement of the American Bible Society, plus a historical time line. Includes detailed coverage of the society's ongoing work.

Dwight, Henry Otis. *The Centennial History of the American Bible Society.* 2 vols. New York: Macmillan, 1916. A detailed account of the background, founding, and first century of the society. Gives excellent coverage to the individuals involved in the founding.

Nord, David Paul. *Faith in Reading: Religious Publishing and the Birth of Mass Media in America.* New York: Oxford University Press, 2004. Argues that the American Bible Society was central to the creation of an American mass media. Bibliographical references and index.

Wosh, Peter J. *Spreading the Word: The Bible Business in Nineteenth Century America.* Ithaca, N.Y.: Cornell University Press, 1994. Puts the American Bible Society in the context of other social movements. Covers organizational changes and historical shifts; concludes with an epilogue entitled "From Missionary Basis to Business Basis? Isaac Bliss's Strange Lament."

SEE ALSO: 1804: British and Foreign Bible Society Is Founded; Apr. 6, 1830: Smith Founds the Mormon Church; 1835: Finney Lectures on "Revivals of Religion"; Apr. 3, 1860-Oct. 26, 1861: Pony Express Expedites Transcontinental Mail; Apr. 12, 1861-Apr. 9, 1865: U.S. Civil War; 1870-1871: Watch Tower Bible and Tract Society Is Founded; Oct. 30, 1875: Eddy Establishes the Christian Science Movement.

RELATED ARTICLES in *Great Lives from History: The Nineteenth Century, 1801-1900:* William Carey; James Fenimore Cooper.

1810's

December, 1816
RISE OF THE COCKNEY SCHOOL

"Cockney School" is a term assigned by Blackwood's Magazine *to a coterie of English writers and artists centered on Leigh Hunt. Conservative Tories attacked them for their vulgarity, loose metrics, and Cockney rhymes and considered them as political as well as artistic radicals whose aesthetic and sociopolitical theories bordered on sedition.*

LOCALE: London, England
CATEGORY: Literature

KEY FIGURES
Leigh Hunt (1784-1859), radical English writer and editor of *The Examiner* and other periodicals
John Keats (1795-1821), English poet
William Hazlitt (1778-1830), English critic and essayist
Percy Bysshe Shelley (1792-1822), English poet
John Gibson Lockhart (1794-1854), contributor to *Blackwood's Magazine* and editor of the *Quarterly Review*, 1825-1853

SUMMARY OF EVENT

In 1811, the radical writer and editor Leigh Hunt began formulating his new poetics. Instead of ascribing to French school poetics, he advocated those of the Italian school and the poetics of the Italian Renaissance and the English writers Geoffrey Chaucer, William Shakespeare, Edmund Spenser, and John Milton. He included notions of "a freer spirit of versification" and the use of "actual" language—not far from William Wordsworth's "language of the common man."

In December of 1816, Hunt published a review essay, "Young Poets," in the *Examiner*, announcing the formation of a new school of poetry and introducing Percy Bysshe Shelley, John Keats, and John Hamilton Reynolds. It was soon followed in 1817 by William Hazlitt's edited volume *The Round Table: A Collection of Essays on Literature, Men, and Manners.* This "new school" shared a belief that poetics and politics of the new generation had to progress beyond those of the older generation of poets such as Wordsworth, Samuel Taylor Coleridge, and Robert Southey, whom Hazlitt had dubbed the Lake School. He objected to their sociopolitical beliefs, finding that those who had been idealistic in the early days of the French Revolution (1789) had become conservative and reactionary.

The anxiety felt by the cultural establishment concerning Jacobinism, anticlericalism, and other social and political threats extended to periodical literature. Because of advances in print technology and an expanding middle-class readership, periodical literature was flourishing. Whereas quarterly periodicals had been addressed to well-educated readers, the new "magazines" sought to gain wider audiences without losing their older reading public. Among those who were writing for these new readers were Leigh Hunt and his suburban London associates. Conservatives regarded these writers as radicals, whose unorthodox lifestyles, subversiveness, and aesthetic assaults on tradition threatened to undermine established culture.

Leigh Hunt. (Hulton Archive/Getty Images)

In October, 1817, John Gibson Lockhart, writing as "Z," launched a series of articles in *Blackwood's Magazine* attacking Hunt and other writers. He challenged Hunt's qualifications to found any school, his aesthetic and political pretensions, his lack of taste, and his vulgarity. Lockhart labeled Hunt a "man of little education" who knew no Latin or Greek, who read no great French authors yet denigrated French literature, and who had to read both classical and contemporary authors in translation. Pointing to Hunt's presumptions, Lockhart called his coterie the Cockney School and designated Hunt its "chief Doctor and Professor." Of Hunt's *The Story of Rimini* (1816), a poem that crystallized Cockney aesthetics, Lockhart charged that it amounted to nothing but "pretence, affectation, finery, and gaudiness." Even in an age of caustic wit, Lockhart's essays were exceptionally vitriolic.

One may ask what Hunt had done to deserve such opprobrium and why Lockhart was so hysterical. It had to do with the print revolution, social class, politics, literary gatekeeping, and suburban population growth. According to Lockhart, Hunt was not a gentleman. British writers had always been men of rank and, as such, would evince no "vulgarity" in their work. Not so Hunt, whose lack of station and breeding and his "low habits"—according to Lockhart—were apparent in whatever he did. Lockhart regarded Hunt as a Londoner whose nature poetry derived merely from a city dweller's acquaintance with gardens rather than from true rural landscapes. He charged that Hunt's poetry could be appreciated only by other Londoners—"the young attorneys and embryo-barristers around town." What Lockhart regarded as Hunt's worst "sin," however, was his lack of "religious" and "patriotic feeling." In Lockhart's eyes, Hunt was guilty of the dreaded anticlericalism and radicalism that he detected in the Cockney School—always excepting the aristocratic Byron and Shelley. In short, the Cockneys were usurping the cultural preeminence of the educated upper classes.

Lockhart seemed equally disconcerted by what he saw as the "moral depravity" of the Cockney School. Referring to Hunt's *The Story of Rimini*, he charged that its indecency would undermine the institution of marriage. He also contrasted Hunt's license with Wordsworth's "dignified purity of thought." Of Hunt's connections with Lord Byron and Thomas Moore, Lockhart was especially ungenerous, regarding the association as "unsuitable" for both. Moore, a gentleman, could not possibly esteem someone of so little breeding as Hunt. Lockhart was also upset with Hunt's dedicating of a book

HUNT'S POETICS

In his preface to The Story of Rimini, *excerpted below, Leigh Hunt—the man at the center of the Cockney School, and its most vilified member—explained his ideas about the nature of poetry and the proper way critically to evaluate it.*

Poetry, in its highest sense, belongs exclusively to such men as Shakespeare, Spenser, and others, who possessed the deepest insight into the spirit and sympathies of all things; but poetry, in the most comprehensive application of the term, I take to be the flower of any kind of experience, rooted in truth, and issuing forth into beauty. All that the critic has a right to demand of it, according to its degree, is, that it should spring out of a real impulse, be consistent in its parts, and shaped into some characteristic harmony of verse. Without these requisites (apart from fleeting and artificial causes), the world will scarcely look at any poetical production a second time; whereas, if it possess them, the humblest poetry stands a chance of surviving not only whatever is falsely so called, but much that contains, here and there, more poetical passages than itself; passages that are the fits and starts of a fancy without judgment—the incoherences of a nature, poetical only by convulsion, but prosaic in its ordinary strength.

Source: Leigh Hunt, *Selected Writings*. Edited by David Jesson-Dibley (New York: Routledge, 2003), p. 13.

social change and the amelioration of the oppressed. The sociopolitical radicalism of the Cockneys represented a dogged determination on the part of many second-generation Romantics to maintain revolutionary ideals and to eschew the disillusionment and resultant conservatism of the older generation. Hunt set as the Cockney agenda the democratization of poetry and the Cockney aesthetic of "cheerfulness" and "sociality."

The Tory establishment saw almost everything that the Cockneys did as a challenge to tradition, especially the Cockneys' poetic theory and practice. Their poetics seemed unabashedly luxuriant and luxurious, sensual and personal in a rather public way; their writing was disturbing. Z noted "Cockney rhymes" and "jargon" with disdain. Instead of respecting the boundaries of the traditional poetic form, which used closed couplets as Alexander Pope had with two lines of rhymed iambic pentameter providing impact at the close of the second line, Cockneys enjambed the couplets, running over the second lines, as though writing rhymed blank verse without the magisterial tone and appropriate subject matter. They also violated "standard" vowel sounds in verse (or so it seems from the distance of two centuries). They introduced the trivial and the mundane into letters at a time when the subject matter of Romanticism was reaching ever more toward the sublime.

Cockney poetics, which Hunt deemed "free and idiomatic," injected common descriptions of experience and common disruptions of literary language in ways that most jarred conservative sensibilities. One contemporary critic labeled Hunt's writing style "confectionary." It would be a misconception, however, to think of the Cockneys as a coherent school. Byron's early castigation of Keats's work is well known, though Byron came to admire Keats, believing his early writing "spoilt by Cockneyfying and Suburbing."

At a time when the subject matter of what was regarded as the greatest poetry was the sublime and affecting forms of nature, elevating nature to the status of a deity, the Cockneys were seen as worse than urban—they were *suburban*, centered on Hunt's Hampstead residence north of central London. Being suburban at that

to Byron, whom he regarded as "the most nobly born of English Patricians, and one of the first geniuses whom the world ever produced." He regarded Hunt's act as so audacious that it incited public disgust and called Hunt "a paltry cockney newspaper scribbler" who should have minded his station.

Within six months of Lockhart's attack, Hunt published *Foliage* (1818). Prefaced by a statement advocating greater personal, political, and aesthetic freedom, this book was an essential document in the formation of the Cockney School. Its preface announced the school's agenda, and its sonnets named people and places to announce the school's membership.

Hunt may not have been born an English aristocrat or a "gentleman," but to Lockhart and others, his purported radicalism may have been even worse than his birth into the amorphous middle class. At the time Lockhart attacked Hunt, Great Britain had been at war with France for two decades, and the memory of the French Revolution's Reign of Terror had not faded. The English Tory establishment feared Jacobinism and any social protests that smacked of antigovernment sentiment. *Blackwood's Magazine* called Hunt "the most fierce democrat and demagogue."

Hunt, Keats, Byron, and Shelley were young and idealistic at the time of Lockhart's attacks. They advocated

time meant many things. With socioeconomic changes, the population of England had increased geometrically, causing urban overcrowding and migration to the suburbs. Historically, the suburbs of London had hardly been enclaves of gentility, so the fact that Hunt, Keats, and their fellows were from the suburbs allowed Z to cast them as unsophisticated on one hand and as lacking in country virtues on the other.

"Nature" in Cockney life and literature was redolent not of Grasmere or Windemere but of the home garden. In the suburbs, newly comfortable middle-class families could live in a degree of affluence that, for Z, came dangerously close to rivaling that of their social betters. In his third essay, Z accused Hunt of an intent "to spread the infection of a loathsome licentiousness," asserting that the Cockneys, through their lifestyle, aesthetics, and politics, would bring down the very time-honored institutions of English life.

By the 1830's, anti-Cockney sentiment was dissipating, possibly due to the passage of reforming legislation that averted in Great Britain the threat of political upheaval occurring on the Continent. Nevertheless, "Cockney" remained a pejorative term. By midcentury, it had come to refer merely to working-class Londoners born within the sound of Bow Bells.

SIGNIFICANCE

Cockney cockiness—in blending colloquialisms and slang with the rhetorical registers of Chaucer, Shakespeare, Spenser, Milton, and the Renaissance Italians, in intruding the profane and ridiculous into the sacred and sublime—may have incurred the wrath of conservative Tory periodical culture. However, it may also be seen as a breakthrough that led to the poetics of Robert and Elizabeth Barrett Browning and later to the juxtapositions of modernism, evident in T. S. Eliot's intermingled voices in *The Waste Land* (1922). Keats's early imitations of Italian Renaissance models gave him the foundation on which to write some of the greatest lyrics in the English language. Hunt was long marginalized, but he is now re-

garded as a seminal figure in second-generation Romanticism.

—Donna Berliner

FURTHER READING

Cox, Jeffrey. *Poetry and Politics in the Cockney School: Keats, Shelley, Hunt and Their Circle*. Cambridge, England: Cambridge University Press, 1998. Cox makes a case for Romantics as coterie writers.

Dawson, P. M. S. "Byron, Shelley, and the 'New School.'" In *Shelley Revalued: Essays from the Gregynog Conference*, edited by Kelvin Everest. Totowa, N.J.: Barnes & Noble, 1983. Discusses the relationship of aristocratic writers to the Cockney School.

Jones, Elizabeth. "The Cockney School of Poetry: Keats in the Suburbs." In *The Persistence of Poetry: Bicentennial Essays on Keats*, edited by Robert M. Ryan. Amherst: University of Massachusetts Press, 1998. Discusses the suburban phenomenon in English literary history.

Roe, Nicholas, ed. *Leigh Hunt: Life, Poetics, Politics*. New York: Routledge, 2003. An essential collection of articles on Leigh Hunt that also provides a valuable bibliography.

Wu, Duncan. "Keats and the 'Cockney School.'" In *The Cambridge Companion to Keats*, edited by Susan J. Wolfson. New York: Cambridge University Press, 2001. Observes Keats as a Cockney writer, although an ambivalent one.

SEE ALSO: 1807: Bowdler Publishes *The Family Shakespeare*; 1807-1850: Rise of the Knickerbocker School; July 14, 1833: Oxford Movement Begins; Fall, 1848: Pre-Raphaelite Brotherhood Begins; July, 1881-1883: Stevenson Publishes *Treasure Island*.

RELATED ARTICLES in *Great Lives from History: The Nineteenth Century, 1801-1900:* Lord Byron; Samuel Taylor Coleridge; John Keats; Percy Bysshe Shelley; William Wordsworth.

1817
RICARDO IDENTIFIES SEVEN KEY ECONOMIC PRINCIPLES

The leading classical economic theorist, David Ricardo systematized the study of economics by identifying the most basic economic principles, and his theories played an important role in Great Britain's repeal of restrictive economic laws.

LOCALE: England
CATEGORIES: Economics; business and labor

KEY FIGURES

David Ricardo (1772-1823), British financier and economic theorist

Adam Smith (1723-1790), Scottish economic theorist

John Ramsay McCulloch (1789-1864), Scottish economist, statistician, and friend of James Mill and David Ricardo

James Mill (1773-1836), Scottish utilitarian propagandist and theorist

John Stuart Mill (1806-1873), son of James Mill and an economic theorist best known for *Principles of Political Economy*

SUMMARY OF EVENT

Two of the most influential figures in the history of economic theory are Karl Marx (1818-1883), who is associated with the development of communist theory, and John Maynard Keynes (1883-1946), whose best-known economic theory concerns deficit spending and argues that it is the government's responsibility to control and regulate fluctuations in the economy. A third major figure is David Ricardo, the foremost classical economist, who published his main theories in 1817. Classical economic theory is based on the principles of individual liberty, which allow people to use their own initiative to acquire property and wealth. According to classical economic theory, the best way for the government to encourage accumulation of wealth is to follow laissez-faire policies.

Adam Smith, the first of the major classical economists, began to examine economic theory in *An Inquiry into the Nature and Causes of the Wealth of Nations* (1776). Ricardo followed Smith, bringing a new level of order and a strong theoretical foundation. James Mill and John Ramsay McCulloch, both friends of Ricardo, helped to spread Ricardian economic theory through their own writings. The last of the school was Mill's son, John Stuart Mill, who continued the process of system-

atizing economic thought in *Principles of Political Economy*, which he first published in 1848.

Known as a theorist's theorist, Ricardo began his career as a stockbroker and began dabbling in economic theory in 1799. In 1813, he retired from his stockbroker work a wealthy man and devoted the remainder of his life to economics, including a period of four years of service when he represented Gloucestershire in Great Britain's Parliament. He died in Gloucestershire in 1823 at the age of fifty-one.

Chronologically, Ricardo falls between Adam Smith and John Stuart Mill. Classical economic thought dominated the field from the late eighteenth to the late nineteenth century, with Ricardo's influence covering the span from the 1820's to the 1850's. Ricardo was influenced by Adam Smith, and he in turn influenced Mill. Ricardo's life spanned the close of the age of mercantilism and the rise of capitalism. In the former age, nations calculated their wealth by the amounts of gold they held. Gold came largely from trade, which was enhanced by possession of overseas colonies. Smith's theory based the wealth of a nation on the value of the goods it produced, a theory that encouraged reinvestment of at least a portion of the wealth created to create more wealth.

Ricardo's interest in economics came after he read Adam Smith's *The Wealth of Nations*. Although Ricardo's ideas have long since been regarded as outmoded, he was the first person to systematize the study of economics. Through his work he inspired both those, such as David Hume, who supported laissez-faire economic policy that advocated separating government and economics and those who opposed it, favoring instead government control of the economy, as in communism, a theory developed by Karl Marx.

Ricardo thought inductively, working from abstract principles to establish economic laws. For example, he saw that population was increasing, a fact that resulted in more humans competing for resources. As population expanded, people needed to produce more food through more intensive methods of farming and through increasing the amount of land under production. As technology improved, so would people's ability to increase food production, but since population would continue to rise, there would be no increase in surplus production, thus keeping the majority of the population at a subsistence level.

David Ricardo. (Library of Congress)

Whereas Smith's writings emphasized a nation's ability to produce, those of Ricardo focused on the distribution of resources among the three major classes: landowners, capitalists, and workers. In his major treatise, *On the Principle of Political Economy and Taxation*, first published in 1817, Ricardo worked to establish a theory of wealth. His book soon became the definitive work in economics, replacing Smith's *The Wealth of Nations*. Ricardo changed the direction of economic thought when he argued that the fundamental purpose of studying economics was to determine the appropriate relationships among these three groups.

Ricardo's basic principle was the wage fund theory, in which he argued that the available amount of money was fixed. This theory built upon the laissez-faire assumptions that free and unlimited exchanges of labor existed in a self-regulating market economy. Laissez-faire economic theory, which is fundamental to the classical economists, argued that the economic laws of supply and demand needed to be allowed to function freely without outside interference. In such an economic climate, Ricardo argued, as did the other classical economists, to take money for poverty relief was to withhold it from the

industrious, an action that would reduce the standard of living for all workers, thus hurting, rather than helping, the poor.

Each of Ricardo's three groups had its own unique source of capital. Landlords received income from rents charged for the use of real property. The income of the capitalists came from profits and interest on investments. Laborers earned their funds from their labor. Of these three groups, Ricardo had the least use for landlords, whom he characterized as parasites. Their income, rent, rose simply because they held the title to an increasingly valuable factor of production—the land. Because landlords needed only to continue to hold the land to earn a living, it could be argued that they provided nothing to the advancement of society. Associated with rent was Ricardo's "law of diminishing returns." Land produces food through the application of capital and labor. As more capital and labor are applied, more food can be produced. There comes a point, however, when additional capital and labor will not result in a proportional increase in production, and that point represents his law of diminishing returns.

Laborers were in the unfortunate position, Ricardo argued, of always living at a subsistence level. In his "iron law of wages" theory, nothing could be done to raise the level of compensation for workers above the minimum. Although wages might rise in the short term, he theorized, such an increase would in turn create an increase in population that would tend to depress wages, returning them to their subsistence level. Further adding to the plight of wage earners, profits and wages represented opposite interests. Ricardo argued that, because there existed a finite amount of money, the only way wages could rise would be if profits declined. To use more money to pay wages would result in lower profits, which would be harmful because fewer people would invest their time and talent in creating new ventures. Further adding to the plight of labor was the increasing industrialization of society. More machinery resulted in lower production costs, allowing capitalists to set aside more funds for investment.

Beyond explaining relationships among rent, capital, and labor, Ricardo's other main area of interest focused on the trade among nations. In nineteenth century Great Britain, the Corn Laws imposed tariffs on imported grains. Ricardo argued that such tariffs were self-defeating, favoring a system of free trade among nations. Free trade would encourage nations to specialize in the areas in which they excelled, thus increasing their production and thereby their wealth.

In his theory of comparative advantage, Ricardo argued that as each nation found its own productive specialization, it could produce its special commodity for its own people and then export the surplus to others at a cost lower than that of other nations. It could then exchange its special commodity with other nations for goods that it could not produce for itself at an advantageous price. For example, as Britain industrialized, it would be in a position to export surplus industrial goods, thus creating a profit, while it imported food for its growing population. Ricardo's work contributed to Parliament's repeal of the Corn Laws, which established a long period of free trade in Great Britain.

SIGNIFICANCE

In addition to fostering free trade, Ricardo's writing helped bring to an end many of Britain's intrusive economic policies. By popularizing Adam Smith's policy of laissez-faire, Ricardo was instrumental in the simplification of England's taxation. Further, his influence was felt in the repeal of the Navigation Acts, which symbolized government control of the economy and stood as one of the main causes of the American Revolution (1775-1783).

—*Duncan R. Jamieson*

FURTHER READING

Blaug, Mark. *Ricardian Economics: A Historical Study.* New Haven, Conn.: Yale University Press, 1958. Blaug studies the rise and fall of Ricardian economics in England, focusing on both its successes and its failures.

Cameron, Rondo. *A Concise Economic History of the World.* New York: Oxford University Press, 1993. A valuable survey placing classical economics and David Ricardo in an appropriate historical context.

Churchman, Nancy. *David Ricardo on Public Debt.* New York: Palgrave, 2001. Study of Ricardo's ideas about public debt that places those ideas in the context of his other economic theories.

Henderson, John P., and John B. Davis. *The Life and Economics of David Ricardo.* Edited by Warren J. Samuels and Gilbert B. Davis. Boston: Kluwer Academic, 1997. Comprehensive intellectual biography, recounting Ricardo's early years, career, economic theories, and relationships with Thomas Malthus and other classical economists.

Hollander, Samuel. *The Economics of David Ricardo.* Toronto: University of Toronto Press, 1979. Hollander puts Ricardo's theories in perspective relative to the work of Adam Smith and the other classical economists.

Landreth, Harry, and David C. Colander. *History of Economic Thought.* Boston: Houghton Mifflin, 1994. An excellent introduction that places Ricardo and classical economics in perspective.

Ricardo, David. *The Principles of Political Economy and Taxation.* Introduction by Michael P. Fogarty. London: J. M. Dent & Sons, 1969. Although difficult for nonspecialists, this treatise is Ricardo's main work in the field of political economy.

SEE ALSO: 1824: British Parliament Repeals the Combination Acts; 1833: British Parliament Passes the Factory Act; 1839: Blanc Publishes *The Organization of Labour*; Sept. 2, 1843: Wilson Launches *The Economist*; June 15, 1846: British Parliament Repeals the Corn Laws; Feb., 1848: Marx and Engels Publish *The Communist Manifesto*; 1859: Mill Publishes *On Liberty*; 1867: Marx Publishes *Das Kapital*.

RELATED ARTICLES in *Great Lives from History: The Nineteenth Century, 1801-1900:* Thomas Robert Malthus; Karl Marx; James Mill; John Stuart Mill; David Ricardo.

1810's

c. 1817-1828
ZULU EXPANSION

In one of the most significant indigenous revolutions in African history, Shaka transformed the petty Zulu chiefdom into the most powerful African state in Southern Africa and launched expansionist wars that changed the map of the subcontinent.

ALSO KNOWN AS: Mfecane
LOCALE: Zululand, South Africa
CATEGORIES: Expansion and land acquisition; wars, uprisings, and civil unrest

KEY FIGURES

Shaka (c. 1787-1828), Zulu king, r. c. 1817-1828
Dingiswayo (c. 1770-c. 1818), paramount chief of the Mthethwa
Zwide (d. 1826), paramount chief of the Ndwandwe
Dingane (c. 1795-1840), brother of Shaka, whom he assassinated and succeeded as king

SUMMARY OF EVENT

At the turn of the nineteenth century, the Zulu were a small, clan-centered group of Northern Nguni-speaking people who had settled in what later became known as Zululand, on the northeast coast of South Africa. Since arriving there several hundred years earlier, the Zulu had established a thriving pastoral and agricultural society that was surrounded by other Northern Nguni clans, including the increasingly aggressive and expansionist Mthethwa and Ndwandwe states.

Burgeoning populations, ever-greater pressures on territorial resources. and opportunities to trade with European merchants on the coast sparked higher levels of competition and conflict. Traditional southeast warfare in the region had been relatively bloodless, consistently mainly of intimidating rituals that emphasized taunting and athleticism and ended with the seizure of cattle and human hostages. The chieftains Zwide of the Ndwandwe and Dingiswayo of the Mthethwa fought against each other and reduced the surrounding peoples to client or tributary status.

The Zulu fell under the sway of the Mthethwa, and Dingiswayo took under his wing Shaka, the young son of the Zulu chief Senzangakona. He raised Shaka to become one of his principal military commanders. After Senzangakona died, Dingiswayo helped install Shaka as Zulu chief around 1817, and bonds between the Mthethwa and Zulu were strengthened. However, when Zwide's Ndwandwe invaded the Mthethwa, the Zulu mobilized

but refrained from fighting. The Ndwandwe defeated the Mthethwa, killing Dingiswayo. Shaka and his friendless Zulu were next. The Zulu army fought in its traditional way and held its own against the Ndwandwe, but saw the invaders ravage its homeland in the Mfolozi Valley.

Shaka responded to this setback by drastically reorganizing the Zulu military. He extended the period of service, replaced javelins with long-bladed stabbing spears for close-quarter combat, and integrated allies and defeated warriors directly into his units. Many of his neighbors joined him in the face of the Ndwandwe threat. Others who remained aloof, such as Phathakwayo ka-Khondolo of the Qwabe, were killed and their people forcibly absorbed into the new kingdom. Still others, such as Mzilikazi's Khumalo, migrated across the Drakensberg Mountains to escape Shaka's new order.

Idealized portrait of Zulu founder-king Shaka from Nathaniel Isaacs's 1836 book, Travels and Adventures in East Africa. *(Arkent Archive)*

ZULU EXPANSION AND THE MFECANE

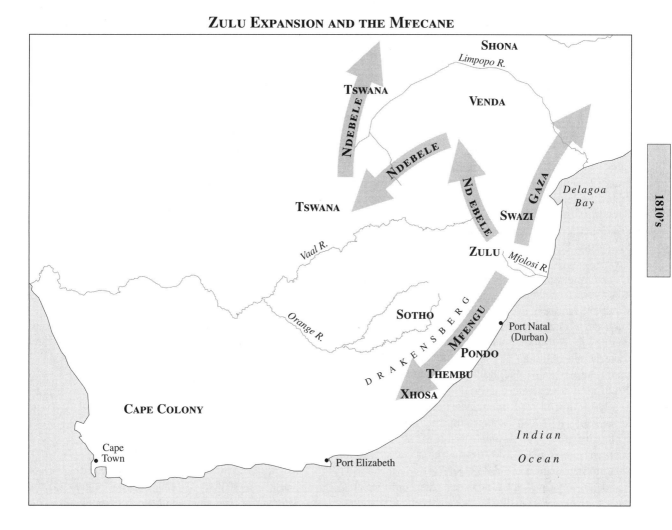

Shaka's personal ruthlessness and success established his power and authority but gained him powerful enemies as well. In 1818, the Ndwandwe attacked the Zulu again, and the still inferior Zulu fought them off and repaired the extensive damage to their territory. Meanwhile, Shaka's army grew stronger. When Zwide invaded again in 1819, Shaka's army not only repulsed the Ndwandwe but aggressively pursued them into their own lands. The Zulu sacked Zwide's capital and pushed his armies north beyond the Phongolo River. Zulu power—and that of Shaka—was at an unprecedented height for the region. Ndwandwe tributaries became Zulu tributaries, and Shaka built military compounds along his northern frontier to protect it from further aggression.

Shaka next considered war against the Mabhudu and Thembe peoples. The Mabhudu people had organized the region's first powerful and centralized kingdom dur-

ing the 1790's, and with the Thembe they controlled the trading network that filled Portuguese ships at Delagoa Bay to the north of Zululand. However, Shaka held his hand, knowing that the Mabhudu were powerful and that a war on his northern frontier would probably draw Zwide's Ndwandwe against him. Shaka instead attacked the Ngwane (later known as Swazi) and Chunu to his west and south, in the Mzimkulu River basin and the shadow of the Drakensberg Mountains.

Farther south, the Thembu and Mpondo, who were themselves regional aggressors, also drew Zulu attention. Shaka sensed that Zulu success depended upon continuous expansion and military victory, which enriched his warriors, his reputation, and his personal war chest. However, Zulu success could also come in the form of new and powerful European allies. In 1795, the British had replaced the Dutch as rulers of the Cape Colony and

271

were now slowly sending out feelers along the Indian Ocean coast. Naval lieutenant Francis Farewell and the trader Henry Francis Fynn established the first British colony in Port Natal (Durban) in 1824, duly recognizing—if not always understanding—the role they would play as clients of the Zulu.

After Zwide died in 1826, the Ndwandwe were led by his son, Sikhuyana. This new chieftain was known to support Shaka's many internal enemies—disgruntled family members, minority tribal leaders, and Zulu who had grown tired of constant war. Shaka, in turn, supported Sikhuyana's brother and rival, Somaphunga. In September of 1826, the Zulu and Ndwandwe fought a decisive battle at the izinDolowane Hills. In that battle Shaka first employed his new British clients and their firearms.

The Zulu shattered Ndwandwe power by using their new tactical formation known as the horns of the bull, in which the army extended its flanks around enemy forces and then closed in and crushed them. After three Zulu charges, the Ndwandwe warriors fled, and the remaining women and children, as well as the wounded, were killed. Somaphunga then replaced his brother, and the Ndwandwe were reduced to Zulu tributaries.

Shaka utilized his British clients and their weapons again in early 1827 in his attack on the Bheje people of Khumalo in the rough mountain terrain of his new northwestern frontier. In late 1827 the Zulu capital was moved south to kwaDukuza in the Port Natal area as Shaka had decided to treat with the British regarding Zulu expansion southward toward the Cape Colony and into the European sphere of influence. James King led the mission, which failed not least because Shaka decided to attack the Mpongo across the boundary Mzimkhulu River. Although it was merely a raid for cattle and other prizes to placate bored warriors, the attack soured Zulu relations with the colonial authorities. In August, 1828, the Zulu struck out against the refugee Ngwane peoples, scattering—and enraging—them. Shortly afterward, Shaka abruptly shifted his axis of campaign again and ordered the army northward in a raid on the Gaza people near Delagoa Bay, while he stayed at home. Shaka's brothers Mhlangana and Dingane found the army's absence an opportunity to murder the increasingly unstable Shaka on September 24, 1828.

SIGNIFICANCE

The last campaign left Dingane in control and the Zulu army shrunken, demoralized, disease-ridden, and unvictorious. Shaka's system of total warfare devastated the Natal region and left its peoples in a state of utter confusion and often dire poverty. Cattle, which were central to Nguni life, were depleted, and agriculture all but ceased in many parts of Natal. The Zulu wars displaced entire tribal groups, and while some found new homes on the high veld, others were left little more than refugees, helpless at the hands of more powerful tribes. Other displaced peoples, such as the Tlokwa, became piratic hordes that lived off plunder. Some of the surviving tribal groups adopted Zulu tactics and aggression and established themselves as local bully states. The social, political, and economic disruption rippled out from the Zulu homeland in a vast chain of disturbances that became known as the Mfecane.

Zulu victories did, however, help create a modern Zulu consciousness and identity that has survived into the twenty-first century. It also served to crystallize the kingdoms of the Swazi, the Sotho, and the Gaza, changing the political landscape of the region. Under the increasingly despotic Dingane the Zulu kingdom survived, despite serious challenges from other African states and Europeans. The Zulu Kingdom remained the strongest independent African state in South Africa until it was finally conquered by the British in 1879.

—*Joseph P. Byrne*

FURTHER READING

Beck, Roger. *The History of South Africa*. Westport, Conn.: Greenwood Press, 2000. General history of South Africa that contains a good chapter on the Mfecane era and the rise of the Zulu Kingdom.

Hamilton, Carolyn, ed. *The Mfecane Aftermath: Reconstructive Debates in Southern African History*. Bloomington: Indiana University Press, 1996. Collection of essays on a revisionist theory of the Mfecane disturbances advanced by the historian Julian Cobbing.

Knight, Eric, and Angus McBride. *Zulu, 1816-1906*. Oxford, England: Osprey, 1995. Short but well-illustrated discussion of the Zulu way of war and its influence on the kingdom's expansion.

Laband, John. *The Rise and Fall of the Zulu Nation*. London: Arms and Armour Press, 1997. The first several chapters cover the period of Shaka and his immediate successors, while the rest chronicle the fate of this kingdom. Contains a full discussion of Zulu culture and the changing role of warfare within it.

Omer-Cooper, J. D. *The Zulu Aftermath: A Nineteenth-Century Revolution in Bantu Africa*. London: Longmans, 1966. Standard history of the rise of the Zulu

Kingdom that traces its impact on surrounding societies.

Ritter, E. A. *Shaka Zulu*. New York: Penguin Books, 1985. Reprint of a classic biography of Shaka that presents a clear, if sometimes exaggerated, picture of Zulu culture. Relies heavily on the myths and traditions surrounding Shaka.

Sutherland, Jonathan, and Diane Canwell. *The Zulu Kings and Their Armies*. Barnsley, England: Pen & Sword Military, 2005. Essentially a military history of the nineteenth century Zulu people, with special attention to the reorganization of the Zulu army under Shaka.

Westley, David. *The Mfecane: An Annotated Bibliography*. Madison: African Studies Program, University of Wisconsin-Madison, 1999. Brief bibliographical guide to the Mfecane and the early Zulu Kingdom.

SEE ALSO: 1835: South Africa's Great Trek Begins; 1865-1868: Basuto War; Jan. 22-23, 1879: Battles of Isandlwana and Rorke's Drift; Jan. 22-Aug., 1879: Zulu War; Oct., 1893-October, 1897: British Subdue African Resistance in Rhodesia.

RELATED ARTICLES in *Great Lives from History: The Nineteenth Century, 1801-1900:* H. Rider Haggard; Paul Kruger; Lobengula; Shaka.

January 18, 1817-July 28, 1821
SAN MARTÍN'S MILITARY CAMPAIGNS

In stark contrast to Símon Bolívar's fiery and explosive military campaigns in the northern Spanish colonies of South America, José de San Martín's more measured initiatives and methodical approach secured the independence of Latin America's Southern Cone region and, before he retired from the scene in favor of Bolívar, went far toward securing the liberation of Peru from colonial Spanish rule.

LOCALE: Argentina; Chile; Peru

CATEGORIES: Wars, uprisings, and civil unrest; colonization; government and politics; expansion and land acquisition

KEY FIGURES

José de San Martín (1778-1850), South American revolutionary leader

Simón Bolívar (1783-1830), Venezuelan Creole revolutionary leader and later ruler of Gran Colombia, 1822-1830

Bernardo O'Higgins (1778-1842), Chilean general and liberal dictator, 1817-1823

Manuel Blanco Encalada (1790-1876), Argentine naval officer and later president of Chile, 1826

Thomas Cochrane (1775-1860), British naval veteran who commanded the Chilean navy, 1818-1822

Juan Martín de Pueyrredón (1776-1850), Argentine general and supreme director of Argentina, 1816-1819

Mariano Osorio (1777-1819), governor-general of Chile, 1814-1816

Casimiro Marcó del Pont (1770-1819), last governor-general of Chile, 1816-1817

Rafael Maroto (1783-1853), Spanish commander at the Battle of Chacabuco

SUMMARY OF EVENT

A native of the country that was to become Argentina, José de San Martín was taken by his parents to Spain at an early age and acquired considerable military experience by the time he returned to Buenos Aires in 1812. Meanwhile, he entered the Spanish army in 1789 at the age of eleven and served in campaigns in Morocco, southern France, and Portugal. From 1808 to 1811, he saw action during the Peninsular War (1808-1815) against the French occupiers of Spain, rising to the rank of lieutenant colonel. San Martín grew disillusioned by politics and favoritism within the Spanish army, which he believed discriminated against soldiers who, like himself, were not born in Spain. He returned to South America and fell in with the liberal revolutionary movement in Argentina, soon joining the revolutionary army at Buenos Aires as a lieutenant colonel.

On May 25, 1810, an independent governing junta was named to supplant the viceregal government of Rio de La Plata at Buenos Aires and to form a new state. From there, the forces of this new state of Argentina had fanned out in an attempt to clear Spanish troops from the region. The Army of the North was organized under the command of General Manuel Belgrano and tried to carry the fight into the Spanish stronghold of Upper Peru (present-day Bolivia). Belgrano was defeated in 1813,

José de San Martín. (Library of Congress)

precipitating his replacement (1814) by San Martín, who had gained notice through his victory over royalist forces at San Lorenzo de Parana on February 3, 1813.

Now a general, San Martín differed with leaders of the new Argentine government over their plans of direct attack on Upper Peru. Instead, he envisioned an indirect approach across the Andes Mountains and into the captaincy general of Chile. Rather than directly disobey orders, he played for time, perhaps feigning ill health. In 1814, the government acceded to the general's request to be allowed to resign his command of the Army of the North and to be reassigned to command of Argentine forces in Cuyo Province, whose capital at Mendoza was located at the foot of the Andes. In 1816, San Martín benefited from a change in the political climate. On May 3 of that year, Juan Martín de Pueyrredón was named supreme director of Argentina and, as he secretly agreed with San Martín's plan, officially designated San Martín's expeditionary force as the Army of the Andes, signing his regime's approval to its commander's plans.

San Martín embarked upon the lengthy, painstaking process of planning his audacious blow. His plan called for him to march his army across the mountains during the midst of the Andean summer after thoroughly reconnoitering the area and setting up a network of agents and fifth columnists. Relying on the elements of stealth and speed, he would surprise Spanish forces in Chile. Once Chile was secured, it could be used as a base from which to invade Peru. San Martín received invaluable assistance from exiled Chilean revolutionaries, who had been driven out in defeat at the hands of royalist General Mariano Osorio at the Battle of Rancagua. First, San Martín had to resolve a feud between two factions among the Chileans, one led by Bernardo O'Higgins and the other by José Miguel Carrera and his brothers Juan and Luis. Deciding in favor of O'Higgins, he appointed the Chilean to command the left wing of the Army of the Andes.

On January 18, 1817, San Martín led three columns totaling 3,550 troops through separate mountain passes; they had accomplished the crossing by February 8. By February 12, San Martín had completely routed the army of Colonel Rafael Maroto at the Battle of Chacabuco and had swept Governor-General Casimiro Marcó del Pont out of the capital of Santiago. Although Marcó del Pont retired, former Governor-General Mariano Osorio rallied the royalists and inflicted a humiliating defeat on San Martín at Cancha Rayada on March 19, 1818. However, San Martín was able to reorganize his army in an astonishingly short time, and his victorious attack against Osorio at Maipu on April 5, 1818, secured Chile's independence.

With his ally O'Higgins at the helm as Chile's supreme director (a post that San Martín had declined for himself), the victorious liberator formulated his plans for a seaborne assault on the Viceroyalty of Peru. To accomplish this, Chile had to build a navy from scratch, a task undertaken with dramatic success by the twenty-nine-year-old Manuel Blanco Encalada. After little more than a year, a fleet was ready to sail. All that was lacking was a seasoned commander, but that gap was filled—for a price—by the British sailor-of-fortune Thomas Cochrane. Cochrane was immediately given command of the Chilean navy and proceeded to ravage the Peruvian coast and Spanish shipping, even seizing the important port of Valdivia in February, 1820.

On August 20, 1820, the Chilean expeditionary force sailed out of Valparaiso aboard Cochrane's ships under the overall command of San Martín. On September 8, a landing was made at Pisco. Sporadic fighting was interrupted by two cease-fire periods, during which abortive attempts were made by the Spanish colonial regimes of two separate viceroys (Joaquín de Pezuela and José de la

Serna, respectively) to persuade San Martín to withdraw. The talks foundered over San Martín's insistence on no less than total independence, and royal troops evacuated the viceregal capital at Lima on July 6, 1821. San Martín marched into the city six days later. Complete independence was proclaimed on July 28, and San Martín was named protector of Peru.

By late 1821, Simón Bolívar, San Martín's counterpart in northern South America, had successfully liberated Venezuela, Colòmbia, and Ecuador. Meanwhile, San Martín's power and prestige were on the wane after his triumphs in July. Admiral Cochrane had absconded with ships and treasury funds after a salary dispute with the protector, and royalist forces were still defiant, firmly entrenched in the interior of the country, twice outnumbering his own army. San Martín's natural caution, which was aggravated by a debilitating disease—probably tuberculosis—and by the opium treatment he underwent for it, engendered criticism and a questioning of his ultimate resolve. His consistent support for the establishment of a constitutional monarchy under a European prince also provoked growing opposition.

Reaching the conclusion that only cooperation with Bolívar afforded a chance for victory over the remaining royalists, San Martín, in November of 1821, proposed a meeting with the Liberator. This meeting with Bolívar marked the end of San Martín's military activity, for when it occurred at Guayaquil on July 26-27, 1822, Bolívar did not hide his resentment of San Martín or his reluctance to share credit. San Martín, who was tired of the limelight and anxious to end the conflict, resigned from his political office and from military command and retired to private life, leaving Bolívar to secure independence for the rest of Peru.

SIGNIFICANCE

Although low-key in his approach and far less remembered than the more theatrical Simón Bolívar, José de San Martín and his southern campaigns of liberation were nonetheless just as crucial as those in the north. Without the efforts of this southern liberator, the achievement of total independence for South America would certainly have taken far longer to be realized. It may possibly not have been completed at all. San Martín spent the last decades of his life a reclusive exile in Eu-

rope, and he never attempted to shape the political destiny of the nations he helped create.

—*Raymond Pierre Hylton*

FURTHER READING

Graham, Richard. *Independence in Latin America: A Comparative Approach*. New York: McGraw-Hill, 1994. In terms of comparative leadership, the author rates San Martín well, but not as highly as he does Bolívar.

Harvey, Robert. *Liberators: Latin America's Struggle for Independence, 1810-1830*. Woodstock, N.Y.: Overlook Press, 2000. Interestingly written, contains a reasonably thorough character analysis, and discusses the role of the United States in the South American independence struggles.

Herring, Hubert. *A History of Latin America from the Beginnings to the Present*. New York: Alfred A. Knopf, 1967. Older generalist work whose insights have stood the test of time rather well. The author is more sympathetic to San Martín and sees Bolívar's ego as having sabotaged any potential for unified action in Peru.

Robertson, William Spence. *The Rise of the Spanish-American Republics as Told in the Lives of Their Liberators*. New York: Free Press, 1965. Contains the most detailed analysis of San Martín's complex character and strategy, and his controversial monarchical leanings.

Rodriguez O., Jaime E. *The Independence of Spanish America*. New York: Cambridge University Press, 1998. The author is more critical of San Martín than most and sees him as having lost his sense of direction after the liberation of Lima.

SEE ALSO: May 2, 1808-Nov., 1813: Peninsular War in Spain; Sept. 16, 1810: Hidalgo Issues El Grito de Dolores; Sept. 16, 1810-Sept. 28, 1821: Mexican War of Independence; Mar., 1813-Dec. 9, 1824: Bolívar's Military Campaigns; Sept. 7, 1822: Brazil Becomes Independent; Jan., 1833: Great Britain Occupies the Falkland Islands.

RELATED ARTICLES in *Great Lives from History: The Nineteenth Century, 1801-1900:* Simón Bolívar; José de San Martín; Bernardo O'Higgins.

1810's

November 5, 1817-June 3, 1818
THIRD MARATHA WAR

The Third Maratha War was the last of three major conflicts between the British East India Company and the Marathas, the most powerful indigenous force in India. It ended with the Marathas being disarmed, robbed of their ruler, and incorporated into the British subsidiary alliance system: With this victory, the British had destroyed every powerful state in India except for the Sikhs in the Punjab.

ALSO KNOWN AS: Third Anglo-Maratha War; Third Marāthā War

LOCALE: Central India

CATEGORIES Wars, uprisings, and civil unrest; colonization; expansion and land acquisition

KEY FIGURES

Bājī Rāo II (1775-1851), peshwa of the Marathas, r. 1796-1818

Muḍhōjī II (1796-1840), Maratha chief of Nagpur, r. 1816-1818

Raghuji III (1808-1853), Maratha chief of Nagpur, r. 1818-1853

Malhār Rāo Holkar II (1801-1834), Maratha chief of Indore, r. 1811-1833

First Marquis of Hastings (Francis Rawdon-Hastings; 1754-1826), governor-general of India, 1813-1823

Mountstuart Elphinstone (1779-1859), British resident at Poona, 1811-1819

SUMMARY OF EVENT

The three Maratha Wars of 1775-1782, 1803-1805, and 1817-1818 were part of the campaign of the British to dominate India. The Marathas were Hindu inhabitants of the state of Maharashtra who had been made into a great power under Śivajī (1627/1630-1680). The Marathas were a powerful confederation based in Poona (now Pune), Gwalior, Indore, Berar, and Baroda and headed by a peshwa (prime minister) at Poona. By 1749, the peshwaship had become a hereditary office. During the Napoleonic Wars (1793-1815), Great Britain sent the first marquis of Hastings to India as governor-general and commander in chief of the Indian army. He was ordered to establish total British control of India and to prevent the French from reestablishing any foothold in the subcontinent. Fulfilling his assignment entailed engaging in wars against the Gurkhas in Nepal in the north (1814-1816) and against the Pindaris (1817) and Marathas (1816-1818) in central India.

United and under strong leadership, the Maratha states constituted a powerful political and military force, but petty jealousies and personal rivalries between leaders divided them and frequently led to civil war. These internal divisions benefited the British, who normally supported one candidate in a succession struggle in the hope of acquiring more territory if their candidate won or if a civil war afforded other opportunities to annex land. The Marathas were also susceptible to bribes, and the British spent a considerable amount of money buying alliances with various Maratha chieftains. It has been argued that bribery was the key to Britain's success against the Marathas, who often had greater numbers of troops and superior artillery to the British.

The Treaty of Bassein of 1802 forced the peshwa to join the British subsidiary system, a series of alliances with subordinated states through which Britain administered its control over India. A representative of the British Empire, known as a "resident," was established at Poona. The British resident was supported by troops, and he interfered increasingly in the Maratha peshwa's affairs of state.

In 1816, Gangadhar Shastri, an emissary of the state of Baroda, was murdered in Poona. His murderer, Trimbakji Danglia, was a minister of Peshwa Bājī Rāo II. The peshwa was forced by Mountstuart Elphinstone, the British resident at Poona, to hand over Trimbakji to the British, but Trimbakji escaped on September 12, 1816, and the peshwa claimed he did not know where he was. Bājī Rāo also increased the size of his army and prepared to attack the British. Elphinstone responded by forcing the peshwa to sign the Treaty of Poona (June 13, 1817).

Among other punitive measures, the eighteen-article treaty called for the abolition of the Maratha Confederacy, the handing over of Konkan and Ahmadnagar Fort to the British, and the maintenance of five thousand British cavalry, three thousand infantry, and military equipment at Maratha expense. It was a humiliating treaty that considerably reduced Bājī Rāo's moral authority and economic resources, but the peshwa ratified it because he believed he did not have the arms to defeat the British. However, neither Bājī Rāo nor other Maratha leaders could accept this degrading pact, and they gathered troops near Poona.

Some commentators believe that Elphinstone put intolerable pressure on the peshwa deliberately in order to force a war. In any event, on November 5, 1817, the peshwa's military adviser, Bapu Gokhale, and his troops burned down the British residency at Poona. Meanwhile, twenty-six thousand Maratha troops with fourteen guns unsuccesfully attacked a small force of twenty-eight hundred British troops at Kirkee, near Poona. These attacks constituted the casus belli (justification for war) for the Third Maratha War. General Lionel Smith arrived at Kirkee and on November 15 defeated Bapu Gokhale at the Battle of Yeravda. The peshwa fled for his life, going from state to state seeking support from the Maratha chiefs. This was the beginning of a drawn-out series of battles between the British and various Maratha states.

The Maratha leaders Malhār Rāo Holkar II and Muḍhōjī II agreed to support Bājī Rāo II against the British, but other Marathas shunned him. Muḍhōjī attacked the resident at Nagpur, but the British took up a position on a ridge at Sitabaldi and defeated the Nagpur forces on November 27, 1817. With reinforcements arriving a few days later, the British forced Muḍhōjī to surrender. He lost his position as Nagpuri chief within four months. His successor fared no better, however: On December 16, 1818, the Nagpur army, now led by Raghuji III, was utterly defeated.

Malhār Rāo Holkar, meanwhile, was defeated at the Battle of Mahidpur in December, 1817, and forced to sign the Treaty of Mandasor the following month. Indore became part of the subsidiary alliance system. In the Battle of Asti, on February 20, 1818, Bapu Gokhale was again defeated in a hotly contested battle. On April 17, the peshwa was defeated, and by May he had been deserted by large numbers of his troops. Bājī Rāo II surrendered on June 3, 1818. In the treaty that followed, the British again imposed very harsh terms. The peshwa was forced to give up for himself and his descendants all claims to the peshwaship and leadership of the Maratha Confederacy. He was granted a pension of 800,000 rupees per year and forced to live in isolation in the north of India at Bithur, near Kanpur. There, under the watchful eyes of the British commissioner of Bithur, he was prevented from organizing any further Maratha resistance to British colonial power in India.

SIGNIFICANCE

The third and final Maratha war was of major importance to the history of India. It removed the last powerful indigenous force capable of challenging British authority in central India or in other areas of the subcontinent. The Maratha states became princely states. The British now controlled some three hundred states in India through a system of British residents and troops in those states'

capitals. Only the Sikhs, confined west of the River Sutlej in the Punjab, could present any significant opposition to the British, and they were broken in 1849. With the defeat of the Marathas in 1818, India became a British dominion.

—Roger D. Long

FURTHER READING

Banga, Indu. "The Punjab Under Sikh Rule: Formation of a Regional State." In *History and Ideology: The Khalsa over Three Hundred Years*, edited by J. S. Grewal and Indu Banga. New Delhi, India: Tulika Books, 1999. A discussion of the formation of the last indigenous state in India left outside British control after the Third Maratha War.

Choksey, R. D. *Mountstuart Elphinstone: The Indian Years, 1796-1827*. Bombay: Popular Prakashan, 1971. A good study of Elphinstone that includes a number of his journal entries. The chapter "Elphinstone and Bajirao II" covers the former's period as British resident at Poona.

Cooper, Randolf G. S. *The Anglo-Maratha Campaigns and the Conquest of India: The Struggle for Control of the South Asian Military Economy*. Cambridge, England: Cambridge University Press, 2003. While Cooper's case study is of the Second Maratha War, his study is important for an understanding of the Third Maratha War as well. He argues that the British were victorious not for military reasons but because of their superior financial resources.

Gadre, Prabhakar. *Bhosle of Nagpur and East India Company*. Jaipur: Publication Scheme, 1994. Provides a comprehensive study of Nagpur, explaining why the British campaign in the region was unexpectedly short and conclusive.

Gordon, Stewart. *The Marathas, 1600-1818*. Cambridge, England: Cambridge University Press, 1993. One of the volumes of the New Cambridge History of India series; offers a comprehensive but short introduction to Maratha history, administrative practice, and especially geopolitics. Essential reading to understand the complicated Maratha polity.

Sardesai, G. S. *New History of the Marathas*. Vol. 3. Bombay: Phoenix, 1946-1948. Comprehensive history of the Marathas that was produced in both Marathi and English. Sardesai's three volumes in English, which he condensed from his eight-volume work of more than four thousand pages, are considered the authoritative account of the history of the Marathas. The Third Maratha War is covered in volume 3.

Varma, Sushama. *Mountstuart Elphinstone in Maha-rashtra, 1801-1827: A Study of the Territories Conquered from the Peshwas.* Calcutta, India: K. P. Bagchi, 1981. Chapter 3 of this useful study covers Mountstuart's tenure as resident at Poona from 1811 to 1817.

SEE ALSO: 1839-1842: First Afghan War; Apr., 1848-Mar., 1849: Second Anglo-Sikh War; May 10, 1857-July 8, 1858: Sepoy Mutiny Against British Rule.
RELATED ARTICLE in *Great Lives from History: The Nineteenth Century, 1801-1900:* Ranjit Singh.

November 21, 1817-March 27, 1858
SEMINOLE WARS

Three protracted wars between Seminole Indians and the U.S. military over four decades were a continuation of the U.S. policy of containment and relocation of Native Americans from east of the Mississippi to reservations west of the Mississippi.

ALSO KNOWN AS: Florida Wars
LOCALE: Florida
CATEGORIES: Wars, uprisings, and civil unrest

KEY FIGURES
Sam Jones (Arpeika; 1760-1860), Mikasuki shaman
Wildcat (Coacoochee; c. 1810-1857), Seminole war
  leader
Osceola (Billy Powell; c. 1804-1838), Seminole war
  leader
Jumper (Ote Emathla; c. 1790-1838), Seminole war
  leader
Billy Bowlegs (Holatamico; c. 1810-1859), Seminole
  war leader
Andrew Jackson (1767-1845), general, first U.S.
  governor of Florida, president of the United States,
  1829-1837
Thomas Sidney Jesup (1788-1860), commander of the
  army in Florida, 1836-1838
Micanopy (c. 1780-1849), Seminole chief
Zachary Taylor (1784-1850), commander of the army
  in Florida, 1838-1840, president of the United
  States, 1849-1850

SUMMARY OF EVENT
The conflicts known as the First, Second, and Third Seminole Wars were never declared wars on the part of the U.S. government. The collectively known Seminole Wars were a continuation of U.S. policy to contain Native American populations east of the Mississippi and remove them to reservations west of the Mississippi, a policy that resulted in the Indian Removal Act of 1830. The wars also might be seen as early battles fought over the jurisdiction of runaway slaves that would eventually escalate into the Civil War (1861-1865).

The First Seminole War was preceded by years of border disputes along the Florida-Georgia border, climaxing in the destruction of Fort Negro on the Apalachicola River. Built by the British in 1815 and turned over to a band of runaway slaves on the British departure from Florida, Fort Negro proved an obstacle in the supply route to Fort Scott in Georgia. When a U.S. vessel was fired upon from the fort, Andrew Jackson ordered General Edmund Gaines to destroy the fort. A hot cannonball, fired from the expedition led by Lieutenant Colonel Duncan Clinch, landed in a powder magazine, blowing up the fort and killing 270 of its 344 occupants.

Neamathla, the village chief of Fowltown, reacted to the destruction and death by warning General Gaines that if U.S. soldiers tried to cross the border into Florida, they would be annihilated. A gunfight between U.S. soldiers and Neamathla's Seminoles on November 21, 1817, is considered the opening salvo of the First Seminole War. This conflict, ending with Andrew Jackson's occupation of the city of Pensacola in May, 1818, led to the Adams-Onís Treaty of 1819, in which Spain ceded the territory of Florida to the United States.

The 1823 Fort Moultrie Creek Treaty restricted Seminole settlements to a reservation of four million acres north of Charlotte Harbor and six small reservations for north Florida chiefs. The Seminoles agreed not to make the reservations a haven for escaped slaves. The 1830 enactment of the Indian Removal Act mandated that all Indians be encouraged to trade their eastern land for western land. If they failed to do so, they would lose the protection of the federal government.

In May, 1832, U.S. commissioner James Gadsden convened a meeting with the Seminole chiefs at Payne's Landing. What transpired at the meeting has been the subject of much political and scholarly controversy. All that is certain is that a treaty was signed on May 9, 1832, in which the chiefs agreed that a delegation would travel to inspect the lands in the territory that later became Oklahoma, and, if the lands were satisfactory, the Seminoles would agree to move west as a part of the Creek allocation. The ambiguity of who "they" were—the chiefs or their tribal councils—and the peculiar stipulation that the Seminoles would be absorbed by their longtime enemies, the Creeks, put the validity of the treaty into question. There have been allegations that bribery and coercion were used to get the Seminoles to sign the treaty. All of the chiefs whose names were on the treaty later repudiated it.

An exploratory party left for Oklahoma in October, 1832, and returned to Fort Gibson, Arkansas, in March, 1833, where they entered into a series of negotiations. Again, there have been allegations of coercion and forged marks on the Fort Gibson Treaty, by which the chiefs agreed that the Seminoles would move west within three years.

In October, 1834, Indian agent Wiley Thompson brought the chiefs together to discuss plans for a spring removal. The Seminoles gathered in their own council after Thompson's initial meeting, and strong opposition to migration emerged, especially from the Seminole war leader Osceola. Relations deteriorated and skirmishes increased between the government and Seminoles throughout 1835, culminating in the outbreak of war in December. The two most notable incidents occurred on December 28. Ote Emathla, also known as Jumper, and a warrior known as Alligator led 180 warriors in ambushing a relief column under the command of Major Francis Dade. Only 3 of the 108 soldiers escaped slaughter in the fierce battle that followed. Meanwhile, Osceola led sixty warriors in an attack on Fort King with the express purpose of killing Thompson, who had imprisoned Osceola in chains earlier in the year.

The army was in disarray during most of 1836. General Winfield Scott immediately began to feud with General Gaines. General Call was put in charge of the troops until November, when General Thomas S. Jesup arrived in Florida and assumed the command until 1839. Jesup's command in Florida was crucial for the outcome of the Seminole Wars. The general had persuaded a large number of chiefs and their tribes to emigrate on the condition

1810's

Seminole attack on a federal block house. (Library of Congress)

that they would be accompanied by their African American allies and slaves. When opposition arose among landowners claiming that the Seminoles harbored runaway slaves, a compromise was reached: Only those black people who had lived with the Seminoles before the outbreak of the war would be permitted to go.

More than seven hundred Seminoles had gathered at Fort Brooke north of Tampa by the end of May, 1837. On the night of June 2, Osceola and the Mikasuki shaman Sam Jones (Arpeika) surrounded the camp with two hundred warriors and spirited away nearly the entire population.

The defection caused a drastic shift in Jesup's tactics; no longer did he feel any compunction about using trickery to gain his ends. In September, General Joseph Hernandez captured King Philip, Yuchi Billy, Wildcat, and Blue Snake in the vicinity of St. Augustine and imprisoned them at Fort Marion. When Osceola and Coa Hadjo sent word to Hernandez that they were willing to negotiate, he set up a conference near Fort Peyton. Jesup ordered him to violate the truce and capture the Indians. News of Osceola's capture spread through the nation, and when he was transferred to Fort Moultrie in Georgia, George Catlin visited him and painted his portrait. His death on January 30, 1838, enshrined him as a martyr to the Indian cause.

After Wildcat escaped from Fort Marion on November 29, 1837, he headed south to join bands led by Jumper, Jones, and Alligator. The largest and last pitched battle of the war was fought on the banks of Lake Okeechobee on December 25. Colonel Zachary Taylor commanded eleven hundred men against approximately four hundred Indians. The Indians finally retreated from the two-and-a-half-hour battle, leaving 26 killed and 112 wounded and having sustained 11 killed and 14 wounded.

In February, 1838, further treachery at Fort Jupiter netted more than five hundred Seminoles. Persuasion and mopping-up operations sent many of the remaining Seminole leaders, including Micanopy, the chief, on the westward migration. Jesup's tenure in Florida, which had resulted in the capture, migration, or death of more than twenty-four hundred Indians, ended in May, 1838, when General Taylor took over command of the Florida forces. Taylor remained in Florida for another two years, during which time operations were carried out against scattered bands of Indians throughout the peninsula.

General Alexander MacComb, the commanding general of the army, came to Florida in April, 1839, and declared the war over when he concluded an agreement with the Seminoles, who agreed to withdraw south of the Peace River by July 15, 1839, and remain there until further arrangements were made. Although a guarded trading post was set up on the Caloosahatchee River, the Indians learned that they were not to be allowed to stay in Florida. Chekika, the chief of the Spanish Indians, led an attack and destroyed the post in July. After he led a raid on Indian Key in August, 1840, Chekika was surprised in the Everglades and executed.

The commands of General Walker K. Armistead and General William J. Worth saw the final years of the Second Seminole War. Following the successful policy of deceiving chiefs who came to negotiate, most notably Wildcat, and through continuing guerrilla warfare, the army managed to remove all but about six hundred of Florida's Indians, who were restricted to a temporary reservation south of the Peace River because Congress refused to continue to fund any further campaigns in 1842. The Second Seminole War was more costly than all of the other Indian wars combined. Nevertheless, new settlers came to the interior of Florida, which had been made accessible by the mapping, exploration, and road-building entailed by the wars. The military had gained skill in guerrilla warfare and an understanding of the need for interservice cooperation, and the federal government learned to exercise its power to convert economic power into military strength.

Between 1842 and the outbreak of the Third Seminole War in 1855, the Seminoles kept to the reservation and followed the dictates of regulations imposed upon them. They remained adamant in their opposition to removal until Secretary of War Jefferson Davis declared that, if they did not leave voluntarily, the military would remove them by force.

In December, 1855, a patrol investigating Seminole settlements in the Big Cypress Swamp was attacked by a band of forty Seminoles led by Billy Bowlegs and Oscen Tustenuggee, marking the first skirmish of the war that was dubbed Billy Bowlegs's War. It was a war of skirmishes, raids, and harassment against small settlements, both white and Seminole, and was to be the last of the Florida wars.

SIGNIFICANCE

A treaty signed on August 7, 1856, which granted the Seminoles more than two million acres in Indian Territory separate from the Creek allotment, along with a generous financial settlement, was the catalyst to the end of the conflict in Florida. A government offer of money in return for removal was accepted on March 27, 1858.

Bowlegs and his band left Florida in May, and two other bands left the following February. Only the Muskogee band led by Chipco, hidden north of Lake Okeechobee, and Jones's Mikasuki band, buried deep in the Everglades, a remnant of one hundred to three hundred persons, remained in relative peace in Florida, the ancestors of twentieth century Seminoles.

—Jane Anderson Jones

FURTHER READING

Covington, James W. *The Seminoles of Florida.* Gainesville: University Press of Florida, 1993. The most thorough history of the Seminoles in Florida, which devotes six chapters to the Seminole Wars.

Knetsch, Joe. *Florida's Seminole Wars, 1817-1858.* Mount Pleasant, S.C.: Arcadia, 2003. Part of Arcadia's Making of America series. The author examines the Seminole Wars, pairing historical images with a comprehensive narrative. Includes maps, sketches, paintings, and battle plans.

Mahon, John K. *History of the Second Seminole War, 1835-1842.* Rev. ed. Gainesville: University Press of Florida, 1985. Describes the battles and leaders, the problems of military organization and ordnance, and Seminole culture and history in the period of the Second Seminole War.

Missall, John, and Mary Lou Missall. *The Seminole Wars: America's Longest Indian Conflict.* Gainesville: University Press of Florida, 2004. A history of the three Seminole wars, examining their causes and significance in American history.

O'Brien, Sean Michael. *In Bitterness and in Tears: Andrew Jackson's Destruction of the Creeks and Seminoles.* Guilford, Conn.: Lyons Press, 2005. Engagingly written history of Andrew Jackson's role as a military commander in the Creek War of 1813-1814 and the First Seminole War of 1818.

Tebeau, Charlton W. "The Wars of Indian Removal." In *A History of Florida.* Rev. ed. Coral Gables, Fla.: University of Miami Press, 1980. This chapter in a standard Florida history covers the Seminole Wars.

Tour of the Florida Territory During the Seminole (Florida) Wars. Comprehensive Web site on the Seminole Wars maintained by Christopher D. Kimball. Includes maps of the battle areas by county, a narrative by Kimball, a list of forts, and links to related documents. http://tfn.net/~cdk901/index.html. Accessed January, 2006.

Wickman, Patricia R. *Osceola's Legacy.* Tuscaloosa: University of Alabama Press, 1991. A study of the life and myth of Osceola, based on a survey of artifacts and documents from the time period.

Wright, J. Leitch. *Creeks and Seminoles: The Destruction and Regeneration of the Muscogulge People.* Lincoln: University of Nebraska Press, 1986. An examination of the culture of the Creeks and Seminoles, and their Spanish, British, and African connections.

SEE ALSO: July 27, 1813-Aug. 9, 1814: Creek War; Feb. 22, 1819: Adams-Onís Treaty Gives the United States Florida; 1830-1842: Trail of Tears; May 28, 1830: Congress Passes Indian Removal Act; Feb. 6, 1861-Sept. 4, 1886: Apache Wars; Aug., 1863-Sept., 1866: Long Walk of the Navajos; June 27, 1874-June 2, 1875: Red River War; June 15-Oct. 5, 1877: Nez Perce War.

RELATED ARTICLES in *Great Lives from History: The Nineteenth Century, 1801-1900:* George Catlin; Jefferson Davis; James Gadsden; Andrew Jackson; Osceola; Winfield Scott; Zachary Taylor.

1818-1854
SEARCH FOR THE NORTHWEST PASSAGE

Between the end of the Napoleonic Wars and the beginning of the Crimean War, Great Britain's Royal Navy searched for the elusive Northwest Passage through the North American continent to the Pacific Ocean. The British hoped that the discovery of such a navigational shortcut would prove Britain's scientific and maritime superiority.

LOCALE: Arctic Ocean; northern Canada
CATEGORIES: Exploration and discovery; science and technology

KEY FIGURES
Sir John Franklin (1786-1847), four-time Arctic navigator, whose 1845 disappearance led to the eventual discovery of the passage
Sir Robert John Le Mesurier McClure (1807-1873), who discovered the Northwest Passage during his search for Franklin
Sir William Edward Parry (1790-1855), English navigator who charted the major entrances into the eastern Arctic
James Clark Ross (1800-1862), English explorer who discovered the magnetic North Pole
John Rae (1813-1893), Hudson's Bay Company surveyor who found the first evidence of Franklin's fate

SUMMARY OF EVENT
After the Napoleonic Wars ended in 1815, the leaders of Great Britain's Royal Navy were not eager to reduce their navy's size to reflect the budgetary restrictions of peacetime. Instead, Second Secretary of the Admiralty John Barrow (1804-1845) rekindled national interest in the discovery of a northwest passage to find employment for idle officers and their men, and to offer them chances for promotion. Icebergs, scurvy, and the challenges of survival in the Arctic became the navy's new enemies, and British officers and sailors went north in an attempt to claim the government's £20,000 reward for discovery of a passage between the North Atlantic and North Pacific.

In 1818, Lieutenant William Edward Parry, who would become England's favorite Arctic hero during the nineteenth century, sailed as second-in-command of a two-ship expedition under Commander John Ross. When the *Isabella* and *Alexander* set sail for Davis Strait, Ross's nephew, Midshipman James Clark Ross, was also

aboard; he would be ranked with Parry as another eminent polar explorer of the period. Although the expedition lasted only one summer, the elder Ross considered the expedition a success because he had determined that Lancaster Sound, which the ships were to sail through on their way to the Pacific, was blocked by an impressive mountain range. This mountain range, on which Ross staked his reputation, turned out to be a mirage, which Parry—who disagreed with Ross's "discovery"—later proved by sailing through it during his first command in 1819. Parry thus became the new Admiralty favorite; John Ross was never again offered a navy appointment.

Although Parry no doubt sailed during fortuitous seasons of open water, he also distinguished himself as a leader on his four expeditions. In 1819-1820, Parry commanded the first overwintering expedition in the Arctic, during which he kept his crews entertained by daily exercises, reading classes, and theatrical performances. Parry's first command established his reputation as an exemplary captain: Not only did he disprove his former superior's discovery of a mountain range but he also went on to chart the principal routes into the Arctic from the Atlantic—Barrow Strait, Wellington Channel, Prince Regent Inlet, and Viscount Melville Sound.

During his second command (1821-1823), Parry made great advancements in overland exploration technology, experimenting with person- and dog-hauled sledges for island surveying. As Parry's northern experience increased, however, his success diminished: His second voyage was unable to push its way through the ice and into the network of Arctic islands; his third voyage, of 1824-1825, ended with the abandonment of one of his two ships. His fourth voyage, in 1827, attempted to reach the North Pole but ended almost before it began, as the ice was too thick for Parry's bluff ships to sail through.

On each of Parry's expeditions was James Clark Ross, who had accompanied his uncle to the Arctic in 1818. Refusing to choose sides over the dispute of the fictional mountain range, the younger Ross continued to sail with both Parry and his uncle, thereby becoming the century's most experienced Arctic explorer. With Parry, Ross distinguished himself as a surveyor and a sledder, and this experience paid off when, in 1831, he became the first to record the location of the magnetic North Pole. Ironically, Ross made this remarkable discovery when second-in-command of a private expedition, commanded by his ostracized uncle, John Ross. Although the younger Ross received a reward for his discovery, his uncle remained outside the Admiralty circle of favored explorers.

John Franklin was the third explorer whose career began with the first expeditions, though his beginnings were less impressive than those of Parry. Franklin, second-in-command of another 1818 expedition, never even reached North America: He and Commander David Buchan were forced to return to England after encountering violent weather off the Greenland coast. Despite this early failure, Franklin, like Parry, became an Admiralty favorite and accepted command of a small overland expedition to explore the Arctic coast adjacent to the mouth of the Coppermine River. This expedition was a failure on a much grander scale.

Taking the five English explorers and fifteen Canadian voyagers over more than 5,500 miles of territory—much of which had already been charted—from 1819 to 1822, the expedition met with disaster in the fall of 1821. Nine members of the party died from starvation, and two died from violent encounters. Undeterred, Franklin set out in 1825 in command of his second overland expedition, which lasted until 1827. Although less dramatic, this survey was more successful. Franklin and his men charted the Arctic coastline east and west of the Mackenzie River delta, solving a large and important piece of the puzzle of the northern mainland coast.

THE NORTHWEST PASSAGE

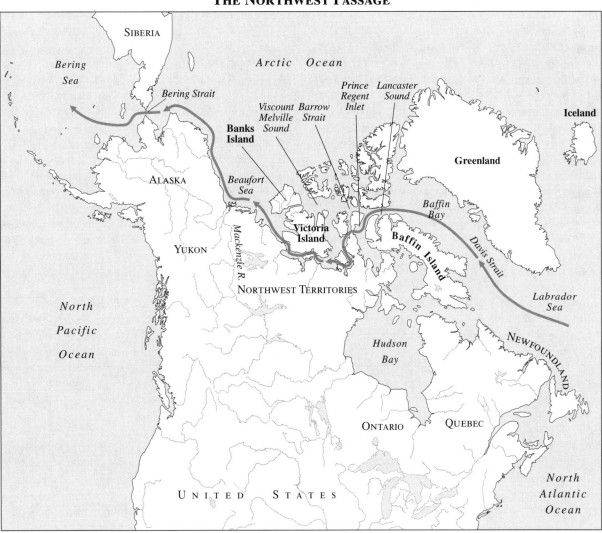

The British Admiralty was not the only institution interested in charting the passage at the time; the Hudson's Bay Company also sent surveyors north to discover possible routes through the Arctic. Its best explorer was John Rae, who surveyed the northern mainland coast. Rae's unparalleled success was, in no small part, due to his respect for, and adoption of, indigenous practices. He traveled with small parties, lived off the land, wore fur, walked great distances, and even gained weight in the land where Franklin's men had starved. Although his opinions about routes were sought by members of the navy, Rae remained on the periphery of the Admiralty community, preferring his own style of travel to the navy's more cumbersome methods. His skill as a surveyor, however, would figure prominently in the mystery that was to instigate the second wave of searches in the 1840's and 1850's—the disappearance of Franklin's third expedition.

Commanding the *Erebus* and *Terror* in 1845, Franklin and his 128 officers and crew intended to sail through the remaining blank space on the map and solve the puzzle of the passage. They were never heard from again. In the decade that followed, more than thirty ships went in search of the missing sailors. The search parties were sponsored by the British and American governments, and by private and public subscription. Ironically, many of the most impressive geographical discoveries in the Arctic were made during the search for Franklin and his crew—concern for their fellow adventurers took them down passages and through archipelagos they might not otherwise have explored.

Indeed, one such explorer was Captain Robert John Le Mesurier McClure, who, in his efforts to search for Franklin from the west, was the first to chart the Northwest Passage. Separated from McClure's ship before he entered the western Arctic, McClure's superior officer, Captain Richard Collinson, also discovered the Northwest Passage, but he arrived in England too late to claim the prize.

Although the passage was officially discovered in 1854, the search for Franklin continued until 1859. The perceived connection between rewards dispensed for geographical discovery and those available for discovery of Franklin was disturbing to many, most notably Franklin's widow, Jane, Lady Franklin. She rightly noted the dwindling enthusiasm for the search as money, intended for expeditions that discovered news of the missing sailors, was dispensed instead for new geographical discoveries. Forced to fund her own expedition to discover the truth of her husband's fate, Lady Franklin sent her own

ship, the *Fox*, under the command of Captain Francis Leopold McClintock, to the one area left not searched (identified by Rae in 1854).

In 1859 members of the *Fox*, sledging across King William Island, discovered that Franklin, too, had discovered a passage in 1847, though no sailor from the expedition had lived to tell the tale. In 1859, when the *Fox* returned to England, the saga of British Arctic exploration was over.

SIGNIFICANCE

The search for the Northwest Passage was and continues to be significant as a testament to human curiosity and scientific endeavor. Even in 1818 the passage was acknowledged to have no commercial value, but its "objective" exploration over the next forty years helped shape the way in which the growing fields of science and geography defined the world.

—*Erika Behrisch*

FURTHER READING

Atwood, Margaret. *Strange Things: The Malevolent North in Canadian Literature.* Oxford, England: Clarendon Press, 1995. Includes a twentieth century perspective on Sir John Franklin, acknowledging the continued fascination with his disappearance.

Berton, Pierre. *The Arctic Grail: The Quest for the North West Passage and the North Pole, 1818-1909.* Toronto: McClelland and Stewart, 1988. A popular account of Arctic expeditions.

Cooke, Alan, and Clive Holland. *The Exploration of Northern Canada, 500-1920: A Chronology.* Toronto: Arctic History Press, 1978. A comprehensive list of all attempts to explore and chart the Canadian Arctic.

David, Robert G. *The Arctic in the British Imagination, 1818-1914.* Manchester, England: Manchester University Press, 2000. A historical look at the Arctic's definition as a place of imperial interest.

Ross, M. J. *Polar Pioneers: John Ross and James Clark Ross.* Montreal: McGill-Queen's University Press, 1994. A detailed overview of the Rosses' personalities and their expeditions.

Savours, Ann. *The Search for the North West Passage.* New York: St. Martin's Press, 1999. A compendious chronicle of Arctic exploration from the sixteenth to the twentieth century, containing several contemporary maps and illustrations.

Spufford, Francis. *I May Be Some Time: Ice and the English Imagination.* London: Faber & Faber, 1996. An examination of the Arctic's popularity in nineteenth century British culture, and the establishment of the Arctic explorer as a new brand of hero.

SEE ALSO: May 14, 1804-Sept. 23, 1806: Lewis and Clark Expedition; Sept. 8, 1810-May, 1812: Astorian Expeditions Explore the Pacific Northwest Coast;

1820-early 1840's: Europeans Explore the Antarctic; 1872: Dominion Lands Act Fosters Canadian Settlement; 1893-1896: Nansen Attempts to Reach the North Pole.

RELATED ARTICLES in *Great Lives from History: The Nineteenth Century, 1801-1900:* Sir John Franklin; Sir James Clark Ross; Charles Wilkes.

1819
SCHOPENHAUER PUBLISHES *THE WORLD AS WILL AND IDEA*

Arthur Schopenhauer's The World as Will and Idea *gave rise to a pessimistic strand of German Romantic philosophy, introduced Europe to several concepts drawn from Eastern philosophy, and provided a major and well-reasoned response to the philosophy of Immanuel Kant.*

ALSO KNOWN AS: *Die Welt als Wille und Vorstellung*
LOCALE: Leipzig, Saxony (now in Germany)
CATEGORY: Philosophy

KEY FIGURES
Arthur Schopenhauer (1788-1860), German philosopher
Immanuel Kant (1724-1804), German philosopher
Richard Wagner (1813-1883), German opera composer

SUMMARY OF EVENT
Arthur Schopenhauer published *Die Welt als Wille und Vorstellung* (1819; *The World as Will and Idea*, 1883-1886, 3 volumes) at a time when European philosophy was still attempting to grasp the implications of a new concept of the human mind, thought, and understanding that had been developed by Immanuel Kant. Himself responding to the theories of David Hume (1711-1776), Kant had distinguished two distinct aspects of reality: phenomenal reality, or the world as it appears to the human mind, and noumenal reality, or the world as it really is. Kant had asserted that there was a nearly absolute gap between phenomena and noumena, such that the noumenon, or the "thing in itself" (*Ding an sich*), was not directly knowable. Only its phenomenal appearance could be known.

Thus, on the level of perception, human beings in Kant's system were permanently divorced from the ultimate reality. Kant did, however, believe that humans

could make contact with the noumenal on the level of practice, because they were capable of making moral decisions that recognized and agreed with the objective moral world of freedom and justice. Nevertheless, in Kant's description of everyday experience, each person's experience of the world was really an experience of his or her mental conception of the world; it was never a true encounter with the world itself.

Kant's theories were designed to solve a version of what has come to be known as the "mind/body problem" that became particularly important in the wake of Sir Isaac Newton's model of a universe governed by physical laws. If all physical objects, including the human

Arthur Schopenhauer. (R. S. Peale/J. A. Hill)

SCHOPENHAUER ON REPRESENTATION

The central term in Arthur Schopenhauer's work—and in that of many other nineteenth century German philosophers—was Vorstellung, *or representation (also translated as "idea"). The German word connotes even more strongly than its English equivalent that representations are intermediaries between the world and the perceiving mind, and this notion of mediation between mind (or subject) and world (or object) was the foundation of German Idealism in general and of Schopenhauer's Idealism in particular.*

"The world is my representation": this is a truth valid with reference to every living and knowing being, although man alone can bring it into reflective, abstract consciousness. If he really does so, philosophical discernment has dawned on him. It then becomes clear and certain to him that he does not know a sun and an earth, but only an eye that sees a sun, a hand that feels an earth; that the world around him is there only as representation, in other words, only in reference to another thing, namely that which represents, and this is himself. If any truth can be expressed *a priori*, it is this; for it is the statement of that form of all possible and conceivable experience, a form that is more general than all others, than time, space, and causality, for all these presuppose it. While each of these forms, which we have recognized as so many particular modes of the principle of sufficient reason, is valid only for a particular class of representations, the division into object and subject, on the other hand, is the common form of all those classes; it is that form under which alone any representation, of whatever kind it be, abstract or intuitive, pure or empirical, is generally possible and conceivable. Therefore no truth is more certain, more independent of all others, and less in need of proof than this, namely that everything that exists for knowledge, and hence the whole of this world, is only object in relation to the subject, perception of the perceiver, in a word, representation.

Source: Arthur Schopenhauer, *The World as Will and Representation.* Translated by E. F. J. Payne (New York: Dover, 1966), vol. 1, p. 3.

---

body, are determined by laws, Kant wanted to know, how can the human mind be capable of free will and yet be fundamentally linked to the body? The division of the world into two different levels of reality—phenomena and noumena—was a crucial step in Kant's overall system, designed to explain how the free mind could relate to the law-governed body. It created a different problem, however: If human minds could never have direct, unmediated contact with physical reality (bodies), how could these minds form ideas about external reality that have any sort of validity? Kant believed that he had solved this problem in his Three Critiques, but most philosophers of mind who came after him seem to have disagreed, since they have all tried to find their own answers to the problem. Schopenhauer's answers have been greatly influential.

When Schopenhauer published *The World as Will and Idea*, he saw his work as both a development of

Kant's theories and an artfully constructed solution to the epistemological problems raised by those theories. Officially published in 1819 (even though the first copies appeared in December of the previous year), *The World as Will and Idea* would be revised and enlarged by Schopenhauer twice in his lifetime (in 1844 and 1854). Its impact was not immediate. Largely ignored by the academic and artistic community until the 1840's and 1850's, the work began to be met with widespread acclaim only near the end of Schopenhauer's life, when its author suddenly was celebrated as a great visionary. In the treatise's original four-volume format, the first and third volumes dealt with Kant's concept of phenomenal understanding, which Schopenhauer termed the "world as idea" (*Vorstellung*; properly, "representation"). The second and fourth volumes presented Schopenhauer's proposed solution to the problems that he believed Kant had raised for philosophy, a solution that Schopenhauer termed the "world as will" (*Wille*).

According to Schopenhauer's view of the world, will—which should be viewed as closer to the English concepts of "desire" and "craving" than to the sort of conscious volition implied by the term "will"—is a universal principle found in all of nature. It is not only the characteristic feature of human existence but may also be seen in animals (which, lacking human rationality, respond to their world purely out of will), plants (which turn toward the sun, put forth leaves, and develop roots as a means of satisfying their needs), and even inanimate objects (for which such forces as gravity and the laws of thermodynamics may be viewed as an impersonal sort of will).

In Kantian terms, Schopenhauer's concept of the will provided a direct point of contact between the mind and the physical universe, since human desires, needs, and longings always occur in the mind even though they are directed toward some external body. For instance, a human being may develop will (for example, a desire for water) if there is thirst, desire for food if there is hunger, desire for air if a room is stifling, and similar desires in any of a number of different situations. On the other hand, no one would ever say that they long for or need the square root of negative two or the space-time continuum in the same way. The latter are mental constructs rather than physical bodies, and the will is always a mental state directed toward the physical universe. Seen in this light, therefore, Kant's perceived dichotomy between mental concepts and physical objects did not exist in Schopenhauer's depiction of the world. The bridge between them was the will.

If Kant's division between phenomena and noumena did not exist for Schopenhauer, what Schopenhauer did regard as a central challenge for philosophy was the essentially tragic view of human existence implied by his own theory of the world. In other words, he believed, since the characteristic quality of all nature is the will, existence is necessarily frustrating for the human consciousness. Throughout all of life, as soon as one desire is satisfied, another desire appears; permanent satisfaction is never possible. In addition, even when satisfied, the same desire will eventually return. Food, water, sexual gratification, sleep, and other human needs must be addressed on a regular basis, and a perfect state of happiness will never be possible.

Even worse, according to Schopenhauer, was the suffering produced in the mind because certain desires could never be satisfied, compelling human beings to experience life as a wearisome cycle of ordeal characterized by endless longing. The only cessation to the will, Schopenhauer believed, was that which was suggested by several Eastern philosophies: the cessation of all human desire, particularly that which occured in death and the obliteration of the human consciousness. By introducing to the West such concepts as nirvana (the complete extinction of all desire), *The World as Will and Idea* played a major role in the European discovery of Buddhist thought and helped pave the way for such works as Eugène Burnouf's *Introduction à l'histoire du bouddhism indien* (1844; *Legends of Indian Buddhism*, 1911) and Karl Friedrich Köppen's *Die Religion des Buddha und ihre Entstehung* (1857; the religion of the Buddha and its origin).

Schopenhauer's view of human understanding and his pessimistic view of existence influenced a broad range of philosophers, including Karl Robert Eduard Von Hartmann (1842-1906), Henri Bergson (1859-1941), and Hans Vaihinger (1852-1933). Schopenhauer's pessimism stands in marked contrast to the materialist, utopian, and optimistic philosophies of such figures as Karl

Marx, Robert Owen, and Charles Fourier, who represent an entirely separate strain of philosophy. Perhaps most distinctly, the impact of *The World as Will and Idea* may be seen in the later works of Richard Wagner, such as *Tristan und Isolde* (1859; Tristan and Isolde) and *Parsifal* (1882), as well as in the works of poets and novelists such as Charles Baudelaire, Stéphane Mallarmé, and Joris-Karl Huysmans.

SIGNIFICANCE

Schopenhauer's publication of *The World as Will and Idea* initiated a major new direction in Romantic philosophy. First, by attempting to answer several of the key questions that Kant had proposed in such works as *Kritik der reinen Vernunft* (1781; *Critique of Pure Reason*, 1838), Schopenhauer redirected the approach of many nineteenth century philosophers away from Kant's obscure and highly complex Idealism to a more readily comprehended, all-encompassing philosophy that suited the needs of many intellectuals and artists of the late Romantic age. Second, by popularizing many of the ideas that Schopenhauer had encountered in Buddhist and Hindu authors, *The World as Will and Idea* introduced many Europeans to Eastern philosophy for the first time and helped begin to forge an integration between Eastern and Western philosophic ideas. Third, Schopenhauer's influence on such cultural figures as Wagner, Baudelaire, and others carried his pessimistic Romantic philosophy into such fields as music and literature, where they were encountered by entirely new audiences.

—*Jeffrey L. Buller*

FURTHER READING

Coplestone, Frederick Charles. *Arthur Schopenhauer: Philosopher of Pessimism*. New York: Barnes & Noble Books, 1975. A classic work exploring both Schopenhauer's philosophy and its influence on the Romantic age.

Magee, Bryan. *The Philosophy of Schopenhauer*. Oxford, England: Oxford University Press, 1997. An excellent and thorough analysis of every aspect of Schopenhauer's philosophy, presented in language that a general reader will be able to understand.

Tanner, Michael. *Schopenhauer*. New York: Routledge, 1999. A very brief and accessible overview of Schopenhauer for the non-philosopher.

SEE ALSO: Apr., 1807: Hegel Publishes *The Phenomenology of Spirit*; 1824: Ranke Develops Systematic History; 1826-1842: Young Germany Movement;

Feb., 1848: Marx and Engels Publish *The Communist Manifesto*; 1867: Marx Publishes *Das Kapital*; 1886: Rise of the Symbolist Movement; 1900: Freud Publishes *The Interpretation of Dreams*.

RELATED ARTICLES in *Great Lives from History: The Nineteenth Century, 1801-1900:* Charles Baudelaire; Georg Wilhelm Friedrich Hegel; Karl Marx; Robert Owen; Arthur Schopenhauer; Richard Wagner.

1819-1820
IRVING'S *SKETCH BOOK* TRANSFORMS AMERICAN LITERATURE

After winning its independence from Great Britain, the United States slowly began to develop a new, unique, and non-European identity in both its politics and its culture. With his clever satires of the "old ways" and his relaxed comic prose, best exemplified in The Sketch Book of Geoffrey Crayon, Gent., *Washington Irving led America to a new and optimistic literature and a new age of journalism.*

LOCALE: New York, New York
CATEGORY: Literature

KEY FIGURE
Washington Irving (1783-1859), American writer

SUMMARY OF EVENT

At the beginning of the nineteenth century, New York City's population tripled, from 100,000 to 300,000 persons, and the city took over Philadelphia's role as the commercial and cultural capital of the United States. This shift also caused a change in political power from wealthy Dutch landowners from the Hudson Valley to European immigrants and hardworking young American-born men who became self-made capitalists and entrepreneurs in New York City. The United States began to look for its own identity in both literature and politics after gaining independence from Great Britain.

As New York City became the center for American business and politics, it also became the center for a new journalism. During the early years of the nineteenth century, the standard for American literary magazines was the Philadelphia *Port Folio*, edited by Harvard-educated Joseph Dennie (1768-1812). However, it increasingly found competition in many new and short-lived magazines that arose in New York. Many young men in business and law decided to try their hand at writing, and the growing number of literary journals and newspapers in New York created a demand for short stories, light verse, tales, and satirical prose.

Washington Irving was the first American-born writer to achieve literary credibility in both the United States and England. Born in 1783, the year that the United States became independent, he studied law but turned to writing satirical prose. He first published "The Letters of Jonathan Oldstyle, Gent." anonymously in his brother Peter Irving's newspaper, *The Morning Chronicle*. Irving then collaborated with another brother, William Irving, as well as James Kirke Paulding, to write entertaining sketches and essays to "instruct the young and reform the old." These were published in a series of pamphlets titled *Salmagundi: Or, The Whim-Whams of Opinions of Launcelot Langstaff, Esq. and Others* (1807).

Although the United States was enjoying its new independence, there was a feeling among many young men that the country was being run much in the same way as it had been under Britain, and that the men of established families were still making the rules and keeping the

Washington Irving. (R. S. Peale/J. A. Hill)

wealth. In Irving's eyes it was time to celebrate freedom and a new and more egalitarian government. Irving put his ideas into writing as he brazenly attacked the status quo in his first real literary success, *A History of New York* (1809).

Irving's *A History of New York* is a comic history of the city's Dutch colonization and politics that lampoons the Dutch governors of New Amsterdam and their exploits, along with President Thomas Jefferson. Irving cleverly embellished Dutch history with whimsical facts and comical caricatures and at the same time lent a spurious credibility to his history by basing it on the journals of the fictional Diedrich Knickerbocker. Knickerbocker was cleverly introduced to the public in a series of newspaper articles as a gentleman who had recorded Dutch history over his lifetime, had left his journal in a boardinghouse, and had somehow disappeared. In reality Diedrich Knickerbocker was a pen name that Irving used to set himself apart from the story that was being told.

ICHABOD CRANE

One of Washington Irving's most famous characters was Ichabod Crane, the protagonist of "The Legend of Sleepy Hollow." Crane was one of a new breed of protagonists invented by Irving, Sir Walter Scott, and other early nineteenth century authors often now referred to as "the common man." Rather than being inherently interesting or worthy of depiction in a story or novel, such protagonists are everyday people to whom something extraordinary happens. Reproduced below is the initial description of Ichabod Crane.

In this by-place of Nature there abode, in a remote period of American history—that is to say, some thirty years since—a worthy wight of the name of Ichabod Crane, who sojourned, or, as he expressed it, "tarried," in Sleepy Hollow for the purpose of instructing the children of the vicinity. He was a native of Connecticut, a State which supplies the Union with pioneers for the mind as well as for the forest, and sends forth yearly its legions of frontier woodmen and country schoolmasters. The cognomen of Crane was not inapplicable to his person. He was tall, but exceedingly lank, with narrow shoulders, long arms and legs, hands that dangled a mile out of his sleeves, feet that might have served for shovels, and his whole frame most loosely hung together. His head was small, and flat at top, with huge ears, large green glassy eyes, and a long snip nose, so that it looked like a weathercock perched upon his spindle neck to tell which way the wind blew. To see him striding along the profile of a hill on a windy day, with his clothes bagging and fluttering about him, one might have mistaken him for the genius of Famine descending upon the earth or some scarecrow eloped from a cornfield.

Source: Washington Irving, "The Legend of Sleepy Hollow." *The Sketch Book of Geoffrey Crayon, Gent.* Rev. ed. (New York: G. P. Putnam, 1848).

Irving served in the War of 1812, a conflict that many believed finally gave the United States true freedom from Britain and a stronger desire to create a unique American identity. Afterward, he spent seventeen years visiting England and the Continent. In 1819-1820, he published *The Sketch Book of Geoffrey Crayon, Gent.* He released the collection of stories, tales, and essays in seven installments in order to gauge the public's response to it. When he saw that the collection was a success, he republished it as a book that contained thirty-two sketches. Of the four sketches about American subjects, two became Irving's most famous stories, "Rip Van Winkle" and "The Legend of Sleepy Hollow." Drawing on German folklore, both tales were unique in that Irving set them in America with a new kind of literary hero who would come to be known as "the common man."

The Sketch Book of Geoffrey Crayon, Gent. was well received by English and American readers alike. Indeed, it was such a success that Irving became regarded as the first American writer. *The Sketch Book of Geoffrey Crayon, Gent.* revealed Irving's ability to show reverence toward the literature of the old country while simultaneously showing enthusiasm for a new literature set in a new land. His stories often use contrasts between the old and the new and between the natural and the supernatural. For example, the village in which "Rip Van Winkle" is set is located between a real river and the "fairy mountains" of the Catskills. Irving also blends fact and fancy, past and present.

A rather lazy character living in America before the American Revolution, Rip Van Winkle is of Dutch decent. When Rip goes into the woods to escape from his wife's badgering, he meets men in Dutch costumes with whom he drinks. He then settles down to take a nap but sleeps for twenty years and misses the Revolution, He thus awakens to a new land and a new life. Although Rip is initially confused, he easily adjusts to the new society he finds. He also discovers that in this new society he now has new status, even though he is merely a common person. Rip's name may be an acronym for the well-known epitaph "rest in peace" (R.I.P.)—an indication that the story lays the old ways to rest.

Irving's relaxed style was a significant change from the literature of the Enlightenment in England and Europe. His tales are typically frame stories in which his narrators recount tales stories that are told to them. This technique—which Mark Twain later employed to good effect—allows Irving to exaggerate and include fantasy and gothic qualities, while freeing him from taking responsibility for his stories' validity. *The Sketch Book of Geoffrey Crayon, Gent.* uses Irving's old friend Diedrich Knickerbocker's journals to validate its tales.

Although Washington Irving went on to write bulky novels on George Washington, Christopher Columbus, and the Moorish conquest of Granada, his later writings never received the kind of acclaim enjoyed by *The Sketch Book of Geoffrey Crayon, Gent*. In fact, his later works lacked the freshness and humor of his earlier works. Nevertheless, his early writings inspired a group of authors and journalists to set their own stories in America, to look to common people for their heroes, and to be proud of the new country and society that they were forming. Fittingly, these new writers became known as the Knickerbocker school.

SIGNIFICANCE

The primary significance of Washington Irving as an author lay in his development of a unique literature based in American settings that was respected internationally. His informal prose style departed from the more formal and structured literary style of the Old World. His use of fictitious frame narrators allowed him to entertain readers through exaggeration and wonderment. Irving might also be called the first American humorist with his contributions of satire and humor in *Salmagundi* and *A History of New York*.

Irving's early writings inspired New York writers from diverse backgrounds and writing styles to call themselves the Knickerbockers. From 1810 to 1840, these writers contributed articles, stories, and tales for New York's literary magazines and newspapers, basing their writings on the new independent country in which they and the new culture and form of politics that they were developing. Irving also influenced the writing styles of such major literary figures as Nathaniel Hawthorne, Henry Wadsworth Longfellow, and Mark Twain,

as well as countless other writers and students of literature during the nineteenth century. Irving's legacy can be seen in the name of the modern New York Knickerbocker basketball team and the continued popularity of "Rip Van Winkle" and "The Legend of Sleepy Hollow," both of which have been immortalized in films.

—*Toby Stewart*

FURTHER READING

Aderman, Ralph, ed. *Critical Essays on Washington Irving*. Boston: G. K. Hall, 1990. Anthology of contemporary reviews of Irving's work and twentieth century essays on his art and literary debts.

Gardner, Jared. *Master Plots*. Baltimore: Johns Hopkins University Press, 1998. Discusses the relationship between the development of American literature and the creation of a national identity in the United States.

Loving, Jerome. *Lost in the Customhouse: Authorship in the American Renaissance*. Iowa City: University of Iowa Press, 1993. Excellent critique of "Rip Van Winkle" that details Irving's influence on the writers who followed him.

Spiller, Robert. *The Cycle of American Literature*. New York: Free Press, 1967. Discusses the political, religious, and economic issues that influenced the development of literature in the United States. Examines authors from the nineteenth century to the twentieth century.

Tuttleton, James W., ed. *Washington Irving: The Critical Reaction*. New York: AMS Press, 1993. Useful collection of modern essays on Irving's literary works. Includes a chronology of his life.

SEE ALSO: 1807-1850: Rise of the Knickerbocker School; Dec. 15, 1814-Jan. 5, 1815: Hartford Convention; c. 1830's-1860's: American Renaissance in Literature; 1880's: Brahmin School of American Literature Flourishes; Dec., 1884-Feb., 1885: Twain Publishes *Adventures of Huckleberry Finn*.

RELATED ARTICLES in *Great Lives from History: The Nineteenth Century, 1801-1900:* Nathaniel Hawthorne; Washington Irving; Henry Wadsworth Longfellow; Henry David Thoreau.

1819-1833
BABBAGE DESIGNS A MECHANICAL CALCULATOR

Charles Babbage designed an early form of the mechanical calculator that could produce accurate mathematical tables. In 1833, he completed a portion of a machine that could automatically compute and print table values. He later perfected this work and produced a primitive device that anticipated the electronic computers of the late twentieth century.

LOCALE: London, England
CATEGORIES: Mathematics; inventions; engineering

KEY FIGURES
Charles Babbage (1791-1871), English mathematician
Joseph Clement (1779-1844), English machinist

SUMMARY OF EVENT

Charles Babbage wanted to master numbers mechanically. His mathematical work and research required the use of the many mathematical tables of his era, but these tables were riddled with errors, and so he set out to produce tables that were more accurate. As early as 1812, Babbage began to think about the possibilities for a newly designed mechanical calculator, and in 1819, he started to work seriously on the project.

Large mathematical tables on multiplication, logarithms, and other functions were used heavily at the beginning of the nineteenth century. Tables reduced the tedious work of complex calculations and provided ready references. Teams of calculators—the term for people performing simple arithmetic tasks—worked over long periods to produce results, which were then gathered and given to a typesetter, who would set the figures and print the tables. This procedure left much room for error, not only in computation but also in copying and typesetting.

Mechanical calculators had been performing additions and multiplication by means of continual additions, but the calculators were hand cranked, and their accuracy and practical use had been restricted by a lack of precision engineering. Babbage, facing the same mechanical and mathematical problems, decided to use the method of "differences" and to have his machine not only perform the computations but also set the type to avoid the human error of transferring the figures from machine to writing to print.

Table makers had used a "tool" called the method of differences when constructing tables of polynomial function values. This tool could eliminate the difficult

operations of multiplication and division by replacing them with simple additions. For a polynomial function such as $f(x) = 3x + 1$ (see table), note the differences between each adjacent value of $f(x)$ when evaluated for successive values of x. Thus, one finds the constant differences. In complex functions, it may be necessary to calculate the differences of differences (or second differences) before finding a constant difference. To evaluate a function for many values of x in a table, it is simpler to do so by adding the constant difference to the difference above, then adding that difference to the one above it, and so on, until reaching the function value.

VALUES AND DIFFERENCES FOR $f(x) = 3x + 1$					
$x =$	1	2	3	4	5
$f(x) =$	4	7	10	13	16
differences =	3	3	3	3	3

In 1822, Babbage completed a small working model with spare parts in his basement. The model calculated six-digit numbers and could evaluate functions with a constant second difference. Babbage called his machine the "difference engine." It could store a series of numbers and perform addition with those numbers. The stored numbers stood for the polynomial value, its first difference, second difference, and so on. The machine added each difference to the next higher one until it reached the polynomial value. In using the method of differences for his machine, Babbage needed only to mechanically replicate addition, not multiplication.

While Babbage had managed to build the working model on his own, a full-size engine required the development of more precision engineering, which would be costly. Using his model, he asked the Royal Society for help with petitioning the government for funds to build a full-scale machine. In 1823, he received £1,500 and agreed to put up £3,000 to £5,000 of his own funds. He hired the machinist Joseph Clement to help develop new techniques and depended on him for all the practical mechanical work. Babbage designed the parts for the difference engine, and he and Clement designed and created tools to make those parts. The team followed a pattern of

Charles Babbage. (Library of Congress)

design, toolmaking, and redesign, a process that created great advances in the toolmaking trade. Clement trained numerous machinists in his workshop and disseminated new methods throughout the industry in Great Britain.

Babbage had expected the government to refund his portion of the research and development costs upon completion. However, that part of the bargain was forgotten by 1827. Through pressure from some of Babbage's friends, the government eventually gave him some additional funds. A pattern of work stoppages began, however, when Babbage's personal funds ran out. He had to let go of trained personnel. When he did receive additional funds, he rehired and often had to retrain the same workers.

Babbage's work also was delayed when he and Clement broke off their association. Clement had established a successful machinist shop and had many customers besides Babbage. Babbage had expected Clement to move his shop, and the engine, to a location near Babbage's home, but Clement declined. The ownership of the tools that they had designed for the construction of the machine belonged to Clement, and he took those tools and the designs with him.

During the work stoppage after Clement's departure,

Babbage conceived an idea for an "analytical engine." His design included the prescient use of punched cards to control or program the machine. He adapted the programming (control mechanism) on Jacquard looms to mechanical mathematical calculation. Technically, Babbage's system was identical to that of Jacquard—punched cards to control the action of small, narrow, circular metal rods that in turn governed the actions required to weave or calculate (by controlling positions of cogwheels). Babbage designed this engine with five basic parts—the store, mill, control, input, and output—which remained the basic units found in electronic computers of one century later.

Babbage tried to persuade the government that it would take less time and money to construct the new design than to finish the old one. They debated his proposal for more than eight years, and eventually the government told Babbage no more money would be forthcoming.

The government had paid a total of £17,000 while Babbage had contributed £20,000. For this financial outlay, the government received a portion of a larger machine in 1833 that could calculate tables for functions with two or three orders of difference; what Babbage delivered was a crude form of the more modern calculator. A full machine, if built, would have been 10 feet high, 10 feet wide, and 5 feet deep, and would have seven vertical steel axles, each of which would have eight brass wheels. The axles each represented one of six orders of differences, with the seventh representing the value of the function. Each of the wheels would have the digits 0 to 9 engraved around the circumference, and the wheel's position would designate which number it represented.

Babbage had designed his machine to be as error-free as possible. The machine would include mechanisms to handle problems such as wheels getting out of place. The printing capability of this machine set it apart from earlier machines. The mechanism created a stereotyped plate for the printing presses and removed human typesetting errors.

SIGNIFICANCE

Charles Babbage wrote up plans for an improved difference engine in 1849 and attempted to get the government to construct it; the government refused. In his design work for a second difference engine (Difference Engine No. 2) and for the analytical engine, Babbage was far ahead of his time. His designs included many of the elements of the computers built one hundred years later. Yet, the development of the machines meant frustration, financial loss, and ultimate failure on a personal level.

The main impact of Babbage's difference engine was perhaps indirect. In the process of designing his mechanical calculator, his demands and his work with Joseph Clement set new, higher standards of precision for the mechanical engineering field. Standards of toolmaking advanced greatly through the work of Clement and his apprentices, which included the toolmaking industry pioneer Joseph Whitworth. Furthermore, Babbage's struggle with the British government between 1823 and 1848 over funds set an example for future relations between scientific researchers and government finance.

—*Linda Eikmeier Endersby*

FURTHER READING

Ashworth, William J. "Charles Babbage, John Herschel, and the Industrial Mind." *Isis* 87 (1996): 629-653. Analyzes Babbage's mathematical thought processes.

Babbage, Charles. *Passages from the Life of a Philosopher*. Edited by Martin Campbell-Kelly. Piscataway, N.J.: IEEE Press, 1994. Babbage's personal reminiscences regarding the design and development of the mechanical calculators and other projects.

Babbage, Henry P., ed. *Babbage's Calculating Engines: A Collection of Papers Relating to Them—Their History, and Construction*. Los Angeles: Tomash, 1982. Facsimile reprint of 1889 edition published in London, with a new introduction by Allan G. Bromley. Contains thirty-three items, most of them assembled by Charles Babbage before his death. Additions and editing provided by his youngest son.

Collier, Bruce. *The Little Engines That Could've: The Calculating Machines of Charles Babbage*. New York: Garland, 1990. A good account of Babbage's struggles to develop his calculator.

Hyman, Anthony. *Charles Babbage: Pioneer of the Computer*. Princeton, N.J.: Princeton University Press, 1982. A standard biography with a rich account of Babbage's life and times.

Lindgren, Michael. *Glory and Failure: The Difference Engines of Johann Muller, Charles Babbage and Georg and Edvard Scheutz*. Cambridge, Mass.: MIT Press, 1990. Provides a detailed exploration of similar work being done in the field during Babbage's time.

Swade, Doron. *The Difference Engine: Charles Babbage and the Quest to Build the First Computer*. New York: Viking Press, 2001. A short and readable account of Babbage's work on the difference engine and on the attempt to build his design in the late twentieth century.

SEE ALSO: 1847: Boole Publishes *The Mathematical Analysis of Logic*; June 23, 1868: Sholes Patents a Practical Typewriter; 1899: Hilbert Publishes *The Foundations of Geometry*; 1900: Lebesgue Develops New Integration Theory.

RELATED ARTICLES in *Great Lives from History: The Nineteenth Century, 1801-1900:* Niels Henrik Abel; Charles Babbage; Countess of Lovelace; Ottmar Mergenthaler.

1810's

February 22, 1819

ADAMS-ONÍS TREATY GIVES THE UNITED STATES FLORIDA

One of the most important treaties in U.S. history, this agreement resolved almost all conflicts between the United States and Spain, gave the United States Florida, settled the boundaries between the Louisiana Territory and Spanish possessions to the west, and signaled the entry of the United States as a world power.

ALSO KNOWN AS: Transcontinental Treaty
LOCALE: Washington, D.C.; Madrid, Spain
CATEGORIES: Diplomacy and international relations; expansion and land acquisition

KEY FIGURES
John Quincy Adams (1767-1848), U.S. secretary of state and later president, 1825-1829

Luis de Onís (1762-1827), Spanish minister to the United States, 1809-1819

James Madison (1751-1836), president of the United States, 1809-1817

James Monroe (1758-1831), Madison's secretary of state and president of the United States, 1817-1825

Ferdinand VII (1784-1833), king of Spain, r. 1808, 1814-1833

Andrew Jackson (1767-1845), commander of the U.S. military expedition into Florida in 1818 and later president, 1829-1837

SUMMARY OF EVENT

After the War of 1812, the United States intensified its efforts to resolve long-standing disputes with Spain.

Spanish difficulties with the United States had entered a critical new phase during the undeclared U.S. naval war with France that lasted from 1798 to 1800. As an ally of France at that time, Spain had permitted its ships to assist in ransacking U.S. commerce on the high seas and allowed the French to seize U.S. ships in Spanish ports. The United States later demanded compensation from Spain for the loss of these vessels and cargoes. In 1802, the Spanish suspended the right of the United States to deposit and transfer goods at New Orleans, which was then under Spanish rule, damaging U.S. commerce in the trans-Appalachian West. Although the Treaty of San Lorenzo of 1795—which was also known as the Pinckney Treaty—between the United States and Spain had guaranteed U.S. deposit rights and prohibited privateering by either nation upon the other, the Spanish balked at paying compensation for its transgressions, leaving the dispute unresolved in 1805.

The U.S. purchase of Louisiana from France in 1803 complicated Spanish-American relations. The French had obtained the territory from Spain in the Treaty of San Ildefonso of 1800. By that agreement, France had pledged not to transfer Louisiana to another power without first offering to restore the territory to Spain. The Spanish thus considered the U.S. purchase of the territory to be illegal and continued to demand its return until 1818. Meanwhile, the United States quickly defined Louisiana's boundaries, part of which ran along two adjacent Spanish provinces, Texas and West Florida. U.S. claims to the latter territory were dubious at best, and Spanish rights to western and central Texas were solidly founded upon the chain of Spanish forts and missions that had established there before 1800. East Texas, however, was largely unsettled and would become the crux of the dispute after the War of 1812.

U.S. interest in Spanish territory also extended to areas to which the United States could make no plausible legal claims. East Florida was one such area, and the United States negotiated continuously for its purchase, beginning in the 1790's. U.S. government leaders believed that possession of Florida would give the United States command of the Gulf of Mexico and secure from foreign interference the trade that passed through the Mississippi River. After 1808, U.S. prospects for acquiring both West and East Florida improved greatly: Napoleon had invaded Spain, diverting most of that nation's resources to a life-or-death struggle against France.

In the summer of 1810, the United States colluded in the successful rebellion of settlers in the Baton Rouge region of West Florida. Later during that same year, the area was legally annexed to the United States up to the Pearl River and later became part of the state of Louisiana. After the United States went to war with Great Britain in 1812, the U.S. government came under domestic pressure to use the opportunity to expand at Spain's expense. In the spring of 1813, Congress authorized the occupation of Mobile, the principal Spanish port in the section of West Florida between the Pearl and Perdido Rivers. The Spanish responded to U.S. aggression by allowing the British to use Pensacola as a base, and by assisting the Creek Indians in their 1813-1814 war against the United States. The War of 1812 thus dramatically illustrated U.S. vulnerability: In the hands of Spain, Florida had become a yawning gap in the coastal defenses of the United States—a highway through which the interior of the country could be penetrated easily.

After the United States concluded the Treaty of Ghent with Great Britain in early 1815, the acquisition of East Florida became the prime goal of U.S. foreign policy. Spain recognized that it had only two choices to avoid a shameful abandonment of the region: to gain the support of a European ally, or to attain a semblance of honor in the affair by winning from the United States favorable territorial concessions west of the Mississippi. At first, the Spanish were successful in securing the support of the British, who warned the United States against further encroachments on their neighbors.

Bolstered by Britain's encouragement, Luis de Onís, Spain's minister to the United States, successfully sparred with his counterpart, Secretary of State James Monroe, throughout 1815 and 1816. The Spaniard demanded the return of Louisiana and West Florida to Spain and protested against American supplying of revolutionaries fighting against Spain in Spain's Central and South American colonies and American support of the privateers operating out of Baltimore that preyed on Spanish shipping. Soon, Spain had developed its own list of financial claims against the United States and was demanding compensation. President James Madison declined to intensify the diplomatic struggle, because delay only aided the United States, which was growing stronger, as Spain was growing weaker.

The inauguration of former secretary of state James Monroe as president in March, 1817, placed the negotiations in impatient, decisive hands. Monroe was determined to push the Spanish to an agreement and appointed a secretary of state, John Quincy Adams, who shared his views. In the fall of 1817, the U.S. cabinet decided to adopt a new attitude toward Spain, a decision that resulted in the dispatch of an army under the command of

Major General Andrew Jackson into Florida—ostensibly to pursue Seminoles who were raiding in retaliation for the destruction of one of their villages.

Jackson's orders from Washington were ambiguous: He was authorized to enter Florida to punish the Seminoles but was forbidden to attack them if they sheltered under a Spanish fort. At the same time, he was also enjoined to adopt the measures necessary to end the conflict. After Jackson was actually in Florida, he discovered evidence of Spanish aid to the Seminoles. Relying on the discretion allotted to him, he judged that only the capture of Spanish forts would end the conflict. Jackson accordingly adopted these "necessary measures" by seizing St. Marks and Pensacola, effectively wresting Florida from Spain.

Although the U.S. administration would later deny having intended that Jackson should take such extreme action, Adams used the military pressure to force the Spanish to retreat from their extreme negotiating positions. International conditions also encouraged Spain to accommodate U.S. demands. By early 1818, Great Britain had made it clear that it would not risk war with the United States by seeking to enforce mediation of Spanish-American disputes. European commitments and dangers had caused the British to reconsider their support for Spain and to seek détente with the United States. In the summer, Great Britain agreed to negotiate with the United States over all outstanding issues. These talks resulted in the Convention of 1818. The British-American rapprochement thus ended Spanish pretensions to power.

Negotiations between the United States and Spain resumed in the fall of 1818, after the United States had agreed to restore the forts to the Spanish. Near the end of the year, the two nations agreed upon a western boundary that went up the Sabine River from its mouth and continued north to the Red River, zigzagged westward along the Red and Arkansas Rivers, followed the crest of the Rocky Mountains to the forty-second parallel, and then turned westward to the Pacific Ocean.

On February 22, 1819, Adams and Onís signed the treaty that bears their names. It embodied the compromise western boundary and resolved nearly all the disputes between their two nations. The Spanish retained Texas but gave up claims to the Oregon Country. Spain ceded all its territory east of the Mississippi to the United States. Both nations renounced their claims for damages, although the United States agreed to assume the claims of its citizens against Spain up to a maximum of five million dollars.

Adams successfully avoided guaranteeing that the United States would not recognize the Latin American nations claiming independence from Spain. At first, King Ferdinand VII of Spain refused to ratify the treaty because the United States had failed to provide such guarantees. However, a January, 1820, revolution in Spain brought to power a liberal regime whose leaders were inclined to accommodate the United States. France and Russia, who feared that the Spanish-American quarrel threatened world peace, pressured the new Spanish government to settle. Spain finally ratified the treaty in October, 1820, and the Adams-Onís Treaty (also known as the Transcontinental Treaty) became effective on February 22, 1821.

SIGNIFICANCE

The Adams-Onís Treaty was crucial to determining the course of North American history. It signified the decay of Spanish power in the New World and provided conclusive evidence of British acquiescence in limited United States expansion. The acquisition of Florida strengthened the United States materially and enhanced its national security by closing a gap in its coastal defenses. Spain's recognition of U.S. rights in Oregon signaled the beginning of the role of the United States as a global power. Resolving problems with Spain largely freed the United States from European entanglements for several decades.

The treaty also played a decisive role in modern Seminole history. By replacing stagnant Spanish rule with that of a demographically and economically expanding United States, the treaty ensured that the Seminoles could not long remain in possession of their lands. Their removal westward almost inevitably followed during the 1830's.

—Michael S. Fitzgerald

FURTHER READING

Bemis, Samuel F. *John Quincy Adams and the Foundations of American Foreign Policy.* New York: Alfred A. Knopf, 1949. Detailed examination of Adams's role in the treaty negotiations, strongly emphasizing the continentalism in his thinking.

Brooks, Philip C. *Diplomacy and the Borderlands: The Adams-Onís Treaty of 1819.* Berkeley: University of California Press, 1939. This highly detailed account of the negotiations unfortunately emphasizes legal aspects of the treaty so strongly that the book obscures the role of power in determining the treaty's final shape.

Cox, Isaac J. *The West Florida Controversy, 1798-1813: A Study in American Diplomacy.* 1918. Reprint. Gloucester, Mass.: Peter Smith, 1967. Although inadequate in several respects, this study provides an excellent summary of the development of Spanish-American disputes before 1815.

Griffin, Charles C. *The United States and the Disruption of the Spanish Empire, 1810-1822.* New York: Columbia University Press, 1937. Stresses the domestic and international context of the negotiations. Analysis of U.S. public opinion illuminates United States decision making.

Missall, John, and Mary Lou Missall. *The Seminole Wars: America's Longest Indian Conflict.* Gainesville: University Press of Florida, 2004. Study of the three Seminole wars that examines their causes and significance in American history, including the U.S. acquisition of Florida from Spain.

Remini, Robert V. *Andrew Jackson.* 3 vols. Baltimore: Johns Hopkins University Press, 1998. The first volume of this major biography covers Jackson's role in territorial expansion, including his pivotal role in the U.S. acquisition of Florida.

Weeks, William E. *John Quincy Adams and American Global Empire.* Lexington: University Press of Kentucky, 1992. A balanced account of the treaty negotiations, which includes the role of U.S. expansionism and aggression. Unlike some earlier historians, Weeks does not regard the Florida cession as the almost inevitable result of Spanish decay.

SEE ALSO: May 9, 1803: Louisiana Purchase; May 14, 1804-Sept. 23, 1806: Lewis and Clark Expedition; June 18, 1812-Dec. 24, 1814: War of 1812; July 27, 1813-Aug. 9, 1814: Creek War; c. 1815-1830: Westward American Migration Begins; Feb. 17, 1815: Treaty of Ghent Takes Effect; Nov. 21, 1817-Mar. 27, 1858: Seminole Wars; 1838-1839: Aroostook War; Aug. 9, 1842: Webster-Ashburton Treaty Settles Maine's Canadian Border; June 15, 1846: United States Acquires Oregon Territory; May 8, 1871: Treaty of Washington Settles U.S. Claims vs. Britain.

RELATED ARTICLES in *Great Lives from History: The Nineteenth Century, 1801-1900:* John Quincy Adams; Andrew Jackson; James Monroe.

March 6, 1819
MCCULLOCH V. MARYLAND

In this landmark decision, the U.S. Supreme Court recognized the doctrine of implied powers, which gave the federal government broad authority over state governments and irrevocably established the principle of federal supremacy.

LOCALE: Washington, D.C.
CATEGORIES: Laws, acts, and legal history; government and politics

KEY FIGURES
James W. McCulloch (fl. early nineteenth century), cashier in the Baltimore branch of the Second Bank of the United States
Thomas Jefferson (1743-1826), secretary of state under President George Washington and later president of the United States, 1801-1809
Alexander Hamilton (1755-1804), secretary of the Treasury, 1789-1795
John Marshall (1755-1835), chief justice of the United States, 1801-1835
Luther Martin (1748-1826), attorney general of Maryland and chief counsel for Maryland

William Pinkney (1764-1822), counsel for McCulloch and the Second Bank
Daniel Webster (1782-1852), U.S. senator and counsel for McCulloch and the Second Bank
William Wirt (1772-1834), U.S. attorney general and counsel for the Second Bank

SUMMARY OF EVENT
From the time of its framing in 1787, the U.S. Constitution has stirred controversy over the nature of the union that it created and the extent of federal authority. The Civil War (1861-1865) would in 1865 settle certain outstanding questions as to the nature of the union, but a more articulate consideration of the problem was provided by the Supreme Court of the United States in 1819 in the landmark case of *McCulloch v. Maryland.*

The arguments surrounding the case were as old as the Constitution itself. Although the Constitutional Convention of 1787 had considered and rejected the proposal that Congress be empowered to charter corporations, a classic constitutional debate took place during the first administration of President George Washington over the question of chartering the First Bank of the United States. In memoranda they wrote at the president's request, Secretary of the Treasury Alexander Hamilton and Secretary of State Thomas Jefferson presented diametrically opposed advice on the question of whether the president should approve the bill chartering the First Bank of the United States. Hamilton urged a broad interpretation of the Constitution's "necessary and proper" clause, contending that Congress had the power to make all laws that it considered expedient or convenient. Jefferson insisted on a stricter interpretation of that clause, which, he argued, authorized Congress to pass only those laws that were necessary to give effect to its specifically delegated powers.

Washington took Hamilton's advice, and the bank was chartered in 1791. The bank's charter expired in 1811, and the adverse economic impact of the War of 1812, coupled with the abuses and irresponsibility of state-chartered banks, led to the chartering in 1816 of the Second Bank of the United States. The chartering of the First Bank of the United States had prompted a movement in favor of a constitutional amendment to restrict Congress's powers under the "necessary and proper" clause, and the chartering of the Second Bank of the United States led many states to adopt laws designed to suppress the bank's operations.

Hostility toward the bank rested on a number of factors. First, it was regarded as a Federalist-controlled enterprise, much of whose stock was held by foreign investors. Moreover, the operations of the First Bank of the United States had tended to undercut the success of the state banks, and many blamed the bleak economic conditions following the War of 1812 on the policies of the First Bank of the United States. Champions of the new bank regarded renewal of its charter as the only hope of improving economic conditions.

In certain states, antibank sentiment was rampant. Indiana, Illinois, Tennessee, Georgia, North Carolina, Kentucky, Ohio, and Maryland adopted laws designed to curtail or prohibit the operation of the Bank of the United

---

MARSHALL'S OPINION IN *MCCULLOCH V. MARYLAND*

U.S. Supreme Court chief justice John Marshall wrote the majority opinion, excerpted here, for the Court in the case of McCulloch v. Maryland.

If any one proposition could command the universal assent of mankind, we might expect it would be this—that the Government of the Union, though limited in its powers, is supreme within its sphere of action. This would seem to result necessarily from its nature. It is the Government of all; its powers are delegated by all; it represents all, and acts for all. Though any one State may be willing to control its operations, no State is willing to allow others to control them. The nation, on those subjects on which it can act, must necessarily bind its component parts. But this question is not left to mere reason; the people have, in express terms, decided it by saying, "this Constitution, and the laws of the United States, which shall be made in pursuance thereof," "shall be the supreme law of the land," and by requiring that the members of the State legislatures and the officers of the executive and judicial departments of the States shall take the oath of fidelity to it. The Government of the United States, then, though limited in its powers, is supreme, and its laws, when made in pursuance of the Constitution, form the supreme law of the land, "anything in the Constitution or laws of any State to the contrary notwithstanding.". . .

The Court has bestowed on this subject its most deliberate consideration. The result is a conviction that the States have no power, by taxation or otherwise, to retard, impede, burden, or in any manner control the operations of the constitutional laws enacted by Congress to carry into execution the powers vested in the General Government. This is, we think, the unavoidable consequence of that supremacy which the Constitution has declared.

We are unanimously of opinion that the law passed by the Legislature of Maryland, imposing a tax on the Bank of the United States is unconstitutional and void.

States. The momentum of the antibank movement was encouraged by the mismanagement and fraud of the managers of the Second Bank of the United States. The growing anxiety over the deteriorating state of the economy made an appeal to the courts an attractive way of settling the question of the legitimacy of the state burdens that were being imposed on the bank's operations. This was the immediate motivation for the litigation that led to *McCulloch v. Maryland.*

John James, an agent of the state of Maryland, called on James W. McCulloch, the cashier of the Baltimore branch of the bank, and demanded that McCulloch comply with the state law. The Maryland law, adopted in February, 1818, required all banks chartered outside Maryland to pay a tax of one hundred dollars on all notes issued or, alternatively, to pay an annual sum of fifteen thousand dollars into the state's treasury. McCulloch refused to comply with this prohibitive state law. When he was prosecuted for his refusal, the Maryland courts ruled against him. In September, 1818, his case was appealed to the U.S. Supreme Court.

The Supreme Court heard arguments in the case for nine days. Appearing on behalf of the bank were Attorney General William Wirt, William Pinkney, and Daniel Webster. Luther Martin, the fiery attorney general of Maryland who had expedited the bringing of the case to the Supreme Court; Joseph Hopkinson; and Walter Jones were the lawyers appearing for Maryland.

On March 6, 1819, the Supreme Court handed down its decision, only three days after completion of arguments and while there was much activity in Congress aimed at revoking the bank's charter. The opinion by Chief Justice John Marshall is regarded by most scholars as his most important pronouncement in constitutional law and the one most important to the future of the United States. The Constitution, said Marshall, established a truly national government that "is emphatically and truly a government of the people. In form and in substance it emanates from them, its powers are granted by them, and are to be exercised directly on them, and for their benefit."

Much of the remainder of Marshall's opinion is an extension and application of this "national" theory of the Constitution's foundations. Sovereignty is divided between federal and state governments. When state power conflicts with national power, the former must yield because national sovereignty is supreme. The judiciary, Marshall wrote, is constitutionally required to construe Congress's enumerated powers broadly. The "necessary and proper" clause, sometimes called the "elastic" clause, was designed to empower Congress to exercise its delegated powers by any convenient and expedient methods not prohibited by the Constitution itself. Marshall found that the "necessary and proper" clause gave rise to what have come to be called "implied powers":

> A constitution, to contain an accurate detail of all the subdivisions of which its great powers will admit, and all of the means by which they may be carried into execution, would partake of the prolixity of a legal code, and could scarcely be embraced by the human mind. It would probably never be understood by the public. Its nature, therefore, requires that only its great outlines should be marked, its important objects designated, and the minor ingredients which compose those objects be deduced from the nature of the objects themselves.

By focusing on the ends sought to be achieved by the Constitution's framers, Marshall ensured that Congress neither overstepped its bounds nor was denied any pow-

ers involved with its responsibilities. That flexible approach allowed Congress to select the means by which to implement its powers. Both the spirit and the language of the Constitution supported that view. The Framers had "omitted to use any restrictive term which might prevent its receiving a fair and just interpretation. In considering this question, then, we must never forget, that it is a constitution we are expounding."

SIGNIFICANCE

McCulloch v. Maryland was the Supreme Court's earliest and most renowned implied powers case. In its ruling, the Court upheld the constitutionality of the federal government to incorporate a national bank in Baltimore. In doing so, it accomplished three important goals: It clarified the power of state taxation and congressional authority in economic policy making, reinforced the principles of U.S. federalism, and specified that the necessary and proper clause of the Constitution grants Congress certain implied powers that extend beyond its enumerated powers.

After the *McCulloch* decision, the implied powers were used to expand and contract governmental power in *Gibbons v. Ogden* in 1824 and in *United States v. Lopez* in 1995. Although many cases decided by the Court have dealt with economic policies, the Court has also addressed crime prevention programs, federalism cases, and the implied powers of the presidency. Indeed, the majority of presidential powers are based on authority implicit in such enumerated, yet vague, powers as the commander in chief and executive power clauses of the Constitution.

During the twentieth century, Supreme Court justice Felix Frankfurter asserted that Marshall's words were the most important ever uttered by a United States judge, acknowledging an expansive source of power and an extension of that power beyond those expressly named sources. "Let the end be legitimate, let it be within the scope of the Constitution, and all means are appropriate, which are plainly adopted to that end, which are not prohibited, but consist with the letter of the Constitution, are constitutional. . . ." As a precedent for future assertions of national authority, the opinion asserted that legitimate uses of national power took priority over state authority and that the "necessary and proper" clause was a broad grant of national authority.

Luther Martin had insisted in his argument that even if Congress had the authority to establish the Bank of the United States, a state could still levy the tax in question. Marshall rejected his argument and laid down the general principle that the central government had constitutional power to "withdraw any subject from the action" of the states. "The power to tax," he declared, "involves the power to destroy." To permit Maryland to tax the bank's operations would place all federal programs at the mercy of the states. This facet of the *McCulloch* opinion gave rise to the doctrine of intergovernmental tax immunity.

— *James J. Bolner, updated by Marcia J. Weiss*

FURTHER READING

Barron, Jerome A., and C. Thomas Dienes. *Constitutional Law in a Nutshell.* 2d ed. St. Paul, Minn.: West, 1991. A compact reference on the law for those with a legal or political science background.

Cox, Archibald. *The Court and the Constitution.* Boston: Houghton Mifflin, 1987. The former U.S. solicitor general and Watergate special prosecutor chronicles issues and debates in each era of constitutional history.

Gunther, Gerald, ed. *John Marshall's Defense of McCulloch v. Maryland.* Stanford, Calif.: Stanford University Press, 1969. A compilation of the debates surrounding Marshall's decision. Contains the newspaper battle with ideological opponents of the Supreme Court, as well as Marshall's replies. Introduction by the editor.

Johnson, Herbert A. *The Chief Justiceship of John Marshall, 1801-1835.* Columbia: University of South Carolina Press, 1997. Excellent biography of Marshall that closely examines his work on the Supreme Court.

Lewis, Thomas T., and Richard L. Wilson, eds. *Encyclopedia of the U.S. Supreme Court.* 3 vols. Pasadena, Calif.: Salem Press, 2001. Comprehensive reference work on the Supreme Court that contains substantial discussions of *McCulloch v. Maryland*, implied powers, John Marshall, and many related subjects.

McCloskey, Robert G. *The American Supreme Court.* 2d ed. Revised by Sanford Levinson. Chicago: University of Chicago Press, 1994. A detailed treatment of the Marshall Court. Contains additional resources in a bibliographical essay.

Smith, Jean E. *John Marshall: Definer of a Nation.* New York: Henry Holt, 1996. One of the best biographies of Marshall yet published.

SEE ALSO: Feb. 24, 1803: *Marbury v. Madison*; Mar. 16, 1810: *Fletcher v. Peck*; Apr., 1816: Second Bank of the United States Is Chartered; Mar. 2, 1824: *Gibbons v. Ogden*; July 10, 1832: Jackson Vetoes Rechartering of the Bank of the United States.

RELATED ARTICLES in *Great Lives from History: The Nineteenth Century, 1801-1900:* Nicholas Biddle; John Marshall; Daniel Webster.

May, 1819
UNITARIAN CHURCH IS FOUNDED

The founding of the Unitarian Church in the midst of the Unitarian Controversy, a religious debate between liberal and orthodox Congregationalists, marked the birth of a leading institution of religious and social reform in the United States.

LOCALE: Boston, Massachusetts

CATEGORIES: Religion and theology; organizations and institutions

KEY FIGURES

Hosea Ballou (1771-1852), Universalist minister of Portsmouth, New Hampshire

Lyman Beecher (1775-1863), pastor of Boston's Park Street Church

William Ellery Channing (1780-1842), known as the Apostle of Unitarianism, pastor of Federal Street Church, Boston

Charles Chauncy (1705-1787), pastor of Boston's First Church

Dorothea Dix (1802-1887), social reform leader

Ebenezer Gay (1696-1787), minister of a liberal church in Hingham, Massachusetts

Jonathan Mayhew (1720-1766), pastor of West Church, Boston

Jedidiah Morse (1761-1826), minister at Charlestown, Massachusetts, and founder of *The Panoplist*

Joseph Priestley (1733-1804), founder of Philadelphia's first Unitarian church

Jared Sparks (1789-1866), Unitarian minister and editor of *The Unitarian*

Joseph Tuckerman (1778-1840), Boston minister-at-large

Henry Ware (1764-1845), Hingham, Massachusetts, minister and Harvard College professor of divinity

SUMMARY OF EVENT

The roots of Unitarianism go back to sixteenth century Spain and the teachings of Michael Servetus (1511-1553). Unitarianism in the United States developed from an independent movement resulting from a split in the Congregationalist churches in Massachusetts during the nineteenth century.

In May, 1819, William Ellery Channing, the pastor of Boston's Federal Street Church, traveled to Baltimore to preach at the ordination of a Unitarian minister, Jared Sparks. His sermon, "Unitarian Christianity," was a landmark in the founding of the Unitarian Church of the United States. Channing delivered his sermon in the midst of the Unitarian Controversy, a religious debate between liberal and orthodox Congregationalists, which had begun officially in 1805 when Henry Ware was appointed Hollis Professor of Divinity at Harvard College, but which reached back into the early eighteenth century. Religious liberalism, or Arminianism as it was called, emerged in the 1730's as a reaction against the rigorous Calvinism of men such as Jonathan Edwards and Samuel Hopkins. In the prerevolutionary period, Charles Chauncy, the pastor of Boston's First Church, and Jona-

William Ellery Channing. (Library of Congress)

than Mayhew, the pastor of Boston's West Church, were the foremost Arminian spokesmen, preaching anti-Trinitarianism, the benevolence of God, and human ability in salvation. Other denominations besides Congregationalists were affected by the liberal impulse.

During the early 1780's, anti-Trinitarian views were heard in King's Chapel, which subsequently broke away from the Church of England. This established the first Universalist Church in the United States in 1785. However, other ministers preached anti-Trinitarian views. One of the earliest was Ebenezer Gay, who passively expressed his views in church by simply omitting fundamental Calvinist beliefs from his sermons. Joseph Priestley, an early English Unitarian, began preaching in Philadelphia in 1794 after fleeing persecution in his homeland and established a Unitarian church in that city. Universalists such as Hosea Ballou of Portsmouth, New Hampshire, also embraced the liberal theology.

Liberalism was particularly strong in Boston and among Congregationalists, and it was within that denomination that the Unitarian Controversy occurred. At the beginning of the nineteenth century, orthodox Congregationalists, led by such men as Jedidiah Morse, minister at Charlestown, Massachusetts, and Lyman Beecher, the pastor of Park Street Church, Boston, tried to fight the tide of liberalism. Morse founded *The Panoplist* to proselytize "the faith once delivered to the saints" and succeeded in uniting Hopkinsians and Old Calvinists in a common front against the liberals. When the Hollis Chair of Divinity at Harvard College became vacant in 1803, orthodox Congregationalists attempted to get a moderate Calvinist appointed. When Ware was appointed, they gave up Harvard as lost to heterodoxy and founded their own seminary at Andover in 1808. Gaining the chair eventually led the Unitarians to take their first organizational step: the founding of Harvard Divinity School.

The decade following Ware's appointment at Harvard saw a hardening of the lines between orthodox and liberal Congregationalists. Liberals—who preferred that title to the "Unitarian" label that their opponents had fastened on them—steadily gained strength, spreading their views by way of pulpit and press. The orthodox intensified their attack. In 1815, Morse distributed a pamphlet entitled *American Unitarianism*, a chapter from a British work that argued that New England liberals were Unitarians in the English sense, meaning that they avowed merely the humanity of Jesus. Morse also published a review of the pamphlet in *The Panoplist*, which denounced liberal Congregationalists as heretics secretly conspiring to overthrow the true faith and called for their expulsion from the Congregational church.

As the leader of the Boston liberals, Channing answered *The Panoplist* attack by a public letter to Samuel C. Thacher, minister of the New South Church. This letter brought a reply from Samuel Worchester of Salem, who defended the review. A long pamphlet debate between Channing and Worchester followed, with the issue shifting from *The Panoplist* review to the more general question of the nature of Unitarianism. As the theological differences became clearer, liberals began to accept the once unpopular term "Unitarian," although they expanded and elaborated on its meaning.

It was in this context of bitter theological debate that Channing decided in 1819 to deliver the now-famous Baltimore sermon, which laid the foundation for the Unitarian Church in the United States. "Unitarian Christianity" provided a comprehensive statement of the beliefs of U.S. Unitarians, as well as an eloquent defense of their faith. Unitarians, Channing declared, interpreted the Scriptures by "the constant exercise of reason" and rejected any theological doctrines repugnant to reason and moral sense. Thus they believed in the unity of God, rejecting the "irrational and unscriptural doctrine of the Trinity." They also rejected the Calvinist God, worshiping instead a God who was "infinitely good, kind, and benevolent." Such a God offered salvation not to a few elect, but to all.

Unitarians also rejected doctrines of natural depravity and predestination, not only because of their "unspeakable cruelty" but also because such doctrines were adverse to God's "parental character." Channing concluded his sermon on a conciliatory note, saying,

> We have embraced this system not hastily or lightly, but after much deliberation, and we hold it fast, not merely because we believe it to be true, but because we regard it as purifying truth, as a doctrine according to godliness,

---

"UNITARIAN CHRISTIANITY"

In 1819, pastor William Ellery Channing delivered what is likely the most important sermon in Unitarian history. Also known as the "Baltimore Sermon," Channing's words came at the height of debates between liberal Christians and Orthodox Calvinists within Congregationalist churches of the United States. The liberals would soon take the name "Unitarian."

To all who hear me, I would say, with the Apostle, Prove all things, hold fast that which is good. Do not, brethren, shrink from the duty of searching God's Word for yourselves, through fear of human censure and denunciation. Do not think, that you may innocently follow the opinions which prevail around you, without investigation, on the ground, that Christianity is now so purified from errors, as to need no laborious research. There is much reason to believe, that Christianity is at this moment dishonored by gross and cherished corruptions. If you remember the darkness which hung over the Gospel for ages; if you consider the impure union, which still subsists in almost every Christian country, between the church and state, and which enlists men's selfishness and ambition on the side of established error; if you recollect in what degree the spirit of intolerance has checked free inquiry, not only before, but since the Reformation; you will see that Christianity cannot have freed itself from all the human inventions, which disfigured it under the Papal tyranny. No. Much stubble is yet to be burned; much rubbish to be removed; many gaudy decorations, which a false taste has hung around Christianity, must be swept away; and the earth-born fogs, which have long shrouded it, must be scattered, before this divine fabric will rise before us in its native and awful majesty, in its harmonious proportions, in its mild and celestial splendors This glorious reformation in the church, we hope, under God's blessing, from the progress of the human intellect, from the moral progress of society, from the consequent decline of prejudice and bigotry, and, though last not least, from the subversion of human authority in matters of religion, from the fall of those hierarchies, and other human institutions, by which the minds of individuals are oppressed under the weight of numbers, and a Papal dominion is perpetuated in the Protestant church.

Source: "Unitarian Christianity." May 5, 1819. American Unitarian Conference.

---

as able to "work mightily" and to "bring forth fruit" in them that believe. . . . We see nothing in our views to give offence, save their purity, and it is their purity which makes us seek and hope their extension through the world.

Despite its conciliatory tone, Channing's sermon made reconciliation between liberal and orthodox Congregationalists even less likely than before. Separation of Unitarians from Congregationalists and vice versa became commonplace, as one or the other group (usually the latter) within a church withdrew to form a new society. Unitarian organization was slow and met with resistance from within, but in May, 1825, the American Unitarian

Association was founded "to diffuse the knowledge and promote the interests of pure Christianity." This was the final act of separation that divided Unitarians and Congregationalists into two denominations and ended the long theological conflict that had begun more than a quarter of a century earlier. In 1961, the denomination merged with the Universalist Church to form the Unitarian Universalist Association.

SIGNIFICANCE

The impact of Unitarianism reaches far beyond the splitting of the Congregationalist church. The Unitarians became leaders in promoting social progress. Dorothea Dix, one of Channing's own parishioners, spent most of her lifetime seeking to improve living conditions for the mentally ill. Joseph Tuckerman, a minister-at-large of Boston, not only brought Unitarian teachings to the city's poor but also worked hard to bring practical help to them through personal visits and counseling. Tuckerman's work generated similar endeavors in other cities. The examples of Dix, Tuckerman, and other early Unitarians sparked reforms in education, health, and women's rights.

—Anne C. Loveland,
updated by Pamela Hayes-Bohanan

FURTHER READING

Buehrens, John, and F. Forrester Church. *Our Chosen Faith: An Introduction to Unitarian Universalism.* Boston: Beacon Press, 1989. Describes the philosophies and histories of Unitarians and Universalists. Includes information on famous Unitarians and Universalists and provides a chronology of the faith.

Elgin, Kathleen. *The Unitarians: The Unitarian Universalist Association.* New York: David McKay, 1971. Some background on Unitarian history in general, but mainly discusses Dorothea Dix and her work with the mentally ill.

Harris, Mark W. *Historical Dictionary of Unitarian Universalism.* Lanham, Md.: Scarecrow Press, 2004. A comprehensive resource that includes an editor's introduction, a list of acronyms, a chronology, and bibliographical references.

Mead, Frank S. "Unitarian Universalist Association." In *Handbook of Denominations in the United States*, edited by Frank S. Mead, Samuel S. Hill, and Craig D. Atwood. 12th ed. Nashville, Tenn.: Abingdon Press, 2005. Provides a brief history of Unitarian Universalism. Discusses the church in the late twentieth century and its philosophies.

Robinson, David. *The Unitarians and the Universalists.* Westport, Conn.: Greenwood Press, 1985. A comprehensive history of Unitarian Universalism in the United States and its impact. Includes a biographical dictionary of Unitarian Universalist leaders.

Wright, Conrad. *The Beginnings of Unitarianism in America.* 1955. Reprint. Hamden, Conn.: Archon Books, 1976. Discusses the early roots of Unitarianism in America, from 1735 to 1805, and the events leading to the split in the Congregational churches.

_____. *The Unitarian Controversy: Essays on American Unitarian History.* Boston: Skinner House Books, 1994. Articles on the Unitarian Controversy by a leading Unitarian scholar. One article is entitled "The Channing We Didn't Know."

SEE ALSO: 1820's-1850's: Social Reform Movement; Apr. 6, 1830: Smith Founds the Mormon Church; 1835: Finney Lectures on "Revivals of Religion"; 1836: Transcendental Movement Arises in New England; 1870-1871: Watch Tower Bible and Tract Society Is Founded; Oct. 30, 1875: Eddy Establishes the Christian Science Movement.

RELATED ARTICLES in *Great Lives from History: The Nineteenth Century, 1801-1900:* Olympia Brown; William Ellery Channing; Dorothea Dix; Ralph Waldo Emerson; Nathaniel Hawthorne; Harriet Martineau; Frederick Denison Maurice; Theodore Parker; Elizabeth Palmer Peabody; Rammohan Ray.

May 22-June 20, 1819
SAVANNAH IS THE FIRST STEAMSHIP TO CROSS THE ATLANTIC

In traveling from the state of Georgia to Liverpool, England, the steamship Savannah *established that steam power could be utilized on the open seas. Although the converted packet ship was outfitted only with auxiliary steam equipment and conducted much of its voyage under sail, its voyage is recognized as the first steam-assisted transatlantic crossing.*

LOCALE: Atlantic Ocean, between Savannah, Georgia, and Liverpool, England

CATEGORIES: Transportation; engineering; trade and commerce

KEY FIGURES

Moses Rogers (1779-1821), captain of the *Savannah*

William Scarbrough (1776-1838), principal owner of the *Savannah*

Stephen Vail (1780-1864), foundry owner and entrepreneur

Stevens Rogers (1789-1868), sailing master and first officer of the *Savannah*

SUMMARY OF EVENT

The transatlantic voyage of the *Savannah* was set in motion by a small group of businessmen who gambled that steam power could profitably increase the efficiency of transport on the open seas and thereby revolutionize international commerce. Veteran steamboat captain Moses Rogers had envisioned an oceangoing steam-powered ship as a natural extension of riverboat technology. He had hoped that a successful crossing would conclusively demonstrate that the future use of steamships was inevitable. Established merchants in the shipping industry, however, doubted the practicability of the enterprise.

Rogers was uniquely qualified to lead such an undertaking, as he had been captain of the steamboat *Phoenix* on its 1809 voyage from New York to Philadelphia, which was the first coastal steam-assisted voyage. He continued throughout his career to be an innovator in the design and sailing of steam vessels, and eventually became partial owner and captain of the *Charleston*, which was launched in 1817 to establish steamboat service between Charleston, South Carolina, and Savannah, Georgia. Rogers soon made connections with a major financial figure of Savannah, William Scarbrough, and with the owner and operator of the Speedwell Iron Works of Morristown, New Jersey, Stephen Vail, who had been visiting Savannah. The three men combined resources to

mastermind the *Savannah* project, with Rogers as captain and engineer, Scarbrough as the primary financial advocate, and Vail as supervisor of the ship's partial conversion from sail to steam.

The future use of steam power to propel oceangoing vessels had been discussed in shipping circles for a number of years, and speculation had increased in the wake of the success of steamboat lines running on coasts and rivers. These operations had added convenience and reliability to passenger service and shipping. Packets, or vessels sailing by scheduled departure and arrival times, were also new and popular innovations. Savannah investors were persuaded that converting a sailing ship by adding a steam engine and dual paddle wheels would free it from the vagaries of wind propulsion. Thus, subscriptions to the Savannah Steamship Company sold rapidly when offered in May of 1818, and the company received official corporate status later that year.

The ship purchased by the company was built in the shipyard of Samuel Crockett and William Fickett in New York City and launched in 1818, sailing south to Elizabethtown, New Jersey, not far from the Speedwell Foundry in Morristown, where it docked for conversion. Almost from the beginning, frightening rumors about the ship circulated among observers, who were shocked by its appearance. A large opening in the deck awaited boiler installation, and holes in the sides of the ship had been left for the paddle wheels. The ship, now officially the *Savannah*, was nicknamed "Fickett's steam coffin." Veteran mariners feared that the firing of boilers in a wooden ship would prove disastrous at sea.

The *Savannah* had begun life as a conventional three-masted, 320-ton ship, registered at approximately 98 feet long and 26 feet wide. Its relatively small size indicates that it was originally intended as a coastal rather than as an oceangoing ship. The conversion from sail to steam, a process in which the engine, boilers, and paddle wheels had to be built specifically for the *Savannah*, proved extremely difficult. Design errors and manufacturing failures necessitated the recasting of several crucial parts. The project fell behind schedule, and to avoid the possibility of further delays because of icy conditions, Rogers ordered the *Savannah* to return in December of 1818 to New York, where the conversion was completed.

The *Savannah* was unique. It was equipped with one of the largest steam engines of the times, had specially designed collapsible paddle wheels that could be taken in during major storms, and had a tilted smokestack that could swivel to avoid setting fire to the sails. In addition, no expense had been spared in the decoration of passenger cabins, which featured ornamental wood paneling and full-length mirrors.

The *Savannah* sailed south to what would be its home port of Savannah, Georgia, at the end of March, 1819. Captain Rogers had recruited as sailing master a friend and distant cousin named Stevens Rogers. Although the two were respected seamen, it had been nearly impossible to hire a crew because of fears about the seaworthiness of the *Savannah*. Also, few passengers joined the voyage. On the trip south, Stevens Rogers recorded in the ship's log the times and hours sailed under steam, providing evidence that the steam equipment functioned well; but the *Savannah*'s overall travel time proved unimpressive.

Throughout the conversion and subsequent trip south, official reports hailed the *Savannah* as a commendable experiment, although with little apparent effect. Free passage was offered to U.S. president James Monroe for a trip from Charleston to Savannah, but he agreed only to visit the ship briefly in the latter port. Reluctant passengers and merchants refused to book space on the *Savannah* for its transatlantic voyage, all but eliminating hope for a successful commercial venture. In fact, William Scarbrough, the *Savannah*'s owner, along with other Savannah merchants, had been shipping cargo on competing ships. President Monroe, however, indicated that after the transatlantic voyage the ship might be useful in naval operations. Rumors also circulated that the *Savannah* would be sold to Czar Alexander I of Russia, who had negotiated with inventor Robert Fulton for an oceangoing steamship.

On May 22, 1819, the *Savannah* departed for Liverpool, England, with plans to continue on to St. Petersburg, Russia. There were no recorded passengers, nor was there freight on board. On the voyage across the Atlantic, the *Savannah* proceeded under steam power for eighty to one hundred hours, was in sight of the coast of Ireland by June 16, and arrived in Liverpool on June 20, completing the passage in twenty-nine days. Thirty-day passages by sail between New York and Liverpool were fairly common at that time. The *Savannah* then continued on to St. Petersburg, Russia, with stops in Sweden, Norway, and Denmark, and eventually returned to Savannah, Georgia.

Although the voyage had been successfully completed, and although the ship's design and accomplishments were highly praised throughout its sojourns in Europe, the *Savannah* failed to make money for its investors. A devastating fire in Savannah added to the troubles of the Savannah Steamship Company, forcing the firm into bankruptcy. The U.S. Congress refused to purchase the ship, so it was sold at auction. The new owner removed the *Savannah*'s machinery and converted into a packet sailing ship. It sailed until running aground on Fire Island in 1821.

SIGNIFICANCE

Although the conversion of the *Savannah* is well documented, its transatlantic voyage is not. In later years the *Savannah*'s accomplishments appeared so unimportant to Americans that Stevens Rogers gave the detailed log to a visiting Englishman. Records of the ship's machinery and appearance were also lost until, in 1930, it was discovered that a French citizen, Jean-Baptiste Marestier, had drawn its outline and written a description of it in his 1824 book *Mémoire sur les bateaux á vapeur des Etats-Unis d'Amerique* (1824; *Memoir on Steamboats of the United States of America*, 1957) while it was docked in the Washington Navy Yard for congressional evaluation.

On the whole, Europeans were more interested in ocean steamships than were Americans, who preferred to invest in packet sailing ships. These packet lines came to monopolize the Atlantic shipping industry, but the development of steamship technology continued in Europe. The arrival in 1838 of the *Sirius* and the *Great Western* in New York, both having made the transatlantic crossing fully under steam, marked the beginning of a new era. British steamship lines thus dominated service on the Atlantic for many years, in part because of an American fascination with the advancement of clipper ships.

The daring of the *Savannah* experiment was later recognized by Americans, however, and May 22, its transatlantic departure date, is celebrated as National Maritime Day in the United States.

—*Margaret A. Dodson*

FURTHER READING

Historic Speedwell, Morristown, N.J. http://www .morrisparks.net/speedwell/home.html. Web site of Historic Speedwell, the site of the *Savannah*'s conversion. Includes a summary of the ship's history and the history of the Speedwell Iron Works. Accessed December, 2005.

Braynard, Frank O. *S.S. Savannah, the Elegant Steam Ship*. Athens: University of Georgia Press, 1963. Definitive history of the steamship *Savannah*.

Cavanaugh, Cam, Barbara Hoskins, and Frances D. Pingeon. "S.S. *Savannah.*" In *At Speedwell in the Nineteenth Century.* Morristown, N.J.: Speedwell Village, 1981. Brief history of the Vail family, the Speedwell Iron Works, and the *Savannah.* Includes black-and-white photographs and illustrations.

Chapelle, Howard Irving. *The Pioneer Steamship "Savannah": A Study for a Scale Model.* Washington, D.C.: Smithsonian Institution Press, 1961. Describes the process used in constructing an accurate model of the *Savannah.*

Dubois, Muriel L., and Miriam Butts. *Industrial Revolution Comes to America.* Amawalk, N.Y.: Jackdaw, 2001. Portfolio of illustrations, facsimiles, and maps placing the invention of the *Savannah* in context.

Evans, Harold. *They Made America.* New York: Little, Brown, 2004. Provides the historical context of early steam propulsion in the United States.

Ridgely-Nevitt, Cedric. *American Steamships on the At-lantic.* Newark: University of Delaware Press, 1981. Concludes that the *Savannah* was a problematic auxiliary steam vessel and a commercial failure.

Sloan, Edward W. "Moses Rogers." *American National Biography.* New York: Oxford University Press, 1999. A biography of *Savannah* captain Moses Rogers.

SEE ALSO: Aug. 17, 1807: Maiden Voyage of the *Clermont*; c. 1845: Clipper Ship Era Begins; 1847: Hamburg-Amerika Shipping Line Begins; Aug. 22, 1851: *America* Wins the First America's Cup Race; Jan. 31, 1858: Brunel Launches the SS *Great Eastern*; Mar. 9, 1862: Battle of the *Monitor* and the *Virginia*; June 20, 1895: Germany's Kiel Canal Opens; July 2, 1900: Zeppelin Completes the First Flying Dirigible.

RELATED ARTICLES in *Great Lives from History: The Nineteenth Century, 1801-1900:* Robert Fulton; Cornelius Vanderbilt.

1810's

December 11-30, 1819
BRITISH PARLIAMENT PASSES THE SIX ACTS

After the Peterloo Massacre of August, 1819, the Tory administration of the second earl of Liverpool proposed a series of measures designed to stifle radical dissent (by regulating public assembly, speech, and the press), to speed up trials, and to ban military drilling. Acting quickly, the Tories in Parliament passed six such measures over the opposition of the Whigs.

LOCALE: London, England

CATEGORIES: Laws, acts, and legal history; government and politics; civil rights and liberties

KEY FIGURES

First Viscount Sidmouth (Henry Addington; 1757-1844), British home secretary, 1812-1822

Second Earl of Liverpool (Robert Banks Jenkinson; 1770-1828), British prime minister, 1812-1827

Henry Hunt (1773-1835), British social reformer and popular speaker

William Cobbett (1763-1835), British writer, political commentator, social reformer, and publisher

SUMMARY OF EVENT

During the Regency period (1811-1820) of the reign of George III (r. 1760-1820)—when his son, the future George IV, ruled Great Britain as prince regent—the British government feared the development of radicalism and possible insurrection in the nation similar to the excesses of the French Revolution and the Napoleonic era in France (1789-1815). Unprecedented problems caused by the disruption of traditional patterns of life that were due to the Agricultural and Industrial Revolutions, war with France and the United States, demobilization of soldiers and sailors after the defeat of Napoleon I in 1815, and a tremendous increase in population had produced significant strains in Great Britain's economy, society, and government.

These strains spurred many to call for political and social reform and emboldened others to pursue radical solutions to the country's problems. Episodes such as the actions of the Luddites, the Spa Fields Riot (1816), the March of the Blanketeers (1817), and the Pentrich Rising (1817) had caused the second earl of Liverpool's government to pass the Seditious Meetings Act (1817) and suspend the right of habeas corpus (1817) in order to prevent what was feared might be a large-scale rebellion. Both of these measures lasted only until 1818, however.

The immediate impetus for the passage of the Six Acts in December, 1819, was the Peterloo Massacre of August, 1819, in which local officials in Manchester at-

---

THE SIX ACTS

Training Prevention Act (60 George III cap. 1): Limited the use of government agents within radical groups, forbade civilians from drilling or training to use weapons. Violators received two years imprisonment and seven years transportation (or forced exile).

Seizure of Arms Act (60 George III cap. 2): Empowered justices of the peace and other local officials to search people and property for weapons and to confiscate such weapons. Also restricted the use of government agents.

Seditious Meetings Act (60 George III cap. 6): Restricted the right of people to assemble. Any meeting of more than fifty people required approval of the local sheriff or magistrate, who could change the time and date of the meeting. Any meeting to deal with a matter involving "Church and State" had to be held at the local level only. It also banned the use of flags and drums in demonstrations, which could be dispersed after fifteen minutes.

Blasphemous and Seditious Libels Act (60 George III cap. 4): Provided severe penalties for possession of materials judged to be "blasphemous" and "seditious"—fourteen years transportation.

Misdemeanours Act (60 George III cap. 8): Created conditions for quicker trials and convictions, so that justice would not be delayed.

Newspaper and Stamp Duties Act (60 George III cap. 9): Applied taxes or duties to a wide range of printed materials, including works that contained only opinion, such as pamphlets.

---

tempted to arrest the social reformer Henry Hunt during a massive outdoor meeting of between forty and eighty thousand people. The actions of the authorities and the panicked crowd resulted in eleven deaths and hundreds of injuries. Calls for an investigation of the local authorities' behavior were rejected.

The home secretary, the first Viscount Sidmouth, expressed regret that Parliament had not been summoned in order to enact measures to prevent disturbances such as the one at Peterloo. When Parliament met on November 23, 1819, Sidmouth presented a set of measures in the House of Lords that the government had prepared for consideration. The proposals were based upon the belief that reform meetings constituted in principle a "treasonable conspiracy" against George III, the Church, and property. They set forth a set of provisions that should be enacted to regulate such meetings. Sidmouth continued his presentation with a statement to the effect that an individual convicted of "blasphemous or seditious libel" a second time should suffer imprisonment or banishment and that other publications should be subject to the tax due on newspapers. Because unauthorized military drilling posed a potential danger, Sidmouth outlined measures to ban such practices and allow local authorities to seize weapons. The same program was presented to the House of Commons.

Parliament moved swiftly. The Tory Party held the majority in both houses of Parliament, with the Whig Party in opposition, and between December 11 and 30, 1819, the Six Acts—as they came to be called—were passed over the protests of the Whig leadership, which claimed that they were "an attack" on the British constitution and that the measures were not necessary and might drive some to more extreme measures. However, a number of rank-and-file Whigs supported the proposals.

Under the Six Acts, British subjects could no longer arm themselves, train in the use of arms, or gather and discuss political matters freely. Trials were to be held more speedily, and seditious libel and blasphemy were to be punished more severely. Moreover, the tax on publications was greatly increased. Inexpensive publications costing less than sixpence that appeared at least once every twenty-six days were now charged a four pence tax, an extremely heavy amount. Those who produced such works had to put up some form of security as a type of bond, £300 in London and £200 in other cities. Much of the primary source information for the measures came from the radical journalist William Cobbett's publications, the *Political Register*, established in 1802, and *Parliamentary Debates*, established in 1803.

SIGNIFICANCE

The year 1819 saw the high water mark of political reaction in England, although Prime Minister Liverpool's government did not resort to the suspension of habeas corpus rights as it had in 1817. The Cato Street Conspiracy of February, 1820, an attempt by radical revolutionaries to assassinate the British cabinet, appeared to demonstrate the need for the Six Acts, but as economic conditions improved and some reform measures were enacted in the 1820's and 1830's, fear of insurrection waned.

Recent scholarship has drawn attention to the fact that the Six Acts may not have been as repressive as was once thought. The Seditious Meetings Act was repealed in

1824. Several others were allowed to lapse, and the Blasphemous and Seditious Libels Act proved difficult to enforce, because juries often refused to render guilty verdicts for offenses charged under it. The Training Prevention Act seemed to be a responsible measure and is still in force today, as is the Seizure of Arms Act. Collectively, the Six Acts helped provide a degree of stability in a society that possessed no internal police force, although for some very conservative Tories the measures did not go far enough.

—*Mark C. Herman*

FURTHER READING

Cookson, J. E. *Lord Liverpool's Administration: The Crucial Years, 1815-1822*. Hamden, Conn.: Archon Books, 1975. The first major reassessment of this prime minister's government provides a backdrop for understanding the origins and passage of the Six Acts.

Gash, Norman. *Lord Liverpool: The Life and Political Career of Robert Banks Jenkinson, Second Earl of Liverpool, 1770-1828*. Cambridge, Mass.: Harvard University Press, 1984. An important biography that assesses the motivations of Liverpool's administration in introducing and securing passage of the Six Acts.

Plowright, John. *Regency England: The Age of Lord Liverpool*. London: Routledge, 1996. A short work that argues persuasively that the Six Acts were not as repressive as previous works have described them to be.

Sack, James L. *From Jacobite to Conservative: Reaction and Orthodoxy in Britain, c. 1760-1832*. Cambridge, England: Cambridge University Press, 1993. Places the turmoil in England and the Six Acts within the context of a shift toward political reform.

Smith, Robert A. *Late Georgian and Regency England*. Cambridge, England: Cambridge University Press, 2004. Provides information essential for understanding the context in which the Six Acts were passed.

Stevenson, John. *Popular Disturbances in England, 1700-1870*. 2d ed. London: Longman, 1992. A major work of interpretation with ample material on the Regency disturbances that prompted passage of the Six Acts.

SEE ALSO: Jan., 1802: Cobbett Founds the *Political Register*; Feb. 23, 1820: London's Cato Street Conspirators Plot Assassinations; 1824: British Parliament Repeals the Combination Acts; May 9, 1828-Apr. 13, 1829: Roman Catholic Emancipation; June 4, 1832: British Parliament Passes the Reform Act of 1832; 1843: Carlyle Publishes *Past and Present*; Aug., 1867: British Parliament Passes the Reform Act of 1867.

RELATED ARTICLES in *Great Lives from History: The Nineteenth Century, 1801-1900:* William Cobbett; Charles Grey; Second Earl of Liverpool.

1820's

CHINA'S STELE SCHOOL OF CALLIGRAPHY EMERGES

Influenced by the discoveries of ancient artifacts, Qing Dynasty artists created new Chinese art styles based on ancient forms of inscription. A group of calligraphers who formed the Stele School borrowed designs from ancient stone carvings on columns, or steles, and from bronze bowls and other artifacts and blended these old forms and methods with modern methods in calligraphy.

LOCALE: China
CATEGORY: Art

KEY FIGURES

Bao Shichen (Pao Shih-ch'en; 1775-1855), civil servant, calligrapher, and art historian
Deng Shiru (Teng Shih-ju; 1743-1805), founder of the Stele School

Qianlong (1711-1799), Chinese emperor, r. 1736-1795, and art collector
Ruan Yuan (1764-1849), first scholar to describe the Stele School
Yi Bingshou (1754-1815), calligrapher and teacher
Zhao Zhiqian (1829-1884), calligrapher and painter

SUMMARY OF EVENT

During the last third of the Qing Dynasty (1644-1912), Chinese scholars took a renewed interest in their country's ancient stone and bronze carvings and engravings as archaeologists uncovered countless artifacts that had been hidden from view for centuries. Calligraphers also took note, particularly of the newly uncovered ancient stone monuments that are called stelae in English, after the Latin word for stone pillars. Drawing on the stelae for inspiration, the calligraphers created a new style of artistic writing, or calligraphy, that fused ancient and more modern scripts. The movement to create these new forms was later called the Stele School in English, after the singular Greek word for stela, *stele* (pronounced STEE-lee).

Qianlong, the fourth emperor of China's Qing Dynasty, was a passionate art collector. Using his imperial powers, he amassed a great collection of important works, including porcelains, bronzes, rare books, calligraphy, and many early paintings. For many years artists were not able to study China's early works and thus learn from them because Qianlong gathered so much of the country's important work. Landscape painters, especially, were disadvantaged by the collection, because, traditionally, they had found their inspiration for new works by studying older works. As Qianlong's reign continued, Chinese painting began to stagnate as an art form, and other forms, including calligraphy, took on greater importance. At the same time, Chinese intellectuals were increasingly denied active roles in government, so many of them, too, changed their focus to scholarly research on China's antiquities. Qianlong was himself a moderately skilled calligrapher, and he had gathered an extensive collection of early examples. This collection was guided by his own taste, and as he encouraged scholars to study and write about this collection, his views came to shape what was valued and what was not.

Under Qianlong's influence, scholars reexamined Confucian texts. Classical education at the end of the eighteenth century had been based heavily on eleventh and twelfth century commentaries on the writings of Confucius (551-479 B.C.E.), the ancient Chinese sage whose philosophies have informed much of Chinese thought for more than two millennia. Rather than rely on these commentaries, scholars began to search for as much of the original ancient texts as possible. To find the most authentic versions of the texts, epigraphic studies examined ancient inscriptions that had been carved into the stone monuments called stelae, as well as bronze engravings, old books and manuscripts, and other objects. Qianlong's reign, and the reigns of his successors Jiaqing and Daoguang, saw the unearthing of many stelae that had been buried for centuries.

Deng Shiru was one of the first calligraphers to study the stelae and to move toward a truly new style combining formal qualities of the ancient inscriptions with new artistic techniques. Working at the end of the eighteenth century, Deng focused his attention on the stelae produced during the Northern Wei period (386-534). Because he had wealthy patrons who supported him, he was able to spend long periods studying individual objects and the rubbings of objects. He copied them repeatedly until he mastered their scripts. Most significantly, he wrote scholarly treatises about what he learned, passing his discoveries to the next generation. In one of his most important works, the *Four Styles Album* (*Siti tie*), he broke with tradition by combining brush techniques from various scripts. Tradition dictated the strict description of each character in each different script, giving no value to the unique variations and combinations from individual calligraphers.

At the beginning of the nineteenth century, most Chinese calligraphers received formal training that involved reproducing master works of calligraphy from copybooks or model books. These copybooks included tracings and copies of older works. Students copied and recopied the models until they mastered every stroke of every character, leaving little room for innovation. As calligraphers became more familiar with and attracted to stele inscriptions, a new style of calligraphy developed, which was modeled after the stele inscriptions.

The mathematician and astronomer Ruan Yuan wrote several academic texts about calligraphy, including *On the Northern and Southern Schools of Calligraphy* (1823; *Nanbei shupai lun*) and *On the Northern Stelae and Southern Album* (1823; *Beipai nantie lun*), comparing the calligraphy produced in northern China, which was based on stelae, and that produced in southern China, which was based on copybooks. Ruan was thus the first scholar to formally describe a division of calligraphy into two branches, and to describe the Stele School as a separate and worthy movement. For this reason, some scholars consider the 1820's to be the beginning of the Stele School. Ruan owned nearly five hundred inscribed bronze vessels that dated from the year 1600 B.C.E., and he based much of his study of calligraphy on objects in his own collection.

Bao Shichen was the first art historian to celebrate the work of Deng Shiru. Bao's treatise *Oars of the Boat of Art* (1829; *Yizhou shuangji*) praised Deng and influenced others, including Wu Rangzhi (1799-1870) and Yi Bingshou, to pattern their calligraphy on stelae instead of copybooks. Bao was a skilled calligrapher, but he was better known as a theorist. He wrote about the significance of the stelae even as he would produce most of his own work in the copybook style.

A generation after Bao Shichen saw the arrival of Zhao Zhiqian, a civil servant and an artist who was fascinated with ancient artifacts. He had become interested in stelae through his epigraphic studies of ancient inscriptions. In 1863, on a trip from Shanghai to Beijing, where he took part of the national civil service examination, he began to make copies in calligraphy of carved stelae from the Northern Wei period, as Deng Shiru had done. Working in a new "square brush" style that imitated the stele carvings, Zhao produced calligraphy that was more angular than was his previous work. Influenced by the theories of Ruan and Bao, Zhao developed his own brush strokes and effects.

Although calligraphers had studied the stelae for more than half a century and had produced work influenced by them, Zhao's work was the first to capture the attention of other artists in great numbers. After Zhao's example, the Stele School became something of a fad, although Zhao himself abandoned the new style near the end of his life.

SIGNIFICANCE

Breaking with tradition, Zhao Zhiqian created important work in more than one medium. He carried some of the aesthetic ideals of the Stele School into painting, creating flower paintings that blended old and new effects, and he demonstrated new directions for modern artists working in traditional genres. The commonplace format of paired hanging scrolls can also be traced to the Stele School.

The new approaches to calligraphy coming out of the Stele School influenced Chinese art into the twenty-first century. Calligraphers influenced by the Stele School include Qian Juntao, who has amassed a large collection of work from the Qing and has patterned his own work on that of Deng Shiru. Other inspired calligraphers include Wu Rangzhi, Zhao Zhiqian, and Hua Rende, whose work frequently pairs his own texts with rubbings of stelae and other carvings, demonstrating the range of possibilities available to artists inspired by the scholarship of the Stele School and its willingness to blend old and new forms.

—*Cynthia A. Bily*

FURTHER READING

Fu, Shen C. Y. *Traces of the Brush: Studies in Chinese Calligraphy*. New Haven, Conn.: Yale University Art Gallery, 1977. An analysis of the calligrapher's dependence on a firm grasp of tradition in cultivating a personal style. Many black-and-white illustrations.

Harrist, Robert E., Jr., and Wen C. Fong. *The Embodied Image: Chinese Calligraphy from the John B. Elliott Collection*. Princeton, N.J.: Art Museum, Princeton University, 1999. An exhibition catalog, lavishly illustrated, which includes analysis of the scholarship of Ruan Yuan and examples of Stele School work.

Hearn, Maxwell K. "Art in Late Nineteenth-Century Shanghai." *Bulletin of the Metropolitan Museum of Art* 58, no. 3 (Winter, 2001): 10-13. A brief exploration of Zhao Zhiqian as a transitional figure who borrowed from traditional styles to create new forms.

Hummel, Arthur W. *Eminent Chinese of the Ch'ing Period, 1644-1912*. 2 vols. Washington, D.C.: Library of Congress, 1943-1944. The first biographical dictionary in any language to cover this period, with brief but thorough entries.

Nishibayashi, Shoichi. "Copybook and Stele Studies of the Qing Dynasty." In *Chinese Calligraphy*, edited by Yujiro Nakata and translated by Jeffrey Hunter. New York: Weatherhill/Tankosha, 1983. A 238-page history of calligraphy in China, part of the History of the Art of China series.

SEE ALSO: 1823-1831: Hokusai Produces *Thirty-Six Views of Mount Fuji*; 1831-1834: Hiroshige Completes *The Tokaido Fifty-Three Stations*.
RELATED ARTICLE in *Great Lives from History: The Nineteenth Century, 1801-1900:* Hiroshige.

1820's

1820's-1830's
FREE PUBLIC SCHOOL MOVEMENT

After tentative moves toward public education during the late eighteenth century, American states started acting on the principle of government responsibility for educating all their citizens during the 1820's, and the notion that education is a responsibility of democratic governments began to spread.

ALSO KNOWN AS: Free School Movement
LOCALE: United States
CATEGORIES: Education; government and politics

KEY FIGURES

Henry Barnard (1811-1900), editor of the *American Journal of Education* and commissioner of public schools in Connecticut and Rhode Island
James G. Carter (1795-1849), Massachusetts educational reformer
DeWitt Clinton (1769-1828), governor of New York, 1817-1822, 1825-1828
Edward Everett (1794-1865), governor of Massachusetts, 1836-1840
Horace Mann (1796-1859), secretary of the Massachusetts Board of Education, 1837-1848
Thaddeus Stevens (1792-1868), leader of free-school supporters in the Pennsylvania House
Calvin Wiley (1819-1887), first superintendent of common schools in North Carolina

SUMMARY OF EVENT

The free public school movement of the late 1820's and the 1830's had its roots in the late eighteenth century, when a number of U.S. states drafted constitutions containing clauses urging public aid to education. Nevertheless, the idea that education was a government responsibility, rather than a responsibility of families, churches, and philanthropy, took hold only gradually. Teaching was generally done by low-paid and untrained young men who regarded teaching as a temporary occupation. It was not until the early nineteenth century that states began enacting laws leading to the establishment of public, or common, schools. Even then, however, government schools were generally created primarily for pauper children. Moreover, although most states eventually established permanent school funds to supplement local support of schools, few states resorted to direct taxation as a means of financing education.

The free school movement should be understood within the context of Jacksonian democracy and the re-

form movement of which it was a part. Free public schools were one of many organized efforts for self-improvement which also included such other notable developments as the lyceum movement for adult education, lending library societies and associations, literary societies, and debating societies. During the first three decades of the nineteenth century, religious and philanthropic institutions were more active than state governments in promoting free public schooling. The Sunday school movement contributed significantly to the growth of interest in public education. Even more important were the efforts of philanthropists working through benevolent societies. The Free School Society of the City of New York, later reorganized as the Public School Society of New York, was typical of such efforts, as was the Philadelphia Society for the Establishment and Support of Charity Schools. Nevertheless, like existing state-supported institutions, these schools were mainly for the benefit of children of the poor.

Not until the late 1820's and the 1830's were demands heard for the establishment of a system of free public schooling open to all. In some larger cities, workingmen's parties called upon their state legislatures to establish public schools. Thus the workingmen of Boston declared in 1830 that "the establishment of a liberal system of education, attainable by all, should be among the first efforts of every lawgiver who desires the continuance of our national independence." At the same time, a number of educational reformers, influenced by the social reform movement which swept over the United States during the 1830's and 1840's, began to promote the cause of free public schooling.

James G. Carter of Massachusetts wrote newspaper articles and pamphlets suggesting improvements in the educational system of his state. As a member of the Massachusetts House and chairman of the Committee on Education, Carter drafted the bill creating the Massachusetts Board of Education in 1837. Horace Mann, who was named secretary of the board, left a promising legal and political career to dedicate himself to what he called "the supremest welfare of mankind upon the earth." During his twelve years on the board, Mann sustained a concerted campaign on behalf of public education. Largely as a result of efforts by Carter and Mann, Massachusetts led the way in establishing a system of public schooling.

Mann's celebrated "annual reports" were perhaps the single most important factor in bringing the concept of universal free education to the national political agenda. In Mann's 1848 annual report, he argued that "nothing but Universal Education can counterwork this tendency to the domination of capital and the servility of labor." Mann saw education as "the great equalizer of the conditions of men—the balance wheel of the social machinery. . . . It does better than to disarm the poor of their hostility toward the rich; it prevents being poor." Although Mann's hopes for the impact of education may seem hyperbolic, his leadership on the board of education and his annual reports resulted in significant and tangible results, including a lengthened school year, increased teacher salaries, the establishment of the first state-supported normal school to train teachers, and an organized state association for public school teachers.

In Connecticut and Rhode Island, Henry Barnard promoted the public school cause. In the South and West, where obstacles to free public schools were greater than in New England, other educational reformers worked to establish systems of public education and to improve facilities and teacher training. Calvin Wiley made North Carolina the center of educational reform in the South. Caleb Mills called for the establishment of a public school system in a series of six annual "addresses" to the Indiana legislature. In neighboring Ohio, Calvin Stowe, a founder of the Western Literary Institute and College of Professional Teachers, contributed to the development of free public schools through his accounts of the Prussian educational system.

The efforts of educational reformers in promoting free schooling were aided by a number of politicians, including Governors DeWitt Clinton of New York, Edward Everett and Marcus Morton of Massachusetts, and George Wolf of Pennsylvania. The New York Whig leader William H. Seward justified state support of common schools on much the same grounds as other internal improvements. In Pennsylvania, Thaddeus Stevens invoked humanitarian and democratic notions in support of a state law supporting public education. A young Whig legislator, Stevens provided the leadership to pass the 1834 state school law in Pennsylvania that allowed for universal free schools. Opposing forces had argued strongly that free education should be provided only for the very poor. Robert Rantoul, Jr., the first Democratic member of the Massachusetts Board of Education, was another spokesman for free schooling. Publicists and editors, such as George Bancroft, William Cullen Bryant, and William Leggett, also lent their voices to the campaign for "universal education."

By 1850, the movement for free public schooling had largely achieved its basic objectives. The principle of public support for common schools was generally accepted throughout the union. For example, by midcentury, every state had established some type of permanent school fund. Moreover, every state except Arkansas had experimented with taxation as a means of school support. Taxation was not universally accepted and school tax laws were repealed in some states, but a precedent had been established that would serve as a basis for a unified system of compulsory taxation. Accompanying the principle of public support was the principle of public control of education. By 1850, according to historian Lawrence Cremin, "the people . . . largely controlled the schools which they had instituted with public funds." Thus the middle of the nineteenth century marked the end of the initial phase of the campaign for free public schooling, during which the essential groundwork was laid, and the beginning of a second phase of expansion and development was made.

SIGNIFICANCE

Despite the tangible advances that occurred during these decades, American free public schools remained in a stage of infancy: There were virtually no compulsory attendance laws, school terms remained relatively short and susceptible to manipulation by the local farming seasons and other factors, the quality and extent of the school curriculum varied widely, teaching methods remained based on rote memorization, and discipline often depended heavily on corporal punishment. Free public education had become the norm only in Massachusetts and a few areas of the North. An 1827 Massachusetts law stipulated that every town of five hundred families or more had to create a public high school. That law led to the creation of more than one hundred Massachusetts public high schools by 1860; however, only two hundred public high schools existed in all of the rest of the country at that time.

Through the rest of the nineteenth century and indeed into the twentieth century, the issue of free public schools continued to have opponents as well as supporters. Although the supporters might articulate that employers needed literate workers, and social theorists strongly supported the idea that a society founded upon the notion of universal suffrage needed universal public education in order to ensure well-informed voters, there remained critics—including many taxpayers who did not want to educate other people's children—who considered education strictly a private concern. Although the Sunday school movement had helped to publicize the idea of free education, many religious groups wanted to maintain their own schools without public funds and also without public advice and consent in their own specialized curricula.

—*Anne C. Loveland, updated by Richard Sax*

FURTHER READING

Butts, R. Freeman, and Lawrence A. Cremin. *A History of Education in American Culture*. New York: Henry Holt, 1953. Comprehensive survey of American education that includes a dialectical discussion concerning how the free school movement developed from various crosscurrents in educational thought.

Downs, Robert B. *Horace Mann: Champion of Public Schools*. Boston: Twayne, 1974. Biography that emphasizes Mann's influence on the concept of public education in the United States.

Gibbon, Peter H. "A Hero of Education." *Education Week* 21, no. 38 (May 29, 2002): 33. Brief profile of Horace Mann that covers his views on education and his efforts to improve public schools.

Good, Harry G., and James D. Teller. *A History of American Education*. 3d ed. New York: Macmillan, 1973. Chapter 5, "From Private Schools to State Systems," includes a lengthy discussion of the Free School Society of New York City, which later became the Public School Society.

Gutek, Gerald L. *Historical and Philosophical Foundations of Education: A Biographical Introduction*. 4th ed. Englewood Cliffs, N.J.: Prentice Hall, 2004. Useful general historical overview of education in the United States that includes biographies of Horace Mann and other pioneers in public education.

McClellan, B. Edward, and William J. Reese, eds. *The Social History of American Education*. Urbana: University of Illinois Press, 1988. Collection of seventeen essays, arranged chronologically. Michael Katz's article, "The Origins of Public Education: A Reassessment," provides an intellectual context for the free school movement.

Spring, Joel. *The American School, 1642-1990*. 2d ed. New York: Longman, 1990. Spring's informed, though politically slanted, argument shows how the common school movement developed from the premise that education is a panacea for a society with failing families and an oppressive factory culture.

SEE ALSO: 19th cent.: Development of Working-Class Libraries; 1813: Founding of McGill University; 1820's-1850's: Social Reform Movement; May, 1823: Hartford Female Seminary Is Founded; 1828-1842: Arnold Reforms Rugby School; Nov., 1828: Webster Publishes the First American Dictionary of English; Mar. 2, 1867: U.S. Department of Education Is Created; Oct. 4-6, 1876: American Library Association Is Founded.

RELATED ARTICLES in *Great Lives from History: The Nineteenth Century, 1801-1900:* George Bancroft; Henry Barnard; DeWitt Clinton; Horace Mann; Thaddeus Stevens.

1820's-1850's
SOCIAL REFORM MOVEMENT

A wave of religious and philanthropic movements, collectively known as the social reform movement, worked for humanitarian and democratic reforms that included abolition, temperance, woman suffrage, and wider access to education.

LOCALE: Northeastern and western United States
CATEGORIES: Social issues and reform; organizations and institutions; education

KEY FIGURES
Ralph Waldo Emerson (1803-1882), former Unitarian minister who was a central figure in the Transcendental movement
Lyman Beecher (1775-1863), pastor of Boston's Park Street Church
Elihu Burritt (1810-1879), pacifist editor of the *Advocate of Peace and Universal Brotherhood*
Dorothea Dix (1802-1887), reformer concerned especially with the treatment of the mentally ill
Charles Fourier (1772-1837), French social theorist whose doctrine of communitarian living was embraced by many American reformers
Thomas Hopkins Gallaudet (1787-1851), founder of the first free American school for the hearing impaired
William Lloyd Garrison (1805-1879), abolitionist editor of *The Liberator*
Samuel Gridley Howe (1801-1876), educator who founded the Perkins School for the Blind
Horace Mann (1796-1859), champion of free public education

Theodore Dwight Weld (1803-1895), founder of the American Anti-Slavery Society and organizer of the group "Seventy"

SUMMARY OF EVENT

In 1841, Ralph Waldo Emerson declared, "In the history of the world the doctrine of Reform had never such scope as at the present hour." The wave of reform that swept over much of the United States from the 1820's to the 1850's seemed to prove Emerson's theory that the human being is "born . . . to be a Reformer, a Remaker of what man has made; a renouncer of lies; a restorer of truth and good, imitating that great Nature which embosoms us all, and which sleeps no moment on an old past, but every hour repairs herself." In those decades, people enlisted in a variety of causes and crusades, some of which were of a conservative nature, while others challenged basic institutions and beliefs.

The antebellum reform movement was partly a response to economic, social, and political changes following the War of 1812. Such changes provoked feelings of anxiety in the United States, generating anti-Mason, anti-Roman Catholic, and anti-Mormon crusades. However, change also generated a feeling of optimism and confirmed the almost universal faith in progress that characterized early nineteenth century Americans. Reformers came from two groups: religious reformers and the wealthy who felt obligated to help the less fortunate.

Evangelical religion played an important role in the origins of the reform movement. The shift from the Calvinistic doctrine of predestination to more democratic teachings that emphasized humankind's efforts in achieving salvation nourished ideas of perfectionism and millenarianism. Not only could individuals achieve "perfect holiness" but the world itself, as evidenced by the movements of reform, was improving and moving toward the long-awaited thousand-year reign of the Kingdom of God on Earth.

In addition to evangelicalism, the legacy of the Enlightenment and the American Revolution—the natural rights philosophy and the faith in humanity's ability to shape society in accordance with the laws of God and nature—was a stimulus to reform. So was the nineteenth century's romantic conception of the individual. "The power which is at once spring and regulator in all efforts of reform," Emerson wrote, "is the conviction that there is an infinite worthiness in man, which will appear at the call of worth, and that all particular reforms are the removing of some impediment."

Samuel Gridley Howe. (Library of Congress)

Antebellum reformers attacked a variety of evils. Dorothea Dix urged humane treatment for the mentally ill; Thomas Gallaudet and Samuel Gridley Howe founded schools for the hearing impaired and the blind. Prison reform engaged the efforts of some, and a campaign to abolish imprisonment for debt made slow but sure progress in the pre-Civil War period. Horace Mann championed common schools, and free public schooling gradually spread from New England to other parts of the United States. Elihu Burritt, the "learned blacksmith," urged the abolition of war and related evils. Communitarians, inspired by religious or secular principles, withdrew from society to found utopian experiments such as Oneida, Amana, Hopedale, Ephrata Cloister, and New Harmony. The communitarian teachings of French social theorist Charles Fourier inspired such experiments as Brook Farm, the North American Phalanx of Red Bank, New Jersey, and the Sylvani Phalanx of northeastern Pennsylvania. Lucretia Mott, Elizabeth Cady Stanton, Lucy Stone, and others championed higher education, the suffrage, and legal and property rights for women.

Temperance and abolition were the two most prominent secular crusades of the period. Both of them passed through several phases, moving from gradualism to immediatism and from persuasion to legal coercion. The temperance movement began with an appeal for moderation in the consumption of alcoholic beverages and shifted by the late 1820's to a demand for total abstinence. The Reverend Lyman Beecher's *Six Sermons*, published in 1826, were instrumental in effecting this shift to total abstinence; the "teetotal" position was further popularized during the 1840's by the Washington Temperance Society of reformed "drunkards" (alcoholics) and the children's Cold Water Army.

Similar to the temperance movement, the abolition, or antislavery, movement moved from a position favoring gradual emancipation and colonization during the 1820's, to a demand for immediate abolition of the sin of slavery. William Lloyd Garrison's *Liberator* and Theodore Dwight Weld's "Seventy" preached the immediatist doctrine, and it was adopted by the American Anti-Slavery Society, which had been founded in 1833. During the 1840's, some temperance and antislavery reformers, disillusioned by the lack of results from education and moral suasion, turned to politics as a means of achieving their goals. Some abolitionists supported the Liberty and Free-Soil Parties, and later the Republicans, and sought legislation preventing the extension of slavery into the territories. Temperance advocates succeeded in getting statewide prohibition and local option laws passed in a number of states during the early 1850's.

In most cases, the vehicle of reform was the voluntary association. Virtually every movement had a national organization, with state and local auxiliaries, which sponsored speakers, published pamphlets, and generally coordinated efforts in behalf of its cause. Although such societies were often rent by factionalism, they proved remarkably effective in arousing the popular conscience on the moral issues of the day. By 1850, for example, there were almost two thousand antislavery societies with a membership close to 200,000, compared to about five hundred such societies in 1826.

SIGNIFICANCE

Although most of the reform movements had their largest following in the northeastern and western parts of the United States, their impact was not confined to those sections. Southerners, although hostile to abolitionism and other radical causes, were receptive to pleas for educational and prison reform and for better treatment of the insane and the blind. The temperance crusade made considerable headway in the South. Thus, to a greater or lesser degree, depending on the particular cause, the antebellum social reform movement was a truly national phenomenon.

—*Anne C. Loveland, updated by Geralyn Strecker*

FURTHER READING

Foster, Lawrence. *Women, Family, and Utopia: Communal Experiments of the Shakers, the Oneida Community, and the Mormons*. Syracuse, N.Y.: Syracuse University Press, 1991. An intriguing study of religion, sexuality, and women's roles in utopian living.

Griffin, Clifford S. *Their Brothers' Keepers: Moral Stewardship in the United States, 1800-1865*. New Brunswick, N.J.: Rutgers University Press, 1960. Views the antebellum reform movement as an essentially conservative effort by wealthy reformers attempting to preserve social stability, sobriety, and order.

Guarneri, Carl J. *The Utopian Alternative: Fourierism in Nineteenth-Century America*. Ithaca, N.Y.: Cornell University Press, 1991. Evaluates the influence of Charles Fourier's communitarianism on the growth of utopian living in the United States.

Holloway, Mark. *Heavens on Earth: Utopian Communities in America, 1680-1880*. 2d rev. ed. New York: Dover, 1966. Discusses the general characteristics of utopian communities and describes several important examples.

Mandelker, Ira L. *Religion, Society, and Utopia in Nineteenth-Century America*. Amherst: University of Massachusetts Press, 1984. Discusses both the social tensions that caused a need for utopian communities and the internal tensions that caused most of them to fail.

Nye, Russel B. *William Lloyd Garrison and the Humanitarian Reformers*. Boston: Little, Brown, 1955. Explains Garrison's role in the greater humanitarian reform movement, as well as his involvement with abolition groups.

Tyler, Alice Felt. *Freedom's Ferment: Phases of American Social History to 1860*. 1944. Reprint. Freeport, N.Y.: Books for Libraries Press, 1970. Surveys major reform efforts in the context of political, economic, and social conditions in the United States. The conclusions have been challenged by later works, but this remains a valuable, comprehensive study of reform.

SEE ALSO: Mar. 2, 1807: Congress Bans Importation of African Slaves; Spring, 1814-1830: Communitarian Experiments at New Harmony; May, 1819: Unitarian Church Is Founded; 1820's-1830's: Free Public School Movement; c. 1830-1865: Southerners Advance Proslavery Arguments; Dec., 1833: American Anti-Slavery Society Is Founded; July 19-20, 1848:

Seneca Falls Convention; July 6, 1853: National Council of Colored People Is Founded; Apr. 9, 1866: Civil Rights Act of 1866; Sept. 18, 1889: Addams Opens Chicago's Hull-House; Feb. 17-18, 1890: Women's Rights Associations Unite.

RELATED ARTICLES in *Great Lives from History: The Nineteenth Century, 1801-1900:* Bronson Alcott; Dorothea Dix; Ralph Waldo Emerson; Charles Fourier; William Lloyd Garrison; Octavia Hill; Samuel Gridley Howe; Horace Mann; Lucretia Mott; Robert Owen.

1820
JESUITS ARE EXPELLED FROM RUSSIA, NAPLES, AND SPAIN

The expulsion of the Jesuits from Russia, Naples, and Spain in 1820 contributed to increased secularism, to a century of European revolution, and ultimately to the emergence of socialism and communism.

LOCALE: Russia; Naples (now in Italy); Spain
CATEGORIES: Religion and theology; government and politics

KEY FIGURES
Clement XIV (Giovanni Ganganelli; 1705-1774), Roman Catholic pope, 1769-1774, who suppressed the Jesuits in 1773
Pius VII (Barnaba Gregorio Chiaramonti; 1742-1823), Roman Catholic pope, 1800-1823, who reinstated the Jesuits in 1814
Karl Marx (1818-1883), German political philosopher
Napoleon I (1769-1821), emperor of France, r. 1804-1814, 1815

SUMMARY OF EVENT
The members of the Society of Jesus, or Jesuits, were expelled from Russia, Naples, and Spain—all in the year 1820. Their expulsion from these and many other European countries and the laws passed against the Jesuits greatly reduced their power, led to the loss of their wealth, and drastically lowered their numbers. In turn, this lessening of Jesuitical influence within the courts of Europe increased the shift in world power from religious to secular and contributed to a century of revolution that ultimately led to the emergence of socialism and communism in the early twentieth century.

Although it was originally founder Saint Ignatius Loyola's plan that Jesuits would act as missionaries, from the sixteenth century on the members of the religious order came deeply to influence the world's politics and to gain recognition as the world's premier educators. Known for high intellectualism, rigorous loyalty to the pope, and absolute defense of Catholic dogma, for centuries the Jesuits were a great aid to the Roman Catholic Church, and their missions, colleges, and seminaries gained worldwide recognition. Indeed, the Jesuits were referred to as the "schoolmasters of Europe." However, in time the zeal and enormous effectiveness of the Jesuit Order provoked fear, jealousy, and hostility among other religious orders, and their increasing wealth, political power, and incredible ability to command the loyalty of Catholics throughout the world caused increasing concern among European rulers.

The rise of secularism, which had contributed to the 1773 suppression of the Jesuits, was greatly influenced by the highly secular philosophes, or philosophers, of the eighteenth century French Enlightenment. In particular, Voltaire and the encyclopedists attracted strong ruling-class support. In their move to rid the world of religious education, these liberal literati, who indeed were radically opposed to Christianity itself and sought to replace God with philosophy and reason, agreed that the first step toward their secular aims must be the destruction of the Jesuits. Many European Catholic sovereigns were also opposed to the Jesuits. On August 16, 1773, the Franciscan pope Clement XIV, dreading the loss of the Papal States, yielded to the demands of the Bourbon court and issued his brief *Dominus ac Redemptor*, which suppressed and disbanded the Society of Jesus throughout Europe.

In 1814, Pius VII lifted the order of suppression by the bull *Solicitudo omnium ecclesiarum*, in which he reinstated the Jesuits. However, the nineteenth century postrevolutionary heirs to the Enlightenment lived in a different world than the one in which the Society of Jesus had last existed, more than forty years earlier. Many among the French aristocracy, which had supported the Jesuits' initial suppression, had lost their heads to the guillotine, and despite their formal reinstatement, the Jesuits could never hope to regain anywhere near their earlier power.

The anticlericism fostered during the 1789 French Revolution created a backlash, as the Reign of Terror under Robespierre, the subsequent rise of Napoleon, and the Napoleonic Wars engendered a heightened sense of conservatism throughout Europe . By 1820, though, all of Europe found itself in the turbulent throes of revolution, and anticlericism gained even greater force. In the few short years since their reinstatement, the Jesuits had come to be viewed by many as evil incarnate, and they were often made scapegoats for events beyond their control. They were finally expelled from Russia, Naples, and Spain in 1820.

Although Empress Catherine the Great of Russia had ignored the 1773 suppression order—and indeed had provided Russian refuge for the homeless priests—her successor, Czar Alexander I, refused to allow their presence. In 1820, he ousted more than two hundred Jesuits. Scholars have since maintained that this action contributed to the ensuing century of revolution and the ultimate dominance of communism in twentieth century Russia.

In Spain, the Jesuits were expelled in the insurrection of Major Rafael del Riego, who forced King Ferdinand VII to swear to a modern constitution. Allowed to return in 1823, the Jesuits were blamed for a cholera epidemic in 1843; they were removed by a mob chanting "Death to Jesuits." Fourteen Jesuits and dozens of other priests were killed. This event forced the remaining Jesuits to flee to South America, where they became successful missionaries and educators.

In Italy, the Jesuits alternately suffered rejection and acceptance throughout much of the nineteenth century. While they were expelled from Naples in 1820, they were allowed back in 1836, only to be driven out again by the revolution of 1848. They were able to return when peace was restored, but they were once again suppressed throughout Italy, even in Rome, as late as 1871. Problems in Italy arose partly over papal conflict with the Jesuits, which had begun in 1769 after a conclave, heavily influenced by European Catholic sovereigns, elected Clement XIV to the papacy. Clement was elected partly on the strength of his promise to expel the Jesuits.

Pius VI had succeeded Clement XIV in 1775 and instigated further reforms designed to make the state and not the church supreme. He had supported the reform plans of the ruler of the Holy Roman Empire, Joseph II, that had included the closure of monasteries and government appointments of clergy. However, when Pius rejected reforms in 1791, the French annexed the papal property at Avignon and Venaissin. When Pius then spoke out against Louis XVI's execution by the revolutionary government, Napoleon attacked the Papal States in 1802 and removed the pope from Rome. Napoleon forced the next pope, Pius VII, to crown him emperor in Paris in 1804—only to take the crown from the pope's hands at the last minute and crown himself. Napoleon took the Papal States in 1809 and Rome in 1814. After Napoleon's downfall in 1814, Pius returned to Rome and restored the Jesuits. However, he found the anti-Jesuitical sentiment of Europe so extreme that the pope himself oversaw their 1820 expulsions.

Pope Pius VII. (Library of Congress)

SIGNIFICANCE

The suppression of the Jesuits corresponded with the decline of the temporal power of the Roman Catholic Church and of the pope in particular—one of the turning points in the history of Christianity. Today, scholars maintain that the Jesuits' suppression and exclusion originated in misinformation developed during the secularizing efforts of the French and disseminated in the lands in which the revolution took root. The Jesuits had always been seen as the pope's independent and sometimes military support. However, after their suppression, for all intents and purposes the Church came to be in the hands of Europe's secular rulers. The balance of power between religious and secular institutions, which had for centuries been fairly stable in Europe, was now turned topsy-turvy.

The consequences were a century of revolution and conflict and the ultimate rise of socialism and communism in the early twentieth century.

The nineteenth century suppression of the Jesuits also contributed to changes in European philosophy. Without the Jesuits to help keep tabs on teachings that could be construed as heretical, philosophies such as that of Immanuel Kant—who had instituted the "Copernican turn inward," centering philosophy on the mind rather than on God—were able to gain traction. Opposing Kant's idealist view was the materialism of Karl Marx, who was highly influential in the development of communism and who denounced religion as evil and promoted a world without God. Subsequently, in opposition to Marx, a radical form of individualism that saw the mind, and not God, as creator, spread across the West. Thus, both of the major poles of nineteenth century intellectual debate treated religion as somewhat irrelevant, as their arguments instead focused on idealism versus materialism and individualism versus collectivism.

—*M. Casey Diana*

FURTHER READING

Barthel, Manfred. *Jesuits: History and Legends of the Society of Jesus.* New York: Quill, 1987. Overview of five hundred years of Jesuit history.

Martin, Malachi. *Jesuits.* New York: Simon & Schuster, 1988. Reveals the behind-the-scenes story of the "new" worldwide Society of Jesus and the historical alliances and compromises that emerged during the nineteenth century.

Paris, Edmond. *The Secret History of the Jesuits.* New York: Chick, 1983. Scholarly work that provides a comprehensive overview of Jesuit history, highlighting the order's role as the political arm of the Roman Catholic Church.

Wright, Jonathan. *God's Soldiers—Adventure, Politics, Intrigue, and Power: A History of the Jesuits.* New York: Doubleday, 2004. British historian Wright writes a succinct, highly balanced historical account of the intrigue and controversy surrounding the Jesuit Order in the Roman Catholic Church.

SEE ALSO: July 2, 1820-Mar., 1821: Neapolitan Revolution; Jan. 12, 1848-Aug. 28, 1849: Italian Revolution of 1848; Feb., 1848: Marx and Engels Publish *The Communist Manifesto*; Feb. 22-June, 1848: Paris Revolution of 1848; Mar. 3-Nov. 3, 1848: Prussian Revolution of 1848; Dec. 8, 1854: Pius IX Decrees the Immaculate Conception Dogma; Dec. 8, 1864: Pius IX Issues the Syllabus of Errors; Dec. 8, 1869-Oct. 20, 1870: Vatican I Decrees Papal Infallibility Dogma; 1871-1877: Kulturkampf Against the Catholic Church in Germany; May 15, 1891: Papal Encyclical on Labor.

RELATED ARTICLES in *Great Lives from History: The Nineteenth Century, 1801-1900:* Alexander I; Leo XIII; Karl Marx; Pius IX.

1820's

1820-early 1840's
EUROPEANS EXPLORE THE ANTARCTIC

European explorations of the Antarctic in the first half of the nineteenth century confirmed the existence of Antarctica, mapped much of the continent's surroundings, fostered competing claims to the territory, contributed valuable scientific data on the largely unknown region, and contributed to the decimation of its seal and whale populations.

LOCALE: Antarctica

CATEGORIES: Exploration and discovery; environment and ecology; geography

KEY FIGURES

Fabian Gottlieb von Bellingshausen (1778-1852), Russian naval officer

Nathaniel B. Palmer (1799-1877), Connecticut sealer

Edward Bransfield (1785-1852), British naval officer

James Weddell (1787-1834), British whaler and explorer

Sir James Clark Ross (1800-1862), British explorer

Jules-Sébastien-César Dumont d'Urville (1790-1842), French naval officer

Charles Wilkes (1798-1877), head of the U.S. Exploring Expedition of 1838-1842

SUMMARY OF EVENT

The coldest and most isolated continent, Antarctica is surrounded by the world's stormiest seas and by thick masses of floating ice. Nineteenth century Antarctic exploration had its basis in commercial enterprises, most notably the sealing and whaling industry, which searched the region for new hunting grounds. Most explorers believed that a larger southern continent existed, even before one became known. This continent had been called Terra Australis Incognita (unknown southern land).

British Captain James Cook completed the first circumnavigation of Antarctica during his voyage of 1768-1775. He circumnavigated the Antarctic Circle three times but never spotted the mainland. He noted the large numbers of seals and whales in the region, which later sparked commercial interest. As outlying islands were stripped of their seal populations, commercial explorers began pushing farther south to find new hunting grounds.

Controversy surrounds the question of who first discovered the actual continent of Antarctica. The American sealer Nathaniel B. Palmer, Russia's Fabian Gottlieb von Bellingshausen, and Great Britain's Edward Bransfield and their countries all laid claim to its discovery. It is possible that other sealers sighted the Antarctic Peninsula earlier, but their records have been lost.

The Russian aristocrat and naval officer Fabian Gottlieb von Bellingshausen commanded Russia's first government-sponsored Antarctic expedition, commissioned by Czar Alexander I in 1819. Bellingshausen left Russia in 1820 with the ships *Vostok* and *Mirnyi*, closely follow-

ing Captain James Cook's eighteenth century course. Bellingshausen circumnavigated the Antarctic Circle and was the first since Cook to survey the region extensively. He spotted the Finibul Ice Shelf, the first sighting of the Antarctic continent, but the ice stopped his southerly progress. He also discovered Peter I Island, the most southerly land known at the time, and named Alexander Coast (now Alexander Island). He also encountered the American expedition under Palmer. Bellingshausen created excellent maps and charts that were published several years later.

The British Royal Navy sent Bransfield to the Antarctic region aboard the *Williams* in 1820 to chart the south Shetland Islands and nearby areas. William Smith served as Bransfield's pilot on this first official British expedition to Antarctica. Bransfield charted the coastline and harbors, collected science specimens, took meteorologic and magnetic readings, and then claimed the continent in the name of King George III. He sighted Livingston Island; landed on King George Island; discovered Deception Island, Tower Island, and the Bransfield Strait; and spotted the mountains of the Antarctic Peninsula, calling them Trinity Land. He also discovered Gibbs, O'Brien, Elephant Seal, and Clarence Islands, and was the first person to sail into the Weddell Sea. Controversy sur-

Charles Wilkes's Antarctic expedition. (C. A. Nichols & Company)

rounded his claims to spotting the Antarctic continent because his ship's logbook was later lost.

The Connecticut sailor Palmer commanded the sealing ship *Hero* when it sailed to the Antarctic region in 1820. He sighted Trinity Land, which was the second sighting of the Antarctic continent, observing a land mass and an inland mountain range. The United States named the land Palmer Peninsula, the British referred to it as Graham Land, and other nations referred to it as the Antarctic Peninsula. Palmer also discovered McFarlane Strait and Yankee Harbor but left the area because it had few seals or whales.

Although Bellingshausen, Bransfield, and Palmer spotted the mainland of Antarctica, no explorer in the first half of the nineteenth century reached the continent itself because of the nearly impenetrable ice fields that surrounded it. Within the next decade and a half, sealers continued to search for new hunting grounds. The British whaling firm Enderby Brothers underwrote many of these expeditions. These expeditions discovered new islands and mapped many miles of coastline, helping define the new continent's outlines. One of the voyages found a potential passage through the packed ice that later would be followed by famed explorers such as Sir James Clark Ross, Carsten Egeberg Borchgrevink, Robert Falcon Scott, Sir Ernest Shackleton, and Roald Amundsen.

February 7, 1821, marked what some historians believe is the first recorded landing on the Antarctic continent, by a crew from an American sealing ship under the command of Captain John Davis. Other historians credit Borchgrevink's British expedition of 1899 as the first to set foot on the Antarctic continent. In 1821, an officer and ten men of the British sealing ship *Lord Melville* wintered on King George Island after their ship had been driven away by a storm, stranding them. They were the first to endure an Antarctic winter. In 1821, sealers George Powell and Palmer discovered the South Orkney Islands. James Weddell took part in sealing expeditions in 1820-1821 and 1821-1822. He was interested as much in science and discoveries as in sealing. In 1823, he explored the South Orkney Islands, and that same year, he reached the Weddell Sea, the farthest south anyone has explored and a feat that would not be repeated for another eighty years.

In the 1830's, the British, French, and Americans launched scientific expeditions and also voyages to reach the farthest southern point possible. They sought new land and the location of the south magnetic pole and established that Antarctica was indeed a continent. The

French naval expedition headed by Jules-Sébastien-César Dumont d'Urville and Charles Hector Jacquinot, in the *Astrolabe* and *Zelee*, sailed from 1837 to 1840. They charted parts of the Antarctic Peninsula and came within four miles of the continent. They named the land they saw Adlie Land, claiming it for France, and measured the earth's magnetism in southern waters.

Lieutenant Charles Wilkes and the U.S. Exploring Expedition sailed in 1838 under the aegis of the U.S. Navy in order to chart the southern seas. Wilkes charted several hundred miles of new coastland, including Cape Hudson and the Shackleton Ice Shield, but he could not reach the south magnetic pole because of thick ice. The U.S. expedition's work marked a milestone in American science and helped establish U.S. claims to parts of the continent.

In 1839, the British sent Sir James Clark Ross with the ships *Erebus* and *Terror* to find the south magnetic pole; he had already found the north magnetic pole in 1831. Ross changed course after hearing of the French and American expeditions and discovered that the most accessible area of the coast lay in what became known as the Ross Sea. He spotted the Admiralty Mountains, which had been the most southerly land known. He claimed Victoria Land (Possession Island) for Great Britain and discovered Franklin Island and Mount Erebus, an active volcano on Ross Island. He was stopped by what became known as the Ross Ice Shelf. Ross discovered that the magnetic pole had to be accessed by land, not sea. His scientific crew also spotted a number of new fish species.

SIGNIFICANCE

After the expeditions of the first half of the nineteenth century, most Antarctic exploration was abandoned for the rest of the century. The seal and whale populations had been greatly reduced and there was little commercial interest in the land itself. The John Franklin expedition of 1845, sent by the British to find the fabled Northwest Passage through the Arctic region, disappeared, drawing explorers back to the Arctic to discover the expedition's fate.

In 1895, the Sixth International Geographical Congress sought to revive Antarctic exploration, beginning a new age of exploration in the region. The advent of the whaling industry in the beginning of the twentieth century also helped reinvigorate interest in the continent. The "heroic age" of Antarctic exploration lasted from 1894 until 1941 and included the famous and tragic race for the South Pole in 1911-1912 between Scott of Britain

1820's

and Amundsen of Norway. This period, marked by geopolitical interest in exploring and laying claim to the last uncharted territory on Earth, also witnessed the first systematic scientific exploration of the continent.

—*Marcella Bush Trevino*

FURTHER READING

Gurney, Alan. *Below the Convergence: Voyages Towards Antarctica, 1699-1839.* New York: W. W. Norton, 1977. Chronicles the major voyages of discovery and exploration as well as everyday life and problems encountered during the expeditions.

_____. *The Race to the White Continent: Voyages to the Antarctic.* New York: W. W. Norton, 2000. Explores the American, French, and British expeditions launched between the years 1837 and 1842 and discusses their significance.

Markham, Clements R. *The Lands of Silence: A History of Arctic and Antarctic Exploration.* 1921. Reprint. Mansfield Centre, Conn.: Martino, 2005. A classic overview of exploration in the Antarctic and Arctic regions.

Mills, William J., ed. *Exploring Polar Frontiers: A Historical Encyclopedia.* Santa Barbara, Calif.: ABC-Clio, 2003. A useful overview of key figures and expeditions.

Rosove, Michael H. *Let Heroes Speak: Antarctic Explorers, 1772-1922.* Annapolis, Md.: Naval Institute Press, 2000. Covers the period from Cook's 1772 expedition to Shackleton's final voyage in 1922. Includes extensive notes, a bibliography, and an index.

SEE ALSO: Sept. 7, 1803: Great Britain Begins Colonizing Tasmania; Apr. 5, 1815: Tambora Volcano Begins Violent Eruption; 1818-1854: Search for the Northwest Passage; 1893-1896: Nansen Attempts to Reach the North Pole.

RELATED ARTICLES in *Great Lives from History: The Nineteenth Century, 1801-1900:* Sir John Franklin; Sir James Clark Ross; Charles Wilkes.

c. 1820-1860
COSTUMBRISMO MOVEMENT

Borrowing on a Spanish word for custom or practice, the costumbrismo *movement provided a stylistic and thematic thread through nineteenth century art forms in both Spain and Latin America. The best-known* costumbristas *were Spanish literary figures who focused on the everyday manners and customs of specific social or provincial milieus.*

LOCALE: Spain; Spanish America
CATEGORIES: Literature; theater

KEY FIGURES

Sebastián Miñano y Bedoya (1779-1845), author of the first *costumbrista* work
Manuel Bretón de los Herreros (1796-1873), Spanish dramatist
Cecilia Böhl von Faber (Fernán Caballero; 1796-1877), best-known Spanish female conservative *costumbrista*
Serafín Estébañez Calderón (El Solitario; 1799-1867), Andalusian lawyer, linguist, journalist, and writer
Ramón de Mesonero Romanos (1802-1882), Spanish businessman and writer
Ventura de la Vega (1807-1865), Argentine-born Spanish actor and dramatist
Mariano José de Larra (Fígaro; 1809-1837), Spanish liberal writer and critic
Pedro Antonio de Alarcón (1833-1891), Spanish humorist
José María de Pereda (1833-1906), Spanish novelist
Vicente Medina y Tómas (1866-1937), Spanish journalist, soldier, schoolteacher, and poet
José María Gabriel y Galán (1870-1905), Spanish schoolteacher and poet

SUMMARY OF EVENT

Rooted in prior Spanish literary movements and tied to the concurrent socioeconomic and political aspects of the Hispanic world, the *costumbrismo* movement reached its zenith around the middle third of the nineteenth century. The independence of South American nations and the continuing decline of Spain fostered a focus on specific surroundings and situations and a conservative, or defensive, versus liberal, or critical, paradigm. Overlapping with both Romanticism and realism in terms of time period and orientation, with a degree of continuity throughout the century, the influence of *costumbrismo* shows up in all the literary genres. However, the points at which one movement leaves off and another begins or continues are not well defined, and assigning writers to specific categories is often debatable.

The two main types of *costumbrista* literature are *artículos* (articles), satirical or critical looks at reality that were frequently published in periodicals, and *cuadros* (pictures), picturesque examinations highlighting local color that were usually published in essay or short-story form. These works typically feature realistic descriptions of characters, manners, and customs; emphasize discourses on social background, rather than plot; and use short-story frameworks and dialogue to point up aspects of society. Such works were published on both sides of the Atlantic, but most of the works best known outside their own areas describe Castilian and Spanish Andalusian landscapes. They are frequently set in rural areas far from urban centers.

The first work considered *costumbrista* was Sebastián Miñano y Bedoya's *Cartas de un pobrecito holgazán* (1820; letters of a poor loafer). However, the child prodigy Mariano José de Larra is considered the best-known literary figure to represent the conflict and ferment of that era. Although Larra wrote in all genres, including literary criticism, particularly theatrical criticism, he combined his journalistic and literary endeavors with his politically and philosophically liberal agenda. He is best known for moralizing and reformist works that he wrote under his pseudonym, Fígaro, or El Pobrecito Hablador (the Poor Little Talker). He was a fervent anti-Carlist and had a sad personal life, ending in suicide, that makes him seem more suited to the Romantic tradition. However, he had no nostalgia for the past and was an astute observer of traditional institutions who voiced his opinions and concerns using irony and satire. He wanted Spain to modernize and was an idealist who believed that both Spain and its population could better themselves.

Other writers tended to follow more limited, objective, and picturesque approaches that used local color and details without ideological overlays and revealed a preference for the past. For example, Ramón de Mesonero Romanos, a Madrid businessman who became a writer, was an observer of scenes. He launched the first illustrated newspaper and retained many aspects of the eighteenth century neoclassical style in his works. Other notable prose writers in the movement included Pedro Antonio de Alarcón, best known for *El sombrero de tres picos* (1874; *The Three-Cornered Hat*, 1886), and Armando Palacio Valdés, a literary critic, novelist, and writer of short stories.

Larra and Mesonero Romanos wrote mostly about urban life, but the majority of the *costumbristas* focused on rural milieus. For example, Serafín Estébañez Calderón, writing under the pseudonym El Solitario, wrote about the traditions of his native Andalusia in southern Spain, incorporating folklore, local color, and archaic effects. Another Andalusian, Salvador Rueda, wrote poetry, novels, short stories, and dramas featuring a similar provincial ambience. *Costumbrista* writings by Larra, Mesonero Romanos, and others made extensive references to Andalusia and often portrayed scenes with Andalusian flamenco music and dancing. For example, Estébañez Calderón's *Esceñas andaluzas* (1847; Andalusian scenes) contains two stories so dedicated, mentioning mythical singers of the time, El Planeta and El Fillo, and describing aspects of flamenco.

Cecilia Böhl von Faber was the best-known conservative woman *costumbrista*. She wrote under the male pseudonym of Fernán Caballero and is remembered mostly for her novel *La gaviota* (1849; *The Seagull*, 1867). She was also a journalist and short-story writer. Another conservative novelist, José María de Pereda, was the most rigidly regional and reactionary *costumbrista*. He focused on the mountains of his native Santander in northern Spain.

The best-known poets of the *costumbrista* movement are Vicente Medina y Tómas and José María Gabriel y Galán, from Murcia and Extremadura respectively. Both were schoolteachers who shared a rural orientation. Medina, a journalist and soldier, published in newspapers and wrote regionalistic, rustic poetry in simple language with dialect about the soul and spirit of the people. His writings featured primitive elemental aspects, rather than picturesque aspects of regions. Gabriel became a provincial farmer whose poetry featured landscapes, rustic sayings, and the use of dialect in treating the simplicity of rural life.

In *costumbrista* theater, Manuel Bretón de los Herreros was the first Spanish dramatist to move from imitating the famous neoclassicist Leandro Fernández de Moratín (1760-1828) toward realistic comedies of manners and drama of social satire. Ventura de la Vega, who was born in Argentina but taken to Spain at an early age, also imitated Fernández de Moratín in his early writings. An actor, lecturer, and socially critical dramatist, he developed the modern *zarzuela* from a short musical dramatic form from earlier centuries.

SIGNIFICANCE

Costumbrismo set the stage for both Romanticism and realism in Spain and Pereda's rural-versus-urban dichotomy influenced the later civilization-versus-barbarism

1820's

literary theme in Latin America. Furthermore, Pereda's personal progression from sketch to novel helped set the stage for the realistic novels of manners of the late nineteenth century and laid the groundwork for regional novels, the first examples of which were a string of *cuadros* with flimsy plots. Those regional and realistic novels grew out of the *artículos de costumbre* and the realistic novels of earlier centuries and had little foreign influence, as they relied on their own portrayed traditions.

Romanticism, somewhat time-delayed in Spain, may have been so since *artículos*, essays in fictional form, already fulfilled the purpose of fiction. Some critics believe that Romanticism was delayed in Spain due to the socially repressive nature of King Fernando VII's reign, which seemed to tolerate the critical *artículos* as nonthreatening. The same critics cite as evidence for their theory the attitudinal shift after the death of Fernando and the establishment of a liberal government.

—Debra D. Andrist

FURTHER READING

Chandler, Richard E., and Kessel Schwartz. *A New History of Spanish Literature*. Baton Rouge: Louisiana State University Press, 1961. Although somewhat dated and often fragmented in its coverage of the broad field of Spanish literature, this survey contains a useful overview of the *costumbrismo* movement and its writers.

Franco, Jean. *An Introduction to Spanish American Literature*. 1969. Reprint. New York: Cambridge University Press, 1994. The first four chapters of this survey cover Latin American literature during the time period generally associated with *costumbrismo*. The next four chapters cover the corresponding social milieu associated with Spanish *costumbrismo*.

Montesinos, José. *Introducción a una historia de la novela en España, en el siglo XIX*. Valencia: Editorial Castalia, 1955. Important Spanish-language work that ties the nineteenth century's movements together chronologically, thematically, and stylistically.

Rodríguez Rubí, Tomás, et al. *Los españoles pintados por sí mismos, 1843-4*. Vols. 1-2. Madrid: Gaspar y Roig, 1851. Published at the zenith of the *costumbrista* movement, this seminal volume contains forty-nine articles by members of the movement, as well as Romantics, such as the Duque de Rivas, José de Zorrilla y Moral, and Juan Hartzenbusch.

Schurlknight, Donald E. *Spanish Romanticism in Context: Of Subversion, Contradiction, and Politics—Espronceda, Larra, Rivas, Zorrilla*. Lanham, Md.: University Press of America, 1998. Explains Spain's nineteenth century literary movements and characteristics within a sociopolitical setting.

Silver, Philip W. *Ruin and Restitution: Reinterpreting Romanticism in Spain*. Nashville, Tenn.: Vanderbilt University Press, 2005. Study of Spanish literature that redefines nineteenth century literary movements.

SEE ALSO: c. 1830's-1860's: American Renaissance in Literature; c. 1865: Naturalist Movement Begins; c. 1869: Golden Age of Flamenco Begins; Oct., 1889-Apr., 1890: First Pan-American Congress.
RELATED ARTICLES in *Great Lives from History: The Nineteenth Century, 1801-1900:* Carolina Coronado; Rubén Darío.

February 23, 1820

LONDON'S CATO STREET CONSPIRATORS PLOT ASSASSINATIONS

The Cato Street Conspiracy was the climactic event in the conflict between the forces of reaction and reform that emerged in England during the years after the defeat of Napoleon I in 1815. Twenty conspirators plotted to assassinate the political leadership of England, but the plot was discovered and thwarted. Parliament enacted the repressive Six Acts, which increased governmental powers against sedition, after the scope of the conspiracy was revealed.

LOCALE: London, England

CATEGORIES: Terrorism and political assassination; laws, acts, and legal history; wars, uprisings, and civil unrest

KEY FIGURES

Arthur Thistlewood (1774-1820), English revolutionary who organized the Cato Street Conspiracy

William Cobbett (1763-1835), English political writer who founded the *Political Register*

Henry Hunt (1773-1835), English political activist and advocate of parliamentary reform

Hannah More (1745-1833), English writer, feminist, and philanthropist

Second Earl of Liverpool (Robert Banks Jenkinson; 1770-1828), British prime minister, 1812-1827

SUMMARY OF EVENT

After the collapse of Napoleon I's French armies at Waterloo and the finalization of the treaties that emerged at the Congress of Vienna in 1815, England looked forward to a period of peace and a return to normalcy. The generation of war, however, caused extensive changes in England's economy and in the nation's political attitudes. Almost one-half million British troops were demobilized without support and found themselves in a society that already had high unemployment and a low standard of living. During the years immediately following the war, the government of the prime minister, the second earl of Liverpool, failed to recognize the extent of the domestic problems and the expectations of the people. Liverpool and most of his ministers were hostile to the Enlightenment ideas that demanded social change; British leadership was interested in returning to pre-war conditions—the Great Britain and the Europe of the ancien régime—and looked upon change and reform as revolutionary and related to the disastrous French experiment of the previous generation.

During the war years, there were indications that forces of change and reform were emerging in Britain. On the political right were the Luddites, who appeared in 1812, constituting a secret, anti-industrial sect that supported the values of labor among craftsmen, particularly the making of textiles. Luddites despised and feared the machine age and the disappearance of their livelihoods. On the political left were reformers such as Robert Owen, a factory owner and utopian socialist, who argued in publications such as *New View of Society: A New View of Society* (1813) that capitalist owners had an obligation to assume responsibility for the well-being of their workers and their families.

Liverpool's government was not sympathetic to any of these calls for reform. By mid-1815, Britain was in an economic depression, a situation aggravated by passage of the protectionist Corn Law of 1815, which forbade the importation of foreign grain until that grain reached the so-called "famine price" of eighty shillings per quarter. Supporters of the Corn Law argued that the law would provide support for British agriculture, which had lost most of its foreign markets after the peace in Europe. Suffering high unemployment and shouldering the effects of the Corn Law, the general populace could not afford the increased price, leading to widespread hunger in Britain during 1815-1816.

The situation was further aggravated in 1816 when Parliament eliminated the 10 percent income tax that had been enacted to support the costs of the war with France; most of this tax burden fell on those with high incomes. Concurrently, Parliament enacted new duties on many articles. This "sales tax" led to higher prices, harming the general populace, which was not prepared or able to pay the tax. Organized opposition to these measures and conditions began in 1816. William Cobbett, who had a national following based on his *Political Register*, was an advocate for radical political, economic, and social reform. Along with other radicals, such as Henry Hunt, Cobbett believed that the fundamental structure of government needed changing, so that it would reflect the people's needs and aspirations.

On December 2, 1816, a group of radicals gathered a crowd at Spa Fields, north of London, to discuss political change. Exchanges between the crowd and police resulted in violence and several arrests. Hannah More, a contemporary feminist reformer and writer, later argued that no gains would be achieved by "breaking of win-

1820's

323

Executions of the Cato Street conspirators outside London's Newgate Prison. (Hulton Archive/Getty Images)

paper tax, new powers of search and seizure for the government, prohibition of training in fire-arm use, and restrictions on public meetings. All these measures were clear violations of traditional English freedoms.

The government's policies and actions inflamed the radical militants, who, with twenty men under the leadership of Arthur Thistlewood, entered into a secret plot to assassinate the entire British cabinet during a dinner meeting at the home of the earl of Harrowby in Grosvenor Square, London, on February 23, 1820. Through informants, police learned of the plot and, as the conspirators were leaving a building on Cato Street, they arrested many of those involved; the next day several others were arrested. In the sensational trial that followed, five of the conspirators, including Thistlewood, were sentenced to death, and the others received extensive prison sentences. The Cato Street Conspiracy failed, the reformers were discredited, and the Six Acts were enacted.

SIGNIFICANCE

The Cato Street Conspiracy demonstrated the extent of the political polarization that developed during the five postwar years in Britain. In its aftermath the repressive Six Acts became law, significantly restricting traditional freedoms. These measures reflected the sentiments of those—the landowners and aristocrats—who associated calls for reform with revolution. They feared that weakness in dealing with the reformers would result in a revolution in Britain comparable to the French Revolution (1789).

A younger generation of leaders—Robert Peel, Earl Grey, and others—recognized the need for some reforms in order to address dangerous economic, political, and social conditions and to unite the country; they did not fear change and adopted a more progressive approach to governing. Although assassination attempts were directed at British leaders during the nineteenth century, a plan as ambitious as the failed Cato Street Conspiracy would not surface again in Britain until the mid-twentieth century.

—*William T. Walker*

dows, or breaking of laws." As a result of the Spa Fields Riot, Cobbett's activities were restricted. He migrated to the United States in 1817 but returned to England in 1819. Hunt scheduled a public address at St. Peter's Field in Manchester for August 16, 1819, to call for reforms in government and society. A struggle broke out between police and a few in the crowd, leading police to an unwarranted cavalry charge into the crowd. Scores of people were wounded and eleven died in what is called the Peterloo Massacre of 1819. Liverpool's government immediately suspended the writ of habeas corpus and restricted meetings and activities it believed were seditious.

The crisis between the old order and its challenger had reached a new level of intensity. In an effort to curtail the spread of radicalism and violence in December, 1819, the Liverpool government presented the repressive Six Acts. These acts required quick trials on charges of misdemeanors, registration of all newspapers, a new news-

FURTHER READING

Anand, Vidya, and Francis A. Ridley. *The Cato Street Conspiracy*. London: Medusa Press, 1977. An adequate introduction to the forces that resulted in the conspiracy and the crisis of Regency England.

Chandler, James K. *England in 1819: The Politics of Literary Culture and the Case of Romantic Historicism*. Chicago: University of Chicago Press, 1998. An important scholarly work that places the conspiracy within the context of the literature of dissent and reform.

Gash, Norman. *Lord Liverpool: The Life and Political Career of Robert Banks Jenkinson, Second Earl of Liverpool, 1770-1828*. Cambridge, Mass.: Harvard University Press, 1985. Still the best biography of Liverpool. Includes an excellent chapter on his government postwar policies that contributed to the conspiracy.

Plowright, John. *Regency England: The Age of Lord Liverpool*. New York: Routledge, 1996. An excellent study of British politics during the early nineteenth century. Plowright provides a well-written and provocative section on the 1815 to 1820 period that culminated in the conspiracy and the Six Acts.

Reid, Robert. *The Peterloo Massacre*. London: William Heinemann, 1989. An excellent account of the massacre in Manchester, the suppression of the protesters, and the subsequent trials that contributed to the origins of the conspiracy.

Shelley, Percy Bysshe. *The Mask of Anarchy*. New York: Woodstock Books, 1990. Written in 1819 as *The Masque of Anarchy* by the contemporary English poet, in remembrance of the massacre in Manchester. Reprint of the 1832 edition.

Stanhope, John. *The Cato Street Conspiracy*. London: Jonathan Cape, 1962. An excellent authoritative study of the Cato Street Conspiracy that is balanced, based on the effective use of primary sources, and well written.

Wilkinson, George Theodore. *An Authentic History of the Cato Street Conspiracy: With the Trials at Large of the Conspirators, for High Treason and Murder*. New York: Arno Press, 1972. Based on extensive use of primary sources, this history of the conspiracy is valuable even with its sensational statements and implications. Originally published in 1820.

SEE ALSO: Jan., 1802: Cobbett Founds the *Political Register*; Mar. 11, 1811-1816: Luddites Destroy Industrial Machines; Sept. 15, 1814-June 11, 1815: Congress of Vienna; June 18, 1815: Battle of Waterloo; Nov. 20, 1815: Second Peace of Paris; Dec. 11-30, 1819: British Parliament Passes the Six Acts; June 4, 1832: British Parliament Passes the Reform Act of 1832.

RELATED ARTICLES in *Great Lives from History: The Nineteenth Century, 1801-1900:* Thomas Carlyle; William Cobbett; George IV; Second Earl of Liverpool; Robert Owen; Sir Robert Peel; Percy Bysshe Shelley.

March 3, 1820
MISSOURI COMPROMISE

By allowing Missouri to enter the union as a slave state, while Maine entered as a free state, this congressional measure helped preserve the delicate balance between northern and southern sectional interests for more than three decades.

LOCALE: Washington, D.C.

CATEGORIES: Laws, acts, and legal history; civil rights and liberties

KEY FIGURES

Henry Clay (1777-1852), Speaker of the U.S. House of Representatives

James Tallmadge (1778-1853), representative from New York

Jesse Burgess Thomas (1777-1853), senator from Illinois

James Monroe (1758-1831), president of the United States, 1817-1825

SUMMARY OF EVENT

Between 1818 and 1819, representatives from both Missouri and Maine petitioned the U.S. Congress to admit their territories to the union as states. The Missouri Territory had been created from the Louisiana Purchase (1803) and was promised constitutional protection. However, Congress could not decide if the right of property applied to the institution of slavery. The question at issues was whether slavery should be allowed in Missouri and the rest of the Louisiana Purchase, or did Congress have the moral responsibility to rectify the issue of slavery that had been avoided since the Constitutional Convention of 1787. It would take three sessions of Congress between 1818 and 1821 before Missouri was fully admitted as a state. The issue of slavery sparked by the ensuing debate spread throughout the country and threatened to cause disunion between the northern and southern regions of the United States.

At the time Missouri and Maine applied for statehood, the union had exactly eleven free states and eleven slave states. This political balance had been achieved since 1789 by alternately admitting slave and free states, whose status was determined by each state's geographical location and its region's past history with regard to slavery. This arrangement ensued that each section of the country had an equal number of senators, and it attempted to equalize representation in the House of Representatives through the three-fifths clause.

The three-fifths clause, added to the final draft of the Constitution in 1789, allowed slave states to count each slave as three-fifths of a person to balance their representative power against that of the more densely populated North. Nevertheless, the North had a majority of representatives in Congress (105 to 81). Missouri's admission as a free or slave state therefore became an important issue in the very body that would resolve it. Missouri threatened either to extend the influence of the industrial free North in the Senate or to provide the majority to the agrarian slaveholding South.

In 1818, the boundaries of Missouri Territory were approximately the same as those of the modern state, and the territory was estimated to contain two thousand to three thousand slaves. Slavery in Missouri was a historical by-product of prior French and Spanish colonial policies. Representatives from Missouri reasoned that slavery should be allowed to continue there as it had in other territories that had been granted statehood since 1789.

In February, 1819, the House of Representatives responded to this debate by adopting an amendment that Representative James Tallmadge of New York proposed to attach to the bill allowing Missouri to frame a state constitution. The two clauses in the Tallmadge amendment would restrict the expansion of slavery in Missouri and provide that all children born to slaves would become free at the age of twenty-five. Both clauses of his amendment passed the House. Southern senators were shocked by the bitterness of the debate in the House and the ability of the North to muster votes. They saw the Tallmadge amendment as the first step in eliminating the expansion of slavery in the nation as a whole. Voting along sectional lines, the Senate rejected both clauses.

THE CONSTITUTION AND THE ADMISSION OF NEW STATES

The U.S. Constitution's rules for the admission of new states to the Union are outlined in these two brief paragraphs, which make up the whole of Article IV, section 3.

New States may be admitted by the Congress into this Union; but no new State shall be formed or erected within the Jurisdiction of any other State; nor any State be formed by the Junction of two or more States, or Parts of States, without the Consent of the Legislatures of the States concerned as well as of the Congress.

The Congress shall have Power to dispose of and make all needful Rules and Regulations respecting the Territory or other Property belonging to the United States; and nothing in this Constitution shall be so construed as to Prejudice any Claims of the United States, or of any particular State.

Congress then adjourned until December 6, 1819. During the interim period, Maine framed a constitution and applied for admission to the union as a free state. Maine had originally been incorporated into the Massachusetts Bay Colony in 1691 but had started to agitate for separate statehood during the War of 1812. Its application for statehood as a free state seemed to provide a possible solution to the Missouri debate that threatened the stability of the young nation.

On February 18, 1820, the Senate Judiciary Committee joined the Missouri and Maine measures and the Senate passed both Maine's and Missouri's applications for statehood but without mentioning slavery. This infuriated Maine, which had, as part of Massachusetts, outlawed slavery in 1780. What should have been a routine confirmation of new states became part of the most explosive issue to face the country. Maine was to be allowed to separate from Massachusetts and gain statehood, so long as Congress approved its application by March 4, 1820, or its nine counties would revert to Massachusetts. Even so, many of Maine's constituency urged that Maine's application fail so that slavery would not spread into Missouri.

Senator Jesse Burgess Thomas of Illinois offered a compromise amendment to the Senate bill that would admit Missouri as a slave state with the proviso that the remaining territories in the Louisiana Purchase above 36° 30′ north latitude, Missouri's southern border, would be free of slavery. The northern-controlled House responded by rejecting Thomas's amendment and instead passed a proviso prohibiting the further introduction of slavery anywhere in the United States. The result was polarization along sectional lines. In turn, the Senate struck out the antislavery provision and added the Thomas amendment. Thus began the final debate over whether slavery would be allowed to expand.

Senator Rufus King of New York continued the debate by stating that Congress, under Article IV, section 3 of the Constitution, was empowered to exclude slavery from the territory and to make slavery an issue for statehood. "New states *may be* admitted by the Congress into this Union." A precedent had been established under in the Northwest Ordinance of 1787, which forbade slavery in lands above the Ohio River. Therefore, in the minds of many of the northern congressmen, they should take this opportunity to eliminate slavery from any point west of the Mississippi. In response, Senator William Pickering of Maryland argued that because the United States was made up of equal numbers of slave and free states, Missouri should be allowed to determine its own fate.

Missouri responded with anger and frustration, asserting that the issue was not about slavery but rather the issue of state sovereignty. Congress had delayed Missouri's admission for several years. Missouri, like other states, had the right to choose its own property laws. In Missouri, as well as the rest of the South, the issue swung from one dealing with slavery to one dealing with property rights and the equality of states within the United States. These issues captured the attention of citizens throughout the country and led to heated debates on all levels. For the first time, slavery was being justified and defended as a good way of life not only by southern politicians but also by the southern clergy. Would the country be influenced by restrictionists who sought to control this institution, or would states' rights be preserved?

A compromise was eventually reached, between the two houses, in a conference formed to break the deadlock. Speaker of the House Henry Clay of Kentucky stated that he would not support Maine's admission unless Missouri was admitted without restrictions. The Senate took the House bill and inserted the Thomas amendment. On March 3, 1820, the House under Clay's leadership voted to admit Maine as a free state and Missouri as a slave state and restricted slavery north of 36° 30′. It is interesting to note that seven of Maine's nine representatives in the Massachusetts state delegation voted against Maine's admission so that their state would not be used to provide a solution to the slavery issue.

Missouri continued to be an issue when it presented a state constitution in November, 1820. As if to get the fi-

nal word, the Missouri constitutional convention had incorporated into its constitution a provision excluding free blacks and mulattoes from the state. This provision incited the antislavery factions in the Senate and House and threatened to destroy the fragile compromise. A "Second Missouri Compromise" was needed that would state that Missouri would not gain admission as a state unless its legislature assured Congress that it would not seek to abridge the rights of citizens. The Missouri legislature agreed to this in June, 1821. On August 10, 1821, President James Monroe admitted Missouri as the twenty-fourth state. After waiting a short time, Missouri's state legislature sought to have the last say when it approved statutes forbidding free blacks from entering the state.

SIGNIFICANCE

The Missouri Compromise would stand until Congress's passage of the Kansas-Nebraska Act in 1854. Until that time, the Missouri Compromise served to mark a clear delineation between the growing regional and sectional problems of the North and South and made states' rights the rallying cry for the South until the Civil War (1861-1865). In 1857, Missouri would again become the focus of a national debate on slavery when the Dred Scott case reached the U.S. Supreme Court, whose ruling nullified the principles of the Missouri Compromise.

—Vincent Michael Thur

FURTHER READING

Brown, Richard H. *The Missouri Compromise: Political Statesmanship or Unwise Evasion?* Boston: D. C. Heath, 1964. Contains primary source material showing views of contemporary leaders and varying perspectives of historians.

Clark, Charles E. *Maine: A Bicentennial History.* New York: W. W. Norton, 1977. Condensed overview of Maine history.

Cunningham, Noble E., Jr. *The Presidency of James Monroe.* Lawrence: University Press of Kansas, 1996. Study of the major domestic and foreign policy issues that Monroe faced during his two terms in office, including the Missouri Compromise.

Hurt, R. Douglas. *Agriculture and Slavery in Missouri's Little Dixie.* Columbia: University of Missouri Press, 1992. A study of the political and legal impact of the Missouri Compromise during the antebellum era in a seven-county area along the Missouri River.

McPherson, James M. *The Battle Cry of Freedom: The Civil War Era.* Oxford, England: Oxford University Press, 1988. Definitive perspective on the sectional

1820's

differences leading up to and through the Civil War era.

Moore, Glover. *The Missouri Controversy, 1819-1821.* Gloucester, Mass.: Peter Smith, 1967. A significant monograph on the political compromise that signaled nineteenth century sectional controversies during the antebellum era.

Nagel, Paul C. *Missouri: A Bicentennial History.* New York: W. W. Norton, 1977. Condensed overview of Missouri history by a leading historian.

Nash, Gary B., ed. *The American People: Creating a Nation and a Society.* 2d ed. New York: Harper & Row, 1990. Overview of American history that places the Missouri Compromise in a national historical context.

Shankman, Kimberly Christner. *Compromise and the Constitution: The Political Thought of Henry Clay.* Lanham, Md.: Lexington Books, 1999. Examination of the political thinking of the man who was Speaker of the House of Representatives at the time of the Missouri Compromise.

SEE ALSO: May 9, 1803: Louisiana Purchase; Mar. 2, 1807: Congress Bans Importation of African Slaves; Dec. 1, 1824-Feb. 9, 1825: U.S. Election of 1824; Jan. 19-27, 1830: Webster and Hayne Debate Slavery and Westward Expansion; Jan. 29-Sept. 20, 1850: Compromise of 1850; May 30, 1854: Congress Passes the Kansas-Nebraska Act; May, 1856-Aug., 1858: Bleeding Kansas; Mar. 6, 1857: *Dred Scott v. Sandford*; June 16-Oct. 15, 1858: Lincoln-Douglas Debates.

RELATED ARTICLES in *Great Lives from History: The Nineteenth Century, 1801-1900:* Henry Clay; James Monroe; Roger Brooke Taney.

April 24, 1820
CONGRESS PASSES LAND ACT OF 1820

Enacted in response to mounting federal budget needs, the Land Act of 1820 laid the basis for transferring public domain lands in former Indian lands to individual U.S. citizens over the next two decades.

LOCALE: Washington, D.C.
CATEGORIES: Laws, acts, and legal history; expansion and land acquisition; economics

KEY FIGURES

Alexander Hamilton (1755-1804), secretary of the Treasury, 1789-1795, who advocated using proceeds of land sales to reduce the federal debt
Albert Gallatin (1761-1849), secretary of the Treasury, 1801-1814, who organized the system of Land Offices
William Henry Harrison (1773-1841), victor in the Battle of Tippecanoe, which opened Indiana to Euro-American settlement
Anthony Wayne (1745-1796), Army general who forced American Indians to cede large parts of the Old Northwest

SUMMARY OF EVENT

From their beginnings, Great Britain's North American colonies were colonies of settlement. By the time of the Revolutionary War (1775-1783), most of the good agricultural land in the original thirteen colonies had been turned into farms by the settlers, and many settlers were eager to move west of the Alleghenies, to the area later known as the Old Northwest. To ensure the friendship of the Native American societies in that region, the British forbade settlement. With British defeat in the Revolutionary War, the unsettled area now belonged to the thirteen colonies, where pressure to open it to settlement was overwhelming.

In 1785, the Confederation Congress began deliberations about how to arrange the transfer of land in the Old Northwest, as well as portions of the Old Southwest, acquired by the 1783 Treaty of Paris with Great Britain. Several principles were agreed on: Before settlement and transfer of title, the land would have to be ceded by treaty with the Native Americans; the land would have to be surveyed, in square township units, and sale would be by portions of the surveyed townships; and the proceeds of sales would be applied to the federal debt. These principles were embodied in the Ordinance of 1785, which continued to bind the federal government after the adoption of the Constitution in 1789.

In addition to pressure from would-be settlers, the federal government owed obligations to thousands of veterans of the Revolutionary War who had been promised land grants in lieu of pay during the war. Many veterans had received scrip, redeemable in grants from the public domain. As a result, the federal government attempted to begin surveying the land. After a modest portion of land was mapped, it was to be subdivided into townships and offered for sale.

In 1784, 1785, and 1786, treaties had been negotiated with some of the Indian tribes by which the tribes ceded much of western New York and western Pennsylvania and large portions of southern Ohio to the United States. In Congress a belief prevailed that this laid the foundation for surveying and subsequent settlement by Euro-Americans. However, some of the Indians refused to accept the treaties, and they fought battles with federal troops during the early 1790's. The Indians won the first battle in 1791 but in 1794 they lost to a force commanded by General Anthony Wayne at the Battle of Fallen Timbers. Wayne then ravaged the Indian settlements in northern Ohio and forced the Indians to accept the Treaty of Greenville (1795), by which they accepted confinement to a reservation in northwestern Ohio and ceded the rest of Ohio, as well as parts of Indiana, Illinois, and a small part of Michigan, to the United States.

In the region known as the Old Southwest—which would become the states of Mississippi and Alabama, as well as parts of western Georgia—numerous treaties were concluded with the local tribes. These treaties defined tribal lands and opened up significant lands for Euro-American settlement, mostly in the southern portions of the area.

Meanwhile, Alexander Hamilton, the secretary of the Treasury, began organizing the system that would administer sales of the land. According to the Ordinance of 1785, the land was to be sold at auction for at least one dollar per acre after being surveyed. Sales were to be administered by the Department of the Treasury, and surveying was to be supervised by the U.S. geographer (a post abolished in 1796 and replaced by the surveyor general). Surveys were to be of townships in six-square-mile units. In 1796, the price was raised to two dollars per acre, but plots of 640 acres were allowed. However, sales on this scale proved disappointing.

In 1800, William Henry Harrison induced Congress to change the terms of sale. Sales of smaller parcels were allowed, and purchasers were permitted to make their payments on the installment plan over four-year periods. Simultaneously, Albert Gallatin, the new secretary of the Treasury, put in place an organization of land offices located in the areas to be sold. In 1812, these offices were subordinated to a General Land Office that supervised the local offices. They increased rapidly in number as more land was surveyed and put up for sale. This rearrangement of the system, particularly the inclusion of

purchases on credit, laid the basis for a large land boom between 1812 and 1819.

The land boom revealed the weakness of the system created in 1800. Purchases on credit were hard to monitor because of the limited clerical help in the local land offices and in the General Land Office. Also, Congress passed a number of relief acts after 1800, extending the time limits on credit purchases. By 1820, only about one-third of the purchase price of the lands recorded as sold had been collected. Federal finances were in perilous shape after the War of 1812, which had raised the federal debt to new heights. Since receipts from land sales, along with tariff receipts, were the only sources of federal income, and as the South opposed any increases in tariff, reform of the sales of public lands was needed.

SIGNIFICANCE

Passed by Congress on April 24, 1820, the Land Act abolished credit purchases on land, requiring full payment in cash. However, prices were reduced from $2 to $1.25 per acre, and those who still owed money on previous credit purchases were given more time to complete their payments. Purchasers who still owed money would be allowed to surrender part of the land they had bought to cover the remaining debt due. Although this law dealt with some of the problems in the system of selling off the public domain, it failed to still criticism, for the public lands issue had become deeply enmeshed in sectional politics, which would determine subsequent modifications.

—Nancy M. Gordon

FURTHER READING

Carstensen, Vernon, ed. *The Public Lands: Studies in the History of the Public Domain.* Madison: University of Wisconsin Press, 1963. This book remains a standard source for the most controversial issues associated with the public lands.

Clark, Thomas D., and John D. W. Guice. *Frontiers in Conflict: The Old Southwest, 1795-1830.* Albuquerque: University of New Mexico Press, 1989. An account of the difficulties with the tribes of the Old Southwest and the problems in securing their acceptance of Euro-American settlement.

Gates, Paul W. *History of Public Land Law Development.* Washington, D.C.: Zenger, 1968. This large compendium of information, written for the Public Land Law Review Commission, is the ultimate source of information on the land laws.

Hurt, Douglas. *The Ohio Frontier: Crucible of the Old Northwest, 1726-1830.* Bloomington: Indiana Uni-

1820's

versity Press, 1996. Comprehensive study of the early settlement of Ohio, which was one of the territories affected by the Land Act of 1820.

North, Douglas C., and Andrew R. Rutten. "The Northwest Ordinance in Historical Perspective." In *Essays on the Economy of the Old Northwest*, edited by David C. Klingaman and Richard K. Vedder. Athens: Ohio University Press, 1987. The most useful of several chapters relating to the disposition of the public domain.

Rohrbough, Malcolm J. *The Land Office Business: The Settlement and Administration of American Public Lands, 1789-1837*. New York: Oxford University Press, 1968. The best detailed history of the operation of the various land offices.

Sword, Wiley. *President Washington's Indian War: The Struggle for the Old Northwest, 1790-1795*. Norman: University of Oklahoma Press, 1985. A detailed account of the conflict with the American Indians to free up the Northwest Territory for Euro-American settlement.

SEE ALSO: May 28, 1830: Congress Passes Indian Removal Act; Sept. 4, 1841: Congress Passes Preemption Act of 1841; May 20, 1862: Lincoln Signs the Homestead Act; July 2, 1862: Lincoln Signs the Morrill Land Grant Act; 1879: Powell Publishes His Report on the American West; Feb. 8, 1887: General Allotment Act Erodes Indian Tribal Unity.

RELATED ARTICLES in *Great Lives from History: The Nineteenth Century, 1801-1900:* Thomas Hart Benton; Henry Clay; Albert Gallatin; William Henry Harrison.

July 2, 1820-March, 1821
NEAPOLITAN REVOLUTION

Inspired by political changes in France and Spain, the Neapolitan Revolution forced King Ferdinand I to accept a constitutional government but was quickly suppressed by the Austrian military. Nevertheless, its underlying goal of Italian self-government was realized forty years later with the establishment of an independent Italian state.

LOCALE: Naples (now in Italy)
CATEGORIES: Government and politics; wars, uprisings, and civil unrest

KEY FIGURES
Ferdinand I (1751-1825), Bourbon king of the Two Sicilies, 1816-1825
Metternich (1773-1859), Austrian foreign affairs minister
Guglielmo Pepe (1783-1855), Italian soldier who led the revolution
Morelli (fl. early nineteenth century), army lieutenant who followed Pepe
Minichini (fl. early nineteenth century), radical Roman Catholic priest
Viscount Castlereagh (Robert Stewart; 1769-1822), British foreign secretary, 1812-1822

SUMMARY OF EVENT
The Neapolitan Revolution of 1820 followed shortly after a similar revolt in Spain and preceded revolutionary disturbances in northern Italy. The year 1820 was a year of crisis for the system of peace and security that had been initiated at the Congress of Vienna in 1815 and carried through Italy by Prince Metternich, the Austrian minister of foreign affairs. The causes of the Neapolitan revolt go back to that Congress, at which the victorious allies had restored Ferdinand I to the kingdom of the Two Sicilies under the principle of "legitimacy." Like other Italian rulers, Ferdinand was indebted to Metternich for his restored throne and thereby wedded to the forces of reaction. By a secret treaty, Ferdinand promised to uphold his absolutist convictions, maintain the status quo, and accept changes only with the consent of Austria. Any revolt against Ferdinand's rule was therefore a revolt against Austria. In order to consolidate his power, Ferdinand restored loyal Bourbonists to honored positions in his state, and until 1817, he depended upon the Austrian army to protect this throne.

Since the Bourbon restoration meant the end of French domination and a return to peace, Ferdinand's return to Naples was initially greeted with enthusiasm. There were, however, elements of dissatisfaction. Two groups, the Muratists and the Carbonari, were immediately alienated but remained representative of the forces of change. The Muratists were originally the loyal followers of Joachim Murat, the brother-in-law of Napoleon I whom Napoleon had made king of Naples. These followers envied the honored positions given to the

Bourbonists, whom they considered to be a feudal privileged class without experience or enlightenment. Hoping to be knighted as peers of the realm and honored as an enlightened nobility, the Muratists longed for a constitution similar to the conservative charter that Louis XVIII had allowed the French people to have.

The Carbonari, or "charcoal burners," were members of a mysterious secret society, an offshoot of freemasonry, which sough to end French rule in Naples. When Ferdinand was restored to power after the Napoleonic Wars, the society split. Some members eagerly accepted Ferdinand, while others pressed for an end to Austrian influence and for social and economic reforms. The Carbonari also wanted a constitution like the Spanish constitution of 1812, which had been drawn up during the revolt against the rule of Joseph Bonaparte in Spain, as amended by the revolutionary government of Spain in 1820. The Carbonari, however, wanted their constitution for the kingdom of Naples to be modeled after the liberal French constitution of 1791.

The effectiveness of the Carbonari was limited by their lack of organization, unified doctrines, and concerted plans of action. To the small proprietors, Carbonarism meant parceling out of the large estates; while to peasants who were normally loyal to the monarchy, it meant land ownership. To all members, Carbonarism signified patriotism. Under the illusion that the Muratists were sympathetic to a liberal constitution, the Carbonari clung to the hope that men such as the Muratist soldier Guglielmo Pepe would channel their enthusiasm and put an end to Bourbon rule. This enthusiasm, which displayed republican tendencies at times, was to become the dynamic of the revolutionary movement.

Between 1815 and 1820, King Ferdinand followed a policy that both alienated and strengthened the dissatisfied factions. When he brought Muratists into his government, they took orders from the Bourbonists. Many Muratist generals, for example, were given commands in the army, which was headed by an Austrian, General Nugent, and a Royal Council of loyal Bourbonists, thereby accentuating the privileges of the Bourbonists.

On the other hand, the Carbonari, victims of an inconsistent policy of persecution, grew in strength as a result of a tax policy initiated by the Italian minister of finance, and many Carbonarist plots and disturbances developed. The Salerno Lodge, the most active, approached Pepe

Metternich, the Austrian minister of foreign affairs. (Library of Congress)

with a plan for revolution under his leadership. He discreetly refused, only to become a major figure after the revolution began.

Meanwhile, the Spanish Revolution of March, 1820, encouraged revolutionary activity in Naples. The government reacted with further suppression, a policy that was difficult to implement through a Muratist-led army. Ferdinand wanted to warn Austria of the impending revolution but was advised that the situation was not serious. Then on July 2, 1820, a Carbonarist-inspired mutiny successfully captured the city of Nola. Led by the radical priest Minichini and Lieutenant Morelli, a follower of Pepe, the mutiny spread throughout the district.

The revolutionary forces enjoyed instant success, thanks to the confusion at Naples, the army loyal to the Muratist leaders, and a militia heavily influenced by the Carbonari. The revolution surprised not only the rest of Europe but also Ferdinand, his court, and, in many ways, the forces of victory—the Carbonari, the Muratists, and the constitutionalists. Because Naples was ostensibly the prosperous capital of a relatively contented kingdom, there was little or no anticipation of the revolution. The Carbonari had attracted cautious vigilance, but they were hardy a powerful force for change. When the Carbonari did manage to stage a major revolt, the monarchy, confused and surprised, was unable to coordinate a counteroffensive. Minichini and Morelli, the leaders of the mutiny at Nola, were pleasantly surprised at the ease with which their revolt gained momentum.

The Carbonari never really completed a comprehensive plan for revolution. By the time the news of their uprising had spread throughout the other lodges, their revolt was a success. Unable to foresee the meaning of the revolt at Nola, Pepe hesitated for two days in Naples before assuming command. The Muratist generals, on the other hand, were also apprehensive about the mutiny because they found themselves in command of forces that they seemed to fear rather than respect. Thus both the court and the constitutionalists were caught unaware as events swiftly climaxed with Pepe's march on Naples, the king's apparent acceptance of the revolution as a fait accompli, and the formation of a provisional government under the leadership of the Muratist generals, who were ill-prepared for their new political responsibilities.

Pepe himself assumed command of the revolutionary district, marched back to Naples, and sent a deputation to the king. Ferdinand took to his bed, appointed his son vicar-general, and agreed to everything. While the Spanish constitution of 1812, freedom of the press, and other reforms were being proclaimed, the king sent a letter to Metternich condemning the revolution and appealing for intervention.

After a relatively bloodless week of revolution, the Bourbon regime had passed from an absolute to a constitutional monarchy. Three main forces emerged during the following months: the Muratist-dominated ministry, the Carbonarist-dominated parliament, and the king. Since the revolution never reached the intensity of a popular uprising, the majority of the people were generally indifferent. Conscious of the threat of intervention by the allies, the Muratists reported the events to the other courts of Europe not as a revolutionary change but as a sort of governmental reorganization. Although the Carbonari constituted a minority in the new parliament, they were able to appeal to the lower classes as they stressed the revolutionary significance of the constitutional government.

Torn between loyalty to the new government and objections to the Carbonarist left-of-center position, the Muratists were weakened by internal conflicts and factionalism. While the Muratists represented moderation and the Carbonari symbolized radicalism, the king plotted with Metternich for a return to absolute government, capitalizing on Muratist and Carbonarist differences, especially on the need to seek allies through diplomacy and to engage in the practical work of reform. The confusion was compounded by the rise of a revolution within the revolution—the Sicilian revolt for autonomy—and civil war followed. From the beginning, the revolution was threatened by intrigue, radical plotting, civil war, and subsequent inability to form a workable coalition. As the only leader who appeared to transcend narrow factional lines, Pepe refused to assume political leadership. Whichever way the revolution went, Metternich was determined to restore Ferdinand to absolute power.

At the time that revolution had broken out in Naples, the allies had already decided to meet at Troppau in order to take up the issue of revolution in Spain. Metternich's plan was to work through the Quadruple Alliance. Great Britain, represented by Viscount Castlereagh, the foreign secretary, favored Austrian intervention, but because of the possibility that the general principle of collective intervention to put down revolution might be contrary to future British interests, Great Britain could not support collective action. Castlereagh refused to sign the Troppau Protocol, in which the other allies refused recognition to all governments that were products of revolution. Specific means for intervention were put off until the January 11, 1821, meeting at Laibach, which Ferdinand was invited to attend.

By then, events in Naples had developed to the point that any workable coalition among the various factions appeared to be impossible. However, the members of the Neapolitan parliament trusted the king when he promised to represent the constitutional position at the Laibach Conference—a meeting that spelled doom to the Neapolitan Revolution. Metternich had little difficulty in convincing the allies of the necessity of sending an Austrian army to Naples. When news of this decision reached Naples, Pepe took command of the Neapolitan army to defend the revolution. With the Austrian army on the border on March 7, 1821, Pepe's army moved north to cross into the Papal States and took the offensive, only to suffer what was to be called the Rout of Rieti. Pepe's efforts were in vain, as the Austrian army once again restored the Bourbon regime of Ferdinand.

The opposition to Bourbon rule, divided against itself, could not withstand the Austrian invasion. Imprisonment, exile, and censorship accompanied the restoration.

Although it put an end to the civil war, the constitutional government was unable to work out practical reform. The Muratist ministry was never in full sympathy with the Spanish constitution, which ushered in a parliament vulnerable to a radical minority. On the other hand, the Carbonari encouraged factionalism and lacked the necessary leadership. Although foreign intervention was almost inevitable, the internal weaknesses of the revolutionary government paved the way for Metternich's easy victory.

SIGNIFICANCE

The significance of the Neapolitan Revolution of 1820 may best be seen in the context of a struggle between the forces of reaction, led by the Quadruple Alliance, and the forces of self-government. The revolt in Naples was part of a larger picture, one that included periodic revolution in northern Italy, as well as revolts in Spain, Greece, France, Belgium, and Poland.

The desire for self-government, as symbolized in the Neapolitan Revolution of 1820, continued to be a strong force in world history through the twentieth century. Although the forces of reaction won a temporary victory in Italy, they were unable to withstand the progress of liberalism once it was wedded to the powerful sentiments of nationalism. Thus, the Neapolitan desire for self-government became an Italian desire and, forty years later, emerged into reality as an independent Italian state.

—*Christopher J. Kauffman, updated by Carl Rollyson*

FURTHER READING

Acton, Harold. *The Bourbons of Naples, 1734-1825.* Vol. 1. London: Methuen, 1956. Offers a story, sympathetic to Ferdinand, of the revolutionary events as viewed from the palace at Naples.

Croce, Benedetto. *History of the Kingdom of Naples.* Reprint. Chicago: University of Chicago Press, 1970. Reprint of 1925 edition that makes available in English a classic work by one of Italy's most renowned writers, praised for his analytical and dramatic style.

Especially relevant is chapter 4, "The Age of Revolutions and the End of the Kingdom."

Davis, John A., ed. *Italy in the Nineteenth Century, 1796-1900.* New York: Oxford University Press, 2000. Collection of essays on a variety of aspects of nineteenth century Italian history.

DiScala, Spencer M. *Italy from Revolution to Republic: 1700 to the Present.* 3d ed. Boulder, Colo.: Westview Press, 2004. Useful overview of modern Italian history that places the Neapolitan Revolution in a broad perspective.

Nicholson, Harold. *The Congress of Vienna: A Study in Allied Unity, 1812-1822.* New York: Grove Press, 2000. Reprint of a classic text first published in 1947 that provides a comprehensive narrative of the negotiations at the Congress and the power struggle among Castlereagh and other participants.

Romani, George T. *The Neapolitan Revolution of 1820-1821.* Evanston, Ill.: Northwestern University Press, 1950. Concentrates primarily on narrating the events leading up to the revolution and the story of the revolution itself.

Schroeder, Paul W. *The Transformation of European Politics, 1763-1848.* Oxford, England: Clarendon Press, 1994. A sweeping, magisterial history. See especially part 3 of chapter 13, "Revolution in Spain and Italy, 1820-1821."

SEE ALSO: May 2, 1808-Nov., 1813: Peninsular War in Spain; Apr. 11, 1814-July 29, 1830: France's Bourbon Dynasty Is Restored; Sept. 15, 1814-June 11, 1815: Congress of Vienna; 1820: Jesuits Are Expelled from Russia, Naples, and Spain; Oct. 20-30, 1822: Great Britain Withdraws from the Concert of Europe; Jan. 12, 1848-Aug. 28, 1849: Italian Revolution of 1848; Mar. 17, 1861: Italy Is Proclaimed a Kingdom.

RELATED ARTICLES in *Great Lives from History: The Nineteenth Century, 1801-1900:* Viscount Castlereagh; Metternich.

1820's

November 6, 1820
AMPÈRE REVEALS MAGNETISM'S RELATIONSHIP TO ELECTRICITY

André Ampère was the first scientist to describe the mathematical relationships between electricity and magnetism, or electrodynamics. His findings led to the modern understanding of light waves and radio waves and to the development of the telegraph.

LOCALE: Paris, France
CATEGORIES: Physics; science and technology; mathematics; radio and television

KEY FIGURES
André-Marie Ampère (1775-1836), French mathematician and physicist
Hans Christian Ørsted (1777-1851), Danish physicist
Félix Savary (1797-1841), French mathematician
Jean-Baptiste Biot (1774-1862), French mathematician and physicist
Félix Savart (1791-1841), French mathematician and physicist
François Arago (1786-1853), French physicist

SUMMARY OF EVENT

The magnetic compass was invented by the Chinese, who used lodestone, a naturally occurring magnetic material, in water compasses to guide ships as early as the eleventh century. Until the early nineteenth century, it was believed that only naturally occurring iron or lodestone was magnetic. In 1820, Danish physicist Hans Christian Ørsted performed a series of science demonstrations in his home for a group of his friends and students. First, Ørsted demonstrated that electric currents caused wires to heat up. He also planned to demonstrate magnetism and mounted a compass needle on a wooden stand. While performing his heating demonstration, Ørsted noticed that each time the electric current was turned on, the compass needle moved, suggesting that the electric current in the wire caused the deflection of the magnetic needle. This experiment provided the first demonstration that there was a relationship between electricity and magnetism.

François Arago, a French physicist and astronomer, reported on Ørsted's discovery at a meeting of the Academy of Sciences in Paris in September, 1820. Arago repeated Ørsted's experiments at an academy meeting and began his own research on the relationship between electricity and magnetism. Just one week later, Arago showed that the passage of an electric current through a cylindrical spiral of copper wire caused it to attract iron filings as if it were a magnet. As soon as the current was turned off, the iron filings fell from the wire. Arago's demonstration was the first use of an electromagnet, a magnet that functions because of the passage of current through a coiled wire.

Another French physicist, André Ampère, a professor of mathematics at the École Polytechnique in Paris, was fascinated by Arago's report of Ørsted's research. Although Ampère was primarily a mathematician, he also worked in a variety of other fields, including metaphysics, physics, and chemistry. He tried not only to repeat and extend Ørsted's experiments but also to develop mathematical laws describing the relationship between electricity and magnetism. Ampère is not recognized as a methodical experimentalist but is known for having brilliant flashes of insight that he pursued to logical conclusions. Within a few weeks, Ampère demonstrated various electrical and magnetic effects to the academy. He recognized that if a current in a wire exerted a magnetic force on a compass needle, then two current-carrying wires should each produce a magnetic field, and the magnetic fields of these wires should interact. By the end of September, 1820, Ampère demonstrated these interactions, observing that two parallel, current-carrying wires are attracted to each other if both currents are in the same direction, and that they repel each other when the two currents flow in opposite directions.

Ampère's discoveries allowed him to design and build an instrument called a galvanometer to measure the flow of electricity. A simple galvanometer is a compass with a conducting wire wrapped around it. When the wire carries an electrical current—as when a wire connects battery terminals—then the current that flows in the wire produces a magnetic field that deflects the compass needle. The stronger the current the larger the deflection of the needle; the position of the needle indicates the amount of current flowing in the wire. Ampère's invention of the galvanometer led him to perform quantitative experiments on the relationship between the amounts of current flowing in pairs of wires and the strength of the magnetic forces between them. This work was critical in the formulation of the equations that relate electricity to magnetism.

Ampère was not the only person who reacted quickly to Arago's report of Ørsted's discovery. Jean-Baptiste Biot and his assistant, mathematician Félix Savart, conducted experiments on electromagnetism and reported to the Paris academy in October, 1820. This led to Biot-Savart's law, which relates the intensity of the magnetic field set up by a current flowing through a wire to the distance from the wire. Another French experimenter who worked on magnetism at that time was Siméon-Denis Poisson, who treated magnetism as a phenomenon completely separate from electricity. Ampère continued his own work as well, describing his law for the addition of "electrodynamical forces" to the academy on November 6, 1820.

During the next few years Ampère was assisted by Félix Savary, who performed many experiments and helped Ampère write up the results. Ampère's most important publication on electricity and magnetism, *Théorie des phénomènes électro-dynamiques* (1826; theory of electrodynamic phenomena), describes four of his experiments and contains the mathematical derivation of the electrodynamic force law. Physicists now refer to one of Ampère's mathematical relationships as Ampère's law, an equation relating the electric current flowing through wires to the strength of the resulting magnetic fields at any distance from the wires.

Ampère also attempted to explain the natural magnetism of compass needles. He knew that when current flows through circular loops of wire, it creates magnets much like those of magnetic compass needles. Noting this, Ampère proposed that each atom of iron contains electric current, turning the atom into a small magnet. In iron magnets, these atomic magnets line up in the same direction, so their total magnetic forces are cumulative.

SIGNIFICANCE

André Ampère's discoveries, as well as François Arago's work, had immediate and practical applications. Once it was discovered that current-carrying wires generate magnetism, it was a simple matter to bend wires into coils that stack many loops of wire on top of one another and strengthen the overall magnetic effect. This finding led to the development of the electromagnet. In 1823, English electrical engineer William Sturgeon wrapped eighteen turns of copper wire around a bar, producing an electromagnet that could lift twenty times its own weight. In 1829, Joseph Henry used insulated wire on his electromagnet, allowing the wires to come closer together without shorting. By 1831, he demonstrated an electromagnet that could lift a ton of iron.

The electromagnet is also the basis for the operation of the telegraph, the first practical means for instant communication over long distances. Samuel F. B. Morse developed the idea of an electromagnetic telegraph in 1832.

Although Morse constructed an experimental version in 1835, the first practical telegraph system was a line from Baltimore to Washington, D.C., that did not begin operation until 1844.

Ampère's discovery also provided an explanation for the earth's magnetic field, arguing that natural lodestone in the earth loses its magnetism at high temperatures, and temperature is known to increase with depth in the earth. A circulating electric current in the earth's core is believed to generate the earth's magnetic field. Finally, the discovery of the link between electricity and magnetism was fundamental to the later understanding of electromagnetic waves, including light waves and radio waves. In 1864, James Clerk Maxwell demonstrated that the connection between the electric and the magnetic forces involved a constant, the velocity of light in a vacuum. The idea that light was an electromagnetic phenomenon evolved from Maxwell's work, which led to the discovery of radio waves, the development of the theory of relativity, and much of twentieth century physics. The fundamental unit of electric current was named the ampere in honor of Ampère's contributions to electromagnetism.

—*George J. Flynn*

FURTHER READING

Asimov, Isaac. *Understanding Physics: Light, Magnetism, and Electricity*. New York: Signet Books, 1966. This volume in Asimov's history of physics includes a chapter on electromagnetism describing Ampère's discoveries and their practical applications.

Darrigol, Oliver. *Electrodynamics from Ampère to Einstein*. New York: Oxford University Press, 2000. A 532-page exploration of the development of electrodynamics, beginning with Ampère's experiments and the formulation of this new field during the early 1820's. A well-documented and well-illustrated account of how Ampère's work, and that of his successors, paved the way for Einstein's theory of relativity.

Hofmann, James R., David Knight, and Sally Gregory Kohlstedt, eds. *André-Marie Ampère: Enlightenment and Electrodynamics*. New York: Cambridge University Press, 1996. A 420-page biography of Ampère, describing his significant contributions to mathematics, chemistry, and physics as well as his development of the new field of electrodynamics.

SEE ALSO: c. 1801-1810: Davy Develops the Arc Lamp; 1814: Fraunhofer Invents the Spectroscope; Oct., 1831: Faraday Converts Magnetic Force into Electricity; May 24, 1844: Morse Sends First Telegraph

Message; 1850-1865: Clausius Formulates the Second Law of Thermodynamics; Nov. 9, 1895: Röntgen Discovers X Rays; June, 1896: Marconi Patents the Wireless Telegraph; Nov. 16, 1896: First U.S. Hydroelectric Plant Opens at Niagara Falls; 1900: Wiechert Invents the Inverted Pendulum Seismograph; Dec. 14, 1900: Articulation of Quantum Theory.

RELATED ARTICLES in *Great Lives from History: The Nineteenth Century, 1801-1900:* The Becquerel Family; William Fothergill Cooke and Charles Wheatstone; Thomas Alva Edison; Michael Faraday; Joseph Henry; James Clerk Maxwell; Samuel F. B. Morse; Wilhelm Conrad Röntgen; George Westinghouse.

March 7, 1821-September 29, 1829
GREEKS FIGHT FOR INDEPENDENCE FROM THE OTTOMAN EMPIRE

In their fight for independence from the Ottoman Turks, the Greeks launched the first successful national revolution during the 1820's, forming an independent state after defeating the Turks.

ALSO KNOWN AS: Greek Revolution; Greek War of Independence

LOCALE: Greece

CATEGORIES: Wars, uprisings, and civil unrest; government and politics

KEY FIGURES

Ibrāhīm Paṣa (1789-1848), leader of the Egyptian invasion of Greece, 1825-1828

Ioánnis Antónios Kapodístrias (1776-1831), first president of Greece, 1827-1831

Theódoros Kolokotrónis (1770-1843), Greek military leader, 1821-1829

Mahmud II (1785-1839), sultan of the Ottoman Empire, r. 1808-1839

Aléxandros Mavrokordátos (1791-1865), president of the Greek National Assembly, 1822

Otto I (Otto of Wittelsbach; 1815-1867), king of Greece, r. 1832-1862

Alexander Ypsilantis (1792-1828), Greek military leader, 1821

SUMMARY OF EVENT

The Greek war of independence from the Ottoman Empire was the culmination of a long historical process that began after the Turks conquered Greece in the fifteenth century and was completed in 1829. For almost four centuries, the Turks ruled over Greece. Turkish rule was generally harsh and became corrupt and even brutal, particularly when the empire began to decline in the eighteenth century.

During the first centuries of their rule over Greece, however, the Turks allowed the Greeks to use their own

language and to exercise their own Orthodox faith. The Greek patriarch of Constantinople (now Istanbul) became the political and spiritual head of all Orthodox Christians in the Balkans. Likewise, a small segment of educated Greeks, known as the Phanariotes, acquired high positions in the Ottoman administration and government. The Greek merchants, too, gradually dominated much of the commerce and trade in the Ottoman Empire. Economic prosperity and intellectual and literary revival in the eighteenth century led to a resurgence of Greek national consciousness. The desire of the Greeks to free themselves from Turkish rule was further stimulated by the French Revolution (1789) and Napoleon and by the rebellion of Ali Pasha of Jannina against the sultan in 1820.

The Greek struggle for independence entered a new phase with the creation of the secret organization of the Philiké Hetairía, or friendly society, in 1814 in the southern Russian city of Odessa. The society's expressed goal was to organize a revolution to free Greece from the Ottoman Empire. Prince Alexander Ypsilantis, a former aide-de-camp of Czar Alexander I of Russia, was chosen head of the Hetairía. Initially, the revolt broke out in the Romanian principalities, where Greek influence was strong and Greek Phanariote princes, appointed by the sultan, ruled them. On March 7, 1821 (February 23 according to the Julian calendar), Ypsilantis crossed the Pruth River from southern Russia into Jassy, the capital of Moldavia (then part of the Ottoman Empire), and called the Greeks to arms. However, Turkish forces entered the Romanian principalities and defeated Ypsilantis's army. He fled to Austria, where he was imprisoned and died in Vienna in 1828.

Simultaneously, a second revolt broke out in the Peloponnesus on March 25, 1821. This day (according to the Julian calendar), is Greece's Independence Day. For the next nine years, the Greek struggle for independence experienced a period of war, internal civil strife, foreign intervention, and finally victory.

The Greek revolution can be conveniently divided into three phases. In the first phase, 1821 to 1824, the revolt spread rapidly throughout the Peloponnesus, central Greece, and the Aegean islands. Within a short time, the Greeks seized several fortresses, towns, and villages, defeating the isolated Turkish forces. However, the conflict was marked from the beginning by a rash of violence and brutality by both sides. The massacre of Turks in Greece set the tone of violence for the war, turning it into a religious conflict. Sultan Mahmud II ordered the hanging in 1821 of Gregory V, the Greek Orthodox patriarch of Constantinople, and several high church officials, arousing indignation and sympathy for the Greek cause among liberals and intellectuals in Europe and the United States.

A pro-Greek movement, known as Philhellenism, gave moral and financial support to the Greek revolutionaries. Volunteers from Europe and the United States came to Greece and joined the Greek struggle. The most notable among them was the English poet Lord Byron, who fought against the Turks and died in Greece in 1824.

The Greeks, in the meantime, fought not only against the Ottoman Turks but also among themselves in a civil war involving various rival political factions competing for power and control of the central government. In 1822, there were two governments: one on mainland Greece, led by the military chieftain Theódoros Kolokotrónis, and the other at the island of Hydra, off the coast of eastern Peloponnesus, headed by Aléxandros Mavrokordátos. Efforts to form a central government failed to resolve the political crisis. Civil war broke out in 1823 and continued throughout 1824, undermining the war efforts against the Turks.

The turning point of the revolution came during the second stage, 1825 to 1827. When the Turks failed to defeat the Greeks both on land and sea, Sultan Mahmud II appealed for military aid to Muḥammad ʿAlī Pasha, the viceroy of Egypt, then a tributary state of the sultan. The viceroy sent a naval force under the command of his stepson, Ibrāhīm Paşa, who landed in southern Peloponnesus

British destruction of the Ottoman fleet in the Battle of Navarino. (Francis R. Niglutsch)

in February of 1825 and began a sweeping campaign to the north, burning and pillaging towns and villages and dispersing the Greek forces. Meanwhile, a temporary reconciliation among the various Greek political and military factions was concluded in 1827. A national assembly met in April and approved a new republican constitution. Count Kapodístrias was elected the first president of the Greek Republic.

The third period, 1827 to 1829, saw the direct involvement of the European powers Great Britain, Russia, and France. They viewed the Greek revolution as a threat to the European balance of power. The fall of the Ottoman Empire would create a power vacuum, but which of the powers would fill it? At the outset, the European powers maintained strict neutrality, hoping for a Turkish victory over the Greeks. However, they eventually intervened in the Greek-Turkish conflict because of the growing European public opinion in favor of the Greeks and because the continuation of the war affected their economic interests in the Mediterranean.

In April of 1826, Great Britain and Russia signed the Protocol of St. Petersburg, which provided for mediation of the conflict on the basis of establishing an autonomous Greece but tributary to the sultan. The Turks, however, flushed with their recent military successes, refused mediation, while the Greeks accepted it. In July of 1827, France joined the two powers and signed the Treaty of London, which called for an immediate armistice between the two belligerents. If one of the parties were to refuse mediation, the powers would intervene militarily to end hostilities between the Turks and Greeks. The Turks declined allied mediation, thus compelling the powers to dispatch a combined naval force to the Greek waters with orders to avoid hostilities unless provoked.

The allied warships met the Turko-Egyptian fleet at the narrow Bay of Navarino (Pylos) in southwest Peloponnesus. A Turkish soldier fired and killed a British officer. This incident precipitated the naval Battle of Navarino in October of 1827, in which nearly the entire Turko-Egyptian fleet was destroyed. Navarino was a major turning point in ensuring Greek independence.

Appalled by the action of the allied powers, Sultan Mahmud II proclaimed a holy war on Russia, the historical adversary of the Turks. In turn, Czar Nicholas I retaliated by declaring war on the Ottoman Empire in April, 1828. The Russian army reached the outskirts of Constantinople in September, 1829, and forced the Turkish government to sign the Treaty of Adrianople. By the terms of the treaty the sultan recognized the independence of Greece.

SIGNIFICANCE

In February of 1830, Britain, Russia, and France signed the London Protocol, which negated the republican constitution and declared Greece an independent kingdom under the guarantee of the three allied powers. They offered the crown to Prince Otto (who became Otto I), the son of the king of Bavaria. Otto arrived at Nafplion, the provisional capital of Greece, in February of 1833, and Greece began its modern existence as an independent kingdom under a foreign dynasty.

—*James J. Farsolas*

FURTHER READING

Brewer, David. *The Greek War of Independence: The Struggle for Freedom from Ottoman Oppression and the Birth of the Modern Greek Nation.* Woodstock, N.Y.: Overlook Press, 2001. A useful survey of the Greek struggle against the Ottoman Empire.

Clogg, Richard. *A Short History of Modern Greece.* 2d ed. New York: Cambridge University Press, 1986. A summary of the history of Greece from the fall of Byzantium, through the war of independence, and to the major political events in the twentieth century.

_____, ed. *The Struggle for Greek Independence: Essays to Mark the 150th Anniversary of the Greek War of Independence.* Hamden, Conn.: Archon Books, 1973. A collection of scholarly articles dealing with different issues of the war of Greek independence.

Crawley, Charles W. *The Question of Greek Independence: A Study of British Policy in the Near East, 1821-1833.* Reprint. New York: Howard Fertig, 1973. First published in 1930, Crawley's book remains the standard work on British and European diplomacy during the Greek war of independence.

Dakin, Douglas. *The Greek Struggle for Independence, 1821-1833.* Berkeley: University of California Press, 1973. A thorough and balanced account of the domestic affairs and European diplomatic involvement in the Greek revolution.

Fleming, K. E. *The Muslim Bonaparte.* Princeton, N.J.: Princeton University Press, 2000. A scholarly work addressing how modern Greece, in the context of European history, came under a surrogate form of colonial control—in which Greek history and culture became colonized.

MacKenzie, David, ed. *Violent Solutions: Revolutions, Nationalism, and Secret Societies in Europe to 1918.* Lanham, Md.: University Press of America, 1996. An account of the underground groups that fomented revolutions and movements for independence in modern

Europe. Chapter 8 discusses the Greek revolution, Greece under Turkish rule, and Philiké Hetairía, the secret revolutionary society.

Roesse, David E. *In Byron's Shadow: Modern Greece in English and American Literature from 1770 to 1967.* New York: Oxford University Press, 2001. Discusses the beginnings of the Greek war of independence against Ottoman rule.

Woodhouse, Christopher M. *The Battle of Navarino.* Chester Springs, Pa.: Dufour Editions, 1965. This work provides a detailed account of the events leading to naval battle in 1827 and the defeat of the Turko-Egyptian fleet by the combined British, Russian, and French warships.

_____. *The Greek War of Independence: Its Historical Setting.* Reprint. New York: Russell & Russell, 1975. A concise analysis of the origin, the course of the revolution, and the recognition of Greece's independence in 1832.

SEE ALSO: 1803-1812: Elgin Ships Parthenon Marbles to England; Oct. 20-30, 1822: Great Britain Withdraws from the Concert of Europe; Apr. 26, 1828-Aug. 28, 1829: Second Russo-Turkish War; Sept. 24, 1829: Treaty of Adrianople; 1832-1841: Turko-Egyptian Wars; 1863-1913: Greece Unifies Under the Glücksburg Dynasty; Apr. 24, 1877-Jan. 31, 1878: Third Russo-Turkish War; Jan. 21-May 20, 1897: Greco-Turkish War.

RELATED ARTICLES in *Great Lives from History: The Nineteenth Century, 1801-1900:* Alexander I; Ali Paşa Tepelenë; Lord Byron; Muḥammad ʿAlī Pasha; Nicholas I; Alexander and Demetrios Ypsilantis.

September, 1821
SANTA FE TRAIL OPENS

The opening of the Santa Fe Trail extended American commerce to the Mexican-ruled Southwest, helped to disintegrate the Indian frontier, and paved the way for the later U.S. occupation of the Southwest.

LOCALE: Southwestern United States

CATEGORIES: Transportation; expansion and land acquisition; trade and commerce

KEY FIGURES

William Becknell (1787/1788-1856), trailblazer credited with opening the Santa Fe route for trade purposes

Jacob Fowler (1765-1850) and

Hugh Glenn (1788-1833), traders who sold goods in Santa Fe in 1821

Thomas James (1782-1847), St. Louis merchant who traded on the Santa Fe Trail

SUMMARY OF EVENT

During the early years of the nineteenth century, Santa Fe was an isolated Spanish outpost fifteen hundred miles from the center of Spanish authority in Mexico City. Its inhabitants possessed an abundance of silver, furs, and mules, but they suffered from a lack of fabricated goods. Traders on the Missouri frontier were eager to obtain products from Santa Fe in exchange for inexpensive textiles, cutlery, utensils, and a wide variety of other items. The mutual advantage of trade was obvious, but venture-some traders arriving in Santa Fe between 1804 and 1820 were forcefully reminded that the Spanish Empire was not open to foreigners. Those who failed to heed the warnings had their property confiscated, and some were imprisoned. Mexico's overthrow of Spanish rule, which was achieved in 1821, brought an end to Spanish restrictions on commerce in New Mexico, which became a northern province of the Republic of Mexico.

The Mexican War of Independence and the Panic of 1819 in the United States intensified the need for commerce between the United States and Mexico. For years, Mexico had suffered from currency depletion, as its mineral wealth was shipped to faraway Spain. The revolution, which lasted more than a decade, further weakened the Mexican economy. At the same time, the Panic of 1819 worsened a currency shortage in the western United States. Adventurers hoped to trade durable goods in New Mexico for precious metals, easing their fiscal plight.

In the long run, the conditions that prompted trade did not produce economic equality. Between 1821 and 1846, the Santa Fe Trail, which connected Independence, Missouri, and Santa Fe, served as a conduit of economic and social change. Mexican officials lacked the personnel to regulate the northern border, so smuggling was rife. North-south trade within Mexico was reoriented to an east-west trade along the Santa Fe Trail, resulting in a further loss of Mexican wealth. Euro-American mer-

Contemporary illustration of a wagon train approaching the town of Santa Fe on the Santa Fe Trail. (Courtesy, Museum of New Mexico)

chants married Mexican and Indian women, contributing to the social diversity of the Southwest. Euro-American entrepreneurs displaced many Mexican merchants who earlier had traded in New Mexico.

The initial exchange along the Santa Fe Trail occurred in September, 1821, when William Becknell and his band of thirty men, who had been catching horses near Raton, New Mexico, learned of Mexican independence and proceeded to Santa Fe, where the party exchanged their supplies for silver dollars. The exchange was lucrative: One investor in Becknell's expedition reaped a return of nine hundred dollars on a sixty-dollar investment.

Even before Euro-Americans learned how profitable the Santa Fe trade could be, other trading parties followed Becknell. Thomas James of St. Louis reached Santa Fe in December, 1821, and spent the winter there attempting to persuade its citizens to buy his drab cotton fabrics. Another party, led by Jacob Fowler and Hugh Glenn, reached Santa Fe and enjoyed a profitable business. Fowler had first scouted the Sangre de Cristo Mountains to the north and concluded that a profitable fur trade could be developed.

During the following spring, William Becknell and a score of men returned to Santa Fe with three wagons of merchandise. Becknell thus gained celebrity as the founder of the Santa Fe trade. Knowing that it would be difficult to ascend Raton Pass with heavily laden wagons, Becknell pioneered a new direct route to Santa Fe from the Arkansas River Crossing through the Cimarron Desert, a route known as the Cimarron Cutoff.

By 1824, wagons were being used extensively on the trail, and the numbers of people and amounts of goods increased steadily each year until 1838, despite many difficulties. Hazards included the problems of conducting wagon trains across treeless plains and desert terrain and the chances of attack by Kiowas and Comanches, who resented having their homelands invaded. Upon arriving in Santa Fe, traders had to pay import taxes that sometimes ran as high as 60 percent of the value of their goods. To avoid paying taxes, traders often resorted to bribery. In 1839, the Mexican government moved to counter cheating by imposing a flat tax of five hundred dollars per wagon. This measure merely encouraged traders to use larger wagons, which they often overloaded. Nevertheless, despite the taxes and uncertainties, the average wagon train earned a profit of between 10 and 40 percent.

SIGNIFICANCE

In the total economy of the American West, the value of the Santa Fe trade was minimal, averaging only $130,000 a year between 1822 and 1843. The best year was 1841, when the value of trade goods reached $450,000. The trade was temporarily stopped by the Mexican government between 1843 and 1844 but was revived during the Mexican War and attained a wartime peak value of $1,752,250 in 1846. The business continued after the war, not as an international trade but as a means of supplying U.S. military forces in the Southwest. Trade was also brisk during the Civil War (1861-1865), and the Santa Fe Trail continued to be used for commercial purposes until the railroad era.

This military commerce resulted from the U.S. policy of trying to maintain a permanent American Indian frontier along the western boundary of Missouri, while simultaneously trying to guarantee the plains region to the tribes and encouraging and protecting traders who were intruding upon Indian domains. Major Stephen Cooper had led a company of thirty traders to Santa Fe in 1823. Two years later, the federal government appropriated thirty thousand dollars to mark the route within the limits of the United States and to seek concessions from the tribes guaranteeing safe passage to the traders. However, the markings were made of earthen and stone mounds and were placed upon the little used and longer Mountain Route that ascended the Arkansas River to Bent's Fort near La Junta, Colorado, thence south to Santa Fe, rather than along the Cimarron Cutoff.

Fort Leavenworth was established in 1827, principally to guard the trail, but the following year, Native Americans attacked the caravans headed for Santa Fe. Several traders were killed, others were robbed, wagons were abandoned when the animals drawing them were killed, and at least one party had to walk home. Military escorts were provided at government expense in 1829, 1834, and 1843 to protect the traders as far as the United States boundary. After the Mexican War, additional forts were erected. These forts not only helped to secure trade over the Santa Fe Trail but also provided new markets for agricultural products raised in the Southwest.

The Santa Fe trade not only initiated the disintegration of the permanent Indian frontier but also turned the attention of the United States toward the Mexican territory in the Southwest. Reports from traders dispelled the illusion of Mexican military power and demonstrated the ease with which the United States might take over the region. In addition, Santa Fe traders assisted in destroying the concept that the Great Plains were the Great American Desert.

—W. Turrentine Jackson,
updated by Edward R. Crowther

FURTHER READING

Coues, Elliot, ed. *The Journal of Jacob Fowler, 1821-1822*. New York: Frances P. Harper, 1898. The classic work describing how Fowler and Hugh Glenn followed the course of the Arkansas River and secured permission to trap and trade in Mexican territory in 1821.

Dary, David. *The Santa Fe Trail: Its History, Legends, and Lore*. Reprint. New York: Penguin Books, 2002. Engagingly written account of the full history of the Santa Fe Trail.

DeBuys, William. *Enchantment and Exploitation: The Life and Hard Times of a New Mexican Mountain Range*. Albuquerque: University of New Mexico Press, 1985. Details the social and economic changes of the lower Rockies after the opening of trade between Mexico and the United States along the Santa Fe Trail.

Field, Matthew C. *Matt Field on the Santa Fe Trail*. Edited by John E. Sunder. Norman: University of Oklahoma Press, 1960. A vivid memoir of an able journalist who spent the summer of 1839 on the Santa Fe Trail and in the settlements of New Mexico.

Gregg, Kate L. *The Road to Santa Fe*. Albuquerque: University of New Mexico Press, 1952. A definitive account of the survey and marking of the Santa Fe Trail by the U.S. government, 1825-1827. Includes the journals and diaries of George Champlin Sibley and others.

Hall, Thomas D. *Social Change in the Southwest, 1350-1880*. Lawrence: University Press of Kansas, 1989. Details the impact of marriage and commerce on family units in the Rio Grande region.

Magoffin, Susan S. *Down the Santa Fe Trail and into Mexico: The Diary of Susan Shelby Magoffin, 1846-1847*. Edited by Stella M. Drumm. Rev. ed. New Haven, Conn.: Yale University Press, 1962. The account of an observant young woman who accompanied her husband, a veteran Santa Fe trader, to New Mexico and south to Chihuahua City during the Mexican War.

Moorhead, Max L. *New Mexico's Royal Road: Trade and Travel on the Chihuahua Trail*. Norman: University of Oklahoma Press, 1958. A scholarly and interpretive study emphasizing the nature and importance

1820's

of trade between Santa Fe and Chihuahua City and explaining its relationship to the Santa Fe Trail.

Simmons, Marc, and Hal Jackson. *Following the Santa Fe Trail: A Guide for Modern Travelers*. Rev. ed. Santa Fe, N.Mex.: Ancient City Press, 2001. Modern travel book that follows the historic Santa Fe Trail, providing numerous photographs, maps, and directions that make it easy to connect historical sites with modern locations.

Vestal, Stanley. *The Old Santa Fe Trail*. Boston: Houghton Mifflin, 1939. A popular account that attempts to recapture the experience of those who traveled to Santa Fe.

Young, Otis. *The First Military Escort on the Santa Fe Trail, 1829*. Glendale, Calif.: Arthur H. Clark, 1952.

Synthesizes available source materials to describe the attacks made on caravans traversing the Santa Fe Trail in 1828.

SEE ALSO: July 15, 1806-July 1, 1807: Pike Explores the American Southwest; Apr. 6, 1808: American Fur Company Is Chartered; 1822-1831: Jedediah Smith Explores the Far West; May, 1842-1854: Frémont Explores the American West; June 30, 1846-Jan. 13, 1847: United States Occupies California and the Southwest; Jan. 19-Feb. 3, 1847: Taos Rebellion; 1867: Chisholm Trail Opens.

RELATED ARTICLES in *Great Lives from History: The Nineteenth Century, 1801-1900:* Kit Carson; Zebulon Pike; Jedediah Smith.

1822-1831
JEDEDIAH SMITH EXPLORES THE FAR WEST

During Jedediah Smith's brief career as a fur trapper and trader, he led several major exploratory expeditions into the Far West and helped open new routes across the continent to the Pacific Ocean.

LOCALE: Region between Mississippi River and Pacific coast

CATEGORIES: Expansion and land acquisition; exploration and discovery

KEY FIGURES

Jedediah Smith (1799-1831), partner in the Rocky Mountain Fur Company and a pathfinder to California

William H. Ashley (1778-1838), military officer who sent Smith on his first expedition to the Pacific

Harrison G. Rogers (d. 1828), quartermaster of Smith's expedition who wrote a chronicle of its journey

José María de Echeandia (d. 1852?), Mexican governor of California, 1825-1831

John McLoughlin (1784-1857), buyer for the Hudson's Bay Company at Fort Vancouver

SUMMARY OF EVENT

A native of Chenango County, New York, Jedediah Smith learned to read and write before he and his family moved to St. Louis in 1816. There he soon became interested in fur trapping and began his trapping career in Missouri in 1822 when he was about twenty-three years

old. Over the next decade, long before the Southwest was ceded to the United States, Smith would twice traverse the country and help open the region to American settlement.

Smith's career shows both entrepreneurship and adventure. His first trek to the Pacific coast began in 1822, after he had read a notice in the *Missouri Gazette and Public Advertiser* of U.S. Army general William H. Ashley's plan to hire one hundred men to ascend the Missouri River to work at its headwaters for one to three years. By November, Smith and twelve companions had reached the mouth of the Musselshell River in Blackfoot country. Eight returned east before winter snows cut off transportation routes, while Smith and four others wintered there. The following year, Smith joined an expedition that followed the South Platte River to cross the Continental Divide at what became known as Bridger Pass. From there, they crossed the mountains of northern Colorado, the Great Basin, and the Green River Canyon. Smith continued on to the Pacific.

In 1825, Smith joined forces with Ashley, and a year later he joined with David E. Jackson and William L. Sublette to buy out Ashley and form the Rocky Mountain Fur Company—an enterprise that would become one of the most famous fur-trading companies. Smith and his partners were better trappers and traders than those of John Jacob Astor's American Fur Company. However, they generally suffered greater losses to Native Americans.

During the late summer of 1826, Smith arrived at the rendezvous of the Rocky Mountain Fur Company located at the Great Salt Lake, loaded with goods from the East. His express purpose was to explore the territory south and west of the lake while his partners conducted the fall hunt. Smith and a party of sixteen men left the lake in mid-August, traveled southwest to Utah Lake, and then, by way of the Sevier River, crossed a mountain range to the Virgin River, which they followed to the Colorado River. There, they crossed to the Colorado's east bank and then rode through the Black Mountain country of Arizona for four days before reaching an area occupied by the Mojave tribe.

After resting with the Mojave for more than two weeks and collecting information about the surrounding territory, Smith's party set out across the Mojave Desert on November 10, 1826. They were guided by two Native Americans who had fled from a Spanish mission in Southern California. Although their exact course for this stage of the journey is unclear, they undoubtedly traveled westward along the earlier Native American trade routes, which were much the same as those later followed by the Santa Fe Railroad. They crossed the Sierra Madre range (later known as the San Gabriel Mountains), probably using Cajon Pass, and camped a short distance from the San Gabriel Mission. Completion of this journey made Smith's party the first U.S. expedition to travel overland through the Southwest to California.

Although Mexican law forbade their presence in California, Smith and his men were hospitably received by the Franciscan monks at the mission. Governor José María de Echeandía, however, viewed the American traders as intruders and purposely delayed answering a letter from Smith requesting permission to journey through the province. After waiting ten days for a reply, Smith went to San Diego to plead with the governor in person. Mollified by Smith's action and his gift of beaver skins, Echeandía finally agreed not to imprison Smith and his men for violating the border, on condition that they leave California in the direction from which they had come.

Smith ignored the governor's instructions and led his party—minus two men who succumbed to the charms of California mission life—back through the Cajon Pass. From there, they went either west across the Tejon or north across the Tehachapi Pass into the San Joaquin Valley. Leaving his men behind to trap beaver, Smith, Silas Gobel, and Robert Evans ascended the middle fork of the Stanislaus River to cross the towering Sierra Nevada. On May 20, 1827, the three men began an eight-day trek across the mountains near Ebbetts Pass to the headwaters of the Walker River, which flowed into Walker Lake. Almost nothing is known of Smith's route across the Great Basin, but he probably went east to the vicinity of what became Ely, Nevada, then northeast to the Great Salt Lake, where he and his associates arrived in June after a punishing journey.

After a brief rest, Smith set out with nineteen men in mid-July to rejoin his hunters in California, as he had promised. Retracing his route of the previous year, the party arrived at the Mojave villages, where Indians surprised and killed ten of Smith's company. The remainder abandoned most of their belongings and traveled as fast as they could across the desert to the San Gabriel Mission. Meanwhile, Smith rejoined the hunters he had left in the San Joaquin Valley. The necessity for obtaining food and supplies caused him then to go to the San José Mission, where he was arrested and placed in jail and denied access to Governor Echeandía for a time. He was finally permitted to talk with Echeandía in Monterey, but only the intervention of several American merchant ship captains prevented his being sent to a Mexican prison. He was forced to post a thirty-thousand-dollar bond to guarantee his departure from California within two months.

From Monterey, Smith's route took him northward to the head of the Sacramento River, then west, probably along the Trinity River to the coast, and northward to the Umpqua River in Oregon. While Smith's party was encamped on this stream, local Indians attacked them. Only Smith and two of his men survived, and all their furs were stolen. Among the dead was Harrison G. Rogers, the expedition's clerk and quartermaster. When Smith had returned to the Great Salt Lake the year before, he had left Rogers in charge of the party in the San Joaquin Valley, and Rogers had kept a journal of his experiences.

The three survivors made their way north to Fort Vancouver, the Hudson's Bay Company's post on the Columbia River, where Dr. John McLoughlin, the chief factor, gave them aid and sent a party to regain the captured furs, which he subsequently purchased for twenty thousand dollars. The act was a generous one, for Smith himself had no means of transporting the large collection of furs back to the Great Salt Lake. However, McLoughlin exacted a promise that the Rocky Mountain Fur Company would not again penetrate the Northwest. In the spring of 1828, Smith and one companion made their way to Pierre's Hole on the western side of the Teton Mountains, where they rejoined Smith's partners, Jackson and Sublette.

1820's

In 1830, Smith sold his interest in the Rocky Mountain Fur Company. The following year, Comanche warriors killed him at a watering hole on the Sante Fe Trail as he was traveling to Taos. He was only thirty-two years old.

SIGNIFICANCE

Smith's achievement was his exploration of a new route from the Great Salt Lake southwest into California. His expeditions made the first crossing of the Sierra and opened another route across the Great Basin desert to the Great Salt Lake. In marching to the Columbia River, his men were the first American party to explore the great interior valleys of California. They opened a north-south route and made known California's potential for U.S. traders and settlers. Smith thus became the first U.S. explorer to mark both a central and a southern route across the continent to the Pacific.

—W. Turrentine Jackson,
updated by Duncan R. Jamieson

FURTHER READING

Dale, Harrison C., ed. *The Ashley-Smith Explorations and the Discovery of a Central Route to the Pacific, 1822-1829*. Rev. ed. Glendale, Calif.: Arthur H. Clark, 1941. First published in 1918, this monograph was for years the standard account of Jedediah Smith's activities. Opened new vistas on the fur trade history and emphasized the interrelationship between trading and exploration.

Douthit, Nathan. *A Guide to Oregon South Coast History: Traveling the Jedediah Smith Trail*. Corvallis: Oregon State University Press, 1999. Practical travel guide to Oregon's southern coast with considerable information on local ethnography and history written by a professional historian. The second section of the book retraces Smith's 1828 route.

Morgan, Dale L. *Jedediah Smith and the Opening of the West*. 1953. Reprint. Lincoln: University of Nebraska Press, 1994. A good biography of Smith that is also a history of the mountain men and their experiences. Despite limited factual information, Morgan dispels some of the myths surrounding Smith's experiences.

Neihardt, John G. *Splendid Wayfaring: The Exploits and Adventures of Jedediah Smith and the Ashley-Henry Men*. 1970. Reprint. Lincoln: University of Nebraska Press, 1990. Analyzes the Ashley-Smith explorations.

Smith, Alson J. *Men Against the Mountains: Jedediah Smith and the South West Expedition of 1826-1829*. New York: John Day, 1965. A popular, well-written book, carefully based on the scholarly accounts of Dale, Morgan, and Sullivan.

Smith, Jedediah Strong. *The Southwest Expedition of Jedediah S. Smith: His Personal Account of the Journey to California, 1826-1827*. Edited by George R. Brooks. 1977. Reprint. Lincoln: University of Nebraska Press, 1989. These accounts, by the explorer himself, are supplemented by a bibliography and an index.

Sullivan, Maurice S. *The Travels of Jedediah Smith*. Lincoln: University of Nebraska Press, 1992. Originally published in 1934 using materials from Smith's surviving journals, this book has long been considered the definitive reference on Smith's life and travels.

White, Richard. *"It's Your Misfortune and None of My Own": A History of the American West*. Norman: University of Oklahoma Press, 1991. A scholarly, readable narrative that places Smith in the history of the West.

Wood, Raymund F., ed. *Jedediah Smith and His Monuments: Bicentennial Edition, 1799-1999*. Rev. ed. Stockton, Calif.: Jedediah Smith Society, 1999. Collection of documents and illustrations relating to Smith's explorations published as part of the celebration of the bicentennial of his birth. Includes a folding map of his travels.

SEE ALSO: May 14, 1804-Sept. 23, 1806: Lewis and Clark Expedition; July 15, 1806-July 1, 1807: Pike Explores the American Southwest; Apr. 6, 1808: American Fur Company Is Chartered; Sept. 8, 1810-May, 1812: Astorian Expeditions Explore the Pacific Northwest; Sept., 1821: Santa Fe Trail Opens; May, 1842-1854: Frémont Explores the American West; Feb. 4, 1846: Mormons Begin Migration to Utah; Mar. 2, 1853-1857: Pacific Railroad Surveys; 1867: Chisholm Trail Opens; 1879: Powell Publishes His Report on the American West.

RELATED ARTICLES in *Great Lives from History: The Nineteenth Century, 1801-1900:* John Jacob Astor; Zebulon Pike; John Wesley Powell; Jedediah Smith; David Thompson.

1822-1874
EXPLORATION OF NORTH AFRICA

European interest in advancing geographical and scientific knowledge, expanding trade, spreading Christianity, and abolishing the slave trade prompted European explorers to examine the interior of northern Africa closely during the nineteenth century.

LOCALE: North Africa
CATEGORIES: Exploration and discovery; geography

KEY FIGURES

Walter Oudney (1790-1832), Scottish doctor, botanist, and explorer
Hugh Clapperton (1788-1827), British naval officer and explorer
René-Auguste Caillié (1799-1838), French explorer
James Richardson (1806-1851), British minister, explorer, and antislavery agent
Heinrich Barth (1821-1865), German scholar and explorer
Adolf Overweg (1822-1852), German geologist, astronomer, and explorer
Gustav Nachtigal (1834-1885), German physician, diplomat, and explorer
Friedrich Gerhard Rohlfs ((1831-1896), German soldier and explorer

SUMMARY OF EVENT

At the beginning of the nineteenth century, much of the coast of North Africa remained under the nominal control of Turkey's Ottoman Empire, but piracy, European imperialism, and the Ottomans' own inefficiency were weakening the empire's grasp. The interior regions of North Africa—across which stretched the vast and forbidding Sahara Desert—remained a mystery to Europeans and Ottomans alike. During the early 1820's, a handful of adventurous Europeans, supported by their governments and private organizations, set out to investigate the Sahara's secrets.

In 1822, the Scottish doctor and botanist Walter Oudney, British naval lieutenant Hugh Clapperton, and British army officer Dixon Denham went south from the Mediterranean port of Tripoli, which is now in Libya, hoping to chart the course of the largest river in West Africa, the Niger. After a delay of several months in the oasis of Marzuq, they reached Lake Chad on February 4, 1823. Immense but shallow, Lake Chad now connects the corners of modern Niger, Nigeria, Cameroon, and Chad. The expedition was to disprove the theory that wa-

ters of the Niger flowed into Lake Chad and from there connected to the Nile, but not before the death of Oudney in January, 1824.

Located on the upper Niger River in what is now Mali, Timbuktu was a lure for numerous explorers. Believed to be a fabulously wealthy center of commerce and culture, the city had excited the imagination of Europeans for centuries. Like most sites in and near the Sahara, however, it was accessible only by camel caravans, whose leaders guarded the secrets of their routes closely. The shipwrecked American sailor Robert Adams had apparently been taken to the city as a captive in 1811, but his account of his adventures was dismissed at the time. The Scottish explorer Gordon Laing reached Timbuktu in 1826 but was killed soon after leaving the city—an early example of the hostility that strangers, especially Christians, would arouse among the predominantly Muslim peoples of the Sahara.

Hoping to resolve the mystery of the city, the Geographical Society of Paris announced a prize in 1825 to be awarded to the first person to bring back an authentic firsthand account of Timbuktu. The offer was to spur Frenchman René-Auguste Caillié to greater efforts. Although Caillié's first two attempts at exploration had been ended by illnesses, he returned to West Africa in 1824 planning to disguise himself as an Arab traveler. The French government of Senegal refused its support, however, and Caillié went to work instead in the adjacent British colony of Sierra Leone. It was there that he learned of the society's prize.

In mid-1827, Caillié set out with a caravan, pretending to be an Egyptian. After enduring nearly a year of illness and physical privation, he reached the fabled city in late April, 1828. After remaining for only two weeks, he joined another caravan, but his companions' suspicions of his true identity led him to desert the group. Caillié eventually reached Tangier, Morocco, in August and returned to France, where he duly collected the Geographical Society's award. However, his description of Timbuktu—which contained little more than a collection of mud dwellings—was disappointing to geographers and the general public alike.

The next man to explore the region was a member of Britain's Anti-Slavery Society. The British Protestant minister James Richardson intended to spread Christianity and to help abolish the slave trade. His first important expedition, in 1845, took him across what is today Libya,

The West African city of Timbuktu in 1828, from a drawing by René-Auguste Caillié. (Hulton Archive/Getty Images)

navigate the lake, but he, too, died on September 27, 1852.

Barth was meanwhile reconnoitering the Benue and Shari Rivers, determining that the former emptied into the Niger River and the latter into Lake Chad. Intending next to head east, Barth instead received instructions from the expedition's sponsors to proceed west to Timbuktu. The trip was a dangerous one, but Barth disguised himself as a Muslim holy man and reached the city on September 7, 1853. He appears to have been in danger the entire time that he was in Timbuktu, and he managed to leave only in May, 1854. In August, 1855, he reached Tripoli by returning past Lake Chad.

Two other Germans, Friedrich Gerhard Rohlfs and Gustav Nachtigal, built on Barth's achievements, carrying out extensive explorations of North Africa during the latter part of the nineteenth century. Rohlfs had already made two abortive attempts to reach Timbuktu in 1862, and became the first European to visit the oasis of Touat and the first since Caillié to visit Tafilet—both places that are now in Algeria. In 1865, he undertook a far more ambitious expedition. Departing from Tripoli, he crossed the Sahara to Lake Chad. He then followed the Benue and Niger Rivers downstream. In the process, he became the first European to cross the African continent from the Mediterranean to the Gulf of Guinea, the arm of the Atlantic Ocean lying south of the bulge of West Africa.

During the following decades, Rohlfs's interests shifted to the eastern Sahara. When the German colonial office asked him to visit the Kingdom of Bornu, on the southwest side of Lake Chad, on a diplomatic mission, he urged his government to send fellow countryman Gustav Nachtigal in his place. A doctor whose lung problems had led him to seek the dry climate of North Africa, Nachtigal gladly undertook the mission. He departed from the Mediterranean coast in February, 1869, passed through Marzuq, and paid a perilous visit to the oasis of Tibesti (now in Chad). Nachtigal eventually reached Bornu, which his diplomatic skills allowed him to use as a base for further exploration over the next few years. On the final leg of these journeys, he traveled eastward to Khartoum on the Nile River, which he reached in 1874.

from Tripoli, southwest to the oases of Ghudamis and Ghat. After compiling copious notes on the societies of the region and its caravan routes, Richardson returned to Tripoli two years later.

Richardson's next venture was the sonorously titled English Mixed Scientific and Commercial Expedition, an ambitious expedition undertaken to encourage commerce, extend scientific knowledge, and combat slavery. Richardson was accompanied by the German scholar Heinrich Barth, who had already traveled throughout the Middle East, and the German scientist Adolf Overweg. Their expedition set out from Tripoli in early 1850, stopping at Marzuq and Agadez (now in Niger). Near the latter the three men separated, with Richardson, whose relations with his German companions had soured, setting out to the southeast for Lake Chad.

Meanwhile, Barth continued going south into what is now Nigeria, while Overweg made for the town of Maradi (now in Niger). The three explorers had agreed to join up again on the southwestern shore of Lake Chad, but Richardson contracted a tropical disease and died on March 4, 1851. Overweg rejoined Barth as planned, and the two made extensive surveys of the lake region. Overweg became the first known European to circum-

SIGNIFICANCE

North Africa's European explorers displayed a keen desire to share their discoveries with the rest of the world by recording their experiences and observations in often encyclopedic detail. Barth's account of his ten-thousand-mile, six-year journey, *Reisen und entdeckungen in Nord- und Central-Afrika in den jahren 1849 bi 1855* (1857-1858; *Travels and Discoveries in North and Central Africa*, 1859), describes his identification of prehistoric and Roman habitations, the sophisticated customs and occasional hostility of the native peoples, and the nearly unbearable heat of the desert. Nachtigal produced an equally extensive record in *Saharâ und Sûdân* (1879-1881; *Sahara and Sudan*, 1971-1975).

By the time Nachtigal's work was published, the broad outlines of North African geography had been established, paving the way for European imperial ambitions. Nachtigal's later career illustrates this shift clearly, as he joined the Kolonialverein, an organization devoted to the encouragement of German colonization. He was also later involved in the sometimes forceful establishment of colonies in western and southwestern Africa.

Although Caillié and Barth confirmed the fabled Timbuktu's squalor, its name has remained a byword for remoteness and romance. It is a reminder of the powerful attraction of the unknown in human history and affairs.

—*Grove Koger*

FURTHER READING

Gardner, Brian. *The Quest for Timbuctoo.* New York: Harcourt, Brace & World, 1968. Brief and easily readable survey of American, British, and European attempts to reach the city. Map, black-and-white illustrations, chronology, brief bibliography.

La Gueriviere, Jean de. *The Exploration of Africa.* Woodstock, N.Y.: Overlook Duckworth, 2003. At-

tractively illustrated volume that emphasizes French explorers, some of whom are little known to English readers. Map, bibliography, numerous illustrations.

McLynn, Frank. *Hearts of Darkness: The European Exploration of Africa.* New York: Carroll & Graf, 1992. Continent-wide survey emphasizing the mechanics of exploration and the darker aspects of the explorers' personalities. Illustrations, maps, bibliographical essay.

Porch, Douglas. *The Conquest of the Sahara.* New York: Alfred A. Knopf, 1984. Popular history of French exploration and conquest in North Africa, including an account of Caillié's journey. Map, bibliography.

Sattin, Anthony. *The Gates of Africa: Death, Discovery, and the Search for Timbuktu.* New York: St. Martin's Press, 2005. History of the African Association and the expeditions it sponsored in the northern half of the continent. Illustrations, maps, chronology, bibliography.

SEE ALSO: Summer, 1801-Summer, 1805: Tripolitan War; May 4, 1805-1830: Exploration of West Africa; Mar. 22, 1812: Burckhardt Discovers Egypt's Abu Simbel; 1814-1879: Exploration of Arabia; June 14-July 5, 1830: France Conquers Algeria; 1832-1847: Abdelkader Leads Algeria Against France; 1848-1889: Exploration of East Africa; Sept. 13, 1882: Battle of Tel el Kebir; Mar. 13, 1884-Jan. 26, 1885: Siege of Khartoum; Nov. 15, 1884-Feb. 26, 1885: Berlin Conference Lays Groundwork for the Partition of Africa.

RELATED ARTICLES in *Great Lives from History: The Nineteenth Century, 1801-1900:* Sir Richard Francis Burton; Mary Kingsley; John Hanning Speke; Henry Morton Stanley.

1820's

September 7, 1822
BRAZIL BECOMES INDEPENDENT

Fearing a return to their former subservient colonial status in the wake of the exiled Portuguese king's return to Lisbon, Brazilian elites supported the Portuguese prince regent in claiming independence from the mother country. Unlike the Spanish South American colonies, which were becoming independent republics, Brazil remained a monarchy ruled by the Portuguese house of Braganza until 1889.

LOCALE: Brazil

CATEGORIES: Government and politics; colonization; expansion and land acquisition

KEY FIGURES

John VI (1767-1826), king of Portugal, r. 1816-1826

Pedro I (1798-1834), first emperor of independent Brazil, r. 1822-1831

José Bonifácio de Andrada e Silva (c. 1763-1838), Brazilian statesman

Maria I (1734-1816), queen of Portugal, r. 1777-1816

Napoleon I (1769-1821), emperor of France, r. 1804-1814, 1815

Joseph Bonaparte (1768-1844), king of Naples, r. 1806-1808, king of Spain, r. 1808-1813, and brother of Napoleon I

SUMMARY OF EVENT

The Napoleonic Wars in Europe sparked independence movements in Latin America. When Napoleon I's brother Joseph Bonaparte was placed on the throne of Spain, Spaniards in Spain and in America viewed him as a usurper; they established governing boards to hold power until the legitimate king was restored. The situation in Portugal, however, was quite different, for the Portuguese crown did not fall prey to Napoleon's armies. Instead, protected by the Britain's Royal Navy, the royal family of Portugal, accompanied by thousands of nobles, sailed to Brazil in November, 1807. Because Queen Maria I suffered from diminished mental capacity, her son John had become prince regent in 1799, and it was he who presided over affairs of state.

The arrival of the Portuguese court in Brazil transformed politics, culture, and society in the colony. One of the first acts of the prince regent was to open the ports of Brazil to trade with friendly nations. Three hundred years of mercantilist trade restrictions quickly crumbled. With the arrival of foreign merchants, the principal ports of Brazil became much more cosmopolitan, and resi-

dents benefited from the new economic opportunities that resulted.

Prince John quickly set about transforming Rio de Janeiro into the center of the Portuguese empire. He had brought the royal treasury with him from Lisbon, and he created a bank in Brazil to handle royal finances. He also brought the first printing press to the colony and established the first universities in Brazil. Although it was sometimes difficult for Brazilians in the capital city to adjust to the presence of such a large group of Portuguese nobles, the advantages of the royal presence far outweighed any logistical problems created by that presence. Brazilians of all social classes, including slaves, came to relish their much easier access to the monarch.

While at first some of the Portuguese nobles resented being away from their land and family in Europe, the royals adjusted well to their new life. Even after Napoleon's defeat at Waterloo in 1815, which meant they could safely return to Lisbon, they appeared to be in no hurry to leave the colony. In an attempt to normalize this unique situation, the prince regent elevated Brazil to the status of kingdom in 1815, making the colony equal to its mother country. When Queen Maria I died one year later and the prince regent became King John VI, he still refused to leave Brazil. For the first time ever, the new king was crowned not in Lisbon but in America. Brazilians delighted in the pomp and splendor of the coronation. It must have become clear to the Portuguese in Europe that Brazil's new status might become permanent. In 1817, King John contracted the marriage of his elder son Pedro to Archduchess Leopoldina, a daughter of the Austrian emperor. The wedding was celebrated in Brazil.

Five years after Napoleon's defeat, chafing under a regency controlled by the British, Portuguese citizens in Europe longed for the return of their king. Meanwhile, the Spanish colonies in South America were engaged in wars to free themselves from European control. Patriot armies led by José de San Martín marched northwestward, while the armies of Simón Bolívar headed south. It was clear to John that political peace was the key to ensuring the continued prosperity of Brazil. Because he was married to Carlota Joaquina, a Spanish princess, he was well aware of events in the neighboring Spanish-speaking regions of South America. It seemed to him politically expedient to remain in Brazil.

Portugal was not immune to the constitutionalist spirit sweeping Europe. In 1820, a military revolt in Porto urged the king to adopt constitutional rule. Back in Brazil, crowds in Rio de Janeiro spilled into the streets in support of a constitution as well. Finally, John determined that he must return to Lisbon and deal with the changing political climate. In February, 1821, after thirteen years in Brazil, he quietly sailed back to Europe. His son Pedro, the heir to the Portuguese throne, stayed behind as regent of Brazil. When the liberal Portuguese representative assembly (the Côrtes) insisted in January, 1822, that the prince also return to Europe, he refused. Clearly, he had cast his lot with Brazil. Some of Pedro's Brazilian advisers, including José Bonifácio de Andrada e Silva, urged him formally to break political ties with Portugal before separatist movements in Brazil brought about the colony's independence despite him.

So it was that on September 7, 1822, while traveling in the province of São Paulo in an effort to respond to the concerns of citizens there, Pedro received news that the Portuguese côrtes had taken measures limiting his authority in Brazil and moving toward reinstating Brazil's colonial status. Upon reading the letter containing this news, he unsheathed and raised his sword, proclaiming, "Independence or death." This moment, on the banks of the Ipiranga River in the province of São Paulo, marked Brazil's independence from Portugal.

Although making this personal declaration of independence a reality was not achieved without some bloodshed, the land and naval battles in Brazil's war for independence were much less costly than those fought in Spanish America, partly because the British supported Brazil's separation from Portugal. The question of what kind of government would rule the new nation was also resolved quickly. The man who proclaimed Brazilian independence, who was also the heir to the Portuguese throne, became Pedro I, the constitutional emperor of Brazil.

The road to establishing an independent nation, however, proved rocky at times. Unsatisfied with a European monarch, Brazilians clamored for a Brazilian-born king during the late 1820's. In 1831, Pedro abdicated the throne of Brazil in favor of his five-year-old son, who had been born in Brazil. The ten years that followed, in which Brazilian regents conducted the affairs of government, witnessed separatist rebellions throughout Brazil. When Pedro II came into his own as emperor in 1840, at the age of fourteen, he inherited a deeply divided empire. By the early 1850's, however, most of the violence had subsided and Brazil emerged as the largest and most politically stable independent nation in South America.

SIGNIFICANCE

Brazil's relatively peaceful transition from colony to independent empire could not have been accomplished had the colony not served temporarily as the center of the Portuguese empire. The transfer of the court reinforced, for Brazilians, the importance of monarchy. Even when constitutionalism prevailed, it did so under a monarchy. The support of the British, along with fears of slave rebellion, help to explain the nature of Brazil's unusual independence movement. Although independence was not achieved without some problems, the politics of independent Brazil were marked by the presence of stable, recognized dynastic rulers at a time when neighboring Spanish-speaking republics were witnessing multiple—frequently violent—transitions in government. The fact that politics were fairly stable and that the British were intent on trading with independent Brazil also meant that economic recovery came swiftly. Only in the last third of the century did unresolved issues connected to slavery, latifundia (large agricultural estates), and monoculture bring about the collapse of the empire and the proclamation of a republic in 1889.

—*Joan E. Meznar*

FURTHER READING

Barman, Roderick J. *Brazil: The Forging of a Nation, 1798-1852*. Stanford, Calif.: Stanford University Press, 1988. An engagingly written history of the political process whereby Brazil was transformed from a colony of Portugal into a stable independent empire. Demonstrates that the process was complex and the end result was not a foregone conclusion.

Bethell, Leslie. "The Independence of Brazil." In *Brazil: Empire and Republic, 1822-1930*, edited by Leslie Bethell. Cambridge, England: Cambridge University Press, 1989. An excellent discussion of the events that led to Brazil's separation from Portugal, with attention to the role of Great Britain.

Haring, C. H. *Empire in Brazil: A New World Experiment with Monarchy*. Cambridge, Mass.: Harvard University Press, 1958. A classic account of the independence of Brazil and its position as the only independent monarchy in the Americas.

Kraay, Hendrick. *Race, State, and Armed Forces in Independence-Era Brazil: Bahia, 1790's-1840's*. Stanford, Calif.: Stanford University Press, 2002. Focusing on one of Brazil's major slave-holding regions, the author describes the transformation of Brazil's military forces during the wars for independence.

Schultz, Kirsten. *Tropical Versailles: Empire, Monar-

1820's

chy, and the Portuguese Royal Court in Rio de Janeiro, 1808-1821*. New York: Routledge, 2001. An insightful discussion of how the arrival of the Portuguese court in Rio de Janeiro changed local society. Demonstrates how the presence of African slaves in Brazil gave a unique dimension to relations between the monarch and his subjects, slavery having been abolished earlier in Portugal.

Vale, Brian. *Independence or Death: British Sailors and Brazilian Independence, 1822-1825*. London: I. B. Tauris, 1996. Shifts the focus of the wars for independence to the Atlantic Ocean, describing the important role of Great Britain's Lord Cochrane and his sailors in securing Brazil's separation from Portugal.

SEE ALSO: Sept. 16, 1810: Hidalgo Issues El Grito de Dolores; Sept. 16, 1810-Sept. 28, 1821: Mexican War of Independence; Mar., 1813-Dec. 9, 1824: Bolívar's Military Campaigns; Jan. 18, 1817-July 28, 1821: San Martín's Military Campaigns; 1828-1834: Portugal's Miguelite Wars; Jan., 1833: Great Britain Occupies the Falkland Islands; June 16, 1855-May 1, 1857: Walker Invades Nicaragua; May 1, 1865-June 20, 1870: Paraguayan War.

RELATED ARTICLES in *Great Lives from History: The Nineteenth Century, 1801-1900:* Simón Bolívar; Napoleon I; Pedro I; Pedro II; José de San Martín.

October 20-30, 1822
GREAT BRITAIN WITHDRAWS FROM THE CONCERT OF EUROPE

Great Britain's withdrawal from the Concert of Europe—the diplomatic, political, and military cooperation between European powers—weakened the use of collective diplomacy by the great powers to settle disputes and maintain peace without appealing to collective military intervention.

ALSO KNOWN AS: Congress of Verona
LOCALE: Verona, Italy
CATEGORY: Diplomacy and international relations

KEY FIGURES
Henry Brougham (1778-1868), Whig leader of the opposition in Great Britain's House of Commons
Viscount Castlereagh (Robert Stewart; 1769-1822), British foreign secretary and leader of the House of Commons until August 12, 1822
George Canning (1770-1827), Castlereagh's successor as British foreign secretary and leader of the House of Commons, 1822-1827
François-René de Chateaubriand (1768-1848), French representative at the Congress of Verona
Second Earl of Liverpool (Robert Banks Jenkinson; 1770-1828), Tory prime minister of Great Britain, 1812-1827
Metternich (1773-1859), Austrian foreign affairs minister
Duc de Montmorency-Laval (1766-1826), French foreign minister who represented France at the Congress of Verona

Duke of Wellington (Arthur Wellesley; 1769-1852), Brtish representative at the Congress of Verona

SUMMARY OF EVENT
The difference of viewpoint between Great Britain and Russia that eventually split the Concert of Europe was even evident at the Congress of Vienna in 1815. There, Viscount Castlereagh, the British foreign secretary, successfully resisted attempts by Czar Alexander I to intervene in the internal affairs of other countries. Castlereagh had taken the position that the Quadruple Alliance had been formed to prevent Napoleon I from returning to the throne of France, to guarantee international boundaries, and to preserve European peace. He did concede that Austria had a special right to intervene in Italy and Germany because they were Austrian spheres of influence.

Beyond his concession, however, Castlereagh probably believed that nonintervention best served British interests; he conjectured that intervention would only stir up nationalism, and that the British parliament would not back any interventionist plans. When Alexander proposed the Holy Alliance, a list of idealistic promises based on goodwill and Christian principle, Castlereagh refused to sign for Great Britain. Instead, he dismissed that alliance as "a piece of sublime mysticism and nonsense."

Castlereagh departed from the traditional British "balance of power" concept and took a more widely international view. He saw maintenance of a political equilibrium in Europe as essential to preserving the peace and maintaining British interests. He hoped that a series of congresses would lead to peaceful settlements of disputes and that Great Britain could serve in a conciliatory role, but basically, Castlereagh preferred to follow a policy of nonintervention in continental affairs unless peace demanded it. The only justification for such collective intervention was a revived military threat from France. Anything less could be handled through diplomatic channels at regular congresses.

Many British people did not agree with Castlereagh's policy of cooperation with the continental powers. It was difficult to convince the British public of the necessity for an active foreign policy, characterized by high taxes and continued military expenditures, during peacetime. The reactionary attitudes of Austria and Russia were not popular in Great Britain, especially when Liberalism began to revive after 1820. The Whigs argued for the balance of power concepts, as did some of the Tories. The Liberals thought that Britain should oppose the suppression of continental Liberals by repressive monarchs.

In 1820 the inherent contradictions between British and Russian policies became clearer because of liberal revolts in Spain and Naples. The Spanish Revolution of 1820 came first, but a crisis was avoided when Metternich agreed with the arguments of Castlereagh and the duke of Wellington against the joint intervention that Alexander I sought. The subsequent revolt in Naples, however, created a more serious problem. Alexander I was so alarmed that he completely gave up his liberal tendencies. Metternich was also concerned with the threat to Austrian hegemony in Italy, and decided that he needed Alexander's support. Prussia as usual followed Austria's lead. A distinctly reactionary and interventionist turn had been given to the Concert of Europe.

A conference called to discuss the Italian problem met at Troppau on October 29, 1820. Austria, Russia, and Prussia attended, while Great Britain and France only sent observers without power to act. This action by the British represented a partial break in the Concert of Europe. On November 19, Alexander I persuaded the delegates to write the Troppau Protocol, which justified interference in the internal affairs of other nations to prevent revolutions.

In response to the Troppau Protocol, Castlereagh circulated a strong protest to concert members, which, while admitting Austria's right to intervene in Italy because of its hegemony, objected to military intervention in internal affairs by the Concert of Europe as a group.

Viscount Castlereagh. (Library of Congress)

Some attempts were made by Metternich to conciliate Castlereagh when they met in Hanover in the autumn of 1821. Metternich supported Castlereagh's policy of opposing Russian intervention on behalf of the Greeks in revolt against Turkey, and Castlereagh agreed to send a representative to the congresses at Vienna and Verona the next year. Difficulties centered on the continuing Spanish unrest and the Latin American revolt against Spain. Castlereagh committed suicide on August 12, 1822, however, and was succeeded as foreign secretary by George Canning.

Like Castlereagh, Canning favored nonintervention, but unlike Castlereagh, he had not been involved in creating the peace. He did not see the value of the Concert of Europe and believed that British interests often lay with revolution rather than legitimacy. Canning maintained that British national interests, not any international considerations, should guide British foreign policy. The duke of Wellington was sent as the British representative to the Congress of Verona. With him, he carried a memorandum, drawn up by Castlereagh before his death, which stated that Great Britain would prefer "rigid abstinence" from internal interference in Spain. He also carried a protest against the Russian closing of the Bering

Sea. Noninterference was also to be the British policy in Greece and Latin America.

The Congress of Verona opened on October 20, 1822, and it became absorbed in the Spanish problem, which had grown acute. The extreme liberals were in power in Spain and King Ferdinand VII was virtually their prisoner. The continental powers (Russia, Austria, Prussia, and France), prodded by Czar Alexander, agreed to intervene in Spain to restore the king to power. Represented by its foreign minister, duc de Montmorency-Laval, and François-René de Chateaubriand, France argued successfully to be allowed to restore royal power in Spain. The other continental powers—Russia, Austria, and Prussia—agreed to withdraw their ambassadors from Spain as a form of moral persuasion and support of France.

When the British prime minister, the second earl of Liverpool, and the Tory cabinet heard of this agreement, they ordered Wellington to announce to the congress on October 30 that Great Britain refused to be a party to the intervention and refused to withdraw its ambassador from Madrid. This statement was tantamount to withdrawing from the Concert of Europe because it put Britain in clear and public opposition to the policies of the Concert of Europe. This move, supported by Whig opposition leader Henry Brougham and his followers, was popular in England because Great Britain feared French Bourbon ambitions and the reconquest of the Spanish colonies in America.

SIGNIFICANCE

Britain's withdrawal from the Concert of Europe was important as a significant diplomatic shift away from international cooperation and closer to the more nationalistic British foreign policy of maintaining the balance of power in "splendid isolation." At the time, it was as much a shift in style, since Canning continued cooperation with Austria and supported the concert in condemning the Greek revolt. Canning did not, however, endorse intervention in Spain.

The withdrawal of Great Britain weakened the Concert of Europe considerably, especially in western Europe. Deprived of the influence of its most liberal member, the eastern members of the concert followed a more reactionary and interventionist policy. Congresses did meet occasionally after the Congress of Verona to settle such important questions as the Greek and Belgian revolts, but the congress idea had received a mortal blow. British withdrawal from the Concert of Europe ultimately represented a diplomatic revolution.

—James H. Steinel, updated by Michael J. Galgano

FURTHER READING

Clarke, John. *British Diplomacy and Foreign Policy, 1782-1865: The National Interest*. London: Unwin Hyman, 1989. Surveys the role of domestic politics in shaping foreign policy and diplomacy in a period of growing professionalism.

Elrod, Richard. "The Concert of Europe: A Fresh Look at an International System." *World Politics* 28 (January, 1976): 159-174. Sees the Concert of Europe as crucial to maintaining European security and stability, and downplays the significance of British withdrawal.

Hinde, Wendy. *Castlereagh*. London: Collins, 1981. A clear biography with a good discussion of the withdrawal from the Concert of Europe.

Palmer, Alan W. *Metternich*. New York: Harper & Row, 1972. An excellent English-language biography of the Austrian statesman.

Schroeder, Paul W. "The Nineteenth-Century International System: Changes in the Structure." *World Politics* 39 (October, 1986): 1-26.

_____. "The Nineteenth Century System: Balance of Power or Political Equilibrium?" *Review of International Studies* 15 (April, 1989): 135-154. Two articles that connect European stability to the success of the Concert of Europe, with diplomacy by conference and political equilibrium replacing balance of power.

Temperley, Harold W. *The Foreign Policy of Canning, 1822-1827: England, the Holy Alliance, and the New World*. London: Frank Cass, 1966. Although dated (it was originally published in 1924), Temperley's work remains the fullest account of Canning's policies.

Webster, Charles K. *The Foreign Policy of Castlereagh, 1815-1822*. 2d ed. London: Bell, 1963. Standard analysis of Castlereagh's policies and achievements. Less sound on Metternich's contributions.

SEE ALSO: Sept. 15, 1814-June 11, 1815: Congress of Vienna; Nov. 20, 1815: Second Peace of Paris; July 2, 1820-Mar., 1821: Neapolitan Revolution; Mar. 7, 1821-Sept. 29, 1829: Greeks Fight for Independence from the Ottoman Empire; July 29, 1830: July Revolution Deposes Charles X; Aug. 25, 1830-May 21, 1833: Belgian Revolution; Feb. 22-June, 1848: Paris Revolution of 1848; Mar. 3-Nov. 3, 1848: Prussian Revolution of 1848.

RELATED ARTICLES in *Great Lives from History: The Nineteenth Century, 1801-1900:* Henry Brougham; George Canning; Viscount Castlereagh; François-René de Chateaubriand; Second Earl of Liverpool; Metternich; Napoleon I; Duke of Wellington.

1823-1831
HOKUSAI PRODUCES *THIRTY-SIX VIEWS OF MOUNT FUJI*

Hokusai's woodblock print series Thirty-Six Views of Mount Fuji *is an amalgamation of the* ukiyo-e *style of artistry and of his own perspectives. Hokusai's work, greatly influential in the world of Japanese printmaking, also inspired the development of Impressionist and other modern art styles of western Europe.*

ALSO KNOWN AS: *Fugaku sanjūrokkei*
LOCALE: Edo (now Tokyo), Japan
CATEGORY: Art

KEY FIGURES
Hokusai (Katushika Hokusai;1760-1849), Japanese
    print artist
Tokugawa Ieyasu (1543-1616), shogun of Japan,
    r. 1603-1616
Hiroshige (1797-1858), Japanese print artist
Suzuki Harunobu (1725?-1770), Japanese print artist
Félix Bracquemond (1833-1914), French printmaker
    and designer

SUMMARY OF EVENT
Japanese print artist Katushika Hokusai's 1823-1831 woodblock print series *Thirty-Six Views of Mount Fuji* (*Fugaku sanjūrokkei*) was based on the artist's own unique perspective of the popular nineteenth century *ukiyo-e* style of woodblock printing in Japan. This series of prints is regarded as one of the most influential in the history of art. Later Japanese and European artists, inspired by Hokusai's style, merged traditional Japanese imagery with popular culture in a unique style especially for the common individual.

The capital city of Edo (now Tokyo) was under the power of the Tokugawa shogunate (1615-1868). Shogun Tokugawa Ieyasu was a fan of fairs and lively entertainment such as kabuki theater and of activities that included erotic and risqué displays from the pleasure quarters of the Yoshiwara, or Floating World, district. The Tokugawa period marked the beginning of a peaceful era after nearly four hundred years of civil unrest in Japan. The renewed interest in cultural activities in lieu of militarism led to a rising middle class that produced and sold everyday goods and wares.

Detailed views of city life were popularized under the term *ukiyo-e*, or images of the floating world, at the beginning of the Tokugawa period. *Ukiyo-e* embodies the Japanese ideal that life is fleeting, or impermanent, and

that the elements of everyday life are ephemeral and transitory; life, therefore, should be pleasurable. As the primary artistic medium of *ukiyo-e*, woodblock prints met the artistic desires of a large urban capital such as Edo while remaining cost-effective. Woodblock prints were inexpensively produced and reproduced for about the cost of a laborer's meal, and they offered a means for individualism in a heavily populated region. Advancements in woodblock design allowed for beautifully polychromatic prints called *nishiki-e* (brocade pictures), a process invented by Suzuki Harunobu in 1765.

The rise of the merchant class led to the popularization of a genre of art that embraced everyday activities through boldly colored depictions of actors, scenes of daily life, tea houses, legendary characters, courtesans, and the surrounding landscape so treasured by the Japanese. Censorship of subject matter deemed inappropriate by government authorities was enforced starting around 1801. As a result, the subject of woodblock prints metamorphosed into a hybrid of traditional Japanese imagery of historical figures with the energy of the urban city in the form of panoramic cityscapes and landscapes. This omniscient artistic viewpoint developed out of a long tradition of landscape imagery seen in Japanese painting. Traveling opportunities outside the country, previously prohibited, were reinstated after 1820, which heightened popular interest in scenery and in souvenirs of favorite locales.

Hokusai was familiar with bustling big cities and was known as a master of Japanese landscape imagery. His *Thirty-Six Views of Mount Fuji* was inspired by the beauty of the natural environment. The forty-six prints (thirty-six original views and ten added later) captured the steadfast nature of Mount Fuji as it faced all types of weather and seasonal conditions. All but one of the forty-six images illustrate the interaction between humans and the immortal Mount Fuji.

The two most popular images from the series are *The Great Wave off Kanagawa* and *South Wind, Clear Dawn* (also known as *Red Fuji*), which display the effects of a great storm and the renewal of nature after a storm, respectively. Although the subjects are imbued in nature and its effects, each image has its own sense of order and balance, often despite an asymmetrical composition. *The Great Wave* was colored with Prussian blue, adding vibrancy to the image of a colossal wave about to capsize a boat of frightened seafarers; the viewer's perspective is similar to one of the seafarers, as if Hokusai intended to place his viewer desperately out at sea at the mercy of nature. Hokusai originally outlined all of the prints with Prussian blue ink because of the pigment's popularity in Europe at the time.

South Wind, Clear Dawn, on the other hand, was a unique production because it used a stark, angular outline of the mountain and three basic colors, named for the red glow of the mountain often seen in the morning light of summer months, hence the image's other name, *Red Fuji*. *South Wind, Clear Dawn* was the only image of the series that did not include a human element, leaving a very powerful impression of nature. Despite its simple means, *South Wind, Clear Dawn* was incredibly popular; it was favored among the series and remains a significant image in the history of printmaking.

The focus on Mount Fuji, a clear cultural landmark, stemmed from Shinto beliefs in a harmonious connection between humans and the nature spirits called *kami*.

Mount Fuji was regarded as an immortal monument of nature that was constant despite the changing years, turning seasons and variances in atmosphere. Hokusai furthered this concept by blending an ancient spiritual belief of the immortal mountain with the modern cultural identity of Japan. Many of Hokusai's patrons were Shinto believers who had been making their journey to Mount Fuji.

Hokusai completed *Thirty-Six Views of Mount Fuji* at the age of seventy-one. His focus on an image of immortality was not coincidental but rather an expression of his desire to continue on in his career for as long as possible. Hokusai's younger contemporary, Hiroshige, also made a name for himself as a woodblock-print artist by following in Hokusai's footsteps by developing the landscape genre. Hokusai's influence is especially evident in Hiroshige's multi-image series of local scenery in and around Edo, *Meisho Edo Hyakkei* (1856-1858; one hundred views of Edo).

Hokusai's Boy Viewing Mount Fuji. (AP/Wide World Photos)

SIGNIFICANCE

Thirty-Six Views of Mount Fuji is perhaps the most widely recognized print series in history. Hokusai's body of work is credited with influencing European artists such as the Impressionists and Post-Impressionists. The Impressionists, including Claude Monet, painted objects as they appeared to the senses, using the effects of sunlight, especially, to convey with unmixed colors and dabbed brush strokes what the eye actually sees.

Hokusai's works also introduced western Europeans to the value of Japanese prints. With the exception of the Dutch, the general Western audience had limited knowledge of Japanese artistic abilities until the nineteenth century. Half a world away, views of the Japanese countryside and reflections of an urban city in a tradition-oriented society managed to bring to Europeans, the French in particular, a sense of fascination and newfound affinity for Japanese works, called *japonisme* in French. French printmaker and designer Félix Bracquemond was one of the first to credit artists such as Hokusai for his interest in asymmetrical viewpoints. Bracquemond helped make Japanese prints popular in Europe, which in turn inspired the abstract elements of modern art history.

—*Emilie B. Fitzhugh Sizemore*

FURTHER READING

Carpenter, John T., ed. *Hokusai and His Age: Ukiyo-e Painting, Printmaking, and Book Illustration in Late Edo Japan.* Amsterdam: Hotei, 2005. Examines a full range of Hokusai's work as well as the world of Edo Japan during his lifetime. Illustrations.

Dunn, Charles. *Everyday Life in Traditional Japan.* Rutland, Vt.: Charles E. Tuttle, 1969. A survey of the lifestyles, events, and expectations of various classes of individuals in traditional Japanese culture.

Forrer, Matthi. *Hokusai: Mountains and Water, Flowers and Birds.* New York: Prestel, 2004. A brief look at Hokusai's artistry. Illustrations.

Guth, Christine. *Art of Edo Japan: The Artist and the City, 1615-1868.* New York: Harry N. Abrams, 1996. Provides an excellent overview of the variety of artworks in Japan, including traditional art forms like painting and printing as well as cultural arts such as theater and tea ceremonies.

Nagata, Seiji. *Hokusai: Genius of the Japanese Ukiyo-e.* New York: Kodansha International, 1995. Examines Hokusai's extensive history of artistic production, including the various periods within his own career.

Newland, Amy, ed. *The Commercial and Cultural Climate of Japanese Printmaking.* Hotei Academic European Studies on Japan 2. Amsterdam: Hotei, 2004. A scholarly study of the socioeconomic aspects of *ukiyo-e* printmaking. Provides a unique account of the social and economic conditions under which *ukiyo-e* artists created their works.

Ray, Deborah Kogan. *Hokusai: The Man Who Painted a Mountain.* New York: Farrar, Straus and Giroux, 2001. A 34-page book written especially for younger readers. Illustrations.

Sansom, George. *A History of Japan: 1615-1867.* Stanford, Calif.: Stanford University Press, 1963. Examination of the political structure and social development of Japan under Shogun Tokugawa Ieyasu.

Whitford, Frank. *Japanese Prints and Western Painters.* New York: Macmillan, 1977. Discusses the influence of Japanese woodblock prints on European painting during the nineteenth century. Contains color plates.

SEE ALSO: 1820's: China's Stele School of Calligraphy Emerges; 1831-1834: Hiroshige Completes *The Tokaido Fifty-Three Stations.*

RELATED ARTICLES in *Great Lives from History: The Nineteenth Century, 1801-1900:* Paul Cézanne; Paul Gauguin; Vincent van Gogh; Hiroshige; Henri de Toulouse-Lautrec.

1820's

May, 1823
HARTFORD FEMALE SEMINARY IS FOUNDED

Catharine Beecher's Hartford Female Seminary was one of the earliest institutions to offer nontraditional studies for the intellectual development of women and helped to create the teachers who were needed in the opening of the West.

LOCALE: Hartford, Connecticut
CATEGORIES: Education; organizations and institutions; women's issues

KEY FIGURE
Catharine Beecher (1800-1878), pioneer in women's education

SUMMARY OF EVENT

Hartford Female Seminary, which Catharine Beecher founded in May, 1823, and incorporated in 1827, was the second major female seminary to promote the higher education of women. It offered young women a comprehensive education aimed at more than "finishing" them for a successful social life and, ultimately, invented the profession of teaching and trained women in it. When Beecher and her sister Mary opened the seminary in 1823, it was located above a harness shop at the corner of Kinsley and Main Streets in Hartford, Connecticut, and only seven pupils. It soon moved to more spacious quarters in the basement of the North Church. By 1826, the school had nearly one hundred pupils, and Catharine Beecher sought more permanent quarters.

Beecher knew many of Hartford's most influential citizens through her family connections, her friendship with writer and former teacher Lydia Sigourney, and her membership in Hartford's First Congregational Church. She appealed to business and religious leaders for subscriptions to her school. After they refused her, she undertook a religious revival for the daughters and wives of the city's elite families, and then appealed to them. Eventually, she raised $4,850 by selling ninety-seven stock subscriptions to forty-five women at prayer meetings in her home.

Beecher obtained a legislative charter for her seminary, which by 1827 had its own building on Pratt Street with a capacity for 150 pupils and eight teachers. Its board of trustees comprised the city's leading religious and financial men. Thomas Day served as president for twenty years, followed by the Reverend Joel Hawes, who served until 1867. The building, which was planned by Beecher and architect Daniel Wadsworth, contained a

lecture room and six recitation rooms. In 1862, the trustees decided that better facilities were needed and built a large addition containing a gymnasium, several recitation rooms, a music room, and a studio for art classes. The number of pupils increased from 39 to 203 in the period 1861-1868. By 1888, however, the trustees determined that falling enrollments necessitated closing the school. They voted for its dissolution and sold the building to the Good Will Club for seventeen thousand dollars, of which more than nine thousand dollars was needed to pay off indebtedness.

The dissolution of the school followed by ten years the death of its founder. Catharine Beecher was born on September 6, 1800, in East Hampton, Long Island, New York, the first child of the prominent Congregationalist minister Lyman Beecher and Roxanna Foote Beecher. The family soon moved to Litchfield, Connecticut, where Catharine attended a leading school for girls, Miss Sarah Pierce's Female Academy. She also studied music and drawing in Boston. When her mother died in 1816, she helped her Aunt Esther run her father's household until he remarried a year later. She then taught briefly in New London, met the young but eminent Yale professor Alexander Fisher and, after hesitating, agreed to marry him. However, Fisher was drowned in a shipwreck on his way to a one-year tour of European universities, leaving Beecher with a legacy of two thousand dollars and the determination never to marry.

An invitation to spend the winter with Fisher's parents in Franklin, Massachusetts, gave Beecher an opportunity to read Fisher's papers and books on mathematics and physics. She discovered that her education had not been as rigorous as his, but that she was capable of understanding the topics treated in his materials. She studied algebra, geography, chemistry, and physics. During that period, she also struggled with serious theological concepts, as she tried to reconcile her father's stern religious belief in Fisher's lost spiritual state with her own feelings of justice and fairness.

These events, together with the need of a school in Hartford, encouraged Beecher to start the seminary and influenced not only the development of that school but also her numerous writings on the subject of education and women. The seminary, like several others started around the same time, had as its goal not only to adapt but also to improve on the curriculum of men's colleges. Beecher believed that women had two closely intertwined honorable professions: homemaker and teacher. Mothers were teachers and should be trained as such. Beecher viewed homemaking as a profession that, in order to be done well, required scientific and technical training. She and the heads of the other women's seminaries saw a new profession for women, that of the female educator, both inside and outside the home. Beecher also believed that women should teach women. She set up her schools so that the teachers, who were women, would be co-equal with the school administrators (who often were men, at least in the beginning) in the matter of forming policy and curriculum.

Although Beecher herself spent only a few years at the seminary she created, it was run according to her philosophies of education. Its course of studies included subjects such as drawing, music, and French—subjects that were considered proper for young ladies and enabled them to become accomplished wives for the rising middle class. The curriculum also included subjects that were taught in the men's colleges: geography, rhetoric, ancient history, Euclid's geometry, Abercrombie's mental philosophy, Comstock's philosophy and chemistry, Abercrombie's moral feelings, Comstock's botany, Hedge's logic, Paley's theology, Blake's astronomy, Sullivan's political book, Butler's analogy, and Latin and Greek.

The school was soon divided into primary, junior, and senior classes. The primary division included girls from the ages of six to about twelve years old, who were taught reading, writing, spelling, grammar, composition, and arithmetic. The regular course consisted of five divisions, each with specific courses. A supplementary course was also offered, which was open to students whether or not they had attended the seminary previously. It included extensive courses in music, drawing, and painting, intended for personal accomplishment or teaching. There was also a department of physical culture, reflecting Beecher's lifelong battle against the confining clothing and physical restraints of her period. Here, too, Beecher's struggle between her essentially feminist feelings and her dedication to the customs of her time are evident: The catalog notes that the purpose of physical culture for young ladies is "first, bodily health and its reflex influence on mental ability; next, a graceful, erect and elastic carriage."

At that time, teachers were needed in the new schools being built in the opening western territories. This need provided jobs for the graduates of the female seminaries and also gave Beecher an opportunity to move west when her father took a pastorate in Cincinnati, Ohio, in 1831. She had some success starting a number of schools, which were essentially normal schools, in Illinois, Wisconsin, and Iowa. In 1847, she founded the National Board of Popular Education and, in 1852, the American Women's Education Association. She also was the author of a large number of essays, articles, and books.

Beecher's first important educational presentation was in 1829, when she was still at the Hartford Female Seminary. It was part of her continuing effort to raise endowments for her school and to set a pattern of endowments for women's schools, so that their existence would not be so precarious. Beecher correctly foresaw that without an endowment, no lasting system of schooling could be maintained. In spite of continued efforts throughout her life, she was never successful. The lack of an endowment, the increasing popularity of the public Hartford High School, and the founding of well-endowed colleges for women at Poughkeepsie, New York, Wellesley and Northampton, Massachusetts, and elsewhere, were responsible for the demise of her school.

Beecher was principal of her school until 1831, when she resigned because of poor health and left for Cincinnati with her father. She was replaced temporarily by the Reverend Thomas Hopkins Gallaudet. In 1832, John P. Brace of Litchfield, nephew of Miss Pierce and head teacher at her school, started a thirteen-year term, with women assistants. From 1845 until the school's closing in 1888, most of the principals were women.

SIGNIFICANCE

Beecher's school differed from the Latin grammar schools that were common in New England during the early nineteenth century by offering a practical curriculum that revolved around domestic sciences and by strenuously attempting to cast household work in a favorable light. Her school was one of four similar institutions created during the same period in Connecticut and Massachusetts. The others included the Troy Female Seminary, which was later renamed the Emma Willard School after its founder. It was founded in Troy, New York, in 1821. Zilpah Polly Grant founded a female seminary in Ipswich, Massachusetts, in 1828, and Mary Lyon founded one in South Hadley, Massachusetts, in 1837 that later became Mount Holyoke College. Beecher's and Grant's seminaries did not survive, but Mount Holyoke College and Emma Willard School have endured into the twenty-first century.

—*Erika E. Pilver*

FURTHER READING

Boydston, Jeanne, Mary Kelley, and Anne Margolis. *The Limits of Sisterhood: The Beecher Sisters on Women's*

1820's

Rights and Woman's Sphere. Chapel Hill: University of North Carolina Press, 1988. Letters and other writings of Catharine Beecher, Harriet Beecher Stowe, and Isabella Beecher Hooker. Includes brief but comprehensive and valuable introductions to the book and to each section.

Martin, Jane Roland. *Reclaiming a Conversation: The Ideal of the Educated Woman.* New Haven, Conn.: Yale University Press, 1985. Presents an imaginary conversation with Beecher and philosophers and other educators from other times.

Rugoff, Milton. *The Beechers: An American Family in the Nineteenth Century.* New York: Harper & Row, 1981. Probing study of the lives of Lyman Beecher and his many prominent children. Valuable for details of their lives.

Sklar, Kathryn Kish. *Catharine Beecher: A Study in American Domesticity.* New York: W. W. Norton, 1976. Puts Beecher's history, philosophy, and accomplishments into context.

Solomon, Barbara Miller. *In the Company of Educated Women.* New Haven, Conn.: Yale University Press, 1985. Explains the educational settings of, and philosophies about education for, women over time.

White, Barbara A. *The Beecher Sisters.* New Haven, Conn.: Yale University Press, 2003. Fascinating joint biography of Catharine Beecher and her sisters, Harriet Beecher Stowe, the author of *Uncle Tom's Cabin,* and Isabel Beecher, a leader in the women's movement.

SEE ALSO: 1813: Founding of McGill University; 1820's-1830's: Free Public School Movement; Dec. 3, 1833: Oberlin College Opens; Nov. 8, 1837: Mount Holyoke Female Seminary Opens; Sept. 26, 1865: Vassar College Opens; Mar. 2, 1867: U.S. Department of Education Is Created.
RELATED ARTICLES in *Great Lives from History: The Nineteenth Century, 1801-1900:* Catharine Beecher; Henry Ward Beecher; Sarah and Angelina Grimké; Mary Lyon; Harriet Beecher Stowe; Emma Willard.

October 5, 1823
WAKLEY INTRODUCES *THE LANCET*

Thomas Wakley founded the medical journal The Lancet *to expose corruption in the unregulated British medical profession, to advocate for reforms in metropolitan hospitals, and to share news of medical discoveries, treatments, and advances. In the twenty-first century,* The Lancet *remains one of the world's leading medical journals.*

LOCALE: London, England
CATEGORIES: Health and medicine; journalism

KEY FIGURES
Thomas Wakley (1795-1862), physician and founding editor of *The Lancet*
William Cobbett (1763-1835), author and social reformer
Sir Astley Cooper (1768-1841), physician

SUMMARY OF EVENT

Thomas Wakley, the youngest of eleven children, was born in Membury, Devon, on July 11, 1795. At the age of ten, his father allowed him to join the British East India Company as a midshipman, but he quickly found the naval life unstable and he returned to Taunton, where he studied pharmacology. In Taunton, Wakley encountered his first brush with discrimination in the medical profession as doctors routinely discounted the work of the pharmacists upon whom they relied for making medicines. At the age of twenty-two, Wakley was admitted to the Royal College of Surgeons in London, and he apprenticed at the United Hospitals of St. Thomas and St. Guys near London Bridge before opening his own practice in London.

During his medical education, Wakley was sensitive to forms of corruption in the medical profession, including doctors' practice of nepotism, carelessness during surgeries, and doctors' beliefs that they formed an exclusive group and were not servants of the people. Wakley's outrage against these practices and attitudes would lead his drive to reform the entire medical profession, using *The Lancet* and his skill at public speaking as his principal tools.

Wakley was already a controversial figure; when he turned his attention to editing and writing *The Lancet*, his reputation as the "sailor doctor" preceded him. In May of 1820, he was rumored to have been the surgeon who had beheaded the members of the failed Cato Street Conspiracy, an attempt to overthrow the British parliament. Wakely was assaulted in his own home and left for dead when his house was set ablaze. It was not long after this incident, on October 5, 1823, that Wakley left private medical practice and began *The Lancet* with the financial support of his father-in-law, the merchant Joseph Goodchild. Wakely had married Elizabeth Goodchild on February 5, 1820.

Wakley probably was inspired to found *The Lancet* by the success of *The New England Journal of Medicine and Surgery*, founded in 1811 in Boston by Walter Channing, a leader in medical care for women. When the first issue of *The Lancet* appeared, there was one English medical journal with a good reputation, *The Medico-Chirurgical Review*, a monthly started in 1816. *The Medical and Physical Journal*—another monthly, started in 1799—would end publication in 1833. In 1827, just four years into *The Lancet*'s existence, a group of doctors who had sued Wakley for articles he had published about their malpractice started a third magazine, *The Medical Gazette*, which in 1839 became a part of *The Medical Times*.

The Lancet was a unique journal because Wakley, as editor, did not limit the journal's contents to medical news. He also published his own editorials, which called for reform in the education of doctors and in the practice of medicine. He also attacked doctors for malpractice and fully reported how their patients died as a result of a given doctor's poor care. Wakley also included, in the first two years of his weekly paper, chess games and theater reviews. Such content reflected his belief that chess offered good mental training for young medical students. In time, however, he decided to shift the focus of *The Lancet* to reporting on medical breakthroughs, effective treatments for diseases (including rabies), and areas of the medical profession in need of reform.

The first issue of *The Lancet* included a detailed statement of purpose written by Wakley. The mission statement was not especially controversial, as it laid out the aims of the new periodical as being devoted to teaching and informing the public about the practice of medicine. Wakley had also published lectures by one of his teachers at the United Hospitals, Sir Astley Cooper. This type of editorial content was more controversial because students typically paid £15 for a professor's medical lectures. When Wakley reprinted the lecture without permission—although he did not violate copyright law—he did take from Cooper the chance to make money from his own intellectual property. Instead of suing Wakley, however, Cooper met with him and gave him permission to publish some of his lectures as long as his name did not appear with the article; Cooper did not want to be associated with a weekly medical news journal.

To fill the pages of *The Lancet*, Wakley used copies of

medical lectures he owned, his own rhetorical skills to write editorials, and a cadre of reporters to write about hospital news. Because he had many enemies, Wakley was sued for what was presumed to be infringement of copyright and for libel, as he exposed medical incompetence in graphic detail in the pages of his publication. Every lawsuit he won increased the reputation of the journal, and within two years of its founding, it came to focus solely on medical news (domestic and foreign) and had editorials that were focused on the profession.

Wakley's reporters were frequently ejected from the hospitals they attempted to cover, and Wakley himself was assaulted several times because of his viewpoints. He also was a leading consumer advocate and had the most successful medical news organ of the nineteenth century, having driven three other medical periodicals out of print. He attracted journalists and doctors who could write well and who shared his views on political and social reform. From 1836 to 1839, for example, Wakley debated in Parliament and in the pages of *The Lancet* the cruelty of military floggings, and although reform was not achieved until 1881, Wakley raised public awareness of the practice from a medical standpoint, thus providing intellectual arguments that his readers could use to shape their opinions and influence their electoral choices. Although his attack on nepotism in the Royal College of Surgeons did not end the practice, he did provoke a series of reforms deemed beneficial that were outlined in numerous issues of *The Lancet*.

Within two years, *The Lancet* had four thousand subscribing readers and sold for the reasonable price of six pence per copy. It attracted readers from many fields, not just medicine, and as its reputation grew, it attracted a variety of contributors as well. The best-known contributor in Wakley's day was William Cobbett, a poet and social reformer. Cobbett and Wakley remained friends until Cobbett's death in 1835. Cobbett had influenced Wakley to some degree and, in 1826, encouraged him to move his printing and publishing of *The Lancet* from the firm of G. L. Hutchinson in London's Strand to Mills, Jowett, and Mills (Cobbett's own printer and bookseller), located on Fleet Street.

Wakley focused on a stable set of topics that would dominate the rest of his life and his careers as editor of *The Lancet*, as Middlesex coroner, and as a member of Parliament from Finsbury. He found that *The Lancet* alone could not be the sole reform tool, as he had envisioned. While he could use the journal to motivate the public (he actually was happy and eager to be sued by those whose malpractice he exposed, as such suits were

1820's

signs that his message was being received), he still felt that he needed a better method of effecting changes in laws that affected the lives of all those needing medical help, particularly the poor.

In 1836, Wakley published a pamphlet in support of eliminating the Stamp Tax, which led to a reduction in the tax from four pence to one or two pence, according to the paper's size. Still, most of the issues Wakley addressed in his parliamentary career were drawn from his passion for medical reform and for the professionalization of the medical field. In 1839, soon after he was elected coroner of Middlesex, he published a series of eight rules that governed his practices as coroner.

In 1852, Wakley retired from Parliament. He died on May 16, 1862, while on a holiday in Madeira, Spain. He was buried in Membury.

SIGNIFICANCE

The Lancet has been in continuous publication since 1823. The journal gave its founder, Thomas Wakley, a means to raise public awareness about medical malpractice, about the need to reform the Royal College of Surgeons, about poor medical practice, and about poor medical education. He also argued that coroners should be qualified as doctors. Wakley's efforts, largely accomplished through the pages of *The Lancet*, effected major civil reforms. Under Wakley's editorship, *The Lancet* lived up to its symbolic name, as Wakley used it to pierce the comfortable and corrupt lives of physicians and drain the wounds that for so long had plagued the medical profession.

—Beverly E. Schneller

FURTHER READING

Digby, Anne. *Making a Medical Living: Doctors and Patients in the English Market for Medicine, 1720-1911*. New York: Cambridge University Press, 2002. Traces the commercialization of medicine in Great Britain from the mid-eighteenth century, beginning with the first volunteer hospital and ending in 1911 with the institution of national health insurance. Good general context for understanding Wakley and the medical profession of his times.

Hostettler, John. *Thomas Wakley: An Improbable Radical*. Chichester, England: Barry Rose Law, 1993. This life of Wakley draws on the contemporary account by Sir Samuel Squire Sprigge and includes newer insights and explanations of Wakley's political career.

Sprigge, Sir Samuel Squire. *The Life and Times of Thomas Wakley*. 1897. Reprint. Introduction by Charles G. Ronald. Huntington, N.Y.: Robert E. Kreiger, 1974. The earliest biography of Wakley. Chapter 25 summarizes his achievements with *The Lancet* during its first decade.

SEE ALSO: 1816: Laënnec Invents the Stethoscope; Oct. 16, 1846: Safe Surgical Anesthesia Is Demonstrated; May, 1847: Semmelweis Develops Antiseptic Procedures; 1867: Lister Publishes His Theory on Antiseptic Surgery; Jan. 23, 1897: "Aspirin" Is Registered as a Trade Name.

RELATED ARTICLES in *Great Lives from History: The Nineteenth Century, 1801-1900:* Elizabeth Blackwell; William Cobbett; Joseph Lister; Sir William Osler; Ignaz Philipp Semmelweis.

December 2, 1823
PRESIDENT MONROE ARTICULATES THE MONROE DOCTRINE

During his state of the union address, U.S. president James Monroe outlined a doctrine of European nonintervention in Western Hemispheric affairs that would become a centerpiece of American foreign policy over the next two centuries.

LOCALE: Washington, D.C.
CATEGORY: Diplomacy and international relations

KEY FIGURES

James Monroe (1758-1831), president of the United States, 1817-1825
John Quincy Adams (1767-1848), Monroe's secretary of state and later president, 1825-1829
Alexander I (1777-1825), czar of Russia, r. 1801-1825
Viscount Castlereagh (Robert Stewart; 1769-1822), British foreign secretary
George Canning (1770-1827), Castlereagh's successor as foreign secretary
Metternich (1773-1859), Austrian chancellor
Auguste-Jules-Armand-Marie de Polignac (1780-1847), French ambassador to Great Britain
Richard Rush (1780-1859), U.S. minister to Great Britain

SUMMARY OF EVENT

On December 2, 1823, President James Monroe delivered his annual message to the U.S. Congress. Although most of his remarks concerned domestic matters that were soon forgotten, his foreign policy declaration became the cornerstone of U.S. policy in the Western Hemisphere. "The American Continents," he declared, "by the free and independent condition which they have assumed and maintain, are henceforth not to be considered as subjects for future colonization by a European power." The president then turned to European colonial policy in the New World:

1820's

Cartoon published at the time of a border dispute between Venezuela and Great Britain's Guiana colony that depicts Uncle Sam defending the Western Hemisphere against European imperialists. The original caption reads, "Keep off! The Monroe Doctrine must be respected." (Library of Congress)

With the existing Colonies or dependencies of any European power, we have not interfered, and shall not interfere. But with the Governments who have declared their independence, and maintained it, and whose Independence we have, on great consideration, and on just principles, acknowledged, we could not view any interposition for the purpose of oppressing them, or controlling in any other manner, their destiny, by any European power, in any other light than as the manifestation of an unfriendly disposition toward the United States.

Monroe's message contained three main points outlining the new role of the United States as defender of the Western Hemisphere. First, he announced to Europe that the United States would oppose any attempt to take over any independent country in the Western Hemisphere (the no-transfer principle). Second, he promised that the United States itself would abstain from becoming involved in purely European quarrels (nonintervention). Third, Monroe insisted that European states not meddle in the affairs of the New World countries. In other words, Monroe declared that the United States would not take sides in European disputes, but in return, Europe would not be permitted to tamper with the internal and continental affairs of the Western Hemisphere.

Monroe's bold message offered no immediate threat to such nations as Great Britain and France because in 1823 the United States lacked the power to enforce its self-proclaimed role as protector of the Western Hemisphere. Fortunately for the United States, however, Great Britain desired just such a policy as Monroe suggested. The British Royal Navy, not Monroe's declaration, would maintain the independence of Latin America. It would not be until 1852 that anyone referred to Monroe's declaration as the Monroe Doctrine, and it was not until the twentieth century that the United States was powerful enough to enforce international acceptance of the Monroe Doctrine.

Even so, Monroe's words reflected the change in unfriendly relations between the United States and Great Britain that had led to the War of 1812. The explanation lies in the decisions made at the Congress of Vienna in 1815. Napoleon had been defeated; Prussia, Russia, Austria, France, and Great Britain set out to turn the clock back, through establishing a Quintuple Alliance to undo the damage wrought by Napoleon's ambition. The establishment of the alliance led to the Concert of Europe, which sponsored four congresses between 1818 and 1822. The congresses created the modern system of conference diplomacy, although their various participants failed to agree on Europe's future.

Autocratic reactionaries hampered the Quintuple Alliance's effectiveness from the beginning. Czar Alexander I of Russia led the way, persuading the monarchs of Austria and Prussia to join him in the Holy Alliance, which dedicated itself to upholding autocratic rule. Great Britain chose not to join, but continued to be a member of the Quintuple Alliance. As a member of that alliance, Britain seemed to support a policy of reestablishing monarchy and opposing revolution. By refusing to join the Holy Alliance, however, the British avoided appearing as the bastion of the conservative reactionaries. When put to the test, Britain's actions proved that it favored a system of monarchy and a European balance of power, but not systematic oppression of revolution in others parts of the world.

The "other parts of the world" in question were primarily the newly independent states of the Western Hemisphere—most of which had thrown off Spanish colonial rule. Spain demanded the return of its New World colonies. In 1820, when Prince Metternich, the Austrian architect of reaction, suggested that the Concert of Europe had a sacred duty to crush revolution, Britain protested. Metternich's proposal would have meant sending an army to Latin America to overthrow the new republics. Britain distinguished between a European balance-of-power system, in which revolution would not be permitted, and a colonial empire in the New World where revolution would be allowed to occur. In addition, Spain had monopolized trade with its colonies; only as independent republics could the former colonies maintain a profitable trade with the British.

Czar Alexander also tried to extend his interests in North America. Through an imperial decree on September 14, 1821, Russia claimed territory on the northern Pacific coast, as far south as the fifty-first parallel—well into Oregon Country—by insisting that all foreign ships must remain a substantial distance from the coast that far south. Secretary of State John Quincy Adams vigorously opposed the Russian decree, citing the U.S. principle of noncolonization. Russia never enforced its decree.

Viscount Castlereagh, the British foreign secretary, decided that Spanish claims to its former colonies in the New World were less important to Great Britain's interests than profitable trade with the newly independent nations. Accordingly, the British began devising an arrangement with the United States that would prevent European powers from taking new, or regaining old, colonies in the Western Hemisphere. In August, 1823, George Canning, Castlereagh's successor, suggested to Richard Rush, the U.S. minister to Great Britain, that the two countries jointly declare that they would oppose further colonization of the New World. Rush was reluctant to agree to such a bold move without consulting his own superior, Secretary of State Adams.

Meanwhile, Canning began a series of discussions with Prince Auguste-Jules-Armand-Marie de Polignac, the French ambassador in London, seeking some guarantee that France would not help Spain regain its lost colonies in the New World. On October 12, 1823, the ambassador gave Canning the specific assurances he wanted, in a document known as the Polignac Memorandum.

France's promise to Great Britain—not the American Monroe Doctrine—ended any chance of Spain regaining its colonies in the New World. Unaware of the Polignac Memorandum, Adams advised Monroe against a joint noncolonization declaration with the British. Instead, he suggested that the United States make a unilateral declaration opposing further European colonization in the Western Hemisphere. The resulting declaration came in the president's message to Congress in December, 1823.

MONROE DOCTRINE

In his State of the Union address of December 2, 1823, President James Monroe asserted that the Western Hemisphere was off limits to European colonization and that the United States would refrain from intervening in the affairs of Europe. He warned that any movement toward the West, to the Americas in general, would be considered an act of aggression against the United States and would be met with resistance.

[T]he American continents, by the free and independent condition which they have assumed and maintain, are henceforth not to be considered as subjects for future colonization by any European powers. . . .

In the wars of the European powers in matters relating to themselves we have never taken any part, nor does it comport with our policy so to do. It is only when our rights are invaded or seriously menaced that we resent injuries or make preparation for our defense. With the movements in this [Western] hemisphere we are of necessity more immediately connected, and by causes which must be obvious to all enlightened and impartial observers. The political system of the allied powers is essentially different in this respect from that of America. This difference proceeds from that which exists in their respective Governments; and to the defense of our own, which has been achieved by the loss of so much blood and treasure, and matured by the wisdom of their most enlightened citizens, and under which we have enjoyed unexampled felicity, this whole nation is devoted. We owe it, therefore, to candor and to the amicable relations existing between the United States and those powers to declare that we should consider any attempt on their part to extend their system to any portion of this hemisphere as dangerous to our peace and safety. With the existing colonies or dependencies of any European power we have not interfered and shall not interfere. But with the Governments who have declared their independence and maintained it, and whose independence we have, on great consideration and on just principles, acknowledged, we could not view any interposition for the purpose of oppressing them, or controlling in any other manner their destiny, by any European power in any other light than as the manifestation of an unfriendly disposition toward the United States. In the war between those new Governments and Spain we declared our neutrality at the time of their recognition, and to this we have adhered, and shall continue to adhere, provided no change shall occur which, in the judgment of the competent authorities of this Government, shall make a corresponding change on the part of the United States indispensable to their security.

SIGNIFICANCE

Since 1823, President James Monroe's message has gained much greater significance as the United States has grown militarily stronger. During the U.S. Civil War (1861-1865), France established a puppet government under the Austrian archduke Maximilian in Mexico. By invoking the Monroe Doctrine and threatening invasion in 1867, the United States ensured the collapse of Maximilian's regime. In December, 1904, President Theodore Roosevelt added a corollary to the Monroe Doctrine, in which he stated that the United States would not interfere with Latin American nations that conducted their affairs with decency. Should they fail to do so, the United States would then intervene and exercise international police power to ensure the stability of the Western Hemisphere. In 1930, President Herbert Hoover formally repudiated the Roosevelt Corollary by revealing the publication of a document known as the Clark Memorandum adjuring any right of the United States to intervene in Latin America. Henceforth, the Monroe Doctrine was to be applied only as originally intended— to protect Latin America from European intervention.

Since 1930, however, the United States has repeatedly found reasons for intervening in the affairs of other countries in the Western Hemisphere. In 1965, for example, President Lyndon B. Johnson ordered U.S. troops into the Dominican Republic to prevent a takeover of that country by a communist government, although the official justification for that action was the protection of U.S. citizens and property. The same justification was used by President Ronald Reagan in 1983 to invade the tiny island nation of Grenada. In 1989, President George Bush used hemispheric stability and his war on drugs to invade Panama and capture Panamanian dictator Manuel Noriega, who he declared was an international drug trafficker.

—*David H. Culbert, updated by William Allison*

FURTHER READING

Alvarez, Alejandro. *The Monroe Doctrine: Its Importance in the International Life of the States of the New World*. Buffalo, N.Y.: William S. Hein, 2003. A publication of the Carnegie Endowment for International Peace, this substantial volume considers the impact of the Monroe Doctrine on the modern nations of the Western Hemisphere.

Bartlett, Christopher J. "Castlereagh, 1812-1822." In *The Makers of British Policy: From Pitt to Thatcher*, edited by T. G. Otte. New York: Palgrave, 2002. Essay on the last decade of Castlereagh's life, when he was British foreign secretary.

Bemis, Samuel Flagg. *The Latin American Policy of the United States: An Historical Interpretation*. New York: W. W. Norton, 1967. Best account to date of Secretary of State John Quincy Adams's role in forming the Monroe Doctrine.

Cunningham, Noble E., Jr. *The Presidency of James Monroe*. Lawrence: University Press of Kansas, 1996. Study of the most important policy issues with which Monroe dealt during his two-term presidency, with considerable attention to the Monroe Doctrine.

Donovan, Frank Robert. *Mr. Monroe's Message: The Story of the Monroe Doctrine*. New York: Dodd, Mead, 1963. A narrative history of the formulation of the Monroe Doctrine in the context of the domestic and international situation of the United States at the time.

Klimenko, Michael. *Alexander I, Emperor of Russia: A Reappraisal*. Tenafly, N.J.: Hermitage, 2002. Full biography of Czar Alexander I by a professor of Russian history.

May, Ernest R. *The Making of the Monroe Doctrine*. Cambridge, Mass.: Belknap Press of Harvard University Press, 1975. Stresses the domestic side of the Monroe Doctrine.

Rappaport, Armin, ed. *The Monroe Doctrine*. New York: Holt, Rinehart and Winston, 1964. A solid history of the impact of the Monroe Doctrine on U.S. foreign policy through the early 1960's, when the United States was attempting to intervene in Cuba.

Ronfeldt, David F. *Rethinking the Monroe Doctrine*. Santa Monica, Calif.: Rand, 1985. Discussion of the long-term implications of the Monroe Doctrine.

Smith, Gaddis. *The Last Years of the Monroe Doctrine, 1945-1993*. New York: Hill & Wang, 1994. Attack on abuses of the Monroe Doctrine by the United States since the end of World War II.

SEE ALSO: Nov. 20, 1815: Second Peace of Paris; Oct. 20-30, 1822: Great Britain Withdraws from the Concert of Europe; June 15, 1846: United States Acquires Oregon Territory; Oct. 31, 1861-June 19, 1867: France Occupies Mexico; Oct., 1889-Apr., 1890: First Pan-American Congress.

RELATED ARTICLES in *Great Lives from History: The Nineteenth Century, 1801-1900:* John Quincy Adams; Alexander I; George Canning; Viscount Castlereagh; Maximilian; Metternich; James Monroe.

1824
BRITISH PARLIAMENT REPEALS THE COMBINATION ACTS

*Motivated by a fear of revolution, the government of
William Pitt the Younger passed the Combination Acts
in 1799 and 1800, outlawing trade unions or any form
of collective bargaining in Great Britain. In 1824,
active organizing by proponents of unions led
Parliament to repeal the acts.*

ALSO KNOWN AS: Combination Laws
LOCALE: London, England
CATEGORIES: Laws, acts, and legal history;
government and politics; business and labor; social
issues and reform; civil rights and liberties

KEY FIGURES
Joseph Hume (1777-1855), parliamentary leader of the
repeal effort
William Huskisson (1770-1830), president of the
British Board of Trade
William Pitt the Younger (1759-1806), British prime
minister, 1783-1801, 1804-1806
Francis Place (1771-1854), British tailor who organized
the campaign for repeal of the Combination Acts

SUMMARY OF EVENT
The last decade of the eighteenth century was a time of
turmoil in Europe. The French Revolution of 1789, rapidly fluctuating prices, and the beginnings of the Industrial Revolution had combined to create social and economic uncertainty. Manufacturing workers, both those
in factories and those still in small workshops, sought
ways to improve their lives, particularly through collective action. They sought to improve the wages and hours
they worked, but they were beset by legal obstacles, including laws regulating or forbidding collective action
by workers in individual industries. Workers continued
to band together despite these laws, and the government
of William Pitt the Younger, fearful that such combinations could become the basis for a political revolution,
passed the Combination Acts of 1799 and 1800, forbidding the formation of workers' collective organizations
and threatening them with prosecution.

At the time the Combination Acts were passed, there
were already many laws and rules directed at workers'
combinations. If a group organized a strike that resulted
in work already contracted being left unfinished, its
members could be prosecuted for breach of contract, particularly because the old apprenticeship rules forbade
leaving work unfinished. Under the common law, more-

over, such workers could also be prosecuted for conspiracy. The result was that many trade unions went underground, meeting in secret and keeping their membership
lists secret. The greatest obstacle to legal action against
unions was that, under existing law, an employer had to
instigate proceedings before the authorities could intervene.

A second factor behind the industrial unrest of the
period was the rapid technological change then occurring, which, by 1810, had begun to spark riots and other
mob actions protesting the introduction of labor-saving
machinery. This unrest, commonly referred to as "Luddism" (from the name of a possibly mythical leader of the
protest movement, King Ludd), was particularly violent
in the Nottingham region, among the makers of stockings. Stocking manufacturers were introducing machines called stocking frames in their factories, greatly
increasing their output without any increase in the number of employees. Indeed, in some cases, the increase in
productivity led manufacturers to eliminate jobs. Several
of the new machines were destroyed by Luddite mobs,
until a law passed in 1812 made frame breaking a capital
offense. Similar protests occurred in the West Riding of
Yorkshire when cloth manufacturers introduced gig
mills and shearing frames, which increased productivity
in "cropping," or finishing, cloth. Meanwhile, in southern Lancashire, cotton cloth weavers began to protest the
introduction of new, more productive looms.

In response to this industrial unrest, Parliament undertook to modernize the laws on the books governing labor relations. The most important of these was the Statute of Artificers, governing apprenticeships, which dated
back to Elizabethan times. Such laws were modernized
to respond not only to unrest but also to new economic
thinking, sparked in particular by the work of Adam
Smith and David Ricardo, who espoused the view that
the market was the only force that could properly determine the price of labor. Thus, the old rules that restrained
production, such as those governing apprenticeships,
needed to go. The Statute of Artificers was accordingly
repealed in 1814.

At the same time, despite the restrictions on the formation of unions, activists such as Francis Place, a self-
educated tailor who exercised a profound influence on
labor relations, began to change public opinion. Place believed that workers ought to have the right to organize
unions in order to gain equivalence in their relations with

1820's

365

THE SELECT COMMITTEE REPORTS ON THE COMBINATION ACTS

The Select Committee of the House of Commons on the Combination Laws issued a set of resolutions on May 21, 1824, recommending that Parliament repeal the Combination Acts of 1799 and 1800 and that the common law be altered to permit peaceful meetings of workers or employers. The first six of these resolutions are reproduced below.

1. That it appears, by the evidence before the Committee, that combinations of workmen have taken place in England, Scotland and Ireland, often to a great extent, to raise and keep up their wages, to regulate their hours of working, and to impose restrictions on the masters, respecting apprentices or others whom they might think proper to employ; and that, at the time the evidence was taken, combinations were in existence, attended with strikes or suspension of work; and that the laws have not hitherto been effectual to prevent such combinations.
2. That serious breaches of the peace and acts of violence, with strikes of the workmen, often for very long periods, have taken place, in consequence of, and arising out of the combinations of workmen, and been attended with loss to both the masters and the workmen, and with considerable inconvenience and injury to the community.
3. That the masters have often united and combined to lower the rates of their workmen's wages, as well as to resist a demand for an increase, and to regulate their hours of working; and sometimes to discharge their workmen who would not consent to the conditions offered to them; which have been followed by suspension of work, riotous proceedings, and acts of violence.
4. That prosecutions have frequently been carried on, under the Statute and the Common Law against the workmen, and many of them have suffered different periods of imprisonment for combining and conspiring to raise their wages, or to resist their reduction, and to regulate their hours of working.
5. That several instances have been stated to the Committee, of prosecutions against masters for combining to lower wages and to regulate the hours of working; but no instance has been adduced of any master having been punished for that offence.
6. That the laws have not only not been efficient to prevent combinations either of masters or workmen, but, on the contrary, have, in the opinion of many of both parties, had a tendency to produce mutual irritation and distrust, and to give a violent character to the combinations, and to render them highly dangerous to the peace of the community.

Source: A. Aspinall and E. Anthony Smith, eds. *1783-1832.* Vol. 11 in *English Historical Documents* (New York: Oxford University Press, 1959), pp. 752-754.

By the 1820's, despite or perhaps because of the fact that the national government was dominated by the Tories, who chiefly represented landowners, conditions had become ripe for action on the Combination Acts. Parliament was receiving petitions from groups of workers asking for the right to organize unions. Radical members of Parliament were able to exploit the division in Parliament between the majority Tories, who supported landowners, and the Liberals, who supported industrial employers. These radicals, under the leadership of Joseph Hume and working closely with Francis Place, began to introduce legislation that would abolish the Combination Acts and free the workers to organize legally.

When Hume stated his intention to introduce a bill abolishing the Combination Acts, the Tory-controlled government, through William Huskisson, the president of the Board of Trade, agreed to appoint a select committee of the House of Commons to look into the issue. By carefully selecting the witnesses appearing before the committee, Hume and Place were able to ensure that the committee only heard testimony supporting repeal. A bill repealing the Combination Acts was then introduced into the House of Commons by Joseph Hume, and—perhaps because of the careful preparation of the testimony before the committee—it passed in the 1824 session, almost without discussion. The 1824 law did more than repeal the statutes prohibiting collective bargaining: It also abolished the common law rule against conspiracies as applied to unions—perhaps its most important feature. It freed unions as well from prosecution if they called a strike that prevented the completion of work under contract.

SIGNIFICANCE

The law of 1824 legalizing union activity unleashed a wave of union actions in Great Britain. Notably in Scotland, coal miners created a union embracing workers at

employers, although he doubted that negotiated wages could be sustained if they departed markedly from the prevailing wage determined by the market. Place was particularly influential in publicizing the conditions of labor and in organizing groups asking for repeal of the Combination Acts and the legalization of trade unions.

many mines. This union was able to negotiate substantial wage increases, through strikes or the threat of strikes, in some cases boosting wages by as much as 80 percent. The owners responded by hiring "blacklegs," or non-union workers, but they aroused public opinion sufficiently that Parliament was inspired to revise the legislation of 1824. The revised law of 1825 restored the application of the common law against conspiracies to unions and employers in some circumstances, but it left in place the right of the unions to negotiate with respect to wages and hours. Merely belonging to a union was no longer an illegal act. Thus, unions were freed from the risk of prosecution, though their members were not necessarily free from the possibility of legal action being taken against them. Under the still existing Masters and Servants Law, individual workers could be prosecuted for leaving a task unfinished. As long as unions did not attempt to "intimidate" employers, however, they were free to exist.

The repeal of the Combination Acts in 1824, even with the modification in 1825, recognized that the relations between workers and employers would henceforth be determined by collective action rather than the individual relationships that had defined the rules governing masters and apprentices from the Middle Ages. The new laws reflected the arrival of the Industrial Revolution, which grouped together workers in factories rather than the small workshops that had previously dominated British labor. These new laws and their resulting rules and regulations dominated labor relations in Great Britain until a more liberal regime was introduced after 1870.

—*Nancy M. Gordon*

FURTHER READING

Halévy, Élie. *The Liberal Awakening, 1815-1830*. Vol. 2 in *A History of the English People in the Nineteenth Century*. Translated by E. I. Watkin. 2d rev. ed. New York: Peter Smith, 1949. This volume of Halévy's classic history of Britain during the nineteenth century contains numerous details of the fight to repeal the Combination Acts.

Harris, Ron. "Government and the Economy, 1688-1850." In *The Cambridge Economic History of Modern Britain*, edited by Roderick Floud and Paul Johnson. 3 vols. Cambridge, England: Cambridge University Press, 2004. Contains a short section under "Regulation" that neatly summarizes British law on unions.

Miles, Dudley. *Francis Place, 1771-1854: The Life of a Remarkable Radical*. New York: St. Martin's Press, 1988. This comprehensive biography of Francis Place is indispensable for understanding the complex public relations campaign that led up to the repeal.

Rule, John, ed. *British Trade Unionism, 1750-1850*. London: Longman, 1988. This compilation of a variety of articles dealing with the development of trade unions during this period contains some useful details.

Stevenson, John. *Popular Disturbances in England, 1700-1832*. 2d ed. London: Longman, 1992. Traces the role of worker protests leading up to the imposition of the Combination Acts in 1799 and 1800.

Thompson, E. P. *The Making of the English Working Class*. New York: Vintage Books, 1963. The classic Marxist treatment of modern British history; contains many useful details.

Woodward, E. L. *The Age of Reform, 1815-1870*. Oxford, England: Clarendon Press, 1939. Full of useful details, particularly regarding the process of reform in Parliament.

SEE ALSO: Dec. 11-30, 1819: British Parliament Passes the Six Acts; May 9, 1828-Apr. 13, 1829: Roman Catholic Emancipation; June 4, 1832: British Parliament Passes the Reform Act of 1832; 1833: British Parliament Passes the Factory Act; Aug. 14, 1834: British Parliament Passes New Poor Law; Sept. 9, 1835: British Parliament Passes Municipal Corporations Act; June 15, 1846: British Parliament Repeals the Corn Laws; Aug., 1867: British Parliament Passes the Reform Act of 1867; June 2, 1868: Great Britain's First Trades Union Congress Forms; Jan., 1884: Fabian Society Is Founded; Dec. 6, 1884: British Parliament Passes the Franchise Act of 1884; Aug. 3, 1892: Hardie Becomes Parliament's First Labour Member.

RELATED ARTICLES in *Great Lives from History: The Nineteenth Century, 1801-1900:* Second Earl of Liverpool; Sir Robert Peel; Francis Place; David Ricardo.

1820'S

1824
PARIS SALON OF 1824

A national, government-sponsored exhibition and prize competition, the Salon of 1824 launched three artists of widely varying styles who would become world famous: John Constable, Eugène Delacroix, and Jean-Auguste-Dominique Ingres.

LOCALE: Le Palais du Louvre, Paris, France
CATEGORY: Art

KEY FIGURES
John Constable (1776-1837), English landscape
　　painter
Eugène Delacroix (1798-1863), French painter
Jean-Auguste-Dominique Ingres (1780-1867), French
　　painter
Charles X (1757-1836), king of France, r. 1824-1830

SUMMARY OF EVENT
The art exhibition known as the Paris Salon, or simply the Salon, began in the seventeenth century. It was at first both intermittent and variable in location and format, but it became a permanent, regular event beginning in 1737. The Salon of 1824 proved particularly noteworthy, because it represented the coming to prominence of three radically different European artists, each of whom would go on to be recognized as a nineteenth century master. More than one thousand paintings, juried and accepted by the royal commission, were displayed at the 1824 Salon.

One of John Constable's entries, *The Hay Wain*, won a gold medal in the overall competition. The painting—a tranquil, pastoral scene of a draught horse, a farmer, and a hay wagon cooling its wheels in a pond during a pause in the harvest—featured an extended view of a sumptuous, dewy landscape. It seemed to offer a nostalgic retreat from the dawning Industrial Revolution to a bygone rural era. Constable had left his native village of East Bergholt, Suffolk, sometime before rich landowners in the area took advantage of the enclosure laws to claim the commons for themselves and to drive off the gleaners and subsistence farmers. Thus, his compositions of the village were doubly nostalgic, truer to his memories than to the current state of his first home.

French painters and critics, unaware of recent British social history, focused on Constable's painterly technique. He was unmatched in representing luminous, moist atmospheres over fields (just as J. M. W. Turner, who painted from a boat, was unrivaled in treating light

and atmosphere over open water). Constable's original title for *The Hay Wain*, *Landscape: Noon*, strongly suggests that light was his main subject, as it would be the main subject half a century later in Claude Monet's series studying the façade of a cathedral, a lily pond, or a haystack at different times of day.

In 1821, Constable had begun to use subtly juxtaposed touches of white and contrasting primary colors. His fame in France had increased the same year, when the French fantasist and travel writer Charles Nodier praised Constable's *The Hay Wain* in *Promenade de Dieppe aux montagnes d'Écosse* (1821; *Promenade from Dieppe to the Mountains of Scotland*, 1822). To create a market for Constable's work in France, the dealer John Arrowsmith arranged for *The Hay Wain*, *The View on the Stour Near Dedham*, and a view of Hampstead Heath to be shown at the Paris Salon of 1824, where all three aroused great interest.

Meanwhile, Jean-Auguste-Dominique Ingres, back in France after spending sixteen years studying and painting in Italy, had accepted a commission for a painting of Louis XIII, who had reigned near the height of royal absolutism in the seventeenth century. Shrewdly avoiding the unintended unfavorable connotations of the original plan to depict Louis XIII praying before a Pietà—a depiction of Mary mourning over Christ's body—(which would suggest royal repentance), Ingres instead portrayed the king dedicating his reign to the Blessed Virgin. The painting was an ideal opening wedge, allowing the artist to reenter the French art market and find wealthy, prominent patrons.

Eugène Delacroix, finally, had three compositions accepted for exhibition at the Salon of 1824. The most impressive of these, *Scène des massacres de Scio: Familles grecques attendant la mort ou l'esclavage* (*Scene of the Massacre at Chios: Greek Families Awaiting Death or Slavery*, commonly known as *The Massacre at Chios*), benefited from competition among wealthy collectors interested in the work. A composite scene of Turkish overlords raping, enslaving, and slaughtering innocent civilian populations on the Greek island of Scio, Delacroix's painting was quietly purchased by Charles X's curator even before it was publicly displayed—and without the king's knowledge. This irregular, unprecedented action was intended to help mend the revolutionary breach of twenty-five years that had long deprived the French monarchy of its former role as the major patron of the arts and guardian of France's national heritage.

Delacroix's heavily muscled nude figures in distorted poses—noteworthy at the 1822 Salon in *Dante et Virgile aux enfers* (*The Barque of Dante*)—derived from Michelangelo, the painter of the Sistine Chapel's ceiling at the Vatican. This merely stylistic similarity to the papally chosen painter provided Delacroix with undeserved theocratic credentials in the eyes of the French court, credentials congenial to the conservative Charles X, who claimed to rule by divine right. The choice proved fortuitous nonetheless, as Delacroix's illustrations of the great literary classics of the Western tradition—including those of William Shakespeare, Johann Wolfgang von Goethe, and Sir Walter Scott—would increase enormously by association the prestige of the new French monarchy.

The Massacre at Chios was not yet the mature work of a master: Its secondary compositional elements were somewhat awkward and were overly derivative of Delacroix's inspirations, Théodore Géricault's *Raft of the Medusa* and recent neoclassical art glorifying Napoleon and his empire. These shortcomings, however, were compensated by the painting's topical interest as a sympathetic commentary on the Greeks oppressed by their Turkish masters and fighting for independence. Although the Greeks were Christians and the Turks were Muslims, Charles X would have preferred to continue supporting the established Turkish government, with which he and earlier French leaders had had longstanding relations. Public opinion, though, was spurred in 1824 by the death of George Gordon, Lord Byron, while fighting for the Greek cause and by Delacroix's painting. It finally pushed the French government into supporting the Greeks, who won independence in 1830. Delacroix thus anticipated Pablo Picasso's anti-fascist protest painting, *Guernica*, shown in Paris in 1937.

SIGNIFICANCE

The great painters unveiled at the Salon of 1824 participated not only in the rarefied world of art but in the realm of French politics and ideology as well. Charles X's newly established monarchy sought to legitimize itself by bridging the twenty-five-year gap created by the French First Republic and First Empire to connect the new king with the traditional monarchy in the eyes of the people. The French monarchic succession had gone unbroken since the eighth century, before it was interrupted by the French Revolution (1789) and Napoleon's regime (1804-1815), and Charles's political success depended on inserting himself in the established tradition to acquire the dignity of his forebears. A major focus of this effort to connect the king with history was historical painting, which created a public record of the past while simultaneously glorifying French rulers.

In addition to participating in this process, Ingres's *Le Vœu de Louis XIII* (*The Vow of Louis XIII*) linked the monarchy to the Roman Catholic Church, whose aegis provided absolute monarchs with the semblance of divine approval. Moreover, although Delacroix did not render obeisance to established religion, he shared with Ingres an at least implicit homage to the established European powers. Both Delacroix's and Ingres's work engaged in orientalism—an ideology that rendered the East exotic, mysterious, and otherworldly—for example in the highly sexualized depiction of the Maghreb and the Middle East in the guise of female sex slaves. They thus helped represent the continuing French conquest of North Africa as being justified by the decadence of that region. The motif of European dominance, depicted simultaneously in representations of Europe as invader and as voyeur, linked the Napoleonic expeditions at the turn of the nineteenth century to the expansive dream of a French manifest destiny in North Africa.

Jean-Auguste-Dominique Ingres. (Library of Congress)

1820's

These two painters would sustain a fierce rivalry embodied in their divergent, neoclassical and Romantic, styles for forty more years (although Delacroix rejected the label of "Romantic"). Delacroix's intensely kinetic compositions and figures, as well as his rough finish, contrasted starkly with Ingres's static, neoclassical compositions and shiny, unctuous surfaces. Delacroix's implicit painterly challenge to the existing order was overlooked because of the intriguing vitality and originality of his work. His *Liberty Leading the People*, a paean to the July Revolution of 1830, appeared only after the constitutional monarchy sought by that uprising had become a fait accompli. He won major government commissions until the end of his life.

Meanwhile, to French eyes, the ideological "innocence" of the English landscape painter John Constable allowed viewers in the Louvre Museum to focus on his outstanding painterly qualities. His impressionistic effects in outdoor scenes anticipated the Barbizon School of the 1830's and the Impressionist movement in the last quarter of the nineteenth century, as well as the pointillists, such as Georges Seurat, who followed.

—*Laurence M. Porter*

FURTHER READING

Bishop, Peter. *An Archetypal Constable: National Identity and the Geography of Nostalgia*. Madison, N.J.: Fairleigh Dickinson University Press, 1995. Uses the Jungian concept of "archetype" to argue that Constable's paintings helped create a British national identity by portraying imagined landscapes that defined "home" and, by extension, "self" for British subjects.

Bryson, Norman. *Tradition and Desire: From David to Delacroix*. Cambridge, England: Cambridge University Press, 1984. Seminal poststructuralist reading of French art and history; chapters 4 and 5 discuss Delacroix.

Duncan, Carol. "Ingres's *Vow of Louis XIII* and the Politics of the Restoration." In *The Aesthetics of Power: Essays in Critical Art History*. Cambridge, England: Cambridge University Press, 1993. Situates Ingres's painting against the sociopolitical anxieties and tensions of its time.

Fraser, Elisabeth A. "Family as Nation in the *Massacres of Chios*," In *Delacroix, Art, and Patrimony in Post-Revolutionary France*. New York: Cambridge University Press, 2004. Sees a correspondence between Delacroix's need to establish his artistic genealogy and Charles X's need to establish his monarchic lineage: For both figures, patrimony was crucial, and their needs converge in the production and reception of Delacroix's major paintings of the 1820's.

Grigsby, Darcy Grimaldo. *Extremities: Painting Empire in Post-Revolutionary France*. New Haven, Conn.: Yale University Press, 2002. Reads the *Massacres at Chios* as part of the French colonial project of the nineteenth century.

Lambert, Ray. *John Constable and the Theory of Landscape Painting*. Cambridge, England: Cambridge University Press, 2005. Reveals Constable's extensive knowledge of aesthetic theory and the ways in which that knowledge influenced his own paintings.

Siegfried, Susan L. "Ingres and the Theatrics of History Painting." *Word and Image* 16, no. 1 (2000): 58-76. Examines Ingres's deployment of theatrical tropes in the composition of his paintings.

Stendhal. *Salons*. Edited by Stéphane Guégan and Martine Reid. Paris: Gallimard, 2002. Includes Stendhal's extensive review of the Salon of 1824. In French.

Vaughan, William. *John Constable*. London: Tate, 2002. Seeks to show Constable and his work in a new light by juxtaposing his paintings with his letters and other writing.

SEE ALSO: 1801: Emergence of the Primitives; c. 1830-1870: Barbizon School of Landscape Painting Flourishes; July 29, 1830: July Revolution Deposes Charles X; Oct.-Dec., 1830: Delacroix Paints *Liberty Leading the People*; Mar. 12, 1832: *La Sylphide* Inaugurates Romantic Ballet's Golden Age; May 15, 1863: Paris's Salon des Refusés Opens; Feb. 20, 1872: Metropolitan Museum of Art Opens; Apr. 15, 1874: First Impressionist Exhibition; Late 1870's: Post-Impressionist Movement Begins; 1892-1895: Toulouse-Lautrec Paints *At the Moulin Rouge*.

RELATED ARTICLES in *Great Lives from History: The Nineteenth Century, 1801-1900:* John Constable; Eugène Delacroix; Jean-Auguste-Dominique Ingres; Stendhal; J. M. W. Turner.

1824
RANKE DEVELOPS SYSTEMATIC HISTORY

Ranke's first historical study transformed the discipline of history by claiming that historians could produce scientifically objective accounts of the past by following a properly systematic historiographic methodology. Ranke's prolific writing and teaching over the next six decades would earn him recognition as the founder of scientific history.

LOCALE: Berlin, Prussia (now in Germany)
CATEGORY: Historiography

KEY FIGURES

Leopold Ranke (1795-1886), German historian who was later ennobled as Leopold von Ranke
Barthold Georg Niebuhr (1776-1831), German historian
Georg Wilhelm Friedrich Hegel (1770-1831), German philosopher of history
Metternich (1773-1859), Austrian politician and diplomat

SUMMARY OF EVENT

While completing his studies in theology and classics at the University of Leipzig when he was twenty years old, Leopold Ranke (who would become Leopold von Ranke in 1865) ceased to be a citizen of Saxony and became instead a citizen of Prussia. Such was the decision of the Congress of Vienna (1814-1815), which transferred Ranke's native Thuringia from Saxony to Prussia. This transfer reinforced Ranke's belief that it was political matters above all else that affected people's lives and the course of history.

Upon graduation, Ranke took a position in the Prussian grammar school system at Frankfurt. In order to improve his knowledge of history, which consisted largely of ancient history, Ranke conducted research and wrote. His love of ancient history caused him to read Barthold Georg Niebuhr's work *Römische Geschichte* (1811-1812; *The Roman History*, 1827), which pioneered scientific history by using available documents to discuss Rome from its founding to the Punic Wars (264-146 B.C.E.). Niebuhr's work exposed as fables many previously held beliefs about Rome's historical development. Ranke too became determined to trust only original sources rather than use the work of other authors.

The result of this determination was Ranke's first book, *Geschichte der romanischen und germanischen Völker von 1494 bis 1514* (1824; *History of the Latin and*

Teutonic Nations from 1494 to 1514, 1887). The study was such an immediate success that it earned him a professorship at the University of Berlin the following year. Ranke's work was very different from that of his contemporaries. He used a wide variety of primary sources, including memoirs, letters, diplomatic dispatches, and eyewitness accounts, to analyze the struggle between the French and the Habsburgs for domination of Italy.

Ranke selected this narrowly defined topic as the subject of his first major study, because he regarded it as an important turning point in history. As in all his subsequent writings, Ranke's emphasis was on political history and international developments. Writing in a graphic narrative style, he intended to transport his readers to another time and place, transforming them as nearly as possible into witnesses of history and allowing them to observe the unfolding of events firsthand. There was drama in the French-Habsburg power struggle for dominance in Italy, and Ranke allowed that drama to structure his account, detailing a series of events that built up to a historical climax.

Ranke studiously avoided using dull and often incorrect information from textbooks or secondary sources. Attached at the end of his work as an appendix was a critique of history as it had been written thus far and a set of recommendations as to how it should be written in the future. It was in this appendix that Ranke defined his new scientific approach to history. He denounced the fiction of the past as mere literary creation and enthroned fact in its place. History, he asserted, rested on particulars, not general laws or preconceived concepts. He rejected moralizing upon events in the past based on the values of the present, insisting instead that the historian's mission was simply to demonstrate objectively the way things actually were at a particular point in time.

Individuals and past societies, for Ranke, had to be understood in their own terms, and all historical facts that led to such an understanding had to be derived from and documented by sources. Thus, Ranke insisted that the historian must locate documents, critically sift through the information they contain, collect the objective facts that can be distilled from them, and piece these facts together to reconstruct a logical sequence of events. Such critical investigation would result in conclusions that would have scientific validity. These conclusions were not enough, however: Ranke also argued that the historian must use his "God-given talents" to present the ma-

1820's

371

Leopold von Ranke. (Library of Congress)

terial in an artistic way, capturing the interest and imagination of a reader. Hence, a historian was not only a critical investigator but also a writer. A historian's work could be a literary masterpiece, yet the use of facts would make it a nonfictional masterpiece.

Ranke's second work, *Fürsten und Völker von Süd-Europa im sechszehnten und siebzehnten Jahrhundert* (1827-1836, 4 volumes; *Sovereigns and Nations of Southern Europe, in the Sixteenth and Seventeenth Centuries: More Commonly Known as Ranke's History of the Popes, and of the Spanish and Ottoman Empires*, 1843), used a variety of archival sources, paramount among which was the correspondence of Venetian diplomats about the struggle between the expanding Ottoman Empire and Spain for hegemony in the Mediterranean. This correspondence had been unavailable to other historians: It was Metternich's active intervention on Ranke's behalf that allowed him to gain access to archives in Vienna and Italy.

The material Ranke obtained in these archives formed the basis of wonderful narratives about the popes, whom he viewed more as pragmatic political leaders than as re-

ligious figures. The use of stories and the unfolding of intimate details also acted to render the character and behavior of the popes as intriguing as the histories they inhabited. In all instances, Ranke attempted to be a dispassionate observer and an objective analyst. If any conclusions were to be drawn, it was the reader who was to draw them. Ranke merely sought to provide the details, both positive and negative, upon which those conclusions would be based. Key events or turning points were not to be declared as such: They were only hinted at by the degree of attention and detail Ranke provided in his descriptions of them. This same objectivity was brought to bear in Ranke's *Deutsche Geschichte im Zeitalter der Reformation* (1839-1847; *History of the Reformation in Germany*, 1845-1847), aiding his analysis of what was still a delicate topic.

Ranke's scholarly production was voluminous. He completed fifty-four volumes and wrote nine volumes of an uncompleted universal history, which he worked on during the last ten years of life. He produced voluminous studies of the House of Brandenberg, sixteenth and seventeenth century France, and seventeenth century England. These national histories brought into focus a theme continually found in Ranke's work that the evolution of history led to the development of unique nation-states. The nation-state was the idea or theme of the age. In this, Ranke appropriated the concept of zeitgeist, or spirit of the age, first skillfully employed in the philosophy of Georg Wilhelm Friedrich Hegel. In determining the nature of the zeitgeist, Ranke insisted on following the path of particulars rather than beginning with an overarching a priori assumption. Ranke's writings about political developments of the past ultimately led him to conclusions about how the major states of Europe had developed to their then-present forms.

SIGNIFICANCE

In both quality and quantity, Leopold von Ranke can be regarded as the Western world's leading historian for the second half of the nineteenth century. His writings changed the status of the historian from a glorified storyteller to a scientist and literary artist. His teaching at the University of Berlin from 1825 to 1871 was equally impactful and related to the scientific methodology espoused in his seminal 1824 work. Ranke's students plunged into primary-source archival research and were strictly trained in their professor's scientific method. Ranke demanded footnotes and bibliographies, so any researcher could easily find a mentioned source. He pioneered the use of the seminar method, so his students could challenge one another's conclusions. From these approaches developed the idea that historical works had to stand the test of time to prove their authority and had to withstand challenges of other historians working from the same evidence, as well as new sources of evidence. Ranke trained more than two generations of leading German historians. His scientific history was further developed by such notables as Friedrich Meinecke and Max Lenz. These German historians in turn influenced the way history was researched, taught, and written in other European countries and the United States.

Ranke's narrow focus on political history and the policies of important political leaders remained a common bias among most historians until social and cultural history began to flourish in the 1960's. In part, this bias was a by-product of the types of sources historians could work with in government archives. Today, there are still a large number of historians who believe that the use of historical facts carefully distilled from primary source documents enables them to ascertain objective truths and that history is the mother of the social sciences. There are many others, however, who embrace the lessons of deconstruction, poststructuralism, and other movements that emphasize that narrative is inherently biased, and as soon as facts are used to tell a story they cease to be objective. Ranke's *History of the Latin and Teutonic Nations from 1494 to 1514*, then, can be viewed as having launched history into the modern age, in part by providing the founding terms of a debate that is still raging.

—*Irwin Halfond*

FURTHER READING

Bentley, Michael. *Modern Historiography: An Introduction*. New York: Routledge, 1999. Excellent background information; chapter 4 is devoted to Ranke. References and index.

Gilbert, Felix. *History: Politics or Culture? Reflections on Ranke and Burckhardt*. Princeton, N.J.: Princeton University Press, 1990. A comparative analysis of two fathers of modern history and the clash between Ranke's political history and Jacob Burckhardt's cultural history. Footnotes and bibliography.

Iggers, Georg G. *Historiography in the Twentieth Century: From Scientific Objectivity to the Postmodern Challenge*. Middleton, Conn.: Wesleyan University Press, 2004. The first three chapters treat Ranke's scientific historical influence, along with that of other German historians.

Iggers, Georg G., and James Powell, eds. *Leopold von Ranke and the Shaping of the Historical Discipline*. Syracuse, N.Y.: Syracuse University Press, 1990. A collection of essays by leading historians evaluating different aspects of Ranke's influence. Includes thirty-five pages of bibliographical references.

Krieger, Leonard. *Ranke: The Meaning of History*. Chicago: University of Chicago Press, 1971. A good starting point for interpreting Ranke's work. Footnotes and bibliography.

SEE ALSO: Apr., 1807: Hegel Publishes *The Phenomenology of Spirit*; 1819: Schopenhauer Publishes *The World as Will and Idea*; 1835-1836: Strauss Publishes *The Life of Jesus Critically Examined*; 1843: Carlyle Publishes *Past and Present*.

RELATED ARTICLES in *Great Lives from History: The Nineteenth Century, 1801-1900:* Jacob Burckhardt; Georg Wilhelm Friedrich Hegel; Metternich; Theodor Mommsen; Barthold Georg Niebuhr; Leopold von Ranke.

1820's

February 20, 1824
BUCKLAND PRESENTS THE FIRST PUBLIC DINOSAUR DESCRIPTION

Basing his conclusions mainly on a few fossil teeth and a jawbone that had been unearthed near Oxford, England, William Buckland published the first scientific description of an extinct land reptile, or dinosaur, giving it the genus name Megalosaurus.

LOCALE: London, England
CATEGORIES: Biology; science and technology

KEY FIGURES
William Buckland (1784-1856), English clergyman, geologist, and paleontologist
Robert Plot (1640-1696), English naturalist
James Hutton (1726-1797), Scottish geologist
Georges Cuvier (1769-1832), French comparative anatomist and paleontologist
Gideon Mantell (1790-1852), English physician and paleontologist
James Parkinson (1755-1824), English physician and geologist
Richard Owen (1804-1892), English anatomist and paleontologist

SUMMARY OF EVENT
Dinosaur fossils have been uncovered for thousands of years, but before the nineteenth century, the fossils were thought to be the bones of still-living animal species such as elephants, crocodiles, and fish. The idea that there had once existed life forms that had become extinct received little, if any, credence, mainly because Western religions maintained that the earth was young and that God would not allow his creations to become extinct.

It was not until the early nineteenth century, with the rapid development of the new science of geology, that views began to change. In 1795, Scottish geologist James Hutton posited that the earth was far older than the approximately six thousand years suggested in the Bible's Book of Genesis. Hutton's concept, known as uniformitarianism, attributed the features of Earth's crust to natural processes acting over long time periods, rather than to catastrophic events such as a biblical flood.

The earliest scientific documentation of dinosaurs was made in 1677 by an Englishman, Robert Plot, the first person to publish an illustration of a dinosaur bone. He incorrectly identified the bone as belonging to an elephant, however, and therefore cannot be credited with the first scientific description of a dinosaur. As geology was developing as a science during the early nineteenth

century, so, too, was vertebrate paleontology, the study of fossils of animals having backbones. In France, comparative anatomist Georges Cuvier was pioneering a new approach to the interpretation of fossils, using his knowledge of the anatomy of living animals to try to understand prehistoric ones. He maintained that fundamental laws governed animal structure, and that all the parts of an animal are interdependent and must function together for that creature to survive. Thus, for example, a carnivore's teeth, jaws, limbs, and other body parts are geared toward eating meat. Building from this principle, Cuvier established that there were past life forms that had become extinct.

Before it was known that dinosaurs existed, fossils in England were being unearthed. The fossils included those of extinct, giant reptiles, marine animals such as ichthyosaurs and plesiosaurs, and a flying creature, pterodactyl, all dating to the Mesozoic era (248 million to 65 million years ago). Scientists then found a new kind of creature, similarly ancient.

Some time before 1818, William Buckland, a clergyman and professor of geology at Oxford University, obtained some bones that included several fossil vertebrae, part of a thigh bone, and a piece of jaw with a few teeth from slate quarries at Stonesfield, about twelve miles north of Oxford, in south-central England. The English surveyor and geologist William Smith (1769-1839), who had mapped the geological strata of England, had shown that the strata in which the bones were found by Buckland dated to the mid-Jurassic period of the Mesozoic. (Scientists have since determined that Jurassic strata are 206 million to 144 million years old.)

In 1818, Cuvier examined the Stonesfield fossils. He knew that, although the leg bones bore some resemblance to those of mammals, no fossils of mammals had been found that were from the Jurassic. In addition, Cuvier noted the teeth did resemble, but were much larger than, those of a monitor lizard, an existing, carnivorous, terrestrial reptile. Cuvier therefore concluded that the fossils belonged to a previously unknown and gigantic carnivorous land reptile. The fossils were too fragmentary to provide a clear idea of the animal's appearance, however.

Buckland waited six years to publish the discovery of the Stonesfield fossils. Meanwhile, duirng the early 1820's, English physician-paleontologist Gideon Mantell unearthed teeth from another great land reptile from strata dating to the early Cretaceous period (beginning 144 million years ago), in Sussex, England. Mantell observed that the teeth of this creature differed from those of the carnivore discovered by Buckland. Mantell concluded that his creature was a plant eater, or herbivore.

Finally, on February 20, 1824, Buckland announced the discovery of the Stonesfield fossils in a paper read to the Geological Society of London. Based mainly on the teeth and lower jawbone, he described the creature as an extinct, giant, carnivorous, terrestrial "lizard." He named the animal megalosaurus, drawing on the Greek words *megalo*, for great, and *saurus*, for lizard. It was the largest land reptile, living or extinct, to be identified up to that time. Buckland, however, did not invent the name megalosaurus. James Parkinson published that name in 1822 but did not include a description of the animal referred to, so he did not receive credit. Scientists now know that megalosaurus was up to thirty feet long, ten feet in height, and weighed one ton or more. It is classified in the theropod group of dinosaurs.

Later in 1824, the Geological Society published Buckland's description of megalosaurus in its journal *Transactions of the Geological Society*. The following year, Mantell formally announced the discovery of the first giant, extinct, land-dwelling, herbivorous reptile, which he named iguanodon. Although Buckland's and

Georges Cuvier. (National Archives)

Mantell's announcements constituted the earliest published scientific descriptions of dinosaurs, these creatures had not yet been recognized as belonging to a distinct group and the term "dinosaur" had not yet been invented.

In 1842, English paleontologist Richard Owen reviewed the fossil evidence of the three species of large, extinct, land reptiles that had by then been confirmed by multiple specimens: megalosaurus, iguanodon, and a species that Mantell had discovered in 1833, hylaeosaurus. Noting the similarity in hip structure, Owen placed all three in a previously unrecognized order or suborder of reptiles. Owen called this new category the *dinosauria*, from the Greek *dino*, meaning fearfully great, and *saur*, lizard. Up to that time, eight other fossil reptiles had been named that would later be transferred to the *dinosauria* category. An important distinguishing characteristic of dinosaurs is that their legs are tucked in beneath their bodies, providing greater support than the legs of other reptiles, which project from the sides. Thus, dinosaurs, generally, had been able to walk and run more efficiently than had other reptiles.

SIGNIFICANCE

William Buckland's scientific description of the fossils of a long-extinct, giant, terrestrial reptile launched paleontology, the scientific study of past life as known from fossilized elements. The full significance of the early dinosaur discoveries came only after many years, however. The initial import of the discoveries was that they added to the mounting tally of species that had become extinct, and they established that giant reptiles had once roamed the land. The discoveries grew in significance when Richard Owen recognized these fossil reptiles as belonging in a new, separate taxonomic category called dinosaurs.

Later, the hunt for dinosaurs spread from Great Britain to the United States, then to the rest of the world. Paleontologists unearthed fossils of many new species, revealing that dinosaurs were a very large, diverse, and important group of animals. Eventually, scientists determined that many dinosaurs were intelligent and some nested colonially and cared for their young. As of the early twenty-first century, more than one thousand species of dinosaurs had been discovered, and scientists anticipated the discovery of many new genera and species.

Dinosaurs dominated life on land for approximately 160 million years, spanning much of the Mesozoic era, from the late Triassic period to the end of the Cretaceous period. Their dominance gave the Mesozoic its epithet,

1820's

the "age of reptiles." At the end of the Cretaceous, dinosaurs—or at least most of them—became extinct. Many paleontologists believe that these creatures left a living legacy: birds. Mounting evidence during the late twentieth and early twenty-first centuries indicates that birds descended from a small, carnivorous dinosaur.

—Jane F. Hill

FURTHER READING

Buckland, William. "Notice on the Megalosaurus or Great Fossil Lizard of Stonesfield." *Transactions of the Geological Society* 1, ser. 2 (1824): 390-396. The first published scientific description of a dinosaur.

Cadbury, Deborah. *Terrible Lizard: The First Dinosaur Hunters and the Birth of a New Science.* New York: Henry Holt, 2001. Details the drama surrounding the early dinosaur discoveries.

Farlow, James O., and M. K. Brett-Surman, eds. *The Complete Dinosaur.* Indianapolis: Indiana University Press, 1997. Chapters 1 and 2 of this comprehensive volume treat early dinosaur discoveries.

Larson, Edward J. *Evolution: The Remarkable History of a Scientific Theory.* New York: Modern Library, 2004. A broad overview that includes discussion of early dinosaur fossilists.

McGowan, Christopher. *The Dragon Seekers: How an Extraordinary Circle of Fossilists Discovered the Dinosaurs and Paved the Way for Darwin.* Cambridge, Mass.: Perseus, 2001. Describes early discoveries of dinosaurs and the debate over the origin of species.

Spalding, David A. E. *Dinosaur Hunters: Eccentric Amateurs and Obsessed Professionals.* Rocklin, Calif.: Prima, 1993. Chapter 2 discusses the early British fossilists.

SEE ALSO: 1809: Lamarck Publishes *Zoological Philosophy*; 1830's-1840's: Scientists Study Remains of Giant Moas; July, 1830: Lyell Publishes *Principles of Geology*; 1861: *Archaeopteryx Lithographica* Is Discovered.

RELATED ARTICLES in *Great Lives from History: The Nineteenth Century, 1801-1900:* Louis Agassiz; Georges Cuvier; Sir Edwin Ray Lankester; Sir Charles Lyell.

March 2, 1824
GIBBONS V. OGDEN

In supporting the federal license of a steamboat operator who challenged a state monopoly, the U.S. Supreme Court expanded federal control of commerce and laid the basis for many future Court rulings on commerce.

LOCALE: Washington, D.C.

CATEGORIES: Laws, acts, and legal history; transportation; trade and commerce

KEY FIGURES

Robert Fulton (1765-1815), inventor and builder of steamboats

Thomas Gibbons (1757-1826), wealthy Georgia lawyer and steamboat company owner

John Marshall (1755-1835), chief justice of the United States

William Johnson (1771-1834), associate justice of the Supreme Court

James Kent (1763-1847), chief justice and chancellor of New York

Robert R. Livingston (1746-1813), amateur scientist and speculator in steamboats

Aaron Ogden (1756-1839), entrepreneur, former governor of New Jersey, and steamboat company owner

Daniel Webster (1782-1852), Gibbons's chief attorney and later a U.S. senator

SUMMARY OF EVENT

In order to provide the commercial relations of the United States with a sense of orderliness and uniformity that had been lacking before 1787, the U.S. Constitution empowered Congress to "regulate Commerce with foreign Nations, and among the several States, and with the Indian Tribes." Congress almost immediately took advantage of this power in the field of foreign commerce by providing for the regulation of ships and commerce from foreign countries and by enacting the National Coasting Licensing Act in 1793 for the licensing of vessels engaged in coastal trade. However, the Constitution was silent as to the meaning and scope of the commerce power. It was left to the Supreme Court, thirty years later, to make the first national pronouncement regarding domestic commerce in the case of *Gibbons v. Ogden.*

The catalyst for this decision was the development of the steamboat as a means of commercial transportation. This was accomplished in August of 1807, when Robert Fulton and Robert R. Livingston made a successful voyage up the Hudson River from New York to Albany. In April of 1808, the legislature of the state of New York responded to this success by giving Fulton and Livingston a monopoly to operate steamboats on New York waters for a period not to exceed thirty years. All other steam-powered craft were forbidden from navigating New York streams unless they were licensed by Fulton and Livingston. Any unlicensed vessels that were captured were to be forfeited to the same two men. A similar grant was obtained from the legislature of Orleans Territory in 1811, thus conferring upon Fulton and Livingston control over the two great ports of the United States, New York City and New Orleans.

As a practical matter, the commercial potential of steam transportation was too great to be left to the devices of two men. Rival companies soon came into being, and a commercial war reminiscent of the old Confederation era erupted. The state of New Jersey authorized owners of any boats seized under New York law to capture New York boats in retaliation. Connecticut would not allow Livingston and Fulton's boats to enter its waters. Georgia, Massachusetts, New Hampshire, Vermont, and Ohio enacted "exclusive privilege" statutes for operators of steamboats on their own waters. Finally, a number of New York citizens defied the state law and operated unlicensed steam vessels up the Hudson River. Among these was a man named Thomas Gibbons, who had a license granted under the federal Coasting Licensing Act of 1793. He was operating in competition with a former partner, Aaron Ogden, who had secured exclusive rights from Livingston and Fulton to navigate across the Hudson River between New York and New Jersey.

As early as 1812, the New York Court of Errors and Chief Justice James Kent, one of the most prominent U.S. jurists, had issued a permanent injunction against intruders on the Fulton-Livingstone monopoly. Gibbons persisted in the face of this injunction because he had a federal license, and Ogden sought a restraining order in New York Court of Chancery. Kent, who by then was state chancellor, upheld the monopoly once again, reasoning that a federal coasting license merely conferred national character on a vessel and did not license it to trade, especially in waters restricted by state law. In short, there was no conflict between the act of Congress and the actions of New York State, for the power to regu-

New York State chief justice James Kent. (Library of Congress)

late commerce was a concurrent one, existing on both the federal and state levels. Nevertheless, Gibbons persisted in appealing to the New York Court of Errors, where Kent's decision was upheld. This set the stage for his final appeal to the U.S. Supreme Court.

It was expected that Gibbons's case would be heard during the 1821 term of the Court, but for technical reasons it was delayed until February, 1824. The oral arguments lasted four and one-half days that, by all accounts, resulted in a great social and political occasion as well as one of the great moments in U.S. constitutional history. Among the distinguished attorneys presenting the case was Daniel Webster, champion of a strong national government and the best-known orator of his time. Webster opened his argument in sweeping terms by contending that the statutes of New York, and by implication all exclusive grants of others states, violated the U.S. Constitution: "The power of Congress to regulate commerce is complete and entire," he argued. Individual states have no concurrent powers in this area; the federal government's domain is exclusive. Webster left no doubt that commerce included navigation. Opposing counsel necessarily wished to limit the notion of commerce to traffic or to the buying and selling of commodities, which would not include navigation. The regulation of New

York, he contended, was a matter of internal trade and navigation, the province of the states.

The case before the Court, however, dealt with far more than the conflict between New York State law and a federal coasting licensing act. In the weeks immediately preceding and during the argument in *Gibbons v. Ogden*, Congress was debating whether it had the power to build roads and canals, a debate in which the association of slavery with national control over commerce became apparent. If Congress could legislate over matters of internal commerce, it could easily prohibit the slave trade. Furthermore, Marshall's earlier decisions, particularly in *McCulloch v. Maryland* (1819) and *Cohens v. Virginia* (1821), were under fire in Congress, from the president, and in the press.

In a sense, the forces arguing the two sides of the *Gibbons* case represented national power and the potential for emancipation (some would add those who supported the protective tariff) on one hand, and, on the other, state sovereignty and the fear of emancipation (with some free trade proponents)—a not altogether logical set of alliances. It was in this context, however, that one month later, on March 2, 1824, John Marshall delivered the decision of the Court.

Typically, the opinion was a broad one, loaded with gratuitous comments or representations, and not typically as nationalistic as expected, or as Webster would have desired. Marshall began by agreeing with Webster's definition of commerce:

> Commerce, undoubtedly, is traffic, but it is something more; it is intercourse. It describes the commercial intercourse between nations, and parts of nations, in all its branches, and is regulated by prescribing rules for carrying on that intercourse. The mind can scarcely conceive a system for regulating commerce between nations, which shall exclude all laws concerning navigation, which shall be silent on the admission of the vessels of the one nation into the ports of the other and be confined to prescribing rules for the conduct of individuals, in the actual employment of buying and selling, or of barter.

What did the Constitution mean when it said that Congress had the power to regulate such commerce among the several states?

> The word "among" means intermingled with. A thing which is among others is intermingled with them. Commerce among the States cannot stop at the external boundary line of each State, but may be introduced into the interior.

After having laid the logical groundwork for claiming complete and exclusive federal power to regulate such commerce, which was Webster's argument, Marshall then retreated, stating:

> It is not intended to say that these words comprehend that commerce which is completely internal, which is carried on between man and man in a State, or between different parts of the same State, and which does not extend to or affect other States. . . . Comprehensive as the word "among" is, it may very properly be restricted to that commerce which concerns more States than one. . . .

The federal power over commerce was not exclusive, as Webster maintained, although in this instance, the state law was in violation of the federal coasting act. The one concurring opinion in the case given by Associate Justice William Johnson, ironically a Republican appointed by Thomas Jefferson, was stronger and more nationalistic than Marshall's. Johnson contended that the power of Congress "must be exclusive; it can reside but in one potentate; and hence, the grant of this power carries with it the whole subject, leaving nothing for the state to act upon."

For Marshall, if it was clear that the "acts of New York must yield to the Law of Congress," it was also evident that the "completely internal commerce of a state, then, may be considered as reserved for the state itself." The nationalist chief justice had unwittingly laid the basis for a multitude of legal perplexities by making a distinction between intrastate and interstate commerce (terms he did not use); and it would fall to less subtle judicial minds to interpret this as meaning commerce that does not cross state lines. Lest anyone misunderstand his position on the general enumerated powers of the Congress and on the theory of strict construction of the Constitution adopted by Ogden's counsel and by Chancellor Kent, Marshall concluded his opinion with these words:

> Powerful and ingenious minds, taking, as postulates, that the powers expressly granted to the government of the union are to be contracted, by construction, into the narrowest possible compass, and that the original powers of the states are retained, if any possible construction will retain them, may, by a course of well digested, but refined metaphysical reasoning, founded on these premises, explain away the construction of our country, and leave it a magnificent structure indeed, to look at, but totally unfit for use. They may so entangle and perplex the understanding, as to obscure principles which were before thought quite plain, and induce doubts where, if the

mind were to pursue its own course, none would be perceived. In such a case, it is peculiarly necessary to recur to safe and fundamental principles. . . .

In other words, the courts should construe the Constitution and the powers of Congress broadly.

In immediate practical terms, Marshall finally had rendered a popular decision. The steamboat monopoly had come to an end, and state fragmentation of commerce was prevented. *Gibbons v. Ogden* was the first great antitrust decision given at a time when monopolies were decidedly unpopular. Lost in the public euphoria over the end of "exclusive grants," save to a few Jeffersonian Republicans, was the fact that Marshall had made the Supreme Court the future arbiter of matters involving congressional power over commerce and intervention into state police and taxing powers. In so doing, he had struck one more blow for a broad view of the Constitution and of national power. Only when steam came to be used for land transportation would the full commercial implications of the Gibbons decision be clear. If, as many maintain, half of the Constitution is the commerce clause (the other half being the due process clause of the Fourteenth Amendment), the *Gibbons v. Ogden* case has been correctly termed the "emancipation proclamation of American commerce."

SIGNIFICANCE

Chief Justice John Marshall's opinion in *Gibbons v. Ogden* provided the starting point for all subsequent interpretations of the Constitution's commerce clause. Initially, Marshall's conception was demanded by the needs of a developing nation and an expansive approach to federal authority. The breadth and elastic nature of his definition of commerce, however, justified the extensive commercial enterprises in which the national government has been engaged since, including regulation of new forms of commercial activity brought about by technological changes, inventions, and advances in communications and transportation. During the twentieth century, the commerce power was used to justify various types of economic legislation (interstate and intrastate), including a presidential wage and price freeze under the Economic Stabilization Act of 1970 and noneconomic matters such as civil rights, kidnapping, and pollution control.

Further refinements of the definition of commerce and the types of activities that it encompasses evolved in a series of cases. Since 1937, the commerce clause has been understood to permit congressional regulation of intrastate activities that have a close and substantial relation to interstate commerce, so that their control is essential for protection from burdens and obstruction. In *United States v. Lopez* (1995), for example, the Supreme Court held that a purely intrastate activity is subject to congressional regulation only if it "substantially affects" interstate commerce. The case dealt with enactment of a 1990 criminal law banning possession of a gun within one thousand feet of a school. According to the Court, such noncommercial enterprise was unrelated to commerce, however broadly it is defined.

—*Cecil L. Eubanks, updated by Marcia J. Weiss*

FURTHER READING

Baxter, Maurice G. *The Steamboat Monopoly: "Gibbons v. Ogden," 1824.* New York: Alfred A. Knopf, 1970. A narrative and assessment of the case in which the Supreme Court had its first opportunity to interpret the commerce clause of the Constitution.

Faulkner, Robert K. *The Jurisprudence of John Marshall.* Princeton, N.J.: Princeton University Press, 1968. A comprehensive critique of Marshall's juridical thought. Places *Gibbons v. Ogden* in perspective with regard to Marshall's legal philosophy.

Frantz, John P. "The Reemergence of the Commerce Clause as a Limit on Federal Power: *United States v. Lopez.*" *Harvard Journal of Law and Public Policy* 19, no. 1 (Fall, 1995): 161-174. A scholarly analysis of the *Lopez* case within the framework of the commerce clause, discussing its evolution.

Lewis, Thomas T., and Richard L. Wilson, eds. *Encyclopedia of the U.S. Supreme Court.* 3 vols. Pasadena, Calif.: Salem Press, 2001. Comprehensive reference work on the Supreme Court that contains substantial discussions of *Gibbons v. Ogden, United States v. Lopez,* John Marshall, the commerce clause, and many related subjects.

Levinson, Isabel Simone. *"Gibbons v. Ogden": Controlling Trade Between States.* Springfield, N.J.: Enslow, 1999. Concise analysis of the *Gibbons* case and its legal ramifications.

Newmyer, R. Kent. *John Marshall and the Heroic Age of the Supreme Court.* Baton Rouge: Louisiana State University Press, 2001. Examination of Marshall's legal philosophy, with analyses of many Court decisions.

_____. *The Supreme Court Under Marshall and Taney.* Arlington Heights, Ill.: Harlan Davidson, 1968. Contains detailed information and presents Marshall's philosophy. Places *Gibbons v. Ogden* and the commerce power in historical context.

1820's

Schwartz, Bernard. *A History of the Supreme Court*. New York: Oxford University Press, 1993. Comprehensive in scope, this scholarly work details the Marshall Court and its influence on U.S. politics and society.

Smith, Craig R. *Daniel Webster and the Oratory of Civil Religion*. Columbia: University of Missouri Press, 2005. Biography focusing on Webster's legendary rhetorical ability, which he employed in the *Gibbons* case.

SEE ALSO: Feb. 24, 1803: *Marbury v. Madison*; Aug. 17, 1807: Maiden Voyage of the *Clermont*; Mar. 16, 1810: *Fletcher v. Peck*; Mar. 6, 1819: *McCulloch v. Maryland*; Mar. 18, 1831, and Mar. 3, 1832: Cherokee Cases; Feb. 4, 1887: Interstate Commerce Act.

RELATED ARTICLES in *Great Lives from History: The Nineteenth Century, 1801-1900:* Robert Fulton; James Kent; John Marshall; Joseph Story.

May 7, 1824
FIRST PERFORMANCE OF BEETHOVEN'S NINTH SYMPHONY

One of the greatest and most frequently performed orchestral works, Ludwig van Beethoven's Ninth Symphony added a chorus and vocal soloists to the orchestra to sing verses from Friedrich Schiller's "Ode to Joy." By stretching the definition of a symphony, it inspired further experimentation by other composers throughout the nineteenth century.

LOCALE: Vienna, Austria
CATEGORY: Music

KEY FIGURES
Ludwig van Beethoven (1770-1827), German composer
Friedrich Schiller (1759-1805), German dramatist and historian
Michael Umlauf (1781-1842), conductor of the Ninth Symphony's first performance

SUMMARY OF EVENT
The first performance of Ludwig van Beethoven's Ninth Symphony on May 7, 1824, in the Kärntnerthor Theater in Vienna, Austria, was greeted with enthusiasm by the audience. It is unlikely, however, that any of those in attendance recognized the lasting impact the work would have upon musical history. The Ninth Symphony was a massive work, the longest symphony written up to its time, and it uniquely added a chorus and vocal soloists to the orchestra in the finale. The text, setting verses of Friedrich Schiller's poem "An die Freude" (1786; "Ode to Joy"), speaks of universal brotherhood in the symphony's jubilant conclusion.

One of the greatest composers in European history, Beethoven was baptized on December 17, 1770, in Bonn, Cologne (now in modern Germany), and first studied with his father, a musician for the local elector.

He studied with several other composers before settling permanently in 1792 in Vienna, where he soon came to favor with local aristocrats as an accomplished performer on the piano. His first important compositions were piano sonatas, and over his career he also wrote concertos, string quartets, an opera, and many other works, but he is perhaps best known for his nine symphonies. Beethoven often pushed the boundaries set by previous composers, such as by adding trombones, piccolo, and contrabassoon to the finale of his Fifth Symphony—all instruments never before employed in a symphony.

The greatest crisis in Beethoven's life arose in 1802, as he confronted a growing loss of his hearing. While visiting the town of Heiligenstadt seeking a cure for his deafness, he wrote a letter to his brothers—intended to be read after his death—expressing his anguish at losing a sense so important for a musician. This letter, later known as the Heiligenstadt Testament, marked a turn in Beethoven's life, after which he accepted this handicap and overcame it. Several of his works, including the Ninth Symphony, have a theme of triumph over adversity, with darker sections in the early part of the work giving way to bright sections at the end.

The genesis of the Ninth Symphony came about over a number of years, as evidenced by ideas that Beethoven wrote for this work and most of his others in his composition sketchbooks. He began considering setting Schiller's "Ode to Joy" to music as early as 1792, according to a letter written by a Bonn law professor to Schiller's wife, although no sketches of the time confirm this date. The earliest sketches of music Beethoven eventually employed in the Ninth Symphony were written in 1815, with additional sketches being added up to 1818. He began writing the Ninth Symphony in earnest in 1823 and finished in the spring of 1824.

Ludwig van Beethoven (at keyboard) with several friends. (P. F. Collier and Son)

1820's

The Ninth Symphony is divided into four movements, or sections, as was typical of symphonies of the time, but there are a number of innovative aspects of the work. In the first movement, instead of the traditional opening theme beginning the work, the music gradually unfolds from silence and builds into an outbreak of the dark, forceful theme in a minor key. The remainder of the movement contains some of the most complex interplay of themes found in the classical period. The second movement, while incorporating dance music typical of an inner symphonic movement, creates a dynamic interchange of various rhythms and meters that transcends the expected rhythmic stability of a dance movement. The third movement's variations on two themes, instead of only one, is a form found only in one previous Beethoven symphony, his fifth.

The final movement of the Ninth Symphony is unlike any other symphonic movement written up to its time. The movement itself is as long as most of the entire symphonies that preceded it, and its structure has been interpreted in multiple ways by multiple scholars. The opening section presents and seemingly rejects the music of

the first three movements, before introducing variations on the "Ode to Joy" theme in the orchestra. Only after these variations have been introduced do the soloists and full choir join with the orchestra, singing verses of Schiller's poem. Beethoven's addition of singers to the orchestra in a symphony was unprecedented, and, like the new instruments added to the Fifth Symphony, it indicated his independence in expanding the limits of the genre. The combined performing forces alternate and then join together for a powerful and thrilling conclusion to the work.

The first performance of the Ninth Symphony on May 7, 1824, also included an overture and portions of a mass by Beethoven. The orchestra and chorus only had two full rehearsals together before the performance, although the chorus, orchestra, and soloists had all practiced separately as well. The conductor for the performance was Michael Umlauf, the music director for the Kärntnerthor Theater, but Beethoven stood next to him on stage. Although he was almost totally deaf at that time, Beethoven was present to indicate the beginning tempos, or speed, for each movement; he apparently gestured and conducted portions along with Umlauf as well. At the conclusion of the symphony, the soprano soloist had to indicate for Beethoven to turn around to see the applause of the audience that he could not hear.

The large audience was enthusiastic for the first performance of the Ninth Symphony, as were newspaper reviews, although some indicated problems they attributed to the performers having insufficient time to learn such difficult music. Financially, the performance barely broke even in spite of the full auditorium, because paying the large number of performers took most of the box office receipts. Another performance later that month was poorly advertised, and only half the seats were filled, resulting in a financial loss. Nevertheless, the artistic greatness of the work assured it a long life, and the Ninth Symphony entered the orchestral repertoire, where it has been performed thousands of times since its premiere.

SIGNIFICANCE

The legacy of Beethoven's Ninth Symphony has been far-reaching. Many composers of the nineteenth century were both inspired by and apprehensive about the work, concerned whether they could ever match the grand conception of such an all-encompassing composition. The Schiller verses espousing the brotherhood of mankind resonated with the ideals of the Romantic movement, and the work as a whole also became a potent symbol for nineteenth century nationalistic movements, especially in Germany.

During the twentieth century, the Ninth Symphony became a ceremonial work, performed often at the opening of new concert halls and as the opening or concluding work of a symphony's concert season. It was also performed as part of the ceremonies of many Olympic Games. In December, 1989, in celebration of the fall of the Berlin Wall, Leonard Bernstein conducted the Ninth Symphony with an orchestra made up of musicians from both East and West Germany and the Allied forces in concerts on both sides of Berlin. Bernstein substituted the word *Freiheit* (freedom) for the word *Freude* (joy) in Schiller's text to align more closely the significance of Beethoven's work with the modern political event. Bernstein's concerts were broadcast to an audience of millions in thirty-six countries. An arrangement of the "Ode to Joy" theme serves as the anthem of the European Union, and the melody has been heard in numerous films and television productions. Beethoven's Ninth Sym-

phony has a rich cultural legacy and is destined to remain as one of the supreme achievements in Western music.

—R. Todd Rober

FURTHER READING

Buch, Esteban. *Beethoven's Ninth: A Political History*. Translated by Richard Miller. Chicago: University of Chicago Press, 2003. Examines the contradictory ways in which the work has been used since its premiere, from nationalistic propaganda to celebratory hymn.

Cook, Nicholas. *Beethoven: Symphony No. 9*. Cambridge, England: Cambridge University Press, 1993. A thorough examination of the work, its first performance, and its reception history.

Kinderman, William. *Beethoven*. Berkeley: University of California Press, 1995. A detailed analysis of Beethoven's music in the context of his life; includes many musical examples.

Levy, David. *Beethoven: The Ninth Symphony*. Rev. ed. New Haven, Conn.: Yale University Press, 2003. An analysis of the work that considers both its original cultural context and its later reception up to 2003.

Lockwood, Lewis. *Beethoven: The Music and the Life*. New York: W. W. Norton, 2003. A clear overview that places Beethoven's life and music into context in an evocative way that is understandable for the non-musician.

Solomon, Maynard. *Beethoven Essays*. Cambridge, Mass.: Harvard University Press, 1988. An engaging series of essays, including ones on the Ninth Symphony and Schiller, that explores the psychological meanings of Beethoven's music.

SEE ALSO: Apr. 7, 1805: Beethoven's *Eroica* Symphony Introduces the Romantic Age; Mar. 12, 1832: *La Sylphide* Inaugurates Romantic Ballet's Golden Age; Aug. 13-17, 1876: First Performance of Wagner's Ring Cycle; Dec. 22, 1894: Debussy's *Prelude to the Afternoon of a Faun* Premieres.
RELATED ARTICLES in *Great Lives from History: The Nineteenth Century, 1801-1900:* Ludwig van Beethoven; Johannes Brahms; Anton Bruckner; Frédéric Chopin; Antonín Dvořák; Engelbert Humperdinck; Franz Liszt; Felix Mendelssohn; Franz Schubert; Clara Schumann; Robert Schumann; Johann Strauss; Richard Wagner; Carl Maria von Weber.

December 1, 1824-February 9, 1825
U.S. ELECTION OF 1824

The fierce competition in this election among four Republicans split the Republican Party into National Republicans and Democratic Republicans.

LOCALE: Washington, D.C.
CATEGORY: Government and politics

KEY FIGURES

John Quincy Adams (1767-1848), winner of the 1824 election and president of the United States, 1825-1829

Andrew Jackson (1767-1845), loser of the 1824 election and later president, 1829-1837

Henry Clay (1777-1852), losing candidate who became secretary of state under Adams

William Harris Crawford (1772-1834), candidate who had to withdraw from the election for health reasons

John C. Calhoun (1782-1850), secretary of war in the Monroe administration and a presidential candidate in 1824 who withdrew

Martin Van Buren (1782-1862), New York politician who supported Jackson and later became the eighth president, 1837-1841

SUMMARY OF EVENT

By the 1820's, the Federalist Party had ceased to exist, and the dubiously named Era of Good Feelings was coming to a close. Five men in the Republican Party wanted to succeed the fifth president of the United States, James Monroe. At issue in the minds of some was an impending conflict over slavery that seemed closer as a result of the Missouri Compromise of 1820, which "locked in" the states of the slave South to minority status—in the Senate in the short term, and in the House in the longer term. The Missouri Compromise had mandated that all territories becoming states above the 36°30′ parallel had to be free states, but that those below the line could be free or slave. Martin Van Buren of New York and William H. Crawford of Georgia had formulated a plan to create a new political party, in which loyalty to the party would be rewarded with political jobs—a practice that became known as the spoils system. A key test of party allegiance would be the willingness of candidates to avoid discussions of slavery, thus instituting a "gag" on all debate of slavery at the national level.

Crawford was the selection of a rump congressional caucus; his candidacy ended, however, when he suffered a stroke in mid-campaign, temporarily derailing Van Buren's plans for a political party and removing its most logical leader. Crawford had been supported by Monroe and Thomas Jefferson, and claimed to be the only true heir of the Jeffersonian tradition in the race. Born in Virginia and a resident of Georgia, Crawford represented the large plantation interests. He advocated the strict construction of the Constitution and emphasized states' rights.

Of the other four men running for president, Henry Clay of Kentucky put forth the most positive program. With his American System, which involved high protective tariffs and federally supported internal improvements, Clay sought to consolidate the different sections of the country behind him. At the time, Clay had no appreciation of the potential for a mass party such as that entertained by Crawford and Van Buren.

Andrew Jackson of Tennessee was the most popular choice and the nation's premier military hero. He was

1820's

John Quincy Adams. (White House Historical Society)

JOHN QUINCY ADAMS'S INAUGURAL ADDRESS

President Adams used his inaugural address of March 4, 1825, to comment on the effect that the closely contested election of 1824 might have on his presidency.

Fellow-citizens, you are acquainted with the peculiar circumstances of the recent election, which have resulted in affording me the opportunity of addressing you at this time. You have heard the exposition of the principles which will direct me in the fulfillment of the high and solemn trust imposed upon me in this station. Less possessed of your confidence in advance than any of my predecessors, I am deeply conscious of the prospect that I shall stand more and oftener in need of your indulgence. Intentions upright and pure, a heart devoted to the welfare of our country, and the unceasing application of all the faculties allotted to me to her service are all the pledges that I can give for the faithful performance of the arduous duties I am to undertake. To the guidance of the legislative councils, to the assistance of the executive and subordinate departments, to the friendly cooperation of the respective State governments, to the candid and liberal support of the people so far as it may be deserved by honest industry and zeal, I shall look for whatever success may attend my public service; and knowing that *"except the Lord keep the city the watchman waketh but in vain,"* with fervent supplications for His favor, to His overruling providence I commit with humble but fearless confidence my own fate and the future destinies of my country.

---

convention was generally adopted within the next decade.

The greatest difficulty for the nominees was a lack of clear issues. Even before his stroke, Crawford could not state clearly that the goal of his campaign was to create institutional barriers to stifle debate about a moral issue. All the candidates were for tariff reform, although Adams termed his tariff policy cautious and Jackson called his judicious. Both Adams and Clay, neo-Federalists, supported the American System, although Adams outstripped Clay in his support of internal improvements. To those issues, Jackson added an attack on the caucus system and supported the right of the people to choose their presidential electors directly.

As there were no real political differences among the candidates, the contest quickly became one of personalities. There was little campaigning, and most of the excitement was provided by the press. With Crawford's physical infirmity virtually eliminating him, Adams assumed the favorite's position. He was expected to gain from the split in the South and West between Clay and Jackson.

In the election held on December 1, 1824, Jackson received the greatest number of popular votes, but not a majority. The electoral vote count was ninety-nine votes for Jackson, eighty-four for Adams, forty-one for Crawford, and thirty-seven for Clay. As no candidate had received a majority, the choice of the president was passed to the House of Representatives, which would vote by states. Clay was eliminated from the race because of the constitutional stipulation that the House should choose from among only the three candidates receiving the highest electoral totals.

The real choice was between Adams and Jackson, but Clay was in a unique position. As Speaker of the House, he could control many of the votes there, and he was forced to choose between two men, both of whom he heartily disliked. There was only one logical choice for Clay, however, as he considered Jackson unfit for the presidency. On the other hand, Clay supported Adams's nationalist public policies because he was a supporter of the American System, which had arisen out of a need to rebuild the nation after the War of 1812. Under the American System, the federal government was to as-

also the only candidate supported outside his own section, appealing not only to citizens in the West but also to small farmers in the South and laborers in the East. Much of his popularity came from his reputation as a fighting general—the first general since George Washington to seek the presidency. John Quincy Adams of Massachusetts, secretary of state in the Monroe administration, was the choice of conservative New Englanders. Although his statesmanship and personal honesty were admitted by all, his lack of tact and charm and his unwillingness to become involved in the rough-and-tumble of politics prevented him from gaining a popular following. John C. Calhoun of South Carolina soon withdrew rather than face such formidable opposition for the presidency and became the sole vice presidential candidate.

Without a true modern party structure, complete with primaries and other nominating apparatus, candidates were nominated by the congressional caucuses. The caucus system had picked all presidential candidates prior to 1824, by which time it came under attack for its undemocratic features and for giving Congress too much power. Crawford was the last candidate nominated by the caucus: State legislatures nominated the other candidates, and this new device continued in use until the nominating

sume certain state debts incurred during the war, establish a uniform national money supply, and provide tariff protections for budding industries competing with established foreign (mainly British) imports.

Clay agreed to meet with Adams to discuss "public affairs." Although both men later denied that any deal was made, Clay was able to deliver several states into the Adams camp, notably his own state of Kentucky, whose electors had been instructed to vote for Jackson. In the House election of February, 1825, Adams received thirteen votes to seven for Jackson and four for Crawford.

After the House vote, rumors of a "corrupt bargain," or deal, between Clay and Adams became rampant. In January, an anonymous letter had appeared in the *Philadelphia Columbian Observer* charging that Clay had sold out to Adams in return for his appointment as secretary of state. Clay immediately denied the charge and published a card challenging his accuser to a duel. However, no duel was never fought and no proof of the bargain was ever provided. Nevertheless, one of Adams's first acts as president was to appoint Clay as his secretary of state. Thus, according to the Jacksonians, was the "corrupt bargain" consummated. Jackson wrote to one of his supporters.

> So you see the Judas of the West has closed the contract and will receive his thirty pieces of silver.... Was there ever witnessed such barefaced corruption in any country before?

Jackson and his supporters believed that he had been cheated out of the presidency because he had refused to bargain with Clay. Jackson, they contended, was the obvious popular choice and should have been named president. Many believed that Congress had been morally bound to elect him. The election left both Adams and Clay discredited in the eyes of many. Jackson resigned his Senate seat and returned to Tennessee, where he was nominated as that state's presidential candidate in 1828. By that time, Van Buren had refocused his party strategy around Jackson, whom he would support in 1828. The election of 1824 actually served to pair a vastly popular candidate with a formidable new political machine run out of Albany. Jackson and Van Buren recognized the power of the press and incorporated "news" papers into political propaganda.

SIGNIFICANCE

The election of Adams in 1824 terminated the succession of the "Virginia dynasty" in the Republican Party. Dur-

ing Adams's administration, the Jeffersonians split into two wings: the Adams-Clay wing, whose adherents went by the name of National Republicans; and the Jackson wing, whose membership became known as the Democratic Republicans, or simply Democrats. Adams was caught in the middle of this partisan strife, and, unwilling or unable to engage in personal politics, lost popular support and was eventually defeated by Jackson in the campaign of 1828.

—*Cecil L. Eubanks, updated by Larry Schweikart*

FURTHER READING

Baxter, Maurice G. *Henry Clay and the American System.* Lexington: University Press of Kentucky, 1995. Penetrating examination of Clay's views on economic development and his impact upon American government.

Brown, Richard H. "The Missouri Crisis, Slavery, and the Politics of Jacksonianism." *South Atlantic Quarterly* 65, no. 1 (Winter, 1966): 55-72. A classic article, asserting that the Jacksonian Party was formed well before the "corrupt bargain" out of fear that the Missouri Compromise would undo the fragile truce that had kept the nation together.

Calhoun, John C. *The Papers of John C. Calhoun.* Edited by Frank M. Merriwether, et al. 28 vols. Columbia: University of South Carolina Press, 1959-2003. An ambitious project, consisting of Calhoun's papers from 1801 to 1850, with skillful editorial comment integrated throughout.

Eaton, Clement. *Henry Clay and the Art of American Politics.* Boston: Little, Brown, 1957. A short biography of Clay that analyzes Clay's decision in 1824, arguing that there was no corrupt bargain.

Ellis, Richard E. *Andrew Jackson.* Washington, D.C.: CQ Press, 2003. Masterful study of Jackson's life, career, policies, and the impact of his presidency.

McCormick, Richard P. *The Second American Party System: Party Formation in the Jacksonian Era.* Chapel Hill: University of North Carolina Press, 1966. Uses statistical analysis of election returns to examine changes in the political party system during this era.

Niven, John. *Martin Van Buren: The Romantic Age of American Politics.* New York: Oxford University Press, 1983. A detailed look at the "little magician," focusing on his political machinations in New York and his contributions to the party structure.

Remini, Robert V. *The Life of Andrew Jackson.* New York: Harper & Row, 1988. A one-volume condensed version of Remini's three-volume biography, against

1820's

which all others are measured. Highly sympathetic toward "Old Hickory."

Watson, Harry L. *Andrew Jackson vs. Henry Clay: Democracy and Development in Antebellum America.* Boston: Bedford/St. Martin's, 1998. Dual biography, describing the two men's conflicting visions for the future of the United States. Includes reprints of twenty-five primary documents, including speeches and letters.

SEE ALSO: Feb. 17, 1801: House of Representatives Elects Jefferson President; Sept. 25, 1804: Twelfth Amendment Is Ratified; Mar. 3, 1820: Missouri Compromise; Dec. 3, 1828: U.S. Election of 1828; Dec. 2, 1840: U.S. Election of 1840.

RELATED ARTICLES in *Great Lives from History: The Nineteenth Century, 1801-1900:* John Quincy Adams; John C. Calhoun; Henry Clay; Andrew Jackson; James Monroe; Martin Van Buren.

1825-1830
GREAT JAVA WAR

To exploit the natural resources of Indonesia, the Netherlands built roads to haul cash crops from rural areas to coastal ports. After plans were made for a road to cross over the sacred property of a sultan's son, the son mobilized a guerrilla force to drive the Dutch from central Java. His effort was crushed, however, after a five-year struggle. The conflict would be the last major Javanese resistance to the Dutch during the nineteenth century.

LOCALE: Java, Dutch East Indies (now Indonesia)
CATEGORIES: Wars, uprisings, and civil unrest; colonization; indigenous people's rights

KEY FIGURES
Pangeran Dipo Negoro (c. 1785-1855), son of a sultan of Jogjakarta
Léonard du Bus de Gisignies (1780-1849), commissioner general of Dutch East Indies, 1826-1830
Hendrik Merkus de Kock (1779-1845), lieutenant governor-general and general of the Dutch army in the Dutch East Indies, 1826-1830
Mangkubumi (d. 1877), sultan as Hamengkubuwana VI, r. 1855-1877
Hamengkubuwana (1818-1855), sultan during the Great Java War, r. 1822-1855
Godert Alexander Gerard Philip van der Capellen (1778-1848), Dutch East Indies commissioner-general, 1816-1819, and governor-general, 1819-1826

SUMMARY OF EVENT
During the sixteenth century, the Dutch began establishing colonies around the world to control the lucrative trade in valuable commodities. Dutch traders set up

headquarters on the island of Java in the Indonesian archipelago, then known as the Dutch East Indies and part of the largest possession for the Dutch. The Javanese people had developed a complex, hierarchical civilization that included sultans in charge of courtly arts, Islamic spiritual leaders, and aristocrats who held political power. Accordingly, some Javanese resented the intrusion of the Dutch, who, in turn, sought to subdue the local population by supporting local leaders, by establishing Dutch colonial administrators in key governmental positions, and by employing military force against uprisings.

The Dutch divided Java into a number of residencies headed by a Dutch administrator. Each residency was subdivided into a number of regencies, which were formally headed by a Javanese regent assisted by a Dutch official. Regencies, which were subdivided into districts and subdistricts, included several hundred villages. The regents cooperated with the Dutch because they could skim profits from cash crops (cinnamon, coffee, cotton, indigo, pepper, rice, silk, sugar, tea, and tobacco), which were harvested by plantation workers; in turn, the regents continued to tax their subjects for rice and for labor.

Meanwhile, Chinese workers were being imported as higher-level bureaucrats, professionals, and plantation managers, and cooperative Javanese aristocrats and former government officials were being demoted to mid-level bureaucrats. Furthermore, the Dutch employed loyal Javanese and Christians from elsewhere in the archipelago to maintain colonial order. The rest of the population consisted of disaffected aristocrats, small-scale landowners, spiritual leaders, petty traders, and peasants. Surakarta and Yogyakarta remained independent states outside the Dutch colonial system.

When the French armies under Napoleon I conquered the Netherlands in 1795, the Dutch king asked the British to assume temporary control of its East Indies colony. The British, however, who occupied a portion of Yogyakarta in 1812, tried to disrupt the regency system and to abolish the court system that separated indigenous peoples from foreigners. The British had no interest in the cash-crop export economy, and they paid for the administration of the colony by a system of taxation. After Napoleon's defeat in 1814, the Netherlands resumed control of the archipelago, but the local population was not entirely happy to see the Dutch return. Members of the local elite were in debt when the Dutch resumed demands for tax revenues, and the Dutch reinstituted the regency system, the cash-crop economy, and segregated courts.

In 1825, the Netherlands appointed Léonard du Bus de Gisignies the commissioner general of the Dutch East Indies, with a mandate to reduce the deficit in expenses of the East Indies colonial administration. When he arrived, there were numerous grievances because of the policies of his predecessor, Godert Alexander Gerard Philip van der Capellen. In 1824, van der Capellen had abolished the contracts of land tenancy, which gave tenants not only the use of the land but also control over farmers on the land, which left the economic system in chaos. Tolls were newly being levied for movement across the border between government and indigenous land.

In 1825, the Dutch planned to build a road across a piece of property that contained a sacred tomb. The road would have been an unwelcome intrusion, according to the owner of the property, Yogyakarta's prince Pangeran Dipo Negoro, whom the Dutch had passed over when they appointed Hamengkubuwana the new sultan of Yogyakarta in 1822. Accordingly, Dipo Negoro recruited his friend Mangkubumi to organize a guerrilla force of approximately 100,000 soldiers to keep the Dutch out of the Javanese heartland. Dipo Negoro's success in raising the army came out of his broad appeal to all classes of Javanese. He and Mangkubumi had been appointed coguardians of the sultan, who was only seven years old in 1825.

As a member of the upper aristocracy, Dipo Negoro could successfully argue that the Dutch were reducing traditional rulers to mere cogs in the wheels of the colonial administration. His appeal to commoners was based on his childhood experience of living in a rural village with his grandmother. The religious leaders accepted his authority because he was well versed in Islamic teachings and also claimed to have experienced a mystical vision in which the goddess of the southern ocean promised that he would become a future king. In a sense, the war was a jihad against the Dutch, and Dipo Negoro was considered to be a messiah.

One day in 1825, Dipo Negoro's guerrilla force appeared in Jogyakarta while the Dutch army was out of town. Gaining widespread support from the indigenous population, the rebels massacred Europeans and Chinese plantation farmers. The Dutch carried the young sultan away to safety during the disorder. General Henrik Merkus de Kock was then ordered to central Java but had too few troops to stop the insurrection, though he persuaded the ruler of Surakarta to refrain from joining the insurgency.

With muskets and other instruments of warfare from corrupt Dutch officials, from British and American gunrunners, and from local arms manufacturers, the Javanese guerrillas were at first victorious in attacking the Dutch in the jungles, because the conventional forces of the Dutch were large and immobile. De Kock crushed the insurgency by using the fortress system, in which small units of mobile troops were posted in various forts for hit-and-run raids.

In 1829, Mangkubumi deserted to the Dutch, and in 1830 Dipo Negoro sued for peace. Dipo Negoro offered to end the insurgency if the Dutch would name him sultan, but, instead, Dipo Negoro was arrested, thus depriving the insurgency of an indispensable leader. He was first exiled to Manado in northern Sulawesi and then to Makasar (now Ujung Pandang), where he died. In all, the Dutch employed 50,000 troops but suffered only 1,000 deaths. When the war ended, more than 15,000 Javanese soldiers and 200,000 Javanese civilians (7 percent of the population) lost their lives, mostly from famine and disease.

SIGNIFICANCE

Victory for the Dutch in the Great Java War led to the opening up of new land for commercial exploitation, which substantially reduced the domains of Yogyakarta and Surakarta. The sultans, though, were compensated for their losses. The next governor-general took note of the grievances and implemented new policies that shared more of the profits with the indigenous elite, thereby increasing contentment within the aristocracy, enriching European officials and Chinese middlemen, and increasing productivity, such that the Netherlands enjoyed larger profits.

Javanese plantation workers, however, were exploited even more than in the past, and they were so overworked that they had neither energy nor time to grow their own food, thereby ushering in an era of epidemics and famine. The discontent of the masses resulted ultimately in an anticolonial movement that gained momentum during the twentieth century.

Dipo Negoro's resistance in the first half of the nineteenth century was glorified and he became celebrated as the first anticolonial, nationalistic hero of the later struggle for independence. Indonesia became independent in 1948.

—*Michael Haas*

FURTHER READING

Eng, Pierre van der. *The "Colonial Drain" from Indonesia, 1823-1890*. Canberra: Economics Division, Research School of Pacific Studies, Australian National University, 1993. An economic analysis of the Dutch exploitation of Indonesia's resources, proving that the colony operated at a net loss for the colonial power.
Hall, D. G. E. *A History of South-East Asia*. 4th ed. New York: St. Martin's Press, 1981. Chapter 30 provides a brief account of the causes and conduct of the Great Java War.
Ricklefs, M. C. *A History of Modern Indonesia Since c. 1200*. 3d ed. Stanford, Calif.: Stanford University Press, 2001. The most authoritative historical account of Indonesia, covering the Srivijaya Empire to the end of the twentieth century.
Van Der Kroef, Justus M. "Prince Diponegoro: Progenitor of Indonesian Nationalism." *Far Eastern Quarterly* 8 (August, 1949): 424-450. A biography of the charismatic Indonesian who organized, led, and then surrendered in the Great Java War.

SEE ALSO: Aug. 13, 1814: Britain Acquires the Cape Colony; Apr. 5, 1815: Tambora Volcano Begins Violent Eruption; 1854-1862: Wallace's Expeditions Give Rise to Biogeography; Aug. 27, 1883: Krakatoa Volcano Erupts.

September 27, 1825
STOCKTON AND DARLINGTON RAILWAY OPENS

England's Stockton and Darlington Railway was the first public railroad in the Western world to carry both passengers and freight behind steam locomotives. The British railroad system grew rapidly and eventually replaced horse-drawn carts and canals as primary transportation methods for coal, iron ore, and other commodities.

LOCALE: Northern England
CATEGORIES: Transportation; trade and commerce; engineering

KEY FIGURES

Timothy Hackworth (1786-1850), engineering superintendent on the Stockton and Darlington Railway
Edward Pease (1767-1858), leading Quaker financier of the railroad
George Stephenson (1781-1848), engineer who designed the first locomotive used on the railroad
Robert Stephenson (1803-1859), George Stephenson's son, and engineer who built rolling stock for the railroad

SUMMARY OF EVENT

Stockton and Darlington are two small communities in the county of Durham, in northern England, in the valley of the Tees River. The river flows into the North Sea a short distance to the east of Stockton. Small port facilities existed at Stockton, and Darlington was a commercial center for the growing trade in coal. Coal had been used since Elizabethan days for heating buildings, especially in London. The north of England contained many coal deposits, and by the nineteenth century they were being steadily exploited, especially in areas near water transport: The Tees River was ideal for coal transport.

As early as the eighteenth century surface coal deposits had already been mined in the area, and coal mining became increasingly an underground operation. This posed a great technical problem: The mines tended to fill with water. Engineers and others, throughout the eighteenth century, tried to find a solution to the problem. One solution was the steam engine, which came to be used primarily to pump water out of mines, and their use spread widely. These engines were being steadily improved, and it was not long before they were used to mine coal.

The first solution to the problem of transporting coal to consumers was to expand the reach of navigable water by building canals. Irregular countryside, though, including many hills and valleys, was a burden to functioning canals. Locks were extremely expensive and slow to move traffic, and many engineers opted instead to go overland around these obstacles to reach the canals. Soon, a number of tracks were built between mines and canals or rivers to accommodate rail carts, which could move heavy products such as coal comparatively easily when pulled by horses. Because the countryside around Stockton and Darlington was full of hills and valleys, it would be too expensive to build and maintain canals in the area. This combination of geography and prohibitive cost led to the development of the Stockton and Darlington Railway.

The area around Stockton and Darlington was the home ground of one of the pioneers in the use of steam engines, George Stephenson, so when the owners of local coal mines wanted better, more cost-efficient transport for their coal, they turned to Stephenson. The leading transportation proponent was one of the many leading Quaker businessmen in Darlington, Edward Pease. Pease had visited a mine where Stephenson was using a steam engine to remove coal, and he was enormously impressed. He persuaded his fellow Quaker businessmen to authorize the development of a railroad to pick up the Tees Valley coal and transport it to Stockton, where it could be loaded onto vessels and carried to London.

The contemporary model for the railroad was the canal, and canals required legislative authorization. Proponents were required to have assembled 80 percent of the financing before asking Parliament for authorization. Pease and his numerous relatives and friends in the Quaker community were prepared to put up the money, after a survey had been done suggesting a railroad could be built for less than £100,000, half the amount a canal would have cost. Pease persuaded Stephenson to lay out the line, and on the basis of his route, legislation was passed in the spring of 1821. Minor changes were made in subsequent laws, but the biggest change, the third modification, specifically authorized the use of steam locomotives.

In its final version, the line was to extend twenty-five miles, and the railroad in steeper terrain was to run along

BRITISH RAILWAY NETWORK AROUND 1840

small branches of lines navigated by horse-drawn cars or along inclined planes, where the coal cars would be moved by stationary steam engines. Although passenger transport was authorized, it was clear that the major business envisaged by the promoters of the Stockton and Darlington was the movement of coal.

Opening day for the new venture was scheduled for July 29, 1825. Anticipation led to large crowds. A new steam locomotive named Locomotion, which was designed by George Stephenson and his son Robert, was hoisted onto the tracks and hitched to one passenger car and twenty-one new coal cars. The locomotive successfully pulled the train to Stockton, with pauses along the way, at an average rate of four miles per hour (as skeptics noted, no better than the rate of horses). Within a few years, however, comparative cost figures had been compiled and it was found that locomotives were significantly cheaper than horses.

The Stockton and Darlington was, in a very real sense,

an experiment, and as such it encountered difficulties in its first years. The engines—the company soon possessed four of them—proved to have insufficient power, forcing pauses in the runs. The company hired a local engineer, Timothy Hackworth, to superintend operations; he proved to be an important contributor, devising some of the technical improvements—such as increased steam pressure, improved wheels, and direct linkage of the steam power to the wheels—which eventually led to engines of his own design that had the necessary pulling power.

There also were initial problems with the tracks. George Stephenson was a strong advocate of wrought iron rails, and the first years of the Stockton and Darlington proved he was right. The portion of the early track that was not wrought iron had to be replaced. Furthermore, because the line was a single track, with just a few sidings, train scheduling proved very difficult, especially as independent operators of horse-drawn passenger cars also used the lines. This soon led to centralized operations for both passenger and freight trains and to the use of locomotives only. The problem of a single line was soon solved, as a second line was constructed during the early 1830's.

The success of the Stockton and Darlington inspired many imitators. To preserve its monopoly, the line built extensions, the most important of which was the line to Middlesbrough, a new city, on the coast where the Tees River entered the North Sea, created by the railroad company. The company built new port facilities at Middlesbrough that could handle far more coal traffic than the older quays at Stockton. Lines also were extended to the west to Yorkshire. Eventually, the Stockton and Darlington came to be the dominant line in the county of Durham.

Despite its difficulties, the Stockton and Darlington was a financial success from the beginning. Its freight revenues rose from £14,455 in 1826-1827 to £57,819 in 1832-1833. By 1842-1843, its gross revenues were just under £100,000. By the late 1830's, the company had been paying an annual dividend to the original investors (the shares were increased from 675 to 1,000 in 1827) of around 15 percent. However, the company was in the habit of financing extensions of the line with borrowed money, leading the company to difficult times in the 1850's. These troubles required new legislation that authorized recapitalization.

The character of the company's business changed, too. It was overwhelmingly a coal line during the 1830's and 1840's, but the 1850's and 1860's saw the line carry increasing quantities of iron ore because of growing demand for iron products. New sources of iron ore were discovered in and around Durham at that time, so the Stockton and Darlington was able to ride this new business successfully.

What had been a large enterprise with a monopoly in its own backyard in the 1830's gradually became a niche railroad as the entire country was covered by railroads. The Stockton and Darlington management recognized this, and during the late 1850's the company began negotiations with the North Eastern Railway, which absorbed the Stockton and Darlington in 1863. Stockton and Darlington management was highly regarded, so the railroad continued operating as a semi-independent division of the North Eastern Railway for a number of years.

SIGNIFICANCE

The successful operation of the Stockton and Darlington Railway marked the beginning of the railroad age in the Western world. The lines freed up commercial development, which had been constrained by the difficulties of land transport, especially of large, bulky commodities. The canal system functioned as a short-term solution, but railroads proved their endurance.

—*Nancy M. Gordon*

FURTHER READING

Clapham, J. H. *An Economic History of Modern Britain: The Early Railway Age.* Cambridge, England: Cambridge University Press, 1939. A still-useful classic on the impact of the railroad on the economy of Great Britain.

Hoole, K. *A Regional History of the Railways of Great Britain.* Dawlish, England: David & Charles, 1965. A multivolume work. Vol. 4 examines the railroads of northeastern England.

Kirby, Maurice W. *The Origins of Railway Enterprise: The Stockton and Darlington Railway, 1821-1863.* New York: Cambridge University Press, 1993. A first-rate work on the history of the Stockton and Darlington Railway.

Raistrick, Arthur. *Quakers in Science and Industry.* New York: Augustus Kelley, 1968. Makes clear the pivotal role played by the Quaker community in developing the railroad in England.

Rolt, L. T. C. *George and Robert Stephenson: The Railway Revolution.* Westport, Conn.: Greenwood Press, 1977. Reveals how important George Stephenson was in the initial phases of the railroad.

SEE ALSO: Mar. 24, 1802: Trevithick Patents the High-Pressure Steam Engine; Jan. 7, 1830: Baltimore and Ohio Railroad Opens; July 21, 1836: Champlain and St. Lawrence Railroad Opens; Nov. 10, 1852: Canada's Grand Trunk Railway Is Incorporated; Mar. 2, 1853-1857: Pacific Railroad Surveys; Jan. 10, 1863: First Underground Railroad Opens in London; Apr., 1869: Westinghouse Patents His Air Brake; May 10, 1869: First Transcontinental Railroad Is Completed.

RELATED ARTICLES in *Great Lives from History: The Nineteenth Century, 1801-1900:* Andrew Carnegie; Jay Cooke; Rudolf Diesel; George Stephenson; Richard Trevithick.

October 26, 1825
ERIE CANAL OPENS

By providing an economical transportation route between the Great Lakes and the Atlantic coast, the Erie Canal advanced the economic development of the Old Northwest, solidified New York City's place as the center of American commerce, and inspired other states to build their own canal systems.

ALSO KNOWN AS: Clinton's Wonder; Clinton's Ditch
LOCALE: Between Albany and Buffalo, New York
CATEGORIES: Transportation; trade and commerce; engineering

KEY FIGURE
DeWitt Clinton (1769-1828), governor of New York, 1817-1821 and 1825-1828

SUMMARY OF EVENT

During the antebellum period, coastal cities in the United States engaged in strenuous competitions for the commercial wealth of the expanding West. Before progress could be made in weaving the sections together into a single economic unit, difficulties had to be overcome concerning the accessibility of markets. For example, in 1815, the Old Northwest was without convenient access to the markets of the East Coast. Farmers and merchants were forced to send their products to market by way of the Ohio and Mississippi Rivers to New Orleans and from there to the East Coast. Farmers in the area of Pittsburgh found it cheaper to ship their goods over that long, circuitous route than to send them overland to Philadelphia or New York, even though that was a far shorter distance. Al-though the federal government had completed the National Road from Cumberland, Maryland, to Wheeling, Virginia, in 1817 it was still uneconomical to ship bulky farm produce over that route.

Construction on the canal begn in 1817, with different sections of the canal assigned to different contractors. The canal took eight years to complete and was considered the construction marvel of its day. Indeed, some people considered it the eighth wonder of the world. However, it was built without the aid of a single professional engineer. Most of the canal was excavated by hand, with the help of horse-, oxen-, and mule-powered scrapers. Malaria and dysentery plagued the workers, most of whom were recent immigrants. In 1825, when

1820's

Governor DeWitt Clinton and other dignitaries riding the first passenger boat on the Erie Canal. (Library of Congress)

the canal opened its waterway, it was 4 feet (1.2 meters) deep, had eighteen aqueducts and eighty-three locks, and rose to an elevation of 568 feet (173 meters) between the Hudson River and Lake Erie. Construction costs were more than seven million dollars, but within a few years, the revenue from tolls brought more than one million dollars each year into the state coffers.

On October 26, 1825, the canal officially opened when the canal barge *Seneca Chief* left Buffalo with New York governor DeWitt Clinton and other dignitaries for the first trip down the canal. As the barge left Buffalo, cannoneers stationed along the way fired relay shots to notify people in New York that the canal was open. Stopping at most towns along the canal made the first journey a slow one, but on November 4 Clinton stood on the front of his barge and poured a keg of Lake Erie water into the Atlantic, celebrating "the wedding of waters."

The canal's opening reduced the cost of shipping freight from northwestern New York to the coast from one hundred dollars per ton to only six dollars per ton. During the first decade of its operation, the Erie Canal played a large part in the development of the south shore of Lake Erie. Areas in the northwestern part of New York, now provided with access to markets in New York City, increased in population and productivity. The canal added an all-water route to the northern portions of the Old Northwest and accelerated the growth of that region, which encompassed the area around the Great Lakes and between the Ohio and Mississippi Rivers. The resulting growth in population caused an expansion of production to meet the needs of the new immigrants. They, in turn, were able to increase the amount of farm produce available to the East. Their presence also augmented the demand for the importation of eastern manufactured goods.

Perhaps the most important consequence of Clinton's Wonder, as the canal soon came to be known, was the stimulus it gave to other regions, in both the East and the West, to emulate the success of New York by building

THE ERIE CANAL

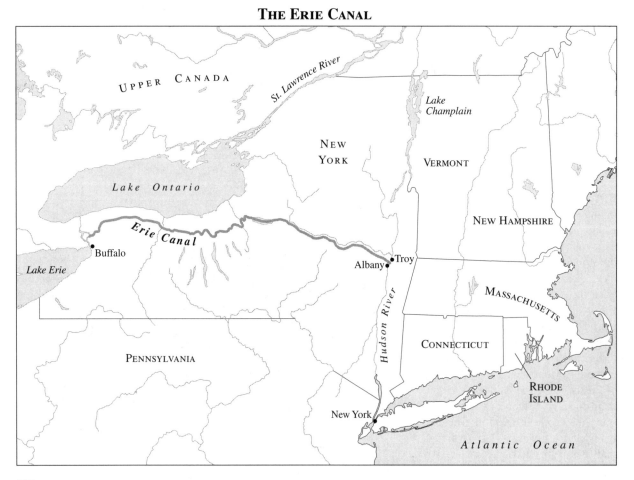

canals of their own. During the 1830's, Ohio started building canals, and Indiana and Illinois followed later. All three states used canals to link their interior regions to the Great Lakes-Erie Canal system. Ohio's canals connected Cincinnati with Toledo and Cleveland. In Indiana, the Wabash and Erie Canal connected Toledo and Terre Haute, while in Illinois, the Illinois and Michigan Canal connected Chicago with the lush lands along the Illinois River. As a consequence of the opening of these waterways, interior arms were opened up and production rose, for farmers now had new routes on which to send their produce to markets. Construction of the canals also caused many American Indian tribes to be removed to reservations west of the Mississippi River.

The effects of the Erie Canal in the East were equally momentous. The canal solidified the position of New York City as the greatest emporium in the nation. Other eastern cities, such as Philadelphia and Baltimore, could not afford to sit still while New York monopolized the western trade. If they were to survive as commercial centers, they had to develop their own connections with the West. Pennsylvania began building a system of canals and waterways between Philadelphia and Pittsburgh and followed it with the Pennsylvania Railroad. Baltimore undertook two major improvements: construction of the Baltimore and Ohio Railroad and the Chesapeake and Ohio Canal. Farther north, Boston constructed a canal across to Albany, hoping to intercept some of the western trade.

This vigorous and deadly competition in the East was not without effects on the established Mississippi River system. Cities functioning as parts of the lake system competed not only with one another but also with cities that formed part of the river system. For example, Toledo and Cleveland engaged in commercial warfare with Cincinnati and Louisville; St. Louis, especially in the 1850's, felt the impact of the Illinois and Michigan Canal in its struggle with Chicago. Downstream, New Orleans was sensitive to any events that impinged on the trade of St. Louis, Cincinnati, and Louisville.

Expanding railroads added a new dimension to the struggle, and their development overlapped and went beyond the era of the great canals. By the 1850's, the competition initiated by the construction of the Erie Canal had entered a new phase. A struggle involving three transportation systems and a host of cities and towns had evolved. Cities that had pinned their hopes on the canals were bypassed by the railroad. Cities bid against one another, mortgaging their futures for the privilege of becoming rail hubs. Smaller towns with exalted visions of

"FIFTEEN YEARS ON THE ERIE CANAL"

The construction of the Erie Canal caught the popular imagination, as it symbolized both American ingenuity and the labor necessary to put that ingenuity into action. Such labor is emphasized in the 1905 folk song "Low Bridge, Everybody Down: Or, Fifteen Years on the Erie Canal," by Thomas S. Allen, excerpted below.

I've got an old mule and her name is Sal,
Fifteen years on the Erie Canal,
She's a good old worker and a good old pal,
Fifteen years on the Erie Canal.
We've hauled some barges in our day,
Filled with lumber, coal and hay—
And every inch of the way I know
From Albany to Buffalo.

Low bridge, everybody down,
Low bridge! We're coming to a town!
You can always tell your neighbor, you can always
   tell your pal
If you've ever navigated on the Erie Canal.

We'd better look around for a job, Old Gal,
Fifteen years on the Erie Canal.
You bet your life I wouldn't part with Sal,
Fifteen years on the Erie Canal.
Giddap there, Gal, we've passed that lock,
We'll make Rome 'fore six o'clock-
So one more trip and then we'll go
Right straight back to Buffalo.

Low bridge, everybody down;
Low bridge, I've got the finest mule in town.
Once a man named Mike McGintey tried to put over
   Sal,
Now he's way down at the bottom of the Erie Canal.

Oh! where would I be if I lost my pal?
Fifteen years on the Erie Canal,
Oh, I'd like to see a mule as good as Sal,
Fifteen years on the Erie Canal.
A friend of mine once got her sore,
Now he's got a broken jaw,
'Cause she let fly with her iron toe
And knocked him in to Buffalo.

Low bridge, everybody down;
Low bridge, I've got the finest mule in town.
If you're looking for trouble, better stay away,
She's the only fighting donkey on the Erie Canal.

Source: Poets' Corner.

1820's

their economic potential rose and then fell, succumbing to the economic power of more dynamic and luckier competitors.

SIGNIFICANCE

The first major effort to open an economic commercial connection between the West and East occurred with the construction of New York's Erie Canal. The 363-mile-long canal connected Albany on the Hudson River with Buffalo on Lake Erie. Skeptics at first called the canal "Clinton's Ditch" after its most consistent advocate, New York governor DeWitt Clinton. However, after the canal opened, skepticism quickly evaporated, as the canal had a direct and cumulative effect on the nation in general and the Northwest in particular.

To keep up with competition from other transportation sources, the Erie Canal was enlarged to a depth of 7 feet (2.1 meters) in 1862. In time, the Champlain, Oswego, and Cayuga-Seneca canals branched off from the Erie, adding canal access to other cities and lakes. This new system of canals was renamed the New York State Canal System. Dredging continued to deepen the canals, and minimum depths of 12 feet (3.66 meters) were the norm by the mid-twentieth century. Early in the twenty-first century, plans were under way to deepen New York's canals to 16 feet throughout the entire canal system.

—John G. Clark, updated by Russell Hively

FURTHER READING

Albion, Robert G. *The Rise of New York Port, 1815-1860*. New York: Charles Scribner's Sons, 1939. Evaluates the factors, including the Erie Canal, that led to the commercial leadership of New York City.

Baida, Peter. "The Admirable Three Millions." *American Heritage* 39, no. 5 (July/August, 1988): 16-20. Tells how William James turned sixty thousand dollars into three million dollars through land investments prior to the completion of the Erie Canal.

Bernstein, Peter L. *Wedding of the Waters: The Erie Canal and the Making of a Great Nation*. New York: W. W. Norton, 2005. Engagingly written history of the Erie Canal that considers it in the broad context of nineteenth century American history and demonstrates its impact on national development.

Cornog, Evan. *The Birth of Empire: DeWitt Clinton and the American Experience, 1769-1828*. New York: Oxford University Press, 1998. Comprehensive and well-regarded biography that emphasizes Clinton's political accomplishments and how they affected New York City and the state as a whole.

Goodrich, Carter. *Government Promotion of Canals and Railroads, 1800-1890*. New York: Columbia University Press, 1960. A study of federal, state, and local government aid and encouragement of internal improvements, including an enlightening analysis of state efforts.

Hecht, Roger W. *The Erie Canal Reader, 1790-1950*. Syracuse, N.Y.: Syracuse University Press, 2003. Collection of fiction, poetry, essays, and other works about the Erie Canal written over the course of its history.

Meyer, Balthaser H. *History of Transportation in the United States Before 1860*. Reprint. Washington, D.C.: Peter Smith, 1948. A reference work containing facts and information regarding all the major early road, canal, and railroad developments in the nation.

Shaw, Ronald E. *Erie Water West: A History of the Erie Canal, 1792-1854*. Lexington: University Press of Kentucky, 1966. A complete history of the canal from its conception to completion, and its first twenty-nine years of operation.

SEE ALSO: Aug. 17, 1807: Maiden Voyage of the *Clermont*; 1811-1840: Construction of the National Road; c. 1815-1830: Westward American Migration Begins; Jan. 7, 1830: Baltimore and Ohio Railroad Opens; July 21, 1836: Champlain and St. Lawrence Railroad Opens; Nov. 17, 1869: Suez Canal Opens; June 20, 1895: Germany's Kiel Canal Opens.

RELATED ARTICLES in *Great Lives from History: The Nineteenth Century, 1801-1900:* DeWitt Clinton; Robert Fulton; Benjamin Henry Latrobe; Thomas Telford.

December 26, 1825
DECEMBRIST REVOLT

The uprising that Russia's Decembrist revolt sparked failed; however, it inspired later reformers and revolutionaries seeking social, economic, and political changes in Russia.

LOCALE: St. Petersburg, Russia
CATEGORIES: Social issues and reform; wars, uprisings, and civil unrest

KEY FIGURES

Alexander I (1777-1825), czar of Russia, r. 1801-1825
Constantine Pavlovich (1779-1831), grand duke; Alexander's brother and ostensible heir
Nicholas I (1796-1855), czar of Russia, r. 1825-1855
Mikhail Bestuzhev-Ryumin (1801-1826), leader of the St. Petersburg revolt
Nikita Muravyov (1796-1843) and
Yevgeny Obolensky (1796-1865), leaders of the Northern Society
Sergey Trubetskoy (1790-1860),
Kondraty Ryleyev (1795-1826) and
Peter Kakhovsky (1797-1826), members of the Northern Society
Sergey Muravyov-Apostol (1796-1826), leader of military uprising in the south
Pavel Pestel (1793-1826), army colonel and radical leader of the Southern Society

SUMMARY OF EVENT

The Decembrist Revolt of 1825 was Russia's first modern revolution. Many later Russian revolutionaries, including the Bolsheviks, traced their origins to the young aristocrats who revolted in St. Petersburg on December 26, 1825 (December 14 on the Julian calendar then in use in Russia). The roots of the revolt go back a century earlier to the westernizing efforts of Peter the Great, and the subsequent gradual spread of the Enlightenment to Russia. The French invasion of Russia in 1812, and Russia's victory over Napoleon, also contributed to the growth of Russian patriotic sentiment.

All these factors encouraged a demand for reform and progress. Czar Alexander I became a national hero after the Napoleonic Wars, and educated Russians believed that freedom for Europe would mean freedom for Russia. However, it was not to be. When peace in 1815 did not bring reforms, groups of young men began to discuss what should be done. These men were the flower of Russia's educated class; many of them had been officers dur-

ing the war of liberation, some had served with occupation forces in France in the years after Napoleon's defeat. Others were intellectuals. All were imbued with the progressive ideas of the European Enlightenment and wished to dedicate their efforts to the improvement of their homeland.

The objectives of the reformers included the abolition of serfdom, termination of the hated military colonies, shorter enlistment terms for soldiers in the Russian army (from the existing twenty-five years), and the end of widespread corruption in government bureaus. These idealists also sought political and social rights in a written constitution, reduction of the power of the autocratic czarist government, guaranteed civil liberties—such as trial by jury—and a better system of land distribution and ownership.

Around 1816, several people established a secret organization to plan Russia's future. Their Union of Salvation was the first of several secret bodies from which the Northern and Southern Societies ultimately sprang. Based in St. Petersburg, the Union of Salvation began with a membership of twenty. Later groups included the Union of Welfare (1818), the Southern Society (1821), the Northern Society (1822), and the Society of United Slavs (1823). The organizational forms and many of the principles which these groups followed were drawn from European secret societies, including the Masonic Order, whose combination of absolute secrecy, mystic ritual, and humanitarianism was especially appealing.

The first Russian reformist societies were nonrevolutionary, although individual members spoke of regicide and rebellion. A few naïvely believed they could bring about reforms simply by reporting abuses to the czar. However, as Russia drifted toward reaction, the secret societies not only proliferated but also turned toward revolutionary activism. Attempts to cooperate and establish centralized direction for the movement failed. By 1825, the Northern Society in St. Petersburg and the Southern Society, located at Tulchin in the Kiev Military district, were the most important groups. Nikita Muravyov, a moderate constitutionalist, led the Northern Society, and Colonel Pavel Pestel headed the Southern Society.

The Northern Society favored a constitutional system with the czar as a limited monarch. Pestel, the leader of the Southern Society, was the most widely educated political theorist among the Decembrists and also the most radical. Even Pestel, however, feared a social revolution,

Coronation of Czar Nicholas I. (Francis R. Niglutsch)

cow, although the public remained ignorant of the transaction. When word of Alexander's death reached St. Petersburg, Nicholas ordered that the country take the oath of allegiance to Constantine, although he knew of Constantine's abdication. Constantine, who was married to a Roman Catholic Polish aristocrat and living in Warsaw, refused to accept the crown and refused to return to the capital to explain the situation publicly. Nicholas had no choice but to replace the original oath with an oath to himself as czar.

The problem with Nicholas's accession was that to the public he appeared to be a usurper. Since Constantine was more popular with the troops than Nicholas, there was real danger of a mutiny. As rumors of this situation circulated through St. Petersburg, the Northern Society saw its chance. The new oath was to be sworn on December 14, and the leaders met on December 25 (December 13 on Russia's Julian calendar) to plan their strategy. Yevgeny Obolensky, Sergey Trubetskoy, Peter Kakhovsky, and Kondraty Ryleyev decided to make their move.

None of the plotters was a professional revolutionary, and by modern standards they were all inept. Moreover, since Nikita Muravyov was out of the city, there was no designated leader. Their plan was simple, but it depended on the willingness of several regiments to follow their officers in a mutiny, and the officers' willingness to lead them. The Decembrists badly overestimated their support, and they had only a vague idea of how the actual seizure of power would occur. These deficiencies doomed the rebellion in the capital on December 26 from the start.

Approximately three thousand soldiers obeyed their officers participating in the conspiracy in St. Petersburg, but Nicholas mustered fifteen thousand soldiers to oppose them. Rebel and loyal troops were in position on opposite sides of Senate Square by mid-morning on December 26. The rebels shouted for the "true" czar, Constantine, and a crowd gathered to watch. Shouts and slogans were exchanged, but there was little bloodshed. Finally, toward sunset Nicholas ordered his artillery to fire into the rebellious soldiers. An estimated seventy to

and he planned only to stage a coup d'état that would destroy the czar and the imperial family and establish a revolutionary dictatorship to prepare Russia for a highly centralized "republican" government. Pestel's ideas had a totalitarian ring to them, and his models were drawn from revolutionary French thought.

The revolutionary societies found their opportunity when Czar Alexander I died unexpectedly in faraway Taganrog in southern Russia on November 19, 1825. His legal successor was his brother Grand Duke Constantine Pavlovich. However, in January of 1822, Constantine had secretly abdicated his claim to the throne in favor of a younger brother, Nicholas. Documents ratifying the abdication were deposited both in St. Petersburg and Mos-

eighty fatalities resulted, and the revolt quickly collapsed.

The uprising in the south was equally unsuccessful. Pestel, leader of the Southern Society, was arrested on December 25 before news from St. Petersburg reached him of events there. Sergey Muravyov-Apostol therefore began the rebellion in the region near Kiev, but the one army unit that did mutiny was defeated soon afterward. The government had known of the secret societies for years; the night before the uprising, Nicholas was warned that it would happen.

SIGNIFICANCE

After the revolt, the police rounded up the leaders, and the investigation began at once. The Decembrists confessed fully and freely, and during the next four months the government collected a vast quantity of data concerning both the revolutionary societies and the conditions that produced them. When the investigation was completed, a seventy-two-man court was formed with M. M. Speransky as its moving spirit, and this court evaluated the evidence and passed sentence on the rebels. The five adjudged most guilty were sentenced to be drawn and quartered, and thirty-one others were sentenced to be hanged. Nicholas commuted the latter sentences to exile and imprisonment and substituted hangings for the barbarous first sentences. In all, 579 men were indicted, and 121 received sentences. On July 21, 1826, Pestel, Sergey Muravyov-Apostol, Kondraty Ryleyev, Mikhail Bestuzhev-Ryumin, and Peter Kakhovsky were hanged. More than one hundred others were sent to Siberia, where the last "Decembrist" died in 1892. Several wives were allowed to accompany their convicted husbands into exile.

Effects of the Decembrist uprising resulted in even greater suppression of liberal and reform movements in Russia, and a strengthening of the authoritarian rule of Czar Nicholas I. The execution of the Decembrist leaders profoundly shocked liberal elements of Russian society, and their sacrifice became a living part of the memory of the Russian revolutionary tradition.

—Roderick E. McGrew, updated by Taylor Stults

FURTHER READING

Barratt, Glynn. *The Rebel on the Bridge: A Life of the Decembrist Baron Andrey Rozen, 1800-84*. Athens: Ohio University Press, 1976. Biography of a Northern Society member.

Evreinov, Ludmila. *Alexander I, Emperor of Russia: A Reappraisal*. 2 vols. New York: Xlibris, 2001. The author maintains her book differs from previous biographies because she has based her conclusions on diplomatic correspondence, Russian laws, and other previously untapped primary sources of information.

O'Meara, Patrick. *The Decembrist Pavel Pestel: Russia's First Republican*. New York: Palgrave Macmillan, 2004. Well-researched biography of one of the Decembrist Revolt's leading ideologues.

Mazour, Anatole G. *The First Russian Revolution: The Decembrist Revolt*. Berkeley: University of California Press, 1937. Although somewhat dated, Mazour's work remains the essential account on the topic.

_____. *Women in Exile: Wives of the Decembrists*. Tallahassee, Fla.: Diplomatic Press, 1975. Sympathetic account of those who followed their husbands to Siberia.

Raeff, Marc. *The Decembrist Movement*. Englewood Cliffs, N.J.: Prentice-Hall, 1966. A helpful account of the event along with source materials.

Ulam, Adam. *Russia's Failed Revolutionaries: From the Decembrists to the Dissidents*. New York: Basic Books, 1981. Excellent account of the history of Russian revolutionary movements.

Yarmolinsky, Avrahm. *The Road to Revolution: A Century of Russian Radicalism*. New York: Macmillan, 1959. Broad assessment of the revolutionary and reform movements during the nineteenth century, including the Decembrists.

Zetlin, Mikhail. *The Decembrists*. New York: International Universities Press, 1958. Study of the revolt emphasizing the personalities of its leaders; includes their exile years in Siberia.

SEE ALSO: 1840's-1880's: Russian Realist Movement; Mar. 3, 1861: Emancipation of Russian Serfs; Jan. 22-Sept., 1863: Russia Crushes Polish Rebellion.

RELATED ARTICLES in *Great Lives from History: The Nineteenth Century, 1801-1900:* Alexander I; Aleksandr Herzen; Nicholas I; Mikhail Mikhaylovich Speransky.

1820's

c. 1826-1827
FIRST MEETINGS OF THE PLYMOUTH BRETHREN

Several small groups of people in England and Ireland—dissatisfied with both Roman Catholicism and the established Anglican Church—banded together to form what would become known as the Plymouth Brethren. While the Brethren never attracted great numbers of adherents, their theology influenced the beliefs and practices of many other British Christians.

LOCALE: England; Ireland
CATEGORIES: Organizations and institutions; religion and theology

KEY FIGURES

John Nelson Darby (1800-1882), Irish clergyman, prolific writer, and a founder of the Plymouth Brethren

Anthony N. Groves (1795-1853), Brethren missionary and attorney

Benjamin Wills Newton (1807-1899), early Brethren leader who was often in conflict with Darby over doctrine

Edward Cronin (1801-1882), a dentist and Brethren founder who converted from Roman Catholicism

John Bellett (1795-1864), a Brethren founder and dentist

George Müller (1805-1898), Lutheran clergyman and early Brethren leader

Francis Hutchinson (1802-1833), a founding member of the Plymouth Brethren

SUMMARY OF EVENT

The Plymouth Brethren originated in reaction to organized Christianity in Europe during the 1820's, particularly the Church of England (Anglican Church). The group's members sought a simpler, truer form of Christianity, one not tied to the state. They believed that an ideal community of faith would emulate what they perceived as the dynamic spirit of the early Church, rather than the rigid hierarchy and clerical or priestly control that developed later.

There is some debate as to exactly when, where, and by whom the first gathering of the Plymouth Brethren was organized. Several small groups with similar concerns about the state of the Christian faith met independently around 1826-1827 in both England and Ireland. These later merged into one, becoming known as the Plymouth Brethren during the early 1830's. One of these groups, naturally enough, was meeting in Plymouth,

Devon, England, by 1831, while at least one other had begun in Ireland. The best known early and influential members included John Nelson Darby, Edward Cronin, Anthony N. Groves, John Bellett, Francis Hutchinson, and Benjamin Wills Newton.

One credible version of the Brethren foundation story states that one group formed around Cronin and another around Bellett and that these two clusters came together at Hutchinson's home. Long before these clusters formed, though, other similar groups of Christians gathered to worship simply and without clergy while seeking the spiritual gifts they read about in the New Testament, such as speaking in tongues, healing, and visions of future events. Such supernatural gifts were seen as a sign of the imminent return of Christ. The desire to witness the return of the Messiah also gave such Christian enclaves a strong interest in studying unfulfilled prophecies set forth in the Book of Daniel, in the Old Testament, and Revelation, in the New Testament. Prophecy conferences such as the 1833 conference held in Powerscourt in Darby's home county of Wicklow, Ireland, helped solidify the Brethren into a cohesive whole.

Darby's role as founder of the Plymouth Brethren is questionable. It is unclear who, if anyone, solely deserves that title, and Darby was at any rate little more than an occasional visitor to the Brethren's meetings at first. However, when an injury kept him convalescing in Dublin, Darby became a more active participant and eventually became key to the movement. It was Darby's leadership that contributed to the uniqueness of the Brethren, carving for the movement a place in history while many similar groups simply faded away after their founders' deaths. Ultimately, Darby broke from the established Church and went on to write forty lengthy books about Brethren theology and prophecy studies.

The Brethren rejected the notion that only a member of the clergy could lead a religious service. In fact, the group condemned the notion of an ordained priesthood as being unbiblical. This condemnation came despite the fact that Darby, the group's most prolific and prominent member, was an Anglican clergyman, and George Müller, another influential early Brethren member, was a Lutheran pastor. Darby, Müller, and other Brethren felt strongly that spiritual gifts and leadership should be open to the laity and that God, rather than humans, should call forth leaders within a community. Within Brethren gatherings, priestly acts such as preaching or even "breaking of the bread" (Communion) could be performed by those who felt called, rather than trained and paid professional clerics. Brethren espoused egalitarianism not only in their religious practices but also in their social lives, as in the case of an English peer who made a point of eating with his servants. They also detested rent pews, a system common to the established Church in which the wealthy would pay for exclusive access to particular pews in a church. This effectively limited poor people's access to church seating or marked them as charity cases when they had to sit in designated free pews.

Studying biblical prophecy became an important element of Brethren life. Naturalist and author Edmund Gosse's autobiography, *Father and Son: A Study of Two Temperaments* (1907), even talks about prophecy discussion being a favorite family pastime during his childhood. Gosse's father led a Brethren congregation in England and was torn between his Brethren faith's distrust of science, particularly evolution, and his own strong interest in biology.

In addition to prophecy study, an empowered laity, and an egalitarian spirit, another important Brethren theme was unity. This ideal, however, was far from a reality, even within the early Brethren leadership. For example, Newton pressed for excluding or separating from apostates, while Darby vied for openness and forbearance. The two also disagreed on details about Christ's return. The issue of openness versus exclusion later led to a split, with the two camps becoming known as the Open Brethren and the Exclusive Brethren. Other splits over doctrinal issues followed.

SIGNIFICANCE

The Plymouth Brethren never became a large or popular group, yet it was important at its founding, and its ideas and foci continue to affect religious life in Great Britain and elsewhere. Darby's prophecy speculations, for example, fueled premillennialist expectations that Christ would soon return to gather the true Christians before the apocalyptic end of the world. This line of thinking continues to be part of religious and popular culture today, as seen in the popularity of apocalyptic fiction such as Tim LaHaye and Jerry B. Jenkins's Left Behind series. Darby's systematizing of dispensationalism (a theory of biblical eras, such as the era of Adam or the era of Abraham) has earned him a place of honor among premillennialists and those who study biblical prophecy. Darby argued that God gives humanity a particular responsibility in each era.

— *Elizabeth Jarnagin*

FURTHER READING

Baumgartner, Frederic J. *Longing for the End: A History of Millennialism in Western Civilization.* New York: Palgrave, 2001. Examines how expectations of Christ's return and other religious end-of-world scenarios have played out in the culture and history of various nations and groups.

Bayless, Robert. *My People: The History of Those Christians Sometimes Called Plymouth Brethren.* Wheaton, Ill.: Harold Shaw, 1995. In addition to discussing prominent Brethren figures such as Darby and Newton, the author looks at Brethren history from the standpoint of less well-known practitioners of the faith.

Callahan, James Patrick. *Primitivist Piety: The Ecclesiology of the Early Plymouth Brethren.* Lanham, Md.: Scarecrow Press, 1997. Looks at the distinction in Brethren thought between primitivism and restorationism, as well as providing a thoroughly documented look at early Brethren history and the group's place in the broader elements of British Evangelicalism such as millenarianism and prophecy conferences.

Enns, Paul. *The Moody Handbook of Theology.* Chicago: Moody Press, 1989. Provides basic outline and charts about various types of Christian theology, including dispensational, all from a fairly conservative evangelical viewpoint

Gosse, Edmund. *Father and Son.* Reprint. New York: Penguin Books, 1989. A thoughtful recounting of a man's life growing up as the son of a naturalist and devout leader of a Plymouth Brethren congregation in Victorian England

Rowdon, Harold H. *The Origins of the Brethren: 1825-1850.* London: Pickering & Inglis, 1967. Provides a good entry-level look at the group's early years by primarily focusing on key relationships between founding members such as Darby and Newton, as well as Müller and Craik.

Ryrie, Charles C. *Dispensationalism Today.* Chicago: Moody Press, 1965. Explains the origins of dispensationalism, including Darby's role in its formation. Lists the various dispensations, or eras in Christian history.

Smith, Nathan DeLynn. *Roots, Renewal, and the Brethren.* Pasadena, Calif.: Hope, 1986. The author is a Christian educator and Brethren member. His book, originally a doctor of ministry thesis, opens with a brief, historical look at the group's formation and proceeds into a critique of some current practices.

1820's

Stunt, Timothy C. F. "Benjamin Wills Newton." In *Oxford Dictionary of National Biography*. Vol. 40. Oxford, England: Oxford University Press, 2004.

_____. "John Nelson Darby." In *Oxford Dictionary of National Biography*, vol. 15, pp. 117-118, Oxford, England: Oxford University Press, 2004. These entries provide a quick glimpse at the lives and careers of two key Brethren founders, as well as offering lists of additional readings.

Turner, W. G. *John Nelson Darby*. 1901. Reprint. London: Chapter Two, 1986. Short, laudatory biography written less than a generation after Darby's death, relies heavily on associates' reminiscences, as well as

excerpts from Darby's own writings, primarily letters and hymns.

SEE ALSO: 1804: British and Foreign Bible Society Is Founded; July 14, 1833: Oxford Movement Begins; Oct. 9, 1845: Newman Becomes a Roman Catholic; 1870-1871: Watch Tower Bible and Tract Society Is Founded; Oct. 30, 1875: Eddy Establishes the Christian Science Movement.

RELATED ARTICLES in *Great Lives from History: The Nineteenth Century, 1801-1900:* Alexander Campbell; Henry Edward Manning; Frederick Denison Maurice; John Henry Newman; E. B. Pusey; John Russell.

1826-1842
YOUNG GERMANY MOVEMENT

Poet Heinrich Heine, novelist Karl Gutzkow, and dramatist Georg Büchner were the central figures of Young Germany, a movement that influenced German literature, philosophy, popular culture, and sociopolitical theory in the 1830's and helped sow the seeds for the radical politics of the 1840's that led to the revolutions of 1848.

LOCALE: Germany

CATEGORIES: Cultural and intellectual history; literature; philosophy

KEY FIGURES

Karl Gutzkow (1811-1878), German novelist, dramatist, and critic

Heinrich Heine (1797-1856), German poet and social critic

Georg Büchner (1813-1837), German dramatist

Ludolf Wienbarg (1802-1872), German writer, critic, and literary theorist

Ferdinand Freiligrath (1810-1876), German poet

Ludwig Börne (Lob Baruch; 1786-1837), German satirist, journalist, and critic

Christian Dietrich Grabbe (1801-1836), German dramatist

Henri de Saint-Simon (1760-1825), French socialist philosopher

Georg Wilhelm Friedrich Hegel (1770-1831), German philosopher

SUMMARY OF EVENT

After the Congress of Vienna (1814-1815) established a new European conservative order designed mostly by

Metternich, monarchs throughout Europe vigorously persecuted the revolutionary ideals that had found expression under Napoleon I. Nationalism increased dramatically in reaction to Napoleon's unsuccessful attempt to create a pan-European empire. In Germany, student fraternities called *Burschenschaften* promoted militarism and an extreme, almost fanatic, nationalism. Similarly, outside the schools and universities, the athletic clubs (*Turnvereine*) were thinly disguised nests of political dissatisfaction and their members (*Turner*) were often nationalistic politically but liberal socially.

In 1819, Karl Ludwig Sand, a member of the *Burschenschaft* at the University of Erlangen, assassinated August von Kotzebue, a prominent German author and diplomat, whom Sand believed was a spy for Russia and therefore a traitor to Germany. Directly as the result of this murder, the Prussian monarchy imposed the Carlsbad Decrees, which suppressed the *Burschenschaften* and the *Turnvereine* and marked the beginning of harsh and intimidating censorship in Germany. These laws remained in effect from 1819 until the people forced their repeal in 1848.

It was during that time of political repression and censorship that the movement that would come to be known as Young Germany (*junges Deutschland*) arose. Young Germany developed out of German Romanticism but rejected most Romantic premises. It could be regarded as an uneasy synthesis of Romanticism and nationalism. Romanticism is often interpreted as an apolitical movement, yet its aim of liberating the human spirit from the conventions of society, the tyranny of government, and the pressures of religion was taken over and given a political slant by Young Germany. Like Romanticism, Young Germany emphasized freedom, but while some Romantic writers took freedom to be essentially a state of mind, for Young Germany the concept of freedom was entirely political. Ferdinand Freiligrath began his poetic career by imitating the Romantic style of Victor Hugo but soon moved toward producing overtly political poetry and gained a reputation as an agitator.

Heinrich Heine was Germany's first political poet and the founder of the Young Germany movement in literature. In 1826, he began to shift his formerly Romantic inclinations toward a more political emphasis with the first volume of *Reisebilder* (1826-1831, 4 volumes; *Pictures of Travel*, 1855), a collection of poems about the political and social alienation of a restless spirit. The movement was only loosely aligned, however, and it was unnamed until 1834, when Ludolf Wienbarg coined the term "Young Germany" in *Aesthetische Feldzüge: Dem jungen Deutschland gewidmet* (aesthetic campaigns: dedicated to young Germany).

Henri de Saint-Simon advocated a type of socialism based on nondogmatic Christianity and the hard facts of natural science. His thought closely resembled the later philosophy of secular humanism and lent great energy to the Young Germany movement, which, although clearly nationalistic, was also liberal, egalitarian, socialist, democratic, and even proto-feminist. Heine and most subsequent Young Germans were also influenced by Georg Wilhelm Friedrich Hegel's philosophy of history, but Hegel cannot be considered the intellectual godfather of the movement that Saint-Simon was. Hegel was one of the first Romantic philosophers to insist that abstract knowledge was inseparable from politics—for him, understanding the world accurately and forming the perfect society are synonymous projects—but from his earliest interpreters onward he has often been misconstrued as an individualist. Under this interpretation, he was too individualistic for Young Germany. Some Young Germans, like Karl Gutzkow, had studied under Hegel at the University of Berlin, and all of them knew Hegel's philosophy well enough.

The Young Germans advocated the emancipation of the Jews, who could not then hold office or be admitted to most professions in Germany unless they allowed themselves to be baptized. Ludwig Börne changed his name from Lob Baruch when he converted to Lutheranism in 1818, and Heine insincerely went through the motions of baptism in 1825 so that he could practice law. Christian Dietrich Grabbe, one of the few anti-Semites among the Young Germans, wrote such fine historical dramas and

Heinrich Heine. (Library of Congress)

tragedies in verse that even Heine admired him.

In 1834, Georg Büchner, a graduate student in medicine and zoology at the University of Giessen who was involved in underground revolutionary activities, narrowly avoided arrest for writing an anonymous subversive pamphlet, *Der Hessische Landbote* (1834; with Friedrich Ludwig Weidig; *The Hessian Courier*, 1963). The next year, he wrote an inflammatory play about the squelched ideals of the French Revolution (1789), *Dantons Tod* (pb. 1835, pr. 1902; *Danton's Death*, 1927), which Gutzkow helped him to publish in a censored version. He fled in March, 1835, to Strasbourg, France, where he wrote a novel, *Lenz* (1839; English translation, 1963), a light comedy, *Leonce und Lena* (wr. 1836, pb. 1850, pr. 1895; *Leonce and Lena*, 1927), and his doctoral dissertation on the skull nerves of fish. He settled in Zürich, Switzerland, where he died of typhus at twenty-four. Büchner's unfinished masterpiece, the poignant, socially conscious drama *Woyzeck* (wr. 1836, pb. 1879, pr. 1913; English translation, 1927), appeared posthumously and eventually became a celebrated opera by Alban Berg, *Wozzeck* (pr. 1925).

The court in Mannheim jailed Gutzkow for ten weeks in 1835 to punish him for his eloquent attack on traditional religion and marriage in *Wally: Die Zweiflerin* (1835; *Wally the Skeptic*, 1974). Authorities used Gutzkow's case as an excuse to crack down on a broader category of literary works that might threaten the political order. On December 10, 1835, the Frankfurt Bundestag banned all writings by the members of Young Germany. Most of the authors attached to the movement experienced time either in prison or in exile. Other major Young German works include Heine's *Buch der Lieder* (1827; *Book of Songs*, 1856), Grabbe's *Don Juan und Faustus* (pr., pb. 1829; *Don Juan and Faust*), Grabbe's *Napoleon: Oder, Die hundert Tage* (pb. 1831, pr. 1869; *Napoleon: Or, the hundred days*), Börne's *Briefe aus Paris* (1832-1834, 6 vols.; letters from Paris), Heine's *Die romantische Schule* (1836; *The Romantic School*, 1876)—itself an expansion of his *Zur Geschichte der neueren schönen Literatur in Deutschland* (1833; *Letters Auxiliary to the History of Modern Polite Literature in Germany*, 1836)—Freiligrath's *Gedichte* (1838; *Poems*, 1949), as well as *Gedichte eines Lebendigen* (1841, 1843, 2 vols.; poems of a living man) by Georg Herwegh (1817-1875), *Madonna* (1835) by novelist and critic Theodor Mundt (1808-1861), and *Das junge Europa* (1833-1837, 5 vols.; young Europe) by the German writer and dramatist Heinrich Laube (1806-1884).

SIGNIFICANCE

The period in Germany between the fall of Napoleon (1815) and the revolutions that began in March, 1848, is called the *Vormärz* ("Before March"). More specific, the label refers to the intense prerevolutionary spirit that appeared after the ascension in 1840 of Prussian king Frederick William IV and his reactionary minister of education, Johann Albrecht Friedrich Eichhorn, replacing the more enlightened King Frederick William III and his relatively liberal minister of education, Baron Karl vom Stein zum Altenstein. The Ministry of Education held tremendous power in Prussia, determining university appointments, enforcing the Carlsbad Decrees, setting the cultural agenda, protecting Christian orthodoxy, and sending out networks of spies among the intelligentsia. Literate Germans tolerated Altenstein but detested Eichhorn.

The Young Germans are to be distinguished from the Young Hegelians, who used Hegel's dialectical logic and philosophy of history as the basis of their social philosophy and political theory. Young Hegelianism began in 1835 with David Friedrich Strauss and ended in 1846 with Karl Schmidt; it included Bruno Bauer, Edgar Bauer, Max Stirner, Moses Hess, Ludwig Feuerbach, Arnold Ruge, Friedrich Engels, and Karl Marx and formulated many of the philosophical ideas that emerged in the 1848 revolutions and beyond. Both Young Germany and Young Hegelianism were leftist political movements, but the former was literary and nationalistic, while the latter was philosophical and internationalistic.

Both the Young Germans and the Young Hegelians came under Eichhorn's particular scrutiny. Their demise was due as much to his persecution of them as to

---

ENGELS ON YOUNG GERMANY

In 1839, German political philosopher Friedrich Engels wrote a letter, excerpted below, in which he defended the members of the Young Germany movement from the many critics of their aesthetic and political agenda.

These noble people accused Young Germany of wanting the emancipation of women and the restoration of the flesh and wanting as a side-line to overthrow a couple of kingdoms and become Pope and Emperor in one person. Of all these charges, only the one concerning the emancipation of women (in the Goethean sense) had any grounds, and it could only be brought against Gutzkow, who later disavowed the idea (as high-spirited, youthful over-haste). Through their standing by one another, their aims became more and more sharply defined; it was the "ideas of the time" which came to consciousness in them. These ideas of the century (so Kühne and Mundt said) are not anything demagogic or anti-Christian as they are made out to be, but are based on the natural right of every man and extend to everything in the present conditions which conflicts with it. Thus these ideas include: above all, participation by the people in the administration of the state, that is, constitutional matters; further, emancipation of the Jews, abolition of all religious compulsion, of all hereditary aristocracy, etc. Who can have anything against that? The Evangelische Kirchen-Zeitung and Menzel have it on their consciences that they have so cried down the honour of Young Germany. As early as 1836-37, among these writers, who were bound together by unity of purpose, but not by any special association, the idea was clear and definite; by the high quality of their writing they won for themselves the recognition of the other, mostly wretched, writers and attracted all the young talents to themselves.

naturally disintegrative factors within each movement. While Young Germany faded away after about 1842 and Young Hegelianism disappeared abruptly in 1846, they each contributed much to the ferment that erupted in 1848. Young Germany also laid the groundwork for psychological realism and social commentary in the literature of the late nineteenth and early twentieth centuries.

—*Eric v.d. Luft*

FURTHER READING

Butler, Eliza Marian. *Saint-Simonian Religion in Germany: A Study of the Young German Movement.* New York: H. Fertig, 1968. Gives an account of Saint-Simon's theory and shows how it influenced Heine, Laube, Gutzkow, Mundt, and Wienbarg.

Clason, Christopher R. "Young Germany." In *A Concise History of German Literature to 1900,* edited by Kim Vivian. Columbia, S.C.: Camden House, 1992. A clear and concise treatment by the chair of the Department of Modern Languages at Oakland University.

Hohendahl, Peter Uwe. *Building a National Literature: The Case of Germany, 1830-1870.* Ithaca, N.Y.: Cornell University Press, 1989. A standard and frequently cited work by a leading scholar in the field.

Sagarra, Eda. *Tradition and Revolution: German Literature and Society, 1830-1890.* New York: Basic Books, 1971. Includes a detailed evaluation of Young Germany in the context of the sociopolitical and literary culture of this sixty-year period.

Sammons, Jeffrey L. *Six Essays on the Young German Novel.* Chapel Hill: University of North Carolina Press, 1975. Includes a noteworthy interpretation of *Wally the Skeptic.*

Stern, Joseph Peter. *Idylls and Realities: Studies in Nineteenth-Century German Literature.* New York: Ungar, 1971. A selective overview of the era, discussing only Büchner and Heine among the Young Germans.

SEE ALSO: Apr., 1807: Hegel Publishes *The Phenomenology of Spirit*; Sept. 15, 1814-June 11, 1815: Congress of Vienna; 1819: Schopenhauer Publishes *The World as Will and Idea*; Feb., 1848: Marx and Engels Publish *The Communist Manifesto*; Mar. 3-Nov. 3, 1848: Prussian Revolution of 1848.

RELATED ARTICLES in *Great Lives from History: The Nineteenth Century, 1801-1900:* Friedrich Engels; Georg Wilhelm Friedrich Hegel; Heinrich Heine; Karl Marx; Metternich; Napoleon I; Henri de Saint-Simon.

1820's

1828-1834
PORTUGAL'S MIGUELITE WARS

When Miguel usurped the Portuguese throne from his niece Maria II, his action prompted a civil war between the conservative absolutist Miguel and Maria's father, the liberal constitutionalist Emperor Pedro I of Brazil. The war concluded in 1834, when Miguel was defeated and exiled and Maria II was restored to the throne.

ALSO KNOWN AS: War of the Two Brothers
LOCALE: Portugal
CATEGORIES: Wars, uprisings, and civil unrest; government and politics

KEY FIGURES

Pedro I (1798-1834), son of John VI of Portugal, first emperor of Brazil, r. 1822-1831, and king of Portugal, r. 1826

Maria II (Maria da Glória; 1819-1853), daughter of Pedro I and queen of Portugal, r. 1826-1828, 1834-1853

Miguel (1802-1866), brother of Pedro I and Portuguese pretender

SUMMARY OF EVENT

The occupation of numerous European countries during the early nineteenth century by Napoleon I resulted in the overthrow of various royal regimes. With Napoleon's defeat, these regimes were restored. However, while conservatives sought the restoration of absolutist regimes just as they had been before the Napoleonic Wars, liberals urged the establishment of constitutional monarchies, with written charters defining royal and parliamentary rights and responsibilities.

The debate over constitutional monarchy occurred in Portugal under circumstances distinctly different from those that obtained in the rest of Europe. After Napoleon's invasion of the country in 1807, the Portuguese monarchy had fled to Brazil, establishing that colony as the seat of the royal government. Long after the defeat of

Napoleon, however, John VI lingered in Brazil. By 1821, the Portuguese parliament demanded that the king return and that he agree to the establishment of a liberal constitution for the country. The king acceded to these demands. In departing, however, he left his elder son and heir, Prince Pedro, in Brazil as the colony's regent. He took his younger son, Prince Miguel, back to Portugal with him.

The following year, Pedro declared the independence of Brazil and was crowned as its first emperor, granting the country a constitution. In 1826, John VI died and Pedro was acclaimed as king of Portugal. Under the terms of the new Brazilian constitution, however, Pedro was not allowed to become the sovereign of any other state so long as he ruled Brazil. Therefore, after granting the country a liberal constitution, he abdicated the Portuguese kingship and placed his daughter on the throne as Maria II, arranging at the same time that his brother (her uncle) should marry her and become regent of the country.

Reactionary forces opposed such a compromised regime and supported Miguel to become king in his own right. They overthrew Maria II in 1828. These forces included Miguel's mother, the Infanta Carlota Joaquin, daughter of the king of Spain, and reactionary European courts opposed to the moderate constitutional measures John VI had allowed. The northern trading city of Porto became a center of liberal constitutionalism opposed to the new regime. An uprising there, however, was suppressed by the *miguelistas*, the supporters of Miguel, who then pursued a general persecution and exiling of liberals.

Some constitutionalists fled to England or to the island of Terceira in the Atlantic Portuguese archepelago of the Azores. The *miguelistas* attempted to suppress this nucleus of liberal opposition in the Azores, but they failed. The liberal constitutionalists made the Azores their stronghold. Meanwhile, in 1831, in the midst of the anti-liberal campaign, Pedro was forced to abdicate the Brazilian throne. He decided to return to Portugal and restore his daughter as queen. To place her back on the throne, however, Pedro would have to invade Portugal. He prepared for this invasion by augmenting the liberal armed forces on the Azore Islands. With British and French support, Pedro assembled an army of almost eight thousand men, including foreign mercenaries.

In 1832, Pedro invaded Portugal, attacking in the north at Porto, where constitutionalist sympathy remained strong. The invasion was successful, occupying the city in a few days. Although the absolutist forces were larger and better equipped, Pedro's army had the advantage of surprise. The *miguelistas* had not been prepared for an invasion at Porto, because they had expected such an action to occur at the southern capital, Lisbon. The *miguelistas* had sufficient force, however, to lay a powerful siege on Porto. They bombarded the city throughout the autumn and winter and blocked supplies of food from entering it. Plague ravaged the city during the winter. Porto, nonetheless, held out for a year. To weaken the hold of their besiegers, the liberals organized a naval expedition to the south of the country during the summer of 1833. Off the coast of the Algarve and then on the Tagus River, near Lisbon, they defeated the absolutist naval forces. These defeats demoralized the absolutists, and desertions resulted. Liberal guerrilla uprisings occurred in other parts of the country. Finally, the liberals occupied Lisbon, the *miguelistas* fled, and Pedro entered the capital at the end of July.

During September of 1833, the absolutists attempted unsuccessfully to retake Lisbon, and they continued to lay siege to Porto. However, suffering further military defeats, by the spring of 1834 Miguel surrendered to the now victorious Pedro. The treaty ending the war was signed at Évora-Monte on May 26, 1834. Miguel left for exile in Italy in June, and Maria II returned to Lisbon and was reestablished as queen by September.

SIGNIFICANCE

The end of the Miguelite Wars witnessed many misfortunes. By the autumn of 1834, Pedro, residing at the royal palace where he had been born in 1798, died of tuberculosis. The Portuguese economy, after years of war and internal conflict, was in ruins. The country was extensively indebted to foreign powers. Moreover, since Pedro and Miguel were both now gone from the Portuguese political scene, the nation's liberal and conservative forces, which continued at odds, had to reconcile themselves by making political compromises without their former leaders to guide them.

The legacy of the war created a fragile nucleus for parliamentary government in Portugal. The constitutionalist conflict was not a democratic debate but rather one between competing elites. On one side lay the traditional aristocracy, landed gentry, and religious hierarchy; on the other side rose a growing class of wealthy urban merchants, professionals, and the newly ennobled. The latter relied on foreign intellectual and financial support, so popular opinion came to associate Portuguese liberalism with external influence and the incursion of alien forces in the national character. The alienation of the majority of Portuguese from the limited economic, political, and cultural franchise of liberalism gave a powerful weight to authoritarian and corporate forces in Portugal. These came to the fore and dominated most of the country's modern history until the last decades of the twentieth century.

—*Edward A. Riedinger*

FURTHER READING

Anderson, James Maxwell. *The History of Portugal.* Westport, Conn.: Greenwood Press, 2000. A volume for general readership that describes events of early nineteenth century Portugal, from the end of Napoleonic occupation to the beginning of the constitutionalist period, within the context of the country's larger history.

Birmingham, David. *A Concise History of Portugal.* 2d ed. Cambridge, England: Cambridge University Press, 2003. Noted British historian provides a succinct account of cultural contradictions and the uneven development of constitutionalism within the larger context of Portugal's political history.

Bragança Cunha, Vicente de. *Eight Centuries of Portuguese Monarchy: A Political Study.* New York: J. Pott, 1911. Places the monarchs involved in the Miguelite Wars in relation to the Portuguese sovereigns who preceded and followed them.

Cardozo, Manoel S. "Review of *D. Pedro IV e D. Miguel 1826-1834.*" *The Hispanic American Historical Review* 21, no. 4 (November, 1941): 632-634. This review of a book on the parallel lives of Manuel and Pedro includes this remark of the former regarding the latter, "My brother and I were both unfortunate. On his side was intelligence without honor; on mine, honor without intelligence."

D'Auvergne, Edmund Basil Francis. *The Coburgs: The Story of the Rise of a Great Royal House.* London: S. Paul, 1911. One chapter provides the biography of Maria II of Portugal, who was married to Prince Ferdinand of Saxe-Coburg-Gotha.

Lambert, Francis J. D. *The Cortes and the King: Constitutional Monarchy in the Iberian World.* Glasgow: University of Glasgow, Institute of Latin American Studies, 1981. Traces the development of critical constitutional relations between the monarchy and the parliament in nineteenth century Portugal.

Macaulay, Neill. *Dom Pedro: The Struggle for Liberty in Brazil and Portugal, 1798-1834.* Durham, N.C.: Duke University Press, 1986. The final sections of this biography detail the political and military campaigns of Pedro I to restore his daughter, Maria II, to the Portuguese throne.

Manchester, Alan K. "The Paradoxical Pedro: First Emperor of Brazil." *The Hispanic American Historical Review* 12, no. 2 (May, 1932): 176-197. Examines the contradictory character of Pedro within the context of the final denouement of his life, restoring his daughter to the throne of Portugal.

Marques, A. H. Oliveira de. *History of Portugal.* Vol 2. New York: Columbia University Press, 1972. The opening section traces political differences and military developments between the opposing forces in the Miguelite Wars, doing so within the wider context of data and trends on social and economic features of the period.

Rocha, António da Silva Lopes. *Injust Proclamation of His Serene Highness the Infante Don Miguel as King of Portugal....* London: R. Greenlaw, 1829. Contemporary Portuguese volume, translated into English, denouncing the juridical claims of Manuel to the throne of Portugal.

SEE ALSO: Sept. 16, 1810-Sept. 28, 1821: Mexican War of Independence; Sept. 7, 1822: Brazil Becomes Independent; Jan., 1833: Great Britain Occupies the Falkland Islands; May 1, 1865-June 20, 1870: Paraguayan War.

RELATED ARTICLES in *Great Lives from History: The Nineteenth Century, 1801-1900:* Pedro I; Pedro II.

1820's

1828-1842
Arnold Reforms Rugby School

In the years after his death, Dr. Thomas Arnold came to be regarded as the most innovative educator of his generation. This posthumous fame, due in large part to the testimonies of former students and friends, permanently associated the name of this headmaster of Rugby School with nineteenth century educational reform.

Locale: Rugby, Warwickshire, England
Category: Education

Key Figures
Thomas Arnold (1795-1842), English headmaster of
　　Rugby School, 1828-1842
Thomas Hughes (1822-1896), English writer
Arthur Penrhyn Stanley (1815-1881), English writer,
　　editor, and dean of Westminster

Summary of Event
Born on June 13, 1795, Thomas Arnold was the son of a customs official stationed on the Isle of Wight. When he was six years old, his father suddenly died of a heart attack—just as Thomas would die the day before his own forty-seventh birthday in 1842. Educated at Warminster and Winchester, Arnold was elected a scholar at Corpus Christi College, Oxford University, in 1811, when he was only sixteen. Three years later, he earned a first-class degree (the equivalent of an A average) in classics and received a fellowship at Oriel College, Oxford, in 1815. In 1818, he was ordained as a deacon in the Church of England, and in 1820 he married Mary Penrose. The Arnolds had five sons and four daughters; their most famous child was Matthew Arnold, the poet and essayist.

In 1828, Thomas Arnold received the degrees of bachelor of divinity and doctor of divinity; that same year, he was appointed headmaster of Rugby School. His only previous experience teaching was coaching a small number of students seeking a place at either Oxford or Cambridge. Other than his own experience as a student, Arnold had no real practical knowledge of education. He was, however, an intensely religious man who believed he had a mission to help reform the morals of the aristocracy and of the rising middle class through education based on Christian principles. At times, Arnold approached this calling with the zeal and intensity of a seventeenth century Puritan. For the next fourteen years, he would exhort successive generations of students to follow the course he had set for himself.

Arnold was an innovator in the area of interdisciplinary studies. While the curriculum at Rugby School was broadened to include work in mathematics, the sciences, and modern foreign languages, half of the academic program still was grounded in the classics. Arnold's primary goal as headmaster was the promotion of "Christian education" as the cornerstone of the future. He also sought to mold gentlemen from the boys who were sent to him from every stratum of British society. Creating a climate in which first-class scholars might thrive was not half as important to him as fashioning an atmosphere in which the youngsters under his control might be transformed into models of manly virtue. While he recognized the value of exercise, Arnold was not an advocate of games—such as Rugby football—as tools for building character.

At times, the system of forcing younger boys to perform all manner of domestic duties for older students (known as "fagging") had amounted at Rugby School to institutionalized sadism. While Arnold approved of the system in principle, he sought to transform it to serve the greater good. The most able and mature older boys were appointed as prefects and given the responsibility of

Thomas Hughes, author of the novel Tom Brown's Schooldays, *which immortalized Rugby School.* (Library of Congress)

training and supervising the younger boys within the framework of the fagging system. In addition to their teaching duties, the school's masters were expected to monitor and advise the prefects. By integrating the older boys into the administrative structure of the school, Arnold was able to gain greater control over the whole student body in a manner that was soon copied in other schools throughout the kingdom. As masters left Rugby to assume the leadership of other schools, they duplicated Arnold's managerial system in their new situations.

In 1841, Arnold was appointed Regius Professor of Modern History at Oxford. The position required him to deliver eight public lectures a year, so Arnold was able to remain at Rugby School as headmaster and still fulfill his duties at Oxford. He was able to deliver only one lecture, however, before his untimely death from a heart condition in June, 1842. After his death, Arnold's accomplishments and aspirations might have faded into obscurity had it not been for the devotion of his former students to his memory and to what they considered his legacy. In 1844, the Reverend Arthur Penrhyn Stanley published *The Life and Correspondence of Thomas Arnold, D.D.*, but it was *Tom Brown's School Days* (1857) by Thomas Hughes that created the popular legend of Dr. Thomas Arnold.

In the latter book, Tom Brown and his best friend Harry East, typical English schoolboys subjected to the countless temptations of youth, are transformed into models of Christian manhood by the benevolent presence of Dr. Arnold and the friendship of the saintly George Arthur. As in all good quest literature, the heroes must overcome some form of corruption or evil—in this case, Harry Flashman, a vicious bully. It is ironic that this enemy of chastity, virtue, and Dr. Arnold has become the antihero of a series of delightful modern novels by George MacDonald Fraser.

Tom Brown's School Days was an instant success with young readers but also, and most especially, with their parents. Hughes created, in his Rugby School, an idealized representation of the perfect public school, one that emphasized the wholesome comradeship of the playing field, solid scholarly achievement, and manly Christianity under the leadership of a faculty dedicated to the boys in their charge. Hughes's picture of education reassured the rising middle class that their sons matriculating at public schools would be entering a safe environment where they could master the lessons that would fit them someday to share in the governance and moral leadership of a great empire. His novel also transformed the rough-and-tumble game of Rugby football into a character-

building exercise for would-be gentlemen. Thus, the game and the school would be forever linked in the public mind.

In 1896, with the placement of a bust of Dr. Thomas Arnold in Westminster Abbey, that Valhalla of Victorian respectability, the legend of the headmaster who transformed British education was complete. In seeking to honor their beloved headmaster, Stanley and Hughes created a myth that was enhanced by the heroism displayed in two world wars by the men who were nurtured by the system to which Arnold contributed.

SIGNIFICANCE

Dr. Thomas Arnold became a symbol of reform in the British educational system during the mid-nineteenth century. His fourteen-year tenure as the headmaster of Rugby School was arguably no more innovative than those of many of his contemporaries who headed Great Britain's leading public schools during the same period. Indeed, many of the men who served under him as masters were actually more creative than he was when they left his tutelage to assume the leadership of other public schools.

The reputation of Thomas Arnold as the dean of Victorian educators was in large part created by the popularity of two works published by former students in the years immediately after his death: Stanley's laudatory 1844 biography and Hughes's 1857 autobiographical novel. Thomas Arnold was a pivotal, if often unseen, character in the latter work's fictional portrayal of Rugby School, and this rather sentimental novel has never been out of print since its publication. A film version of *Tom Brown's School Days*, produced in 1940 and starring Sir Cedric Hardwicke as the mythic headmaster, served to enhance the reputation of Arnold, who has become a symbol of everything humane and innovative in modern British education.

—*Clifton W. Potter, Jr.*

FURTHER READING

Chandos, John. *Boys Together*. New Haven, Conn.: Yale University Press, 1984. Study of English public schools from 1800 to 1860; deals in depth with Dr. Arnold's tenure as the headmaster of Rugby School and with the enhancement of his posthumous reputation as the innovator who helped transform British private education.

Copley, Terence. *Black Tom: Arnold of Rugby, the Myth and the Man*. London: Continuum, 2002. Examines Arnold's life and his influence as an educator, theologian, and churchman. Provides a more balanced view than previous uncritical biographies on one hand and cynical mythbreakers on the other.

Hughes, Thomas. *Tom Brown's School Days.* Reprint. Holicong, Pa.: Wildside Press, 2004. Novel based on the personal experiences of the author; its celebration of the life and work of Dr. Arnold is extraordinary in its innocence and candor.

McCrum, Michael. *Thomas Arnold, Headmaster: A Reassessment.* Oxford, England: Oxford University Press, 1989. Biography of Arnold that evaluates him and his educational reforms within the framework of his own time.

Simpson, J. B. Hope. *Rugby Since Arnold: A History of Rugby School from 1842.* New York: St. Martin's Press, 1967. Fascinating study of the men who built upon the reputation of Arnold and transformed the very fabric of that most British of institutions—the public school.

SEE ALSO: 19th cent.: Development of Working-Class Libraries; 1820's-1830's: Free Public School Movement.

RELATED ARTICLES in *Great Lives from History: The Nineteenth Century, 1801-1900:* Matthew Arnold; Thomas Arnold.

February 21, 1828
CHEROKEE PHOENIX BEGINS PUBLICATION

The Phoenix *was both the first Native American newspaper and the first published in a Native American language. While struggling to survive under constant harassment from white Georgians, the paper served as a source of Cherokee pride and helped guide the Cherokee nation through a period of tumultuous changes.*

LOCALE: New Echota, Cherokee Nation, Georgia
CATEGORIES: Journalism; indigenous people's rights

KEY FIGURES

Sequoyah (c. 1770-1843), Cherokee author of the syllabary that made the written language of the Cherokees possible
Elias Boudinot (Buck Watie; c. 1803-1839), nephew of Major Ridge and editor of the *Cherokee Phoenix*
John Ross (1790-1866), elected principal chief of Cherokees during the removal debate
Samuel A. Worcester (1798-1859), Protestant missionary to the Cherokees

SUMMARY OF EVENT

The *Cherokee Phoenix*, the first Native American newspaper, began on February 21, 1828, as the Cherokee nation created institutions and built its new capital at New Echota in Georgia. The Cherokee people lived on a reservation in northwestern Georgia after ceding their lands in several southeastern states. There they created their own governing institutions. Following European models, they wrote a constitution, established a legislature, and built schools and churches.

While Georgia passed laws stripping Cherokees of their rights, the Cherokees used every peaceful means of protest, including the printing press. When the *Cherokee Phoenix* published editorials against the laws, white Georgians stole the newspaper's printing press and jailed its staff. Cherokees fought against their removal from Georgia through the press, the courts, and Congress.

The newspaper's editor, Elias Boudinot, a college-educated missionary and clerk of the Cherokee National Council, wrote in both Cherokee and English, hoping the newspaper would help Native Americans to improve their living conditions and their image in the larger white society. During that era, newspaper editors were often advocates, and political parties and other special interests often subsidized their publications. The *Cherokee Phoenix* received its support from the National Council, white Christian missionaries, and fund-raising efforts by Boudinot and other Cherokee leaders. The possibility of improving a people's image through their newspapers was another premise of early nineteenth century journalism, especially among political parties and town boosters. As the First Amendment to the U.S. Constitution protected freedom of the press from federal government harassment, the Native American press expected to be free from restraint, despite its subsidy from the National Council.

The *Cherokee Phoenix* also depended upon the Cherokee language, for which a writing system had been invented by a young Cherokee genius, Sequoyah, a few years earlier. Sequoyah had been born around 1770 of a Cherokee mother and a white drifter. He recognized that his people were at a disadvantage compared to the whites, who had a printed and written language. Despite having no formal education, Sequoyah grew up to become the only person in history known to have created a written language single-handedly. His eighty-six-character syllabary, using syllables instead of individual letters as a basic form, allowed the easy translation of the traditionally oral Cherokee language into written form. Assembling words from these sounds proved easier than doing it from the twenty-six letters of the English alphabet. White observers were astonished at the speed with which young people learned to write their language. Cherokee children learned as much language in a few days as English children learned of their language in one or two years. Thanks to Sequoyah's syllabary, most of the Cherokee nation became literate in a matter of months.

In its prospectus, the biweekly *Cherokee Phoenix* promised that it would provide laws and public documents of the Cherokee nation; accounts of manners, customs, and the progress of the nation in education, religion, and "the arts of civilized life"; the interesting news of the day; and miscellaneous articles to promote learning among the Cherokees. The Reverend Samuel A. Worcester, a Protestant missionary to the Cherokees, provided essential support for the newspaper.

When the newspaper acquired its printing press, two white printers came with it from New England, where special typefaces had to be made to accommodate Sequoyah's syllabary. The printers set type on the hand press by taking detailed instructions from Worcester instead of learning the language. The printing office also published translations of the Bible into Cherokee. While trying to build an independent state within Georgia, the Cherokees received support from missionaries, Whig Party leaders, and ultimately the U.S. Supreme Court in its 1832 *Worcester v. Georgia* ruling, one of the so-called Cherokee cases.

The *Worcester* case began when Samuel A. Worcester and another missionary refused to sign a loyalty oath that Georgia required of white people who worked among Native Americans. The missionaries were arrested and convicted, but Worcester successfully appealed his case to the U.S. Supreme Court, which ruled the Georgia law unconstitutional. President Andrew Jackson refused to enforce the Court's decision. Meanwhile, the U.S. Congress passed the Indian Removal Act of 1830, setting

Sequoyah with the syllabary that he developed for the Cherokee language. (National Museum of the American Indian, Smithsonian Institution)

up the process of forcing the Cherokees to move to Indian Territory, in what are now parts of Oklahoma and Kansas.

Reflecting his missionary-school background, Boudinot editorialized that Cherokees could become civilized and showed a condescending attitude toward Native Americans and other ethnic groups who did not accept Christian assumptions of progress. At first, Boudinot strongly editorialized against removal, despite the growth of individual acts of violence against Cherokees. As a relative of the Ridge family that eventually concluded that getting the best terms for removal was better than resistance, Boudinot signed the removal treaty without approval of the National Council.

Boudinot resisted pressure from Georgians, whose legislature in 1829 stripped Cherokees of their civil rights. Under the new laws, whites could easily commit crimes against Cherokees in the knowledge that Indians could not testify against them in court. Despite a Supreme Court decision supporting the Cherokees, Jackson refused to intervene. "Full license to our oppressors, and every avenue of justice closed against us," the *Cherokee Phoenix* said. "Yes, this is the bitter cup prepared for us

BOUDINOT ON GEORGIAN HARASSMENT

On January 8, 1831, Elias Boudinot published this editorial in the Cherokee Phoenix.

The Georgians have again made another warlike irruption into the nation, of which the following particulars may be relied upon as substantially correct.

A company of twenty-five armed men from Carrol County, under the command of one Major Bogus, came into the neighborhood of Hightower, about two weeks since, for the purpose of arresting a number of Cherokees. On their way to Beanstick's they came across two lads, utterly unknown to them. On seeing such an armed force making towards them, the lads fled towards the river, and plunged into the water. Some of the Company pursued them to the bank of the river, and fired at them as they were swimming, and, it is said, came very near shooting one of them. They then went to Beanstick's and arrested his son Joseph. Here they wheeled about, and after parading about the neighborhood with characteristic bravery, marched towards Georgia. They soon discovered that they had mistaken their prisoner Joseph, for one Moses Beanstick, for whom it seems they had a warrant. But it made not a cent's difference with them, for they took him on into Carrol. He had not returned on last Monday.

Our feelings are not in a proper state to allow us to make comments upon such proceedings. Will the Congress of the United States permit its citizens to invade us in a warlike manner in time of peace?

---

by a republican and religious government—we shall drink it to the very dregs." A year later, the newspaper reported harassment, arrests, and threats of physical harm to its staff members. After the newspaper protested the postmaster's sale of liquor to American Indians to encourage violent incidents, the postmaster retaliated by cutting off the newspaper's mail service. The move left the *Cherokee Phoenix* without its source of supplies and exchange papers. "This new era," Boudinot wrote, "has not only wrested from us our rights and privileges as a people, but it has closed the channel through which we could formerly obtain our news. By this means the resources of the *Phoenix* are cut off." The newspaper said Native Americans had become more dependent upon sympathetic whites.

The *Cherokee Phoenix* covered basic issues within the Cherokee nation, including acculturation and Christianity. In its pages, national leaders debated how the new Cherokee government should be organized and how elections should be conducted. While political candidates argued election issues, the newspaper proclaimed the need for national unity. Leaders debated the division of the legislature into two houses and the political system into two parties. The newspaper said all Cherokees must keep "the preservation of ourselves as a free and sovereign people" as their primary goal. The National Council approved a punishment of one hundred lashes against people who formed organizations to foster disunity among the Cherokees.

Violent conflicts between whites and Cherokees became so common that many feared for the safety of Native Americans who remained in the Southeast. Friends seeking to protect Native Americans and enemies seeking to eliminate them came together to remove the Five Civilized Tribes to land west of the Mississippi. Because early voluntary removals had proved so disastrous to the Cherokees and the Choctaws, those remaining in Georgia vowed to remain on their native land. The Cherokees' elected principal chief, John Ross, ordered Boudinot to suppress news of dissension within the National Council over the removal issue; instead, the editor was to present a united front of Cherokee resistance against white encroachment.

Boudinot resigned from the paper in 1832, revealing that he could not manage it without a free discussion of important issues. "I should think it my duty to tell them the whole truth. I cannot tell them that we shall be reinstated in our rights when I have no such hope." Ross appointed his brother-in-law, Elijah Hicks, to succeed Boudinot, but Hicks lacked Boudinot's journalistic experience and rhetorical power.

Meanwhile, outside pressures continued. In 1833, the postmaster sent letters to the *Cherokee Phoenix*'s exchanges, stating that the newspaper had been discontinued. The paper's publication became erratic, and in 1834, Hicks suspended publication. His parting editorial asked readers not to give up the fight. "Although our enemies are numerous we are still in the land of the living and the JUDGE of all the earth will impart the means for the salvation of our suffering Nation."

SIGNIFICANCE

Although Boudinot had campaigned against removal, he gave up the fight and signed the Treaty of Echota in 1835, agreeing to removal. Three years later, the U.S. Cavalry forced Cherokee people from their Georgia homes and forced them to walk to Indian Territory (now Oklahoma). Cherokees, who had agreed to removal as self-preservation, saw four thousand men, women, and children die along this winter "Trail of Tears." For his involvement with the treaty faction, Boudinot was killed by Ross supporters in 1839, though Ross himself was not involved.

In 1844, Worcester and printer John F. Wheeler, both of whom had served prison time in Georgia for their work on the *Cherokee Phoenix*, helped the Cherokees start the *Cherokee Advocate*. Based in the new Cherokee capital of Tahlequah, the *Advocate* continued free distribution and publication in both Cherokee and English. As the official paper of the Cherokee nation, the *Advocate* had editors who were selected by the National Council. The first editor was William Potter Ross, the nephew of John Ross. Like the *Phoenix*, the *Advocate* worked to assimilate Cherokees, provide news, and defend Indian rights. Except for a suspension during the Civil War, the paper continued as an official mouthpiece of whatever party was in power. The paper ended with tribal government in 1906.

—William E. Huntzicker

FURTHER READING

Danky, James P., ed. *Native American Periodicals and Newspapers, 1828-1982.* Westport, Conn.: Greenwood Press, 1984. Comprehensive overview of the history of Native American newspapers.

Hoig, Stan. *Sequoyah: The Cherokee Genius.* Oklahoma City: Oklahoma Historical Society, 1995. Full biography of Sequoyah, who created the Cherokee syllabary.

Jahoda, Gloria. *The Trail of Tears.* New York: Wings Books, 1995. Narrative of the forced removal and resettlement of the Cherokees west of the Mississippi River.

Luebke, Barbara P. "Elias Boudinot, Indian Editor: Editorial Columns from the *Cherokee Phoenix*." *Journalism History* 6 (1979): 48-51. Discusses Boudinot's conflicts as editor of the *Cherokee Phoenix*.

McLoughlin, William G. *Cherokees and Missionaries, 1789-1839.* New Haven, Conn.: Yale University Press, 1984. Study of the missionaries, who played such an important role in supporting the Cherokees.

Murphy, James E., and Sharon M. Murphy. *Let My People Know: American Indian Journalism, 1828-1978.* Norman: University of Oklahoma Press, 1981. A history of Native American journalism that includes some discussion of the *Cherokee Phoenix*.

Perdue, Theda, ed. *Cherokee Editor: The Writings of Elias Boudinot.* Knoxville: University of Tennessee Press, 1983. Brief biographical introduction to Boudinot, with reproductions of important documents in the history of the *Cherokee Phoenix* and Boudinot's fundraising.

Riley, Sam G. "The *Cherokee Phoenix:* The Short, Unhappy Life of the First American Indian Newspaper." *Journalism Quarterly* 53, no. 4 (Winter, 1976): 666-671. Discusses Boudinot's editorial dilemmas and political pressure.

1820's

SEE ALSO: 1830-1842: Trail of Tears; Jan. 19-27, 1830: Webster and Hayne Debate Slavery and Westward Expansion; May 28, 1830: Congress Passes Indian Removal Act; Mar. 18, 1831, and Mar. 3, 1832: Cherokee Cases; Feb. 8, 1887: General Allotment Act Erodes Indian Tribal Unity.

RELATED ARTICLES in *Great Lives from History: The Nineteenth Century, 1801-1900:* John Ross; Sequoyah.

April 26, 1828-August 28, 1829
SECOND RUSSO-TURKISH WAR

Angered by Turkish refusals to live up to past treaties and taking advantage of Turkish preoccupations in Greece, Russia's Czar Nicholas I sent armies against Turkish possessions in northeastern Anatolia and the eastern Balkan region. After disasters on both fronts, the Turkish sultan sued for peace. The decidedly pro-Russian terms were embodied in the Treaty of Adrianople.

LOCALE: Southeastern Caucasus; eastern Balkans
CATEGORY: Wars, uprisings, and civil unrest

KEY FIGURES

Nicholas I (1796-1855), Russian czar, r. 1825-1855
Mahmud II (1785-1839), Ottoman sultan, r. 1808-1839
Ivan Fyodorovich Paskevich (1782-1856), Russian
    viceregent of the Caucasus and field marshal
Peter Wittgenstein (1769-1843),
    Russian count and field marshal
Johann von Diebitsch (1785-1831),
    Russian general

SUMMARY OF EVENT

When Nicholas I ascended the throne of the Russian Empire in 1825, he inherited from his brother the problem of what to do about the Ottoman Empire, with whom Russia had been at war intermittently since the early eighteenth century. Turkish defeats in the war of 1806-1812 released its grip on the Danubian territories of Walachia and Moldavia, and native revolts in Serbia and Greece were further undermining Turkish power in the Balkans.

Nicholas did not want to destroy Turkey, which would have invited an onslaught by European imperialists, but he did want to enhance his positions to both the east and west of the dying giant. In his role as czar, Nicholas also presented himself as the guarantor of Christian Orthodoxy in the Balkans, ruling as he did from Moscow, the Third Rome. The antagonistic activities of Sultan Mahmud II in the Danubian territories added fuel to the fire, as Nicholas was far less forgiving than his brother had been. The Greek War of

Independence (1821-1829) made allies of Russia, France, and Great Britain through the Protocol of St. Petersburg (1826) and the Treaty of London (1827), both of which dedicated the trio to supporting Greek independence.

On March 24, 1826, Nicholas sent an ultimatum to the sultan insisting on Ottoman compliance with aforementioned treaties and, especially, the Treaty of Bucharest (1812). Facing a revolt of his Janissary corps and international intervention in Greece, Mahmud acceded to Nicholas's demands and signed the Treaty of Akkerman (1826). With the Russians distracted by a war with Persia, and both the French and British engaged in changes of government, Mahmud publicly repudiated the Treaty of Akkerman at the end of 1827.

The victories of General Ivan Fyodorovich Paskevich in Persia led to the Treaty of Turkmanchai (1828) and

Turks surrendering Varna to the Russians. (Francis R. Niglutsch)

Russia's occupation of the old western khanates of Erivan and Nakhichevan. The Russians under Paskevich now had direct access to the Ottoman Empire's border. Meanwhile, Nicholas sent the Russian Second Army, under the aging field marshal Peter Wittgenstein, to a jumping off point in Russian-controlled Bessarabia, control of which it had gained in 1812. The czar declared war on the Ottomans on April 26, 1828, and the Russian armies immediately marched on Turkish positions.

In the east, Paskevich advanced from Tiflis with 25,000 men and 200 cannons. The troops covered 350 miles in just four months and defeated some 80,000 Turkish troops in battle. In late June, 12,000 Russian cavalry and infantry besieged the fortress city of Kars, which was defended by Emin Pasha, who commanded some 15,000 men and 165 cannons. On July 5 the city fell. The Russians lost about 600 men in the fighting and the Ottomans suffered nearly 5,000 casualties and captives. One month later, Paskevich laid siege to Akhaltsikhe with 110,000 men and 70 guns. At the end of the three-week siege, the 40,000-man garrison surrendered, with both sides losing numbers very similar to those at Kars. By the onset of winter, Paskevich had also reduced Anapa, Ardahan, Poti, and Bayazid, before settling down in Georgia.

General Johann von Diebitsch planned Wittgenstein's 1828 campaign. The object was to occupy Moldavia, Walachia, and the Dobruja, and to seize the fortress cities of Varna and Shumen. With some 94,000 men, Wittgenstein crossed the Pruth and quickly occupied the Danubian territories. He stopped to await the delighted czar, who joined the army at Braila on May 7. They crossed the Danube near Isaccea and divided the army among multiple sieges. The Turks, led by Hussein Paşa, fielded an army of some 150,000 men who defended the Balkan region vigorously and intelligently. On October 12, Prince Menshikov captured Varna after a three-month siege, at a cost of 5,000 of his 35,000 men. Shumen, however, remained in Turkish hands and the advance had clearly stalled.

As the season turned, Nicholas returned to St. Petersburg to consult with his council of war, which recommended that Wittgenstein be replaced with Diebitsch. For his part, Mahmud replaced Hussein Paşa with the grand vizier Mustafa Reşid Paşa in the Balkans.

Come spring, 1829, Paskevich seized Erzerum and aimed his army toward Trebizond. In the west, Diebitsch energized his Russian army, now possibly 114,000 strong. The fortress of Silistria and its 16,000-man garrison was first to fall, after a forty-four day siege (June 25). Mean-

while, Reşid and Diebitsch met at Kulevcha on June 11, and the Russians held the field. Supported by the Black Sea fleet, the Russians marched southward rapidly and largely without opposition. Burgas fell on July 12 and the way to Adrianople (Edirne) and Constantinople (Istanbul), the Ottoman capital, lay wide open. The mere threat of attack caused Adrianople to surrender on August 20, and a week later the sultan sued for peace. Terms were dictated and a treaty signed in Adrianople in September.

Even with the lopsided Russian victories, the czar lost a total of nearly 140,000 men on both fronts, most of whom died of disease. Ottoman casualties, also mainly from disease, amounted to about 80,000 men.

SIGNIFICANCE

Czar Nicholas I was able to dictate terms that ensured a Russian presence that would be deeply embedded on Turkey's western and northeastern borders while leaving the so-called "sick man of Europe," the Ottoman Empire, largely intact and capable of continuing. By ceding Georgia and other Caucasian territories, and the eastern shores of the Black Sea, Sultan Mahmud II virtually guaranteed future border wars.

Russia's sponsorship of Moldavia and Walachia merely underlined the terms of previous treaties, but its insistence on Serbian autonomy under Turkish suzerainty and Greek autonomy with tributary status created a new role for Russia as guarantor of southern Slavic (and Orthodox) independence. Russia's fleeting alliance with France and Great Britain in support of Greek independence would prove short-lived as Nicholas's aims to control the straits between the Black Sea and the Mediterranean became ever clearer.

—*Joseph P. Byrne*

FURTHER READING

Allen, W. E. D. *Caucasian Battlefields: A History of the Wars on the Turco-Caucausian Border 1828-1921.* Richmond, Surrey, England: Curzon Press, 2002. Opens with a detailed discussion of the eastern front and the victories of Paskevich.

Brewer, David. *The Greek War of Independence.* New York: Overlook, 2001. Provides important background to the Turkish preoccupation and Russian religious and ethnic goals in the southern Balkans.

Curtis, John Shelton. *The Russian Army Under Nicholas I, 1825-1855.* Durham, N.C.: Duke University Press, 1965. Discusses Nicholas's early reign, helping to explain why the Russians were so successful against the Turks.

1820's

Lincoln, W. Bruce. *Nicholas I: Emperor and Autocrat of All the Russias*. Evanston: Northern Illinois University Press, 1989. A standard biography in English that paints a fine picture of the czar's military and diplomatic intentions.

Saunders, David. *Russia in the Age of Reaction and Reform, 1801-1881*. New York: Longman, 1992. A general history of Russia that places the war in the context of Russia's nineteenth century territorial expansion and developing pan-Slavism.

SEE ALSO: 1808-1826: Ottomans Suppress the Janissary Revolt; Mar. 7, 1821-Sept. 29, 1829: Greeks Fight for Independence from the Ottoman Empire; Sept. 24, 1829: Treaty of Adrianople; 1832-1841: Turko-Egyptian Wars; 1840's-1880's: Russian Realist Movement; Oct. 4, 1853-Mar. 30, 1856: Crimean War; Apr. 24, 1877-Jan. 31, 1878: Third Russo-Turkish War.

RELATED ARTICLES in *Great Lives from History: The Nineteenth Century, 1801-1900:* George Canning; Nicholas I; Alexander and Demetrios Ypsilantis.

May 9, 1828-April 13, 1829
ROMAN CATHOLIC EMANCIPATION

In 1828, the British parliament repealed two seventeenth century laws that had disenfranchised Roman Catholics and Protestant Dissenters in Great Britain. In 1829, Parliament passed the Emancipation Act, making it possible for British and Irish Roman Catholics to vote, to enter the universities, and to hold public, political, and military offices.

ALSO KNOWN AS: Catholic Relief Act; Emancipation Act of 1829; Repeal of the Test and Corporation Acts

LOCALE: London, England

CATEGORIES: Laws, acts, and legal history; government and politics; religion and theology; social issues and reform; civil rights and liberties

KEY FIGURES

Daniel O'Connell (1775-1847), Irish leader of agitation for emancipating Catholics

John Russell (1792-1878), chief Liberal and reformer and later prime minister of Great Britain, 1846-1852, 1865-1866

Duke of Wellington (Arthur Wellesley; 1769-1852), Tory prime minister, 1828-1830

Sir Robert Peel (1788-1850), Tory home secretary, 1822-1827, leader of the House of Commons, 1828-1830, and later prime minister, 1834-1835, 1841-1846

George IV (1762-1830), king of Great Britain, r. 1820-1830

Sir Francis Burdett (1770-1844), English Radical supporter of Catholic emancipation

First Earl of Eldon (Sir John Scott; 1751-1838), leader of the extreme reactionary Tories, known as ultras, who were strongly opposed to all non-Anglicans

Sir Henry William Paget (Marquis of Anglesey; 1768-1854), lord lieutenant of Ireland, 1828-1829, 1830-1833

Twelfth Duke of Norfolk (Bernard Edward Howard; 1765-1842), Catholic leader of the English nobility

SUMMARY OF EVENT

Roman Catholics in Great Britain and Ireland suffered serious political, social, economic, and religious restrictions from the time of the Reformation into the early nineteenth century. Many restrictions on them remained in effect in 1825. Catholics were, for example, forbidden by law to hold political office, either elective or appointive, or any high military post; they could not enter the universities, and they were forced to pay tithes to the Church of England. Dissenters—Protestants who objected to the doctrine of the Church of England—were technically in a similar position because of the Test and Corporation Acts. These acts, however, were a mere formality, since Parliament annually passed an amnesty for Dissenters who violated them.

In England and Scotland, Catholics had no right to vote, though in Ireland they had been able to vote but not hold office since 1793. The English and Scottish Catholics were a small minority but included some influential nobility, including the twelfth duke of Norfolk, traditional leader of the English nobility. On the other hand, the Irish Catholics were an overwhelming majority except in Ulster (modern Northern Ireland), but they were largely oppressed tenants of Protestant English landlords who owned most of the Irish land. The problem of Catholic rights was inseparably bound up with Ireland, and both the strong opposition to and the eventual success of Catholic emancipation was a result of its link with the so-called Irish Question. There was enough anti-Roman Catholic prejudice in England, however, to block several attempts to separate the issues by giving votes only to English Catholics.

The agitation for Catholic rights in Ireland had been going on since the late eighteenth century. The Act of Union of Great Britain and Ireland was passed in 1801 with the understanding that Catholic emancipation would follow, but the British government had backed down in the face of opposition from King George III. Catholic relief bills proposed by Liberal Irish Protestants such as Henry Grattan and William Conyngham Plunket were introduced a number of times and came close to passage. In 1821, for example, one such bill passed the House of Commons but was defeated in the House of Lords. Since these bills included a government veto over appointments to Catholic bishoprics, however, they remained unacceptable to the Irish Catholic bishops. There was considerable support for Catholic emancipation among many prominent English statesmen, such as George Canning, Henry Brougham, John Russell, and Sir Francis Burdett.

A new and decisive element was added by the appearance of the Catholic Association in 1823. It was led by Daniel O'Connell, a Catholic lawyer and skillful political leader. By 1825, the Catholic Association was a well-established mass organization with chapters in almost every parish. It commanded the loyalty of most Irish Catholics and the support of the Catholic Church. The association was funded through the collection of "Catholic rent," a call for each Catholic in Ireland to contribute a small amount to finance the Catholic campaign for emancipation. In a little more than a year, the Catholic Association amassed a fund of some sixteen thousand pounds to be used for securing favorable press coverage, lobbying, and legal aid.

O'Connell carefully avoided violence, but the British parliament still suppressed the association. It was immediately reformed, however, as an "educational and charitable" association to evade the law. In 1825, Sir Francis Burdett's Emancipation Bill passed the House of Commons, but the bill was rejected by the House of Lords through the influence of King George IV.

In 1826, the Catholic Association showed its power by electing a man of their choice, Henry Villiers Stuart, in place of George Beresford, the powerful Protestant landlord. The elections of 1826 in Great Britain, however, aroused anti-Catholic prejudices and returned

Daniel O'Connell. (Library of Congress)

some strongly anti-Catholic members, so that Burdett's bill failed to pass the Commons by four votes in 1827. Another apparent setback for the Catholic cause was the formation, in August of 1827, of the ministry of Sir Robert Peel and the duke of Wellington, which included the chief leaders of the anti-Catholic party, especially Sir Robert Peel himself.

Backed by several Protestant Dissenter organizations, John Russell introduced a bill to repeal the Test and Corporation Acts. Over strong opposition led by the first earl of Eldon, the Repeal of the Test and Corporation Acts was passed on May 9, 1828, and Dissenters were allowed to hold public and political offices without fear of penalty. Although this repeal only removed an irritating formality, it made the Catholic ban seem even more inconsistent, as Russell intended. Later that month, Burdett's Emancipation Bill passed the Commons by a majority of six votes, but it was again defeated in the House of Lords, although by a smaller margin than in 1825 and only by Wellington's plea to postpone the question.

The final impetus for passage of the Emancipation Act was provided by a by-election in County Clare, Ireland, in June, 1828. O'Connell stood for election against

---

A NEW PARLIAMENTARY OATH

The Catholic Relief Act did away with the requirement for members of Parliament to take the Oaths of Allegiance and Supremacy, both of which required the espousal of anti-Catholic ideology as a sign of allegiance to the Crown of the United Kingdom. Upon passage of the 1829 act, the following alternative oath was instituted. It could be sworn by any peer in the House of Lords or any member elected to the House of Commons who was unwilling to take the other oaths.

I A.B. do sincerely promise and swear, That I will be faithful and bear true Allegiance to his Majesty King George the Fourth, and will defend him to the utmost of my Power against all Conspiracies and Attempts whatever, which shall be made against his Person, Crown, or Dignity; and I will do my utmost Endeavour to disclose and make known to His Majesty, His Heirs and Successors, all Treasons and traitorous Conspiracies which may be formed against Him or Them:

And I do faithfully promise to maintain, support, and defend, to the utmost of my Power, the Succession of the Crown, which Succession, by an Act, intituled An Act for the further Limitation of the Crown, and better securing the Rights and Liberties of the Subject, is and stands limited to the Princess Sophia, Electress of Hanover, and the Heirs of her Body, being Protestants; hereby utterly renouncing and abjuring any Obedience or Allegiance unto any other Person claiming or pretending a Right to the Crown of this Realm: And I do further declare, That it is not an Article of my Faith, and that I do renounce, reject, and abjure the Opinion, that Princes excommunicated or deprived by the Pope, or any other Authority of the See of Rome, may be deposed or murdered by their Subjects, or by any Person whatsoever: And I do declare, That I do not believe that the Pope of Rome, or any other Foreign Prince, Prelate, Person, State, or Potentate, has or ought to have any Temporal or Civil Jurisdiction, Power, Superiority, or Pre-eminence, directly or indirectly, within this Realm. I do swear, That I will defend to the utmost of my Power the Settlement of Property within this Realm, as established by the Laws; And I do hereby disclaim, disavow, and solemnly abjure any Intention to subvert the present Church Establishment, as settled by Law within this Realm: And I do solemnly swear, That I never will exercise any Privilege to which I am or may become entitled, to disturb or weaken the Protestant Religion or Protestant Government in the United Kingdom: And I do solemnly, in the Presence of God, profess, testify, and declare, That I do make this Declaration, and every Part thereof, in the plain and ordinary Sense of the Words of this Oath, without any Evasion, Equivocation, or mental Reservation whatsoever. So help me GOD.

---

sary, thus introducing the threat of civil war.

Catholic Ireland now stood organized and united behind O'Connell, who urged avoidance of violence. It was obvious, however, that his revolutionary organization would be hard to restrain if he were rejected from Parliament and if nothing were done about Catholic emancipation. Sir Henry William Paget, the lord lieutenant of Ireland, urged concessions and doubted that violence could be prevented for long. Even George Dawson, an anti-Catholic Ulsterman and brother-in-law of Peel, urged the need for emancipation.

By autumn of 1828, Wellington and Peel were convinced of the necessity of a Catholic emancipation bill, but the king's strong opposition prevented action until February 5, 1829, when the King's Address from the Throne proposed Catholic emancipation. Peel introduced the Catholic Relief Bill into the House of Commons on March 5. The bill proposed to grant to Catholics the right to hold most public offices, except those of commander in chief, lord chancellor, regent, lord lieutenant of Ireland, and a few others. On the other hand, the bill restricted the Catholic Church in several ways: The Jesuits were to be expelled, religious orders could not receive property by bequest, and clerical robes could not be worn on public streets. Two other restrictive bills were introduced at the same time. One suppressed the Catholic Association again, and the other raised the property qualifications for voting in Ireland to reduce the number of Catholic voters. These two bills passed easily, since the Liberal supporters of Catholic emancipation believed they were the necessary price for securing passage of the main Catholic Relief Bill.

The debate on the Catholic Relief Bill was bitter, as was the opposition to the Tory party leadership by many rank-and-file Tories who believed that they had been betrayed. Peel lost his seat in a by-election and had to be re-

William Vesey Fitzgerald, a popular Protestant landlord and a supporter of Catholic emancipation. O'Connell was overwhelmingly elected to a parliamentary seat that he could not legally take. It was now obvious to the British government that the Catholic Association could control elections in Ireland. The situation became more tense as Ulster Protestants formed Brunswick Clubs on the model of the Catholic Association. These groups let it be known that they were prepared to use force, if neces-

turned from a pocket borough, while Wellington had to fight a duel to protect his good name after being publicly accused of having insidious plans to introduce "popery" in Britain. Nevertheless, Wellington and Peel pushed the Catholic Relief Bill through rapidly. It passed the House of Commons on March 30 by a vote of 320 to 142 and the House of Lords on April 11 by 111 to 109. The bill was signed into law by the king on April 13. The defeated anti-Catholic group obtained a manner of revenge shortly after by excluding O'Connell on the ground that he was elected before the bill had been passed, although several English Catholic peers had already been admitted to the House of Lords and one Catholic had been elected and seated in the House of Commons. O'Connell might have been admitted, for he made a convincing and well-received speech on his own behalf, but he staunchly refused to take the oath of supremacy; the final vote was 190 to 116 against him.

SIGNIFICANCE

The Catholic Relief Act gave Catholics of the British Isles most political rights and gave the Irish a role in British politics. Irish gratitude, however, was largely nullified by the accompanying restrictions on the Catholic Church, the Catholic Association, and the Irish franchise, as well as by the exclusion of O'Connell from Parliament. O'Connell's successful methods, however, set an example for future Anglo-Irish political agitation. Combined with the 1828 Repeal of the Test and Corporation Acts, the Catholic Relief Act removed almost all legal religious discrimination against Christians who did not subscribe to the doctrines of the Church of England.

—*James H. Steinel, updated by Cynthia A. Bily*

FURTHER READING

Bartlett, Thomas. *The Fall and Rise of the Irish Nation: The Catholic Question, 1690-1830.* Savage, Md.: Barnes & Noble Books, 1992. Explores two centuries of response by the British and Irish governments to the call for Catholic emancipation, and the struggle as a uniting force for the Catholic community. The Emancipation Acts themselves appear in the epilogue of this thorough history.

Gwynn, Denis. *The Struggle for Catholic Emancipation.* London: Longmans, Green, 1928. Focuses mainly on emancipation in Ireland, but also useful for its coverage of England. Gwynn praises O'Connell for his ability, his character, and his self-sacrifice, while conceding that some of the ideas often ascribed to O'Connell were really suggested by his subordinates.

Hinde, Wendy. *Catholic Emancipation: A Shake to Men's Minds.* Oxford, England: Basil Blackwell, 1992. Covers January, 1828, through April, 1829, when the Catholic Question seemed most likely to result in civil war, and examines how the British government averted that crisis. Includes contemporary political cartoons.

Lee, Nicholas, ed. *The Catholic Question in Ireland, 1762-1829.* 8 vols. Bristol, England: Thoemmes Press, 2000. Set of twelve major primary sources on the Catholic Question collected in eight volumes; an invaluable research aid for anyone working on the period.

Machin, G. I. T. *The Catholic Question in English Politics, 1820 to 1830.* Oxford, England: Clarendon Press, 1964. Focuses more on the British than on the Irish aspects of the controversy, emphasizing the crises the Catholic question caused for the British government. There is also a good analysis of the various bases of anti-Catholic feeling in British society.

Mansergh, Danny. *Grattan's Failure: Parliamentary Opposition and the People of Ireland, 1779-1800.* Dublin: Irish Academic Press, 2005. Provides the late eighteenth century background to the fight for Catholic emancipation in the first three decades of the nineteenth century.

O'Ferrall, Fergus. *Catholic Emancipation: Daniel O'Connell and the Birth of Irish Democracy, 1820-1830.* Dublin: Gill & Macmillan, 1985. An exploration of O'Connell's background and his role in liberating Irish Catholics. O'Ferrall has previously published an extensive biography of O'Connell.

Reynolds, James A. *The Catholic Emancipation Crisis in Ireland, 1823-1829.* New Haven, Conn.: Yale University Press, 1954. An excellent study of the Irish aspects of Catholic emancipation.

Taylor, William Cooke. *Reminiscences of Daniel O'Connell: During the Agitations of the Veto Emancipation and Repeal.* Edited by Patrick Maume. Dublin: University College Dublin Press, 2005. This biography, originally published shortly after O'Connell's death, is based on eyewitnesses' accounts and O'Connell's memoirs and articles. Although Taylor sympathized with O'Connell's struggle for Catholic liberation, he argues that O'Connell's abusive oratory hindered emancipation.

SEE ALSO: 1804: British and Foreign Bible Society Is Founded; Dec. 11-30, 1819: British Parliament Passes the Six Acts; June 4, 1832: British Parliament

1820's

Passes the Reform Act of 1832; July 14, 1833: Oxford Movement Begins; Oct. 9, 1845: Newman Becomes a Roman Catholic; July 26, 1858: Rothschild Is First Jewish Member of British Parliament.

RELATED ARTICLES in *Great Lives from History: The Nineteenth Century, 1801-1900:* Henry Brougham; George Canning; George IV; Daniel O'Connell; Sir Robert Peel; John Russell; Duke of Wellington.

November, 1828
WEBSTER PUBLISHES THE FIRST AMERICAN DICTIONARY OF ENGLISH

Publication of Noah Webster's American dictionary was an important step in the movement to assert the cultural independence of the United States from Europe.

LOCALE: New Haven, Connecticut

CATEGORIES: Cultural and intellectual history; education

KEY FIGURES

Samuel Johnson (1709-1784), English lexicographer

Noah Webster (1758-1843), author of *An American Dictionary of the English Language*

Charles Merriam (1803-1880) and

George Merriam (1806-1887), brothers who purchased the rights to publish Webster's dictionary

Timothy Dwight (1752-1817), Connecticut Wit and president of Yale College, 1795-1817

SUMMARY OF EVENT

Although the United States achieved its political independence from Great Britain in 1783, in many respects the new nation remained a cultural colony of Europe. This influence was particularly evident in what was regarded as "high" culture. Literature and the fine arts in the United States were largely derivative and subservient to European, especially British, standards. Although it was natural that a provincial country would follow the cultural leadership of the metropolitan centers of its mother country, U.S. nationalism after the American Revolution (1775-1783) demanded a national culture that would reflect American themes, roots, and ideals.

A literary group known as the Connecticut, or Hartford, Wits, although still imitative of British and continental styles, strained to give the United States a unique and distinguished literature. Long after political independence had been achieved, Ralph Waldo Emerson and other writers continued to call for cultural independence. However, despite Walt Whitman's path-breaking poetry during the 1850's, the nature of U.S. cultural relations with Europe remained a contentious matter well into the twentieth century. One strong force for, and cogent symbol of, the recurrent plea for a national culture that did stand out was Noah Webster's publication of *An American Dictionary of the English Language* in November, 1828.

Born in Connecticut in 1758, Webster graduated from Yale College when he was twenty years of age. As a Yale graduate and member of Hartford's Friendly Club, he associated with artist John Trumbull, writers Theodore and Timothy Dwight, and other Connecticut Wits. Webster's own early contributions toward elevating American culture were as an educator, a function that his lexicographical career continued on a broader scale. His biographers have regularly accorded him titles such as Schoolmaster of America and Schoolmaster of the Republic. In that role, he was the author of *A Grammatical Institute of the English Language* (1787), eventually a three-volume textbook for schoolchildren. The first part of this series became famous as the "Blue-Backed Speller." According to one biographer, no other book, except the Bible, played a more important role in unifying the United States. Parts 2 and 3 of Webster's work, a grammar and a reader, also did much to mold American self-identity.

Webster's concern with language usage stemmed partly from his conviction that language was an important national bond. He believed that linguistic independence should follow political independence, with the gradual evolution of a distinct American dialect of English. He was eager to accelerate the process leading to that end, not only through the sanctioning and encouragement of American usages but also through his advocacy of a reformed American spelling.

At one time, adopting a reformed phonetic alphabet seemed to Webster the best way to render the United States culturally independent of Great Britain. He enlisted the support of the venerable statesman Benjamin Franklin in a plan to have the Confederation Congress promulgate the new alphabet. Although Webster came to realize that radical changes could not win support, he remained the advocate of spelling reform, as in the removal of silent or unnecessary letters. His authority did eventually support such minor deviations of American English from the parent tongue as the omission of the *u* in words such as "honour" and "colour." He also defended distinctly American pronunciations and variations. Although Webster lived in comparatively insular Connecticut, he grasped that the ethnically and racially multicultural populations in Britain's other North American colonies had infused English with a mixture of indigenous, African, and non-English European vocabulary and sentence structure.

An American Dictionary of the English Language was the logical culmination of Noah Webster's career. Prior to his lexicography, three shorter American dictionaries had appeared, but most people in the United States still depended primarily on British dictionaries, such as Samuel Johnson's famous work. For Webster, however, Johnson's effort was unsatisfactory. Not only did it fail to fit American needs, but also, Webster believed, its author was frequently mistaken in etymology. Webster himself was well qualified by training and temperament to compile a dictionary. His learning was broad: He had practiced law, written about epidemic diseases, conducted laboratory experiments, and studied business conditions. He delighted in etymological investigations, and eventually learned more than twenty other languages to understand the roots and interrelationships of English. He was undoubtedly the first notable comparative philologist in the United States. Finally, Webster possessed extraordinary diligence and patience in the compilation and investigation of words.

As a Federalist through much of the period during which he was preparing the dictionary, Webster had political and social goals for his linguistic reforms. The democratization of politics and society under the Jeffersonians upset him. Believing humans to be intrinsically evil and in need of hierarchical control, Webster, like many other early nineteenth century reformers, longed to establish a "benevolent empire" that would embrace order, sobriety, and other values of an emerging middle class. Language, Webster surmised, would be an important agent in this movement, because words and phraseology modified people's thought patterns and behavior.

1820's

Late nineteenth century montage honoring Noah Webster for his contributions to American education. (Library of Congress)

Although he reveled in Americanisms, Webster worried that the expanding frontier regions, the areas that fueled such language additions, undercut any compact vision of order and would continually support the Jeffersonians. By codifying spelling and grammar and loading his dictionary definitions with his own euphemisms and values, Webster hoped to introduce a purity into U.S. culture that would combat what he perceived as impending chaos. Starting in 1808, when he himself became a convert to the rampant Second Great Awakening and calmed his fears about human depravity, Webster added an evangelical fervor to his vision. Order would still be necessary to fulfill the millennial mission of the United States. The dictionary reflected his religious hopes as much as his nationalism.

In 1806, Webster launched his crusade with the publication of a *Compendious Dictionary of the English Language*, which had five thousand more entries than were found in the best English dictionaries. The following year, he brought out an abridgment for classroom use. Another two decades remained before *An American Dictionary of the English Language* would come from the press. When that dictionary finally appeared in 1828, it listed seventy thousand words—twelve thousand more than the then current edition of Johnson's dictionary. It also included an introduction in which Webster expounded on his ideas about language and etymology. He made use of a preface to assert the parity of American English with the British standard and to defend the American statesman James Madison, jurist James Kent, writer Washington Irving, and others as authorities equal to the best British masters of the language.

SIGNIFICANCE

Webster's dictionary soon became the lexicographical benchmark in the United States. Webster's own anti-British attitudes softened over time, but he continued to celebrate American achievements as rivaling those of Europe. After his death in 1843, George and Charles Merriam purchased the publishing rights to his lexicon. Since that time, the Merriam-Webster company and others have published many successive editions of the work, from time to time making significant revisions. Nevertheless, the name of Noah Webster remains closely identified with the campaign to validate American English that he began and boosted in the eighteenth and nineteenth centuries, and the name Webster has become virtually synonymous with American dictionaries.

—*Michael D. Clark, updated by Thomas L. Altherr*

FURTHER READING

Ellis, Joseph J. *After the Revolution: Profiles of Early American Culture*. New York: W. W. Norton, 1979. The best short introduction to Webster's major contribution to American intellectual independence. Places Webster in the context of postrevolutionary cultural ebullience, along with painter Charles Willson Peale, novelist Hugh Henry Brackenridge, and dramatist William Dunlap.

Micklethwait, David. *Noah Webster and the American Dictionary*. Jefferson, N.C.: McFarland, 2000. Examination of Webster's life that describes his publications and the methods that influenced his creation of a new American dictionary.

Moss, Richard J. *Noah Webster*. Boston: Twayne, 1984. Examines Webster's use of linguistics and his role as a literary figure.

Rollins, Richard M. *The Long Journey of Noah Webster*. Philadelphia: University of Pennsylvania Press, 1980. This slim but provocative treatise explores Webster's personal traits as indices of his literary and linguistic endeavors.

Spencer, Benjamin T. *The Quest for Nationality: An American Literary Campaign*. Syracuse, N.Y.: Syracuse University Press, 1957. Webster appears frequently in this study of literary nationalism, which is concerned primarily with the nineteenth century.

Unger, Harlow Giles. *Noah Webster: The Life and Times of an American Patriot*. New York: John Wiley & Sons, 1998. Comprehensive biography, recounting Webster's many accomplishments as a teacher, philosopher, orator, political leader, and editor as well as a lexicographer.

Webster, Noah. *Noah Webster: On Being American— Selected Writings, 1783-1828*. Edited by Homer Babbidge. New York: Frederick A. Praeger, 1967. Provides most of the pertinent essays on Webster's linguistic nationalism.

SEE ALSO: 1807-1850: Rise of the Knickerbocker School; 1819-1820: Irving's *Sketch Book* Transforms American Literature; 1820's-1830's: Free Public School Movement; Mar. 2, 1867: U.S. Department of Education Is Created.

RELATED ARTICLES in *Great Lives from History: The Nineteenth Century, 1801-1900:* Ralph Waldo Emerson; William Holmes McGuffey; Noah Webster; Walt Whitman.

December 3, 1828
U.S. ELECTION OF 1828

The election of Andrew Jackson, in his second campaign against John Quincy Adams, coincided with the birth of a new political party system and introduced the trappings of modern political campaigns.

ALSO KNOWN AS: Election of Andrew Jackson
LOCALE: United States
CATEGORY: Government and politics

KEY FIGURES

Andrew Jackson (1767-1845), president of the United States, 1829-1837
John Quincy Adams (1767-1848), president of the United States, 1825-1829
William Harris Crawford (1772-1834), co-creator of the party system
Henry Clay (1777-1852), Kentucky congressman
Martin Van Buren (1782-1862), co-creator of the party system and later the president, 1837-1841

SUMMARY OF EVENT

The political campaign that culminated in the December 3, 1828, presidential election was among the bitterest in U.S. history. It is also one of the most discussed and analyzed, in part because it symbolized a number of practices and trends that were developing in American society. The 1828 contest followed on the heels of the famous election of 1824 and matched the same two major candidates—John Quincy Adams, who was now the incumbent president, and Andrew Jackson. The contest in 1824 also had included William H. Crawford, then secretary of war, and Henry Clay, a congressman from Kentucky. When no candidate in that election received a majority in the electoral college, the selection went to the House of Representatives. There, Clay threw his support and electors behind Adams, who named him secretary of state immediately after taking office. Jackson and his supporters complained about the "corrupt bargain" that cost Jackson the election and vowed to return in 1828.

More important than the so-called corrupt bargain, however, was the formation of a new political party system, first conceived in the wake of the Missouri Compromise by the Georgian Crawford and the New York politician Martin Van Buren as a way to stifle further political debate over slavery. The Missouri Compromise had built into the process by which territories became states a permanent disadvantage for the slave-holding South: Every northern territory that became a state had to be free, but territories below 36°30′ could choose to be free or slave. Therefore, the South soon would be outvoted in both houses of Congress. Crawford and Van Buren thought they had found a way to demand neutrality of politicians on the issue of slavery through the discipline of a new party system based on political jobs or other party rewards, called spoils. Individual politicians, from presidential candidates down to local candidates, had an incentive to refrain from taking a position on slavery in return for party support, money, and coverage from the numerous party newspapers.

Crawford's sudden ill health removed him from the 1824 contest too late for Van Buren to find another acceptable candidate to head the new organization. Jackson's popularity made him the perfect vehicle for the Little Magician—as Van Buren was known—and the 1828 election was the appropriate time to introduce the new party system. Henry Clay's so-called American System differed little from the policies of the sitting president, Adams. Jackson's campaign focused on the personality of the general, and Adams contrasted Jackson's lowbrow, commoner image to his own well-bred, educated, and experienced persona.

The campaign developed into one of the greatest contests of mudslinging in U.S. political history. No charge, however inaccurate or unfounded, seemed too extreme for the zealous campaigners. Each candidate was the target of vicious slander, as charges of murder, adultery, and pandering were slung back and forth. Adams was portrayed as a monarchist, the darling of the old Federalists, and a profligate spender who presided over a corrupt squadron of insiders and officeholders who lived in undemocratic luxury at the voters' expense. The hoary details of the corrupt bargain—that marriage between "the Puritan and the black-leg"—were dredged up repeatedly by the Jacksonians. Meanwhile, Jackson himself fared no better. His enemies portrayed him as a hot-tempered, overly ambitious, would-be tyrant, who had lived in sin with his beloved Rachel, and who appealed to the basest emotions of King Mob.

Changes in the organization of political parties and Van Buren's emphasis on getting out the vote made the outcome a foregone conclusion. Adams's supporters still operated under the assumption that small groups of elites selected the president. However, Van Buren's machine understood, and even directed, the new mass politics that

1820's

421

had evolved. Several developments made new mass parties practical: Requirements that voters own property had been lifted in most states, allowing far more men to vote than ever before. Newspapers, which were little more than political propaganda organs, had expanded greatly in number and influence, and the caucus system of selecting candidates or other spokespersons for the parties gave way to nominating conventions. With a popular candidate, such as Jackson, who appealed to the newly enfranchised voters at the top of the ticket, debates over issues were relatively unimportant. The only question was who would get out the vote. To that end, Van Buren's machine—which was divided into state, county, city, and precinct suborganizations—easily outclassed the stodgy Adams's campaign apparatus.

Jackson won 647,286 popular and 178 electoral votes to the 508,064 popular and 83 electoral votes of Adams. Adams carried only the New England section plus New Jersey, Maryland, and Delaware. It was a resounding victory for the general, but it was neither a triumph of democracy over aristocracy nor an economic revolution. Van Buren's spoils system merely replaced Adams's elites with a new group named by Jackson. With the expansion of the size of government ensured by every election (since it was necessary always to get out more of the vote than one's opponent did), those in power had more power and privilege than ever before. As for an economic revolution, economic gulfs continued to widen during the Jacksonian era.

SIGNIFICANCE

Van Buren—and to a lesser extent Jackson—saw the election as ensuring the continuation of the union by removing the threat of a civil war over slavery. It seemed that voters and candidates could be persuaded to put party loyalty over personal opinions on slavery. That attitude was especially critical in the North, where antislavery sentiments ran high. The new party, called the Democratic Republicans (or simply, Democrats), appeared to be able to contain the debate over slavery by electing candidates who would refuse to deal with it. As one author concluded, the system could survive as long as it could elect "northern men with southern principles." In the process, however, neither Van Buren nor Jackson appreciated the twofold dynamic inherent in the new system, one that increased the scope and authority of the federal government and a second that increased the power of the presidency within that government. In fact, Jackson's presidency produced more vetoes than all six previous administrations put together. The party discipline over

slavery could not survive either an antislave president or a Congress dominated by northern men of northern principles, which was exactly what it got in the election of 1860.

—Larry Schweikart

FURTHER READING

Brown, Richard. "The Missouri Crisis, Slavery, and the Politics of Jacksonianism." *South Atlantic Quarterly* 65, no. 1 (Winter, 1966): 55-72. Shows that the second political party system was conceived as a response to the Missouri Compromise. Maintains that Van Buren and Crawford designed a political organization that would reward party loyalty with jobs, requiring the party faithful to limit or avoid discussion of slavery.

Ellis, Richard E. *Andrew Jackson*. Washington, D.C.: CQ Press, 2003. Broad study of Jackson's entire life—his military and political careers, his policies, and the impact of his presidency.

Formisano, Ronald P. *The Transformation of Political Culture: Massachusetts Parties, 1790's-1840's*. New York. Oxford University Press, 1983. Uses Massachusetts as a test case to examine the changes in party organization and structure that led to the evolution of national parties.

McCormick, Richard P. "New Perspectives on Jacksonian Politics." *American Historical Review* 65, no. 2 (January, 1960): 288-301. Uses voter participation statistics to show that the election of 1828 was not a popular revolution and that the true revolution did not occur until 1840, when a Whig was elected.

Marshall, Lynn L. "The Strange Stillbirth of the Whig Party." *American Historical Review* 72, no. 2 (January, 1967): 445-468. A classic study of party organization by the Jacksonians and of the Whigs' ill-fated response. Explains the centralizing tendencies of the spoils system and the nationalization of elections.

Niven, John. *Martin Van Buren: The Romantic Age of American Politics*. New York: Oxford University Press, 1983. A thorough account of the life of the Little Magician, offering a detailed look at Van Buren's political life in New York, although appreciating the role slavery played in national politics.

Remini, Robert V. *Andrew Jackson*. 3 vols. Baltimore: Johns Hopkins University Press, 1998. New edition of Remini's nearly definitive biography of Jackson, whose election campaigns are covered in the second and third volumes.

_____. *The Election of Andrew Jackson*. Philadelphia:

J. B. Lippincott, 1963. This concise treatment of the election by a historian sympathetic to Jackson emphasizes the rise of democratic forces and the "common man" over traditional elites.

_____. *John Quincy Adams*. New York: Times Books, 2002. Brief study of Adams's long public career.

Schlesinger, Arthur M., Jr. *The Age of Jackson*. Boston: Little, Brown, 1945. A Pulitzer Prize-winning study that views Jackson as a hero. Portrays the election in terms of democratic reaction to elites; more economic in its analysis than Remini's book.

Schweikart, Larry. "Jacksonian Ideology, Currency Control, and 'Central Banking': A Reappraisal." *The Historian* 51, no. 1 (November, 1988): 78-102. Uses Jackson's war on the Bank of the United States to show the effect of the spoils system and the new party organization on the growth of government. Argues that the policies and organizational dynamic of the Jacksonians, regardless of their rhetoric, resulted in greater power accruing to the federal government and to the president in particular.

Sibley, Joel H. *Martin Van Buren and the Emergence of American Popular Politics*. Lanham, Md.: Rowman & Littlefield, 2002. Study of the growing popular participation in political parties after the War of 1812 that focuses on Van Buren's role in this development.

SEE ALSO: Feb. 17, 1801: House of Representatives Elects Jefferson President; Sept. 25, 1804: Twelfth Amendment Is Ratified; Dec. 1, 1824-Feb. 9, 1825: U.S. Election of 1824; Nov. 24, 1832-Jan. 21, 1833: Nullification Controversy; Apr. 14, 1834: Clay Begins American Whig Party; Mar. 17, 1837: Panic of 1837 Begins; Dec. 2, 1840: U.S. Election of 1840.

RELATED ARTICLES in *Great Lives from History: The Nineteenth Century, 1801-1900:* John Quincy Adams; Andrew Jackson; Martin Van Buren.

1829-1836
IRISH IMMIGRATION TO CANADA

Between 1829 and 1836, Irish immigration to Canada reached its highest volume and broadest extent up till that time. By the mid-1830's, Irish settlements of various sizes stretched from Newfoundland and the other maritime provinces through Lower Canada and into the hinterlands of Upper Canada.

LOCALE: Eastern Canada

CATEGORIES: Immigration; colonization; expansion and land acquisition

KEY FIGURE

Peter Robinson (1785-1838), Canadian politician who brought many Irish to Canada during the mid-1820's

SUMMARY OF EVENT

The mass exodus of Irish people to North America during the nineteenth century represented the culmination of more than three hundred years of frequent disruptions and upheavals in Ireland. The English conquest of the island in the sixteenth century had installed a new ruling class of loyal English gentry on lands seized from the native Irish and redistributed by the British government. Then, in the seventeenth century, the English crown had relocated to the northern Irish province of Ulster some 200,000 Presbyterian farmers and laborers from Lowland Scotland. The Scots were intended to counterbalance a native Roman Catholic populace hostile to English rule. Presbyterians and Catholics clashed repeatedly, even as both camps suffered harsh government penalties because of their refusal to join the official Anglican Church. Meanwhile, Ireland remained among the poorest countries in Europe.

During the 1790's, however, French military campaigns across continental Europe began to disrupt the normal patterns of trade. The disruption of trade patterns was beneficial to the Irish economy. Great Britain, for example, cut off from its customary continental markets, found in Ireland the main source of the meat, grain, and butter it required for domestic consumption. As a result, the landed estates, small farms, and market towns of Ireland thrived. For a time, the Irish economy boomed: Both employment and population soared.

This prosperity ended abruptly with the fall of France's Napoleon I in 1815. Great Britain promptly reconnected with its broader continental markets, and the Irish economy again sank into depression. Furthermore, as the growing of grain for export became less profitable, many Irish landowners switched from tillage to the grazing of animals, which required far less labor and therefore resulted in massive unemployment. Likewise, the early Industrial Revolution introduced to Ireland several commercial linen factories, which undercut the local domestic weaving of linen goods, especially among Presbyterian populations in Ulster. Some two-thirds of the Irish population was composed of landless laborers living in hovels and surviving primarily on potatoes. Meanwhile the population of Ireland, which was five million in 1800, had ballooned to six and a half million in just fifteen years.

In Ireland after 1815, then, the steep rise in population conspired with severely constricted job opportunities and the oppressive policies of the English government to induce mass emigration. There was a long history of European colonization of the New World. Another chapter in this history was opened during the early nineteenth century, as thousands of dissatisfied and frustrated Irish, both Protestants and Catholics, looked for a new life overseas. Many Europeans saw North America as a domain of mythic proportions, where free land abounded and the opportunities were unlimited.

Great Britain's American colonies had won their independence by 1783, and an estimated sixty thousand Americans still loyal to the British crown were deported to Canada. A number of Irish were among these Loyalists, who settled mainly in the new province of Quebec, recently seized from France. By 1815, British North America consisted of Lower Canada (Quebec), Upper Canada (the future Ontario), and a number of island colonies, such as Newfoundland and New Brunswick in the Gulf of St. Lawrence. The vast prairie lands to the west of Ontario remained too remote for substantial development. In sum, British North America in 1815 consisted of small clusters of farming and fishing villages scattered across the island colonies in the Gulf of St. Lawrence, along with modest farms strung along the lower St. Lawrence River Valley.

Around 1820, this situation began to change dramatically, as immigration from Ireland to the New World surged. During the initial period of this wave of immigration, 1820-1835, close to half a million Irish immigrants arrived in North America, about 60 percent of whom landed in Canada. Immigrants had to travel there almost exclusively on English sailing boats rigged to carry timber, which the ships picked up in the New World and transported back to Britain on their return trips. The voyage to Canada could last up to ten weeks and proved at times grueling for the ten to twenty fare-paying passengers. The traffic in emigrants to Canada further accelerated in 1827, when the British government cut the fare to

Canada in half while leaving the cost of passage to the United States at a high level. This fare disparity led many Irish immigrants to come first to Canada before going on to America.

With a few exceptions, the immigrants traveled at their own expense, without government assistance. The typical Irish immigrant was a young farmer who was not destitute but had some modest savings, supplemented by the sale of tenant rights to his small Irish farm. Ordinarily, he had enough after the expenses of the voyage to find land, build a shelter, and obtain the seeds and implements necessary to sow his crops. He had also to sustain his family until the first harvest. Securing a permanent source of food was the first priority of the immigrant. Artisans, including displaced weavers from Ulster, also found their niche in the more settled areas.

The bulk of these pioneers—up to 60 percent—were Protestants, although Protestants represented only 25 percent of the population of Ireland. Most of them came from the Scots-Irish Presbyterian counties of Ulster, adjacent to the ports of Derry and Belfast where empty timber boats bound for Canada could dock. As a rule, the ties of the Scots-Irish to Ireland, to which their ancestors had come only recently, proved less strong than those of the native Irish Catholics, whose ancestral ties to the land extended over many hundreds of years.

It soon became evident that the small maritime provinces of the St. Lawrence Gulf could not accommodate the influx of new arrivals after 1820. Particularly during the period of greatest volume, from 1829 to 1836, more than twice as many immigrants passed on to Lower and Upper Canada as settled in the maritime colonies. This trend toward moving inland only increased after 1836. With Quebec as the gateway, Upper Canada quickly became a primary destination because of its rumored abundance of fertile land. Upper Canada retained its almost exclusively rural character until well after mid-century.

The Peterborough Experiment offered a notable exception to the norm of Irish Canadian colonization without government aid. During the mid-1820's, a Canadian official named Peter Robinson was commissioned by the English government to recruit a substantial number of destitute Irish Catholic farm laborers from the southern Irish county of Cork for transplanting to Upper Canada. The authorities had the double motive of relieving population pressure in County Cork and providing a cadre of loyal Irish-Canadian militias to defend Canada from further American incursions, as during the War of 1812.

Catholic and Protestant churches soon appeared in Upper Canada to provide a greater sense of continuity and spiritual community to the frontier settlers. Fraternal lodges like the Orange Order proved very popular among the Scots-Irish population. Meanwhile, by the mid-1830's the outlines of a future nation were clearly visible in British North America. It was already a very diverse and vital society, extending from the teaming fisheries of the Grand Banks of Newfoundland, through a nascent urbanized, French-speaking Quebec, to the bountiful farm lands and lumber camps of Upper Canada. The imprint of the Irish pioneers would be indelible on the new confederation.

SIGNIFICANCE

The Irish settlement of Canada during the early nineteenth century contrasted sharply in several respects with the parallel experience of Irish immigrants in the United States. During the 1820's and 1830's, Irish immigrants came to Canada in significantly greater numbers than to the United States. It was in these years that the predominantly rural character of the Canadian Irish lifestyle was established. Most immigrants lived by farming, fishing, hunting, cutting timber, or laboring on public projects like canals. There was no widespread urbanization in the land until the later nineteenth century.

In the United States, on the other hand, the period of mass Irish immigration occurred during the Irish Famine (1845-1854). A large percentage of emigrants during the famine years were landless laborers, virtually destitute in many cases and certainly much poorer than the small farmers who had emigrated to Canada one or two decades earlier. Furthermore, the landless, Catholic Irish in the United States tended to gravitate much more to urban settings than did their landowning Canadian counterparts, and Catholicism became almost synonymous with Irish ancestry in many U.S. locales.

In short, the American model for Irish immigration history during the early nineteenth century cannot be applied to the Canadian scene without major modifications. Each setting had its unique evolution that should be examined in its own terms.

—*Donald Sullivan*

FURTHER READING

Houston, Cecil J., and William J. Smyth. *Irish Emigration and Canadian Settlement: Patterns, Links, and Letters*. Toronto: University of Toronto Press, 1990.

Well-written analysis and synthesis of Irish emigration to British North America. Stresses the diversity of the early Irish settlements in the Canadas.

Mannion, John. *Irish Settlements in Eastern Canada: A Study of Cultural Transfer and Adaptation*. Toronto: University of Toronto Press, 1974. Comparative study of early Irish settlements in Ontario, New Brunswick, and Newfoundland. Based on extensive field interviews.

Miller, Kerby A. *Emigrants and Exiles: Ireland and the Irish Exodus to North America*. New York: Oxford University Press, 1985. Especially valuable for the discussion of the ambiguous Irish attitudes toward overseas emigration and the cultural shock many Irish experienced on arrival.

Moran, Gerard. *Sending Out Ireland's Poor: Assisted Emigration to North America in the Nineteenth Century*. Portland, Oreg.: Four Courts Press, 2004. Examines assisted emigration and the debates surrounding it both before and after the Irish Famine, as well as the fates of the impoverished Irish emigrants once they arrived in North America.

Scally, Robert J. *The End of Hidden Ireland: Rebellion, Famine, and Emigration*. Oxford, England: Oxford University Press, 1995. The first half of this book vividly describes the conditions and problems encountered in pre-Famine Ireland.

SEE ALSO: 1840's-1850's: American Era of "Old" Immigration; Feb. 10, 1841: Upper and Lower Canada Unite; May 6-July 5, 1844: Anti-Irish Riots Erupt in Philadelphia; 1845-1854: Great Irish Famine; Apr. 25, 1849: First Test of Canada's Responsible Government; June, 1866-1871: Fenian Risings for Irish Independence; 1872: Dominion Lands Act Fosters Canadian Settlement; 1873: Ukrainian Mennonites Begin Settling in Canada; 1892: America's "New" Immigration Era Begins; Jan. 1, 1892: Ellis Island Immigration Depot Opens; 1896: Immigrant Farmers Begin Settling Western Canada.

RELATED ARTICLES in *Great Lives from History: The Nineteenth Century, 1801-1900:* George Brown; Anna Jameson; Sir John Alexander Macdonald; Alexander Mackenzie; William Lyon Mackenzie; Napoleon I; Thomas Talbot.

1820's

September 24, 1829
TREATY OF ADRIANOPLE

The Treaty of Adrianople was the first in a series of nineteenth century treaties through which the Slavic peoples of the Balkan peninsula gained their independence from the Turkish-ruled Ottoman Empire.

LOCALE: Adrianople, Turkey
CATEGORIES: Diplomacy and international relations; wars, uprisings, and civil unrest

KEY FIGURES

Karageorge (1762-1817), leader of the first Serbian uprising who founded Serbia's Karageorgević dynasty
Miloš Obrenović (1780-1860), leader of second Serbian uprising who founded Serbia's Obrenović dynasty
Muḥammad ʿAlī Pasha (1769-1849), ruler of Egypt
Alexander I (1777-1825), czar of Russia, r. 1801-1825
Nicholas I (1796-1855), czar of Russia, r. 1825-1855

SUMMARY OF EVENT

After capturing Constantinople in 1453, the Ottoman Turks extended their empire into Europe by marching up through the Balkan peninsula and subjecting local inhabitants to Ottoman rule. The peak of their advance into Europe was marked by their siege of Vienna in 1683, followed by their defeat by a European army that ended their advance. In the centuries that followed, Europeans gradually retook the lands conquered by the Ottoman Turks until, by 1913, Turkey's European territories had been reduced to a small hinterland surrounding Constantinople. The Treaty of Adrianople was an important stage in this reconquest of the Balkans by European Christians.

With the end of their military advance into Europe, the character of the Ottoman regime began a slow decline that lasted for more than two centuries. The top administrative posts in the empire were generally reserved for Muslims, and only Muslims (or, in the case of the famous Janissaries, Muslim converts from Christianity) could serve in the army. For governing some of the outlying regions, the Ottoman rulers adopted a semifeudal system, under which estates were granted to individuals who assumed some administrative responsibilities in the territory. Increasingly, however, this system became corrupt, as appointees bought their appointments and then sought to recoup their expenses by exploiting the inhabitants of the area.

In situations in which the Ottoman rulers could not find suitable parties to carry out local administrative duties, they relied on the Greek Orthodox Church, to which they turned over many civil responsibilities, often including tax collection. Even ecclesiastical positions were frequently purchased.

As corruption in the Ottoman Empire increased, the lot of ordinary Christian peasants under Ottoman rule worsened. The legal system was effectively reserved for Muslims, so Christians had little hope of legal redress. Many Christians held their lands as sharecroppers, turning over more than 50 percent of their crops to their landlords. When their financial burdens became more than they could handle, they often fled into the mountains to join bands of brigands who supported themselves by raiding the countryside. The lack of law and order, the corruption of the administration, both local and central, and the possibility of help from outside, from either Austria or Russia, finally prompted some of the subject peoples of the Ottoman Empire to rebel during the early decades of the nineteenth century.

The first Ottoman subjects to rebel during the early years of the nineteenth century were the Serbs. Living at a great distance from Constantinople, separated from the capital by difficult mountainous terrain, and encouraged by the Austrians, Serbian peasants under the leadership of Karageorge broke out into revolt in 1804. Their revolt was quickly suppressed, and their leader fled first to Austria and then to Russia. Although Russia at first denied assistance to the rebels, relations between Russia and Turkey soon deteriorated, and Russia declared war on Turkey in 1809.

When Napoleon launched his ill-fated attack on Russia in 1812, however, it became important for Russia's Czar Alexander I to concentrate on protecting his homeland. In the Treaty of Bucharest signed between Turkey and Russia in 1812, the Ottoman government agreed to grant autonomy to the Serbians. However; as Russia's position grew more precarious with the advance of Napoleon I's army into Russia, the Turks ignored the terms of the treaty. The Turks made Miloš Obrenović, a native Serbian, the leading local official, or *knez*, in Serbia. In November of 1815, they recognized him as the principal *knez* in Serbia. Shortly thereafter, Obrenović arranged the murder of Karageorge when the latter sought to return home. This act led to a lethal feud between the two Serbian families that would later supply monarchs for the Serbian throne.

Meanwhile, the British had entered the picture. They wanted to ensure that no great power would become dominant in the eastern Mediterranean because such a power might threaten their position in India, so they had established a major naval presence in the area. In the postwar settlement of 1815, they acquired a protectorate over the Ionian islands as well as the island of Malta, which became a permanent major base for the British Royal Navy.

By the 1820's, unrest among the Christian inhabitants of the Ottoman Empire had spread to the Greeks. For more than a century, the Greeks had occupied a privileged position within the empire. Thanks to their exceptional ability to master foreign languages, they had supplied most of the lesser government officials. They were avid traders and had built extensive commercial ties throughout the empire, particularly with the north shore of the Black Sea, even after this area had been ceded by the Ottoman government to Russia.

In 1821, Greeks living in the province of Moldavia-Wallachia began to rebel against Ottoman rule but were quickly put down by the Turks. Meanwhile, however, Greeks living in the Morea, part of classical Greece, had begun a more effective revolt. Turkish authorities responded by massacring Greeks throughout their empire, particularly Greeks living in Constantinople. Even the patriarch of the Greek Orthodox Church was hanged. In January of 1822, the leaders of the revolt in the Morea proclaimed an independent Greece. In June of that same year, a motley Greek navy was able to defeat the Turkish navy. Under pressure from numerous classical enthusiasts in Great Britain, not least the poet Lord Byron, the British government recognized the independence of Greece and lent the rebels money.

The Ottoman government looked about for help and found it in its semiautonomous ruler in Egypt, Muḥammad ʿAli Pasha. Between 1825 and 1827, an army trained in European methods of warfare and commanded by Ali's son Ibrahim completely suppressed the Greek revolt in the Morea.

In the 1827 Treaty of London, Great Britain, France, and Russia agreed to impose a settlement of the Greek situation on Turkey, but the Ottoman government refused the great powers' offer of mediation. In October, the British responded by destroying the Turkish navy at Navarino Bay. In January, 1828, Russia declared war on Turkey, and a Russian army began marching toward Constantinople. By August, the Russians had reached Adrianople, just north of Constantinople. On September 24, 1829, the Turks signed the Treaty of Adrianople.

SIGNIFICANCE

The Treaty of Adrianople confirmed the autonomy of Serbia, Moldavia-Wallachia, and Greece (in the 1830 Treaty of London, Britain, France, and Russia agreed to total independence for Greece). Russia withdrew its army from the Balkans and restored the area to Turkish control. However, it collected a large indemnity from Turkey and confirmed its possession of parts of the Caucasus that it had recently occupied. The settlement revealed Turkey's weakness to all the world. It would not be long until other ethnic groups in the Balkans would win their independence.

—*Nancy M. Gordon*

FURTHER READING

Brewer, David. *The Greek War of Independence.* New York: Overlook, 2001. Useful survey of the Greek struggle against the Ottoman Empire.

Castellan, Georges. *History of the Balkans: From Mohammed the Conqueror to Stalin.* Translated by Nicholas Bradley. Boulder, Colo.: East European Monographs, 1992. Although the translation is often poor and there are typographical errors, this is a useful survey of Balkan history.

Djordjevic, Dimitrije, and Stephen Fischer-Galati. *The Balkan Revolutionary Tradition.* New York: Columbia University Press, 1981. Djordjevic discusses the revolutionary movements of the seventeenth through the nineteenth centuries and the formation of states in the Balkans.

Fahmy, Khaled. *All the Pasha's Men: Mehmed Ali, His Army, and the Making of Modern Egypt.* New York: Cambridge University Press, 1997. Examines the military reforms and recruitment policies of Muḥammad ʿAli, whose army suppressed the Greek revolt in the Morea.

Jelavich, Barbara. *History of the Balkans.* 2 vols. New York: Cambridge University Press, 1983. Authoritative survey of Balkan history by a leading American authority on the subject.

Jelavich, Charles, and Barbara Jelavich. *The Establishment of the Balkan National States, 1804-1920.* Seattle: University of Washington Press, 1977. Detailed account of the gradual elimination of Turkish control in the Balkans.

Roesse, David E. *In Byron's Shadow: Modern Greece in English and American Literature from 1770 to 1967.* Oxford, England: Oxford University Press, 2001. Discusses the beginnings of the Greek War of Independence against Ottoman rule in the context of English-language literature.

1820's

Stavrianos, L. S. *The Balkans, 1815-1914*. New York: Holt, Rinehart and Winston, 1965. Compact account of Balkan history that is well suited for students.

SEE ALSO: 1808-1826: Ottomans Suppress the Janissary Revolt; Mar. 7, 1821-Sept. 29, 1829: Greeks Fight for Independence from the Ottoman Empire; Apr. 26, 1828-Aug. 28, 1829: Second Russo-Turkish War;

1863-1913: Greece Unifies Under the Glücksburg Dynasty; May, 1876: Bulgarian Revolt Against the Ottoman Empire; Jan. 21-May 20, 1897: Greco-Turkish War.

RELATED ARTICLES in *Great Lives from History: The Nineteenth Century, 1801-1900:* Alexander I; Lord Byron; Nicholas I; Muḥammad ʿAlī Pasha; Alexander and Demetrios Ypsilantis.

December 4, 1829
BRITISH ABOLISH SUTTEE IN INDIA

Suttee, the Hindu custom of widows burning themselves to death on their dead husbands' funeral pyres, was frequently practiced in India from ancient times until the nineteenth century, when a British governor-general outlawed it. However, the British prohibition did not end the practice completely, and Hindu resentment of the prohibition has been considered a contributing cause of the Sepoy Mutiny of 1857.

ALSO KNOWN AS: Widow burning; sati; *sahamaran*; *satidaha*; *jauhar brata*
LOCALE: British India (now Republic of India)
CATEGORIES: Religion and theology; anthropology; women's issues; social issues and reform; laws, acts, and legal history

KEY FIGURES
William Bentinck (1774-1839), governor-general of Bengal in 1827 and governor-general of India in 1833, who abolished suttee in 1829
Rammohan Ray (1772-1833), Hindu religious leader and reformer who worked for the abolition of suttee
Radhakanta Deb (1784-1867), leader of conservative Hindus opposing the abolition of suttee

SUMMARY OF EVENT
In many ancient cultures, women—especially favorite wives and concubines—were buried, either voluntarily or by force, with their dead husbands or lords. The voluntary self-immolation of wives and concubines after the deaths of their husbands and lovers was a custom of the Hindus of India that began in ancient times. The Hindu epic *Mahabharata* (second millennium B.C.E.) mentions the practice, and foreign observers of Hinduism remarked on this custom as early as the fourth century B.C.E.

Derived from the Sanskrit adjective *sat* (good or true), sati, or the more common term "suttee," means the "ideal woman." In India, suttee was the practice whereby Hindu women would immolate themselves along with the corpses of their husband—an act also called *sahamaran*, or dying together. When the women could not burn themselves with their husbands' bodies during their cremation, they would commit suicide later on funeral pyres while holding objects belonging to their dead husbands—an act called *anumaran*, or dying later. In some Hindu communities women were buried alive with their dead husbands, believing that by so doing, they were guaranteed great rewards and pleasures in the afterlife. Such acts brought fame to the families of the women and their husbands. Huge crowds assembled to watch the suttee (or *satidaha*, the burning of a suttee), and the ashes of the pyres as well as the ground where the *satidaha* occurred were treasured as holy relics. Often memorial pillars, or *satisthambhas*, were erected on the spots with the suttees' handprints.

The reasons behind suttee are diverse. In addition to wishing to follow their husbands to the afterlife, some women wanted to avoid living as widows. Hindu widows were forbidden any type of pleasurable activity and lived lives of constant toil unless they were independently rich. The relatives of some rich widows forced them to undergo suttee to obtain their property, and there is evidence that some women were administered drugs to overcome their resistance. In some royal families, especially among the Rajputs in west-central India, women committed communal death by fire (*jauhar brata*) to avoid falling into the hands of victorious enemies, generally Muslim conquerors.

From the earliest available records, relatives and local rulers, including Muslim rulers and the British in India, tried to dissuade women, without force, from performing suttee. It was rare to see the forced rescue of a woman by the British. Job Charnock (d. 1693), the English merchant who founded Calcutta, is said to have rescued and then married a Hindu widow preparing for suttee. Jules Verne's popular novel *Le Tour du monde en quatre-vingts jours* (1873; *Around the World in Eighty Days*, 1873), describes its protagonist, Phineas Fogg, saving Princess Aouda from forced immolation on her dead husband's funeral pyre.

In 1757, the British established a political foothold in Bengal in eastern India and started to increase their holdings. The first few governors-general of the British East India Company followed a policy of least interference with the customs of the local people. They had no specific policies against *satidaha*, and local British magistrates were advised to dissuade, but not force, a widow from committing suttee. In 1813, a Brahman priest, addressing the religious basis of suttee after being asked to do so by the British government, answered that suttee was indeed a part of the Hindu religion.

In 1815, the British government began keeping accounts of how many *satidahas* occurred within its territory and found that the practice was prevalent in all Hindu castes and was particularly common in the district of Calcutta, which had a high number of educated and wealthy Hindus. The police were ordered to attend all such acts and to stop the immolations if the women were children or were pregnant, unwilling, or drugged. *Satidahas* often occurred before local authorities could arrive, but conspirators sometimes faced fines or corporal punishment. Published figures show that in 1824 there were 335 *satidahas* in fifteen districts; the local police attended 255 (76 percent). Of 433 *satidahas* in 1825, the police attended 391 (90 percent). In most cases, therefore, the acts seem to have been voluntary.

The British were in control of territories on the north-

1820's

Indian widow practicing suttee by burning herself to death on her husband's funeral pyre during the mid-nineteenth century. (Hulton Archive/Getty Images)

BRITISH RESOLUTION OUTLAWING SUTTEE

The following is excerpted from Sati Regulation XVII of the Bengal Code, passed and enacted in 1829 by officials of the government of British India declaring as illegal the practice of suttee.

The practice of suttee, or of burning or burying alive the widows of Hindus, is revolting to the feelings of human nature; it is nowhere enjoined by the religion of the Hindus as an imperative duty; on the contrary a life of purity and retirement on the part of the widow is more especially and preferably inculcated, and by a vast majority of that people throughout India the practice is not kept up, nor observed: in some extensive districts it does not exist: in those in which it has been most frequent it is notorious that in many instances acts of atrocity have been perpetrated which have been shocking to the Hindus themselves, and in their eyes unlawful and wicked. The measures hitherto adopted to discourage and prevent such acts have failed of success, and the governor-general in council is deeply impressed with the conviction that the abuses in question cannot be effectually put an end to without abolishing the practice altogether. Actuated by these considerations the governor-general in council, without intending to depart from one of the first and most important principles of the system of British government in India, that all classes of the people be secure in the observance of their religious usages, so long as that system can be adhered to without violation of the paramount dictates of justice and humanity, has deemed it right to establish the following rules, which are hereby enacted to be in force from the time of their promulgation throughout the territories immediately subject to the president of Fort William.

The practice of suttee, or of burning or burying alive the widows of Hindus, is hereby declared illegal, and punishable by the criminal courts. . . .

It is hereby declared, that after the promulgation of this regulation all persons convicted of aiding and abetting in the sacrifice of a Hindu widow, by burning or burying her alive, whether the sacrifice be voluntary on her part or not, shall be deemed guilty of culpable homicide, and shall be liable to punishment by fine or by both fine and imprisonment, at the discretion of the court of circuit, according to the nature and circumstances of the case, and the degree of guilt established against the offender; nor shall it be held to be any plea of justification that he or she was desired by the party sacrificed to assist in putting her to death.

---

a change in government attitude concerning Indian customs. Bentinck was strongly influenced by British utilitarianism and introduced many reforms in the interest of the people. He admitted Indians to important office, fostered communication and education, and revised the system of landholding.

Less tolerant, however, of Indian customs, Bentinck abolished suttee by law in 1829, making it a punishable criminal act. Three years later an attempt to overturn the law failed in an appeal to the Privy Council, the ultimate Court of Appeals in Great Britain. He was helped by a determined group of Hindus spearheaded by Rammohan Ray, an independently wealthy Hindu reformer who knew Arabic, Persian, Hindi, Bengali, Sanskrit, and English. Ray was a pioneer in promoting female education and was also one of the earliest authors in Bengali and one of the first Hindus to travel overseas, which orthodox Hindus considered a sin.

Born into an orthodox Hindu Brahman family, Ray was later disowned by his immediate family because of his apostasy. He had read the Qurʾān and the Bible and became a monotheist. Reading the Hindu scriptures showed him that Hinduism was originally monotheistic. From the old Sanskrit texts he found that women traditionally had a much

ern side of the Ganges River that extended from Bengal to Delhi and smaller tracts on the southeastern and southwestern coasts of India. The extent to which suttee was in practice in the rest of the country has not been recorded. The number of women who committed the act was minuscule compared to the overall population. Each act was greatly admired by a section of the native Hindu population, though the majority of the Hindus were against the practice.

Missionaries, along with some local people, voiced their disapproval of this custom, but to little effect. With the arrival of William Bentinck as the governor-general of Bengal (later governor-general of India) in 1827 came

more exalted position in society. All these factors led him to start working actively for the improvement of a woman's place in contemporary Hindu society.

Ray is said to have become convinced of the need to abolish suttee also after seeing his elder brother's wife die on the pyre of her husband, but this is an unsubstantiated claim. Ample documentation exists, however, that Ray attended many *satidāhas* in and around Calcutta trying to dissuade widows from committing suicide. Starting in 1812 he wrote a number of pamphlets in Bengali, Hindi, and English, arguing that suttee was not advocated in the scriptures; rather, widows were advised by scripture to live chaste and fruitful lives. The scriptures even advocated widow remarriage. Another great Hindu reformer, Ishvar Chandra Vidyasagar, tried to make Hindu widow remarriage legal in 1856.

Ray was joined by a group of progressive Hindus who actively worked for the legal abolition of suttee. The conservative Hindus banded together to oppose the reform, claiming suttee was an established aspect of their religious practices. Ray was publicly reviled and was threatened with personal harm, including death, but he persisted in his efforts.

Bentinck, who arrived in Calcutta as governor-general in 1833, solicited the opinions of many, including Ray, about *satidaha*. In the end, he decided to abolish the practice legally in Bengal on December 4, 1829. Within six months suttee was abolished in Bombay and Madras. Prior to enacting the law, Bentinck summarized his reasons to his council in a document dated November 8, 1829. In turn, the conservative Hindus, under the leadership of Radhakanta Deb, sent a petition to Bentinck, who politely refused their appeal. The conservatives, in July, 1832, then sent English barrister (lawyer) Francis Bathie to England to persuade the Privy Council to remove the law. (Ray also was in London at the time and attended the sessions.) The application to repeal the law was turned down, however, and *satidaha* remained a criminal offense of culpable homicide.

SIGNIFICANCE

William Bentinck changed the British policy of noninterference toward *satidaha* with a great deal of care. He made extensive enquiries, especially about the possible effect on the Indian elements of the British army. He was reassured that there would be no significant adverse reactions. The Sepoy Mutiny of 1857 is said to have been fueled by suttee's abolition, though no one has explained why this opposition came twenty-eight years later.

While *satidaha* was legally stopped in British India, its practice continued in the princely states for another fifty years or so. Even after India's independence from Britain, occasional isolated instances still occurred in orthodox Hindu areas such as Rajputana and Madhya Pradesh. While the vast majority of Indians and Hindu monks decry suttee, a small minority of fundamentalists and monks still consider suttee to be legitimate religious practice. In one twentieth century case, a woman was forced to descend from the pyre by police in 1985. A temple was built for her, and she is now revered as a living suttee. In 1987 a young woman committed suttee, with tremendous repercussions. The state governor of Rajasthan was forced to promulgate an ordinance banning

suttee because the 1829 act "was [considered to be] only a regulation passed by the East India Company and could not apply to the present case." In June, 2005, a seventy-five-year-old woman allegedly performed suttee on the funeral pyre of her eighty-year-old husband.

—*Ranes C. Chakravorty*

FURTHER READING

Basham, A. L., ed. *A Cultural History of India*. Oxford, England: Clarendon Press, 1975. Contains thirty-five essays discussing almost every aspect of India's history from ancient times to the present. Provides a broad intellectual and social context in which Ray and other reformist thinkers worked.

Cassels, N. G. Bentinck. "Humanitarian and Imperialist: The Abolition of Sati." *Journal of British Studies* 5, no. 1 (November, 1965): 77-87. A well-documented paper on Bentinck's role in the abolition of suttee.

Collet, Sophia Dobson. *Raja Rammohun Roy*. Edited by D. K. Biswas and P. C. Ganguli. 4th ed. Calcutta, India: Sadharan Brahmo Samaj, 1988. Details Ray's role in the abolition of suttee.

Crawford, S. Cromwell. *Ram Mohan Roy: Social, Political, and Religious Reform in Nineteenth Century India*. New York: Paragon, 1987. Discusses the differences between Bentinck's and Ray's approaches to the abolition of suttee and gives a modern analysis of their roles.

James, Lawrence. *Raj: The Making and Unmaking of British India*. New York: St. Martin's Press, 1998. A history of British rule in India, including administration and policies.

Narasimhan, Sakuntala. *Sati: Widow Burning in India*. New York: Doubleday, 1992. A detailed description of *satidaha* as it has been practiced throughout history. Includes the complete text of Bentinck's minutes to his council, as well as of the act. Well illustrated.

Roy, Rammohun [Rammohan Ray]. "Abstract of the Arguments Regarding the Burning of Widows, Considered as a Religious Rite." In *The English Works of Raja Rammohun Roy*, edited by Jogendra Chunder Ghose and translated by Tuhfatul Muwahhiddin. 1934. Reprint. New Delhi, India: Cosmo, 1982. The first English circular on abolishing suttee, first published in 1830.

_____. "Counter-Petition to the House of Commons to the Memorial of the Advocates of the Suttee." In *The English Works of Raja Rammohun Roy*, edited by Jogendra Chunder Ghose and translated by Tuhfatul Muwahhiddin. 1934. Reprint. New Delhi, India:

1820's

Cosmo, 1982. Ray's petition to the British House of Commons.

Sen, Mala. *Death by Fire: Sati, Dowry, Death, and Female Infanticide in Modern India.* New Brunswick, N.J.: Rutgers University Press, 2002. A detailed discussion of the 1987 *satidaha* in Rajasthan.

Twain, Mark. *Following the Equator.* 1896. Reprint. New York: Oxford University Press, 1996. Twain spent several months in India and was fascinated by its cultures. He was particularly interested in suttee, which he vividly describes in several chapters. Chapter 48 includes an extended anecdote about a Hindu

widow's struggle to obtain permission to perform suttee.

SEE ALSO: Apr. 10, 1802: Lambton Begins Trigonometrical Survey of India; Apr., 1848-Mar., 1849: Second Anglo-Sikh War; May 10, 1857-July 8, 1858: Sepoy Mutiny Against British Rule; Jan. 25, 1884: Indian Legislative Council Enacts the Ilbert Bill; 1885: Indian National Congress Is Founded.

RELATED ARTICLES in *Great Lives from History: The Nineteenth Century, 1801-1900:* First Marquis of Dalhousie; Dadabhai Naoroji; Rammohan Ray.

1830's-1840's
SCIENTISTS STUDY REMAINS OF GIANT MOAS

Up until modern times, giant wingless moa birds had roamed New Zealand for millions of years. The Maori peoples, who settled the island around the first millennium, hunted moas to extinction. English settlers, along with missionaries and scientists, who settled the land during the early nineteenth century, collected moa bones for scientific study. No confirmed sightings of the living bird were reported, but the bird's bones were displayed with much fanfare in British museums.

LOCALE: New Zealand

CATEGORIES: Environment and ecology; biology; exploration and discovery; science and technology

KEY FIGURES

William Colenso (1811-1899), British evangelist

George Grey (1812-1898), British explorer and lieutenant governor of New Zealand, 1845-1854 and 1861-1868

Johann Franz Julius von Haast (1824-1887), German geologist, surveyor-general of Canterbury, 1861-1871

Richard Owen (1804-1892), scientist and curator

Richard Taylor (1805-1873), English missionary, botanist, and geologist

SUMMARY OF EVENT

Giant moa birds were hunted to the point of extinction by the Maori peoples sometime before the European colonization of New Zealand during the early nineteenth century. After English settlement of the island, settlers, scientists, and missionaries found scattered remains of the

bird. Tall tales of the enormous moa, much bigger than the better-known ostrich, caught the imagination of not only scientists but also the general public, who gawked at moa skeletons upon their display in British museums.

With leg joints as tall as an adult human and necks more than one meter (three feet) in length, all topped by a tiny head, moa skeletons reached three meters in height. Similar to all ratites (flightless birds such as the ostrich, emu, rhea, cassowary, and kiwi), moas had flat breastbones and lacked the keel needed to attach wings strong enough to fly. Long ago, moas had lost even the vestigial wings that the other ratites still possess.

Large numbers of moa bones (called subfossils because they have not undergone the mineral changes needed to transform them into fossils) were recovered from moa butchering and processing sites soon after the arrival of British immigrants during the early nineteenth century. When the first moa bone, a femur fragment fifteen centimeters (nearly six inches) in length arrived in England in 1839, John Rule took it to Richard Owen, a professor at the Royal College of Surgeons in London. Following exhaustive comparisons with bones from various mammals and birds, Owen concluded that the bone belonged to a bird he estimated to be three meters tall and belonging to the same order—the Struthioniformes—as the ostrich. He called the bird Dinornis, which he indicated meant "surprising bird."

British scientists and missionaries became aware of the moa during the late 1830's and 1840's, and moa remains were collected by Europeans throughout the nineteenth century. Within New Zealand, missionaries William Colenso, Richard Taylor, and William Williams all

GIANT MOA FOSSIL SITES IN NEW ZEALAND

became moa enthusiasts. Colenso and Taylor both sought recognition for being the first European to have discovered the moa in 1839. Taylor, in his book *Te Ika a Maui: Or, New Zealand and Its Inhabitants* (1855), referred to finding the remains of extinct "giraffe-like birds."

Most of the three hundred known moa-butchering and food-preparation sites were excavated in the second half of the nineteenth century. More than sixty species of moa were described through studies of bones retrieved from these sites. The largest known moa kill site was at the mouth of the Waitaki River, where scientists estimated that between twenty thousand and ninety thousand moas were butchered and processed.

Through most of the nineteenth century, a number of people believed that a few moas continued to survive in the rugged terrain of New Zealand's South Island. Scattered reports of moa sightings from sailors and tourists have continued into the twenty-first century, but at the time British settlement began during the early nineteenth century, two hundred years earlier, there was no scien-

tific evidence to confirm any surviving moas.

It remains unclear exactly when the giant moa became extinct, although many scientists think that most moas were gone before 1500. Colenso contended that Maori oral tradition contained only sparse reference to moas, and he concluded from this that moas had died off generations earlier. Throughout his sojourns in New Zealand, George Grey collected moa bones for Richard Owen. Grey and Richard Taylor spoke to a Maori elder at Waingongoro in 1866, who recounted hunting giant moas in his youth. The elder was able to point out the ovens his hunting party used to cook their kill; upon excavation, Grey and Taylor found large numbers of moa bones in the oven.

Johann Franz Julius von Haast was the first scientist to study the moa in New Zealand. In 1859, Haast excavated in Glenmark Swamp (North Canterbury), where he found more than one thousand moa skeletons, along with bones of other extinct birds. Haast then determined that a large eagle, *Harpagornis moorei* (better known as Haast's eagle), having a 2.9 meter wingspan, weighing between ten and fourteen kilograms (twenty-two to thirty pounds), and with a flapping rather than soaring flight, had once preyed upon moas in the forests. By 1870, Haast had opened the Canterbury Museum, which displayed moa remains, including a 3.5-meter skeleton. Research on moa extinction moved from England to the growing number of scientific institutions in New Zealand.

SIGNIFICANCE

The giant moa thrived in New Zealand's forests prior to the arrival of humans in the region, preyed upon only by the Haast's eagle. When humans arrived, they killed moas weighing up to 250 kilograms (about 550 pounds) for food and destroyed large portions of the moas' forest habitat. Scientific and public interest in moas has grown considerably since the mid-nineteenth century, when museums began displaying the huge skeletons of female giant moas.

1830's

433

Modern research reveals the strange distribution of living ratites (ostrich, emu, cassowary, kiwi, and rhea), found only in Africa, Australia, New Guinea, New Zealand, and South America, which strengthens the theory of continental drift. Scientists postulate that ratites were primitive bird forms that shared a common ancestor prior to the breakup of the supercontinent Gondwana. Scientists have also concluded that these flightless birds, confined to widely dispersed landmasses, underwent significant evolutionary development and were only distantly related to each other.

With the modern advent of DNA analysis, all living and recently extinct members of the ratite group of birds were sequenced, with results that surprised most scientists. One of the first discoveries made through DNA studies was that ratite dispersal occurred more recently than the time of the powerful movements of Earth's plates that separated Gondwana. The moa birds arrived in New Zealand long before kiwis, which migrated from Australasia to New Zealand relatively recently. DNA analysis also determined that the kiwi of New Zealand were more closely related to the Australian cassowary than to the moa. Both the cassowary and kiwi are in danger of extinction sometime in the twenty-first century.

DNA studies from many different moa bones indicate that there were only eleven species of moa. Scientists determined that a very large size difference existed between mature male and female moas within a single species; females were about one-and-a-half times larger than males. DNA studies also indicate that moa species developed separately on the North and South Islands of New Zealand.

Scientists of the twenty-first century have speculated on how quickly the Maori eliminated the moa. Some concluded that all moas disappeared within two centuries of human arrival in New Zealand, while other scientists favor a theory involving three separate moa-hunting periods during perhaps a four-century time period. Those advocating extremely fast disappearance of all moas point to evidence of overkill, in which only the one-meter-long "drumstick" legs were removed from moa kills, leaving whole carcasses.

—*Anita Baker-Blocker*

FURTHER READING

Lambert, David, Craig Millar, and Leon Huynen. "Ancient DNA Solves Sex Mystery of Moa." *Australian Science* (September, 2004): 14-16. Written especially

Reconstructed skeleton of a giant moa. (Hulton Archive/Getty Images)

for general readers, this brief article describes how scientists used DNA analysis to determine that female and male moas of the same species differed in size.

Taylor, Richard. *Te Ika a Maui: Or, New Zealand and Its Inhabitants.* London: Wertheim & Macintosh, 1855. Facsimile ed. Wellington, New Zealand: Read, 1974. A contemporary work that examines the natural history of New Zealand.

Wolfe, Richard. *Moa: The Dramatic Story of the Discovery of a Giant Bird.* New York: Penguin Books, 2003. Written as a history of the Maori and the European colonization of New Zealand. Discusses the role humans played in the extinction of the moa and examines the nineteenth century scientists who built their reputations studying and describing the bird.

Worthy, T. H., Richard N. Holdaway, and Rod Morris. *The Lost World of the Moa.* Indianapolis: Indiana University Press, 2002. An examination of New Zealand's flora and fauna. Begins with Cretaceous dinosaur fossils but focuses on the changes brought about by the arrival of the Maori in the first millennium. The best book about moas and other extinct and endangered species of New Zealand.

SEE ALSO: Dec. 6, 1801-Aug., 1803: Flinders Explores Australia; Feb. 20, 1824: Buckland Presents the First Public Dinosaur Description; 1854-1862: Wallace's

Expeditions Give Rise to Biogeography; Nov. 24, 1859: Darwin Publishes *On the Origin of Species*; Mar., 1868: Lartet Discovers the First Cro-Magnon Remains.

RELATED ARTICLES in *Great Lives from History: The Nineteenth Century, 1801-1900:* John James Audubon; Georges Cuvier; Charles Darwin; Sir Edwin Ray Lankester.

c. 1830's-1860's
AMERICAN RENAISSANCE IN LITERATURE

Taking its name from a phrase coined by F. O. Matthiessen in 1941, the American Renaissance was an era that saw the publication of the most significant works of nineteenth century American literature. Major writers of the period developed a distinctly American literature that used the vernacular language of the young republic to describe the uniqueness of its people, cultures, and geographies.

LOCALE: Northeastern United States
CATEGORIES: Literature; philosophy

KEY FIGURES
Ralph Waldo Emerson (1803-1882), essayist, lecturer, and poet
Margaret Fuller (1810-1850), philosopher and essayist
Nathaniel Hawthorne (1804-1864), novelist and short story writer
Herman Melville (1819-1891), novelist, short story writer, and poet
Edgar Allan Poe (1809-1849), poet and essayist
Henry David Thoreau (1817-1862), essayist and naturalist
Walt Whitman (1819-1892), poet and essayist

SUMMARY OF EVENT
The literature of the American Renaissance marks the fulfillment of what Ralph Waldo Emerson called for in *The American Scholar* (1837), his watershed Phi Beta Kappa speech at Harvard College: an indigenous American literature that would describe the people, language, and cultures of the United States in the middle decades of the nineteenth century. As early as 1850, Herman Melville, in "Hawthorne and His Mosses," could argue that such a distinctively American literatus already existed in Nathaniel Hawthorne, an argument confirming the pro-

ductivity of the period and the development of a unique American literary identity.

During the middle decades of the twentieth century, a Harvard professor named F. O. Matthiessen coined the term "American Renaisssance" with the publication of his eponymous critical text in 1941. He strictly limited the term to the period between 1850 and 1855. These years undeniably mark the most significant years of the movement, which saw the publication of masterpieces of

Margaret Fuller. (Library of Congress)

American literature such as Hawthorne's *The Scarlet Letter* (1850), Herman Melville's *Moby Dick: Or, The Whale* (1851) and *Pierre: Or, The Ambiguities* (1852), Henry David Thoreau's *Walden: Or, Life in the Woods* (1854), and Walt Whitman's *Leaves of Grass* (1855). It is reasonable, however, to begin an examination of the period in the decade of the 1830's, the decade when Hawthorne, who had recently graduated from Bowdoin College, began to write and later publish his short stories, collected in *Twice-Told Tales* (1837, expanded 1842) and in *Mosses from an Old Manse* (1846). Also, Edgar Allan Poe's short stories and poems began to appear in East Coast periodicals in the 1830's, culminating with the publication of *Tales of the Grotesque and Arabesque* (1840). Poe's international reputation, which came after his early, untimely, and suspicious death in 1849, came principally from the publication four year earlier by Wiley & Putnam of his work *The Raven, and Other Poems* (1845).

The young American republic continued to grapple with divisive issues, most notably slavery and the tariff, which often split along regional lines. The subgenre of the slave narrative developed at that time. *The Narrative of the Life of Frederick Douglass, an American Slave, Written by Himself* (1845) and Harriet Jacobs's *Incidents in the Life of a Slave Girl* (1861) are the best known of a number of antebellum slave narratives that poignantly describe slavery in the United States that would require a civil war to correct.

Slave narratives express only one area of the complex cultural matrix of issues that affected American life at midcentury and that the writers of the American Renaissance attempted to describe. Even though the writers were concentrated in the northeast, they all showed an appreciation for the changing frontier line that defined the American West, including issues of westward expansion, imperialism, foreign affairs, America's diplomatic place in the world, and the treatment of American Indians. At the same time writers were look-

ing West, they were well aware of the influences of British Romantic thought from across the Atlantic, which emphasized the primacy of the individual artist.

Another phenomenon of the American Renaissance was the changing understanding of the role of women in society. One can easily trace a line from Mary Wollstonecraft's *A Vindication of the Rights of Women* (1792) to Margaret Fuller's *Woman in the Nineteenth Century* (1845) to the Seneca Falls (New York) women's rights convention of 1848 to view the expanding role of women in American life and literature.

There was no collective interplay between all of the American Renaissance writers, but there were occasional and worthwhile interactions, perhaps most notably Ralph Waldo Emerson's tutelage of Henry David Thoreau. Although the patrician Emerson and the plebe-

---

LEAVES OF GRASS

Walt Whitman's collection of poems, Leaves of Grass *(1855), remains central to any course in American literature, and the work epitomizes the American literary Renaissance. Two excerpts from the collection follow:*

I SAW IN LOUISIANA A LIVE-OAK GROWING
I saw in Louisiana a live-oak growing,
All alone stood it and the moss hung down from the branches,
Without any companion it grew there uttering joyous leaves of dark green,
And its look, rude, unbending, lusty, made me think of myself,
But I wonder'd how it could utter joyous leaves standing alone there without its
    friend near, for I knew I could not,
And I broke off a twig with a certain number of leaves upon it, and twined
    around it a little moss,
And brought it away, and I have placed it in sight in my room,
It is not needed to remind me as of my own dear friends,
(For I believe lately I think of little else than of them,)
Yet it remains to me a curious token, it makes me think of manly love;
For all that, and though the live-oak glistens there in Louisiana solitary in
    a wide flat space,
Uttering joyous leaves all its life without a friend a lover near,
I know very well I could not.

THE COMMONPLACE
The commonplace I sing;
How cheap is health! how cheap nobility!
Abstinence, no falsehood, no gluttony, lust;
The open air I sing, freedom, toleration,
(Take here the mainest lesson—less from books—less from the schools,)
The common day and night—the common earth and waters,
Your farm—your work, trade, occupation,
The democratic wisdom underneath, like solid ground for all.

Source: Walt Whitman, *Leaves of Grass* (Brooklyn: author, 1855).

Walt Whitman. (Library of Congress)

1857, a work that did not receive significant notice for a full century. Spending most of his last two decades as a customs-house officer in New York City, Melville published some short Civil War poems and a lengthy narrative poem called *Clarel: A Poem and Pilgrimage in the Holy Land* (1876), and he wrote *Billy Budd, Foretopman* in the last three years of his life, but the text was not discovered and published until 1924. Therefore, it would be quite accurate to classify Melville as an American Renaissance writer.

Emerson continued to write essays and poetry throughout his life, but his reputation was established through his signature essays of the 1830's. Whitman also continued to write poetry and to augment *Leaves of Grass* through the revised editions that were published up to the 1892 "deathbed" edition. His notable contributions to American letters, however, are the first (1855) edition of *Leaves of Grass* and some of his post-Civil War essays, especially *Democratic Vistas* (1871).

SIGNIFICANCE

The American Renaissance established American literature as an equal player in the pantheon of world literature. The seminal texts of the era—especially Hawthorne's *The Scarlet Letter*, Melville's *Moby Dick*, and Whitman's *Leaves of Grass*—remain part of the canon of American and world literatures.

The antebellum slave narratives fix in time a compelling social dilemma that contributes to both the historical and literary traditions of the nation. Talented African American writers such as Frederick Douglass and Harriet Jacobs, whose literary subjects reflected their life experiences, would in future generations be freed from the physical and intellectual limits of slavery. In a similar manner, Margaret Fuller's philosophical treatise on the condition of women helped forge a new agenda for female artistic productivity.

—*Richard Sax*

FURTHER READING

Abrams, Robert E. *Landscape and Ideology in American Renaissance Literature: Topographies of Skepticism.* New York: Cambridge University Press, 2003. Abrams describes how mid-nineteenth century American writing incorporated new concepts of space and landscape as a means of negotiating certain chaotic dilemmas of antebellum American culture.

Brooks, Van Wyck. *The Flowering of New England, 1815-1865.* 1936. Reprint. Boston: Houghton Mifflin, 1981. This elegant narrative, which won the Pu-

ian Whitman kept their geographic and intellectual distance for most of their careers, Emerson recognized the power and vision of Whitman's 1855 edition of *Leaves of Grass* and wrote a laudatory letter to Whitman, who treasured it for the rest of his life. The letter included the memorable sentence, "I greet you at the beginning of a great career, which yet must have had a long foreground somewhere, for such a start."

Herman Melville and Nathaniel Hawthorne were often solitary writers, but as neighbors in the Berkshire Mountains in the summer of 1850, they were, nonetheless, personal and professional friends at a time of remarkable literary productivity for both. Their Monument Mountain climb in early August of that year is perhaps the best-known nineteenth century "picnic" in American literary history.

Like many other eras of literary productivity, the American Renaissance was relatively short-lived. Poe died in 1849, and Fuller drowned in 1850. Thoreau died in 1862, and Hawthorne died in 1864, though Hawthorne spent much of his last decade principally as a diplomat rather than a writer. Although Melville lived until 1891, he essentially stopped working as a full-time writer after publishing *The Confidence Man: His Masquerade* in

litzer Prize and the National Book Award, describes how New England authors defined and created a national literature.

Grey, Robin, et al., eds. *The Complicity of Imagination: The American Renaissance, Contests of Authority, and Seventeenth-Century English Culture*. New York: Cambridge University Press, 1997. This collection of essays investigates seventeenth century English allusions in the works of Emerson, Fuller, Melville, and Thoreau.

Grossman, Jay. *Reconstituting the American Renaissance: Emerson, Whitman, and the Politics of Representation*. Durham, N.C.: Duke University Press, 2003. A discussion of the American Renaissance through the differing ways that Emerson and Whitman viewed the political efficacy of their literary productions.

Lewis, R. W. B. *The American Adam: Innocence, Tragedy, and Tradition in the Nineteenth Century*. 1955. Reprint. Chicago: University of Chicago Press, 1975. Traces the Adamic myth in American thought and literature of the period 1820 to 1860.

Matthiessen, F. O. *American Renaissance: Art and Expression in the Age of Emerson and Whitman*. 1941. Reprint. New York: Oxford University Press, 1968. The first, and an enduring, study of the America literary Renaissance of the mid-nineteenth century, emphasizing the importance of the particular poets who defined an age.

Reynolds, David S. *Beneath the American Renaissance: The Subversive Imagination in the Age of Emerson and Melville*. Cambridge, Mass.: Harvard University Press, 1989. Examines the products of popular culture (from 1820 to 1855) to argue how such influences as reform literatures, religious evangelical style, and popular fiction were "beneath" the creative process of many texts of the period.

Versluis, Arthur. *The Esoteric Origins of the American Renaissance*. New York: Oxford University Press, 2001. An analysis of the influence of the Euro-American discovery of Asian religions on American Transcendentalism and on the American Renaissance.

SEE ALSO: 1807-1850: Rise of the Knickerbocker School; 1819-1820: Irving's *Sketch Book* Transforms American Literature; 1820's-1850's: Social Reform Movement; c. 1820-1860: *Costumbrismo* Movement; 1836: Transcendental Movement Arises in New England; 1851: Melville Publishes *Moby Dick*; 1870's: Aesthetic Movement Arises; 1880's: Brahmin School of American Literature Flourishes; Dec., 1884-Feb., 1885: Twain Publishes *Adventures of Huckleberry Finn*; Nov. 8, 1900: Dreiser Publishes *Sister Carrie*.

RELATED ARTICLES in *Great Lives from History: The Nineteenth Century, 1801-1900:* Ralph Waldo Emerson; Margaret Fuller; Nathaniel Hawthorne; Herman Melville; Edgar Allan Poe; Henry David Thoreau; Walt Whitman.

1830-1842
TRAIL OF TEARS

The removal to the western Indian Territory of the Five Civilized Tribes was one of the most tragic developments in U.S. history.

ALSO KNOWN AS: Indian Removal
LOCALE: Southeastern United States
CATEGORIES: Human rights; atrocities and war crimes; indigenous people's rights

KEY FIGURES
Andrew Jackson (1767-1845), seventh U.S. president, 1829-1837
John Ross (1790-1866), principal chief and antiremoval leader of the Cherokees
Levi Colbert (1790?-1834), Chickasaw chief who tried to ease the burden of removal

Menewa (c. 1765-1865), Creek chief who strongly defended his people's rights
Osceola (c. 1804-1838), militant Seminole leader who violently resisted removal
Pushmataha (1764-1824), principal chief of the Choctaws and an able negotiator

SUMMARY OF EVENT
Soon after the American Revolution ended in 1783, demands began for the removal of all Native Americans from the southeastern part of the new United States. After a brief renewal of violent resistance, led by warriors such as Dragging Canoe of the Cherokees and Alexander McGillivray of the Creeks, most tribes were peaceful but firm in their efforts to remain in their ancestral lands.

Artist Robert Lindneux's painting Trail of Tears *is somewhat misleading, as most of the Indians forced to move made their arduous journey on foot.* (Wollaroc Museum, Bartlesville, Oklahoma)

The exception was the Seminoles in Florida. Many early treaties were negotiated to persuade these tribes to move west voluntarily. When the desired result was not achieved, Congress passed the Indian Removal Act in 1830, paving the way for forced removal. President Andrew Jackson, an old foe of the southeastern tribes, signed the bill, which became law on May 28, 1830.

The first tribe to experience forced removal was the Choctaw of southeastern Mississippi. Preliminary treaties with the Choctaws, whose population was about twenty-three thousand, began with the Treaty of Mount Dexter in 1805. Individual Choctaws had been encouraged to incur debts at government trading posts that were beyond their ability to pay. At Mount Dexter, Choctaw leaders were forced to cede four million acres of their land in return for the cancellation of those debts. The first exchange of Choctaw land for land in the Indian Territory west of the Mississippi River was approved by the Treaty of Doak's Stand in 1820. Pushmataha, the principal chief and able diplomat of the Choctaws, negotiated this treaty with General Andrew Jackson. However, since white settlers already occupied much of the new Choctaw land, the treaty had little effect.

The Treaty of Dancing Rabbit Creek, signed on Sep-

tember 27, 1830, was the first negotiated under the Indian Removal Act. It provided for the exchange of all Choctaw land for land in the Indian Territory. Choctaw acceptance of this treaty was facilitated by intratribal conflicts and by the duplicity of the self-proclaimed Choctaw spokesperson, Greenwood Leflore. By the end of 1832, about two-thirds of the Choctaws had emigrated to their new homes. Most others migrated over the next twenty years. A few, including Greenwood Leflore, remained in Mississippi.

The Choctaw removal became a pattern for the removal of the remaining tribes in the Southeast. The next to experience the process were the twenty-three thousand Creeks of eastern Alabama. Led by Menewa and other chiefs, the Creeks bitterly resisted removal. In 1825, Menewa carried out the execution for treason of William McIntosh, a half-breed chief who had favored removal. By 1831, Creek chiefs such as Eneah Micco, although vigorously protesting the invasion of their land by white squatters, realized that only removal could save their people from destruction. The Treaty of Washington, signed on March 24, 1832, provided for complete removal to the Indian Territory. Although the generous provisions of this treaty soon were ignored, conditions in

TRAIL OF TEARS, AFTER 1830

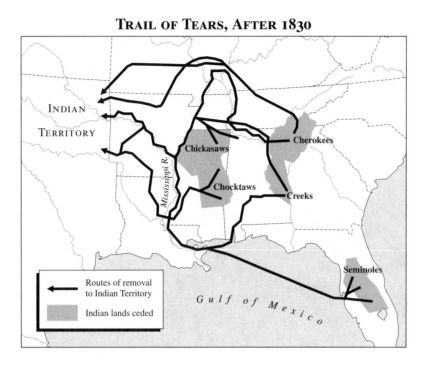

the Creek Nation became intolerable and they began their sad trek to the West.

Creek migration was interrupted in May, 1836, by reprisal raids against white settlements. This action brought in the U.S. Army, with orders to forcibly remove all Creeks from Alabama. By 1838, the removal was complete. An ironic footnote is that during the course of their removal, several hundred Creek men were impressed into the army for service against their Seminole cousins in Florida.

The least controversial of the Trail of Tears removals was that of the five thousand Chickasaws from the northern parts of Mississippi and Alabama. For thirty years, the government worked to transform the Chickasaws from a hunting society into an agricultural society that would require less land. By 1830, the process seemed complete, but the result had been widespread poverty. It also produced friction between the "full-bloods" who resisted the process and the "part-bloods" who favored it.

The Chickasaw removal process was initiated by the Treaty of Pontotoc Creek in 1832. It was agreed that the Chickasaws would move west when suitable land could be obtained. Finding such land was difficult, however, with the best possibility being part of the Choctaw domain already established. Levi Colbert, the most prominent of several Chickasaw chiefs, was ill and not present when the Treaty of Pontotoc Creek was signed. He pro-

tested the use of coercion by General John Coffee, the leading government negotiator, to get the other chiefs to sign. However, he cooperated with the removal process in order to secure the best possible land and to ease the burden on his people. The Chickasaw removal followed the signing of the Treaty of Doaksville in January, 1837. Land was secured and most of the tribe moved during that same year. Unlike other tribes, they were able to take most of their possessions with them, and few died along the way. However, after arrival in the Indian Territory, they faced the typical problems of intertribal conflicts, substandard food, and a smallpox epidemic.

In 1830, about sixteen thousand Cherokees still lived on their ancestral lands in northern Georgia and southeastern Tennessee. Their removal, first called the "trail where they cried," is the source of the name Trail of Tears. The federal government's efforts to remove the Cherokees began with the signing of the Georgia Compact in 1802, when President Thomas Jefferson agreed to seek reasonable terms for removing the Cherokees in a peaceful manner. In 1828, when gold was discovered on Cherokee land in Georgia, the process was facilitated, but not on the reasonable terms that had been stipulated by Jefferson. The state of Georgia nullified Cherokee laws and incorporated a large portion of the Cherokee Nation. The Cherokees responded with a legal defense led by their democratically elected principal chief, John Ross, who took their case to federal court. Although a decision by Chief Justice John Marshall favored the Cherokees, President Jackson refused to enforce it.

A small group of proremoval Cherokees, led by Major Ridge, signed the New Echota Treaty in December, 1835. Following ratification by the U.S. Senate in May, 1836, the entire tribe had two years to move to the Indian Territory. John Ross and the majority protested the treaty and refused to move. Forced removal began in June, 1838. When the journey ended in March, 1839, four thousand unmarked graves had been left behind along the route. About one thousand Cherokees escaped removal by fleeing into the southern Appalachian Mountains. The final tragedy of Cherokee removal was the murder in the Indian Territory of the proremoval leaders who had reluctantly signed the treaty.

The Seminoles of central Florida, descendants of Creeks who had moved there to escape harassment in the eighteenth century, provide the last chapter in the Trail of Tears. Their population of about six thousand people included many African Americans, both freemen and runaway slaves from the southern states. The desire to cut off that escape route for slaves had been part of the incentive for Jackson's invasion and the resulting acquisition of Florida from Spain in 1819 under the Adams-Onís Treaty. The demand to move the Seminoles to the Indian Territory soon followed.

In 1832, an unauthorized group of Seminoles signed the Treaty of Payne's Landing, declaring that all would give up their land and move west. Opposition to the treaty was led by Osceola and Cooacoochee (Wildcat). The result was the Second Seminole War, in 1835. Seminoles captured during that war were immediately sent to the Indian Territory. By 1842, the war was over and the remaining Seminoles slowly migrated west. By 1856, the only Seminoles left in Florida were those in the nearly inaccessible swamps of the Everglades.

SIGNIFICANCE

The Trail of Tears removals rank among the most tragic episodes in United States history. The policies of three American leaders reveal the changing attitudes on how to best accomplish the removals. After Thomas Jefferson's peaceful persuasion and reasonable terms failed, John C. Calhoun, as secretary of war under President James Monroe, favored educating Native Americans to accept the need for removal. In the end, it was Andrew Jackson's policy of forced removal that completed the distasteful task.

—Glenn L. Swygart

FURTHER READING

DeRosier, Arthur. *The Removal of the Choctaw Indians.* Knoxville: University of Tennessee Press, 1970. Discusses removal circumstances. Includes maps and portraits.

Ehle, John. *Trail of Tears: The Rise and Fall of the Cherokee Nation.* New York: Doubleday, 1988. Covers Cherokee history from 1770 to 1840. Details the intratribal conflicts relating to removal policy.

Foreman, Grant. *Indian Removal: The Emigration of the Five Civilized Tribes of Indians.* Norman: University of Oklahoma Press, 1932. Surveys the treaties and leaders of removal. Maps and illustrations.

Gibson, Arrell. *The Chickasaws.* Norman: University of Oklahoma Press, 1971. Puts removal in context with Chickasaw history from the eighteenth century to 1907.

Jahoda, Gloria. *The Trail of Tears.* New York: Wings Books, 1995. Sympathetic history of the forced removal and resettlement of the Cherokees to west of the Mississippi River.

Missall, John, and Mary Lou Missall. *The Seminole Wars: America's Longest Indian Conflict.* Gainesville: University Press of Florida, 2004. Fascinating study of the three Seminole wars that examines their causes and their impact in U.S. history.

Remini, Robert V. *Andrew Jackson.* 3 vols. Baltimore: Johns Hopkins University Press, 1998. Nearly definitive biography of the most fervid and effective advocate of Indian removal.

Williams, Jeanne. "The Cherokees." In *Trails of Tears: American Indians Driven from Their Lands.* Dallas, Tex.: Hendrick-Long, 1992. Puts Cherokee removal in the context of the similar experiences of the Comanches, Cheyennes, Apaches, and Navajos.

Wright, J. Leitch. *Creeks and Seminoles: The Destruction and Regeneration of the Muscogulge People.* Lincoln: University of Nebraska Press, 1986. Discusses removal and resettlement in the West. Extensive bibliography.

SEE ALSO: July 27, 1813-Aug. 9, 1814: Creek War; Nov. 21, 1817-Mar. 27, 1858: Seminole Wars; Feb. 22, 1819: Adams-Onís Treaty Gives the United States Florida; Feb. 21, 1828: *Cherokee Phoenix* Begins Publication; May 28, 1830: Congress Passes Indian Removal Act; Mar. 18, 1831, and Mar. 3, 1832: Cherokee Cases; Sept. 4, 1841: Congress Passes Preemption Act of 1841; Apr. 30, 1860-1865: Apache and Navajo War; Feb. 6, 1861-Sept. 4, 1886: Apache Wars; Aug., 1863-Sept., 1866: Long Walk of the Navajos.

RELATED ARTICLES in *Great Lives from History: The Nineteenth Century, 1801-1900:* John C. Calhoun; Andrew Jackson; Osceola; John Ross.

1830's

c. 1830-1865
SOUTHERNERS ADVANCE PROSLAVERY ARGUMENTS

During the early 1830's, southern apologists for slavery began changing their tactics from defending the institution to aggressively arguing its virtues. New proslavery arguments strengthened intellectual bonds among southerners, who saw slavery as a moral institution, in opposition to northern abolitionists.

LOCALE: Southern United States

CATEGORIES: Human rights; economics; social issues and reform; civil rights and liberties

KEY FIGURES

Thomas R. Dew (1802-1846), professor of political economy at Virginia's William and Mary College

William Lloyd Garrison (1805-1879), abolitionist leader and editor of *The Liberator*

John C. Calhoun (1782-1850), South Carolina senator and political theorist

George Fitzhugh (1806-1881), Virginia writer and social philosopher

James Henry Hammond (1807-1864), South Carolina senator

Josiah Nott (1804-1873), physician and author

Thornton Stringfellow (1788-1869), Baptist minister of Culpepper County, Virginia

SUMMARY OF EVENT

During the decades preceding the U.S. Civil War (1861-1865), southerners advanced a wide range of arguments and theories—some old, some new—to justify the institution of chattel slavery. The distinctiveness of proslavery thinking during those years lay less in its content than in its tone or spirit. Defenders of the South's "peculiar institution" were no longer on the defensive; their mood was no longer apologetic. Unlike most of their predecessors, they did not merely tolerate slavery; they defined it as a moral institution and many glorified it. They took the offensive on behalf of slavery partly in response to the attacks of northern abolitionists. Perhaps the primary objective of their aggressive proslavery campaign was to dispel the doubts of southerners as to the justice of slavery and to offer compelling proof to nonslaveholders and slaveholders alike that slavery found sanction in religion, science, and morality, that it constituted an essential part of a civilized economic and political order.

After 1830, proslavery discourse borrowed from a variety of sources, many of which had been used before calls for immediate abolition posed a new threat to slavery. Proslavery apologists pointed to the existence of slavery during biblical times and throughout most of history. They also called attention to the notion of entailment, which blamed the introduction of slavery on the British and predicted social catastrophe if slavery were to be abolished.

These arguments continued to dominate the thinking of most proslavery writers during the 1830's, as evidenced, for example, in the scholar Thomas R. Dew's *Review of the Debate in the Virginia Legislature of 1831 and 1832* (1832). Although Dew's tract was once treated as the first work of the new proslavery discourse, later historians have seen it as the culmination of the earlier, less affirmative phase of proslavery writing in the South. Dew's work, which was widely read, asserted that slavery was a preferred way of compelling efficient labor in the hot-climate states of the lower South. This view was the harbinger of the notions of perpetual slavery developed by later southern apologists.

Historians have traditionally understood post-1830 proslavery arguments as reactions to the launching of William Lloyd Garrison's journal *The Liberator*, which marked the beginning of the immediate-abolition movement, as well as the fear spawned by Nat Turner's slave rebellion in Southampton County, Virginia. Both events occurred in 1831, but other issues intensified proslavery writing and abolitionist discourse during the 1830's.

Proslavery polemics seem to have escalated along a continuum, rather than suddenly appearing after 1831. Two interrelated themes characterized this escalation of southern proslavery. The first was a reaction to the abolitionist mail campaign of 1835, in which northern abolitionists attempted to flood the South with literature arguing that slavery was immoral. In response, southern ministers and denominations took the lead in denouncing the moral foundations of abolitionists. Virulent antiabolitionism became a major feature—perhaps the single constant—in southern proslavery thought. Southerners denounced abolitionism as incendiary, a wanton and dangerous interference with southern safety. Southerners construed abolitionists as intent upon fomenting rebellion among southern slaves, and were also infuriated by the Congress's gag rule, which persuaded northerners that southerners would trample on the First Amendment or any other right to preserve slavery.

The second theme involved a defense of slavery more ideological in tone, which blended biblical literalism with conservative social theories, some of which were quite popular among New England Federalists during the early nineteenth century. This strain of thinking challenged industrial economics and modern reform movements, asserting that a stratified social order produced the best possible society. A heavy lace of paternal imagery, which threaded together honor and social responsibility, gave ornamentation to this new proslavery fabric. In the hands of the South Carolina politician John C. Calhoun, this two-pronged argument proved that slavery was not an evil, as the abolitionists claimed, but

> a good—a positive good . . . a great blessing to both races, [and] great stay of the union and our free institutions, and one of the main sources of the unbounded prosperity of the whole.

Typical of thinkers who championed this phase of proslavery writing was Thornton Stringfellow, a Baptist minister of Culpepper County, Virginia, whose *Brief Examination of Scripture Testimony on the Institution of Slavery* (1841) argued that slavery enjoyed "the sanction of the Almighty in the Patriarchal Age . . . that its legality was recognized . . . by Jesus Christ in his kingdom; and that it is full of mercy." Godly southerners, Stringfellow maintained, should withdraw from abolitionists, whose moral notions must originate from some source other than the Bible.

In a speech before the U.S. Senate in 1858, James Henry Hammond of South Carolina held that African American slaves provided the "mud-sill" of society, whose labor was necessary but whose mean estate made essential their exclusion from the political process. Slavery was essential to free "that other class which leads progress, civilization and refinement" for more enlightened endeavors. Fortunately, the senator observed, the South had found African Americans perfectly adapted to serve as the

> very mud-sill of society and of political government . . . a race inferior to her own, but eminently qualified in tem-

SLAVERY IN THE UNITED STATES AND ITS TERRITORIES, C. 1860

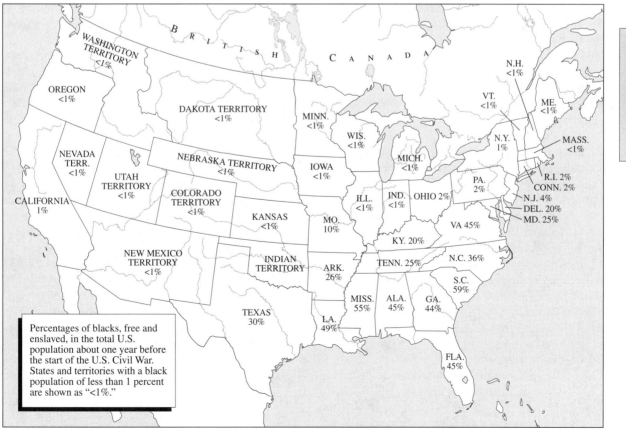

Percentages of blacks, free and enslaved, in the total U.S. population about one year before the start of the U.S. Civil War. States and territories with a black population of less than 1 percent are shown as "<1%."

per, in vigor, in docility, in capacity to stand the climate, to answer all her purposes.

During the 1850's, other southern writers embraced even more extreme proslavery theories. However, these views attracted more interest from historians in the twentieth century than they did from nineteenth century advocates. For example, Henry Hughes, of Port Gibson, Mississippi, drew upon the infant discipline of sociology to buttress his proslavery views. He described slavery as "Ethical Warranteeism," in which slaves labored for masters in return for food, clothing, and shelter. Josiah Nott, of Mobile, Alabama, embraced the theory of polygenesis, holding in *Types of Mankind* (1854) that Africans had arisen from a separate creation and were not *Homo sapiens*.

Others compared southern slavery with free labor in the North. In *Sociology of the South* (1854) and *Cannibals All!* (1857), for example, Virginian George Fitzhugh suggested that the northern states would have to adopt some form of slavery to control the immigrant working classes, or else face moral and social chaos. Free labor, he asserted, produced class warfare in the North, while slavery permitted social harmony in the South. Southern masters had moral obligations toward, and were predisposed to kind treatment of, their slaves. Northern factory owners discarded their laborers at whim.

SIGNIFICANCE

Most southerners adhered to the less extreme proslavery argument based on the Bible and the ancient Greek philosopher Plato. The proslavery argument became a justification for the entire southern way of life, whose culture, social structure, and economy were believed to depend upon the institution of slavery. Its ubiquity helped bind southerners together and produced the remarkable degree of unity among them in the days following the election of Abraham Lincoln in 1860 and his call for troops in April, 1861. Undoubtedly, the intensity and unanimity with which southerners defended slavery had much to do with the fact that they had come to identify the system of slavery with southern society as a whole and with their place in the union.

—*Anne C. Loveland, updated by Edward R. Crowther*

FURTHER READING

Cain, William E., ed. *William Lloyd Garrison and the Fight Against Slavery: Selections from "The Liberator."* Boston: Bedford Books of St. Martin's Press, 1995. Selections from the abolitionist newspaper that

helped to galvanize proslavery advocates. Cain's introduction provides historical background on slavery and the abolition movement in the United States and the events in Garrison's career.

Faust, Drew Gilpin. *The Ideology of Slavery: Proslavery Thought in the Antebellum South, 1830-1860.* Baton Rouge: Louisiana State University Press, 1981. Excellent anthology of proslavery writings, augmented by a thoughtful introductory essay.

Freehling, William W. *The Road to Disunion: Secessionists at Bay, 1776-1854.* New York: Oxford University Press, 1990. Shows clearly the complex uses southerners made of proslavery thinking and why a degree of intellectual unity was vital in a South divided against itself.

Jenkins, William S. *Pro-Slavery Thought in the Old South.* Chapel Hill: University of North Carolina Press, 1935. One of the oldest monographs on proslavery thinking, this book remains a useful starting point for the study of the subject.

Snay, Mitchell. *Gospel of Disunion: Religion and Separatism in the Antebellum South.* New York: Cambridge University Press, 1993. Illustrates how significant proslavery thinking was in southern clerical thought and how that created a great degree of intellectual unity in the South.

Stauffer, John. *The Black Hearts of Men: Radical Abolitionists and the Transformation of Race.* Cambridge, Mass.: Harvard University Press, 2002. Study of the interracial alliance that linked John Brown, Frederick Douglass, and others in the struggle to abolish slavery.

Tise, Larry E. *Proslavery: A History of the Defense of Slavery in America, 1701-1840.* Athens: University of Georgia Press, 1987. Shows that proslavery thinking existed in both northern and southern states, and explains well the subtle shifts in southern proslavery thought after 1830.

Young, Jeffrey Robert, ed. *Proslavery and Sectional Thought in the Early South, 1740-1829: An Anthology.* Columbia: University of South Carolina Press, 2006. Collection of thirteen representative texts showing the development of proslavery arguments from colonial times to the early national South. Includes tracts, sermons, lectures, and petitions.

SEE ALSO: 1820's-1850's: Social Reform Movement; Jan. 19-27, 1830: Webster and Hayne Debate Slavery and Westward Expansion; Jan. 1, 1831: Garrison Begins Publishing *The Liberator*; Aug. 21, 1831: Turner

Launches Slave Insurrection; Dec., 1833: American Anti-Slavery Society Is Founded; Dec. 3, 1847: Douglass Launches *The North Star*; 1852: Stowe Publishes *Uncle Tom's Cabin*; June 16-Oct. 15, 1858: Lincoln-Douglas Debates; July, 1859: Last Slave Ship Docks at Mobile; Jan. 1, 1863: Lincoln Issues

the Emancipation Proclamation; Dec. 6, 1865: Thirteenth Amendment Is Ratified.

RELATED ARTICLES in *Great Lives from History: The Nineteenth Century, 1801-1900:* John Brown; John C. Calhoun; Frederick Douglass; William Lloyd Garrison.

c. 1830-1870
BARBIZON SCHOOL OF LANDSCAPE PAINTING FLOURISHES

Inspired by masters of the Dutch golden age and by Romantic art from England, the landscape painters of France's Barbizon school opposed academic tradition by advocating plein air painting and naturalism in art. The painters concentrated on natural scenes and life in rural France and showed concern for environmental preservation. Their attention to changing light and atmospheric conditions inspired the development of Impressionism.

LOCALE: Barbizon, France
CATEGORY: Art

KEY FIGURES

Théodore Rousseau (1812-1867), French landscape painter
Jean-François Millet (1814-1875), French genre and landscape painter
Jules Dupré (1811-1889), French landscape painter
Constant Troyon (1810-1865), French landscape painter
Narcisse-Virgile Diaz de la Peña (1807-1876), French painter
Charles-François Daubigny (1817-1878), French landscape painter
Charles Jacque (1813-1894), French landscape painter, printmaker, and illustrator

SUMMARY OF EVENT

During the early nineteenth century, the French art establishment was governed to a large extent by classical doctrine founded on the principles of order, clarity, and harmony. Institutions such as the École des Beaux-Arts (school of art) and its state-sponsored salons showed a marked preference for heroic themes laden with historical, religious, or mythological symbolism. The Italianate style of landscape painting, with its stock ruins and Arcadian vistas, had become a standard feature in academic art, but it relied less on the direct observation of nature than on mastery of idealized space and composition.

Leading teachers and critics of academic art generally advocated some direct study of nature in the early stages of composition, mainly through sketches or preliminary studies; however, it was still generally expected that the major portion of an artist's work be conducted in a studio. The practice of outdoor painting called plein air painting was not yet common. Only later did the introduction of oil-based paint in tubes and lighter equipment, portable easels in particular, allow artists to wander the countryside more freely in search of inspiration. The creation of a Prix de Rome for landscape painting in 1817 ultimately led to a greater appreciation for the genre and provided an incentive for young artists to develop their skills in the study of nature.

During the 1820's and 1830's, as Romanticism was coming to fruition in French art and literature, the public's growing interest in regional and national history fueled a buoyant market for illustrated travel books. A growing number of artists, inspired by the Dutch landscapists of the seventeenth century and by expositions of English Romantic art in the French capital, set out to discover the spirit of rural France and the beauty of its natural surroundings. One favorite destination, given its convenient proximity to Paris, was the humble farming community of Barbizon, located on the edge of the forest of Fontainebleau in north-central France. Artists looking to escape the noise and pollution of the cities traveled to Barbizon on vacation, immersing themselves in nature and observing the local inhabitants at work.

The now-famous Auberge Ganne, established in Barbizon by a former stonecutter and his wife sometime around 1824, provided inexpensive lodging and served as a meeting place not only for avant-garde landscape painters but also for sculptors and writers. By mid-century, the village had become easily accessible by rail, increasing the village's ability to attract a wide spectrum of artists. A detailed list of clients maintained by the owners of the Auberge Ganne between 1848 and

1830's

1861 identifies scores of artists who came to visit, some from Germany, Switzerland, and from as far away as America.

The leading members of the Barbizon school were Théodore Rousseau, Jules Dupré, Constant Troyon, Charles-François Daubigny, Narcisse-Virgile Diaz de la Peña, Charles Jacque, and Jean-François Millet. Rousseau first visited Barbizon around 1828, before settling there permanently in 1846. He gained notice as a landscape painter during the early 1830's, exhibiting at the Parisian salons of 1831, 1833, 1834, and 1835. However, his liberal political leanings and opposition to classical standards in art led to his exclusion from subsequent salons until the fall of the July Monarchy in 1848.

During the 1850's and 1860's, at the height of Rousseau's popularity, his radical naturalism found expression in rapid brushwork, rough textures, and subdued colors. His paintings, many of them now preserved in major museums throughout Europe and the United States, present an assortment of wooded vales, forest clearings, ponds under cloudy skies, marshes, quaint hamlets, and isolated farms often cloaked in melancholy. Genuinely concerned with the progressive destruction of France's forests, Rousseau initiated a campaign resulting in the creation of national land preserves in the forest of Fontainebleau in 1852 and 1853.

Felled trees are common in the work of Jules Dupré and Constant Troyon. Both artists had become acquainted with Rousseau during the early 1830's and later accompanied him to remote sites to paint. Dupré's *Landscape with Cattle* of 1837, featuring a severed trunk in its central foreground, illustrates the artist's dismay at the destruction of trees. Like other Barbizon painters, Dupré and Troyon were profoundly influenced by Dutch Baroque art, which had gained popularity among liberals for its egalitarian spirit. After a trip to the Netherlands and Belgium in 1847, where he admired paintings by Albert Cuyp (1620-1691) and Paulus Potter (1625-1654), Troyon specialized in large-scale landscapes with livestock.

It appears that Charles-François Daubigny did not spend a substantial amount of time in Barbizon, but nonetheless he made trips with Rousseau and Dupré to Valmondois and L'Île-Adam, which are north of Paris, in 1846. River landscapes became a dominant feature in his art. In 1857, he set up a studio and living quarters on a boat so that he could devote himself to plein air painting along the Seine, Marne, and Oise Rivers. His *Evening on the Oise* (1863) and *On the Banks of the Oise* (1864) are typical of his style.

Narcisse-Virgile Diaz de la Peña made regular trips to the forest of Fontainebleau and spent time with Rousseau in 1837. His choice of subjects varied considerably over the years, ranging from provocative nudes and mythological allegories to the Barbizon-styled landscapes for which he is best remembered. Like Rousseau, he was attentive to the effects of light and atmosphere on his subjects. Various landscapes of the 1860's, including *Landscape with a Pine Tree* (1864) and *Heights of Le Jean de Paris* (1867), suggest the influence of Dutch painter Jacob van Ruisdael (1628-1682) on his style.

Jean-François Millet moved to Barbizon in 1849, as did Charles Jacque, who specialized in painting barnyard scenes and livestock. Both men were influenced by Dutch art. Millet's realist paintings of French peasants, including *The Sower* (c. 1850), *The Gleaners* (1857), and *Man with a Hoe* (1860-1862), were, however, wrought with controversy. While Millet's paintings appealed to socialists and liberals as a tribute to the humblest members of French society, conservatives saw in them the nefarious seeds of revolution. After the mid-1860's, Millet turned to landscape painting in the fashionable Barbizon style.

SIGNIFICANCE

Despite its nostalgic appeal, the term "Barbizon school" remains a problematic one for art historians. Not all artists associated with the school were primarily landscape painters, and personal styles varied considerably. All of these artists, however, were affected by the urban-industrial revolution that was transforming not only the French landscape but also French society. The Barbizon circle of artists, sensing the dangers of unbridled progress, intuitively looked to the heartland of rural France for social, moral, and artistic sustenance. The stolid peasant figures, for example, that populate Millet's art are pendants to the massive oaks and solitary pines common in paintings by Rousseau and Dupré. Peasants and trees, both at odds with the destructive forces that surround them, are at once symbols of stability and loss.

After the Paris Revolution of 1848, the Barbizon painters set the tone in French landscape painting. Art collectors in the United States were particularly eager to purchase their paintings, and this sometimes led to bidding wars between French and American buyers. One of the founders of the Rhode Island School of Design, American painter William Morris Hunt (1824-1879), was a great admirer of the Barbizon school and did much to promote its appreciation within the United States. The Barbizon painters also contributed to the development of

French Impressionism by championing the practice of plein air painting, by reducing their field of vision, and by demonstrating the advantageous use of short brush strokes and dabs of paint.

—*Jan Pendergrass*

FURTHER READING

Adams, Steven. *The Barbizon School and the Origins of Impressionism.* London: Phaidon Press, 1994. Presents the evolution of French landscape painting from the neoclassical era to late nineteenth century Impressionism. Discusses to what extent the Barbizon painters influenced the Impressionist movement. Includes numerous full-color prints.

Bouret, Jean. *The Barbizon School and Nineteenth Century French Landscape Painting.* Greenwich, Conn.: New York Graphic Society, 1983. Examines the lives and careers of eight leading Barbizon painters. A good source of anecdotal information.

Burmester, Andreas, Christoph Heilman, and Michael Zimmermann, eds. *Barbizon: Malerei der Natur Natur der Malerei.* Munich, Germany: Klinkhardt & Biermann, 1999. An important collection of articles on the Barbizon school of painters. Texts in English, French, and German.

Herbert, Robert L. *Barbizon Revisited: Essay and Catalogue.* New York: Clarke and Way, 1962. A critical survey of Barbizon landscape painting from the 1820's to the late 1870's. Includes monochrome and color reproductions.

Sillevis, John, and Hans Kraan, eds. *The Barbizon School.* The Hague, Netherlands: Haags Gemeentemuseum, 1985. A collection of thirteen articles, with special emphasis on Dutch and Flemish influences.

Thomas, Greg M. *Art and Ecology in Nineteenth-Century France. The Landscapes of Théodore Rousseau.* Princeton, N.J.: Princeton University Press, 2000. Examines the importance of ecological themes in Rousseau's art, and uncovers similar themes in the art of Dupré, Diaz de la Peña, Jacque, and Millet.

SEE ALSO: 1801: Emergence of the Primitives; 1824: Paris Salon of 1824; Fall, 1848: Pre-Raphaelite Brotherhood Begins; 1855: Courbet Establishes Realist Art Movement; Apr. 15, 1874: First Impressionist Exhibition; Late 1870's: Post-Impressionist Movement Begins.

RELATED ARTICLES in *Great Lives from History: The Nineteenth Century, 1801-1900:* Gustave Courbet; Paul Gauguin; Pierre-Auguste Renoir.

January 7, 1830
BALTIMORE AND OHIO RAILROAD OPENS

The first long-distance railroad line in the United States, the Baltimore and Ohio line began slowly but helped to launch a national mania for railroad construction that within a few decades revolutionized transportation throughout the country.

LOCALE: Baltimore, Maryland
CATEGORIES: Transportation; expansion and land acquisition; engineering

KEY FIGURES
Philip Evan Thomas (1776-1861), prosperous Baltimore merchant and promoter of the railroad
Evan Thomas (fl. early nineteenth century), Philip's brother, a Baltimore businessman
Peter Cooper (1791-1883), industrialist who built the early steam locomotive *Tom Thumb*
John Eager Howard (1752-1827), prominent Baltimore resident

Jonathan Knight (1789-1864), mathematician and chief engineer of the railroad
Stephen Harriman Long (1784-1864), army officer who oversaw surveying
Charles Carroll (1737-1832), last surviving signer of the Declaration of Independence

SUMMARY OF EVENT
The quickening pace of American life achieved a new momentum during the early national period. The westward movement acquired a national character as New Englanders pushed into the Ohio Valley and Virginians filled up Kentucky and Tennessee. The eastern seaboard, with its cities and port facilities, turned to the West for its food, and the grain-producing hinterland responded with increased production. Improved forms of transportation were required to bring the produce of the interior to the coast. Enterprising businessmen, pooling their capital resources, engaged in canal building and railroad con-

Peter Cooper's experimental locomotive Tom Thumb *racing against a horse in August, 1830.* (Hulton Archive/Getty Images)

struction. Private initiative, in the absence of a consistent government policy of promoting public works, laid the foundation of a national transportation system. This transportation system began with canals, but regions without navigable waterways had to find another method. Railroads provided the answer.

The development of transportation in the early national period took three forms: canals, roads, and railroads. Built in areas of accessible rivers and lakes, canals were by far the cheapest transportation system. Horse-drawn canal barges could move heavy bulk commodities inexpensively, and the cost of canal maintenance was negligible. After the Erie Canal opened in 1825, Buffalo and New York City became entrepôts for western trade. The Morris Company Canal, under construction from 1824 to 1832, eventually connected New York Harbor to the mouth of the Lehigh River and served to bring Lehigh coal to the seaboard. Other canals were enthusiastically promoted, with the expectation of reaping huge profits from the western trade. Smarting from the success of New York's Erie Canal, Pennsylvania constructed the

Pennsylvania Portage and Canal System between 1826 and 1840. However, this elaborate system of cable portages and short canals was a dismal failure. High construction costs and competition from railroads rendered this bold scheme obsolete before it opened.

The construction of roads had a much longer history. The Philadelphia-Lancaster Turnpike, completed in 1794, encouraged road building in other areas. In New England and the middle states, where distances between towns were relatively short, toll roads were constructed feverishly during the 1790's and early nineteenth century. Nevertheless, road transportation was more expensive than canal transportation. High freight costs precluded the movement of bulk commodities, and overland transportation declined rapidly with the rise of canals. By 1821, six hundred miles of new turnpike construction had been authorized, and nearly four thousand miles stood completed. The old National Road, connecting Cumberland, Maryland, and Wheeling, on the Ohio River, fell into neglect after the opening of the Erie Canal. By 1825, the turnpike boom had passed.

Railroads, the third form of transportation, required the assistance of more advanced technology. In 1825, the Stockton and Darlington Railway opened in England. The railroad's potential for the United States quickly was recognized. Within a few years, railroad construction in the United States surpassed that in Great Britain. Short-line railroads were first, but with the incorporation of the Baltimore and Ohio Railroad in 1827, long-distance rail transportation for goods and passengers became a reality in the United States.

Baltimore's decision to sponsor a railroad into the interior was, in essence, a manifesto in its struggle with New York City for commercial supremacy on the East Coast. By 1827, Baltimore boasted a population of eighty thousand people, of whom nearly two-thirds earned their livings in commerce and related industries. The completion of the Erie Canal threatened Baltimore's prosperity. Other planned canals, such as the Chesapeake and Ohio Canal, were also threats to the port of Baltimore. The National Road, which had played a significant role in Baltimore's commercial success up until that time, could not compete with New York's all-water route. Hence, the idea of a railroad, an ambitious and fiscally dangerous scheme at best, soon found influential supporters in Baltimore's business community.

Discussion preceded organization. At a dinner party held at the Baltimore home of Colonel John Eager Howard in 1826, the scheme for a railroad linking Baltimore with the Ohio Valley was first discussed. Evan Thomas, an influential member of Baltimore's business elite, who was to become the first president of the new railroad, had just returned from England, where he had viewed the operations of the Stockton and Darlington Railway. Thomas was enthusiastic about the new enterprise, and he succeeded in arousing the interest of a few business leaders with his vivid descriptions of the English railroad. Most business leaders, however, remained reticent, and their cautious attitude prevented immediate action. Evan's brother, Philip Evan Thomas, now took up the cause. As a prosperous merchant who felt threatened by New York City's ascendancy, Philip Thomas began pushing the idea at every available gathering. When New York City appeared to be running away with the western trade, Baltimore businessmen began to panic. The ideas of the Thomas brothers, so quietly received in 1826, aroused unbridled enthusiasm during the early months of 1827.

At a dinner party held at the home of George Brown on February 2, 1827, the Thomas brothers presented a discourse on the relative advantages of a railroad trade route to the West. Twenty-five businessmen attended this affair, representing a good portion of Baltimore's business elite. After the discourse, a committee was appointed to investigate the feasibility of the scheme. One week later, the committee reported that immediate steps should be taken to construct a railroad between the city of Baltimore and a suitable point on the Ohio River. The report further suggested that a company be formed and a charter of incorporation be obtained from the legislature. Business leaders received the report and took action immediately. A large edition of the report was published in pamphlet form and distributed publicly. News of the plan quickly spread beyond city limits, and throughout the state of Maryland tongues were wagging. When a formal petition for a charter of incorporation was submitted to the Maryland State legislature on February 27, 1827, little opposition arose. The bill for incorporation passed easily the next day, and America's first significant experiment in railroad building was under way.

The charter of the Baltimore and Ohio Railroad Company provided for a capital stock of three million dollars to be raised by the public sale of fifteen thousand shares at one hundred dollars per share. Ten thousand shares were reserved for subscription by the state of Maryland, and five thousand for subscription by the city of Baltimore. When ten thousand shares had been purchased, the corporation would be declared established and all its rights and privileges would take effect immediately. The fiscal organization of the Baltimore and Ohio Railroad transformed the city of Baltimore and the state of Maryland into a private corporation, and the citizens of the state into a public enterprise.

When the stock offer was made, an enthusiastic public responded. Money flowed into the company coffers. Parents took out stock in their children's names, and a wave of speculation swept the state. The stock books were opened on March 20, 1827, at the Farmers Branch Bank in Frederick and the Mechanics Bank in Baltimore. Twelve days later, the books were closed. The Baltimore and Ohio Railroad stock was distributed among twenty-two thousand individuals; almost every white family in the state had a stake in the company. Private enterprise had created a public utility. In effect, the building of the Erie Canal forced the leaders of Baltimore to accept the challenge of an experimental mode of transportation, whereas other cities pursued abortive and costly experiments with canal construction in inappropriate locations.

The actual construction of the line awaited the solution of many engineering problems. Americans were novices in railroad building, but what they lacked in

1830's

practical experience they more than made up for with energy. The federal government possessed the only major repository of engineering knowledge, and the management of the Baltimore and Ohio Railroad raided the government for talent. Colonel Stephen Harriman Long was recruited from the Army, and Jonathan Knight, a well-recognized mathematician, came from the National Road project. Engineers were sent to England to study the British system, and preliminary surveys were made to determine the best route to follow. Problems arose, but public impatience goaded the bureaucracy to action.

By the summer of 1828, enough progress had been made to allow a symbolic gesture. The historic significance of America's first long-distance railroad was clearly seen. The citizens of Maryland believed themselves to be upon the threshold of a new era. To ensure a conspicuous place in later history books, the management of the Baltimore and Ohio Railroad sought to commemorate the occasion with the laying of a cornerstone. To perform this symbolic act, they chose Charles Carroll, the last surviving signer of the Declaration of Independence. In a ceremony preceded by parades and speeches on July 4, 1828, Carroll laid the cornerstone for the first interstate railroad in the United States.

Two years later, on January 7, 1830, the Baltimore and Ohio Railroad opened its line from Pratt Street through to Carrolton Viaduct for public riding. Four rail cars, pulled by teams of horses, with a total seating capacity of 120 persons, made the first run. Although it would not be until the 1850's when the trains actually reached Ohio, the thirteen-mile initial line from Baltimore to Ellicott's Mills quickly became a showcase of early U.S. railroading.

Peter Cooper, who owned a Baltimore iron foundry, built the *Tom Thumb*, a diminutive steam locomotive. In an experimental trial on August 28, 1830, it hauled thirty-six people at speeds up to eighteen miles per hour. The railroad's directors were impressed, and with the help of Baltimore engine builders, the railroad was transformed into a true steam-operated railroad during the 1830's.

As the railroad expanded, the need for technological improvements became evident. Only a year after the railroad began operation, Jonathan Knight, the railroad's chief engineer, said the comfort of the passenger carriages had to be improved by mounting them on springs to improve ride quality. In addition, sheets of timetables, called "Arrangements of Trains," were posted in stations for the edification of travelers. Ridership and freight tonnage increased. Service improvements caused more use.

All acted to feed industrial growth. The need for improved railroad equipment spawned support industries to serve it.

SIGNIFICANCE

The beginning of long-distance railroads was inauspicious, but the potential for public rail transportation created a railroad mania throughout the nation. Schemes for railroad construction took the public imagination by storm. By 1833, the South Carolina Canal and Railroad Company had completed its line from Charleston to Hamburg, South Carolina. In 1836, the Erie and Kalamazoo Railroad connected Toledo, Ohio, with Adrian Township, in the Michigan Territory. Between 1840 and 1860, an additional twenty-eight thousand miles were added to the nation's railroad system. The growth of railroads allowed the absorption of immigrants both on the coast and in the interior. At the same time, westward expansion resulted in the displacement of the American Indian population there.

More efficient steam engines soon replaced the smoking teakettle contraptions of the earlier years, and as horsepower per tonnage increased, freight costs dropped dramatically. What had begun as a private enterprise by Baltimore merchants to save their city became a national institution. The railroad soon came to dominate internal transportation, but more important, the railroad created a need for corporate organization on a large scale. The phenomenal growth of American industry in the second half of the nineteenth century cannot be understood without reference to the impact of the railroads upon American economic life.

—*John G. Clark, updated by Stephen B. Dobrow*

FURTHER READING

Douglas, George H. *All Aboard! The Railroad in American Life.* New York: Paragon House, 1992. Examines how the railroad has shaped the lives of Americans and the communities in which they live.

Faith, Nicholas. *The World the Railways Made.* New York: Carroll & Graf, 1991. Examines the effects of railroads on society on a worldwide basis.

Fishlow, Albert. *American Railroads and the Transformation of the Antebellum Economy.* Cambridge, Mass.: Harvard University Press, 1965. A controversial interpretation of the effect of railroad expansion on the economy of the pre-Civil War United States.

Hornung, Clarence. *Wheels Across America.* New York: A. S. Barnes, 1959. A graphic history of vehicular transportation in North America.

Hungerford, Edward. *The Story of the Baltimore and Ohio Railroad*. 2 vols. New York: G. P. Putnam's Sons, 1928. Traces the history of the Baltimore and Ohio Railroad as an example of corporate institutional growth.

Ross, David. *The Willing Servant: A History of the Steam Engine*. Stroud, England: Tempus, 2004. A history of the steam engine and its impact on society. Ross begins his chronicle with Trevithick's invention of the first steam engine during the early nineteenth century.

Stover, John F. *American Railroads*. Chicago: University of Chicago Press, 1961. This general history of U.S. railroads places the founding of the Baltimore and Ohio Railroad in historical perspective.

SEE ALSO: Mar. 24, 1802: Trevithick Patents the High-Pressure Steam Engine; 1811-1840: Construction of the National Road; c. 1815-1830: Westward American Migration Begins; September 27, 1825: Stockton and Darlington Railway Opens; Oct. 26, 1825: Erie Canal Opens; July 21, 1836: Champlain and St. Lawrence Railroad Opens; Nov. 10, 1852: Canada's Grand Trunk Railway Is Incorporated; Mar. 2, 1853-1857: Pacific Railroad Surveys; May 10, 1869: First Transcontinental Railroad Is Completed.
RELATED ARTICLES in *Great Lives from History: The Nineteenth Century, 1801-1900:* Leland Stanford; Cornelius Vanderbilt.

January 19-27, 1830

WEBSTER AND HAYNE DEBATE SLAVERY AND WESTWARD EXPANSION

One of the most famous debates in U.S. political history, the Senate confrontation between Daniel Webster and Robert Young Hayne crystallized the issues separating the slave and free states in the context of westward expansion and intensified the struggle between states' rights and nationalism.

LOCALE: Washington, D.C.
CATEGORY: Government and politics

KEY FIGURES

Robert Young Hayne (1791-1839), South Carolina senator
Daniel Webster (1782-1852), Massachusetts senator who was known as a great orator
John C. Calhoun (1782-1850), vice president of the United States under Jackson
Samuel Augustus Foot (1780-1846), Connecticut senator
Thomas Hart Benton (1782-1858), Missouri senator

SUMMARY OF EVENT

In December, 1829, Connecticut senator Samuel A. Foot presented a resolution to the U.S. Senate suggesting the imposition of a temporary restriction on sales of public land. Under his resolution, only lands already surveyed and placed for auction were to be sold. Foot's resolution was seemingly inoffensive, but it precipitated America's most famous debate during the first month of the following year.

A liberal policy on distributing land to settlers was considered vital for the continued growth of the West. When Foot presented his resolution, Senator Thomas Hart Benton, who represented the West as a senator from Missouri, jumped to his feet to attack it as a barefaced attempt to keep emigrant laborers out of the West and force them to remain in the East as industrial wage-slaves. Eastern efforts to check the development and prosperity of the West were nothing new, according to Benton, who called Foot's resolution another sign of the hatred of the East toward the West that had so often plagued the forum of national politics. Benton concluded by saying that the hope of the West lay "in that solid phalanx of the South," which in earlier times had saved that section when in danger.

Southern political leaders were anxious to make an alliance with western politicians to secure their support for the slavery issue. The South also was interested in alliance with the West because southern politicians saw the growing population and economic clout of the North and thought that westward expansion of slaveholding societies would help redress the North-South balance. This was imperative in light of the fact that the Missouri Compromise of 1820 had unearthed fundamental tensions between the free and slave states. An alliance between southern planters and western farmers could more than offset the eastern manufacturing interests in controlling the federal government. The hope for such a combination led South Carolina's Senator Robert Y. Hayne to step forward and take up the fight.

Hayne offered southern support to the West and deftly

shifted the argument from land to state sovereignty. If the eastern proposals were put into effect, he said, the price of land would increase. The income derived from the sale of the higher-priced land would provide a "fund of cor-ruption" that would add to the power of the federal government and correspondingly reduce the independence of the states. Preaching strict constructionist and states' rights views against federal intervention, the South Carolinian declared that "the very life of our system is the independence of the states and there is no evil more to be deprecated than the consolidation of government."

In the course of his remarks, Hayne made a bitter attack upon New England and what he regarded as that section's disloyalty during the War of 1812. His remarks incensed Senator Daniel Webster from Massachusetts, who rose to defend his state and section: "Sir . . . I deny that the East has at anytime shown an illiberal policy toward the West." Fearful that he might further alienate the West, Webster ignored Benton and addressed his remarks to Hayne. Attacking the southerner's views on the consolidation of government, Webster deplored the tendency of some "habitually [to] speak of the Union in terms of indifference and even disparagement," and then challenged Hayne to meet him on the grounds of states' rights versus national power.

Thus, a discussion that had started on the subject of public-land policy shifted to a debate over the nature and meaning of the federal Union. Both nationalism and state sovereignty were debated by two of their most capable champions. Hayne was an able lawyer, a skilled debater, and a splendid orator. Tall and graceful, with cordial and unaffected manners, he was the epitome of the southern aristocrat. As the defender of the South and the advocate of that section's doctrines, Hayne stood second only to his mentor and fellow statesman, John C. Calhoun, then the vice president.

Webster was considered the country's greatest orator. Further, he was a man of commanding presence, with a large head, dark and penetrating eyes,

---

EXTRACTS FROM THE WEBSTER-HAYNE DEBATES

Daniel Webster made his reputation as an orator in a series of debates with Robert Hayne over the questions of federal public lands, slavery, the southern states, and other topics. Hayne, in his second speech to the Senate, excerpted here, speaks of Webster's earlier denunciation of slavery in the South.

Was the significant hint of the weakness of slaveholding states, when contrasted with the superior strength of free states, like the glare of the weapon half drawn from its scabbard,— intended to enforce the lessons of prudence and of patriotism, which the gentleman [Webster] had resolved, out of his abundant generosity, gratuitously to bestow upon us? Mr. President [of the Senate], the impression which has gone abroad of the weakness of the south, as connected with the slave question, exposes us to such constant attacks, has done us so much injury, and is calculated to produce such infinite mischiefs, that I embrace the occasion presented by the remarks of the gentleman of Massachusetts, to declare that we are ready to meet the question promptly and fearlessly. It is one from which we are not disposed to shrink, in whatever form or under whatever circumstances it may be pressed upon us.

We are ready to make up the issue with the gentleman, as to the influence of slavery on individual or national character on the prosperity and greatness, either of the United States or of particular states.

The following excerpt is part of Daniel Webster's reply to Hayne.

I spoke, Sir, of the Ordinance of 1787, which prohibits slavery, in all future times, northwest of the Ohio, as a measure of great wisdom and foresight, and one which had been attended with highly beneficial and permanent consequences. I supposed that, on this point, no two gentlemen in the Senate could entertain different opinions. But the simple expression of this sentiment has led the gentleman [Hayne], not only into a labored defence of slavery, in the abstract, and on principle, but also into a warm accusation against me, as having attacked the system of domestic slavery now existing in the Southern States. For all this, there was not the slightest foundation, in any thing said or intimated by me. I did not utter a single word which any ingenuity could torture into an attack on the slavery of the South. I said, only, that it was highly wise and useful, in legislating for the Northwestern country while it was yet a wilderness, to prohibit the introduction of slaves; and I added, that I presumed there was no reflecting and intelligent person, in the neighboring State of Kentucky, who would doubt that, if the same prohibition had been extended, at the same early period, over that commonwealth, her strength and population would, at this day, have been far greater than they are. If these opinions be thought doubtful, they are nevertheless, I trust, neither extraordinary nor disrespectful. They attack nobody and menace nobody. And yet, Sir, the gentleman's optics have discovered, even in the mere expression of this sentiment, what he calls the very spirit of the Missouri question! He represents me as making an onset on the whole South, and manifesting a spirit which would interfere with, and disturb, their domestic condition.

and a deep and resonant voice. It has been said that no man could be as great as Daniel Webster looked. Indeed, his countenance was so overpowering and his oratorical style so effective that even trivial and commonplace statements sounded profound when presented by the "god-like Daniel." Webster brought to his speeches not only a political viewpoint, but a philosophical and conceptual weight that impressed his listeners.

During an age when political debates were loved by the American people, this battle between two brilliant speakers attracted wide attention. The Senate chamber, a small semicircular room in which only forty-eight members sat, was crowded to capacity and the galleries were packed. At one time, so many congressmen came to listen that the House of Representatives could not conduct its own business.

Hayne answered Webster with a slashing defense of states' rights as it had been outlined by Calhoun. He spoke with logic and eloquence as Calhoun looked down from the Speaker's chair, smiling and occasionally nodding his approval. Hayne's defense was based upon the Virginia and Kentucky Resolves of 1798, and he asserted that each state, while assenting to the federal Constitution, reserved the right to interpret that document within its own borders; that is, the people of any state, if they believed themselves offended, could declare an act of the federal government null and void. Otherwise, Hayne continued, the federal government would have the capacity to "proscribe the limits of its own authority," and this made government without any restriction of its powers. The states and the people would be entirely at the mercy of the federal government.

In what has been called the greatest speech ever made in the Senate, Webster upheld the doctrine of nationalism. A state could not, he said, annul an act of Congress except "upon the ground of revolution." He believed that the Constitution, as the supreme law of the land, was created by the people, not the states. The primary question, Webster maintained, was not the right of revolution against oppression, but that of determining whose prerogative it was to decide on the constitutionality of the laws. For him there was only one answer: The Constitution was the nation's highest law, and the ultimate appeal lay with the Supreme Court. He ended his endeavor with this peroration:

Daniel Webster replying to Robert Young Hayne during their debate on the Senate floor. (C. A. Nichols & Company)

When my eyes shall be turned to behold for the last time the sun in heaven, may I not see him shining on the broken and dishonored fragments of a once glorious Union; on states dissevered, discordant, belligerent; on a land rent with civil feuds, or drenched, it may be, in fraternal blood! Let their last feeble and lingering glance rather behold the glorious ensign of the republic, known and honored throughout the earth, still full high advanced, its arms and trophies streaming in their original lustre, not a strip erased or polluted, nor a single star obscured, bearing for its motto, no such miserable interrogatory as "What is it all worth?" nor those words of delusion and folly, "Liberty first and Union afterwards": but everywhere . . . that other sentiment, dear to every true American heart, —Liberty and Union, now and forever, one and inseparable!

SIGNIFICANCE

The *Philadelphia Gazette* summed up the result of the debate: "The opposition party generally contend that Mr.

Webster overthrew Mr. Hayne; while, on the other hand, the result is triumphantly hailed by the friends of the administration as a decisive victory over the eastern giant." It would be a mistake to see the Webster-Hayne debate solely as part of the buildup to the Civil War (1861-1865). This assumption would be purely the product of historical hindsight. Contemporary observers might well have seen the debate as being between Jacksonian Democrats, with their southern and western base, and the emerging Whig Party, which championed national unity above all. Regardless of who may have won, the debate clarified the issues and intensified the struggle between states' rights and nationalism. It furnished both North and South with powerful arguments and thus accentuated the ardor with which each defended its cause.

—*John H. DeBerry, updated by Nicholas Birns*

FURTHER READING

Baxter, Maurice G. *One and Inseparable: Daniel Webster and the Union.* Cambridge, Mass.: Harvard University Press, 1984. Thoughtful exposition of Webster's fundamental philosophy of national unity.

Chambers, William Nisbet. *Old Bullion Benton, Senator from the New West: Thomas Hart Benton, 1782-1858.* New York: Russell & Russell, 1970. Examines Benton's role in the debate and the general question of the West's role in the slavery and states' rights debates.

Current, Richard Nelson. *Daniel Webster and the Rise of National Conservatism.* Boston: Little, Brown, 1955. Places Webster in the context of the rise of the Whig Party and its nationalist ideology.

Petersen, Merrill D. *The Great Triumvirate: Webster, Clay, and Calhoun.* New York: Oxford University Press, 1987. Examines Webster's relations with his legislative colleagues and his pivotal role in the debates of the United States about itself; highly recommended.

Smith, Craig R. *Daniel Webster and the Oratory of Civil Religion.* Columbia: University of Missouri Press, 2005. Biography of Daniel Webster that closely examines his famous oratory ability.

Smith, Page. *The Nation Comes of Age: A People's History of the Ante-bellum Years.* New York: McGraw-Hill, 1981. Entertaining general history of the period. Asserts the Webster-Hayne debates presaged the Civil War.

SEE ALSO: c. 1815-1830: Westward American Migration Begins; Mar. 3, 1820: Missouri Compromise; c. 1830-1865: Southerners Advance Proslavery Arguments; Nov. 24, 1832-Jan. 21, 1833: Nullification Controversy; Apr. 14, 1834: Clay Begins American Whig Party.

RELATED ARTICLES in *Great Lives from History: The Nineteenth Century, 1801-1900:* Thomas Hart Benton; John C. Calhoun; Henry Clay; Daniel Webster.

March 3, 1830
HUGO'S *HERNANI* INCITES RIOTING

The opening run of Victor Hugo's play Hernani *was accompanied by rioting and by a major quarrel known as the "battle of* Hernani*" between adherents of Romanticism and supporters of classicism.* Hernani *called for the liberation of theater from the constraints of neoclassical drama. The dispute also had political implications, as the two groups represented opponents and supporters, respectively, of the conservative Restoration Monarchy in France.*

LOCALE: Paris, France
CATEGORIES: Theater; literature

KEY FIGURES
Victor Hugo (1802-1885), French playwright
Stendhal (1783-1842), French writer
Théophile Gautier (1811-1872), French Romantic poet
Madame de Staël (1766-1817), French writer
François-René de Chateaubriand (1768-1848), French writer

SUMMARY OF EVENT
The so-called "battle of *Hernani*" was probably the most visible manifestation of a generational struggle between proponents of the established norms of classicism and advocates of the fresh and dynamic Romanticism. In many ways, this conflict constituted a nineteenth century version of the late seventeenth century literary quarrel (*querelle des Anciens et des Modernes*) between the ancients and the moderns. To show what was at stake in this newest quarrel, one has to take a brief look at what led to the quarrels and the rioting at the Comédie Française in 1830.

At the beginning of the nineteenth century, in an unstable social, cultural, and political context that was still attempting to cope with the loss of a century-old order known as the ancien régime, the works of two major writers, both opposed to the current imperial system of government, proved groundbreaking for the birth of French Romanticism: François-René de Chateaubriand's *Le Génie du Christianisme* (1799, 1800, 1802; *The Genius of Christianity*, 1802) and *René* (1802; English translation, 1813), as well as Madame de Staël's *De la littérature considérée dans ses rapports avec les institutions sociales* (1800; *A Treatise on Ancient and Modern Literature*, 1803) and *D'Allemagne* (1813; *Germany*, 1813).

Chateaubriand had insisted on conservative religious values paired with the introduction of a new sensibility into literature through themes such as melancholy, or the central role of dreams and passions. Staël had been strongly influenced by a pan-European Romanticist movement that was reflected in authors such as Johann Wolfgang von Goethe, Friedrich Schiller, and Lord Byron; hence the attempt to liberate art and literature from the restrictive catalog of the famous neoclassical rules, a catalog that still dominated the cultural landscape in France, particularly in the field of the drama, the noblest of all genres.

The young generation of French writers (the Jeunes-France) happily embraced a concept that proclaimed the collapse of the old literary order as a direct and inevitable consequence of the collapse of the old political order: "A new kind of art for a new nation," as Hugo put it so eloquently in his preface to *Hernani* on March 9, 1830.

An essential premise for the battle of *Hernani* was the consolidation of two opposing tendencies among the young Romantics. Initially, Hugo belonged to a rather conservative group known as the Cénacle that had met at the Arsénal library around 1824 and published the monthly magazine *La Muse française*. Other prominent members included Alfred de Musset, Alfred de Vigny, Alphonse de Lamartine, Gérard de Nerval, Alexandre Dumas, *père*, and Honoré de Balzac. More liberal ideas were defended by the likes of Stendhal, Prosper Mérimée, and Charles-Augustin Sainte-Beuve in their journal *Le Globe*.

Inspired by the first Romantic manifesto, Stendhal's *Racine et Shakespeare* (part 1, 1823; part 2, 1825; *Racine and Shakespeare*, 1962), Hugo's stance, as well as that of Chateaubriand, shifted more and more toward the liberal position of *Le Globe* and thus helped reconcile the two movements. One famous line in the preface to *Hernani*

Victor Hugo. (Library of Congress)

illustrated this new attitude: "Romanticism . . . is nothing else but liberalism in literature." This shift was completed in 1827, as Hugo wrote the prototype of the Romantic drama, the virtually "unstageable" *Cromwell:* Some 6,400 stanzas, 62 characters, and various stage settings made it impossible to produce. Its preface, however, actually written after the play, was to become the major theory of Romanticism, a theory that *Hernani* was to illustrate three years later.

Hugo's major claim was basically to value aesthetics and realism, as well as complete artistic and creative freedom over the restrictive rules of neoclassicism. In concrete terms, he called for an abandonment of the three unities (time, place, and action) as well as the *bienséance*, a mixture of linguistic registers (in particular of lyrical and everyday language) as well as of styles, especially of the sublime and the grotesque, and a loosening of the rules of versification. Such changes were meant to create a theater that appealed to a broader segment of the population; the modern theater adapted to its age what the preface to *Hernani* called for explicitly.

The composition of *Hernani* was directly related to Hugo's fury about the banning of his previous play, *Marion De Lorme*, on August 13, 1829. The playwright

1830's

455

would follow this with a completed *Hernani*, finished in less than one month. On October 5 the play was enthusiastically received by the Comédie Française actors, who even renounced on their customary vote and accepted the play by acclamation. As was to be expected, censors objected to certain lines but refrained from banning *Hernani*. The censors did, however, play a crucial role in the upcoming "battle," as one of them leaked passages from the play to Hugo's anti-Romanticist opponents.

Hugo seemed not only aware of this plot but also seemed deliberately to provoke the proponents of the old order by turning the play into a showcase for his Romantic doctrine. The enjambment that breaks the Alexandrine in the two opening verses, a clear breach of neoclassical rules, set the tone from the very beginning. The *bienséance* was also disregarded in the opening scene as the king of Spain was ridiculed by being obliged to hide in a closet to escape detection on his visit to Dona Sol, the play's love interest. In general, the action, including violence and death, was actually put on stage and not merely reported by eyewitnesses, as had been the classical norm. This innovation infringed on the supremacy of language; the latter had to share the spotlight with the visual spectacle. Moreover, the unities of time and place were utterly disregarded.

The playwright was well prepared for the expected negative reaction at the opening performance: He bought a significant number of tickets for the first three performances to ensure that his supporters outnumbered his opponents. Led by Théophile Gautier, who had been clad in his revolutionary red vest, the Jeunes-France carried the day in the shouting matches staged during each of those three performances. Rioting did not erupt until the fourth of the initial thirty-nine shows on March 3, the run being interrupted by the July Revolution, as the actors deemed it more prudent to not stage the play.

SIGNIFICANCE

From a commercial point of view, *Hernani* was a big success and regularly sold out a Comédie Française that usually played to empty seats during that time period in its history. The sellouts continued even after the performances of *Hernani* resumed in 1836, although the rioting had ended. Italian composer Giuseppe Verdi made the play into an opera called *Ernani* (1844).

Hernani's literary impact was more complex, however. The Romantic drama did not replace its neoclassical predecessor as the dominant genre, as was underlined by the failure of Hugo's last play, *Les Burgraves* (1843). Hugo's program, which could be summarized as "toler-

ance and liberty" in art as well as in politics, a slogan from the preface to *Hernani*, was more easily fulfilled in a former minor genre that, thanks to its creative energy and artistic freedom, asserted itself as the dominant genre during the nineteenth century: the novel, which was best suited to French society after the ancien régime. So Hugo's vision had come true and his attack of neoclassical drama had indeed resulted in neoclassicism's replacement, albeit by a more "prosaic" genre in which Hugo distinguished himself much more than in the field of Romantic theater.

—*Bernd Renner*

FURTHER READING

Barricelli, Jean-Pierre. "Percept and Concept: From Hugo's *Hernani* to Verdi's *Ernani*." In *Le Rayonnement international de Victor Hugo*, edited by Francis Claudon. Vol. 1. New York: Peter Lang, 1989. A study of the relationship between Hugo's play and Verdi's opera.

Carlson, Marvin. "*Hernani*'s Revolt from the Tradition of French Stage Composition." *Theater Survey: The American Journal of Theater History* 13, no. 1 (1972): 1-27. Paints a general picture of *Hernani*'s impact, with particular emphasis on the technical aspects involved in staging a play at the time.

Halsall, Albert. *Victor Hugo and the Romantic Drama.* Toronto: University of Toronto Press, 1998. The author puts Hugo's play in the larger context of his theatrical production and focuses on the aesthetic revolt conveyed through *Hernani*.

Porter, Laurence. *Victor Hugo.* New York: Twayne, 1999. Concise, general study of Hugo. Devotes a chapter to his work in theater. Conclusion explores Hugo's work in music and his reception in popular culture.

SEE ALSO: Feb. 20, 1816: Rossini's *The Barber of Seville* Debuts; Feb. 6, 1843: First Minstrel Shows; 1850's-1880's: Rise of Burlesque and Vaudeville; Mar. 3, 1875: Bizet's *Carmen* Premieres in Paris; Aug. 13-17, 1876: First Performance of Wagner's Ring Cycle; 1879: *A Doll's House* Introduces Modern Realistic Drama; Oct. 22, 1883: Metropolitan Opera House Opens in New York.

RELATED ARTICLES in *Great Lives from History: The Nineteenth Century, 1801-1900:* Honoré de Balzac; Sarah Bernhardt; François-René de Chateaubriand; Gaetano Donizetti; Alexandre Dumas, *père*; Victor Hugo; Stendhal; Giuseppe Verdi.

April 6, 1830
SMITH FOUNDS THE MORMON CHURCH

One of many American religious leaders who sprang up during the Second Great Awakening, Joseph Smith offered something unique: another testament of Christ in an ancient history written on golden plates that he claimed to find and translate. His Book of Mormon became the basis of what is generally regarded as the first entirely new religion founded in the United States.

ALSO KNOWN AS: Church of Jesus Christ of Latter-day Saints

LOCALE: Fayette, New York

CATEGORIES: Religion and theology; organizations and institutions

KEY FIGURES

Joseph Smith (1805-1844), founder and first president of the Church of Jesus Christ of Latter-day Saints

Oliver Cowdery (1806-1850), Smith's scribe in the translation of the Book of Mormon

Sidney Rigdon (1793-1876), Campbellite preacher who converted to Mormonism and became an important leader

Hyrum Smith (1800-1844), older brother of Smith who replaced Cowdery as associate president of the church

Brigham Young (1801-1877), Vermont farmer who succeeded Smith as president of the church

SUMMARY OF EVENT

The Erie canal, begun in 1817, opened western New York to more settlement. Seeking a better life, people moved to the frontier faster than organized churches could follow, although many would have welcomed the comfort, assurance, and constancy promised by religion. To meet this need, preachers traveled the frontier holding revivals and camp meetings with such a great effect that the period from the 1790's to the 1830's became known as the Second Great Awakening. In western New York the flames of religious excitement swept the region from the Adirondacks to Lake Erie so many times that the region became known as the Burned-Over District.

Dissatisfied with most of the organized religions, "seekers" sought a return to what they regarded as the Primitive Gospel that had been taught in the New Testament. The young New Yorker Joseph Smith, both his grandfathers, and both his parents were seekers. Smith later claimed that when he had been a teenager, he saw a vision in which God the Father and his son, Jesus Christ, appeared before him. Many people in New York's Burned-Over District claimed to have had similar visions, but Smith went further. He also claimed that God told him that all earthly churches had gone astray, but that if he were faithful, he would be instrumental in restoring the true church.

Smith also claimed that in preparation for that great task, an angel visited him and showed him where gold plates were buried in a nearby hill. Supposedly these plates contained the history of an ancient Middle Eastern people who had come to the Western Hemisphere, along with the fullness of Christ's gospel. Through the "gift and power of God," Smith translated the plates and published them as the Book of Mormon, after the name of the ancient prophet who wrote most of the history. Smith's followers regard the Book of Mormon as a second witness for Christ, alongside the Bible.

The laws of the state of New York required a minimum of six people to begin a church. On April 6, 1830, about fifty-five people met in the home of Peter Whitmer, Sr., in Fayette, New York. The six who were the first official members were Joseph Smith Jr.; Oliver Cowdery, who had transcribed Smith's dictation of the Book of Mormon; Joseph's brother Hyrum Smith; Peter Whitmer, Jr.; Samuel H. Smith; and David Whitmer. Smith and Cowdery then ordained each other as the first and second elders of the new church. The church was called Church of Christ until 1838, when its name was lengthened to Church of Jesus Christ of Latter-day Saints. From that time, the church's members called themselves Saints, although they would become better known to outsiders as "Mormons."

Biographer Robert V. Remini describes Smith as "a man of compelling charisma, charm, and persuasiveness, a man absolutely convinced that his religious authority came directly from God." Many of his relatives, friends, and neighbors joined his new church. He also sent out missionaries to preach in surrounding areas. One of Smith's most important converts was Sidney Rigdon, a fiery and prominent Campbellite preacher who had congregations in Kirtland and Mentor, Ohio. Rigdon and many of his parishioners joined the new church, and Rigdon eventually became a close counselor to Smith. Within its first year, the new church had about five hundred members in and around Fayette, New York, and another one hundred members around Kirtland, Ohio.

In New York, some of Smith's neighbors took him to

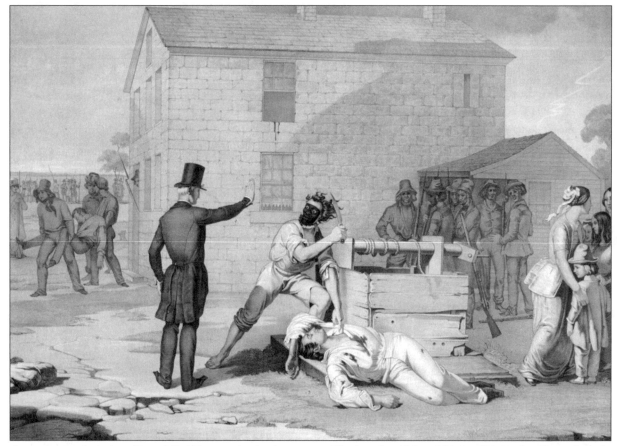

Contemporary depiction of Joseph Smith's assassination by an angry Illinois mob, which took him and his brother Hyrum from the Carthage jail in which they were held after Smith destroyed the press of a Nauvoo newspaper whose critical reporting he would not tolerate. (Library of Congress)

court, attempting to prove that he was a fraud who had deceived the Latter-day Saints. After that effort failed, Smith's enemies began to harass his church's members, interrupting their meetings and threatening Smith and others with bodily harm. In the spring of 1831, Smith led his family and hundreds of his followers to Kirtland, Ohio, where he hoped they would be safer.

Hundreds of Smith's followers were willing to give up their homes and follow him for many reasons, including their conviction that to do so was God's will, for they believed Smith to be God's prophet. They also believed they were separating themselves from the wicked in preparation for Christ's return and millennial reign. Indeed, Latter-day Saints regarded the persecution that they suffered as a sign that they were correct in their beliefs, for they believed that persecution was the heritage of the faithful. Many of Smith's followers were of hardy pioneer stock and had the skills, industry, and tempera-

ment that enabled them to leave their old homes, trek through the wilderness, and establish new communities.

At first, the new church prospered in Kirtland, where its members built their first temple. After a few years, however, internal strife split the church, and Smith again moved, this time leading his followers to a region near Independence, Missouri, where Smith hoped to establish the permanent headquarters of the church. Other church members had been developing a community there since the early 1830's, but the growing influx of Mormons worried their neighbors, who feared that Mormons would soon control local political offices, stir up the Indians against them, and interfere with their slaves. After seeing their crops and homes burned, some Mormons retaliated in kind, giving Missouri's governor an excuse to have the militia drive the Mormons from the state.

Citizens of Illinois regarded the mistreatment of Mormons in Missouri as barbaric and welcomed them to their own state, hoping that they would help develop their economy. In 1839, thousands of Mormons fled to Illinois, where they founded the city of Nauvoo along the Mississippi River. There they built farms, houses, shops, brick-making kilns, public buildings, and a beautiful temple on a hill overlooking the river. Meanwhile, the church sent missionaries to England, where they made thousands of converts, most of whom emigrated to the United States to join their fellow church members. By 1842, Nauvoo was the tenth largest city in the United States. Illinois's legislature granted Nauvoo a generous charter that incorporated the city and established a municipal court system, a university, and a militia called the Nauvoo Legion.

SIGNIFICANCE

As the power of Mormons grew, their non-Mormon neighbors increasingly worried that they would lose their own political power. They regarded Mormons as different and therefore a people to be feared—a concern that grew along with rumors that Mormon men practiced polygamy. Displeased with the candidates for president of the United States in 1844, Smith decided to run for the presidency himself and to put the Mormon persecutions before the nation. Some enemies feared that Smith might win by some fluke, and they decided that Smith and the Mormons had to be stopped while that was still possible.

On June 27, 1844, fourteen years after Smith organized his church, he and his brother Hyrum were murdered by an Illinois mob. By that time, the church claimed more than 35,000 members. With the death of Smith, the church's enemies thought the church would fall apart. Instead, most of the Mormons followed their new leader, Brigham Young, west to the territory that would became Utah. Unmolested by its enemies, the church thrived in Utah and maintained one of the most aggressive missionary programs of any church. By the early twenty-first century, the church claimed more than twelve million members throughout the world. Although the church's success testifies to the work and perseverance of the Mormons themselves, it also demonstrates the growing acceptance of religious and cultural diversity in the United States.

—*Charles W. Rogers*

FURTHER READING

Arrington, Leonard J., and Davis Bitton. *The Mormon Experience*. 2d ed. Chicago: University of Illinois Press, 1992. Scholarly account of the church from its founding to the late twentieth century by two nationally recognized Mormon historians.

Bringhurst, Newell G., ed. *Reconsidering No Man Knows My History: Fawn M. Brodie and Joseph Smith in Retrospect*. Logan, Utah: Utah State University Press, 1996. Collection of essays by both Mormons and non-Mormons who draw on new research to evaluate Brodie's biography of Smith.

Brodie, Fawn M. *No Man Knows My History: The Life of Joseph Smith, the Mormon Prophet*. New York: Alfred A. Knopf, 1946. Controversial study of Smith by a distinguished biographer who was a former Mormon herself. Although highly regarded by scholars, the biography rankles Mormons because of Brodie's dismissal of Smith as a fraud who wrote the Book of Mormon in the hope of profiting from it and became a church leader almost by accident. Brodie's 1971 revision of this book adds a psychoanalytic interpretation of Smith's actions that suggests he may not have been an impostor who used fantasy to resolve his own identity conflict.

Bushman, Richard Lyman. *Joseph Smith: Rough Stone Rolling*. New York: A. A. Knopf, 2005. Sympathetic biography of Smith by a prominent Mormon historian who credits the church's survival to the strong organizational structure that Smith gave to it.

Dunn, Scott C. "Spirit Writing, Another Look at the Book of Mormon." *Sunstone* 10, no. 5 (June, 1985): 16-26. Dunn examines some similarities between the dictation of the Book of Mormon and "spirit" or "automatic" writing.

Remini, Robert V. *Joseph Smith*. New York: Viking/Penguin, 2002. Brief, well-written, and well-researched account of Smith's life by a nationally acclaimed historian of the Jacksonian era.

SEE ALSO: May 8, 1816: American Bible Society Is Founded; 1820's-1850's: Social Reform Movement; 1835: Finney Lectures on "Revivals of Religion"; Feb. 4, 1846: Mormons Begin Migration to Utah; 1870-1871: Watch Tower Bible and Tract Society Is Founded; Oct. 30, 1875: Eddy Establishes the Christian Science Movement.

RELATED ARTICLES in *Great Lives from History: The Nineteenth Century, 1801-1900:* Sir Richard Francis Burton; Alexander Campbell; Joseph Smith; Brigham Young.

1830's

May 28, 1830
CONGRESS PASSES INDIAN REMOVAL ACT

This federal legislation began the forced resettlement of sixty thousand eastern Native Americans to lands west of the Mississippi River—a traumatic blow to Indian societies that caused untold suffering and changed the cultural map of Native America.

LOCALE: Southeastern United States; Indian Territory
CATEGORIES: Expansion and land acquisition; laws, acts, and legal history; indigenous people's rights

KEY FIGURES
Andrew Jackson (1767-1845), seventh U.S. president, 1829-1837
John Marshall (1755-1835), chief justice of the United States, 1801-1835
Major Ridge (c. 1771-1839), Cherokee leader who reluctantly signed the removal treaty
John Ridge (c. 1803-1839), son of Major Ridge who opposed removal
Elias Boudinot (Buck Watie; c. 1803-1839), nephew of Major Ridge and editor of the *Cherokee Phoenix*
John Ross (1790-1866), elected principal chief of the Cherokees
Samuel A. Worcester (1798-1859), missionary to the Cherokees

SUMMARY OF EVENT
Members of the so-called Five Civilized Tribes—Choctaw, Chickasaw, Cherokee, Seminole, and Creek—established independent republics with successful governments. Adapting to the culture of their white neighbors, they became farmers, miners, and cattle ranchers. Some had plantations and even owned slaves. They built schools and churches, wrote constitutions, and established independent governments. However, despite their achievements, they learned a bitter lesson: Whites wanted their land, not their assimilation into Euro-American society.

As a local militia leader and politician, Andrew Jackson negotiated the acquisition of fifty million acres of Indian land in Georgia, Alabama, Tennessee, and Mississippi even before he became president of the United States. By the time he became president in 1829, the Cherokees had lost their land outside Georgia, and their neighbors had grown increasingly jealous of Cherokee success. For generations, Cherokees had provided a textbook picture of Jefferson's ideal nation of farmers. For example, Sequoyah, a young man of Cherokee and white

blood, invented a phonetic alphabet, or syllabary, that enabled almost every member of his nation to become literate within a few months. To ensure that they held their remaining land, Cherokees made the sale of any additional land to whites a capital offense.

Violent conflicts between whites and Indians became so common that many friends and enemies alike advocated removal of the Cherokees to the west to protect Cherokees from white citizens who routinely attacked them. In 1817, some Cherokees exchanged land in North Carolina for space in Arkansas. Within two years, six thousand had moved voluntarily. However, their move only worsened Cherokee problems. By 1821, the Cherokees were at war with the Osages who had been in Arkansas Territory already, and both groups fought whites who continued to move onto their land.

These early voluntary removals proved so disastrous that the Cherokees and Choctaws remaining in Georgia vowed to stay on their native land. Although President James Monroe proposed removal again in 1825, neither Monroe nor his successor, John Quincy Adams, could get a removal measure through Congress. Only the enthusiasm of President Jackson got removal approved on a close vote in 1830. In 1829, Jackson admitted that the five Indian republics had made "progress in the arts of civilized life," but he said American Indians occupied land that whites could use. Beyond the Mississippi River lay enough land for Native Americans and their descendants to inhabit without interference "as long as grass grows or water runs in peace and plenty."

Meanwhile, the Georgia state legislature extended its power over the Cherokee nation and stripped Native Americans of civil rights. These laws forbade anyone with American Indian blood to testify in court against a white man, annulled contracts between Native Americans and whites, and required oaths of allegiance to Georgia from white people living among American Indians. The laws also prevented Native Americans from holding meetings or digging for gold on their own land.

Instead of going to war, the Cherokees hired two prominent Washington lawyers and went to the U.S. Supreme Court with a series of legal actions that became known as the Cherokee cases. They lost their first case, challenging Georgia for hanging a Cherokee man convicted under Cherokee law. The second case, *Worcester v. Georgia* (1832) challenged the Georgia loyalty oath that was designed to remove teachers, missionaries, and other whites from the reservation. The Reverend Samuel A. Worcester and other missionaries among Cherokees refused to sign the loyalty oath, despite public humiliation, abuse, and imprisonment.

Chief Justice John Marshall declared Georgia's re-

pressive laws unconstitutional. American Indian nations, Marshall said, were "domestic dependent nations" that were entitled to have independent political communities without state restrictions. President Jackson, who had built his reputation by fighting Indians in the South, sug-

TRIBAL-LANDS IN INDIAN TERRITORY IN 1836

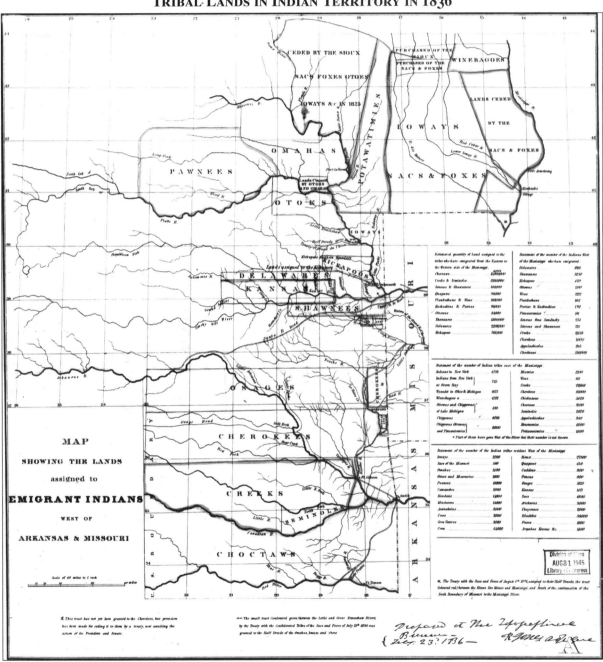

ANDREW JACKSON ON INDIAN REMOVAL

In his last state of the union address, on December 5, 1836, President Andrew Jackson touched on the removal of Native Americans to Indian Territory—a policy that he had strongly advocated.

. . . The national policy, founded alike in interest and in humanity, so long and so steadily pursued by this Government for the removal of the Indian tribes originally settled on this side of the Mississippi to the W[est] of that river, may be said to have been consummated by the conclusion of the late treaty with the Cherokees. The measures taken in the execution of that treaty and in relation to our Indian affairs generally will fully appear by referring to the accompanying papers. Without dwelling on the numerous and important topics embraced in them, I again invite your attention to the importance of providing a well-digested and comprehensive system for the protection, supervision, and improvement of the various tribes now planted in the Indian country.

The suggestions submitted by the Commissioner of Indian Affairs, and enforced by the Secretary, on this subject, and also in regard to the establishment of additional military posts in the Indian country, are entitled to your profound consideration. Both measures are necessary, for the double purpose of protecting the Indians from intestine war, and in other respects complying with our engagements with them, and of securing our western frontier against incursions which otherwise will assuredly be made on it. The best hopes of humanity in regard to the aboriginal race, the welfare of our rapidly extending settlements, and the honor of the United States are all deeply involved in the relations existing between this Government and the emigrating tribes. I trust, therefore, that the various matters submitted in the accompanying documents in respect to those relations will receive your early and mature deliberation, and that it may issue in the adoption of legislative measures adapted to the circumstances and duties of the present crisis. . . .

gested that Georgia could ignore the Court's decision, as he, not the Supreme Court, controlled the army.

Congress also took up Georgia's cause by passing the Indian Removal Act on May 28, 1830. It began a process of exchanging Indian lands in the twenty-four existing states for new lands west of the Mississippi River. In 1834, Congress established Indian Territory—which is now a major part of Oklahoma—as a permanent reservation. The Cherokee leader Major Ridge and his family, who had been among the strongest opponents of removal, and Cherokee lobbyists, including John Ridge, celebrated their Supreme Court victory in *Worcester*. However, they had incorrectly thought Whigs in Congress would prevail against Jackson's removal policy.

The federal removal law did not specify that Native Americans could be forced to move, but the Ridge family and the Cherokee newspaper editor Elias Boudinot began to see the move as necessary to protect Cherokees from increasing violence. Principal Chief John Ross, however, still resisted removal. Believing that removal was in their nation's best interest, the Ridge family signed a removal treaty without approval of the tribal council.

Many Indians resisted removal from their ancient homelands. The Alabama Creeks were forcibly removed, some of them in chains. Choctaws were forced out of Mississippi in winter and given no opportunity to carry provisions against the cold. Some were tricked into getting drunk and signing away their possessions. Others signed away their lands, believing the promises of government officials. Forced marches of Creeks, Choctaws, and Cherokees brought sickness, starvation, and death to thousands of people during the 1830's.

The Cherokees faced a special horror. Georgia's repressive laws had created a climate of lawlessness. Whites could steal land, and Cherokees could not testify in court against them. In one notorious case, two white men dined in the home of a family whose father was part Cherokee. In the evening, the parents left temporarily and the guests forced the children and their nurse from the home and set it on fire, destroying the house and all of its contents. The men were arrested, but a judge dismissed the case because all the witnesses were part Cherokee. Only pure-blooded whites were allowed to testify in court.

Finally, Jackson's successor, President Martin Van Buren, ordered General Winfield Scott, with about seven thousand U.S. soldiers and state militia, to begin the forced removal on May 26, 1838. Soldiers quietly surrounded each house to surprise its occupants, according to James Mooney, a researcher who interviewed the participants years later. Under Scott's orders, the troops built stockades to hold people while being prepared for the removal. "From these," Mooney wrote,

squads of troops were sent to search out with rifle and bayonet every small cabin hidden away in the coves or by the sides of mountain streams, to seize and bring in as prisoners all the occupants, however or wherever they might be found. Families at dinner were startled by the sudden gleam of bayonets in the doorway and rose up to be driven with blows and oaths along the weary miles of trail that led to the stockade.

Men were taken from their fields, children from their play. "In many cases, on turning for one last look as they crossed the ridge, they saw their homes in flames." Some scavengers stole livestock and other valuables, even before the owners were out of sight of their homes. "Systematic hunts were made by the same men for Indian graves, to rob them of the silver pendants and other valuables deposited with the dead." Some sympathetic soldiers allowed one family to feed their chickens one last time, and another to pray quietly in their own language before leaving their home.

Within a week, the troops had rounded up more than seventeen thousand Cherokees and herded them into concentration camps. In June, the first group of about one thousand began the eight-hundred-mile journey. Steamboats took them on the first leg down the Tennessee River. The oppressive heat and cramped conditions on the boats fostered disease and caused many deaths. Then the Cherokees walked the last leg of the trip to beyond the western border of Arkansas. Because of the heat, Cherokee leader John Ross persuaded General Scott to delay the largest removal until fall. Thus, the largest procession—about thirteen thousand people—started on the long overland march in October, 1838. Most walked or rode horses; others drove 645 wagons.

Dozens of people died of disease, starvation, or exposure on each day of the journey. Before it was over, more than four thousand Cherokees died on the journey that the survivors named the Trail of Tears. The procession reached the Mississippi River opposite Cape Girardeau, Missouri, in the middle of winter. Most had only a single blanket to protect themselves from the winter winds as they waited for the river ice to clear. In March, 1839, they reached their destination in Indian Territory. Many were buried along the road, including Chief John Ross's wife, Quatie Ross, who died after giving up her blanket to a sick child in a sleet- and snowstorm. Her death left Ross to grieve both his wife and his nation.

In his last message to Congress, President Jackson said he had settled the Native American problem to everyone's satisfaction and saved the race from extinction by placing them "beyond the reach of injury or oppression." Native Americans would now share in "the blessings of civilization" and "the General Government will hereafter watch over them and protect them." Between

1778 and 1871, 370 treaties stipulated land cessions to whites. Jackson ridiculed the idea of making treaties with Native Americans and called the idea of treating American Indians as separate nations an absurd farce.

By the end of June, 1838, Georgians could boast that no Cherokees remained on their soil, except in the stockade. Sixty thousand members of the five Indian republics had been removed to beyond the Mississippi River. In the process, as many as fifteen thousand men, women, and children died of starvation and disease. The Choctaws had moved in 1832; the Chickasaws in 1832-1834, the Seminoles in 1836, and the Creeks in 1836-1840. In June, 1839, members of the Ross faction, in revenge for the law that John Ridge signed into effect, murdered John Ridge, Major Ridge, and Elias Boudinot for their signing a removal treaty selling Cherokee land.

SIGNIFICANCE

Although nineteenth century controversies surrounding removal focused on the Five Civilized Tribes, the small but numerous bands of Indians living in the north were also subject to removal. With the exception of some who migrated to Canada, their fates differed little materially from that of the southern tribes, and many also were forced to relocate several times before reaching their final destinations.

The impact of removal on Indian culture was demoralization and destruction. Shifts in geographical locations often eroded their culture and rendered subsistence patterns obsolete. In addition, Indians often faced hostile welcomes from western tribes. Ultimately, treaties were broken by the U.S. government as the whites' inexorable population growth and westward movement stimulated their interest in even the most marginal Indian lands.

—*William E. Huntzicker, updated by the editors*

FURTHER READING

Decker, Peter R. *"The Utes Must Go!": American Expansion and the Removal of a People*. Golden, Colo.: Fulcrum, 2004. Study of three centuries in the history of the Utes, with particular attention to the federal government policies forcing their removal from Colorado, New Mexico, and Wyoming.

Foreman, Grant. *Indian Removal: The Emigration of the Five Civilized Tribes of Indians*. 2d ed. Norman: University of Oklahoma Press, 1953. The classic and most comprehensive history of removal.

Green, Michael D. *The Politics of Indian Removal: Creek Government in Crisis*. Lincoln: University of Nebraska Press, 1982. Well-researched history of

1830's

removal as it affected the Creek nation.

Guttmann, Allen. *States' Rights and Indian Removal: "The Cherokee Nation v. the State of Georgia."* Boston: D. C. Heath, 1965. Brief documentary history of the Cherokees' legal struggle to keep their land.

Jahoda, Gloria. *The Trail of Tears*. New York: Wings Books, 1995. Sympathetic history of the forced removal and resettlement of the Cherokees to west of the Mississippi River.

McLoughlin, William G. *After the Trail of Tears: The Cherokees' Struggle for Sovereignty, 1839-1880*. Chapel Hill: University of North Carolina Press, 1993. Study of the social, cultural, and political history of the Cherokees during the first four decades after they were moved to Oklahoma.

_____. *Cherokee Renascence in the New Republic*. Princeton, N.J.: Princeton University Press, 1983. Cherokee history up through the removal crisis.

_____. *Cherokees and Missionaries, 1789-1839*. New Haven, Conn.: Yale University Press, 1984. Thorough and well-documented history of missionary involvement among the Cherokees in the period leading up to their removal.

Mooney, James. *Historical Sketch of the Cherokee*. Chicago: Aldine, 1975. A valuable study by a contemporary who interviewed people involved.

Moulton, Gary E. *John Ross, Cherokee Chief*. Athens: University of Georgia Press, 1978. Biography of the Cherokee leader at the time of removal.

Remini, Robert V. *The Legacy of Andrew Jackson: Essays on Democracy, Indian Removal, and Slavery*. Baton Rouge: Louisiana State University Press, 1988. The leading biographer of Andrew Jackson reflects on his significance to these issues.

Wallace, Anthony F. C. *The Long, Bitter Trail: Andrew Jackson and the Indians*. New York: Hill & Wang, 1993. Brief overview of the removal policies, the Trail of Tears, and the implications of both for U.S. history.

Wilkins, Thurman. *Cherokee Tragedy: The Ridge Family and the Decimation of a People*. Rev. ed. Norman: University of Oklahoma Press, 1986. Discusses the prominent family of Cherokee leaders.

SEE ALSO: July 27, 1813-Aug. 9, 1814: Creek War; Nov. 21, 1817-Mar. 27, 1858: Seminole Wars; Apr. 24, 1820: Congress Passes Land Act of 1820; Feb. 21, 1828: *Cherokee Phoenix* Begins Publication; 1830-1842: Trail of Tears; Mar. 18, 1831, and Mar. 3, 1832: Cherokee Cases; Sept. 4, 1841: Congress Passes Preemption Act of 1841; Apr. 30, 1860-1865: Apache and Navajo War; Feb. 6, 1861-Sept. 4, 1886: Apache Wars; Mar. 3, 1871: Grant Signs Indian Appropriation Act; June 27, 1874-June 2, 1875: Red River War; Feb. 8, 1887: General Allotment Act Erodes Indian Tribal Unity.

RELATED ARTICLES in *Great Lives from History: The Nineteenth Century, 1801-1900:* Andrew Jackson; Belva A. Lockwood; John Ross; Sequoyah.

June 14-July 5, 1830
FRANCE CONQUERS ALGERIA

France took the first step in its annexation of northwest Africa when it conquered Algeria. In the process, it forced a complete restructuring of Algerian society.

LOCALE: Algeria

CATEGORIES: Colonization; expansion and land acquisition; wars, uprisings, and civil unrest

KEY FIGURES

Abdelkader (1808-1883), emir of Algeria, r. 1834-1847

Louis-Auguste-Victor de Bourmont (1773-1846), commander in chief of the Army of Africa, 1830, and leader of the French invasion

Charles X (1757-1836), king of France, r. 1824-1830

Bertrand Clauzel (1772-1842), commander in chief of the Army of Africa, 1830-1831, marshal, 1831-1835, and governor of Algeria, 1835-1837

Joseph Collet (fl. early nineteenth century), rear admiral and commander of the French naval squadron in Algiers in 1827

Hussein ben Hassan (fl. early nineteenth century), governor of Algiers, 1818-1830

Louis-Philippe (1773-1850), king of France, r. 1830-1848

Mahmud II (1785-1839), sultan of the Ottoman Empire, r. 1808-1839

SUMMARY OF EVENT

From 1579 until the early nineteenth century, France's relations with Algiers were strained. However, its con-

French bombardment of Algiers.

quest of the city and the surrounding countryside in the summer of 1830 was its first decisive military incursion into the western portion of North Africa. This step was to lead eventually to its control of a broad strip of territory stretching from Tunisia to the Atlantic coast of Morocco.

The immediate pretext for France's attack came on April 30, 1827, when the dey (governor) of Algiers, Hussein ben Hassan, either tapped or struck (depending on conflicting accounts) visiting French consul Pierre Deval with a fly whisk. The incident may simply have been intended to indicate by the dey that their interview was at an end, or it may have constituted, as the French chose to interpret it, a "horrible and scandalous outrage." Behind this seemingly trivial event lay another, equally trivial but long-standing disagreement over a minor debt.

The incident found both countries in politically weakened condition. Hussein ben Hassan controlled only the city of Algiers and the nearby countryside directly. The remainder of the northern region of what is today Algeria was divided into three provinces; each was ruled by an official who was appointed by the dey but who was otherwise autonomous and whose authority seldom extended beyond the populated areas. Although the prov-

inces were nominally part of the Ottoman Empire, in practice they did little but forward taxes to the Ottoman capital of Constantinople.

King Charles X of France was anxious to deflect attention from domestic problems, and so seized upon the fly-whisk incident. Announcing publicly that he was eradicating Algerian privateering, Charles quickly dispatched a naval squadron under the command of Rear Admiral Joseph Collet. Collet reached the port of Algiers on June 11. After taking the consul and other French citizens on board, he set up a naval blockade.

Through the next three years, Sultan Mahmud II of the Ottoman Empire tried in vain to persuade Dey Hussein ben Hassan to come to terms with the French. He was supported in these efforts by the British, who were anxious to maintain a balance of power in the Mediterranean and to protect their own interests. In March of 1830, Mahmud sent an emissary, a former grand mufti (judicial official) of Algiers who had since retired to Turkey, to insist that Hussein ben Hassan make peace. By that time the French government, in ever-increasing need of a distraction from its internal affairs, had decided to launch a direct invasion. The emissary's ship was intercepted and turned back before it reached Algiers. On May 11, a fleet of six hundred French ships set sail from the Mediterranean port of Toulon and, delayed by a storm, reached the African coast on June 12 some distance from Algiers.

Earlier, under orders from Napoleon Bonaparte, an engineer named Boutin had surreptitiously visited Algeria in 1808 to prepare detailed plans for a projected French invasion. Although that invasion never took place, the plans were preserved, and it was in large part thanks to these plans that the French force of 34,000 troops commanded by General Louis-Auguste-Victor de Bourmont triumphed in 1830. Hussein ben Hassan had assembled a larger force of 43,000 soldiers, including a number called in from the neighboring provinces at the last minute, but he proved unable to match the superior organization and firearms of the French.

Bourmont landed his first troops on June 14 on the peninsula of Sidi Fredj west of Algiers, defeated the Algerians in decisive battles on June 19 and June 24-25, and by June 29 had reached the city. French artillery began heavy bombardment on July 4, and Algiers surrendered the next day. Hussein ben Hassan was allowed to depart into exile with his entourage and a fraction of his fortune. All the while patriotic French civilians watched the military action from pleasure boats anchored offshore.

After winning the war, France proved unable to establish a satisfactory peace, either at home or abroad. Within weeks of the victory in Algiers, the so-called July Revolution toppled the government of Charles X, and the king was replaced by his cousin Louis-Philippe as a constitutional monarch. Like his former enemy Hussein ben Hassan, Charles slipped into exile. The new government consisted of opponents of the Algerian expedition who now, ironically, found themselves unable to act on their convictions. Doubts about the Algerian invasion had been based on the belief that France should expend its energy and money in Europe, not abroad. In fact an official commission later concluded that the French effort had been a mistake, but that to withdraw would be an unacceptable blow to national pride.

General Bourmont had expected all the Ottoman provinces of Algeria to surrender in a matter of weeks, but early French behavior in Algiers enraged the population. The victorious Christian soldiers pillaged the Muslim city, desecrating many of its holy places and cemeteries. The treasury was looted, ostensibly to cover the cost of the expedition.

Upon learning of the July Revolution, General Bourmont made plans to return to France to fight for the restoration of Charles, but when his troops refused to follow

him, he fled into exile in Spain. Replacing him was Bertrand Clauzel, who took advantage of the new French government's ambivalence by pursuing further military campaigns and by initiating the wholesale seizure of Algerian land and property. So unpopular did these measures prove that Clauzel himself was soon replaced.

SIGNIFICANCE

In all, eight military commanders or governors were to administer French Algeria during its first decade of existence, one of whom was responsible for massacring an entire tribe, including women and children. The 1834 report of the African Commission of the French Chamber of Deputies acknowledged that the country had "outdone in barbarity the barbarians" it had set out to civilize. Nevertheless, that same year the French made official their conquest and vowed to continue their colonization.

In the aftermath of the French invasion, Algerian resistance came to center on a powerful and charismatic figure. Abdelkader became chief of a confederation of tribes in western Algeria in 1832, and soon assumed leadership of the entire Algerian resistance movement. By 1840, he controlled two-thirds of Algeria and was able to attack, but not reconquer, Algiers itself. French citizens disillusioned with their country's record in Algeria championed his cause, and he enjoyed at least the unofficial support of Great Britain. His surrender in 1847 marked the end of any significant threat to French rule for a century.

—Grove Koger

FURTHER READING

Abun-Nasr, Jamil M. "The Emergence of French Algeria." In *A History of the Maghrib.* Cambridge, England: Cambridge University Press, 1971. A detailed survey of the early years of French occupation and resulting Algerian resistance. The "Maghrib" of the title refers to Libya, Tunisia, Algeria, and Morocco.

Adamson, Kay. *Political and Economic Thought and Practice in Nineteenth-Century France and the Colonization of Algeria.* Lewiston, N.Y.: Edwin Mellen Press, 2002. A historical study of the significance of the colonization of Algeria on its colonizers: the French. Focuses on the political-economic aspects of French colonization.

Clancy-Smith, Julia A. *Rebel and Saint: Muslim Notables, Populist Protest, Colonial Encounters (Algeria and Tunisia, 1800-1904).* Berkeley: University of California Press, 1994. Abdelkader is included in this examination of the religious beliefs and political actions of prominent Muslims and their followers. Analyzes Algerian resistance to, and accommodation with, French colonists.

Danziger, Raphael. *Abd al-Qadir and the Algerians: Resistance to the French and Internal Consolidation.* New York: Holmes & Meier, 1977. Discusses organized resistance to French conquest and the role of an early "rebel" leader and national hero. Still the best modern treatment in English.

King, John. "Arms and the Man: Abd el-Kader." *History Today* 40 (August, 1990): 22-28. Profiles Abdelkader and examines evidence that this key figure was covertly armed by the British.

Laurie, G. B. *The French Conquest of Algeria.* London: Hugh Rees, 1909. A seriously dated work in its outlook, but still the most complete account in English of French military action in Algeria through 1857.

Morsy, Magali. "The French Conquest of Algeria." In *North Africa, 1800-1900: A Survey from the Nile Valley to the Atlantic.* London: Longman, 1984. An examination of French military action and policy from 1830 through 1847. A subsequent chapter, "Algeria in an Imperial Design," extends the examination into the late nineteenth century.

Naylor, Phillip Chiviges, and Alf Andrew Heggoy. *Historical Dictionary of Algeria.* 2d ed. Metuchen, N.J.: Scarecrow Press, 1994. A lengthy introduction surveys key aspects of Algerian history, and individual entries profile most of the important individuals and events involved in the French period.

Singer, Barnett, and John Langdon. *Cultured Force: Makers and Defenders of the French Colonial Empire.* Madison: University of Wisconsin Press, 2004. The authors reassess the nature of French imperialism by focusing on the lives and careers of French leaders in African and Asian colonies.

Spencer, William. "The French Conquest." In *Algiers in the Age of the Corsairs.* Norman: University of Oklahoma Press, 1976. A survey of French relations with Algeria, concluding with an account of the blockade and the invasion. Earlier chapters of Spencer's history emphasize the predominant role of privateering in the city's history.

SEE ALSO: May 4, 1805-1830: Exploration of West Africa; 1822-1874: Exploration of North Africa; 1832-1841: Turko-Egyptian Wars; 1832-1847: Abdelkader Leads Algeria Against France; 1848-1889: Exploration of East Africa; Nov., 1889-Jan., 1894: Dahomey-French Wars.

RELATED ARTICLES in *Great Lives from History: The Nineteenth Century, 1801-1900:* Abdelkader; Ali Paşa Tepelenë; Louis Faidherbe; Muḥammad ʿAlī Pasha.

July, 1830
LYELL PUBLISHES *PRINCIPLES OF GEOLOGY*

Lyell's Principles of Geology *launched a fundamental change in the science of geology by rejecting catastrophic geological change and helping to free the discipline from the restrictions of religion, thereby drastically expanding the earth's age and making Darwinian evolution conceptually possible.*

LOCALE: London, England

CATEGORIES: Geology; earth science; science and technology

KEY FIGURES

Charles Lyell (1797-1875), English naturalist and founder of uniformitarianism

Charles Darwin (1809-1882), English naturalist who developed the theory of evolution through natural selection

James Hutton (1726-1797), Scottish physician and naturalist

Comte de Buffon (Georges-Louis Leclerc; 1707-1788), French naturalist who opposed mingling science and theology

SUMMARY OF EVENT

Charles Lyell developed the theory of uniformitarianism as a determined effort to separate geology from the biblical view of creation and place it on the same footing as the general sciences. His theory was part of a tradition dating back to the seventeenth century French mathematician René Descartes, who tried to detach astronomy from religion by arguing that existence was composed of thinking substance (spirit) and extended substance (matter), and that theology was only concerned with the spirit and should be excluded from investigations of nature. Uniformitarianism also reflected the Cartesian view that physical change was the result of law-bound matter in motion.

The claim that matter was law-bound and outside the proper area of theologians worked its way from cosmology into geology in the works of a noted French naturalist, the comte de Buffon. A believer in the Enlightenment and a great admirer of the early eighteenth century English physicist Isaac Newton, who had convincingly demonstrated that matter was indeed law-bound, Buffon sharply criticized the mixing of science with religion. Theologians, he insisted, should confine themselves to Scripture, while naturalists should rely on accurate observations of natural occurrences.

Buffon's arguments, advanced in the first volume of his *Natural History, General and Particular* (1749), were largely rejected by his contemporaries and immedi-

Charles Lyell. (Library of Congress)

ate successors. Over the next half century, geological speculation was dominated by such late eighteenth and early nineteenth century catastrophists as Jean-Étienne Guettard, Nicolas Desmarest, Abraham Gottlob Werner, and Georges Cuvier. All these naturalists accepted intellectual limits imposed upon them by the Bible, although they might disagree about the importance of the various upheavals that shaped the features of the earth. Guettard and Desmarest were vulcanists, convinced that underground fires and the volcanoes they produced played an important and previously underappreciated role in earth history. Werner and Cuvier, on the other hand, were neptunists, convinced that a primeval earth-spanning ocean (followed, after the rise of continents, by catastrophic floods) largely determined the shape of the physical environment.

Buffon's challenge to a biblical view of creation was renewed in a more effective way by the Scottish physician and naturalist James Hutton, whose *Theory of the Earth* (1795) contained key uniformitarian principles. Hutton was not a consistent uniformitarian and did not try to separate science from religion, for he viewed continental uplift as a cataclysmic event and saw geological processes as proof of the workings of Divine Providence. The earth's ecosystem, he claimed, floated on an enormous sea of magma and was meant to be self-maintaining through constant renewal; it was part of God's plan for humankind.

However, if Hutton incorporated Deist elements into his theory, he also rejected biblical creationism. He insisted that the present was the key to an understanding of the past, that geological change could, and should, be explained in terms of the ordinary actions of natural forces acting normally. That view, which emphasized the slow actions of temperature, wind, and water on land forms, automatically required an extension of the earth's age that seemed to contradict the account of Earth's creation in the Bible's Book of Genesis.

A full-blown uniformitarianism finally appeared in July of 1830, when the English geologist Charles Lyell produced the first volume of his *Principles of Geology*. With impressive consistency, Lyell insisted on explaining geological change strictly in terms of known physical agents operating at current levels of force. The earth had been sculpted by the interplay of water and heat—as he expressed it, by aqueous and igneous phenomena. Through the erosion cycle, the action of water tended to level the earth. The raising or depressing of the earth's surface was caused by volcanoes and earthquakes, which were themselves products of the earth's enormous internal heat. Furthermore, the cycles of raising and lowering, of construction and destruction, tended to proceed at the same approximate rates. Even volcanoes, the most violent natural force considered by Lyell, produced about the same amount of lava from eruption to eruption. This meant that the surface of the earth—or, more exactly, the successive surfaces of the earth—remained in roughly the same general condition throughout its enormously long history.

Lyell's work was more impressive than that of Hutton for several reasons. Unlike Hutton's work, it was thoroughly documented and tightly argued. Moreover, its unrelieved insistence on uniformity and regularity within the bounds of familiar phenomena was solidly within the Newtonian tradition and, therefore, fit the current model of good science. Finally, Lyell went beyond Hutton by incorporating organic and well as inorganic change into his theory. He flatly rejected progressiveness in the fossil record. However, he did believe that organic remains were vital evidence of fluctuating geologic and climatic conditions, for ecological change would be marked by shifting species distributions, mass extinctions, and a certain amount of species mutability.

The *Principles of Geology* immediately touched off a dispute over the rate of geological change known as the Uniformitarian-Catastrophist Debate. That dispute soon flowed into the question of whether change was progressive or whether the earth remained in structural equilibrium, in a sort of Lyellian steady state. In both cases, the controversy promoted further research, especially in potentially revealing areas such as mountain-building.

Lyell's views were partly invalidated by later research, which found that intermittent cataclysmic episodes did, in fact, interrupt the normal flow of uniform forces and that the fossil record was, indeed, progressive. However, if he represented a philosophic extreme, he still occupied a prominent place in the development of modern geology. In undermining the legitimacy of a linkage between earth history and scriptural belief, in careful, extensive documentation of generalizations, and in searching for regularity in geological processes, his theory helped push that emerging discipline toward maturation.

Lyell's work was also crucial to the development of Charles Darwin's theory of evolution. Darwin was deeply impressed by *Principles of Geology*, which he read carefully during his famous voyage around the world on HMS *Beagle* during the early 1830's. As he later noted, Lyell's insights allowed him to see the natural world through different lenses. Uniformitarianism

prepared the ground for Darwin's later work in several ways. First, any notion of evolution in small increments required freedom from rapid, catastrophic change and a vast time span within which to operate. Lyell's theory provided Darwin with both of these conditions.

Darwin also found that his observations of the fossil record supported Lyell's conclusions about the correlation between species distribution, climate, and geography. That increased awareness of paleoecology deepened his understanding of the ways living plants and animals were distributed and allowed him to make connections between the living conditions of past and present life forms. Finally, Lyell's geologic uniformitarianism provided a model for Darwin's vision of the gradual modification of species. Darwin was unaware of the breakthrough in genetics achieved by the Austrian monk and botanist Gregor Mendel and could not accurately describe the way characteristics were transmitted from parents to offspring. Nevertheless, he conceived of biological change in a Lyellian, uniformitarian manner. It was gradual, steady, and cumulative, reacting to known forces operating in known ways.

SIGNIFICANCE

Lyell's work is significant primarily because of the way it furthered Cartesian values in two emerging disciplines. In geology, his uniformitarianism further distanced science from theology and promoted the fundamental notion of René Descartes that the natural world was formed by law-bound matter in motion. In biology, it advanced the Cartesian definition of life as highly organized law-bound matter in motion by freeing geological time from scriptural bonds. In both cases, Lyell's uniformitarianism accelerated the rise of modern scientific disciplines.

—*Michael J. Fontenot*

FURTHER READING

Bolles, Edmund Blair. *The Ice Finders: How a Poet, a Professor, and a Politician Discovered the Ice Age.* Washington, D.C.: Counterpoint, 1999. Lively narrative of how naturalist Louis Agassiz, Charles Lyell, and poet Elisha Kent Kane collaborated to create public acceptance for the existence of an ice age.

Dalrymple, G. Brent. *The Age of the Earth.* Stanford, Calif.: Stanford University Press, 1991. Places Lyell's concerns about the antiquity of the earth in fullest possible context, stretching from ancient beliefs to radiometric dating

Gould, Stephen Jay. *Time's Arrow, Time's Cycle: Myth and Metaphor in the Discovery of Geological Time.*

1830's

Cambridge, Mass.: Harvard University Press, 1987. Provides an extensive treatment of Lyell's ideas and carefully analyzes the different ideas subsumed under the general umbrella of uniformitarianism.

Greene, John C. *The Death of Adam: Evolution and Its Impact on Western Thought*. Ames: Iowa State University Press, 1959. Places Lyell's influence on nineteenth century science in perspective and traces the connections between Lyell's and Darwin's thoughts on species migration.

Greene, Mott T. *Geology in the Nineteenth Century: Changing Views of a Changing World*. Ithaca, N.Y.: Cornell University Press, 1982. Taking a broad perspective, Greene evaluates Lyell's contributions and offers the view that Hutton's work laid the foundations of modern geology.

Klaver, J. M. I. *Geology and Religious Sentiment: The Effect of Geological Discoveries on English Society and Literature Between 1829 and 1859*. New York: Brill, 1997. Study of Lyell's scientific and religious views about world antiquity and how they were received by theologians, philosophers, poets, and novelists.

Lyell, Charles. *Principles of Geology, Being an Attempt to Explain the Former Changes of the Earth's Surface by Reference to Causes Now in Operation*. 3 vols. London: John Murray, 1830-1833. First of many editions of Lyell's landmark work, which is remarkably easy to read, as it is written in an open and accessible style.

Rudwick, Martin J. S. *George Cuvier: Fossil Bones and Geological Catastrophes—New Translations and Interpretations of the Primary Texts*. Chicago: University of Chicago Press, 1997. Study of the French naturalist Cuvier, whose writings on animal fossils and natural catastrophes anticipated modern research into mass extinctions and the study of fossils as records of plant and animal life that help to date the age of the earth.

Wilson, Leonard G. *Charles Lyell*. 2 vols. New Haven, Conn.: Yale University Press, 1972. This sizable biography places Lyell in the scientific context of his times and provides a detailed account of his work and personal life.

SEE ALSO: 1809: Lamarck Publishes *Zoological Philosophy*; Apr. 5, 1815: Tambora Volcano Begins Violent Eruption; Feb. 20, 1824: Buckland Presents the First Public Dinosaur Description; 1854-1862: Wallace's Expeditions Give Rise to Biogeography; Aug., 1856: Neanderthal Skull Is Found in Germany; Nov. 24, 1859: Darwin Publishes *On the Origin of Species*; 1871: Darwin Publishes *The Descent of Man*; Aug. 27, 1883: Krakatoa Volcano Erupts; July, 1897-July, 1904: Bjerknes Founds Scientific Weather Forecasting; 1900: Wiechert Invents the Inverted Pendulum Seismograph.

RELATED ARTICLES in *Great Lives from History: The Nineteenth Century, 1801-1900:* Georges Cuvier; Charles Darwin; Sir Charles Lyell.

July 29, 1830
JULY REVOLUTION DEPOSES CHARLES X

France's July Revolution ousted the Bourbon king Charles X and his Ultraroyalist advisers because of their failure to accept the principles of civil equality and other ideals established by the revolution of 1789.

ALSO KNOWN AS: Les Trois Glorieuses (the Three Glorious Days),

LOCALE: Paris, France

CATEGORIES: Government and politics; wars, uprisings, and civil unrest

KEY FIGURES

Charles X (1757-1836), king of France, 1824-1830
Louis-Philippe (1773-1850), Duke of Orléans and later king of the French, r. 1830-1848

François-René de Chateaubriand (1768-1848), Romantic writer and conservative politician
Marquis de Lafayette (1757-1834), liberal politician who played an important role in the French Revolution
Auguste-Jules-Armand-Marie de Polignac (1780-1847), Ultraroyalist politician
Adolphe Thiers (1797-1877), liberal politician

SUMMARY OF EVENT

After the long, exhausting years of the Napoleonic Wars, the French people passively accepted the restoration of the Bourbon monarchy in 1814-1815. At first, there was relief that the long years of warfare had at last come to an

July revolutionists manning the barricades in Paris. (Francis R. Niglutsch)

end, but there was also apprehension that the political, social, and economic gains made during the French Revolution (1789) might be lost. The moderate constitutional regime established by Louis XVIII reassured many French people.

During the 1820's, the monarchy began to drift to the right at the same time that the French nation was moving to the left. Only the highly restricted suffrage and various changes to election laws enabled the factions of the right to maintain a majority in the Chamber of Deputies. By July of 1830, the political situation had reached the breaking point, and a brief, relatively bloodless revolution overthrew the Bourbons and established a new, more liberal monarchy.

Political tensions intensified in 1824, when Louis XVIII died and the throne passed to his brother, who became Charles X. The last surviving brother of the executed King Louis XVI, Charles was an extreme conservative. Throughout the years of the French Revolution (1789) and the First Empire, Charles had been the rallying point around whom the most violent antirevolu-

tionary forces gathered. He had originally fled France in July, 1789, just as the revolution was beginning, and had remained abroad, condemning all changes in France, until Napoleon's abdication in 1814. Although his ultimate goal was to restore the Old Regime (*l'ancien régime*) to France, he did not at first take drastic measures, which would have antagonized the moderate and liberal opposition. Nevertheless, his government began shifting to the right. The liberal left was in opposition from the outset of Charles's reign, which began with a five-hour medieval coronation at Rheims.

It was not until the moderates and one wing of the conservatives went into opposition, however, that Charles was driven from the throne. Two royal policies had the effect of alienating all political opinion except that of the extreme right. One was a marked trend toward enlarging the power of the nobility; the other, a trend toward increasing clerical influence in government. By 1829-1830, many conservatives who had loyally supported Louis XVIII and his Charter of 1815 had moved into opposition of Charles X and his Ultraroyalist supporters.

Soon after Charles's coronation, the Chamber of Deputies, controlled by the Ultraroyalists, passed laws to indemnify the émigré nobles for the loss of their property during the revolution. To finance this indemnity, interest paid on government bonds was reduced from 5 to 3.5 percent, and the difference of more than one-half billion francs was paid to the nobility who had abandoned their property when they fled France during the 1790's. The upper bourgeoisie owned most of the bonds and lost much of their anticipated interest. Other critics believed the windfall should have been used to defray government debts, not reward people who had often fought in foreign armies against France. On the other hand, the transaction had the positive effect of settling the nagging issue of émigré claims to lands they had abandoned, since they accepted the money as compensation. Nevertheless, no group outside the nobility favored this action. The middle classes also protested in 1827, when the king dissolved the National Guard, the citizen militia that was not under the control of the regular military officials.

Meanwhile, the growing influence of the Church also caused apprehension in some quarters. The Ultramontane faction of Roman Catholics who surrounded Charles X were widely perceived as abandoning the historical positions of the Roman Catholic Church in France, known as Gallicanism. Church control was extended over many tax-supported institutions of education, leading to dismissals of liberal instructors and prohibitions of certain subjects. The 1826 Law of Sacrilege instituted the penalty of mutilation followed by death for anyone convicted of committing, inside churches, certain acts defined as sacrilegious. No one was actually charged with such acts, but this linking of the power of the state to the religious beliefs of a minority of the population contributed to the formation of a majority coalition against the throne. Elections in November, 1827, resulted in a liberal majority in the Chamber, forcing the king to dismiss his Ultraroyalist ministers. For a time, Charles attempted to steer a moderate course between the liberals and Ultraroyalists, but this effort had the effect of leaving both sides dissatisfied.

An impatient man, Charles was not politically adept. Convinced of his royal prerogative, he appointed a new Ultraroyalist prime minister, even though he knew that he did not have majority support in the Chamber. Popularly dubbed the "Ultra of the Ultras," Prince Auguste-Jules-Armand-Marie de Polignac was totally unacceptable to the Chamber, whose majority claimed the right to approve or disapprove the ministers. The Charter of 1815 did not specifically grant the Chamber this function, but

such ministerial responsibility had been practiced since 1816. The opposition began to consolidate, rallying around traditional heroes, such as the marquis de Lafayette, and inspired by new leaders, such as Adolphe Thiers.

Early in 1830, a hostile Chamber of Deputies met and voted an address to Charles denouncing his new ministry. In his response, the king, who recalled that his brother Louis XVI had been criticized for yielding to the National Assembly in 1789, took a hard line and dissolved the Chamber of Deputies without replying to their address. The election that followed returned an even greater majority opposing the king. Once again, Charles answered by dissolving the National Assembly. This time, the king was determined to have his own way. He altered the Charter of 1815 in such a manner as to ensure an Ultra majority in the Chamber of Deputies by stripping the bourgeoisie of their right to vote and imposing a strict censorship on the press. The result of his action, however, was not what he had expected.

Previously faithful royalists now abandoned the regime, including the great Romantic writer René de Chateaubriand, who insisted that freedom of expression must be preserved. Republicans, Bonapartists, and others who had always been excluded from parliamentary channels of dissent began to organize and show their opinion in the only way left them, illegally and violently. On July 26, 1830, a few small demonstrations erupted in Paris. On the following day, barricades were constructed in the working-class sections of the city. By July 28, Paris was in complete rebellion, with students and workers demanding the reestablishment of a republic. Charles X attempted to negotiate, offering to abdicate in favor of his ten-year-old grandson. The next day, he gave up his throne. Lafayette and other leaders were won over by the liberal deputies and the bourgeoisie to support a new, more liberal royal dynasty under Louis-Philippe, the duke of Orléans.

SIGNIFICANCE

Although Louis-Philippe was a direct descendant of King Louis XIII (1601-1643), his ideas and actions seemed in keeping with those of the French middle classes. The new king's father had been an eager participant in the early stages of the French Revolution (1789) until perishing in the Reign of Terror. Louis-Philippe himself had fought in French armies against the Austrians and Prussians before emigrating in 1793. His elevation to a new throne reassured many French citizens who feared that establishment of a republic might result in opposition from foreign governments or in Jacobin extremism.

The new regime was controlled by the upper middle class, who dominated the Chamber of Deputies. Although the masses had no voice in the government, the new order was a further step in the direction of representative government and was tolerated for eighteen years. Had King Charles X and his Ultraroyalist supporters been more flexible and willing to make concessions to the middle classes, French political institutions might have evolved in the manner and direction of those of Great Britain; instead, French institutions changed through revolutionary processes and resulted in a thoroughly democratic republican government by the end of the nineteenth century.

—*John G. Gallaher, updated by Sharon B. Watkins*

FURTHER READING

Alexander, Robert. *Re-writing the French Revolutionary Tradition: Liberal Opposition and the Fall of the Bourbon Monarchy*. New York: Cambridge University Press, 2003. Broad study of the revolutionary tradition in French politics between 1815 and 1830 that looks at all classes of French citizens.

Howarth, T. E. B. *Citizen King*. London: Eyre & Spottiswoode, 1967. This is a clear, readable account of the life and times of Louis-Philippe, who succeeded Charles X as king of France.

Kroen, Sheryl. *Politics and Theater: The Crisis of Legitimacy in Restoration France, 1815-1830*. Berkeley: University of California Press, 2000. Exploration of politics in postrevolutionary France, as seen through the prism of theater, with a focus on Molière's play *Tartuffe* (1664), which enjoyed renewed popularity during the 1820's.

Magraw, Roger. *France, 1815-1914: The Bourgeois Century*. New York: Oxford University Press, 1986. The July Revolution is viewed as a further step by the bourgeoisie toward political and social dominance in France.

Marrinan, Michael. *Painting Politics for Louis Philippe: Art and Ideology in Orleanist France, 1830-1848*. New Haven, Conn.: Yale University Press, 1988. A fascinating account of the use of art as political propaganda during the July monarchy.

Pinkney, David. *The French Revolution of 1830*. Princeton, N.J.: Princeton University Press, 1972. This work is one of the most complete and objective accounts in English.

Rader, Daniel L. *The Journalists and the July Revolution in France: The Role of the Political Press in the Overthrow of the Bourbon Restoration, 1827-1830*. The Hague, Netherlands: Nijhoff, 1973. Rader explains how journalists helped end a regime that attempted to limit freedom of expression.

SEE ALSO: Dec. 2, 1804: Bonaparte Is Crowned Napoleon I; Apr. 11, 1814-July 29, 1830: France's Bourbon Dynasty Is Restored; Nov. 20, 1815: Second Peace of Paris; Oct. 20-30, 1822: Great Britain Withdraws from the Concert of Europe; 1824: Paris Salon of 1824; Aug. 25, 1830-May 21, 1833: Belgian Revolution; Oct.-Dec., 1830: Delacroix Paints *Liberty Leading the People*; Feb. 22-June, 1848: Paris Revolution of 1848; Dec. 2, 1852: Louis Napoleon Bonaparte Becomes Emperor of France.

RELATED ARTICLES in *Great Lives from History: The Nineteenth Century, 1801-1900:* François-René de Chateaubriand; Napoleon I; Adolphe Thiers.

1830's

August 25, 1830-May 21, 1833
BELGIAN REVOLUTION

Dissatisfaction with Dutch rule prompted a Belgian revolt that led to the creation of a new nation with a constitutional monarchy.

LOCALE: Belgium

CATEGORIES: Wars, uprisings, and civil unrest; government and politics

KEY FIGURES

William I (Prince Willem Frederik of Orange; 1772-1843), king of the Netherlands, r. 1815-1840

Louis-Philippe (1773-1850), king of France, r. 1830-1848

Leopold I (1790-1865), first king of the Belgians, r. 1831-1865

Charles Rogier (1800-1885), Belgian revolutionary leader who led the provisional government

Lord Palmerston (Henry John Temple; 1784-1865), British foreign secretary, 1830-1834, 1835-1841, and 1846-1851

SUMMARY OF EVENT

After the victory of revolutionary France over the Austrians at Fleurus in 1793, the Austrian Netherlands, which included what is now Belgium. became an appendage of revolutionary France. Under Napoleon's rule, economic development was encouraged that would provide the foundations for Belgium's industrial revolution. By reopening to commerce the important Scheldt River, which had been closed by the Dutch after their revolt splintered the old Spanish Netherlands, Napoleon also laid the basis for the resurgence of Antwerp, and the great impact which that would have on Belgium.

The powers at the Congress of Vienna were anxious to remove the vacuum along France's northern frontier that had attracted French aggression from the time of Louis XIV. To buttress the area, they ceded Belgium's eastern cantons—Eupen, Malmedy, and St. Vith—to Prussia, and the rest of Belgium was amalgamated with Holland. It was believed that the commercial economy of the Netherlands would complement the increasingly manufacturing-oriented economy of Belgium.

However, the Belgians themselves became increasingly dissatisfied, and the new construct lasted only about fifteen years. The Dutch king William I was Calvinist and conservative. He succeeded in alienating Flemish Roman Catholics, the French-speaking Walloons, and the liberals. Dutch became the official language except within the French-speaking Walloon districts. The Dutch were favored in the civil service. Although Belgium had nearly twice the population of the Netherlands, it assigned the same number of representatives in the States General. Finally, passions were driven to a fever pitch by a series of bad harvests and by a crisis of overproduction that crippled the textile industry of Verviers, Liège, and Tournai.

Efforts by the government to limit freedom of the press in Belgium encouraged Belgian writers, at considerable risk, to heap criticism upon their Dutch masters. Much of this criticism was directed against the government's policy of burdening the Belgians with half of Holland's huge national debt. Especially galling to the Belgians was the fact that the government sought to meet this debt by levying taxes on two of the primary necessities of life, flour and meat. These outrageous taxes touched every household and thereby helped to arouse the whole Belgian nation against Dutch rule.

This growing opposition consisted of individuals and groups with widely divergent perspectives, but of particular importance was the catalytic impact of the growing population of young Belgian professionals and intelligentsia, who believed that their future prospects were blocked by the Dutch and antiliberal character of William's regime. The opposition demanded ministerial responsibility, equal access to employment, and freedom of education and the press. However, their demand for a truly democratic parliamentary regime would have meant the dominance in the Netherlands of Belgium, with its rapidly increasing population.

The revolution of July, 1830, in neighboring France abruptly terminated the reign of Charles X and heightened tensions in Belgium. The explosion came on August 25, 1830, with the performance of Daniel Auber's *La Muette de Portici* at Théâtre de la Monnaie in Brussels. The singing of the patriotic ballad "Amour sacré de la Patrie" (sacred love of fatherland) brought the audience to its feet and into the streets. The demonstration at the opera led to an explosion by the desperate and exasperated proletariat of Brussels. The bourgeois liberals had not foreseen this and were terrified by the specter of anarchy. They were willing to accept an autonomous administration with William's oldest son Frederick, the prince of Orange, as viceroy.

Were it not for the timidity of Frederick, Dutch authority could have been easily restored on September 1 with the six thousand Dutch troops under his command. The discomfort of the moderates was such that the second Dutch effort on September 23 also would have succeeded had it not been for insufficient Dutch resolve. A provisional government was set up under Charles Rogier, independence was proclaimed on October 4, and a national congress was summoned to draw up a constitution. The very election for a Belgian congress on November 3 demonstrated the lack of enthusiasm for complete separation from the Dutch. Of the forty-six thousand eligible voters, only thirty thousand voted. Many did not vote because of the absence of antirevolutionary and pro-union candidates. Of those who voted, one-third cast blank protest votes.

The stubborn refusal of William to accept the division of his kingdom transformed the Belgian independence movement into an international issue that was to plague Europe for almost a decade. William hoped that Austria, Russia, and Prussia would help him restore the union. Despite the sympathy of those conservative countries, however, no assistance was forthcoming.

Following the Dutch bombardment of Antwerp on October 27, the British called for a conference of the great powers, which met in London and ordered an armistice on November 4. On November 10, the Belgian congress declared the House of Orange deposed but expressed its support for a constitutional hereditary monarchy. Lord Palmerston, who had just taken over the British foreign office, had two goals: to prevent Belgium from falling under the control of France, and to prevent the outbreak of war. Louis-Philippe, who was consolidating his power in France, was inclined to follow the lead of Great Britain. Russia, which was confronted with a Polish insurrection, and Prussia, saddled with war debt, reluctantly acquiesced to this alteration of the Vienna settlement. On December 20, the London Conference declared the dissolution of the kingdom of the Netherlands, and recognized Belgium's independence on January 20, 1831.

When the Belgian congress chose the second son of Louis-Philippe, the duke of Nemours, to be king of Belgium on February 3, 1831, the French king heeded the warnings of Palmerston and repudiated the offer. The Belgian congress proceeded to draw up a very liberal constitution patterned on the unwritten constitution of Britain. Finally, on June 4, it chose Prince Leopold of Saxe-Coburg as king. An excellent and politic choice, Leopold was not only talented and capable but as the widower of Princess Charlotte of England and the uncle of Victoria—the future queen of Britain—had an English con-

nection. By marrying the daughter of Louis-Philippe in 1832, Leopold also established a French connection.

King William was dissatisfied with the settlement drawn up in London. After he crossed the new Belgian frontier on August 2 and defeated a makeshift Belgian force, a French army, with British approval, forced his army to retire. With William still resisting and refusing to evacuate Antwerp, a combined British and French naval force in conjunction with a French army expelled the Dutch from Belgium. On May 21, 1833, the Dutch were compelled to agree to an indefinite armistice, which, in effect, recognized Belgium's independence. Finally, on April 19, 1839, William accepted a settlement that recognized a frontier which, with the exception of Limburg and Luxembourg, was basically the frontier of 1790.

SIGNIFICANCE

The grand duchy of Luxembourg, which had been assigned to the Dutch king by the Congress of Vienna, also revolted in 1830 and sought to join Belgium. The Prussian garrison placed in Luxembourg City by the Congress maintained order in the city and its surroundings. The Treaty of London divided the duchy. Although the Belgians claimed all of Luxembourg, only the larger western (French-speaking) section was added to Belgium as the province of Luxembourg. The smaller Lettisch-speaking area remained under William as the grand duchy of Luxembourg. The Belgians also received half of the province of Limburg, but Maastricht remained Dutch. The Scheldt River was declared open to the commerce of both countries and the national debt was divided between the two.

According to article VII of the settlement, Belgium was declared an "independent and perpetually neutral state" with this neutrality guaranteed by the signatory powers. This guarantee became the infamous "scrap of paper" disregarded by the Germans when they invaded Belgium in 1914.

—*Edward P. Keleher, updated by Bernard A. Cook*

FURTHER READING

Aronsen, Theo. *Defiant Dynasty: The Coburgs of Belgium*. Indianapolis: Bobbs-Merrill, 1968. Chatty history of the Belgian dynasty that contains a chapter on the first Belgian king, Leopold I.

Carson, Patricia. *The Fair Face of Flanders*. Ghent, Belgium: E. Story-Scientia, 1974. Contains a brief history of the revolution, its causes, its course, and the international reaction.

Chambers, James. *Palmerston: "The People's Darling."*

1830's

London: John Murray, 2004. Comprehensive biography of Viscount Palmerston, the British diplomat who played a decisive role in the achievement of Belgian independence.

Cook, Bernard A. *Belgium: A History*. New York: Peter Lang, 2002. Broad survey of Belgian history.

De Meeüs, Adrien. *History of the Belgians*. Translated by G. Gordon. New York: Frederick A. Praeger, 1962. General history of Belgium that includes a lengthy, detailed, and interesting interpretive treatment of the Belgian Revolution and its aftermath.

Kossmann, E. H. *The Low Countries, 1780-1940*. Oxford, England: Clarendon Press, 1978. This general history of the Low Countries provides a clear and insightful summary of the Belgian Revolution and the regime to which it gave birth. Kossmann points out the inchoate nature of the protests at their outset in August, 1830.

Thomas, Daniel. *The Guarantee of Belgian Independence and Neutrality in European Diplomacy, 1830's-1930's*. Kingston, R.I.: D. H. Thomas, 1983. Extensive study of the London Conference that secured both independence and neutrality for Belgium.

Van Houtte, J. A. "The Low Countries." In *The New Cambridge Modern History*, edited by C. W. Crowley. Vol. 9. Cambridge, England: Cambridge University Press, 1965. Chapter 16 clearly describes the religious and linguistic issues that alienated the Belgians from William.

Witte, Els, Jan Craeybeckx, and Alain Meynen. *Political History of Belgium from 1830 Onwards*. Translated by Raf Casert. Brussels: VUB University Press, 2000. General history of Belgium, from the nation's founding in 1830 through the late twentieth century.

SEE ALSO: Apr. 11, 1814-July 29, 1830: France's Bourbon Dynasty Is Restored; Sept. 15, 1814-June 11, 1815: Congress of Vienna; Nov. 20, 1815: Second Peace of Paris; Oct. 20-30, 1822: Great Britain Withdraws from the Concert of Europe; July 29, 1830: July Revolution Deposes Charles X.

RELATED ARTICLES in *Great Lives from History: The Nineteenth Century, 1801-1900:* Leopold II; Lord Palmerston.

October-December, 1830
DELACROIX PAINTS *LIBERTY LEADING THE PEOPLE*

Eugène Delacroix's Liberty Leading the People, *his only historical painting inspired by a contemporary event, became the quintessential symbol of heroic and egalitarian struggle for liberty, but it was also a reflection of the artist's desire to paint for his country and thus participate in the July Revolution deposing Charles X.*

LOCALE: Paris, France
CATEGORY: Art

KEY FIGURES
Eugène Delacroix (1798-1863), French Romantic painter
Charles X (1757-1836), king of France, r. 1824-1830
Louis-Philippe (1773-1850), king of France, r. 1830-1848

SUMMARY OF EVENT
On July 26, 1830, the French king Charles X suspended freedom of the press, dissolved the Chamber of Deputies, and restricted the right to vote. In direct protest to the king's oppressive measures, the people took to the streets. Three days of violence ensued, resulting in one thousand deaths and widespread destruction, as well as the fall of the Bourbon Dynasty, which had been restored to power after Napoleon I's defeat at Waterloo in 1815. Historically referred to as the July Revolution or Les Trois Glorieuses (the Three Glorious Days), the riots of July 27-29 led to Charles X's abdication on August 2, 1830, and the accession of Louis-Philippe to a republican throne as the "king of the French people." The young painter Eugène Delacroix was moved by the battle scene he had witnessed firsthand near the Pont d'Arcole in Paris to paint an allegory representing this historical moment, *Liberty Leading the People*.

Nineteenth century viewers easily recognized the setting and members of society among the crowd represented in Delacroix's passionate work. At a distance of only a few months, Delacroix recreated from memory the stirring sensation of the Three Glorious Days when the spirit of Liberty, the central figure in his painting, led French people from different walks of life to unite in revolt. Amid billowing clouds of smoke, the profile of Notre Dame Cathedral emerges in the painting as the topographical

Eugène Delacroix's Liberty Leading the People. *(North Wind Picture Archives)*

backdrop for the revolution. One can readily identify various personages on the basis of their characteristic outfits, including a factory worker with a saber, a bourgeois foreman with a gun, and a tradesman kneeling at Liberty's feet. In the background, one may also discern a student from the prestigious engineering college L'École Polytechnique by his tipped hat. Victims on opposing sides of the rebellion lie prostrate in the foreground: at left, the body of a male combatant of the people; at right, two soldiers of the royal guard who attempted to suppress the insurrection. To Liberty's immediate right, a young boy brandishing arms recalls the students from the Latin Quarter who joined in the victorious uprising.

The painting takes its name from the figure who occupies the center of the work, a young woman dressed like the people boldly standing barefoot at the top of a barricade formed by the cadavers of revolutionaries. Soiled and with breasts bared, she proudly waves the revolutionary tricolor flag with which her red Phrygian cap indicates a clear allegiance. Delacroix's arresting transformation of the classical nude into a modern allegorical symbol outraged many nineteenth century art critics yet captivated his contemporaries. He elevated the figure of a working-class woman into Liberty incarnate.

In a letter to his brother Charles dated October 12, 1830, Delacroix announced that he had undertaken a modern subject, *A Barricade*, and with this project, the otherwise noncombatant painter had taken up artistic arms on behalf of his country. Exceptionally political in the context of Delacroix's generally apolitical oeuvre, *Liberty Leading the People* portrayed in both realistic and allegorical ways the "glorious" victory of the people that brought Louis-Philippe to power. The title of the painting squarely situated the work in a specific historical context, whereas Delacroix's symbol of Liberty raised questions about his aesthetics and eventually about the politics of his painting.

The composition of the painting is united through a

pyramidal construction. The base of the pyramid, composed by cadavers lying side by side, forms a triangle that is anchored at right by the foot of the boy accompanying Liberty and at left by the butt of the bourgeois personage's rifle. The spectator's eye is directed upward to the flag, held high above the barricade. In striking contrast to the classical compositional stability of the work, along with the play of light and shadows, Delacroix's mixing of brilliant colors and earth tones evokes movement and emotion in ways associated with Romanticism. Interweaving the real and the ideal, *Liberty Leading the People* expressed the sensibility of an era rife with contradictions.

Delacroix's thoroughly Romantic canvas was first presented at the Salon of 1831, and it earned the artist the Legion of Honor. The new king, Louis-Philippe, was initially impressed by the dynamism and ardor of the painting and acquired it for the Palais du Luxembourg. In a matter of months, however, the increasingly conservative July regime viewed the political implications of Delacroix's composition with suspicion. Delacroix had captured for generations to come the revolutionary impetus that precipitated Louis-Philippe's reign, a universal passion for liberty that threatened any monarch's authority.

By 1832, Louis-Philippe ordered that *Liberty Leading the People* be stored out of public view. The painting was returned to Delacroix in 1839, most likely because the director of fine arts at the time, Edmond Cavé, was a friend of the artist. The controversial work was again requested from Delacroix after the Paris Revolution of 1848 and exhibited at the Luxembourg until 1850, after which time the canvas, once again considered charged with subversive potential, was stored. By way of a direct appeal to Napoleon III, Delacroix succeeded in having *Liberty Leading the People* included in the retrospective dedicated to him at the Exposition Universelle of 1855. It was not until 1861, however, that Delacroix's painting was reinstated at the Luxembourg Museum and transferred to the Louvre Museum in 1874. In 2003, France's minister of culture announced plans to decentralize Delacroix's work of art, removing it from Paris to a provincial location. The fate of Delacroix's masterpiece has yet to be determined.

SIGNIFICANCE

The aesthetic weight and political meaning of Eugène Delacroix's *Liberty Leading the People* was apparent in his day. Publicly honored and rejected in succession for his choice and treatment of a politically indeterminate historic moment, Delacroix rightly saw 1830 emblem-

atically as a time of tension and indecision about the future of liberty in a postrevolutionary culture. Criticized for his figure of Liberty, a living type taken from contemporary life that did not hark back to classical mythology, the Romantic Delacroix, wittingly or not, prepared the way for realism.

To reconsider Delacroix's illustration of a scene of contemporary history today is to appreciate more fully his inspired use of color to evoke real sensation, which the poet Charles Baudelaire deemed visionary during the nineteenth century. With *Liberty Leading the People*, Delacroix successfully negotiated his formal classical heritage and his expressive Romantic tendencies. The aesthetic ambivalence of his allegorical picture continues to inspire new readings of his artistic genius. A painting that gained popular currency, as suggested by its use on the one-hundred-franc bill in 1979 and on a postage stamp in 1982, *Liberty Leading the People* is a singular cultural archive of a principal chapter in French history and a unique monument to the rich history of French art.

—*Adrianna M. Paliyenko*

FURTHER READING

Fraser, Elisabeth A. *Delacroix, Art, and Patrimony in Post-Revolutionary France*. New York: Cambridge University Press, 2004. A close treatment of Delacroix's relationship to the Bourbon Restoration, traced in relation to his early art, which set the stage for the political significance of *Liberty Leading the People*.

Jobert, Barthélémy. *Delacroix*. Princeton, N.J.: Princeton University Press, 1998. A careful reappraisal of Delacroix's place in cultural history that treats stages of the painter's visionary work and the conditions under which he created particular works, including *Liberty Leading the People*.

Prideaux, Tom. *The World of Delacroix, 1798-1863*. New York: Time, 1966. A detailed account of Delacroix's historical moment that relates the complexity of his artistic genius to the tension between his classical and Romantic tendencies.

Roger-Marx, Claude, and Sabine Cotté. *Delacroix's Universe*. Translated by Lynn Michelman. Woodbury, N.Y.: Barrons, 1970. A thematic study of Delacroix's drawings, sketches, and pastels for his majors works, including *Liberty Leading the People*, with selections from his writings.

Wiseman, Mary. "Gendered Symbols." *The Journal of Aesthetics and Art Criticism* 56, no. 3 (1998): 241-249. A detailed analysis of gendered readings of *Liberty Leading the People* that exposes their reliance upon familiar conceptions of the feminine and opens up a new way of thinking about Delacroix's use of allegory.

Wright, Beth Segal, ed. *The Cambridge Companion to Delacroix*. New York: Cambridge University Press, 2001. A collection of essays that provide an overview of Delacroix's life and work and analyses of the painter's canvases, thoughts, and influence.

SEE ALSO: 1801: Emergence of the Primitives; Mar., 1814: Goya Paints *Third of May 1808: Execution of the Citizens of Madrid*; Apr. 11, 1814-July 29, 1830: France's Bourbon Dynasty Is Restored; 1824: Paris Salon of 1824; July 29, 1830: July Revolution Deposes Charles X; Feb. 22-June, 1848: Paris Revolution of 1848; 1855: Courbet Establishes Realist Art Movement; May 15, 1863: Paris's Salon des Refusés Opens; Apr. 15, 1874: First Impressionist Exhibition; Late 1870's: Post-Impressionist Movement Begins; 1892-1895: Toulouse-Lautrec Paints *At the Moulin Rouge*; 1893: Munch Paints *The Scream*.

RELATED ARTICLES in *Great Lives from History: The Nineteenth Century, 1801-1900:* Charles Baudelaire; Eugène Delacroix; Napoleon I; Napoleon III.

November 29, 1830-August 15, 1831
FIRST POLISH REBELLION

Despite the apparent successes of the partial integration of Poland into the Russian Empire, many Poles still sought independence for their homeland. Their first significant rebellion enjoyed a brief success, but the Poles themselves were too divided to withstand Russia's reassertion of military control.

LOCALE: Congress Poland
CATEGORY: Wars, uprisings, and civil unrest

KEY FIGURES
Nicholas I (1796-1855), czar of Russia and king of Poland, r. 1825-1855
Constantine (1827-1892), son of Nicholas I and commander of the Polish army
Józef Chłopicki (1771-1854), Polish conservative who was made the military dictator
Adam Jerzy Czartoryski (1770-1861), Polish conservative leader
Johann von Diebitsch (1785-1831), German-born commander of Russian forces
Joachim Lelewel (1786-1861), Polish historian and radical leader
Ksawery Drucki Lubecki (1779-1846), chancellor of Poland
Maurycy Mochnacki (1804-1834), Polish radical leader and writer
Ivan Fyodorovich Paskevich (1782-1856), commander of Russian forces and later viceroy of Poland

SUMMARY OF EVENT
Vulnerably situated in the center of Europe and hemmed in by the growing assertiveness of Prussia and the impe-

rial power of Austria and Russia, Poland weakened itself during the eighteenth century through its internal dissension. It even temporarily vanished from the map of Europe when its three powerful neighbors partitioned it in 1772, 1793, and 1795, with Russia gaining the largest share. Many Poles continued to dream of resurrecting an independent Poland, and some revolted against Russian authority in 1794. However, large numbers of Poles also became absorbed into the governing structure of partitioned Poland. After Napoleon I's defeat in 1815, the Congress of Vienna established a Polish kingdom, which was given the name "Congress Poland," but placed it under the personal administration of the Russian czar.

Russia's position in Congress Poland, where Czar Nicholas I ruled as king in accordance with the Vienna settlement, seemed secure by 1829. Apparently reconciled to Russian rule, Poles prospered under the Russian-appointed chancellor, Prince Ksawery Drucki Lubecki. An entire generation of Polish émigrés had fought on Napoleon's side in his wars against Russia, and they had become influenced by French revolutionary ideas. These Polish radicals hoped that the spirit of revolution in France would spread across Europe, eventually liberating their country from foreign control. The Polish army, commanded by Nicholas's brother Grand Duke Constantine, was the kind of superbly disciplined military machine that Nicholas loved. Indeed, he prized the Poles enough to use only Russian units in his war against Turkey in 1828. In that campaign, Field Marshal Johann von Diebitsch's troops had marched to the gates of Constantinople. The Russian triumph was been costly, but Nicholas spared his magnificent Poles from what would have been heavy casualties.

After Russia's triumph in Turkey, Russian security quickly vanished. Rebellion erupted in France in July, 1830, and soon spread. Desiring to check the revolutionary threat, Nicholas alerted his Polish units for war, but the events of November 29, 1830, destroyed the czar's plan. A number of Polish army officers who despised Constantine's strict disciplinary methods and resented missing opportunities for glory in the war against the Turks helped students to execute a coup d'état. Constantine immediately withdrew from Warsaw. Arguing that the rebellion was strictly a Polish affair, he prevailed on Nicholas to delay any reaction until the Poles recovered their senses. Later, with Nicholas's approval, Constantine withdrew all Russian forces from Poland and permitted the Polish units that had remained with him to return to Warsaw. He hoped that such measures would avoid bloodshed.

Deep historical feelings had caused the Polish rebellion. Poland's nobility had never completely abandoned hope of restoring the independent Polish state, which had been dominated by an aristocratic oligarchy until its disappearance in the late eighteenth century partitions. Since 700,000 Poles were numbered among the nobility, this attitude constantly endangered Russian control. Romanticism inspired educated Poles to revive their anti-Russian national heritage. Tension between Roman Catholic Poles and Orthodox Christian Russians intensified nationalistic animosity.

Polish students, impressed by their culture's romantic emphasis on individual military valor, were hostile toward the Russians and older Poles who accepted Russian influence as economically progressive. Poles traditionally had sought French support for their independence and claimed to admire French republicanism. Rumors that the czar would order Polish troops to march against the new French Republic angered them. Secret nationalist organizations, aware that the police had discovered them, exploited this tense situation to launch what proved to be a premature coup on November 29, 1830.

The Polish revolutionary movement had numerous weaknesses. From its inception, it was divided into a radical wing led by Maurycy Mochnacki and Joachim Lelewel, and a conservative wing led first by Lubecki and later by Prince Adam Jerzy Czartoryski. The conservatives appointed General Józef Chłopicki military dictator on December 1, but their control of the movement was weak. Moreover, aristocratic dominance of the insurrection alienated the Polish serfs. In the long run, the Poles

could scarcely hope for military victory. Russian superiority in manpower and equipment would eventually be overwhelming, and the Russians were far more united than the Poles. At best, the Poles could only hope for early victories, an anti-Russian revolt in West Russia where the nobility was Polish, or foreign intervention.

Following Constantine's advice, Czar Nicholas responded to the revolt cautiously. He conferred with Lubecki in St. Petersburg on December 26, 1830, offering the Poles general amnesty in exchange for their submission, but refusing to guarantee Poland's constitution of 1815. The Polish radicals merely became more adamant. On January 16, 1831, they forced Chłopicki to resign after he had argued that war with Russia would be futile. Czartoryski's new coalition government failed to curb rising nationalism. The Poles deposed Nicholas as their titular king and demanded restoration of the 1772 boundaries, including West Russia. Nicholas then decided to fight.

On February 7, 1831, Diebitsch's Russians entered Poland. The Poles won the initial skirmishes but were shattered in the first major battle at Grochów on February 24. Panic then developed in Warsaw. Wary that a long campaign might increase foreign diplomatic pressure, Nicholas urged that Warsaw be taken. However, Diebitsch decided to rest and provision his army at some distance from the Polish capital. The front remained relatively static for two months. The Poles, fearing a major engagement far from Warsaw, awaited foreign intervention or widespread revolt in West Russia. Cholera ravaged the Russian army, killing thirteen thousand soldiers. General Jan Skrzynecki, the Polish commander, finally attacked the Russians and was thoroughly defeated at Ostrolenka on May 26. Diebitsch, who was himself to die of cholera early in June, again allowed the Poles to escape.

Field Marshal Ivan Paskevich, Nicholas's new commander, was ordered to crush the insurgents quickly. In July and August, he cautiously blockaded Warsaw while Russian reinforcements poured into Poland. The Poles refused Nicholas's final offer of amnesty on July 29, but their already sharp political divisions worsened under the tension produced by an apparently inevitable Russian victory. On August 15, a mob toppled the Czartoryski government and murdered some Russian prisoners. Both Polish disunity and Russian military superiority made Paskevich's storming of Warsaw on September 5 almost anticlimactic. The Polish rebellion had already ended.

Nicholas punished rebels in Congress Poland less severely than the Poles who, as Russian citizens, had rebelled in West Russia. Thousands of the former group became voluntary exiles, although an amnesty issued on October 20 pardoned all Poles in Congress Poland except those involved in the massacre of Russian prisoners on August 15. Some estates in Congress Poland were confiscated and given to Russian officers. West Russian Polish insurgents suffered execution, imprisonment, or exile to Siberia. Finally, on February 26, 1832, Nicholas promulgated the Organic Statute, which restricted the rights Poles had enjoyed under the constitution of 1815. Paskevich, named viceroy under the new system, began a systematic campaign against Polish nationalism.

SIGNIFICANCE

With the failure of the Polish rebellion, Poland became virtually an integral part of Russia. Thousands of Poles began emigrating—many of them to Paris, which then became the focal point of Polish nationalist agitation. In spite of crushing defeats the idea of an independent Poland survived—if only as an improbable, romantic aspiration. The slim hope that either Great Britain or France would intervene on the behalf of the Poles was extinguished in the 1830-1831 Polish rebellion.

The uprising illustrated that Polish shortcomings were as damaging to the Polish cause as Russian strength. However, this lesson escaped many bitter Poles who blamed the failure of 1830-1831 on poor or "treasonous" generals. The failure of Polish leaders to heal the divisions plaguing the nationalist movement would cause another rebellion to fail in 1863.

—*Wayne D. Santoni, updated by Carl Rollyson*

FURTHER READING

Biskupski, Mieczyslaw B. *The History of Poland*. Westport, Conn.: Greenwood Press, 2000. Solid general history of Poland, whose political transformations have been at least as great as those of any nation in Europe.

Chapman, Tim. *The Congress of Vienna: Origins, Processes, and Results*. London: Routledge, 1998. Study of the proceedings at the international peace conference that created Congress Poland, with attention to the long-term consequences of the conference's decisions.

Curtiss, John Shelton. *The Russian Army Under Nicholas I, 1825-1855*. Durham, N.C.: Duke University Press, 1965. In addition to providing biographies of both Diebitsch and Paskevich, this superb work contains information on the military aspects of the Polish revolution and offers reasons for Diebitsch's reluctance to crush the Poles quickly.

Davies, Norman. *God's Playground: A History of Poland*. New York: Columbia University Press, 1984. This two-volume study remains one of the most up-to-date, reliable, and readable histories of Poland in English.

_____. *Heart of Europe: A Short History of Poland*. New York: Oxford University Press, 1984. Works backward from the events during the early 1980's to eighteenth century Poland, emphasizing those factors that were most important in shaping the country's present.

Halecki, Oskar, with additional material by A. Polonsky. *A History of Poland*. London: Kegan Paul, 1978. Standard work on Polish history. Contains especially useful maps.

Kagan, Frederick W. *The Military Reforms of Nicholas I: The Origins of the Modern Russian Army*. New York: St. Martin's Press, 1999. Thorough and scholarly study of Nicholas's reign and reorganization of the Russian army during the period of the first Polish rebellion. Most suitable for scholars.

Kukiel, Marian. *Czartoryski and European Unity, 1770-1861*. Princeton, N.J.: Princeton University Press, 1955. Kukiel praises the great Polish conservative statesman, concentrating on his foreign policy.

Wandyc, Piotr S. *The Lands of Partitioned Poland, 1795-1918*. Seattle: University of Washington Press, 1996. Excellent overview of the many partitions and realignments of Poland from the late eighteenth century through the end of World War I.

SEE ALSO: Sept. 15, 1814-June 11, 1815: Congress of Vienna; Jan. 22-Sept., 1863: Russia Crushes Polish Rebellion.

RELATED ARTICLES in *Great Lives from History: The Nineteenth Century, 1801-1900:* Napoleon I; Nicholas I.

1830's

1831
MAZZINI FOUNDS YOUNG ITALY

*Giuseppe Mazzini's founding of Young Italy gave the
fragmented Italian unification movement a clear focus,
stronger organization, and eager recruits.*

ALSO KNOWN AS: Giovane Italia
LOCALE: Piedmont, in northern Italy
CATEGORIES: Government and politics; organizations
and institutions

KEY FIGURES

Giuseppe Mazzini (1805-1872), revolutionary
spokesperson for liberal nationalism and Italian
unification
Count Cavour (1810-1861), prime minister of
Sardinia-Piedmont, 1852-1861
Giuseppe Garibaldi (1807-1882), revolutionary soldier
who led the popular struggle for Italian unification
Victor Emmanuel II (1820-1878), king of Sardinia-
Piedmont, r. 1849-1861, and first king of Italy,
r. 1861-1878

SUMMARY OF EVENT

The Risorgimento was the long process whereby the six
governments that shared the Italian peninsula in 1815
eventually disappeared, as a single unitary kingdom of
Italy arose. Among the various political and military
leaders who emerged during this process, the names of
three tower above all others: Giuseppe Mazzini, Count
Cavour, and Giuseppe Garibaldi. In assessing the complex relationships among these three men, one might label Mazzini the spiritual inspiration, Cavour the careful
statesman, and Garibaldi the popular soldier—a spirit, a
mastermind, and a sword who fomented revolutionary
change and founded modern Italy.

Giuseppe Mazzini was, perhaps, an unlikely revolutionary hero. Born into a comfortable professional family in the northern Italian port city of Genoa in 1805, he
was a rather sickly child who spent much time in the
company of books and adults. Nevertheless, the studious
youth absorbed revolutionary ideas from his reading
about the French Revolution (1789) and from the reform-
minded adults around him. Genoa had been a part of Napoleon I's French Empire and had undergone numerous
progressive reforms. Those reforms were abolished after
1815, when the Congress of Vienna placed much of northern Italy under the control of the conservative houses of
Savoy (Piedmont) and of Habsburg (Austria). Middle-
class liberals such as the Mazzinis' circle quickly began

to yearn for the days of "liberty, equality, and fraternity"
once more.

As early as 1821, sporadic revolts began in northern
Italy against the control of Piedmont and Austria. Mazzini thus grew up in an atmosphere filled with political
dissent and resentment against the German-speaking foreigners in Vienna whose armies crushed Italian aspirations toward self-government. Intellectually, Mazzini
began to combine opposition to all existing governments, desire for political freedom, and Italian nationalism into one noble cause. From the time he was in his
early twenties, he wore only black clothing, expressing
his mourning over the loss of Italian freedoms. In 1830,
he joined the secret conspiratorial society of the Carbonari, a loosely organized group of liberal and radical
revolutionaries. He attended illegal meetings, distributed
banned newspapers, procured weapons, and took part in
riotous antigovernment demonstrations.

A passion for Italy became the driving force of Mazzini's life. He was arrested and spent six months impris-

Giuseppe Mazzini. (Library of Congress)

oned in a local fortress. During this enforced solitude, he pondered Italy's future and realized his life's calling: to dedicate himself to the mission of freeing Italy. To that end, he took as his motto "God and the People." He believed that God had intended humankind to find individual freedom by combining in nationhood. Once all peoples had achieved political liberties and combined into national communities, they would pursue humanitarian goals and live in peace with one another.

Mazzini charged that earlier revolutionaries, such as the Carbonari, had failed because they overemphasized individual rights and freedoms. He now exhorted Italians to emphasize duty, the sacred duty to make Italy a single nation under one government. These ideas illustrated major themes of the liberal variety of nationalism that dominated the first half of the nineteenth century. To Mazzini and his followers, nationalism ultimately meant cooperation among all peoples, not competition or warfare. These views reflect the powerful influence of the Romantic movement and of contemporary utopian socialism, with its stress on cooperation and community values. Unlike many other liberals, Mazzini had strong faith in the masses of the people and believed they would rise up and overthrow the "tyrants" oppressing Italy. He was a firm republican and even when the king of Piedmont lent his prestige and power to the unification movement, Mazzini opposed monarchy and rejected the leadership of Piedmont.

Mazzini reserved for Italy a special place among nations. Just as Rome had been the center of a great empire in antiquity and the center of Christianity, during the Middle Ages, Mazzini expected Italy again to lead Europe forward. Soon after his release from prison, he established in 1831 a new revolutionary society that he called Young Italy (*Giovane Italia*). He expected Young Italy, armed with his messianic message and personal direction, to succeed where the Carbonari had failed. Young Italy had one goal: unification of all Italians in a single republican government with civil and political freedom for all.

Mazzini worked to harness the energies of youth to his dream; Young Italy primarily recruited young middle-class men who bravely (and illegally) went forth to proselytize among all classes of Italians. He poured forth nearly one hundred volumes of writings to provide inspiration and propaganda for his troops. He also urged his followers to action. Young Italy prepared for uprisings and guerrilla warfare by stockpiling weapons and organizing recruits in cells of ten, with officers whose titles reflected those of the ancient Roman army.

After government officials discovered Mazzini's activities, they exiled him. He left Italy at the age of twenty-seven and spent most of his remaining years in exile, chiefly in Great Britain, where popular opinion favored his cause. However, critics charged that Mazzini soon lost contact with Italian realities and that his mystical doctrines were impractical. Nevertheless, his influence was widespread and his personal dedication inspired thousands, including Garibaldi, to take direct action.

Mazzini personally participated in the tumultuous events in Rome during the Italian Revolution of 1848 and skillfully led the Roman republic until it was defeated by foreign troops. From Britain, his ideology spread to non-Italians and he blessed the creation of Young Hungary, Young Germany, and Young Europe. He advocated the formation of twelve independent countries in Europe to satisfy the national aspirations of major ethnic groups with recognized histories and cultures.

Italy was ultimately unified under the direction of Cavour and Victor Emmanuel II of Savoy, with assistance from Garibaldi and the Italian people. Cavour obtained assistance from foreign governments, first France and then Prussia, to expel the Austrians and then gradually fit the separate pieces of Italian territory together between 1859 and 1870. However, Mazzini insisted that Italians acting alone must fulfill their divine duty. He was disappointed that his fellow Italians accepted a monarchy and assistance from foreigners. He bitterly resented the papacy's determined opposition to all forms of Italian unification and regretted that millions of Italians nevertheless remained faithful to the pope. He became convinced that both liberals and socialists had abandoned their ideals and adopted grasping materialism. His burning devotion to his original ideals never wavered, but most Italians accepted Piedmont's achievements.

SIGNIFICANCE

Mazzini remained in exile even after the kingdom of Italy was firmly established and he had been elected to its parliament by grateful citizens. Later, however, he returned to Italy under a false name, stubbornly remaining an outlaw and revolutionary. Such behavior gave some credence to the suggestions that he was ignorant of true conditions in Italy and unrealistic in his goals. Even so, the inspired zeal and persistent agitation of the Young Italy organization that he had created had prepared the foundation for the emergence of a united Italy. As Mazzini hoped, the masses did sometimes rise up against repression, the people adopted the Italian nationalist cause, and the new Italian state was unitary, not federated, and

1830's

possessed a liberal, constitutional government. Mazzini's blueprint was not followed in every detail, but none could deny he was a major architect of modern Italy.

—*Sharon B. Watkins*

FURTHER READING

Albrecht-Carrié, René. *Italy from Napoleon to Mussolini*. Rev. ed. New York: Columbia University Press, 1966. A readable account of Italian history from 1796 that places Mazzini into the broad context of the Risorgimento.

Di Scala, Spencer. *Italy from Revolution to Republic: 1700 to the Present*. 3d ed. Boulder, Colo.: Westview Press, 2004. General history of modern Italy that includes a section on the Risorgimento.

Griffith, Gwilym O. *Mazzini: Prophet of Modern Europe*. Reprint. New York: Howard Fertig, 1970. A solid, reliable biography that sees Mazzini as a principal source of nationalism.

Mack Smith, Denis, ed. *The Making of Italy, 1796-1870*. New York: Walker, 1968. This volume combines documents from the past with a modern commentary linking the events discussed; interesting selections from Mazzini's writings.

_____. *Mazzini*. New Haven, Conn.: Yale University Press, 1994. Written by a well-known specialist in Italian history, this account of Mazzini and his work is full of narrative detail and analysis.

Riall, Lucy. *The Italian Risorgimento: State, Society, and National Unification*. London: Routledge, 1994. Scholarly study of the Risorgimento movement, with considerable attention to Mazzini's role.

Roberts, William. *Prophet in Exile: Joseph Mazzini in England, 1837-1868*. New York: Peter Lang, 1989. This work combines Mazzini's personal story with that of his work abroad.

Salvemini, Gaetano. *Mazzini*. Translated by I. M. Rawson. New York: Collier Books, 1957. Biography that provides a thorough explanation of Mazzini's thought and doctrines.

Sarti, Roland. *Mazzini: A Life for the Religion of Politics*. Westport, Conn.: Praeger, 1997. Biography exploring the relationship between Mazzini's life and his ideas.

SEE ALSO: Jan. 12, 1837: Mazzini Begins London Exile; Jan. 12, 1848-Aug. 28, 1849: Italian Revolution of 1848; Dec. 8, 1854: Pius IX Decrees the Immaculate Conception Dogma; May-July, 1860: Garibaldi's Redshirts Land in Sicily; Mar. 17, 1861: Italy Is Proclaimed a Kingdom.

RELATED ARTICLES in *Great Lives from History: The Nineteenth Century, 1801-1900:* Count Cavour; Giuseppe Garibaldi; Vincenzo Gioberti; Giuseppe Mazzini.

1831-1834
HIROSHIGE COMPLETES *THE TOKAIDO FIFTY-THREE STATIONS*

One of Japan's most popular artists of his day, Hiroshige published fifty-five woodblock prints depicting scenes found along the fifty-three towns and checkpoints of the Tokaido, or main highway, of Edo, Japan. The series became an immediate best seller and is still regarded as one of the finest examples of the ukiyo-e genre of printmaking.

ALSO KNOWN AS: *Tōokaidōo gojusan no uchi*
LOCALE: Japan
CATEGORY: Art

KEY FIGURES
Hiroshige (1797-1858), *ukiyo-e* printmaker noted for his sensitive and detailed landscapes
Hokusai (1760-1849), noted printmaker of the nineteenth century

Utagawa Toyohiro (1773-1829), teacher of Hiroshige
Tokugawa Ienari (1733-1841), shogun of Japan, r. 1787-1837
Jippensha Ikku (1765-1831), playwright and novelist of comic fiction

SUMMARY OF EVENT
The mid-nineteenth century saw the zenith of *ukiyo-e*, a genre of woodblock print popular during Japan's Edo period (1600-1868). *Ukiyo-e*, pictures of the floating world, were typified by their bright garish colors depicting famous high-ranking courtesans, or geisha, well-known kabuki actors, theater scenes, landscapes, and illustrations for sex manuals. *Ukiyo-e* was an art form intended for mass consumption, and prints were available in albums or single sheets. One of the most famous

and best-selling collections was Hiroshige's 1831-1834 *Tōokaidōo gojusan no uchi* (*The Tokaido Fifty-Three Stations*, 1926).

The son of a firefighter, Hiroshige was born in 1797 in Edo (now Tokyo). He was given the name Utagawa Hiroshige one year after he began studying with the well-known master Utagawa Toyohiro at the age of fourteen. Between 1825 and 1858, Hiroshige produced more than 5,400 color woodblock prints, including nine hundred scenes of Edo alone. In his lifetime, he likely supervised and designed five thousand more prints, or about two per week for forty-five years.

Japan's Edo period was a time of relative peace and calm. After centuries of intermittent civil war, the Tokugawa family gained control of the islands and established the shogunate, ruling in the name of the emperor, who held cultural legitimacy but not much political power. Because of little actual fighting, members of the samurai warrior class gradually became bureaucrats and administrators. Farmers and artisans, no longer plagued by lawless marauding armies, devoted themselves to production. For most areas of the country, the population increased, as did the quality of life of the people.

The most significant development of Edo times, however, was the establishment of a merchant culture. Towns sprang up around the castles of the various local vassal warlords, and prosperity led to the establishment of an urban middle class. Skilled laborers, craftsmen, artisans, and other service providers were required to support the idle samurai, who now wrote poetry, cultivated the arts, and practiced scholarship as much as swordsmanship. By 1800, Edo had a population of more than one million, and Osaka (a major business center) and Kyoto (the imperial capital) had more than 300,000 inhabitants between them. An urban merchant class of *chonin*, or townsmen, arose with the commercialization of the rural economy.

The *chonin*, and some of the idle samurai, established a fledging bourgeois culture of consumption and entertainment. Tea houses and pleasure quarters were found in every city. Popular art forms—such as the kabuki theater, romance and adventure novels, and illustrated volumes of comic pictures—widely proliferated. Woodblock printing allowed for the mass production and

Hiroshige's 1857 woodblock print Plum Estate, Kameido, from his "One Hundred Famous Views of Edo." (AP/Wide World Photos)

inexpensive distribution of picture books and illustrated novels and stories. In essence, then, *ukiyo-e* was the visual documentation of this ephemeral "floating world" of pleasure of the townsmen lifestyle.

Hiroshige lived during the reign of Tokugawa Ienari, the eleventh shogun. The time was one of good harvests, economic stability, and the absence of political strife (though this would change during the late 1830's when crop failures, famine, and Ienari's increasing corruption weakened the government). The Tokaido road connected the residence of the Tokugawa shogun with the emperor's palace in Kyoto. Many traveled the Tokaido as local warlords sent their families back and forth for yearlong "visits" to Edo—where the shogun could keep a close eye on them, gaining leverage against any warlord with political ambitions. Thousands traveled the road as porters for these entourages, as religious pilgrims, as merchants or traders, or as adventurers. Jippensha Ikku immortalized some of these travels in a popular serialized satirical novel called *Dōchū hizakurige* (1802-1822; *Hizakurige: A Shanks' Mare Tour of the Tokaido*, 1952), an account of two wanderers who had increasingly outlandish and bawdy escapades.

Travel along the Tokaido usually took about two weeks. About every two or three hours by foot was a *shukuba machi* (postal town), an official settlement established by the government to cater to travelers needs and to regulate who was going where. There were fifty-three such stations along the Tokaido.

By 1832, Hiroshige was a minor official in the shogun's fire department. During that year he accompanied a troop taking a horse that Ienari was presenting to the emperor. As more and more people were becoming familiar with the Tokaido through their own travels or through popular literary accounts (such as that of Jippensha Ikku), and, as woodblock prints were often sold on street corners much like souvenir post cards, Hiroshige and his publisher, Hoeido Takenouchi, realized that the sketches of his trip would make quite profitable reproductions.

In *The Tokaido Fifty-Three Stations*, Hiroshige extended the development of the landscape form initiated by Hokusai, the other great *ukiyo-e* master of the time. Hiroshige's lighting and texture was more subtle, however, as was his use of weather to convey mood and atmosphere. The prints in the series demonstrated Hiroshige's knowledge of Western realism and perspective, and often his coloring mimicked the brush strokes of a painting.

SIGNIFICANCE

The immediate success of *The Tokaido Fifty-Three Stations* made Hiroshige an overnight sensation, and the work led to great demand for other series of travel scenes of the Tokaido. Hiroshige made some four dozen other series of Tokaido themes, the majority consisting of fifty or more prints. He catered to all tastes and age groups, from depictions of the Tokaido's famous rivers to its famous bedrooms. Other artists tried, without much success, to duplicate his scenes, but no one was ever as popular or as critically acclaimed. Even Hiroshige only rarely exceeded the genius shown in the original series published by Hoeido. For example, his depictions, in collaboration with Eisen Ikeda (1790-1848), of the Kiso-

kaido, the alternative inland route from Edo to Kyoto, was less popular though still full of artistic merit. The work was published as *Kiso kaidō rokujūkyūtsugi* (sixty-nine stations of the east-west highway through the central mountains) in 1834-1842, and an English introduction and presentation of the artwork was published in 1922.

Hiroshige's landscapes had a more universal appeal than the prints of other artists who specialized in kabuki actors, famous beautiful women, or erotica. While some say that the painter Hokusai may have been more inventive, Hiroshige was by far the most popular *ukiyo-e* artist, ever, in terms of sales.

Nineteenth century Japanese woodblock prints were the most advanced means of mass color reproduction anywhere until the advent of color photography decades later. When Japan was opened to international commerce during the late nineteenth century, Westerners became enchanted with Japanese art and curios of all kinds. Hiroshige's prints were among the most popular. His works were on display at the Paris Expositions of 1855, 1876, and 1878. Young Vincent van Gogh, studying in Paris in 1870, owned and copied numerous Hiroshige prints, and other Western artists, such as James McNeill Whistler, Claude Monet, and many Impressionists, were influenced by Hiroshige's compositional ideas or imagery.

Hiroshige died in 1858. Ironically, it was around that time that Hiroshige's Edo—the floating world of the townsmen and travelers—began to disappear with Japan's rapid industrialization. As one art critic noted, Hiroshige was the last Japanese *ukiyo-e* artist to work entirely within the conventions of the genre. His work is one of the last—and most complete and romantic—accounts of Edo culture.

—*James Stanlaw*

FURTHER READING

Bicknell, Julian. *Hiroshige in Tokyo: The Floating World of Edo*. San Francisco, Calif.: Pomegranate Art Books, 1994. A well-illustrated description of Hiroshige's work in the context of Edo culture. Includes a chapter on the fifty-three stations of the Tokaido.

Blood, Katherine L., James Douglas Farquhar, Sandy Kita, and Lawrence E. Marceau. *The Floating World of Ukiyo-e: Shadows, Dreams, and Substance*. New York: Harry N. Abrams, 2001. A colorful look at *ukiyo-e* and the floating world of Edo, Japan. An excellent resource published in association with the Library of Congress. See the companion Library of

Congress Web site at http://www.loc.gov/exhibits/ukiyo-e/. Accessed January, 2006.

Fahr-Becker, Gabriele. *Japanese Prints*. Cologne, Germany: Taschen, 1999. A common example of the many general collections of Japanese prints, but Fahr-Becker places Hiroshige in his artistic context and provides many detailed examples.

Forrer, Matthi. *Hiroshige: Prints and Drawings*. London: Royal Academy of Arts, 1997. A collection of some 140 color illustrations, with essays by Hiroshige scholars Henry D. Smith II and Juzo Suzuki.

Michener, James. *The Floating World*. New York: Random House, 1954. A classic anecdotal account of the history of *ukiyo-e* by an American author and Japanese print collector. Michener's insightful chapter on Hiroshige contains an interesting discussion on how and why the color of one print was altered in various editions.

Narazaki, Muneshiuge. *Hiroshige: The 53 Stations of the Tokaido*. Tokyo: Kodansha, 1969. Probably the best discussion of this print series for students and general readers. All fifty-five pictures are presented in color and analyzed individually.

Salter, Rebecca. *Japanese Woodblock Printing*. Honolulu: University of Hawaii Press, 2001. This book, by a Western woodblock printer who studied in Japan, covers the making of Japanese woodblock prints. She describes in detail the creation of several of Hiroshige's prints and how their special qualities were achieved.

Stanley-Baker, Joan. *Japanese Art*. London: Thames and Hudson, 2000. An accessible historical overview of the Japanese visual arts, copiously illustrated with an extensive bibliography.

Woodblock Prints of Ando Hiroshige. http://www.hiroshige.org.uk/. This comprehensive site includes images of Hiroshige's work from both the fifty-three and sixty-nine stations series of prints. Also includes online versions of books from 1922 and 1925 that introduce Japanese printmaking to Western readers. Provides links to topic-related Web sites. Accessed January, 2006.

SEE ALSO: 1820's: China's Stele School of Calligraphy Emerges; 1823-1831: Hokusai Produces *Thirty-Six Views of Mount Fuji*.

RELATED ARTICLES in *Great Lives from History: The Nineteenth Century, 1801-1900:* Paul Cézanne; Paul Gauguin; Vincent van Gogh; Henri de Toulouse-Lautrec.

January 1, 1831
GARRISON BEGINS PUBLISHING *THE LIBERATOR*

During an era when abolitionist newspapers proliferated in northern states, William Lloyd Garrison's The Liberator *stood out as the most radical and uncompromising advocate of immediate abolition of slavery.*

LOCALE: Boston, Massachusetts
CATEGORIES: Journalism; social issues and reform

KEY FIGURES
William Lloyd Garrison (1805-1879), abolitionist leader and editor of *The Liberator*
Arthur Tappan (1786-1865), first president of the American Anti-Slavery Society
Lewis Tappan (1788-1873), leader of church-oriented abolitionists
Maria Weston Chapman (1806-1885), journalist and associate of Garrison
James Forten (1766-1842), African American abolitionist and financial backer of *The Liberator*
Benjamin Lundy (1789-1839), Quaker abolitionist
Wendell Phillips (1811-1884), orator and Garrison's associate

SUMMARY OF EVENT
William Lloyd Garrison and his newspaper were products of the era of religious revival known as the Second Great Awakening, which transformed Protestant theology in the United States. The Awakening engendered moral reform movements in New England and other parts of the North during the early decades of the nineteenth century. Unlike their Calvinist predecessors, those who engaged in moral reform assumed that human beings, by their actions, could create a perfect society and bring about the millennial return of Jesus Christ. In his perception of the sinfulness and criminality of slaveholding, which he believed deprived both slaves and masters of a chance for salvation, Garrison went beyond most reformers of his time.

William Lloyd Garrison. (Library of Congress)

Garrison was born in Newburyport, Massachusetts, in 1805. Deserted by his seafaring father at the age of three, he was raised in poverty by his devout Baptist mother, who instilled in him her own strict moral code. At thirteen years of age, he apprenticed as a printer at the *Newburyport Herald*, where he learned the newspaper business. By 1828, he was in Boston, working as the editor of *The National Philanthropist*, which supported the temperance movement. Garrison also supported what he and others perceived to be the antislavery efforts of the American Colonization Society (ACS), which had been founded in 1817. As the dominant antislavery organization of the 1820's, the ACS advocated the gradual abolition of slavery, combined with the transportation of free black Americans to Africa.

In 1828, Garrison's decision to join Quaker abolitionist Benjamin Lundy in Baltimore as coeditor of Lundy's weekly, *The Genius of Universal Emancipation*, led to *The Liberator* and a more radical antislavery movement. In Baltimore, Garrison observed slavery in practice. Influenced by members of Baltimore's African American community, he came to believe that gradualism would

never end the "peculiar institution." African American influences also led Garrison to conclude that the ACS perpetuated a racist assumption that black and white people could not live together as equals in the United States, and he came to oppose the society's "colonization" goals.

Garrison's increasing militancy made cooperation with the more conservative Lundy difficult. Garrison's radicalism also led to his imprisonment for libel in Baltimore and to his decision to return to New England to begin his own antislavery newspaper. On January 1, 1831, he published the first issue of *The Liberator* in Boston. In that inaugural issue, Garrison proclaimed his conversion to immediate, not gradual, abolition of slavery. Harshly condemning slaveholders as sinners and thieves, he pointed out that one did not ask sinners to stop sinning gradually or require that thieves gradually stop committing crimes. Christian morality and justice, he insisted, required that slaveholders immediately and unconditionally free their bondspeople.

Garrison was not the first to advocate immediate emancipation. What was different about him was his rejection of moderation and his linkage of immediatism with a demand that the rights of the formerly enslaved be recognized in the United States. In his most famous statement, Garrison proclaimed,

I am in earnest—I will not equivocate—I will not excuse—I will not retreat a single inch—AND I WILL BE HEARD.

Garrison's launching of *The Liberator* is also significant for its reflection of biracial cooperation in the antislavery movement. Although Garrison, like other white abolitionists, never entirely escaped the racial prejudices of his time, he and his newspaper enjoyed the strong support of African Americans. Wealthy black abolitionist James Forten of Philadelphia provided crucial financial support to *The Liberator* in its early years. During the same period, Garrison employed black subscription agents, and three-quarters of the newspaper's subscribers were black. In Boston, where white antiabolition sentiment could produce violent confrontations, Garrison enjoyed the physical protection of African Americans.

Meanwhile, Garrison and *The Liberator* played an essential role in the formation of the American Anti-Slavery Society (AASS). Founded in December, 1833, under the leadership of Garrison and New York City businessmen Arthur and Lewis Tappan, the AASS united immediate abolitionists in the United States through most of the 1830's. Reflecting the pacifistic views of Garrison, the Tappans, and others, the society pledged in its Declaration of Sentiments—modeled on the Declaration of Independence—to use peaceful means to bring about the immediate, uncompensated emancipation of all U.S. slaves, without colonization.

Promoted by *The Liberator*, dozens of other anti-slavery newspapers, and thousands of antislavery pamphlets, the AASS grew rapidly. By 1838, it claimed a membership in the North of approximately 250,000 people in 1,350 local affiliates. At the same time, however, internal tensions were tearing the AASS apart. The essential problem was that Garrison and his closest New England associates, including Maria Weston Chapman, Wendell Phillips, and Henry C. Wright, had concluded that the spirit of slavery had so permeated the nation that the North, as well as the South, had to be fundamentally changed.

Although other abolitionists were reaching similar conclusions during the late 1830's, many of them objected to the specific policies advocated in the columns of *The Liberator* to effect those changes. In particular, an increasingly unorthodox Garrison antagonized church-oriented abolitionists by his wholesale condemnation of organized religion. He also seemed to threaten traditional concepts of patriarchy by his championing of women's rights and, specifically, female equality within the AASS. He appeared to threaten government through his advocacy of nonresistance, the pacifist doctrine that physical force is never justified, even in self-defense or on behalf of law and order. He frustrated those who desired a separate abolitionist political party by condemning political parties as inherently corrupt.

As a result of these tensions, the abolitionist movement splintered in 1840. Garrison, his New England associates, and a few others throughout the North retained control of the AASS, but the great majority of abolitionists left the organization. Lewis Tappan began the American and Foreign Anti-Slavery Society, which, until 1855, maintained a church-oriented antislavery campaign. Politically inclined abolitionists organized the Liberty Party. By the 1850's, a majority of non-Garrisonian abolitionists had come to support the Republican Party, which advocated neither immediate abolition nor equal rights for African Americans.

During the 1840's and 1850's, Garrison used *The Liberator* and other forums to promote anticlericalism, women's rights, and nonresistance, as well as immediate emancipation and equal rights for African Americans.

GARRISON'S DECLARATION OF SENTIMENTS

The Declaration of Sentiments, excerpted below, represented the manifesto of the American Anti-Slavery Society. Modeled on the Declaration of Independence, it put forward both the rationale and the objectives of the society.

More than fifty-seven years have elapsed, since a band of patriots convened in this place [Philadelphia], to devise measures for the deliverance of this country from a foreign yoke. The corner-stone upon which they founded the Temple of Freedom was broadly this—'that all men are created equal; that they are endowed by their Creator with certain inalienable rights; that among these are life, LIBERTY, and the pursuit of happiness.' At the sound of their trumpet-call, three millions of people rose up as from the sleep of death, and rushed to the strife of blood; deeming it more glorious to die instantly as freemen, than desirable to live one hour as slaves. They were few in number—poor in resources; but the honest conviction that Truth, Justice and Right were on their side, made them invincible.

We have met together for the achievement of an enterprise, without which that of our fathers is incomplete; and which, for its magnitude, solemnity, and probable results upon the destiny of the world, as far transcends theirs as moral truth does physical force.

In purity of motive, in earnestness of zeal, in decision of purpose, in intrepidity of action, in steadfastness of faith, in sincerity of spirit, we would not be inferior to them.

Their principles led them to wage war against their oppressors, and to spill human blood like water, in order to be free.

Ours forbid the doing of evil that good may come, and lead us to reject, and to entreat the oppressed to reject, the use of all carnal weapons for deliverance from bondage; relying solely upon those which are spiritual, and mighty through God to the pulling down of strong holds.

Their measures were physical resistance—the marshalling in arms—the hostile array—the mortal encounter. Ours shall be such only as the opposition of moral purity to moral corruption—the destruction of error by the potency of truth—the overthrow of prejudice by the power of love—and the abolition of slavery by the spirit of repentance.

Source: William Lloyd Garrison, *Selections from the Writings of W. L. Garrison* (Boston: R. F. Wallcut, 1852).

1830's

Although he and his former AASS colleagues remained in agreement on many points, there was also considerable mutual antagonism. Chances for reconciliation among them diminished in 1842, when Garrison began to call on the people of the North to dissolve the union. He argued that it was northern support that kept slavery in existence in the South, implying that, when the North withdrew its support through disunion, the slaves could free themselves. His abolitionist critics responded that disunion was tantamount to the North's divorcing itself from the slavery issue.

When the South, rather than the North, initiated disunion in 1860 and 1861, however, changing circumstances caused Garrison to draw back from some of his more radical positions. He compromised his pacifism and his opposition to party politics by supporting Republican president Abraham Lincoln's war to preserve the union and free the slaves. After the war ended successfully for the North and slavery was formally abolished by the Thirteenth Amendment on December 18, 1865, Garrison, old, tired, and seeking vindication, announced that his work was done—although it was clear that black equality had not been achieved with the end of slavery. The last issue of *The Liberator* rolled off its press on December 29, 1865.

SIGNIFICANCE

Publication of abolitionist William Lloyd Garrison's weekly newspaper, *The Liberator*, helped to transform the antislavery movement in the United States. It symbolized the beginning of a radical effort to abolish slavery and secure equal rights for African Americans throughout the country. Garrison stood out as one of the most uncompromising advocates of emancipation. Early in his career, he was often vilified and sometimes even physically attacked. However, with the achievement of emancipation in 1865, Garrison was seen as a prophetic hero, and he is now regarded as one of the most influential antislavery voices of the nineteenth century.

—*Stanley Harrold*

FURTHER READING

Abzug, Robert H. *Cosmos Crumbling: American Reform and the Religious Imagination.* New York: Oxford University Press, 1994. Demonstrates Garrison's radicalism in the context of early nineteenth century U.S. Protestantism.

Friedman, Lawrence J. *Gregarious Saints: Self and Community in American Abolitionism, 1830-1870.* New York: Cambridge University Press, 1982. A study of relationships among abolitionists. Includes a description of Garrison's circle of abolitionists and his leadership style.

Garrison, William Lloyd. *William Lloyd Garrison and the Fight Against Slavery: Selections from "The Liberator."* Edited with an introduction by William E. Cain. Boston: Bedford Books of St. Martin's Press, 1995. Collection of forty-one selections from Garrison's newspaper dealing with slavery issues. Cain's introduction provides historical background on slavery and the abolition movement in the United States and the events in Garrison's career.

Mayer, Henry. *All on Fire: William Lloyd Garrison and the Abolition of Slavery.* New York: St. Martin's Press, 1998. Biography of William Lloyd Garrison that places his life within the broader context of the abolitionist movement.

Newman, Richard S. *The Transformation of American Abolitionism: Fighting Slavery in the Early Republic.* Chapel Hill: University of North Carolina Press, 2002. Scholary study of the early years of the abolition movement.

Rogers, William B. *"We Are All Together Now": Frederick Douglass, William Lloyd Garrison, and the Prophetic Tradition.* New York: Garland, 1995. Describes how Douglass and Garrison drew on the tradition of biblical prophecy in their struggle against slavery, intemperance, and the oppression of women and minorities.

Stewart, James Brewer. *William Lloyd Garrison and the Challenge of Emancipation.* Arlington Heights, Ill.: Harlan Davidson, 1992. A brief biography that explores the personal choices that initiated and maintained Garrison's career as an abolitionist.

SEE ALSO: 1820's-1850's: Social Reform Movement; c. 1830-1865: Southerners Advance Proslavery Arguments; Aug. 21, 1831: Turner Launches Slave Insurrection; Dec., 1833: American Anti-Slavery Society Is Founded; Dec. 3, 1833: Oberlin College Opens; Dec. 3, 1847: Douglass Launches *The North Star*; c. 1850-1860: Underground Railroad Flourishes; 1852: Stowe Publishes *Uncle Tom's Cabin*; Dec. 6, 1865: Thirteenth Amendment Is Ratified.

RELATED ARTICLES in *Great Lives from History: The Nineteenth Century, 1801-1900:* Mary Ann Shadd Cary; Frederick Douglass; Charlotte Forten; William Lloyd Garrison; Sarah and Angelina Grimké.

March 18, 1831, and March 3, 1832
Cherokee Cases

Although these two U.S. Supreme Court rulings on cases involving the Cherokees and the state of Georgia had little practical impact on those cases, they would serve to limit the sovereignty of all Native American tribes by placing them under federal protection.

Also known as: *Cherokee Nation v. Georgia* and
  Worcester v. Georgia
Locale: Washington, D.C.
Categories: Indigenous people's rights; laws, acts, and legal history

Key Figures

Andrew Jackson (1767-1845), president of the United States, 1829-1837
John Marshall (1755-1835), chief justice of the United States, 1801-1835
George Gilmer (1790-1859), governor of Georgia, 1829-1839
Jeremiah Evarts (1781-1831), missionary and legal expert on Native American affairs
Sequoyah (c. 1770-1843), Cherokee man who created the syllabary for the Cherokee language
Daniel Webster (1782-1852), Massachusetts senator who supported the Cherokees
William Wirt (1772-1834), congressman and presidential candidate who served as Cherokee legal counsel
Samuel A. Worcester (1798-1859), Protestant missionary to the Cherokees

Summary of Event

In 1823, the U.S. Supreme Court made its first notable ruling that helped to define the relationship between the federal government and Native Americans. *Johnson v. McIntosh*, the case under review, concerned disputed land titles. The Court ruled that the federal government was, in effect, the ultimate landlord over Native Americans, who were thus the government's tenants. Chief Justice John Marshall and the Court majority thus ruled that the federal government was responsible for Native American affairs, including the protection of Native American peoples against state actions, which often materially affected Native American lives and property.

The Supreme Court considered the *Johnson* case at a time when the federal government and the states were locked in disputes about where the U.S. Constitution intended ultimate sovereignty to reside. Federal authority

seemed unsure, and Georgia contemplated removing its Cherokee and Creek peoples from the northern and western portions of the state. To legitimate its plans, Georgia charged that when it had agreed, in 1802, to cede its western land claims to the federal government, the latter had agreed to invalidate Native American titles to those lands and then return the lands to the state. However, the federal government never followed through, and Georgia had had to deal with the presence of a sovereign Native American state within its borders.

Land-hungry as a result of expansive pressures from the cotton culture, Georgians themselves initiated steps to remove Native Americans, primarily Cherokees. They denied the relevance of federal treaties with the Cherokees and threatened to use force against federal troops if they were dispatched to protect the tribe. Andrew Jackson's election as president in 1828 accelerated Georgia's actions to begin removing the Cherokees, because Jackson, a veteran Indian fighter who deemed Native Americans "savages," was a strong proponent of removal.

In December, 1828, the Georgia legislature added Cherokee lands to a number of Georgia counties. Far from being "savages," the Cherokees who protested this action had become a successful farming people. Thanks to a syllabary produced by their own Sequoyah, they were literate and produced their own newspaper, the *Cherokee Phoenix*. In response to the Georgia action, they instantly assembled a distinguished delegation to appeal to Congress for assistance. Their course was applauded by a host of congressmen and public officials—including Daniel Webster and William Wirt—who proclaimed Georgia's legislation unjust, on moral as well as legal grounds.

In December, 1829, Georgia's legislature went even further by enacting a comprehensive law that essentially nullified all Cherokee laws. Further aggravating the Cherokees' plight was the discovery of gold on Cherokee land in western Georgia during the following year. A gold rush flooded Cherokee land with white gold seekers, whose presence violated Cherokee treaties. Under great pressure, Georgia governor George Gilmer claimed the gold as state property and threatened to oust the Cherokees forcibly. Having failed in Georgia's courts, the Cherokees, as a last peaceful resort and encouraged by missionaries such as Jeremiah Evarts and public officials such as Webster and Wirt, appealed to the U.S. Supreme Court under Article III, section 2 of the Constitution, which gave the Court original jurisdiction in cases brought under treaties or by foreign nations.

In *Cherokee Nation v. Georgia*, Chief Justice Marshall, who had been sympathetic to Cherokee claims but also was aware of Jackson's hostility toward both Native Americans and the Supreme Court, dismissed the case on March 18, 1831. Marshall asserted that the Court lacked the jurisdiction to halt Georgia's sequestration, or legal seizure, of Cherokee lands. In making that ruling, Marshall defined the relationship of the Cherokees—and, by inference, all other Native American tribes—to the federal government as that of a "domestic, dependent nation," rather than a sovereign one.

On March 3, 1832, however, Marshall modified his earlier ruling while deciding *Worcester v. Georgia*. The *Worcester* case arose from a Georgia law enacted in 1831 that forbade whites from residing on Cherokee lands without a state license. The law was aimed primarily at white missionaries who were encouraging Cherokee resistance to removal. Under its new law, Georgia arrested, convicted, and sentenced two unlicensed missionaries, Samuel Worcester and Elizur Butler, whom the American Board of Commissioners for Foreign Missions promptly defended by engaging William Wirt as their counsel. Wirt then was running as a vice presidential candidate for the National Republican Party and as a presidential candidate for the Anti-Masonic Party. Therefore, he hoped for a decision that would embarrass Jackson.

Because the plaintiff in *Worcester* was a white missionary and the defendant the state of Georgia, the Supreme Court had clear jurisdiction in this case. Without overruling his *Cherokee Nation* decision, Marshall ruled that the Georgia law was unconstitutional and therefore void, because it violated treaties, as well as the commerce and contract clauses of the U.S. Constitution. Furthermore, Marshall declared, Georgia's laws violated the sovereignty of the Cherokee nation, and, in this case, the Court was constrained to define relationships between Native Americans and a state. The ruling overturned Worcester's and Butler's convictions but did nothing to save the Cherokees from eventual removal from their homeland.

SIGNIFICANCE

As historians and legal scholars later observed, the Cherokee cases advanced two contradictory descriptions of Native American sovereignty. In *Cherokee Nation v. Georgia*, Marshall delineated the dependent relationship of Native American tribes to the federal government. In *Worcester*, sympathetically stressing historic aspects of

Native American independence, nationhood, and foreignness rather than their domestic dependency, he defined the relationship of Native American tribes to the states. Together, these decisions suggested that although Native American tribes lacked sufficient sovereignty to claim political independence and were therefore wards of the federal government, they nevertheless possessed sufficient sovereignty to guard themselves against intrusions by the states, and that it was a federal responsibility to preserve that sovereignty. In subsequent years, these conflicting interpretations were exploited by both the federal government and Native Americans to serve their own purposes.

Marshall's pronouncements were one thing; making them effective was yet another thing. President Jackson who, as chief executive, was the only party capable of enforcing the Court's decision, chose to ignore it. Instead, Jackson threw federal troops into the removal of Cherokees and others of the so-called Five Civilized Tribes to the newly created Indian Territory beyond the Mississippi River. The resulting tragedy became known as the Trail of Tears.

—*Mary E. Virginia*

FURTHER READING

Deloria, Vine, Jr., and Clifford M. Lytle. *The Nations Within*. New York: Pantheon Books, 1984. Traces the past and weighs the future of Native American sovereignty, from the Doctrine of Discovery through the shift from tribal and federal notions of self-government to self-determination.

Guttmann, Allen. *States' Rights and Indian Removal: "The Cherokee Nation v. the State of Georgia."* Boston: D. C. Heath, 1965. Brief documentary history of the Cherokees' legal struggle to keep their land.

McLoughlin, William G. *Cherokees and Missionaries, 1789-1839*. New Haven, Conn.: Yale University Press, 1984. Study of the missionaries, who played such an important role in supporting the Cherokees.

Prucha, Francis Paul. *American Indian Treaties*. Berkeley: University of California Press, 1994. Unravels the political anomaly of the treaty system, a system devised according to white perspectives that made the relationships between Native Americans and the federal government unlike the legal and political relationships of any other two peoples.

_____. *The Great Father*. Vol. 1. Lincoln: University of Nebraska Press, 1984. A masterful, detailed analysis of historical relationships—political, economic, and social—between the federal government and Native Americans through cultural changes affecting both groups, from the Revolutionary War to 1980. Chapter 2 discusses the Cherokee cases and American Indian removal.

Remini, Robert V. *Andrew Jackson*. 3 vols. Baltimore: Johns Hopkins University Press, 1998. Nearly definitive biography of the most fervid and effective advocate of Indian removal.

_____. *The Legacy of Andrew Jackson: Essays on Democracy, Indian Removal, and Slavery*. Baton Rouge: Louisiana State University Press, 1988. The leading biographer of Andrew Jackson discusses Jackson's role in Indian removal and other social and political issues of his time.

Satz, Ronald N. *American Indian Policy in the Jacksonian Era*. Lincoln: University of Nebraska Press, 1974. Excellent coverage of the Cherokee cases; also clarifies the complex political climate in which the cases developed around conflicts between the Jackson administration, Georgia, and the Cherokees.

Wallace, Anthony F. C. *The Long, Bitter Trail: Andrew Jackson and the Indians*. New York: Hill & Wang, 1993. Brief overview of the removal policies, the Trail of Tears, and the implications of both for U.S. history.

Williams, Robert A. *The American Indian in Western Legal Thought*. New York: Oxford University Press, 1990. Starting with the thirteenth century notion that the West had a mandate to conquer the earth, this intriguing study explores the laws that evolved to legitimate this mandate, specifically as the mandate was interpreted by Spanish, English, and U.S. laws regarding relations with Native Americans.

SEE ALSO: Mar. 2, 1824: *Gibbons v. Ogden*; Feb. 21, 1828: *Cherokee Phoenix* Begins Publication; 1830-1842: Trail of Tears; May 28, 1830: Congress Passes Indian Removal Act; Sept. 4, 1841: Congress Passes Preemption Act of 1841; 1876: Canada's Indian Act; Feb. 8, 1887: General Allotment Act Erodes Indian Tribal Unity; Mar. 28, 1898: *United States v. Wong Kim Ark*.

RELATED ARTICLES in *Great Lives from History: The Nineteenth Century, 1801-1900:* Andrew Jackson; Belva A. Lockwood; John Ross; Sequoyah; Daniel Webster.

May, 1831-February, 1832
TOCQUEVILLE VISITS AMERICA

During a nine-month tour of the United States, the young Frenchman Alexis de Tocqueville gathered the material that he would use to write Democracy in America—*a classic analysis of American social and political institutions that still offers insights into modern American institutions.*

LOCALE: United States
CATEGORIES: Historiography

KEY FIGURES
Alexis de Tocqueville (1805-1859), French magistrate, political philosopher, and historian
Gustave de Beaumont (1802-1866), French magistrate who accompanied Tocqueville on his travels
Andrew Jackson (1767-1845), president of the United States, 1829-1837

SUMMARY OF EVENT
In May, 1831, two young Frenchmen, Alexis de Tocqueville and Gustave de Beaumont, arrived in the United States. Both were magistrates whose official purpose in coming to the New World was to study the U.S. prison system and penal reforms. However, there was another and more important reason for their visit: They wanted to observe democracy at first hand. The experience of France's July Revolution of 1830 had convinced the two aristocrats, especially Tocqueville, that history was moving toward equality and democratic institutions. A study of the United States, where such conditions already had been reached, would provide an important lesson for the future. As Tocqueville observed, it was not

> merely to satisfy a legitimate curiosity that I have examined America; my wish has been to find there instruction by which we may ourselves profit. . . . I confess that, in America, I saw more than America; I sought there the image of democracy itself, with its inclinations, its character, its prejudices, and its passions, in order to learn what we have to fear or to hope from its progress.

The travelers' path, which took them to a number of cities and states, included an exploration of the Michigan wilderness north of Detroit, visits to pioneer cabins, and

WHY TOCQUEVILLE WROTE *DEMOCRACY IN AMERICA*

In his introduction to Democracy in America, *excerpted below, Alexis de Tocqueville explained the source of his fascination with U.S. society and his motives for writing a book about that society.*

Amongst the novel objects that attracted my attention during my stay in the United States, nothing struck me more forcibly than the general equality of conditions. I readily discovered the prodigious influence which this primary fact exercises on the whole course of society, by giving a certain direction to public opinion, and a certain tenor to the laws; by imparting new maxims to the governing powers, and peculiar habits to the governed. I speedily perceived that the influence of this fact extends far beyond the political character and the laws of the country, and that it has no less empire over civil society than over the Government; it creates opinions, engenders sentiments, suggests the ordinary practices of life, and modifies whatever it does not produce. The more I advanced in the study of American society, the more I perceived that the equality of conditions is the fundamental fact from which all others seem to be derived, and the central point at which all my observations constantly terminated.

I then turned my thoughts to our own hemisphere, where I imagined that I discerned something analogous to the spectacle which the New World presented to me. I observed that the equality of conditions is daily progressing towards those extreme limits which it seems to have reached in the United States, and that the democracy which governs the American communities appears to be rapidly rising into power in Europe. I hence conceived the idea of the book which is now before the reader. . . .

Source: Alexis de Tocqueville, *Democracy in America*, translated by Henry Reeve. (New York: D. Appleton, 1904). Introduction.

a steamboat ride down the Mississippi River to New Orleans. The travelers not only experienced diverse features of the American landscape but also formed impressions of the different peoples living in American society and the relations among the different races. Some of Tocqueville's impressions were more favorable than others. For example, he was disconcerted by some of his experiences with Native Americans whom he met. These included encounters with a group of Iroquois in Buffalo and a group of Choctaws traveling down the Mississippi River to a forced resettlement in Arkansas ordered by President Andrew Jackson. Believing it was inevitable that the Native American way of life would succumb to the influences and policies introduced to the United States by European immigrants and their descendants, Tocqueville wrote in one of the many notebooks he kept that "the Indian races are melting in the presence of European civilization like snow in the presence of the sun."

The travelers returned to France after a nine-month tour of the United States, After they drafted their official report on the U.S. prison system and submitted it to their government, they began to write their separate analyses of the U.S. system. Beaumont set down his reflections in *Marie: Ou, L'Esclavage aux États-Unis* (1835), a study of race relations in the United States in the form of a novel. Although *Marie* contained many penetrating observations, the fictional approach and somewhat limited scope of the book accounted for its modest reception. By contrast, Tocqueville's work, a panoramic view of U.S. civilization, won greater recognition and praise.

Tocqueville's *De la démocratie en Amérique* (1835, 1840; *Democracy in America*, 1835, 1840) revealed "the image of democracy"—and of Jacksonian America as well—that Tocqueville had discovered during his travels in the United States. For the young Frenchman, the most striking characteristic of U.S. democracy was "the general equality of condition among people." In Tocqueville's view, equality of condition was "the fundamental fact from which all others seem to be derived, and the central point at which all my observations constantly terminated." Issued in two parts, his book analyzed the effect of this phenomenon on U.S. civilization.

In the first part of *Democracy in America*, published in both French and English in 1835, Tocqueville analyzed the U.S. political system, describing the workings of township, state, and federal governments, and commenting on the roles of political parties, newspapers, and public associations. The key principle governing the operation of the system, Tocqueville declared, was the principle of the sovereignty of the people, outgrowth of equality of condition. "The people reign in the American political world as the Deity does in the universe," he observed. Among the advantages of democratic government, Tocqueville cited the fact that it "brings the notion of political rights to the level of the humblest citizens." In addition, democratic government creates "an all-pervading and restless activity" that, although it makes for less methodical and skillful public administration than other forms of government, is nevertheless more productive: "if it does fewer things well, it does a greater number of things."

The chief disadvantage of democratic government, in Tocqueville's view, stemmed from the "unlimited power of the majority in the United States." He believed that its effect on public opinion was particularly harmful. Tocqueville's observations on the relations between African Americans and Euro-Americans in northern states such as Pennsylvania, where slavery was outlawed, helped to contribute to this conclusion. Although the freedom of African Americans was legally recognized, Tocqueville saw that the force of public opinion concerning African Americans had created conditions under which black and white people did not mix as social equals. Moreover, African Americans often did not feel comfortable taking part in the political process, although they were legally entitled to participate. His reflections on "the tyranny of the majority," its sources and consequences, constitute one of the major themes of *Democracy in America*.

Tocqueville published the second part of his work in 1840. In that part, his approach was more philosophical. Although he often illustrated his remarks by referring to his experience in the United States, he was concerned primarily with revealing the universal principles of democracy and showing their effect on intellectual and social life. He was less concerned with the politics of democracy than with the culture shaped by widespread equality of condition.

In the course of his analysis, Tocqueville pointed out the difficulty of reconciling equality and liberty. Equality of condition nurtured a preference for equality over liberty, he observed. "Democratic communities have a natural taste for freedom," he explained,

> left to themselves, they will seek it, cherish it, and view any privation of it with regret. But for equality their passion is ardent, insatiable, incessant, invincible; they call for equality in freedom; and if they cannot obtain that, they still call for equality in slavery.

Paradoxically, although liberty was threatened by equality of condition, it nevertheless remained people's best protection: "to combat the evils which equality may produce, there is only one effectual remedy: namely, political freedom," Tocqueville declared. He also emphasized the leveling tendency inherent in democracy. Equality of condition produced a monotonous uniformity of manners and opinions. Under democracy, individualism gave way to conformity. "As the conditions of men become equal among a people," Tocqueville observed,

individuals seem of less and society of greater importance; or rather every citizen, being assimilated to all the rest, is lost in the crowd, and nothing stands conspicuous but the great and imposing image of the people at large. This naturally gives the opinion of the privileges of society and a very humble notion of the rights of individuals; they are ready to admit that the interests of the former are everything and those of the latter nothing.

SIGNIFICANCE

During the early nineteenth century, Tocqueville was one of a number of notable European visitors to the United States who included Charles Dickens and Frances Trollope. However, his unbiased yet friendly approach and the accuracy of his observations distinguished him, in the eyes of the people of the United States, from what one contemporary newspaper called "our common herd of travelers." *Democracy in America* exerted a considerable influence on American thought during the nineteenth century, and the twentieth century witnessed a revival of interest in the work. More than 170 years after its original publication, Tocqueville's work still offers valuable and penetrating insights into the nature of U.S. democracy and ranks as one of the classics of political philosophy.

—Anne C. Loveland,
updated by Diane P. Michelfelder

FURTHER READING

Beaumont, Gustave de. *Marie: Or, Slavery in the United States—A Novel of Jacksonian America.* Translated by Barbara Chapman. Baltimore: Johns Hopkins University Press, 1999. New translation of the novel that Beaumont wrote after returning home from the United States with Tocqueville in 1835.

Drolet, Michael. *Tocqueville, Democracy, and Social Reform.* New York: Palgrave Macmillan, 2003. Study of Tocqueville's writings on such diverse social issues as prison reform, pauperism, and the problems of abandoned children.

Hereth, Michael. *Alexis de Tocqueville: Threats to Freedom in Democracy.* Translated by George Bogardus. Durham, N.C.: Duke University Press, 1986. Argues that Tocqueville was not simply interested in describing and commenting on the fundamental principles of democracy, but also was committed to their further development.

Mancini, Matthew. *Alexis de Tocqueville.* New York: Twayne, 1994. A brief but insightful account of Tocqueville's writings. Discusses *Democracy in America* and looks especially carefully at Tocqueville's views of Native Americans and slavery.

1830's

Pierson, George W. *Tocqueville and Beaumont in America*. New York: Oxford University Press, 1938. Lively and thorough reconstruction of Tocqueville and Beaumont's visit to the United States, based on published and unpublished sources. An abridged edition of this book, *Tocqueville in America* (Gloucester, Mass.: Peter Smith, 1969), reduced sections on women and Native and African Americans as "matters of lesser interest."

Reeves, Richard. *American Journey: Traveling with Tocqueville in Search of "Democracy in America."* New York: Simon & Schuster, 1982. Retraces Tocqueville's journey across the United States a century and a half later. Engagingly weaves Tocqueville's reflections with commentary on current social conditions in places visited by Reeves and interviews with prominent U.S. citizens.

Schleifer, James T. *The Making of Tocqueville's "Democracy in America."* Chapel Hill: University of North Carolina Press, 1980. An informative, scholarly work that argues that the ideas found in *Democracy in America* took shape from Tocqueville's notes, drafts of his manuscripts, and his readings of works by others, such as the *Federalist* papers.

Tocqueville, Alexis de. *Democracy in America*. Translated by Arthur Goldhammer. New York: Library of America, 2004. New translation of Tocqueville's classic work on American institutions.

_____. *Journey to America*. Rev. ed. Edited by J. P. Mayer and translated by George Lawrence. Garden City, N.Y.: Doubleday, 1971. Presents the fourteen notebooks Tocqueville kept on his tour of the United States to record his interviews and observations, which served as the basis for his reflections in *Democracy in America*.

Wolin, Sheldon S. *Tocqueville Between Worlds: The Making of a Political and Theoretical Life*. Princeton, N.J.: Princeton University Press, 2001. A distinguished political philosopher, Wolin examines Tocqueville's political life by tracing the development of his theories about democracy and other political issues.

SEE ALSO: July 29, 1830: July Revolution Deposes Charles X; 1859: Mill Publishes *On Liberty*.

RELATED ARTICLES in *Great Lives from History: The Nineteenth Century, 1801-1900:* Charles Dickens; Andrew Jackson; Alexis de Tocqueville; Frances Trollope.

Summer, 1831
MCCORMICK INVENTS THE REAPER

Cyrus McCormick's invention of the earliest commercially successful mechanical reaper dramatically reduced the need for labor and made large-scale wheat production possible.

LOCALE: Walnut Grove, Virginia

CATEGORIES: Agriculture; inventions; manufacturing; government and politics; science and technology

KEY FIGURES

Cyrus Hall McCormick (1809-1884), inventor of the reaper

John Deere (1804-1886), manufacturer who introduced the steel plow in 1837

Obed Hussey (1792-1860), inventor of a competing reaper

John H. Manny (1825-1856), manufacturer of farm implements

SUMMARY OF EVENT

Wheat is a crop that historically presented a special challenge to farmers because of its short harvest period. After

it ripens, its husks begin to open and begin rotting if they are not harvested within ten days. Before the development of mechanical harvesters, farmers had to be careful not to plant more wheat than they could harvest with the limited supply of labor available to them. Labor shortages on American farms made the development of mechanical reapers a pressing need during the early nineteenth century.

Cyrus Hall McCormick is generally credited with the invention of the first reaper containing the basic elements that are still used in modern reaping machines. Other inventors in the United States and Great Britain produced working models of mechanical reapers before McCormick did, but none of their inventions proved commercially successful. For example, in Great Britain, Thomas Brown manufactured and marketed a mechanical reaper before 1820, but its sales were slow because farm labor in Britain was more plentiful and cheaper than in the United States, and because British farms typically had small fields that made the use of mechanical reapers difficult.

McCormick developed his reaper on a twelve-hundred-

Painting by Bernarda Bryson (1903-2004) of Cyrus McCormick standing in front his reaper, while holding a newspaper with the headline "Boom in Wheat!" (Library of Congress)

acre family farm of Walnut Grove in Virginia's Shenandoah Valley. The problem of a mechanical reaper had intrigued McCormick's father, Robert McCormick, who had attempted to build one several times. Robert McCormick used tools and materials available in the farm's blacksmith shop and did not succeed. During the summer of 1831, however, his son Cyrus built a reaper that performed successfully. The younger McCormick then set the invention aside for several years to pursue other business interests. It was not until 1834, after a failed attempt to market a hemp-breaking machine invented by his father, that Cyrus resumed work on the reaper and applied for a patent.

McCormick's reaper revolutionized grain farming in the United States. Prior to its invention, the methods used in harvesting grain had not changed in thousands of years. Harvesting was done with hand-held scythes and cradles, with teams of rakers and binders following behind. As workers with scythes or sickles cut the grain,

other workers raked the fallen stalks, and binders gathered the stalks into bundles known as sheaves. The sheaves then were stacked into piles (shocks) to await collection into wagons.

Harvesting was backbreaking work and resulted in much waste. According to technology historian Harold Livesay, in 1830 a crew of six laborers—one worker cutting the wheat with the others following behind, raking and binding—could harvest only two acres per day. During the 1840's, the McCormick reaper could handle between ten and fifteen acres per day and required fewer binders following behind. The substantial savings in labor allowed a relatively small workforce to at least triple the acreage harvested.

By 1839, when McCormick started advertising his machine, other reapers already had entered the market. A former sailor from Maine, Obed Hussey, had patented a mechanical reaper in 1833 and had been selling reapers for several years. Hussey was McCormick's first serious competitor. In 1840, McCormick sold only two reapers; both of them broke down, so he returned to his workshop to improve his reaper's design. In 1842, he sold six machines; in 1843, twenty-nine.

During this initial period, most of the reapers in use were in the eastern states, although McCormick's machines had been built in Ohio. McCormick had visited the prairie states, however, and knew that was where the reaper would be in highest demand, as farming, particularly the production of grain crops, was moving west. In 1848, McCormick moved to Chicago and built a factory to manufacture reapers. This location offered several advantages. Transportation from Chicago was already good and was getting better with the construction of new railroad lines in Illinois and west of the Mississippi River. Also, Illinois and Wisconsin were becoming the major grain-producing states, and the broad, level wheatlands of the West could employ mechanical reapers more efficiently than the smaller and often hilly and rocky wheatlands of the East.

McCormick's reaper factory in Chicago helped make that city a center for the manufacture of agricultural machinery in the United States. During 1849, the first full year that McCormick manufactured machines in Chicago, his factory produced fifteen hundred reapers. By 1858, sales of his reaper had made McCormick a millionaire.

Mechanization of farming brought many changes to American agriculture. In 1830, the total wheat crop of the United States had amounted to approximately 40 million bushels. Within nine years, this figure doubled, and in 1860 it exceeded 170 million bushels. During the 1830's, New York, Pennsylvania, and Virginia were major wheat-producing states, but the center of the wheat-growing area moved steadily westward. In 1839, the Old Northwest produced 31 percent of the nation's crop; in 1849, 37 percent; and in 1859, 46 percent. A reason for the dramatic increase in wheat production was the introduction of the McCormick reaper.

As the domestic economy grew, stimulated by the immigration of large numbers of Europeans after the late 1840's, the demand for wheat and other grains increased proportionately. From 1846 to 1860, prices were fairly high, and farmers throughout the states of Ohio, Indiana, Illinois, and Wisconsin expanded their acreage in wheat. Before the U.S. Civil War (1861-1865), wheat was the most important cash crop in the northern agricultural economy, and by 1860 it was the most important cash crop in the United States. Its importance was largely the result of the growth of the domestic economy rather than of the entrance of American grain and flour into European markets. The development of a nationwide transportation system of canals and railroads allowed farmers in formerly isolated regions to participate in the market economy. Crops such as wheat that had been prohibitively expensive to transport by wagon were transported cheaply and easily by rail.

SIGNIFICANCE

The reaper had a significant impact prior to and during the Civil War (1861-1865). Reapers sold by McCormick and his strongest competitor, John H. Manny, were common in northern Illinois and southern Wisconsin during the 1850's. One authority estimated that more than seventy thousand reapers and mowers were in operation west of the Appalachians by 1858. By 1860, about 70 percent of the wheat harvested in that area was cut by machine. By 1864, about 250,000 reapers and mowers were in use in the North, enough to provide machines for 75 percent of all northern farms of more than a hundred acres. A significant number of these machines came from the growing production lines of Cyrus H. McCormick. His profits from sales in 1856 reached three hundred thousand dollars; between 1868 and 1870, annual sales were double what they had been during the war, and the factory on the Chicago River produced eight thousand reapers and mowers for harvest each year.

The mechanization of agriculture and the establishment of Chicago as a center of production came just in time to service the movement of the center of grain production into the trans-Mississippi country. The semiarid prairies of Kansas, Colorado, and Nebraska demanded farming on a large scale. Machinery was necessary. Similarly, the movement of wheat into the bonanza farms of California required machinery. The inventive genius of McCormick, Hussey, Manny, John Deere, and others made it possible to prepare, seed, tend, and harvest thousand-acre wheat farms with relatively small workforces. McCormick did for wheat what Eli Whitney had done for cotton.

—John G. Clark,
updated by Nancy Farm Mannikko

FURTHER READING

Brands, H. W. *Masters of Enterprise: Giants of American Business from John Jacob Astor and J. P. Morgan to Bill Gates and Oprah Winfrey.* New York: Free Press, 1999. Collection of brief biographies of twenty-five American entrepreneurs, including Cyrus McCormick.

Casson, Herbert Newton. *Cyrus Hall McCormick: His*

Life and Work. Freeport, N.Y.: Books for Libraries Press, 1971. Definitive biography of McCormick.

Collins, Edward John T. *Sickle to Combine: A Review of Harvesting Techniques from 1800 to the Present Day*. Reading, England: Museum of English Rural Life, 1969. Brief but comprehensive discussion of the evolution of mechanization in agriculture.

Hoseason, David. *Harvesters and Harvesting, 1840-1900*. London: Croom Helm, 1982. Agricultural history focusing on changes in the workforce as farming became more mechanized.

Isern, Thomas D. *Bull Threshers and Bindlestiffs: Harvesting and Threshing on the North American Plains*. Lawrence: University Press of Kansas, 1990. Includes a concise history of the development of harvesting equipment in North America. Highly accessible; clear illustrations.

Livesay, Harold C. *American Made: Men Who Shaped the American Economy*. Boston: Little, Brown, 1979. Contains a concise, lively account of the life of Cyrus McCormick and the company he founded.

McCormick, Cyrus. *The Century of the Reaper: An Account of Cyrus Hall McCormick, the Inventor of the Reaper* . . . Boston: Houghton Mifflin, 1931. Uncritical biography of the inventor of the McCormick reaper by his grandson of the same name. Written to celebrate the centennial anniversary of the invention.

Wendel, Charles H. *One Hundred Fifty Years of International Harvester*. Osceola, Wis.: Motorbooks International, 1993. History of the company that McCormick founded, containing descriptions of the various pieces of farm machinery the firm manufactured and sold.

SEE ALSO: Oct. 14, 1834: Blair Patents His First Seed Planter; 1840: Liebig Advocates Artificial Fertilizers; July 2, 1862: Lincoln Signs the Morrill Land Grant Act; 1894-1895: Kellogg's Corn Flakes Launch the Dry Cereal Industry.

RELATED ARTICLES in *Great Lives from History: The Nineteenth Century, 1801-1900:* Johnny Appleseed; Cyrus Hall McCormick.

August 21, 1831
TURNER LAUNCHES SLAVE INSURRECTION

Although Nat Turner's slave rebellion in Virginia was quickly suppressed, it was the first American slave uprising to achieve even brief success and consequently sent a shockwave through the South that resulted in new repressive legislation restricting the rights and movements of slaves.

LOCALE: Southampton County, Virginia
CATEGORIES: Atrocities and war crimes; wars, uprisings, and civil unrest

KEY FIGURES
Nat Turner (1800-1831), Virginia slave and Baptist minister
Cherry Turner (fl. 1820's), Turner's wife

SUMMARY OF EVENT

So far as is known, Turner spent his entire life as a slave in his native Southampton County, where he had been born on the plantation of Benjamin Turner, from whom he got his surname. His mother appears to have been a native African, who taught him at an early age to believe that he possessed supernatural powers. He was both a mystic and oriented toward religion. In addition to possessing those traits, he could read, and historians have surmised that he learned this skill from the Turner family. Turner became a Christian through the instruction of his grandmother Bridget. He read the Bible and became a Baptist preacher. Because of his mysticism, his ability to read, and his activities as a minister, he gained considerable influence over his fellow slaves.

Benjamin Turner's son Samuel Turner inherited ownership of Nat during a time of economic depression in Virginia. He hired a new overseer, who drove the slaves to work harder. In response, Nat ran away. After eluding capture for thirty days, Nat turned himself in to his owner. His return went unpunished, but in the days that followed, Nat saw that his own freedom could not be realized without his people's freedom.

During the early 1820's, Nat married another slave, named Cherry, with whom he had three children. Cherry would later conceal coded maps and lists that Turner used in his revolt, which experts have never been able to decode. When Samuel Turner died in 1822, Nat's family was broken up and sold to different families. Nat went to a neighboring farmer, Thomas Moore, and was sold again, to Joseph Travis, in 1831.

Nat Turner thought of himself as an instrument of God. Between 1825 and 1830, he gained respect as a traveling neighborhood preacher. He became deeply religious, fasting and praying in solitude. In his own mind he had been ordained—like the prophets of old—to perform a special mission. He professed that God communicated with him through voices and signs in the heavens. On May 12, 1828, he heard a "great noise" and saw "white spirits" and "black spirits" battling.

In February, 1831, an unusual blueness in the atmosphere caused by a solar eclipse convinced Nat that God was announcing that the time had come for slaves to attack their white masters. Turner communicated this message to his band of followers. The rebellion began on August 21, when Turner and seven other slaves murdered everyone in the Travis family. Twenty-four hours after the rebellion began, the rebel band numbered seventy-five slaves. Over the next two days, the rebels killed another fifty-one white people. Despite the growing scale of the rebellion, no evidence exists to indicate that Turner's movement was a part of any larger scheme.

Turner next directed his attack toward the county seat, Jerusalem, and the weapons in its armory, but he never made it. The white community responded promptly, and with its overpowering force of armed slave owners and militia, it routed the poorly armed slaves on the second day of the rebellion. Although Turner eluded capture for

six weeks, he and all the rebels were eventually killed or captured and later executed. Hundreds of other slaves who did not participate in the rebellion were also slain by terrified members of the white community. Turner's court-appointed attorney, Thomas Gray, recorded Turner's "confessions" on November 1, and on November 11, 1831, Turner was hanged. Gray later remarked on Turner's intelligence and knowledge of military tactics.

SIGNIFICANCE

Although Turner's revolt took place in a relatively isolated section of Virginia, the uprising caused the entire South to tremble. Many white southerners called for more stringent laws to regulate slaves' behavior, such as making it a crime to teach a slave to read or write. Turner's revolt coincided with the blossoming of the abolition movement in the North, for the rebellion occurred during the same year that William Lloyd Garrison began his unremitting assault on slavery. Although no one has been able to demonstrate that abolitionist activity influenced Turner, white southerners were horrified at the seeming coincidence. They described abolitionists as persons who wanted not only to end slavery but also to encourage a massacre of southern whites. The white South stood as one against any outside interference with its system.

While white people throughout the South looked anew at slavery, in no place did they look more closely

Contemporary depiction of Turner's rebellion. (Library of Congress)

NAT TURNER'S CONFESSION

In Thomas Gray's The Confessions of Nat Turner, *the author recounts his visit with the rebel leader in prison and the statement that he gave detailing his background and motives, as well as his account of the insurrection he led. In the following excerpt, Turner claims to have divinely granted powers of prophecy that aided him in planning the insurrection.*

Agreeable to his own appointment, on the evening he was committed to prison, with permission of the jailer, I visited NAT on Tuesday the 1st November, when, without being questioned at all, he commenced his narrative in the following words:

SIR, - You have asked me to give a history of the motives which induced me to undertake the late insurrection, as you call it . . . In my childhood a circumstance occurred which made an indelible impression on my mind, and laid the ground work of that enthusiasm, which has terminated so fatally to many, both white and black, and for which I am about to atone at the gallows. It is here necessary to relate this circumstance—trifling as it may seem, it was the commencement of that belief which has grown with time, and even now, sir, in this dungeon, helpless and forsaken as I am, I cannot divest myself of. Being at play with other children, when three or four years old, I was telling them something, which my mother overhearing, said it had happened before I was born—I stuck to my story, however, and related some things which went, in her opinion, to confirm it—others being called on were greatly astonished, knowing that these things had happened, and caused them to say in my hearing, I surely would be a prophet, as the Lord had shewn me things that had happened before my birth. And my father and mother strengthened me in this my first impression, saying in my presence, I was intended for some great purpose, which they had always thought from certain marks on my head and breast.

Source: Thomas R. Gray, *The Confessions of Nat Turner: The Leader of the Late Insurrection in Southampton, Va.* (1831). Turner's Confession.

West Virginia during the Civil War), an area of few slaves, could not agree on a specific plan to accomplish their purpose.

Virginia's defenders of slavery countered by boasting of Virginia's economic well-being and the good treatment and contentment of their slaves. Referring to the well-established belief in the sanctity of private property, they denied that the legislature had any right to meddle with slave property.

The Virginia legislature decided not to tamper with slavery. It rebuffed those who wanted to put Virginia on the road to emancipation. After the slavery debates, white southerners no longer seriously considered any alternative to slavery. In the aftermath of Turner's revolt and Virginia's debate, the South erected a massive defense of its peculiar institution. That defense permeated southern politics, religion, literature, and science. Nat Turner's revolt—the only successful slave uprising in the South—heralded and confirmed the total southern commitment to black slavery. However, Turner left a profound legacy: Slaves would fight for their freedom. Turner's rebellion later helped inspire twentieth century black activists, including Marcus Garvey and Malcolm X.

—*William J. Cooper, Jr.,*
updated by Marilyn Elizabeth Perry

1830's

than in Virginia. The state's 1831-1832 legislative session saw the most thorough public discussion of slavery in southern history before 1861. Only four months after Turner's revolt, the state legislature appointed a committee to recommend to the state a course of action in dealing with slavery. Virginians opposed to slavery made their case. They argued that slavery was a prime cause of Virginia's economic backwardness; that it injured white manners and morals; and that, as witnessed by Turner's revolt, it was basically dangerous. Although they also said that abolition would benefit the slaves, they primarily maintained that white Virginians would reap the greatest rewards, as former slaves, after a gradual and possibly compensated emancipation, would be removed from the state. These abolitionists, most of whom were from western Virginia (which separated and became

FURTHER READING

Bisson, Terry. *Nat Turner*. Los Angeles: Melrose Square, 1988. An easy-to-read account of Nat Turner's life and motivations.

Blassingame, John W. *The Slave Community: Plantation Life in the Antebellum South*. New York: Oxford University Press, 1979. A detailed account of slave culture and community life.

French, Scot. *The Rebellious Slave: Nat Turner in American Memory*. Boston: Houghton Mifflin, 2004. Analysis of Turner's legacy that examines how he has been depicted in popular culture. Describes how Turner's image has changed from the immediate aftermath of his rebellion to more recent debates.

Gray, Thomas R. *The Confessions of Nat Turner: The Leader of the Late Insurrection in Southampton, Va.*

1831. Reprint. Miami: Mnemosyne, 1969. Contains Turner's own account of his revolt, as given to an official of the court that tried him.

Greenberg, Kenneth S., ed. *The Confessions of Nat Turner and Related Documents*. New York: St. Martin's Press, 1996. Includes the text of Turner's confessions to Thomas R. Gray and other historical documents from the time period.

_____. *Nat Turner: A Slave Rebellion in History and Memory*. New York: Oxford University Press, 2003. Collection of essays about Turner, including an exploration of his relationship with the black community in Southampton County, Virginia, and the role of women in his insurrection.

Styron, William. *Confessions of Nat Turner*. New York: Random House, 1967. A controversial novel that aimed to show an understanding of Turner's revolt and the institution of slavery but was sharply attacked by African American intellectuals.

Tragle, Henry Irving. *The Southampton Slave Revolt of 1831: A Compilation of Source Material*. Amherst: University of Massachusetts Press, 1971. Reprints primary source material: newspaper accounts, trial records, and other documents written at the time of the revolt.

SEE ALSO: c. 1830-1865: Southerners Advance Pro-slavery Arguments; Jan. 1, 1831: Garrison Begins Publishing *The Liberator*; Aug. 28, 1833: Slavery Is Abolished Throughout the British Empire; Dec., 1833: American Anti-Slavery Society Is Founded; July 2, 1839: *Amistad* Slave Revolt; Oct. 16-18, 1859: Brown's Raid on Harpers Ferry.

RELATED ARTICLES in *Great Lives from History: The Nineteenth Century, 1801-1900:* Henri Christophe; Frederick Douglass; William Lloyd Garrison; Nat Turner.

October, 1831
FARADAY CONVERTS MAGNETIC FORCE INTO ELECTRICITY

By converting magnetic force into electricity through careful experiments, Michael Faraday reinforced the belief of scientists in a field theory that would explain the relationships among light, electricity, and magnetism and helped to make possible the development of modern electric generators.

LOCALE: London, England
CATEGORIES: Physics; science and technology; mathematics

KEY FIGURES
Michael Faraday (1791-1867), British scientist who became director of the Royal Institution laboratory in 1825
André-Marie Ampère (1775-1836), French scientist who studied the connection between electricity and magnetism
Sir Humphry Davy (1778-1829), British scientist and director of London's Royal Institution
Hans Christian Ørsted (1777-1851), Danish scientist who sought to find a connection between electricity and magnetism
James Clerk Maxwell (1831-1879), Scottish physicist who extended Faraday's work

SUMMARY OF EVENT
Early in the nineteenth century, scientists who studied heat, light, electricity, and magnetism sought unifying features that would link these phenomena together. They did so because their experimental evidence contradicted the established principles of Newtonian science, which treated these phenomena as separate and distinct subjects acting as straight-line forces between centers of bodies. The experiments of nineteenth century scientists suggested that these forces exerted their influence as waves acting through some medium. With this evidence, physicists began to think in terms of a field of forces rather than straight-line effects. This growing belief in a field theory benefited from the influential nineteenth century German *Naturphilosophie* school of philosophy, which sought a unity in nature to prove that a *Weltseele*, a world spirit or force, was the sole power in place in nature.

Naturphilosophie strongly influenced the Danish scientist Hans Christian Ørsted while he was doing his graduate studies in Germany. When he returned to Denmark, Ørsted embraced this belief in the unity of forces and sought demonstrable evidence of a link between electricity and magnetism. In 1813, he published results of an experiment that demonstrated that an electrical current moving through a wire deflected a compass needle.

A few years later, during the early 1820's, French scientist André-Marie Ampère found that a circular coil of wire carrying a current acted like a magnet and that current moving in parallel wires caused an attraction or repulsion depending on the direction of the current in the wires. Ampère's work showed that electricity and magnetism were clearly related.

These experimental results intrigued two members of London's Royal Institution, Humphry Davy, its director, and his assistant, Michael Faraday, who repeated and extended Ørsted's work in 1820 and 1821. The Royal Institution had been founded in 1799 to spread scientific knowledge and conduct scientific experiments. It was thus befitting for Faraday to conduct a series of experiments treating electromagnetism, and he published a compendium of existing knowledge about the field in his "Historical Sketch of Electromagnetism" in late 1821 and early 1822. This review of the subject heightened Faraday's interest in seeking a unity of nature's forces.

In his search for unity, Faraday brought a theoretical construct shaped by *Naturphilosophie* and his theological beliefs grounded in the small fundamentalist sect

Michael Faraday demonstrating an electrical apparatus in a bookshop. (Hulton Archive/Getty Images)

known as the Sandemanians. His religious beliefs instilled in him the notion that nature derived from a single force: God. As he investigated nature, he sought an economy to, and unity of, nature that endorsed those beliefs. During the 1820's, he conducted experiments to confirm the relationships among electricity, heat, light, and magnetism.

At the Royal Institution, Faraday had a basement laboratory in which he investigated many developing scientific concepts. There, in 1821, he demonstrated that a bar magnet rotated around a wire carrying a current and postulated that circular lines of force accounted for the path of that motion. These results, producing electromagnetic rotation, set in place a continuing effort by Faraday over many years to use experimental methods to discover the connections between electricity and magnetism. In doing so, he held steadfast to the principle that sound scientific theories must rely on strong experimental evidence. Faraday constantly revised his theories through experi-

ment with a superb talent that combined preceptual, conceptual, and laboratory-based information to generate new knowledge. He recorded his laboratory investigations meticulously in a diary he kept over a forty-year period. It is a rich source of information about his speculations in the world of science and his ingenuity in explaining theories with elegant and carefully planned public demonstrations and lectures.

A skilled experimentalist, Faraday continually addressed the issue of electromagnetism during the 1820's. By 1824, he believed that a magnet should act on an electrical current, just as Ørsted had demonstrated that an electrical current acted on a magnet. With Faraday's many duties at the Royal Institution, where he became director of the laboratory in 1825, and his private work as a consulting scientist, he turned to the issue repeatedly but sporadically for years. Finally, in 1831, he began a series of experiments, which continued from August to November, in which he focused on electromagnetic induction.

During those four months, Faraday conducted 135 experiments to test his hypothesis that electricity could be induced by magnetic substances. His first success came in late August, when he arranged two separate coils of wire, insulated from each other, around opposite sides of an iron ring and suspended a magnetic needle over this ring. He then introduced a current in one wire coil and detected an induced current in the second wire coil on the ring—the magnetic needle oscillated. This experimental evidence confirmed his long-held belief that electricity was related to magnetism: The movement of electrical current in a coil of wire produced a current in another coil when these two coils were linked by a magnetic material.

Although Faraday's experiment confirmed most of his expectations, it also had one surprising result. Faraday had assumed that the induced current in the second coil would be continuous; instead, he discovered that it was transient—he obtained a pulse of current, not a continuous flow. However, the evidence of his August, 1831, experiment convinced him that electromagnetic induction was a fact, and this led him to conduct several more tests over the next few months building on the evidence of his first researches. By mid-October of 1831, he was producing an electric current directly from a magnet itself by the reciprocal motion of a magnet in and out of a cylindrical helix.

The key to this process lay in Faraday's strong belief in a field composed of lines of force: Continuous electricity was produced only when a conductor was moved through a magnetic field cutting the lines of force. An experiment conducted in late October, 1831, confirmed this: Faraday rotated a copper disc between the poles of a powerful electromagnet and obtained a continuous current. These results provided him with the experimental evidence he needed to prove his theory of the unity of forces between electricity and magnetism. On November 24, 1831, he presented those findings to the Royal Society in a series of lectures titled *Experimental Researches in Electricity*. In this public setting, Faraday demonstrated the reciprocal linkage between magnetism and electricity.

SIGNIFICANCE

With this brilliant experimental work, Faraday established the scientific principles that resulted in the development of electric generators, or dynamos. These devices became the foundation of a new electrical technology using generators and motors as a new power source in the latter half of the nineteenth century. His work also reinforced the unity principles of *Naturphilos-*

ophie and convinced many nineteenth century physicists that electricity, magnetism, and light were interrelated. Further, Faraday's experimental evidence provided a foundation for James Clerk Maxwell, a distinguished British physicist, to analyze electromagnetic forces propagated through space. Maxwell's resulting equations became the basis for field theory and provided unifying mathematical statements for the observations of electromagnetic forces studied by experimentalists such as Ørsted and Faraday.

Faraday's work represents the importance of careful, thorough experimentation in nineteenth century physics. Although Faraday held strong convictions about the nature of forces, he tested those notions in the laboratory and constantly revised his interpretations of events based on his experimental results. The Royal Institution, his scientific and personal home for almost forty years, provided the framework and facilities for his ongoing research. His special skill in devising definitive experiments allowed him to discover electromagnetic induction and to explain it to the scientific community in elegant ways. In doing so, he was a founder of the scientific world of field theory and the technological world of electrical power.

—*H. J. Eisenman*

FURTHER READING

Agassi, Joseph. *Faraday as Natural Philosopher.* Chicago: University of Chicago Press, 1971. Agassi portrays Faraday as an adventuresome thinker rather than an experimental genius.

Cantor, Geoffrey. *Michael Faraday: Sandemanian and Scientist: A Study of Science and Religion in the Nineteenth Century.* New York: St. Martin's Press, 1991. Cantor provides a thorough analysis of Faraday's scientific work emphasizing the linkages between that work and Faraday's Sandemanian religion.

Gooding, David, and Frank A. J. L. James, eds. *Faraday Rediscovered: Essays on the Life and Work of Michael Faraday, 1791-1867.* New York: Macmillan, 1985. Several contemporary Faraday scholars provide new insights into Faraday's methods and achievements.

Hamilton, James. *A Life of Discovery: Michael Faraday, Giant of the Scientific Revolution.* New York: Random House, 2002. Biography focusing on Faraday's life, including his relationships with friends and colleagues, and less on his scientific discoveries.

Mahon, Basil. *The Man Who Changed Everything: The Life of James Clerk Maxwell.* Chichester, England: Wiley, 2003. Sympathetic biography of the physicist who extended Faraday's work that explains Maxwell's scientific work.

Thomas, John Meurig. *Michael Faraday and the Royal Institution: The Genius of Man and Place.* Bristol, England: Institute for Physics, 1997. Description of Faraday's life, work, and legacy by the director of Great Britain's Royal Institution. Well illustrated and easy for nonscientists to understand.

Williams, L. Pearce. *Michael Faraday: A Biography.* New York: Basic Books, 1965. This thorough biography by a noted historian of science places Faraday and his achievements within the context of nineteenth century science.

_____. *The Origins of Field Theory.* New York: Random House, 1966. This cogent treatment of field theory provides a context for understanding Faraday's

work within the larger framework of nineteenth century field physics.

SEE ALSO: c. 1801-1810: Davy Develops the Arc Lamp; 1802: Britain Adopts Gas Lighting; Nov. 6, 1820: Ampère Reveals Magnetism's Relationship to Electricity; 1850-1865: Clausius Formulates the Second Law of Thermodynamics; Oct. 21, 1879: Edison Demonstrates the Incandescent Lamp; Nov. 9, 1895: Röntgen Discovers X Rays; Nov. 16, 1896: First U.S. Hydroelectric Plant Opens at Niagara Falls; Dec. 15, 1900: General Electric Opens Research Laboratory.

RELATED ARTICLES in *Great Lives from History: The Nineteenth Century, 1801-1900:* Sir Humphry Davy; Michael Faraday; Joseph Henry; James Clerk Maxwell.

1832-1841
TURKO-EGYPTIAN WARS

Struggles between the declining Ottoman Empire and Egypt reshaped power in the Middle East and opened the Eastern Question, an international diplomatic concern over how Europe should respond to the possible breakup of the Ottoman Empire.

LOCALE: Egypt, Palestine, Syria, and Anatolia
CATEGORIES: Wars, uprisings, and civil unrest; government and politics; expansion and land acquisition

KEY FIGURES
Ibrāhīm Paṣa (1789-1848), commander of the Egyptian army
Muḥammad ʿAlī Pasha (1769-1849), viceroy of Egypt, r. 1805-1848
Mahmud II (1785-1839), Ottoman sultan, r. 1808-1839
Lord Palmerston (Henry John Temple; 1784-1865), British foreign minister

SUMMARY OF EVENT
"Destiny caresses the few and molests the many." This Turkish proverb seems appropriate to describe the 1832 to 1841 war between Egypt and the Ottoman Empire. The war featured major campaigns that taxed both nations and killed thousands, but in the end benefited only a single family.

Although technically an Ottoman vassal, Egypt's *wali* (governor), Muḥammad ʿAlī Pasha (also known as

Mehmed Ali), enjoyed de facto independence from 1805. His numerous economic and military reforms created a European-style military machine, *al-nizam al-jadid* (new model army), which made the *wali* more powerful than his nominal overlord, Sultan Mahmud II. After participating in the failed Ottoman campaign to maintain control of Greece (1821-1829), sultan and *wali* fell out over questions of compensation for Egypt's significant contributions. At issue was the Ottoman province of Syria, whose economic and strategic assets were of great interest to Muḥammad ʿAlī Pasha. In 1831, he demanded Syria as a reward for past support of the Ottoman Porte (government). Ottoman intransigence led to war.

On paper, the Ottoman military seemed strong. A British report from 1832 listed 60,000 to 100,000 soldiers, eleven ships-of-the-line, and ten frigates. In reality, Ottoman troops had a terrible reputation. They were unable to end internal rebellions such as the Wahhābī movement in Arabia, or the more recent Greek insurrection, and had just lost a war with Russia.

Egyptian troops, who numbered slightly more than sixty thousand, were polar opposites. Under the leadership of Muḥammad ʿAlī's favorite son, Ibrāhīm Paṣa, these men enjoyed a string of victories that stretched from the Sudan to Arabia. Ibrāhīm took twenty-six thousand of these veterans into Palestine in the fall of 1831. They captured Jaffa on November 26, and a day later,

Egyptian scouts were outside the walls of Acre.

Despite a long siege and spirited defense, Egyptian troops stormed the city on May 27, 1832. Next, Ottoman provincial forces were crushed at Homs. Egyptians dubbed this "the defeat of the eight pashas" because so many high-ranking Ottoman officials participated in this July 8 struggle. Victory was sweet, for as one eyewitness wrote, the loot included enough sugar and coffee "to supply a city." Next, the Egyptians attacked twenty thousand Ottoman soldiers commanded by Hussein Bey. Dug into the heights of Bilan, they occupied a formidable position. Yet, on July 29, Ibrāhīm's sixteen thousand men stormed the Syrian Gates and destroyed yet another Ottoman army.

Egyptian victories, plus Ibrāhīm's proclamation for a reduction of taxes for local Christians and Jews, garnered support for the invaders. Local notables such as Mount Lebanon's Baṣīr II quickly joined Ibrāhīm and contributed militia forces to maintain law and order. With his rear secure, the Egyptian commander marched into Anatolia, while Ottoman authorities rushed to create a new army. Under the grand vizier, Muḥammad ʿAlī Pasha, the

British foreign minister Lord Palmerston. (R. S. Peale/J. A. Hill)

506

army numbered almost fifty thousand troops of indifferent quality. With less than thirty thousand men, Ibrāhīm faced the Ottomans at Konia on December 21. The grand vizier personally led a cavalry charge and was captured; as his men found out, they fled the field. This was the decisive battle of the campaign, as it eliminated the last significant Ottoman force between Ibrāhīm and Constantinople. (According to military historian David Nicolle, Konia also marked the first use of cigarettes in the Middle East, when Egyptian troops captured large quantities of Turkish tobacco, but finding no pipes, rolled it with cartridge paper instead.)

Ibrāhīm wrote to his father that after Konia, an advance on the imperial capital of Constantinople was "as easy as a drink of water." Possibly so, but the Egyptian blitzkrieg ended when a great power threw its support behind the sultan. Strangely, the support came from Russia, a traditional foe of the Ottomans. For the Russians, the support was realpolitik, as they had no desire to see inefficient Ottoman leadership replaced by the more dynamic Muḥammad ʿAlī Pasha. The Ottoman perspective is summed up by a Turkish diplomat who explained that "a drowning man will grasp a serpent." This confluence resulted in twelve thousand Russian soldiers landing to defend Constantinople, and in 1833, the signing of the Treaty of Hunkar Iskelesi. The treaty led to a defensive alliance between Russia and the Ottoman Empire.

Ibrāhīm now needed a drink stronger than water, for Russian intervention had saved Mahmud. In May of 1832, Ibrāhīm accepted the Convention of Kutahia, which placed Syria under Egyptian control, but the convention was worded in a style that suggested it was more a truce than a definitive peace treaty.

Hunkar Iskelesi allowed the Russians to request closure of the Dardanelles (narrow strait between Europe and Asia) for any cause. It increased tremendously Russian influence in the Levant, and it alarmed both England and France. Initially, this did not register with Muḥammad ʿAlī Pasha, who told an American diplomat that he would never leave Syria, "as long as I have a soldier and a dollar." Prophetic words, for by the mid-1830's, an Egyptian Levant was anathema to England. Lord Palmerston, who served as foreign minister from 1830 to 1834, and again from 1835 to 1841, actively opposed Egyptian efforts to hold Syria permanently. "I hate Mehmed Ali," wrote Palmerston, "he is an ignorant barbarian. . . . His boasted civilization of Egypt is humbug!" Palmerston established connections between England, the Ottoman Empire, and Austria, all aimed at thwarting Egypt.

With great-power backing, Mahmud built a new army and sought revenge. Mehmed Ḥāfiẓ Paşa, the Ottoman commander for Anatolia, fed Mahmud's desires by greatly underestimating Egyptian potential, while overestimating Syrian resistance to Ibrāhīm's authority. He also overvalued his own troops, whom eyewitness Helmuth von Moltke described as equipped with "Russian jackets, French regulations, Belgian weapons, Turkish caps, Hungarian saddles, English swords, and instructors from every nation." Yet despite this hodgepodge of gear and training, the Prussian advisory team also pressed for an invasion of Syria. So with encouragement from all sides, Mahmud ordered a renewal of hostilities in 1839.

During the spring of 1839, Mehmed Ḥāfiẓ Paşa crossed the Syrian frontier. He brought eighty thousand men, plus specific orders to avoid battle in the open and to fight only from behind fixed defenses. Ibrāhīm, with seventy-five thousand troops, marched toward the invaders, and the two armies met at Nezib on June 24-25, 1839. Prussian advice to the contrary, this turned out to be another Ottoman disaster. The Egyptians smashed their adversaries and were again poised to march on an undefended Constantinople.

After Nezib, the Ottoman Empire unraveled. Mahmud II died on June 30, 1839, and as political infighting surged, the empire's last major military force, its navy, defected to Muḥammad ʿAlī Pasha. On July 14, the Ottoman navy sailed into Alexandria harbor, instantly making Egypt a major naval power in the Mediterranean. The Ottoman Empire was as close to collapse as after the disaster at Ankara in 1402, when Tamerlane defeated Ottoman sultan Bayezid I in a battle over Anatolia.

Ibrāhīm was ready again to march on Constantinople, until Great Britain and Austria intervened and with Prussia and Russia swinging toward intervention as well. Russia, for example, unilaterally abrogated Hunkar Iskelesi to appease Palmerston. The Europeans demanded Ibrāhīm halt his advance and enter negotiations for a permanent settlement with the Ottomans. France remained ambivalent under the government of Adolphe Thiers, which encouraged Muḥammad ʿAlī Pasha to consider possible backing from a great power. This ended when Thiers was replaced by François Guizot in October, leaving Egypt bereft of friends.

Led by Palmerston, a European coalition now demanded an end to the war. Muḥammad ʿAlī Pasha listened, but he refused their offer of Syria for his lifetime only. He ordered Ibrāhīm to repel all invaders, but by summer, 1840, Palmerston had created a powerful coalition, the Convention for the Pacification of the Levant.

Austrian and British naval units then attacked the coast of Palestine and, in a spectacular bombardment, leveled the fortress of Acre on November 1-2, 1840. As Royal Marines and Austrian sailors landed up and down the coastline, local rebels increased their activities, so that with the destruction of Acre, Ibrāhīm had no option but retreat into Egypt. Recognizing that his Syrian Empire was gone, Muḥammad ʿAlī Pasha accepted an Ottoman *firmin* (decree) of February 13, 1841, which, backed by the powers, allowed Muḥammad ʿAlī Pasha and his family to hold Egypt in perpetuity. It also required, however, his surrender of all other Middle Eastern holdings and recognition of the Porte as Egypt's suzerain.

SIGNIFICANCE

The Ottoman-Egyptian Wars played a critical role in shaping nineteenth century Middle Eastern history. First, the wars firmly established the Eastern Question, an international diplomatic issue that led to the Crimean War (1853-1856) and the Russo-Turkish War (1877-1878), and played a part in the Ottoman entry into World War I on the side of the Central Powers.

Second, continual Ottoman defeats in the 1830's helped push through the *Tanzimat* reforms (government reorganizations) that copied some of those already begun in Egypt. Finally, although Ibrāhīm's army was unable to hold Syria, the hard-fighting *al-nizam al-jadid* secured Egypt for the Muḥammad ʿAlī Pasha Dynasty, and a member of that dynasty sat on the Egyptian throne until the revolution of 1952.

—John P. Dunn

FURTHER READING

Fahmy, Khaled. *All the Pasha's Men: Mehmed Ali, His Army, and the Making of Modern Egypt*. New York: Cambridge University Press, 1999. A complex look at Egyptian military affairs, arguing against Mehmed Ali's role as the founder of modern Egypt.

Mishaqa, Mikhayil. *Murder, Mayhem, Pillage, and Plunder: The History of Lebanon in the Eighteenth and Nineteenth Centuries*. Translated and edited by W. M. Thackston, Jr. Albany: State University of New York Press, 1988. Tremendous coverage by an eyewitness on the Egyptian occupation of Syria in the 1830's.

Nicolle, David. "Nizam-Egypt's Army in the Nineteenth Century." *Army Quarterly and Defense Journal* 108, no. 1 (January, 1978): 69-78; and 108, no. 2 (April, 1978): 177-187. A quick look at the making of the Egyptian army and its campaigns.

1830's

SEE ALSO: 19th cent.: Arabic Literary Renaissance; 1811-1818: Egypt Fights the Wahhābīs; Mar. 1, 1811: Muḥammad ʿAlī Has the Mamlūks Massacred; Mar. 7, 1821-Sept. 29, 1829: Greeks Fight for Independence from the Ottoman Empire; Apr. 26, 1828-Aug. 28, 1829: Second Russo-Turkish War; June 14-July 5, 1830: France Conquers Algeria; Oct. 4, 1853-Mar. 30, 1856: Crimean War; 1863-1913: Greece Unifies Under the Glücksburg Dynasty; Apr. 24, 1877-Jan. 31, 1878: Third Russo-Turkish War.

RELATED ARTICLES in *Great Lives from History: The Nineteenth Century, 1801-1900:* Muhammad ʿAbduh; Jamāl al-Dīn al-Afghānī; The Mahdi; Muḥammad ʿAlī Pasha; Lord Palmerston; Adolphe Thiers.

1832-1847
ABDELKADER LEADS ALGERIA AGAINST FRANCE

After France began colonizing parts of North Africa in 1830, Algerian tribes united in resistance under Abdelkader, who created an army to fight the French in a holy war that would last fifteen years.

LOCALE: Algeria
CATEGORIES: Wars, uprisings, and civil unrest; colonization; expansion and land acquisition

KEY FIGURES
Abdelkader (ʿAbd al-Qādir; 1808-1883), emir of Mascara
Charles X (1757-1836), Bourbon king of the French, r. 1824-1830
Louis-Alexis Desmichels (1779-1849), commander of French forces in Algeria
Camille Alphonse Trézel (1780-1860), Desmichels's successor as commander
Thomas-Robert Bugeaud (Duc d'Isly; 1784-1849), French governor-general of Algeria, 1840-1847

SUMMARY OF EVENT
During the centuries leading up to the 1830's, Algeria was ruled by the Ottoman Empire, which was based in Turkey. The Turkish government had established a system of keeping order and collecting taxes by offering financial incentives to tribes in Algeria. The early part of the nineteenth century saw tensions rise as Turkish rulers dramatically raised taxes. A number of small rebellions broke out, but none was strong enough to challenge Ottoman rule. The people of Algeria did not mount a united opposition. Their centuries-old lifestyle kept them divided into tribes, some of which were nomadic and others sedentary. This division, along with other cultural and linguistic differences, made it difficult for the Algerians to resist outside control of the area.

Meanwhile, across the Mediterranean Sea, the increasingly autocratic policies of France's King Charles X were becoming highly unpopular among his subjects. Charles hoped that a military expedition that expanded France's influence in North Africa would help him regain support from his people. On June 14, 1830, French forces began landing on the Algerian coast, from which they marched inland unopposed. About three weeks later, the governor, or dey, of Algiers surrendered Algeria's major port city to the French. Despite this success in North Africa, Charles X was driven from his throne in July.

The new liberal French government that replaced Charles then found itself in control of a North African colony that it did not want, and it faced a growing debate over the question of whether France should expand its Algerian holdings or simply withdraw from North Africa. Algeria's economic potential did not appear to justify expending more resources to conquer the entire country, but many people in France believed that great riches were to be found in Algeria's interior. Also, many French people believed that colonization would convey the advantages of their own superior civilization to Algeria's peoples. In June, 1834, the French government decided to remain permanently in Algeria and issued a decree creating a federal position of governor-general in Africa.

During the early years of France's occupation of Algeria, the power of Abdelkader's family grew, paving the way for his rise to power. His family was one of the most prominent in the Oran province. In 1831, the French occupied Oran and relieved of his position Hasan Bey, the leader appointed under the Turkish regime. Moroccan troops then used Oran as grounds for opposing the French, and in the spring of 1832, Muhi al-Din, Abdelkader's father, was named deputy to the sultan of Morocco for all of Oran. Tribal leaders repeatedly offered Abdelkader the position of emir, but he refused. Instead, he agreed to lead a jihad against France. After his son had campaigned for two years, Muhi al-Din swore allegiance to his son, and Abdelkader was named *emir al-mu'minin*—the commander of the believers. That office afforded Abdelkader many political advantages. By that time, several nomadic tribes had already sworn their loyalty to him. Others were attracted to his banner when he issued a pronouncement against the invasion of Christian Europeans, accepting the challenge of uniting Algeria's Muslims against French occupation.

Many tribes accepted Abdelkader's leadership without dissent, but others feared that accepting him as a leader would cost them not only power within their tribes, but also money and property. At the same time, however, some Algerians did not regard France as a serious threat to their country. Considering the consolidation of central power a priority, Abdelkader named some of the men who resisted his leadership to positions in his newly established government. Although his influence in Oran remained tenuous, Abdelkader was the primary leader of Algerian resistance to French occupation between 1832 and 1834.

In late 1833, members of the Borjia tribe captured a French officer and four soldiers, later killing one of the soldiers. The French demanded their safe return. Abdelkader refused, and the French commander in Algeria, General Louis-Alexis Desmichels, began exchanging letters of negotiation with the emir. Abdelkader finally agreed to release the prisoners on the condition that the French enter into a peace treaty with him. In 1834, he accepted a treaty, under which he recognized the French conquest of much of northern Algeria in return for French recognition of his authority in Oran. He then began to train and equip his army according to French models—a practice that helped him overtake tribes that had not previously sworn allegiance to him. Unknown in France until 1836, Abdelkader also signed a second, secret treaty at the same time that granted him more economic and local power. Desmichels abided by the terms of both treaties, recognizing Abdelkader's power in Oran. Whenever Abdelkader disapproved of French actions, Desmichels was quick to accommodate him.

In 1835, after Desmichels's tendency to acquiesce to Abdelkader became apparent, he was replaced by General Camille Al-

phonse Trézel, who was less cooperative with Abdelkader. Hostilities between Abdelkader and the French soon resumed. Abdelkader won an important early battle against the French, but both sides scored victories. Gradually, Abdelkader gained more strength. In 1837, when a new French governor-general, Thomas-Robert Bugeaud, arrived in Algeria, Abdelkader signed a new peace agreement, the Treaty of Tafna. In return for acknowledging French suzerainty in the coastal regions, most of the hinterland was left under Muslim control. Nevertheless, fighting resumed in 1839 and continued until 1847. Abdelkader commanded eighty thousand men, but the French committed ever larger numbers of troops to the war. Under Bugeaud's command, a large French force began a systematic conquest of the interior, driving Abdelkader into Morocco, where he enlisted the aid of the sultan.

Despite Abdelkader's successes, his power over the Algerians had long been underestimated by the French. His charisma and ability to unite warring tribes under the banner of jihad supported his authority domestically, and

French soldiers in Algeria. The figure at the left wears the uniform of an infantry soldier; the figure at the right is a chasseur, *a member of light cavalry or mounted infantry.* (Library of Congress)

his familiarity with the terrain and use of Western military tactics and arms made him a formidable adversary in battles against occupying French forces. During the first decade of French occupation, Abdelkader managed to restrict the French largely to coastal towns. However, as the conflict continued into the 1840's, the French began to gain strongholds inland and expanded the conflict into the west, where they conquered Morocco in 1844. Now under French control, the sultan of Morocco could no longer offer refuge to Algerians, seriously hampering Abdelkader's ability to mount significant military operations. On August 14, 1844, Bugeaud decisively defeated him at the Battle of Isly. Abdelkader's armies continued fighting, but the French remained strong and gradually took advantage of divisions within Abdelkader's army.

In 1846, Abdelkader failed in an attempt to take Algiers. While he was fleeing toward Morocco, he defeated a Moroccan army sent to intercept him but lost his last strongholds in Algeria in the process. Fearful of losing his own position, the sultan of Morocco sent his own army against Abdelkader, forcing the latter back into Algeria in 1847. Abdelkader then realized the hopelessness of his position. When he surrendered to the French general Christophe Lamoriciere on December 21, he negotiated for a safe passage and exile to Acre or Alexandria. However, France did not honor Lamoriciere's promise and confined Abdelkader in French prisons for four years. Afterward, Abdelkader settled in Damascus, Syria, where he died in 1883.

SIGNIFICANCE

Abdelkader's wars against France between 1832 and 1847 marked the most powerful native resistance to European imperial forces in Africa during that period. For fifteen years, he united much of a naturally divided country under his rule and established the first pan-Algerian state. He was a skillful diplomat who used treaties with France to strengthen his position relative to both the Ottoman Empire and numerous local tribes. He was also a brilliant warrior who early recognized the necessity of using Western technology in fighting the French. Although France eventually prevailed in Algeria, Abdelkader's rule established a model of resistance to European imperialism. During the twentieth century, he was hailed as one of the great early African state builders. During the twenty-first century, he became recognized as an early exponent of Islamic rule and resistance to Western modernism.

—Tessa Li Powell

FURTHER READING

Abun-Nasr, Jamil M. *A History of the Maghrib in the Islamic Period.* Cambridge, England: Cambridge University Press, 1987. Broad look at the history of the Maghrib people from the time of the Roman Empire until independence in 1951; touches briefly on the French colonization of Algeria.

Adamson, Kay. *Political and Economic Thought and Practice in Nineteenth-Century France and the Colonization of Algeria.* Lewiston, N.Y.: Edwin Mellen Press, 2002. Exploration of the significance of the colonization of Algeria on its colonizers that focuses on political-economic aspects of French colonization.

Danziger, Raphael. *Abd al-Qadir and the Algerians: Resistance to the French and Internal Consolidation.* New York: Holmes & Meier, 1977. Detailed portrayal of Abdelkader's rise to power, consolidation of Algerian tribes, and Algerian conflicts with the French. Offers detailed accounts of battles and Abdelkader's administration and military staff.

Naylor, Phillip Chiviges, and Alf Andrew Heggoy. *Historical Dictionary of Algeria.* 2d ed. Metuchen, N.J.: Scarecrow Press, 1994. This book's lengthy introduction surveys key aspects of Algerian history, and individual entries profile most of the important individuals and events involved during the French period.

Swain, J. E. "The Occupation of Algiers in 1830: A Study in Anglo-French diplomacy." *Political Science Quarterly* 48, no. 3. (September, 1933): 359-366. Brief examination of the interaction between Great Britain and France as they wrestled for control of the Mediterranean region.

Vandervort, Bruce. *Wars of Imperial Conquest in Africa, 1830-1914.* Bloomington: Indiana University Press, 1998. Details the struggle for control in Africa as European forces moved to expand their empires.

Willis, Michael. *The Islamist Challenge in Algeria: A Political History.* New York: New York University Press, 1996. Discusses the importance of Abdelkader's resistance to French imperialism in brief summary; the text focuses mainly on post-1962 Algeria.

SEE ALSO: 1822-1874: Exploration of North Africa; June 14-July 5, 1830: France Conquers Algeria; Feb. 22-June, 1848: Paris Revolution of 1848.

RELATED ARTICLES in *Great Lives from History: The Nineteenth Century, 1801-1900:* Abdelkader; Louis Faidherbe; Samory Touré.

March 12, 1832
LA SYLPHIDE INAUGURATES ROMANTIC BALLET'S GOLDEN AGE

The golden age of Romantic ballet, inaugurated by Filippo Taglioni's La Sylphide, *was a short-lived yet intense period of artistic creation. For close to twenty years, ballerinas reigned supreme at the Paris Opera, delighting their public with authentic folk dances imported from exotic locales and ethereal pointe work set against supernatural backdrops.*

LOCALE: Paris, France
CATEGORY: Dance

KEY FIGURES
Filippo Taglioni (1777-1871), Italian choreographer
Marie Taglioni (1804-1884), Italian ballerina
Adolphe Nourrit (1802-1839), French operatic tenor
   and ballet scenarist
Charles Ciceri (1782-1868), costume and set designer
   at the Paris Opera
Jean Coralli (1779-1854), chief ballet master at the
   Paris Opera, 1831-1845
Jules Perrot (1810-1892), French dancer,
   choreographer, and ballet master
Carlotta Grisi (1819-1899), Italian prima ballerina
Fanny Cerrito (1817-1909), Italian prima ballerina
Lucile Grahn (1819-1907), Danish prima ballerina

SUMMARY OF EVENT
The emergence of *ballet d'action*, or dramatic panto-mime ballet, during the second half of the eighteenth century helped establish professional dance as an independent theatrical art. Performers progressively abandoned the use of masks, cumbersome hoopskirts, and elevated heels in favor of more natural attire and greater freedom of movement. During France's First Republic and throughout the Napoleonic era, the male virtuoso dancer tended to dominate the stage with dazzling leaps and spectacular pirouettes while pantomime served to advance the plot. Greek and Roman legends were common themes; costumes were elaborate and stage machinery complex. This remained the case until the early 1830's, when Romanticism invested French ballet with new vigor, and the ballerina, embodiment of the artist's quest for the infinite and unattainable, came to the forefront of public attention.

Various organizational changes at the Paris Opera helped set the stage for Romantic ballet. Between 1826 and 1831, three of the institution's leading ballet masters, Pierre Gardel, Jean-Louis Aumer, and Louis Jacques Jessé Milon, went into retirement, leaving the field open to a younger generation of talented choreographers receptive to emerging trends in literature, art and music. Gardel, in particular, had been a mainstay of French neoclassical ballet for more than forty years.

After the fall of the Bourbon monarchy in 1830, the Paris Opera, previously under royal supervision, was transformed into a private enterprise. It was endowed with public funding and placed under the capable financial direction of Louis Désiré Véron, founder of the literary magazine *Revue de Paris* (Paris review). Upon assuming his functions in 1831, Véron promptly hired dancer-choreographer Jean Coralli as ballet master and retained Marie Taglioni, daughter of Italian choreographer Filippo Taglioni, as the opera's star ballerina.

By then, work had already begun on the production of Giacomo Meyerbeer's grand opera-ballet, *Robert le diable* (Robert the demon), which premiered on November 21, 1831. Marie Taglioni was renowned for her pointe work (that is, her ability to dance on the tips of her toes), and the third act of *Robert le diable* incorporated a ballet scene, the so-called Dance of the Nuns, that was designed as a vehicle to showcase Taglioni's skill at dancing on pointe. The white-clad *corps de ballet*, dancing in the midnight decor of an eerie graveyard bacchanal, formed an integral part of the opera's narrative design and revealed to a delighted Parisian audience the direction in which Romantic ballet would evolve. Such scenes are now commonly referred to as *ballet blanc*, or white ballet, spectacles.

The first major success in Romantic ballet, *La Sylphide* (the sylph), opened at the Paris Opera on March 12, 1832. (Note that this ballet is not related to Michel Fokine's 1908 ballet, *Les Sylphides*.) Adolphe Nourrit, who had sung the part of Robert in Meyerbeer's opera a few months earlier, adapted the libretto for *La Sylphide* from a popular short story by French novelist Charles Nodier. Marie Taglioni performed the title role, and her father, Filippo, provided choreography. The ballet's narrative was set in two locales, one a material world of daylight and reason, the other a supernatural realm of enchantment and dream. It told the timeless story of a Scottish gentleman lured away from his betrothed by the haunting apparition of a beautiful yet elusive sylph on the day of his proposed marriage. Following the sylph into a dimly lit forest, he attempted to ensnare her in a magic veil yet succeeded only in precipitating her destruction.

*Marie Taglioni (standing), Carlotta Grisi, Lucile Grahn, and Fanny Cerrito
in an early production of* La Sylphide. *(Hulton Archive/Getty Images)*

Taglioni's graceful pointe work and diaphanous skirt, innovations linked to the Romantic era, served to underscore the mysterious, ephemeral qualities of the title character, helping make her a central element of the narrative. Costume designer Charles Ciceri, working in collaboration with painter Eugène Lami, designed the ballerina's virginal white dress, establishing it not only as a standard costume of ballet's Romantic era, but also as its most conspicuous emblem. The universal appeal of the dress's neo-Grecian design made it a perfect match for the otherworldly sensation of *ballet blanc*, allowing it to cross national borders with ease and combine with just about any form of regional decor. The introduction of gas lighting at the Paris Opera, yet another of the era's innovations, gave designers the ability to create new and convincing illusions on stage. Its cerulean radiance, once perfected by the addition of colored glass media, was particularly well suited to evoke the supernatural ambiance of the Romantic white ballet.

Soon after the premier of *La Sylphide*, ballets featuring ethnic color, exotic locale, supernatural beings, and human passion became the rage. Austrian ballerina Fanny Elssler, Taglioni's principal rival for the public's affection, pioneered the use of authentic national dance in *Le Diable boiteux* (1836; the lame devil), *La Gypsy* (1839; the gypsy) and *La Tarentule* (1839; the tarantella). The Italian Carlotta Grisi achieved no less fame in ballets by master choreographers Jean Coralli, Jules Perrot, and Joseph Mazilier, notably in *Giselle* (1841), *La Péri* (1843; the peri), *Esmeralda* (1844), and *Le Diable à quatre* (1845; the devil to pay). Fanny Cerrito, renowned for her shadow dance in the ballet *Ondine* (1841), later shared the stage with Marie Taglioni, Carlotta Grisi, and Lucile Grahn in *Pas de quatre* (1845; dance for four), produced by Perrot at Her Majesty's Theatre in London.

Driven by theatrical success, Romantic ballet promoted the ballerina by placing its emphasis on technique, buoyancy, and grace, rather than spectacular leaps and bounds. To an ever greater extent, male dancers served on stage as mere *porteurs* (lifters) whose primary function was to raise the ballerina to greater heights. Leading female dancers toured Europe and distant continents, performing to enthusiastic crowds in Paris, London, Milan, Vienna, Copenhagen, Saint Petersburg, Moscow, and the Americas. A significant number of them also attained recognition in the field of choreography. Thérèse Essler, the Austrian ballerina Fanny Essler's elder sister, stands out for her production of *La Volière* (the aviary) at the Paris Opera in 1838. Fanny Cerrito staged performances in Vienna, Rome, and London during the 1840's and danced the title role in *Gemma*, one of her own creations, before a Parisian audience in 1854. Marie Taglioni's oriental fantasy *Le Papillon* (the butterfly), written for her pupil Emma Livry, premiered at the Paris Opera in 1860.

SIGNIFICANCE

By the late 1840's—once choreographers and dancers had thoroughly explored the finite variations that *ballet blanc* and national folk dances could offer—the golden age of Romantic ballet came to an end, at least in France and England. A steady decline in box-office receipts and the rising popularity of dance and music halls in the post-Romantic era indicated that the creative artistic fever first displayed in *La Sylphide* and perfected in *Giselle* had run its course. The only truly remarkable success in French ballet during the Second Empire was Arthur Saint-Léon's comic ballet, *Coppélia* (1870), based on a short story by E. T. A. Hoffmann.

During the last decades of the nineteenth century, St. Petersburg under the artistic direction of Marius Petipa surpassed Paris and London as the undisputed capital of classical dance. Placing greater emphasis on the unity of music and dance and relying less on pantomime, Petipa not only breathed new life into old favorites such as *Coppélia*, *Giselle*, *Le Diable à quatre*, and *La Sylphide* but also cast exciting new ballets in the familiar Romantic tradition of lyric fantasy and national dance (*Sleeping Beauty* in 1890, *The Nutcracker* in 1892, and *Swan Lake* in 1895). Romantic ballet, refined to the tastes of modern audiences, has demonstrated over and again the depth of its artistic vision and its vitality as an independent theatrical art.

—Jan Pendergrass

FURTHER READING

Bremser, Martha, Larraine Nicholas, and Leanda Shrimpton, eds. *International Dictionary of Ballet*. 2 vols. Detroit: St. James Press, 1993. Contains detailed biographies and iconographic resources on major figures in nineteenth century ballet.

Cohen, Selma Jeanne, ed. *International Encyclopedia of Dance*. 6 vols. New York: Oxford University Press, 1998. Biographies on important figures; articles on ballet technique, scenic design, lighting, music, notation, libretti, costumes, prints, and drawings.

Foster, Susan Leigh. *Choreography and Narrative: Ballet's Staging of Story and Desire*. Bloomington: Indiana University Press, 1996. Discussion of narrative ballet from Marie Sallé's *Pygmalion* (1734) to the first staging of *Giselle* (1841).

Garafola, Lynn, ed. *Rethinking the Sylph: New Perspectives on the Romantic Ballet*. Hanover, N.H.: Wesleyan University Press, 1997. Articles by thirteen specialists.

Guest, Ivor. *Ballet Under Napoleon*. London: Dance Books, 2002. Discussion focused on the first two decades of the nineteenth century.

_____. *The Romantic Ballet in England*. London: Phoenix House, 1954. Examines the development of ballet in England during the first half of the nineteenth century.

_____. *The Romantic Ballet in Paris*. London: Pitman, 1966. Essential reading focused on the period 1820-1847.

Lee, Carol. *Ballet in Western Culture: A History of Its Origins and Evolution*. New York: Routledge, 2002. Includes sections on Romantic and post-Romantic ballet in western Europe and Russia.

SEE ALSO: 1802: Britain Adopts Gas Lighting; Apr. 7, 1805: Beethoven's *Eroica* Symphony Introduces the Romantic Age; 1824: Paris Salon of 1824; Jan. 2, 1843: Wagner's *Flying Dutchman* Debuts; Jan. 27, 1895: Tchaikovsky's *Swan Lake* Is Staged in St. Petersburg.

RELATED ARTICLES in *Great Lives from History: The Nineteenth Century, 1801-1900:* Edgar Degas; Léo Delibes; Fanny Elssler; Jacques Offenbach; Peter Ilich Tchaikovsky.

1830's

June 4, 1832
BRITISH PARLIAMENT PASSES THE REFORM ACT OF 1832

The Reform Act altered the system of political representation in Great Britain by extending the franchise to members of the middle class and middle-class controlled cities, thus increasing their influence within Parliament, while weakening the power of both the peers and the monarchy.

LOCALE: London, England

CATEGORIES: Laws, acts, and legal history; social issues and reform

KEY FIGURES

Thomas Attwood (1783-1856), middle-class leader of the Birmingham Political Union

William Cobbett (1763-1835), prominent radical journalist and supporter of reform

Second Earl Grey (1764-1845), Whig prime minister, 1830-1834, who forced the Reform Bill of 1832 through Parliament

Sir Robert Peel (1788-1850), Tory opponent of the Reform Bill in the House of Commons

Francis Place (1771-1854), London organizer of agitation for reform

Lord John Russell (1792-1878), prominent Liberal leader who advocated reform

Duke of Wellington (Arthur Wellesley, or Wesley; 1769-1852), former prime minister and Tory opponent of the Reform Bill in the House of Lords

William IV (1765-1837), king of England, r. 1830-1837

SUMMARY OF EVENT

Through almost a century and a half, the mechanism of Great Britain's unwritten constitutional structure had remained unaltered. The counties and boroughs of England, Wales, and (after 1707) Scotland were represented in the House of Commons by the same numbers of members as at the time of William and Mary in the late seventeenth century, even though Britain's population had grown greatly and shifted geographically.

Each borough retained its own particular tradition for choosing its representatives. "Pocket boroughs" voted at the beck and call of their wealthy patrons; corporation boroughs were in the careful hands of small groups of leading town fathers. Democratic boroughs, such as Preston, experienced violent electioneering, since their entire adult male populations possessed the vote. The

borough franchise was a matter of local "liberty" and custom rather than of parliamentary statute.

The English county franchise, on the other hand, was somewhat more uniform; since 1432, each forty-shilling freeholder (the owner of land worth that much in annual rental) had had the right to vote. By the early nineteenth century, this provision would have created virtual universal manhood suffrage in the counties if the vast majority had been freeholders. Most residents were leaseholders, tenants, or day laborers and were thus excluded from the franchise. This exclusion was the result of the enclosure movement of the previous century, which had deprived many of their land.

This diverse system had come under repeated attack during the later years of the eighteenth century. Some reformers argued simply that the democratic element of the "mixed" British constitution, the House of Commons, ought to be made more democratic and more obviously and justly representative of the population, while the aristocratic and monarchal elements represented in the House of Lords and the king should be allowed to retain their due influence on the government. A reform bill embodying significant changes in borough representation and franchise requirements came close to success during the 1780's. The outbreak of the French Revolution in 1789 led to more extreme proposals; men such as Thomas Paine, Joseph Priestley, and William Godwin demanded not only that the House of Commons be democratized but also that the House of Lords and the Crown itself ultimately be abolished.

The French Revolution (1789) briefly inflamed the British reform spirit, only to squelch it after the worst abuses of the revolution became known. Calls for reform became associated with the guillotine and France's Reign of Terror. When Britain and France went to war in 1793, a strong political reaction against reform set in. As an embattled island, standing at times alone against the Napoleonic empire, Britain seemed to require political stability rather than change. Thus, the social processes that literally altered the British landscape and contributed greatly to the ultimate military triumph in 1815 remained unreflected in the country's political structure. By 1820, however, reform was once again before the public consciousness and political radicals, moderate Whigs, and ambitious industrialists all clamored in a multitude of ways for a fundamental change in the political system.

The practical problem was that if a far-reaching political shift were to come about, barring revolution, it had to take place inside Parliament itself, and that would require members of Parliament to vote themselves out of power. This situation explains, as readily as any abstract principle, why men who had tackled other difficult political questions were unwilling to take on a measure of general political reform. However, if nothing were done, there was the intermittent fear that the patience of the unenfranchised—especially members of the new industrial classes—might wear out and that the nineteenth century, like the seventeenth, would become a century of revolution.

Opposition to the old electoral system arose gradually from several overlapping sources. Democratic radicals, such as William Cobbett, Sir Francis Burdett, and Daniel O'Connell, favored wide suffrage and had the support from the workers. Benthamite utilitarians, such as Joseph Hume and James Mill, sought a more "rational" system. Whig-Liberals, such as Lord Russell and Earl Grey, and progressive Tories, such as Lord Chandos, desired a more representative House of Commons. Finally, middle-class leaders, such as Thomas Attwood and Fran-

cis Place, sought a wider political role for the rising industrial middle class.

Several events led to increase the hitherto lagging agitation. One of these events was the 1829 crisis over Roman Catholic emancipation, which weakened Wellington's Tory government by alienating diehard anti-Catholics and further crumbling the fragile structure of English political parties. Catholic emancipation also brought Daniel O'Connell and his Irish pro-Reform followers into Parliament.

The success of O'Connell and the success of his Catholic Association's methods of mass agitation led advocates of parliamentary reform to form similar groups. The July Revolution of 1830 in France and similar revolts on the Continent moved many British people to push for reform in order to avoid revolution in Great Britain. This fear was increased by a few minor outbreaks in England itself. The death of King George IV in June of 1830 also removed an implacable foe of reform.

Wellington's flat opposition to reform and his statement that the existing representation system could not be improved helped to cause the fall of his government on November 15, 1830. Earl Grey, the Whig leader, formed a new government that included the progressive Tory Canningite faction. Since reform had long been a Whig platform, a Reform Bill of some type was certain and a committee was set up to prepare such a bill.

On March 1, 1831, Lord John Russell's committee presented the First Reform Bill to the Commons. It disenfranchised all boroughs with fewer than two thousand inhabitants and cut in half the representation of the boroughs with fewer than four thousand inhabitants. The 168 seats abolished by these means were allotted to large cities such as Manchester, Birmingham, and London, and to some of the larger counties. Qualifications for the franchise were standardized to include male adults who rented or owned quarters worth ten pounds in the boroughs or owned property worth forty shillings in the counties. This last provision increased the number of voters, especially those of the middle classes, in some areas but also disenfranchised poorer voters in some places.

New extraparliamentary organizations urging acceptance of reform included the Political Unions, modeled after O'Connell's Catholic Association, which were organized throughout England and Scotland, especially in the large cities. The first and most important was the Birmingham Union led by Thomas Attwood and supported by Cobbett and Burdett. It was dominated by middle-class elements, but it was also supported by radicals, workers, utilitarians, and some progressive Tories. The

King William IV. (Library of Congress)

London organization led by Francis Place was also influential. A certain amount of friction developed between the Political Unions and the Whigs over some of the provisions of the Reform Bill and over stern Whig suppression of unrest.

In the parliamentary debates on the bill, the Tories, led by Sir Robert Peel, argued that the bill's provisions would destroy the aristocracy and lead to revolution, middle-class control, and universal suffrage. Some radicals objected that the bill did not go far enough, since it excluded workers and did not provide for the secret ballot. The Whigs defended their bill by claiming that it was a reasonable reform that would protect the aristocracy from more revolutionary changes. The First Reform Bill passed its second reading in the House of Commons by a single vote. When a Tory motion against reducing the number of seats passed, Grey dissolved Parliament and called for new elections.

In the heated political campaign that followed, elements advocating reform won a sweeping victory, and the Tories lost more than one hundred seats in Parliament. Consequently, a similar Second Reform Bill was introduced on June 24, 1831, and passed by more than one hundred votes, although a Tory amendment giving the vote to tenant-farmers, often dependent on aristocrats, was passed over government opposition. However, the House of Lords rejected the bill on October 8, 1831. The action of the House of Lords unleashed a wave of protest from the Political Unions and some outbreaks of violence.

The Whig government then introduced a Third Reform Bill, which saved a few smaller boroughs and allowed some freemen without property to retain their votes. This bill passed the Commons by a larger margin, 324 to 162, and was sent up to the Lords. There it passed its second reading by nine votes, but an amendment was carried that would have split the enfranchising clauses from the disenfranchising clauses on the final vote. Earl Grey then asked King William IV to create enough peers to pass the bill through the Lords. However, the king instead demanded Grey's resignation and asked Wellington to form a new government. This demand was greeted with widespread opposition and threats of revolution from the Political Unions if Wellington were to return to office. However, Wellington could not form a ministry, and the king was forced to recall Grey. With the threat of having new peers created hanging over them, the House of Lords finally passed the Reform Bill on June 4, 1832, by a considerable margin, and it received the royal assent on June 7.

The effects of the Reform Act of 1832 were not as radical as many of its supporters had hoped or its opponents had feared. The total electorate was increased by only 50 percent. The middle classes and middle-class-controlled cities were largely enfranchised and increased their influence in Parliament. Although some workers maintained their votes, the working classes on a whole lost both votes and influence. The aristocracy also lost some power, but the increased rural vote, which they controlled, maintained their dominant role in politics.

The end of the so-called rotten boroughs lessened political corruption to some extent. The redistribution of seats removed the most glaring inequities, but it came nowhere near equalizing districts. The organized, popular-based agitation of the Political Unions set a precedent for future political activity. The Reform Act strengthened the Whigs, but the continually growing middle-class influence transformed their party into the Liberal Party. Despite the intention that the Great Reform Bill, or Victorian Compromise, would be final, the Reform Act was only the first step toward eventual universal suffrage and democracy.

The monarchy lost much prestige and power as a result of the Reform Act because three successive kings had not been able to unite the nation behind their own view of government. The crystallization of an increasingly disciplined two-party parliamentary system also weakened the monarchy. In a Parliament composed of numerous small factions with no deep ideological issues dividing them and many members owing their jobs to royal favor, the king had much room to maneuver. By contrast, with party organizations stronger and party leaders more clearly defined, the king had much less choice.

By engaging the electorate, by imposing uniform franchise requirements, and by instituting a system of registering electors, the Reform Act encouraged not only the strengthening of the parliamentary party but also the beginning of a national party organization. The more clearly the House of Commons could be seen to reflect the will of the British people, the less plausible could a monarch oppose it in the name of the "true" interests of his or her subjects. Thus the Reform Bill clearly weakened the political influence of the monarch.

The bill also had a comparable effect upon the House of Lords. The course of the struggle had demonstrated that, in a showdown, the House of Commons was the more powerful of the two chambers as well as the arena in which the more vital political personalities engaged in debate. The bill had also very much limited the influence that the peers could exercise as borough mongers with numerous House of Commons seats at their disposal.

At the same time that the Reform Bill had weakened the prestige of king, peers, and gentry, it had notably strengthened the position of the new custodians of commercial and industrial wealth. They now shared with old-line oligarchs the rule of the kingdom. The fundamental political imbalance caused by industrialization had largely been rectified, and it is no coincidence that these elements would reshape British politics in their own images.

SIGNIFICANCE

It was the peaceful manner in which the bill was passed by the force of public opinion and extraparliamentary agitation that made the Reform Bill a landmark toward full democracy. Perhaps the ultimate significance of the bill lies in that it was passed at all, and without revolution. It proved, as Peel and Wellington had rightly predicted, the first act of the play and not the last. However, within a very short time it was accepted by even diehard Tories who had dreaded its passage. Radicals, Whigs, and Tories had all learned one crucial lesson, which was to apply repeatedly during the century that followed. When the object was reform, it was possible in the last resort to gain fundamental change peacefully. Henceforth, whatever the grievance, political agitation was not merely a legitimate but also a practical means to achieve reform. The battle might be long and the opposition strong but, provided the grievance was real and enough people truly wanted change, a remedy by means of legislation rather than revolution was possible.

—*James H. Steinel, updated by Kevin B. Vichcales*

FURTHER READING

Arnstein, Walter L. "Reform or Revolution." In *Britain Yesterday and Today: 1830 to the Present.* Lexington, Mass.: D. C. Heath, 1994. This chapter provides a concise narrative of the issues surrounding the 1832 Reform Act and places the act into a historical context of British and European development.

Burton, Anthony. *William Cobbett, Englishman: A Biography.* London: Aurum Press, 1997. Biography of one of the leading radical supports of the Reform Act.

Dinwiddy, John R. *From Luddism to the First Reform Bill: Reform in England, 1810-32.* New York: Oxford University Press, 1986. This work places the Reform Act into the context of working-class struggle for rights within British society. As such it provides a critical assessment of the Reform Act.

Jupp, Peter. *British Politics on the Eve of Reform: The Duke of Wellington's Administration, 1829-1830.* New York: St. Martin's Press, 1998. Analysis of the British monarchy, office of prime minister, Parliament, and other political institutions on the eve of Britain's adoption of the Reform Act of 1832.

Parry, Johnathon P. *The Rise and Fall of Liberal Government in Victorian Britain.* New Haven, Conn.: Yale University Press, 1993. Identifies the Reform Act as the precursor of the rise of Liberal government in Britain and asssesses the act and its provisions in terms of their influence on the political composition of British government and as a model for further reform during the early and middle Victorian period.

Phillips, John A., and Charles Wetherell. "The Great Reform Act of 1832 and the Political Modernization of England." *The American Historical Review* 100 (April, 1995): 411-436. Details the impact of the Reform Act of 1832 on the development of political parties during the nineteenth century.

Scherer, Paul. *Lord John Russell: A Biography.* Selinsgrove, Pa.: Susquehanna University Press, 1999. Scholarly biography of the great Liberal leader who supported the Reform Act and later served as prime minister during a period of further reforms.

Seymour, Charles. *Electoral Reform in England and Wales.* London: Oxford University Press, 1925. Despite its age, Seymour's work remains the most thorough and extensive study of the provisions of the Reform Act. It takes the provisions of the Reform Bill, point by point, discussing the old electoral law, the debates, and the new provisions.

Smith, E. A., ed. *Reform or Revolution? A Diary of Reform in England, 1830-2.* Wolfeboro Falls, N.H.: Alan Sutton, 1992. Focuses on the critical period 1830 through 1832 during which the Reform Bill was before the British parliament. It provides a critical analysis of the events surrounding the passage of the act and detailed coverage of the most important questions of reform raised by the act.

SEE ALSO: Dec. 11-30, 1819: British Parliament Passes the Six Acts; Feb. 23, 1820: London's Cato Street Conspirators Plot Assassinations; 1824: British Parliament Repeals the Combination Acts; May 9, 1828-Apr. 13, 1829: Roman Catholic Emancipation; 1833: British Parliament Passes the Factory Act; Sept. 9, 1835: British Parliament Passes Municipal Corporations Act; May 8, 1838-Apr. 10, 1848: Chartist Movement; June 15, 1846: British Parliament Repeals the

1830's

Corn Laws; Aug. 28, 1857: British Parliament Passes the Matrimonial Causes Act; Aug., 1867: British Parliament Passes the Reform Act of 1867; Dec. 6, 1884: British Parliament Passes the Franchise Act of 1884.

RELATED ARTICLES in *Great Lives from History: The Nineteenth Century, 1801-1900:* William Cobbett; Charles Grey; Sir Robert Peel; John Russell; Duke of Wellington; William IV.

July 10, 1832
JACKSON VETOES RECHARTERING OF THE BANK OF THE UNITED STATES

Andrew Jackson's impassioned campaign against rechartering the national bank succeeded and had the result of helping to spur a period of economic growth and spiraling inflation.

LOCALE: Washington, D.C.; Philadelphia, Pennsylvania

CATEGORIES: Banking and finance; trade and commerce; government and politics

KEY FIGURES

Andrew Jackson (1767-1845), president of the United States, 1829-1837

Thomas Hart Benton (1782-1858), Missouri senator who opposed the bank

Nicholas Biddle (1786-1844), president of the Second Bank of the United States

Henry Clay (1777-1852), Kentucky senator who supported the bank

Roger Brooke Taney (1777-1864), secretary of the Treasury, 1833-1834

Martin Van Buren (1782-1862), governor of New York and later president, 1837-1841

Daniel Webster (1782-1852), Massachusetts senator who supported the bank

SUMMARY OF EVENT

If the importance of political events is measured by the intensity of feeling aroused and the vigorous debate engendered among contemporaries, then Andrew Jackson's war against the Second Bank of the United States stands out as one of the critical issues of the antebellum period of American history. It is a comparatively simple task to describe the sequence of events that led to the destruction of the bank and to list the people involved on both sides of the struggle. It is difficult, however, to explain motivations, such as why Jackson unleashed such a violent attack, what the motives of his supporters were, and why Nicholas Biddle, the bank's presi-

dent, took up the challenge when he did. It is also necessary to consider the net effect of the struggle on the nation.

Contemporary caricature depicting President Andrew Jackson as a despotic "King Andrew" because of his inflexible opposition to the Bank of the United States. (Library of Congress)

In 1828, it appeared that the Bank of the United States had regained general favor throughout the nation. Opposition had not been entirely eliminated, but the success of the bank under Biddle, combined with the vitality of the economy, which was entering into a period of high prosperity, provided antibank elements with little ammunition with which to press their attack. Nevertheless, the resentment of interests such as the state bankers existed, awaiting only an opportunity to strike at the national bank. Moreover, memories of the bank's errors during the depression of the early 1820's had not been entirely erased. Martin Van Buren, the governor of New York, had opposed the bank in 1826, and Senator Thomas Hart Benton of Missouri still regarded the institution as a "monster" and a monopoly that should be destroyed. They could do little by themselves, but they were prepared to respond to the call of a more prominent champion of the people against the bank interests—President Andrew Jackson.

Jackson's previous public career as a military general, planter in Tennessee, judge, senator, speculator, and bank-stock owner provided no foreknowledge of the position that he was to take on the Bank of the United States. When Jackson took office, Biddle, who was from a prosperous Philadelphia family, was reasonably sure that he and the president could reach an agreement concerning the bank. In Jackson's first annual message to Congress in December, 1829, he questioned the constitutionality of the bank while also charging that the bank had failed to establish a uniform and sound currency. In his second message, he treated the bank more harshly, but neither message demoralized Biddle. During that same year, Jackson had written to Biddle,

> I do not dislike your bank any more than all banks. But ever since I read the history of the South Sea Bubble [which had defrauded thousands of eighteenth century British investors] I have been afraid of banks.

In 1830, neither Jackson nor Biddle wished to make the bank an issue in the election of 1832. Biddle believed that compromise was possible.

At that point, it appears that the supporters of Jackson and of Biddle convinced the two men that the issue could not be postponed. The bank's charter was valid until

---

JACKSON QUESTIONS THE BANK OF THE UNITED STATES' CONSTITUTIONALITY

In his first state of the union address, on December 8, 1829, President Andrew Jackson argued against the renewal of the Bank of the United States' charter on constitutional grounds. He asked Congress to pass laws establishing a more acceptable financial institution to function in place of that bank.

The charter of the Bank of the United States expires in 1836, and its stock holders will most probably apply for a renewal of their privileges. In order to avoid the evils resulting from precipitancy in a measure involving such important principles and such deep pecuniary interests, I feel that I can not, in justice to the parties interested, too soon present it to the deliberate consideration of the Legislature and the people. Both the constitutionality and the expediency of the law creating this bank are well questioned by a large portion of our fellow citizens, and it must be admitted by all that it has failed in the great end of establishing an uniform and sound currency.

Under these circumstances, if such an institution is deemed essential to the fiscal operations of the Government, I submit to the wisdom of the Legislature whether a national one, founded upon the credit of the Government and its revenues, might not be devised which would avoid all constitutional difficulties and at the same time secure all the advantages to the Government and country that were expected to result from the present bank. . . .

1836, but Senators Henry Clay and Daniel Webster, who performed legal work for the bank, viewed the bank issue as one that could seriously damage Jackson's chances for reelection in 1832. For reasons still not thoroughly explained, Biddle succumbed to their urgings and agreed to apply for recharter prior to the election. Under the pressure of his antibank advisers, Jackson had drifted to a position that made compromise with Biddle unlikely.

A bill for recharter passed in the Senate on June 11 and passed in the House on July 3, 1832. Jackson vetoed it on July 10, and the bank's supporters could not muster the votes to override his veto. The veto message has been praised and condemned by the advocates and detractors of Jackson. The veto did not deal with the bank as an economic institution but as a vehicle by which the special interests, "the rich and powerful . . . bend the acts of government to their selfish purposes." According to Jackson, the bank was irresponsible: It favored the rich against the poor, and it was not compatible with democratic self-government. Jackson seized upon the bank as a symbol of special privileges for the wealthy. He questioned the bank's constitutionality, large number of foreign stockholders, and favoritism for its friends in Congress. He commented, "Many of our rich men have not been content with equal protection and equal benefits, but have besought us to make them richer by act of Congress." The bank became a major issue in the election of 1832, in which Jackson won a convincing victory over Henry Clay.

Jackson considered the 1832 election results as a mandate to escalate his war against the Bank of the United States. Not satisfied that the bank would pass from the scene in 1836, Jackson decided to destroy it at once. In spite of opposition from Congress, Jackson determined to withdraw government deposits from the bank. After dismissing two secretaries of the Treasury who balked at this action, Jackson appointed a third, Roger Brooke Taney, who suspended the deposits of federal funds in the bank and placed them in various state-chartered banks around the country. The bank reacted to this diminution of its resources by calling in its loans and restricting its credit operations. At that point, Biddle became so obsessed with the threat to the bank that he seems to have forgotten that the bank had a responsibility to the public. Biddle's policies were more severe than the situation required, but he was determined to demonstrate the power of the bank and thus force its recharter. Jackson had accused the bank of irresponsibility in 1832, and during the period 1834-1836, Biddle's activities substantiated Jackson's charge. The bank lost much support during the last two years of its national charter.

SIGNIFICANCE

President Andrew Jackson struck at the Bank of the United States at a moment when the nation could least afford to lose it. The economy was entering a boom cycle. Land sales were mounting rapidly, specie was scarce, credit was overextended, state banks proliferated, their printing presses poured out paper money, and prices rose. Deprived of federal deposits, the Bank of the United States could no longer restrain the manufacture of credit and currency by state banks. It also could not enter the specie market with strength. Although it is impossible to say that the destruction of the Bank of the United States caused the Panic of 1837 and the resultant depression, the severity of both might have been alleviated greatly and the depression shortened had the bank continued to function under a national charter.

—*John G. Clark, updated by Joseph Edward Lee*

FURTHER READING

Bodenhorn, Howard. *A History of Banking in Antebellum America: Financial Markets and Economic De-*velopment in an Era of Nation-Building. New York: Cambridge University Press, 2000. Examination of American banking policies in the years leading up to the Civil War, with attention to the Bank of the United States.

Brown, Marion A. *The Second Bank of the United States and Ohio, 1803-1860: A Collision of Interests.* Lewiston, N.Y.: Edwin Mellen Press, 1998. Study of conflicts between the Second Bank of the United States and the state of Ohio.

Govan, Thomas P. *Nicholas Biddle: Nationalist and Public Banker, 1786-1844.* Chicago: University of Chicago Press, 1959. Well-written biography that provides rich background information on the development of the Second Bank of the United States.

Hammond, Bray. *Banks and Politics in America, from the Revolution to the Civil War.* Princeton, N.J.: Princeton University Press, 1957. Argues that Jackson and the bank's allies were all capitalists, but the Jacksonians favored rapid development while the Bank of the United States was more cautious.

Kaplan, Edward S. *The Bank of the United States and the American Economy.* Westport, Conn.: Greenwood Press, 1999. Broad economic study of the role of the Bank of the United States in American economic history.

Remini, Robert V. *Andrew Jackson and the Course of American Empire.* 3 vols. New York: Harper & Row, 1977-1984. Provides a thorough background on Jackson, his political rise, and the issues, such as multification, that are identified with the age of Jackson.

Schlesinger, Arthur M. *The Age of Jackson.* Boston: Little, Brown, 1953. This beautifully written book suggests that Nicholas Biddle personified privilege, and that by attacking the bank, Jackson was championing democracy.

Sharp, James R. *The Jacksonians Versus the Banks: Politics in the States After the Panic of 1837.* New York: Columbia University Press, 1970. Examines the ruinous aftereffects of the demise of the national bank and the rise of untrustworthy state banks.

Watson, Harry L. *Liberty and Power: The Politics of Jacksonian America.* New York: Noonday Press, 1990. Analyzes the political forces that elevated the bank battle to the level of the primary issue in the 1832 presidential campaign.

SEE ALSO: Apr., 1816: Second Bank of the United States Is Chartered; Mar. 6, 1819: *McCulloch v. Maryland*; Apr. 14, 1834: Clay Begins American Whig Party;

Mar. 17, 1837: Panic of 1837 Begins; Aug. 1, 1846: Establishment of Independent U.S. Treasury; Feb. 25, 1863-June 3, 1864: Congress Passes the National Bank Acts.

RELATED ARTICLES in *Great Lives from History: The Nineteenth Century, 1801-1900:* Thomas Hart Benton; Nicholas Biddle; Henry Clay; Andrew Jackson.

November 24, 1832-January 21, 1833
NULLIFICATION CONTROVERSY

Responding to federal tariffs on imports that damaged South Carolina's economy, the state of South Carolina advocated a theory of nullification, by which sovereign states could ignore unacceptable federal laws. The federal government prevailed on the issue of nullification but eased its tariff levels, allowing both sides to claim victory.

ALSO KNOWN AS: Tariff of 1832; Tariff of Abominations

LOCALE: South Carolina; Washington, D.C.

CATEGORIES: Trade and commerce; government and politics

KEY FIGURES

John C. Calhoun (1782-1850), vice president of the United States, 1825-1832, and later senator from South Carolina

Henry Clay (1777-1852), senator from Kentucky

Andrew Jackson (1767-1845), president of the United States, 1829-1837

SUMMARY OF EVENT

By the late 1820's, the southeastern section of the United States was economically depressed. Most of its fiscal ailments were blamed on the protective Tariff of 1828, which protected the North against competition for its textile goods but limited the South's disposing of its agricultural commodities on world markets. While the South languished, the industrial Northeast flourished. In fact, the soil in the oldest southern states was badly depleted, which meant that the region could not compete on equal terms with the newer states in the Gulf region. Leadership in the fight against the tariff fell to South Carolina, whose planter aristocrats enjoyed political power and where the relative decline in prosperity was the greatest.

The keys to South Carolina's defiance against the tariff were its racial demography and a very conservative political structure, different from that of its slaveholding neighbors. In 1830, South Carolina was the only state with a absolute majority of black people. Most of the black population was concentrated on the sea islands and tidal flats south of Charleston. The low-country planters controlled state politics. Very high property qualifications for holding office kept power in the hands of the planter elite. This elite controlled the state legislature, which appointed most officials and therefore had tremendous leverage on public opinion in the state.

South Carolina was primarily a cotton-producing state and had experienced a collapse of cotton prices in the Panic of 1819, falling production because of soil erosion, competition from cotton produced on cheaper and more fertile western lands, and an exodus of its white population. Up-country slaveholders incurred heavy losses when upland cotton prices fell 72 percent by 1829, and they were receptive to the argument of the antitariff advocates—the so-called Nullifiers—who blamed the tariff for their plight. Tariff rates had increased as much as 50 percent by 1828, and the Nullifiers argued that these high tariffs caused prices on domestic manufactured goods to rise, while potentially limiting export markets for agricultural goods. In effect, they argued, the tariffs penalized one class of people for the benefit of another. Along with the tariff issue, there was the issue of slavery. The leaders of nullification were rice and sea-island cotton planters whose greater fear was not losing cotton profits but losing control over their African American majority.

South Carolina's most eloquent spokesman was John C. Calhoun, who by the late 1820's had completed his philosophical change from ardent nationalist to states' rights advocate. Calhoun then advocated the ultimate in states' rights thinking—a belief in, and support of, the doctrine of nullification, first stated by Thomas Jefferson and James Madison in the Virginia and Kentucky Resolves of 1798. In 1828, while running as a vice presidential candidate, Calhoun anonymously wrote the "South Carolina Exposition and Protest." This essay protested against the Tariff of 1828, known as the Tariff of Abominations by southerners because of its high protective duties. Calhoun's authorship of this document remained secret, and for four years South Carolina did not act upon it, hoping that President Andrew Jackson would work for a lower tariff. The "Exposition" and a later paper called "A Disquisition on Government" explained Calhoun's doctrine of nullification.

Contrary to popular belief, Calhoun's theory did not advocate secession; rather, he believed that nullification would prevent the disruption of the union. Calhoun saw nullification as an antidote to secessionist feelings. The basic tenets of his argument were that sovereignty was, by its very nature, absolute and indivisible. Each state was sovereign, and the union was a compact among the states. Each individual state entered into an agreement with the others, and the terms of this covenant went into the U.S. Constitution.

The Constitution provided for a separation of powers between the states and the federal government, but not a division of sovereignty. Sovereignty was not the sum of a number of governmental powers but the will of the political community, which could not be divided without being destroyed. The states had been sovereign under the Articles of Confederation, and they had not given up their supreme authority when they joined the new union.

Since the union had been created by the states, and not vice versa, it logically followed that the creator should be more powerful than its creation. As the federal government was not supreme, it could exercise only those powers given it by the states, as embodied in the Constitution. Should it exceed these powers, the measures enacted would be unconstitutional.

Calhoun's theory raised the question of who was to be the arbiter of constitutionality. Certainly not the U.S. Supreme Court, as it was an instrument of the federal government: If the federal government were not sovereign, then one of its branches could not be sovereign. Supreme authority therefore rested solely in the people of the states. When a state believed that a federal law exceeded the delegated powers of Congress, that state could declare the law null and void and prevent its enforcement within its own boundaries.

When passing on the constitutionality of a law of the federal government, the state acted through a convention called for the express purpose of considering this question, for this was the only way in which the people of a state could give expression to their sovereign will. This action, however, should be taken only as a last resort to protect its rights. Congress could then counter by offering an amendment authorizing the powers that the state contested. If the amendment were not ratified, the law was to be annulled, not only for the state in question but also for the entire nation. Should the amendment pass, the dissatisfied state would have to yield or secede—it could not remain in the union without accepting the amendment. Thus, the final arbiter would be the same power that created the Constitution, the people of the states. Calhoun was sure that this theory would prevent secession, for if three-fourths of the states were to speak against one state, that state would be unlikely to secede.

After simmering for four years, the issue of nullification erupted in 1832 over a new tariff. In December, 1831, President Andrew Jackson recommended to Congress a downward revision of the tariff and the elimination of the worst features of the Tariff of Abominations. Such a bill finally was pushed through on July 14, 1832, but the new tariff was not low enough to satisfy southern planters. Although some of the so-called "abominations" in the tariff bill were removed, the general level of the duties was only slightly lower. The greatest reductions were made on noncompetitive manufactured items, and the protective makeup of the tariff hardly had been changed.

By mid-1832, the South Carolina extremists were ready to put the nullification theory into action. Many de-

John C. Calhoun. (Courtesy, University of Texas at Austin)

JACKSON ON TARIFF REDUCTION AND NULLIFICATION

In his state of the union address of December 4, 1832, President Andrew Jackson spoke at length on the need to retire the public debt. He held out the possibility of tariff reduction, but at the same time he warned against states trying to exert their own sovereignty in violation of federal laws.

In effecting this [budget] adjustment it is due, in justice to the interests of the different States, and even to the preservation of the Union itself, that the protection afforded by existing laws to any branches of the national industry should not exceed what may be necessary to counteract the regulations of foreign nations and to secure a supply of those articles of manufacture essential to the national independence and safety in time of war. If upon investigation it shall be found, as it is believed it will be, that the legislative protection granted to any particular interest is greater than is indispensably requisite for these objects, I recommend that it be gradually diminished, and that as far as may be consistent with these objects the whole scheme of duties be reduced to the revenue standard as soon as a just regard to the faith of the Government and to the preservation of the large capital invested in establishments of domestic industry will permit. . . .

It is my painful duty to state that in one quarter of the United States opposition to the revenue laws has arisen to a height which threatens to thwart their execution, if not to endanger the integrity of the Union. What ever obstructions may be thrown in the way of the judicial authorities of the General Government, it is hoped they will be able peaceably to overcome them by the prudence of their own officers and the patriotism of the people. But should this reasonable reliance on the moderation and good sense of all portions of our fellow citizens be disappointed, it is believed that the laws themselves are fully adequate to the suppression of such attempts as may be immediately made. Should the exigency arise rendering the execution of the existing laws impracticable from any cause what ever, prompt notice of it will be given to Congress, with a suggestion of such views and measures as may be deemed necessary to meet it. . . .

power of a single state to annul a federal law was "incompatible with the existence of the union, contradicted by the letter of the Constitution, unauthorized by its spirit, inconsistent with every principle on which it was founded, and destructive to the great object for which it was formed." He called nullification an "impractical absurdity" and concluded that "disunion by armed force is treason." This "Proclamation to the People of South Carolina" received the enthusiastic support of nationalists.

Although Jackson was bold, he was also conciliatory. In his fourth annual message to Congress, in December, 1832, he promised to press for further reduction of the hated tariffs. This was repeated later the same month when the president issued a proclamation to the people of South Carolina. On January 16, 1833, Jackson sent a message to Congress reviewing the circumstances in South Carolina and recommending measures that would enable him to cope successfully with the situation. Tension mounted as the Senate passed the Force Bill in February. This measure authorized Jackson to use the U.S. Army and Navy to enforce the federal laws, if necessary. On January 21, South Carolina politicians agreed to postpone execution of the state's nullification ordinance until after Congress adjourned in March.

In fulfilling his promise to see that the tariffs were reduced, Jackson did his best to see that legislation giving him full power to force obedience to the laws was accompanied by bills to reduce the tariffs. While the Force Bill was being debated, Henry Clay brought forward a new compromise tariff bill calling for the gradual reduction of tariff duties over the next ten years. By 1842, the tariff was not to exceed 20 percent. South Carolinians waited anxiously to see what would happen, for it was already apparent that no other southern states were coming to its aid, and it would have to fight it out alone. Calhoun, who had resigned the vice presidency after the passage of the Tariff of 1832 and had been elected immediately to the Senate, objected to the Force Bill but feared that strong

1830's

nounced the Tariff of 1832 as unconstitutional and oppressive to the southern people. In the subsequent state election that fall, the States' Rights and Unionist parties made the tariff and nullification the chief issues. When the States' Rights Party won more than two-thirds of the seats in the legislature, it promptly called for a state convention. The convention met in November, 1832, and by a vote of 136 to 26 adopted an Ordinance of Nullification on November 24. Under that ordinance, the Tariffs of 1828 and 1832 were both declared null and void. After February 1, 1833, the tariff duties were not to be collected, and should the federal government attempt to collect them forcibly, South Carolina would secede from the union.

Jackson met this challenge in typical fashion. On December 10, 1832, he boldly proclaimed that the Constitution formed a government, not a league, and that the

opposition might hurt the chances of reconciliation that were presented by the Compromise Tariff. He and Clay worked to push the new tariff bill through Congress, and on March 2, 1833, Jackson signed into law both the Force Bill and the Compromise Tariff of 1833.

SIGNIFICANCE

After the Compromise Tariff was passed, South Carolina repealed its own Ordinance of Nullification; however, in a last gesture of defiance, the state convention declared the Force Bill null and void. Jackson ignored this final face-saving move on the part of South Carolina, for the Force Bill was irrelevant while the tariff duties were being collected.

Both sides claimed victory. Nationalists declared that the power of the federal government had been upheld by both the president and Congress, while South Carolina asserted that nullification had proved an effective method of sustaining states' rights. However, the failure of any other southern state to rally to South Carolina's defense showed that the doctrine of nullification was unpopular, and from that time forward, militant southerners looked to the doctrine of secession as their best redress of grievances.

—*John H. DeBerry, updated by Bill T. Manikas*

FURTHER READING

Bancroft, Frederic. *Calhoun and the South Carolina Nullification Movement*. Baltimore: Johns Hopkins University Press, 1928. A brief historical and critical study of Calhoun and the nullification controversy as a political event in Jackson's administration, and of the events leading up to and following it.

Bartlett, Irving H. *John C. Calhoun: A Biography*. New York: W. W. Norton, 1993. Scholarly biography, tracing Calhoun's evolution from ardent nationalist to advocate of sectionalism and nullification.

Boucher, Chauncey S. *The Nullification Controversy in South Carolina*. Chicago: University of Chicago Press, 1916. A detailed monograph relating the story of nullification, as found in contemporaneous newspapers, manuscripts, and writings of the participants.

Calhoun, John C. *The Papers of John C. Calhoun*. Edited by Frank M. Merriwether, et al. 28 vols. Columbia: University of South Carolina Press, 1959-2003. Collection of all of Calhoun's surviving papers, which include many documents on the subject of nullification.

Capers, Gerald M. *John C. Calhoun: Opportunist*. Gainesville: University Press of Florida, 1960. Depicts Calhoun as a Machiavellian politician willing to sacrifice friends, family, and principles to become president.

Coit, Margaret L. *John C. Calhoun*. Boston: Houghton Mifflin, 1950. A Pulitzer Prize-winning biography that presents Calhoun as a statesman and a family man—a farmer at heart, but a politician in practice.

Freehling, William. *Prelude to Civil War: The Nullification Controversy in South Carolina, 1816-1836*. New York: Harper & Row, 1965. Comprehensive study of the crisis that marked Calhoun's shift from nationalism to sectionalism. Includes a good description of his reluctant participation in the event and provides a penetrating analysis of the significance of nullification.

Remini, Robert V. *Andrew Jackson*. 3 vols. Baltimore: Johns Hopkins University Press, 1998. Nearly definitive biography that treats every aspect of Jackson's presidency in some detail.

Smith, Page. *The Nation Comes of Age: A People's History of the Ante-bellum Years*. New York: McGraw-Hill, 1981. Chapter 5 emphasizes the themes of slavery and the extension of democracy.

SEE ALSO: Dec. 3, 1828: U.S. Election of 1828; Jan. 19-27, 1830: Webster and Hayne Debate Slavery and Westward Expansion; Apr. 14, 1834: Clay Begins American Whig Party; Mar. 17, 1837: Panic of 1837 Begins; Dec. 4, 1867: National Grange Is Formed.

RELATED ARTICLES in *Great Lives from History: The Nineteenth Century, 1801-1900:* Henry Clay; John C. Calhoun; Andrew Jackson; Daniel Webster.

1833
BRITISH PARLIAMENT PASSES THE FACTORY ACT

Great Britain's Factory Act prohibited the employment of young children and required some schooling for the youngest allowed to be employed. By creating a system of factory inspectors, the law ensured enforcement of its regulations.

LOCALE: London, England

CATEGORIES: Laws, acts, and legal history; business and labor; government and politics; social issues and reform

KEY FIGURES

Anthony Ashley Cooper (Lord Ashley; 1801-1885), English member of Parliament, 1826-1851, and later the seventh earl of Shaftesbury, 1851-1885

Sir John Cam Hobhouse (1786-1869), member of Parliament

Michael Thomas Sadler (1780-1835), member of Parliament who sponsored early factory legislation

Richard Oastler (1789-1861), English propagandist for factory legislation

David Ricardo (1772-1823), English economist

Adam Smith (1723-1790), Scottish economist

SUMMARY OF EVENT

Machinery was introduced into the production of goods in the late eighteenth and early nineteenth centuries in what is known as the Industrial Revolution. The rise of industrialization entailed to the widespread establishment of factories, especially in northern England and southern Scotland. To tend the machinery, large workforces were required. Many of the workers were children, some less than ten years old, working often twelve to fifteen hours per day. The gradual realization of the impact of these conditions sparked a movement for reform that led to the Factory Act of 1833.

Parliament, in 1802 and 1819, had already passed laws prohibiting the employment of young children in factories, particularly at night. These laws lacked an enforcement mechanism, however. At the same time, new economic theories propounded by Adam Smith and David Ricardo argued that free markets should determine who was employed and under what conditions, and these views gained widespread acceptance in England in the first half of the nineteenth century. Workers, it was contended, were free agents who could determine whether or not to work at the wages and under the conditions offered.

As the factories expanded, however, the need for workers grew continuously, particularly in the textile factories. Children, often employed by adult workers themselves, formed a very large part of the labor force. Most British subjects agreed that children were not free agents in the way that adult laborers were and that it was therefore appropriate to pass laws governing the employment of children. According to some estimates, as many as two-thirds of those employed in textile factories were children, earning between one-sixth and one-third the wages of adults. Many of these children were taken from orphanages in London and other large cities, the orphanage directors being glad to rid themselves of children for whom no other adult was responsible. As these circumstances became known, they inspired outrage in many circles in England, especially those affiliated with evangelical churches.

A large public campaign was sparked by the letters of Richard Oastler to many newspapers in northern England, especially the *Leeds Mercury*. Oastler pilloried the factory owners, who, he said, profited from the work of "thousands of little children . . . sacrificed at the shrine of avarice." Oastler's words led to efforts to legislate against the hiring of very small children. Sir John Cam Hobhouse, a radical member of Parliament from Westminster, introduced a bill in 1831 prohibiting the employment of children up to age eighteen in cotton textile mills for more than twelve hours per day. Hobhouse's bill did not win support, though, and the task was passed on to Michael Thomas Sadler, member of Parliament for a small borough in Yorkshire.

Sadler, himself a Tory (a conservative), won widespread support among the landowning classes, who elected many members of Parliament and who had no hesitation in reining in the industrialists establishing the new factories. Just at the moment when Sadler might have succeeded at passing factory-reform legislation, however, the electoral process was transformed by the Reform Act of 1832, and Sadler lost his seat. Leadership was passed to another Tory, Anthony Ashley Cooper (known as Lord Ashley until he succeeded to the earldom of Shaftesbury in 1851). Lord Ashley introduced legislation similar to that proposed by Hobhouse. However, the opponents of factory reform, now with stronger representation in Parliament, succeeded in sidetracking Ashley's proposal by requiring a royal commission to examine the subject. The commission, meeting between

MAJOR PROVISIONS OF THE FACTORY ACT OF 1833

1. No worker could be younger than nine years old.
2. Employers had to have a medical certificate or proof of age on file for each child worker.
3. Children between the ages of nine and thirteen could work no more than nine hours per day.
4. Children between the ages of thirteen and eighteen could work no more than twelve hours per day.
5. Children could not work at night.
6. Children were to be provided with two hours of schooling per day.
7. A total of four factory inspectors were to be appointed to enforce the law throughout the United Kingdom.

March and June of 1833, traveled the country to investigate the problem, and as they did so, many public demonstrations, staged mostly by workers, occurred. The workers hoped that a law to restrict the working hours of children would have the effect of restricting their own hours as well.

The report of the royal commission modified the proposal advanced by Hobhouse in 1831 and proposed instead to restrict the application of the law to young children. Legislation to enact the recommendations of the commission was proposed and voted into law as the Factory Act. The act completely prohibited employing children under the age of nine, and those between nine and thirteen years old were allowed to work no more than eight hours per day or forty-eight hours per week. Furthermore, the law required that such children must attend school at least two hours per day, and in effect it required any factory owners who employed children to create and maintain schools, since a system of government schools did not then exist in England. Most important, the law created a system of factory inspectors, appointed by the national government so that they would be less subject to local influences, with the right to enter any factory.

The Factory Act of 1833 was just a beginning. It was agreed to reluctantly by the Whig government that had been elected to the first reformed Parliament in 1833, but its effects were somewhat limited. Some textile factories were exempt from the application of the law, including those producing silk or lace, and the number of inspectors for the entire country was exactly four, so although they were able to carry out inspections, they could not revisit many sites. Finally, although the workers who had played a large part in the demonstrations had hoped that

the law would enact the "ten-hour day," long a worker objective, it did not do so. The Factory Act was the first step in a long campaign that did, eventually, restrict the hours of employment in factories.

Lord Ashley, sponsor of the Factory Act of 1833, sponsored a select committee of Parliament in 1840 to examine the operation of the act. The most important witness before the committee was Francis Horner, one of the first four factory inspectors appointed. Horner's testimony showed that legislation of this kind could indeed make a profound difference: He asserted that the law had virtually banned children from factories in Scotland. Ashley sponsored new legislation, passed in 1844, requiring that dangerous machinery be fenced in and that the working day of women and children older than thirteen be restricted to twelve hours. Horrific stories of women and children employed in coal mines had led to the Mines Act of 1842, which forbade the employment of women or children under the age of ten in mines.

SIGNIFICANCE

The most important feature of the Factory Act of 1833 was the inclusion of a government enforcement mechanism. The factory inspectors, appointed by the national government, grew in number over the years and were the first stage in assembling a bureaucracy monitoring the conditions of work that has since become widely accepted. Despite the continued reign of free market economic theory, practicality dictated some control over the actions of employers. Moreover, the campaign for the Factory Act of 1833 showed that public demonstrations could, in fact, bring about legislative action to solve widely perceived social problems.

—*Nancy M. Gordon*

FURTHER READING

Evans, Eric J. *The Forging of the Modern State: Early Industrial Britain, 1785-1870*. New York: Longman, 1996. Contains much useful information about the development of legislation and the bureaucracy supervising the growth of factories. A basic source.

Fay, C. R. *Round About Industrial Britain, 1830-1860*. Toronto: University of Toronto Press, 1952. Contains a number of useful details about the act.

Halevy, Elie. *History of the English People, 1830-1841:*

The Triumph of Reform. London: Ernest Benn, 1950. Although an older work, it is a classic and contains extensive details on the parliamentary maneuvering that led to the passage of the act.

Morgan, Kenneth. *The Birth of Industrial Britain: Social Change, 1750-1850.* Harlow, England: Pearson/Longman, 2004. Contains a compact summary of the efforts to control employment through legislative action.

Thomis, Malcolm I. *Responses to Industrialisation: the British Experience, 1780-1850.* Newton Abbot, England: David & Charles, 1976. Focuses on the early developments.

Tuttle, Carolyn. *Hard at Work in Factories and Mines: The Economics of Child Labor During the British Industrial Revolution.* Boulder, Colo.: Westview Press, 1999. Subjects much of the material cited by those arguing about the employment of children to careful quantitative scrutiny.

SEE ALSO: 1817: Ricardo Identifies Seven Key Economic Principles; 1824: British Parliament Repeals the Combination Acts; May 9, 1828-Apr. 13, 1829: Roman Catholic Emancipation; June 4, 1832: British Parliament Passes the Reform Act of 1832; Aug. 14, 1834: British Parliament Passes New Poor Law; Sept. 9, 1835: British Parliament Passes Municipal Corporations Act; Aug., 1867: British Parliament Passes the Reform Act of 1867; June 2, 1868: Great Britain's First Trades Union Congress Forms; Aug. 3, 1892: Hardie Becomes Parliament's First Labour Member.
RELATED ARTICLES in *Great Lives from History: The Nineteenth Century, 1801-1900:* Edwin Chadwick; Charles Grey; Robert Owen; David Ricardo.

January, 1833
GREAT BRITAIN OCCUPIES THE FALKLAND ISLANDS

Following the sack of a small Argentine settlement on the Falkland Islands by the United States, the British reasserted an old claim to the islands, establishing a permanent naval base and civilian settlement. Argentina never ceded its claim to the islands, but Great Britain afterward retained continuous control of the small archipelago.

ALSO KNOWN AS: Malvinas Islands
LOCALE: Falkland Islands, South Atlantic Ocean
CATEGORIES: Expansion and land acquisition; colonization; wars, uprisings, and civil unrest; diplomacy and international relations

KEY FIGURES
Louis Vernet (d. 1835), German-Argentinean entrepreneur
Louis-Antoine de Bougainville (1729-1811), French explorer
Robert Fitzroy (1805-1865), British naval officer and explorer
Silas Duncan (1788-1834), American naval officer
Juan Manuel de Rosas (1793-1877), dictator of Argentina, r. 1829-1852

SUMMARY OF EVENT
Lying at 51 degrees south latitude, three hundred miles east off the coast of South America, the treeless, wind-swept Falkland Islands have periodically assumed importance in the annals of history. In the 1970's, discovery of potentially very large though currently unexploitable oil reserves in the territorial waters of the Falklands sparked a conflict culminating in the Falkland Islands War between Great Britain and Argentina in 1982. Suddenly, the question of their rightful ownership became important, and the tangled history of territorial claims to the islands became worthy of scrutiny.

The Falklands supported no aboriginal inhabitants before the coming of Europeans. Esteban Gomez, sailing with Ferdinand Magellan's fleet, may have sighted the islands in 1520. British and Dutch explorers also reported them before 1600. An Englishman, John Strong, landed and conducted surveys in 1690 but did not attempt settlement. The earliest claim to the islands based on occupation is therefore that of the French.

In 1763, Louis-Antoine de Bougainville obtained backing from the French government to establish a colony on East Falkland, relocating settlers who had been expelled from Acadia at the close of the Seven Years' War. Spain objected, citing the Treaty of Utrecht (1714), and in 1767 France conceded, withdrawing its colonists and accepting monetary compensation. The Spanish occupied the abandoned French outpost, and from 1767 until about 1800 they maintained a small military presence on East Falkland. This lapsed during the Napoleonic Wars.

1830's

527

THE FALKLAND ISLANDS

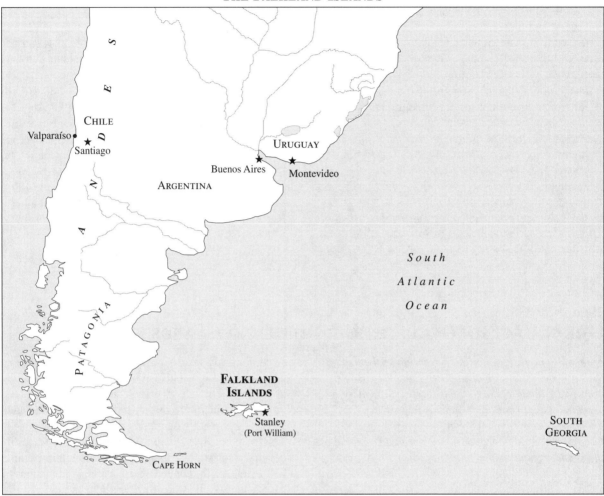

Meanwhile, unbeknown to the French, Great Britain was developing a settlement and naval station on West Falkland. Founded in 1765, Port Egmont was to serve as a provisioning station for ships rounding Cape Horn. Because uncertain relations between Spain and Britain periodically closed South American ports, having a safe harbor on the Falklands became essential to British expansion into the Pacific.

In 1770, Spain seized Port Egmont and expelled the British, citing the agreement with France. The British maintained that that agreement applied only to East Falkland. In 1771, a British naval force retook West Falkland, meeting no opposition. In 1774, faced with more urgent naval matters elsewhere, Britain withdrew from its base, albeit without relinquishing its claims.

From 1800 until 1820, the Falklands were abandoned

to feral cattle and to seal hunters of several nations. Meanwhile, the Spanish colonies proclaimed their independence. During the long process of consolidation and establishment of boundaries for the newly independent states, a naval officer in the service of Buenos Aires landed at Port Louis in 1820. He claimed the Falklands for his employers and left a garrison there. In 1826, the newly constituted Republic of Argentina granted a charter to Louis Vernet, a German-born immigrant, to found a settlement. By 1831, this settlement was a viable concern, with about one hundred civilian inhabitants cultivating the soil and exploiting wild cattle.

Conflicts arose between Vernet and sealers who wantonly slaughtered seals and cattle. To combat this behavior, the Argentine government officially appointed Vernet governor and empowered him to seize offenders.

In 1831, after repeatedly warning American sealers to stay away, he seized one of their ships and sent the crew to Buenos Aires for prosecution. America responded predictably. A gunboat under the command of Captain Silas Duncan attacked and sacked Port Soledad, formerly Port Louis. The U.S. government backed his actions, refusing to compensate Vernet.

In 1832, the British reviewed the situation in the Falkland Islands and Argentina. The infant Republic of Argentina was engaged in a civil war, as its dictator, Juan Manuel de Rosas, consolidated his power. Thus, though Argentina arguably had a legitimate territorial claim, it lacked the ability to enforce it. Moreover, given the record of aggressive American territorial expansion and the rivalry between Britain and America over whale fisheries and access to markets on the Pacific coast of South America, the British viewed the attack on Port Soledad as a possible prelude to American occupation. They therefore dispatched the warship *Clio*, which arrived in January of 1833. Finding Port Soledad apparently deserted, the British declared the Falklands to be without effective sovereignty and raised the British flag over the islands. Argentina disputed the claim, as Vernet's agent was still present, along with some of the settlers and a few troops.

When Robert Fitzroy arrived in the HMS *Beagle* in 1834, he discovered the same vacuum. Gauchos had murdered Vernet's agent, and the remaining settlers fled in terror at the approach of any ship. Fitzroy made his usual meticulous survey of the coastline and physical features of the Falklands while the ship's naturalist, Charles Darwin, cataloged the flora and fauna. Fitzroy's recommendations, which included establishing a penal colony, helped convince the Admiralty and the British government that the Falklands were worth developing on economic grounds.

An act of Parliament in 1842 established the Falklands as a Crown Colony and appointed a governor. In 1843, the seat of government was moved from Port Louis to Port William, which was renamed Stanley. The Falkland Islands Company, founded in 1851, oversaw the transition of the economy from exploitation of feral cattle to raising sheep for wool. During the latter half of the nineteenth century, the economy of the Falklands rested on three legs: wool, servicing ships rounding Cape Horn, and the whaling industry. Administratively part of the Falklands, the remote Antarctic island of South Georgia housed the factories processing whale carcasses, while Stanley served as the commercial hub of the industry. The population of the Falkland Islands rose steadily,

from perhaps 50 in 1833, to 287 in 1851, 2,043 in 1901, and a high of 2,392 in 1931. In 1980, 1,813 people lived on the four thousand square miles of territory, along with one-half million sheep.

SIGNIFICANCE

Construction of the Panama Canal reduced the importance of the Falkland Islands as a port of call, and the whaling industry became extinct. This left wool as the sole basis of the economy. By the middle of the twentieth century, the Falklands appeared to have outlived their usefulness as a territorial possession. In the 1970's, however, geologists discovered the South Atlantic oil field. Most of this field lay beneath deep water, in some of the stormiest seas on earth, precluding its immediate exploitation. It was clear, however, that major oil reserves lay within the territorial waters of the Falkland Islands.

When Leopoldo Galtieri seized control of the Argentine government in 1981, he found a country whose sovereignty was compromised by British control of its economic sector. His strategy for combating this situation included reasserting Argentina's long-dormant claim to the Falklands, first through negotiation and pleas to the United Nations. In 1982, when negotiation seemed fruitless, Galtieri mounted a full-scale military invasion of Las Islas Malvinas (the Spanish name of the islands, derived from the old French name, Les Malouines). The British elected to fight back, reinvading and retaking the islands after a brief but intense contest in which 236 British soldiers and 655 Argentineans were killed. Economic considerations played an important role in their decision to resist Galtieri. However, the British were also able to point to the interests of the English-speaking Falkland islanders, mostly of British descent, who had no desire to live under an Argentine dictatorship. The failure of the Argentine invasion was a key factor in the downfall of Galtieri and return of Argentina to civilian rule.

Had the British not seized control of the Falklands in 1832, the islands' history would undoubtedly have been different. Viewing the turbulent history of Argentina during the dictatorship of Rosas, it is hard to imagine that country developing the islands successfully or preventing other countries from exploiting them piecemeal. Occupation by the United States, or, later in the century, by Germany could have heralded more aggressive attempts to establish hegemony in southern South America. Thus, in terms of international commerce during the nineteenth century and environmental preservation in the present day, British occupation had far-reaching consequences.

—Martha A. Sherwood

1830's

FURTHER READING

Burgess, James Bland. *Letters Lately Published in the Diary on the Subject of the Present Dispute with Spain Under the Signature of Verus*. London: B. Kearsley, 1790. An earlier view of Britain's claims.

Fitzroy, Robert. *Narrative of the Surveying Voyages of His Majesty's Ships "Adventure" and "Beagle" Between the Years 1826 and 1836*. Vol. 2. London: Henry Colburn, 1839. Reprint. New York: AMS Press, 1966. Fitzroy presents the captain's view of the *Beagle*'s famous voyage of exploration, with much discussion of naval strategy.

Gibran, Daniel K. *The Falkland War: Britain Versus the Past in the South Atlantic*. Jefferson, N.C.: McFarland, 1998. Includes historical background of the 1982 Falklands war and an economic history of the islands.

Hoffman, Fritz L., and Olga Mingo Hoffman. *Sovereignty in Dispute: The Falklands/Malvinas, 1493-1982*. Boulder, Colo.: Westview Press, 1984. Defends Argentine claims; good diplomatic history for the nineteenth century.

Matthew, H. C. G., and Brian Harrison, eds. *Oxford Dictionary of National Biography: From the Earliest Times to the Year 2000*. New York: Oxford University Press, 2004. Good entry on Fitzroy.

SEE ALSO: Mar., 1813-Dec. 9, 1824: Bolívar's Military Campaigns; Jan. 18, 1817-July 28, 1821: San Martín's Military Campaigns; Sept. 7, 1822: Brazil Becomes Independent; 1828-1834: Portugal's Miguelite Wars; June 16, 1855-May 1, 1857: Walker Invades Nicaragua; May 1, 1865-June 20, 1870: Paraguayan War.

RELATED ARTICLE in *Great Lives from History: The Nineteenth Century, 1801-1900:* Charles Darwin.

July 14, 1833
OXFORD MOVEMENT BEGINS

The Oxford Movement opposed liberal and evangelical trends within the Church of England. It sought to reestablish the high moral and devotional level of the early Christian Church and insisted that the Church of England was a divine institution rather than merely an arm of the state. The Oxford Movement had a long-lasting influence on Anglican doctrine and practice, as well as on Victorian art, architecture, and literature.

ALSO KNOWN AS: Tractarian Movement
LOCALE: Oxford, England
CATEGORIES: Religion and theology; social issues and reform; literature

KEY FIGURES

John Keble (1792-1866), Anglican priest, poet, and professor of poetry at Oxford

John Henry Newman (1801-1890), Anglican vicar and later a Roman Catholic priest and cardinal

E. B. Pusey (1800-1882), Anglican priest and professor of Hebrew at Oxford

Richard Hurrell Froude (1803-1836), Anglican priest, Oxford fellow, and close friend of Newman

SUMMARY OF EVENT

The first decade and a half of the nineteenth century saw relatively little internal political strife in Great Britain:

As long as the British were threatened with invasion by France, they united behind their monarch. However, after Napoleon I was defeated in 1815, reformers again felt free to agitate for social and political change. Among their grievances was the fact that members of the Church of England (Anglican Church) enjoyed rights and privileges denied to Roman Catholics, who were in the majority in Ireland, and to Dissenting Protestants, whose numbers were increasing rapidly.

The Corporation Act of 1661 and the Test Act of 1671 excluded anyone from public office who would not take Communion in the Church of England. In 1828, a nervous Tory government repealed these acts, and the following year it moved on to full Catholic emancipation, which meant that Roman Catholics could now sit in Parliament. However, it was the passage of the Irish Church Temporalities Bill, abolishing ten Irish bishoprics, that prompted Oxford's professor of poetry, John Keble, to ascend the pulpit of the University Church, St. Mary's, on July 14, 1833, and preach a sermon on what he called England's "National Apostasy." Thus began the Oxford Movement.

Keble's fears for the Church were shared by two other young Oriel College dons, Richard Hurrell Froude and John Henry Newman, and by a number of older High Church clergy who lived in the Oxford area. However, at their first meeting, it became clear that this group could not agree on a strategy. Instead of working through a society, committees, and petitions, the younger men wanted to reach a wider audience by publishing a series of lively essays by various writers that would awaken the clergy and the laity to the dangers the Church was facing. The first of these *Tracts for the Times* was published on September 1, 1833. Over the next eight years, ninety tracts were published, twenty-four of them written by Newman. It was from these tracts that the movement took its other name, the Tractarian Movement.

The three founders of the Oxford Movement were delighted when one of Oxford's preeminent scholars, E. B. Pusey, agreed to write a tract. However, at first Pusey was far more sympathetic to the Protestant reformers than were the other Tractarians; it was not until 1837 that his theological views were clearly in harmony with those of the others. Ironically, after Newman left the Anglican Church for Roman Catholicism in 1845, it was Pusey who took his place as leader of the movement.

There were a number of principles on which the Tractarians agreed. One was that the authority of the Church of England rested not upon the state but instead upon the Apostolic Succession, passed down from Christ through his apostles to the present-day bishops. The Tractarians found their ideal in the Church as it was in the fourth and fifth centuries, before it split and before both Rome and Geneva corrupted Christian doctrine and practice. As Newman defined it, Anglicanism was the embodiment of the early Church; it was also the *via media*, or middle way, between Roman Catholicism and Calvinism.

The Tractarians believed that the early Church had had a spirituality that Christianity had since lost. In order to recapture that holiness, they suggested that the Church abandon the notion that to be a clergyman, one need only be a gentleman. Regardless of social class, the Tractarians argued, it should be a man's devotional life and his capacity for dedicating himself to his parishioners that made him worthy of ordination. Moreover, the Eucharist should once again be made the central service in the Church; in order to accomplish that goal, communi-

---

"NATIONAL APOSTASY"

John Keble's sermon "National Apostasy," excerpted below, was first delivered on July 14, 1833, at St. Mary's Church, Oxford. His condemnation of liberalism and religious tolerance constituted the founding moment of the Oxford, or Tractarian, Movement.

One of the most alarming, as a symptom, is the growing indifference, in which men indulge themselves, to other men's religious sentiments. Under the guise of charity and toleration we are come almost to this pass; that no difference, in matters of faith, is to disqualify for our approbation and confidence, whether in public or domestic life. Can we conceal it from ourselves, that every year the practice is becoming more common, of trusting men unreservedly in the most delicate and important matters, without one serious inquiry, whether they do not hold principles which make it impossible for them to be loyal to their Creator, Redeemer, and Sanctifier? Are not offices conferred, partnerships formed, intimacies courted,—nay, (what is almost too painful to think of,) do not parents commit their children to be educated, do they not encourage them to intermarry, in houses, on which Apostolical Authority would rather teach them to set a mark, as unfit to be entered by a faithful servant of Christ?

I do not now speak of public measures only or chiefly; many things of that kind may be thought, whether wisely or no, to become from time to time necessary, which are in reality as little desired by those who lend them a seeming concurrence, as they are, in themselves, undesirable. But I speak of the spirit which leads men to exult in every step of that kind; to congratulate one another on the supposed decay of what they call an exclusive system. . . .

The point really to be considered is, whether, according to the coolest estimate, the fashionable liberality of this generation be not ascribable, in a great measure, to the same temper which led the Jews voluntarily to set about degrading themselves to a level with the idolatrous Gentiles? And, if it be true anywhere, that such enactments are forced on the Legislature by public opinion, is APOSTASY too hard a word to describe the temper of that nation?

1830's

---

cants must be educated as to the real meaning of the sacrament, which to all the Tractarians was more than a memorial and to some of them was very close to the Roman doctrine of the real presence. Another change they advocated was the reestablishment of private confession.

At first, British High Church clergymen saw the Tractarians as merely a younger version of themselves. However, they changed their minds when they read a volume of Froude's writings that Newman and Keble had assembled after his death. They were shocked that an Anglican priest would consistently attack the great Protestant reformers and just as consistently justify the Roman Catholic Church. Now the High Church priests began to suspect what the Evangelicals had contended from the beginning: that the Oxford Movement sought to take the Church of England back to Rome. Already, a number of Tractarians had converted to Roman Catholicism; in 1845, they were followed by the acknowledged leader of the Oxford Movement, John Henry Newman.

Newman's conversion dealt such a blow to the Tractarians that traditionally 1845 has been given as the date the Oxford Movement ended. However, though the inner circle at Oxford mourned the loss of their friend, many of the clergymen and laity who had been influenced by Tractarian ideas were little affected by Newman's action. In fact, the removal of a leader who for some years had made more moderate Anglicans uneasy was to them a relief, because it enabled them to pursue the less radical goals of the movement.

SIGNIFICANCE

The effects of the Oxford Movement were felt within the Church of England throughout the rest of the nineteenth century and into the twentieth. The Tractarians' criticisms of the clergy led to the selection of better educated, more dedicated priests, who would not only set a moral example for their parishioners but could also explain basic theological concepts in terms the laity could understand. Once that task had been accomplished, it became possible to introduce meaningful ceremonials, including the use of candles, the wearing of Eucharistic vestments, and even the burning of incense. Even more important was the fact that within a generation or two, the Eucharist became much more widely recognized as the central service of the Church.

These church reforms were not universal. Certainly, there were many parishes where ceremonial practices would not be tolerated. However, members of the Church of England acquired the option of attending Anglo-Catholic churches and even of joining Anglican monastic communities. They retain those options to this day, lending support to the claims of the Church, and of the worldwide Anglican Communion, that it is both truly universal and truly free.

The Oxford Movement also influenced literature, art, and architecture. The works of the novelist Charlotte Mary Yonge, for example, all reflect her Tractarian views, and the views of the movement led architect Augustus Welby Northmore Pugin to insist that only the Gothic style was appropriate for a Christian church. The Arts and Crafts movement, associated with the designer William Morris, utilized medieval motifs, and medieval subjects dominated the art and the the literary works of his friends in the Pre-Raphaelite Brotherhood and even

the works of the literary giant Alfred, Lord Tennyson. Thus, largely because of the Oxford Movement's idealization of the medieval Church and, by extension, of the medieval period, the Gothic revival that had begun in the middle of the eighteenth century lasted well into the Victorian period.

—*Rosemary M. Canfield Reisman*

FURTHER READING

Chadwick, Owen. *The Spirit of the Oxford Movement: Tractarian Essays.* Cambridge, England: Cambridge University Press, 1990. Includes an important essay entitled "The Mind of the Oxford Movement."

Church, R. W. *The Oxford Movement: Twelve Years, 1833-1845.* 1891. Reprint. McLean, Va.: IndyPublish.com, 2004. An early nineteenth century Oxonian describes events as he observed them. A classic account.

Faught, C. Brad. *The Oxford Movement: A Thematic Study of the Tractarians and Their Times.* University Park: Pennsylvania State University Press, 2003. Utilizing a new approach to the subject, the author of this work shows how the movement affected English society in five important areas.

Herring, George. *What Was the Oxford Movement?* London: Continuum, 2002. A useful, brief study, including charts demonstrating the long-lasting effects of the movement.

Nockles, Peter B. *The Oxford Movement in Context: Anglican High Churchmanship, 1760-1857.* Cambridge, England: Cambridge University Press, 1996. Traces the movement back to earlier High Churchmanship.

Reed, John Shelton. *Glorious Battle: The Cultural Politics of Victorian Anglo-Catholicism.* Nashville, Tenn.: Vanderbilt University Press, 2000. A sociologist argues that what began as a counterculture movement was eventually absorbed by the Victorian establishment.

SEE ALSO: 1804: British and Foreign Bible Society Is Founded; Dec., 1816: Rise of the Cockney School; c. 1826-1827: First Meetings of the Plymouth Brethren; May 9, 1828-Apr. 13, 1829: Roman Catholic Emancipation; 1835-1836: Strauss Publishes *The Life of Jesus Critically Examined*; Oct. 9, 1845: Newman Becomes a Roman Catholic; Fall, 1848: Pre-Raphaelite Brotherhood Begins; Nov. 5, 1850: Tennyson Becomes England's Poet Laureate.

RELATED ARTICLES in *Great Lives from History: The Nineteenth Century, 1801-1900:* William Morris; Napoleon I; John Henry Newman; Augustus Welby Northmore Pugin; E. B. Pusey; Alfred, Lord Tennyson; Charlotte Mary Yonge.

August 28, 1833
SLAVERY IS ABOLISHED THROUGHOUT THE BRITISH EMPIRE

The abolition of slavery throughout the British Empire freed more than 800,000 slaves and contributed significantly to the worldwide abolition movement.

ALSO KNOWN AS: Abolition of Slavery Act; Emancipation Act

LOCALE: London, England

CATEGORIES: Human rights; laws, acts, and legal history; civil rights and liberties; social issues and reform

KEY FIGURES

Granville Sharp (1735-1813), founder of the British abolition movement

William Wilberforce (1759-1833), member of Parliament who led agitation in the House of Commons after 1787 against the slave trade and founded the Anti-Slavery Society in 1823

Thomas Fowell Buxton (1786-1845), leader in the House of Commons of the antislavery movement

Henry Brougham (1778-1868), leader in the House of Lords of the antislavery movement

George Canning (1770-1827), British foreign secretary and leader of the House of Commons, 1822-1827, and prime minister in 1827

Charles Grey (1764-1845), Whig prime minister, 1830-1834

Joseph Sturge (1793-1859), abolitionist and founder of the Agency Committee

SUMMARY OF EVENT

The abolition of slavery throughout the British Empire was the culmination of the great antislavery movement in Great Britain. The first planned British effort to eradicate slavery began as early as 1765, when Granville Sharp, a civil servant, sought to gain the freedom of Jonathan Strong, a runaway slave who had incurred a severe beating from his owner. Although Sharp's attempt failed, he remained committed to the abolition of slavery in England. The initial legislation that served as a precursor to the eventual abolition of slavery in Great Britain and the British colonies occurred in 1807. Specifically, the abolition of the British slave trade on March 25, 1807, was the first stage in the struggle that continued until the institution of slavery was finally eradicated throughout the empire.

Opponents of the British slave trade calculated that their victory would gradually lead to the end of slavery and that the condition of existing slaves would improve when slave owners could no longer replenish their supplies of unpaid labor and would have to increase their paid labor forces. It was hoped that such amelioration of the slaves' condition would eventually lead to emancipation.

By 1823, however, the hopes of the humanitarians, and others, were at a low point. Aside from moral and ethical prohibitions against slavery, there was a growing disaffection with slavery by those who asserted that the British economy was undergoing transition as steam power was gradually replacing human power. Consequently, these critics of slavery emphasized that the institution of slavery was detrimental to the British economy as there were an increasing number of industries that had a need for raw materials from foreign markets rather than slaves. Thus, slaves had lost their value as they were replaced by industrialization in England. For example, when the British slave trade was abolished in 1807, the reaction in Liverpool—which had thrived on the slave trade—was characterized by terror, because residents expected a major decline in their standard of living.

Despite the ban on the slave trade in the colonies, illicit importation continued. One reason illegal slave trading continued was the fact that penalties for violating the trading ban were only monetary fines. The slave trade was so profitable that slave traders could easily pay the fines. Even after slave trading became a felony offense, British slave traders developed new means of circumventing the law. The slave trade thus continued, and the condition of the slaves did not show marked improvements. Attempts at change had been disregarded or resisted by slave owners and colonial legislatures, especially in areas such as the West Indies where plantation agriculture was performed primarily by black slaves. In reaction to the continued existence of these problems, abolitionists decided to attack the institution of slavery itself, hoping that the emancipation of slaves in the British Empire would set a pattern for other countries.

There were, however, critics—particularly from other countries—who believed that the British were hypocritical and selective in their quest to abolish slavery. The British had derived innumerable benefits from their domination of the slave trade for many years, and they had also financed the Industrial Revolution from the unpaid labor of black slaves. Critics also maintained that the British campaign to eradicate slavery in the West Indies ignored their earlier dependence and profits derived from slave-maintained sugar and cotton plantations in these colonies. Moreover, they argued that the British continued to use these colonial goods to purchase slaves in Africa. Further, they cited another inconsistency stating that while the British were boycotting the slave-grown products of the West Indies, Britain's economy depended greatly on cotton that was produced from the labor of black slaves in the United States.

In January, 1823, the Society for the Gradual Mitigation and Abolition of Slavery Throughout the British Dominions—better known as the Anti-Slavery Society—was formed. The leadership of the society was impressive. The duke of Gloucester, a nephew of the late King George III, served as president, and the society's vice presidents included five peers and fourteen members of the House of Commons. William Wilberforce and Thomas Clarkson, who had spearheaded the drive against the slave trade, were nominally officers, but actual leadership fell to younger men, such as Henry Brougham and Thomas Foxwell Buxton, who were also members of Parliament.

The Anti-Slavery Society was to be the parent organization to numerous societies. By means of its monthly journal, the *Anti-Slavery Monthly Reporter* edited by Zachary Macaulay, important speeches and documents relating to the cause were summarized and local societies were kept informed. In addition, pamphleteering was used in the society's attempt to marshal public support and generate pressure on Parliament.

The abolition campaign in Parliament began on May 5, 1823, when Thomas Buxton moved that slavery, "repugnant alike to the British constitution and Christian principles," should be gradually abolished. He presented a two-part plan for abolition: All children born to slaves after a certain date were to be free, and reform measures were to be instituted for those who were then slaves. The first part of the plan would mean the eventual extinction of slavery; the second part would limit the authority of owners over the slaves they already held, extend personal rights not previously held by slaves, and generally improve the physical condition of slaves.

George Canning, the leader of the House of Commons, replying to Buxton's plan for the government, evaded the first part of Buxton's motion but was in agreement with the second part. He then presented resolutions that would effectively and decisively ameliorate the condition of the slaves and prepare them for freedom "at the earliest period . . . consistent with the welfare of the slaves themselves and a fair and equitable consideration of the state of property." Canning made it clear that re-

forms would be introduced in the Crown Colonies and recommended to the colonies's legislative bodies. Buxton then withdrew his own motion, and Canning's resolutions were carried.

These resolutions, providing for the amelioration and eventual abolition of slavery, formed the basis of government policy almost up to the time of the Emancipation Act of 1833. Numerous orders in council that gradually became more specific were founded upon them. The object of the orders in council was to improve the slaves' position by altering slave codes in the colonies. The use of the whip and the flogging of women were prohibited; evidence presented by slaves, under certain regulations, was allowed in law courts; facilities for manumission were to be established; and facilities for the moral and religious instruction of slaves were to be encouraged.

During the seven years following the Canning proposals, the government's policy was shown to be ineffective. There was strong opposition to the government policies in Britain's West Indies colonies on the grounds that only such resistance would save their property. It was claimed that the cultivation of sugar was impossible without slavery, as freed slaves would work only hard enough to maintain themselves at a subsistence level. Orders in council consequently encountered considerable colonial resistance and were enforced only with great reluctance. Moreover, in the period after 1826, Parliament's attention was absorbed by domestic issues, such as the removal of political restrictions on Nonconformists and Roman Catholics and the parliamentary reform movement.

By 1830, it was apparent that the gradual emancipation policy of the government would never work. Despite the fact that the Anti-Slavery Society enthusiastically approved a motion for the immediate abolition of slavery in the British colonies in May, 1830, political events in Great Britain once again pushed the question of slavery to the side. In 1831, voters expressed dissatisfaction with the more conservative policies of the duke of Wellington's ministry by returning a Whig government under the leadership of Charles Grey. The new Whig government was more in sympathy with the objectives of the antislavery movement, and Lord Brougham, leader of the Anti-Slavery Society, served as Lord Chancellor in the cabinet.

Parliamentary reform nevertheless remained the question of the hour, even under the sympathetic Whig government. One attempt was made to resurrect the policy of amelioration. A strict order in council, designed to reform slave codes in the Crown Colonies, was enacted, accompanied by the promise of lower duties on sugar to encourage the colonial legislatures to enforce the order. Even this order in council was resisted by the planters, who anticipated that the Whig government would probably initiate more severe measures against slavery in the future.

The case against slavery, meanwhile, was being argued more extensively than ever before. Agitation was sharpened in June, 1831, with the formation of the Agency Committee by younger and more zealous abolitionists such as George Stephens and Joseph Sturge. Believing that nothing effectual would be accomplished in Parliament without first increasing the "pressure from without," younger abolitionists decided to inform the public mind by means of antislavery lectures given throughout the country by agents of the committee who were independent of the parent society.

Events moved rapidly in the reformed Parliament that met in February, 1833. Disturbed by the omission of the slavery issue from King William IV's speech opening Parliament, Buxton was determined to press the issue. Parliament was bombarded with petitions containing 1.5 million signatures, antislavery delegates from every local center were summoned to a convention at Exeter Hall on April 18, 1833, and a body of more than three hundred men proceeded to Downing Street to address the prime minister. When Buxton rose in the Commons to move for immediate emancipation, the government promised to present its plan on April 23, 1833. Additional time was needed to gather further information and seek a compromise with opposing elements. On May 14, 1833, Edward Stanley, the colonial secretary, rose to explain the principles of the government's abolition proposals. Surveying the past history of the question, Stanley noted that public opinion would no longer countenance delay on the issue.

Noting that previous parliamentary pressures had had no effect on the colonial legislatures, Stanley proposed a plan that would free not only future generations of slaves but also the current generation, while it would at the same time prevent any possible dangers from immediate emancipation. The plan included two key provisions. First, all children who were born after the act, or who were under the age of six, would be free. Second, existing slaves would be placed in an intermediate stage of apprenticeship, which would last no longer than twelve years. Apprentices would be cared for by their former masters and would devote three-fourths of their labor to their former masters, the last fourth being contracted out as a free labor system with part of the proceeds used as compensation to the planters. Compensation to the slave owners was to be in the form of a fifteen-million-pound loan to the West Indian group. This sum, equal to the ten-year net profits on the cultivation of sugar, rum, and coffee, would compensate the owners for the one-fourth wages they would have to pay under the apprentice system. Debates and consultations on the proposal began with Stanley calling for the adoption of the scheme in five motions.

When the motions appeared before Parliament as a bill, several changes were introduced as the proposals passed through the House of Commons. The alterations were necessary to achieve both abolitionist support and West Indian planter acceptance. The apprentice period was reduced from twelve to six years for agricultural workers and from six to four years for nonagricultural workers. This alteration was demanded by the abolitionists who were repelled by the apprenticeship concept. To secure the acceptance of slave owners, the loan was changed to a twenty-million-pound gift as compensation for property loss. The revised bill subsequently passed the House of Commons and was sent to the House of Lords, where a few nonsubstantive changes were made. The bill received the royal assent on August 28, 1833, and thus became law.

SIGNIFICANCE

The emancipation of some 800,000 slaves in the British Empire was a remarkable triumph for the abolitionists. It was also a triumph that would give impetus to the case of slave emancipation throughout the world, particularly in the United States, where emancipation was finally achieved with the ratification of the Thirteenth Amendment in 1865.

—*Thomas D. Riethmann, updated by K. Sue Jewell*

FURTHER READING

Barclay, Alexander. *A Practical View of the Present State of Slavery in the West Indies*. Reprint. Miami, Fla.: Mnemosyne, 1969. Originally published in 1828, this work contains a detailed discussion of slave labor in the West Indies and the British slave trade to these islands during the late eighteenth and mid-nineteenth centuries.

Barclay, Oliver. *Thomas Fowell Buxton and the Liberation of Slaves*. York, England: Sessions, 2001. Biography of Buxton that emphasizes his seminal role in Great Britain's abolition movement.

Coupland, Reginald. *The British Anti-Slavery Movement*. London: Frank Cass, 1964. This book presents a classic statement of the humanitarian perspective in

1830's

the antislavery movement by an authority on empire history.

Drescher, Seymour. *The Mighty Experiment: Free Labor Versus Slavery in British Emancipation.* New York: Oxford University Press, 2002. Examination of the British debates over emancipation that argues that neither abolitionists nor proslavery advocates sincerely believed that free labor would ultimately be more economically profitable than slavery.

Mathieson, William Law. *British Slave Emancipation, 1838-1849.* New York: Octagon Books, 1967. Originally published in 1932, this complement to Mathieson's book on abolition (below) represents a further statement on the antislavery campaign and its aftermath.

_____. *British Slavery and Its Abolition, 1823-1838.* New York: Octagon Books, 1967. Originally published in 1926, this book surveys the first part of the antislavery campaign along the lines of Coupland's school of thought, which emphasizes the humanitarian aspect of the movement.

Mellor, George R. *British Imperial Trusteeship, 1783-1850.* London: Faber & Faber, 1951. This work contains a succinct treatment of the antislavery movement in its survey of British relations with dependent peoples, including Indians, Africans, the Maoris, and Australian Aborigines.

Sheridan, Richard. *Sugar and Slavery: An Economic History of the British West Indies.* Kingston, Jamaica: University of West Indies Press, 2000. Detailed history of the important role that slavery played in the sugar industry, which provided the mainstay of the economies of Britain's Caribbean colonies.

SEE ALSO: Mar. 2, 1807: Congress Bans Importation of African Slaves; 1820's-1850's: Social Reform Movement; Aug. 21, 1831: Turner Launches Slave Insurrection; Dec., 1833: American Anti-Slavery Society Is Founded; July 26, 1847: Liberia Proclaims Its Independence; Mar. 3, 1861: Emancipation of Russian Serfs; Nov., 1862: Slave Traders Begin Ravaging Easter Island; Jan. 1, 1863: Lincoln Issues the Emancipation Proclamation; Oct. 7-12, 1865: Morant Bay Rebellion; Dec. 6, 1865: Thirteenth Amendment Is Ratified; 1873-1897: Zanzibar Outlaws Slavery.

RELATED ARTICLES in *Great Lives from History: The Nineteenth Century, 1801-1900:* Sir Thomas Fowell Buxton; George Canning; Samuel Ajayi Crowther; Charles Grey.

September 3, 1833
BIRTH OF THE PENNY PRESS

The birth of the penny press in New York City launched a revolution in journalism that began the proliferation of mass-circulation newspapers that popularized new technologies and consumerism.

LOCALE: New York, New York
CATEGORIES: Journalism

KEY FIGURES
Benjamin Henry Day (1810-1889), founder and editor of the *New York Sun*
James Gordon Bennett (1795-1872), founder and editor of the *New York Herald*

SUMMARY OF EVENT
In the Western world of the early nineteenth century, literacy was a sign of privilege, denied to many by the restrictions of tradition, custom, and economics. Even in the United States, ostensibly the most egalitarian and democratic nation of the Western community, free pub-

lic education was merely a dream in many sections and communities, and only limited reading materials existed for literate citizens who could not afford to own personal libraries. Free public libraries were to a large extent unavailable, and even newspapers were generally priced beyond the means of middle- and lower-class purchasers. In fact, the wealthy believed that because they were leaders of society, the press should cater to their interests. A subscription to a newspaper was a sign of status that was associated with the fine clothing, gracious dwellings, expensive carriages, and other appurtenances of the upper class.

The newspapers that served upper-class readers naturally catered to their interests and pretensions. Mercantile and political topics took up most of the papers' space; in fact, many of the journals were devoted exclusively to one or the other of these subjects. However, in both mercantile and political areas, the United States was in the throes of change by the early 1830's. The economic world was being revolutionized through rapid technological change. Bringing about improved communication, transportation, and manufacturing technologies, the Industrial Revolution was also spawning a new laboring class that was becoming conscious of its group identity and eager for institutions and leaders that would serve and reflect its interests. In the Democratic Party of Andrew Jackson, many laborers believed that they had found a defender. However, although both the Whigs and the Democrats had newspapers that endorsed their general positions, no journals catered to the interests of the working class, whose literacy rate was steadily rising.

It was not only the workers themselves who were aware of this deficiency. The Industrial Revolution had vastly increased the scale of business and manufacturing operations. By 1830 it had precipitated a considerable shift from an individualistic, handicraft, self-sufficient economy toward one in which the individual was dependent upon specialized producers for many of the staples of life. These producers in turn were increasingly aware of their need to reach potential consumers through advertising. Newspapers offered an obvious solution. However, during the early 1830's, the average circulation of the eleven six-cent dailies published in New York was only about seventeen hundred copies each. These low circulation figures are not surprising, as each of these journals charged between six and ten dollars per year in advance for a subscription—more money than most skilled workers earned in a week. It should thus be clear that a large, untapped audience for aggressive advertisers existed. What was needed was newspapers priced for working-class readers.

Into this vacuum stepped Benjamin Henry Day, a former employee of Massachusetts's *Springfield Republican* and compositor for the *New York Evening Post*. On September 3, 1833, he launched the *New York Sun*, the harbinger of a new era of journalism. Priced at only one cent per copy, the *Sun* was the first truly successful penny newspaper in the United States. However, it was not the initial venture along these lines. The *Illustrated Penny Magazine*, published in London, had sold in large quantities in America since 1830, and several efforts to found penny papers in Philadelphia, New York, and Boston had failed earlier. Benjamin Day's *Sun* appropriated the techniques utilized by these earlier journals. It was smaller, both in length and in actual page size, than most older newspapers; it cost only one cent per copy; and readers could get it without having to buy subscriptions. The *Sun* was sold on the sidewalks of New York by newsboys, despite the indignation of citizens and rivals who charged

James Gordon Bennett. (Library of Congress)

that the lads were being led into lives of vice and degradation.

The *Sun*'s innovations were not, however, simply in the areas of merchandising, size, or even price. Day brought a new style to journalism. His newspaper was breezy, even flippant, and it ignored politics and purely mercantile concerns in order to concentrate on local color, human-interest stories, and sensationalism. Finally, it carried a large volume of advertising, particularly of the "help wanted" variety. Indeed, the rise of advertising coincided with the rise of wide-circulation newspapers. The formula proved most effective. By 1836, the *Sun* had a circulation of some thirty thousand copies a day, making it by far the largest-selling newspaper in the United States.

The sensationalism in the *Sun* provoked criticism, but it sold newspapers and inspired many imitators. Undoubtedly the most significant of these was the project of James Gordon Bennett, who launched the *New York Her-*

ald on May 6, 1835. Some scholars regard the *Herald* as the first truly modern newspaper. Like the *Sun*, Bennett's *Herald* sold for a penny and attracted a mass audience through a heady combination of sensationalism, trivia, local gossip and news, advertisements, and even vulgarity. The *Herald* was, however, more broadly based. As it gained circulation, it also began to publish political essays, foreign commentaries and news, and commercial and financial information. Thus, in a sense, Bennett united the coverage and approach of the penny press with the specialized functions of the older "class," party, and mercantile newspapers.

By the 1840's, the *Herald* was the most aggressive and comprehensive of American journals. On the eve of the Civil War (1861-1865), it had a daily circulation of some sixty thousand, outstripping even the *Sun* and leading its other American competitors as well. Furthermore, while it was fashionable to regard Bennett as the *enfant terrible* of American journalism, his influence on other newspapers was profound, since they either aped the *Herald* or consciously reacted against it stylistically.

SIGNIFICANCE

The *Sun*, the *Herald*, and their many imitators wrought profound changes in American journalism and in the lives of countless American citizens as well. They took the newspaper out of the hands of the privileged few and brought the news and entertainment to an entire social and economic class which the older six-cent daily newspapers had scarcely touched. This was in itself a democratic force, as common workers were now able to receive information at first hand, instead of getting news after it filtered down through the mercantile and educated classes.

Politicians and parties could no longer limit themselves to expressions through the "party press." Thus, the penny papers made them more responsive to their lower- and middle-class constituents. Furthermore, they broadened the concept of news through a greater emphasis on sensational items, such as sex and crime, increased local coverage, and the inclusion of feature and human-interest stories. Finally, as they achieved size and power, the penny newspapers fought viciously for circulation, and in the course of their intense competition greatly speeded up the gathering and publication of news items. In their efforts to scoop competitors, the new newspapers used and glamorized steamboats, railroads, the telegraph, and other devices that so significantly altered American development. The penny press gave the United States its first genuinely popular journalism and

illuminated the path to the future in many areas of American life.

—*John H. DeBerry*

FURTHER READING

Bergmann, Hans. *God in the Street: New York Writing from the Penny Press to Melville*. Philadelphia: Temple University Press, 1995. A history of American writing and intellectual life during the early nineteenth century.

Carlson, Oliver. *The Man Who Made the News: James Gordon Bennett*. New York: Duell, Sloan and Pearce, 1942. A detailed account of the journalistic story of the *New York Herald*, as well as of Bennett's life.

Crouthamel, James L. *Bennett's "New York Herald" and the Rise of the Popular Press*. Syracuse, N.Y.: Syracuse University Press, 1989. Study of the journalistic methods that Bennett used to make the *New York Herald* the largest and most prosperous newspaper in the United States.

Emery, Edwin. *The Press and America: An Interpretive History of Journalism*. 2d ed. Englewood Cliffs, N.J.: Prentice-Hall, 1962. Contains three well-written chapters on the background and development of the penny press and popular journalism.

Lee, James Melvin. *History of American Journalism*. Rev. ed. New York: Houghton Mifflin, 1923. Although old, this volume contains some interesting information in a chapter titled "Beginnings of the Penny Press."

Mott, Frank L. *American Journalism: A History, 1690-1960*. 3d ed. New York: Macmillan, 1962. This standard history of American journalism contains an excellent chapter on the penny press of the 1830's.

Nevins, Allan. *The Evening Post: A Century of Journalism*. 1922. Reprint. New York: Russell & Russell, 1968. This history of one of the new penny newspapers' older six-cent rivals has an excellent section on the *Sun*, the *Herald*, and the influence of Bennett.

O'Brien, Frank M. *The Story of the "Sun," New York, 1833-1928*. 1928. Reprint. New York: Greenwood Press, 1968. A rare account of the *Sun*'s establishment, full of anecdotes and trivia, if short on analysis of the paper's importance.

Payne, George Henry. *History of Journalism in the United States*. New York: D. Appleton, 1920. An old text, but its chapters titled "Penny Papers and the *New York Sun*" and "James Gordon Bennett and the *Herald*" are still valuable.

Trimble, Vance H. *The Astonishing Mr. Scripps: The*

Turbulent Life of America's Penny Press Lord. Ames: Iowa State University Press, 1992. A biography of Edward Wyllis Scripps (1854-1926), of the famous Scripps publishing family, which founded numerous newspapers and newspaper leagues.

Turner, Hy B. *When Giants Ruled: The Story of Park Row, New York's Great Newspaper Street.* New York: Fordham University Press, 1999. History of journalism in New York City that concentrates on the century during which the *Herald* and other newspapers were located on Park Row.

SEE ALSO: Jan. 1, 1831: Garrison Begins Publishing *The Liberator*; Dec. 3, 1847: Douglass Launches *The North Star*; Sept. 18, 1851: Modern *New York Times* Is Founded; 1880's-1890's: Rise of Yellow Journalism; 1895-1898: Hearst-Pulitzer Circulation War.

RELATED ARTICLES in *Great Lives from History: The Nineteenth Century, 1801-1900:* James Gordon Bennett; Joseph Pulitzer; Edward Wyllis Scripps; John Walter II.

September 29, 1833-1849
CARLIST WARS UNSETTLE SPAIN

Sparked by questions over the legality of Spain's law of succession, the Carlist Wars metamorphosed into a clash over the country's political and social future. The wars pitted guerrilla forces of the monarchist, Roman Catholic, and traditionalist conservatives backing the would-be king against the army, which was loyal to the socially progressive liberals favoring the queen. Also, the wars forever altered public perceptions of the traditional powers of Spain, the monarchy and the Catholic Church.

ALSO KNOWN AS: Seven Years' War (First Carlist War); Spanish Civil War

LOCALE: Spain

CATEGORIES: Wars, uprisings, and civil unrest; government and politics

KEY FIGURES

Ferdinand VII (1784-1833), king of Spain, r. 1813-1833

Don Carlos (1788-1855), brother of Ferdinand VII and pretender to the throne as Charles V

María Cristina (1806-1878), princess of Bourbon-Two Sicilies, queen consort of Spain, 1829-1833, and queen regent of Spain, r. 1833 to 1840

Isabella II (1830-1904), queen of Spain, r. 1833-1868, and daughter of Ferdinand and María Cristina

Baldomero Espartero (1793-1879), commander in chief of the army, victor in the First Carlist War, and regent of Spain, r. 1841-1843

SUMMARY OF EVENT

Immediately upon King Ferdinand VII's death on September 29, 1833, his brother Don Carlos, the self-proclaimed Charles V, challenged both the right of three-year-old Isabella II to the Spanish throne and the regency of her mother, María Cristina. While Charles disputed the legality of Ferdinand's change (with the Pragmatic Sanction of 1789) of the ancient Salic succession law to favor his daughter, other Carlists (supporters of Carlos's claim to the throne) impugned the character of Ferdinand's widow, claiming that Ferdinand had bequeathed the crown to his brother but that she had suppressed that fact and even forged her dead husband's name to a decree recognizing Isabella as heir.

María Cristina had secretly remarried a commoner, a former sergeant of the royal guard, shortly after Ferdinand's death, and her new husband was given the title of duke. Because they had several children together, the news of their marriage eventually leaked and made her very unpopular with most of the public, no matter their political propensities.

Carlist support and associated guerrilla warfare had begun by 1834 in the mostly rural, and politically and religiously traditional, northeast of Spain, and it swelled to civil war proportions over much more than succession. Regional jealousies and competitiveness and Roman Catholic regard for traditional hierarchies fanned the flames. Within months, the Carlist volunteers organized into a small field army, albeit without the same general public support and resources of the government forces. The Quadruple Alliance of Great Britain, France, and Portugal with the Spanish government, concluded on April 22, 1834, affirmed Isabella's legitimacy and rejected Charles's claim, leading to the stationing of British and French troops in Spanish territory to help contain the Carlists in the north. The Carlists were so much more

Procession at the wedding of Isabella, whose 1846 marriage triggered the Second Carlist War. (Francis R. Niglutsch)

defense-oriented than offense-oriented that they were unable to make more than regional inroads by 1837. That year, however, the government forces were nearly paralyzed by mutiny and the Carlists came close to seizing Madrid, the capital.

Crucially, the government forces had sided with María Cristina and Isabella. While most of the army and its officers refrained from intervening in politics, some had become involved in either moderate or progressive liberalism. This led to a pattern of military intervention and leadership in politics—sometimes outright, sometimes subtle—by army liberals in favor of more representative policies and by those who felt it was their patriotic duty to side with the liberal cause with which the established national government was becoming identified. Many officers, who were mostly middle class, poorly paid, and frustrated with governmental disorganization, favored the modernization and new opportunities promised by liberals. Military leaders filled the institutional vacuum between Ferdinand's absolutism and the poor organization and weakness of the liberals.

The two main rival political factions, the moderates and progressives, could agree on nothing, and so a seesaw of opposing governments, rewritten constitutions, changing suffrage requirements, and power struggles ensued over the next several years, punctuated by attempts at land and social reform.

In the meantime, Charles made mistakes and had much bad luck. He was not good at military command; some of his best officers were killed. As the traditionalists were worn down by attrition and government forces closed in, a split developed among his supporters, the fanatical apostolic elements and the more practical regional traditionalists. A professional general commanding the main Carlist force accepted the Convention of Vergara in August, 1839, which promised no reprisals, to incorporate Carlist officers in the regular army and to respect Basque privileges. The last fighting ended when Carlist forces in the east were ousted in 1840. Charles's claim was later revived, unsuccessfully, by his heirs in 1860, 1869, and 1872.

General Baldomero Espartero, who commanded the government forces in the north during the final campaign in 1839, dominated the Spanish army in the First Carlist

War. He, too, became embroiled in the progressive/moderate seesaw. At this point, the queen regent tried to gain his support by promising to name him prime minister. Civil unrest forced the appointment of Espartero as prime minister and ultimately drove María Cristina to abdicate the regency in 1840. Widespread knowledge of the queen regent's remarriage and doubts about the sincerity of her support for her liberal ministers and their policies eventually caused even the army to call for her resignation.

The seesaw continued. Although María Cristina had gone into permanent exile in France, she fomented insurrections against Espartero in 1841, 1842 and 1843; Espartero was the dictatorial head of government during that time. Public sentiment turned against Espartero as did the majority in the Cortes, Spain's parliament. His regime was toppled in 1843 because of his reprisals against the provinces that had most strongly supported the Carlists, reneging on the promise to respect regional privileges, and dissolving the Cortes, acts that were opposed within many of Spain's garrisons. General Ramón María Narváez led opposing troops from Valencia and seized Madrid, and Espartero fled to England. Isabella, though just thirteen years old, was declared of age and made the head of the Spanish government.

Carlism had not died after its military defeat, however. Although the dynastic issue remained the central Carlist claim, what really kept the movement alive was the strength of religious traditionalism and the insistence on regional identity and privileges. Interference by Great Britain and France and the marriage of Isabella in 1846 triggered the Second Carlist War (1846-1849). Because it was poorly organized and lacking coordination, it was even less of a challenge to Madrid than was the first war. Again the centers of action lay in the north, in Catalonia, Navarre, and the Basque Country.

General Narváez was appointed chief minister in 1847 in order to cope with the Carlists, which he did. The so-called Second Carlist War was no more than a rising of rural Catalonia, not yet integrated into the liberal social and economic system. The liberal regime in Madrid tended to usurp local privileges without offering the advantages of a modern central government.

When revolution forced Isabella II from her throne in 1868, she joined her mother in exile. In 1870, she renounced the throne in favor of her son, Alfonso XII. His supporters made it clear that neither his mother nor his grandmother could play an active role in the effort to restore the monarchy. When Alfonso XII regained the Spanish crown in 1874, María Cristina and Isabella II were permitted to return to Spain as visitors but were denied permission to live there permanently or exercise influence in the Spanish government.

SIGNIFICANCE

The traditional powers of Spain, the monarchy and the Roman Catholic Church, were never the same after the Carlist Wars. Both fomented their own opposition. As overreaching, overweening institutions, they inspired their liberal foes. The monarchy, ever fickle and self-serving, irrevocably revealed its ugly faults to its subjects, undercutting the traditional respect for its divine right to rule. The Church's sacred and secular influence was deeply undercut by its dogged, and often violent, refusal to modernize and to share power and resources. Also, the clergy was seriously affected in terms of numbers and commitment. The Vatican's argument with the Spanish crown over the naming of bishops resulted in more and more Spanish sees remaining vacant, and many monks and priests of uncertain vocation left the Church. It has been estimated that during the first decades of liberalism approximately one-third renounced their vows altogether.

The liberals, too, revealed their petty power rivalries and their disregard for the people. Moderates and progressives, all liberals, agreed on nothing and put the government and the people through enormous hardships and confusion as they fought, literally and figuratively, over dominance, constitutions, suffrage, resources, and influence. They managed to undermine their own ideals because their excesses contributed to the longevity as well as revival of traditionalism, which seemed to be losing much of its support.

Certainly the Carlist Wars of the nineteenth century planted the seeds of the even more significant Spanish Civil War of 1936-1939, which continued to pit the traditionalists and the progressives against each other, this time under different guises: Falangista/fascist (nationalist and traditionalist) and republican (leftist and progressive).

—Debra D. Andrist

FURTHER READING

Barahona, Renato. *Vizcaya on the Eve of Carlism: Politics and Society, 1800-1833.* Reno: University of Nevada Press, 1989. A study of the political and social conditions in Vizcaya, a Basque province of Spain, and how these conditions led to Basque support for the Carlist movement.

Barton, Simon. *A History of Spain.* New York: Palgrave

Macmillan, 2004. A comprehensive overview of Spanish history, from ancient times to the twenty-first century. Includes discussion of the Carlist Wars. Maps, chronology, glossary, selected bibliography, and index.

Carr, Raymond, ed. *Spain: A History.* New York: Oxford University Press, 2000. Carr has gathered a selection of essays that provide an excellent overview of the political climate in Spain before, during, and after Isabella's thirty-five year reign.

Flynn, M. K. *Ideology, Mobilization, and the Nation: The Rise of Irish, Basque, and Carlist Nationalist Movements in the Nineteenth and Early Twentieth Centuries.* New York: St. Martin's Press, 2000. Flynn recounts the general evolution of nationalism in west-ern Europe by the nineteenth century, then describes the rise of nationalism among the Carlists and Basques in Spain as examples of this movement.

Holt, Edgar. *The Carlist Wars in Spain.* London: G. P. Putnam's Sons, 1967. This evenhanded analysis of the three Carlist Wars has an epilogue covering events up to 1965 and includes illustrations, a map, and a bibliography.

SEE ALSO: May 2, 1808: Dos de Mayo Insurrection in Spain; Sept. 30, 1868: Spanish Revolution of 1868; 1876: Spanish Constitution of 1876.

RELATED ARTICLES in *Great Lives from History: The Nineteenth Century, 1801-1900:* Don Carlos; Isabella II.

December, 1833
AMERICAN ANTI-SLAVERY SOCIETY IS FOUNDED

The foundation of the American Anti-Slavery Society reflected a new and more militant trend in the abolitionist movement, away from nonviolent gradualism and toward radical immediatism.

LOCALE: Philadelphia, Pennsylvania
CATEGORIES: Human rights; civil rights and liberties; organizations and institutions

KEY FIGURES

Elizur Wright (1804-1885), one of the founders of the American Anti-Slavery Society

Arthur Tappan (1786-1865), first president of the American Anti-Slavery Society

Lewis Tappan (1788-1873), leader of church-oriented abolitionists

William Lloyd Garrison (1805-1879), abolitionist leader and editor of *The Liberator*

Frederick Douglass (1817?-1895), former slave and the editor of *The North Star*, an abolitionist paper

Sojourner Truth (c. 1797-1883), former slave, abolitionist, and a compelling orator

Harriet Tubman (c. 1820-1913), fugitive slave and leading black abolitionist

James Gillespie Birney (1792-1857), American antislavery leader and presidential candidate for the Liberty Party

Theodore Dwight Weld (1803-1895), American Anti-Slavery Society agent

SUMMARY OF EVENT

The tumult of reform and revivalism that swept over the northern and western areas of the United States during the 1830's and 1840's produced a number of voluntary associations and auxiliaries. Perhaps the most important of these was the American Anti-Slavery Society (AASS), which was founded by Elizur Wright and others in December, 1833. Sixty delegates gathered in Philadelphia to form the national organization, electing Arthur Tappan, a wealthy New York businessman, as president. They also approved a Declaration of Sentiments, drawn up by William Lloyd Garrison, Samuel May, and John Greenleaf Whittier, that called for immediate, total, and uncompensated abolition of slavery through moral and political action. In signing the declaration, the delegates pledged themselves to

> do all that in us lies, consisting with this declaration of our principles, to overthrow the most execrable system of slavery that has ever been witnessed upon earth . . . and to secure to the colored population of the United States, all the rights and privileges which belong to them as men and Americans.

Like other reform societies of the day, the AASS organized a system of state and local auxiliaries, sent out agents to convert people to its views, and published pamphlets and journals supporting its position. The society grew rapidly. By 1838, it claimed 250,000 members and 1,350 auxiliaries.

Before the 1830's, most opponents of slavery advocated moderate methods such as gradual and "compensated" emancipation—which would have granted remunerations to former slave owners. Some abolitionists favored resettlement of free African Americans to Liberia in West Africa by the American Colonization Society, which had been founded in 1817. The formation of a national organization based on the principle of immediatism, or immediate and total emancipation, symbolized the new phase that antislavery agitation entered during the early 1830's—radical, uncompromising, and intensely moralistic.

The shift to immediatism had several causes, including the failure of moderate methods; the example of the British, who abolished slavery in their empire in 1833; and, probably most important, evangelical religion. Abolitionists of the 1830's inherited from earlier antislavery reformers the notion that slavery was a sin. This notion, coupled with the contemporaneous evangelical doctrine of immediate repentance, shaped the abolitionist doctrine of immediate emancipation.

Given the influence of evangelical doctrines and methods, it is not surprising that abolitionists emphasized moral suasion over political methods. The demand for immediate emancipation was a purely moral demand: Abolitionists were calling for immediate repentance of the sin of slavery, an action that they believed would necessarily lead to emancipation itself. They hoped to persuade people to emancipate the slaves voluntarily and to form a conviction of guilt as participants in the national sin of slavery. In effect, abolitionists were working for nothing less than a total moral reformation.

The AASS represented the union of two centers of radical abolitionism, one in Boston, the other based around Cincinnati. William Lloyd Garrison, the key figure among New England abolitionists, began publishing *The Liberator* in 1831 and soon organized the New England Anti-Slavery Society, based on the principle of immediate abolition. Garrisonian abolitionists galvanized antislavery sentiment in the Northeast, where they were later aided by the New York Anti-Slavery Society, which was founded by William Jay, William Goodell, and brothers Lewis and Arthur Tappan in 1834. Meanwhile, the West also was shifting from gradualism and colonization to radical abolitionism. In the West, Western Reserve College and Lane Seminary were seedbeds for the doctrine of immediate emancipation. Theodore Dwight

Sojourner Truth. (Library of Congress)

Weld, a young man who had been converted to evangelical Christianity by Charles Grandison Finney, organized a group of antislavery agents known as the Seventy, who preached the gospel of immediatism throughout the Midwest.

Although leadership in the antislavery movement remained predominantly white, free African Americans were a significant vital force in the movement as well. Prior to 1800, the Free African Society of Philadelphia and black spokespersons such as astronomer Benjamin Banneker and church leader Richard Allen had denounced slavery in the harshest terms. By 1830, fifty black-organized antislavery societies existed, and African Americans contributed to the formation of the AASS in 1833.

Black orators, especially escaped slaves such as Frederick Douglass and Sojourner Truth, moved large audiences with their impassioned and electrifying oratory. African Americans also helped run the Underground Railroad, through which Harriet Tubman alone led more than three hundred slaves to freedom. Generally, African American abolitionists shared the nonviolent philosophy of the Garrisonians, but black anger often flared because

DECLARATION OF THE NATIONAL ANTI-SLAVERY CONVENTION

In addition to a manifesto, the American Anti-Slavery Society, founded by abolitionists in December, 1833, in Philadelphia, articulated its political position with its Declaration of Sentiments, excerpted here.

We have met together for the achievement of an enterprise, without which, that of our fathers is incomplete, and which, for its magnitude, solemnity, and probable results upon the destiny of the world, as far transcends theirs, as moral truth does physical force.

In purity of motive, in earnestness of zeal, in decision of purpose, in intrepidity of action, in steadfastness of faith, in sincerity of spirit, we would not be inferior to them. . . .

Their grievances, great as they were, were trifling in comparison with the wrongs and sufferings of those for whom we plead. Our [founding] fathers were never slaves—never bought and sold like cattle—never shut out from the light of knowledge and religion—never subjected to the lash of brutal taskmasters.

But those, for whose emancipation we are striving,—constituting at the present time at least one-sixth part of our countrymen,—are recognized by the laws, and treated by their fellow beings, as marketable commodities—as goods and chattels—as brute beasts;—are plundered daily of the fruits of their toil without redress;—really enjoy no constitutional nor legal protection from licentious and murderous outrages upon their persons;—are ruthlessly torn asunder—the tender babe from the arms of its frantic mother—the heart-broken wife from her weeping husband—at the caprice or pleasure of irresponsible tyrants;—and, for the crime of having a dark complexion, suffer the pangs of hunger, the infliction of stripes, and the ignomy of brutal servitude. They are kept in heathenish darkness by laws expressly enacted to make their instruction a criminal offence.

These are the prominent circumstances in the condition of more than two millions of our people, the proof of which may be found in thousands of indisputable facts, and in the laws of the slaveholding States.

Hence we maintain—

That, in view of the civil and religious privileges of this nation, the guilt of its oppression is unequalled by any other on the face of the earth;—and, therefore,

That it is bound to repent instantly, to undo the heavy burden, to break every yoke, and to let the oppressed go free. . . .

Source: William Lloyd Garrison, "Declaration of Sentiments" (December 14, 1833).

SIGNIFICANCE

The late 1830's marked the high point of the movement for immediate abolition through moral suasion. Abolitionism, like other crusades of the time, was hard hit by the Panic of 1837, which reduced funds and distracted attention away from reform. At the same time, abolitionists faced an internal challenge as the AASS divided into radicals and moderates. One issue causing the split was women's rights. Moderate abolitionists tolerated and even welcomed women in the society, so long as their activities were confined to forming auxiliary societies, raising money, and circulating petitions. They refused, however, the request that women be allowed to speak in public on behalf of abolitionism or to help shape the AASS's policies. They also wanted to prevent abolitionism from being distracted or diluted by involvement with any other secondary reform. At the Anti-Slavery Convention of 1840, Garrison and a group of radical followers used the issue of women's rights to capture the organization for themselves. When they succeeded in appointing a woman to the society's business committee, moderates and conservatives seceded and formed another organization, the American and Foreign Anti-Slavery Society.

Another issue that divided abolitionist ranks was that of political action. Some abolitionists, convinced that political action, not merely moral suasion, was necessary to effect emancipation, formed the Liberty Party in 1840 and nominated James Gillespie Birney for president of the United States. During the 1840's and 1850's, a small group of abolitionists, some of them militant "come-outers" such as Garrison and Wendell Phillips, continued to rely on moral suasion. The majority of abolitionists, however, moved gradually into the political arena, where they became involved in the Free-Soil movement and other aspects of the sectional conflict leading to the Civil War (1861-1865).

—*Anne C. Loveland, updated by Sudipta Das*

of the racism they found within the antislavery ranks. Influenced by tactical and race considerations, white abolitionist leaders such as Garrison and Weld limited their African American counterparts to peripheral roles or excluded them from local organizations. Discriminatory policies within the AASS glaringly contradicted the organization's egalitarian rhetoric.

FURTHER READING

Abbott, Richard H. *Cotton and Capital: Boston Businessmen and Antislavery Reform, 1854-1868*. Amherst: University of Massachusetts Press, 1991. Examines the activities and ideology of a group of Bostonian businessmen who fostered abolition. Meticulously researched and annotated.

Chesebrough, David B. *Frederick Douglass: Oratory from Slavery*. Westport, Conn.: Greenwood Press, 1998. Biographical study that emphasizes Douglass's oratory skills and techniques, which were central to Douglass's effectiveness as an abolitionist leader.

Clinton, Catherine. *Harriet Tubman: The Road to Freedom*. New York: Little, Brown, 2004. Meticulously detailed biography that places Tubman's life within the context of the abolitionist movement and the nineteenth century American South.

Filler, Louis. *The Crusade Against Slavery, 1830-1860*. New York: Harper & Row, 1960. Comprehensive treatment of the people and groups who made up the antislavery movement and the relation of the movement to other reform activities of the period. Excellent bibliography.

Friedman, Lawrence J. *Gregarious Saints: Self and Community in American Abolitionism, 1830-1870*. New York: Cambridge University Press, 1982. Fresh and challenging analysis of the antislavery movement, written from a psychological perspective and focusing on the movement's first-generation immediatists.

Kraut, Alan M., ed. *Crusaders and Compromisers. Essays on the Relationship of the Antislavery Struggle to the Antebellum Party System*. Westport, Conn.: Greenwood Press, 1983. These essays broke new ground by concentrating on politics, juxtaposing the antislavery crusaders to the national political struggles before the Civil War. An excellent anthology.

Larson, Kate Clifford. *Bound for the Promised Land: Harriet Tubman, Portrait of an American Hero*. New York: Ballantine, 2004. Comprehensive account of the life of the heroic conductor of the Underground Railroad. Based in part on new sources, including court records, contemporary newspapers, wills, and letters.

McKivigan, John R. *The War Against Proslavery Religion: Abolitionism and the Northern Churches, 1830-1865*. Ithaca, N.Y.: Cornell University Press, 1984. Corrects a number of old interpretations and offers new insights into the impact of antislavery crusaders on northern churches and major Northeast denominations. Based on primary sources; reflects more recent scholarship.

Perry, Lewis, and Michael Fellman, eds. *Antislavery Reconsidered: New Perspectives on the Abolitionists*. Baton Rouge: Louisiana State University Press, 1979. Fourteen original, thought-provoking essays based on a variety of interpretive and methodological approaches. Attempts to see abolition in the context of the larger society of which it was a part.

Rogers, William B. *"We Are All Together Now": Frederick Douglass, William Lloyd Garrison, and the Prophetic Tradition*. New York: Garland, 1995. Describes how Douglass and Garrison drew on the tradition of biblical prophecy in their struggle against slavery, intemperance, and the oppression of women and minorities.

Thomas, John L. *The Liberator: William Lloyd Garrison*. Boston: Little, Brown, 1963. In tracing Garrison's career, the author surveys not only the antislavery movement but also the many other reforms in which the well-known editor was engaged.

SEE ALSO: Mar. 2, 1807: Congress Bans Importation of African Slaves; Apr. 9, 1816: African Methodist Episcopal Church Is Founded; 1820's-1850's: Social Reform Movement; c. 1830-1865: Southerners Advance Proslavery Arguments; Jan. 1, 1831: Garrison Begins Publishing *The Liberator*; Aug. 21, 1831: Turner Launches Slave Insurrection; Dec. 3, 1833: Oberlin College Opens; July 2, 1839: *Amistad* Slave Revolt; Dec. 3, 1847: Douglass Launches *The North Star*; c. 1850-1860: Underground Railroad Flourishes; 1852: Stowe Publishes *Uncle Tom's Cabin*; July 6, 1853: National Council of Colored People Is Founded; July, 1859: Last Slave Ship Docks at Mobile; Dec. 6, 1865: Thirteenth Amendment Is Ratified.

RELATED ARTICLES in *Great Lives from History: The Nineteenth Century, 1801-1900:* Frederick Douglass; William Lloyd Garrison; Sojourner Truth; Harriet Tubman.

1830's

December 3, 1833
OBERLIN COLLEGE OPENS

Oberlin College was the first coeducational institution of higher education in the United States—graduating the first woman in the United States to be ordained to the Christian ministry—and was a center of theological training for students of all races.

ALSO KNOWN AS: Oberlin Collegiate Institute
LOCALE: Lorain County, Ohio
CATEGORIES: Education; organizations and
   institutions; women's issues

KEY FIGURES

James Bradley (fl. early nineteenth century), first
   African American enrolled in the Oberlin system
Antoinette Brown Blackwell (1825-1921), pioneer
   theology graduate of Oberlin
Charles Grandison Finney (1792-1875), U.S.
   revivalist, teacher, and later president of the college
John J. Shipherd (1802-1844) and
Philo Penfield Stewart (1798-1868), cofounders of the
   community of Oberlin, Ohio, and the Oberlin
   Collegiate Institute
Theodore Dwight Weld (1803-1895), member of
   Finney's "holy band" of evangelists
Charles Stuart (1783-1865), close friend of Weld and
   largely responsible for Weld's antislavery
   enthusiasm
Arthur Tappan (1786-1865) and
Lewis Tappan (1788-1873), wealthy New York City
   merchants and philanthropists

SUMMARY OF EVENT

In 1825, the celebrated Presbyterian revivalist Charles Grandison Finney appeared in Utica, New York, where he recruited twenty-two-year-old Theodore Weld into his "holy band" of evangelists. Weld, who enrolled in the Oneida Institute in Whitesboro, New York, to prepare for the ministry, also became an exponent of emancipation. Weld's devotion to the antislavery movement was inspired by his close friend, Charles Stuart, a Utica schoolteacher and member of Finney's holy band, who was an avid opponent of slavery.

In 1830, Weld met Arthur and Lewis Tappan, New York City merchants and philanthropists who were financing Finney's revival movement. Weld sought to persuade them to establish a theological seminary for preparing Finney's converts for the ministry. In 1831, Arthur Tappan agreed to Weld's suggestion and asked

him to find a suitable site for the proposed seminary. Weld selected the already established Cincinnati's Lane Theological Seminary, which Tappan pledged to endow. He also helped appoint well-respected scholars to its faculty. Most of the students who enrolled in the school were Finney's converts. The Lane Seminary instantly became a center of debate on the slavery question, as Weld's students demanded immediate emancipation.

Weld's tenure at Lane Seminary proved to be of short duration. Cincinnati was so close to the slave area and so dependent on southern trade that the trustees of the seminary ordered all discussion of the explosive slavery issue to cease immediately. Faced with that administrative injunction, Weld and most of his students who opposed slavery withdrew from the school, establishing their own seminary in Cumminsville, Ohio.

The Reverend John J. Shipherd, a Presbyterian minister, and Philo Penfield Stewart, who had been a missionary to the Choctaw Indians, had founded the community of Oberlin in Lorain County, Ohio. In 1832, Shipherd and Stewart conceived a plan to establish the community that they hoped would also serve as the site for a theological school. Shipherd wanted such an institution because, as he observed in 1832, "The growing millions of the Mississippi Valley are perishing through want of well-qualified minister and teachers."

On December 3, 1833, the Oberlin Collegiate Institute—named in honor of Jean F. Oberlin, an Alsatian clergyman, educator, and philanthropist—opened its doors. The school was founded on Oberlin's "manual labor plan," which had gained popularity at American seminaries during the late 1820's. Strict adherence to a program of manual labor was believed to be a panacea for both the physical and moral ills that threatened students while attending school. Original plans for Oberlin contemplated only a college preparatory program. After consulting with his colleagues, however, Shipherd decided that the college should offer a collegiate curriculum, including a department of theology. He then invited Weld and the "Lane rebels" to join Oberlin.

Moved by the prospect of having, in a single institution, a school for the Lane rebels, a place to educate African Americans, and a platform from which to promote abolition, Tappan financially supported Oberlin, as he had Lane Seminary, saving the school from financial collapse. Weld's students were placed under the tutelage of Charles Grandison Finney, who, in 1835, was invited by the trustees of Oberlin to establish the department of theology at the school. The prospects of bringing both the slavery issue and African American students to the school aroused a storm of opposition in the community, leading to six unsuccessful attempts in the Ohio state legislature to revoke the college's charter. In 1835, Oberlin's trustees, under the threat of losing the Tappans' financial support, approved admission of students "without respect to color" by a margin of one vote. In 1836, James Bradley, an African American, was admitted to the Sheffield Manual Labor Institute, a branch preparatory school established by Oberlin.

From Oberlin's opening in 1835, the trustees approved the admission of women, although initially restricting them to the preparatory program. The event heralded the beginning of collegiate-level coeducation for women in the United States. In September, 1837, Oberlin gained distinction as the first coeducational institution to offer the degree of bachelor of arts to women. Four women who had completed Oberlin's preparatory program were then admitted to the regular curriculum as freshmen. Three of them, Mary Hosford, Mary Kellog, and Caroline Mary Rudd, received bachelor of arts degrees in 1841.

"The work of female education," Stewart wrote in 1837,

> must be carried on in some form, and in a much more efficient manner than it has hitherto, or our country will go to destruction. For I believe that there is no other way to secure success to our great moral enterprises than to make prevalent the right kind of education for women.

Despite Stewart's enthusiasm, however, fewer than six other colleges in the country followed Oberlin's example before the Civil War (1861-1865).

Oberlin restricted women by refusing to allow them to address mixed audiences, thus preventing them from presenting their graduation orations. Admission to the theological seminary also was barred to women. However, in 1847, Antoinette Brown (later Blackwell) and Lettice Smith began attending classes in the Theological Institute as "resident graduates pursuing the theological course." Both completed the course. Smith married, but Brown, denied ordination at Oberlin, persisted until she was ordained over the church at South Butler, New York, thus becoming the first woman in the United States ordained to the Christian ministry.

Oberlin's first commencement exercises took place on September 14, 1836, when more than two thousand people witnessed fifteen men graduate from the Theological Institute. In the 1841 commencement, three of the four female students who had entered the freshman class in 1837 received the bachelor of arts degree, along with their nine male classmates. Those three women were the first women in the country to be awarded bachelor's degrees in a collegiate program identical in content to that required of male students pursuing the same degree.

1830's

Faculty and student body of Oberlin College in front of the college's Memorial Hall in 1906. (Library of Congress)

547

SIGNIFICANCE

During its first years, the Oberlin Collegiate Institute, formally renamed Oberlin College in 1850, was primarily a religious school. Finney had agreed to teach there in order to train evangelists, and he believed that the conversion of sinners was prerequisite to the millennium that, when attained, would permit other reforms to come about. In his commencement address of 1851, Finney reminded graduates that they had been educated in what he referred to as "God's College." As a member of Oberlin's faculty, and then as president of the school between 1851 and 1866, Finney endeavored to preserve that emphasis. Oberlin emerged from its first years of existence as the nation's first coeducational institution of higher education based on the traditional curriculum, and as a vibrant center of theological training.

—John G. Clark, updated by Ralph L. Langenheim, Jr.

FURTHER READING

Fletcher, Robert S. *A History of Oberlin College from Its Foundation Through the Civil War*. 2 vols. Oberlin, Ohio: Oberlin College Press, 1943. A solid, incisive study of Oberlin's role and place in nineteenth century intellectual life.

Hosford, Frances Juliette. *Father Shipherd's Magna Charta: A Century of Coeducation in Oberlin College*. Boston: Marshall Jones, 1937. Relates accomplishments of various women students and women educators at Oberlin.

Lasser, Carol. *Educating Men and Women Together: Coeducation in a Changing World*. Urbana: University of Illinois Press, in conjunction with Oberlin College, 1987. Symposium on coeducation, with many references to Oberlin's influence.

Lasser, Carol, and Marlene Merrill, eds. *Friends and Sisters: Letters Between Lucy Stone and Antoinette Brown Blackwell, 1846-93*. Chicago: University of Illinois Press, 1987. Letters of Lucy Stone and her personal thoughts, views on women's rights, and half-century friendship with Antoinette Brown Blackwell, Oberlin graduate.

_____. *Soul Mates: The Oberlin Correspondence of Lucy Stone and Antoinette Brown, 1846-1850*. Oberlin, Ohio: Oberlin College, 1983. Letters between two feminists and abolitionists provide insight regarding Oberlin's influence in these movements

Tewksbury, Donald G. *The Founding of American Colleges and Universities Before the Civil War, with Particular Reference to the Religious Influences Bearing upon the College Movement*. New York: AMS Press, 1965. A general survey placing Oberlin's emergence in context.

Woodson, Carter G. *The Education of the Negro Prior to 1861*. New York: Arno Press, 1968. A general survey of African Americans and education.

Woody, Thomas. *A History of Women's Education in the United States*. 2 vols. New York: Octagon Books, 1966. A general survey of women and education.

SEE ALSO: Jan., 1804: Ohio Enacts the First Black Codes; 1813: Founding of McGill University; 1820's-1850's: Social Reform Movement; May, 1823: Hartford Female Seminary Is Founded; Jan. 1, 1831: Garrison Begins Publishing *The Liberator*; Dec., 1833: American Anti-Slavery Society Is Founded; 1835: Finney Lectures on "Revivals of Religion"; Nov. 8, 1837: Mount Holyoke Female Seminary Opens; Jan. 1, 1857: First African American University Opens; Sept. 26, 1865: Vassar College Opens.

RELATED ARTICLES in *Great Lives from History: The Nineteenth Century, 1801-1900:* Catharine Beecher; Mary Lyon; Lucy Stone.

January 1, 1834
GERMAN STATES JOIN TO FORM CUSTOMS UNION

The coming together of most of the German states in a customs union was an important first step in the unification of Germany.

ALSO KNOWN AS: Zollverein
LOCALE: German states (now Germany)
CATEGORIES: Trade and commerce; government and politics

KEY FIGURE

Friedrich von Motz (1775-1830), Prussian finance minister and principal architect of the customs union

SUMMARY OF EVENT

When the European great powers gathered in Vienna in 1814-1815 to redraw the map of Europe following their defeat of Napoleon I, one of their most important tasks was to decide what to do with Germany. Before the Napoleonic Wars, Germany had consisted of more than three hundred separate principalities, tied loosely together in the Holy Roman Empire, which was presided over by the ruler of the Habsburg lands as Holy Roman Emperor. However, Napoleon had forced the last Holy Roman Emperor, Francis II, to give up the imperial crown, and Francis had become Francis I, emperor of Austria. There was no thought of reviving that medieval relic, the Holy Roman Empire.

The alternative solution devised by the powers was the creation of a German Confederation, embracing the two leading German powers, Austria and Prussia, and the more than three hundred German principalities that had either survived Napoleon by bowing to his will, or had played a part in the defeat of Napoleon. The multitude of tiny independent principalities that had existed before Napoleon had reconstructed Germany into satellites for his siblings were combined into thirty-eight different states. Perhaps the most important innovation introduced at the Congress of Vienna was the assignment to Prussia of a substantial block of territory in the west of Germany, along the Rhine River. However, the original Prussia remained intact and was separated from the new Prussia on the Rhine. The overriding motive for this arrangement was to make Prussia the defender of Germany against any future Napoleon. History was to validate this decision, but in ways the other powers had not anticipated.

The founding document of the Germanic Confederation made provision for economic cooperation among the members of the confederation in article 19, which authorized the members of the confederation to devise new arrangements over the levying of customs duties and particularly transit duties, to reduce the number of imposts by common consent. This provision proved meaningless, however, as common consent could never be secured.

Meanwhile, faced with the need for reviving government finance and developing a governmental system that incorporated the new Rhineland territories of Prussia, Prussian finance minister Friedrich von Motz had determined that the best way to achieve this goal was to create a single tariff for all of Prussia, collected on the borders. This was not an easy task, because the territorial arrangements of the Congress of Vienna had given Prussia an extremely long frontier, deriving in part from bringing together the two halves of Prussia: the old, eastern half and the new western half in the Rhineland. This meant high expenses in policing this lengthy frontier. At the same time, there was an urgent need to reorganize government finances, and customs dues were the principal source of revenue. Under the plan introduced by Motz, all internal dues were abolished and duties were collected only on the frontier. In general the duties were moderate, established to discourage smuggling, encourage trade, and, at the same time, generate needed revenue.

Prussia introduced a new tariff in 1818. Raw materials were generally admitted free of duty. Items for consumption within Prussia were charged moderate rates, varying between 10 and 30 percent. The lower figure applied to manufactured items; the higher duties fell on tropical products. One unusual feature of the tariff was that the duties were all specific, that is, so much per item or per unit of weight or volume. This contrasted with the customs tariffs of many other countries, whose duties were *ad valorem*, that is, specified percentages of the products' values. The effect of the Prussian system was that when prices fell, as many did in the postwar years, duties rose in proportion to the value of imports, since they did not change with the products' prices.

Although the reconstruction of the map of Germany by the great powers in Vienna in 1815 had eliminated many minute principalities, a significant number of small German states still existed. Between 1818 and 1834, eight of these small territories surrounded by Prussia agreed to join the Prussian customs system. Prussia took over the collection of duties and distributed revenues on the basis of population. The participation of these small states greatly simplified the collection of customs duties.

A major advance occurred in 1828, when Hesse-Darmstadt agreed to join the Prussian customs system. Hesse-Darmstadt badly needed financial reform and particularly needed new revenue. By agreeing to join the customs system of Prussia, Hesse-Darmstadt was entitled to a portion of the total customs revenue of the Prussian system in the proportion of its population to Prussia's western provinces, those in the Rhineland. The arrangement differed from that with the small enclaves in that Hesse-Darmstadt officials, rather than Prussian customs agents, collected duties on the borders of Hesse-Darmstadt with other states. This treaty was the first of a series concluded over the next five years that brought much of the rest of Germany into the Prussian customs system which, from January 1, 1834, was called the Zollverein, or customs union.

Meanwhile, the southern German states, notably Bavaria and Württemberg, the two largest states after Austria, formed their own customs union in 1828. Revenues were to be distributed generally according to the proportion of population. In 1833, Bavaria and Württemberg agreed to a formal merger with the Prussian customs system, effective January 1, 1834.

Meanwhile, Prussia had hit on a method to make joining the customs system more attractive to the smaller states. It agreed to build roads through these states, largely at Prussian expense. This offer unleashed a large increase in road building in Germany that helped enormously to strengthen commercial ties among the various states.

SIGNIFICANCE

By 1833, almost all the smaller states of Germany had joined the Prussian customs system. The agreements by which the various states joined entitled them to representation at the conferences of the Zollverein in ways that generally reflected their relative sizes and economic importance. Although conferences were supposed to meet annually, they actually met at irregular intervals. During the three decades between 1834 and 1863, fifteen conferences were held. Unanimity for any changes in the tariff or other regulations of the Zollverein was required.

By 1834, most of Germany enjoyed a large measure of economic unity, a unity that was to make possible strong economic growth in the decades ahead. The only German state never to join was Austria, and its refusal to come to terms with the Zollverein was to have fateful political consequences in the twentieth century.

—*Nancy M. Gordon*

FURTHER READING

Alter, Peter. *The German Question and Europe: A History*. London: Arnold, 2000. Survey of two centuries of history of German unification that considers Germany's changing place in Europe.

Clapham, J. H. *The Economic Development of France and Germany, 1815-1914*. Cambridge, England: Cambridge University Press, 1936. Although old, this work is still the most useful comprehensive treatment.

Davis, John R. *Britain and the German Zollverein, 1848-66*. New York: St. Martin's Press, 1997. Study of British-German relations that explores misunderstanding between the two great European powers.

Henderson, W. O. *The Industrial Revolution on the Continent*. London: Frank Cass, 1961. Provides a brief treatment of the formation of the Zollverein.

_____. *The Zollverein*. London: Frank Cass, 1959. First published in 1938, this is the most nearly definitive account of the Zollverein.

Kitchen, Martin. *The Political Economy of Germany, 1815-1914*. London: Croom Helm, 1978. The first two chapters deal with the Zollverein.

Nipperdey, Thomas. *Germany from Napoleon to Bismarck*. Princeton, N.J.: Princeton University Press, 1996. Contains a brief discussion of the formation of the Zollverein.

SEE ALSO: June 8-9, 1815: Organization of the German Confederation; Mar. 3-Nov. 3, 1848: Prussian Revolution of 1848; Sept. 12, 1848: Swiss Confederation Is Formed; 1866-1867: North German Confederation Is Formed; Jan. 18, 1871: German States Unite Within German Empire.

April 14, 1834
CLAY BEGINS AMERICAN WHIG PARTY

The creation of the Whig Party strengthened the two-party system in American politics and accentuated the sectional divisions that were to lead to the U.S. Civil War.

LOCALE: United States

CATEGORIES: Government and politics; organizations and institutions

KEY FIGURES

John C. Calhoun (1782-1850), vice president of the United States, 1829-1832, and senator from South Carolina

Henry Clay (1777-1852), Kentucky senator and leading Whig politician

Andrew Jackson (1767-1845), president of the United States, 1829-1837

Martin Van Buren (1782-1862), vice president under Jackson an successful Democratic candidate for president in 1836

William Henry Harrison (1773-1841), military hero, former senator, Whig candidate for president in 1836, and successful candidate in 1840

Daniel Webster (1782-1852), Massachusetts senator and Whig candidate for president in 1836

Hugh Lawson White (1773-1840), Tennessee senator and Whig candidate for president in 1836

SUMMARY OF EVENT

The emergence of the Whigs as a national party would have advanced more rapidly had there been a single over-riding issue or outstanding leader to rally around. Since there was neither, the opponents of the Democrats were a hodgepodge of malcontents, an "organized incompatibility" with only one unifying theme: an undying hatred of Andrew Jackson. They disliked the seventh president of the United States, whom they dubbed King Andrew I because of his ostensibly ruthless and dictatorial manner, and they slowly drew together into the Whig Party. They gave themselves the name "Whigs" because they ostensibly opposed tyranny and monarchy, as did the English Whigs. The name "Whig" became official when Senator Henry Clay gave it his stamp of approval in a speech that he delivered before the Senate on April 14, 1834; however, the name had been used unofficially for at least two years prior to then.

The old Federalists and the National Republicans who opposed Jackson in 1828 were later joined by many who had supported Jackson in that election but had turned against him over his positions on such divisive matters as his attack on the Second Bank of the United States and the South Carolina nullification controversy. These desertions were serious jolts to the Democratic Party and strengthened the ranks of a coalescing opposition. This opposition was strongest among the high-tariff merchants and manufacturers in the Northeast, wealthy planters in the South, and western farmers who desired internal improvements.

If there were common ideological denominators to the Whig Party, they were support for property rights and interest in government's capacity to build and improve the nation's institutions. Thus, there was both a conservative and a progressive side to the Whig Party. Like the earlier Federalists, the Whigs tended to represent the financial and business establishment. Unlike the Federalists, the Whigs understood the impetus toward westward expansion that was seizing the United States during the 1830's.

The Whigs also became champions of small businessmen—a class that might later have been called the *petit bourgeois*. Their constituency often included entrepreneurs who were in what is now the Midwest and mid-South, who were seeking prosperity and wanted a strong government, friendly to business, to ensure that they got what they sought. The Whig Party did not have the common touch of the Democrats, but it was never so thoroughly a captive to southern, slaveholding interests as its counterparts. Indeed, it was out of the Whig Party that the Republican Party, the primary antislavery party, would later emerge. The Whig Party eventually split, over slavery among other things. During its less-than-thirty-year existence, it elected two presidents and maintained the idea that the U.S. party system consisted of two equally strong but ideologically opposed parties, both representing a broad range of interests.

After a time of local party building, the Whigs first tested their national strength in the presidential campaign of 1836. Either Kentucky's Henry Clay, the glamorous "Harry of the West," or Daniel Webster, the eloquent Massachusetts defender of the union, would have seemed a logical choice to head the ticket. However, their positions on issues were too well known. In addition, the two men were bitter rivals whose differences threatened to split the infant party. Furthermore, many southern states' rights Whigs looked to John C. Calhoun

Henry Clay. (Library of Congress)

for leadership. However, although Calhoun joined Clay and Webster in their hatred of Jackson, he never truly considered himself a Whig.

With so many diverse elements, agreement about a candidate or a platform was impossible. Consequently, the party held no national nominating convention in 1836. Instead, Whig strategy was to run several candidates from the different sections of the nation. These candidates included Daniel Webster of Massachusetts; William Henry Harrison of Ohio, who had been a military hero in the Indian wars; and Hugh Lawson White of Tennessee, who, it was alleged, had killed a Cherokee chief with his own hands and thus gained credence and acclaim among frontier settlers. The Whigs did not expect that any one of their candidates would receive a majority in the electoral college. However, they hoped to draw enough votes away from the Democratic candidate to prevent him from receiving a majority. The election would then be thrown into the House of Representatives, where a Whig would have a good chance of being chosen.

This multipronged strategy was deemed foolhardy by many at the time and did not augur well for the Whigs'

chances in the 1836 election. Leaving nothing to chance, Jackson used his prestige and party organization to win the Democratic nomination for his own vice president, Martin Van Buren, on the first ballot. The Whigs selected Hugh Lawson White of Tennessee, William Henry Harrison of Ohio, and Webster as their standard-bearers. The grand strategy backfired, because the Whig candidates split the anti-Jackson vote and enabled the well-disciplined Democrats to put Van Buren in office easily.

The new president inherited a multitude of problems and had been in office only three months when the Panic of 1837 occurred. New York banks suspended specie payments, other banks and businesses began to fail, unemployment rose, and railroads and canals were abandoned as the panic evolved into a lengthy depression. This condition was caused by many things, including Jacksonian financial measures, especially the bank war and the Specie Circular; ravaging of the wheat crop by the Hessian fly; overspeculation in land; and easy credit, which left most Americans in debt. Labor, the backbone of the Democratic Party, suffered heavily, and by late 1837, 90 percent of the eastern factories were closed. The lingering depression hit the farmers of the South and West hardest, adding stress to their status as debtors.

Following the typical political thinking of the day, Van Buren did little to fight the depression, and his administration ended under a cloud of gloom. Opposition came not only from the Whigs but also from dissident Democrats. The political impact of the depression was immediately apparent as Whig strength rapidly increased.

Voters became Whigs for various reasons. Westerners, caught between their needs and resentments, were badly divided on both the banking and internal improvement issues. Southerners were equally divided between those who, like Calhoun, saw in Van Buren's Independent Treasury sound Democratic policy and those who, like John Tyler of Virginia, still bitterly resented the Democratic administration's attack on nullification. In the Northeast, conservative business interests who called for wider government activity became more sharply divided from the working groups and farmers than ever before. New political alignments were emerging, and the Democrats, as the party in power, suffered the most from these new developments.

SIGNIFICANCE

In the election of 1840, the Whigs showed the extent to which they had learned the lessons of popular appeal. When they nominated the old western military hero, William Henry Harrison, rather than Webster or Clay, and placed Tyler, an anti-Jackson Democrat, on the ticket as the vice presidential candidate, the Whigs demonstrated their political sophistication. By proclaiming the true democratic qualities of their candidates—exemplified by such slogans as "Tippecanoe and Tyler Too" and "Log Cabins and Hard Cider"—and refusing to write a platform, they allowed dissatisfied elements in all sections to assume that they would gain their ends.

The Whigs' populist campaign in 1840 led almost inevitably to some distortions of the truth. Harrison, for example, was said to have been born in a log cabin, proving his humble origins; in fact, he had been born on a Virginia plantation. The U.S. electorate either did not know this fact or preferred to forget it; they accorded Harrison great popularity. Van Buren, though tainted by the economic depressed, was sullenly renominated by the Democrats and was immediately denounced by the Whigs as an aristocrat of the worst sort. The campaign that developed was all sound and fury, slogan and vituperation. More than any other, the 1840 campaign may be said to have set the tone for what later came to typify presidential campaigns. An emphasis on image and personality rather than ideology and a premium placed on the skillful use of the mass media would from then on be necessary to elect a party candidate president of the United States. Issues were forgotten or ignored as the glamorous Harrison was elected. The rise of the Whigs was now a fact of political life.

—*John H. DeBerry, updated by Nicholas Birns*

FURTHER READING

Baxter, Maurice G. *Henry Clay and the American System.* Lexington: University Press of Kentucky, 1995. Thorough examination of Clay's politics, views on economic development, and impact upon American government.

Brown, Thomas. *Politics and Statesmanship: Essays on the American Whig Party.* New York: Columbia University Press, 1985. An important collection that surveys the American Whig Party from various informative perspectives.

Howe, Daniel Walker. *The Political Culture of the American Whigs.* Chicago: University of Chicago Press, 1979. Discusses the ideology and social affiliations of the Whig Party.

McCormick, Richard P. *The Second American Party System.* Chapel Hill: University of North Carolina Press, 1966. Shows how the Whigs fit into the structure of mid-nineteenth century U.S. politics.

Peterson, Merrill D. *The Great Triumvirate: Webster, Clay, and Calhoun.* New York: Oxford University Press, 1987. Examines three important Whig senators of the nineteenth century.

Sibley, Joel H. *Martin Van Buren and the Emergence of American Popular Politics.* Lanham, Md.: Rowman & Littlefield, 2002. Political biography of the winner of the 1836 presidential election that examines the development of partisan politics in decades leading up to Van Buren's election.

Watson, Harry L. *Andrew Jackson vs. Henry Clay: Democracy and Development in Antebellum America.* Boston: Bedford/St. Martin's, 1998. Dual biography, describing the two men's conflicting visions for the future of the United States. Includes reprints of twenty-five primary documents, including speeches and letters.

Widmer, Ted. *Martin Van Buren.* New York: Times Books, 2005. Unflattering political biography of Van Buren by a former adviser to president Bill Clinton.

SEE ALSO: Nov. 7, 1811: Battle of Tippecanoe; Dec. 3, 1828: U.S. Election of 1828; Jan. 19-27, 1830: Webster and Hayne Debate Slavery and Westward Expansion; July 10, 1832: Jackson Vetoes Rechartering of the Bank of the United States; Nov. 24, 1832-Jan. 21, 1833: Nullification Controversy; Mar. 17, 1837: Panic of 1837 Begins; Dec. 2, 1840: U.S. Election of 1840; July 6, 1854: Birth of the Republican Party.

RELATED ARTICLES in *Great Lives from History: The Nineteenth Century, 1801-1900:* John C. Calhoun; Henry Clay; Andrew Jackson; Millard Fillmore; Martin Van Buren; Daniel Webster.

1830's

August 14, 1834
BRITISH PARLIAMENT PASSES NEW POOR LAW

Passage of the new Poor Law by the British parliament represented the culmination of fifty years of experimentation in poor relief; it sought to make relief more stringent, more centralized, and more in tune with a capitalist labor market.

ALSO KNOWN AS: Poor Law Amendment Bill of 1834
LOCALE: England; Wales
CATEGORIES: Laws, acts, and legal history; social issues and reform; economics

KEY FIGURES
Sir Edwin Chadwick (1800-1890), utilitarian who became first secretary of the Poor Law Commission
Benjamin Disraeli (first earl of Beaconsfield; 1804-1881), Tory politician who opposed passage of the Poor Law Amendment Bill
John Fielden (1784-1849), leading Radical who opposed the new Poor Law
Richard Oastler (1789-1861), humanitarian Tory who led the Anti-Poor Law League
Feargus Edward O'Connor (1794-1855), Chartist editor of the *Northern Star*
Nassau William Senior (1790-1864), classical Liberal economist who led the Poor Law Study Commission
John Charles Spencer (1782-1845), Whig leader who piloted the Poor Law Amendment Bill through Parliament
John Walter II (1776-1847), editor of *The Times* of London

SUMMARY OF EVENT
England's first Poor Laws for poor relief dated from the Reformation period and were based on local parish support. The spirit and application of the laws had varied, as had the degree of central control. Some parishes treated the poor in a humanitarian way, while others were harsh. The Industrial Revolution and the Napoleonic Wars had brought serious new economic problems to Great Britain's poor. The plight of the agricultural laborers had become desperate by the late 1790's because of low wages caused by general agricultural distress.

This situation resulted in the humanitarian but unsound Speenhamland system, which began at Speenhamland, near Newbury, Berkshire, England, in 1795. Under that system, the government supplemented wages of the poor from parish taxes in order to maintain a living wage for workers. The Speenhamland system was most common in the rural parishes of southern England, but on occasion periodic unemployment in industrial districts also required extensive expenditures. The system led to a number of serious problems and abuses such as the growth of pauperism, idleness, illegitimacy, and general demoralization of character. It also subsidized farmers who hired only laborers on relief since they could then pay them lower wages. The system also encouraged workers to get on the relief roles in order to be hired.

The huge and rapidly increasing costs of the Speenhamland system finally caused a rising demand for change. More than 50 percent of local English property tax revenues were going for poor relief. Some rural parishes in the south were near ruin because of the high cost of the system. The situation was aggravated by the Law of Settlement, which caused the parishes in which men were born or apprenticed to support them when they were out of work. That law encouraged factory employers to send their unemployed workers back to their original parishes when business slackened.

Another cause for change was the appearance of new economic theories, such as utilitarianism, with its ideas of centralization and "the greatest happiness of the greatest number." Others included Malthusianism, with its emphasis on the danger of overpopulation among the poor, and Manchester liberalism, with its insistence on economic individualism and laissez-faire. From different perspectives, they all condemned existing practices of dealing with the poor. A further source of alarm in 1830 was a series of disturbances in rural areas where workers demanded allowances as a right.

A Royal Commission, appointed shortly after the Whigs took office in 1830, issued a report on the Poor Laws after two years of study. This Poor Law Study Commission was dominated by economists of the utilitarian and Malthusian type, most notably Nassau William Senior and Edwin Chadwick. The commission recommended that relief be abolished for the able-bodied, who should be forced to live in workhouses if they were destitute. The commission also proposed that relief payments should be considered loans to be repaid. The administration should be centralized in the national government, and parishes should be grouped into unions for more efficiency and freedom from local influences. Moreover, workhouses were to be made as unattractive as possible to discourage idleness. Separate workhouses were to be provided for the old, the sick, and children. In the matter of illegitimate children, searches for fathers were to cease, and mothers were to be held responsible and sent to workhouses with their children. The commission apparently followed the preconceived theories of its leading members without studying the problems in depth or even gathering statistics to any great extent.

From the commission's report came the Poor Law Amendment Bill of 1834, sponsored by the Whig government. It proposed to set up a centralized administrative structure and authorized the building of workhouses. While generally allowing only "indoor" or workhouse relief, an amendment added by the duke of Wellington authorized the continuation of "outdoor" relief outside workhouses if it was considered necessary. The bill did not adopt all the recommendations of the Poor Law Study Commission, but most members of Parliament assumed that those recommendations would be put into effect.

Sponsored by Viscount Althorp in the House of Lords and by John Charles Spencer in the House of Commons, the Poor Law Amendment Bill moved through Parliament in fewer than four months in mid-1834 because of politicians' fear of popular resentment. Most Whig and Tory landowners supported the bill in the hope that it would reduce the high costs of relief. Most Radicals and Liberals supported it as a Benthamite step toward a more efficient centralized government and as an expression of liberal economic theories. The chief opposition to the bill came from a small group of humanitarian Tories and democratic Radicals. Much of the press, especially *The Times* of London, edited by John Walter II, bitterly attacked the bill, but its vagueness made it a hard target to hit. Besides the humanitarian opposition, many believed that the centralized method of poor relief that it would impose was unconstitutional. As a concession to this view, the bill's life was limited to five years, and it passed into law.

After the bill was passed on August 14, 1834, new Poor Law commissioners were appointed to control all aspects of social welfare previously handled by different agencies. The first secretary of the commission, Edwin Chadwick, an efficient but harsh and insensitive bureaucrat, strove to make the workhouses as undesirable to live in as possible so that they would become refuges only to those facing starvation. The goal was to make the standard of living in workhouses worse than that of

the poorest paid laborers. However, during the 1830's wages were often near the starvation level anyway. Therefore, to discourage workers from entering workhouses, deliberately harsh regulations were drawn up.

In practice, the new Poor Law proved considerably less centralized than Chadwick and the utilitarians intended. During the implementation of the statute beginning in the autumn of 1834, the itinerant assistant commissioners traveling throughout the countryside ran up against the reality of well-entrenched local elites. Peers and gentry insisted that the organizing of poor law unions (groupings of parishes) conform as much as possible to the boundaries of their landed estates. Local leaders tended to take a leading part on the new boards of guardians as well, with the result that the Poor Law Commission in London had to negotiate the terms of the reform with them.

Benjamin Disraeli rising to give his first speech in Parliament. (Francis R. Niglutsch)

Such matters as workhouse dietaries and the granting of outdoor relief varied from union to union and were frequently at variance with commission directives. Nevertheless, the peers, gentry, and prosperous farmers who dominated most boards of guardians in the south and the Midlands—the first region formed into poor law unions—agreed with the general tenor of the reform. Scattered pockets of resistance by the poor arose. These ranged from protest meetings to physical attacks on the new workhouses that were under construction. However, these disturbances were effectively countered by military force and by the importation of London Metropolitan Police.

Regulations within the workhouses were similar to those of prisons, and for this reason workers called them "Bastilles," after the notorious Paris prison that was stormed and later razed during the French Revolution (1789). Members of families who entered workhouses were separated and not allowed to visit one another, total silence was enforced at meals, inmates were seldom allowed to go outside, and attempts were even made to prevent funeral services. Among the types of work provided were stone-crushing and bone-grinding. The sick, the insane, and the depraved were often not separated.

Applying the new system to the rural south was comparatively easy because good harvests in 1834 and 1835 reduced poverty levels. The commissioners also reduced unemployment by using their power to transport workers to districts where there was work. Although the commissioners found it necessary to continue some outdoor relief, they quickly wiped out the allowance system and destroyed most of the abuses of the old system.

When the Poor Law Commission began to organize unions in the industrial north in 1837, it met a fierce storm of protest because an industrial depression had thrown large numbers of workers out of work. The abuses of the allowance system had never been common in the north, and there was little need for such a radical reform because most unemployment was involuntary and caused by business cycles. Mass worker protests and riots erupted throughout the north, and in some areas humanitarian manufacturers, such as John Fielden, prevented the introduction of the new Poor Law. The opposition became organized into the Anti-Poor Law League led by Tories Robert Oastler and J. R. Stephens, and aided by John Walter and *The Times*. The Chartists in the north, led by Feargus Edward O'Connor, the editor of the *Northern Star*, joined in the attack. These protests forced the commissioners to continue extensive outdoor relief.

Parliamentary opposition also grew, led by Tories

such as Benjamin Disraeli and John Walter, and Radicals such as John Fielden. However, Tory, Whig, and Radical leaders remained in favor of the new Poor Law. The opposition had some effect, causing one-year extensions of the act until 1842, when the law was finally extended for five full years. At that time, a number of concessions were made. In the workhouses, undesirables were segregated, older husbands and wives were permitted to live together, more freedom to go outside was allowed, silent meals were ended, and children could see their parents daily. Finally, Poor Law Employment Yards were set up as alternatives to workhouses, especially in northern industrial areas.

Conditions in the Andover Workhouse in 1846 led to a special investigating commission, which returned a scathing report. Consequently in 1847, when the Poor Law was up for renewal, the Poor Law Commission was abolished and replaced by a Poor Law Board directly responsible to a cabinet minister. Chadwick resigned, and certain improvements were made. Serious and basic problems remained, but many of the harshest features were softened.

SIGNIFICANCE

The Poor Law Amendment Bill of 1834 is significant as an extreme government reaction to an extreme economic problem. It was a harsh system and has often been cited as an argument against welfare programs. On the more positive side, the new Poor Law did succeed in correcting most of the earlier abuses and served as a foundation for later improvements. It also represented the temporary triumph of the economic theories of the Manchester Liberals, especially in its utilitarian and Malthusian aspects. However, even in their triumph, these theories showed their limitations, especially their inhumanitarian effects. The Poor Law Commission also represented a pioneer attempt in modern centralized administration. The worker antagonism which the new Poor Law aroused contributed to the rise of the Chartist movement.

—*James H. Steinel, updated by Anthony Brundage*

FURTHER READING

Brundage, Anthony. *The Making of the New Poor Law: The Politics of Inquiry, Enactment, and Implementation, 1832-1839*. New Brunswick, N.J.: Rutgers University Press, 1978. A detailed account of the background, parliamentary proceedings, and difficulties of implementation of the new Poor Law.

Chadwick, Edwin. *Edwin Chadwick: Nineteenth Century Social Reform*. Edited by David Gladstone.

5 vols. London: Routledge/Thoemmes Press, 1997. Collection of a wide range of the writings of the first secretary of the Poor Law Commission.

Dean, Mitchell. *The Constitution of Poverty: Toward a Genealogy of Liberal Governance.* London: Routledge, 1990. Wide-ranging discussion of the economic and social theory behind Great Britain's nineteenth century poor law system.

Driver, Felix. *Power and Pauperism: The Workhouse System, 1834-1884.* New York: Cambridge University Press, 1993. Close examination of the controversial workhouse system established by the new Poor Law, bringing to bear geographic and spatial modes of analysis.

Finlayson, Geoffrey. *Citizen, State, and Social Welfare in Britain, 1780-1930.* Oxford, England: Clarendon Press, 1994. Places the new Poor Law in a wider context by considering the relationship between the public and private sectors of poor relief in Britain.

Hamlin, Christopher. *Public Health and Social Justice in the Age of Chadwick: Britain, 1800-1854.* Cambridge, England: Cambridge University Press, 1998. Well-researched and detailed account of British efforts to improve public health through construction of public works during the early nineteenth century.

Poynter, J. R. *Society and Pauperism: English Ideas on Poor Relief, 1795-1834.* London: Routledge & Kegan Paul, 1969. Excellent analysis of the intellectual background behind the new Poor Law of 1834.

Rose, Michael E., ed. *The Poor and the City: The English Poor Law in Its Urban Context, 1834-1914.* New York: St. Martin's Press, 1985. Collection of incisive essays on social, political, and economic aspects of urban poor relief, and relations between poor law authorities and organized charity.

Wood, Peter. *Poverty and the Workhouse in Victorian Britain.* Wolfeboro Falls, N.H.: Alan Sutton, 1991. Excellent survey of all aspects of poor relief, in both rural and urban communities, under the new Poor Law.

SEE ALSO: 1824: British Parliament Repeals the Combination Acts; May 9, 1828-Apr. 13, 1829: Roman Catholic Emancipation; 1833: British Parliament Passes the Factory Act; May 8, 1838-Apr. 10, 1848: Chartist Movement; June 15, 1846: British Parliament Repeals the Corn Laws; Mar., 1852-Sept., 1853: Dickens Publishes *Bleak House*; 1864: Hill Launches Housing Reform in London; Aug., 1867: British Parliament Passes the Reform Act of 1867; Dec. 4, 1867: National Grange Is Formed; Aug. 3, 1892: Hardie Becomes Parliament's First Labour Member.

RELATED ARTICLES in *Great Lives from History: The Nineteenth Century, 1801-1900:* Edwin Chadwick; Benjamin Disraeli; Charles Grey; Sir George Gilbert Scott.

1830's

October 14, 1834
BLAIR PATENTS HIS FIRST SEED PLANTER

Henry Blair's corn and cotton seed planters helped advance the agricultural revolution of the early nineteenth century in the United States at a time when most African Americans were enslaved and when free blacks were fighting for the basic rights of citizenship. Until his first patent in 1834, only one other African American inventor—Thomas L. Jennings—had applied for and received a patent.

LOCALE: Maryland
CATEGORIES: Inventions; agriculture; science and technology

KEY FIGURES
Henry Blair (1804-1860), African American inventor
Thomas L. Jennings (1791-1859), American inventor

SUMMARY OF EVENT

Born in Montgomery County, Maryland, and living and working at a time and place hostile to people of African American descent, Henry Blair is the only inventor described as "a colored man" in the records of the U.S. Patent Office. His corn seed planter, patented on October, 14, 1834, allowed farmers to plant more corn in a shorter period of time. The corn planter, which was pulled by horses or oxen, dropped individual kernels of corn into furrows, which were then automatically covered with earth as a farmer walked behind the planter. Blair's cotton planter, patented two years later in 1836, was equally instrumental to the agricultural revolution that began in the United States during the first half of the nineteenth century.

It was earlier thought that Blair was the first African

The invention of the cotton gin had an ironic effect. It was designed to save human labor; however, by making it much cheaper to separate seeds from cotton, the gin made cotton-growing more profitable and thereby had the effect of requiring more human labor—typically slave labor—to grow and pick cotton. (C. A. Nichols & Company)

American to receive a patent, but Thomas L. Jennings, a free black tailor living in New York City, patented a dry-cleaning process in 1821. Along with the products of other inventors, such as John Deere (who invented a steel plow that allowed for the cultivation of the midwestern prairies), Blair's planters led to significant increases in American farm production.

Little is known about Blair's early life, but it is assumed that he was a free man, as enslaved people were not allowed to obtain patents. It is also evident that he could not read or write because he signed his patents with an *X*. His experiences in antebellum American society (before the Civil War) likely were similar to those of many other free blacks who lived in the South: plagued by continual fear and intimidation. The percentage of free blacks in the antebellum South actually declined during the period between 1815 and 1860. During the colonial period and immediately following the Revolutionary War (1775-1783), many enslaved Americans either were granted freedom by their masters (who sometimes

felt guilty about their ownership of slaves, given the egalitarian rhetoric of the revolutionary period) or were able to purchase their own freedom as well as the freedom of family members.

After the invention of the cotton gin by Eli Whitney in 1793, however, the changing agricultural economy made it more difficult for slaves to gain their freedom. The cotton gin made it economically feasible to separate the seeds from raw cotton and allowed for more and cheaper cotton to reach the world's textile markets. Cloth manufacturers in England and the northeastern United States could process as much cotton as the American South could produce. Because slaves were the primary source of labor in the southern states, they were also in greater demand. When the cost of slave labor increased, people who had earlier been able to purchase their own freedom were priced out of their own "market." Masters were less willing to let go of their slaves, whose monetary value increased throughout the first half of the nineteenth century.

The free blacks who lived in the South during this period faced increasing dangers of enslavement or re-enslavement. Unscrupulous slave catchers often abducted free blacks and claimed that they were escaped slaves. Restrictions on the movements of free blacks during the antebellum period also grew more severe. Particularly after the planned Denmark Vesey slave rebellion of 1822 in South Carolina and the Nat Turner Rebellion (1831) in Virginia, slave owners (and their supporters in the government) required free blacks to carry manumission papers and to register with local authorities. The education of enslaved people was prohibited. The inability to acquire an education made it difficult for African Americans to enter and progress in the professions; however, the lack of an education did not prevent Blair from capitalizing on his knowledge of the mechanical arts. Fearing that free blacks might aid in the escape of slaves to the northern states or Canada, the Maryland legislature passed an 1841 act that prohibited their possession of abolitionist literature; conviction under the act carried a prison sentence of ten to twenty years.

It is often assumed that slavery in Maryland was not as harsh as in states of the Deep South. Some point to the presence of the Quakers (particularly along the state's eastern shore) as a factor that might have lessened the severity of the institution. According to Frederick Douglass, a leading abolitionist from Maryland who escaped from slavery, the institution was just as harsh in Maryland as it was in other states. Even though the physical climate and work conditions were not as difficult as in the Deep South, enslaved people and free blacks in Maryland suffered from the constant fear that they or their family members could be sold to the cotton plantations of Mississippi and Alabama. For abolitionist Harriet Tubman, also a Maryland resident and a slave, these fears became reality. When she was twenty-eight years old she learned that she and other members of her family were to be transported to the South. She had been married for five years to John Tubman, a free black man. After an unsuccessful first try at escape, she eventually escaped to the North and then returned many times to the South to help more than three hundred slaves escape as well.

It is not clear why Blair continued to reside in Maryland, given its increasingly hostile and unsafe environment. Like many free blacks in the antebellum South, he may have had enslaved family members in the area. In any case, he was able to continue his work as an inventor while living under conditions that required constant vigilance and care.

The information that is available about Blair and other African American inventors is largely based upon the work of Henry Baker, an assistant patent examiner in the federal Patent Office during the late nineteenth century. At the turn of the century, the Patent Office sent letters to patent attorneys, newspaper editors, and prominent African Americans to gather information about black inventors. Baker compiled the information and followed leads, publishing his results in the four-volume work *The Colored Inventor: A Record of Fifty Years* (1913). His research was used to select inventions for exhibition at the New Orleans Cotton Centennial in 1890, the Chicago Columbian Exposition in 1893, and the Atlanta Southern Exposition in 1895.

SIGNIFICANCE

Henry Blair's work as an inventor in antebellum Maryland marks him as both an innovative mechanic and a brave human being. Laboring as a successful farmer in a social climate that engendered fear and anxiety in both free and enslaved African Americans, he was able to produce and receive patents for two important inventions: a corn planter in 1834 and a cotton planter in 1836. In doing so, he was only the second African American to have registered a patent in the United States.

Blair pioneered the way for other African Americans such as George Washington Carver, an agricultural scientist who worked during the late nineteenth century and early twentieth century, as his inventions, and those of others such as Eli Whitney, Cyrus McCormick, and John Deere, helped American farmers increase production and efficiency. Blair's contributions are all the more remarkable because he worked and succeeded in a repressive, prejudiced, and discriminatory social climate.

—*Kay J. Carr*

FURTHER READING

Baker, Henry E. *The Colored Inventor.* 1913. Reprint. New York: Arno Press, 1969. A patent examiner's research into African American patent holders. Brief at twelve pages.

Sluby, Patricia Carter. *The Inventive Spirit of African Americans: Patented Ingenuity.* Westport, Conn.: Praeger, 2004. American patent examiner and agent Sluby explores the history of African American patent holders and their inventions. Includes discussion of Henry Blair.

Weber, Gustavus A. *The Patent Office: Its History, Activities, and Organization.* Baltimore: Johns Hopkins University Press, 1924. A general history of the U.S. Patent Office.

1830's

Whitman, T. Stephen. *Price of Freedom: Slavery and Freedom in Baltimore and Early National Maryland.* New York: Routledge, 2000. The history of slaves and free blacks in antebellum Baltimore and Maryland.

SEE ALSO: Summer, 1831: McCormick Invents the Reaper; Aug. 21, 1831: Turner Launches Slave Insurrection; 1840: Liebig Advocates Artificial Fertilizers.
RELATED ARTICLES in *Great Lives from History: The Nineteenth Century, 1801-1900:* Frederick Douglass; Cyrus Hall McCormick; Harriet Tubman; Nat Turner.

1835
FINNEY LECTURES ON "REVIVALS OF RELIGION"

In his delivery of a series of lectures to his Chatham Chapel congregation in New York City, Charles Grandison Finney preached of the need for a revivalist religion in the United States. He was the leading light of the Second Great Awakening, and his lectures were the definitive statement about conversion and New Light Christianity.

LOCALE: New York, New York
CATEGORY: Religion and theology

KEY FIGURES
Charles Grandison Finney (1792-1875), leading preacher during the Second Great Awakening
Lyman Beecher (1775-1863), pastor of Boston's Park Street Church

SUMMARY OF EVENT
Charles Grandison Finney did not intend to become one of the most influential religious figures in American history. Born in 1792 in Warren, Connecticut, he was moved by his parents when he was two years old to the newly settled frontier community of Oneida County in western New York. As with the case with many New Englanders of the late eighteenth century, the Finneys were in search of fertile lands to replace those that had been worn out by decades of farming in their home states. Finney's parents were not well educated or even religious, but Finney himself was able to attend a common school in his youth, and he received a basic education. As a child he aspired to the profession of law and traveled in his twenties to Adams, New York, to study for the profession. When he was twenty-nine years old, he experienced a religious conversion that would prove pivotal to the course of his life.

Already profoundly uncertain of his relationship to God, Finney left his house one morning in 1821 to take a walk. In his memoirs, he later wrote,

I turned to go up into the woods, I recollect to have said, "I will give my heart to God, or I never will come down from [the woods]." I had gone into the woods after an early breakfast; when I returned to the village, I found it was dinner time.

Finney recalled that during that day he had prayed to God and was converted to a personal Christianity. He said that he was profoundly affected by the experience, explaining that waves of love flowed through his body. The next day, he quit his legal study and vowed to become a minister of religion.

By the end of 1823, Finney was licensed to preach as a Presbyterian minister. He was sent by the Female Mission Society of Western New York to serve as a missionary to Jefferson County, a community of upstate New York, where the increasingly industrial and commercial economy—brought on, in part, by the opening of the Erie Canal in 1825—caused many families to abandon their traditional structures and adopt middle-class characteristics.

From the beginning of his career, Finney avoided the traditional emphasis placed by preachers that tortuous fate awaited nonbelievers. He downplayed notions of predestination and assured his listeners that they could achieve salvation by truly repenting and embracing Jesus Christ as their savior.

During the first half of the nineteenth century many Americans were experiencing personal anxiety over the social upheaval caused by basic changes to the nation's economy. Christian ministers such as Finney helped to allay the fears of many people by preaching the possibility of personal salvation. The nation was transferring from a mainly agrarian economy to one in which commercialism and industrialism accounted for more and more opportunities for employment. The changes in the economy, in turn, created changes in the country's social structure, causing much consternation among the people.

"WHAT A REVIVAL OF RELIGION IS"

In "What a Revival of Religion Is," the first lecture in his series on the topic, Charles Finney explained the fundamental concept underlying his theological model.

A "Revival of Religion" presupposes a declension. Almost all the religion in the world has been produced by revivals. God has found it necessary to take advantage of the excitability there is in mankind, to produce powerful excitements among them, before He can lead them to obey. Men are so sluggish, there are so many things to lead their minds off from religion and to oppose the influence of the Gospel, that it is necessary to raise an excitement among them, till the tide rises so high as to sweep away the opposing obstacles. They must be so aroused that they will break over these counteracting influences, before they will obey God.

Look back at the history of the Jews, and you will see that God used to maintain religion among them by special occasions, when there would be a great excitement, and people would turn to the Lord. And after they had been thus revived, it would be but a short time before there would be so many counteracting influences brought to bear upon them, that religion would decline, and keep on declining, till God could have time, so to speak, to convict them of sin by His Spirit, and rebuke them by His providence, and thus so gain the attention of the masses to the great subject of salvation, as to produce a widespread awakening. Then the counteracting causes would again operate, religion would decline, and the nation would be swept away in the vortex of luxury, idolatry, and pride. There is so little principle in the Church, so little firmness and stability of purpose, that unless it is greatly excited, it will go back from the path of duty, and do nothing to promote the glory of God. The state of the world is still such, and probably will be till the millennium is fully come, that religion must be mainly promoted by means of revivals.

Source: Charles Grandison Finney, *Lectures on Revivals of Religion* (New York: Lord, 1835).

Second Great Awakening. A similar period of intense revivalism had taken place during the middle of the eighteenth century. In that period, called the First Great Awakening, preachers such as Jonathan Edwards, George Whitefield, and Gilbert Tennent had participated in proliferating religious sects in colonial America.

Finney was the leading figure in the Second Great Awakening. First in Jefferson County and then in Utica and Rome in New York, he attracted tremendous numbers of people to revival meetings that met for days on end. He was called to a ministry in Rochester, New York, in 1830; his tenure there led to an intense revivalism that affected the entire community. Shops and factories were closed so workers from all walks of life could attend his lectures and sermons.

Hundreds of people gave up the consumption of alcohol and experienced conversions after hearing Finney speak. He told his followers that they could achieve salvation by simply rejecting sin. His sermons were long, and they appeared unplanned; in them, he promoted controversial methods, referring to individuals as sinners and advocating that people could and should totally eradicate sins in their lives. He also allowed women to pray in public at prayer meetings, used colloquial speech in his sermons, and advocated immediate church membership for converts.

Finney's messages and methods of conversion were denounced by many traditional members of the clergy. In 1827, orthodox members of the Presbyterian Church tried to limit his appeal by questioning his liberal theology, but Finney had enough support from powerful clergymen such as Lyman Beecher to escape the criticism of the conservatives. Finney went on to preach in Philadelphia and Boston and answered a call to the ministry in New York City. It was there, in 1835, that he delivered his lectures on "Revivals of Religion," which were published the same year and with the same name. The work explains the reasons for revivalism and the need for baptism to achieve salvation. His methods, while still controversial, were wildly popular among great numbers of Americans for many decades.

In 1835, Finney began working as a teacher of pasto-

1830's

Increasing numbers of families, for example, which had traditionally lived and worked together on farmsteads, were moving to towns and small cities. Fathers worked in shops and factories and were kept away from their families during the day. Fathers, therefore, had less personal opportunity to interact with their children; mothers were forced to take upon the responsibility of solely raising children.

Historians have pointed to these social changes, as well as others, to explain the tendency among many Americans in the first half of the nineteenth century to seek religion for relief from a growing sense of social and personal anxiety. The religious revivalism that was so prominent during this period has come to be called the

ral theology at the newly founded Oberlin College and Theological Seminary in Ohio. He later served as the president of Oberlin College, from 1851 to 1866. He published two books from his lectures on systematic theology and wrote his autobiography. He retired from the ministry in 1872 and died in 1875 at the age of eighty-two.

SIGNIFICANCE

Charles Grandison Finney may have been responsible for the conversions of one-half million Americans between 1825 and 1850. He appealed to people from all economic strata and preached a form of salvation that threatened the doctrines of the traditional Christian churches.

Finney and his supporters were responsible for creating an American style of religion that was theologically egalitarian and emphasized individual responsibility. Revivalism stressed the necessity of immediate conversion and church membership, even though the American Protestant tradition had insisted upon the primacy of predestination and the power of an elite elect.

—Kay J. Carr

FURTHER READING

Finney, Charles Grandison. *Lectures on Revivals of Religion: The Complete Restored Text, 1868*. Edited by Richard Friedrich. Fenwick, Mich.: Alethea in Heart Ministries, 2003. Complete text of Finney's 1835 lectures. Also available online through the Christian Classics Ethereal Library, Calvin College. http://www.ccel.org/f/finney/. Accessed January 26, 2006.

Johnson, Paul. *A Shopkeeper's Millennium: Society and Revivals in Rochester, New York, 1815-1837*. New York: Hill and Wang, 2004. An excellent examination of the effects of revivalism in the community of Rochester under Finney's ministry.

Miller, Perry. *The Life of the Mind in America, from the Revolution to the Civil War*. New York: Harcourt, Brace, & World, 1965. A classic work and an overview of the period of the Second Great Awakening by one of America's leading intellectual historians.

Perciaccante, Marianne. *Calling Down Fire: Charles Grandison Finney and Revivalism in Jefferson County, New York, 1800-1840*. Albany: State University of New York Press, 2003. An examination of a community during the Second Great Awakening.

Russel, Garth M., and Richard A. G. Dupuis. *The Original Memoirs of Charles G. Finney*. Grand Rapids, Mich.: Zondervan, 2002. A reprint of Finney's own accounts of his conversion and work as a revivalist preacher.

SEE ALSO: Apr. 9, 1816: African Methodist Episcopal Church Is Founded; May 8, 1816: American Bible Society Is Founded; May, 1819: Unitarian Church Is Founded; Apr. 6, 1830: Smith Founds the Mormon Church; 1835-1836: Strauss Publishes *The Life of Jesus Critically Examined*; 1870-1871: Watch Tower Bible and Tract Society Is Founded.

RELATED ARTICLES in *Great Lives from History: The Nineteenth Century, 1801-1900:* Alexander Campbell; Dwight L. Moody.